P9-CRG-538

Research Methods for Social Work

Third Edition

Allen Rubin
University of Texas at Austin

Earl Babbie
Chapman University

Brooks/Cole Publishing Company

I(T)P® An International Thomson Publishing Company

Pacific Grove • Albany • Belmont • Bonn • Boston • Cincinnati • Detroit • Johannesburg • London
Madrid • Melbourne • Mexico City • New York • Paris • Singapore • Tokyo • Toronto • Washington

Sponsoring Editor: *Lisa Gebo*
Marketing Team: *Jean Thompson, Deborah Petit*
Editorial Assistant: *Terry Thomas*
Production Coordination: *The Book Company*
Production Editor: *Jamie Sue Brooks*
Manuscript Editor: *Elizabeth Judd*

Permissions Editor: *Carline Haga*
Cover and Interior Design: *Donna Davis*
Illustrations: *Lotus Art*
Typesetting: *Thompson Type*
Cover Printing: *Phoenix Color Corp.*
Printing and Binding: *Quebecor, Fairfield*

SPSS and SPSS/PC+ are registered trademarks of SPSS Inc.

For more information, contact:

BROOKS/COLE PUBLISHING COMPANY
511 Forest Lodge Road
Pacific Grove, CA 93950
USA

International Thomson Publishing Europe
Berkshire House 168–173
High Holborn
London WC1V 7AA
England

Thomas Nelson Australia
102 Dodds Street
South Melbourne, 3205
Victoria, Australia

Nelson Canada
1120 Birchmount Road
Scarborough, Ontario
Canada M1K 5G4

International Thomson Editores
Seneca 53
Col. Polanco
11560 México, D. F. México

International Thomson Publishing GmbH
Königswinterer Strasse 418
53227 Bonn
Germany

International Thomson Publishing Asia
221 Henderson Road
#05–10 Henderson Building
Singapore 0315

International Thomson Publishing Japan
Hirakawacho Kyowa Building, 3F
2-2-1 Hirakawacho
Chiyoda-ku, Tokyo 102
Japan

Printed in the United States of America.

10 9 8 7 6 5 4 3 2 1

Library of Congress Cataloging-in-Publication Data

Rubin, Allen
    Research methods for social work / Allen Rubin, Earl Babbie. — 3rd ed.
        p.   cm.
    Includes bibliographical references (p.   ) and index.
    ISBN 0-534-26388-7
    1. Social service—Research—Methodology.   I. Babbie, Earl R.
II. Title.
HV11.R84   1997
361'.0072—dc20   96-17903

Dedication

To our children

ANNIE RUBIN

JOSH RUBIN

DAVID RUBIN

AARON BABBIE

ARA VALLASTER

Contents in Brief

Contents in Detail

PART 2

Problem Formulation and Measurement 89

PART 3

The Logic of Research Design 227

PART 4

Quantitative and Qualitative Modes of Observation 341

PART 6

The Social Context of Research 545

APPENDIXES

Preface

We have been delighted with the success of the first two editions of this text. In this third edition, we continued to revise the book significantly in an effort to keep up with advances in the field and in response to many excellent suggestions by instructors who provided extremely helpful, thorough, and thoughtful reviews of the previous editions. Our revisions are far too extensive to sum up in a few paragraphs, so we have provided a chapter-by-chapter summary of the major changes that distinguish this edition from the second edition. The most significant changes to this edition are:

- Expanded coverage of content on qualitative inquiry

- New illustrations of how qualitative and quantitative methods can be integrated

- Increased acknowledgment of epistemological approaches other than positivism and postpositivism

- Demonstrations of connections between epistemology and research methods

We believe that one of the most important features of this text has always been its comprehensiveness and depth of coverage, and with each new edition we have sought to strengthen its comprehensiveness. According to most of the feedback we receive, instructors like the depth and comprehensiveness this book provides. Research content can be difficult for students to grasp. We think that their comprehension is aided not by a simplistic approach, but by explaining things in depth and using multiple examples to illustrate the complex material and its relevance for practice. Moreover, taking this approach enhances the value of the book to students in the long run. Students seem to agree. Rather than reselling the book at the end of the semester, many students choose to keep it for their professional libraries. This text's comprehensive coverage of the range of research methodologies and all phases in the research process—particularly its expanded coverage of qualitative methods, its chapters on data analysis and statistical procedures, and its many illustrations of practice applications (including a new practice-oriented study guide)—also represents our effort to help courses reflect current curriculum policy statements guiding the accreditation standards of the Council on Social Work Education (CSWE).

CHAPTER-BY-CHAPTER FEATURES OF THE NEW EDITION

Chapter 1: Human Inquiry and Science

This chapter's most significant changes have been epistemological. They include:

- New sections on postmodern and other views of reality and idiographic and nomothetic models of understanding

- Expansion of the overview of quantitative and qualitative methods of inquiry, including improved connections to epistemology

The added epistemological material made the chapter quite lengthy, so we moved the section on "The Foundations of Social Science" to Chapter 2, where it seems to fit better. We hope that with these modifications Chapter 1 now sets the stage better for a more balanced approach to quantitative and qualitative methods and for considering the remaining chapters within the context of alternative epistemological paradigms.

Chapter 2: Theory and Research

Major revisions and expansion to achieve a better balance are further reflected in Chapter 2. In this connection, the most significant revision in this chapter is:

- Expanded coverage of paradigms—comparing and contrasting positivism, postpositivism, interpretivism, and the conflict paradigm—and showing the research implications of the alternative paradigms and how each paradigm is reflected in subsequent chapters

In the previous edition, this chapter began with a look at the "traditional" model of science, which some colleagues felt might be misconstrued as implying that a deductive, quantitative approach was always the preferred model. To avoid giving this impression, we now begin the chapter by exploring the role of theory in social work research and practice. We have moved up our discussion of practice models and then discuss paradigms, not in the context of deductive theory construction as in the previous edition, but before we take up inductive and deductive methods. In expanding our coverage of alternative paradigms, we have attempted to alert readers in advance that as they read certain subsequent chapters they may see one approach reflected more than others, but in other chapters, the emphasis may switch. This way, we hope to avoid unintentionally implying that there is only one correct model of inquiry or only one acceptable epistemological approach. Following the expanded section on paradigms is the section moved from Chapter 1 in the previous edition. This section, formerly called "The Foundations of Social Science," is now called "Theory in Research." After this comes the material on inductive and deductive systems (headed "Two Logical Systems"), which is now introduced in a way that attempts to ensure that readers do not think that one is valued over the other.

Chapter 3: The Ethics and Politics of Social Work Research

Several colleagues made excellent suggestions—which we have implemented—for improving this chapter. One was to move up to the beginning of the chapter the major historical examples that catapulted ethics to the research agenda (that is, the Holocaust and the Tuskegee experiment). Another was to reinstall the section on the Tearoom Trade study. New material was also added on the controversial book *The Bell Curve,* as a recent illustration of political and ideological issues connected to research and race.

Chapter 4: Problem Formulation

The most notable changes in this chapter are:

- Examples of qualitative inquiry infused throughout the chapter

- A box discussing the similarities and differences between quantitative and qualitative research proposals

Other changes to this chapter deal with the at times fuzzy distinction between exploratory and explanatory research purposes, understanding and predicting as research purposes, an elaboration of the advantages and disadvantages of panel studies, and a new box that helps clarify the distinctions between cross-sectional, cohort, trend, and panel studies.

Chapter 5: Conceptualization and Operationalization

Throughout this chapter we have added brief reminders regarding the distinctions between quantitative and qualitative research in regard to conceptualization and operationalization. We also added:

- A section on "A Qualitative Perspective on Operational Definitions"

- A box illustrating the qualitative perspective and its complementarity with a quantitative perspective

We have added this qualitative material without dropping any quantitative material; for example, we have significantly expanded our listing of reference volumes for existing quantitative scales.

Chapter 6: Measurement

Again, we attempted to add a qualitative perspective without sacrificing any of the preexisting quantitative content. This has been achieved through:

- A new section at the end of the chapter examining the role of reliability and validity in qualitative research

Chapter 7: Constructing Measurement Instruments

In the previous edition, Chapter 7 focused exclusively on quantitative instruments, and we alerted students to material in later chapters covering the construction of qualitatively oriented instruments. In this edition, we have added quite a bit of material on constructing qualitative measures, most notably the following:

- Content on qualitative interviewing (moved from Chapter 12), including an illustration of a standardized open-ended interview schedule

- A box comparing quantitative and qualitative approaches to asking people questions.

We've also added a little more on culturally sensitive measurement in this chapter (as well as in the previous chapter).

Chapter 8: The Logic of Sampling

Most instructors seem to like this chapter as it is, although some recognize the need to say more about the circumstances under which the reliance on available subjects can be justified and about the implications of using available-subjects sampling in experiments. We have responded to that need in this edition. Other suggestions implemented in this edition include an elaboration of the explanation of Figure 8-6 (on the progression of sampling distributions) and an elaboration of factors influencing sample size (such as the number of variables). In keeping with our effort to add more qualitative/quantitative balance in this edition, we considered adding substantial content on qualitative sampling methods to this chapter. However, in view of the chapter's existing length and complexity, we opted to expand our coverage of qualitative sampling in Chapters 12 and 13, which focus on qualitative methods and already-covered qualitative sampling.

Chapter 9: Causal Inference and Group Designs

Given its topic, this chapter has been inescapably quantitative in focus and remains that way. The most significant changes to this chapter are:

- New sections on practical pitfalls in implementing group designs in agency settings and mechanisms for avoiding or alleviating those pitfalls, including the use of qualitative methods for that purpose

- A new box on the use of qualitative methods in experimental and quasi-experimental studies

Another new section provides an illustration of a quasi-experiment in social work (in a child welfare agency)—one that illustrates the nonequivalent control group design, a time-series component, and the practical pitfalls mentioned above. Other additions to this chapter include an elaboration in the chapter introduction of a framework for understanding the functions of these designs, clarification regarding the limited feasibility of blind raters in social work research, and a new section pointing out ways control groups are not denied services.

Chapter 10: Single-Subject Designs

The main change in this chapter is:

- A new section on the use of qualitative methods in single-case evaluation

Chapter 11: Survey Research

The most significant new feature in this chapter is:

- A box illustrating the complementarity of quantitative survey methods and qualitative methods and how combining the two enables us to benefit from the strengths of survey research while offsetting its weaknesses

We have also extended the discussion of the advantages and disadvantages of surveys with respect to external validity and sample size and internal validity and the time dimension. In the introduction, we have elaborated the historical context of surveys specifically in social work, giving more attention to the social survey movement and its precursors.

Chapter 12: Qualitative Research Methods

Our effort to achieve a better balance between qualitative and quantitative inquiry in this edition is reflected primarily in the qualitative content infused in chapters that previously were more quantitatively focused. We have also expanded our coverage of qualitative inquiry in this chapter by including the following:

- More content on ethnography

- A new section on relating to subjects

- Identification of additional computer programs for processing qualitative data

- Ways to look for patterns when analyzing qualitative data

- A new section on research ethics in field research

- An indication in the title of each illustration noting the particular qualitative methods emphasized in that illustration

- Three new illustrations, covering such methods as case study interviews, grounded theory, feminist research, and oral life history

- An extensive annotated list of additional readings at the end of the chapter, reflecting the emerging spate of literature and interest in qualitative inquiry

Chapter 13: Unobtrusive Research: Quantitative and Qualitative Methods

New material in this chapter includes a new section on conceptualization and the creation of code categories in content analysis, a new section on problems of validity in analyzing existing data, and a new box illustrating the use of existing data to assess the relative degree of suffering in nations around the world.

Chapter 14: Processing Data

We've updated this chapter a bit in regard to time-sharing, microcomputers, and the Internet (which we discuss at length in our new Appendix H). We've also deleted most of our discussion of outdated technology involving punched cards and counter-sorters.

Chapter 15: Interpreting Descriptive Statistics and Tables

Two major changes have been made in this chapter. They are:

- An extended discussion of the elaboration model so as to clarify the concepts of interpretation and suppressor variables

- A new section discussing how qualitative methods can be used to enhance the interpretation of descriptive statistics and how descriptive statistics can be used to enhance the interpretation of qualitative data

Chapters 16 and 17: Inferential Data Analysis

Feedback from colleagues suggested the need to change the sequencing of some of the material in these two chapters. Meta-analysis was moved from Chapter 16 to Chapter 17. Statistical power analysis was moved up to the beginning of Chapter 17. The section on the application of inferential statistics to single-subject designs was moved to a new Appendix I. Reference to a new Appendix J was added to enhance understanding of effect-size values in connection to z scores. Mention of the Bonferroni adjustment has been added regarding running multiple bivariate tests of significance. The most significant revision to these two chapters comes at the end of Chapter 17, where we have added:

- A box illustrating how combining qualitative and quantitative inquiry can help alleviate some problems in inferential data analysis

Chapter 18: Program Evaluation

In this final chapter we have continued to seek a better qualitative/quantitative balance. The most significant changes are:

- A section on process evaluation, including comments on the use of quantitative and qualitative methods in process evaluations
- Acknowledgment of qualitative sampling and qualitative interviewing in needs assessment
- A section on the use of the qualitative method involving focus groups in needs assessment
- A box on combining quantitative and qualitative methods in program evaluation

The other noteworthy revisions to this chapter extend and qualify our discussion of the politics of program evaluation. So that readers will not get the impression that program evaluation is almost always corrupted by political influences, we have added some comments to help readers develop a savvy, yet not cynical, outlook about the potential for corrupting influences as well as the potential for conducting objective and useful evaluations. A practice example, on an evaluation of a federally funded family preservation program, has been added to further illustrate how external evaluators are not immune to political forces. That example also is used in pointing out that following the steps we've recommended to anticipate and prevent resistance to program evaluation will not guarantee success; things can still go awry.

Appendixes

Four of the appendixes in this edition are new, as follows:

- Appendix G replaces our previous two appendixes on SPSS. In the previous edition we had separate SPSS appendixes for IBM compatible computers and for the Macintosh. The new appendix covers both types of computers. It also covers spreadsheet-style data entry and SPSS for Windows (which were missing in the previous edition).
- Appendix H, "Social Work Research and Cyberspace," shows readers how to use the Information Superhighway for research as well as other purposes.
- Appendix I covers the material applying inferential statistics to single-subject designs, which was moved out of Chapter 17.
- Appendix J displays effect-size values in z-score terms in connection with the proportion under normal curve exceeded by the effect-size value. We hope this display will facilitate understanding of the meaning and utility of effect sizes, since it shows, for any effect-size value, what proportion of control group outcomes are exceeded by the mean experimental group outcome.

We are very excited about this new edition of *Research Methods for Social Work* and think that the extensive amount of material that we have added will meet the needs of instructors and students seeking to keep up with advances in the field, seeking clearer and more thorough explanations of challenging concepts, and—in particular—seeking a better balance between qualitative and quantitative content. We hope you will find this new edition useful. We would like to receive any suggestions you might have for improving this book further. Please write to us in care of Brooks/Cole Publishing Company, 511 Forest Lodge Road, Pacific Grove, California 93950, or e-mail us at arubin@mail.utexas.edu.

ANCILLARY PACKAGE

Practice-Oriented Study Guide

Unlike our previous two editions, this edition is accompanied by a *Practice-Oriented Study Guide,* which parallels the organization of the main text but emphasizes its application to practice. It is designed to enhance student comprehension of the text material and to focus on applying that material to problems students are likely to encounter in social work practice. Each chapter of the *Practice-Oriented Study Guide* lists behavioral objectives for applying the chapter content to practice, a chapter summary that focuses on practice applications, multiple-choice review questions generally asked in the context of practice applications (with answers in an appendix accompanied by page references to the relevant text material), exercises involving practice applications that can be done in class (usually in small groups) or as homework, and practice-relevant discussion questions. In addition to enhancing student learning of research content, we hope that this *Study Guide* will significantly enhance the efforts we have made in the main text to foster student understanding of the relevance of research to practice and their consequent enthusiasm for re-

search. We also expect that this *Study Guide* will be helpful to instructors by providing them with practice-relevant exercises that can be done in class or as homework.

Instructor's Manual

As with previous editions, an *Instructor's Manual* mirrors the organization of the main text, offering our suggestions of teaching methods. Each chapter of the *Instructor's Manual* lists an outline of relevant discussion, behavioral objectives, teaching suggestions and resources, and test items. This *Instructor's Manual* is set up to allow instructors the freedom and flexibility needed to teach research methods courses.

The test questions for each chapter include approximately 15 to 20 multiple-choice items, 10 to 12 true-false items, and several essay questions that may be used for exams or to stimulate class discussion. Page references to the text are given for the multiple-choice and true-false questions. Test items are also available on disk in DOS, Macintosh, and Windows formats.

Data Disk

We have sought to provide up-to-date computer—and particularly microcomputer—support for students and instructors. Because there are now many excellent programs for analyzing data, we have provided data to be used with those programs. Specifically, we are providing data from the National Opinion Research Center's *General Social Survey,* offering students a variety of data from 1000 respondents around the country in 1980 and 1990. The disk is available on request to adopters of the text, in Macintosh and both IBM formats (3½″ or 5¼″ disk).

ACKNOWLEDGMENTS

We owe special thanks to the following colleagues who reviewed this edition and made valuable suggestions for improving it: Ram A. Cnaan, University of Pennsylvania; Kevin De Weaver, University of Georgia; Joan E. Esser-Stuart, University of Alabama; Trudy Festinger, New York University; Jane Gilgun, University of Minnesota; Jo Knox, University of Texas at Arlington; Lois Millner, Temple University; Trudy Ann Mitchell-Gilkey; Teresa Morris, California State University, San Bernardino; Cathy Pike, University of South Carolina at Columbia; Paul R. Raffoul, University of Houston; Albert R. Roberts, Rutgers University; Sylvia Rodriguez-Andrew, San Jose State University; Phyllis Solomon, University of Pennsylvania; Tony Tripodi, Ohio State University; and Joseph Wronka, Springfield College.

Additional thanks to Jeff Jacques for his assistance in presenting the most recent version of Appendix G and the data disk.

Thanks also go to Lisa Gebo, Social Work Editor at Brooks/Cole Publishing Company, who came up with some great ideas and offered immense support and guidance in helping us complete the rather extensive and challenging improvements for this edition. She deserves a great deal of the credit for what we think is the most valuable new feature of this new edition: its approach to integrating quantitative and qualitative methods. We also appreciate the efforts of her editorial assistant, Terry Thomas, and of Jamie Sue Brooks, senior production editor at Brooks/Cole, who went far beyond routine expectations in providing assistance. Dustine Davidson at The Book Company, our production service, has our thanks for her excellent work and attention to all the details of design and production.

Allen Rubin
Earl Babbie

The Importance of Social Work Research

Most social work students read research methods texts for only one reason—it is required. What's worse, it is required in a course they never wanted to take in the first place—a research course. Like many other students, you may be wondering why research courses are required for social work students. There is so much to learn about how to help people, and you are probably itching to learn it. Research methodology might be important for academic sociologists and psychologists, but with your still not fully developed skills in the art of helping, you might ask, "Why use up so much of social work education on research methods?"

To many social work students research seems cold, aloof, and mechanistic. These probably are not the types of qualities that attracted you to the social work field. Social work tends to be associated with qualities like warmth, involvement, compassion, humanism, and commitment. There are many social problems for you to tackle out in the real world, and you are probably eager to take action. In fact, your unique background, which perhaps spurred you to become a social worker, may have already led you to identify what particular problem area you are particularly eager or suited to deal with. You want to get on with it, but first you must clear this research hurdle. Welcome to the club!

You might be surprised at the proportion of social work researchers who started out feeling just the way you do. They may have entered the field wanting to become clinical practitioners, administrators, social planners, or community organizers, with no inkling whatsoever that someday they would become researchers. But somewhere along the way they discovered that our field lacks the knowledge base needed to achieve our humanistic

objectives and that without that knowledge base our good intentions are not enough. That is, they realized that we will be more effective practitioners when we learn more about what interventions really help or hinder the attainment of our noble goals. Thus, out of their compassion and commitment to change, they decided to put their efforts where they thought those efforts ultimately would do the most to help the people they cared about— in building our knowledge base.

Social work research and social work researchers are a breed apart from traditional stereotypes of academic research. Their aim is not to produce knowledge for knowledge's sake, but to provide the practical knowledge that social workers need to solve the problems they confront day in and day out. Ultimately, their aim is to give the field the information it needs to alleviate human suffering and promote social welfare. Thus, social work research seeks to accomplish the same humanistic goals as does social work practice, and like practice, social work research is a compassionate, problem solving, practical endeavor.

At this point you might say, "Okay, that's nice, but the odds that I am going to do research are still mighty slim." Very few social workers ever become researchers in the strict sense. But the odds are that during your career you will encounter numerous situations where you will use your research expertise and perhaps wish you had more of it. For example, you may be supervising a clinical program whose continued funding requires that you conduct a scientific evaluation of the effects it is having on clients. You may be a direct service practitioner who wants to use single-subject design methodology to evaluate scientifically your own effectiveness or the effects certain interventions are having on your clients. You may be a community organizer or planner who, as a guide to resource development, wants to conduct a scientific survey to assess the greatest needs extant in a community. You may be an administrator who, in order to be accountable to the public, must provide scientific documentation of whether your program is delivering the amount and type of service it was intended to deliver.

Chances are, though, that you remain skeptical. After all, this is a research text, and its authors may be expected to exaggerate the value of learning research methods. You might be thinking, "Even if I accept the notion that social work research is valuable, I still believe that the researchers should do their thing, and I'll do mine." But what will you do? The field remains quite uncertain as to what really works in many practice situations.

In 1973, Fischer jolted the social work profession with a review of the experimental research that had been conducted up to that point on the effectiveness of social casework. Only 11 studies met his selection criteria for inclusion in the review, which required that they be conducted in the United States after 1930, include a comparison of social work treatment groups with no-treatment or an alternative treatment group, and involve primarily professional caseworkers as providers of the social work treatment. Of the six studies that compared social work treatment to no-treatment, none found a significant effect for social work treatment. Of the five studies that compared social work treatment to an alternative form of treatment, three found little or no significant differences favoring social work, and two had methodological limitations that rendered their findings inconclusive. Based on this review, Fischer concluded that casework was not effective (Fischer, 1973).

Not surprisingly, many social workers did not like Fischer's conclusion. Some questioned the adequacy of the research methodology of the studies he reviewed. Others criticized the clarity or appropriateness of the interventions evaluated in the reviewed studies (Blythe and Briar, 1987). One such critic was Wood, who in 1978 published a review of 22 studies that included some of the studies Fischer reviewed as well as some others. (Her selection criteria were somewhat broader than Fischer's.) Yet the studies in Wood's review, too, tended to find that direct social work practice was not effective. Wood attempted to go beyond a general conclusion of ineffectiveness. She did so by postulating what was wrong with those interventions that had negative outcomes and what practice principles could be derived from those with more positive outcomes. But the overall thrust of the findings of the studies reviewed by Wood was much the same as in Fischer's review and provided little basis for optimism about direct practice effectiveness (Wood, 1978).

A more optimistic note was struck by Reid and Hanrahan (1982), who reviewed 22 experimental evaluations of direct practice effectiveness published between 1973 and 1979. All but a few of these more recent studies contained some positive findings about practice effectiveness. More grounds for optimism about the eventual development of effective interventions were provided by one of the authors of this text (Rubin, 1985), who reviewed 12 experiments published between 1978 and 1983. Unlike the earlier reviews, Rubin's review did not require that the evaluated interventions be delivered by social workers, and therefore his findings did not bear upon the debate as to whether direct social work practice had already achieved a sufficient degree of effectiveness. But since all of the studies he reviewed evaluated interventions attempting to achieve objectives that social workers strive to achieve, and since they all were delivered to clientele that concern the social work profession, his findings did bear upon the prospects for social workers ultimately to incorporate effective interventions in their practice. Of the 12 studies he reviewed, six had positive outcomes and sound research methods, three had positive outcomes but some questionable research methods, and three had equivocal outcomes.

Why the big difference between the findings of the newer and older studies (that is, between the older ones reviewed by Fischer and by Wood and the newer ones reviewed by Reid and Hanrahan and by Rubin)? Among the various proposed answers to this question, one is most prevalent. In many of the older studies, the evaluated interventions tended to be unspecific; casework could cover a variety of unexplicated methods. Implicitly some of the studies seemed to assume that the intervention could be defined as whatever a trained social worker does and that therefore when a group of trained social workers intervenes they are delivering the same (or at least a comparable) intervention. In contrast, the newer studies evaluated interventions that were well-explicated and highly specific about the problems they sought to resolve, the goals they sought to accomplish, and the procedures used to achieve those goals (Briar, 1987; Blythe and Briar, 1987).

The reviews just mentioned imply that it is not enough simply to be a trained social worker and therefore assume that whatever you do will be effective. If you approach your practice with that attitude, much of what you do might be ineffective. It makes a great deal of difference which particular interventions and procedures you employ to achieve which particular objectives with which particular types of clientele or problems. Moreover, social work practice consists largely of interventions and procedures that have not yet received adequate testing. Even those that have been evaluated and had positive outcomes may need additional testing before the evidence is sufficient to resolve prevailing doubt as to their effectiveness. Despite the grounds for optimism provided by the recent research reviews about the eventual development of effective forms of direct social work practice, this doubt is not likely to be resolved soon. In the face of this reality, knowledge of research methods becomes practice knowledge, too. For if we cannot say that whatever trained social workers do has demonstrated effectiveness, then learning how to recognize when particular interventions for particular prac-

tice situations have been supported by adequate scientific evidence becomes at least as important a guide to practice as is learning existing general practice methods that, despite being in vogue, may not always be effective.

But, you might ask, why can't we just let the researchers produce the needed studies and then tell the practitioners the results? Then the practitioners would only have to focus on the practice aspects of those interventions that receive adequate scientific support. In an ideal world that might not be a bad idea. But the real world is a lot messier. There is a vast range in the quality of social work research (as well as applied research in allied disciplines relevant to social work) that gets produced and published. Some of it is excellent; some of it probably should never have been accepted for publication. This unevenness has a variety of causes. Attributing it to varying degrees of competence in researchers is only a partial explanation. Many weak studies get produced not because their authors knew no better but because agency constraints would not permit them to conduct a stronger study. For example, later in this book you will learn the value of assigning clients to experimental and control conditions when assessing the effectiveness of interventions. During control conditions the interventions being tested are withheld from clients. Many agencies will not permit the use of control conditions in clinical research. (There are various practical reasons for this constraint—reasons we'll be examining in this text.) Consequently, researchers are faced with a dilemma: Either do the study under conditions of weak scientific rigor or forego doing the study. With no better alternative available, and in the belief that some limited evidence may be better than no evidence, they often will opt to do the study.

This situation means that if social work practitioners are going to be guided by the findings of social work research studies, they need to understand social work research methods well enough to discriminate those studies with adequate scientific methodologies and, therefore, credible findings, from those whose methodologies are so weak that their findings have little credibility. It also means that the quality of the social work research that gets produced ultimately depends not just on the methodological expertise of the researchers but also on the research knowledge of practitioners and the practice knowledge of researchers. Without a partnership between practice-oriented researchers and methodologically informed practitioners, there is not likely to be a climate of support in agencies for the type of research our field desperately needs—research that is on the one hand responsive to the real needs of agency practitioners and on the other hand done under conditions that permit an adequate level of methodological rigor. Even if you never produce any research, an understanding of research methods will help you critically utilize research produced by others, communicate with researchers to help ensure that their work is responsive to the needs of practice, and ultimately help foster an agency environment conducive to carrying out good and relevant studies.

Earlier we discussed the value of understanding research methods to be able to discriminate which studies are sufficiently credible to guide your practice. Another reason why social workers need to be able to critically evaluate the methodologies of published research is that researchers from outside social work occasionally publish findings that attack the entire social work profession and social welfare enterprise. These authors are not necessarily politically inspired or out to harm the people we care about. They may care about the people we are trying to help just as much as we do and may sincerely believe that social workers and social welfare policies are hurting them. These authors and their research often receive much notoriety in the popular media and are commonly cited by opponents of public welfare spending. A notable example is Charles Murray's book *Losing Ground* (1984), in which Murray compiled masses of data to argue that public social welfare programs developed to help the poor have actually hurt them more than helped them. Another is Christopher Lasch's work, such as *Haven in a Heartless World* (1977), which argued that social workers deliberately usurp parental functions and, in so doing, weaken families and exacerbate various social problems.

If books like these are correct in their logic and conclusions, then we commonly hurt the people we are trying to help and exacerbate the problems we are trying to alleviate. And if their logic or research methodology is faulty and their conclusions therefore erroneous, then it is our responsibility to the people we serve (which includes the public) to have the research expertise that enables us to point this out. Therefore, it is not necessarily out of a concern for professional self-preservation but out of our concern for our clients that we be able to consider arguments and evidence of these critics on equal grounds—not as a profession of anti-scientific practitioners whose disregard for methodological principles forces us to let others decide for us whether our clients would be better off if we all went out of business. Indeed, if we are unable to do so, then we really do not quality to call ourselves "professionals" in the first place.

Being professional involves a number of things. One is that we strive to make sure that we provide our clients the most effective services available. How do we do that? Do we just ask our supervisors what they think is best? That may be a starting point, but the practitioner who just conforms to ongoing practices without keeping abreast of the latest research in his or her field is not doing all possible to see that his or her clients get the best possible service. Indeed, well-established, traditional social work services have often been found to be ineffective, as indicated in the reviews of practice effectiveness mentioned earlier.

Given the frequency with which social work services have been found to be ineffective and the recent emergence of studies identifying new interventions that appear to be effective, failure to keep abreast of the research in one's field is a serious matter. In the face of the scarcity of findings supporting the efficacy of social work intervention, and in particular the lack of support for the notion that whatever trained social workers do is effective, we cannot justify disregarding the latest research with the rationalization that we are too busy helping people. If our services have not been tested for their effects on clients, the chances are that we are not really helping anyone. If that is the case, then who benefits from our blind faith in conventional, but untested, practice wisdom? Not our clients. Not those who pay for our services. Not society. Do we? In one sense, perhaps. That is, it is less work for us if we just unquestioningly perpetuate ongoing practices. That way we do not make any waves. We do not have to think as much. Not reading research means there is one less task in our daily grind. In the long run, however, practitioners who keep up on the research, and who consequently know they are doing everything possible to make sure they are providing the best possible services to their clients, might experience more job satisfaction and be less vulnerable to burnout.

But the main reason to utilize research is not to meet our own needs to be professional or for job satisfaction. The main reason is compassion for our clients. It is because we care about helping our clients that we seek scientific evidence about the effects of the services we are providing them or of alternative services that might help them more. If the services we provide are not effective, and if others are, then we are harming our clients by perpetuating our current services. That is, we are wasting their time (and perhaps money) allowing their problems to go on without the best possible treatment and, by our inattentiveness to the literature, denying them a service opportunity that has a better chance of helping them.

This point can be illustrated using an example of a highly regarded and often cited piece of social work research in the field of mental health. During the 1970s, Gerard Hogarty (an MSW-level social worker) and his associates conducted a series of field experiments on the effectiveness of drug therapy and psychosocially oriented social casework in preventing relapse and in enhancing community adjustment in the aftercare of formerly hospitalized patients suffering from schizophrenia (Hogarty, 1979). They found that drug therapy alone was very effective in forestalling relapse, but it had no effect on community adjustment. Social casework by itself had no influence on relapse. The best results on community adjustment were found for those patients who received drug therapy *and* social casework combined. However, the group of patients who received social casework alone, and no drugs, fared worse than the group who received no treatment whatsoever! Hogarty and his associates reasoned that this was due to the tendency of people suffering from schizophrenia to be unable to cope with the increased cognitive stimulation and expectations associated with psychosocial casework. The physiologic effects of drug therapy, among other benefits, improved their ability to handle the stimulation of psychosocial casework and benefit from it. But without the drug therapy, they were better off without the casework!

Now suppose that at the time this research was published you were a practitioner or an administrator in an aftercare program whose caseload consisted primarily of persons with the diagnosis of schizophrenia. Chances are that program may have been traditionally oriented toward emphasizing drug treatment without an intensive casework component like the one Hogarty and his associates evaluated. Perhaps there was no comprehensive social treatment effort, or perhaps there was an untested one that did not resemble the above tested one. If so, then your services may have been making no impact on your clients' levels of community adjustment. Had you utilized the research, you would be in a much better position to realize this and do something to improve it. On the other hand, perhaps the emphasis in your program was on a psychosocial casework approach like the one Hogarty and his colleagues evaluated, but with little or no systematic effort to ensure that patients were taking prescribed psychotropic drugs. In that case, the preceding findings would have suggested that your program may have been having a harmful effect on some clients, but one which could be turned into a beneficial effect if you had bothered to utilize the research and modified your services in keeping with its findings (that is, by adding a systematic drug therapy component or by monitoring medication compliance more persistently).

The preceding example illustrates rather clearly that understanding research methods, to be able to utilize research discriminatingly, has much to do with basic social work values like caring and compassion. The practitioner who goes through the trouble of understanding and using such research exhibits more concern for the welfare of his or her clients, and ultimately is more helpful to clients, than the one who justifies not taking that trouble on the basis of erroneous stereotypes about research. To better understand this point, sometimes it helps to put yourself in the shoes of the client system. Suppose a beloved member of your immediate family were to develop schizophrenia. Imagine the family trauma and concern that would ensue. Now, suppose that relative were being released to an aftercare program after a period of hospitalization. Imagine the anxiety you and the rest of your family would have about your loved one's prospective plight in the community. Now imagine the outrage you would feel if, after your relative had to be rehospitalized for failing to adjust in the community, you were to learn of Hogarty's research and discover that your relative received only social casework or only drug therapy (but not the two in combination) because the program staff never bothered to utilize the research. How compassionate would those staff members seem to you? Chances are, the adjectives you might use to describe them would sound more like the ones that they might use to describe research (cold, uncaring, aloof, mechanistic, dehumanized, and so on).

But studies on the effects of social work interventions comprise just one prominent example of useful social work research. A long list of other examples of completed research studies could be cited to convey the value of research to social work and why it is important for students preparing to become social work practitioners to know research methods so they can utilize and contribute to the production of such research. Many of these studies will be cited as illustrations of the methodological concepts addressed throughout this text.

Countless examples also can be cited of additional topics on which you, in your chosen practice role, may someday want to see research findings. Only a few will be cited here, as follows: Why do so many of your agency's clients terminate treatment prematurely? What types of clients do and do not drop out of treatment? What reasons do they give? What services did they receive? How satisfied were they with those services? What proportion of time do practitioners in your agency spend on different practice roles? Do they spend too much time performing functions from which they derive relatively high gratification and too little time on functions that are less attractive but more needed by clients? What characteristics of social service volunteers best predict how long they will continue to volunteer? What can you do to orient them, train them, or reward them that will be the most effective in reducing volunteer turnover? In what part of your target community or region should you locate your outreach efforts? Where are you most likely to engage hard-to-reach individuals such as the homeless or recent immigrants? Why do so many homeless individuals refuse to stay in shelters, sleeping instead on the streets? What are their experiences when they stay in a shelter, and what is staying in a shelter like from their point of view? What proportion of your target population does not understand English? Why are so few ethnic minorities being served by your agency? What does your agency mean to them; what is the agency atmosphere like from their viewpoint? As we have implied, we could go on and on. But you get the idea; the possibilities are endless.

The value to practitioners of learning research methods is not limited to the utilization of research studies. Practitioners will also find value in utilizing research methods as part of their face-to-face contact with people, especially for purposes of treatment planning. For example, in the assessment phase practitioners collect clinical data from various individuals. The research concepts they learn regarding such topics as sources of measurement error, reliability and validity, and the principles of sampling will help them evaluate the quality and meaning of the clinical data they collect and will help them plan to collect those data in ways that enhance their quality. Practitioners need to examine the conditions and situations under which they collect information as part of their practice in the same way and for the same reasons as when one systematically collects data as part of a formal research study.

Finally, there is the question of ethics. Ethics is one of the most important concerns of social workers as they consider research, and it is a topic that is discussed throughout this book. One argument as to why research is important to social work practitioners is that the Code of Ethics of the National Association of Social Workers refers to social workers' responsibility to contribute to the knowledge base of the profession. In short, our professional association does not consider us completely ethical unless we try to help develop the knowledge base.

The Code of Ethics also refers to our responsibility for utilizing the knowledge base as part of our practice, a theme that has been emphasized throughout this prologue. When we utilize research discriminatingly, we help uphold and advance the values and mission of the profession and thus are more ethical in our practice than we would be if we did not so utilize research. But social work students nevertheless quite commonly approach the area of research methodology with considerable skepticism about the ethics of many research studies. We will be addressing those ethical concerns in various chapters of the book, not just in the chapter devoted entirely to ethics. We hope that by the time you finish reading this book, you will have a better understanding not only of the ethical dilemmas involved in social work research but also of the reasons why our professional code of ethics bears upon our responsibility to understand, utilize, and contribute to research.

Perhaps more than ever before, social work research offers an opportunity for all social workers to make a difference in the problems they will confront. Attempting to understand research methods can be challenging and at times frustrating. We invite you to take on this challenge and stick with it. Perhaps you will understand some concepts more than others. That is okay. If some chapters set you back, be resilient. Remember, the ultimate reason you are required to read this book is because you care about helping people!

PART

1

An Introduction
to Inquiry

1
Human Inquiry and Science

2
Theory and Research

3
The Ethics and Politics of Social Work Research

Science is a word everyone uses. Yet people's images of science vary greatly.
For some, science is mathematics; for others, it is white coats and laboratories.
The word is often confused with technology or equated with challenging high
school or college courses.

Science is, of course, none of these things per se. It is difficult, however,
to specify exactly what science is. Scientists would disagree on the proper definition. For the purposes of this book, we will look at science as a method of
inquiry—a way of learning and knowing things about the world around us.
Contrasted with other ways of learning and knowing about the world, science

has some special characteristics. We'll examine these traits in this opening set of chapters.

Dr. Benjamin Spock, the renowned author-pediatrician, begins his books on child care by assuring new mothers that they already know more about child care than they think they do. We want to begin this book on social work research methods on the same note. It will become clear to you before you've read very far that you *do* know a great deal about the practice of social scientific research already. In fact, you've been conducting scientific research all your life. From that perspective, the purpose of this book is to assist you in sharpening skills you already have and perhaps to show you some tricks that may not have occurred to you.

Part 1 is intended to lay the groundwork for the rest of the book by examining the fundamental characteristics and issues that make science different from other ways of knowing things. In Chapter 1, we'll begin with a look at natural human inquiry, the sort of thing you've been doing all your life. We'll see some of the ways people go astray in trying to understand the world around them, and we'll summarize the primary characteristics of scientific inquiry that guard against those errors.

Chapter 2 deals specifically with social scientific inquiry, the structure and creation of social scientific theories, and the links between theory and research. The lessons of Chapter 1 are applied in the study of human social behavior. You will discover that, although special considerations arise in studying people, the basic logic of all science is the same.

In Chapter 3 we'll examine some of the special considerations that arise in studying people. This chapter will establish an ethical and political context for the discussions of research methods in the remaining chapters.

The overall purpose of Part 1 is to construct a backdrop against which to view more specific aspects of research design and execution. By the time you complete Part 1, you should be ready to look at some of the more concrete aspects of social work research.

CHAPTER

Human Inquiry
and Science

What You'll Learn in This Chapter

We'll examine the way people learn about their
world and the mistakes they make along the way.
We'll also begin to see what makes science
different from other ways of knowing things.

INTRODUCTION

This book is about knowing things. Although you will probably come away from the book knowing some things you don't know right now, our primary purpose is to assist you in looking at *how* you know things, not at what you know. Let's start by examining a few things you probably know already.

You probably know you have to breathe to live. Obviously, if you stopped breathing, you'd die. You probably also know it's cold on the dark side of the moon, and you know people speak Chinese in China.

How do you know? If you reflect on it for a minute, you'll see you know these things because somebody told them to you and you believed what you were told. You may have read in the *National Geographic* that people speak Chinese in China, and that made sense to you, so you didn't question it. Perhaps your physics or astronomy instructor told you it was cold on the dark side of the moon, or maybe you read it in *Newsweek*. That's how you know.

Some of the things you know seem absolutely obvious to you. If asked how you knew you have to breathe to live, you'd probably say, "Everybody knows that." There are a lot of things everybody knows. Everybody knows the world is round, for example. Of course, at one time, everyone "knew" the world was flat. Much of what you know is a matter of agreement and belief. Little of it is based on personal experience and discovery. A big part of growing up in any society, in fact, is the process of learning to accept what everybody around you "knows" is so. If you don't know the same things, you can't really be part of the group. If you were to seriously question whether you have to breathe to live, you'd quickly find yourself set apart from other people.

Although it's important for you to see that most of what you know is a matter of believing what you've been told, there's nothing wrong with you in that respect. That's simply the way we've structured human societies. The fundamental basis of knowledge is agreement. Because you couldn't learn all those things through personal experience and discovery alone, we've set things up so you can simply believe what others tell you.

There are other ways of knowing things, however. In contrast to knowing things through agreement, it is also possible to know things through direct experience—through observation. If you dive into a glacial stream flowing down through the Canadian Rockies, you don't need anyone to tell you it's cold. You notice that all by yourself. The first time you stepped on a thorn, you knew that hurt even before anyone told you.

TWO REALITIES

Ultimately, you live in a world of two realities. Part of what you know could be called your *experiential reality:* the things you know as a function of your direct experience. Another part could be called your *agreement reality:* things you consider real because you've been told they're real, and everyone else seems to agree they are real. The first is a product of your own experience; the second is a product of what people have told you. The problem is that both seem very real.

Let's take an example. Imagine you've come to a party. It's a high-class affair, and the drinks and food are excellent. In particular, you are taken by one of the appetizers the host brings around on a tray. It's a breaded, deep-fried appetizer with an especially zesty taste. You have a couple, and they are delicious! You have more. Soon you are subtly moving around the room so as to be wherever the host arrives with a tray of these nibblies.

Finally, you can't contain yourself any more. "What are they?" you ask. "How can I get the recipe?" And the host lets you in on the secret: "You've been eating breaded, deep-fried *worms*!" Your response is dramatic: your stomach rebels, and you promptly throw up all over the living room rug. Awful! What a terrible thing to serve guests!

The point of the story is that both feelings about the appetizer would be very real. Your initial liking for them was certainly real, but so was the feeling you had when you found out what you'd been eating. It should be evident, however, that the feeling of disgust you had when you discovered you were eating worms would be strictly a product of the agreements you have with those around you that worms aren't fit to eat. That's an agreement you began the first time your parents found you sitting in a pile of dirt with half of a wriggling worm dangling from your lips. You learned worms were not kosher in our society when they pried your mouth open and reached down your throat in search of the other half of the worm.

Aside from the agreements we have, what's wrong with worms? They are probably high in protein and low in calories. Bite-sized and easily packaged, they are a distributor's dream. They are also a delicacy for some people who live in societies that lack our agreement that worms are disgusting. Some people might love the worms but would be turned off by the deep-fried breadcrumb crust.

Reality, then, is a tricky business. How can you really know what's real? People have grappled with that question for thousands of years. Science is one of the strategies that have arisen out of that grappling.

Science offers an approach to both agreement reality and experiential reality. Scientists have certain criteria that must be met before they will accept the reality of something they haven't personally experienced. In general, an assertion must have both *logical* and *empirical* support: it must make sense, and it must align with observations in the world. Why do earthbound scientists accept the assertion that it's cold on the dark side of the moon? First, it makes sense, since the surface heat of the moon comes from the sun's rays. Second, the scientific measurements made on the moon's dark side confirm the expectation. So, scientists accept the reality of things they don't personally experience—they accept an agreement reality—but they have special standards for doing so.

More to the point of this book, however, science offers a special approach to the discovery of reality through personal experience. It offers a special approach to the business of inquiry. *Epistemology* is the science of knowing; *methodology* (a subfield of epistemology) might be called "the science of finding out." This book is an examination and presentation of social science methodology applied to social work, and we're going to concern ourselves with how that methodology helps solve problems in social work and social welfare. In the remainder of this chapter, we're going to look at inquiry as an activity. We'll begin by examining inquiry as a natural human activity. It is something we have engaged in every day of our lives. Next, we'll look at some kinds of errors we make in normal inquiry, and we'll conclude by examining what makes science different. We'll see some of the ways science guards against the common human errors in inquiry.

NATURAL HUMAN INQUIRY

Practically all people, and many nonhuman animals as well, exhibit a desire to predict their future circumstances. We seem quite willing, moreover, to undertake this task using *causal* and *probabilistic reasoning*. First, we generally recognize that future circumstances are somehow *caused* or conditioned by present ones. We learn that getting an education will affect how much money we earn later in life and that swimming beyond the reef may bring an unhappy encounter with a shark. Sharks, on the other hand, may learn that hanging around the reef may bring a happy encounter with unhappy swimmers. As students we learn that studying hard will result in better examination grades.

Second, people, and seemingly other animals, also learn that such patterns of cause and effect are *probabilistic* in nature: the effects occur more often when the causes occur than when the causes are absent—but not always. Thus, students learn that studying hard produces good grades in most instances, but not every time. We recognize the danger of swimming beyond the reef without believing that every such swim will be fatal. Social workers learn that being abused as children makes people more likely to become abusive parents later on, but not all parents who were abused as children become abusive themselves. They also learn that severe mental illness makes one vulnerable to becoming homeless, but not all adults with severe mental illnesses become homeless.

We will return to these concepts of causality and probability throughout the book. As we'll see, science makes them more explicit and provides techniques for dealing with them more rigorously than does casual human inquiry. It is these qualities that most distinguish science from casual inquiry. What we want to do, then, is to sharpen skills you already have, making you more conscious, rigorous, and explicit in your inquiries.

In looking at natural human inquiry, it is important to distinguish between prediction and understanding. Often, we are able to predict without understanding—you may be able to predict rain when your trick knee aches. And often, even if we don't understand why, we are willing to act on the basis of a demonstrated predictive ability. The racetrack buff who finds that the third-ranked horse in the third race of the day always wins will probably keep betting without knowing, or caring, why it works out that way.

Whatever the primitive drives or instincts that motivate human beings and other animals, satisfying them depends heavily on the ability to predict future circumstances. For humans, however, the attempt to predict is often placed in a context of knowledge and understanding. If you can understand why things are related to one another, why certain regular patterns occur, you can predict even better than if you simply observe and remember those patterns. Thus, human inquiry aims at answering both what and why questions, and we pursue these goals by observing and figuring out.

As we suggested earlier in the chapter, our attempts to learn about the world are only partly linked to direct, personal inquiry or experience. Another, much larger, part comes from the agreed-on knowledge that others give us. This agreement reality both assists and hinders our attempts to find out for ourselves. Two important sources of our secondhand knowledge—tradition and authority—deserve brief consideration here.

Tradition

Each of us inherits a culture made up, in part, of firmly accepted knowledge about the workings of the world. We may learn from others that planting corn in the spring will gain the greatest assistance from the gods, that sugar from too much candy will cause tooth decay, that the circumference of a circle is approximately twenty-two sevenths of its diameter, or that masturbation will blind us. We may test a few of these "truths" on our own, but we simply accept the great majority of them. These are the things that "everybody knows."

Tradition, in this sense of the term, has some clear advantages for human inquiry. By accepting what everybody knows, you are spared the overwhelming task of starting from scratch in your search for regularities and understanding. Knowledge is cumulative, and an inherited body of information and understanding is the jumping-off point for the development of more knowledge. We often speak of "standing on the shoulders of giants"—that is, on the shoulders of previous generations.

At the same time, tradition may be detrimental to human inquiry. If you seek a fresh and different understanding of something that everybody already understands and has always understood, you may be seen as a fool. More to the point, it will probably never occur to you to seek a different understanding of something that is already understood and obvious.

When you enter your first job as a professional social worker, you may learn about your agency's preferred intervention approaches. (If you have begun the field placement component of your professional education, you may have already experienced this phenomenon.) Chances are you will feel good about receiving instructions about "how we do things in this agency." You may be anxious about beginning to work with real cases and relieved that you won't have to choose between competing theories to guide what you do with clients. In conforming to agency traditions you may feel that you have a head start, benefiting from the accumulated "practice wisdom" of previous generations of practitioners in your new work setting. And indeed you do; after all, how many recently graduated social workers are in a better position than experienced agency staff to determine the best intervention approaches in their agency?

But the downside of this situation is that you can become too comfortable conforming to traditional practice wisdom. You may never think to look for evidence that the traditional approaches are really as effective as everyone believes they are or for evidence concerning whether some alternative approaches are more effective. And if you do seek and find such evidence, you may find that agency traditions make your colleagues unreceptive to the new information you have found.

Authority

Despite the power of tradition, new knowledge appears every day. Aside from your personal inquiries, throughout your life you will be the beneficiary of new discoveries and understandings produced by others. Often, acceptance of these new acquisitions will depend on the status of the discoverer. You're more likely to believe the epidemiologist who declares that the common cold can be transmitted through kissing, for example, than to believe a layperson.

Like tradition, authority can both assist and hinder human inquiry. For example, inquiry is hindered when we depend on the authority of experts speaking outside their realm of expertise. The advertising industry plays heavily on this misuse of authority by having popular athletes discuss the nutritional value of breakfast cereals, by having movie actors evaluate the performance of automobiles, and by using other similar tactics. It is better to trust the judgment of the person who has special training, expertise, and credentials in the matter, especially in the face of contradictory

positions on a given question. At the same time, inquiry can be greatly hindered by the legitimate authority who errs within his or her own special province. Biologists, after all, do make mistakes in the field of biology. Biological knowledge changes over time. So does social work knowledge.

A social work–related example of how our knowledge changes over time, and of how traditional wisdom or authorities can be wrong, is discussed by Angus M. Strachan (1986) and Cassandra E. Simon and her associates (1991). Several decades ago authorities in psychoanalysis and family therapy blamed faulty parenting as a prime cause of schizophrenia. They commonly portrayed the mothers of individuals who became afflicted with schizophrenia as "schizophrenigenic mothers" whose cold, domineering, and overprotective behavior did not permit the child to develop an individual identity. Similar prominent ideas in vogue at that time blamed schizophrenia on such factors as parental discord, excessive familial interdependency, and mothers who give contradictory messages that repeatedly put their child in a "double-bind" situation.

Despite a lack of compelling research evidence to support these concepts, they achieved widespread acceptance among mental health practitioners. As a result, clinicians often dealt with the family as a cause of the problem and did not develop treatment alliances with them. Rather than provide support to families, clinicians often acted as the advocate of the client against the harmful influences of the family. Family therapists sought to help the parents see that the problem did not reside in the identified patient, but in a dysfunctional family system. Although family therapists did not intentionally seek to induce guilt or in other ways hurt these parents, many parents nonetheless reported feeling a sense of self-recrimination for their offspring's illness. As you can imagine, this was painful for many parents to "learn," particularly in view of the pain parents normally must live with knowing how ill their once-normal son or daughter has become, and perhaps having to care for the child after he or she has reached adulthood.

If you have recently taken some courses on psychopathology, you probably know that current scientific evidence indicates that genetic and other biological factors play an important role in the causation of schizophrenia. Although environmental stress also may be important, the evidence does not support the notion that treating the schizophrenia as a result of bad parenting is helpful. Indeed, such treatment may be harmful. By inducing guilt among family members, the negative emotional intensity in the family may be exacerbated. This in turn may make it more difficult for family members to provide the proper level of support and stimulation for their sick members, whose vulnerability to relapse seems to be worsened when they are exposed to high levels of environmental stress and overstimulation. Moreover, current theories recognize that undesirable family characteristics may be the *result* of the burden of living with a family member who has schizophrenia rather than the cause of the illness. Consequently, new treatment approaches have been designed (usually called *psychoeducational* approaches) that are aimed at building alliances with families and being more supportive of them.

The point of this review is that knowledge accepted on the authority of legitimate and highly regarded experts can be incorrect, and perhaps harmful, and it is therefore important that social work practitioners be open to new discoveries that might challenge the cherished beliefs of their respected supervisors or favorite theorists. It is also important to keep an open mind about the new knowledge that displaces the old. It, too, may be flawed, no matter how prestigious its founders are. Who knows? Perhaps some day we'll even find evidence that the currently out-of-favor ideas about parental causation of schizophrenia had some merit after all. In light of current evidence, that prospect may seem highly unlikely. But the point is that in taking a scientific approach to knowledge, we try to remain objective and open to new discoveries, no matter how much they may conflict with the traditional wisdom or current authorities. (As we discuss at length else-

where in this chapter and in Chapter 3, being objective may be an impossible ideal to attain; the point here is that we try not to close our minds to new ideas that might conflict with tradition and authority.)

Both tradition and authority, then, are two-edged swords in the search for knowledge about the world. Simply put, they provide us with a starting point for our own inquiry, but they may lead us to start at the wrong point and push us off in the wrong direction.

ERRORS IN PERSONAL INQUIRY

Aside from the potential dangers of tradition and authority, we often stumble and fall down when we set out to learn for ourselves. We are going to mention some of the common errors we make in our casual inquiries and look at the ways science provides safeguards against those errors.

Inaccurate Observation

The keystone of inquiry is observation. We can never understand the way things are without first having something to understand. We have to know *what* before we can explain *why*. On the whole, however, we are sloppy, even unconscious, observers of the flow of events in life. Recall, for example, the last person you talked to today. What kind of shoes was that person wearing? Are you even certain the person was wearing shoes? On the whole, we are pretty casual in observing things, and as a result we make mistakes. We fail to observe things right in front of us and mistakenly observe things that aren't so.

An American tourist in France may be treated rudely by several strangers and conclude that the French are rude, even though the offenders were actually German tourists. A meteor streaking across the sky may be mistaken for a flying saucer and held responsible for the earthquake that occurs the following day.

In contrast to casual human inquiry, scientific observation is a *conscious activity*. Simply making observation more deliberate helps to reduce error.

You probably don't recall, for example, what your instructor was wearing the first day of this class. If you had to guess now, you'd probably make a mistake. If you had gone to the first class meeting with a conscious plan to observe and record what your instructor was wearing, however, you'd have been more accurate.

In many cases, both simple and complex measurement devices help to guard against inaccurate observations. Moreover, they add a degree of precision well beyond the capacity of the unassisted human senses. Suppose, for example, that you had taken color photographs of your instructor that day.

Overgeneralization

When we look for patterns among the specific things we observe around us, we often assume that a few similar events are evidence of a general pattern. Probably the tendency to overgeneralize is greatest when the pressure to arrive at a general understanding is high. Yet it also occurs casually in the absence of pressure. Whenever overgeneralization does occur, it can misdirect or impede inquiry.

Imagine you are a reporter covering an antinuclear demonstration. You have orders to turn in your story in just two hours, and you need to know why the demonstrators are demonstrating. Rushing to the scene, you start interviewing demonstrators, asking them for their reasons. If the first two demonstrators you interview give you essentially the same reason, you may simply assume that the other 3000 are demonstrating for that reason.

The current rage for welfare reform among politicians, pundits, and much of the U.S. electorate today shows many signs of overgeneralization. Mothers on AFDC are stereotyped as being lazy and otherwise characterologically and morally flawed. They are depicted as poor role models and consequently blamed for juvenile crime and a host of other ills. Politicians seeking to reduce welfare spending cite stereotypes like "welfare queens" driving Cadillacs and trading their food stamps for money to buy liquor or other socially unacceptable items. By harping on these stereotypes, they stimulate the public to overgeneralize about welfare recipients and about the extent to which welfare spending is at the root of many social problems.

Scientists guard against overgeneralization by committing themselves in advance to a sufficiently large sample of observations (see Chapter 8). The **replication*** of inquiry provides another safeguard. Basically, this means repeating a study, checking to see if the same results are produced each time. Then the study may be repeated under slightly varied conditions. Thus, when a social work researcher discovers that a particular program of service in a particular setting is effective, that is only the beginning. Is the service equally effective for all types of clients? For both men and women? For both old and young? Among all ethnic groups? Would it be just as effective in other agency settings? This extension of the inquiry seeks to find the breadth and the limits of the generalization about the program's effectiveness.

Totally independent replications by other researchers extend the safeguards. Suppose you read a study that shows an intervention to be effective. Later, you might conduct a study of your own. You would study different clients, and perhaps you'd measure effectiveness somewhat differently. If your independent study produced exactly the same conclusion as the one you read, you would feel more confident in the generalizability of the relationship. If you obtained somewhat different results or found a subgroup of clients among whom it didn't hold at all, you'd have helped save us from overgeneralizing.

Selective Observation

One danger of overgeneralization is that it may lead to selective observation. Once you have concluded that a particular pattern exists and have developed a general understanding of why, you

---

*Words in boldface are defined in the Glossary at the end of the book.

will be tempted to pay attention to future events and situations that correspond with the pattern and ignore those that don't. Racial and ethnic prejudices depend heavily on selective observation for their persistence.

Suppose you were once cheated by a shopkeeper you thought to be Jewish. You might conclude from that one event that Jewish shopkeepers are dishonest. Subsequently, you'd probably take special note of dishonest actions by other Jewish shopkeepers, while ignoring honest Jews and dishonest non-Jews. Some people take special note of all the lazy blacks they come across and ignore energetic blacks and lazy whites. Others notice irrational and emotional women while overlooking stable women as well as unstable men.

The same goes for the way many people not on welfare perceive welfare recipients. Imagine what happens when people with a bias against welfare spending wait in the checkout line at the supermarket behind a mother with a fistful of food stamps. What do you think they are most likely to notice, remember, and discuss later at a cocktail party? The nutritious necessities in the mother's shopping cart? Or the unhealthy and unnecessary items? Likewise, if on their next trip to the supermarket they see another food stamp recipient purchasing nothing but nutritious items, are they as likely to remember that person and discuss them at their next cocktail party?

Selective observation occurs among all of us, not just among people with distasteful prejudices. Social work practitioners who have great compassion for their clients and who do the best they can to help their clients, for example, commonly engage in selective observation in ways that may limit their effectiveness. The practitioner trained to interpret problems in terms of family communication dynamics is apt to look vigilantly for signs of potential communication problems and then magnify the role those problems play in explaining the presenting problem. At the same time, that practitioner is likely to overlook other dynamics, or perhaps to underestimate their impact.

Usually, a research design will specify in advance the number and kind of observations to be made as a basis for reaching a conclusion. If we wanted to learn whether women were more likely than men to support the pro-choice position on abortion, we'd commit ourselves to making a specified number of observations on that question in a research project. We might select a thousand people to be interviewed on the issue. Even if the first ten women supported the pro-choice position and the first ten men opposed it, we'd interview everyone selected for the study and recognize and record each observation. Then we'd base our conclusion on an analysis of all the observations.

There is a second safeguard against selective observation in science that also works against most of the other pitfalls. If you overlook something that contradicts your conclusion about the way things are, your colleagues will notice it and bring it to your attention. That's a service scientists provide to one another and to the enterprise of science itself. The box titled "Popular Press Reporting of Social Science Research" exemplifies the practice of scientists checking on the representativeness of the observations on which research findings are based.

Made-Up Information

Sometimes you just can't ignore the events that contradict your general conclusions about the way things are. Suppose, for example, you had decided that all Jewish shopkeepers were dishonest, and then one of them walked four miles to return the wallet you left on the store counter. What would you do? In our casual, day-to-day handling of such matters, we often make up information that would resolve the contradiction. Maybe the shopkeeper isn't really Jewish after all. Or maybe the shopkeeper was just casing your house with a later burglary in mind.

Perhaps that hard-working and energetic African American at work is just trying to get promoted to a soft executive post. Perversely, people often doubt the general femininity of the woman who is tough-minded, logical, and unemotional in getting the job done. Concluding that she's not really a woman protects the general conclusion that women are irrational and flighty.

In social work practice, we may depict as unmotivated those clients who fail to respond to our cherished intervention model, rather than question the applicability of the model. Or we might say that the intervention would have worked better if we only had more resources and more time to provide it.

Just as we make up probable information in our day-to-day inquiries as a way of explaining away confusion, scientists engaged in scientific inquiry do also. When our scientific observations and analyses don't turn out the way we expect, we often think up reasons to explain away the surprise.

Ex Post Facto Hypothesizing

Suppose you run an outreach program for battered women still living with the batterer, and you have the idea that if your program is successful, soon after entering treatment the battered women should start feeling more positive about themselves as individuals and about their capacity to be less dependent on the batterer. You might test the program's effectiveness by conducting a brief structured interview with clients several times before and after they enter treatment. In the interview, you'd find out (1) how good they feel about themselves and (2) how capable they feel they are of living independently away from the batterer. You'd then examine whether they feel better or more capable after entering treatment than before entering it. But suppose their answers are the opposite of what you expected—that is, suppose they express worse feelings after entering treatment than before. What a disappointment. "Aha!" you might say. "The reason for the negative findings is that before entering treatment the women were unconsciously protecting themselves with the psychological defense mechanism of denial. They expressed better feelings before treatment because they were refusing

to face the dangerous and deplorable situation they were in. Our treatment helped overcome some of this denial and helped them get more in touch with an unpleasant reality they need to face in order to begin trying to change. Therefore, the more 'negative' responses after entering treatment are really more 'positive'! It is good that they are beginning to recognize what bad shape they were in; that's the first step in trying to improve it."

The example we've just described is sometimes called *ex post facto hypothesizing,* and it's perfectly acceptable in science *if it doesn't stop there.* The argument you proposed clearly suggests that you need to test your hypothesis about the program's effectiveness in new ways among a broader spectrum of people. The line of reasoning doesn't prove your hypothesis is correct, only that there's still some hope for it. Later observations may prove its accuracy. Thus, scientists often engage in deducing information, and they follow up on their deductions by looking at the facts again.

Illogical Reasoning

There are other ways of handling observations that contradict our conclusions about the way things are. Surely one of the most remarkable creations of the human mind is "the exception that proves the rule." That idea doesn't make any sense at all. An exception can draw attention to a rule or to a supposed rule, but in no system of logic can it prove the rule it contradicts. Yet we often use this pithy saying to brush away contradictions with a simple stroke of illogic.

What statisticians have called the *gambler's fallacy* is another illustration of illogic in day-to-day reasoning. A consistent run of either good or bad luck is presumed to foreshadow its opposite. An evening of bad luck at poker may kindle the belief that a winning hand is just around the corner, and many a poker player has lost more money because of that mistaken belief. Or, conversely, an extended period of good weather may lead you to worry that it is certain to rain on the weekend picnic.

POPULAR PRESS REPORTING OF SOCIAL SCIENCE RESEARCH

by William R. Todd-Mancillas, Department of Human Communication, Rutgers University

The public learns much about science in newspapers and magazines, but these popular media cannot be relied upon to provide accurate or complete information. Take, for instance, the article written in the *National Enquirer* entitled "Hairy Men Are Smarter." This is how the reporter, Dick Robinson, described the study done by a staff psychiatrist at the St. Louis, Missouri, state hospital:

> Dr. Aikarakudy G. Alias compared the body hair of 117 men in Mensa, an organization of people with extremely high I.Q.'s, with men from the general population and found that the incidence of noticeable body hair is about double in the Mensa members.
>
> Mensa members rated themselves by comparing their body hair with the amount of hair observed on a total of 246 men—105 nude men pictured in *Playgirl* magazine and 141 men photographed on a Miami Beach, FL, public beach.

There are several problems with this brief description of Dr. Alias's study. First, you might wonder why anyone would be interested in doing this study in the first place. Without additional information, the casual reader might get the impression this is just the sort of silly research conducted by many social scientists. But if you were to read Dr. Alias's original research report you would find that this study is only one of several he has conducted attempting to identify physiological signs of personality characteristics. This line of research is based on the known fact that both your skin and brain develop from the same embryonic tissues. Because of their common origin, Dr. Alias thinks (hypothesizes) that features of one of these organs (such as hair on the skin) may vary in a systematic way with features of the other organ (intellectual capacity of the brain). None of this is explained in the brief article appearing in the *National Enquirer*.

The simple fact is that even the best of us get a little funny in our reasoning from time to time. Worse yet, we can get defensive when others point out the errors in our logic.

Although all of us sometimes fall into embarrassingly illogical reasoning in day-to-day life, scientists avoid this pitfall by using systems of logic consciously and explicitly. Chapter 2 will examine the logic(s) of science in more depth. For now, it is sufficient to note that logical reasoning is a conscious activity for scientists, and they usually have colleagues around to keep them honest in that regard as in others.

Ego Involvement in Understanding

The search for regularities and generalized understanding is not a trivial intellectual exercise. It critically affects our personal lives. Our understanding of events and conditions, then, is often

A second problem with popular press stories is that they seldom help the reader to think critically about how the research was done. Take, for instance, the way data were collected in Dr. Alias's study. Mensa members were given a page with nine male torsos arrayed from least to most hairy. Mensa members then identified the torso most closely resembling their own torsos. No similar information was collected for men representing populations with lower IQs. Instead, Dr. Alias compared only Mensa members' self-reports with actual photographs of men shown in *Playgirl* photographs or with photographs of men on a Miami beach. Note that it is possible the Mensa members reported themselves as being hairier than they actually were. It is also possible that for aesthetic reasons *Playgirl* photographers may use male models with only slight-to-moderate as opposed to moderate-to-heavy body hair. In short, since data were not collected the same way for men of average IQ as for men with above average IQ, you simply can't interpret the results without a very large grain of salt.

These aren't the only problems with the study done by Dr. Alias or with the *National Enquirer* account of this study. In fact, when reading any popular press account of behavioral science, you need to be suspicious. Suggestion: Why don't you try making a similar comparison yourself? It only takes three steps: (1) find a newspaper or magazine article describing a study done by a social scientist; (2) write away for the original report; (3) make comparisons between the popular press story and the scientist's report of the study.

Source: "Hairy Men Are Smarter," *National Enquirer,* November 1, 1977, p. 28. "Positive Correlations Between Body Hair and Intelligence . . . ?" (Copy of research report made available through the courtesy of A. G. Alias, M.D.)

of special psychological significance to us. If you lose your job or fail to get a promotion, you may be tempted to conclude that your boss wants to get you out of the way to promote a personal friend. That explanation would save you from examining your own abilities and worth. Any challenge to that explanation, consequently, is also a challenge to your abilities and worth.

In countless ways, we link our understandings of how things are to the image of ourselves that we present to others. Because of this linkage, any disproof of these understandings tends to make us look stupid, gullible, and generally not okay. So we commit ourselves all the more unshakably to our understanding of how things are and create a formidable barrier to further inquiry and more accurate understanding.

Ego involvement in understanding is commonly encountered in social work practice. Naturally, practitioners see it in some of their clients, who may blame others or external circumstances beyond their control for their difficulties, rather than accept responsibility and face up to the way their own behavior contributes to their problems. Practitioners are less likely to see the way their own ego involvement may impede practice. Rather than scientifically reexamine the effectiveness of our own ways of practicing, ways that we may like because we are used to them and because we feel we have special expertise in them, we may tenaciously engage in selective observation, ex post facto hypothesizing, and other efforts to explain away evidence that suggests that perhaps our approach to practice is ineffective.

Social workers who conduct evaluation research frequently confront this form of ego involvement when their evaluations fail to support the efficacy of the programs they are evaluating. Administrators and other practitioners affiliated with programs being evaluated often don't want to be hassled with elegant evaluation research designs, preferring expedience to methodological rigor in the evaluations, and preferring to leave the work of designing and conducting the pain-in-the-neck evaluation to evaluators. But the same folks who initially express disinterest and a lack of expertise in evaluation design, and who say that they don't need a methodologically rigorous design, can become fanatical critics of the methodology of any study whose findings question the efficacy of their program, no matter how rigorous that study may be. Influenced by their ego involvement and vested interests in the unsupported program, administrators and practitioners are capable of grasping at any straw, at magnifying the importance of any trivial methodological imperfection in a study, in order to undermine the methodological credibility of the study. For the same reasons, they are likely not to notice even glaring methodological imperfections in studies whose results they like and are apt to tout those studies as proving the value of their programs. (Chapter 18, on program evaluation, will examine this phenomenon in more depth.)

Administrators and practitioners aren't the only social workers vulnerable to ego involvement in understanding. Being human, program evaluators and other social work researchers are, too. For example, they run the risk of becoming personally involved in and committed to the conclusions they reach in scientific inquiry. Sometimes it's worse than in nonscientific life. Imagine, for example, that you have discovered an apparent cure for cancer and have been awarded the Nobel Prize. How do you suppose you'll feel when somebody else publishes an article arguing that your cure doesn't really work? You might not be totally objective.

A firm commitment to the other norms of science that we have been examining works against too much ego involvement. But if you lack that commitment, you will find that your colleagues can evaluate the critical article more objectively than you can. Ultimately, then, although ego involvement is sometimes a problem for individual scientists, it is less of a problem for science in general.

The Premature Closure of Inquiry

Overgeneralization, selective observation, made-up information, and the defensive uses of illogical reasoning all conspire to produce a premature closure of inquiry. This discussion began with our desire to understand the world around us, and the various errors detailed previously often lead us to stop inquiry too soon.

The anti-Semite who says, "I already understand Jews, so don't confuse me with facts," has achieved a personal closure on the subject. Sometimes this closure of inquiry is a social, rather than an individual, act. For example, the private foundation or government agency that refuses to support further research on a topic that is "already understood" effects closure as a social act, as does the denominational college that prohibits scholarship and research that might challenge traditional religious beliefs. Social workers may do this by refusing to consider evidence that their favored interventions, programs, or policies are not as effective as they would like to believe they are. Feminist or minority group organizations may do this by ruling off limits certain lines of inquiry that pose some risk of producing findings that sexists or bigots could use inappropriately to stigmatize or oppose the advancement of women and minorities. Chapter 3 will examine the ethics of this phenomenon, as well as the impact of politics and ideologies on inquiry, in more depth.

The danger of premature closure of inquiry is obvious. It brings a halt to attempts to understand things before that understanding is complete. If you review the history of human knowledge, however, you will reach a startling conclusion: we keep changing the things we know—even the things we know for certain. In an important sense, then, any closure of inquiry is premature.

It is worth noting, for example, that much of Sigmund Freud's early empirical and theoretical work focused on the disorder known as *hysteria*—very common among women in Victorian Europe. Freud and Josef Breuer (1895) offered powerful breakthroughs in the understanding of hysteria, linking it importantly to the repressed sexuality of the Victorian era.

Freud's observations and theories relating to sexuality are generally acknowledged to have had a long-term and lasting impact on our sexual attitudes and practices. One side effect is that hysteria itself has become very rare. Those cases that do exist today are likely to have some other cause than those Freud and Breuer discovered.

Human social phenomena have a recursive quality less common in other scientific arenas. What we learn about ourselves has an effect on what we are like and how we operate—often canceling out what we learned in the first place. The implication of this is that social science inquiry will always be needed (making it a stable career choice).

At its base, science is an open-ended enterprise in which conclusions are constantly being modified. That is an explicit norm of science. Experienced scientists, therefore, accept it as a fact of life and expect established theories to be overturned eventually. And if one scientist considers a line of inquiry to be completed forever, others will not. Even if a whole generation of scientists closes inquiry on a given topic, a later generation is likely to set about testing the old ideas and changing many of them.

In part, the reward structure of science supports this openness. Although you may have to overcome a great deal of initial resistance and disparagement, imagine how famous you would be if you could demonstrate persuasively that something people have always believed simply isn't true. What if you could *prove* that carbon monoxide was really *good* for people? The potential rewards for astounding discoveries keep everything fair game for inquiry in science.

Mystification

None of us can hope to understand everything. No matter how intelligent or how diligent we may be in our inquiry, there will always be countless events and situations we do not understand. We may never fully understand the origin of the universe; a particular individual may never know why he or she failed calculus in college. A social worker may never fully comprehend why some clients seem to benefit from a group intervention and others do not.

One common response to this problem is to attribute supernatural or mystical causes to the phenomena that humans cannot understand. It is simply asserted that some things are ultimately beyond human comprehension. Quite possibly that may be true of some events and situations; perhaps some things are totally random. Nonetheless, accepting that a phenomenon is ultimately unknowable brings a halt to inquiry, whether the thing is actually knowable or not.

The same comments just made in connection with the premature closure of inquiry can be made about the scientific safeguards against mystification. It is an article of faith in science that everything is knowable, or—waffling slightly—that everything is *potentially* knowable. Even if one scientist is willing to concede that a particular phenomenon is beyond human comprehension, another will recognize the rewards to be gained in making that phenomenon comprehensible. If someone were to publicly announce that we can never hope to understand love, say, that would probably give you an added incentive to find a way to understand it.

The term *mystification* has a pejorative ring, something that we perhaps associate with the Dark Ages. It is hard to imagine professional social work practitioners engaging in mystification. As you continue your education and career in social work, chances are you will encounter some social workers who say something like this: "The effectiveness of social work practice cannot be measured objectively. It is beyond the comprehension of researchers. If we want to know whether a particular approach to social work practice is effective, we can simply rely on the intuition of practitioners. Because they are the closest to the practice arena and to their clients, we should have faith that they are best equipped to know if what they are doing is effective. We will probably never understand how they know that to be true, but we should accept their intuition and judgment, because they are dealing with complex phenomena that are essentially unmeasurable." Is this mystification? Your answer probably depends on your viewpoint about the statement.

To Err Is Human

These, then, are some of the ways that we go astray in our attempts to know and understand the world and some of the ways that science protects its inquiries from these pitfalls. For the most part, science differs from our casual, day-to-day inquiry in two important respects. First, scientific inquiry is a conscious activity. Although we engage in continuous observation in daily life, much of it is unconscious or semiconscious. In scientific inquiry, we make a conscious decision to observe, and we stay awake while we do it. Second, scientific inquiry is more careful than our casual efforts. In scientific inquiry, we are more wary of making mistakes and take special precautions to avoid error.

Nothing we've said should lead you to conclude that science offers total protection against the errors that nonscientists commit in day-to-day inquiry. Not only do individual scientists make every kind of error we've looked at, scientists as a group fall into the pitfalls and stay trapped for long periods of time.

Not long ago, when most of us felt it would be extremely difficult for people to travel to the moon, it was the physicists who could *prove* that such a trip would be *impossible*. We think it had something to do with the weight of the fuel it would take to lift the amount of fuel it would take to lift the amount of fuel it would take. . . . Only the physicists really understood it.

But who put us on the moon in 1969? The physicists! In fact, it was the same physicists who could prove it was impossible. The NASA story provides an excellent illustration of how science operates. The scientists involved were able to view the proven impossibility of going to the moon within a larger context. Given that it's impossible, they asked, how can we do it? Such behavior can call into question the basic meaning of reality.

WHAT'S REALLY REAL?

Philosophers sometimes use the term *naive realism* to describe the way most of us operate in our day-to-day lives. When you sit down at a table to write, you probably don't spend a lot of time thinking about whether the table is "really" made up of atoms, which in turn are mostly empty space. When you step into the street and see a city bus hurtling down on you, that's not the best time to reflect on methods for testing whether the bus really exists. We all live our lives with a view that what's real is pretty obvious—and that view usually gets us through the day.

We do not want this book to interfere with your ability to deal with life on a day-to-day basis. At the same time, however, we hope that the preceding discussions have demonstrated that the nature of "reality" is perhaps more complex than we tend to assume in our everyday functioning. Here are three views of reality that will provide a philosophical backdrop for the discussions of science to follow. Let's look at what are sometimes called *premodern, modern,* and *postmodern* views of reality.

The *premodern* view of reality has guided most of human history. Our early ancestors assumed that they saw things as they *really were.* In fact, this assumption was so fundamental that they did not even see it as an assumption. No cavemom said to her cavekid, "Our tribe makes an assumption that evil spirits reside in the Old Twisted Tree." No, they said, "STAY OUT OF THAT TREE OR YOU'LL TURN INTO A TOAD!"

As human populations increased and unrelated groups ran into each other, they became aware of their diversity. They came to recognize that others did not always share their views of things. Thus, they may have discovered that another tribe didn't buy the wicked tree thing; in fact, the second tribe felt the spirits in the tree were holy and beneficial. The discovery of this diversity in views led members of the first tribe to conclude that "some people I could name are pretty stupid." For them, the tree was still wicked, and they expected some misguided people were going to be moving to Toad City.

What philosophers call the *modern* view—most closely associated with Western industrialized societies—accepts such diversity as legitimate, a philosophical "different strokes for different folks." As a modern thinker, you would say, "I regard the spirits in the tree as evil, but I know others regard them as good. Neither of us is right or wrong. There are simply spirits in the tree. They are neither good nor evil, but different people have different ideas about them."

It is perhaps easier to adopt the modern view in the realm of opinions than in that of "reality." For example, some might regard a dandelion as a beautiful flower, while others only see an annoying weed. To the premoderns, a dandelion has to be either one or the other. If you think it is a weed, it is *really* a weed, though you may admit that some people have a warped sense of beauty. In the modern view, a dandelion is simply a dandelion. It is a plant with yellow petals and green leaves. The concepts "beautiful flower" and "an-

noying weed" are subjective points of view imposed on the plant by different people, just as "good" and "evil" were concepts imposed on the spirits in the tree. Neither "beautiful flower" nor "annoying weed" is a quality of the plant itself.

Philosophers now increasingly speak of a *postmodern* view of reality. In this view, *the spirits don't exist.* Neither does the dandelion. All that's "real" are the images we get through our points of view. Put differently, there's nothing *out there,* it's all *in here.* As Gertrude Stein said of Oakland, "There's no there there."

No matter how bizarre the postmodern view may seem to you on first reflection, there is a certain ironic inevitability to it. Take a moment to notice the book you are reading; notice specifically what it looks like. Since you are reading these words, it probably looks something like Figure 1-1(a).

But does Figure 1-1(a) represent the way your book "really" looks? Or does it merely represent what the book looks like from your current point of view? Surely, Figure 1-1(b), (c), and (d) are equally valid representations of your book. But these views of the book are so different from one another. Which is the "reality"?

As this example should illustrate, there is no answer to the question, "What does the book *really* look like?" All we can offer are the different ways it looks from different points of view. Thus, according to the postmodern view, there is no "book," only various images of it from different points of view. And all the different images are equally "true."

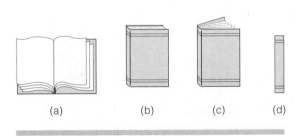

(a) (b) (c) (d)

Figure 1-1 What does the book *really* look like?

Now let's apply this logic to a social situation. Imagine a husband and wife arguing. Figure 1-2(a) shows the wife's point of view about the quarrel. Take a minute to imagine how you would feel and what thoughts you would be having if you were the woman in this drawing. How would you explain later to an outsider—to your best friend, perhaps—what had happened in this situation? What solutions to the conflict would seem necessary or appropriate if you were the woman in this situation? Perhaps you have been in similar situations, and your memories of those events can help you answer these questions.

Now let's shift gears dramatically. What the woman's husband sees is another matter altogether (Figure 1-2(b)). Take a minute to imagine experiencing the situation from his point of view. What thoughts and feelings would you have? How would you tell your best friend what had happened? What solutions would seem appropriate for resolving the conflict?

Now, let's consider a third point of view. Suppose you are an outside observer, watching this interaction between a wife and husband. What would it look like to you now? Unfortunately, we can't easily portray the third point of view with-

out knowing something about the personal feelings, beliefs, past experiences, and so forth that you would bring to your task as "outside" observer. (Though we call you an *outside* observer, you are, of course, observing from *inside* your own mental system.)

To take an extreme example, if you were a confirmed male chauvinist, you'd probably see the fight pretty much the same way the husband saw it. Or, on the other hand, if you were committed to the view that men are generally unreasonable bums, you'd see things the way the wife saw them in the earlier picture.

But consider this. Imagine that you look at this situation and see two unreasonable people, quarreling irrationally with one another—neither of them acting in a way they should be proud of. Can you get the feeling that they are both equally responsible for the conflict?

Or imagine you see two people facing a difficult human situation, each doing the best he or she can to resolve it. Imagine feeling compassion for them and notice the ways each attempts at times to calm things down, to end the hostility, even though the gravity of the problem keeps them fighting anyway.

(a)   (b)

Figure 1-2

Notice how different each of these new views is. Which is a "true" picture of what is happening between the wife and husband? You win the prize if you notice that the personal baggage you brought along to the observational task would again color your perception of what is happening.

This represents a critical dilemma for science and for scientists. While our task is to observe and understand what is "really" happening, we are all human and, as such, we bring along personal orientations that will color what we observe and how we explain it. There is ultimately no way you can totally step outside your humanness to see and understand the world as it "really" is.

Whereas the modern view acknowledges the inevitability of our human subjectivity, the postmodern view suggests there is actually no "objective" reality to be observed in the first place. There are only our different subjective views.

We are going to let you ponder these views on your own for a while. We'll return to this discussion in Chapter 2 when we focus on more specific scientific paradigms. In particular, we'll trace the progress of social scientific thinking from positivism to postpositivism.

What you will see, ultimately, is that (1) established scientific procedures sometimes allow you to deal effectively with the dilemma we've been describing (you can study people and help them through their difficulties without being able to view "reality" directly), and (2) the different philosophical stances we've been discussing suggest a range of possibilities for structuring your research.

Let's turn now to a different philosophical issue underlying scientific inquiry. Then we'll be able to go on to the specific research techniques social scientists use.

DETERMINISM, PROBABILITY, AND CAUSATION

One of the chief goals of the scientist, social or other, is to explain why things are the way they are. And social work practitioners routinely formulate tentative explanations as part of the problem-solving process that they apply to everyday practice dilemmas. Typically, we do that by specifying the causes for the way things are: some things are caused by other things.

The deterministic perspective contrasts with a *freewill* image of human behavior that we take for granted in our daily lives. The fundamental issue is this: Is your behavior the product of your own willpower or the product of forces and factors in the world that you cannot control and may not even recognize? We are going to look at that issue in more depth here. Once we have completed our examination, we'll be in a position to look at the place of causation in social scientific research. We'll start with an example outside the social sciences altogether.

Let's do an experiment. Take a pencil or some other small object, hold it up in the air, and let it go. What happens? It falls down, right? Why does it do that? As you probably learned in high school, one of the laws of the universe is that masses attract with a force reflecting their distance from one another and their masses. In practical terms, we say the gravitational force of the earth pulled the pencil to the ground.

What if the pencil didn't *want* to fall to the ground? That may strike you as a bizarre question, as it should. Obviously, the pencil's feelings—assuming it could have any—make no difference. In fact, if we were to substitute a human being for the pencil, we know that gravity would win out over any feelings that person might have in the matter. The operation of gravity illustrates our commonsense view of cause-and-effect determinism in the world. We accept the limitation that gravity places on our freedom. The deterministic model of explanation is in evidence throughout the natural sciences. Growth, for example, is *caused* by a number of factors. We can affect the growth of plants by varying the amount of light, water, and nutrients they receive. We also know that the rate of growth of human beings is affected by the nutrients they receive. And returning to the "bizarre" question asked earlier, the desire to grow or not to grow is irrelevant—for humans and for plants alike. We acknowledge that nutrition greatly overshadows our free will in the matter. The point of these examples is to show that the natural sciences operate on the basis of a cause-effect, deterministic model, and that model is often applied to human beings as well as to plants and inanimate objects. For the most part, moreover, we accept the deterministic model as appropriate in such cases. We recognize that our free will is limited by certain constraints.

Probabilistic Knowledge

Of course, few things in human behavior can be explained entirely by factors we can identify. The deterministic model, when applied to human behavior, assumes that many factors contribute to the explanation of particular phenomena even if we have not yet discovered all of them. Being poor, for example, is a factor contributing to the causation of homelessness, but being poor, alone, does not cause homelessness. Other factors also come into play, such as the lack of low-income housing, alcoholism or mental disorders, suddenly losing one's job, and so on. We can say with great certainty that being poor makes one *more likely* to be homeless, yet on the other hand we recognize that while poverty contributes to the causation of homelessness, most poor people are not homeless. Thus, when explaining or predicting human behavior, we speak in terms of *probability*, not certainty.

Knowledge based on probability enables us to say that if A occurs, then B is more likely to occur. It does not enable us to say that B will occur, or even that B will probably occur. For example, research into the causation of mental illness has suggested that the offspring of mentally ill parents are about ten times more likely than the rest of the population to become mentally ill. But most children of mentally ill parents never become mentally ill; only about 10% of them do. Because only about 1% of the rest of the popula-

tion ever becomes mentally ill, we can say that having mentally ill parents appears to be one factor that can contribute to the causation of mental illness (perhaps through the transmission of certain genetic combinations that make one biologically more vulnerable to other factors that can contribute to the causation of mental illness). Our ability to say that parental mental illness is a "cause" of mental illness in their offspring is further restricted by the observation that the parents of many mentally ill people were never mentally ill themselves. (Again, genetics offers a possible explanation here.)

Many "causes" that help "determine" human behavior, therefore, are neither necessary nor sufficient for the "effect" that they help to cause. Among many of the homeless, alcoholism may have played a role in causing their homelessness. Yet one can be homeless without ever having been an alcoholic. Alcoholism therefore is not a necessary condition for homelessness to occur. Neither is it a sufficient condition, because alcoholism alone does not produce homelessness.

People who crave certainty may be uneasy with probabilistic knowledge and may therefore spurn the findings of social research. They may prefer the comfort of less complex, nonscientific routes to "understanding," such as freewill notions that we simply choose to do what we do. Alternatively, they may prefer narrow explanations proffered with certainty by supervisors and other authorities. In your social work practice you may find that dealing with uncertainty can be a constant source of uneasiness and anxiety. You may find more relief from this discomfort by latching onto and following unquestioningly the "certain" pronouncements of a guru of a practice dogma than you will in the probabilistic findings of scientific research. Earlier we discussed the risks associated with such reliance on authority. Although escaping from the discomfort of uncertainty may make you feel better, it might lead you further away from the truth, which ultimately is not in the best interests of your clients. But be forewarned (and therefore hopefully forearmed to be better utilizers of research) that most research studies will not give you the kinds of answers that will bring certainty to your practice.

Finding Causes in Social Work Research

When the deterministic model, based on probabilistic knowledge, is used in the social sciences, it is usually so implicit that we may forget the nature of the model we are using. So let us illustrate how social science might proceed with that model. Imagine that you have managed to obtain a large grant to find out the causes of child abuse. That's certainly a laudable aim, and various government and private foundations are often willing to support such research. Let's suppose you receive the money and spend it doing your research. Now you are ready to send your project report off to the foundation. Here's how the report reads:

> After an extensive examination of the subject, we have discovered that some parents abuse their children, and the reason for that is that they want to abuse them. Other parents do not abuse their children, and the reason is that they *don't* want to abuse them.

Obviously, this paragraph would not be a satisfactory conclusion for a research project aimed at finding out what *causes* child abuse. When we look for the causes of child abuse, we look for the reasons: the things that make some parents abusive and others nonabusive. Satisfactory but incomplete probabilistic reasons would include adolescent parenting, stress from socioeconomic difficulties, overcrowded living arrangements, cultural norms and attitudes that tolerate certain forms of violence, physical or mental handicaps or illnesses of the child, and so forth.

Now let's look at the logic of such an explanation a little more closely. What does it say about the people involved in the research conclusion— the subjects of study? Fundamentally, it says that whether they turned out to be abusers resulted from something they did not, themselves, control or choose. It's as though they came to a fork in the road—one turn represents a greater likelihood of child abuse and the other represents a lesser likelihood of child abuse—and they were propelled down one or the other road by forces such as socioenvironmental stress, special characteristics of the child, cultural norms, and similar factors they did not control and perhaps were not even aware of. They turned out to be abusive or nonabusive, or at least became more or less likely to become abusive, for reasons beyond their control.

When social work researchers or other social scientists study juvenile delinquency (or other social problems), the basic model is the same: delinquency is *caused* by factors other than the delinquent's free choice. It is further assumed that those factors can be discovered and perhaps modified, regardless of whether or not the delinquent wants to change.

The same model applies when social work researchers study "nice" behaviors. What are the factors that make a person more likely to become a social service volunteer, such as a Big Brother or Big Sister or a hospice volunteer? If we knew the answer, we could improve the likelihood of success in our volunteer recruitment, screening, and training efforts—so the implicit reasoning goes.

Reasons Have Reasons

Sometimes people protest this reasoning by arguing that individuals personally choose the things that contribute to determining how abusive, delinquent, or altruistic they are. For example, let's say that a particular abusive mother is abusive in large part because as a single, adolescent parent she is emotionally unprepared for parenting, does not know enough about proper child rearing, and lacks socioeconomic resources. Didn't she *choose* to be sexually active, not use contraception, and ultimately keep the baby? Isn't *she,* therefore, the source of the child abuse?

The problem with this view is that reasons have reasons.

Why did she make the choices that resulted in becoming a single, adolescent parent? There may be many reasons for this. Let's say that she had very little self-esteem and that this in turn impeded her propensity to refuse sexual intimacy even in situations where no contraceptive device was available. Perhaps she also immaturely idealized motherhood as a way to gain self-esteem.

But why did she have such low self-esteem in the first place? And why did she see motherhood as the route to higher self-esteem? Perhaps she grew up in a family where socioenvironmental stress made her neglected as a child. Perhaps she had no role models identifying alternative, better opportunities for self-fulfillment.

Clearly we cannot identify all the particular reasons given parents are or are not abusive, but we think you can see that they are that way for reasons, and that those reasons caused the ultimate behavior in question. Moreover, no matter what reason they had at any specific step in the process, their reason would have a reason. The ultimate implication of this discussion is that being abusive, delinquent, altruistic, or anything else can be traced back through a long and complex chain of reasons that explain why someone turned out the way they did.

Recall how silly it seemed to think about whether the pencil wanted to fall when you let go of it. The pencil's feelings had nothing to do with it; gravity caused it to fall. The same thing would have happened to any pencil, so the one we dropped certainly couldn't take any pride in how well it fell. Questions of self-esteem seem unimportant when we are dealing with a pencil being pulled around by gravity.

However, whether a *person* turned out to be abusive or nonabusive seems like a different matter. We know that if you consider yourself to be tolerant or honest or hard-working or a good parent, you feel that such qualities are a reflection of who you are, of the kind of person you are deep down inside. They seem intimately woven into your experience of yourself.

Whenever we undertake explanatory social work research, however—when we set out to discover the causes of child abuse or how to prevent it, for example—we adopt a model of human behavior that assumes people have no more individual freedom of choice than the pencil did. We don't say that, of course, but if you look at the implications of asking "What causes child abuse?" you'll see that it's so.

Determinism in Perspective

As you no doubt know, the issue of determinism and freedom is complex; philosophers have debated it for thousands of years and will probably debate it for thousands more. It is perhaps ultimately one of those "open questions" that is more valuable in the asking than it would be in the answering. We are not going to resolve it here.

Acceptance of a deterministic model does not necessarily imply absolving individuals of legal or moral responsibility for their behavior. It is possible to accept the deterministic model in seeking to understand what causes things, while rejecting it as an excuse to commit acts that harm other people. From time to time most of us do things we feel proud or guilty about. Although we might recognize some of the factors that determined our actions, that usually doesn't eliminate our sense of pride or guilt.

Our purpose in raising the issue of determinism is to engage you with the question and to alert you to its place in social work research. We have observed that when people set out to learn the skills of explanatory social work research, the implicit assumption of determinism disturbs them. Somewhere, new researchers harbor a concern about whether they are learning to demonstrate that *they themselves* have no free will, no personal freedom in determining the course of their own lives. To the extent that this concern grows and festers, it interferes with the learning of analytic skills and techniques. Our purpose in this discussion has been to confront the issue head on rather than leaving it for you to discover later on.

Having said all that, let's clarify and review what is not part of the model. First, social scientists do not *believe* all human actions, thoughts, and feelings are determined, nor do they lead their lives as though they believed that. Second, the deterministic model does not assume that the causal patterns are simple ones, as we've already suggested in the discussions of reasons causing reasons. Nor does the model assume we are all controlled by the same factors and forces: your reasons for majoring in social work were surely somewhat different from those of some of your classmates.

Moreover, the deterministic model lying at the base of explanatory social science does not suggest that we now know all the answers about what causes what, or that we ever will. Realize, however, that this is different from the error of "mystification" discussed earlier.

Finally, we've seen that social science typically operates on the basis of a *probabilistic* causal model. Rather than predicting, for example, that a particular person will become an abusive parent, we say that certain factors make child abuse more or less likely within groups of people. Thus, adolescent parents may be more likely to become abusive than older parents. But this does not mean that all of the former will become abusive and none of the latter will.

To summarize, the kind of understanding we seek as we analyze social work research data inevitably involves a deterministic model of human behavior. In looking for the reasons why people are the way they are and do the things they do, we implicitly assume that their characteristics and actions are determined by forces and factors operating on them. You do not need to *believe* that human beings are totally determined, nor do you have to lead your life as though you were, but when you are looking for explanations in your practice or in your research you will probably find the use of deterministic logic helpful.

The use of deterministic logic in social work research can be complicated by our awareness of concepts about person-in-environment, social systems dynamics, and symbolic interaction theory. The individuals we study are not only influenced by earlier events, but by events that occur at nearly the same time as the behavior in question. That is, individuals' current behaviors can be influenced by the situations they currently are in and the forces and factors that they encounter in those situations. These forces and factors—such as expectations that others have in those situations—can seem to be occurring at the same time that the behavior they are shaping is occurring. Moreover, the individual being studied can influence the actions and expectations of others in a particular social system or situation, and those influences can in turn further influence the individual. Thus, by influencing others, individuals can be seen as influencing themselves to some extent. This is not the same as individuals choosing to be the way they are in a freewill sense, but it complicates the concept of determinism nonetheless.

Things can become even more complicated if we believe that the anticipation of future events can influence current behaviors. For example, individuals who have not yet entered treatment, but know that their first session is the next day, may seem more hopeful or perhaps more apprehensive than they would otherwise feel that day. Similarly, family members about to begin their first family therapy session may be on their best behavior to influence how they will be perceived by the therapist.

We are not saying here that the future can determine the past. Our *belief* that something is going to happen, and not the future event itself (which, due to unexpected factors, might not even occur), is something that has already occurred before the behavior in question occurs. Likewise, when concurrent situational forces, such as the expectations of others, are influencing our behaviors, we perceive those forces before we act. To sum up, our perceptions of concurrent or future forces can precede and influence our behaviors, even though to others it may seem as though effects are preceding causes. It is intuitively illogical to suppose that a cause can produce an effect unless the cause precedes the effect (as we will discuss further in Chapter 9). Consequently, our theoretical concepts regarding social systems dynamics, person-in-environment, and symbolic interactionism make it extremely difficult (some would say impossible) "to distinguish causes from effects" (Rodwell, 1987:238). When, for example, we find that children with provocative behavior problems are more likely than other children to have a conflictual relationship with their mother, we may want to know whether the conflictual relationship caused the behavior problem or whether the child's provocative behavior caused the relationship to sour. Or should we seek to understand both phenomena in terms of concurrent social system dynamics?

Despite this difficulty in distinguishing causes from effects, deterministic thinking can help us when we seek to discover the explanations for human behavior. The fact that our own behavior may influence the forces that in turn influence us does not belie the deterministic perspective, because reasons have reasons. That is, we can look for forces and factors that influenced us to act that way in the first place—going back, if we must, to genetics. As we noted earlier, the deterministic perspective views our behavior as the product of forces and factors beyond our control but does not imply that it will always be easy, or even possible, to distinguish what forces are producing what behaviors.

Two Causal Models of Understanding

As we've seen, social scientists are often interested in understanding and explaining why things are the way they are. In this section, we will discuss two different causal models of understanding: **idiographic** and **nomothetic.** These represent two different ways we can understand human behavior.

The preceding discussions, which probed the multiplicity of reasons that would account for a specific behavior, illustrated the *idiographic* model of explanation. This model aims at explanation through the enumeration of the many, perhaps unique, considerations that lie behind a given action. Of course, we never totally exhaust those reasons in practice. Nevertheless, it is important to realize that the idiographic model is employed frequently in many different contexts.

As an example, let's say we are interested in understanding why a particular young man has become delinquent. If you were his case worker, you would want to learn everything you could about his family situation, his neighborhood, his school environment, his peers, and anything else that might account for his delinquent behavior. Does he live in a broken or dysfunctional family? Does he have delinquent brothers or sisters? Does he belong to a gang? How is he doing in school? Is his family poor? Does he have physical or psychological problems that may contribute to his behavior and your understanding of it? Your purpose in this instance would be to understand this one person as fully as possible, in all his idiosyncratic peculiarities. This is what we call the idiographic model of explanation.

Sometimes social scientists employ a different model of explanation, called the *nomothetic* model. Rather than seeking to understand a particular person as fully as possible, we try to understand a general phenomenon partially. Following up on the previous example, you might be interested in learning about the causes of juvenile deliquency in general. What factors are most important for explaining deliquency among many young people? Let's consider the role of broken homes in causing delinquency.

If you were to study a large number of young people, you would discover a higher incidence of delinquency among those living in broken homes than among those who lived with intact families. This certainly does not mean that broken homes always produce juvenile delinquency or that intact homes always prevent it. As a general rule, however, broken homes are more likely to produce delinquency than intact ones.

Actually, social scientists have discovered what it is about broken homes that increases the likelihood of juvenile delinquency: the lack of adult supervision. Specifically, intact families are more likely to have an adult in the home when the young person gets out of school, and it is the presence of adult supervision that decreases the likelihood of delinquent behavior. In the case of broken homes, there is a greater likelihood that young people will be unsupervised after school and are, therefore, more likely to get into trouble.

Whereas the idiographic model seeks to understand everything about a particular case, through the use of as many causative factors as possible, the nomothetic model seeks a partial understanding of a general phenomenon, using relatively few variables. Notice that the young delinquent we began this discussion with may or may not live in a broken home, and, if he does, that fact may or may not help to account for his delinquency. Taking an idiographic tack, we would want to discover all the particular factors that led that one young man astray. From a nomothetic point of view, we would want to discover those factors, such as lack of adult supervision, that account for many instances of delinquency in general.

The nomothetic model of explanation is inevitably *probabilistic* in its approach to causation. Being able to name a few causal factors seldom if ever provides a complete explanation. In the best of all practical worlds, the nomothetic model indicates there is a very high (or very low) probability or likelihood that a given action will occur whenever a limited number of specified considerations are present. Specifying more considerations typically increases the degree of explanation, but the basic simplicity of the model calls for a balancing of a high degree of explanation with a small number of causal factors being specified.

To illustrate the use of the nomothetic and idiographic models in social work practice, imagine that you are a direct services practitioner who keeps up with the emerging research literature to make sure you provide the most effective services to your clients. You learn of a promising new intervention for trauma survivors. This new intervention, which has been receiving support in several research articles, seems particularly relevant to one of your clients who was a trauma victim and has not been making much progress so far in overcoming posttraumatic stress disorder (PTSD).

The research articles show that the new intervention appears more likely to be effective than alternative treatment approaches. With the new intervention, 70% of trauma survivors have their PTSD symptoms disappear within a few weeks, as compared to only 30% receiving alternative approaches. The new intervention, however, tends to involve more (temporary) emotional discomfort than alternative approaches, because it requires that clients call up vivid images of the traumatic incident. Consequently, you would not want to keep providing the new intervention to your client if it is not working.

The research gives you a nomothetic basis for considering the new intervention. That is, it tells you in probabilistic terms that the new intervention is quite effective in general, but there's no guarantee that it will be effective for your particular client. Perhaps your client is like the 30% who were not helped by the new intervention. The research you've read may give no indication of the variables that make the intervention more or less successful: gender, age, social class, family situation, and so on.

As a social work practitioner, you will be interested in one particular case, and you will want to consider the range of particular characteristics that might influence the intervention's effectiveness. Imagine that your particular client is a young widow, working as a waitress to support her two preschool children, one of whom has a serious learning disability. Are any or all of those factors near the root of your client's PTSD and will they influence the likelihood of the new intervention being successful? This is an example of the idiographic model of causation.

Please be clear that all the contextual variables just discussed in this idiographic example could be and often are examined in nomothetic analyses. Thus, we could study whether young widows, *in general,* suffer PTSD more than, say, married or single women. Similarly, we could undertake a nomothetic examination of the role played by child-rearing in generating PTSD, *in general.* The key difference is that the nomothetic approach looks for causal patterns that occur *in general,* whereas the idiographic approach aims at explaining a single case fully.

You also could take an idiographic approach in finding out if the intervention is effective with your particular client by conducting a single-case design evaluation that would entail measuring your client's PTSD symptoms each day for a week or two and graphing the results before implementing the new intervention. Then you would continue to graph the symptoms after the new intervention begins. Whether the graphed data show a clear amelioration in PTSD symptoms coinciding with the onset of the intervention will indicate whether the intervention appears to be effective for your particular client. In Chapter 10 of this book, on single-subject designs, you will learn more about how to design and conduct idiographic studies like this in your own practice.

QUANTITATIVE AND QUALITATIVE METHODS OF INQUIRY

The discussions of determinism, reality, and different models for understanding illustrate how complex things can get when we examine the philosophical underpinnings of social scientific inquiry. Not all social scientists or social work researchers share the same philosophical assumptions. Some question determinism. Some accept a postmodern view of reality, while others dismiss that view as nonsense. Some social scientists are generally more interested in idiographic understanding, while others are more inclined to the nomothetic view. Moreover, the nature of your professional activities may push you in one direction or in the other. Direct service practitioners, for example, will probably choose an idiographic approach to understanding specific clients, although nomothetic understanding of common causes of social problems may suggest variables to explore in the case of specific clients.

Sometimes differences in philosophical assumptions lead to arguments over which approaches to research are more legitimate than others. Two research approaches that have been the center of much debate in the social work literature since the early 1980s are called *quantitative* methods and *qualitative* methods. **Quantitative methods** emphasize the production of precise and generalizable statistical findings and are generally more appropriate to nomothetic aims. When we want

to verify whether a cause produces an effect in general, we are likely to use quantitative methods. (Sometimes quantitative methods are also used in studies with idiographic aims—especially in idiographic studies employing single-subject designs, as will be discussed in Chapter 10.)

Qualitative research methods emphasize the depth of understanding associated with idiographic concerns. They attempt to tap the deeper meanings of particular human experiences and are intended to generate theoretically richer observations that are not easily reduced to numbers.

During the first half of the 20th century, qualitative methods were commonly employed by sociologists. Social workers at that time often used quantitative methods like social surveys. Of course, direct-service practitioners typically have always relied heavily on a qualitative approach when looking at all the idiosyncratic aspects of a particular client's case. Around the middle of the 20th century, however, the potential for quantitative methods yielding more generalizable conclusions became appealing to social scientists in general. Gradually, quantitative studies were regarded as superior—more "scientific"—and they began to squeeze out qualitative studies.

During the past decade or so, qualitative methods have enjoyed a rebirth of support in the social sciences generally, including social work. In a new swing of the professional pendulum, some have even called quantitative methods obsolete and implored the profession to concentrate on qualitative methods (De Maria, 1981; Heineman, 1981; Ruckdeschel and Faris, 1981; Taylor, 1977). Many scholars, however, do not believe that the two contrasting types of methods are inherently incompatible. In their view, quantitative and qualitative methods—despite their philosophical differences—play an equally important, complementary role in knowledge building, and have done so throughout the history of contemporary social science. Indeed, some of our best research has combined the two types of methods within the same study. One example of this is an inquiry by McRoy (1981) into the self-esteem of transracial and inracial adoptees. Quantitative measurement, using two standardized scales, revealed no differences in levels of self-esteem between the two groups of adoptees on one scale but some differences in the use of racial self-referents on the other scale.

In light of her inconsistent quantitative findings, McRoy used the qualitative approach of open-ended, probing interviews to generate hypotheses on how families were handling issues of racial identity with their adopted children. From her qualitative analysis of the interview data emerged the following tentative factors that might influence how adoptees adjust to racial identity problems: parental attitudes, sibling and peer relationships, role model availability, extended family factors, racial composition of school and community, and experience with racism and discrimination.

Thus, whether we should emphasize qualitative or quantitative research methods may depend on the conditions and purposes of our inquiry. Qualitative methods may be more suitable when flexibility is required to study a new phenomenon about which we know very little, or when we seek to gain insight into the subjective meanings of complex phenomena to advance our conceptualization of them and to build theory that can be tested in future studies. Sometimes, therefore, qualitative research can pave the way for quantitative studies of the same subject. Other times, qualitative methods produce results that are sufficient in themselves. For example, Elliot Liebow's classic study of street-corner life in *Tally's Corner* (1967) needs no further elaboration by statistical analysis. If you read this book, you will come away with a sense of really understanding the quality of life among Liebow's subjects, and you are unlikely to feel the need for statistical data to improve that understanding.

In sum, we want to make it clear that you do not need to choose one camp or the other. Each approach is useful and legitimate. Each makes its unique contribution to inquiry. Each has its own advantages and disadvantages. Each is a set of tools, not an ideology. Researchers need to match the tools they use with the research questions and conditions they face—using quantitative methods for some studies, qualitative methods for others, and both methods combined for still others.

Objectivity and Subjectivity in Scientific Inquiry

A recurrent theme implicit in much of what we have discussed throughout this chapter is the pursuit of objectivity in scientific inquiry. Both quantitative and qualitative methods try to be objective, although they do it in different ways (as we will see in later chapters). It would be misleading, however, to give you the impression that objectivity is easy to achieve or even that its meaning is obvious.

From a premodern point of view, objectivity means observing what's "really there." In contrast, subjectivity would mean that your observations were distorted by the contents of your own mind. As we've seen earlier, however, the modern view essentially says it's impossible to see what's really there, and the postmodern view questions whether there's anything "really" there at all. Thus the first suggests we cannot completely escape our subjectivity, while the latter suggests that subjectivity is all that really exists. How can social workers and other investigators be "objective," then?

Ultimately, there is no way of proving whether there is an objective reality beyond our perceptions, or—if it does exist—whether we are observing it accurately at any given moment. Nonetheless, there is a standard that scientists use in lieu of a direct pipeline to objective reality: *agreement*. As you'll recall from the earlier discussion, agreement is a standard all of us use in everyday life, but scientists have established conscious grounds for such agreements.

In a sense, this whole book is devoted to a discussion of the criteria for reaching scientific agreements, already introduced in the discussion of the foundations of social science. Whereas many of the agreements of everyday life are based in tradition, for example, scientists use standards of rigorous logic and careful observation. When several scientists, using the established techniques of scientific inquiry, arrive at the same conclusion, then, we judge them all to have been objective, to have discovered objective reality.

This is not to suggest that social workers or other social investigators always proceed objectively. Being human, they often fall into the errors of human inquiry discussed earlier.

When social workers devise and test a new intervention approach, for instance, the value of their efforts and the recognition they will receive will be far greater when their findings show that their intervention is effective than when it is shown to be ineffective. Sure, a study about an ineffective intervention may be worth publishing, so that others can learn from and not repeat the "failure," but it is much more gratifying to be able to show the field that you have discovered something that works than it is to discuss why things went wrong.

Because of their vested interests in finding certain results, researchers often devise ways of observing phenomena that attempt to prevent their biases from influencing what is observed. There are many ways they can go about doing this, as we will see in Parts 3 and 4 of this book. For example, they might employ observers who are not given potentially biasing information about the research. They might use paper-and-pencil self-report scales that respondents complete without the researcher's presence. Perhaps they'll look at existing information, like school records, that were collected by others who know nothing of their research. These are just a few examples; we'll examine many more in later chapters. When we do examine these alternatives, we will see that none is foolproof. Every way we choose to observe a phenomenon has some potential for error.

Although we may not know whether one particular observer, or one particular observation method, is really objective, therefore, we assume that objectivity has been achieved when different observers, with different vested interests, agree on what is observed, or when different observational strategies yield essentially the same findings.

We'll close this chapter with an example that illustrates some of the issues we have been discussing concerning objectivity and subjectivity and concerning qualitative and quantitative methods. Suppose a medical social worker wants to assess the psychosocial aspects of hospice care versus standard hospital care for terminally ill patients. Put simply, standard hospital care puts its emphasis on employing medical technology in fighting the disease at all costs, even if the technology entails undesirable costs in quality of life and patient discomfort. Hospice care emphasizes minimizing patients' discomfort and maximizing their quality of life during their final days, even if that means eschewing certain technologies that prolong life but hinder its quality.

Suppose the social worker's prime focus in the study is on whether and how quality of life differs for patients depending on the form of care they receive. In a quantitative study, the social worker might ask the closest family member of each patient to complete a standardized list of interview questions about the degree of pain the patient expressed feeling, the frequency of undesirable side effects associated with medical technology (loss of hair due to chemotherapy, for example), the patient's mood, the patient's activities, and so on. An effort would probably be made to find an instrument that provided scores to each question—scores that could be summated to produce an overall-quality-of-life score. Ideally, it would be an instrument that had been tested elsewhere and seemed to produce consistent data over repeated administrations and with different interviewers. Thus, it would appear to be a measure that seems unaffected by the investigator's predilections or vested interests. If the scores of the hospice-treated patients turn out to be higher than the scores for patients receiving standard medical care, the social worker might conclude that hospice care has a better impact on quality of life than does standard medical care.

Perhaps, however, the social worker is skeptical as to whether the instrument really taps all the complex dimensions of quality of life. The instrument only gives a numerical score—perhaps this is superficial; it tells us little about the ways the two forms of care may differentially affect quality of life and gives us very little understanding of what patients experience and what those experiences mean to them.

As an alternative, the social worker may choose to take a qualitative approach to the inquiry. This might entail spending a great deal of time on the standard and hospice wards that care for terminally ill patients in the hospital. There the social worker might simply observe what goes on and keep a detailed log of the observations. The information in the logs can be analyzed to see what patterns emerge. In Chapter 3 we will examine in depth a study that took this approach (Buckingham and associates, 1976), one in which the investigator actually posed as a terminally ill patient and observed how he was treated differently in the two wards and how this made him feel. Rather than rely on indirect quantitative measures, he decided to experience the phenomenon in a direct fashion. Based on his direct observations and subjective experiences, he was able to discuss in depth how the medical staff on the hospice ward seemed much more sensitive and empathic than those on the other ward, how family members seemed encouraged to be more involved on the hospice ward and the implications this had for personalized care, and how all of this made the patient feel. By subjectively entering the role of the patient, the investigator was able to propose a deep, empathic understanding of how the two forms of care had different implications for quality of life.

But what are the potential pitfalls of the preceding approach? Some might question whether the investigator's previous ties to hospice care, his predilections, and his desire to obtain important findings may have predisposed him to make observations that would reflect favorably on the relative advantages of hospice care. In short, they would be concerned about whether his observations were sufficiently objective. Which of the two studies is preferable, the quantitative or the qualitative one? Actually, both are valuable. Each provides useful information, and each has its own set of advantages and disadvantages in its quest for truth and understanding.

Main Points

- Inquiry is a natural human activity.

- People seek a general understanding of the world around them.

- Much of what we know, we know by agreement rather than by experience.

- Tradition and authority are important sources of understanding.

- When we understand through experience, we make observations and seek patterns of regularities in what we observe.

- In day-to-day inquiry, we often make mistakes. Science offers protection against such mistakes.

- Whereas people often observe inaccurately, such errors are avoided in science by making observation a careful and deliberate activity.

- Sometimes we jump to general conclusions on the basis of only a few observations. Researchers and scientific practitioners avoid overgeneralization through replication, the repeating of studies.

- Once a conclusion has been reached, we sometimes ignore evidence that contradicts that conclusion, only paying attention to evidence that confirms it. Researchers and scientific practitioners commit themselves in advance to a set of observations to be made regardless of whether a pattern seems to be emerging early.

- When confronted with contradictory evidence, all of us make up explanations to explain away the contradictions. Often this involves making assumptions about facts not actually observed. Researchers and scientific practitioners, however, make further observations to test those assumptions.

- Sometimes people simply reason illogically. Researchers and scientific practitioners avoid this by being as careful and deliberate in their reasoning as in their observations. Moreover, the public nature of science means that scientists have their colleagues looking over their shoulders.

- The same support of colleagues protects scientists from being too ego-involved in their conclusions.

- Where people often decide they understand something and stop looking for new answers, researchers and scientific practitioners—as a group—ultimately regard all issues as open.

- Science has no place for the common human conclusion that some things are ultimately unexplainable.

- Explanatory scientific research depends implicitly on the notion of cause and effect.

- Explanatory *social* scientific research depends implicitly on a *deterministic image* of human behavior, at least in part.

- Most explanatory social research utilizes a *probabilistic* model of causation. X may be said to cause Y if it is seen to have *some* influence on Y.

- Objectivity is an important objective of scientific inquiry, but not all scholars agree on how best to attain it.

- Quantitative research methods attempt to produce findings that are precise and generalizable.

- Qualitative research methods emphasize depth of understanding, attempt to subjectively tap the deeper meanings of human experience, and are intended to generate theoretically rich observations.

Review Questions and Exercises

1. Review the common errors of human inquiry discussed in the chapter. Find a magazine or newspaper article, or perhaps a letter to the editor, that illustrates one of those errors. Discuss how a scientist would avoid making that error.

2. Suppose you have been asked to design a research study evaluating the degree of success of a family preservation program that seeks to prevent out-of-home placements of children at risk for child abuse or neglect by providing intensive in-home social work services. Under what conditions might you opt to emphasize quantitative methods or qualitative methods in your design? What would be the advantages and disadvantages of each approach? How and why might you opt to combine both types of methods in the design?

Additional Readings

Babbie, Earl, *Observing Ourselves: Essays in Social Research* (Belmont, CA: Wadsworth, 1986). A collection of essays that expands some of the philosophical issues raised in this book, including objectivity, paradigms, determinism, concepts, reality, causation, and values.

Butterfield, Herbert, *The Origins of Modern Science* (New York: Macmillan, 1960). An excellent, readable history of the development of science that illustrates many of the central issues involved in scientific inquiry. Understanding some of the stages through which science has passed can clarify what it is that now distinguishes scientific from nonscientific inquiry.

Cole, Stephen, *Making Science: Between Nature and Society* (Cambridge, MA: Harvard University Press, 1992). If you are interested in a deeper examination of science as a social enterprise, you may find this a fascinating analysis.

Hoover, Kenneth R., *The Elements of Social Scientific Thinking* (New York: St. Martin's Press, 1992). Hoover presents an excellent overview of the key elements in social scientific analysis.

Toben, Bob, *Space-Time and Beyond* (New York: Dutton, 1975). An absolutely delightful look at the tentativeness of what we know about physical reality. Using a cartoon format, Toben has presented some of the frontier issues of contemporary physics. We've included this book both because it's so much fun and because it fosters a healthy openness as you set about mastering the logic and skills of social science.

Watson, James, *The Double-Helix* (New York: New American Library, 1968). An informal and candid research biography describing the discovery of the DNA molecule, written by a principal in the drama. This account should serve as a healthy antidote to the traditional view of science as totally cool, rational, value-free, and objectively impersonal.

2

Theory and Research

What You'll Learn in This Chapter

You'll see what distinguishes scientific theory from everyday reasoning and how scientific research is linked to theory. This chapter will lay a groundwork for your understanding of the specific research techniques discussed throughout the rest of the book.

INTRODUCTION

Theory plays an important role in social work research, as it does in social work practice. In both practice and research, theory helps us make sense out of diverse observations and see patterns in them. It helps direct our inquiry into those areas that seem more likely to show useful patterns and explanations. It also helps us distinguish between chance occurrences and observations that have value in anticipating future occurrences.

Imagine a colleague tells you that by allowing a young boy to play with small toys in a sandtray and nondirectively commenting to the boy on the themes of the play, she was able to help the boy to better cope with the tragic death of his mother and move on with his life. If you did not study child development theory, and learn about the importance of play in that theory, you might respond with bewilderment, wondering how just letting a boy play and talking to the boy about his play could be a powerful professional intervention. In fact, if you asked your colleague to explain why her intervention worked and she could not explain it, you might be more skeptical about its likelihood of working with your clients than you would be if she could explain it theoretically. Without considering theory, you might flounder around in your practice trying anything and everything anyone tells you in the hope of stumbling on something that seems to work. Then, if something does work with one client, you might continue to apply it indiscriminately with other clients for whom it may be inapplicable.

Suppose you decide to test your colleague's sandplay idea with one of your clients, a girl who has been depressed and withdrawn after witnessing the death of her father in an accident. After several sessions of sandplay, the girl's mother reports to you that the girl has begun to have angry outbursts and spells of intense sobbing for her father. Without theory, you might be inclined to stop the sandplay, fearing that it is having harmful effects. If, on the other hand, you were aware of theory on child development and grieving, you

might interpret the change in the girl's behavior as a necessary, and therefore positive, early step in the grieving process and would not stop the intervention.

Imagine you were conducting research on the effectiveness of the sandplay intervention. If you were operating without theory, you would be likely to encounter analogous problems. You might, for example, measure the impact of the intervention prematurely or look for the wrong indicators of success. Without theory, you might be clueless in designing your study. How long should the intervention last? What is the minimum and maximum age for subjects?

Some research studies are conducted in a less structured and more flexible fashion, in an attempt to minimize the influence of theoretical expectations on what is observed. That is, the researchers may not want their theoretical predelictions to bias their outlook and narrow what they look for. Theory plays a role in these less structured studies as well. Although these studies may be less guided by theory, they typically seek to identify patterns that will help generate new theory. Also, it may be impossible for professionally trained researchers to put aside completely the theoretical frameworks they have learned. Thus, their prior knowledge of child development theory, and theory on the grieving process, might help them see patterns in mounds of case record data—patterns suggesting that effective interventions with children who have lost a parent seem to involve a stage when the child's anger over the loss gets acted out. Moreover, their prior theoretical knowledge can help them make sense out of observations paradoxically suggesting that effective interventions involve a period during which the problem might appear (to a naive observer) to become exacerbated.

Theories also help researchers develop useful implications from their findings for practice and policy. Suppose a researcher finds that broken homes produce more delinquency than intact homes. Without the use of theory, our understanding of why this is so, and what to do about it, would be rather limited. Suppose, however, that we have a theoretical understanding of why broken homes produce more delinquency, and that two important reasons are lack of supervision and the absence of positive role models. This would improve our position to develop effective social programs, such as after-school mentoring programs, for example.

In this chapter, we are going to explore some of the more specific ways theory and research work hand in hand in the adventure of inquiry into social policy and social work practice. We'll begin by illustrating the interconnections between theory and research in the context of some prominent social work practice models.

SOCIAL WORK PRACTICE MODELS

In social work, we tend to apply existing social science theories in an effort to alleviate problems in social welfare. The models that help us organize our views about social work practice often reflect a synthesis of existing theories. We call them *practice models.*

The social work literature is diverse in what practice models are identified and in how they are labeled. If you have taken other social work courses, you may have encountered the following terms for practice models: *psychosocial, functionalist, problem-solving, cognitive-behavioral, task-centered, case management, crisis intervention, ecological perspective, life model, generalist, empirically based practice, eclectic,* and others. Social work practice models tend not to be mutually exclusive. Many of them, for example, stress the importance of the worker-client relationship and the need to forge a therapeutic alliance.

Each model, if interpreted narrowly, can appear to omit important aspects of practice or perhaps overemphasize things that are not applicable to many types of problems or clients. Certain models, for example, have been portrayed as more applicable to voluntary clients than to involuntary clients or more applicable to clients who want and

can afford long-term treatment geared toward personality change than to those who need immediate, concrete, and short-term help with socioeconomic crises and who are unable or unlikely to utilize long-term treatment. Certain models are sometimes criticized for dealing only with superficial aspects of client problems—of dealing only with symptoms without resolving underlying issues that will perpetuate the problem in other forms. Other models, in contrast, are criticized for overemphasizing unrealistically lofty long-term psychological and curative goals that are not relevant to many clients needing social care, economic assistance, or protective environments.

Over time, partly in response to criticism, particular models tend to expand, encompassing important new areas of research findings and theory. As this happens, distinctions between the models become increasingly blurred. This process is evident in Eda Goldstein's *Encyclopedia of Social Work* (1995) description of the *psychosocial model.* Goldstein describes how the psychosocial model expanded after it came under increasing criticism in the 1960s for being too narrowly psychoanalytic and insufficiently attuned to the needs and strengths of oppressed populations and other diverse target groups. Partially in response to these criticisms, but also in response to emerging new theories and the changing landscape of social work practice, the psychosocial model broadened to encompass a social systems and ecological perspective, factors in cultural diversity, crisis theory and crisis intervention, cognitive theory, biological forces, communications theory, role theory, and the impact of community, organizational, and societal forces. Despite this expansion, however, Goldstein acknowledges that the psychosocial model still emphasizes personality factors more than other models do, and therefore may be more congenial to psychotherapists than are some other models.

We won't delve here into the characteristics of all the various models of social work practice, or into the subtleties of how they are similar and different. You can study that in courses on practice or in courses that introduce you to the profession of social work. Instead, we'll simply illustrate how certain themes can influence the way we choose to research social work problems.

Let's begin by considering the evaluation of an outreach program for battered women who still live with the batterer. In researching the effectiveness of the program, a key issue is what to measure as an indicator of successful program outcome. As its name implies, one of the themes of the *functionalist model* of practice is to use the *function* of the agency as a basis for identifying successful outcomes. Those taking a functionalist approach, therefore, might be guided by the agency's mission in choosing an outcome indicator and in formulating a hypothesis.

Suppose the stated objective of the program is to help the women realize the danger they are in and to leave the batterer. This might imply testing the hypothesis that participation in the program increases the likelihood that battered women will leave the batterer. One might be even more likely to pursue this line of inquiry if one or one's agency was further identified with a feminist model that tended to see women's problems in terms of male oppression. How do you suppose individuals who follow an older and narrower version of the psychosocial model might view this approach? Chances are some would call it short-sighted and superficial. The psychosocial model gives more emphasis to the intrapsychic bases of client problems and to the notion that clients carry over problems from previous relationships, dating back to childhood, into present relationships. Proponents of this model might wonder whether battered women, having left one batterer, would soon find themselves in a relationship with another batterer (or perhaps return some day to the original batterer). If so, then simply leaving the current batterer might not be taken as a sufficient indicator of successful intervention.

Instead, psychosocially oriented investigators might want to measure change in certain personality characteristics and follow clients over a long period to see if they stay out of battering relation-ships. A possible hypothesis here might be: Participation in the program reduces depression and dependency and increases the likelihood of avoiding battering in the future.

Some practitioners who have worked with battered women might find some aspects of that particular psychosocial perspective unacceptable, perceiving that it seems to at least in part "blame the victim" for her plight. They might therefore undertake research to assess whether the prevalence of dysfunctional personality characteristics among battered women, or their difficulties in staying out of a battering relationship, can be seen as normal reactions to having been victimized, rather than part of the explanation for the original victimization. Of course, some psychosocial proponents might be equally likely to pursue this line of research, although they might expect to find the opposite type of results.

Let's consider another illustration, this time looking at the psychosocial model and the cognitive-behavioral model. We'll apply this illustration to the treatment of parents at risk of child abuse. The *cognitive-behavioral model* looks at problems like child abuse in terms of dysfunctional emotions connected to irrational beliefs and the need to restructure cognitions and learn better coping skills and parenting skills. Rather than focusing on long-term personality change and dealing with unresolved issues stemming from the parents' own childhood, this model deals in the present with specific skills, cognitions, and behaviors that can be changed in the short term through behavior modification and cognitive therapy techniques.

When researching the outcome of the treatment of at-risk parents, individuals influenced by this model might do the following. They might administer paper-and-pencil tests that attempt to gauge whether parents have become less angry, have changed their attitudes about normal childhood behaviors that they initially perceived as provocative, and have learned new child-rearing techniques (such as using time-outs and so forth). They might also directly observe the parents with their children in situations that require parenting skills and count the number of times the parents exhibit desirable (praise, encouragement, and so forth) and undesirable (slapping, threatening, and so forth) parenting behaviors.

Those influenced by the psychosocial model might be somewhat skeptical of the adequacy of the preceding approach to researching treatment outcome. In particular, they might doubt whether any observed improvements would last very long after the termination of treatment and whether the parents' ability to give desired test answers or act in an acceptable manner while being observed would really reflect what goes on in the normal home environment when observers aren't present. They might suggest that a better indicator of outcome would be whether parents were actually court-reported for abusive behavior over the longer haul.

Although the foregoing illustration is essentially hypothetical, it bears noting that the bulk of actual research with favorable outcomes has evaluated interventions associated with the cognitive or behavioral models of practice. Most other models have received less research, and their outcomes have not been as consistently favorable. Proponents of some other models often attribute this to the "superficiality" of outcome indicators used in cognitive-behavioral evaluations and the difficulty of assessing the more complex, longer-range goals of their models. We won't resolve this debate here, and we expect it to continue for quite a while. Before we leave this section, let's look at one more hypothetical illustration of how practice models, theory, and research are interconnected.

Suppose a social service agency is concerned about the high incidence of premature termination of treatment among its caseload. How might different practice models influence different hypotheses about the possible causes of this problem?

Those taking a psychosocial approach might hypothesize that staff members with more extensive training in clinical diagnosis and psychotherapy have fewer premature terminations. Those taking a cognitive-behavioral approach might hypothesize that cases that have specific, observable target behaviors entered in the case records as treatment goals are less likely to terminate prematurely. Those taking a functionalist approach, which among other things emphasizes the primacy of the therapeutic relationship, might hypothesize that clients who terminate treatment prematurely will rate the quality of the worker-client relationship lower than clients who do not terminate prematurely.

Finally, let's consider the implications of two related models, the *problem-solving* and *task-centered* models, in this illustration. Each model recommends partializing clients' multiple and long-range problems into a series of steps, treating first the target problem that is both most pressing to the client and has the potential for some quick success. Then additional target problems are addressed, one at a time, in order of their tractability and relevance to the client—saving the most intractable and least relevant in the client's view for the later stages of treatment. Each model also emphasizes the importance of working on objectives that both worker and client agree are important and developing a contract with the client on those objectives, rather than just dealing with the deeper psychodynamic problems that (even if diagnostically sound) may have no relevance to the client.

If you were influenced by these models, what hypotheses about premature terminations might you formulate? Our guess is that you'd hypothesize that cases in which the practitioner partialized target problems and contracted with clients about mutually agreed-on treatment objectives were less likely to terminate prematurely than those in which practitioners did not take these steps.

PARADIGMS

If practice models and theories organize our observations and make sense of them, it must be noted that there is usually more than one way to organize or make sense of things. Different points of view are likely to yield different explanations. Imagine two people who begin working with battered wives: one a radical feminist and the other a firm believer in a right-wing Christian conservative view of traditional family values. They are likely to develop different explanations or select different practice models in their work, particularly in regard to whether the battered wives should be encouraged to leave their husbands or should participate with their husbands in a treatment approach that attempts to preserve the marriage while working on resolving the battering.

No one ever starts out with a completely clean slate to create a practice model or a theory. The concepts that are the building blocks of theory are not created out of nothing. We know that when we mentioned juvenile delinquency as an example of a topic for theory construction, you already had some implicit ideas about it. If we had asked you to list some concepts that would be relevant to a theory of juvenile delinquency, you would have been able to make suggestions. We might say that you already have a general point of view or frame of reference.

A **paradigm** is a fundamental model or scheme that organizes our view of something. Although a paradigm doesn't necessarily answer important questions, it tells us where to look for the answers. And, as we'll see repeatedly, where you look largely determines the answers you'll find.

Thomas Kuhn (1970) referred to paradigms as the fundamental points of view characterizing a science in its search for meaning. While we sometimes think of science as developing gradually over time, marked by important discoveries and inventions, Kuhn said it was typical for one paradigm to become entrenched, resisting any substantial change. Eventually, however, as the shortcomings of that paradigm become obvious, a new paradigm would emerge and supplant the old one. Thus, the view that the sun revolved around the earth was supplanted by the view that the earth revolved around the sun. Kuhn's classic book on the subject is titled, appropriately enough, *The Structure of Scientific Revolutions.*

Social scientists have developed a number of paradigms for use in understanding social behavior. The fate of supplanted paradigms in the social sciences has differed from what Kuhn observed in the natural sciences, however. Natural scientists generally believe that the succession from one paradigm to another represents progress from a false view to a true one. No modern astronomer believes that the sun revolves around the earth, for example.

In the social sciences, on the other hand, theoretical paradigms may gain or lose popularity, but they are seldom discarded altogether. Not unlike social work practice models, the paradigms of the social sciences offer a variety of views, each of which offers insights that others lack—but ignores aspects of social life that other paradigms reveal.

The symbolic interactionist paradigm, for instance, sees social life as a process of interactions among individuals. Coming from this paradigm to address juvenile delinquency, you might focus on the ways young people interact as peers. How do young people gain approval in the eyes of friends? How do juvenile gangs recruit and initiate new members? Or, put differently, how do parents go about providing good or bad role models for their children? These are examples of the kinds of questions you might ask if you were approaching juvenile delinquency from the symbolic interactionist paradigm.

The functionalist or social systems paradigm, on the other hand, focuses on the organizational structure of social life. What are the components of society, and how are those components interrelated? From this paradigm, you might pay special attention to the impact of broad economic conditions on delinquency rates: Does delinquency increase during periods of high unemployment, for example? Or does the increased complexity of modern society make it harder for young people to understand what's right or wrong? Attention might be paid to the causes of failure in social control, the breakdown of law and order.

The conflict paradigm describes social life as a struggle among competing individuals and groups. It is, for instance, a competition between the haves and the have-nots, as in the Marxist "class struggle." From this paradigm, you might see juvenile delinquency as a response of the working class to their oppression by the rulers of society. Or, quite differently, you might see delinquency among young people as a way of competing for status.

The three paradigms we have just mentioned—the symbolic interactionist paradigm, the functionalist or social systems paradigm, and the conflict paradigm—are but a few of a larger list of social science paradigms. Sometimes the distinction between the terms *theory* and *paradigm* is fuzzy, since it is possible for some people to become so enamored of and entrenched in one particular theory that they tend to interpret a wide range of phenomena only in terms of that theory, missing or dogmatically dismissing the alternative insights and perspectives that other theories might offer. Thus, some might depict certain theories—psychoanalytic theory, role theory, behavioral theory, and so on—as paradigms. In this sense, it becomes possible to conceive of social work practice models as operating like paradigms for some social workers.

Four paradigms that currently are the subject of much attention and debate pertaining specifically to how best to conduct research in social work and the social sciences can be called: *positivism, postpositivism, interpretivism,* and the *conflict paradigm*. We say "can be called" because different authors use different labels for these paradigms, and not all authors are consistent in the way they define them. The inconsistent labeling of paradigms can confuse even the most experienced social scientists, and we would encourage you to keep this in mind if the labels we use differ from labels used in other writings you may have read. Let's now examine these paradigms and their research implications.

Early Positivism

When the French philosopher Auguste Comte (1798–1857) coined the term *sociologie* in 1822, he launched an intellectual adventure that is still unfolding today. Most important, Comte identified society as a phenomenon that could be studied scientifically. (Initially, he had wanted to label his enterprise *social physics,* but that term was co-opted by another scholar.)

Prior to Comte's time, society simply *was.* To the extent that people recognized different kinds of societies or changes in society over time, religious paradigms generally predominated in explanations of the differences. The state of social affairs was often seen as a reflection God's will. Or, alternately, people were challenged to create a "city of God" on earth to replace sin and godlessness.

Comte separated his inquiry from religion. He thought that society could be studied scientifically, replacing religious belief with scientific objectivity—basing knowledge on observations through the five senses rather than basing it on belief. Comte felt that society could be understood logically and rationally, and studied as scientifically as biology or physics.

Comte's view was to form the basic foundation for the subsequent development of the social sciences. In his optimism for the future, he coined the term **positivism** to describe this scientific approach—in contrast to what he regarded as negative elements in the Enlightenment. Only in recent decades has the ideal of positivism come under serious challenge, as we'll see later in this discussion.

Postpositivism

We began with Comte's assertion that society could be studied rationally and scientifically. Since his time, the growth of science, the relative decline of superstition, and the rise of bureaucratic structures would all seem to put rationality more and more in the center of social life. As fundamental as rationality is to most of us, however, some contemporary scholars have raised questions about it.

For example, positivistic social scientists have sometimes erred in assuming that humans will always act rationally. We're sure there is ample evidence in your own experience to indicate that this is not the case. And yet, many modern economic models fundamentally assume that people will make rational choices in the economic sector: they will choose the highest-paying job, pay the lowest price, and so on. However, this ignores the power of such matters as tradition, loyalty, image, and many other qualities that compete with reason in the determination of human behavior.

A more sophisticated positivism would assert that we can rationally understand even "irrational" human behavior. Here's an example. In the famous "Asch Experiment" (Asch, 1958), a group of subjects are presented with a set of lines on a screen and are asked to identify the two equal-length lines. If you were a subject in such an experiment, you would find the correct answer pretty obvious in each set of lines. To your surprise, however, you might find the other subjects all agreeing on a different answer!

As it turns out, of course, you would be the only real subject in the experiment—all the others were working with the experimenter—and the purpose would be to see whether you would be swayed by public pressure and go along with the incorrect answer. In one-third of the initial experiments, Asch found his subjects did just that.

Giving in to public pressure like this would be an example of nonrational behavior. Nonetheless, notice that it is possible to study such behavior scientifically. Experimenters have examined the various circumstances that will lead more or fewer subjects to go along with the incorrect answer. Thus, it is possible to study nonrational behavior rationally.

The contemporary challenge to positivism, however, goes beyond the question of whether humans behave rationally. In part, the criticism of positivism challenges the idea that scientists can really be as objective as the ideal image of science assumes. Most scientists would agree that personal feelings can and do influence the problems scientists choose to study, what they choose to observe, and the conclusions they draw from those observations.

Research Implications of Positivism and Postpositivism

Positivist and postpositivist researchers emphasize objectivity, precision, and generalizability in their inquiries. Postpositivist researchers recognize that observation and measurement cannot be as purely objective as the ideal image of science implies, but they still attempt to anticipate and minimize the impact of potential unobjective influences. Like positivist researchers, postpositivists also seek to verify causality and attempt to sort out what really is causing what, using logical procedures to distinguish the separate influences of interrelated variables, but they do so in a more probabilistic sense than positivists. Like positivists, postpositivists believe there is an objective external reality, but they recognize its elusive nature. Instead of attempting to verify universal laws, they examine the conditions under which particular ideas and hypotheses are and are not falsified.

Both positivists and postpositivists use highly structured quantitative research methods, but postpositivists are also likely to employ qualitative methods, recognizing the limitations of relying exclusively on quantitative methods in attempting to understand an elusive social reality. When postpositivists utilize qualitative methods they tend to see their findings as essentially tentative and exploratory in nature, generating new ideas for further testing. Positivist and postpositivist researchers are skeptical about the subjective impressions of other researchers. Indeed, they tend to be skeptical of the conclusions of any individual research study. They see research as a never-ending and self-correcting quest for knowledge involving replications of findings by different investigators. While postpositivist researchers recognize that research is never entirely free from political and ideological values, they believe it is possible to utilize logical arrangements and observational techniques that reduce the impact of one's values on one's findings. They also assume that others can judge the validity of one's findings in light of these mechanisms and can test out the findings in later studies.

Interpretivism

A paradigm that contrasts with positivism, but that is not mutually exclusive with it, can be called *interpretivism*. Interpretive researchers do not focus on isolating and objectively measuring causes, or in developing generalizations. Instead, they attempt to gain an empathic understanding of how people feel inside, seeking to interpret individuals' everyday experiences, deeper meanings and feelings, and idiosyncratic reasons for their behaviors. Interpretive researchers are likely to hang out with people and observe them in their natural settings, where they attempt to develop an in-depth subjective understanding of their lives. Rather than convey statistical probabilities for particular causal processes over a large number of people, interpretive researchers attempt to help readers of their reports sense what it is like to walk in the shoes of the small number of people they study.

Interpretive researchers believe that you cannot adequately learn about people by relying solely on objective measurement instruments that are used in the same standardized manner from person to person—instruments that attempt to remove the observer from the observee in order to pursue objectivity. Instead, interpretive researchers believe that the best way to learn about people is to be flexible and subjective in your approach so that you can try to see the subject's world through the subject's own eyes. It is not enough to simply measure the subject's external behaviors or questionnaire answers. You must probe deeper into the subjective meanings and social contexts of an individual's words or deeds.

Both positivist and interpretive paradigms involve the use of theory, but the function of theory varies across the two paradigms. Whereas in positivist paradigms theory functions to provide broad generalizations about interrelationships among thinly defined causal variables, interpretivist theory provides a richly detailed, idiographic description of how a smaller group of people conduct and interpret their everyday lives. Positivist and postpositivist researchers are likely to test their theories by replicating studies across different samples and seeing if different measurement approaches yield the same findings. Interpretive researchers are more likely to be satisfied with a theory if the people they studied say the theory makes sense to them or if those who read their theory acknowledge its usefulness in helping them better see the world through the eyes of the people studied.

Interpretive researchers may or may not agree with positivists and postpositivists that there is an objective, external social reality that can be discovered. But, regardless of their views on the existence of an objective, external reality, interpretive researchers are more interested in discovering and understanding how people perceive and experience the world on an internal, subjective basis. They further believe that no explanation of social reality will be complete without understanding how people's subjective *interpretations* of reality influence the *creation* of their social reality. A positivist researcher briefly observing each of a large number of homeless women might note their neglect of personal hygiene and may therefore develop recommendations connected to emotional dysfunction or the need for social skills training. An interpretivist researcher, in contrast, would study a small group of homeless women more intensively, would probe deeply into their subjective interpretations of their social reality, and might conclude on this basis that their repugnant odor and appearance is a rational strategy for preventing sexual victimization in what they perceive to be a dangerous social context.

The Conflict Paradigm

The final paradigm we'll consider, like the other paradigms, has been labeled in various ways. Some have called it a Marxist paradigm. Others have called it a feminist paradigm. Labeling it an empowerment paradigm or an advocacy paradigm might also make sense. Regardless of what it is called, the chief distinguishing feature of this paradigm is its focus on oppression and its commitment to use research procedures not for truth seeking, but to empower oppressed groups. Toward that end, investigators committed to this paradigm might use quantitative or qualitative procedures, idiographic or nomothetic approaches, or selected elements of other paradigms.

When researchers in this paradigm use methods that resemble the quantitative studies typically associated with positivism and postpositivism, they are distinguished from positivists and postpositivists by their stance toward their findings. Whereas positivist and postpositivist researchers attempt to minimize the influence of political or ideological values in interpreting their findings and attempt to interpret those findings in a neutral, factual manner, conflict paradigm researchers set out to interpret findings through the filter of their empowerment and advocacy aims.

To illustrate this point, consider the difference between how a postpositivist researcher and a feminist researcher might interpret a finding that male social workers tend to earn more than female social workers, but that this difference diminishes when we compare males and females with the same job responsibilities or years of experience. The postpositivist researcher, particularly one not well versed in women's issues, might conclude that this finding indicates that the probabilistic influence of sexism on salaries in social work is less than many think it is. The feminist researcher, however, might conclude from the same finding that sexism influences salaries via less pay for "women's work" or by the loss of annual increments during child-rearing years. In fact, in light of this thinking, the feminist researcher might not even examine the influence of job responsibilities or years of experience on salaries in the first place.

When conflict paradigm researchers use qualitative methods commonly used by interpretivist researchers, these researchers are distinguished from interpretivists by going beyond the subjective meanings of the people they study and by their attempts to connect their observations to their a priori notion of an unjust, broader objective reality that they are seeking to change. Thus, a feminist researcher guided by the conflict paradigm and taking an interpretive approach in the study of battered women would not stop at seeing reality through the eyes of the battered women, but would additionally address aspects of the feminist's vision of reality that might not be shared by the women being studied. For example, if the battered women deny or minimize the severity of the battering, find excuses for the batterer, or think that they cannot leave the batterer, a feminist researcher might note the discrepancy between their subjective views and the objective reality as seen by the feminist researcher. A feminist researcher also might raise questions about the reasons for these undesirable discrepancies and will attempt to derive recommendations for raising the feminist consciousness of the women and empowering them.

As you read this book, you may notice that it reflects contributions from different paradigms. For example, in chapters on surveys, experiments, and statistics, you will clearly detect elements of positivism and postpositivism. In chapters on qualitative methods and measurement, you may find postpositivist and interpretivist ideas. And throughout the book you will see conflict paradigm contributions, particularly where we discuss the use of social work research to alleviate human suffering and achieve social reform. We will now examine the use of theory in the scientific method. As we discuss that topic, you will see that there is more than one way of using or constructing theory, and that paradigms can influence how one proceeds.

THEORY IN RESEARCH

Although the terms *paradigm* and *theory* are sometimes used interchangeably, there are some important differences between them. Paradigms are general frameworks for looking at life. A theory is a systematic set of interrelated statements intended to explain some aspect of social life or enrich our sense of how people conduct and find meaning in their daily lives. Different people who share the same paradigm may or may not share the same theoretical orientations. For example, some postpositivist social work researchers might seek to verify the effectiveness of interventions rooted in cognitive or behavioral theory, while other postpositivist social work researchers might seek to verify the effectiveness of interventions rooted in psychoanalytic theory.

Science is sometimes characterized as logico-empirical. This awkward term carries an important message: the two pillars of science are (1) logic or rationality and (2) observation. A scientific understanding of the world must make sense and correspond with what we observe. Both of these elements are essential to science.

As a gross generalization, scientific theory deals with the logical aspect of science; research methods deal with the observational aspect. A scientific theory describes the logical relationships that appear to exist among parts of the world, and research offers means for seeing whether those relationships actually exist in the real world. Though too simplistic, perhaps, this statement provides a useful jumping-off point for the examination of theory in research.

Theory, Not Philosophy or Belief

Social scientific theory has to do with what is, not with what should be. We point that out because social theory for many centuries has combined these two orientations. Social philosophers mixed liberally their observations of what happened around them, their speculations about why, and their ideas about how things ought to be. Although modern social scientists may do the same from time to time, it is important to realize that social science has to do with how things are and why.

This means that scientific theory—and, more broadly, science itself—cannot settle debates on value. Science cannot determine whether capitalism is better or worse than socialism except in terms of some set of agreed-on criteria. We could determine only scientifically whether capitalism or socialism most supported human dignity and freedom if we were able to agree on some measures of dignity and freedom, and our conclusion in that case would depend totally on the measures

we had agreed on. The conclusions would have no general meaning beyond that. By the same token, if we could agree that suicide rates, say, or perhaps giving to charity, were good measures of a religion's quality, then we would be in a position to determine scientifically whether Buddhism or Christianity was the better religion. Again, however, our conclusion would be inextricably tied to the criteria agreed on. As a practical matter, people are seldom able to agree on criteria for determining issues of value, so science is seldom of any use in settling such debates. Moreover, people's convictions in matters of value are more nonrational than rational, making science, which deals in rational proofs, all the more inappropriate.

This issue will be considered in more detail in Chapter 18 when we look at evaluation research. As you'll see, social scientists have become increasingly involved in studying programs that reflect ideological points of view, and one of the biggest problems researchers face is getting people to agree on criteria of success and failure. Yet such criteria are essential if social scientific research is to tell us anything useful about matters of value. By analogy, a stopwatch cannot tell us if one sprinter is better than another unless we can agree that speed is the critical criterion.

Thus, social science can assist us in knowing only what is and why. It can be used to address the question of what ought to be only when people agree on the criteria for deciding what's better than something else. Furthermore, this agreement seldom occurs. With that understanding, let's turn now to some of the fundamental bases on which social science allows us to develop theories about what is and why.

Social Regularities

Many things in life seem to be chaotic. Ultimately, social scientific theory aims to determine the logical and persistent patterns of regularity in social life. Lying behind that aim is the fundamental assumption that life is regular, not totally chaotic or random—that if we investigate deeply we can detect patterns in what appears at first to be mere chaos. That assumption, of course, applies to all science, but it is sometimes a barrier for people when they first approach social science.

Certainly at first glance, it would appear that the subject matter of the physical sciences is more regular than that of the social sciences. A heavy object, after all, falls to earth every time we drop it, but a person may vote for a particular candidate in one election and against that same candidate in the next election. Similarly, ice always melts when heated enough, but seemingly honest people sometimes steal. Examples like these, although true, can lead us to lose sight of the high degree of regularity in social affairs.

To begin, a vast number of formal norms in society create a considerable degree of regularity. For example, only persons who have reached a certain age are permitted to vote in elections. In many states, only people with social work degrees and certain amounts of continuing education are allowed to call themselves certified social workers. Such formal prescriptions, then, regulate, or regularize, social behavior.

Aside from formal prescriptions, other social norms can be observed that create more regularities. Registered Republicans are more likely to vote for Republican candidates than are registered Democrats. University professors tend to earn more money than unskilled laborers. Men earn more than women. Whites earn more than blacks. The list of regularities could go on and on.

To review, all science is based on the fundamental assumption that regularity exists in what is to be studied, and we have noted that regularities exist in social life. Therefore, logically, social behavior should be susceptible to scientific analysis. But is that necessarily the case? After all, you probably know an unskilled laborer who earns more than most college professors. Or are those kinds of irregularities worthy of scientific study? So Republicans vote for Republicans more than Democrats do. So what? Isn't that pretty obvious? We don't need scientific theories and research to understand something like that. Three major objections can be raised in regard to the kinds of social regularities we've been looking at,

and those should be dealt with before we proceed. First, some of the regularities may seem trivial; everyone is aware of them. Second, contradictory cases may be cited, indicating that the "regularity" isn't totally regular anyway. And third, it may be argued that the people involved in the regularity could upset the whole thing if they wanted to. Let's handle the business of triviality first, those things that "everybody knows."

The Charge of Triviality   Before the 1970s nobody had ever tested the effects of psychosocially oriented social casework, with and without drug therapy, on the community adjustment of formerly hospitalized patients suffering from schizophrenia. If you asked social workers at that time whether patients who did not receive drug therapy would be better off receiving no service whatsoever or only psychosocial casework, chances are the vast majority would have replied that it was pretty obvious that some service is better than none. If you asked whether the casework without drug therapy would, in general, be harmful, their replies may have been an emphatic "Of course not!" And if you had conducted a study on this that concluded that the casework was indeed not harmful, the field's response may have been a collective yawn accompanied by the charge of triviality—that you merely tested the "obvious" and discovered what everybody already knew.

You may recall from this book's prologue, however, that when a social worker (Gerard Hogarty) actually conducted a series of studies on this issue during the 1970s, his findings showed just the opposite. Patients who received the social casework alone, without drug therapy, fared worse than the patients who received neither drugs nor casework.

Hogarty and his associates continued studying this problem in an effort to make sense of this finding. As we mentioned in the prologue, ultimately they reasoned that people suffering from schizophrenia tend to have great difficulty coping with the cognitive stimulation associated with the casework, and they need the drug therapy to be able to tolerate it. Hogarty's work contributed to the development of theory on the influence of overstimulation on the course of schizophrenia and to the development of psychoeducational family interventions, the effectiveness of which was supported by later research (Simon, McNeil, Franklin, and Cooperman, 1991).

This story shows that testing the obvious is a valuable function of any science, physical or social. All too often, the obvious turns out to be wrong, and apparent triviality is not a legitimate objection to any scientific endeavor. (Darwin coined the phrase *fool's experiment* in ironic reference to much of his own research—research in which he tested things that everyone else already knew.)

What About Exceptions?   The objection that there are always exceptions to any social regularity is also inappropriate. It is not important that a particular woman earns more money than a particular man if men earn more than women overall. The pattern still exists. Social regularities represent probabilistic patterns, and a general pattern need not be reflected in 100% of the observable cases.

This rule applies in the physical sciences as well as in social science. In genetics, for example, the mating of a blue-eyed person with a brown-eyed person will probably result in a brown-eyed offspring. The birth of a blue-eyed child does not challenge the observed regularity, however, since the geneticist states only that the brown-eyed offspring is more likely and, further, that brown-eyed offspring will be born in a certain percentage of the cases. The social scientist makes a similar, probabilistic prediction—that women overall are likely to earn less than men. And the social scientist has grounds for asking why that is the case.

People Could Interfere   Finally, the objection that observed social regularities could be upset through the conscious will of the actors is not a serious challenge to social science, even though there does not seem to be a parallel situation in the physical sciences. (Presumably an object cannot resist falling to earth "because it wants to.") There is no denying that a religious, right-wing

bigot could go to the polls and vote for an agnostic, left-wing radical African American if he or she wanted to upset the political scientist studying the election. All voters in an election could suddenly switch to the underdog just to frustrate the pollster. Similarly, workers could go to work early or stay home from work and thereby prevent the expected rush-hour commuter traffic. But these things do not happen often enough to seriously threaten the observation of social regularities.

The fact remains that social norms do exist, and the social scientist can observe the effects of these norms. When norms change over time, the social scientist can observe and explain these changes. Ultimately, social regularities persist because they tend to make sense for the people involved in them. When the social scientist suggests that it is logical to expect a given type of person to behave in a certain manner, that type of person may well agree with the logical basis for the expectation. Thus, although a religious, right-wing bigot could vote for an agnostic, left-wing radical African American candidate, such a voter would be the first to consider it stupid to do so.

Aggregates, Not Individuals

Social regularities do exist, then, and they are both susceptible to and worthy of theoretical and empirical study. Social scientists primarily study social patterns rather than individual ones. All the regular patterns we've mentioned have reflected the aggregate actions and situations of many individuals.

Sometimes the aggregated regularities are amazing. Consider the birthrate, for example. People have babies for an incredibly wide range of personal reasons. Some do it because their own parents want them to. Some feel it's a way of completing their womanhood or manhood. Others want to hold their marriages together. Still others have babies by accident.

If you have had a baby, you could probably tell a much more detailed, idiosyncratic story. Why did you have the baby when you did, rather than a year earlier or later? Maybe your house burned down and you had to delay a year before you could afford to have the baby. Maybe you felt that being a family person would demonstrate maturity that would support a promotion at work.

Everyone who had a baby last year had a different set of reasons for doing so. Yet despite this vast diversity, despite the idiosyncrasy of each individual's reasons, the overall birthrate in a society is remarkably consistent from year to year. If the rate is 19.1 per 1000 this year, it is likely to be very close to 19.1 per 1000 next year, even though the rate may be gradually rising or declining over a longer period of time. If the birthrate of a society were to be 19.1, 35.6, 7.8, 28.9, and 16.2 in five successive years, demographers would begin dropping like flies.

Social scientific theories dealing with aggregated patterns of behavior seek to explain why these patterns are so regular even when the individuals participating in them may change over time. Their aim is to understand the systems within which people operate, the systems that explain why people do what they do. The elements in such systems are not people but variables.

A Variable Language

The idea of a system composed of variables is somewhat complex, and we want to introduce this subtle aspect of social scientific theory with an analogy that tells the story. The subject of a direct social work practitioner's attention is the client. If the client has a problem, the social worker's purpose is to assist that client in alleviating that problem. By contrast, a social work researcher's subject matter is different: the impact of social services on a social problem, for example. The social work researcher may study the social worker's client, but for the researcher that client is relevant only as one of many recipients of a social service.

That is not to say that social work researchers don't care about real people. They certainly do. Their ultimate purpose in studying social problems or social services is to help people benefit from services or to help alleviate social problems.

But in actual research, clients are directly relevant only for what they reveal about the service or social problem under study. In fact, when a social problem can be studied meaningfully without studying actual clients, social work researchers often do so.

By the same token, social science involves the study of two kinds of concepts: variables and the attributes that compose them. Social scientific theories are written in a variable language, and people get involved only as the carriers of those variables. Here's what social scientists mean by variables and attributes. *Attributes* are characteristics or qualities that describe an object—in this case, a person. Examples include female, Asian, alienated, conservative, dishonest, intelligent, farmer, and so forth. Anything you might say to describe yourself or someone else involves an attribute.

Variables, on the other hand, are logical groupings of attributes. Thus, for example, male and female are attributes, and sex or gender are the variables composed of those two attributes. The variable occupation is composed of attributes such as farmer, professor, and truck driver. Social class is a variable composed of a set of attributes such as upper class, middle class, lower class, or some similar set of divisions.

The relationship between attributes and variables lies at the heart of both description and explanation in science. For example, we might describe a social service agency's caseload in terms of the variable sex by reporting the observed frequencies of the attributes male and female: "The caseload is 60% men and 40% women." An unemployment rate can be thought of as a description of the variable employment status of a labor force in terms of the attributes employed and unemployed. Even the report of family income for a city is a summary of attributes composing that variable: $3124, $10,980, $35,000, and so forth.

The relationship between attributes and variables is more complicated in the case of explanation and gets to the heart of the variable language of scientific theory. Here's a social work practice example, involving two variables: use of contracting and level of client satisfaction. For the sake of simplicity, let's assume that the variable level of client satisfaction has only two attributes: satisfied and dissatisfied.

Now let's suppose that 90% of the clients without contracts are dissatisfied and the other 10% are satisfied. And let's suppose that 30% of the clients with contracts are dissatisfied and the other 70% are satisfied. This is illustrated graphically in the first part of Figure 2-1.

Part 1 of Figure 2-1 illustrates a relationship or association between the variables use of contracting and level of client satisfaction. This relationship can be seen in terms of the pairings of attributes on the two variables. There are two predominant pairings: (1) those who have contracts and are satisfied and (2) those who have no contracts and are dissatisfied. Here are two other useful ways of seeing that relationship.

First, let's suppose that we play a game in which we bet on your ability to guess whether a client is satisfied or dissatisfied. We'll pick the clients one at a time (not telling you which one we've picked) and you have to guess whether the client is satisfied. We'll do it for all 20 clients in the first part of Figure 2-1. Your best strategy in that case would be to always guess dissatisfied, since 12 out of the 20 are categorized that way.

Thus, you'll get 12 right and 8 wrong, for a net success of 4.

Now let's suppose that when we pick a client from the figure, we have to tell you whether the practitioner engaged the client in contracting. Your best strategy now would be to guess dissatisfied for each client without a contract and satisfied for each one with a contract. If you followed that strategy, you'd get 16 right and 4 wrong. Your improvement in guessing level of satisfaction by knowing whether contracting was used is an illustration of what is meant by the variables being related.

Second, by contrast, let's consider how the 20 people would be distributed if use of contracting and level of satisfaction were unrelated to one another. This is illustrated in the second part of Figure 2-1. Notice that half the clients have contracts and half do not. Also notice that 12 of the 20 (60%) are dissatisfied. If 6 of the 10 people in each group were dissatisfied, we would conclude that the two variables were unrelated to each other. Then knowing whether contracting was used would not be of any value to you in guessing whether that client was satisfied.

We're going to be looking at the nature of relationships between variables in some depth in Part 5 of this book. In particular, we'll see some

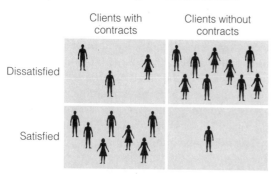

1. Clients are more satisfied with service delivery when their practitioners develop contracts with them.

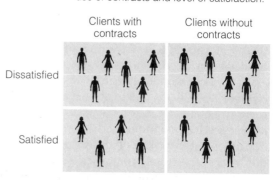

2. There is no apparent relationship between use of contracts and level of satisfaction.

Figure 2-1 Illustration of Relationships Between Two Variables (Two Possibilities)

of the ways relationships can be discovered and interpreted in research analysis. It is important that you have a general understanding of relationships now, however, in order to appreciate the logic of social scientific theories.

Theories describe the relationships that might logically be expected among variables. Often, the expectation involves the notion of causation. A person's attributes on one variable are expected to cause, predispose, or encourage a particular attribute on another variable. In the example just given, it appeared that the use of contracting may have helped cause clients to be more or less satisfied or dissatisfied. It seems that there is something about participating in contracting that leads clients to be more satisfied than if they do not participate in contracting.

The discussion of Figure 2-1 has involved the interpretation of data. We looked at the distribution of the 20 clients in terms of the two variables. In the construction of a theory, we would derive an expectation regarding the relationship between the two variables based on what we know about each. We might postulate, for example, that clients with contracts are more likely to agree with their practitioner about the problem to be worked on and to be motivated to work on that problem than are clients without contracts. Because they are more likely to agree with and be motivated to pursue the goals of the services, it follows that the clients with contracts would be more likely to be satisfied with those services. We might further postulate that a prerequisite of effective treatment is to deal with problems and pursue objectives on which the client and practitioner agree.

Notice that the theory has to do with the two variables, use of contracting and level of client satisfaction, not with people per se. People are, as we indicated before, the carriers of those two variables, so the relationship between the variables can only be seen by observing people. Ultimately, however, the theory is constructed of a variable language. It describes the associations that might logically be expected to exist between particular attributes of different variables.

As we'll discuss in more detail later in the book, use of contracting and level of client satisfaction in this example would be regarded as independent and dependent variables, respectively. These two concepts are implicit in deterministic, causal models. In this example, we assume that levels of satisfaction are determined or caused by something; satisfaction depends on something, hence it is called the *dependent variable*. That which the dependent variable depends on is called the *independent variable;* in this case, satisfaction depends on use of contracting. Although the use of contracting with the clients being studied varies, that variation is independent of level of satisfaction.

TWO LOGICAL SYSTEMS

During your education, you probably have heard someone refer to "*the* scientific method." Actually, it might be more accurate to refer to *two* scientific methods. The two methods are distinguished primarily by the ways they use theory in research. One method is based on *deductive logic;* we'll call it the deductive method. The other is based on *inductive logic;* we'll call it the inductive method. Let's now examine and contrast these two logical systems, beginning with the deductive method.

According to the deductive method, the researcher begins with a theory and then derives one or more hypotheses from that theory to be tested. The next step is to define in specific, observable terms the variables in each hypothesis and the operations to be used in measuring them. The final step is to implement the specified measurements, thus conducting observations of the way things really are and seeing if those observations confirm or fail to confirm the hypotheses. Sometimes this final step involves conducting experiments, sometimes interviewing people, sometimes visiting what you're interested in and watching it.

Figure 2-2 provides a schematic diagram of the deductive model of scientific inquiry, moving from theory to operationalization to observation. In it, we see the researcher beginning with an interest in some problem or an idea about it. For example, the researcher might be concerned about the problem of adolescent runaways. Next comes the development of a theoretical understanding. The theoretical considerations result in a **hypothesis,** or an expectation about the way things ought to be in the world if the theoretical expectations are correct. For example, the researcher might see family dysfunctioning as explaining why adolescents run away, and may use family systems theory to understand family dysfunctioning and what to do about it. In Figure 2-2, this broadly conceived hypothesis is represented by the notation $Y = f(X)$. This is is a conventional way of saying that Y (for example, runaway episodes) is a function of (is in some way affected by) X (for example, family dysfunctioning). At that level, however, X and Y have general rather than specific meanings. From this theoretical understanding one or more specific hypotheses are derived. For example, one could hypothesize that the pro-

vision of family systems therapy will reduce the likelihood of future runaway episodes. Next, those two general concepts must be translated into specific, observable indicators in order to make the hypothesis testable. This is done in the operationalization process. The lowercase y and lowercase x, for instance, represent concrete, observable indicators of capital Y and capital X. In our runaway example, the lowercase y refers to the need to spell out in observable terms exactly what constitutes a runaway episode, and the lowercase x refers to the need to describe in specific terms the substance and processes that comprise the type of family systems theory being tested. Finally, observations aimed at finding out are part of what is typically called **hypothesis testing.**

As we already noted, the deductive method uses what is called *deductive logic* (see **deduction** in Glossary), which is in contrast to *inductive logic* (see **induction** in Glossary). W. I. B. Beveridge, a philosopher of science, describes these two systems of logic as follows:

> Logicians distinguish between inductive reasoning (from particular instances to general principles, from facts to theories) and deductive reasoning (from the general to the particular, applying a theory to a particular case). In induction one starts from observed data and develops a generalization which explains the relationships between the objects observed. On the other hand, in deductive reasoning one starts from some general law and applies it to a particular instance. (1950:113)

The classic illustration of deductive logic is the familiar syllogism "All men are mortal; Socrates is a man; therefore Socrates is mortal." This syllogism presents a theory and its operationalization. To prove it, you might then perform an empirical test of Socrates' mortality. That is essentially the approach discussed as the deductive model.

Using inductive logic, you might begin by noting that Socrates is mortal and observing a number of other men as well. You might then note that all the *observed* men were mortals, thereby arriving at the tentative conclusion that *all* men are mortal.

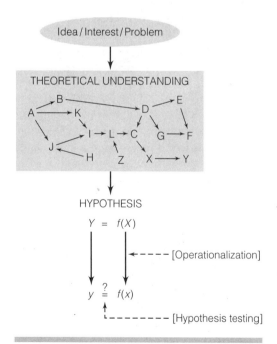

Figure 2-2 The Deductive Image of Science

Figure 2-3 shows a graphic comparison of the deductive and inductive methods. In both cases, we are interested in the relationship between the number of hours spent studying for an exam and the grade earned on that exam. Using the deductive method, we would begin by examining the matter logically. Doing well on an exam reflects a student's ability to recall and manipulate information. Both of these abilities should be increased by exposure to the information before the exam. In this fashion, we would arrive at a *hypothesis* suggesting a positive relationship between the number of hours spent studying and the grade earned on the exam. We say *positive* because we expect grades to increase as the hours of studying increase. If increased hours produced decreased grades, that would be called a *negative* relationship. The hypothesis is represented by the line in Part I(a) of Figure 2-3.

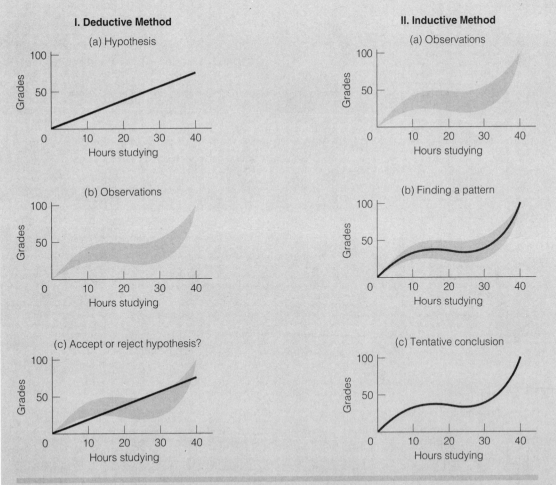

Figure 2-3 Deductive and Inductive Methods

Our next step, using the deductive method, would be to make observations relevant to testing our hypothesis. The shaded area in Part I(b) of the figure represents perhaps hundreds of observations of different students, noting how many hours they studied and what grades they got. Finally, in Part I(c), we compare the hypothesis and the observations. Because observations in the real world seldom if ever match our expectations perfectly, we must decide whether the match is close enough to consider the hypothesis confirmed. Put differently, can we conclude that the hypothesis describes the general pattern that exists, granting some variations in real life?

Now let's turn to addressing the same research question, using the inductive method. In this case, we would begin—as in Part II(a) of the figure—with a set of observations. Curious about the relationship between hours spent studying and grades earned, we might simply arrange to collect some relevant data. Then we'd look for a pattern that best represented or summarized our observations. In Part II(b) of the figure, the pattern is shown as a curved line running through the center of the curving mass of points.

The pattern found among the points in this case suggests that with 1 to 15 hours of studying, each additional hour generally produces a higher grade on the exam. With 15 to about 25 hours, however, more study seems to slightly lower the grade. Studying more than 25 hours, on the other hand, results in a return to the initial pattern: more hours produce higher grades. Using the inductive method, then, we end up with a *tentative* conclusion about the pattern of the relationship between the two variables. The conclusion is tentative because the observations we have made cannot be taken as a test of the pattern—those observations are the *source* of the pattern we've created.

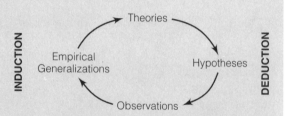

SOURCE: Adapted from Walter Wallace, *The Logic of Science in Sociology* (Chicago: Aldine-Atherton, 1971). Copyright © 1971 by Walter L. Wallace. Used by permission.

Figure 2-4 The Wheel of Science

What do you suppose would happen next in an actual research project? We'd try to find a logical explanation for the pattern discovered in the data, just as Hogarty tried to find a logical explanation for the discovery that the people with schizophrenia who received social casework without drug therapy fared worse than those who received neither drugs nor casework. Eventually, we'd arrive at an explanation—one that would generate further expectations about what should be observed in the real world. Then, we'd look again.

In actual practice, then, theory and research interact through a never-ending alternation of deduction, induction, deduction, and so forth. Walter Wallace (1971) has represented this process nicely as a circle, which is presented in a modified form in Figure 2-4. In the Wallace model, theories generate hypotheses, hypotheses suggest observations, observations produce generalizations, and those generalizations result in modifications of the theory. The modified theory then suggests somewhat modified hypotheses and a new set of observations, which produce somewhat revised generalizations, further modifying the theory. In this model there is clearly no beginning or ending point. You can begin anywhere in examining what interests you. Thus, if we seek to understand and do something about the problem of adolescent runaways, we can begin by deriving hypotheses from family systems theory (or some other theory) and then making observations to test those hypotheses, or we can begin by immersing ourselves in observations of runaways until we are struck by certain consistent patterns that seem to point us in a particular theoretical direction, which in turn will lead to hypotheses and observations.

In summary, the scientific norm of logical reasoning provides a bridge between theory and research—a two-way bridge. (The box entitled "Components of Scientific Theory" illustrates its "bridge" more graphically.) Scientific inquiry in practice typically involves an alternation between deduction and induction. During the deductive phase, we reason *toward* observations; during the inductive phase, we reason *from* observations. Both logic and observation are essential. In practice, both deduction and induction are routes to the construction of social theories. Let's look a little more closely at how each of the two methods operates in that regard.

COMPONENTS OF SCIENTIFIC THEORY

by Michael R. Leming, Department of Sociology, St. Olaf College

According to George Homans, scientific theory is an explanation of a phenomenon by the use of a deductive system of empirical propositions. The three basic components of scientific theory are (1) a conceptual scheme, (2) a set of propositions stating relationships between properties or variables, and (3) a context for verification.

The model of a suspension bridge serves as a good illustration of the relationship between scientific theory's three components. Bridges are constructed out of girders and

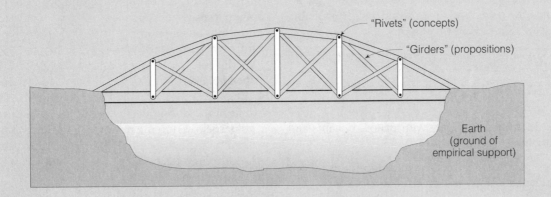

"Rivets" (concepts)

"Girders" (propositions)

Earth
(ground of
empirical support)

rivets and tied into both banks of the river. In similar fashion, a theory consists of concepts ("rivets") and propositions ("girders") tied into an empirical base of support. It is the relationship between the components that makes for a bridge or theory. A disorganized pile of girders and rivets are not sufficient components for what we would call a bridge. Likewise concepts, propositions, and observations are not sufficient in themselves for scientific theory.

Deductive Theory Construction

What's involved in deductive theory construction and hypothesis testing? Although theory construction is not a lockstep affair, the following list of elements in theory construction should organize the activity for you.

1. The first step is to specify the topic. In Chapter 4 we will examine in depth the criteria involved in topic selection in social work research. The topic should have value to the profession, but it should also interest you. It can be broad, such as "What are the explanations for homelessness?" or narrower, as in "What proportion of homeless adults have been previously hospitalized for mental disorders?"

2. Find out what others who have studied your topic have said about it. You can talk to some of these people and read what they and others have written. Appendix A of this book provides guidelines for using the library, and you'll probably spend a lot of your time there.

3. Specify the range of phenomena your theory addresses. Will your theory apply to all homeless people, will it apply only to one gender, only to homeless children, or what?

4. Identify and specify your major concepts and variables.

5. Assemble what is known (propositions) about the relationships among those variables.

6. Reason logically from those propositions to the specific topic you are examining.

As you identify the relevant concepts and discover what has already been learned about them, you can begin creating a propositional structure that explains the topic under study. For the most part, social scientists have not created formal, propositional theories. Still, it is useful to look at a well-reasoned example.

That's enough discussion of the pieces of deductive theory construction. Let's look now at an example of how those pieces fit together in deductive theory construction and empirical research.

An Example of Deductive Theory

The early civil rights movement, beginning in the mid-1950s, was reasonably peaceful outside the deep South, and even there the main acts of violence were perpetrated by whites against blacks. Blacks were, for the most part, nonviolent. All that changed during the summer of 1965. Beginning on August 11, 35 people died and about $200 million in damages were incurred in nearly a week of rioting, burning, and looting in the predominantly black suburb of Watts in Los Angeles.

Although the Watts rioting was triggered by a specific incident involving black residents and white police, that event couldn't account for the extent of the rioting that followed. Most of those who participated in the rioting had nothing to do with the original incident. Who were they, and why did they participate? Many people asked those questions. H. Edward Ransford (1968), a sociologist, was one who suggested an answer.

As he addressed the aftermath of Watts, Ransford found a body of theoretical literature dealing with extreme political behavior. Specifically, previous scholars had linked social isolation and powerlessness to political violence. As he surveyed the violent events of Watts, Ransford found it reasonable to expect that those two variables might lie at the base of participation in the rioting. It made sense to imagine that blacks who were isolated from the mainstream white society would feel they had little opportunity for communication. They would, moreover, have little investment in the system, so it was reasonable to expect that they would be more likely to riot than blacks already participating in the mainstream society.

Similarly, the psychological feeling of being powerless to effect peaceful changes in society should further encourage them to seek violent redress of grievances. Thus, Ransford reasoned that blacks who felt powerless would be more likely to riot than those who felt they already had some chance of improving things.

Ransford, then, had theoretical grounds for expecting that isolation and powerlessness would produce political violence. But that's only half of science, as we've already discussed. Very often, the things that seem to make sense don't turn out to be true. So Ransford undertook a research project to find out if his theoretical expectations were borne out by empirical reality.

Ransford chose to find out if isolation and powerlessness produced violence by interviewing a sample of black residents in Watts. To find out the extent to which the subjects in his study were isolated from the mainstream white society, Ransford had his interviewers ask about contacts with whites in the community. Subjects were asked about contacts with whites at work, in their neighborhoods, in organizations, and in other situations. Other questions probed the extent to which they socialized with whites.

Feelings of powerlessness were measured by other questions in the study. For example, subjects were asked whether they agreed or disagreed with the statement "The world is run by the few people in power, and there is not much the little guy can do about it." Similar statements had been used in previous research projects and had been found to give a good indication of general feelings of powerlessness and alienation.

The answers that subjects gave to all these questions made it possible for Ransford to characterize each in terms of (1) isolation and (2) powerlessness. In the simplest characterization, any particular subject could be described as being high or low in terms of isolation from whites and high or low in the feeling of powerlessness. How did these characterizations relate to participation in the rioting?

It seemed unlikely that many subjects would admit to participating in the actual rioting in Watts, since they might fear criminal prosecution. Therefore, Ransford had his interviewers ask two questions. First, subjects were asked, "Would you be willing to use violence to get Negro rights?" About one-fourth of the subjects said they would be willing. The second question asked if they had ever done so. Only 5% said they had.

If Ransford's theoretical expectations were correct, he should have found that subjects with high isolation and high powerlessness were more likely to report a willingness to use violence and to report actually doing so than those who rated low on isolation and powerlessness. That's exactly what he found. Of the subjects rated high on isolation, 44% said they would be willing to use violence, contrasted with only 17% of those rated low on isolation. Similarly, 41% of those rated high on powerlessness and only 16% of those rated low said they would be willing to use violence. Ransford also found that the reports of actually using violence were strongly related to isolation and powerlessness. Of the 16 people who said they had used violence, for example, all but one scored high on powerlessness, and nearly three-fourths scored high on isolation from whites. Ransford's conclusions regarding the causes of political violence had both logical and empirical support. His theoretical expectations made sense, and their sense was borne out by the facts.

There are two important elements in science, as we've seen: logical integrity and empirical verification. Both are essential to scientific inquiry and discovery. Logic alone is not enough, since what initially seems a logical expectation may not be the case in fact. On the other hand, the mere observation and collection of empirical facts does not provide understanding—the telephone directory, for example, is not a scientific conclusion. Observation, however, can be the jumping-off point for the construction of a social scientific theory, as we now see in the case of inductive theory.

Inductive Theory Construction

Social scientists often begin constructing a theory by observing aspects of social life, seeking to discover patterns that may point to more or less universal principles. Barney Glaser and Anselm Strauss (1967) coined the term *grounded theory* in reference to this inductive method of theory construction. (Here we are referring to qualitative research methods, which we contrasted with quantitative methods at the end of Chapter 1.)

Field research—the direct observation of events in progress (discussed in depth in Chapter 12)—is frequently used to develop theories through observation. A long and rich anthropological tradition has seen this method used to good advantage. Among contemporary social scientists, no one was more adept at seeing the patterns of human behavior through observation than Erving Goffman:

> A game such as chess generates a habitable universe for those who can follow it, a plane of being, a cast of characters with a seemingly unlimited number of different situations and acts through which to realize their natures and destinies. Yet much of this is reducible to a small set of interdependent rules and practices. If the meaningfulness of everyday activity is similarly dependent on a closed, finite set of rules, then explication of them would give one a powerful means of analyzing social life. (1974:5)

In a variety of researches, Goffman uncovered the rules of such diverse behaviors as living in a mental institution (1961) and managing the "spoiled identity" of disfiguration (1963). In each case, Goffman observed the phenomenon in depth and teased out the rules governing behavior. Goffman's research provides an excellent example of qualitative field research as a source of grounded theory. Qualitative field research is not the only method of observation appropriate to the development of inductive theory. A detailed example should illustrate the process of inductive theory construction using quantitative methods. During the 1960s and 1970s, marijuana use on America's college campuses was a subject of considerable discussion in the popular press. Some people were troubled by marijuana's popularity; others welcomed it. What interests us here is why some students smoked marijuana and others didn't. A survey of students at the University of Hawaii (Takeuchi, 1974) provided the data needed to answer that question.

At the time of the study, countless explanations were being offered for drug use. People who opposed drug use, for example, often suggested that marijuana smokers were academic failures who turned to drugs rather than face the rigors of college life. Those in favor of marijuana, on the other hand, often spoke of the search for new values: marijuana smokers, they said, were people who had seen through the hypocrisy of middle-class values. David Takeuchi's (1974) analysis of the data gathered from University of Hawaii students, however, did not support any of the explanations being offered. Those who reported smoking marijuana had essentially the same academic records as those who didn't smoke it, and both groups were equally involved in traditional "school spirit" activities. Both groups seemed to feel equally well integrated into campus life.

There were differences, however:

1. Women were less likely than men to smoke marijuana.
2. Asian students (a large proportion of the UH student body) were less likely to smoke marijuana than non-Asians.
3. Students living at home were less likely to smoke marijuana than those living in apartments.

The three variables independently affected the likelihood of a student's smoking marijuana.

About 10% of the Asian women living at home had smoked marijuana, as contrasted with about 80% of the non-Asian men living in apartments. The researchers discovered a powerful pattern of drug use before they had an explanation for that pattern.

In this instance, the explanation took a peculiar turn. Instead of explaining why some students smoked marijuana, the researchers explained why some *didn't*. Assuming that all students had some motivation for trying drugs, the researchers suggested that students differed in the degree of "social constraints" preventing them from following through on that motivation.

American society has long been more permissive with men than with women when it comes to deviant behavior. Consider, for example, a group of men getting drunk and boisterous. Over the years we have often dismissed such behavior with references to "camaraderie" and "having a good time," whereas a group of women behaving similarly would probably have been regarded with great disapproval. We have had an idiom "Boys will be boys," but no comparable idiom for girls. (Hopefully, this is changing these days.) The researchers reasoned, therefore, that women would have more to lose by smoking marijuana than men would. Being female, then, provided a constraint against smoking marijuana.

Students living at home had obvious constraints against smoking marijuana in comparison with students living on their own. Aside from differences in opportunity, those living at home were seen as being more dependent on their parents—hence more vulnerable to additional punishment for breaking the law.

Finally, the Asian subculture in Hawaii has traditionally placed a higher premium on obedience to the law than other subcultures, so Asian students would have more to lose if they were caught violating the law by smoking marijuana.

Overall, then, a "social constraints" theory was offered as the explanation for observed differences in the likelihood of smoking marijuana. The more constraints a student had, the less likely he or she would be to smoke marijuana. It bears repeating that the researchers had no thoughts about such a theory when their research began. The theory was developed out of an examination of the data.

THE LINKS BETWEEN THEORY AND RESEARCH

Throughout this chapter, we have seen various aspects of the links between theory and research in social scientific inquiry. In the deductive model, research is used to test theories. And in the inductive model, theories are developed from the analysis of research data.

Whereas we have discussed two logical models for the linking of theory and research, actual social scientific inquiries have developed a great many variations on these themes. Sometimes, theoretical issues are introduced merely as a background for empirical analyses. Other studies cite selected empirical data to bolster theoretical arguments. In neither case is there really an interaction between theory and research for the purpose of developing new explanations.

And some studies make no use of theory at all. For example, suppose that social workers in a particular agency need to give a funding source evidence that clients received the types of services the funders intended them to receive and that the clients felt highly satisfied with those services. They could get that evidence by surveying clients. They would conduct that study not to test or to develop theory, but merely for the pragmatic purpose of program maintenance. (Of course, conducting such atheoretical studies that have little or no relevance outside of their pragmatic purposes for a particular agency does little to build social work knowledge. Consequently, some would not call such studies "scientific research," preferring instead to label them with terms like "administrative data gathering.")

There is no simple cookbook recipe for conducting social science research. It is far more open-ended than the traditional view of science would suggest. Ultimately, science rests on three pillars: logic, observation, and theory. As we'll see throughout this book, they can be fit together in many patterns.

Main Points

• A theory is a systematic set of interrelated statements intended to explain some aspect of social life or enrich our sense of how people conduct and find meaning in their daily lives.

• Theory helps us make sense out of diverse observations and see patterns in them.

• Theory helps direct our inquiry into areas that seem more likely to show useful patterns and explanations. It also helps us distinguish between chance occurrences and observations that have value in anticipating future occurrences.

• Theories help researchers develop useful implications from their findings for practice and policy.

• Some major models guiding social work practice today are the psychosocial model, the functionalist model, the problem-solving model, the task-centered model, and the cognitive-behavioral model.

• A paradigm is a fundamental model or scheme that organizes our view of something.

• The social sciences utilize a variety of paradigms that influence the ways research can be done.

• Positivist and postpositivist paradigms emphasize objectivity, precision, and generalizability in research. Postpositivist researchers recognize that observation and measurement cannot be as purely objective as the ideal image of science implies, but they still attempt to anticipate and minimize the impact of potential unobjective influences.

• The interpretivist paradigm emphasizes gaining an empathic understanding of how people feel inside, how they interpret their everyday experiences, and idiosyncratic reasons for their behaviors.

• The conflict paradigm focuses on oppression and uses research procedures to empower oppressed groups.

• Social scientific theory addresses what is, not what should be. Theory should not be confused with philosophy or belief.

• Social science is focused on logical and persistent regularities in social life.

• Social scientists are interested in explaining human aggregates, not individuals.

• An attribute is a characteristic, such as male or young.

• A variable is a logical set of attributes. Sex, for example, is a variable made up of the attributes male and female.

• Although social scientists observe people, they are primarily interested in finding relationships that connect variables.

• Social scientific theory and research are linked through two logical methods:

—*Deduction* involves the derivation of expectations or hypotheses from theories.

—*Induction* involves the development of generalizations from specific observations.

• Science is a process involving an alternation of deduction and induction.

Review Questions and Exercises

1. Consider the possible relationship between use of contracting and client satisfaction. Describe how that relationship might be examined through (a) deductive and (b) inductive methods.

2. Select a research article in some social work journal and classify the relationship between theory and research in that article.

3. List five social work variables and the attributes making up those variables.

Additional Readings

Chavetz, Janet, *A Primer on the Construction and Testing of Theories in Sociology* (Itasca, IL: Peacock, 1978). One of few books on theory construction written expressly for undergraduates. Chavetz provides a rudimentary understanding of the philosophy of science through simple language and everyday examples. She describes the nature of explanation, the role of assumptions and concepts, and the building and testing of theories.

Denzin, Norman K., and Lincoln, Yvonna S. *Handbook of Qualitative Research* (Thousand Oaks, CA: Sage, 1994). Various authors discuss the conduct of qualitative research from the perspective of various paradigms, showing how the nature of inquiry is influenced by one's paradigm. The editors also critique positivism and postpositivism from a postmodern perspective.

Kaplan, Abraham, *The Conduct of Inquiry* (San Francisco: Chandler, 1964). A standard reference volume on the logic and philosophy of science and social science. Though rigorous and scholarly, it is eminently readable and continually related to the real world of inquiry.

Kuhn, Thomas, *The Structure of Scientific Revolution* (Chicago: University of Chicago Press, 1970). An exciting and innovative recasting of the nature of scientific development. Kuhn disputes the notion of gradual change and modification in science, arguing instead that established "paradigms" tend to persist until the weight of contradictory evidence brings their rejection and replacement by new paradigms. This short book is both stimulating and informative.

Lofland, John, and Lofland, Lyn H., *Analyzing Social Settings: A Guide to Qualitative Observation and Analysis* (Belmont, CA: Wadsworth, 1995). An excellent text on how to conduct qualitative inquiry without rejecting the postpositivist paradigm. Also includes a critique of postmodernism.

Reinharz, Shulamit, *Feminist Methods in Social Research* (New York: Oxford University Press, 1992). This book explores a number of social research techniques (for example, interviewing, experiments, and content analysis) from a feminist perspective.

The Ethics and Politics of Social Work Research

What You'll Learn in This Chapter

In this chapter, you'll see something of the social context within which social work research is conducted. As you'll see, ethical and political considerations must be taken into account alongside scientific ones in the design and execution of research.

INTRODUCTION

Before they are able to implement their studies, social workers and other professionals who conduct research involving human subjects confront questions about the ethics of their proposed investigations. They must resolve these questions not only to meet their own ethical standards, but to meet the standards of committees that have been set up to review the ethics of proposed studies and to approve or disapprove the studies' implementation from an ethical standpoint.

Concern about the ethics of research involving human subjects has not always been as intense as it is today. The roots of this concern date back many decades to an era in which studies on human subjects could be conducted with little scrutiny of their ethics, an era in which some research became notorious for its inhumane violations of basic ethical standards. The most flagrant examples were the Nazi atrocities in medical experimentation conducted during the Holocaust.

Another notorious example was the Tuskegee syphilis study that started in 1932 in Alabama. In that study, researchers told several hundred poor black men who were suffering from syphilis that they would receive free treatment for their disease, when in fact there was no intention to treat the disease. Instead, the researchers were merely studying the progress of the disease. Even after penicillin had been discovered as a cure for syphilis, the study continued without providing penicillin or telling the subjects about it. Thirteen journal articles reported the study during this time, but it continued uninterrupted. As reported by James Jones in his book on the Tuskegee experiment, *Bad Blood* (1981:190), "none of the health officers connected with the Tuskegee Study expressed any ethical concern until critics started asking questions." In fact, when a member of the medical profession first objected to the study (in 1965), he got no reply to his letter to the Centers for Disease Control, which read:

> I am utterly astounded by the fact that physicians allow patients with a potentially fatal disease to remain untreated when effective therapy is available. I assume you feel that the information which is extracted from observations of this untreated group is worth their sacrifice. If this is the case, then I suggest that the United States Public Health Service and those physicians associated with it need to reevaluate their moral judgments in this regard.
>
> (JONES, 1981:190)

Jones reports that this letter was simply filed away with the following note stapled to it by one of the authors of one of the articles that reported the study: "This is the first letter of this type we have received. I do not plan to answer this letter."

In December 1965, Peter Buxtun, who was trained as a social worker while in the army, was hired by the Public Health Service as a venereal disease interviewer. Buxtun soon learned of the Tuskegee study from coworkers, and after studying published articles on the study, he became relentless in his efforts to intervene. A series of letters to, and difficult meetings with, high-ranking officials ultimately prompted them to convene a committee to review the experiment, but that committee decided against treating the study's subjects.

Buxtun then went to the press, which exposed the study to the public in 1972. This exposure prompted Senate hearings on the study. Subsequently, in the mid-1970s, the men were treated with antibiotics, as were their wives who had contracted the disease and their children who had it congenitally (Royse, 1991). According to Jones (1981:203), it was the social worker Peter Buxtun—aided by the press—who deserves the ultimate responsibility for stopping the Tuskegee study.

ETHICAL ISSUES IN SOCIAL WORK RESEARCH

When we consider research like the Tuskegee study, it is not hard to find the ethical violations and to agree that the research was blatantly unethical. However, some ethical violations in social work research can be subtle, ambiguous, and arguable. Sometimes there is no "correct" answer to the situation, and people of goodwill disagree.

In most dictionaries and in common usage, ethics is typically associated with morality, and both deal with matters of right and wrong. But what *is* right and what wrong? What is the source of the distinction? For individuals the sources vary. They may be religions, political ideologies, or the pragmatic observation of what seems to work and what doesn't.

Webster's New World Dictionary is typical among dictionaries in defining *ethical* as "conforming to the standards of conduct of a given profession or group." Although the idea may frustrate those in search of moral absolutes, what we regard as morality and ethics in day-to-day life is a matter of agreement among members of a group. And, not surprisingly, different groups have agreed on different codes of conduct. If you are going to live in a particular society, then, it is extremely useful for you to know what that society considers ethical and unethical. The same holds true for the social work research "community."

If you are going to do social work research, you should be aware of the general agreements shared by researchers about what's proper and improper in the conduct of scientific inquiry. The section that follows summarizes some of the more important ethical agreements that prevail in social work research, as well as research in allied fields.

Voluntary Participation and Informed Consent

Social work research often, though not always, represents an intrusion into people's lives. The interviewer's knock on the door or the arrival of a questionnaire in the mail signals the beginning of an activity that the respondent has not requested and that may require a significant portion of his or her time and energy. Participation in research disrupts the subject's regular activities.

Social work research, moreover, often requires that people reveal personal information about themselves—information that may be unknown to their friends and associates. And social work research often requires that such information be revealed to strangers. Social work practitioners also require such information. But their requests may be justified on the grounds that the information is required for them to serve the personal interests of the respondent. The social work researcher cannot necessarily make this claim. Researchers may only be able to argue that the research effort will ultimately help the entire target population of people in need.

A major tenet of medical research ethics is that experimental participation must be *voluntary*. The same norm applies to social work research. No one should be forced to participate. All participants must be aware that they are participating in a study, must be *informed* of all the consequences of the study, and must *consent* to participate in it. This norm is far easier to accept in theory than to apply in practice, however.

Again, medical research provides a useful parallel. Many experimental drugs are tested on prisoners. In the most rigorously ethical cases, the prisoners are told the nature—and the possible dangers—of the experiment; they are told that participation is completely voluntary; and they are further instructed that they can expect no special rewards—such as early parole—for participation. Even under these conditions, it is often clear that volunteers are motivated by the belief that they will personally benefit from their cooperation.

When the instructor in a social work class asks students to fill out a questionnaire that he or she hopes to analyze and publish, students should always be told that their participation in the survey is completely voluntary. Even so, most students will fear that nonparticipation will somehow affect their grade. So the instructor should be especially sensitive to the implied sanctions and make special provisions to obviate them. For example, the instructor could leave the room while the questionnaires are being completed. Or students could be asked to return the questionnaires by mail or to drop them in a box near the door just before the next course meeting.

You should be clear that this norm of voluntary participation goes directly against a number of scientific concerns that we'll be discussing later in this text. One such concern involves the scientific goal of *generalizability*, which is threatened to the extent that the kinds of people who would willingly participate in a particular research study are unlike the people to whom the study seeks to generalize. Suppose the questionnaire assesses student attitudes about the feminization of poverty, and only a minority of students voluntarily participate—those who care the most deeply about feminism and the poor. With such a small group of respondents the instructor would have no basis for describing student attitudes in general, and if he or she did generalize the findings to the entire population of students, the generalizations might be seriously misleading.

Another scientific concern compromised by the norm of voluntary participation and informed consent is the need, in some studies, to conceal the nature of the study from those being observed. This need stems from the fear that participants' knowledge about the study might significantly affect the social processes being studied among those participants. Often the researcher cannot even reveal that a study is being done. Rosenhan (1973), for example, reported a study in which the research investigators posed as patients in psychiatric hospitals to assess whether the clinical staff members of the hospitals, who were unaware of the study, could recognize "normal" individuals (presumably the investigators) who (presumably) did not require continued hospitalization. (The results suggested that they could not.) Had the subjects of that study—that is, the clinical staff members—been given the opportunity to volunteer or refuse to participate, the study would have been so severely compromised that it would probably have been not worth doing. What point would there be to such a study if the clinical staff were aware that the investigators were posing as patients?

But the fact that the norm of voluntary participation and informed consent may be impossible to follow does not alone justify conducting a study that violates it. Was the study reported by Rosenhan justified? Would it have been more ethical not to conduct the study at all? That depends on whether the long-term good derived from that study—that is, regarding the identification, understanding, and possible amelioration of problems in psychiatric diagnosis and care—outweighs the harm done in denying clinical staff the opportunity to volunteer or refuse to participate in the study. The need to judge whether the long-term benefits of a study will outweigh the harm it does by using ethically questionable practices applies to other ethical norms as well, not just voluntary participation, and thus we will be returning to it later. The norm of voluntary participation and informed consent is important. In cases where you feel ultimately justified in violating it, it is all the more important that you observe the other ethical norms of scientific research, such as bringing no harm to the people under study.

No Harm to the Participants

Social work research should never injure the people being studied, regardless of whether they volunteer for the study. Perhaps the clearest instance of this norm in practice concerns the revealing of information that would embarrass them or endanger their home life, friendships, jobs, and so forth. This norm is discussed more fully in the next section.

It is possible for subjects to be harmed psychologically in the course of a study, and the researcher must be aware of the often subtle dangers and guard against them. Research subjects are often asked to reveal deviant behavior, attitudes they feel are unpopular, or personal characteristics they may feel are demeaning such as low income, the receipt of welfare payments, and the like. Revealing such information is likely to make them feel at least uncomfortable.

Social research projects may also force participants to face aspects of themselves that they do not normally consider. That can happen even when the information is not revealed directly to the researcher. In retrospect, a certain past behavior may appear unjust or immoral. The project, then, can be the source of a continuing, personal agony for the subject. If the study concerns codes of ethical conduct, for example, the subject may begin questioning his or her own morality, and that personal concern may last long after the research has been completed and reported.

By now, you should have realized that just about any research you might conduct runs the risk of injuring other people somehow. There is no way for the researcher to guard against all these possible injuries. Yet some study designs make such injuries more likely than others. If a particular research procedure seems likely to produce unpleasant effects for subjects—asking survey respondents to report deviant behavior, for example—the researcher should have the firmest of scientific grounds for doing it. If the research design is essential and also likely to be unpleasant for subjects, you will find yourself in an ethical netherworld and may find yourself forced to do some personal agonizing. Although agonizing has little value in itself, it may be a healthy sign that you have become sensitive to the problem.

Although the fact often goes unrecognized, subjects can be harmed by the analysis and reporting of data. Every now and then, research subjects read the books published about the studies they participated in. Reasonably sophisticated subjects will be able to locate themselves in the various indexes and tables. Having done so, they may find themselves characterized—though not identified by name—as bigoted, abusive, and so forth. At the very least, such characterizations are likely to trouble them and threaten their self-images. Yet the whole purpose of the research project may be to explain why some people are prejudiced and others are not.

Like voluntary participation, not harming people is an easy norm to accept in theory but is often difficult to ensure in practice. Sensitivity to the issue and experience with its applications, however, should improve the researcher's tact in delicate areas of research.

Increasingly, in recent years, social researchers have been getting support for abiding by this norm. Federal and other funding agencies typically require an independent evaluation of the treatment of human subjects for research proposals, and most universities now have human subject committees to serve that evaluative function. Although sometimes troublesome and inappropriately applied, such requirements not only guard against unethical research but can also reveal ethical issues overlooked by the most scrupulous of researchers.

Anonymity and Confidentiality

The clearest concern in the protection of the subjects' interests and well-being is the protection of their identity, especially in survey research. If revealing their survey responses would injure them in any way, adherence to this norm becomes all the more important. Two techniques— *anonymity* and *confidentiality*—assist you in this regard, although the two are often confused.

Anonymity A respondent may be considered anonymous when the researcher cannot identify a given response with a given respondent. This means that an interview survey respondent can never be considered anonymous, since an interviewer collects the information from an identifiable respondent. (We assume here that standard sampling methods are followed.) An example of anonymity would be a mail survey in which no identification numbers are put on the questionnaires before their return to the research office.

As we will see in Chapter 11 (on survey research), assuring anonymity makes it difficult to keep track of who has or hasn't returned the questionnaires. Despite this problem, there are some situations in which you may be advised to pay the necessary price. If you study drug abuse, for example, assuring anonymity may increase the likelihood and accuracy of responses. Also, you can avoid the position of being asked by authorities for the names of drug offenders. When respondents volunteer their names, such information can be immediately obliterated on the questionnaires.

Confidentiality In a *confidential* survey, the researcher is able to identify a given person's responses but essentially promises not to do so publicly. In an interview survey, for instance, the researcher would be in a position to make public the income reported by a given respondent, but the respondent is assured that this will not be done.

You can use a number of techniques to ensure better performance on this guarantee. To begin, interviewers and others with access to respondent identifications should be trained in their ethical responsibilities. As soon as possible, all names and addresses should be removed from questionnaires and replaced with identification numbers. A master identification file should be created linking numbers to names to permit the later correction of missing or contradictory information, but this file should not be available except for legitimate purposes. Whenever a survey is confidential rather than anonymous, it is the researcher's responsibility to make that fact clear to the respondent. Never use the term *anonymous* to mean *confidential*.

As in social work practice, situations can arise in social work research where ethical considerations dictate that confidentiality not be maintained. Suppose in the course of conducting your interviews you learn that children are being abused or that respondents are at imminent risk of seriously harming themselves or others. It would be your professional (and perhaps legal) obligation to report this to the proper agency. Subjects need to be informed of this possibility, before they agree to participate in a study, as part of the informed consent process.

Deceiving Subjects

We've seen that the handling of subjects' identities is an important ethical consideration. Handling your own identity as a researcher can be tricky also. Sometimes it's useful and even necessary to identify yourself as a researcher to those you want to study. You'd have to be a master con artist to get people to participate in a laboratory experiment or complete a lengthy questionnaire without letting on that you were conducting research.

Even when it's possible and important to conceal your research identity, there is an important ethical dimension to be considered. Deceiving people is unethical, and within social research, deception needs to be justified by compelling scientific or administrative concerns. Even then, the justification will be arguable.

Sometimes researchers admit that they are doing research but fudge about why they are doing it or for whom. Suppose you've been asked by a public welfare agency to conduct a study of living standards among aid recipients. Even if the agency is looking for ways of improving conditions, the recipient-subjects are likely to fear a witch hunt for "cheaters." They might be tempted, therefore, to give answers making them seem more destitute than they really are. Unless they provide truthful answers, however, the study will not produce accurate data that will contribute to an effective improvement of living conditions. What do you do? One solution would be to tell subjects that you are conducting the study as part of a university research program—concealing your affiliation with the welfare agency. Doing that improves the scientific quality of the study, but it raises a serious ethical issue in the process.

Analysis and Reporting

As a social work researcher, then, you have a number of ethical obligations to your subjects of study. At the same time, you have ethical obligations to your professional colleagues, and a few comments on those obligations are in order.

In any rigorous study, the researcher should be more familiar than anyone else with the technical shortcomings and failures of the study. You have an obligation to make those shortcomings known to your readers. Even though you may feel foolish admitting mistakes, you should do it anyway.

Negative findings should be reported if they are at all related to your analysis. There is an unfortunate myth in scientific reporting that only positive discoveries are worth reporting (and journal editors are sometimes guilty of believing that as well). In science, however, it is often as important to know that two variables are *not* related as to know that they are. If, for example, an experiment finds no difference in outcome between clients treated and not treated with a tested intervention, it is important for practitioners to know that they may need to consider alternative interventions—particularly if the same null finding is replicated in other studies. And replication would not be possible if the original experiment were not reported.

Similarly, it is important to avoid the temptation to save face by describing your findings as the product of a carefully preplanned analytic strategy when that is not the case. Many findings arrive unexpectedly—even though they may seem obvious in retrospect. So you uncovered an interesting relationship by accident—so what? Embroidering such situations with descriptions of fictitious hypotheses is dishonest and tends to mislead inexperienced researchers into thinking that all scientific inquiry is rigorously preplanned and organized.

In general, science progresses through honesty and openness, and it is retarded by ego defenses and deception. You can serve your fellow researchers—and scientific discovery as a whole—by telling the truth about all the pitfalls and problems you have experienced in a particular line of inquiry. Perhaps you'll save them from the same problems.

WEIGHING BENEFITS AND COSTS

We have noted that ethical considerations in the conduct of social work research often pose a dilemma. The most ethical course of action for researchers to take is not always clearcut. Sometimes it is difficult to judge whether the long-term good to be derived from a study will outweigh the harm done by the ethically questionable practices that may be required in order to have adequate internal validity. Consider, for example, the study in which a team of researchers deceptively posed as hospitalized mental patients, concealing their identity from direct care staff to study whether those staff could recognize their nor-

malcy. Earlier we asked whether the potential benefits of the study—regarding psychiatric diagnosis and care—justified violating the norm of voluntary participation by direct staff. What if the purpose of that study had been to verify whether suspected physical abuse of patients by staff was taking place? Suppose an appalling amount of staff neglect and abuse of patients really was occurring and that the researchers uncovered it. Would the potential benefits to current and future patients to be derived from exposing, and thus hoping to reform, the quality of care outweigh using deception in the research?

If there are alternative ways to conduct the research, ways that can provide equally valid and useful answers to the research question without engaging in ethically questionable research practices, the dilemma would be resolved and an alternate methodology can be chosen. But sometimes no such alternatives appear. If not, then how researchers resolve this dilemma will depend on the values they attach to the various costs and benefits of the research and whether they believe that some ends ever justify some means. No objective formula can be applied to this decision; it is inherently subjective. Some individuals would argue that the end never justifies the means. Others might disagree over which particular ends justify which particular means.

An Illustration: Living with the Dying: Use of Participant Observation

A study by Robert Buckingham and his colleagues (1976) provides one example of where the long-term good to be derived from a study may have justified violating some ethical guidelines. This study, which involved deceiving subjects and not obtaining their informed consent to participate, might be of special interest to students interested in practicing social work in a medical setting or in a hospice organization. (We briefly discussed this study in Chapter 1, and we reexamine it here, particularly in regard to its ethical ramifications.)

Buckingham and his colleagues wanted to compare the value of routine hospital care versus hospice care for the terminally ill. (As we mentioned in Chapter 1, the emphasis in hospice care is on minimizing discomfort and maximizing quality of life, and this might entail eschewing medical procedures that prolong life but hinder its quality. Routine hospital care, in contrast, is more likely to emphasize prolonging life at all costs, even if that requires a lower quality of life for the dying patient. The routine approach is less attentive to the psychosocial and other nonmedical needs of the patient and family.)

Buckingham wanted to observe and experience the treatment of a terminally ill patient in two wards of a hospital: the surgical-care (nonhospice) ward and the palliative-care (hospice) ward. For his observations to be useful, it was necessary that the staff and other patients on his ward not know what he was up to. The steps that he took to carry out his deception are quite remarkable. Before entering the hospital, he lost 22 pounds on a six-month diet. (He was naturally thin before starting his diet.) He submitted himself to ultraviolet irradiation so he would look as if he had undergone radiation therapy. He had puncture marks from intravenous needles put on his hands and arms so he would look as if he had undergone chemotherapy. He underwent minor surgery for the sole purpose of producing biopsy scars. He learned how to imitate the behavior of patients dying with pancreatic cancer by reviewing their medical charts and maintaining close contact with them. Finally, for several days before entering the hospital, he grew a patchy beard and abstained from washing.

Buckingham stayed in the hospital ten days, including two days in a holding unit, four days in the surgical-care unit, and four days in the hospice unit. His findings there supported the advantages of hospice care for the terminally ill. For example, on the surgical-care ward he observed staff communication practices that were insufficient, impersonal, and insensitive. Physicians did not communicate with patients. Staff members in general avoided greeting patients, lacked eye contact with them, and often referred to them by name of their disease rather than by their personal name.

Complacent patients did not receive affection. Negative aspects of the patient's condition were emphasized.

His observations while on the hospice ward, however, were quite different. Staff maintained eye contact with patients. They asked patients questions about what they like to eat and about other preferences. They asked patients how they could be more helpful. They listened to patients accurately, unhurriedly, and empathically. Physicians spent more time communicating with patients and their families. Staff encouraged family involvement in the care process. It is not difficult to see the value of Buckingham's findings in regard to enhancing the care of the terminally ill and their families. In considering whether the benefits of those findings justify Buckingham's particular use of deception, several other aspects of the study might interest you.

Before entering the hospital, Buckingham engaged the hospital's top medical, administrative, and legal staff members in planning and approving the study. The heads of both the surgery ward and the hospice ward also participated in the planning and approved the study. In addition, the personnel of the hospice ward were informed in advance that their unit was going to be evaluated, although the nature of the evaluation was not revealed. Finally, an ad hoc committee was formed to consider the ethics of the study, and the committee approved the study. In light of these procedures and this study's benefits, it may not surprise you to learn that no ethical controversy emerged in response to this study.

Right to Receive Services Versus Responsibility to Evaluate Service Effectiveness

Perhaps the most critical ethical dilemma in social work research pertains to the right of clients in need to receive services and whether the benefit of improving the welfare of clients in the long run ever justifies delaying the provision of services to some clients in the short run. This debate has to do with experimental designs that we will be examining in Part 3. Those designs evaluate the effectiveness of social work interventions by comparing the fates of clients who receive the interventions being evaluated and those from whom we withhold the interventions. Two values are in conflict here: doing something to try to provide immediate help to people in need, and the professional's responsibility to ensure that the services clients receive have had their effects—either beneficial or harmful—scientifically tested.

Some argue that individuals in need should never be denied service for any period or for any research purposes. Others counter that the service being delayed is one whose effects, if any, have not yet been scientifically verified. Otherwise, there would be no need to test it. How ethical, they ask, is it to perennially provide the same services without ever scientifically verifying whether those services are really helping anyone or are perhaps harmful? And if they are potentially harmful, are those who receive them actually taking a greater risk than those who are temporarily denied them until their effects are gauged? Using another medical parallel, would you think your physician was ethical if he or she treated you with a drug while knowing that the beneficial or harmful effects of that drug were as yet untested? If you were being paid to participate in a medical experiment to test the effectiveness of a drug whose benefits and negative side effects were as yet unknown, which group would you feel safer in: the group receiving the drug or the group not receiving it?

One factor bearing on this dilemma is the seriousness of the client's problem. It would be much harder to justify the delay of service to individuals experiencing a dangerous crisis, at risk of seriously harming themselves—suicidal clients, for example—than to those in less critical need. Another factor is the availability of alternative interventions to which the tested intervention can be compared. Perhaps those denied the tested service can receive another one that might prove to be no less beneficial.

If alternative interventions are available, then the conflict between the right to service versus the responsibility to evaluate can be alleviated. Instead of comparing clients who receive a new service being tested to those who receive no service, we can compare them to those who receive a routine set of services that was in place before the new one was developed. This is a particularly ethical way to proceed when insufficient resources are available to provide the new service to all or most clients who seek service. This way, no one is denied service, and the maximum number that resources permit receive the new service.

Another way to reduce the ethical dilemma when resources don't permit providing the new service to every client is to assign some clients to a waiting list for the new service. While they are waiting their turn for the new service, these clients can be compared to the clients currently receiving the new service. Ultimately, everyone is served, and the waiting list clients should be free to refuse participation in the study without being denied services eventually.

NASW CODE OF ETHICS

If decisions about the ethics of research involve subjective value judgments in which we must weigh the potential benefits of the research against its potential costs to research participants, and if we must make those decisions in light of various idiosyncratic factors, then those decisions pose dilemmas for which there may be no right or wrong answers. But researchers can do some things to be as ethical as possible. They can obtain collegial feedback as to the ethics of their proposed research. As mentioned earlier, they can (and perhaps must) obtain approval from a human subjects review committee. They should carefully consider whether there are ethically superior alternatives and strive to ensure that their research proposal is the most ethical one that they can conceive.

To guide them in this endeavor, various professional associations have created and published formal codes of conduct covering research ethics.

E. Scholarship and Research—The social worker engaged in study and research should be guided by the conventions of scholarly inquiry.

1. The social worker engaged in research should consider carefully its possible consequences for human beings.

2. The social worker engaged in research should ascertain that the consent of participants in the research is voluntary and informed, without any implied deprivation or penalty for refusal to participate, and with due regard for participants' privacy and dignity.

3. The social worker engaged in research should protect participants from unwarranted physical or mental discomfort, distress, harm, danger, or deprivation.

4. The social worker who engages in the evaluation of services or cases should discuss them only for the professional purposes and only with persons directly and professionally concerned with them.

5. Information obtained about participants in research should be treated as confidential.

6. The social worker should take credit only for work actually done in connection with scholarly and research endeavors and credit contributions made by others.

Source: Code of Ethics, Part I, Section E, p. 4. Silver Spring, MD: National Association of Social Workers, 1980.

Figure 3-1 Codes Governing Scholarship and Research from the Code of Ethics of the National Association of Social Workers

The relevant codes excerpted from the Code of Ethics of the National Association of Social Workers are illustrated in Figure 3-1. While those codes provide ethical guidelines for conducting research, another section of the codes requires that social workers contribute to the knowledge base of the profession and share research knowledge with their colleagues. That section reminds us that we can violate our ethical responsibilities as professionals not only when we conduct research, but when we refuse to participate in and utilize research. It is worded as follows:

O. Development of Knowledge—The social worker should take responsibility for identifying, developing, and fully utilizing knowledge for professional practice.

1. The social worker should base practice upon recognized knowledge relevant to social work.

2. The social worker should critically examine, and keep current with emerging knowledge relevant to social work.

3. The social worker should contribute to the knowledge base of social work and share research knowledge and practice wisdom with colleagues.

(NASW, 1980, PART V, SECTION O)

FOUR ETHICAL CONTROVERSIES

As you may already have guessed, the adoption and publication of professional codes of conduct have not totally resolved the issue of research ethics. Social scientists still disagree on some general principles, and those who seem to agree in principle debate specifics. In this section, we are going to describe briefly four research projects that have provoked ethical controversy and discussion in recent years. These are not the only controversial projects that have been done; they simply illustrate ethical issues in the real world, and we thought you'd find them interesting and perhaps provocative.

Of the four illustrations of controversial research projects that we examine here, the first two are from social psychology and sociology, and the next two are from social work. The first project examined obedience in a laboratory setting. The second studied homosexual behavior. The third tested whether the decisions made by journal editors on whether or not to publish submitted research papers were biased in favor of publishing studies in which positive findings supported the effectiveness of social work interventions. The fourth was designed to withhold welfare benefits from 800 poor Texans in order to evaluate the effectiveness of a new program intended to wean people from welfare.

Observing Human Obedience

One of the more unsettling clichés to come out of World War II was the German soldier's common excuse for atrocities: "I was only following orders." From the point of view that gave rise to this comment, any behavior—no matter how reprehensible—could be justified if someone else could be assigned responsibility for it. If a superior officer ordered a soldier to kill a baby, the fact of the *order* was said to exempt the soldier from personal responsibility for the action.

Although the military tribunals that tried the war crime cases did not accept the excuse, social scientists and others have recognized the extent to which this point of view pervades social life. Often people seem willing to do things they know would be considered wrong by others, *if* they can cite some higher authority as ordering them to do it. Such was the pattern of justification in the My Lai tragedy of Vietnam, and it appears less dramatically in day-to-day civilian life. Few would disagree that this reliance on authority exists, yet Stanley Milgram's study (1963, 1965) of the topic provoked considerable controversy. To observe people's willingness to harm others when following orders, Milgram brought 40 adult men— from many different walks of life—into a laboratory setting designed to create the phenomenon under study. If you had been a subject in the experiment, you would have had something like the following experience.

You would have been informed that you and another subject were about to participate in a learning experiment. As the result of drawing lots, you would have been assigned the job of "teacher" and your fellow subject the job of "pupil." He would have then been led into another room, strapped into a chair, and had an electrode attached to his wrist. As the teacher, you would have been seated in front of an impressive electrical control panel covered with dials, gauges, and switches. You would have noticed that each switch had a label giving a different number of volts, ranging from 15 to 315. The switches would have had other labels, too, some with the ominous phrases "Extreme-Intensity Shock," "Danger— Severe Shock," and "XXX." The experiment would run like this. You would read a list of word pairs to the learner and then test his ability to match them up. Since you couldn't see him, a light on your control panel would indicate his answer. Whenever the learner made a mistake, you would be instructed by the experimenter to throw one of the switches—beginning with the mildest— and administer a shock to your pupil. Through an open door between the two rooms, you'd hear your pupil's response to the shock. Then you'd read another list of word pairs and test him again.

As the experiment progressed, you'd be administering ever more intense shocks, until your pupil was screaming for mercy and begging for the experiment to end. You'd be instructed to administer the next shock anyway. After a while, your pupil would begin kicking the wall between the two rooms and screaming. You'd be told to give the next shock. Finally, you'd read a list and ask for the pupil's answer—and there would be no reply whatsoever, only silence from the other room. The experimenter would inform you that no answer was considered an error and instruct you to administer the next higher shock. This would continue up to the "XXX" shock at the end of the series.

What do you suppose you would have done when the pupil first began screaming? When he began kicking on the wall? Or when he became totally silent and gave no indication of life? You'd refuse to continue giving shocks, right? Of the first 40 adult men Milgram tested, nobody refused to administer the shocks until the pupil began kicking the wall between the two rooms. Of the 40, 5 did so then. Two-thirds of the subjects, 26 of the 40, continued doing as they were told through the entire series—up to and including the administration of the highest shock.

As you've probably guessed, the shocks were phony, and the "pupil" was another experimenter.

Only the "teacher" was a real subject in the experiment. You wouldn't have been hurting another person, even though you would have been led to think you were. The experiment was designed to test your *willingness* to follow orders, to the point of presumably killing someone.

Milgram's experiments have been criticized both methodologically and ethically. On the ethical side, critics particularly cited the effects of the experiment on the subjects. Many seem to have personally experienced about as much pain as they thought they were administering to someone else. They pleaded with the experimenter to let them stop giving the shocks. They became extremely upset and nervous. Some had uncontrollable seizures. How do you feel about this research? Do you think the topic was important enough to justify such measures? Can you think of other ways in which the researcher might have examined obedience?

Trouble in the Tearoom

The second illustration was conducted by a graduate student and published in a 1970 book called *Tearoom Trade: Impersonal Sex in Public Places.* The researcher, Laud Humphreys, wanted to study the homosexual acts between strangers meeting in public restrooms in parks, called "tearooms" by those who used them for this purpose. Typically, the tearoom encounter involved three people: the two men actually engaged in the homosexual act and a lookout.

To gather observations for his study, Humphreys began showing up at public restrooms and offering to serve as a lookout whenever it seemed appropriate. Humphreys wanted to go beyond his observations as lookout and learn more about the people he was observing. Many of the participants were married men who wanted to keep their homosexuality secret and thus avoid being stigmatized and losing their status in their communities. They probably would not have consented to being interviewed. Instead of asking them for an interview, Humphreys tried to note the license plate numbers of their vehicles and then

track down their names and addresses through the police. Then he visited the men at their homes, disguising himself enough to avoid recognition, and announced that he was conducting a survey. In that fashion, he collected the personal information he was unable to get in the restrooms.

Humphreys' research provoked considerable controversy both within and outside the social scientific community. Some critics charged Humphreys with a gross invasion of privacy in the name of science. What men did in public restrooms was their own business and not Humphreys'. Others were mostly concerned about the deceit involved—Humphreys had lied to the participants by leading them to believe he was only a voyeur-participant. Some were more concerned with Humphreys' follow-up survey than with what he did in public facilities. They felt it was unethical for Humphreys to trace the participants to their houses and to interview them under false pretenses. Still others justified Humphreys' research. The topic, they said, was worth study and could not be studied any other way. They considered the deceit to be essentially harmless, noting that Humphreys was careful not to harm his subjects by disclosing their tearoom activities.

The tearoom trade controversy, as you might imagine, has never been resolved. It is still debated, and it probably will be for a long time, since it stirs emotions and contains ethical issues people disagree about. What do you think? Was Humphreys ethical in doing what he did? Are there parts of the research you feel were acceptable and other parts that were not? Whatever you feel in the matter, you are sure to find others who disagree with you.

Social Worker Submits Bogus Article to Test Journal Bias

The next illustration is the first well-publicized ethical controversy involving a social worker's research. Several articles reported it in national news media, including two stories on it in the *New York Times* (September 27, 1988, pp. 21, 25 and April 4, 1989, p. 21) and one in the *Chroni-*

cle of Higher Education (November 2, 1988, p. A7). The information for this illustration was drawn primarily from those three news articles.

The social worker, William Epstein, hypothesized that journal editors were biased in favor of publishing research articles whose findings confirmed the effectiveness of evaluated social work interventions and biased against publishing research articles whose findings failed to support the effectiveness of tested interventions. To test his hypothesis, Epstein fabricated a fictitious study that pretended to evaluate the effectiveness of a social work intervention designed to alleviate the symptoms of asthmatic children. (Asthma is often thought to be a psychosomatic illness.) Epstein concocted two versions of the bogus study. In one version, he fabricated findings that supported the effectiveness of the intervention; in the other version, he fabricated data that found the intervention to be ineffective.

Epstein submitted the fictitious article to 146 journals, including 33 social work journals and 113 journals in allied fields. Half of the journals received the version supporting the effectiveness of the intervention, and half received the other version. Epstein did not enter his own name as author of his fabricated article; instead, he used a pair of fictitious names.

In his real study, Epstein interpreted his findings as providing some support for his hypothesis that journal editors were biased in favor of publishing the version of the bogus article with positive findings and against publishing the version with negative findings. Among the social work journals, for example, 8 accepted the positive version and only 4 accepted the negative version. Nine journals rejected the positive version, and 12 rejected the negative version. Among the journals in allied fields, 53% accepted the positive version, compared to only 14% that accepted the negative version. A statistical analysis indicated that the degree of support these data provided for Epstein's hypothesis was "tentative" and not statistically significant. After being notified of the acceptance or rejection of his fictitious article, Epstein informed each journal of the real nature of

his study. Later, he submitted a true article, under his own name, reporting his real study, to the *Social Service Review,* a prestigious social work journal. That journal rejected publication of his real study, and its editor, John Schuerman, led a small group of editors who filed a formal complaint against Epstein with the National Association of Social Workers. The complaint charged Epstein with unethical conduct on two counts: (1) deceiving the journal editors who reviewed the bogus article, and (2) failing to obtain their informed consent to participate voluntarily in the study.

Schuerman, a social work professor at the University of Chicago and an author of some highly regarded research articles, recognized that sometimes the benefits of a study may warrant deceiving subjects and not obtaining their informed consent to participate. But he argued that in Epstein's (real) study, the benefits did not outweigh the time and money costs associated with many editors and reviewers who had to read and critique the bogus article and staff members who had to process it.

When an article is submitted for publication in a professional social work journal, it is usually assigned to several volunteer reviewers, usually social work faculty members who do not get reimbursed for their review work. The reviewers do not know who the author is so that the review will be fair and unbiased. Each reviewer is expected to read each article carefully, perhaps two or three times, recommend to the journal editor whether the article should be published, and develop specific suggestions to the author for improving the article. The journal editor, too, is usually a faculty member volunteering his or her own time as part of one's professional duties as an academician. Schuerman noted that in addition to the time and money costs mentioned, there is an emotional cost: "the chagrin and embarrassment of those editors who accepted the [bogus] article" (*New York Times,* September 27, 1988, p. 25).

Epstein countered that journal editors are not the ones to judge whether the benefits of his (real) study justified its costs. In his view, the editors are predisposed to value their own costs very dearly and unlikely to judge any study that would deceive them as being worth those costs. Epstein argued that the journals are public entities with public responsibilities, and that testing whether they are biased in deciding what to publish warrants the deception and lack of informed consent to participate that were necessary to test for that bias.

One might argue that if journal editors and reviewers are biased against publishing studies that fail to confirm the effectiveness of tested interventions, then the field may not learn that certain worthless interventions in vogue are not helping clients. Moreover, if several studies disagree about the effectiveness of an intervention, and only those confirming its effectiveness get published, then an imbalanced and selective set of replications conceivably might be disseminated to the field, misleading the field into believing that an intervention is yielding consistently favorable outcomes when in fact it is not. This could hinder the efforts of social workers to provide the most effective services to their clients, and therefore ultimately reduce the degree to which we enhance the well being of clients.

One could argue that Epstein's study could have been done ethically if he had forewarned editors that they might be receiving a bogus paper within a year and obtained their consent to participate in the study without knowing the specifics of the paper. An opposing viewpoint is that such a warning might affect the phenomenon being studied, tipping off the reviewers in a manner that predisposes them to be on guard not to reveal a real bias that actually does influence their publication decisions.

Some scholars who have expressed views somewhat in sympathy with those of Epstein have argued that journal editors and reviewers exert great influence on our scientific and professional knowledge base and therefore need to have their policies and procedures investigated. Schuerman, who filed the charges against Epstein, agreed with this view, but argued that Epstein's study was not an ethical way to conduct such an investigation. In an editorial in the March 1989 issue of the *Social Service Review,* Schuerman elaborated his

position. He noted that journals have low budgets and small staffs and depend heavily on volunteer reviewers "who see their efforts as a professional responsibility" and receive little personal or professional benefits for their work (p. 3). He also portrayed Epstein's research as "badly conducted," citing several design flaws that he deemed to be so serious that they render the anticipated benefits of the Epstein study as minimal, and not worth its aforementioned costs. Schuerman also cited Epstein as admitting to serious statistical limitations in his study and to characterizing his research as only exploratory. "It is at this point that issues of research design and research ethics come together," Schuerman argued (p. 3). In other words, Schuerman's point is that the methodological quality of a study's research design can bear on its justification for violating ethical principles. If the study is so poorly designed that its findings have little value, it becomes more difficult to justify the ethical violations of the study on the grounds that its findings are so beneficial.

The initial ruling of the ethics board of the National Association of Social Workers was that Epstein had indeed violated research rules associated with deception and failure to get informed consent. It could have invoked serious sanctions against Epstein, including permanent revocation of his membership in the professional association and referral of the case to a state licensing board for additional sanctions. But Epstein was permitted to appeal the decision before any disciplinary action was taken. His appeal was upheld by the executive committee of the association, which concluded that his research did not violate its ethical rules. The committee exonerated Epstein, ruling that the case was a "disagreement about proper research methodology," not a breach of ethics. It did not publicize additional details of its rationale for upholding Epstein's appeal and reversing the initial ruling. Epstein speculated that the reversal may have been influenced by the publicity the case received in the press.

If Epstein's speculation is valid, one might wonder whether the reversal was prompted by the executive committee's sincere judgment that the research really did not violate ethical rules or by expediency considerations, perhaps connected to concerns regarding potential future publicity or other costs. What do you think? What ideas do you have about the two rulings and about the ethical justification for Epstein's study? Which ruling do you agree with? Do you agree with Schuerman's contention that methodological flaws in the research design can bear on research ethics? Is it possible to agree with Schuerman on that issue and still agree with the executive committee that this case was a disagreement about methodology and not a breach of ethics? If, just for the sake of discussion, you assume that Epstein's study had very serious design flaws that prevented the possibility of obtaining conclusive findings, how would that assumption affect your position on the ethical justification for Epstein's study?

"Welfare Study Withholds Benefits from 800 Texans"

The preceding front page headline greeted readers of the Sunday, February 11, 1990, edition of the *Dallas Morning News*. On the next line they read: "Thousands of poor people in Texas and several other states are unwitting subjects in a federal experiment that denies some government help to a portion of them to see how well they live without it."

This was pretty strong stuff, and soon the story was covered on one of the national TV networks. Let's examine it further for our fourth illustration.

The Texas Department of Human Services received federal money to test the effectiveness of a pilot program designed to wean people from the welfare rolls. The program was targeted to welfare recipients who found jobs or job training. *Before* the new program was implemented, these recipients received four months of free medical care and some child care after they left the welfare rolls. The new program extended these benefits to one year of Medicaid coverage and subsidized child care. The theory was that extending the duration of the benefits would encourage recipients to accept and keep entry-level jobs that were un-

likely to offer immediate medical insurance or child care.

The federal agency granting the money attached an important condition. States receiving grants were required to conduct a scientifically rigorous experiment to measure the program's effectiveness in attaining its goal of weaning people from welfare. Some federal officials insisted that this requirement entailed randomly assigning some people to a control group that would be denied the new (extended) program and instead kept on the old program of only four months of benefits. The point of this was to maximize the likelihood that the recipient group (the experimental group) and the nonrecipient (control) group were equivalent in all relevant ways except for the receipt of the new program. If they were, and if the recipient group was weaned from welfare to a greater extent than the nonrecipient group, then it could be safely inferred that the new program, and not something else, caused the successful outcome. (We will examine this logic further in Chapter 9.)

If you have read many journal articles reporting on experimental studies, you are probably aware that many of them randomly assign about one-half of their subjects to the experimental group and the other half to the control group. Thus, this routine procedure denies the experimental condition to about one-half of the subjects. The Texas experiment was designed to include all eligible welfare recipients statewide, assigning 90% of them to the experimental group and 10% to the control group. Thus, only 10% of the subjects, which in this study amounted to 800 people, would be denied the new benefits if they found jobs. Although this seems more humane than denying benefits to 50% of the subjects, the newspaper account characterized the 800 people in the control group as "unlucky Texans" who seemed to be unfairly left out of a program that was extending benefits to everyone else eligible statewide, who numbered in the many thousands. Moreover, the newspaper report noted that the 800 control subjects would be denied the new program for two years to provide ample time to compare outcomes between the two groups. To boot, these 800 "unlucky Texans" were not to be informed of the new program or of the experiment. They were to be told of only the normal four-month coverage.

Advocates of the experiment defended this design, arguing that the control group would not be denied benefits. They would receive routine benefits, and the new benefits would not have been available for anyone in the first place unless a small group was randomly assigned to the routine policy. In other words, the whole point of the new benefits was to test a new welfare policy, not merely to implement one. They further argued that the design was justified by the need to test for unintended negative effects of the new program, such as the possibility that some businesses might drop their child care or insurance coverage for employees, knowing that the new program was extending these benefits. That, in turn, they argued, could impel low-paid employees in those businesses to quit their jobs and go on welfare. By going on welfare and then getting new jobs, they would become eligible for the government's extended benefits, and this would make the welfare program more expensive.

Critics of the study, on the other hand, argued that it violated federal ethics standards such as voluntary participation and informed consent. Anyone in the study must be informed about it and all its consequences and must have the option to refuse to participate. One national think tank expert on ethics likened the experiment to the Tuskegee syphilis study (which we discussed earlier), saying, "It's really not that different." He further asserted, "People ought not to be treated like things, even if what you get is good information."

In the aftermath of such criticism, Texas state officials decided to try to convince the federal government to rescind the control group requirement so that they could extend the new benefits to the 800 people in the control group. Instead of using a control group design, they wanted to extend benefits to everyone and find statistical procedures that would help ferret out program defects (a design that might have value, but which

would be less conclusive as to what really causes what, as we will see in later chapters). They also decided to send a letter to the control group members explaining their special status.

Two days after the *Dallas Morning News* broke this story, it published a follow-up article reporting that the secretary of the U.S. Department of Health and Human Services, in response to the first news accounts, instructed his staff to cooperate with Texas welfare officials so that the project design would no longer deny the new program to the 800 control group members. Do you agree with his decision? Did the potential benefits of this experiment justify its controversial ethical practices?

It probably would not have been possible to form a control group had recipients been given the right to refuse to participate. Who would want to be denied extended free medical and child care benefits? Assuming it were possible, however, would that influence your opinion of the justification for denying them the new program? Do you agree with the expert who claimed that this study, in its original design, was not that different from the Tuskegee syphilis study? What if, instead of assigning 90% of the subjects to the experimental group, the study assigned only 10% to it? That way, the 800 assigned to the experimental group may have been deemed "lucky Texans," and the rest might not have been perceived as a small group of unlucky souls being discriminated against. In other words, perhaps there would have been fewer objections if the state had merely a small amount of funds to test out a new program on a lucky few. Do you think that would have changed the reaction? Would that influence your perception of the ethical justification for the experiment?

DISCUSSION EXAMPLES

Research ethics, then, is an important though ambiguous topic. The difficulty of resolving ethical issues should not be an excuse for ignoring them. To further sensitize yourself to the ethical component in social research, here is a list of real and hypothetical research situations. See if you can find the ethical component in each. How do you feel about it? Do you feel the procedures described are ultimately acceptable or unacceptable? It would be useful to discuss some of these with others in your methods course.

1. A social work professor asks students in a social policy class to complete questionnaires that the instructor will analyze and use in preparing a journal article for publication.

2. After a field study of a demonstration of civil disobedience, law enforcement officials demand that the researcher identify those people who were observed breaking the law. Rather than risk arrest as an accomplice after the fact, the researcher complies.

3. After completing the final draft of a book reporting a research project, the researcher-author discovers that 25 of the 2000 survey interviews were falsified by interviewers—but chooses to ignore that fact and publish the book anyway.

4. Researchers obtain a list of abusive parents they wish to study. They contact the parents with the explanation that each has been selected "at random" from among the general population to take a sampling of "public opinion."

5. A social work doctoral student is conducting dissertation research on the disciplinary styles of abusive parents with toddlers. The parent and child enter a room with toys scattered around it, and the parent is asked to have her child straighten up the toys before playing with them. The parent is told that the researcher will observe her interactions with her child from behind a one-way mirror.

6. In a study of sexual behavior, the investigator wants to overcome subjects' reluctance to report what they might regard as deviant behavior. To get past their reluctance, subjects are asked: "Everyone masturbates now and then; about how much do you masturbate?"

7. A researcher discovers that 85% of the university student body smoke marijuana regularly. Pub-

lication of this finding will probably create a furor in the community. Because no extensive analysis of drug use is planned, the researcher decides to ignore the finding and keep it quiet.

8. To test the extent to which social work practitioners may try to save face by expressing clinical views on matters they are wholly uninformed about, the researcher asks for their clinical opinion regarding a fictitious practice model.

9. A research questionnaire is circulated among clients as part of their agency intake forms. Although clients are not told they must complete the questionnaire, the hope is that they will believe they must—thus ensuring a higher completion rate.

10. A participant-observer pretends to join a group opposing family planning services in order to study it and is successfully accepted as a member of the inner planning circle. What should the researcher do if the group makes plans for:

a. A peaceful, though illegal, demonstration against family planning services?

b. The bombing of an abortion clinic during a time it is sure to be unoccupied?

INSTITUTIONAL REVIEW BOARDS

Earlier in this chapter we noted that one thing researchers can do to ensure that their studies are ethical is to obtain the consent of a human subjects review committee. This type of committee is often called an "institutional review board." Let's just call it by its commonly used acronym, IRB. IRBs became widespread during the 1970s as a result of federal legislation and increased public concern about the ethics of biomedical and behavioral research. Today, all organizations that engage in research and receive federal money are required to have an IRB that reviews the ethics of proposed studies involving human subjects. Investigators in organizations that wish to conduct such studies must get the advance approval of their organization's IRB. This applies to all studies involving human subjects, not just those that receive government funding. IRBs may continue to oversee studies after they are implemented, and they may decide to suspend or terminate their approval of a study.

IRBs vary in the amount and format of material they require to describe the proposed research. In the process of deciding whether to approve a research proposal, an IRB may require that certain modifications be made in order to make the research acceptable. For example, an IRB may require that certain additional information be given to subjects before obtaining their consent to participate, or it may require that you do more to assure subjects that a decision not to participate will not have any adverse consequences for them whatsoever; for example, it will not hinder their future relations with the sponsoring organization. Figure 3-2 reproduces a sample consent form used by the IRB of the University of Texas at Austin. That form addresses many of the ethical concerns we have discussed throughout this chapter, with particular emphasis on voluntary participation based on full information regarding the procedures of the study, potential harm, and anonymity and confidentiality.

Note that the sample consent form does not cover situations in which ethical considerations dictate that confidentiality not be maintained, such as when child abuse is unexpectedly encountered or when respondents are at imminent risk of seriously harming themselves or others. You may need to add this contingency to your consent form. You may also need to assure your participants and your IRB that you will arrange for services to be offered to subjects you encounter who need them.

If you are fortunate enough to have a research instructor who requires that you design and carry out a research project, you may find that you have to get your study approved by your university's IRB before you can begin collecting data. Just what you needed, right? Don't panic yet. Perhaps your study will qualify for an exemption from a full review and you'll therefore be able to obtain approval within a few days. Federal regulations allow IRBs to grant exemptions to certain kinds of studies, although institutions vary considerably in interpreting the federal regulations. Studies that receive these exemptions receive an expedited review. Exempt studies are those that:

1. are conducted as part of normal educational practices, including research on the effectiveness of alternative educational approaches

2. use educational tests with adequate protection of confidentiality

3. use survey or interview procedures or observe public behavior while protecting confidentiality

4. use existing data without violating confidentiality

5. research federal demonstration projects

6. survey or interview elected or appointed public officials or candidates for public office, without violating confidentiality.

The precise wording of the exemptions is much more complicated than this and ought to be available from your IRB. Most student research (with the exception of doctoral dissertations) qualifies for at least one of these exemptions, particularly exemptions 1, 3, or 4. It is important to note that studies that appear to meet one or more of these exemptions might still require a full review if subjects can be identified, if knowledge of their responses could place them at risk of some sort of harm, or if the data are of a sensitive nature. Of course, if your study involves some controversial procedures, such as pretending to faint every time your instructor mentions statistics in order to see whether research instructors are capable of exhibiting compassion—or perhaps to see if this is an effective way to influence exam content—obtaining IRB approval may be problematic (not to mention what it will do to your grade when the instructor reads your report). Other (more realistic) problematic examples include surveys on sensitive topics such as drug abuse or sexual practices

(Title of Study)

You are invited to participate in a study of (state what is being studied). I am a (graduate student/faculty) at The University of Texas at Austin, (Department). (If a student, state how the study relates to your program of work—for example, report, thesis, dissertation.) I/We hope to learn (state what the study is designed to discover or establish). You were selected as a possible participant in this study because (state why and how the subject was selected). You will be one of (give number of subjects being studied) subjects chosen to participate in this study.

If you decide to participate, I/we (or: _____ and associates) will (describe the procedures to be followed, including their purposes, how long they will take, and their frequency. Describe the risks, discomforts, and inconveniences reasonably to be expected, and any benefits reasonably to be expected).

(Describe appropriate alternative procedures that might be advantageous to the subject, if any. Any standard treatment that is being withheld must be disclosed.)

Any information obtained in connection with this study and that can be identified with you will remain confidential and will be disclosed only with your permission. (If you will be releasing information to anyone for any reason, you must state the persons or agencies to whom the information will be furnished, the nature of the information to be furnished, and the purpose of the disclosure.)

Your decision whether or not to participate will not prejudice your future relations with The University of Texas or (identify by name any other institution(s) and/or agency(s)). If you decide to participate, you are free to discontinue participation at any time without prejudice.*

If you have any questions, please ask us. If you have any additional questions later, _____ (in addition, give the address and phone number of your dissertation Chair, if appropriate) will be happy to answer them.

You will be offered a copy of this form to keep.

You are making a decision whether or not to participate. Your signature indicates that you have read the information provided above and have decided to participate. You may withdraw at any time without prejudice after signing this form, should you choose to discontinue participation in this study.**

Figure 3-2 Sample Consent Form (These elements must be included in any Cover Letter)

or surveys on traumatic events that may be painful for respondents to remember.

BIAS AND INSENSITIVITY REGARDING GENDER AND CULTURE

In several chapters of this book you will encounter examples of how gender and cultural bias and insensitivity can hinder the methodological quality of a study and therefore the validity of its findings. Much has been written about these problems in recent years, and some have suggested that when researchers conduct studies in a sexist manner or in a culturally insensitive manner, they are not committing just methodological errors but are also going awry ethically.

The question of ethics arises because some studies are perceived to perpetuate harm to women and minorities. Feminist and minority scholars have suggested a number of ways that such harm can be done. Interviewers who are culturally insensitive can offend minority respondents. If they conduct their studies in culturally insensitive ways, their findings may yield implications for action that ignore the needs and realities of minorities, may incorrectly (and perhaps stereotypically) portray minorities, or may inappropriately generalize

_____   _____
Signature of Participant   Date

_____   _____
Signature of Parent or Legal Guardian   Date
(**NOTE:** This line should not appear on forms that will be given to subjects consenting for themselves.)

_____   _____
Signature of Child   Date
(**NOTE:** Required when child is 7 years of age or older, or a separate Assent Form may be used, when appropriate.)

_____   _____
Signature of Witness (When appropriate)   Date

_____   _____
Signature of Investigator   Date

NOTE: Investigators are requested to use this format to facilitate review of the Consent Form. For special cases see Appendix III.1.D.

If you are collecting your data by means of a mail-out questionnaire you may wish to substitute the following format for these paragraphs. (All information from the Consent Form must be included in your Cover Letter as well.)

*You are under no obligation to participate in the study. Your completing and returning the questionnaire will be taken as evidence of your willingness to participate and your consent to have the information used for purposes of the study.

**You may retain the cover letter and this explanation about the nature of your participation and the handling of the information you supply.

ADDENDUM III: Appendix 1A

Figure 3-2 Sample Consent Form *(continued)*

in an unhelpful way. By the same token, studies with gender bias or insensitivity may be seen as perpetuating a male-dominated world or failing to consider the potentially different implications for men and women in one's research.

Various authors have recommended ways to try to avoid cultural and gender bias and insensitivity in one's research. We will cover some of these recommendations in greater depth in later chapters on methodology, but we'll mention them here as well, in light of their potential ethical relevance. Among the more commonly recommended guidelines regarding research on minorities are the following:

• Spend some time immersing yourself directly in the culture of the minority group(s) that will be included in your study (for example, using participant observation methods described in Chapter 12) before finalizing your research design.

• Engage minority scholars and community representatives in the formulation of the research problem and in all the stages of the research to ensure that the research is responsive to the needs and perspectives of minorities.

• Involve representatives of minority groups who will be studied in the development of the research design and measurement instruments.

• Do not automatically assume that instruments successfully used in prior studies of whites can yield valid information when applied to minorities.

• Use culturally sensitive language in your measures, perhaps including a non-English translation.

• Use in-depth pretesting of your measures to correct problematic language and flaws in translation.

• Use bilingual interviewers when necessary.

• Be attuned to the potential need to use minority interviewers instead of nonminorities to interview minority respondents.

• In analyzing your data, look for ways the findings may differ among different categories of ethnicity.

• Avoid an unwarranted focus exclusively on the deficits of minorities; perhaps focus primarily on their strengths.

In her book *Nonsexist Research Methods*, Margrit Eichler recommends the following feminist guidelines to avoid gender bias and insensitivity in one's research:

• If a study is done on only one gender, make that clear in the title and the narrative and don't generalize the findings to the other gender.

• Don't use sexist language or concepts (for example, males referred to as head of household, while females referred to as spouses).

• Don't use a double standard in framing the research question (such as looking at the work-parenthood conflict for mothers but not for fathers).

• Don't overemphasize male-dominated activities in research instruments (such as by assessing social functioning primarily in terms of career activities and neglecting activities in homemaking and child rearing).

• In analyzing your data, look for ways the findings may differ for men and women.

• Don't assume that measurement instruments used successfully with males are automatically valid for women.

• Be sure to report the proportion of males and females in your study sample.

THE POLITICS OF SOCIAL WORK RESEARCH

At this point you may have gleaned that there may be a fine line between ethical and political issues in social work research. Both ethics and politics hinge on ideological points of view. What is unacceptable from one point of view may be acceptable from another. Thus, we are going to see that people disagree on political aspects of research just as they disagree on ethical ones. As we change topics now, we will distinguish ethical from political issues in two ways.

First, although ethics and politics are often closely intertwined, the ethics of social work research deals more with the methods employed, whereas political issues are more concerned with the practical costs and use of research. Thus, for example, some raise ethical objections to experiments that evaluate the effectiveness of social work services by providing those services to one group of clients while delaying their provision to another group of clients. Those who voice these objections say that the harm done to clients in delaying service provision outweighs the benefits to be derived from evaluating the effectiveness of those services. A political objection, on the other hand, might be that if the results of the evaluation were to suggest that the services were not effective, those negative results might hurt agency funding. Another political objection might be that withholding services would reduce the amount of fees for service or third-party payments received, not to mention the bad publicity that would be risked regarding agency "neglect" of people in need.

The second thing that distinguishes ethical from political aspects of social work research is that there are no formal codes of accepted political conduct comparable to the codes of ethical conduct we discussed earlier. Although some ethical norms have political aspects—for example, not harming subjects clearly relates to our protection of civil liberties—no one has developed a set of political norms that can be agreed on by social work researchers. The only partial exception to the lack of political norms is in the generally accepted view that a researcher's personal political orientation should not interfere with or unduly influence his or her scientific research. It would be considered improper for you to use shoddy techniques or lie about your research as a way of furthering your political views. Although you are permitted to have political views, you are expected to put them aside when you enter the realm of science. It is in this context that science is idealized as apolitical, amoral, and objective.

Objectivity and Ideology

In Chapter 1, we suggested that social research can never be totally objective, since researchers are humanly subjective. Science attempts to achieve objectivity by utilizing accepted research techniques that are intended to arrive at the same results, regardless of the subjective views of the scientists who use them. Social scientists further are urged to seek facts, regardless of how those facts accord with their cherished beliefs or personal politics.

But many scholars do not believe that social research is ever entirely value-free. They argue that values can influence any phase of the research process, such as the selection of a research question, the selection of a sample, or the way a variable is defined. For example, when investigators are evaluating the effectiveness of a program to help battered women, values about family stability or about women's welfare can influence what outcome indicators of program effectiveness are chosen. Those who cherish maintaining family stability may define effectiveness in terms of whether the batterer was reformed, thus enabling the family to stay together safely. Those more concerned about women's rights and safety than about family stability might choose an opposite indicator of program effectiveness, deeming the program effective when it empowers the battered woman to divorce her husband.

In another example, planners working for a state bureaucracy researching the effectiveness of a new state program or policy may focus the research on whether the new approach saves the state money, such as when a new case management program reduces state hospitalization costs for its mentally ill citizens. In their zeal to meet budget-balancing priorities, they may not think to study indicators of client well-being. Perhaps many people in need of hospitalization are worse off under the new program, for example. Clinical researchers, on the other hand, may evaluate the effectiveness of the new program in terms of its impact on the symptomatology or quality of life of the mentally ill individuals, perhaps believing that those concerns are more important than saving taxpayer money on services that are already underfunded and inadequate. In their zeal to maximize client well-being, they may not think to examine the program costs that are required to produce specific increments of benefit to clients.

Here is one more example. Researchers of homelessness may be influenced by their values in the way they define homelessness, which in turn influences whom they include in their sample of homeless individuals. Do the homeless include only people living in the streets? Or do they also include people "doubling up" with friends or relatives or living in squalid, temporary quarters who cannot find a decent place they can afford? It is difficult to make such decisions independent of our values. Researchers who have been active in social action efforts to alleviate homelessness may be predisposed to choose the broader definition, which will indicate a greater number of the homeless; researchers who believe social welfare spending is wasteful and incurs too much dependency among the poor may be predisposed to choose the narrower definition.

Those who believe that social research is never really value-free typically recommend that we should be aware of and describe our values up-front rather than try to kid ourselves or others that we are completely objective. Indeed, not all social scientists agree that researchers should try to separate their values from their research activities. Some have argued that social science and social action cannot and should not be separated. Explanations of the status quo in society, they contend, shade subtly into defenses of that same status quo. Simple explanations of the social functions of, say, discrimination can easily become justifications for its continuance. By the same token, merely studying society and its ills without a commitment to making society more humane has been called irresponsible. Social work has a long tradition of using research as a tool to try to make society more humane. Zimbalist (1977), for example, describes how the profession embraced the social survey movement at the turn of the 20th century as a way to convince society to enact environmental reform to alleviate a host of urban problems. In its overriding concern to spur social reform, the social survey movement was frequently selective in what facts it would present, attempting to "make a case" rather than providing a scientifically disciplined and balanced presentation and interpretation of data.

Social work researchers today may attempt to be more objective than they were a century ago, but their efforts still commonly carry on the tradition of using research findings to spur social action. For example, surveys on homelessness may be conducted in the hope that their findings will influence legislators and their tax-averse constituents to spend more public funds to alleviate homelessness. A social service agency might survey a community to learn of unmet needs that it can try to meet. Survey results might imply the need for new types of agency services and might be used to convince funding sources to grant new money to the agency to help it better address the unmet needs that its research uncovers.

There is nothing wrong with viewing research as a tool that can be used to alleviate human suffering and promote social welfare. Indeed, in the *social work* profession, that is what research is all about. From a scientific standpoint, however, it is one thing to let our values spur us to undertake specific research projects in the hope that the truth we discover will foster the achievement of humanitarian aims. It is quite another to let our values or ideological beliefs spur us to hide from or distort the truth by biasing the way we conduct our research or interpret its findings. If attempting to be completely objective and value-free in the way we conduct research is an impossible ideal, it is risky to kid ourselves into thinking that we are completely neutral. But this does not mean that we shouldn't *try* to keep our beliefs from distorting our pursuit of truth. Being aware of our biases throughout all phases of our research helps us be on guard to minimize their impact on our work. And being up-front in describing our predilections to others better prepares them to evaluate the validity of our findings.

You may find this a bit unsettling. How will we ever know what's true if the goal of being completely objective is so hard to attain and if we are constantly producing new research that disagrees with previous research? In Chapter 1 we noted that science is an open-ended enterprise in which conclusions are constantly being modified. Inquiry on a given topic is never completed, and the eventual overturning of established theories is an accepted fact of life. In light of this, many social work practitioners may simply opt to be guided exclusively by tradition and authority. Rather than utilize research findings to help guide their practice, they merely attempt to conform to the traditional ways of operating in their particular agency or to the ordinations of prestigious, experienced practitioners whom they respect.

In your own professional practice you will be able to decide for yourself whether to utilize research to help guide your practice or whether you want to rely exclusively on alternative sources of knowledge. In making your decision you may want to consider whether various practice authorities are themselves completely objective. With so much potential for bias to distort *everyone's* perceptions of truth, are your efforts to provide the most effective possible service to your clients helped or hindered by relying exclusively on tradition and authority, and by ignoring what various researchers are finding? In recent years there has been increased attention to the ways in which our values and biases can influence our research, thanks in part to the impact of the women's movement on social science. In the box titled "Political Purposes Versus Truth Seeking," two feminist scholars address the conflict between politics and knowledge building, a conflict that can discourage intellectual debate and that may arise inadvertently out of an effort to correct the errors of traditional research. The box illustrates how conducting research for the sole purpose of social change, under conditions of ideologically restricted inquiry, can distort knowledge building and can provide incomplete or distorted knowledge that ultimately hampers one's social change efforts. As you read this box, you may want to relate it to the public media attention being given to the notion of "political correctness" and its implications for freedom of inquiry.

In light of the foregoing discussion, it may not surprise you to learn that some research studies in the social sciences have stimulated considerable controversy about whether their findings represented merely an intrusion of the researcher's own political values. Typically, researchers have denied the intrusion, and the denial has been challenged. Let's look at some examples of the controversies that have raged and continue to rage over this issue.

Social Research and Race   Nowhere have social research and politics been more controversially intertwined than in the area of race relations. Social scientists studied the topic for a long time, and often the products of the social research have found their way into practical politics. A few brief references should illustrate the point.

When the U.S. Supreme Court, in 1896, established the principle of "separate but equal" as a means of reconciling the Fourteenth Amendment's guarantee of equality to blacks with the norms of segregation, it neither asked for nor cited social science research. Nonetheless, it is widely believed that the Court was influenced by the writings of William Graham Sumner, a leading social scientist of his era. Sumner was noted for his view that the mores and folkways of a society were relatively impervious to legislation and social planning. His view has often been paraphrased as "stateways do not make folkways." Thus the Court ruled that it could not accept the assumption that "social prejudices may be overcome by legislation" and denied the wisdom of "laws which conflict with the general sentiment of the community" (Blaunstein and Zangrando, 1970:308).

There is no doubt that Gunnar Myrdal's classic two-volume study of race relations in America titled *An American Dilemma* (1944) had a significant impact on the topic of his research. Myrdal amassed a great many data to show that the position of black Americans directly contradicted American values of social and political equality. And Myrdal did not attempt to hide his own point of view in the matter.

When the doctrine of "separate but equal" was overturned in 1954 (*Brown v. Board of Education of Topeka*), the new Supreme Court decision was based in part on the conclusion that segregation had a detrimental effect on black children. In drawing that conclusion, the Court cited a number of sociological and psychological research reports (Blaunstein and Zangrando, 1970).

For the most part, social scientists in this century have supported the cause of black equality in America. Many have been actively involved in the civil rights movement, some more radically than others. Thus, social scientists have been able to draw research conclusions supporting the cause of equality without fear of criticism from colleagues.

POLITICAL PURPOSES VERSUS TRUTH SEEKING

DuBois's (1983) term "passionate scholarship" reflects the feminist scholar's intent to conduct research for feminist reasons—to document, so as to change, the social conditions of women. Acting on the belief that "the personal is political," feminist researchers expect scholarship on women's lives to have an impact on the socioeconomic structure that determines the status of women (Duelli-Klein, 1983; Mies, 1983). Feminist scholars maintain, validly, that all social science research has such a political context and objectives (Cummerton, 1983; Oakley, 1981) and that feminist scholarship may be different only because it makes these political motivations public. What remains obscure in these declarations are the implications for developing knowledge.

The first such implication centers on questions that are not asked and results that are not wanted. For example, feminist researchers may be reluctant to inquire about the biological determinants of women's potential to achieve, or the intrapsychic factors of women that may contribute to battering relationships, or the possibility that some women provoke sexual harassment. Even though the unwanted response might be part of the truth, feminist researchers do not want to consider answers to such questions because the answers might hinder political action or provoke criticisms from feminist colleagues. Kelly (1978) made a useful distinction between the "fundamental indeterminancy" of the outcomes of research (p. 226) and feminist beliefs and political purposes. The reluctance to consider "undesirable" answers to questions that one's ideology warns one against asking confuses truthseeking with political reform. The issue of restricted inquiry and incomplete results is not new to social science scholarship. Male-oriented research has neglected whole areas of women's lives and, as only one example, failed to engage in inquiries that would have illuminated earlier the imbalance in power between men and women. Feminists cannot rationalize similar discrepancies on their part. Although feminist scholars are open about the

To recognize the solidity of the general social science position in the matter of equality, we need to examine only a few research projects that have produced conclusions disagreeing with the predominant ideological position.

Most social scientists have—overtly, at least—supported the end of even de facto school segregation. Thus, an immediate and heated controversy was provoked in 1966 when James Coleman, a respected sociologist, published the results of a major national study of race and education. Contrary to general agreement, Coleman found little difference in academic performance between black students attending integrated schools and those attending segregated ones. Indeed, such obvious things as libraries, laboratory facilities, and high expenditures per student made little difference. Instead, Coleman reported that family and neighborhood factors had the most influence on academic achievement.

Coleman's findings were not well received by many of the social scientists who had been active in the civil rights movement. Some scholars criticized Coleman's work on methodological grounds,

political motivation of their efforts, they are obligated to understand and deal with the consequent conflict between their political goals and how the "whole truth" about women is to be known. Ironically, by not seeking full answers, including those to politically sensitive questions, feminists will hamper their political efforts as well. They will then be depending on incomplete or distorted knowledge that political opponents can misuse.

A second implication of the motivation toward social reform is that political aims may influence how women are studied. Feminist scholars affirm that research should be conducted for and not just about women. To enlist those who are researched in this good cause, they often seem to have two choices: to study only like-minded, feminist-oriented women or to raise the consciousness of others (Acker, Barry, and Esseveld, 1983).

Luker's (1984) valuable portrayal of activists on both sides of the abortion debate is an instructive example of research that does not choose between these two aims but that places a description of the condition of women, as they are, above social action. (As a matter of fact, Luker's empathic description of anti-abortionists could be useful to the social change efforts of prochoice groups.) Luker's aim was to understand and describe women with diametrically opposite world views. If she had focused only on prochoice activists or had given a distorted view of anti-abortionists, she would have obscured information about contemporary women. The issue is not whether knowledge building or social change is the more valuable. The issue is whether the goal of social change distorts knowledge building.

Source: Naomi Gottlieb and Marti Bombyk, "Strategies for Strengthening Feminist Research," *Affilia*, Summer 1987, pp. 23–35. Used by permission of Sage Publications, Inc.

but many others objected hotly on the grounds that the findings would have segregationist political consequences. The controversy that raged around the Coleman report was reminiscent of that provoked earlier by Daniel Moynihan (1965) in his critical analysis of the black family in America. Another example of political controversy surrounding social research in connection with race concerns the issue of IQ scores of black and white people. In 1969, Arthur Jensen, a Harvard psychologist, was asked to prepare an article for the *Harvard Educational Review,* examining the data on racial differences in IQ test results (Jensen, 1969). In the article, Jensen concluded that genetic differences between blacks and whites accounted for the lower average IQ scores of blacks. Jensen became so identified with that position that he appeared on college campuses across the country discussing it.

Jensen's position has been attacked on numerous methodological bases. It was charged that many of the data on which Jensen's conclusion was based were inadequate and sloppy—there are many IQ tests, some worse than others. Similarly, it was argued that Jensen had not taken social-environmental factors sufficiently into account. Other social scientists raised other appropriate methodological objections.

Beyond the scientific critique, however, Jensen was condemned by many as a racist. He was booed and his public presentations drowned out by hostile crowds. Jensen's reception by several university audiences was not significantly different from the reception received by abolitionists a century before.

A similar reaction erupted in response to a book titled *The Bell Curve,* published in 1994 and coauthored by Charles Murray, a sociologist known as a leading thinker on the political right, and the late Richard J. Herrnstein, a psychologist and distinguished professor at Harvard University. A small portion of the lengthy book argues that ethnic differences in intelligence can be attributed in part (but not exclusively) to genetic factors.

In their book Murray and Herrnstein see intelligence as a crucial factor determining whether Americans will prosper or wind up in an underclass culture of poverty and other social ills. Based on the thesis that intelligence is so hard to change, the book recommends against spending money on a variety of social programs, including those aimed at improving the intellectual performance of disadvantaged youths.

Some critics pointed to serious methodological shortcomings in the procedures and conclusions in the Murray and Herrnstein study. But as with the earlier controversy involving Jensen, what is most germane to this chapter is not the methodological critique of *The Bell Curve,* but its political condemnation. In the criticism of the book, more attention was given to political objections than to the study's serious methodological shortcomings. It was attacked in a *Boston Globe* editorial before it was even published. The *Washington Post* reported that former Education Secretary William Bennett, a conservative supporter and friend of Murray, strongly praised the book but was made nervous by the section on race and intelligence. Because of that section, Bennett reportedly characterized Murray as a "marked man."

The *New Republic* magazine devoted its October 31, 1994, issue to the book. The issue contains a 10-page article by Murray and Herrnstein, based on the section of their book dealing with intelligence and genetics. Preceding that article are 17 pages of editorials, by 20 different authors, about *The Bell Curve* and the Murray and Herrnstein article. Some of the editorials debate whether the magazine was ethical in even considering publishing the article. Most of the editorials sharply attack the article or criticize the magazine's decison to publish it. One depicts Murray and Herrnstein as dishonest. Another portrays them as seeking to justify oppression. Others liken them to racists trying to justify their racism or to bigots practicing pseudo-scientific racism. One of the harsher editorials, titled *Neo-Nazis,* implies that the relevant chapter from Murray and Herrnstein's book is "a chilly synthesis" of the findings of previous works published by neo-Nazis.

In an editorial justifying the decision to publish the Murray and Herrnstein article, on grounds of free inquiry, the magazine's editor argues that the burden of proof for suppressing debate on the topic rests with those seeking to suppress the debate. The editorial argues for judging the issue on scientific and logical grounds, not tarring and feathering the authors by impugning their motives or by associating them with Nazis. The editorial also responds to critics who claim that *The Bell Curve* hurts the feelings of African Americans, especially African American children, who don't want to be called genetically inferior. The editor depicts as itself inherently racist the view that African Americans are vulnerable people who must be shielded from free and open intellectual exchange.

Many social scientists limited their objections to the Moynihan, Coleman, Jensen, and Murray and Herrnstein research to scientific, methodological grounds. The purpose of our account, however, is to point out that political ideology often gets involved in matters of social research. Although the abstract model of science is divorced from ideology, the practice of science is not.

When political and ideological forces restrict scientific inquiry in one area, this can have unfortunate spin-off effects restricting needed inquiry in related areas. Lovell Jones, director of Experimental Gynecology-Endocrinology at the University of Texas M. D. Anderson Cancer Center, provides an illustration. This illustration shows how the political reaction to Jensen's research on intelligence has restricted needed health research about the higher rate of mortality seen in black women with breast cancer as compared to white women with breast cancer.

According to Jones, one plausible factor that might contribute to the higher mortality rate among black women is the fact that black females have more breast tumors that are "estrogen receptor negative," which means that those tumors tend to be more "aggressive." Jones finds it striking that there have been no concrete studies to investigate this possibility, and based on feedback he has received from white research colleagues, he thinks he knows why there have been no studies. His colleagues have told him that they do not want to pursue this line of inquiry because it would be too controversial politically. They say the research would have to delve into racial differences in genetic predispositions to breast tumors. They fear that they would therefore be accused, like Jensen was, of racial bias—if not for their own findings on breast tumors, then for making it easier for other investigators to study more politically sensitive differences in genetic predispositions between blacks and whites (differences connected to intelligence, for example).

Jones further recounts how he was once told by a staff member of a national news program that a spokesperson for the National Cancer Institute suggested that they would prefer that the word *genetics* not be used in commenting on cancer among blacks. In a somewhat related incident, Jones recalls how he once wrote an editorial for a prominent newspaper, an editorial that discussed cancer among minority populations. The paper's editor called him to say that the paper could not run the editorial because it would be accused of racial bias if it did. But when the editor learned that Jones was black, he said, "Well then, we can use it."

Jones also observes that for ten years we have known that white women with a family history of breast cancer have a higher risk of developing breast cancer than do white women with no family history. Jones comments that it stands to reason that the field should have quickly followed up this research by investigating whether the same holds true for black women with and without a family history of breast cancer. But it was not until ten years after the research on white women appeared that the first study on black women came out. Jones attributes this time lapse to the political risk one takes in conducting such research; researchers fear that if they find that the risk of black women getting breast cancer is higher than that of white women, they will be attacked as racists.*

Jones's comments illustrate how politically rooted taboos against certain lines of inquiry may do a disservice to the very people that they seek to protect. What is your opinion about such taboos? Are some or all of them justified? Or is the benefit of ensuring that some research findings will not be misused for harmful purposes outweighed by the risk that such taboos will keep others from conducting much needed research in related areas?

Project Camelot   Among social scientists *Camelot* is a household term in discussions of research and politics. Today, it is frequently referenced

---

*Lovell Jones's comments were presented in part at the Texas Minority Health Strategic Planning Conference, Austin, Texas, July 18, 1991, in his presentation titled "The Impact of Cancer on the Health Status of Minorities in Texas." Jones elaborated on his conference remarks in a telephone conversation with Allen Rubin on July 25, 1991. Some of the material included in his comments is covered in Jerome Wilson, "Cancer Incidence and Mortality Differences of Black and White Americans: A Role for Biomarkers," in Lovell Jones (ed.), *Minorities and Cancer,* 1989, Springer Verlag, pp. 5–20.

with no further description, it is so well known. Irving Louis Horowitz (1967), a man who has criticized government agencies on occasion, said that Project Camelot "has had perhaps the worst public relations record of any agency or subagency of the U.S. government." What provoked such a stir?

On December 4, 1964, the Special Operations Research Office of American University sent an announcement to a number of social scientists about a project being organized around the topic of internal war. The announcement contained, in part, the following description:

> Project *Camelot* is a study whose objective is to determine the feasibility of developing a general social systems model which would make it possible to predict and influence politically significant aspects of social change in the developing nations of the world. Somewhat more specifically, its objectives are:
>
> *First,* to devise procedures for assessing the potential for internal war within national societies;
>
> *Second,* to identify with increased degrees of confidence those actions which a government might take to relieve conditions which are assessed as giving rise to a potential for internal war.
>
> (HOROWITZ, 1967:47)

Of course, few people are openly in favor of war, and most would support research aimed at ending or preventing war. By the summer of 1965, however, with the national debate on Vietnam gaining momentum, Camelot was being hotly argued in social science circles as a Department of Defense attempt to co-opt scientists into a counterinsurgency effort in Chile. Some claimed that the Defense Department intended to sponsor social scientific research aimed at putting down political and potentially revolutionary dissatisfaction in that volatile Latin American nation. Whatever the motivations of the social scientists, it was feared that their research would be used to strengthen established regimes and thwart popular reformist and revolutionary movements in foreign countries.

Many social scientists who had agreed in principle to participate in the project soon felt they were learning a lesson learned decades before them by Robert Oppenheimer and some of the atomic scientists—that scientific findings can be used for purposes that the scientists themselves oppose. Charges and countercharges were hurled around professional circles. Names were called, motives questioned. Old friendships ended. The Defense Department was roundly damned by all for attempting to subvert social research. Foreign relations with Latin America simultaneously chilled and got hot. Finally, under the cloud of growing criticism, Camelot was canceled and dismantled.

It is interesting to imagine what might have happened to Project Camelot had it been proposed to a steadfastly conservative and anticommunist social research community. We think there is no doubt that it would have been supported, executed, and completed without serious challenge or controversy. Certainly war per se was not the issue. There was no serious criticism when the research branch in the army during World War II was developed to conduct research aimed at supporting the war effort, making our soldiers more effective fighters. Ultimately science is neutral on the topics of war and peace, but scientists are not.

Politics in Perspective

The role of politics and related ideologies is not unique to social research. The natural sciences have experienced and continue to experience similar situations. The preceding discussion has three main purposes in a textbook on the practice of social work research.

First, you should realize that science is not untouched by politics. Social science, in particular, is a part of social life. We study things that matter to people, things they have firm, personal feelings about, and things that affect their lives. Scientists are human beings, and their human feelings often show through in their professional lives. To think otherwise would be naive.

Second, you should see that science does proceed even under political controversy and hostility. Even when researchers get angry and call each other names, or when the research community comes under attack from the outside, the job of science gets done anyway. Scientific inquiry persists, studies are done, reports are published, and new things are learned. In short, ideological disputes do not bring science to a halt but simply make it more exciting.

Finally, you should make ideological and political considerations a part of the backdrop you create—a backdrop that will increase your awareness as you learn the various research methods. Many of the established techniques of science function to cancel out or hold in check our human shortcomings, especially those we are unaware of. Otherwise, we might look into the world and never see anything but ourselves—our personal biases and beliefs.

Main Points

• In addition to technical, scientific considerations, social work research projects are likely to be shaped by administrative, ethical, and political considerations.

• What's ethically "right" and "wrong" in research is ultimately a matter of what people agree is right and wrong.

• Scientists agree that participation in research should, as a general norm, be voluntary. This norm, however, can conflict with the scientific need for generalizability.

• Probably all scientists agree that research should not harm those who participate in it, unless they willingly and knowingly accept the risks of harm.

• *Anonymity* refers to the situation in which even the researcher cannot identify specific information with the individuals it describes.

• *Confidentiality* refers to the situation in which the researcher—although knowing which data describe which subjects—agrees to keep that information confidential.

• In some instances the long-term benefits of a study are thought to outweigh their violation of certain ethical norms. But determining whether their ends justify their means is a difficult and often highly subjective process. Nowadays Institutional Review Boards make such determinations in approving studies.

• Bias and insensitivity regarding gender and culture have become ethical issues for many social scientists.

• Guidelines have been proposed by feminist and other scholars.

• Although science is neutral on political matters, scientists are not.

• Even though the norms of science cannot force individual scientists to give up their personal values, the use of accepted scientific practices provides a safeguard against "scientific" findings being the product of bias only.

• Ideological priorities can restrict inquiry out of a fear that certain truths can be misperceived or misused in a manner that will harm certain vulnerable groups; this restriction can lead to incomplete or distorted knowledge building that risks harming the people it seeks to protect.

Review Questions and Exercises

1. Suppose a social work researcher decides to interview children placed for adoption in infancy by their biological parents. The interviewer will focus on their feelings about someday meeting their biological parents. Discuss the ethical problems he or she would face and how those might be avoided.

2. Suppose a researcher personally opposed to transracial adoption wants to conduct an interview survey to explore the impact of transracial adoption on the self-images of adoptees. Discuss the personal-involvement problems he or she would face and how those might be avoided.

Additional Readings

Golden, M. Patricia (ed.), ***The Research Experience*** (Itasca, IL: Peacock, 1976). An excellent collection of pieces about doing research in a social context. The book presents an excerpt from a published report and follows it with a more informal account by the researcher. In several of the informal accounts, you will get an inside view of the way political and ethical issues are involved in social research.

Jones, James H., ***Bad Blood: The Tuskegee Syphilis Experiment*** (New York: Free Press, 1981). This remarkable book provides a fascinating account of the Tuskegee study that we discussed in this chapter. Its account of the history of that study may astound you, and you may be inspired by the tale of a social worker whose relentless efforts over years with public health authorities, and ultimately the press, got the study stopped.

MacRae, Duncan, Jr., ***The Social Function of Social Science*** (New Haven, CT: Yale University Press, 1976). A historical analysis of the interplay of social science and social reform in America. Both the values of the general community and the values of the social scientists themselves are examined.

Ritzer, George (ed.), ***Social Realities: Dynamic Perspectives*** (Boston: Allyn & Bacon, 1974). A lively collection of views regarding political and ethical issues in social science. Ritzer has done an excellent job of presenting widely divergent views regarding the same issue. This book not only portrays "social realities," it will also give you an opportunity to make up your own mind in these matters.

Problem Formulation and Measurement

4
Problem Formulation

5
Conceptualization and Operationalization

6
Measurement

7
Constructing Measurement Instruments

Posing problems properly is often more difficult than answering them. Indeed, a properly phrased question often seems to answer itself. You may have discovered the answer to a question just in the process of making the question clear to someone else. Part 2 considers the structuring of inquiry, which involves posing research questions that are proper from a scientific standpoint and useful from the standpoint of social work and social welfare.

Chapter 4, after providing an overview of the research process, addresses the beginnings of research. It examines some of the purposes of inquiry, sources, and criteria for selecting a research problem, common issues and processes to be considered in sharpening the research question and planning a research study, and the units of analysis in social work research. After reading this chapter, you should see how social work research follows the same problem-solving process as does social work practice.

Chapter 5 deals with specifying what you want to study and the steps or operations for observing the concepts you seek to investigate—a process called conceptualization and operationalization. We're going to look at some of the terms we use quite casually in social work practice—terms like *self-esteem, social adjustment, compassion,* and so forth—and we're going to see how essential it is to get clear about what we really mean by such terms.

Once we have gotten clear on what we mean when we use certain terms, we are then in a position to create measurements of what those terms refer to.

Chapter 6 looks at different types and levels of measurement, common sources of measurement error, and steps we can take to avoid measurement error and assess the quality of our measurement procedures.

Finally, we'll look at the process of constructing some measurement instruments that are frequently used in social work research. Chapter 7 will discuss guidelines for asking questions and the construction of questionnaires, indexes, and scales.

What you learn in Part 2 will bring you to the verge of making controlled, scientific observations. Learning how to make such observations should enhance your work as a social worker even if you never conduct a research study. Practitioners are constantly engaged in making observations that guide their decision making. The more scientific and valid their observations, the better will be the decisions they make based on those observations.

Problem Formulation

What You'll Learn in This Chapter

Here you'll learn about the beginnings of the
research process, the phases of that process, how
to plan a research study, and the wide variety of
choices to be made concerning who or what is to
be studied when, how, and for what purpose.

INTRODUCTION

Social work research, like all scientific pursuits, attempts to find things out. No matter what you want to find out, though, there are likely to be a great many ways of doing it. That's true in social work practice as well.

Suppose, for example, you are administering a social services unit in a state institution for the developmentally disabled and you have a problem with your staff. With the advent of the deinstitutionalization movement, the role expectations you and the public have of your staff have shifted dramatically. Whereas in the past they focused on helping clients and their families adapt to long-term institutional living, now they must focus on discharge planning and case management to help clients get appropriately placed in and to adapt to the community. Your problem is that your staff has become so entrenched in its traditional ways of operating that it is responding inadequately to the new expectations.

You decide that perhaps a good in-service training program might be one way to begin to remedy the problem. Several in-service training programs on case management and discharge planning have been developed, but you are not sure which is most effective or most relevant to your setting. You could, of course, just pick one that has the snazziest brochure and find out by trying it. You could talk to several other social work administrators in similar settings and see what they chose to do and how they felt it turned out. You could read salient journals to see if any of the training programs have had their impacts evaluated.

The same situation occurs in scientific inquiry. Indeed, social work researchers and practitioners follow essentially the same problem-solving process in seeking to resolve social welfare problems. Both practice and research begin with the formulation of the problem, which includes recognizing a difficulty, defining it, and specifying it. Researchers and practitioners then generate, explore, and select alternative strategies for solving the problem. Finally, they implement the chosen approach, evaluate it, and disseminate the findings.

In both practice and research these phases are contingent on one another. Although the logical order is to go from one phase to the next, insurmountable obstacles encountered in any particular phase will prevent moving to the next phase and require returning to a previous phase.

For example, if all the above training programs turn out to be too expensive, then rather than implementing a chosen approach, you would have to go back and generate a different set of alternative strategies. Or, if after implementing and evaluating a training program you found no change in staff behavior, you might consider redefining the problem. Perhaps your institutional reward system—one that does not value community-resource interventions—needs to be revised. As we consider the research process, keep in mind that these same loops back to earlier phases apply. Thus, if after designing an elegant research study we realize that the costs of implementing it would exceed our resources, we would need to return to earlier phases and come up with a study that would be more feasible to implement.

OVERVIEW OF THE RESEARCH PROCESS

• Phase 1: Problem Formulation. A difficulty is recognized for which more knowledge is needed. A question, called the research question, is posed. The research question and its inherent concepts are progressively sharpened to be made more specific, relevant, and meaningful to the field. As this is done the question of feasibility of implementation is always considered. Ultimately the purpose of the research is finalized and the elements of the research, including units of analysis, hypotheses, variables, and operational definitions, are explicated. A critical step in this phase is the literature review.

• Phase 2: Designing the Study. Alternative logical arrangements and data collection methods are considered. Which are selected will depend on the issues addressed in the problem formulation phase. Feasibility is one such issue; the purpose of the research is another. Studies inquiring about causation will require logical arrangements that meet the three criteria for establishing causality that will be discussed in Chapter 9. Other arrangements might suffice for studies seeking to explore or describe certain phenomena.

The term *research design* can have two connotations. One refers to alternative logical arrangements to be selected. This connotes experimental research designs, correlational research designs, and so forth. The other connotation deals with the act of designing the study in its broadest sense. This refers to all the decisions we make in planning the study—decisions not only about what overarching type of design to use, but also about sampling, sources and procedures for collecting data, measurement issues, data analysis plans, and so on.

• Phase 3: Data Collection. The study designed in Phase 2 is implemented. The degree to which this implementation is rigidly structured in advance or is instead a more flexible process open to modification as new insights are discovered depends on the study's purpose and design. Deductive studies that seek to verify hypotheses or descriptive studies that emphasize accuracy and objectivity will require more rigidly structured data collection procedures than will studies using qualitative methods to better understand the meanings of certain phenomena or to generate hypotheses about them.

• Phase 4: Data Processing. Depending on the research methods chosen, a volume of observations will have been amassed in a form that is probably difficult to interpret. Whether the data are quantitative or qualitative, the data processing phase typically involves the classification, or coding, of observations in order to make them more interpretable. The coded information commonly is entered in some computer format: magnetic diskettes, tapes, and so on. However, small-scale studies carried out by social work practitioners, particularly studies involving single-subject de-

signs, may not require computerization. Subsequent chapters will describe some of the ways quantitative, qualitative, and single-subject data are processed or transformed for analysis.

• Phase 5: Data Analysis. The processed data are manipulated for the purpose of answering the research question. Conceivably the analysis will also yield unanticipated findings that reflect on the research problem but go beyond the specific question that guided the research. The results of the analysis will feed back into the initial problem formulation and may initiate another cycle of inquiry. Subsequent chapters will describe a few of the many options available in analyzing data.

• Phase 6: Interpreting the Findings. It will become apparent throughout the rest of this book that there is no one correct way to plan a study and no way to ensure that the outcome of the data analysis will provide the correct answer to the research question. Certain statistical procedures may be essential in order to provide the best possible interpretation of the data, but no mathematical formula or computer will obviate the need to make some judgments about the meaning of the findings. Inevitably we encounter rival explanations of the findings and must consider various methodological limitations that influence the degree to which the findings can be generalized. Consequently, research reports do not end with a presentation of the results of the data analysis. Instead, the results are followed by or included in a thorough discussion of alternative ways to interpret those results, of what generalizations can and cannot be made based on them, and of methodological limitations bearing on the meaning and validity of the results. Finally, implications are drawn for social welfare policy and program development, social work practice and theory, and future research.

• Phase 7: Writing the Research Report. Although writing up our research logically comes at the end of the research process, in practice we write pieces of it as we go along. The components of the research report follow in large part the above phases of the research process. Although the specific terminology of the headings will vary from study to study, typically the report begins with an *introduction* that provides a background to the research problem, informs the reader of the rationale and significance of the study, and reviews relevant theory and research. This introduction is followed by an explication of the conceptual elements of the study, including units of analysis, variables, hypotheses, assumptions, and operational definitions. A *methodology* section delineates in precise terms the design of the study, including the logical arrangements, sampling and data collection procedures, and the measurement approach used. Next come the *results* of the data analysis, which identify the statistical procedures employed, display data in tables, graphs, or other visual devices, and provide a narrative that reports in a technical, factual sense what specific data mean. This is followed by a *discussion* section, which includes the issues identified in Phase 6. Depending on the length of the report and/or its discussion section and whether an abstract was developed, the report might end with a brief summary of the foregoing components that highlights the major findings and conclusions. Appendix B of this book provides further information on the organization of research reports.

Diagramming the Research Process

Ultimately, the research process needs to be seen as a *whole* in order to create a research design. Unfortunately, both textbooks and human cognition operate on the basis of sequential *parts*. Figure 4-1 presents a schematic view of the social work research process. We present this view reluctantly, for it may suggest more of a "cookbook" approach to research than is the case in practice. Nonetheless, it should be useful in picturing the whole process before we launch into the specific details of particular components of research.

At the top of the diagram are problems, ideas, and theories, the possible beginning points for a line of research. The letters (A, B, X, Y, and so on) represent variables or concepts such as sexism, social functioning, or a particular intervention. Thus, the problem might be finding out whether certain interventions are more effective in improving social functioning than others. Alternatively, your inquiry might begin with a specific idea about the way things are. You might have the idea that men in your agency are promoted to supervisory or administrative positions sooner than women and that administrative practices therefore reflect the problem of sexism. We have put question marks in the diagram to indicate that you aren't sure things are the way you suspect they are. Finally, we have represented a *theory* as a complex set of relationships among several variables.

Notice, moreover, that there is often a movement back and forth across these several possible beginnings. An initial problem may lead to the formulation of an idea, which may fit into a larger theory, and the theory may produce new ideas and facilitate the perception of new problems.

Any or all of these three may suggest the need for empirical research. The purpose of such research can be to explore a problem, test a specific idea, or validate a complex theory. Whatever the purpose, a variety of decisions needs to be made, as indicated in the remainder of the diagram.

To make this discussion more concrete, let's take a specific research example. Suppose you are working in a group residential facility for children with behavioral or emotional disorders. A problem is perceived regarding the amount of antisocial behavior occurring in the cottages (residential units). You have the idea that some cottages may have more antisocial behavior than others and that this might have something to do with different styles of behavioral management used by parents in different cottages. You find a framework to pursue your idea further in learning theory. Based on that theory, you postulate that the cottage parents who use behavioral reinforcement contingencies, such as tokens for good behavior that can be accumulated and cashed in for certain special privileges, are the ones whose cottages experience the fewest antisocial behaviors. Or your initial expertise in learning theory may have stim-

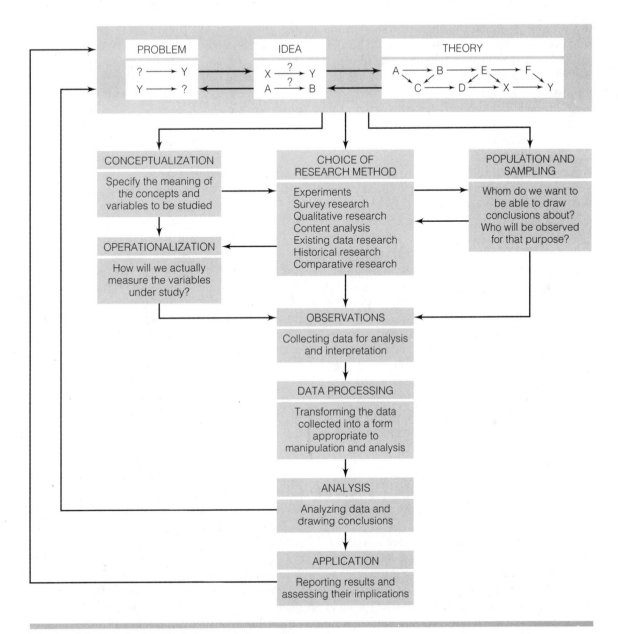

Figure 4-1 The Social Work Research Process

ulated the idea, which in turn may have led you to notice the problem.

Your next step would be to conceptualize what you mean by styles of behavioral management, reinforcement contingencies, and antisocial behav-

ior. Then you would need to specify the concrete steps or operations that will be used to measure the concepts. Decisions must be made about whom to study. Will you study all the residents or cottages in the facility—that is, its population? If not, how will you go about selecting a sample of them? Or do you wish to draw conclusions about group-care facilities in general and therefore conceive of your entire facility as a sample representing a larger population of facilities?

Additional decisions must be made about the choice of a research method. Will you conduct an experiment, randomly assigning children to cottages using different behavioral management styles? Will you conduct a survey, simply interviewing parents about how they attempt to manage behavior and their perception of the frequency of antisocial behaviors in their cottages? Will you do a content analysis of case records to try to sort out the answer to your question? Perhaps you will opt for qualitative methods, observing and discussing in an open-ended manner what goes on in the cottages, rather than attempting to test some precisely defined hypothesis.

Whatever you decide, your next step is to implement that decision, which means conducting your observations. The data you collect will then be processed and analyzed. Suppose in the process of conducting your study you learned that your facility systematically obtains follow-up information from the community about how well discharged youths adjust to the postdischarge community environment. Included in this information are data on juvenile court contacts, school attendance, and school academic performance and conduct. Suppose further that after finding empirical support for your initial idea that different behavioral management styles are associated with different levels of antisocial behavior, and in light of the availability of the above postdischarge data, you get a new idea. You wonder whether the differences you found continue after the child is discharged. That is, you wonder whether the children exposed to the most effective behavioral management styles while they are residents will continue to exhibit less antisocial behavior after they return to the community.

The completion of one research study will have then looped back to generate the research process all over again, this time in connection to social adjustment in the community. Suppose you conduct the new study. If your results are like those of similar research that has been conducted in this problem area, you will find that the type of treatment received while in your program or the gains that children make in your program have little or no bearing on their postdischarge adjustment. That is, you will find no difference in postdischarge adjustment between children who received certain types of behavior management in your program and those who received other types, or between those who exhibited little antisocial behavior prior to discharge and those who exhibited a lot of it (Whittaker, 1987).

Once again you will return to the beginning of the research process. You have a new problem, one that has been identified in the research you just completed. The problem is that what happens in your facility seems to have no bearing on postdischarge outcome. Is your program therefore ineffective? Perhaps, and if so, that would be a whopper of a problem to begin dealing with. But in thinking about this, you get another idea. Perhaps your program is effective as far as it goes and given the resources it has; the problem may be that you need to go further—to intervene in the postdischarge environment. Perhaps it is not reasonable to expect your program to do more than demonstrate its ability to enhance the functioning of children while they are in residence and provide them with a healthy environment for as long as they are there. If society expects you to influence their behavior in the community, it needs to provide your program with the mandate and the resources to intervene in the postdischarge community environment.

Your new idea may be thoughtful and quite plausible, but is it valid? Or is it just a convenient rationalization for the dismal results of your last study? To find out, you begin working on another study. This time your focus will be not on predischarge factors that are associated with adjustment, but on factors in the postdischarge environment associated with it. To what extent are there harmful and beneficial environmental conditions—conditions that perhaps can be influenced by postdischarge social work intervention—that are associated with community adjustment? Suppose the results of your new study confirm such an association. Stop reading for a moment at the end of this sentence and ask yourself whether those results would again return you to the start of a new research process and what the next problem or idea might be.

Okay, have you thought about it? If so, then you probably came up with several new problems or ideas. Chances are that one of them was to test whether certain postdischarge interventions can be implemented effectively to influence environmental conditions and whether those interventions ultimately promote improved community adjustment. Perhaps this could be done on a small, pilot basis if you have funding restraints.

THE RESEARCH PROPOSAL

If you were to undertake a research project—an assignment for this course, perhaps, or even a major study funded by the government or a private foundation—you might very well have to provide a research proposal describing what you intend to accomplish and how. Although some funding agencies (or your instructor, for that matter) may have specific requirements for the elements and/or structure of a research proposal, here are some basic elements you should discuss.

• **Problem or Objective.** What exactly do you want to study? Why is it worth studying? In what ways does the proposed study have significance for practice and policy? Does it contribute to our general understanding of things—to the construction of theories about social problems or their amelioration, for example?

When discussing the importance of the study, cite facts. For instance, if you are proposing to study homelessness, you might want to cite figures from prior studies that assessed the number of homeless individuals in the nation or in a particular city or state. Or you might describe concrete examples taken from prior case studies, so that the subject of your study and its purpose are not vague abstractions. When discussing significant implications for policy or practice, be specific. For example, if you are proposing to study factors that influence school dropout, don't just say vague things like, "By identifying why some children drop out of school and others do not, we can develop new policies and programs to deal with this problem." Spell out specifically what kinds of findings might imply what specific possible policy or program alternatives. Thus, you might say something like the following: "If we find that the absence of positive male role models is an important factor contributing to the dropout problem among males of a particular ethnic group, this may imply the need to hire more male teachers of that ethnicity or to create a special alternative program where such male role models work exclusively with boys on academic material as well as on issues like what it means to be a man. . . ."

It is also important that you know the funding source's priorities before you prepare or submit your proposal. Try to find a funding source whose priorities come closest to the problem you want to study and to the potential significant implications of your study. Then word your problem statement in a manner that emphasizes the degree of fit between your proposed study and the funding source's priorities.

• Literature Review. What have others said about this topic? What theories address it and what do they say? What research has been done previously? Are there consistent findings or do past studies disagree? Are there flaws in the body of existing research that you feel you can remedy? How will your study relate to, yet go beyond, the previous studies? How has the prior work influenced your proposed study, for example, perhaps by implying the need to examine certain variables or to assess them in new ways? Do not cite monotonous, minute details about every relevant study that has ever been done, especially if the body of existing literature is extensive.

Moss (1988) recommends that if the literature is extensive you should concentrate on the most recent findings, yet be sure to include "classic" studies, as well. Moss (1988:434) also recommends that the literature review be "brief enough not to become tedious but extensive enough to inform proposal reviewers about the study's topic."

One way you might try to resolve this conflict is by trying to stick to major themes and to sum up groups of related studies, in a succinct fashion, connecting them to a major theme. For instance, you might say something like this (we'll use fictitious references): "Prior studies on the effectiveness of case management with the severely mentally ill have had inconsistent findings. Four studies (Rubin, 1998; Babbie, 1999; Rubin and Babbie, 2000; Babbie, Rubin, and Freud, 2001) found that it is effective. Three studies (Nietzsche, 1998; Scrooge, 1999; Fischer, 2000) found that it is ineffective. The four studies with positive outcomes all used days hospitalized as the dependent variable, whereas the three studies with negative outcomes all used quality of life as the dependent variable. . . ." If, on the other hand, you have difficulty finding prior studies that are directly relevant to your proposed research, you should cite studies that are relevant in an indirect way (Moss, 1988). Thus, if you find no studies on the effectiveness of case management with the mentally ill, you might look for studies evaluating its effectiveness with other populations, such as the physically or developmentally disabled.

• Subjects for Study. Who or what will you study in order to collect data? First, identify them in general, theoretical terms. Then ascertain more concretely who is available for study and how you will reach them. Will it be appropriate to select a sample? If so, how will you do that? If you will be conducting an exploratory, qualitative study, you will need to use your judgment in identifying and observing variations (such as age, ethnicity, class) among subjects as you go along—ensuring that you have tapped into the range of those variations. If your aim is to conduct a survey for purposes of estimating frequencies of characteristics in the population (for instance, determining the unemployment rate), you will need to select a

probability sample. (Both of these techniques are described in Chapter 8.) Is there is any possibility that your research will have a significant impact on those you study? If so, how will you ensure that they will not be harmed by the research? That should be addressed in your proposal, also.

• Measurement. What are the key variables in your study? How will you define and measure them? Do your definitions and measurement methods duplicate (that's okay, incidentally) or differ from those of previous research on this topic? If you have already developed your measurement device (for example, standardized questionnaire, outline for in-depth interview, observational plan) or will be using something previously developed by others, it might be appropriate to include a copy in an appendix to your proposal.

• Data Collection Methods. How will you actually collect the data for your study? Will you conduct an experiment or a survey? Will you undertake field research, conduct a historical study, or focus on the re-analysis of statistics already created by others?

• Analysis. Give some indication of the kind of analysis you plan to conduct. If you anticipate the use of specific analytic techniques—multiple regression, analysis of variance, and so on—you might say that. Perhaps your intention is to construct ethnographic ideal types representing variations in the phenomenon under study. Say how you will do that. More important, however, is that you spell out the purpose and logic of your analysis. Are you interested in precise description? Do you intend to explain why things are the way they are? Do you plan to account for variations in some quality, for example, why some children are harder to treat than others? What possible explanatory variables will your analysis consider, and how will you know if you've explained variations adequately?

• Schedule. It is often appropriate to provide a schedule for the various stages of research. Even if you don't do this for the proposal, do it for yourself. Unless you have a time-line for accomplishing the several stages of research—and keep in touch with how you're doing—you may end up in trouble.

• Budget. If you are asking someone to give you money to pay the costs of your research, you will need to provide a budget, specifying where the money will go. Large, expensive projects include budgetary categories such as personnel, equipment, supplies, and expenses such as telephones, postage, and so on. Even for a more modest project that you will pay for yourself, it is a good idea to spend some time anticipating any expenses involved: office supplies, photocopying, computer disks, telephone calls, transportation, and so on.

As you can see, if you were interested in conducting a social work research project, it would be a good idea to prepare a research proposal for your own purposes, even if you weren't required to do so by your instructor or a funding agency. If you are going to invest your time and energy in such a project, you should do what you can to ensure a return on that investment. The degree of difficulty you will encounter in preparing a proposal is likely to vary depending on the type of study you plan to conduct. Preparing a proposal for a qualitative study that you will be submitting for funding is likely to be particularly challenging, as is discussed in the box "Similarities and Differences Between Quantitative and Qualitative Research Proposals."

Now that you've had a broad overview of social research, let's move on and learn exactly how to design and execute each specific step. If you have found a research topic that really interests you, it would be useful to keep that topic in mind as you see how you might go about studying it.

PROBLEM IDENTIFICATION

Throughout this book we will be discussing in much greater depth the issues involved in all the phases of the research process. Let's begin with a closer examination of the first phase: problem formulation. This phase commences with the selection of a topic or problem.

Impetus for Topic Selection Because social work is such a diverse profession, possible research topics in the field are virtually endless. They can be in (or perhaps cut across) different problem areas, such as health or mental health, child welfare, gerontology, substance abuse, poverty, mental retardation, crime and delinquency, family violence, and many others. Within one or more problem areas research might focus on individuals, families, groups, communities, organizations, or broader social systems. It might deal with characteristics of a target population, the services social workers provide, the way social workers are supervised or trained, issues in the administration of social welfare agencies, issues in social policy, assessment of client and community needs for purposes of guiding program development or treatment planning, the reasons that prospective clients don't use services, the dynamics of the problems social workers deal with and their implications for service delivery, how adequately social agencies are responding to certain problems and whether they are reaching the target population in the intended manner, attitudes practitioners have about certain types of clients or services, factors bearing on citizen participation strategies and their outcomes, and a host of other topics.

In social work research, as distinguished from social scientific research in other disciplines, the impetus for selecting a topic should come from decisions confronting social service agencies or the information needed to solve practical problems in social welfare. The researcher's intellectual curiosity and personal interests certainly come into play, as they do in all research, but a study is more likely to have value to the social work field (and to be considered social work research) if the topic is selected because it addresses information needed to guide policy, planning, or practice decisions in social welfare. This does not mean that the problem identification process is atheoretical,

SIMILARITIES AND DIFFERENCES BETWEEN QUANTITATIVE AND QUALITATIVE RESEARCH PROPOSALS

The elements of research proposals that we've identified in this book are fairly common, irrespective of the type of research being proposed. Regardless of whether you are proposing a quantitative or qualitative study (or perhaps a blending of the two), you will probably need to begin with a statement of the problem or objective, followed by a literature review, a description of your research methods, and so on. Regardless of which type of study you propose to do, you will have to make a persuasive case as to the importance of the research question and the value of the study. The criteria for a good literature review will also be similar in both types of proposals. Other similarities include the need for a schedule with a realistic time-line, a section covering human subjects review approval, a reasonable budget that anticipates all the various costs you will encounter, and a neat professional appearance that reflects clear and interesting writing and laser printing.

While certain criteria for proposal preparation, like those mentioned above, commonly apply to all research proposals, qualitative methodologists have been identifying ways proposals for qualitative studies differ from proposals for quantitative studies. There appears to be general agreement that qualitative proposals are more difficult to write than quantitative proposals, due mainly to the greater degree of structure and preplanning involved in designing quantitative research. Sandelowski, Davis, and Harris (1989:77), for example, see the preparation of the proposal for a qualitative study as requiring the negotiation of "the paradox of planning what should

not be planned in advance." Likewise, Morse (1994) notes the relatively unstructured, unpredictable nature of qualitative research and the difficulty this presents for writing a proposal that promises exciting results or that is even specific about the types of alternative conclusions the study is likely to generate. These authors point out that the design of qualitative research tends to be in the form of an open-ended starting point from which methods and truth will emerge through encountering subjects in their natural environment, unlike quantitative research, in which the methods and specific alternative findings can be planned and spelled out in detail in advance.

The dilemma for the qualitative researcher, then, is figuring out how to put enough detail about the plan in the proposal to enable potential funders to evaluate the proposal's merits, while at the same time remaining true to the unstructured, flexible, inductive qualitative approach. In the words of Sandelowski and her colleagues, "The most difficult task in preparing the proposal . . . is delineating the method when the investigator can have no definitive method prior to initiating inquiry" (p. 78). This task is even more challenging to the extent that the merits of the proposal will be judged by reviewers who are likely to be more oriented to quantitative research and who expect the precise planning that goes into proposals for quantitative research studies.

One suggestion for preparers of proposals for qualitative studies is to go ahead and describe a plan for sampling and data collection and analysis, but indicate that the plan is only a tentative and initial direction that is open to change as the study proceeds and new insights emerge. Also, the proposal can specify the type of qualitative approach being employed and then describe the general ideas underlying that approach. (Some of the more common qualitative approaches, and their orienting guidelines, are discussed in Chapters 12 and 13 of this book.) Although you will not be able to say in advance exactly what you will do or find, you can convey to reviewers the general principles you will follow in conducting your flexible, emergent inquiry.

The same general idea applies to other qualitative proposal sections that, in a quantitative proposal, would contain a much greater degree of operational specificity. For example, when you discuss sampling, you may not be able to anticipate with the precision of a quantitative proposal the exact number of subjects who will participate in the study and their characteristics. But you can discuss the variety of types of subjects you tentatively think are likely to participate and who you think are likely to supply the most relevant data. You can also describe the general ideas and rationale underlying the qualitative sampling methods you expect to employ. (These methods are discussed in Chapters 8 and 12 of this book.)

Although you may find these suggestions helpful, they won't change the fact that qualitative proposals are more difficult to write and may be reviewed by people more accustomed to reading proposals for quantitative research and to judging proposals according to the canons of quantitative research design.

Since they may be apt to react to your qualitative proposal with puzzlement, it is particularly important that your proposal demonstrate your expertise about qualitative research and ability to carry it out. Make sure that every section of your proposal is well written and that your literature review is adequate. (The literature review in qualitative proposals should perhaps be more extensive than in quantitative proposals, to demonstrate the investigator's expertise, since it may appear as though the funders are being asked to, "Trust me," in qualitative studies more than in quantitative ones.)

Along these lines, it may be helpful to conduct a pilot study on the topic addressed in your proposal and then describe that pilot study in your proposal and submit it as an appendix to the proposal. This will show your commitment and competence. It can also demonstrate how you might go about analyzing the data that might emerge in the proposed study. Of course, being able to refer to previously completed pilot studies will also help your prospects for funding in submitting a proposal for quantitative research, and the two types of proposals are similar in this respect.

While we do not want to understate the similarities between the two types of proposals, or overstate their differences, it is important that anyone planning to prepare a proposal for qualitative research be aware of the special dilemma they face. It is also important for reviewers and board members of funding sources to understand this dilemma and to apply different criteria when reviewing the two types of proposals.

but rather that the ultimate value of the study depends on its applicability to practical social work and social welfare concerns. In fact, by relating the problem to existing theory, we enhance the potential utility of the study, for theory provides a framework that helps others comprehend the rationale for and significance of framing the question in the way we did.

When we say that social work research sets out to solve practical problems in social welfare, the connotation of an "applied" research focus is inescapable. This is in contrast to "pure" research, which connotes the attempt to advance knowledge just for knowledge's sake. But this distinction is not as clear as it first may seem. Although social work research may not aim to advance general social science theory, its findings may still have that effect. Polansky (1975), for example, discusses how a social work research study in which he participated, on "behavioral contagion in children's groups," was cited more frequently in the social psychology literature than in the social work literature (Polansky, Lippitt, and Redl, 1950). By the same token, it is not necessary to have an applied aim in an investigation in order to produce knowledge relevant to solving social welfare problems. Social work has always "borrowed" basic social scientific knowledge advanced by "pure" social research and applied it to practical social welfare concerns.

Is It Social Work Research? Some important studies can transcend disciplinary boundaries and still be valuable as social work research. A study to assess the impact of socioenvironmental family stress on whether children drop out of school, for example, could be done by educational psychologists or sociologists. But if the practical need that provided the impetus for selecting that research problem had to do with informing policymakers about the need to employ school social workers to help alleviate family stress as one way to fight the dropout problem, the study would be of great interest to social workers. The same would apply if the main implication of the study concerned guiding the practice of school social workers, such

as pointing to the need for intensifying interventions aimed at alleviating socioenvironmental sources of family stress or helping families better cope with that stress (as opposed to focusing intervention exclusively on counseling the student).

A study by Royse (1988) exemplifies the sometimes fuzzy distinction between social work research and research associated with other social scientific disciplines. Royse was interested in the degree of predictability of voting precincts with regard to voter support or nonsupport of referenda to continue or to approve new taxes needed to support the provision of human services. His analysis of precinct-by-precinct election returns on such referenda identified certain patterns from which he developed implications for social service administrators and members of planning committees who conduct campaigns to influence the outcome of future elections like these. Would you consider Royse's study to be social work research? Or would you be more likely to associate it with another field—political science, perhaps?

Although Royse's study appears to overlap with political science, and perhaps will be cited by political scientists, we can also call it social work research for three reasons. To begin, Royse was a social work faculty member at the time he reported his study. Also, his study was published in a social work journal, *ARETE* (which is published by the School of Social Work at the University of South Carolina). But perhaps the most important reason to consider it social work research is that the prime purpose of the study was to develop knowledge to guide the practice of social service administrators. What if, however, the same study, with the same implications, was done by a political scientist? Some might still consider it social work research, while others might argue that although its findings are relevant to social workers, it is not social work research. We know of no "correct" answer to this question, and you might understandably feel that it matters little what we call the research. The point is merely to illustrate the difficulty that can arise when we try to distinguish social *work* research from social research, a difficulty connected to the fact that social work traditionally has applied social scientific knowledge, from a variety of disciplines, to social welfare problems.

"So What?" Saying that the identified problem should address the decision-making needs of agencies or practical problems in social welfare does not mean that researchers must ask planners, practitioners, administrators, or other significant social welfare figures to select research problems for them (although getting feedback from those individuals about their needs and priorities is a valuable step in the process). Inspiration for useful research ideas can come from many sources. Sometimes it is something you read. Sometimes it is something you observe in an agency. Sometimes it is something a colleague says to you. Sometimes a neat idea pops into your head from an unknown source.

Whatever the source of the topic, it's important that before you get carried away—before you invest much of your resources in planning to study the topic, before you let your initial enthusiasm or idiosyncratic personal interests wed you too firmly to that topic—you should take steps to ensure that the topic passes the "so what?" test. Passing the "so what?" test means that the study you propose to conduct has clear significance and utility for social work practice or social welfare. Assessing in advance whether your study is likely to be useful and significant means skeptically asking what difference the answer to your research question would make to others concerned about social work practice or social welfare. For example, a proposed study of the social service needs of family caregivers of relatives with HIV/AIDS might have obvious significance for practice or policy. If you asked your professional colleagues for their reactions about the likely value of such a study, they would probably respond with immediate enthusiasm for it. On the other hand, if you were to ask the same colleagues about a study seeking to assess the leisure-time activities of social service agency directors, they might respond by asking "so what?" and wondering whether you might make better use of your time by studying a topic of greater significance for people in need.

Thus, to make a difference to social work practice or social welfare policy, your research question should be *relevant* to the priorities of practice and policy. Relevance, however, is only one of several criteria your research question should meet. Other criteria pertain to how *specific* you are about the question to be answered, whether the question is posed in a way that can be answered by observable evidence, and whether the data needed to answer the question are feasible for the researcher to obtain.

Finally, it is essential that there be *more than one possible acceptable answer* to the research question. This last requirement can be violated in various ways. One would be when feasibility constraints or a system of values make it impossible to implement any changes based on the answer to the research question. Thus, in a fledgling voluntary agency that is constantly struggling to raise enough funds to meet its payroll obligations, there might be little practical value in studying whether increasing the staff-client ratio or travel budget for attending professional conferences would improve staff morale. Another way to violate this requirement would be by posing a tautological research question, a truism in which the answer is a foregone conclusion. An example here would be to see if increasing the proportion of time practitioners spend on certain activities is associated with a decrease in the proportion of time they have left for other activities.

A number of activities are undertaken in the problem formulation phase to ensure that we ultimately will have identified an important research problem and articulated a useful research question. By engaging in these activities we progressively sharpen the original research question and its conceptual elements in line with the above criteria. Or we may reject the original question and formulate a new one that better meets these criteria.

An important step in this process is obtaining critical feedback of colleagues and others to help us more rigorously appraise the utility of the study, the clarity of our ideas, alternative ways of looking at the problem, and pragmatic or ethical considerations that pose potential obstacles to the study's feasibility. It is important to stress to these individuals that you are not looking for their approval and that you want them to try to be critical or skeptical. Otherwise, it is all too expedient for them to think they are currying favor with you by patting you on the back, complimenting you for your initiative and fine mind, and then letting you fall on your face at no cost to themselves.

Feasibility

Other important steps in the problem formulation phase involve compiling the literature review and explicating the conceptual elements of the research problem. Each of these steps will be examined in depth shortly. But first we will consider at greater length some of the issues bearing on the feasibility of research.

Feasibility is a very important topic. Experienced and inexperienced researchers alike find it much easier to conceive of rigorous, valuable studies than to figure out how they can feasibly implement them. One of the most difficult problems confronting researchers is how to make a study feasible without making the research question so narrow that it is no longer worth doing or without sacrificing too much methodological rigor or inferential capacity. Inexperienced researchers commonly formulate idealistic, far-reaching studies and then become immobilized when they find out how much they must scale down their plans in order to have a feasible study. With seasoning we learn how to strike a happy medium. That is, we learn to formulate and appreciate research problems that are not so narrow that they are no longer worth doing, yet at the same time are not so grandiose that they are not feasible.

Selltiz, Wrightsman, and Cook (1976) identify common issues in determining the feasibility of a study, such as its scope, the time it will require, its fiscal costs, ethical considerations, and the cooperation it will require from others. The larger the scope of the study, the more it will cost in time, money, and cooperation. Sometimes the scope is too large because the study seeks to assess more variables than can be handled statistically given the available sample size. *Ethical* issues were examined at length in Chapter 3. A paramount ethical issue bearing on feasibility pertains to whether the value and quality of the research will outweigh any potential discomfort, inconvenience, or risk experienced by participants in the study.

The *fiscal* costs of a study are easily underestimated. Common expenses identified by Selltiz and associates are personnel costs, computer costs for data processing and analysis, travel to collect data, long-distance telephone calls to track down survey nonrespondents who have left town, printing and copying expenses, data collection instruments, and postage. Postage costs are particularly easy to underestimate. Bulky questionnaires may require more stamps than expected, and nonresponse problems may necessitate multiple mailings. And in each mailing we may need to enclose a stamped return envelope. Personnel costs commonly involve the hiring of interviewers, coders, and data entry personnel for computer processing.

Time constraints also may turn out to be much worse than anticipated. Inexperienced researchers in particular may underestimate the time required to recruit participants for the study or to make multiple follow-up contacts urging survey nonrespondents to complete and mail in their questionnaires. Scheduled interviews are often missed or canceled, requiring the scheduling of additional ones. Time may be needed to develop and test data collection instruments, perhaps through several dry runs, before implementing the actual data collection. A great deal of unanticipated time may be needed to reformulate the problem and revise the study based on unexpected obstacles encountered in trying to implement the research. And, of course, time is needed for each additional phase of the research process (that is, data processing and analysis, writing the report, and so forth).

One of the time constraints that can be the most frustrating involves obtaining advance authorization for the study. Approval may need to be secured from a variety of sources, such as agency administrators and practitioners, the agency board, and a human subjects review committee that assesses the ethics of the research. Political squabbles in an agency can delay obtaining approval for a study simply because the battling forces will suspect almost anything that their adversaries support. Administrative turnover also can cause frustrating delays. You may have to delay implementing a study when, after a lengthy period spent involving an executive director in the formulation of the research, that director moves on to another agency.

Sometimes lack of *cooperation* in one setting forces the researcher to seek a different setting in which to implement a study. Agency members in the original setting may be skeptical about research and therefore refuse to authorize it at all. Perhaps they fear that the research findings will embarrass the agency or certain units or staff. Perhaps in the past they have had bad experiences with other researchers who were insensitive to agency needs and procedures. A common complaint is that researchers exploit agencies so they can get the data they need for their own intellectual interests and career needs (doctoral dissertations, for example) and then give nothing back to the agency in terms of useful findings that can help solve agency problems. Some of these agency resistances to research are quite rational, and it is a mistake to treat them lightly or to assume that they are due to the insecurity or ignorance of agency members.

A study that one of the authors of this text (Rubin, 1990) conducted illustrates some of the above points. The study sought to evaluate whether school dropout can be prevented by involving students at high risk for dropping out in a program in which they produce and appear in television shows aired on a local cable TV station. The design included administering paper-and-pencil self-report scales to these students to measure level of self-esteem and willingness to accept responsibility for academic performance. The scales were administered to the students in the classroom setting. Before implementing the study it was necessary to show the scales to school administrators and teachers and to obtain approval for the study from the board of education, from

school principals, and from a university-wide committee on the ethics of human subjects research. Although the scales take only half an hour to administer and seem relatively innocuous, who could blame a school principal or other responsible educators for being reticent to approve the research? In all likelihood some students would talk to their parents about the scales, and from experience educators know all too well the potential this has for parents to become irate over prying into personal issues. In this connection, one of the preconditions for getting the study approved was that parents be informed of the purpose and nature of the study and the scales and that they sign consent forms before their children were involved in the study.

In Chapter 18 (on program evaluation), we will discuss some of the steps researchers can take to try to overcome or prevent agency resistances to research. One important step is to involve all relevant agency figures as early as possible in all phases of problem formulation and research design planning. Interact with them on their ideas about what needs to be done. Don't just pretend to be involving them solely to get their support. Be responsive to what they say, not only in the interaction, but in how you actually formulate the study. If you are responsive to their needs, and if they feel they have made a meaningful contribution to the design of the study, the chances are better that they will find the study useful and will support it. The dialogue also may build a better, more trusting relationship that can dispel some of their anxiety about having a researcher investigate something in their agency. Moreover, it may help them better understand the purpose and necessity for some of the inconveniences your methodology creates.

Before we leave this topic, it is important to note that lack of cooperation can come not only from agency staff and board members, but also from clients or other individuals we hope will be the subjects for our research. Perhaps they will refuse to be observed or interviewed or to respond to a mailed questionnaire (particularly when the data collection procedure is cumbersome or threatening). Even if they are willing to participate, will we be able to find them? Suppose you were trying to carry out a longitudinal study of the homeless mentally ill over a period of years. Imagine how difficult it would be to keep track of them and find them for follow-up interviews (not to mention the difficulty of locating them in the first place for initial interviews). To ensure that your study is sensitive to the needs, lifestyles, and concerns of service consumers, it is important not to overlook representatives of service consumers' groups when involving relevant agency figures in the research planning.

Literature Review

One of the most important steps, not only in the problem formulation phase but in the entire process of designing a study, is the literature review. Although we are discussing this step after discussing feasibility issues, the literature review is completed at no one point in the research process. As the research design evolves, new issues requiring additional investigation of the literature will emerge. Be that as it may, it is usually important to initiate a thorough literature review as early as possible in the research process.

A mistake novice researchers commonly make is to put off their literature review until they have sharpened their research question and come up with a design to investigate it. Research can be done that way, but it is not the most efficient use of time. Doing it that way can result in reinventing the wheel or in failing to benefit from the mistakes and experiences of others. Until we review the literature, we have no way of knowing whether the research question has already been adequately answered, of identifying the conceptual and practical obstacles that others have already encountered in this line of research, of learning how those obstacles have been overcome, and of deciding what lines of research can best build on the work that has already been done in a particular problem area.

Another reason to review the literature early is that it is a prime source for selecting a topic to begin with! What better way to reduce the chances of selecting an irrelevant or outdated topic than by knowing what has already been done in a particular problem area and the implications of that work for future research? What better way to ensure that your study will be valued as part of a cumulative knowledge-building effort regarding that problem, as opposed to being seen as an obscure study that does not seem to address anything that anyone else is addressing or cares about?

Building on prior research does not necessarily imply that your study should never depart radically from previous work or that it should never duplicate a previous study. There may be sound reasons to do either. The point is that you make that decision not in ignorance of the prior research, but in light of it and what your judgment tells you to do. You may wish to repeat a prior study if you think replication is warranted and would be the best contribution you can make. Perhaps your research question has already been answered but the limitations of the methodologies used to investigate it make you skeptical of the validity of the answer currently in vogue. So you might decide to study the same question with a better methodology. On the other hand, you may be inspired to look at the problem in a way no one else ever has. You would do this not just to satisfy your own curiosity, but because after careful consideration of what's been done before you are convinced that this radical departure is precisely what the field needs at this time.

There are countless examples of how an early search of the literature can enrich your study and save you from headaches later on. One common example is that by identifying valid measurement instruments, you can adapt existing measures instead of spending endless hours constructing and testing your own instruments. Another benefit of the literature search is identification of alternative conceptions of the problem or of variables that had not occurred to you.

Suppose you plan to evaluate the effectiveness of a case management program in helping clients recently discharged from psychiatric hospitals adjust to living in the community. It might seem eminently reasonable to select a reduction in the number of days spent in rehospitalization as the indicator of program effectiveness. But a review of the previous research in this area would inform you that some case management programs paradoxically result in an increase in days of rehospitalization. You would learn that in the face of a woefully inadequate system of community-based resources for the chronically mentally ill, clients commonly may need rehospitalization, and effective case managers see that they get what they need.

Had you not done the literature review before implementing your study, you would not have arranged to handle this unforeseen paradox in your design. If your data indeed did show an increase in days of rehospitalization, you would not be able to conclude that this meant your program was effective because in your problem formulation you selected the opposite outcome as the indicator of effectiveness. But having done the literature review early, you were able to avoid this quandary. You did this by selecting alternative indicators of effectiveness, indicators such as the amount of services (other than case management) clients received while in the community, the quality of their living arrangements, whether they received adequate financial support while in the community, and how well they performed basic activities of daily living in the community. In short, the focus was not on whether the program reduced the amount of time they spent in the hospital, but whether it improved their quality of life while in the community.

Some researchers who are using the grounded theory method to construct theory in an inductive fashion (as we discussed in Chapter 2) might opt to delay the literature review until they near the end of the research process. Their reason for doing so would be to avoid being influenced by other people's theories in what they observe or how they interpret what they observe. In Chapter 12 we will discuss some logical pitfalls in conducting this kind of research (along with its advantages). We will see that it requires the researcher to make subjective judgments about what is being observed, and this means that what researchers perceive may be influenced in various ways by the orientations they bring to the research. Not everyone agrees with this point of view, and you should know that it is an issue about which reasonable people can disagree. Gilgun (1991) points out that although some grounded theorists delay the literature review, most grounded theorists do a thorough literature review before beginning their research. Although they want to conduct their observations with their minds as open as possible, they want to start out with an understanding of the current knowledge base and its gaps.

Now that we have established the utility of the literature review, let's briefly examine some common sources for finding the literature that social work researchers typically seek. Appendix A—on using the library—will provide additional information germane to this task. Because so many articles and books are always being published, the best way to begin your review is usually by examining guides to the literature. These guides include abstracts, bibliographies, and indexes.

Abstracts in various fields provide short summaries of published work and indicate where to find the complete publication. Although you might find relevant material in abstracts in the fields of psychology, sociology, urban studies, or public administration, your best bet is probably *Social Work Abstracts* (which previously was called *Social Work Research & Abstracts.*)

Another good place to start is in your library's subject guide. Look under several subjects related to your general field of interest. For example, if you are looking for literature pertaining to the problem of child sexual abuse, don't just look under child sexual abuse. Look also at child abuse, child welfare, and so on. While examining the various references, be on the lookout for any bibliographies, particularly those that are annotated, that others have already compiled on your topic; if you find a good one your search can be expedited a great deal. Also watch for special handbooks that review the literature in an entire field of study.

You might also want to use a computerized search service at your library. With these services you identify a list of key words related to your topic and then receive a computer printout that abstracts published references associated with those key words. But don't rely too much on the "magic" of the computer. Some computerized systems will not have some of the references you need, and even if they do have them, there is no guarantee that the key words you select will match their key words. When using these systems, therefore, be sure to use a very broad list of key words and to use the noncomputerized guides to the literature as well.

Reference libraries can help you identify the proper computerized abstracting services for your particular research project and with compiling lists of key words. Keep in mind, however, that not all such services are free. Their use might add to the fiscal costs of your study.

No matter how thorough you are in using guides to the literature, always remember that there may be a significant time lapse (perhaps as long as a year or two) between the publication of a study and its appearance in one of the guides to the literature. Therefore, it is wise to include routinely in your review a scanning of the tables of contents of recent issues of every professional journal closely related to your topic. This does not take long at all, assuming these journals are easily accessible in your library. When you spot a promising title in the table of contents, read the abstract on the first page of the article; it will tell you what you need to know to decide whether a particular article is sufficiently relevant to your particular focus to warrant your reading it. As you read the specific references you have found, make a list of additional relevant references they cite. This way your bibliography accumulates like a snowball.

Don't just examine journals associated exclusively with social work. Many cross-disciplinary, problem-focused journals are filled with studies relevant to the problems social workers deal with. For example, if you are interested in studies on the effectiveness of social workers in administering mental health and mental retardation programs, look also at journals such as *Administration in Mental Health, American Journal of Mental Deficiency, Mental Retardation,* and *Community Mental Health Journal.* Students tend to be unaware of many of these journals, but that problem is easily remedied by examining the issues of *Social Work Abstracts* from any recent year. Each issue will include a list of the periodicals abstracted for that issue. (The list changes somewhat in each issue.)

How will you know when you have completed your literature review—that you have found all the literature that you need to find? There is no foolproof answer to this question, one that will guarantee that you have not missed any significant work (such as a very recent study in an obscure journal that your library doesn't carry). The best answer to this question is that you have probably reviewed enough literature when, having gone through all of the steps delineated here—including the scanning of the recent issues of all relevant journals—you find that you are already familiar with the references cited in the most recently published articles.

PURPOSES OF RESEARCH

What is learned in the literature review influences another early decision in the research process—determining the purpose of the research. Social work research, of course, serves many purposes. Three of the most common and useful purposes are *exploration, description,* and *explanation.* Although a given study can have more than one of these purposes—and most do—it will be useful to examine them separately because each has different implications for other aspects of research design.

Exploration

Much of social work research is conducted to explore a topic—to provide a beginning familiarity with that topic. This purpose is typical when a researcher is examining a new interest, when the subject of study is relatively new and unstudied, or when a researcher seeks to test the feasibility of undertaking a more careful study or wants to develop the methods to be used in a more careful study.

As an example, let's consider the deinstitutionalization movement in mental health policy. This movement began after drugs that facilitate the control of the symptomatology of mental illness were discovered in 1955. It grew during the 1960s, spurred on by additional pharmacological discoveries, litigation protecting patients' civil rights with respect to involuntary commitment and institutionalization, and the emergence of community mental health programs. During the 1970s state governments, faced with fiscal crises and taxpayer unrest, developed the rationale that federal funding for Medicaid-Medicare and for community mental health centers would permit massive discharges from state-funded psychiatric institutions. While many applauded this movement as restoring the civil liberties of mental patients and letting them live in the least restrictive environment, others feared that this massive "dumping" was premature due to inadequate community facilities to properly care for many discharged patients and that many patients consequently would be significantly harmed by it.

Suppose that you were practicing at that time as a social worker in a mental health planning agency. Or suppose you were a generalist practitioner for a community mental health program. In either case, when your nearby state hospital began discharging patients en masse to the community, you might have sought answers to some critical questions you had about the impact of the new policy and what those answers imply for trying to modify the policy or for program development. You might have wanted to learn about the living conditions of the newly discharged patients. What types of neighborhoods are they living in? Are they living in boarding homes? In halfway houses? With their families? In the streets? Are their living facilities in decent shape? Are the ex-patients getting proper nutrition and medication? Are their finances adequate to meet their subsistence needs? How are they spending their time? What burden does the new policy seem to be im-

posing on their families? How is the community responding? Are neighbors ridiculing or victimizing the ex-patients?

Even if you had never considered yourself a researcher, you might have undertaken an exploratory study to obtain at least approximate answers to some of your questions. Or, in order to devise a questionnaire for a more careful, large-scale survey, you might have conducted relatively unstructured interviews with a small number of ex-patients to provide insights into what questions should be included on the questionnaire and how they should be worded. Exploratory studies are very valuable in social scientific research. They are essential whenever a researcher is breaking new ground, and they can almost always yield new insights into a topic for research. Exploratory studies are also a source of grounded theory, as discussed in Chapter 12.

The chief shortcoming of exploratory studies is that they seldom provide satisfactory answers to research questions. They can only hint at the answers and give insights into the research methods that could provide definitive answers. The reason exploratory studies are seldom definitive in themselves is the issue of representativeness, discussed at length in Chapter 8 in connection with sampling. Once you understand sampling and representativeness, you will be able to know whether a given exploratory study actually answered its research problem or merely pointed the way toward an answer.

Description

A major purpose of many social scientific studies is to describe situations and events. The researcher observes and then describes what was observed. Because scientific observation is careful and deliberate, however, scientific descriptions are typically more accurate and precise than casual descriptions.

In the preceding example on the deinstitutionalization movement, an example of a descriptive study would be a careful, large-scale survey of a representative sample of ex-patients conducted to describe the precise proportion of the discharged population living under certain kinds of arrangements, the proportion properly taking their medications, the frequency with which they are robbed, their average finances, and so on. The U.S. Census is an excellent example of a descriptive social scientific research project. The goal of the census is to describe accurately and precisely a wide variety of characteristics of the U.S. population, as well as the populations of smaller areas such as states and counties.

A Gallup Poll conducted during a political election campaign has the purpose of describing the voting intentions of the electorate. A researcher who computes and reports the number of times individual legislators voted for or against social welfare legislation also has or serves a descriptive purpose. In social work, one of the best-known descriptive studies is the annual canvass of schools of social work conducted by the Council on Social Work Education. It identifies a wide variety of characteristics of students and faculty in every school. By following the report of each annual canvass one can see important trends in social work education, such as increases or decreases in the number of applicants and enrollments at various degree levels, the proportion of women or ethnic minorities enrolled or teaching, and so on.

The foregoing examples of descriptive studies are all quantitative in nature. However, descriptive studies also can be qualitative. The term *description* is used differently in qualitative and quantitative studies. In quantitative studies *description* typically refers to the characteristics of a population, based on quantitative data obtained from a sample of people thought to be representative of that population. The data being described in quantitative studies are likely to refer to surface attributes that can be easily quantified, like age, income, size of family, and so on. In quantitative descriptive studies the objectivity, precision, and generalizability of the description are paramount concerns. We will be examining these considerations in depth in Chapters 6 through 8.

In qualitative studies *description* is more likely to refer to a thicker examination of phenomena and their deeper meanings. Qualitative descriptions tend to be more concerned with conveying a sense of what it is like to walk in the shoes of the people being described—providing rich details about their environments, interactions, meanings, and everyday lives—than with generalizing with precision to a larger population. A qualitative descriptive study of mothers receiving AFDC in states where the levels of AFDC support are lowest, for example, might describe the impact that the inadequate payments have on the daily lives of a small sample of mothers and their children, how they struggle to survive, how their neighbors and welfare workers interact with them, how that makes them feel, and the things they have to resort to in order to provide for their families. A quantitative descriptive study of mothers receiving AFDC, in contrast, would be likely to select a large, representative sample of these mothers and assess things like how long they stay on AFDC, their ages and educational levels, and so on. We will be examining methods for qualitative description in more depth in Chapters 7 and 12.

Explanation

The third general purpose of social scientific research is to explain things. Reporting the voting intentions of an electorate is a descriptive activity, but reporting why some people plan to vote for a tax initiative to fund human services and others against it is an explanatory activity. Reporting why some cities have higher child abuse rates than others is a case of explanation, but simply reporting the different child abuse rates is a case of description. A researcher has an explanatory purpose if he or she wishes to know why battered women repeatedly return to live with their batterers, as opposed to simply describing how often they do. In the preceding example on deinstitutionalization, an explanatory study might look at why some clients have better living conditions than others. Perhaps variations in discharge planning would explain some of the differences. Or the study might look at why some neighborhoods express more opposition to the discharge policy than others. Perhaps more resistance is found in the more residential neighborhoods.

Although it is useful to distinguish the three purposes of research, it bears repeating that most studies will have elements of all three. In our de-institutionalization example, suppose you seek to determine what sort of social work intervention might best enhance the quality of life of the discharged patients. Your study might have exploratory aspects, such as conducting open-ended interviews with social workers about their judgment concerning certain interventions they used that seemed to get the best results and those that got the worst results. It might have descriptive aspects, such as portraying the precise proportion of ex-patients receiving different types of intervention. The same study might have explanatory aspects, such as seeing whether variations in quality of life or rehospitalization are explained in part by the type of social work intervention provided.

Because studies can have more than one purpose, sometimes it is difficult to judge how best to characterize the purpose of a particular study. This is complicated further by the at-times fuzzy distinction between exploratory and explanatory purposes. Suppose, for example, that you develop a program of social support services for family caregivers of persons with HIV/AIDS. Early in this endeavor you learn that some of the caregivers are heterosexual spouses who knew that their spouses had HIV/AIDS before marrying them. In planning support services for this subgroup of caregivers, you believe it is important to understand why they married the person, in light of the potential burden of caregiving and grief that lay ahead.

Because this topic is new and unstudied, because you can obtain only a very small and potentially atypical sample, and because you are seeking only to garner tentative beginning insights into this phenomenon, you may choose to conduct an exploratory study. In your exploratory study, perhaps you will conduct an open-ended interview with five or ten caregivers about their decision to marry their spouse, seeking primarily to understand why they married them and what that might imply for their social support needs. Note that although your study is of an exploratory nature, it also has an explanatory purpose. You are exploring a new phenomenon with the long-range aim of explaining it. Thus, if someone asked you whether your study was exploratory or explanatory, you might have to ponder a while before correctly answering, "Both."

In attempting to differentiate exploratory and explanatory purposes you might also consider two additional research purposes: understanding and predicting. If your study is seeking to develop a beginning understanding of a phenomenon, it is more likely to be exploratory than explanatory, even though it might include questions asking respondents to explain why they did something. On the other hand, your study is more likely to be explanatory to the extent that it seeks to rigorously test out predictions (hypotheses) implied by tentative explanations derived from previous work on the topic. You will see these several research purposes at work in the following discussions of other aspects of research design. One issue closely related to the purpose of your research involves the time period during which your research observations will be conducted. Let's turn now to a consideration of that issue.

THE TIME DIMENSION

Research observations may be made more or less at one time, or they may be deliberately stretched over a long period. If, for example, the purpose of your study is to describe the living arrangements of mentally ill patients immediately after their hospital discharge, you might decide to observe each patient's living arrangements at one predetermined point after their discharge. If, on the other hand, the purpose of your study is to describe how these living arrangements change over time, then you would need to conduct repeated observations of these individuals and their living arrangements over an extended period.

Cross-Sectional Studies

Research studies that study some phenomenon by taking a cross section of it at one time and analyzing that cross section carefully are called **cross-sectional studies.** A cross-sectional study may have an exploratory, descriptive, or explanatory purpose. A single U.S. Census would exemplify a cross-sectional study for descriptive purposes. If you conducted one open-ended, unstructured interview with each client who prematurely terminated treatment in your agency during a specified period—in order to generate insights about why your agency's treatment termination rate is so high—you would be conducting a cross-sectional study for exploratory purposes. If you conducted one structured interview with each of these clients, as well as with clients who completed their planned treatment—in order to test the hypothesis that practitioner-client disagreement about treatment goals is related to whether treatment is completed—then you would be conducting a cross-sectional study for explanatory purposes.

Explanatory cross-sectional studies have an inherent problem. Typically, their aim is to understand causal processes that occur over time, yet their conclusions are based on observations made at only one time. For example, if your cross-sectional study of patients recently discharged from a psychiatric hospital finds that those who are living with their families are functioning better and have less symptomatology than those not living with their families, you would not know whether the differences in functioning or symptomatology between the two groups commenced before or after they entered their current living arrangements. In other words, you wouldn't know whether different living arrangements helped cause differences in functioning and symptomatology or the latter differences help explain placement in particular living arrangements. Although merely finding in a cross-sectional study that such a relationship exists may have significant value, obtain-

ing a better understanding of the causal processes involved in that relationship will require methodological arrangements that we will be discussing later, in chapters on research designs and statistical analysis.

Longitudinal Studies

Studies intended to describe processes occurring over time, and that therefore may conduct their observations over an extended period, are called **longitudinal studies.** An example is a researcher who participates in and observes the activities of a support group for battered women or an advocacy group for families of the mentally ill from the time of its inception to the present. Analyses of newspaper editorials or Supreme Court decisions over time on a subject such as abortion or psychiatric commitment are other examples. In the latter instances, the researcher may conduct observations and analyses at one point in time, but because the study's data correspond to events occurring at different chronological points, the study would still be considered to be longitudinal.

Three special types of longitudinal studies should be noted here. **Trend studies** are those that study changes within some general population over time. One example would be a comparison of U.S. Censuses over time, showing growth in the national population or in specific minority groups. Another example would be an examination of the data generated over the years in the Council on Social Work Education's annual canvasses of schools of social work, perhaps to identify fluctuations over time in the number of social work students specializing in various methods or fields of practice. At the level of a local agency, one could assess whether the types of clients or problems that comprise an agency's caseload are changing over time, and based on that analysis, perhaps make some projections as to what these trends imply for future staffing patterns or in-service training needs.

Cohort studies examine more specific subpopulations (cohorts) as they change over time. Typically, a cohort is an age group, such as the post–World War II baby boom generation, but it can also be based on some other time grouping, such as people whose first episode of schizophrenia occurred during a particular time period after deinstitutionalization policies were implemented. For example, we might be interested in what happens to the incidence of substance abuse among young adults with schizophrenia as they age, since such abuse is particularly dangerous for this group due to the nature of their illness and the prescribed medications they take. In 1980 we might survey a sample of such persons 20–25 years of age and ask them about their use of alcohol or drugs. In 1990 we might survey another sample of such persons 30–35 years of age, and another sample of those 40–45 years of age in 2000. Although the specific set of people would be different, each sample would represent the survivors of the cohort with schizophrenia at the age of 20–25 in 1980.

Panel studies are similar to trend and cohort studies except that the same set of people is studied each time. One example would be a follow-up study of people who graduated with a master's degree in social work during a particular year. We might want to see, for example, whether their attitudes about the value of the research, policy, or administration courses that they were required to take change over time. If appreciation of the value of those courses begins to increase dramatically several years after graduation, as the alumni move into supervisory and administrative positions, this information would be useful to both students and faculty as they discuss whether the curriculum should be revised to make it more relevant to the priorities of current students. Or suppose you wanted to learn how teenage mothers from different ethnic groups adapted to their child-rearing responsibilities. You might arrange to observe and interview a sample of such young mothers over time. You'd be in a position to see what they learned from other family members, the role played by their children's fathers, and so on. By getting to know a specific set of young mothers in depth, you'd be able to understand a wide range of changes occurring in their lives.

Because the distinctions between trend, cohort, and panel studies are sometimes difficult to grasp at first, let's contrast the three study designs in terms of the same variable: social work practitioner attitudes about cognitive-behavioral interventions. A trend study might look at shifts over time among direct-service practitioners in their propensity to use cognitive-behavioral interventions. For example, every five or ten years a new national sample of practitioners could be surveyed.

A cohort study might follow shifts in attitudes among practitioners who earned their social work degrees during a particular era, perhaps between 1990 and 1992. We could study a sample of them in 1993, a new sample of them in 1998 or 2003, and so forth.

A panel study could start with the same sample as the cohort study, but in subsequent surveys it would return to the same individuals, rather than draw a new sample of practitioners who graduated between 1990 and 1992. Notice that only the panel study would give a full picture of shifts in attitudes among specific individuals. Cohort and trend studies would only uncover *net* changes.

Longitudinal studies have an obvious advantage over cross-sectional ones in providing information describing processes over time. But often this advantage comes at a heavy cost in both time and money, especially in a large-scale survey. Observations may have to be made at the time events are occurring, and the method of observation may require many research workers.

Because only panel studies observe the same set of people each time, they offer the most comprehensive data on changes over time and are generally considered the most powerful and accurate of the three longitudinal approaches. However, a chief disadvantage of panel studies is that they are the most formidable of the three approaches to carry out, due to the costs and other difficulties involved in tracking the exact same people over time. A related disadvantage that only affects panel studies is *panel attrition*. Some of the respondents studied in the first wave of the survey may not participate in later waves. The reasons for this are numerous. Some respondents may move away and cannot be found. Some may die. Some may lose interest and simply refuse to participate anymore. This is comparable to the problem of *experimental mortality,* which will be discussed in Chapter 9. The danger is that those who drop out of the study may not be typical, thereby distorting the results of the study. Thus, when Carol S. Aneshensel and her colleagues conducted a panel study of adolescent girls (comparing Hispanics and non-Hispanics), they looked for and found differences in characteristics of survey dropouts among Hispanics born in America and those born in Mexico. Those differences needed to be taken into account to avoid misleading conclusions about differences between Hispanics and non-Hispanics (Aneshensel et al., 1989).

Another potential disadvantage of panel studies is that the process of observing people at an earlier point may influence what they say or do at a later point. For instance, a teenage gang member who earlier expressed intense enthusiasm for gang membership but who now is having second thoughts about it may not admit to having second thoughts so as not to appear inconsistent and unsure of himself, and thus lose face.

You've now seen several purposes that guide social work research, and how they relate to the time dimension. For further clarification of the time dimension, we suggest you examine the box titled "The Time Dimensions and Aging." Let's turn now to a consideration of whom or what you want to study.

UNITS OF ANALYSIS

In social work research, as well as all social scientific research, there is a wide range of variation in what or who is studied. By this, we do not mean the *topics* of research but what are technically called the **units of analysis.** Social scientists most typically have individual people as their units of analysis. You may make observations describing the characteristics of a large number of individual people, such as their genders, ages, regions of birth, attitudes, and so forth. You then aggregate

the descriptions of the many individuals to provide a descriptive picture of the population made up of those individuals.

For example, you may note the age and gender of each individual client in your agency and then characterize the caseload as a whole as being 53% women and 47% men and as having a mean age of 34 years. This is a descriptive analysis of your agency's caseload. Although the final description would be of the agency as a whole, the individual characteristics are aggregated for purposes of describing some larger group. Units of analysis, then, are units that we initially describe for the ultimate purpose of aggregating their characteristics in order to describe some larger group or explain some abstract phenomenon. This concept will become clear when we consider some possible social science units of analysis.

Individuals

As mentioned above, individual human beings are perhaps the most typical units of analysis for social scientific research. We tend to describe and explain social groups and interactions by aggregating and manipulating the descriptions of individuals.

A great variety of individuals may be the unit of analysis for social scientific research. This point is more important than it may seem at first reading. The norm of *generalized understanding* in social science should suggest that scientific findings are most valuable when they apply to *all* kinds of people. In practice, however, social scientists seldom study all kinds of people. At the very least, their studies are typically limited to the people living in a single country, although some comparative studies stretch across national boundaries. Often, our studies are even more circumscribed. When our studies include only certain kinds of people, we must be cautious to generalize our findings only to the same kinds of people. When all the individuals in our study are white males, for example, we should not generalize to non-white males or to females. Suppose we study the factors that influence the behavioral adjustment of children who witness marital violence and that

THE TIME DIMENSION AND AGING

by Joseph J. Leon, Behavioral Science Department, California State Polytechnic University, Pomona

One way to identify the type of time dimension used in a study is to imagine a number of different research projects on growing older in American society. If we studied a sample of individuals in 1990 and compared the different age groups, the design would be termed *cross-sectional*. If we drew another sample of individuals using the same study instrument in the year 2000 and compared the new data with the 1990 data, the design would be termed *trend*.

Suppose we wished to study only those individuals who were 51 to 60 in the year 2000 and compare them with the 1990 sample of 41- to 50-year-old persons (the 41 to 50 age cohort); this study design would be termed *cohort*. The comparison could be made for the 51 to 60 and 61 to 70 age cohorts as well. Now, if we desired to do a panel study on growing older in America, we would draw a sample in the year 1990 and, using the same sampled individuals in the year 2000, do the study again. Remember, there would be fewer people in the year 2000 study because all the 41- to 50-year-old people in 1990 are 51 to 60 and there would be no 41- to 50-year-old individuals in the year 2000 study. Furthermore, some of the individuals sampled in 1990 would no longer be alive in the year 2000.

```
        CROSS-SECTIONAL STUDY              COHORT STUDY
                 1990                  1990          2000
              ↕ 41–50                41–50  ←      41–50
              ↕ 51–60                51–60  ←   →  51–60
              ↕ 61–70                61–70  ←   →  61–70
              ↕ 71–80                71–80      →  71–80


               TREND STUDY                  PANEL STUDY
         1990          2000           1990          2000
        41–50  ←───→  41–50          41–50*  ↘     41–50
        51–60  ←───→  51–60          51–60*   ↘   51–60*
        61–70  ←───→  61–70          61–70*    ↘  61–70*
        71–80  ←───→  71–80          71–80*     ↘ 71–80*
                                                   →  +81*
```

←───→ Denotes comparison
*Denotes same individuals

our findings support the hypothesis that the quality of the parent-child relationship is the most important factor influencing whether or not the child develops a behavioral disorder. If we were unable to get fathers to participate in our study, and thus derived findings solely on the basis of mother-child relationships, we should generalize only to mother-child relationships, and not to parent-child relationships, even if our original intent was to generalize to the latter. We mentioned this issue in Chapter 3, in connection to gender and cultural biases, and we will address it again in Chapter 8, on sampling. We believe that the importance of this principle, and the fact that researchers too frequently violate it, warrants this repeated attention.

Examples of circumscribed groups whose members may be units of analysis—at the individual level—would be clients, practitioners, students, residents, workers, voters, parents, and faculty members. Note that each of these terms implies some population of individual people. The term *population* will be considered in some detail in Chapter 8. At this point, it is enough to realize that studies having individuals as their units of analysis typically refer to the population made up of those individuals.

As the units of analysis, individuals may be characterized in terms of their membership in social groupings. Thus, an individual may be described as belonging to a rich family or to a poor one, or a person may be described as having parents who did or did not graduate from high school. We might examine in a research project whether people whose parents never completed high school are more likely to become school dropouts than those whose parents did complete high school, or whether dropouts from rich families are more likely to have emotional disorders than dropouts from poor families. In each case, the individual would be the unit of analysis—not the parents or the family.

Groups

Social groups themselves may also be the units of analysis for social scientific research. This case is not the same as studying the individuals within a group. If you were to study the members of a street gang in order to learn about gang members, the individual (gang member) would be the unit of analysis. But if you studied all the gangs

in a city in order to learn the differences, say, between big gangs and small ones, between "uptown" and "downtown" gangs, and so forth, the unit of analysis would be the *gang*, a social group.

Families could be the units of analysis in a study. You might describe each family in terms of its total annual income and according to whether or not it had a mentally ill member. You could aggregate families and describe the mean income of families and the percentage with mentally ill members. You would then be in a position to determine whether families with higher incomes were more likely to have mentally ill members than those with lower incomes. The individual *family* in such a case would be the unit of analysis.

Other units of analysis at the group level could be friendship cliques, married couples, parent-child dyads, census blocks, cities, or geographic regions. Each of these terms also implies some population. *Street gangs* implies some population that includes all street gangs. The population of street gangs could be described, say, in terms of its geographical distribution throughout a city, and an explanatory study of street gangs might discover whether large gangs were more likely than small ones to engage in intergang warfare.

Formal social organizations may also be the units of analysis in social scientific research. An example would be social service agencies, which of course implies a population of all social service agencies. Individual agencies might be characterized in terms of their number of employees, annual budgets, number of clients, percentage of practitioners or clients who are from ethnic minority groups, and so forth. We might determine whether privately funded agencies hire a larger or smaller percentage of minority group employees than publicly funded agencies do. Other examples of formal social organizations suitable as units of analysis are churches, colleges, army divisions, academic departments, and supermarkets.

When social groups are the units of analysis, their characteristics may be derived from the characteristics of their individual members. Thus, a family might be described in terms of the age, race, or education of its head. In a descriptive study, then, we might find the percentage of all families that have a college-educated head of family. In an explanatory study, we might determine whether families with a college-educated head have, on the average, more or fewer children than families with heads who have not graduated from college. In each of these examples, however, the family would be the unit of analysis. (Had we asked whether college graduates—college-educated *individuals*—have more or fewer children than their less-educated counterparts, the individual *person* would have been the unit of analysis.)

Social groups (and also individuals) may be characterized in other ways—for instance, according to their environments or their membership in larger groupings. Families, for example, might be described in terms of the type of dwelling unit they reside in, and we might want to determine whether rich families are more likely to reside in single-family houses (as opposed, say, to apartments) than poor families are. The unit of analysis would still be the family.

If all this seems unduly complicated, be assured that in most research projects you are likely to undertake, the unit of analysis will be relatively clear to you. When the unit of analysis is not so clear, however, it is absolutely essential to determine what it is; otherwise, you will be unable to determine what observations are to be made about whom or what.

Some studies have the purpose of making descriptions or explanations pertaining to more than one unit of analysis. In these cases, it is imperative that the researcher anticipate what conclusions he or she wishes to draw with regard to what units of analysis.

Social Artifacts

Another large group of possible units of analysis may be referred to generally as *social artifacts,* or the products of social beings or their behavior. One class of artifacts would include social objects such as books, poems, paintings, automobiles, buildings, songs, pottery, jokes, and scientific discoveries.

Each of these objects implies a population of all such objects: all books, all novels, all biographies, all introductory social work textbooks, all cookbooks. An individual book might be characterized by its size, weight, length, price, content, number of pictures, volume of sale, or description of its author. The population of all books or of a particular kind of book could be analyzed for the purpose of description or explanation.

A social scientist could analyze whether paintings by Russian, Chinese, or American artists showed the greatest degree of working-class consciousness, taking paintings as the units of analysis and describing each, in part, by the nationality of its creator. You might examine a local newspaper's editorials regarding a local university for purposes of describing, or perhaps explaining, changes over time in the newspaper's editorial position on the university; individual editorials would be the units of analysis. Social interactions form another class of social artifacts suitable for social scientific research. Weddings would be an example. Weddings might be characterized as racially or religiously mixed or not, religious or secular in ceremony, resulting in divorce or not, or they could be characterized by descriptions of one or both of the marriage partners. Realize that when a researcher reports that weddings between partners of different religions are more likely to be performed by secular authorities than those between partners of the same religion, the weddings are the units of analysis and not the individual partners to them.

Other examples of social interactions that might be the units of analysis in social scientific research are friendship choices, court cases, traffic accidents, divorces, fistfights, ship launchings, airline hijackings, race riots, and congressional hearings.

Units of Analysis in Review

The purpose of this section has been to stretch your imagination somewhat regarding possible units of analysis for social scientific research. Although individual human beings are typically the units of analysis, that need not be the case. Indeed, many research questions can more appropriately be answered through the examination of other units of analysis.

The concept of the unit of analysis may seem more complicated than it needs to be. It is irrelevant whether you classify a given unit of analysis as a group, a formal organization, or a social artifact. It is essential, however, that you be able to identify what your unit of analysis is. You must decide whether you are studying marriages or marriage partners, crimes or criminals, agencies or agency executives. Unless you keep this point in mind constantly, you run the risk of making assertions about one unit of analysis based on the examination of another.

To test your grasp of the concept of units of analysis, here are some statements from actual research projects. See if you can determine the unit of analysis in each. (The answers are at the very end of this chapter.)

1. Women watch TV more than men because they are likely to work fewer hours outside the home than men. . . . Black people watch an average of approximately three-quarters of an hour more television per day than white people (Hughes, 1980:290).

2. Of the 130 incorporated U.S. cities with more than 100,000 inhabitants in 1960, 126 had at least two short-term nonproprietary general hospitals accredited by the American Hospital Association (Turk, 1980:317).

3. The early TM organizations were small and informal. The Los Angeles group, begun in June 1959, met at a member's house where, incidentally, Maharishi was living (Johnston, 1980:337).

4. However, it appears that the nursing staffs exercise strong influence over . . . a decision to change the nursing care system. . . . Conversely, among those decisions dominated by the administration and the medical staffs . . . (Comstock, 1980:77).

5. In 1958, there were 13 establishments with 1,000 employees or more, accounting for 60 per-cent of the industry's value added. In 1977, the number of this type of establishment dropped to 11, but their share of industry value added had fallen to about 46 percent (York and Persigehl, 1981:41).

6. Though 667,000 out of 2 million farmers in the United States are women, women historically have not been viewed as farmers, but rather, as the farmer's wife (Votaw, 1979:8).

7. The analysis of community opposition to group homes for the mentally handicapped . . . indicates that deteriorating neighborhoods are most likely to organize in opposition, but that upper-middle-class neighborhoods are most likely to enjoy private access to local officials. . . (Graham and Hogan, 1990:513).

8. "This study explores the key dimensions of social work practice position vacancy descriptions and seeks to reflect the changing self-image of modern social work. . . . Which of the major conceptualized dimensions of practice are being emphasized most in position vacancy descriptions published in the profession? Are these position vacancy descriptions and the most emphasized dimensions changing over time? If so, in which directions and to what degree are the position vacancy descriptions and dimensions changing?" (Billups and Julia, 1987:17).

Figure 4-2 gives you a graphic illustration of some different units of analysis and the statements that might be made about them.

The Ecological Fallacy

At this point it is appropriate to introduce briefly two important concepts related to units of analysis: the *ecological fallacy* and *reductionism*. The first of these concepts, the ecological fallacy, means the danger, just mentioned, of making assertions about individuals as the unit of analysis based on the examination of groups or other aggregations. Let's consider a hypothetical illustration of this fallacy.

Suppose like Royse (1988) we are interested in learning something about the nature of electoral support for tax initiatives to fund new human service programs in countywide elections. Let's assume that we have the vote tally for each precinct so that we can tell which precincts gave the referendum the greatest support and which gave it the least. Assume also that we have census data describing some of the characteristics of those precincts.

Our analysis of such data might show that precincts whose voters were relatively old gave the referendum a greater proportion of their votes than precincts whose voters had a younger average age. We might be tempted to conclude from these findings that older voters were more likely to vote for the referendum than younger voters—that age affected support for the referendum. In reaching such a conclusion, we run the risk of committing the *ecological fallacy* because it may have been the younger voters in those "old" precincts who voted for the referendum. Our problem is that we have examined *precincts* as our units of analysis and wish to draw conclusions about *voters*.

The same problem would arise if we discovered that crime rates were higher in cities having large black populations than in those with few blacks. We would not know if the crimes were actually committed by blacks. Or if we found suicide rates higher in Protestant countries than in Catholic ones, we still could not know for sure that more Protestants than Catholics committed suicide.

Notice that very often the social scientist must address a particular research question through an ecological analysis such as those just mentioned. Perhaps the most appropriate data are simply not available. For example, the precinct vote tallies and the precinct characteristics mentioned in our initial example might be easy to obtain, but we may not have the resources to conduct a postelection survey of individual voters. In such cases, we may reach a tentative conclusion, recognizing and noting the risk of committing the ecological fallacy.

Don't let these warnings against the ecological fallacy lead you into committing what we might call an *individualistic fallacy*. Some students approaching social research for the first time have trouble reconciling general patterns of attitudes and actions with individual exceptions they know of. If you know a rich Democrat, for example, that doesn't deny the fact that most rich people vote Republican—as individuals. The ecological fallacy deals with something else altogether—drawing conclusions about individuals based solely on the observation of groups.

Reductionism

A second concept related to units of analysis is *reductionism*. Basically, reductionism refers to an overly strict limitation on the kinds of concepts and variables to be considered as causes in explaining a broad range of human behavior. Sociologists may tend to consider only sociological variables (values, norms, roles); economists may consider only economic variables (supply and demand, marginal value); psychologists may consider only psychological variables (personality types, traumas). For example, what causes child abuse? The psychopathology of the perpetrator? Pathological dynamics in family interaction patterns? Socioeconomic stress? Cultural norms? Abnormalities in the child? Scientists from different disciplines tend to look at different types of answers and ignore the others. Explaining all or most human behavior in terms of economic factors is called *economic reductionism;* explaining all or most human behavior in terms of psychological factors is called *psychological reductionism;* and so forth. Note how this issue relates to the discussion of theoretical paradigms in Chapter 2.

Reductionism of any type tends to suggest that particular units of analysis or variables are more relevant than others. A psychologist or psychiatrist might choose psychopathology of the perpetrator as the cause of child abuse, and thus the unit of analysis would be the individual perpetrator. A family therapist, though, might choose

Units of Analysis

Individuals

Sample Statements

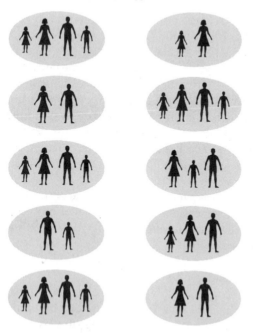

60% of the sample are women

10% of the sample are wearing an eye patch

10% of the sample have pigtails

Families

20% of the families have a single parent

40% of the families have two children

20% of the families have no children

The mean number of children per family is 1.2

Figure 4-2 Illustrations of Units of Analysis

Units of Analysis

Households

Sample Statements

20% of the households are occupied by more than one family

30% of the households have holes in their roofs

10% of the households are occupied by aliens

Notice also that 33%, or 4 of the 12 families, live in multiple-family households with family as the unit of analysis

Figure 4-2 Illustrations of Units of Analysis *(continued)*

families as units of analysis and examine the inter-actional dynamics of family systems. A sociologist might also choose families as the unit of analysis for purposes of examining the degree of socioen-vironmental stress they experience.

Once the foregoing aspects of problem formu-lation have been handled, you are ready to spec-ify and operationally define the variables in your study and, if the study is not purely descriptive, to postulate relationships among those variables (that is, to develop hypotheses). This phase in the research process sets the stage for preparing a measurement strategy and for designing other as-pects of the study. Although it is generally con-sidered part of the problem formulation phase, it is a bridge to subsequent phases. The amount and importance of the material involved in this phase merit examination in a separate chapter, which we will take up next.

Main Points

• Social work research follows essentially the same problem-solving process as does social work practice. Each follows similar phases, and each re-quires that moving on to the next phase is contin-gent upon successfully completing earlier phases. At any point in the process unanticipated obsta-cles may necessitate looping back to earlier phases.

• A good research topic should pass the "so what?" test. Also, it should be specific, capable of being answered by observable evidence, feasible to study, and open to doubt and thus answerable in more than one possible way.

• Conducting the literature review is an impor-tant step in the problem formulation process. Usu-ally, a thorough grounding in the literature should precede, and provide a foundation for, the selec-tion of an important topic.

• Anticipating issues in the feasibility of a study is also an important part of problem formulation. Time constraints, fiscal costs, lack of cooperation,

and ethical dilemmas are essential things to con-sider in planning a study.

• Exploration is the attempt to develop an ini-tial, rough understanding of some phenomenon.

• Description is the precise measurement and re-porting of the characteristics of some population or phenomenon under study.

• Explanation is the discovery and reporting of relationships among different aspects of the phe-nomenon under study. Whereas descriptive stud-ies answer the question "What's so?" explanatory ones tend to answer the question "Why?"

• Cross-sectional studies are those based on ob-servations made at one time.

• Longitudinal studies are those in which obser-vations are made at many times. Such observations may be made of samples drawn from general pop-ulations (trend studies), samples drawn from more specific subpopulations (cohort studies), or the same sample of people each time (panel studies).

• Units of analysis are the people or things whose characteristics social researchers observe, describe, and explain. Typically, the unit of analysis in so-cial research is the individual person, but it may also be a group or a social artifact.

Review Questions and Exercises

1. Consider a problem in social welfare in which you have a special interest (such as child abuse, mental illness, the frail elderly, and so on). For-mulate three different research questions about that problem, each of which would be important for the field to answer and in which, in your opin-ion, a funding agency might be interested. For-mulate each question to deal with a different re-search purpose—one for exploration, one for description, and one for explanation.

2. Look through a social work research journal and find examples of at least three different units of analysis. Identify each unit of analysis and present a quotation from the journal in which that unit of analysis is reported on.

Additional Readings

Hammond, Phillip (ed.), *Sociologist at Work* (New York: Basic Books, 1964). A collection of candid research biographies written by several eminent social science researchers, discussing the studies that made them eminent. A variety of research motivations and designs are illustrated in these honest reports of how the research actually came about and unfolded. Take two chapters every four hours to relieve the discomfort of believing that social science research is routine and dull.

Miller, Delbert, *Handbook of Research Design and Social Measurement* (New York: Longman, 1983). A useful reference book for introducing or reviewing numerous issues involved in design and measurement. In addition, the book contains a wealth of practical information relating to foundations, journals, and professional associations.

Stouffer, Samuel, *Social Research to Test Ideas* (New York: Free Press of Glencoe, 1962). A stimulating and downright inspirational posthumous collection of research articles by one of the giants of social research. In these reports, you will see how an ingenious man formulates an idea, designs the perfect study for testing it, is prevented from conducting the study, and then devises another feasible method for testing the same idea. Especially enlightening are Paul Lazarsfeld's introduction and Chapter 6, in which Stouffer reports on the effects of the Great Depression on the family.

Answers to Units of Analysis Exercise (page 118)

1. individuals
2. cities
3. groups: organizations
4. groups
5. companies
6. individuals
7. neighborhoods
8. artifacts: position vacancy descriptions

Conceptualization and Operationalization

What You'll Learn in This Chapter

In this chapter, you'll discover that many social work terms communicate vague, unspecified meanings. In research we must specify exactly what we mean (and don't mean) by the terms we use to describe the elements of our study.

INTRODUCTION

The preceding chapter described various aspects of the problem formulation phase. If you are doing quantitative research, explicating the conceptual elements of the research comes at the end of the problem formulation phase. Chapter 5 deals with that end stage of problem formulation—the process of moving from vague ideas about what you want to study to being able to recognize and make measurements on what you want to study. This is the conceptualization and operationalization process. It involves refining and specifying abstract concepts (conceptualization) and developing specific research procedures (operationalization) that will result in empirical observations of things that represent those concepts in the real world. This process gets closer to concrete measurements, for operationalization sets the stage for actual data collection. Thus, the present chapter provides the concluding steps of problem formulation and a preview of what is to come in the next chapter on measurement.

As you read this chapter, we'd like you to keep in mind that it applies primarily to quantitative research. Most of it is not applicable to qualitative research. In purely qualitative studies, we do not predetermine specific, precise, objective variables and indicators to be measured. Instead, we emphasize methodological freedom and flexibility so that the most salient variables, and their deeper meanings, will emerge as we immerse ourselves in the phenomena we are studying. In fact, the term *operationalization* is virtually absent from most texts that deal exclusively with qualitative research methods. To help you remember that this chapter applies more to quantitative methods than to qualitative methods, we'll remind you of it at several points throughout the chapter.

CONCEPTUAL EXPLICATION

Once the foregoing aspects of problem formulation (discussed in Chapter 4) have been handled, you are ready to specify and operationally define the variables in your study and, if the study is not purely descriptive, to postulate relationships among those variables (that is, to develop hypotheses). **Variables** are the specific concepts or theoretical constructs we are investigating. Some concepts are relatively easy to observe, such as gender, location of residence, ethnicity, and age. Abstract theoretical constructs are much more difficult to observe and can be assessed only through certain indicators. Examples of such variables would be level of self-esteem, morale of residents in long-term care, level of social functioning, staff burnout, racism, sexism, ageism, homophobia, and so on. We will take up the problem of translating abstract variables into observable terms later in this chapter.

A variable postulated to explain another variable is called the **independent variable.** The variable being explained is called the **dependent variable.** The statement that postulates the relationship between the independent and dependent variables is called the **hypothesis.** Hypotheses, in other words, are tentative statements that predict what we expect to find about the way our variables covary together. A good hypothesis has some of the attributes of a good research question. It should be clear and specific. It should have more than one possible outcome—that is, it should not be a truism. It should also be value-free. And it should be testable.

A third category of variables is termed **extraneous variables.** These variables represent alternative explanations for relationships observed between independent and dependent variables. Suppose, for example, that a study finds that the more social services received by hospital patients, the shorter their life span. That relationship would probably be explained away by the fact that the cases involving the most serious illnesses—particularly terminal illnesses—need to receive more social services. Thus, seriousness of illness might be conceptualized as an extraneous variable that might explain away the relationship between life span and amount of social services received.

Sometimes our studies check on the possibility that the relationship between our independent and dependent variables, or the apparent lack thereof, is misleading—that it is explained away by other variables. When we do that, the variables that we seek to *control* in our design are no longer called extraneous variables, but are now called **control variables.**

If we wanted to check on the possibility that the relationship between life span and amount of social services received is explained away by the fact that the cases involving the most serious illnesses need to receive more social services, we would do the following. First, we would separate all cases into subgroups according to seriousness of illness. For the sake of simplicity, let's assume that we would subdivide them into only two groups: (1) those with life-threatening illnesses, and (2) those whose illnesses are not life threatening. Next, we would assess the relationship between life span and amount of social services received just for those cases with life-threatening illnesses. Then we would do the same just for those cases whose illnesses are not life threatening. Thus, we would be controlling for seriousness of illness by examining whether the original relationship between our independent and dependent variables changes or stays the same for each level of serious illness.

Here is another example. The proportion of reported AIDS cases in the United States is higher among certain ethnic groups than among others. A study reporting that finding might have conceptualized ethnicity as the independent variable and AIDS rate as the dependent variable. But would its finding mean that certain ethnic groups were biologically more susceptible to AIDS or that some other explanation was operating? We might note that the ethnic groups with the higher rates of AIDS are those that also have higher rates of poverty, school dropout, substance abuse, and related social problems. We might therefore suppose that the higher AIDS rates among certain groups are explained, not by biological variables, but by socioeconomic variables that result in greater intravenous drug abuse and less awareness of AIDS prevention among those ethnic groups. To test this out we might examine what happens

to the AIDS rate in each ethnic group when we *control* for the effects of socioeconomic status. In doing this, we would compare the rates of each ethnic group only for particular levels of socioeconomic status. For example, we would compare the poor people in each ethnic group, the middle-class people in each ethnic group, and so on, rather than comparing the groups as a whole. We would thus be using socioeconomic status as a *control variable,* since we would be factoring out its effects in looking at the relationship between ethnicity and AIDS rate. In other words, controlling for a variable means taking each level of that control variable separately and looking at how the original relationship between the independent and dependent variables changes or remains the same within each level of the control variable.

Suppose we wish to conduct an explanatory study to test the hypothesis that case management intervention increases the level of social adjustment of discharged psychiatric patients in the community. Our independent variable would be whether the patient received case management intervention. Our dependent variable would be level of social adjustment.

Also suppose that we suspect that patients referred to case managers are those whose disabilities are the most chronic and whose social adjustment therefore may be most difficult to improve. If that were the case, the effects of the case management services might be masked by the lower capacities for improvement in the case management clients. We would then seek to control for the extraneous variable of degree of chronicity, which we might operationally define as the number of times the individual was admitted as an inpatient to a psychiatric hospital or the total amount of time the individual spent as an inpatient during all psychiatric hospitalizations. We would test the hypothesis by comparing the social adjustment outcome of patients with the same particular degree of chronicity who did and did not receive case management services. We would do this for each degree of chronicity (high, medium, low, and so on) that was included in the operational definition of chronicity.

Suppose we wish to conduct a different explanatory study, this time testing the hypothesis that the amount of citizen participation of neighborhood residents in the early planning of community-based residential facilities for discharged psychiatric patients is associated with the amount of community opposition those facilities ultimately encounter. Our independent variable would be amount of citizen participation in early planning. Our dependent variable would be amount of community opposition encountered.

Suppose we thought that the results of our study might vary according to type of community. Perhaps we expect that more citizen participation leads to less opposition in nonresidential sections of town, but that it backfires in more affluent, residential neighborhoods, leading to more opposition. Then we would control for the variable: type of community. We would look separately at the relationship between amount of citizen participation and amount of opposition in each type of community.

Notice that the way we originally stated our hypothesis did not identify the cause and the effect. Conceivably, the amount of citizen participation that takes place might be less a cause of the amount of opposition than a result of it. For example, some planners might not be inclined to promote citizen participation unless they are compelled to deal with stiff preliminary opposition to their plans. Thus, when they encounter little opposition, they may feel that promoting significant citizen participation is unnecessary or perhaps too risky in the sense that it might stir up resistance among those currently uninvolved and perhaps unaware of the plans. On the other hand, when they encounter stiff opposition to their plans, they might have no choice but to promote citizen participation activities that they had hoped to avoid and that are aimed at overcoming an initially high level of opposition.

In the same sense, there is nothing inherent in a particular concept that makes it an independent, dependent, or control variable in every study that observes it. For example, if one study postulates that amount of citizen participation is the cause of the amount of opposition, then amount of citizen participation is the independent variable and amount of opposition is the dependent variable. But another study could reverse the hypothesis, making amount of citizen participation the dependent variable and amount of community opposition the independent variable. You should also realize that whether a variable is an independent or dependent one does not depend on the sequence in which it is specified in the hypothesis. For example, if we postulate that amount of community opposition will be lowered if we involve citizens in planning, then amount of community opposition is the dependent variable even though it is specified first in the hypothesis. This can be confusing because even though the cause must happen before the effect, putting the effect first in the hypothesis does not mean you are saying that it will happen first.

Types of Relationships Between Variables

Some hypotheses predict positive or negative (inverse) and curvilinear relationships between variables. In a *positive* relationship the dependent variable increases as the independent variable increases (or decreases as the independent variable decreases). That is, both variables move in the same direction. Thus, we might postulate a positive relationship between the amount of symbolic rewards citizens receive for participating in community organizations and the extent to which they participate. We might also postulate a positive relationship between client satisfaction with social services and the extent to which the delivered service focused on the problem or goal for which the client originally sought help (as opposed to a problem or goal that the practitioner chose to work on without involving the client in the decision). The top graph in Figure 5-1 pictorially represents this hypothesized positive relationship.

A *negative*, or *inverse*, relationship means that the two variables move in opposite directions—that is, as one increases, the other decreases. We might postulate a negative relationship between the caseload size of direct-service practitioners

1. POSITIVE RELATIONSHIP

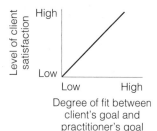

The better the fit between the client's reason for seeking help and the service goal formulated by practitioner, the more the client satisfaction.

2. NEGATIVE RELATIONSHIP

The lower the family income, the higher the level of family stress.

3. CURVILINEAR RELATIONSHIP

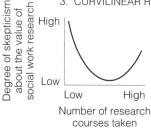

Skepticism decreases as students take more research courses up to a point, but after that skepticism increases as more research courses are taken.

Figure 5-1 Graphic Display of Types of Hypothetical Relationships Between Variables

and their degree of effectiveness because those whose caseloads are too large might be expected to have less time to provide quality services. A negative relationship might also be postulated between family income and level of family stress. The middle graph in Figure 5-1 pictorially represents this hypothesized negative relationship.

A *curvilinear* relationship is one in which the nature of the relationship changes at certain levels of the variables. For example, some social work

educators believe that the students most skeptical about the value of published social work research are those who have either taken many research courses or none at all. Those who have never had a research course may not yet have learned to appreciate research's potential utility. Those with a great deal of knowledge about research might be disillusioned by the many serious methodological flaws they detect in much of the published research. Consequently, those with the least skepticism may be the ones in the middle—those who have enough knowledge to appreciate the value of good research but have not yet critically scrutinized enough of the literature to realize how many published studies are seriously flawed. Educators who believe this notion might hypothesize a U-curve that begins with a negative relationship between the number of courses taken and degree of skepticism about research and ends with a positive relationship between them. That is, the degree of skepticism decreases as more courses are taken up to a certain number of courses, but then after that number it increases as more courses are taken. The bottom graph in Figure 5-1 pictorially represents this hypothesized curvilinear relationship.

OPERATIONAL DEFINITIONS

In quantitative research, before we can implement a study to collect data on our variables, we must first translate those variables into observable terms. The term **operational definition** refers to that translation. That is, it refers to the operations, or indicators, we will use to determine the quantity or qualitative category we observe regarding a particular variable. There are many ways to operationally define abstract variables.

Let's consider an example regarding the concept of social adjustment. Conceptually or theoretically, we might define social adjustment as appropriate performance of one's major roles in life, roles such as parent, student, employee, spouse, and so on. This definition may give us clues about how we might develop an operational definition, but it does not specify precisely what indicators we will observe and the exact categories of social adjustment we will note. One operational definition might be a score on a scale constructed to measure one's level of social adjustment. Another operational definition might be whether an individual is receiving social services aimed at restoring social functioning. That is, those receiving such services would be categorized as having lower levels of social adjustment than others not receiving such services. In an institutional facility for the severely developmentally disabled, our operational definition might identify individuals with higher levels of social adjustment as those whose case records indicate that they were deemed ready to be placed in a sheltered workshop. Operational definitions point the way to how a variable will be measured.

Many students in social work and allied fields have concerns about whether it's possible to measure the stuff of life: love, hate, prejudice, radicalism, alienation, and the like. The answer is yes, it's possible, but it will take a few pages to make that point. Once you see that we can measure anything that exists, we'll turn to the steps involved in doing that.

MEASURING ANYTHING THAT EXISTS

It seems altogether possible that you may have some reservations about the ability of science to measure the really important aspects of human social existence. You may have read research reports dealing with something like liberalism or religion or prejudice, and you may have been dissatisfied with the way the researchers measured whatever they were studying. You may have felt they were too superficial, that they missed the aspects that really matter most. Maybe they measured *religiosity* as the number of times a person went to church, or maybe they measured *liberalism* by how people voted in a single election. Your dissatisfaction would surely have been increased if you found yourself being misclassified

by the measurement system. People often have that experience.

Or you may have looked up the definition of a word like *compassionate* in the dictionary and found the definition wanting. You may have heard yourself muttering, "There's more to it than that." In fact, whenever you look up the definition of something you already understand well, you can probably see ways people might misunderstand the term if they had only that definition to go on.

Earlier in this book, we said that one of the two pillars of science is *observation*. Because this word can suggest a rather casual, passive activity, scientists often use *measurement* instead, meaning careful, deliberate observations of the real world for the purpose of describing objects and events in terms of the attributes composing a variable. If the variable under study were *political party affiliation,* we might consult the list of registered voters to note whether the people we were studying were registered as Democrats or Republicans. In this fashion, we would have measured their political party affiliation.

Although measurement would seem to present a special problem for social science, this section of the chapter makes the point that *we can measure anything that exists.* There are no exceptions. If it exists, we can measure it.

How Do You Know?

To demonstrate to you that social scientists can measure anything that exists, we'd like you to imagine that we are discussing the matter. We'll write the script, but feel free to make substitutions for your side of the dialogue as you see fit. Only one of us will speak for us, so our side of the dialogue follows the word *me.* Here goes:

Me: Social scientists can measure anything that exists.

You: Hah! Betcha can't.

Me: Tell me something that exists, and I'll tell you how to measure it.

You: Okay, let's see you measure prejudice.

Me: Good choice. Now, I'm not willing to waste our time trying to measure something that doesn't exist. So, tell me if it exists.

You: Yes, of course it exists. Everybody knows that.

Me: How do you know prejudice exists?

You: Everybody knows that.

Me: Everybody used to think the world was flat, too. I want to know how you know prejudice really exists.

You: I've seen it in action.

Me: What have you seen that proves prejudice exists?

You: Well, a businessman told me that he'd never hire a woman for an executive position because he thought all women were flighty and irrational. How's that?

Me: Great! That sounds like prejudice to me, so I guess we can assume prejudice exists. I am now prepared to measure prejudice. Ready?

You: Ready.

Me: You and I will circulate quietly through the business community, talking to businessmen about hiring. Whenever a businessman tells us that he would never hire a woman for an executive position because he thinks all women are flighty and irrational, we'll count that as a case of prejudice. Whenever we are not told that, we'll count the conversation as a case of nonprejudice. When we finish, we'll be able to classify all the businessmen we've talked to as either prejudiced or nonprejudiced.

You: Wait a minute! That's not a very good measure of prejudice. We're going to miss a lot of prejudice that way. All we'll measure is blatant prejudice against women in hiring.

Me: I see what you mean. But your comment also means that the situation you described before proves only that blatant prejudice against women in hiring exists. We'd better reconsider whether *prejudice* exists. Does it?

You: Of course it does. I was just giving you one example. There are hundreds of other examples of prejudice.

Me: Give me one that proves prejudice exists.

You: Okay, try this for size. I was in a bar the other night, and two guys—one white and one black—were arguing about politics. Finally, the white guy got so angry, he started using ugly racist language and yelled, "All you blacks are stupid! All of you ought to be sent back to Africa!" Is that prejudiced enough for you?

Me: Suits me. That would seem to prove that prejudice exists, so I'm ready again to measure prejudice. This will be more fun. You and I will split up and start touring bars every night. We'll keep our ears open and listen for a white person using ugly racial epithets and saying, "All you blacks are stupid. All of you ought—"

You: Hold it! I see where this is headed, and that's not going to do it either. A person who said that would be prejudiced, but we're going to classify a lot of prejudiced people as nonprejudiced just because they don't happen to get carried away and speak rashly.

Me: All of which brings me back to my original question. Does prejudice really exist, or have you been just stringing me along?

You: Yes, it exists!

Me: Well, I'm not sure any longer. You persuaded me that businessmen who discriminate against women in hiring exist, because you saw that, and I believe you. You persuaded me that there are people who call black people stupid and say they should all go back to Africa. But I'm not so sure *prejudice* exists. I'd sure like to track it down so I can show you that I can measure it. To be honest, though, I'm beginning to doubt that it really exists. I mean, have you ever seen a prejudice? What color are they? How much do they weigh? Where are they located?

You: What on earth are you talking about?

The point of this dialogue, as you may have guessed, is to demonstrate that *prejudice doesn't exist.* We don't know what a prejudice looks like, how big it is, or what color it is. None of us has ever touched a prejudice or ridden in one. But we do talk a lot about prejudice. Here's how that came about.

As all of us wandered down the road of life, we observed a lot of things and knew they were real through our observations. We heard about a lot of other things that other people said they observed, and those other things seemed to have existed. Someone reported seeing a lynching and described the whole thing in great detail.

With additional experience, we noticed something more. We noticed that people who participate in lynchings are also quite likely to call black people names. A lot of them, moreover, seemed to want women to "stay in their place." Eventually, we began to get the feeling that there was a certain kind of person running around the world that had those several tendencies. When we discussed the people we'd met, it was sometimes appropriate to identify someone in terms of those tendencies. We used to say a person was "one of those who participate in lynchings, call black people names, and wouldn't hire a woman for an executive position." After a while, however, it got pretty clumsy to say all of that, and you had a bright idea: "Let's use the word *prejudiced* as a shorthand notation for people like that. We can use the term even if they don't do all those things—as long as they're pretty much like that."

Being basically agreeable and interested in efficiency, we agreed to go along with the system. That's where *prejudice* came from. It never really existed. We never saw it. We just made it up as a shortcut for talking behind people's backs. Ultimately, *prejudice* is merely a term we have agreed to use in communication: a name we use to represent a whole collection of apparently related phenomena that we've each observed in the course of life. Each of us developed his or her own mental image of what the set of real phenomena we've observed represent in general and what they have in common.

When we say the word *prejudice,* we know it evokes a mental image in your mind, just as it evokes a mental image for us. It's as though we have file drawers in our minds containing thousands of sheets of paper, and each sheet of paper has a label in the upper right-hand corner. One sheet of paper in your file drawer has the term *prejudice* on it, and we have one too. On your sheet are all the things you were told about prejudice and everything you've observed that seemed to be an example of it. Our sheet has what we were told about *prejudice* plus all the things we've observed that seemed to be examples of it.

Conceptions and Concepts

The technical term for those mental images, those sheets of paper in our mental file drawers, is *conception.* Each sheet of paper is a conception. Now, those mental images cannot be communicated directly. There is no way we can directly reveal to you what's written on ours. So we use the *terms* written in the upper right-hand corner as a way of communicating about our conceptions and the things we observe that are related to those conceptions. Let's suppose that Jim is going to meet someone named Pat whom you already know. Jim asks you what Pat is like. Now suppose that you have seen Pat help lost children find their parents and put a tiny bird back in its nest. Pat got you to take turkeys to poor families on Thanksgiving and to visit a children's hospital on Christmas. You've seen Pat weep in a movie about a mother overcoming adversities to save and protect her child. As you search through your mental file drawer, you may find all or most of those phenomena recorded on a single sheet labeled *compassionate* in the upper right-hand corner. You look over the other entries on the page, and you find they seem to provide an accurate description of Pat. So, you say, "Pat is compassionate."

Now Jim leafs through his own mental file drawer until he finds a sheet marked *compassionate*. He then looks over the things written on his sheet, and says, "Oh, that's nice." Jim now feels he knows what Pat is like, but his expectations in that regard reflect the entries on *his* file sheet, not yours. Later, when he meets Pat, he may find that his own, personal experiences correspond to the entries he has on his *compassionate* file sheet, and he'll say you were sure right. Or his observations of Pat may contradict the things he has on his file sheet, and he'll tell you that he doesn't think Pat is very compassionate. If the latter happens, you may begin to compare his notes with yours.

You say, "I once saw Pat weep in a movie about a mother overcoming adversity to save and protect her child." Jim looks at his *compassionate* sheet and can't find anything like that. Looking elsewhere in his file, he locates that sort of phenomenon on a sheet labeled *sentimental*. He retorts, "That's not compassion. That's just sentimentality."

To further strengthen his case, Jim tells you that he saw Pat refuse to give money to an organization dedicated to saving the whales from extinction. "That represents a lack of compassion," he argues. You search through your files and find saving the whales on a sheet marked *environmental activism,* and you say so. Eventually, you compare the entries you have on your respective sheets labeled *compassionate*. You may discover that you have quite different mental images represented by that term.

In the big picture, language and communication only work to the extent that you and Jim have considerable overlap in the kinds of entries you have on your corresponding mental file sheets. The similarities you have on those sheets represent the agreements existing in the society you both occupy. When you were growing up, you were both told approximately the same thing when you were first introduced to a particular term. Dictionaries formalize the agreements our society has about such terms. Each of us, then,

shapes his or her mental images to correspond with those agreements, but because all of us have different experiences and observations, no two people end up with exactly the same set of entries on any sheet in their file systems.

Returning to the assertion made at the outset of this chapter, we *can* measure anything real. We can measure, for example, whether Pat actually puts the little bird back in its nest, visits the hospital on Christmas, weeps at the movie, or refuses to contribute to saving the whales. All of those things exist, so we can measure them. But is Pat really compassionate? We can't answer that question; we can't measure compassion in that sense, because compassion doesn't exist the way those things we just described exist.

Compassion as a *term* does exist. We can measure the number of letters it contains and agree that there are ten. We can agree that it has three syllables and that it begins with the letter C. In short, we can measure the aspects of it that are real.

Some aspects of our conceptions are real also. Whether you have a mental image associated with the term *compassion* is real. When an elementary school teacher asks a class how many know what *compassion* means, those who raise their hands can be counted. The presence of particular entries on the sheets bearing a given label is also real, and that can be measured. We could measure how many people do or do not associate giving money to save the whales with their conception of compassion. About the only thing we cannot measure is what compassion really means, because compassion isn't real. Compassion exists only in the form of the agreements we have about how to use the term in communicating about things that are real.

In this context, Abraham Kaplan (1964) distinguishes three classes of things that scientists measure. The first class is *direct observables:* those things we can observe rather simply and directly, like the color of an apple or the check mark made in a questionnaire. *Indirect observables* require "relatively more subtle, complex, or indirect observations" (1964:55). We note a person's check mark beside *female* in a questionnaire and have indirectly observed that person's sex. History books or minutes of corporate board meetings provide indirect observations of past social actions. Finally, *constructs* are theoretical creations based on observations but which cannot be observed directly or indirectly.

Compassion, then, is an abstraction—a construct that consists of a "family of conceptions" (Kaplan, 1964:49) that include your concepts that comprise compassion, our concepts that comprise it, and the conceptions of all those who have ever used the term. It cannot be observed directly or indirectly, because it doesn't exist. We made it up. All we can measure are the direct observables and indirect observables that we think the term *compassion* implies. IQ is another example. It is constructed mathematically from observations of the answers given to a large number of questions on an IQ test. The other composite measures we'll discuss in Chapter 7 are other examples of constructs.

Conceptualization

Day-to-day communication usually occurs through a system of vague and general agreements about the use of terms. Usually, people do not understand exactly what we wish to communicate, but they get the general drift of our meaning. Although you may not agree completely with us about the use of the term *compassionate,* we're probably safe in assuming that Pat won't pull the wings off flies. A wide range of misunderstandings and conflict—from the interpersonal to the international—is the price we pay for our imprecision, but somehow we muddle through. Science, however, aims at more than muddling, and it cannot operate in a context of such imprecision.

Conceptualization is the process through which we specify precisely what we will mean when we use particular terms. Suppose we want to find out, for example, whether women are more compassionate than men. We can't meaningfully study the question, let alone agree on the answer, without some precise working agreements about the meaning of the term. They are working agreements in the sense that they allow us to work on

the question. We don't need to agree or even pretend to agree that a particular specification might be worth using.

Indicators and Dimensions

The end product of this conceptualization process is the specification of a set of *indicators* of what we have in mind, indicating the presence or absence of the concept we are studying. Thus, we may agree to use visiting children's hospitals at Christmas as an indicator of compassion. Putting little birds back in their nests may be agreed on as another indicator, and so forth. If the unit of analysis for our study were the individual person, we could then observe the presence or absence of each indicator for each person under study. Going beyond that, we could add up the number of indicators of compassion observed for each individual. We might agree on ten specific indicators, for example, and find six present in our study of Pat, three for John, nine for Mary, and so forth.

Returning to our original question, we might calculate that the women we studied had an average of 6.5 indicators of compassion, and the men studied had an average of 3.2. We might therefore conclude on the basis of that group difference that women are, on the whole, more compassionate than men. Usually, it's not that simple.

Often, when we take our concepts seriously and set about specifying what we mean by them, we discover disagreements and inconsistencies. Not only do we disagree, but each of us is likely to find a good deal of muddiness within our own individual mental images. If you take a moment to look at what *you* mean by compassion, you'll probably find that your image contains several *kinds* of compassion. The entries on your file sheet can be combined into groups and subgroups, and you'll even find several different strategies for making the combinations. For example, you might group the entries into feelings and actions.

The technical term for such groupings is *dimension:* a specifiable aspect or facet of a concept. Thus, we might speak of the "feeling dimension" of compassion and the "action dimension" of compassion. In a different grouping scheme, we might distinguish "compassion for humans" from "compassion for animals." Or compassion might center on helping people be and have what *we* want for them or what *they* want for themselves. Still differently, we might distinguish "compassion as forgiveness" from "compassion as pity."

Thus, it would be possible for us to subdivide the concept of compassion according to several sets of dimensions. Specifying dimensions and identifying the various indicators for each of those dimensions are both parts of conceptualization.

Specifying the different dimensions of a concept often paves the way for a more sophisticated understanding of what we are studying. We might observe, for example, that women are more compassionate in terms of feelings, and men are more compassionate in terms of actions—or vice versa. Noting that this was the case, we would not be able to say whether men or women are really more compassionate. Our research, in fact, would have shown that there is no single answer to the question.

The Interchangeability of Indicators

Paul Lazarsfeld (1959), in his discussion of the *interchangeability of indexes,* suggests that we may be able to answer a general question such as whether men or women are the more compassionate—even when we cannot agree on the ultimate or even the best way of measuring it.

Suppose, for the moment, that we have compiled a list of 100 indicators of the concept *compassion* and its various dimensions. Suppose further that we disagree widely on which indicators give the clearest evidence of compassion or its absence.

If we pretty much agree on some indicators, we could focus our attention on those, and we would probably agree on the answer they provided. But suppose we don't really agree on any of the possible indicators. It is still possible for us to reach an agreement on whether men or women are the more compassionate.

If we disagree totally on the value of the indicators, one solution would be to study all of them. Now, suppose that women turn out to be more compassionate than men on all 100 indicators—on all the indicators you favor and on all of ours. Then we would be able to agree that women are more compassionate than men even though we still disagree on what compassion means in general.

The *interchangeability of indicators* means that if several different indicators all represent, to some degree, the same concept, then all of them will behave the same way that the concept would behave if it were real and could be observed. Thus, if women are generally more compassionate than men, we should be able to observe that difference by using any reasonable measure of compassion.

You now have the fundamental logic of conceptualization and measurement. The discussions that follow in this chapter and the next one are mainly refinements and extensions of what we've just presented. Before turning to more technical elaborations on the main framework, however, it may be useful to cover more general topics.

First, we know the previous discussions may not fit exactly with your previous understanding of the meaning of such terms as *prejudice* and *compassion.* We tend to operate in daily life as though such terms have real, ultimate meanings. In the next subsection, then, we want to comment briefly on how we came to that understanding.

Second, lest this whole discussion create a picture of anarchy in the meanings of words, we will describe some of the ways scientists have organized the confusion so as to provide standards, consistency, and commonality in the meaning of terms. You should come away from this latter discussion with a recaptured sense of order—but one based on a conscious understanding rather than on a casual acceptance of common usage.

The Confusion Over Definitions and Reality

Reviewing briefly, our concepts are derived from the mental images (conceptions) that summarize collections of seemingly related observations and experiences. Although the observations and experiences are real, our concepts are only mental creations. The terms associated with concepts are merely devices created for purposes of filing and communication. The word *prejudice* is an example. Ultimately, that word is only a collection of letters and has no intrinsic meaning. We could have as easily and meaningfully created the word *slanderice* to serve the same purpose.

Often, however, we fall into the trap of believing that terms have real meanings. That danger seems to grow stronger when we begin to take terms seriously and attempt to use them precisely. And the danger is all the greater in the presence of experts who appear to know more than you do about what the terms really mean. It's easy to yield to the authority of experts in such a situation.

Once we have assumed that terms have real meanings, we begin the tortured task of discovering what those real meanings are and what constitutes a genuine measurement of them. Figure 5-2 illustrates the history of this process. We make up

1. Many of our observations in life seem to have something in common. We get the sense that they represent something more general than the simple content of any single observation. We find it useful, moreover, to communicate about the general concept.

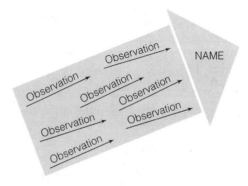

2. It is inconvenient to keep describing all the specific observations whenever we want to communicate about the general concept they seem to have in common, so we give a name to the general concept—to stand for whatever it is the specific observations have in common.

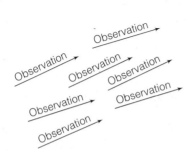

3. As we communicate about the general concept, using its term, we begin to think that the concept is some*thing* that really exists, not just a summary reference for several concrete observations in the world.

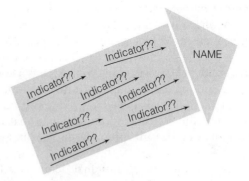

4. The belief that the concept itself is real results in irony. We now begin discussing and debating whether specific observations are "really" sufficient indicators of the concept.

Figure 5-2 The Process of Conceptual Entrapment

conceptual summaries of real observations because the summaries are convenient. They prove so convenient, however, that we begin to think they are real. The process of regarding as real things that are not is called **reification,** and the reification of concepts in day-to-day life is very common.

Creating Conceptual Order

The design and execution of social research requires a clearing away of the confusion over concepts and reality. To this end, logicians and scientists have found it useful to distinguish three kinds of definitions: *real, nominal,* and *operational.* The first of these reflects the reification of terms, and as Carl G. Hempel has cautioned,

> A "real" definition, according to traditional logic, is not a stipulation determining the meaning of some expression but a statement of the "essential nature" or the "essential attributes" of some entity. The notion of essential nature, however, is so vague as to render this characterization useless for the purposes of rigorous inquiry. (1952:6)

The specification of concepts in scientific inquiry depends on nominal and operational definitions. A *nominal* definition is one that is *assigned* to a term. In the midst of disagreement and confusion over what a term really means, the scientist specifies a working definition for the purposes of the inquiry. Wishing to examine socioeconomic status (SES) in a study, for example, we may simply specify that we are going to treat it as a combination of income and educational attainment. In that definitional decision, we rule out many other possible aspects of SES: occupational status, money in the bank, property, lineage, lifestyle, and so forth.

The specification of nominal definitions focuses our observational strategy, but it does not allow us to observe. As a next step we must specify exactly what we are going to observe, how we will do it, and what interpretations we are going to place on various possible observations. All of these further specifications make up the operational definition of the concept—a definition that spells out precisely how the concept will be measured. Strictly speaking, an operational definition is a description of the "operations" that will be undertaken in measuring a concept, as we discussed earlier in this chapter. (This is a good point to remind you that in purely qualitative studies the term *operational definition* rarely if ever appears, since the concepts to be measured and their operational indicators are not spelled out in advance and because the emphasis of the research tends to be placed on deeper subjective meanings rather than on counting observables.)

Pursuing the case of SES, we might decide to ask the people we are studying two questions:

1. What was your total family income during the past 12 months?
2. What is the highest level of school you completed?

Here, we would probably want to specify a system for categorizing the answers people give us. For income, we might use categories such as "under $5000" or "$5000 to $10,000." Educational attainment might be similarly grouped in categories. Finally, we would specify the way a person's responses to these two questions would be combined in creating a measure of SES. Chapter 7, on constructing measurement instruments, will present some of the methods for doing that.

Ultimately, we would have created a working and workable definition of SES. Others might disagree with our conceptualization and operationalization, but the definition would have one essential scientific virtue: it would be absolutely specific and unambiguous. Even if someone disagreed with our definition, that person would have a good idea how to interpret our research results, because what we meant by the term *SES*—reflected in our analyses and conclusions—would be clear.

Here is a diagram showing the progression of measurement steps from our vague sense of what a term means to specific measurements in a scientific study:

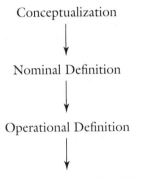

Conceptualization

↓

Nominal Definition

↓

Operational Definition

↓

Measurements in the Real World

Thus, social scientists can measure anything that's real, and they can even do a pretty good job of measuring things that aren't. Granting that such concepts as socioeconomic status, prejudice, and compassion aren't real ultimately, we've now seen that social scientists are able to create order in handling them. It is an order based on utility, however, and not on ultimate truth.

DEFINITIONS AND RESEARCH PURPOSES

Recall from Chapter 4 that two of the general purposes of research are *description* and *explanation*. The distinction between them has important implications for the process of definition and measurement. If you have formed the opinion that description is a simpler task than explanation, you will be surprised to learn that definitions are more problematic for descriptive research than for explanatory research. This point will be discussed more fully in Part 5, but it is important that you have a basic understanding of why it is so before we turn to other aspects of measurement.

The importance of definitions for descriptive research should be clear. If our task is to describe and report the unemployment rate in a city, our definition of *being unemployed* is critical. That definition will depend on our definition of another term: the *labor force*. If it seems patently absurd to regard a three-year-old child as being unemployed, it is because such a child is not considered

a member of the labor force. Thus, we might follow the U.S. Census Bureau's convention and exclude all persons under 14 years of age from the labor force.

This convention alone, however, would not give us a satisfactory definition, because it would count as unemployed such people as high school students, the retired, the disabled, and homemakers. We might follow the census convention further by defining the labor force as "all persons 14 years of age and over who are employed, looking for work, or waiting to be called back to a job from which they have been laid off or furloughed." Unemployed persons, then, would be members of the labor force who are not employed. If a student, homemaker, or retired person is not looking for work, such a person would not be included in the labor force.

But what does "looking for work" mean? Must a person register with the state employment service or go from door to door asking for employment? Or would it be sufficient to want a job or be open to an offer of employment? Conventionally, in survey research "looking for work" is defined operationally as saying "yes" in response to an interviewer's asking "Have you been looking for a job during the past seven days?" (Seven days is the time period most often specified, but for some research purposes it might make more sense to shorten or lengthen it.) In a qualitative, observational study, it might be more appropriate to operationalize this concept in terms of the subject's own perception of whether he or she was looking for work.

We have spelled out these considerations in some detail so that you will realize that the conclusion of a descriptive study about the unemployment rate, for example, depends directly on how each issue is resolved. Increasing the period of time during which people are counted as looking for work would have the effect of adding more unemployed persons to the labor force as defined, thereby increasing the reported unemployment rate. If we follow another convention and speak of the *civilian* labor force and the *civilian* unemployment rate, we are excluding

THE IMPORTANCE OF VARIABLE NAMES

by Patricia Fisher, Graduate School of Planning, University of Tennessee

Operationalization is one of those things that's easier said than done. It is quite simple to explain to someone the purpose and importance of operational definitions for variables, and even to describe how operationalization typically takes place. However, until you've tried to operationalize a rather complex variable, you may not appreciate some of the subtle difficulties involved. Of considerable importance to the operationalization effort is the particular name that you have chosen for a variable. Let's consider an example from the field of Urban Planning.

A variable of interest to planners is citizen participation. Planners are convinced that participation in the planning process by citizens is important to the success of plan implementation. Citizen participation is an aid to planners' understanding of the real and perceived needs of a community, and such involvement by citizens tends to enhance their cooperation with and support for planning efforts. Although many different conceptual definitions might be offered by different planners, there would be little misunderstanding over what is *meant* by citizen participation. The name of the variable seems adequate.

However, if we asked different planners to provide very simple operational measures for citizen participation, we are likely to find a variety among their responses that does generate confusion. One planner might keep a tally of attendance by private citizens at city commission and other local government meetings; another might maintain a record of the different topics addressed by private citizens at similar meetings; while a third might record the number of local government meeting attendees, letters and phone calls received by the mayor and other public officials, and meetings held by special interest groups during a particular time period. As skilled researchers, we can readily see that each planner would be measuring (in a very simplistic fashion) a different *dimension* of citizen participation: extent of citizen participation, issues prompting citizen participation, and form of citizen participation. Therefore, the original *naming* of our variable, citizen participation, which was quite satisfactory from a conceptual point of view, proved inadequate for purposes of operationalization.

The precise and exact naming of variables is important in research. It is both essential to and a result of good operationalization. Variable names quite often evolve from an iterative process of forming a conceptual definition, then an operational definition, then renaming the concept to better match what can or will be measured. This looping process continues (our example above illustrates only one iteration), resulting in a gradual refinement of the variable name and its measurement until a reasonable fit is obtained. Sometimes the concept of the variable that you end up with is a bit different from the original one that you started with, but at least you are measuring what you are talking about, if only because you are talking about what you are measuring!

military personnel; that, too, increases the reported unemployment rate, because military personnel would be employed—*by definition*.

Thus the descriptive statement that the unemployment rate in a city is 3%, or 9%, or whatever it might be, depends directly on the operational definitions used. If that seems clear in this example, it is because there are a number of accepted conventions relating to the labor force and unemployment. Consider how difficult it would be to get agreement about the definitions needed to make the descriptive statement "45% of the students are politically conservative." This percentage, like the unemployment rate, would depend directly on your definition of what is being measured. A different definition might result in the conclusion "5% of the student body is politically conservative."

Ironically, definitions are less problematic in the case of explanatory research. Let's suppose we are interested in explaining political conservatism. Why are some people conservative and others not? More specifically, let's suppose we are interested in whether old people are generally more conservative than young people. What if we have 25 different operational definitions of *conservative,* and we can't agree on which definition is the best one? As we've already seen, this is not necessarily an insurmountable obstacle to our research. Suppose, for example, that we found old people more conservative than young people in terms of *all 25 definitions!* (Recall the earlier discussion of compassion in men and women.) Suppose we found old people more conservative than young people by every reasonable definition of conservatism we could think of. It wouldn't matter what our definition was. We would conclude that old people are generally more conservative than young people—even though we couldn't agree about what a conservative really was.

In practice, explanatory research seldom results in findings quite as unambiguous as this example suggests; nonetheless, the general pattern is quite common in actual research. There *are* consistent patterns of relationships in human social life, and they result in consistent research findings. The

important point here, however, is that such consistency does not appear in a descriptive situation. Changing definitions almost inevitably result in different descriptive conclusions.

The box "The Importance of Variable Names" explores this issue in connection with the variable "citizen participation."

OPERATIONALIZATION CHOICES

As we've just indicated, the social work researcher has a wide variety of options available when it comes to measuring a concept. Although the choices are intimately interconnected, we've separated them for purposes of discussion. Please realize, however, that operationalization does *not* proceed through a systematic checklist.

Range of Variation

In operationalizing any concept, it is essential that you be clear about the range of variation that interests you in your research. To what extent are you willing to combine attributes in fairly gross categories?

Let's suppose you want to measure people's incomes in a study—either collecting the information from records or in interviews. The highest annual incomes people receive run into the millions of dollars, but not many people get that much. Unless you are studying the very rich, it probably wouldn't be worth much to allow for and keep track of extremely high categories. Depending on whom you are studying, you'll probably want to establish a highest income category with a much lower floor—maybe $50,000 or more. Although this decision will lead you to throw together people who earn a trillion dollars a year with "paupers" earning only $50,000, they'll survive it, and that mixing probably won't hurt your research any. The same decision faces you at the other end of the income spectrum. In studies of the general American population, a cutoff of $5000 or less usually works just fine.

In the study of attitudes and orientations, the question of range of variation has another dimension. Unless you're careful, you may end up measuring only "half an attitude" without really meaning to. Here's an example of what we mean.

Suppose you're interested in the views of social work practitioners about transracial adoptions, in which a child, usually of minority ethnicity, is adopted by parents of a different ethnicity. You'd anticipate in advance that some practitioners consider it a great way to find foster parents for children who otherwise would have little chance of being adopted, whereas other practitioners never heard of the concept and have no interest in it. Given that anticipation, it would seem to make sense to ask people how much they favor expanding the use of transracial adoptions. You might give them answer categories ranging from "Favor it very much" to "Don't favor it at all."

This operationalization, however, conceals half of the attitudinal spectrum regarding transracial adoptions. Many practitioners, including minority practitioners concerned about the self-image and stigmatization of minority children raised by white parents in a predominantly white community, have feelings that go beyond simply not favoring it: they are *opposed* to it. In this instance, there is considerable variation on the left side of zero. Some oppose it a little, some quite a bit, and others a great deal. To measure the full range of variation, then, you'd want to operationalize attitudes toward transracial adoptions with a range from favoring it very much, through no feelings one way or the other, to opposing it very much.

This consideration applies to many of the variables we study in social science. Virtually any public issue involves both support and opposition, each in varying degrees. Political orientations range from very liberal to very conservative, and depending on the people you are studying, you may want to allow for radicals on one or both ends. People are not just more or less religious; some are antireligious.

We do not mean that you must measure the full range of variation in any given case. You should, however, consider whether that's needed in the light of your research purpose. If the difference between *not religious* and *antireligious* isn't relevant to your research, forget it. Someone has defined pragmatism by saying "any difference that makes no difference is no difference." Be pragmatic.

Finally, your decision on the range of variation should be governed also by the expected distribution of attributes among your subjects of study. That is what we meant earlier when we said range depends on whom you are studying. In a study of college professors' attitudes toward the value of higher education, you could probably stop at *no value* and not worry about those who might consider higher education dangerous to students' health. (If you were studying students, however. . . .)

Variations Between the Extremes

Precision is a consideration in operationalizing variables. (As we will see in Chapter 6, it also is a criterion of quality in measurement.) What it boils down to is how fine you will make distinctions among the various possible attributes composing a given variable. Does it really matter whether a person is 17 or 18 years old, or could you conduct your inquiry by throwing them together in a group labeled 10 to 19 years old? Don't answer too quickly. If you wanted to study rates of voter registration and participation, you'd definitely want to know whether the people you studied were old enough to vote.

If you are going to measure age, then, you must look at the purpose and procedures of your study and decide whether fine or gross differences in age are important to you. If you measure political affiliation, will it matter to your inquiry whether a person is a conservative Democrat rather than a liberal Democrat, or is it sufficient to know the party? In measuring religious affiliation, is it enough to know that a person is a Protestant, or do you need to know the denomination? Do you simply need to know whether a person is married or not, or will it make a difference to know if he or she has never married or is separated, widowed, or divorced?

There is, of course, no general answer to questions like these. The answers come out of the purpose of your study—the purpose you have in making a particular measurement. We can mention a useful guideline, however. Whenever you're not sure how much detail to get in a measurement, get too much rather than too little. During the analysis of data, it will always be possible to combine precise attributes into more general categories, but it will never be possible to separate out the variations that were lumped together during observation and measurement.

A Note on Dimensions

When people get down to the business of creating operational measures of variables, they often discover—or worse, never notice—that they are not exactly clear about which dimensions of a variable they are really interested in. Here's one example to illustrate what we mean.

Let's suppose we are doing in-depth interviews to determine the attitudes of families toward the long-term care of relatives in nursing homes. Here are just a few of the different dimensions we might examine:

- Do family members think the care their relative receives is adequate?
- How adequate or inadequate do they think the care is?
- How certain are they in their judgment of how adequate or inadequate the care is?
- How do they feel about the inadequacy of nursing home care as a problem in society?
- What do they think causes it?
- Do they think it's inevitable?
- What do they feel should be done about it?
- What are they willing to do personally to improve nursing home care?
- How certain are they that they would be willing to do what they say they would do?

The list could go on and on. How people feel about the adequacy of care in nursing homes has many dimensions. *It's essential that you be clear about which ones are important in your inquiry and direct the interviews appropriately.* Otherwise, you may measure how people feel about it when you really wanted to know how much they think there is, or vice versa.

SOME OPERATIONALIZATION ILLUSTRATIONS

To bring together all the operationalization choices available to the social work researcher and to show you the potential in those possibilities, we want to take a little time to illustrate some of the ways you might address certain research problems. Our purpose here is to stretch your imagination just a bit further and demonstrate the challenge that social work research can present to your ingenuity. To simplify matters, we have not attempted to describe all the research conditions that would make one alternative superior to the others, though you should realize that in a given situation they would not all be equally appropriate. Let's look at specific research questions, then, and at some of the ways you could address them. We'll begin with an example discussed at length earlier. It has the added advantage that one of the variables is reasonably straightforward.

1. *Are women more compassionate than men?*
   a. Select a group of subjects for study. Present them with hypothetical situations that involve someone's being in trouble. Ask them what they would do if they were confronted with that situation. What would they do, for example, if they came across a small child who was lost and crying for his or her parents? Consider any answer that involves helping the child or comforting it to be compassionate, and count whether men or women are more likely to indicate they would be compassionate.

b. Set up an experiment in which you pay a small child to pretend that he or she is lost. Put the kid to work on a busy sidewalk, and count whether men or women are more likely to offer assistance. Be sure to count how many men and women walk by, also, since there may be more of one than the other. If that's the case, simply calculate the percentage of men and the percentage of women who help.

c. Select a sample of people and do a survey in which you ask them what organizations they belong to. Calculate whether women or men are more likely to belong to those that seem to reflect compassionate feelings. To take account of men belonging to more organizations than women in general—or vice versa—do this: For each person you study, calculate the percentage of his or her organizational memberships that reflect compassion. See if men or women have a higher average percentage.

d. Watch your local newspaper for a special feature on some issue involving compassion—the slaughter of baby seals, for example. In the days to follow, keep a record of all letters to the editor on the subject. See whether men or women are the more likely to express their compassion in the matter—making the necessary adjustments for one gender writing more letters to the editor than the other in general.

2. *Is burnout among social workers more likely to occur when they work in public welfare agencies or private family service agencies?*

a. Select a group of public welfare agencies and private family service agencies and then observe and interview the social workers in each agency, asking them to rate how burnt out they feel on a scale from 1 (not at all burnt out) to 10 (extremely burnt out). In addition, you might have each complete an existing scale that measures job satisfaction.

b. Obtain from the personnel records in each of the agencies the number of sick days taken by social workers and how long current and previous social work personnel have worked at the agency. For those no longer working there, do the records show whether they left for another social work job?

c. Survey clients in each agency and ask them how enthusiastic their social worker usually seems to be when seeing them. You might also examine case records to see the extent of process recording done by the social workers.

d. Show up at each agency several times at different points during the workday. How many social workers arrive late or leave early? How many arrive before normal hours or stay late? How many take long lunches? How many skip lunch or work while they eat? How much time do they spend at coffee breaks or socializing with each other? How many are reading the newspaper—especially the employment ads section—or are asleep at their desks?

3. *Are social work students or business administration students better informed about world affairs?*

a. Prepare a short quiz on world affairs and arrange to administer it to the students in a social work class and in a comparable business class. If you want to compare social work and business majors, be sure to ask them what they are majoring in.

b. Get the instructor of a course in world affairs to give you the average grades of social work and business students in the course.

c. Take a petition to social work and business classes that urges that "the United Nations headquarters be moved to New York City." Keep a count of how many in each class sign the petition and how many inform you that the UN headquarters is already located in New York City.

4. *Do people consider New York or California the better place to live?*

   a. Consulting the *Statistical Abstract of the United States* or a similar publication, check the migration rates into and out of each state. See if you can find the numbers moving directly from New York to California and vice versa.

   b. The national polling companies—Gallup, Harris, Roper, and so forth—often ask people what they consider the best state to live in. Look up some recent results in the library or through your local newspaper.

   c. Compare suicide rates in the two states.

5. *Who are the most popular social work instructors on your campus: those who teach practice, research, or policy?*

   a. If your school has a provision for student evaluation of instructors, review some recent results and compute the average ratings given the three groups.

   b. Begin visiting the introductory courses given in each sequence and count the numbers of students attending classes. Get the enrollment figures for the classes you study, and calculate the average absentee rates.

   c. Around Christmas, select a group of faculty in each of the three areas and ask them to keep a record of the numbers of cards and presents they receive from admiring students. See who wins.

   d. Read the obituary column in your campus newspaper every day, and keep a record of all the faculty who are lynched after class by mobs of irate students—taking care to always note their curriculum area. Be sure to adjust your figures to take account of the total number of faculty in each area: the percentages lynched are more appropriate than the numbers lynched.

We could continue moving from the ridiculous to the more ridiculous, but the point of these illustrations has been to broaden your vision of the many ways variables can be operationalized, not necessarily to suggest respectable research projects. When you think about it, absolutely everything you see around you is already an operationalized measure of some variable. Most are measures of more than one variable, so all you have to do is pick the ones you want and decide what they will represent in your particular study. Usually, you will want to use more than one measure for each variable in the inquiry.

The box "The Treatment of Gender in Research" further illustrates the importance of choices researchers must make in operationalizing variables. The guidelines it presents are intended to help sensitize researchers to ways of avoiding gender bias in their research procedures.

OPERATIONALIZATION GOES ON AND ON

Although we've discussed conceptualization and operationalization in quantitative studies as activities that precede data collection and analysis—you design your operational measures before you observe—you should realize that these two processes continue throughout a research project, even after data have been collected and analyzed. Here's what we mean by that.

We have suggested that you measure a given variable in several different ways in your research. That is essential if the concept lying in the background is at all ambiguous and open to different interpretations and definitions. By measuring the variable in several different ways, you will be in a position to examine alternative operational definitions during your analysis. You will have several single indicators to choose from and many ways of creating different composite measures. Thus, you'll be able to experiment with different measures—each representing a somewhat different conceptualization and operationalization—to

THE TREATMENT OF GENDER IN RESEARCH

IV. Operationalizing Major Concepts

A. *In constructing research instruments, such as questionnaires or experimental situations, care should be taken to ascertain that they are equally appropriate for both men and women, as well as for members of various racial groups, and that the reactions of both sexes to research stimuli are identified.* Although often not required, separate versions of the same instrument should be prepared where appropriate. Contextual factors (e.g., sex or race of interviewer) should also be included as a variable in the design and analysis.

B. *Gender-neutral and gender-explicit terminology should be used as appropriate in naming variables or operational measures and discussing findings.* More important, researchers should be fully aware of the implications of using gender-neutral or gender-explicit terms in any particular case. Thus, for example, the term *spouse abuse* should not be substituted for *wife abuse* when one is dealing with victims of abuse who are women and abusers who are men. Despite this, there are occasions when it is advantageous to consider wife abuse within the broader context of spouse abuse. By the same token, the term *parenting* is preferable to *mothering* when it refers to the nurturing behavior of either parent. In addition, the culturally implicit identification of the male with normative and positively valued traits should not bias the way in which concepts are operationalized. For instance, remaining calm and unemotional in a stressful situation is no more "normal," or effective for that matter, than dealing with one's anxieties by expressing them.

C. *Concepts should be operationalized so that eventual empirical identification of any linkages to gender is possible.* For example, by conceptualizing work in terms of paid employment and, more specifically, census categories, many types of work (such as community service and home-based work) are excluded from consideration. Because such work, which is often not compensated, is disproportionately done by women, analyses relying on occupational categories systematically underestimate women's productive activity.

D. *In utilizing secondary sources* (for instance, the National Longitudinal Surveys) *original instruments should be carefully examined to see if they contain biased questions or assumptions.* Thus, for example, data recently collected by the National Center for Health Statistics asked only women how many children they had, presumably because the researchers at NCHS assumed that the presence or absence of children does not affect men's physical or mental health.

Excerpt from pamphlet prepared by members of the 1985 and 1986 Committees on the Status of Women in Sociology, American Sociological Association.

decide which gives the clearest and most useful answers to your research questions.

This doesn't mean you should select the measurement that confirms your expectations or proves your point. That's clearly not appropriate and doesn't do much to advance our understanding of social life. Instead, operationalization is a continuing process, not a blind commitment to a particular measure that may turn out to have been poorly chosen. Suppose, for example, that you decide to measure compassion by asking people whether they give money to charity, and everybody says yes. Where does that leave you? Nowhere. Your study of why some people are more compassionate than others would be in deep trouble unless you had included some other possible measures in designing your observations.

The validity and utility of what you learn in your research doesn't depend on when you first figured out how to look at things any more than it matters whether you got the idea from a learned textbook, a dream, or your brother-in-law.

A QUALITATIVE PERSPECTIVE ON OPERATIONAL DEFINITIONS

Recognizing the risks inherent in trying to pre-determine how to operationally define abstract constructs, we should remember that researchers conducting purely qualitative studies eschew operational definitions. Rather than restrict their observations to predetermined operational indicators, they prefer to let the meanings of little-understood phenomena emerge from their observations. How they do this will be discussed in more detail later in this book; however, we'll elaborate a bit on this issue now.

In qualitative studies the problem of operationally defining variables in advance is threefold. First, we may not know in advance what all the most salient variables are. Second, limitations in our understanding of the variables we think are important may keep us from anticipating the best way to operationally define those variables. Third, even the best operational definitions are necessarily superficial, since they are specified only in terms of observable indicators. Although operational definitions are necessary in quantitative studies, they do not pertain to probing into the deeper meanings of what is observed. These deeper meanings are the purview of qualitative studies.

In a purely quantitative study, we assume that we know enough in advance about a phenomenon to pose a narrow research question about a limited set of variables and to develop precise, objective, observable indicators of those variables that can be counted to answer the research question. In a purely qualitative study, we assume that we need to develop a deeper understanding of some phenomenon and its subjective meanings as it occurs in its natural environment. We take it for granted that we will not be able to develop that richer understanding if we limit ourselves to observable indicators that can be anticipated in advance and counted. In qualitative research, we immerse ourselves in a more subjective fashion in open-ended, flexible observations of phenomena as they occur naturally, and then try to discern patterns and themes from an immense and relatively unstructured set of observations. Also, in qualitative research the social context of our observations is emphasized.

To illustrate the importance of social context, as well as the qualitative perspective, imagine a quantitative study testing the hypothesis that increasing the number of home visits by child welfare practitioners will improve parental functioning and therefore preserve families. Studies like this have been done, and the dependent variable is often operationally defined in quantifiable terms of whether or not (or for how long) children are placed in foster care. A problem with many of these studies is that the increased home visitation might also increase the practitioner's awareness of neglectful or abusive acts by parents. If so, then it is conceivable that any reductions in foster care placement due to improved parental functioning are canceled out by increases in foster care placement due to increased practitioner monitoring. Thus, the hypothesis might not be supported even though the increased home visits are improving service outcomes.

A qualitative inquiry, in contrast, would probe into the deeper meaning and social context of the processes and outcomes in each case. Instead of merely counting the number of placements, it would learn that a foster care placement in one case, and the avoidance of a placement in another case, could both mean that the practitioner has achieved a valuable outcome. Moreover, a qualitative study would observe in detail what practitioners and clients did, probe into the deeper meanings of what was observed, and attempt to discern patterns indicating the conditions under which practitioners appear to be more or less effective.

In describing this qualitative perspective on operational definitions we are not implying that it is a superior perspective (although many qualitatively oriented researchers think it is superior). It is neither superior nor inferior. Neither is it mutually exclusive with a quantitative perspective (although some researchers believe the two perspectives are in conflict). In the foregoing family preservation illustration, for example, a qualitative inquiry could be conducted simultaneously with the quantitative inquiry, and both could be part of the same study. The qualitative component could shed light on why the quantitative hypothesis was not supported. The box "Illustrations of the Qualitative Perspective on Operationalization and Its Complementarity with a Quantitative Perspective" provides two additional examples of this issue.

ILLUSTRATIONS OF THE QUALITATIVE PERSPECTIVE ON OPERATIONALIZATION AND ITS COMPLEMENTARITY WITH A QUANTITATIVE PERSPECTIVE

To further illustrate the qualitative perspective on operationalization, as well as its complementarity with a quantitative perspective, let's reexamine two of the operationalization illustrations presented several pages ago.

1. *Is burnout among social workers more likely to occur when they work in public welfare agencies or in private family service agencies?*

A qualitative study would not pose this research question. Instead of defining *burnout* operationally in terms of one or two observable indicators and then looking at it in relationship to a predetermined independent variable (or set of predetermined independent variables), it might examine the experiences of a small group of social workers in depth and attempt to portray in a richer and deeper sense what it feels like to be burnt out and what it means to the social worker. It might, for example, be in the form of a biography of the career of one or more social workers who are burnt out, perhaps contrasted with a biography of one or more who are not burnt out. Conceivably, the qualitative study could be done in conjuction with a quantitative study. That is, the quantitative component could look at which of the two types of agencies had more burnout, whereas the qualitative component could try to discover the underlying reasons for the quantitative differences.

2. *Who are the most popular social work instructors: those who teach practice, research, or policy?*

A qualitative study would not pose this research question either. Instead of using an operational definition of *popularity* and then seeing if it is related to type of course taught, it might involve observations of all aspects of instructor interactions with students in and out of the classroom, analysis of course materials, and in-depth, open-ended interviews with instructors and students to try to identify what it is that makes instructors popular and what it means to be popular (perhaps popularity does not necessarily imply the most effective instruction). Identifying instructors who appear to be the most popular could be part of a qualitative study, but the point of the study would be to probe deeper into the meaning and experience of their popularity, not to see if a particular operational indicator of their popularity is quantitatively related to another predetermined variable. Rather than report numbers on how popular one group of instructors is compared to another group, a qualitative study might begin by identifying instructors who students generally agree are the most and least popular. It might then provide a wealth of information about each of those instructors, attempting to discern themes and patterns that appear to distinguish popular from unpopular instructors or to provide the field with ideal or undesirable case study types of instructional patterns to emulate or avoid emulating. As with the previous question, the qualitative component of a study could be done in conjuction with a quantitative component. There is no reason why the hypothesis that popularity will be related to curriculum area taught could not be tested as part of a larger study looking qualitatively at the deeper meaning of other aspects of popularity.

SOME MORE EXAMPLES OF OPERATIONALIZATION IN SOCIAL WORK

Throughout this chapter we have discussed how a variety of terms might be operationally defined. Among the terms we considered were: social adjustment, prejudice, compassion, socioeconomic status, being unemployed, looking for work, citizen participation, income, attitudes about transracial adoptions, attitudes about nursing home care, and professional burnout. Some of the terms we discussed were more relevant to social work than others. To make sure that we have presented enough social work examples, we'll examine a few more at this point.

Let's begin with the construct: *marital satisfaction*. Suppose you are conducting a research study, and marital satisfaction is one of your variables. Perhaps you want to see if family therapy increases marital satisfaction, in which case it would be your dependent variable. Or maybe you want to see if higher levels of marital satisfaction among foster parents contribute to successful foster placement, in which case marital satisfaction would be your independent variable. In either study, what are some of the ways you might go about operationally defining marital satisfaction? Would you simply define it as the amount of happiness in a marriage?

That won't do as an *operational* definition because it won't bring you any closer to the *observable* indicators of marital satisfaction. You would merely have substituted one unobservable construct for another. Here are a few options that would be operational.

In the study on foster placement you might simply ask each couple if they have recently sought help for marital problems. You might consider those who say yes to have less marital satisfaction than those who say no. Similarly, you might just ask each couple whether they consider themselves to have a high, medium, or low degree of marital satisfaction. You might understandably have some qualms as to whether the answers you'll get are sufficiently accurate and objective indicators of marital satisfaction, and we are not necessarily recommending either approach. But you should see that either of these would be *operational* definitions.

Alternatively, you might interview each couple about their marriage and count the number of times that either makes a derogatory statement about the marriage or about the spouse. Note that if you go this route you'll have to grapple with the ground rules for considering a statement derogatory. Perhaps you'll just have to leave that to the judgment of the interviewer, and see if an independent observer (perhaps viewing a videotape of the interview) tends to agree with the interviewer's counts. We'll say more about this when we discuss reliability, in the next chapter.

You might ask each spouse to conduct a typical 15-minute conversation while you observe and count the number of times they interrupt one another, raise their voices, or make various physical gestures that seem to indicate frustration or dissatisfaction with the spouse. This can be tricky.

If the couple is disagreeing about an intellectual or political issue (such as foreign policy, for example), perhaps they actually enjoy having heated, animated debates. Although you have an observable definition, you might wonder whether it is really measuring marital satisfaction, and we'll get into that issue as well in the next chapter, when we discuss validity.

Chances are the most expedient operational definition would be to use an existing scale that was devised to measure marital satisfaction. You would ask each person in your study to complete the scale. The higher the score on the scale, the more marital satisfaction. (If both spouses respond, perhaps you will add both scores to get a combined score per couple.) Existing scales that have been constructed to measure certain constructs build the indicators of the construct into the scale. For example, a scale to measure marital satisfaction might ask either spouse how often he or she is annoyed with the spouse, has fun with the spouse, feels he or she can rely on the spouse, wants to be with the spouse, is proud of the spouse, feels controlled by the spouse, resents the spouse, and so on. Each scale item gets a score, and the item scores are summed up for a total score of marital satisfaction. For instance, an individual might get a score of 5 for each positive item (such as feeling proud of spouse) to which he or she responds "always" and for each negative item (such as resenting the spouse) to which the response is "never." If there are twenty items on the scale and the individual responds "always" to every positive item and "never" to every negative item, then the total scale score would be 100. This would indicate that this person had more marital satisfaction than another person who responded "sometimes" to every item, therefore receiving a score of, say, 3 for every item and therefore a total score of 60.

Of course, there are many additional ways one might attempt to operationally define marital satisfaction. For example, if one is doing cross-cultural research, one might compare divorce rates in different geographic areas as one operational indicator of marital satisfaction. Again, this is not to imply that such rates would be a true indicator of the construct, just that they would be operational. Perhaps the culture with the lower divorce rates has no more marital satisfaction, just stricter taboos against divorce.

That's enough for now about marital satisfaction. Let's move on to another example: *parenting skill*. Suppose you want to conduct research to see if your parent education program is effective in improving the parenting skills of parents at risk for child abuse. Or perhaps you want to conduct an exploratory, inductive study to generate hypotheses about what types of people would make the best foster parents. As with marital satisfaction, you have a variety of options for operationalizing the term *parenting skill*. You might begin by making a list of positive parenting behaviors, such as praising, encouraging, modeling, consistency, use of time outs, and so on. Another list might specify undesirable parenting behaviors, such as threatening, slapping, screaming, criticizing, bribing, belittling, and so on. Then you might observe the parents or foster parents in a challenging parenting situation, such as getting children to put away their toys, and count the number of times the parents show positive and negative behaviors. Perhaps you will give them +1 for every positive behavior and −1 for every negative behavior and tally the points to get a parenting skill score.

Chances are you might find the preceding approach too time consuming. As an alternative, therefore, you might simply want the parents to complete an existing self-report scale that purports to measure knowledge and/or attitudes about parenting. Such a scale might ask parents questions about what they would do in various child-rearing situations or how they perceive various normal childhood behaviors that some parents misperceive as provocative.

We'll conclude this section with an example that concerns many social work students: the concept of *social work interviewing skill*. Perhaps you will someday conduct a study to see whether your

agency's in-service training program is effective in improving the interviewing skills of the recently graduated social workers it hires. Or perhaps you will want to see whether there is any difference in entering interviewing skills among social workers who have only MSW degrees, those who have only BSW degrees, and those who have both BSW and MSW degrees. How will you operationally define interviewing skill?

One option would be to have the social workers conduct initial intake interviews with new clients entering the agency (or, alternatively, social workers role playing clients) and then, on completion of each interview, have the clients (or role players) rate how at ease they felt during the interview, how interested the interviewer seemed in them, whether the interviewer seemed to ask the right questions and to understand how they felt, and so on.

Another option would be to list specific behaviors associated with good and bad interviewing, to videotape each interview, and then to count the behaviors. Desirable behaviors might include: maintaining eye contact, giving intermittent positive gestures (smiles, nods, and so on), paraphrasing answers to prompt elaboration, and many more. Undesirable behaviors might include: slouching, yawning, looking at one's watch, passing judgment on answers, and many more. You might add the desirable behaviors and subtract the undesirable behaviors to get a score that would operationalize interviewing skills.

A simpler option might be to have two agency colleagues who are both highly experienced interviewers and supervisors independently view the videotapes and then give an overall rating to each interview (not knowing how the other one rated it)—for example, from poor to excellent, from one to ten, or some such. This option would rely heavily on the judgment of the expert observers, and may or may not prove as useful as the previous option, which used indicators that were more behaviorally specific. In either case, you would want to see if different raters agreed in their ratings; that is, to see if their ratings are reliable—an issue we will discuss in the next chapter.

As another alternative, again we return to the option of using existing paper-and-pencil, self-report scales to obtain the operational definition. An assortment of such scales are available to measure interviewing skill. Typically they present the subject with a case situation and various client statements. The subject then writes down how he or she would respond or selects a response from multiple choices. The responses are scored, and the subject receives a summated score for inter-

viewing skills and/or for certain components of interviewing skill (such as empathy, questioning, and so on).

EXISTING SCALES

In the foregoing examples you can see why the use of existing scales can be a popular way to operationally define variables. They spare researchers the costs in time and money of devising their own measures and provide an option that has been

Aiken, L. R.: 1985 *Psychological Testing and Assessment.* Rockleigh, NJ: Allyn & Bacon.

Anastasi, A.: 1988 *Psychological Testing.* New York: Macmillan.

Andrulis, R. S.: 1977 *Adult Assessment: A Source Book of Tests and Measures of Human Behavior.* Springfield, IL: Thomas.

Beere, C. A.: 1979 *Women and Women's Issues: A Handbook of Tests and Measures.* San Francisco: Jossey-Bass.

Beere, C. A.: 1990 *Sex and Gender Issues: A Handbook of Tests and Measures.* New York: Greenwood Press.

Brodsky, S. L., and Smitherman, H. O.: 1983 *Handbook of Scales for Research in Crime and Delinquency.* New York: Plenum Press.

Buros, O.: 1978 *Eighth Mental Measurements Yearbook.* Highland Park, NJ: Gryphon Press.

Cautela, J. R.: 1981 *Behavior Analysis Forms for Clinical Intervention* (Vol. 2). Champaign, IL: Research Press.

Chun, Ki-Taek, Cobb, S., and French, J. R.: 1975 *Measures for Psychological Assessment: A Guide to 3,000 Original Sources and Their Applications.* Ann Arbor, MI: Institute for Social Research.

Ciarlo, J. A., Brown, T. R., Edwards, D. W., Kiresuk, T. J., and Newman, F. L.: 1986 *Assessing Mental Health Treatment Outcome Measurement Techniques.* Rockville, MD: National Institute of Mental Health (DHHS Publication No. (ADM) 86-1301).

Comrey, A., Barker, T., and Glaser, E.: 1975 *A Sourcebook for Mental Health Measures.* Los Angeles: Human Interaction Research Institute.

Conoley, J. C., and Kramer, J. J.: 1989 *The 10th Mental Measurements Yearbook.* Lincoln, NE: Buros Institute of Mental Measurements.

Corcoran, K. J., and Fischer, J.: 1992 *Measures for Clinical Practice: A Sourcebook* (2nd ed.). New York: Free Press.

Fischer, J., and Corcoran, K.: 1994a *Measures for Clinical Practice: Vol. 1. Couples, Families, Children.* (2nd ed). New York: Free Press.

Fischer, J., and Corcoran, K.: 1994b *Measures for Clinical Practice: Vol. 2 Adults* (2nd ed). New York: Free Press.

Fredman, N., and Sherman, R.: 1987 *Handbook of Measurements for Marriage and Family Therapy.* New York: Brunner/Mazel.

Goldman, B. A., and Busch, J. C.: 1982 *Directory of Unpublished Experimental Measures* (Vol. 3). New York: Human Sciences Press.

Grotevant, H. D., and Carlson, D. I. (Eds.): 1989 *Family Assessment: A Guide to Methods and Measures.* New York: Guilford Press.

Harrington, R. G. (Ed.): 1986 *Testing Adolescents: A Reference Guide for Comprehensive Psychological Assessment Techniques.* Elmsford, NY: Pergamon Press.

Hersen, M., and Bellack, A. S. (Eds.): 1988 *Dictionary of Behavioral Assessment Techniques.* Elmsford, NY: Pergamon Press.

Hudson, W. W.: 1982 *The Clinical Measurement Package: A Field Manual.* Homewood, IL: Dorsey Press.

Hudson, W. W.: 1992 *The WALMYR Assessment Scales Scoring Manual.* Tempe, AZ: WALMYR.

Jacob, T., and Tennebaum, D. L.: 1988 *Family*

Figure 5-3 Some Reference Volumes for Existing Scales That Can Be Used to Operationally Define Variables in Social Work

used successfully to measure the concept in previous studies. Therefore, we'll conclude this chapter with a few comments on finding relevant scales and salient information about them.

The most thorough procedure would be to conduct a literature review on the construct you seek to measure. For example, you might review the literature on marital satisfaction to locate materials that report measures of marital satisfaction. We refer you to Chapter 4 and Appendix A for information on how to conduct a literature review. Of course, this would be a relatively quick litera-

ture review, since the purpose is to locate measures of a construct, not to review all the research on the construct.

One way to expedite the search for measures is to consult reference volumes that list and describe many existing measures. Figure 5-3 lists some volumes that might be useful. Some of these volumes reprint the actual measurement instrument; others describe it and provide additional references on it. Usually they will discuss the quality of the instrument (such as its reliability and validity) and tell you how to obtain the instrument

Assessment: Rationale, Methods, and Future Directions. New York: Plenum Press.

Kestenbaum, C. J., and Williams, D. T. (Eds.): 1988 *Handbook of Clinical Assessment of Children and Adolescents*. Austin, TX: Pro-Ed.

Knoff, H. M.: 1986 *The Assessment of Child and Adolescent Personality*. New York: Guilford Press.

LaGreca, A. M.: 1990 *Through the Eyes of the Child: Obtaining Self-Reports from Children and Adolescents*. Boston: Allyn and Bacon.

Lake, D. G., Miles, M. B., and Earle, R. B., Jr.: 1973 *Measuring Human Behavior: Tools for the Assessment of Social Functioning*. New York: Teachers College Press.

Magura, S., and Moses, B. S.: 1987 *Outcome Measures for Child Welfare Services*. Washington, DC: Child Welfare League of America.

Martin, R. P.: 1988 *Assessment of Personality and Behavior Problems: Infancy Through Adolescence*. New York: Guilford Press.

Mash, E. J., and Terdal, L. G.: 1988 *Behavioral Assessment of Childhood Disorders*. New York: Guilford Press.

McCubbin, H. I., and Thompson, A. I. (Eds.): 1987 *Family Assessment Inventions for Research and Practice*. Madison: University of Wisconsin–Madison.

McDowell, I., and Newell, C.: 1987 *Measuring Health: A Guide to Rating Scales and Questionnaires*. New York: Oxford University Press.

Miller, D. C.: 1983 *Handbook of Research Design and Social Measurement* (4th ed.). New York: Longman.

Mitchell, J. V. (Ed.): 1985 *The Ninth Mental Measurements Yearbook*. Lincoln: University of Nebraska Press.

Mitchell, J.: 1983 *Tests in Print III*. Lincoln, NE: Buros Institute of Mental Measurements.

Ollendick, T. H., and Hersen, M.: 1992 *Handbook of Child and Adolescents Assessment*. Des Moines, IA: Allyn and Bacon.

Quay, H. C., and Werry, J. S. *Psychopathological Disorders of Childhood*. New York: Wiley.

Reynolds, C. R., and Kamphaus, R. W. (Eds.): 1990 *Handbook of Psychological and Educational Assessment of Children*. New York: Guilford Press.

Rutter, M., Tuma, H. H., and Lann, I. S. (Eds.): 1988 *Assessment and Diagnosis in Child Psychopathology*. New York: Guilford Press.

Sattler, J. M.: 1988 *Assessment of Children* (3rd ed.). Brandon, VT: Clinical Psychology Publishing Co.

Scholl, G., and Schnur, R.: 1976 *Measures of Psychological, Vocational, and Educational Functioning in the Blind and Visually Handicapped*. New York: American Foundation for the Blind.

Straus, M., and Brown, B.: 1978 *Family Measurement Techniques: Abstracts of Published Instruments*. Minneapolis: University of Minnesota Press.

Touliatos, J., Perlmutter, B. F., and Straus, M. A. (Eds.): 1990 *Handbook of Family Measurement Techniques*. Newbury Park, CA: Sage.

Walker, D. K.: 1973 *Socioemotional Measure for Preschool and Kindergarten Children*. San Francisco: Jossey-Bass.

Wetzler, S. (Ed.): 1989 *Measuring Mental Illness: Psychometric Assessment for Clinicians*. Washington, DC: American Psychiatric Press.

Figure 5-3 Some Reference Volumes *(continued)*

and more information about it. You will also be informed of whether it is copyrighted, which will indicate whether you must purchase it or use it with the author's permission.

Despite the practical advantages of using existing self-report scales to operationally define variables, not everyone would agree that they are the best way to operationalize a particular variable in a particular study, and there can be difficulties in using them. Consider the preceding example on interviewing skill, for instance. Which measurement approach would give you more confidence that your data adequately reflected practitioners' interviewing skill: their answers to a paper-and-pencil test, or their actual performance in a real face-to-face interview with a client? Many of you, we suspect, would prefer the latter as a more realistic test of the interviewer's skill. At the same time, however, you might opt to use an existing self-report scale in an actual study of interviewing skill, not because you think it is the best measure of that concept, but because you may lack the resources needed to use a preferable measure.

We will be discussing the advantages and disadvantages of using self-report scales in Chapters 6 and 10, how to construct them in Chapter 7, and the advantages and disadvantages of alternative measurement options in Chapters 6, 10, 11, 12 , and 13. These alternative options are evident in the foregoing examples of operational definitions and include: **direct behavioral observation, interviews,** and examining **available records** (such as divorce rates). None of these options provides a foolproof way to operationalize variables. Like the use of **self-report scales,** each is vulnerable to various measurement errors that we'll be addressing shortly, in the next chapter. We'll end this chapter by identifying some of the issues to consider in choosing an existing scale as an operational definition.

Let's begin on a very practical note: How lengthy is the scale? Will it take too long for the subjects in your study to complete? Suppose, for example, a lengthy scale that takes more than an hour to complete was tested on people who were paid $20 to complete the scale. Its success under those circumstances would not be relevant to a study of busy people who were mailed the scale and asked to volunteer that much time—without pay—to complete and mail back the scale.

Another practical question is whether the scale will be too difficult for your subjects to complete. For example, will it be too cumbersome or too complexly worded for them? Suppose you want to study depression among undocumented immigrants from Mexico. Chances are you would not be able to use a scale that was developed to assess depression among American college students, no matter how successful it proved to be with the latter population.

If your study seeks to measure change over time, perhaps before and after receiving a social work intervention, you will need a scale that is sensitive to small changes over relatively short periods. Some clients, after being treated for low self-esteem, for example, might still have very low self-esteem as compared to the rest of the population, but they might have higher self-esteem than they did before the intervention. Some self-esteem scales might be able to detect this movement, while others might not, still simply indicating that these people have much lower self-esteem than the rest of the population.

Two very important issues to be considered in choosing a scale are the scale's reliability and validity. In the next chapter we'll be discussing in depth these two terms, which deal with statistical information on the measurement consistency of instruments and whether they really measure what they intend to measure. For now, we'll just note that the reference literature on existing scales will usually report whatever reliability and validity figures have been established for a particular scale. But interpret those figures with caution. If they are based on studies that tested the instrument on a population very unlike yours, or under study conditions unlike those of your study, they may have no bearing on the suitability of the instrument for your particular study. No matter how reliable and valid the reference literature says a scale may be, you may find that you have to modify it to adapt it to your particular study or that you cannot use it at all. Moreover, the way an instrument's reliability and validity were assessed may have been seriously flawed from a methodological standpoint, thus limiting the value of those figures, no matter how impressively high they may be. Therefore, you may want to go beyond the reference sourcebook that gives an overview of an existing scale, and examine firsthand the studies that reported the development and testing of the scale. With these issues in mind, we are ready to go from the beginning phases of measurement, conceptualization, and operationalization to the broader consideration of measurement in Chapter 6.

Main Points

- Hypotheses consist of independent variables (the postulated explanatory variable) and dependent variables (the variable being explained).

- Relationships between variables can be positive, negative, or curvilinear.

- Extraneous, or control, variables may be examined to see if the observed relationship is misleading.

- Concepts are mental images we use as summary devices for bringing together observations and experiences that seem to have something in common.

- Our concepts do not exist in the real world, so they can't be measured directly.

- It *is* possible to measure the things that our concepts summarize.

- Conceptualization is the process of specifying the vague mental imagery of our concepts, sorting out the kinds of observations and measurements that will be appropriate for our research.

- Operationalization is an extension of the conceptualization process.

- In operationalization, concrete empirical procedures that will result in measurements of variables are specified.

- Operationalization is the final specification of how we would recognize the different attributes of a given variable in the real world.

- In determining the range of variation for a variable, be sure to consider the opposite of the concept. Will it be sufficient to measure religiosity from "very much" to "none," or should you go past "none" to measure "antireligiosity" as well?

- Operationalization begins in study design and continues throughout the research project, including the analysis of data.

- Existing self-report scales are a popular way to operationally define many social work variables, largely because they have been used successfully by others and provide cost advantages in terms of time and money, but scales need to be selected carefully and are not always the best way to operationally define a variable.

- Additional ways to operationalize variables involve the use of direct behavioral observation, interviews, and available records.

- Qualitative studies eschew operational definitions, so that the researchers can immerse themselves in non-predetermined observations into the deeper subjective meanings of phenomena.

Review Questions and Exercises

1. Pick a social work concept, such as child neglect or abuse, quality of life, level of informal social support, and so forth, and specify that concept so that it could be studied in a research project. Be sure to specify the dimensions you wish to include (and those you wish to exclude) in your conceptualization.

2. Specify two hypotheses in which a particular concept is the independent variable in one of the hypotheses and the dependent variable in the other. Try to hypothesize one positive relationship and one negative, or inverse, relationship.

Additional Readings

Miller, Delbert, *Handbook of Research Design and Social Measurement* (New York: Longman, 1983). A useful reference work. This book, especially Part IV, cites and describes a wide variety of operational measures used in earlier social research.

In a number of cases, the questionnaire formats used are presented. Though the quality of these illustrations is uneven, they provide excellent examples of the variations possible.

Wallace, Walter, *The Logic of Science in Sociology* (Chicago: Aldine-Atherton, 1971), Chapter 3. A brief and lucid presentation of concept formation within the context of other research steps. This discussion relates conceptualization to observation on the one hand and to generalization on the other.

Measurement

What You'll Learn in This Chapter

Now we'll go from conceptualization and operationalization, the first steps in measurement, to a consideration of broader issues in the measurement process. After examining alternative levels of measurement, we'll look extensively at measurement error and how to avoid it.

INTRODUCTION

We have come some distance. After asserting that social workers can measure anything that exists, we discovered that many of the things we might want to measure and study really don't exist. Next we learned that it is possible to measure them anyway. We learned that the first step toward doing that is by operationally defining them—that is, we identify the operations, or indicators, that we will use to indicate the presence, absence, amount, or type of the concept we are studying.

We also learned that researchers have a wide variety of options available when they want to operationally define a concept and that it is possible to choose indicators that are imprecise or that represent something other than what they really seek to measure. No matter how we operationally define abstract concepts, and no matter how we go about collecting data on the indicators we select—whether we use self-report scales, available records, interviews, or direct observation—we need to be mindful of the extreme vulnerability of the measurement process to sources of measurement error. We must carefully plan to minimize the likelihood that those errors will occur and then take certain steps to check on the adequacy of our measures. How to do that will be the focus of this chapter.

Before we discuss measurement error, we will examine the four different levels of measurement. Then we will examine common sources of measurement error and different strategies to avoid those errors. Next we will consider the concepts of measurement reliability and validity and how we assess whether our measures are reliable and valid. We will conclude the chapter with an illustration of the foregoing material in a review of a clinical measurement package developed primarily for use by direct-service social work practitioners.

LEVELS OF MEASUREMENT

An attribute, you'll recall, is a characteristic or quality of something. *Female* would be an example. So would *old* or *student*. Variables, on the other hand, are logical sets of attributes. Thus, *sex* or *gender* is a variable composed of the attributes *female* and *male*. The conceptualization and operationalization processes can be seen as the specification of variables and the attributes composing them. Thus, in one of the examples given in the preceding chapter, employment status would be a variable having the attributes *employed* and *unemployed* (and perhaps others to include the other possibilities discussed).

Every variable should have two important qualities. First, the attributes composing it should be *exhaustive*. If the variable is to have any utility in research, you should be able to classify every observation in terms of one of the attributes composing the variable. You will run into trouble if you conceptualize the variable ethnicity in terms of the attributes white, black, Mexican American, or Puerto Rican because some of the people you set out to study may be Asian American, Native American, Cuban, Portuguese, or some other ethnicity. The same could happen if you conceptualized the variable religion in terms of Protestant, Catholic, or Jewish. Some individuals might be Moslem, Hindu, and so on, and some will tell you that they have no religious affiliation. You could make the list of attributes exhaustive by adding *other* and *no affiliation*. Whatever you do, you must be able to classify every observation.

At the same time, attributes composing a variable must be *mutually exclusive*. You must be able to classify every observation in terms of one and only one attribute. Thus, for example, you need to define *employed* and *unemployed* in such a way that nobody can be both at the same time. That means being able to handle the person who is working at a job and looking for work. (You might run across an employed accountant who is looking for the glamour and excitement of being a social worker.) In this case, you might define your attributes so that *employed* takes precedence over *unemployed* and anyone working at a job is employed regardless of whether he or she is looking for something better.

These qualities must be present among the attributes composing any variable. However, attributes may be related in other ways as well. Because of these additional relationships among their attributes, different variables may represent different *levels of measurement.* We are going to examine four levels of measurement in this section: *nominal, ordinal, interval,* and *ratio.*

Nominal Measures

Variables whose attributes have *only* the characteristics of exhaustiveness and mutual exclusiveness are **nominal measures.** Examples of these would be gender, ethnicity, religious affiliation, political party affiliation, birthplace, college major, and hair color. Although the attributes composing each of these variables—*male* and *female* for the variable gender—are distinct from one another and exhaust the possibilities of gender among people, they have none of the additional structures mentioned below.

It might be useful to imagine a group of people being characterized in terms of one such variable and then physically grouped by the applicable attributes. Imagine asking a large gathering of people to stand together in groups according to the states in which they were born: all those born in Vermont in one group, those born in California in another, and so forth. (The variable would be *place of birth;* the attributes would be *born in California, born in Vermont,* and so on.) All the people standing in a given group would share at least one thing in common; the people in any one group would differ from the people in all other groups in that same regard. Where the individual groups formed, how close they were to one another, or how the groups were arranged in the room would be irrelevant. All that would matter would be that all the members of a given group share the same state of birthplace and that each group has a different shared state of birthplace.

To facilitate the collection and processing of data, we assign different code numbers to the different categories, or attributes, of nominal variables. Thus, we might record a 1 to designate male and a 2 to designate female. But, unlike other levels of measurement, with nominal variables the code numbers have no *quantitative* meaning. They simply are a convenient device to record *qualitative* differences.

The word *nominal* comes from the same Latin root used in words like *nominate* and *nomenclature*—words that have something to do with naming. No matter what code number we may assign to them, no matter how high or low that number may be, the code refers only to a name, not an amount. Thus, if in coding ethnicity we assign a 1 to white, a 2 to black, a 3 to Hispanic, a 4 to Asian American, a 5 to Native American, and a 6 to "Other," we are not implying that someone with a higher code number has more of something than someone with a lower code number. An Asian American receiving a code 4 does not have more ethnicity than an African American receiving a code 2. Consequently, when we statistically analyze nominal data we cannot calculate a mean or a median. It would make no sense, for example, to say that the mean (average) ethnicity of an agency with the above six categories of ethnicity was 2.7. Our analysis would be restricted to calculating how many people were in the various categories, such as when we say that 40% of the caseload is white, 30% is black, 20% is Hispanic, and so on.

Ordinal Measures

Variables whose attributes may be logically *rank-ordered* are **ordinal measures.** The different attributes represent relatively more or less of the variable. Variables of this type are social class, racism, sexism, client satisfaction, and the like.

Note that each of these examples would be subject to serious differences of opinion concerning its definition. Many of the ordinal variables used in social scientific research have this quality, but it need not be the case. In the physical sciences, *hardness* is the most frequently cited example of an ordinal measure. We may say that one material (for example, diamond) is harder than another (say, glass) if the former can scratch the latter and not vice versa (that is, diamond scratches glass, but glass does not scratch diamond). By attempting to scratch various materials with other materials, we might eventually be able to arrange several materials in a row, ranging from the softest to the hardest. It would not ever be possible to say how hard a given material was in absolute terms, but only in relative terms—which materials it was harder than and which it was softer than.

Let's pursue the earlier example of grouping the people at a social gathering and imagine that we asked all the people who had graduated from college to stand in one group, all those with a high school diploma (but who were not also college graduates) to stand in another group, and all those who had not graduated from high school to stand in a third group. This manner of grouping people would satisfy the requirements for exhaustiveness and mutual exclusiveness discussed earlier. In addition, however, we might logically arrange the three groups in terms of the relative amount of formal education (the shared attribute) each had. We might arrange the three groups in a row, ranging from most to least formal education. This arrangement would provide a physical representation of an ordinal measure. If we knew which groups two individuals were in, we could determine that one had more, less, or the same amount of formal education as the other; in a similar way, one individual object could be ranked as harder, softer, or of the same hardness as another object.

It is important to note that in this example it would be irrelevant how close or far apart the educational groups were from one another. They might stand 5 feet apart or 500 feet apart; the college and high school groups could be 5 feet apart, while the less–than–high school group might be 500 feet farther down the line. These actual distances would not have any meaning. The high school group, however, should be between the less–than–high school group and the college group or else the rank order would be incorrect.

Another example of ordinal measurement would be to ask clients how satisfied they are with the services they received or to rate the quality of those services. We might ask them whether they are very satisfied, satisfied, dissatisfied, or very dissatisfied. This would tell us the *rank order* of their level of satisfaction, but it would not provide a quantity that allowed us to say that clients at one level of satisfaction were exactly twice as satisfied or three times more dissatisfied than clients at another level of satisfaction. Likewise, if one client rated the quality of the services as excellent and a second client rated them as good, we could say that the first client gave a higher rating to the services, but we could not say precisely how much higher the rating was. For example, we could not say that excellent is one-third better than good or two times better than good, and so on.

As with nominal measurement, we would assign code numbers to represent an individual's rank order. For instance, if clients are rating service quality on an ordinal scale with the categories excellent, good, fair, or poor, the codes might be excellent 4, good 3, fair 2, and poor 1. Unlike nominal measurement, these code numbers would have some quantitative meaning. That is, the code 4 would represent a higher rating than the code 3, and so on. But the quantitative meaning would be imprecise; it would not mean the same thing as having four children as opposed to three, two, one, or no children. Whereas we can say that a parent with four children has four times as many children as a parent with one child, we cannot say that a client who felt the services were excellent (code 4) found them four times better than the client who felt they were poor (code 1). The word *ordinal* is thus connected to the word *order,* and means that we know the order of the categories, only, not their precise quantities or the precise differences between them.

Interval Measures

For the attributes composing some variables, the actual distance separating those attributes does have meaning. Such variables are *interval measures*. For these, the logical distance between attributes can be expressed in meaningful standard intervals. A physical science example would be the Fahrenheit or the Celsius temperature scale. The difference, or distance, between 80 degrees and 90 degrees is the same as that between 40 degrees and 50 degrees. However, 80 degrees Fahrenheit is not twice as hot as 40 degrees Celsius because the zero point in the Fahrenheit and Celsius scales is arbitrary—zero degrees does not really mean lack of heat, nor does –30 degrees represent 30 degrees less than no heat. (The Kelvin scale is based on an *absolute zero,* which does mean a complete lack of heat.)

About the only interval measures commonly used in social scientific research are constructed measures, such as standardized intelligence tests that have been more or less accepted. The interval separating IQ scores of 100 and 110 may be regarded as the same as the interval separating scores of 110 and 120 by virtue of the distribution of observed scores obtained by many thousands of people who have taken the tests over the years. (A person who received a score of 0 on a standard IQ test could not be regarded, strictly speaking, as having *no* intelligence, although we might feel he or she was unsuited to be a college professor or even a college student.)

Ratio Measures

Most of the social scientific variables meeting the minimum requirements for interval measures also meet the requirements for **ratio measures.** In ratio measures, the attributes composing a variable, besides having all the structural characteristics just mentioned, are based on a true zero point. We have already mentioned the Kelvin temperature scale in contrast to the Fahrenheit and Celsius scales. Examples from social work research would include age, length of residence in a given place, number of children, number of service delivery contacts, number of days spent hospitalized, number of organizations belonged to, number of times married, and number of antisocial behaviors.

Returning to the illustration of methodological party games at a social gathering, we might ask people to group themselves by age. All the one-year-olds would stand (or sit or lie) together, the two-year-olds together, the three-year-olds

together, and so forth. The fact that members of a single group share the same age and that different groups have different shared ages satisfies the minimum requirements for a nominal measure. Arranging the several groups in a line from youngest to oldest meets the additional requirements of an ordinal measure and permits us to determine if one person is older than, younger than, or the same age as, another. If we arrange the groups so that they have the same distance between each pair of adjacent groups, we satisfy the additional requirements of an interval measure and will be able to say *how much* older one person is than another. Finally, because one of the attributes included in age represents a true zero (babies carried by women about to give birth), the phalanx of party goers also meets the requirements for a ratio measure, permitting us to say that one person is twice as old as another.

To review this discussion, Figure 6-1 presents a graphic illustration of the four levels of measurement.

Implications of Levels of Measurement

Because it is unlikely that you will undertake the physical grouping of people just described (try it once, and you won't be invited to many parties), we should draw your attention to some of the practical implications of the differences that have been distinguished. Primarily, such implications appear in the analysis of data (discussed in Part 5), but these analytic implications should be anticipated in the structuring of your research project. Certain analytic techniques require variables that meet certain minimum levels of measurement. To the extent that the variables to be examined in your research project are limited to a particular level of measurement—say, ordinal—you should plan your analytical techniques accordingly. More precisely, you should anticipate drawing research conclusions appropriate to the levels of measurement used for your variables. For example, you might reasonably plan to determine and report the mean age of a population under study (add up all the individual ages and divide

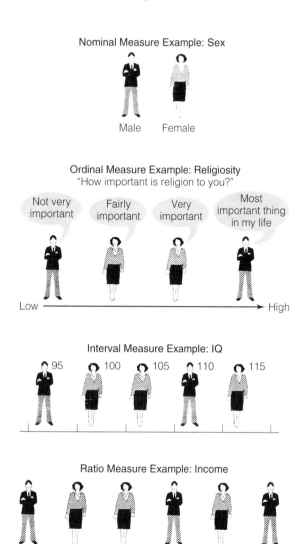

Figure 6-1 Levels of Measurement

by the number of people), but you should not plan on reporting the mean religious affiliation, since that is a nominal variable, and the mean requires interval or ratio-level data. (You could report the *modal*—the most common—religious affiliation.)

At the same time, it is important to realize that some variables may be treated as representing different levels of measurement. Ratio measures are the highest level, then interval, ordinal, and finally nominal, the lowest level of measurement. A variable representing a given level of measurement—say, ratio—may also be treated as representing a lower level of measurement—say, ordinal. Recall, for example, that age is a ratio measure. If you wished to examine only the relationship between age and some ordinal-level variable—say, self-perceived religiosity: high, medium, and low— you might choose to treat age as an ordinal-level variable as well. You might characterize the subjects of your study as *young, middle-aged,* and *old,* specifying what age range composed each of those groupings. Finally, age might be used as a nominal-level variable for certain research purposes. People might be grouped as being born during the depression of the 1930s or not. Another nominal measurement, based on birth date rather than just age, would be the grouping of people by astrological signs.

The analytic uses planned for a given variable, then, should determine the level of measurement to be sought. (Remember that some variables are inherently limited to a certain level.) If a variable is to be used in a variety of ways that require different levels of measurement, the study should be designed to achieve the highest level required. (For instance, if the subjects in a study are asked their exact ages, they can later be organized into ordinal or nominal groupings.)

You need not necessarily measure variables at their highest level of measurement, however. If you are sure you have no need for ages of people at higher than the ordinal level of measurement, you may simply ask people which among several age ranges they belong in: for example, their twenties, thirties, and so forth. Whenever your research purposes are not altogether clear, however, it is advisable to seek the highest level of measurement possible. Although ratio measures can later be reduced to ordinal ones, it is not possible to convert an ordinal measure to a ratio one.

More generally, you cannot convert a lower-level measure to a higher-level one. That is a one-way street worth remembering.

In Chapter 17, when we discuss *parametric* and *nonparametric* statistical tests, we'll be returning to this issue, since parametric statistical procedures require interval- or ratio-level data and nonparametric procedures are needed for ordinal- or nominal-level data.

SINGLE OR COMPOSITE INDICATORS

In presenting so many alternatives and choices for you to make in operationalizing social scientific variables, we realize that we may create a sense of uncertainty and insecurity. You may find yourself worrying about whether you will make the right choices. To counterbalance this feeling, let's add a momentary dash of certainty and stability.

Many social scientific variables have rather obvious, straightforward measures. No matter how you cut it, gender usually turns out to be a matter of male or female: a nominal-level variable that can be measured by a single observation—either looking or asking a question. Although you'll want to think about adopted and foster children, it's usually pretty easy to find out how many children a family has. And although some fine-tuning is possible, for most research purposes the resident population of a country is the resident population of that country—you can look it up in an almanac and know the answer. A great many variables, then, have obvious single indicators. If you can get just one piece of information, you have what you need.

Sometimes, however, there is no single indicator that will give you the measure that you really want for a variable. As discussed in Chapter 5, many concepts are subject to varying interpretations, each with several possible indicators. In these cases, you will want to make several observations for a given variable. You can then combine the several pieces of information you've col-

lected to create a *composite* measurement of the variable in question. Chapter 7, on constructing measurement instruments, discusses ways of doing that, so we'll give you only a simple illustration at this point.

Consider the concept *school performance*. Some young clients do well in school and others don't do so well in terms of their performance in courses. It might be useful to study that, perhaps asking what characteristics and experiences are related to high levels of performance, and many researchers have done just that. How should we measure overall performance? Each grade in any single course is a potential indicator of school performance, but in using any single course grade we run a risk that the one used will not be typical of the student's general performance. The solution to this problem is so firmly established that it is, of course, obvious to you: the *grade point average*. We assign numerical scores to each letter grade, total the points earned by a given student, and divide by the number of courses taken to obtain a composite measure. (If the courses vary in number of credits, adjustments are made in that regard.) It is often appropriate to create such composite measures in social research.

COMMON SOURCES OF MEASUREMENT ERROR

Common sources of measurement error come in two types, systematic error and random error. Let's begin with systematic error.

Systematic Error

Systematic error occurs when the information we collect reflects a false picture of the concept we seek to measure, either because of the way we collect the data or the dynamics of those providing the data. Sometimes our measures really don't measure what we think they are measuring. For example, measuring what people think is the right thing to do will not necessarily reflect what they themselves usually do. When we try to measure likely behavior by collecting data on attitudes or views, we may be making a big mistake. Words don't always match deeds. Some folks who espouse "liberal" views on issues like school busing end up moving to the suburbs or enrolling their children in private schools when it is their own kids who are going to be bused. Many who support the idea of locating residences for the mentally disabled in residential areas would fight efforts to locate one on their block.

Even when measures tap someone's true views, systematic error may occur in thinking that something else (that is, likely behavior) is being measured. Perhaps the most common way our measures systematically measure something other than what we think they are measuring is when **biases** are involved in the data collection. Biases can come in various forms. We may ask questions in a way that predisposes individuals to answer the way we want them to, or we may smile excessively or nod our heads in agreement when we get the answers that support our hypotheses. Or individuals may be biased to answer our questions in ways that distort their true views or behaviors. For instance, they may be biased to agree with whatever we say, or they may do or say things that will convey a favorable impression of themselves. The former bias, agreeing or disagreeing with most or all statements regardless of their content, is called the *acquiescent response set*. The latter bias, the tendency of people to say or do things that will make them or their reference group look good, is called the *social desirability bias*. Most researchers recognize the likely effect of a question that begins "Don't you agree with the president of the United States that . . ." and no reputable researcher would use such an item. Unhappily, the biasing effect of items and terms is far subtler than this example suggests.

The mere identification of an attitude or position with a prestigious person or agency can bias responses. The item "Do you agree or disagree with the statement in our professional code of ethics that . . ." would have a similar effect. We should make it clear that we are not suggesting that such wording will necessarily produce consensus or even a majority in support of the position identified with the prestigious person or agency, only that support would probably be increased over the support that would have been obtained without such identification. Questionnaire items can be biased negatively as well as positively. "Do you agree or disagree with the position of Adolf Hitler when he stated that . . ." is an example.

To further illustrate the ways in which different forms of wording questions can have relatively subtle biasing effects, we may consider Kenneth Rasinski's (1989) analysis of the results of several General Social Survey Studies of attitudes toward government spending. He found that the way programs were identified had an impact on the amount of public support they received. Here are some comparisons:

MORE SUPPORT	LESS SUPPORT
"Halting rising crime rate"	"Law enforcement"
"Dealing with drug addiction"	"Drug rehabilitation"
"Assistance to the poor"	"Welfare"
"Solving problems of big cities"	"Assistance to big cities"
"Improving conditions of blacks"	"Assistance to blacks"
"Protecting social security"	"Social security"

Asking practitioners about their treatment orientations can involve some subtle biases. Suppose you asked them if they agreed that they should try to motivate recently discharged mental patients to take their medications as prescribed. They might be predisposed to agree. It sounds right that patients should take the medicine that their physicians have prescribed for them and that social workers ought to help motivate the disabled to take better care of themselves. But suppose you asked whether they agreed that the principle of self-determination means that they should respect the right of these patients to refuse treatment and should therefore not urge them to take their medications if they don't want to.

As another example of bias, consider the following. In 1989 more than 20 national magazines simultaneously published a questionnaire as part of a survey of opinions on child care and family issues. (We first saw the questionnaire in the February 27, 1989, issue of the *New Republic*.) Readers were encouraged to tear out and complete the questionnaire and return it to "Your Family Matters" at a New York City address. At the top of the questionnaire readers were informed that the survey was being sponsored by the "nonpartisan advocates Child Care Action Campaign and the Great American Family Tour" and that a national cable television channel underwriting the survey would be airing a special documentary, *Hush Little Baby: The Challenge of Child Care*. Also at the top, in large bold letters, was the heading, "TELL THE PRESIDENT YOUR FAMILY MATTERS."

Under this build-up were the questionnaire items, beginning with the following two yes/no items:

1. Do you think the federal government pays enough attention to child care and other family concerns?

2. Do you think family issues should be a top priority for the president and Congress?

Some of the subsequent items asked for opinions about whether various levels of government should develop policies to make child care more available and affordable and should set minimum standards for child care centers.

You may note that there are at least three levels of bias in this survey. At one level, it is not hard for readers to discern in the heading of the questionnaire that the opinions desired by the surveyers are those that call for more government attention to child care and family issues. Indeed the heading instructs the reader to "tell the president your family matters." The second level of bias concerns the issue of who would bother to complete and mail in the questionnaire. People who care deeply about the issue of child care, especially those who strongly believe that more government attention to it is needed, were probably much more likely to respond than those who feel otherwise. (We will examine the latter level of bias—response rate bias—more closely in Chapter 11, on survey research.) The third level of bias has to do with what segments of the population are likely to see the questionnaire in the first place. Chances are that people who subscribe to and read the selected magazines are not representative of the rest of the population in regard to views on child care and family issues, and perhaps are more likely to share the views of the survey sponsors than are the rest of the population. (We will example that type of bias in Chapter 8, on sampling.)

Earlier we noted the potential for the *social desirability bias*. You need to be especially wary of this bias. Whenever you ask people for information, they answer through a filter of what will make them look good. That is especially true if they are being interviewed in a face-to-face situation. Thus, for example, a particular man may feel that things would be a lot better if women were kept in the kitchen, not allowed to vote, forced to be quiet in public, and so forth. Asked whether he supports equal rights for women, however, he may want to avoid looking like a male chauvinist pig. Recognizing that his views might have been progressive in the 15th century but are out of step with current thinking, he may choose to say yes. The main guidance we can offer you in relation to this problem is to suggest that you imagine how you would feel giving each of the answers you offered to respondents. If you'd feel embarrassed, perverted, inhumane, stupid, irresponsible, or anything like that, you should give some serious thought to whether others will be willing

AMERICANS CAUGHT EATING MORE, BUT REPORTING IT LESS

by Mike Toner

Nutritionists have discovered a national fudge factor—one that has more to do with dietary deception than chocolate confection.

Since the 1970s, Americans have been telling government researchers, in survey after survey, that they are eating less. But the average weight, and girth, of the country's population has grown steadily during the same period.

Now, scientists at the U.S. Department of Agriculture say they may have the explanation. When it comes to dietary disclosure, four out of five Americans indulge in what researchers charitably call "underreporting."

Dr. Walter Mertz, director of the USDA's Human Nutrition Center, says it's not that people are trying to fool researchers about what they eat. In a country where the pursuit of thinness is a national obsession, most people apparently are fooling themselves.

Mertz says on the average, people genuinely believe they're eating 18 percent—about 500 calories—less than they actually consume.

A missing cheeseburger a day might not seem like much, but researchers say when these attacks of dietary amnesia are multiplied by month-long studies, factored into dozens of nutritional studies, and extrapolated to the eating habits of 250 million Americans, they leave the nation's nutritional policies on shaky statistical ground.

"The vast majority of food consumption and nutrient intake data used to set national policies comes from individuals' recalling or recording what they ate," Mertz told the a [sic] meeting of the Federation of American Societies of Experimental Biology Thursday in Atlanta.

"If the average person is eating 18 percent more calories than our surveys show, we may be wrong in thinking that they are getting too little of certain nutrients like vitamin B6, zinc, magnesium, and iron. On the other hand, they

to give those answers. The box titled "Americans Caught Eating More, But Reporting It Less" provides an amusing example of the social desirability bias in action. We will have more to say about the social desirability bias later in this chapter and in forthcoming chapters on data collection methods and on single-subject designs.

Cultural Bias Another common source of bias stems from cultural disparities. Intelligence tests, for example, have been cited as biased against certain ethnic minority groups. The argument is posed that children growing up in an economically disadvantaged environment that has different values, opportunities, and speaking patterns are at a disadvantage when they take IQ tests geared to a white, middle-class environment. It is argued, for example, that a minority child may score lower than a white child of equal or lower intelligence simply because the language of the

may also be consuming more fat and cholesterol than we think, too."

To find out what people really eat, USDA researchers selected 266 volunteers from a dozen earlier nutritional studies and fed them exactly what they had reported eating. Most participants lost weight. By adjusting the menu, researchers found that it took an average of 500 additional calories a day to maintain the volunteers' weight—a crude measure of their dietary fudging.

If the results are representative of the U.S. population, Mertz says, men and women are equally likely to "forget" to report the food they consume. Overweight people are more likely than thin ones to forget a few hundred calories—but they were also more likely to overreport.

Nutritionists aren't sure how to deal with Americans' aversion to full dietary disclosure. Some experiments suggest that tightening the rules for reporting actually makes the problem worse.

Mertz says future nutritional surveys may need a team of psychologists to overcome the fudge factor.

"This is not conscious cheating we are seeing," says Mertz. "But people are prone to idealize their weight, and I suspect that many of them are subconsciously motivated to underreport by the belief in our society that maintaining a low body weight contributes to good health."

"In some countries (where) a fat body is a sign of wealth, as it is in India, there is some evidence that people actually overreport what they eat."

Cox News Service (*Austin American Statesman*, Friday, April 26, 1991, pp. 1, 6). Reprinted by permission of Mike Toner.

questions is less familiar or because the questions refer to material things that white, middle-class children take for granted but that disadvantaged children never heard of.

Although this argument is controversial, the potential for cultural bias in measurement is not. Suppose, for example, that you are conducting a survey to see whether recent immigrants to the United States from Asia are less likely to utilize social services than are second- or third-generation Asian Americans. If the recent immigrants, because of language difficulties, don't understand your questions to mean the same thing as do the other groups, then differences in the data between the groups may have less to do with differences in their views on social service utilization than with the systematic language bias in your questions.

Monette, Sullivan, and DeJong (1994) illustrated a similar phenomenon in regard to a study

METHODOLOGICAL PROBLEMS IN THE STUDY OF KOREAN IMMIGRANTS: LINGUISTIC AND CONCEPTUAL PROBLEMS

In most research with non-Westerners, the first obstacle is the language barrier. Since some of our interviewers and the majority of our respondents had difficulty using either spoken or written English, our interview schedules were translated into Korean by the investigators themselves, all of whom are native-born Koreans and bilingual. This translated version was administered to 30 or 40 immigrants as a pretest. On the basis of suggestions and comments given by the respondents, a number of questions were reworded, added, or eliminated. Pretest interviewers also participated in the preparation of the final version. The difficulties of translation between Western and non-Western languages are well known. Many words are just not translatable even literally; for instance, *full-time* or *part-time, random sampling,* or even *community.* As in other Oriental languages, one must also pay a great deal of attention to honorifics when translating from English to Korean.

The most difficult problem, however, was conceptual ambiguity. In our first study, social invitations were used as an index of social assimilation. Our respondents were asked, "How often have you been invited by Americans to their homes in the past year (excluding business-related ones)?" Another question was, "How often have you invited Americans to your home in the past year?" Invitation was translated into Korean as *cho dae.* While the English *invitation* is used to request the presence of a person at a variety of occasions, the Korean *cho dae* means to request the presence of a person at a formal dinner or occasion, usually for a well-prepared entertainment. Thus, *cho dae* has a more restricted meaning than *invitation.* Certainly the problem of conceptual equivalence is paramount. In another study, we investigated marital roles in Korean immigrant families. For our study, we used the instrument which Blood and Wolfe (1960) had developed for their study of American families in the Detroit area. The Korean translation of some terms resulted in negative connotations which could stiffen a Korean man's resistance to the sharing of marital roles (for example, *grocery shopping* or *dish washing*).

The following examples are not necessarily unique to non-Western research. Many respondents reported their family incomes instead of individual incomes. When they were asked, "How often have you changed your residence since you arrived in the Chicago area?" a number of unanticipated questions were raised. Does the frequency of moving in-

of the mental health of Native Americans. In that study, the word *blue* had to be dropped from an instrument measuring depression because *blue* did not mean "sad" among Native Americans.

The same study found that to avoid cultural bias in assessing the utilization of mental health services, traditional healers (what you may call faith healers or spiritualists) had to be added to the list

clude the changes of address before marriage? If so, are we asking for the frequency of the husband's or the wife's moves? Does a move include a change of apartment in the same building? In addition, some of our respondents did not recall how often they moved, and often a husband and wife disagreed.

Our respondents were supposed to answer the question, "How well do you speak English?" with one of the following: (a) fluent; (b) good; (c) fair; (d) poor; (e) not at all. Since this is a self-evaluation of English ability, it is debatable how many of our respondents would actually choose the first or the last category. They would probably exaggerate or underestimate a little to avoid these extremes because this is "normal, polite, and intelligent" Korean behavior. Only six percent of our respondents said they spoke English fluently, while two percent replied that they spoke no English, although many respondents in our first study indicated that English language was their most important problem. The fact that 75 percent of our respondents reported their English speaking ability was "fair" to "good" might be reliable but certainly not valid information.

In our first study we wanted to know if our respondents would like to return to Korea after their retirement. However, the Korean version of the question did not specifically refer to retirement. We did not use the Korean term *twae jik* because the connotation is much narrower than the English word *retirement*. Normally, *twae jik* means disengagement from an official or public position accompanied by a pension or retirement benefit. Disengagement from self-employment is not *twae jik*. The conceptual equivalence of the English retirement, we thought, would be a composite of the following: "When you get old, you won't have to work and can take things easy for the rest of your life." Our question was, "When you get old, would you like to return to Korea and wish to spend the rest of your life there?" No wonder the overwhelming majority (82 percent) of our respondents wanted to go back to their native country and take things easy for the rest of their lives! It turned out that we had asked about their dreams, rather than their plans.

Won Moo Hurh and Kwang Chung Kim, "Methodological Problems in the Study of Korean Immigrants: Conceptual, Interactional, Sampling and Interviewer Training Difficulties," in William T. Liv (ed.), *Methodological Problems in Minority Research* (Chicago: Pacific/Asian American Mental Health Research Center, 1982), pp. 61–80. Used by permission.

of professionals from whom Native Americans might seek help.

In the box titled "Methodological Problems in the Study of Korean Immigrants: Linguistic and Conceptual Problems," two researchers discuss cultural bias and other forms of measurement error in connection to their experiences surveying Korean immigrants in the Chicago area.

Random Error

Unlike systematic errors, **random errors** have no consistent pattern of effects. The effect of random errors is not to bias our measures, but to make them inconsistent from one measurement to the next. This does not mean that whenever data change over time we have random error. Sometimes things really do change, and when they do our measures should detect that change. What it does mean is that if the things we are measuring do not change over time but our measures keep coming up with different results, then we have inconsistencies in measurement, or random error.

Random errors can take various forms. Perhaps our measurement procedures are so cumbersome, complex, boring, or fatiguing that our subjects say or do things at random just to get the measurement over with as quickly as possible. For example, halfway through a lengthy questionnaire full of complicated questions, respondents may stop giving much thought to what the questions really mean or how they truly feel about them.

Another example might be when two raters are recording the number of times a social worker gives an empathic response in a videotaped interview with a client. If the raters are not really sure how to recognize an empathic response when they see one, they may disagree substantially about how many empathic responses they observed in the same videotape. Note the difference between this sort of error and systematic error. If one of the raters was the videotaped social worker's mentor or fiancee and the other rater was the social worker's rival for a promotion, then the differences in the ratings would probably be due to systematic error.

For yet another example of random error, suppose clients who have no familiarity with social service jargon are asked whether they have received brokerage, advocacy, or linkage services. Odds are they would have no idea what those terms meant. Not understanding what they were being asked but not wishing to appear ignorant or uncooperative, they might answer yes or no at random, and they might change their answers the next time they were asked, even though the situation had not changed. That would represent random error. But suppose that even though they had no earthly idea what they were being asked, they suspected that an affirmative response would make them or their social worker look better. If they therefore responded affirmatively to every question just so they would not appear negativistic or get any practitioners in trouble, that would represent systematic error associated with a social desirability bias or acquiescent response set.

Although the term *bias* may sound more insidious than random error or inconsistency in measurement, random error can be a very serious problem. Suppose, for example, that an extremely effective school social work intervention to improve the self-esteem of underachieving third-graders is being evaluated. Suppose further that the measurement instrument selected for the evaluation was constructed for use with well-educated adults and that the researchers evaluating the intervention were unaware of the fact that underachieving third-graders would not understand many of the items on the instrument. This lack of understanding would mean that the children's responses would be largely random and would have little to do with their level of self-esteem. Since many of the answers would be random and have little bearing on self-esteem, the likelihood that the instrument would detect significant increases in self-esteem, even after an effective intervention, would be slim. Random error in measurement, therefore, can make a very effective intervention look ineffective.

An Illustration of Measurement Error

Let's consider an example of potential systematic error connected to the deinstitutionalization movement in mental health. When state officials began to massively discharge chronically mentally disabled individuals after lengthy periods of institutionalization, part of their rationale was that social workers and other direct-care staff employed by federally funded community mental health centers would assure that these individuals got the services they needed to help them adjust to and live adequately in the community. After all, offsetting institutionalization was one of the main formal goals of the community mental health movement.

But before the massive discharges began, community mental health professionals had grown accustomed to a different service model. That model was geared to individuals whose problems were less severe and less chronic. These clients, commonly referred to as the "healthy but unhappy," or the "worried well," were not disabled and tended to desire and receive forms of psychotherapy that are contraindicated for clients whose disabilities are chronic. In the wake of massive state hospital discharges, practitioners who had been trained and were experienced in providing modalities for acute intervention were suddenly expected to provide modalities for the rehabilitation and care of disabled individuals who were less verbal, who had difficulty performing even simple daily living tasks, and who needed case management, brokerage, and advocacy more than in-depth psychotherapy.

Many individuals' self-care skills had atrophied after years of institutionalized dependency. Therefore, many of them needed directive, rehabilitative services to help learn the simple tasks of daily living. For example, they might need someone to accompany them as they first tried to learn how to use public transportation or to shop for groceries. Not only were such tasks difficult for them, but attempting to do them right after discharge could overwhelm them with anxiety and conceivably could exacerbate their symptomatology.

From the standpoint of planning service delivery, the problem was that many community mental health practitioners were not familiar with the needs of chronically mentally disabled individuals. And would those among them who were familiar with these needs be willing to provide services that, in contrast to psychotherapy, might seem very mundane? Moreover, the community mental health staff being relied on to see that these individuals' needs got met often did not have

other community support resources to which they could refer these individuals, and they were likely to perceive modalities for the rehabilitation and care of the chronically disabled a waste of their talents. To assess the extent of this problem in their own agencies or regions, some planners and administrators of state and community mental health programs implemented surveys of community mental health practitioners to measure their attitudes about providing recommended modalities of service to this new target population. Rubin and Johnson (1982) had developed a scale to measure these attitudes and had numerous requests for it for such purposes.

Practitioners indicated on the scale just how important they felt certain service delivery functions were when treating the chronically mentally disabled. But interpreting the meaning of their responses was difficult. All of these social workers might agree that clients would benefit from having someone accompany them to help alleviate their anxiety and enhance their learning when they first set out to take on basic living tasks that could overwhelm them. But does their response mean that they would enthusiastically perform the task themselves if they were on the treatment team assigned to the case? Or does it mean that they think it is a great idea and someone should do it—someone at a lower level of professional status than themselves, perhaps a paraprofessional or a volunteer? Suppose all practitioners working with cases like these fancied themselves to be sophisticated psychotherapists whose expertise would be wasted if they were delivering concrete services but who believed that it was crucial that somebody (else) perform these services. Suppose everyone responded that such concrete tasks were all very important. What will have been measured? If administrators or planners thought the scale measured whether these practitioners were likely to perform the unattractive tasks themselves or how enthusiastic they would be in performing them, they might be making a big mistake. Although the practitioners might think those things are important, perhaps they think someone else should do them. They would also say it is important to keep institutional latrines clean, but that doesn't mean they would do it. And if forced to do those tasks, they might not be very enthusiastic. So even if a uniformly high level of importance were attached to the preceding services, the clients might not really receive them as intended because every practitioner might think that someone else ought to provide them. But suppose that instead of asking how important the tasks were, we asked how likely the practitioners were to perform those tasks themselves. Or suppose we asked how often they already perform those tasks now. If we got positive responses to those questions, then we might have more grounds for optimism about clients receiving those services.

But we still could not be certain that the respondents' deeds would match their words. We have various clichés for this point, such as "Actions speak louder than words." Perhaps the practitioners knew that policymakers and administrators expected them to respond favorably to the questions and therefore, in contrast to their real views, the practitioners just told them what they thought they wanted to hear. This would be a particularly plausible explanation if they thought that their responses were not anonymous. Or, maybe they were simply in an agreeable frame of mind in which they associated negative responses with some sort of negativistic character disorder.

What if, instead of asking the practitioners about the preceding functions, we decided to accompany each of them for a day to observe what they actually do. Perhaps then we would have a better indicator of their attitudes about the referent tasks and their propensity to perform them. Or perhaps we would not. Perhaps the practitioners would act out of character to make a favorable impression on us. Maybe if we asked the clients whether they received the needed services we would get better information. But we wouldn't if we were to ask the questions in a way that the clients didn't understand, for then the clients would give answers that didn't mean what we thought they meant.

We might want to investigate what practitioners actually do by analyzing their case records.

Then we wouldn't have to worry about someone trying to impress us favorably, telling us what we want to hear, or giving answers that didn't really mean what we thought they meant. Or would we? Maybe practitioners exaggerate their records on the amount of time they spend on various activities in the belief that someone might use those records to evaluate their performance. Maybe they resent all the record keeping that is expected of them and therefore are not careful in documenting the tasks they perform. At this juncture you may be thinking, "Egad, what is the point of this example? Are you saying that the measurement process is so fraught with error that research is hardly worth doing?" No, we are not saying that. But we are saying that the measurement process is extremely vulnerable to errors, that we need to be very aware of the potential for these errors to occur, and that we must take steps to deal with them.

AVOIDING MEASUREMENT ERROR

It is virtually impossible to avoid all possible sources of measurement error. Even if all we do is canvass an agency's caseload to describe the proportions of male and female clients of different ages and ethnic groups, chances are we will have some measurement error. For instance, there may be clerical oversights in recording data, coding them, or typing them for computer input. Even relatively concrete concepts like ethnicity can be misunderstood by respondents to surveys. About 20 years ago, for example, the Council on Social Work Education was asked by some of its Native American constituents to change one item on the questionnaire it used in its annual canvass of schools of social work. The item pertained to the ethnicity of faculty members, and the request was to change the category that previously read *American Indian* to read *Native American*. The requested modification was made. In the first year after that change there was a large jump in the number of Native American faculty members reported. In fact, some schools that reported having only white faculty members the year before now reported having only Native American faculty members. Fortunately, by comparing the data to the previous year's report from each school, the measurement error was easy to detect and correct. The clerical staff members who had completed the questionnaire in certain schools thought that the term *Native American* referred to anyone born in the United States, regardless of their ethnicity.

No one should be dissuaded from pursuing research simply because of the inevitability of having some measurement errors. No one expects a study to have perfect measurement, at least not in the field of social scientific research. What matters is that you take steps to minimize any major measurement errors that would destroy the credibility and utility of your findings and to assess how well your measures appear to have kept those errors from exceeding a reasonable level.

Because measurement errors can occur in a myriad of ways, it is not easy to tell you how to avoid them. The sorts of steps you can take depend in large part on the type of data collection methods you use. We will discuss those steps in Chapter 7, on constructing measurement instruments, and in Part 4, when we consider alternative data collection methods in separate chapters. But here is a brief preview of a few of those steps, just to give you an idea of the sorts of things that can be done.

If you are constructing a questionnaire or self-report scale, try to use unbiased wording (to minimize systematic error) and terms that respondents will understand (to minimize random error). Obtain collegial feedback to help spot biases or ambiguities that you may have overlooked. (Because we know what we mean by what we write, it is easy for us to be unaware of ambiguities in our wording.) And be sure to test the questionnaire in a dry run to see if your target population will understand it and not find it too unwieldy.

If you are using people to conduct interviews or rate behaviors they observe, be sure to train them carefully, and make sure that they are con-

sistent in how they perform their tasks. Also attempt to minimize the extent to which they can be influenced by biases. For example, if they are collecting information on how well clients function before and after an intervention as compared to individuals who receive no intervention, try to keep your data collectors blind as to whether any particular measure is being taken before or after the intervention or on whether or not an individual received the intervention.

The box titled "Further Notes on Methodology: Interviewing Asians" shows how researchers studying Asian American minorities in the United States tried to avoid measurement errors associated with interviewer insensitivity to differences in cultural norms.

If your measurement involves direct observation of behaviors, try to arrange the situation so that the client is not keenly aware that observations are occurring and is therefore less likely to act out of character in order to look good. This is known as *unobtrusive observation,* and it is used to minimize the social desirability bias. We will return to the concept of unobtrusive observation in several forthcoming chapters.

If your measurement relies on the use of available records, don't just assume that because an agency values those records, or because they are "official," that they are therefore sufficiently free of error. Talk to agency practitioners and others "in the know" about how carefully or haphazardly records are kept. Probe about any possible reasons why those who enter the data might be influenced by certain biases that reduce your confidence in the validity of what they record.

There are several other data collection steps that are rather generic in nature and whose use cuts across the many data collection alternatives. One such step involves the principle of **triangulation.** Triangulation deals with systematic error by using several different research methods to collect the same information. Since there is no one foolproof method for avoiding systematic measurement error, we can use several imperfect measurement alternatives and see if they tend to produce the same findings. If they do, then we can have more

FURTHER NOTES ON METHODOLOGY:
INTERVIEWING ASIANS

If the successive goals of any scientific inquiry are to describe, explain, and predict, much Asian American research will come under the category of description. An important means of securing this information in its full depth is the intensive face-to-face interview. We ruled out the use of mailed questionnaires for this study because of an astonishingly high rate of nonresponse in other studies of Asian Americans.

It was not an easy task to secure interviews from some of the Asian groups. While Indians and Pakistanis were eager to be interviewed and had a lot to say, members of the Chinese, Korean, and Filipino groups were reluctant to participate. Some of them not only refused to grant interviews but also refused to give names of potential respondents in their ethnic groups. Since we had adopted a snowball approach [Chapter 8] in identifying members of different ethnic groups and the potential respondents in each group, such refusal inordinately delayed completion of the fieldwork. In the interviews we found that the high value of modesty in Asian cultural backgrounds, the gratefulness to America for homes and jobs, a vague fear of losing both in case something went wrong, and the consequent unwillingness to speak ill of the host country, made the Asian American re-sponse to any question about life and work likely to be positive, especially if the interviewer was white. We found that the only way to resolve this critical dilemma was in establishing rapport and checking and rechecking each response. For example, after an extensive account of how satisfying his job was, a male Filipino respondent almost reversed his account as soon as the tape recorder was turned off. In another case, a male respondent from India admitted off-record that life in America was not a bed of roses, even though he had earlier painted a rosy picture.

Aggressive interviewing is not likely to produce the desired results, but may make a respondent timid and constrained. We found that a white male interviewer is unsuitable for interviewing Asian women, not because he is aggressive but because he is likely to be defined as such in terms of cultural norms. Lack of empathy and cultural appreciation on the part of the interviewer, or a chance comment or exclamation which is defined negatively by the respondent may shut off the flow of response. For example, during an interview between a Filipino female respondent and a white female interviewer, the respondent mentioned that her brother was living with her along with her husband and children. The interviewer exclaimed, wondering aloud if her

confidence (but no guarantee) that measurement error is at an acceptable level. If one method yields data that sharply conflict with the data provided by alternative measures, then we have reason to suspect some serious errors somewhere and have some clues as to where they may have occurred. Triangulation requires that the different measures have different potential sources of error. If we ex-husband and children did not mind such an arrangement. Thinking that she had probably committed some cultural "goof," the Filipino respondent just dried up. All her later responses were cut and dried and "correct."

We found that it was most expedient to match a female respondent with a female interviewer from another Asian national background. Sameness of nationality may constrain responses, as respondents may be afraid that confidential information may be divulged. However, it may not be wise for a female Asian to interview an Asian man; the strong patriarchal feeling of Asian men may play a confounding role in their responses. Thus, it would seem that only men would be appropriate interviewers for Asian men.

We recognize, however, that there is no foolproof formula for conducting an interview which would assure its complete integrity. A white man interviewing an Asian man will insure confidentiality, objectivity, and impartiality, but there may be a lack of the cultural appreciation and sensitivity so important for handling sensitive cultural data. On the other hand, an Asian or white female interviewer may provoke boastful responses from an Asian man.

Finally, the most intriguing aspects of in-depth interview situations with Asian Americans is the seeming inconsistency of responses, which may, at times, border on contradiction. It is not uncommon to find Asians simultaneously attracted to and repulsed by some aspect of a person, symbol, value, or system. This way of thought has to be understood in the context of Chinese, Japanese, or Indian philosophic values which view an absolute system of value with uneasiness. This is very different from the typical Western mind which abhors paradoxes and contradictions, or anything that is not clear, well-defined, and determined [Mehta, Asoka, *Perception of Asian Personality*. Calcutta: S. Chand, 1978; Nandi, Proshanta K., "The Quality of Life of Asian Americans in Middle Size Cities: A Neglected Area of Research," in *Bridge* 5(4): 51–53, 59]. This dualism among Asian Americans is likely to pose a major challenge to conventional research techniques in both gathering and interpretation of data.

Nandi, Proshanta K., "Surveying Asian Minorities in the Middle-Sized City," in William T. Liv (ed.), *Methodological Problems in Minority Research* (Chicago: Pacific/Asian American Mental Health Research Center, 1982), pp. 81–92. Used by permission.

pect each measure to be vulnerable to the same sources of error, then consistency among the measures would not really tell us whether that source of systematic error was being avoided.

For instance, suppose we assess practitioner responsivity to the chronically mentally disabled in three ways, as follows: (1) we assess their self-reported attitudes about treating the disabled,

(2) we ask disabled clients about the amount of contact they had with the practitioners and how satisfied they were with the help they received, and (3) we survey case records to tabulate the amount of services practitioners provided to disabled clients. Suppose the practitioners all say that they derive great satisfaction from treating disabled clients but that the case records show that disabled clients usually receive only two or fewer contacts from them and then are no longer followed. Suppose further that the large majority of disabled clients corroborate the case records in terms of the amount of service they received and add that the practitioner seemed impatient with their slowness and disinterested in the problems that they felt were most important. Having triangulated your measures, you would be in a far better position to judge the credibility of your data than if you had used only one of the preceding measures. Moreover, you would be able to avoid the apparent errors inherent in measuring practitioner attitudes, errors that seem to be associated with a social desirability bias, which you would not have been able to avoid had you measured those attitudes and nothing else.

The other generic steps you can take to try to minimize measurement error are closely related to the principle of triangulation. They involve making sure, before you implement the study, that the measurement procedures you will use have acceptable levels of reliability and validity. Reliability and validity are two of the most important concepts you can learn about research methods. Each of these concepts will be discussed thoroughly throughout this chapter.

RELIABILITY

In the abstract sense, *reliability* is a matter of whether a particular technique, applied repeatedly to the same object, would yield the same result each time. Thus, reliability has to do with the amount of random error in a measurement. The more reliable the measure, the less random error in it.

Returning for a moment to the use of the first person singular, suppose that I asked you to estimate how much I weigh. You look me over carefully and guess that I weigh 165 pounds. (Thank you.) Now let's suppose I ask you to estimate the weights of 30 or 40 other people, and while you're engrossed in that, I slip back into line wearing a clever disguise. When my turn comes again, you guess 180 pounds. Gotcha! That little exercise would have demonstrated that having you estimate people's weights was not a very reliable technique.

Suppose, however, that I had loaned you my bathroom scale to use in weighing people. No matter how clever my disguise, you would presumably announce the same weight for me both times, indicating that the scale provided a more reliable measure of weight than guessing.

Reliability, however, does not ensure accuracy. Suppose I've set my bathroom scale to shave five pounds off my weight just to make me feel better. Although you would (reliably) report the same weight for me each time, you would always be wrong due to systematic error (that is, a biased scale).

Here's an example illustrating the problem of reliability. Jeffrey Sacks and his colleagues (1980) focused their attention on Health Hazard Appraisal, a part of preventive medicine. Their purpose was to determine the risks associated with various background and lifestyle factors to make it possible for physicians to counsel their patients appropriately. By knowing patients' life situations, physicians could advise them on their potential for survival and how to improve it. The usefulness of their advice, of course, depended heavily on the accuracy of the information gathered about each subject in the study.

To test the reliability of their information, Sacks and his colleagues had all 207 subjects complete a baseline questionnaire that asked about their characteristics and behavior. Three months later, a follow-up questionnaire asked the same subjects for the same information, and the results of the two surveys were compared. Overall, only 15% of the subjects reported the same information in both studies.

Sacks observes (1980:730): "Almost 10% of subjects reported a different height at follow-up examination. Parental age was changed by over one in three subjects. One parent reportedly aged 20 chronologic years in three months. One in five ex-smokers and ex-drinkers have apparent difficulty in reliably recalling their previous consumption pattern."

Some subjects erased all trace of previously reported heart murmur, diabetes, emphysema, arrest record, and thoughts of suicide. One subject's mother, deceased in the first questionnaire, was apparently alive and well in time for the second. One subject had one ovary missing in the first study, but it was present in the second. In another case, an ovary present in the first study was missing in the second study—and had been for 10 years! One subject was reportedly 55 years old in the first study and 50 years old three months later. You have to wonder if the physician-counselors could have had nearly the impact on their patients as their patients' memories did. Thus, the data collection method was not especially reliable.

Here's another example, a hypothetical one. Let's suppose that we are interested in studying morale among social workers in two different kinds of agencies. One set is composed of public assistance agencies; the other is composed of family service agencies. How should we measure morale? Following one strategy, we could spend some time observing the workers in each agency, noticing such things as whether they joke with one another, whether they smile and laugh a lot, and so forth. We could ask them how they like their work and even ask them whether they think they would prefer their current setting or the other one being studied. By comparing what we observed in the different agencies, we might reach a conclusion concerning which setting produced the higher morale.

Now let's look at some of the possible problems of reliability inherent in this method. First of all, how we feel when we do the observing is likely to color what we see. We may misinterpret what we see. We may see workers kidding each other and think they are having an argument. Or

maybe we'll catch them on an off day. If we were to observe the same group of workers several days in a row, we might arrive at different evaluations on each day. And if several observers evaluated the same behavior, they too might arrive at different conclusions about the workers' morale.

Here's another strategy for assessing morale. Suppose we check the agency records to see how many worker resignations occurred during some fixed period of time. Presumably that would be an indicator of morale: the more resignations, the lower the morale. This measurement strategy would appear to be more reliable: We could count up the resignations over and over and we should keep arriving at the same number.

If you find yourself saying "Wait a minute" over the second measurement strategy, you're worrying about validity, not reliability. Let's complete the discussion of reliability, and then we'll return to validity.

Reliability problems crop up in many forms in social research. Survey researchers have known for a long time that different interviewers get different answers from respondents as a result of their own attitudes and demeanors. If we were to conduct a study of editorial positions on some public issue, we might assemble a team of coders to take on the job of reading hundreds of editorials and classifying them in terms of each's position on the issue. Different coders would code the same editorial differently. Or we might want to classify a few hundred specific occupations in terms of some standard coding scheme, say a set of categories created by the Department of Labor or by the Bureau of the Census. Not all of us would code all those occupations into the same categories. Each of these examples illustrates problems of reliability. Similar problems arise whenever we ask people to give us information about themselves. Sometimes we ask questions that people don't know the answers to. (How many times have you been to church?) Sometimes we ask people about things that are totally irrelevant to them. (Are you satisfied with China's current relationship with Albania?) And sometimes we ask questions that are so complicated that a person who had a clear opinion on the matter might arrive at a different interpretation of the question upon being asked a second time. How do you create reliable measures? There are a number of techniques. First, in asking people for information—if your research design calls for that—be careful to ask only about things the respondents are likely to know the answer to. Ask about things relevant to them and be clear in what you're asking. The danger in these instances is that people will give you answers—reliable or not. People will tell you what they think about China's relationship with Albania even if they haven't the foggiest idea what that relationship is.

Another way to handle the problem of reliability in getting information from people is to use measures that have proven their reliability in previous research. In the case of unreliability generated by research workers, there are several solutions. To guard against interviewer unreliability, it is common practice in surveys to have a supervisor call a subsample of the respondents on the telephone and verify selected pieces of information. Replication works in other situations as well. If you are worried that newspaper editorials or occupations may not be classified reliably, why not have each independently coded by several coders? Those that generate disagreement should be evaluated more carefully and resolved.

Finally, clarity, specificity, training, and practice will avoid a great deal of unreliability and grief. If we were to spend some time with you reaching a clear agreement on how we were going to evaluate editorial positions on an issue—discussing the various positions that might be represented and reading through several together—we'd probably be able to do a good job of classifying them in the same way independently.

Types of Reliability

The type of measurement reliability that is most relevant to a particular study varies according to the purpose and design of the study. If the study involves judgments made by observers or raters, for example, then we need to assess the extent of agreement, or consistency, between observers or raters. This is called **interobserver reliability** or **interrater reliability.** Suppose you are studying whether an in-service training program for paraprofessionals or volunteers increases the level of empathy they express in videotaped role-play situations. To assess interrater reliability you would train two raters; then you would have them view the same videotapes and independently rate the level of empathy they observed in each. If they agree about 80% of the time or more in their ratings, you can assume that the amount of random error in measurement is not excessive. Some would argue that even 70% agreement would be acceptable.

Instead of calculating the percent of agreement, you might want to calculate the correlation between the two sets of ratings. For example, suppose the ratings are on a scale from 1 to 10 and that although the two raters rarely choose the exact same rating, they both tend to give high or low ratings in a consistent fashion. That is, one pair of ratings might be a 9 and an 8, and another pair might be a 2 and a 3. As one rater goes up, the other rater goes up. As one goes down, the other goes down. Although they rarely agree on the exact number, they move up and down together. If so, although the percentage of agreement might be low, the correlation might be high, perhaps above .80. We will discuss correlation later in Part 5. At this point it is sufficient to know that correlations can range from 0 (meaning no relationship—no correlation) to 1.0 (meaning a perfect relationship with no random error). Later we will also discuss how correlations can also be negative, ranging from 0 to −1.0. If the study involves the use of a paper-and-pencil scale that respondents complete to measure certain constructs like self-esteem, depression, job satisfaction, and so on, then there are three ways to assess reliability. The first method is particularly important in studies that seek to assess changes in scale scores over time. It is called **test-retest reliability,** and deals with how *stable* a measure is (that is, how consistent it is over time). If the measurement is not stable over time, then changes that you observe in your study may have less to do with real changes in the phenomenon being observed than with changes in the measurement process.

To assess test-retest reliability, simply administer the same measurement instrument to the same individuals on two separate occasions. If the correlation between the two sets of responses to the instrument is above the .70 or .80 level (the higher the better), then the instrument may be deemed to have acceptable stability. But assessing test-retest reliability can be tricky. What if the individual actually changes between testing and retesting? What if the conditions (time of day and so forth) of the test are different from those of the retest? In assessing test-retest reliability it is important that both tests occur under identical conditions, and the time lapse between test and retest should be long enough that the individuals will not recall their answers from the first testing yet short enough to minimize the likelihood that individuals will change significantly between the two testings.

The second method for testing the reliability of written instruments is called **parallel-forms reliability.** This method requires constructing a second measuring instrument that is thought to be equivalent to the first. It might be a shorter series of questions, and it will always attempt to measure the same thing as the other instrument. Both forms are administered to the same set of individuals, and then we assess whether the two sets of responses are adequately correlated. This method of assessing reliability is extremely rare in social work research because constructing a second instrument and assuring its equivalence to the first is a cumbersome procedure.

The third method for testing the reliability of a written instrument is the most practical and most common. This method assumes that the instrument contains multiple items, each of which is scored and combined with the scores of the other items to produce an overall score. The method assesses the homogeneity of the measure and is called **internal consistency reliability.** In this approach, instead of devising a second, parallel instrument, we simply divide the single instrument into two halves, each of which contains an equal number of items, and then assess the correlation of the total scores of the two halves. Various procedures and formulas have been proposed to separate the items and to calculate the correlation between their subtotals.

The most common and powerful method used today for calculating internal consistency reliability is *coefficient alpha*. The calculation of coefficient alpha is easily done using canned computer software. It is the average of all possible split-half reliabilities. That is, the computer keeps subdividing all the items of an instrument into different halves until the subscore of each possible subdivision of items has been calculated for each subject and correlated with the subscore for the other half. Coefficient alpha equals the average of all these correlations.

We'll return to the issue of reliability more than once in the chapters ahead. For now, however, let's recall that even total reliability doesn't ensure that our measures measure what we think they measure. Now let's plunge into the question of validity.

VALIDITY

In conventional usage, the term *validity* refers to the extent to which an empirical measure adequately reflects the *real meaning* of the concept under consideration. Whoops! We've already committed to the view that concepts don't have any real meaning. Then how can we ever say whether a particular measure adequately reflects the concept's meaning? Ultimately, of course, we can't. At the same time, we've already suggested some of the ways researchers deal with this issue.

To begin, there's something called **face validity.** Particular empirical measures may or may not jibe with our common agreements and our individual mental images associated with a particular concept. We might quarrel about the adequacy of measuring worker morale by counting the number of resignations that occurred, but we'd surely agree that the number of resignations has *something* to do with morale. If we were to suggest that we measure morale by finding out how many books the workers took out of the library during their off-duty hours, you'd undoubtedly raise a more serious objection: that measure wouldn't have any face validity.

Face validity is necessary if a measurement is to be deemed worth pursuing. But it is far from sufficient. In fact, some might argue that technically it is misleading to call it a type of validity at all. Whether a measure has face validity is determined by subjective assessments made by the researcher and/or perhaps by other experts. Having face validity does not mean that a measure really measures what the researcher intends to measure; it only means that it *appears* to measure what the researcher intends to measure.

To illustrate the limited value of face validity, let's consider the development of the paranoia scale in the Minnesota Multiphasic Personality Inventory (MMPI). The MMPI has long been one of the most widely used and highly regarded personality measures. When it was originally developed for clinical assessment purposes it contained nine scales. Each scale contained items to which one can respond either true or false. One of the scales measured paranoia. For each item on this scale a particular answer (either true or false) was scored higher or lower for paranoia. To validate the scale, it was administered to large numbers of people who were and were not diagnosed as paranoid. Items were deemed valid if individuals diagnosed as paranoid tended to answer those items differently than did individuals not diagnosed as paranoid.

Below are several items that were on the paranoia scale. Each item differentiated those with paranoia from those not so diagnosed. Examine each item and see if you can determine which answer, true or false, those with paranoia were more likely to select.

"Most people will use somewhat unfair means to gain profit or an advantage rather than lose it."

"I tend to be on my guard with people who are somewhat more friendly than I had expected."

"I think most people would lie to get ahead."

From a face validity standpoint, we expect that you probably chose "true" as the response more likely to be selected by those with paranoia. Indeed, it seems reasonable to suppose that those with paranoia would be more suspicious of the tendencies of others to cheat them, deceive them, or lie to them. But the opposite was the case! That is, those with paranoia were more likely than normals to answer "false" to the above items (Dahlstrom and Welsh, 1960)! In light of this fact, and with 20/20 hindsight, we might be able to construct a rational explanation of why this occurred, perhaps noting that paranoids have unrealistically high expectations of what other people are like and that with these overly idealistic expectations they set themselves up to feel betrayed and persecuted when people act less nobly. But without the benefit of hindsight, there is a good chance that we would link the face validity of the preceding items to the likelihood that paranoids would more frequently respond "true." If this were the case, and if we relied solely on face validity to determine the scale's quality and its scoring system, then on these items we would be more likely to give a worse (higher) paranoia score to those without paranoia and a better (lower) paranoia score to those with paranoia.

A technically more legitimate type of validity, one that includes elements of face validity, is known as content validity. Content validity refers to the degree to which a measure covers the range of meanings included within the concept. For example, a test of mathematical ability, Carmines and Zeller (1979) point out, cannot be limited to addition alone but would also need to cover subtraction, multiplication, division, and so forth. But like face validity, content validity is established on the basis of judgments. That is, researchers or other experts make judgments about whether the measure covers the universe of facets that make up the concept. Although we must make judgments about face and content validity when constructing a particular measure, it is important to conduct an empirical assessment of the adequacy of those judgments. For no matter how much confidence we may have in those judgments, we need empirical evidence to ascertain whether the measure really indeed measures what it is intended to measure. Evidence about the degree to which a measure is correlated with other indicators of the concept it intends to measure, and with related concepts, pertains to the empirical validity of the measure. The two most widely cited forms of *empirical validity* are criterion-related validity and construct validity.

Criterion-related validity is based on some external criterion. For instance, the validity of the college board is shown in its ability to predict the students' success in college. The validity of a written driver's test is determined, in this sense, by the relationship between the scores people get on the test and how well they drive. In these examples, success in college and driving ability are the *criteria*. In the MMPI example just cited, the criterion was whether an individual was diagnosed as having paranoia. The validity of the MMPI was determined by its ability, on the basis of its scores, to distinguish those diagnosed as paranoid from those without that diagnosis.

Two subtypes of criterion-related validity are *predictive validity* and *concurrent validity*. The difference between these subtypes has to do with whether the measure is being tested according to (1) ability to predict a criterion that will occur in the future (such as later success in college) or (2) its correspondence to a criterion that is known concurrently.

Construct validity is based on the way a measure relates to other variables within a system of theoretical relationships. Let's suppose, for example, that you are interested in studying "marital satisfaction"—its sources and consequences. As part of your research you develop a measure of marital satisfaction, and you want to assess its validity. In addition to developing your measure, you will have also developed certain theoretical

expectations about the way marital satisfaction "behaves" in relation to other variables. For example, you may have concluded that family violence is more likely to occur at lower levels of marital satisfaction. If your measure of marital satisfaction relates to family violence in the expected fashion, that constitutes evidence of your measure's construct validity. If "satisfied" and "dissatisfied" couples were equally likely to engage in family violence, however, that would challenge the validity of your measure.

In addition to testing whether a measure fits theoretical expectations, construct validation can involve assessing whether the measure has *both* convergent validity and discriminant validity.

A measure has *convergent validity* when its results correspond to the results of other methods of measuring the same construct. Thus, if the clients whom clinicians identify as having low levels of marital satisfaction tend to score lower on your scale of marital satisfaction than clients who clinicians say have higher levels of marital satisfaction, then your scale would have convergent validity.

A measure has *discriminant validity* when its results do not correspond as highly with measures of other constructs as they do with other measures of the same construct and when its results correspond more highly with the other measures of the same construct than do measures of alternative constructs.

Suppose, for example, that the results of a measure of depression or self-esteem correspond more closely to clinician assessments of maritally satisfied and dissatisfied clients than do the results of your marital satisfaction scale. Then your scale would not have construct validity even if it had established convergent validity. The idea here is that if your scale were really measuring the construct of marital satisfaction, it should correspond more highly to other measures of marital satisfaction than do measures of conceptually distinct concepts. Likewise, if your scale is really measuring marital satisfaction, it should not correspond more highly with measures of self-esteem or depression than it does with measures of marital satisfaction.

It is possible that a scale that intends to measure marital satisfaction will correspond to another measure of marital satisfaction, and yet not really be a very good measure of the construct of marital satisfaction. If we assume, for example, that people who have low self-esteem or who are depressed are less likely to be maritally satisfied than other people, then a scale that really has more to do with depression or self-esteem than it has to do with marital satisfaction will still probably correspond to a measure of marital satisfaction. The process of assessing discriminant validity checks for that possibility, and thus enables us to determine whether a measure really measures the construct it intends to measure, and not some other construct that happens to be related to the construct in question.

Let's consider another hypothetical example regarding construct validity. Suppose you conceptualized a construct that you termed "battered women's syndrome" and decided to develop a scale to measure it. Let's further suppose that your scale had items about how often the women felt sad, hopeless, helpless, undeserving of a better fate, and similar items that, although you didn't realize it, all had a lot to do with depression and self-esteem.

You administered your scale to women residing in a battered women's shelter and to those with no reported history of battering and found that the two groups' scores differed as you predicted. Thus, you established the scale's criterion-related validity. Then you administered it to battered women before and after they had completed a long period of intensive intervention in a battered women's program and found that, as you predicted, their scores on your scale improved. This gave you theoretically based confidence in the construct validity of your scale, but at that point you realized that depression and low self-esteem were a big part of what you were conceptualizing as a battered women's syndrome. You began to wonder whether improvement on your scale had more to do with becoming less de-

pressed or having more self-esteem than it did with overcoming your notion of a syndrome. So you decided to test your scale's discriminant validity. You repeated the same studies, but this time additionally had the women complete the best scale that you could find on depression and the best scale you could find on self-esteem. Your results showed that battered women improved more on those scales after treatment than they improved on your scale. Moreover, the differences between battered women and women with no history of battering were greater on those scales than on your scale. In addition, you found that the scores on your scale corresponded more highly with the scales on depression and self-esteem than it did with the women's status regarding battering or treatment. In light of this you appropriately concluded that although your scale had criterion-related validity, it had more to do with measuring other constructs like self-esteem and depression than it had to do with measuring your conception of a battered women's syndrome. The following real illustration is intended to clarify this process further, as well as other processes in assessing reliability and validity.

AN ILLUSTRATION OF RELIABLE AND VALID MEASUREMENT IN SOCIAL WORK: THE CLINICAL MEASUREMENT PACKAGE

During the mid-1970s Walter Hudson and his associates began to develop and validate a package of nine short, standardized scales that they designed for repeated use by clinical social workers to assess client problems and monitor and evaluate progress in treatment. The nine scales were collectively referred to as *The Clinical Measurement Package* (Hudson, 1982). Each of the scales was found to have test-retest reliability and internal consistency reliability of at least .90, which is quite high. Each scale also was reported to have high face and empirical validity.

Although each scale measures a different construct, the nine scales are similar in format. Each lists 25 statements that refer to how the client feels about things, and the client enters a number from 1 to 5 beside each statement to indicate how often he or she feels that way. The 25 responses are summed (with reverse scoring for positively worded items) to get the client's total score on the scale (the higher the score, the greater the problem with the construct being measured). The nine constructs that the nine scales were designed to measure are: (1) depression, (2) self-esteem, (3) marital discord, (4) sexual discord, (5) parental attitudes about child, (6) child's attitude toward father, (7) child's attitude toward mother, (8) intrafamilial stress, and (9) peer relationships.

For a discussion of the entire measurement package, readers are referred to the preceding reference (Hudson, 1982). For our purposes in this text, however, let's examine the characteristics of one of the scales and how its reliability and validity were assessed empirically. The scale we will examine is the *Child's Attitude Toward Mother* (CAM) scale, whose reliability and validity were reported by Giuli and Hudson (1977). The CAM scale is reproduced in Figure 6-2 with permission from W. W. Hudson, *The Clinical Measurement Package*, Chicago, Illinois, The Dorsey Press ©1982.

To begin, let's look at how this scale illustrates some of the measurement issues discussed earlier in this chapter. For example, what level of measurement is exemplified by each item? The correct answer is "ordinal," since the 1–5 rankings have a quantitative meaning that is imprecise. What sources of measurement error might most concern you if you were considering using this scale? Notice that you might not be too concerned about the acquiescent response set because some of the items are worded positively and others are worded negatively.

But what about a social desirability bias? Look at items 13 and 20. Would children who hate their mother or feel violent toward her admit to such feelings? Will differences in scale scores really measure differences in these feelings, or will they instead just measure differences in the propensity of children to admit to the socially unde-

sirable feelings they have? We can resolve these questions by assessing the empirical validity of the scale, and we will examine how Giuli and Hudson did so shortly.

But before we consider the validity of the scale, what about its reliability? How vulnerable does the scale appear to be to random error? Will having to select a number from 1 to 5 for each of the 25 items be too cumbersome for children? Are there any words or phrases that they might not understand, like "embarrasses" in item 5, "too demanding" in item 6, or "puts too many limits on me" in item 9? If the scale is too cumbersome, or if it is too difficult to understand, then it will contain too many random errors, which means that measurement will lack consistency and therefore be unreliable.

Giuli and Hudson administered the scale to 664 high school students. To assess the scale's internal consistency reliability, they computed coefficient alpha, which, as noted earlier in this chapter, is the average of all possible split-half reliabilities. They found a very high internal consistency reliability, with a coefficient alpha of .94. To assess the stability of the scale over time, they assessed its test-retest reliability. This was done with a sample of adults enrolled in a graduate-level psychology statistics course. The students completed the scale twice, with a one-week time lapse between the two administrations. The test-retest reliability was .95, which is very high.

To assess the scale's criterion validity, they asked the 664 high school students to indicate whether they were having problems with their mothers. Those who said "yes" had a mean CAM score of 49.9. Those who said they were not having problems with their mother had a mean CAM score of 20.8. This very large and significant difference was interpreted by Giuli and Hudson to mean that the scale has excellent criterion validity because it does so well at differentiating those who acknowledge a problem with their mother from those who deny having such a problem.

But was the scale really measuring the construct of child's attitude toward mother? Perhaps it was really measuring something else, like level

Today's Date _____

CHILD'S ATTITUDE TOWARD MOTHER (CAM)

Name _____

This questionnaire is designed to measure the degree of contentment you have in your relationship with your mother. It is not a test, so there are no right or wrong answers. Answer each item as carefully and accurately as you can by placing a number beside each one as follows:

    1 Rarely or none of the time
    2 A little of the time
    3 Some of the time
    4 A good part of the time
    5 Most or all of the time

Please begin.

1. My mother gets on my nerves.   _____
2. I get along well with my mother.   _____
3. I feel that I can really trust my mother.   _____
4. I dislike my mother.   _____
5. My mother's behavior embarrasses me.   _____
6. My mother is too demanding.   _____
7. I wish I had a different mother.   _____
8. I really enjoy my mother.   _____
9. My mother puts too many limits on me.   _____
10. My mother interferes with my activities.   _____
11. I resent my mother.   _____
22. I think my mother is terrific.   _____
13. I hate my mother.   _____
14. My mother is very patient with me.   _____
15. I really like my mother.   _____
16. I like being with my mother.   _____
17. I feel like I do not love my mother.   _____
18. My mother is very irritating.   _____
19. I feel very angry toward my mother.   _____
20. I feel violent toward my mother.   _____
21. I feel proud of my mother.   _____
22. I wish my mother was more like others I know.   _____
23. My mother does not understand me.   _____
24. I can really depend on my mother.   _____
25. I feel ashamed of my mother.   _____

Figure 6-2 Sample scale from *The Clinical Measurement Package: Child's attitude toward mother.*

of depression or self-esteem, that was related to having problems with parents. To assess the scale's construct validity, each of the 664 high school students also completed scales (from *The Clinical Measurement Package*) that measured depression and self-esteem. The strength of the relationship between each of these measures and whether the student admitted to having problems with his or her mother was then assessed. The CAM score turned out to be much more strongly related to the latter criterion than was either the depression score or the self-esteem score. Giuli and Hudson concluded that these findings supported the construct validity of the CAM scale.

No study in social research is ever perfectly flawless. Even the best ones have some (perhaps unavoidable) limitations. This is just as true for studies assessing measurement reliability and validity as it is for other sorts of studies. Let's consider some possible limitations in the Giuli and Hudson study, for example. Note that reliability was not assessed for children younger than high school age. We cannot fault Giuli and Hudson for that; it is unreasonable to expect them to study every conceivable age group. Finding the resources to do that is extremely difficult. Nevertheless, it would be inappropriate to assume that the same high level of reliability applies to elementary school students, especially those in the lower grades. Perhaps children that young would find the instrument much more difficult to understand or much more cumbersome than did the high school students and therefore would be much less consistent in their responses to it.

Note also the debatable criterion Giuli and Hudson used to separate the students having problems with their mothers from those not having such problems. Like the CAM scale itself, that criterion was vulnerable to a social desirability bias because it relied on students' willingness to acknowledge that they were having problems with their mothers. It is conceivable that those not willing to acknowledge such problems on the CAM scale, due to a social desirability bias, were also unwilling to acknowledge having problems

in a general sense when asked, due to the same bias. If so, then the construct actually being measured might have less to do with real attitudes toward one's mother than with a willingness to acknowledge socially undesirable attitudes. When selecting a criterion measure of the construct in question, it is essential that that criterion be an *independent* measure of the construct, not just a parallel form of the same measure whose validity you are assessing. If it is not—that is, if it seems just as vulnerable in the same way to the same biases as is the measure in question—then instead of measuring validity, you are really measuring parallel-forms reliability.

Giuli and Hudson recognized this problem and conducted a further assessment of the CAM scale's empirical validity. To do this, they obtained a sample of 38 children receiving therapy for a variety of problems. They divided the children into two groups: those known by the therapist to have behaviorally identifiable problems with their mother and those for whom no such problem could be established. The average CAM score for the first group was 54.82, as compared to 14.73 for the latter group. Since the therapists' observations were not vulnerable to the same biases as the CAM scale, the large and significant differences in CAM scores provided stronger grounds for claiming the empirical validity of the CAM scale—that is, for claiming that it really measures attitudes, not just some systematic bias bearing on a person's willingness to acknowledge those attitudes.

RELATIONSHIP BETWEEN RELIABILITY AND VALIDITY

As we noted earlier, although it is desirable that a measure be reliable, its reliability does not ensure that it is valid. Suppose an abusive mother and father were referred by the courts to family therapy as a precondition for keeping their child. As involuntary clients, they might be reluctant to admit abusive behaviors to the therapist, believing that

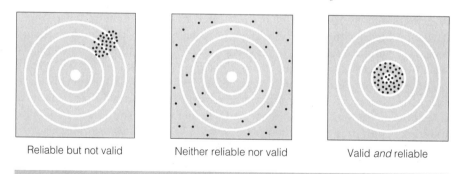

Reliable but not valid   Neither reliable nor valid   Valid *and* reliable

Figure 6-3 An Analogy to Validity and Reliability

such admissions would imperil their maintaining custody of their child. Even if they continued to abuse their child, they might deny it every time the therapist asked them about it. Thus, the therapist would be getting highly reliable (that is, consistent) data. No matter how many times and ways the therapist asked about abusive behaviors, the answer would always be the same.

But the data would not be valid. That is, the answer would not really measure the construct in question; it would not indicate the amount of child abuse that was occurring. Instead, what was really being measured was the reluctance of the parents to convey a socially undesirable image to the therapist.

Figure 6-3 presents a graphic portrayal of the difference between validity and reliability. If you can think of measurement as analogous to hitting the bull's-eye on a target, you'll see that reliability looks like a "tight pattern," regardless of where it hits, because reliability is a function of consistency. Validity, on the other hand, is a function of shots being arranged around the bull's-eye. The failure of reliability in the figure can be seen as random error, whereas the failure of validity is a systematic error. Notice that neither an unreliable nor an invalid measure is likely to be very useful.

A certain tension often exists between the criteria of reliability and validity. Often we seem to face a trade-off between the two. If you'll recall for a moment the earlier example of measuring morale in different work settings, we think you'll

see that the strategy of immersing yourself in the day-to-day routine of the agency, observing what went on, and talking to the workers seems to provide a more valid measure of morale than counting resignations. It just seems obvious that we'd be able to get a clearer sense of whether the morale was high or low in that fashion than we would from counting the number of resignations.

However, the counting strategy would be more reliable. This situation reflects a more general strain in research measurement. Most of the really interesting concepts that we want to study have many subtle nuances, and it's difficult to specify precisely what we mean by them. Researchers sometimes speak of such concepts as having a "richness of meaning." Scores of books and articles have been written on topics such as depression, self-esteem, social support and so on, and they still haven't exhausted the interesting aspects of those concepts.

Yet science needs to be specific to generate reliable measurements. Very often, then, the specification of reliable operational definitions and measurements seems to rob such concepts of their richness of meaning. For example, morale is much more than a lack of resignations; depression is much more than five items on a depression scale.

Developing measures that are reliable and still capable of tapping the richness of meaning of concepts is a persistent and inevitable dilemma for the social researcher, and you will be effectively forearmed against it by being forewarned. Be prepared for it and deal with it. If there is no clear agreement on how to measure a concept, measure it several different ways. If the concept has several different dimensions, measure them all. And above all, know that the concept does not have any meaning other than what we give it. The only justification we have for giving any concept a particular meaning is utility; measure concepts in ways that help us understand the world around us.

RELIABILITY AND VALIDITY IN QUALITATIVE RESEARCH

Much of the preceding discussion of reliability and validity applies most clearly to quantitative research. While much of the basic logic is the same, qualitative researchers may approach the issues somewhat differently. Let's see what some of those differences might be.

In a quantitative study of adolescent depression, the researcher would conceivably administer a standardized depression scale to a sizeable sample of adolescents, perhaps to assess the extent of depression among adolescents or to see if the extent of depression was related to some other variable(s). In planning the study, or in reading about it, a critical issue would be the reliability and validity of the depression scale. But we would know that even the best depression scale is not 100% reliable and valid. Even using the best scale, the study would be dealing with probabilistic knowledge. That is, specific scores would indicate a higher or lower probability that the adolescent is depressed. A good clinical scale would be correct about 90% of the time in depicting an adolescent as depresssed or not depressed, and it would be important to know how often the scale is accurate and how often it is mistaken. But if all we have on each adolescent is quantitative data from a scale score, we will not know which adolescents are being accurately depicted and which are among the 10% or so who are being inaccurately depicted.

In a qualitative study of adolescent depression, the researcher would not rely on a standardized instrument. The researcher would be more likely to study a much smaller sample of adolescents and conduct very extensive and varied direct observations and in-depth interviews with each one of them and their significant others. Perhaps the scope would be limited to a biographical case study of the impact of adolescent depression on one family. Or perhaps the sample would include several families. The sample would be kept small enough to permit the researcher to describe the everyday lives of the subjects in such rich detail that the reader would not question the existence of depression or would simply not care what construct was used to label the observed phenomenon.

Suppose the qualitative report described an adolescent girl whose academic and social functioning began deteriorating gradually after the onset of puberty. After acheiving high grades throughout her previous schooling, she began staying awake all night, sleeping all day, and refusing to go to school. On the days when she did attend school, she was unable to concentrate. Her grades began falling precipitously. She began isolating herself from family and friends and refusing to leave her room. She began expressing feelings of hopelessness about the future and negative thoughts about her looks, intelligence, likability and worthiness. She no longer had the energy to do things she once did well, and started to neglect basic daily tasks associated with cleanliness and grooming. She began wearing the same black clothes every day, refusing to wear any other color. When family or friends reached out to her she became unresponsive or irritable. She displayed no signs of substance abuse but began to wonder if that might make her feel better. She began having thoughts of suicide and started to cut herself. She showed no signs of schizophrenia, such as delusions or hallucinations.

A good qualitative report would depict the above clinical deterioration in a format replete with detailed observations and quotations that would be many pages in length and would leave the reader with a sense of having walked in the shoes of the girl and her family, sensing the girl's depression and agony as well as the burden this placed on the family. The detail of the study and its report would be so rich that if the girl did not score in the depressed range of a standardized scale, the reader would be likely to conclude that this was one of the 10% or so of cases in which the scale got it wrong. The reader might not even care whether the phenomenon described fit best under the rubric of depression or under some other label. Rather than verifying a label for it that could be generalized to others, the study would be geared more to giving the reader a deeper sense of the situation that the girl and her family were struggling with, the ways in which the various family members experienced the situation and the subjective meanings it had for them, and what they felt they needed.

The point of qualitative studies, in other words, is to study and describe things in such depth and detail, and from such multiple perspectives and meanings, that there is less need to worry about whether one particular measure is really measuring what it is intended to measure. In quantitative studies, on the other hand, we are more likely to rely heavily on one indicator, or a few indicators, administered perhaps in a matter of minutes, to determine the degree to which a hypothetical construct applies to a large number of people, and with an eye toward generalizing what we find to an even larger number of people. In such studies, it is critical to assess the reliability and validity of the indicators we use. It is thus possible to recognize the critical role of reliability and validity in quantitative studies while at the same time appreciating the need to take a different perspective on the role of reliability and validity in qualitative studies. In fact, without even attempting to quantitatively assess the validity of in-depth qualitative measurement, one could argue that the directness, depth, and detail of its observations often gives it better validity than quantitative measurement.

We are not, however, saying that the concepts of reliability and validity have no role in qualitative studies. Qualitative researchers disagree on the nature and extent of the role of reliability and validity in their work, and their disagreement is connected to the epistemological assumptions

they make. At one extreme are the researchers who conduct qualitative research without buying into a postmodern rejection of the notion of an objective reality or of our ability to improve or assess our objectivity. These researchers use varied criteria to judge whether the evidence reported in qualitative studies is to be trusted as accurate and unbiased. Some might even compare the qualitative interpretations with data from quantitative measures. To the degree that the quantitative data support the qualitative interpretations, the qualitative material may be seen as more credible.

Some researchers judge the reliability of qualitative interpretations according to criteria that aren't really quantitative, but that resemble the underlying logic of quantitative approaches to reliability. Akin to interobserver reliability in quantitative studies, for example, one might assess whether two independent raters arrive at the same interpretation from the same mass of written qualitative field notes. What distinguishes this from a quantitative approach is that the consistency between the two raters would not be calculated via quantitative indicators such as percentages of agreement or correlations. Instead, one would merely ask whether the two arrived at the same particular overarching interpretation. (Some might argue that this is still a quantitative indicator— that is, agreement is either 100% or zero %.) Akin to internal consistency reliability, one might examine whether different sources of data fit consistently with the researcher's observations and interpretations. Rather than calculate quantitative reliability coefficients, however, one would attempt to illustrate how, on an overall basis, the different sources were in qualitative agreement.

Some researchers use indicators of reliability of a more distinctly qualitative nature. They might, for example, ask the subjects of the research to confirm the accuracy of the researcher's observations. Or the subjects might be asked whether the researcher's interpretations ring true and are meaningful to them. Some judge reliability according to whether the research report indicates ways in which the researcher searched thoroughly for disconfirming evidence, such as by looking for other cases or informants whose data might not fit the researcher's interpretation. They might also ask whether the researcher sufficiently varied the time, place, and context of the observations, and whether the interpretation fit consistently across the observations taken across different times, places, and contexts.

Jane Kronick (1989), a social work professor at Bryn Mawr College, has proposed four criteria for evaluating the validity of qualitative interpretations of written texts. The first is analogous to internal consistency reliability in quantitative research. That is, the interpretation of parts of the text should be consistent with other parts or with the whole text. Likewise, the "developing argument" should be "internally consistent." Second, Kronick proposes that the interpretation should be complete, taking all of the evidence into account. Her third criterion involves "conviction." This means that the interpretation should be the most compelling one in light of the evidence within the text. Fourth, the interpretation should be meaningful. It should make sense of the text and extend our understanding of it.

As in quantitative research, limitations inhere in some of the qualitative approaches to reliability and validity. For instance, the subjects of the research may not confirm the accuracy of a researcher's observations or interpretations because they do not like the way they are portrayed, may not understand the researcher's theoretical perspective, or may not be aware of patterns that are true but which only emerge from the mass of data. A second rater may not confirm the interpretations of the principal investigator because certain insights might require having conducted the observations or interviews and might not emerge from the written notes alone.

While some qualitative researchers disagree about which of the above types of approaches to reliability and validity to use and how to use them, others reject the whole idea of reliability and validity in keeping with their postmodern epistemological rejection of assumptions connected to objectivity. Or they define reliability and validity in terms that are worlds apart from

what other researchers mean by those two words. Sometimes they define reliability and validity in terms that researchers who do not share their epistemological assumptions would perceive as nonscientific or even antiscientific. For instance, some would deem a study valid if a particular group deemed as oppressed or powerless experienced it as liberating or empowering. Thus, rather than define validity in terms of objectivity and accuracy, some define it according to whether findings can be applied toward some political or ideological purpose (Altheide and Johnson, 1994). Others point to writing style as a validity criterion, deeming a study valid if the report is written in a gripping manner that draws the reader into the subjects' worlds so closely that readers feel as though they are walking in the subjects' shoes, recognize what they read to correspond to their own prior experiences, and perceive the report to be internally coherent and plausible (Adler and Adler, 1994). In this connection, some have depicted postmodern qualitative research as blurring the distinction between social science and the arts and humanities (Neuman, 1994). In fact, one recent qualitative study used fictional novels and plays as sources of data for developing insights about the experience of family caregiving of relatives with Alzheimer's disease (England, 1994).

As you encounter the terms *reliability* and *validity* throughout the remainder of this book, they will be used primarily in reference to their quantitative meanings, since these terms are more commonly used in quantitative research. But we will be discussing qualitative research as well in the remaining chapters, and we hope you will keep in mind the distinctive ways reliability and and validity are considered in qualitative research as you read that material.

Main Points

- Nominal measures refer to those variables whose attributes are simply different from one another. An example would be gender.

• Ordinal measures refer to those variables whose attributes may be rank-ordered along some progression from more to less. An example would be the variable *prejudice* as composed of the attributes "very prejudiced," "somewhat prejudiced," and "not at all prejudiced."

• Interval measures refer to those variables whose attributes are not only rank-ordered but also are separated by a uniform distance between them. An example would be IQ.

• Ratio measures are the same as interval measures except that ratio measures are also based on a true zero point. Age would be an example of a ratio measure because that variable contains the attribute *zero years old*.

• A given variable can sometimes be measured at different levels of measurement. Thus, age, potentially a ratio measure, may also be treated as interval, ordinal, or even nominal. The most appropriate level of measurement employed depends on the purpose of the measurement.

• Measurement error can be systematic or random. Common systematic errors pertain to social desirability biases and cultural biases. Random errors have no consistent pattern of effects, make measurement inconsistent, and are likely to result from difficulties in understanding or administering measures.

• Reliability concerns the amount of random error in a measure and measurement consistency. It refers to the likelihood that a given measurement procedure will yield the same description of a given phenomenon if that measurement is repeated. For instance, estimating a person's age by asking his or her friends would be less reliable than asking the person or checking the birth certificate.

• Different types of reliability include interobserver reliability or interrater reliability, test-retest reliability, parallel-forms reliability, and internal consistency reliability.

• Validity refers to the extent of systematic error in measurement—the extent to which a specific measurement provides data that relate to commonly accepted meanings of a particular concept. There are numerous yardsticks for determining validity: face validity, content validity, criterion-related validity, and construct validity. The latter two are empirical forms of validity, whereas the former are based on expert judgments.

• Construct validation involves testing whether a measure relates to other variables according to theoretical expectations. It also involves testing the measure's convergent validity and discriminant validity.

• A measure has *convergent validity* when its results correspond to the results of other methods of measuring the same construct.

• A measure has *discriminant validity* when its results do not correspond as highly with measures of other constructs as they do with other measures of the same construct and when its results correspond more highly with the other measures of the same construct than do measures of alternative constructs.

• The creation of specific, reliable measures often seems to diminish the richness of meaning our general concepts have. This problem is inevitable. The best solution is to use several different measures to tap the different aspects of the concept.

• Studies assessing the reliability and validity of a measure, just like any other type of study, can be seriously flawed. Ultimately, the degree to which we can call a measure reliable or valid depends not just on the size of its reliability or validity coefficient, but also on the methodological credibility of the way those coefficients were assessed. For example, was an appropriate sample selected? Was the criterion of the construct truly independent of the measure being assessed and not vulnerable to the same sources of error as that measure?

• Reliability and validity are defined and handled differently in qualitative research than they are in quantitative research. Qualitative researchers disagree about definitions and criteria for reliability and validity, and some argue that they are not applicable at all to qualitative research. These disagreements tend to be connected to differing epistemological assumptions about the nature of reality and objectivity.

Review Questions and Exercises

1. What level of measurement—nominal, ordinal, interval, or ratio—describes each of the following variables:

a. Agency auspices (public versus private)

b. Attitudes about increased social welfare spending (strongly approve, approve, disapprove, strongly disapprove)

c. Number of students with field placements in social action organizations

2. In a newspaper or magazine, find an instance of invalid and/or unreliable measurement. Justify your choice.

Additional Readings

Carmines, Edward G., and Zeller, Richard A., *Reliability and Validity Assessment* (Beverly Hills, CA: Sage, 1979). In this chapter, we've examined the basic logic of validity and reliability in social science measurement. Carmines and Zeller explore those issues in more detail and examine some of the ways of calculating reliability mathematically.

Denzin, Norman K., and Lincoln, Yvonna S., *Handbook of Qualitative Research* (Thousand Oaks, CA: Sage, 1994). An edited volume of informative and provocative papers discussing the various nonpositivist epistemologies influencing qualitative inquiry and their implications for how qualitative research is conceptualized, carried out, interpreted, and reported. Many of the chapters discuss alternative ways reliability and validity are viewed and handled in qualitative research.

Gould, Julius, and Kolb, William, *A Dictionary of the Social Sciences* (New York: Free Press, 1964). A primary reference to the social scientific agreements on various concepts. Although the terms used by social scientists do not have ultimately "true" meanings, this reference book lays out the meanings social scientists have in mind when they use those terms.

Hudson, Walter, *The Clinical Measurement Package* (Chicago: Dorsey Press, 1982). This field manual describes in detail the nine scales discussed in this chapter that are used by clinical social workers.

Lazarsfeld, Paul, and Rosenberg, Morris (eds.), *The Language of Social Research* (New York: Free Press, 1955), Section I. An excellent and diverse collection of descriptions of specific measurements used in past social research. These 14 articles present extremely useful accounts of actual measurement operations performed by social researchers, as well as more conceptual discussions of measurement in general.

Constructing Measurement Instruments

What You'll Learn in This Chapter

Now that you understand measurement error, its
common sources, and the concepts of reliability
and validity, let's examine the process of
constructing some measurement instruments that
are commonly used in social work research.

INTRODUCTION

The preceding chapter focused on levels of measurement and the broad issue of measurement error. In this chapter we will delve further into measurement methodology by examining the construction of measurement instruments widely used in social work research: questionnaires, interview schedules, and scales. Later in this book we will look at alternative research designs and modes of collecting data. Some of these methodologies will not require the application of the instruments just mentioned, so we will be discussing ways to measure social work variables that don't involve asking people questions or administering written instruments to them. But despite the value of those alternative methodologies, instruments designed to gather data by communicating with people orally or in writing (with questionnaires, interview schedules, and scales) are among the most prominent techniques that social worker researchers use to collect data. As we examine the construction of these types of instruments, it is important to bear in mind that the principles guiding their design will vary, depending on whether the research is primarily qualitative or quantitative. Among the most important objectives in designing quantitative instruments is the avoidance of measurement error. Thus, we seek to construct instruments that are reliable and valid. Among the most important objectives in designing qualitative instruments is probing for depth of meaning from the respondent's perspective. We'll begin our consideration of instrument construction by examining some broad guidelines for asking people questions.

GUIDELINES FOR ASKING QUESTIONS

As we implied above, one of the most common ways that social work researchers operationalize their variables is by asking people questions as a way of getting data for analysis and interpretation. Asking people questions is most commonly associated with survey research, which will be discussed in Chapter 11, but it is also used often in experiments (to be discussed in Chapters 9 and 10) and in qualitative research (Chapter 12). Sometimes the questions are asked by an interviewer, and the list of questions is referred to as an *interview schedule*. Instead of using an interview schedule, some qualitative studies utilize an *interview guide*, which lists topics to be asked about but not the exact sequence and wording of the questions. Sometimes the questions are written down and given to respondents for completion. In that case, we refer to the sets of questions as *questionnaires*, or perhaps as *self-administered questionnaires*.

As we'll see, several general guidelines can assist you in framing and asking questions that serve as excellent operationalizations of variables. There are also pitfalls that can result in useless and even misleading information. This section should assist you in differentiating the two. Let's begin with some of the options available to you in creating questionnaires.

Questions and Statements

The term *questionnaire* suggests a collection of questions, but an examination of a typical questionnaire will probably reveal as many statements as questions. That is not without reason. Often, the researcher is interested in determining the extent to which respondents hold a particular attitude or perspective. If you are able to summarize the attitude in a fairly brief statement, you will often present that statement and ask respondents whether they agree or disagree with it. Rensis Likert has greatly formalized this procedure through the creation of the Likert scale, a format in which respondents are asked to strongly agree, agree, disagree, or strongly disagree, or perhaps strongly approve, approve, and so forth. Both questions and statements may be used profitably. Using both in a given questionnaire gives you more flexibility in the design of items and can make the questionnaire more interesting as well.

Open-Ended and Closed-Ended Questions

In asking questions, researchers have two options. We may ask *open-ended* questions, in which case the respondent is asked to provide his or her own answer to the question. Open-ended questions can be used in interview schedules as well as in self-administered questionnaires. For example, the respondent may be asked, "What do you feel is the most important problem facing your community today?" and be provided with a space to write in the answer or be asked to report it orally to an interviewer.

In an *interview schedule,* the interviewer may be instructed to probe for more information as needed. For instance, if the respondent replies that the most important problem facing the community is "urban decay," the interviewer may probe for more clarification by saying, "Could you tell me some more about that problem?" (We'll discuss this process in greater depth in Chapter 11, on survey research.) Because of the opportunity to probe for more information, open-ended questions are used more frequently on interview schedules than on self-administered questionnaires, although they commonly appear in both formats.

With *closed-ended* questions, the respondent is asked to select an answer from among a list provided by the researcher. Closed-ended questions can be used in self-administered questionnaires as well as interview schedules and are popular because they provide a greater uniformity of responses and are more easily processed. Open-ended responses must be coded before they can be processed for computer analysis, as will be discussed in Chapter 14. This coding process often requires that the researcher interpret the meaning of responses, opening the possibility of misunderstanding and researcher bias. There is also a danger that some respondents will give answers that are essentially irrelevant to the researcher's intent. Closed-ended responses, on the other hand, can often be transferred directly into a computer format.

The chief shortcoming of closed-ended questions lies in the researcher's structuring of responses. When the relevant answers to a given question are relatively clear, there should be no problem. In other cases, however, the researcher's structuring of responses may overlook some important responses. In asking about "the most important problem facing your community," for example, your checklist of problems might omit certain ones that respondents would have said were important.

In the construction of closed-ended questions, you should be guided by two structural requirements. The response categories provided should be *exhaustive:* they should include all the possible responses that might be expected. Often, researchers ensure this by adding a category labeled something like Other (Please specify: _____).

Second, the answer categories must be *mutually exclusive:* the respondent should not feel compelled to select more than one. (In some cases, you may wish to solicit multiple answers, but these may create difficulties in data processing and analysis later on.) To ensure that your categories are mutually exclusive, you should carefully consider each combination of categories, asking yourself whether a person could reasonably choose more than one answer. In addition, it is useful to add an instruction to the question asking the respondent to select the *one best* answer, but this technique is not a satisfactory substitute for a carefully constructed set of responses.

Make Items Clear

It should go without saying that questionnaire items should be clear and unambiguous, but the broad proliferation of unclear and ambiguous questions in surveys makes the point worth stressing here. Often you can become so deeply involved in the topic under examination that opinions and perspectives are clear to you but will not be clear to your respondents—many of whom have given little or no attention to the topic. Or if you have only a superficial understanding of the topic, you may fail to specify the intent of your question sufficiently. The question "What do you think about the proposed residential facility for the developmentally disabled in the community?" may evoke in the respondent a counterquestion: "*Which* residential facility?" Questionnaire items should be precise so that the respondent knows exactly what the researcher wants an answer to.

Avoid Double-Barreled Questions

Frequently, researchers ask respondents for a single answer to a combination of questions. That seems to happen most often when the researcher has personally identified with a complex question. For example, you might ask respondents to agree or disagree with the statement "The state should abandon its community-based services and spend the money on improving institutional care." Although many people would unequivocally agree with the statement and others would unequivocally disagree, still others would be unable to answer. Some would want to abandon community-based services and give the money back to the taxpayers. Others would want to continue community-based services but also put more money into institutions. These latter respondents could neither agree nor disagree without misleading you.

As a general rule, whenever the word *and* appears in a question or questionnaire statement, you should check whether you are asking a *double-barreled question*. See the box titled "Double-Barreled and Beyond" for some imaginative variations on this theme.

Respondents Must Be Competent to Answer

In asking respondents to provide information, you should continually ask yourself whether they are able to do so reliably. In a study of child-rearing, you might ask respondents to report the age at which they first talked back to their parents. Aside from the problem of defining *talking back to parents,* it is doubtful if most respondents would remember with any degree of accuracy.

As another example, student government leaders occasionally ask their constituents to indicate the way students' fees ought to be spent. Typically, respondents are asked to indicate the percentage of available funds that should be devoted to a long list of activities. Without a fairly good knowledge of the nature of those activities and the costs involved, the respondents cannot provide meaningful answers. (Administrative costs will receive little support although they may be essential to the program as a whole.)

One group of researchers examining the driving experience of teenagers insisted on asking an open-ended question concerning the number of miles driven since receiving a license. Although consultants argued that few drivers would be able to estimate such information with any accuracy, the question was asked nonetheless. In response, some teenagers reported driving hundreds of thousands of miles.

Questions Should Be Relevant

Similarly, questions asked in a questionnaire should be relevant to most respondents. When attitudes are requested on a topic that few respondents have thought about or really care about, the results are not likely to be useful. Of course, the respondents may express attitudes even though they have never given any thought to the issue, and you run the risk of being misled.

This point is illustrated occasionally when you ask for responses relating to fictitious persons and issues. In one political poll one of your authors (Babbie) conducted, he asked respondents whether they were familiar with each of 15 political figures in the community. As a methodological exercise, he made up a name: Tom Sakumoto. In response, 9% of the respondents said they were familiar with him. Of those respondents familiar with him, about half reported seeing him on television and reading about him in the newspapers.

When you obtain responses to fictitious issues, you can disregard those responses. But when the issue is real, you may have no way of telling which

DOUBLE-BARRELED AND BEYOND

Even established, professional researchers sometimes create double-barreled questions and worse. Consider this question, asked of Americans in April 1986, at a time when America's relationship with Libya was at an especially low point. Some observers suggested the U.S. might end up in a shooting war with the small North African nation. The Harris Poll sought to find out what American public opinion was.

> If Libya now increases its terrorist acts against the U.S. and we keep inflicting more damage on Libya, then inevitably it will all end in the U.S. going to war and finally invading that country, which would be wrong.

Respondents were given the opportunity of answering "Agree," "Disagree," or "Not sure." Notice the elements contained in the complex statement:

1. Will Libya increase its terrorist acts against the U.S.?

2. Will the U.S. inflict more damage on Libya?

3. Will the U.S. inevitably or otherwise go to war against Libya?

4. Would the U.S. invade Libya?

5. Would that be right or wrong?

These several elements offer the possibility of numerous points of view—far more than the three alternatives offered respondents to the survey. Even if we were to assume hypothetically that Libya would "increase its terrorist attacks" and the U.S. would "keep inflicting more damage" in return, you might have any one of at least seven distinct expectations about the outcome:

responses genuinely reflect attitudes and which reflect meaningless answers to an irrelevant question.

Short Items Are Best

In the interest of being unambiguous and precise and pointing to the relevance of an issue, the researcher is often led into long and complicated items. That should be avoided. Respondents are often unwilling to study an item in order to understand it. The respondent should be able to read an item quickly, understand its intent, and select or provide an answer without difficulty. In general, you should assume that respondents *will* read

items quickly and give quick answers; therefore, you should provide clear, short items that will not be misinterpreted under those conditions.

Avoid Negative Items

The appearance of a negation in a questionnaire item paves the way for easy misinterpretation. Asked to agree or disagree with the statement "The community should not have a residential facility for the developmentally disabled," a sizable portion of the respondents will read over the word *not* and answer on that basis. Thus, some will agree with the statement when they are in

	U.S. will not go to war	War is probable but not inevitable	War is inevitable
U.S. will not invade Libya	1	2	3
U.S. will invade Libya but it would be wrong	—	4	5
U.S. will invade Libya and it would be right	—	6	7

The examination of prognoses about the Libyan situation is not the only example of double-barreled questions sneaking into public opinion research. Here are some questions the Harris Poll asked in an attempt to gauge American public opinion about Soviet General Secretary Gorbachev:

He looks like the kind of Russian leader who will recognize that both the Soviets and the Americans can destroy each other with nuclear missiles so it is better to come to verifiable arms control agreements.

He seems to be more modern, enlightened, and attractive, which is a good sign for the peace of the world.

Even though he looks much more modern and attractive, it would be a mistake to think he will be much different from other Russian leaders.

How many elements can you identify in each of the questions? How many possible opinions could people have in each case? What does a simple "agree" or "disagree" really mean in such cases?

Source: Reported in *World Opinion Update,* October 1985 and May 1986.

favor of the facility, and others will agree when they oppose it. And you may never know which is which.

In a study of civil liberties support, respondents were asked whether they felt "the following kinds of people should be prohibited from teaching in public schools," and were presented with a list including such items as a communist, a Ku Klux Klansman, and so forth. The response categories "yes" and "no" were given beside each entry. A comparison of the responses to this item with other items reflecting support for civil liberties strongly suggested that many respondents gave the answer yes to indicate willingness for such

a person to teach, rather than to indicate that such a person should be prohibited from teaching. (A later study in the series that gave "permit" and "prohibit" as answer categories produced much clearer results.)

Avoid Biased Items and Terms

Recall from the earlier discussion of conceptualization and operationalization that there are no ultimately true meanings for any of the concepts we typically study in social science. *Prejudice* has no ultimately correct definition, and whether a given person is prejudiced depends on our definition of

LEARNING FROM BAD EXAMPLES

by Charles Bonney, Department of Sociology, Eastern Michigan University

Here's a questionnaire I've used to train my students in some of the problems of question construction. These are questions that might be asked in order to test the hypothesis "College students from high-status family backgrounds are more tolerant toward persons suffering mental or emotional stress" (where *status* has been operationally defined as the combined relative ranking on family income, parents' educational level, and father's occupational prestige—or mother's, *if* father not present or employed). Each question has one or more flaws in it. See if you can identify these problems. (A critique of the questionnaire appears at the end of the box.)

Questionnaire

1. What is your reaction to crazy people?

_____

_____

2. What is your father's income? _____

3. As you were growing up, with whom were you living?

_____ both parents

_____ mother only

_____ father only

_____ other (please specify)

4. What is your father's occupation?

_____

(If father is deceased, not living at home, or unemployed or retired, is your mother employed?

_____ yes   _____ no)

5. Did your parents attend college?

_____ yes   _____ no

6. Wouldn't you agree that people with problems should be sympathized with?

_____ yes   _____ no

7. The primary etiology of heterophilic blockage is unmet dependency gratification.

_____ agree

_____ undecided

_____ disagree

8. If a friend of yours began to exhibit strange and erratic behavior, what do you think your response would be?

_____

9. Has *anyone* in your immediate family ever been institutionalized?

_____ yes   _____ no

Critique

The most fundamental critique of any questionnaire is simply, "Does it get the information necessary to test the hypothesis?" While questions can be bad in and of themselves, they can be good only when seen in terms of the needs of the researcher. Good question-naire construction is probably about as much an art as a science, and even "good" questions may contain hidden pitfalls or be made even better when the overall context is considered, but the following flaws definitely exist:

1. Derogatory and vague use of a slang term. Because it's the first question it's even worse: it may contaminate your results either by turn-ing off some people enough to affect your re-sponse rate or it may have a "funneling effect" on later responses.

2. The operational definition of status calls for *family* income, not just father's. Also, it's been found that people are more likely to an-swer a question as personal as income if cate-gories are provided for check-off, rather than this open-ended format.

3. "As you were growing up" is a vague time period. Also, the question is of dubious rele-vance or utility in the current format, al-though it *could* have been used to organize questions 2, 4, and 5.

4. The format (asking about mother's em-ployment only if there's no employed father) may well be sexist. Although it follows the operational definition, the operational defini-tion itself may well be sexist. There are two additional problems. First, a checklist nearly always works better for occupation—open-ended questions often get answers that are too vague to be categorized. Also, in cases where status *will* be measured by mother's occupation, the question only elicits whether or not she's employed at all.

5. Limited measure of educational levels. Also, it's double-barreled: what if one parent attended college and the other didn't?

6. "Wouldn't you agree" is leading the re-spondent. Also, "sympathized" and "prob-lems" are vague.

7. Technical jargon. No one will know what it means. (In fact, *I'm* not even sure what it means, and I wrote it! As close as I can trans-late it, it says, "the main reason you can't get a date is because your folks ignored you.")

8. Asks for speculation regarding a vague, hypothetical situation—which is not always bad, but there's usually a better way. Note, however, that the question is not double-barreled as many have said: it asks only about behavior that is *both* "strange" *and* "erratic."

9. "Institutionalized" is a vague term. Many types of institutionalization would clearly be irrelevant.

that term. This same general principle applies to the responses we get from persons completing a questionnaire.

The meaning of someone's response to a question depends in large part on the wording of the question that was asked. That is true of every question and answer. Some questions seem to encourage particular responses more than other questions. Questions that encourage respondents to answer in a particular way are called **biased.**

In our discussion of the social desirability bias in Chapter 6, we noted that we need to be especially wary of this bias whenever we ask people for information. This applies to the way questionnaire items are worded. Thus, for example, in assessing the attitudes of community residents about a halfway house proposed for their neighborhood, we would not ask if residents agreed with prominent clergy in supporting the facility. Likewise, we would not ask whether they endorsed "humanitarian" proposals to care for the needy in the community. Before moving on to the topic of formatting questionnaires, we'd like to call your attention to the box "Learning from Bad Examples," which illustrates problems in asking questions that we've just discussed.

QUESTIONNAIRE CONSTRUCTION

General Questionnaire Format

The format of a questionnaire is just as important as the nature and wording of the questions asked. An improperly laid out questionnaire can lead respondents to miss questions, can confuse them about the nature of the data desired, and in the extreme, may lead them to throw the questionnaire away. Both general and specific guidelines can be suggested.

As a general rule, the questionnaire should be spread out and uncluttered. Inexperienced researchers tend to fear that their questionnaire will look too long, and as a result, they squeeze several questions onto a single line, abbreviate questions, and try to use as few pages as possible. All

these efforts are ill-advised and even dangerous. Putting more than one question on a line will cause some respondents to miss the second question altogether. Some respondents will misinterpret abbreviated questions. And more generally, respondents who find they have spent considerable time on the first page of what seemed a short questionnaire will be more demoralized than respondents who quickly completed the first several pages of what initially seemed a long form. Moreover, the latter will have made fewer errors and will not have been forced to reread confusing, abbreviated questions. Nor will they have been forced to write a long answer in a tiny space.

The desirability of spreading questions out in the questionnaire cannot be overemphasized. Squeezed-together questionnaires are disastrous whether they are to be completed by the respondents themselves or to be administered by trained interviewers. And the processing of such questionnaires is another nightmare. We'll have more to say about this in Chapter 14.

Formats for Respondents

In one of the most common questionnaire formats, the respondent is expected to check one response from a series. A variety of methods are available. One good option is to provide *boxes* adequately spaced apart. Computer software makes the use of boxes a practical technique these days, or if the questionnaire is to be set in type, this can be accomplished easily and neatly. It is also possible to approximate boxes on a typewriter, however.

If the questionnaire is typed on a typewriter with brackets, excellent boxes can be produced by a left bracket, a space, and a right bracket: [   ]. If brackets are not available, parentheses work reasonably well in the same fashion: (   ). We discourage the use of slashes and underscores, however. First, this technique requires considerably more typing effort, and second, the result is not very neat, especially if the response categories must be single-spaced. Figure 7-1 provides a comparison of the different methods.

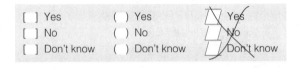

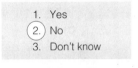

Figure 7-1 Three Answer Formats

Figure 7-2
Circling the Answer

Of the three methods shown, the brackets and the parentheses are clearly the neatest; the slash-and-underscore method looks sloppy. Because every typewriter at least has parentheses, there is no excuse for using slashes and underscores. Another commonly used method is to provide open blanks for check marks. If this method is used, be sure to leave ample vertical space between the blanks. Otherwise, it is often impossible to determine which response was intended because respondents will often enter large check marks.

A very different method might also be considered. Rather than providing boxes to be checked, the researcher might print a code number beside each response and ask the respondent to *circle* the appropriate number (see Figure 7-2). This method has the added advantage of specifying the code number to be entered later in the processing stage (see Chapter 14). If numbers are to be circled, however, you should provide clear and prominent instructions to the respondent because many will be tempted to cross out the appropriate number, which makes data processing even more difficult. (*Note:* The technique can be used more safely when interviewers administer the questionnaires, since they can be specially instructed and supervised.)

Contingency Questions

Quite often in questionnaires, certain questions will be clearly relevant only to some of the respondents and irrelevant to others. In a study of birth control methods, for instance, you would probably not want to ask men if they take birth control pills.

Frequently, this situation—realizing that the topic is relevant only to some respondents—will arise when you wish to ask a series of questions about a certain topic. You may want to ask whether your respondents belong to a particular organization and, if so, how often they attend meetings, whether they have held office in the organization, and so forth. Or you might want to ask whether respondents have heard anything about a certain community issue and then learn the attitudes of those who have heard of it.

The subsequent questions in series such as these are called **contingency questions:** whether they are to be asked and answered is contingent on responses to the first question in the series. The proper use of contingency questions can facilitate the respondents' task in completing the questionnaire because they are not faced with trying to answer questions irrelevant to them.

There are several formats for contingency questions. The one shown in Figure 7-3 is probably the clearest and most effective. Note two key elements in this format. First, the contingency question is isolated from the other questions by being set off to the side and enclosed in a box. Second, an arrow connects the contingency question to the answer on which it is contingent. In the illustration, only respondents answering yes are expected to answer the contingency question. The rest of the respondents should skip it.

It should be noted that the questions shown in Figure 7-3 could have been dealt with in a single question. The question might have read: "How many times, if any, have you smoked marijuana?" The response categories, then, might have read: "Never," "Once," "2 to 5 times," and so forth. Such a single question would apply to all respondents, and each would find an appropriate answer

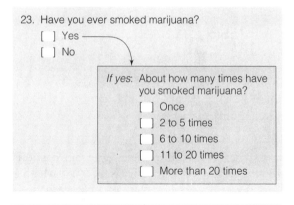

Figure 7-3 Contingency Question Format

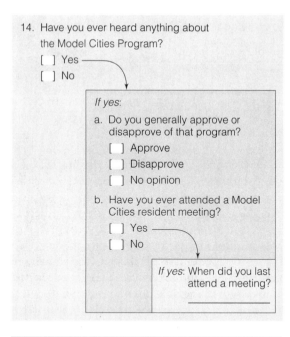

Figure 7-4 Complex Contingency Question

category. Such a question, however, might put some pressure on respondents to report having smoked marijuana, since the main question asks how many times they have smoked it, even though it allows for those cases who have *never smoked marijuana even once*. (The emphases used in the previous sentence give a fair indication of how respondents might read the question.) The contingency question format illustrated in Figure 7-3 should reduce the subtle pressure on respondents to report having smoked marijuana. The foregoing discussion should show how seemingly theoretical issues of *validity* and *reliability* are involved in so mundane a matter as how to put questions on a piece of paper.

Used properly, even rather complex sets of contingency questions can be constructed without confusing the respondent. Figure 7-4 illustrates a more complicated example.

Sometimes a set of contingency questions is long enough to extend over several pages. Suppose you are studying the voting behaviors of poor people, and you wish to ask a large number of questions of individuals who had voted in a national, state, or local election. You could separate out the relevant respondents with an initial question such as "Have you ever voted in a national, state, or local election?" but it would be confusing to place the contingency questions in a box

stretching over several pages. It would make more sense to enter instructions in parentheses after each answer, telling respondents to answer or skip the contingency questions. Figure 7-5 provides an illustration of this method.

In addition to these instructions, it would be worthwhile to place an instruction at the top of each page containing only the contingency questions. For example, you might say, "This page is only for respondents who have voted in a national, state, or local election." Clear instructions such as these spare respondents the frustration of reading and puzzling over questions irrelevant to them as well as increasing the likelihood of responses from those for whom the questions are relevant.

Matrix Questions

Quite often, you will want to ask several questions that have the same set of answer categories. This is typically the case whenever the Likert re-

13. Have you ever voted in a national, state, or local election?

[ ] Yes (Please answer questions 14–25.)

[ ] No (Please skip questions 14–25. Go directly to question 26 on page 8.)

Figure 7-5 Instructions to Skip

17. Beside *each* of the statements presented below, please indicate whether you Strongly Agree (SA), Agree (A), Disagree (D), Strongly Disagree (SD), or are Undecided (U).

	SA	A	D	SD	U
a. What this country needs is more law and order.	[ ]	[ ]	[ ]	[ ]	[ ]
b. The police should be disarmed in America.	[ ]	[ ]	[ ]	[ ]	[ ]
c. During riots, looters should be shot on sight.	[ ]	[ ]	[ ]	[ ]	[ ]
etc.					

Figure 7-6 Matrix Question Format

sponse categories are used. In such cases, it is often possible to construct a matrix of items and answers as illustrated in Figure 7-6.

This format has a number of advantages. First, it uses space efficiently. Second, respondents will probably find it faster to complete a set of questions presented in this fashion. In addition, this format may increase the comparability of responses given to different questions for the respondent as well as for the researcher. Because respondents can quickly review their answers to earlier items in the set, they might choose between, say, "strongly agree" and "agree" on a given statement by comparing their strength of agreement with their earlier responses in the set.

There are some dangers inherent in using this format as well. Its advantages may encourage you to structure an item so that the responses fit into the matrix format when a different, more idiosyncratic, set of responses might be more appropriate. Also, the matrix question format can foster a response set among some respondents: they may develop a pattern of, say, agreeing with all the statements. That would be especially likely if the set of statements began with several that indicated a particular orientation (for example, a liberal political perspective) with only a few later ones representing the opposite orientation. Respondents might assume that all the statements represented the same orientation and, reading quickly, misread some of them, thereby giving the wrong answers. In Chapter 6 we referred briefly to this problem as the *acquiescent response set*. This problem can be reduced somewhat by interspersing positively and negatively worded statements rep-

resenting different orientations and by making all statements short and clear. For instance, in Chapter 6 we noted that the Child's Attitude Toward Mother scale handled this problem by interspersing items like "I resent my mother" and "I hate my mother" with items like "I really enjoy my mother" and "I feel proud of my mother."

Ordering Questions in a Questionnaire

The *order* in which questions are asked can also affect the answers given. First, the appearance of one question can affect the answers given to later ones. For example, if a number of questions have been asked about the dangers of communism to the United States and then a question asks respondents to volunteer (open-ended) what they believe to represent dangers to the United States, communism will receive more citations than would otherwise be the case. In this situation, it is preferable to ask the open-ended question first.

If respondents are asked to assess their overall religiosity ("How important is your religion to you in general?"), their responses to later questions concerning specific aspects of religiosity will be aimed at consistency with the prior assessment. The converse would be true as well. If respondents are first asked specific questions about different aspects of their religiosity, their subsequent overall assessment will reflect the earlier answers.

Some researchers attempt to overcome this effect by randomizing the order of questions. This is usually a futile effort. To begin, a randomized set of questions will probably strike respondents as chaotic and worthless. It will be difficult to answer, moreover, because they must continually switch their attention from one topic to another. And, finally, even a randomized ordering of questions will have the effect discussed previously—except that you will have no control over the effect.

The safest solution is sensitivity to the problem. Although you cannot avoid the effect of question order, you should attempt to estimate what that effect will be. Thus, you will be able to interpret results in a meaningful fashion. If the order of questions seems an especially important issue in a given study, you might construct more than one version of the questionnaire containing the different possible ordering of questions. You would then be able to determine the effects. At the very least, you should pretest your questionnaire in the different forms.

The desired ordering of questions differs somewhat between self-administered questionnaires and interviews. In the former, it is usually best to begin the questionnaire with the most interesting set of questions. The potential respondents who glance casually over the first few questions should want to answer them. Perhaps the questions will ask for attitudes that they are aching to express. At the same time, however, the initial questions should not be threatening. (It might be a bad idea to begin with questions about sexual behavior or drug use.) Requests for duller, demographic data (age, gender, and the like) should generally be placed at the end of a self-administered questionnaire. Placing these questions at the beginning, as many inexperienced researchers are tempted to do, gives the questionnaire the initial appearance of a routine form, and the person receiving it may not be motivated to complete it.

Just the opposite is generally true for interview surveys. When the potential respondent's door first opens, the interviewer must begin gaining rapport quickly. After a short introduction to the study, the interviewer can best begin by enumerating the members of the household, getting demographic data about each. Such questions are easily answered and generally nonthreatening. Once the initial rapport has been established, the interviewer can then move into the area of attitudes and more sensitive matters. An interview that began with the question "Do you believe in God?" would probably end rather quickly.

Instructions

Every questionnaire, whether it is to be completed by respondents or administered by interviewers, should contain clear instructions and introductory comments where appropriate.

It is useful to begin every self-administered questionnaire with basic instructions to be followed in completing it. Although many people these days are pretty familiar with forms and questionnaires, you should begin by telling them exactly what you want: that they are to indicate their answers to certain questions by placing a check mark or an X in the box beside the appropriate answer or by writing in their answer when asked to do so. If many open-ended questions are used, respondents should be given some guidance about whether brief or lengthy answers are expected. If you wish to encourage your respondents to elaborate on their responses to closed-ended questions, that should be noted.

If a questionnaire is arranged into content subsections—political attitudes, religious attitudes, background data—introduce each section with a short statement concerning its content and purpose. For example, "In this section, we would like to know what people around here consider the most important community problems." Demographic items at the end of a self-administered questionnaire might be introduced thus: "Finally, we would like to know just a little about you so we can see how different types of people feel about the issues we have been examining."

Short introductions such as these help make sense out of the questionnaire for the respondent.

They make the questionnaire seem less chaotic, especially when it taps a variety of data. And they help put the respondent in the proper frame of mind for answering the questions.

Some questions may require special instructions to facilitate proper answering. That is especially true if a given question varies from the general instructions pertaining to the whole questionnaire. Some specific examples will illustrate this situation.

Despite the desirability of mutually exclusive answer categories in closed-ended questions, more than one answer may often apply for respondents. If you want a single answer, you should make this clear in the question. An example would be, "From the list below, please check the *primary* reason for your decision to attend college." Often the main question can be followed by a parenthetical note: "Please check the *one* best answer." If, on the other hand, you want the respondent to check as many answers as apply, that should be made clear as well.

When a set of answer categories are to be rank-ordered by the respondent, the instructions should indicate as much, and a different type of answer format should be used (for example, blanks instead of boxes). These instructions should indicate how many answers are to be ranked (for example, all, first and second, first and last, most important and least important) and the order of ranking (for instance, "Place a 1 beside the most important, a 2 beside the next most important, and so forth"). Rank-ordering of responses is often difficult for respondents, however, because they may have to read and reread the list several times, so this technique should only be used in situations where no other method will produce the desired result.

In multiple-part matrix questions, it is helpful to give special instructions unless the same format is used throughout the questionnaire. Sometimes respondents will be expected to check one answer in each *column* of the matrix, and in other questionnaires they will be expected to check one answer in each *row*. Whenever the questionnaire contains both types, it will be useful to add an instruction clarifying which is expected in each case.

We could give you countless other tips and guidelines in connection with questionnaire construction, but this section of this single chapter would soon be longer than the rest of the book. There is also the danger that you'd be bored silly. Somewhat reluctantly, then, we'll complete this discussion with an illustration of a real questionnaire, showing you how some of these comments find substance in practice.

Before turning to the illustration, however, we want to mention a critical aspect of questionnaire design that we will delay discussing until Chapter 14: *precoding*. Because the information collected by questionnaires is typically transformed into some type of computer format, it is usually appropriate to include data processing instructions on the questionnaire itself. These instructions indicate where specific pieces of information will be stored in the machine-readable data files. In Chapter 14, we'll discuss the nature of such storage and point out the kinds of questionnaire notations that would be appropriate. As a preview, however, notice that the following illustration has been precoded with the mysterious numbers that appear near questions and answer categories.

A Composite Illustration

Figure 7-7 is a portion of a 32-page student survey questionnaire developed by University of Hawaii students in 1974. The purpose of the survey was to create a comprehensive file of information about student attitudes and orientations in a variety of areas: politics, religion, education, and others.

Although this questionnaire is rather dated and is not a social work questionnaire, we present it here because it has so many points for you to consider. (Also, it employed no expensive production techniques—it was typed and then photo-offset.) On the whole, it is a pretty good questionnaire. Still, it is not perfect. As you read through the

GENERAL INSTRUCTIONS: Either a pen or pencil may be used to complete this questionnaire. Most of the questions may be answered by simply placing an X in the appropriate box; other questions ask for written-in answers. However, you may write in additional comments whenever you wish to do so. Please ignore the numbers beside the questions and answers; they are for machine tabulation only.

A. POLITICAL ORIENTATIONS

NOTE 1

(1-4, 5/1)

1. Beside each of the statements listed below, please indicate whether you strongly agree (SA), agree (A), disagree (D), strongly disagree (SD), or don't know (DK).

	SA 1	A 2	D 3	SD 4	DK 5
(6-15)					
a. It would be a good thing if the United Nations were someday converted into a world government.	[ ]	[ ]	[ ]	[ ]	[ ]
b. People who defile the American flag should be put in prison.	[ ]	[ ]	[ ]	[ ]	[ ]
c. The United States is too ready to interpret the actions of communist nations as threatening.	[ ]	[ ]	[ ]	[ ]	[ ]
d. The United States is spending too much money on defense	[ ]	[ ]	[ ]	[ ]	[ ]
e. Communism is probably the best form of government for some countries	[ ]	[ ]	[ ]	[ ]	[ ]
f. The Central Intelligence Agency has too much power.	[ ]	[ ]	[ ]	[ ]	[ ]
g. The NLF (Viet Cong) are mostly invaders from North Vietnam.	[ ]	[ ]	[ ]	[ ]	[ ]
h. The United States was justified in using nuclear weapons against Japan in 1945	[ ]	[ ]	[ ]	[ ]	[ ]
i. If it were not for the power of the United States, most nations of the world would be taken over by the communists	[ ]	[ ]	[ ]	[ ]	[ ]
j. We should support our country's policies even when they are wrong.	[ ]	[ ]	[ ]	[ ]	[ ]

NOTE 1: This is not a serious problem, but because the full questionnaire dealt with a variety of topics, it would have been useful to insert a short introductory comment at this point to inform respondents of what was contained in the section. Such introductions would have been even more useful in later sections, where respondents were asked implicitly to switch their thinking to different topics. An appropriate introduction might have been, "In this first section, we are interested in learning how you feel about a variety of foreign and domestic political issues."

Figure 7-7 A Sample Questionnaire

2. In general, how do you feel about each of the following possible U.S. policies regarding the war in Vietnam? Please indicate beside each whether you approve (A), disapprove (D), or don't know (DK).

(16-25)	A 1	D 2	DK 3
a. Maintenance of present level of U.S. military activities	[ ]	[ ]	[ ]
b. Immediate beginning of unilateral withdrawal of U.S. forces	[ ]	[ ]	[ ]
c. Withdrawal of U.S. forces into strategic hamlets in South Vietnam.	[ ]	[ ]	[ ]
d. Bombing of strategic targets in North Vietnam	[ ]	[ ]	[ ]
e. Invasion of North Vietnam by U.S. ground forces	[ ]	[ ]	[ ]
f. Invasion of North Vietnam by South Vietnamese ground forces.	[ ]	[ ]	[ ]
g. Use of nuclear weapons against North Vietnam if recommended by U.S. military leaders	[ ]	[ ]	[ ]
h. Cessation of all U.S. bombing in South Vietnam.	[ ]	[ ]	[ ]
i. Granting U.S. military leaders complete freedom to handle the war as they see fit	[ ]	[ ]	[ ]
j. Continuation of the Paris peace talks	[ ]	[ ]	[ ]

3. As a general rule, do you personally tend to believe or doubt the validity of *official* U.S. government reports regarding the following aspects of the war in Vietnam?

(26-28)	Believe 1	Doubt 2	Don't know 3
a. Reports of enemy casualties.	[ ]	[ ]	[ ]
b. Reports of Viet Cong atrocities	[ ]	[ ]	[ ]
c. Proclamations of U.S. goals in Vietnam.	[ ]	[ ]	[ ]

4. Is there anything else you would like to say about the war in Vietnam? (Additional space is provided at the end of the questionnaire.)
   (29-30)

Figure 7-7 *(continued)*

5. Listed below are some statements people have made regarding the student peace movement in America. Beside each, please indicate whether you strongly agree (SA), agree (A), disagree (D), strongly disagree (SD), or don't know how you feel (DK).

	(31–36)	SA 1	A 2	D 3	SD 4	DK 5
a. Peace demonstrators threaten the peace more than they enhance it	. . .	[ ]	[ ]	[ ]	[ ]	[ ]
b. A person's moral convictions should take precedence over national policies of war	. . . .	[ ]	[ ]	[ ]	[ ]	[ ]
c. Peace demonstrators are primarily interested in personal publicity	. . .	[ ]	[ ]	[ ]	[ ]	[ ]
d. Pacifism is simply not a practical philosophy in the world today	. .	[ ]	[ ]	[ ]	[ ]	[ ]
e. Burning one's draft card should not be considered a crime	. . . .	[ ]	[ ]	[ ]	[ ]	[ ]
f. Peace demonstrators should be drafted and sent to Vietnam	. . . . . .	[ ]	[ ]	[ ]	[ ]	[ ]

6. In November, 1968, two U.S. Marines sought sanctuary on the UH campus as a protest against the war in Vietnam. Which of the following do you believe *should* have been the policy of the university administration?

(37)

    1 [ ] The university should have granted official sanctuary.   <u>NOTE 2</u>

    2 [ ] The university should have permitted them to stay on campus without granting official sanctuary.

    3 [ ] The university should have forced them to leave the campus.

    <u>NOTE 3</u>

7. There has been disagreement recently as to whether the university should permit military recruiters and antidraft counselors to come on the UH campus to talk with students. Do you personally feel the university should permit both, only one, or neither to come on campus to talk with students?

(38)

    1 [ ] Should permit *both* military recruiters and antidraft counselors

    2 [ ] Should permit only *military* recruiters

    3 [ ] Should permit only *antidraft* counselors

    4 [ ] Should permit *neither*

    5 [ ] I don't know

NOTE 2: Because Question 5 has its answer spaces to the right of the answers, it would have been better to follow the same pattern with Questions 6 and 7. Switching the placement of answer spaces on the same page will make data entry somewhat difficult and will increase the likelihood of errors.

NOTE 3: The list of response categories for Question 6 is probably not exhaustive. In fact, some respondents wrote in answers of their own. It would have been better to provide an "Other (Please specify): _____" category for this purpose. (Incidentally, the university administration chose the second alternative, and everything worked out just fine.)

Figure 7-7 *(continued)*

8. Which of the following, if any, do you believe should be sufficient grounds for exemption from military service? (Please check 'yes' if you believe it should be sufficient and 'no' if you believe it should not be sufficient.)

	Yes 1	No 2	Don't know 3
(39-43)			
a. Membership in a religious group with strong pacifist principles	[ ]	[ ]	[ ]
b. Strong personal religious pacifist principles	[ ]	[ ]	[ ]
c. Strong personal moral or philosophical (nonreligious) pacifist principles	[ ]	[ ]	[ ]
d. Strong objections to a particular war	[ ]	[ ]	[ ]
e. Other (Please specify: _____ _____) . . .	[ ]	[ ]	[ ]

9. Have you personally supported the current peace movement in any of the following ways?

	Yes 1	No 2
(44-50)		
a. Attended a peace rally	[ ]	[ ]
b. Participated in a peace march	[ ]	[ ]
c. Written a letter intended for publication.	[ ]	[ ]
d. Spoken at a peace rally	[ ]	[ ]
e. Written a letter to a public official	[ ]	[ ]
f. Campaigned for a peace candidate.	[ ]	[ ]
g. Distributed peace literature.	[ ]	[ ]
h. Participated in *mild* direct action subject to arrest (trespassing, disturbing the peace, etc.)	[ ]	[ ]
i. Participated in *strong* direct action subject to arrest (destruction of property, interfering with military operations, etc.)	[ ]	[ ]
j. Was arrested for peace movement activities	[ ]	[ ]
k. Other (Please specify: _____ _____) . . .	[ ]	[ ]

10. Which government would you prefer to have represented in the United Nations: the Nationalist government on Taiwan or the Communist government on the mainland of China?

(55)   NOTE 4

   1 [ ] Only the Nationalist government on Taiwan
   2 [ ] Only the Communist government on the mainland
   3 [ ] Both governments should be represented

NOTE 4: Rather whimsically, the answer spaces for Question 10 have been placed to the left, whereas those for Questions 11 and 12 are on the right. See Note 2 if you've forgotten why this is a bad idea.

Figure 7-7 *(continued)*

11. Please indicate whether you agree (A), disagree (D), or are undecided (U) about each of the following possible United States' policies toward mainland China.

(56-61)	A 1	D 2	U 3
a. Granting diplomatic recognition to China	[ ]	[ ]	[ ]
b. Seeking economic trade with China.	[ ]	[ ]	[ ]
c. Offering economic aid to China	[ ]	[ ]	[ ]
d. Seeking cultural exchange programs with China .	[ ]	[ ]	[ ]
e. Seeking to contain China militarily.	[ ]	[ ]	[ ]
f. Seeking to destroy China's military power . . .	[ ]	[ ]	[ ]

12. The question of military intervention has come up many times in the past. The following is a list of instances in which the U.S. had to decide whether or not to intervene militarily. In each case, please indicate whether or not you feel the U.S. should have intervened with military force.

(62-72)	Should have intervened 1	Should not have intervened 2	Not sure 3
a. Chinese Communist Revolution, 1948-49	[ ]	[ ]	[ ]
b. Korean conflict, 1950	[ ]	[ ]	[ ]
c. Hungarian revolt, 1956 . . .	[ ]	[ ]	[ ]
d. Bay of Pigs invasion, 1961 .	[ ]	[ ]	[ ]
e. Vietnam buildup, 1964-65 . .	[ ]	[ ]	[ ]
f. Dominican Republic revolt, 1965	[ ]	[ ]	[ ]
g. Rhodesian independence, 1965	[ ]	[ ]	[ ]
h. Greek military coup d'etat, 1965	[ ]	[ ]	[ ]
i. Israeli-Arab conflict, 1967 .	[ ]	[ ]	[ ]
j. Capture of U.S.S. Pueblo, 1968	[ ]	[ ]	[ ]
k. Russian occupation of Czechoslovakia, 1968.	[ ]	[ ]	[ ]

13. In general, how would you characterize your own political orientation? How would you characterize the political orientations of your parents? (Please answer for each.)

(73-75)	Yourself	Your Father	Your Mother
Right radical	1 [ ]	1 [ ]	1 [ ]
Very conservative	2 [ ]	2 [ ]	2 [ ]

Figure 7-7 *(continued)*

	(73-75)	Yourself	Your Father	Your Mother	NOTE 5
Moderately conservative		3 [ ]	3 [ ]	3 [ ]	
Moderately liberal		4 [ ]	4 [ ]	4 [ ]	
Left radical		5 [ ]	5 [ ]	5 [ ]	
Other (Please specify: _____					
_____) . .		6 [ ]	6 [ ]	6 [ ]	
Don't know		7 [ ]	7 [ ]	7 [ ]	

14. Do you normally identify yourself with any particular political party? (Please indicate *which party*, if any, you identify
with.)   NOTE 6
(76)

     1 [ ] Democratic party
     2 [ ] Republican party
     3 [ ] American Independent party
     4 [ ] Peace and Freedom party
     5 [ ] Other (Please specify: _____)
     6 [ ] No party identification, independent

15. Were you eligible to vote in the November, 1968, general
election?   NOTE 7
(77-78)

     1 [ ] Yes**   15a. **If *yes*, did you vote? 1 [ ] Yes
     2 [ ] No   2 [ ] No

16. Whether or not you were eligible to vote in November, 1968,
which of these Presidential candidates, if any, did you
prefer?
(79)

     1 [ ] Hubert Humphrey
     2 [ ] Richard Nixon
     3 [ ] George Wallace
     4 [ ] Eldridge Cleaver
     5 [ ] None of these

(80/R)

NOTE 5: "Very liberal" is missing from the list of response categories. As a result, the spectrum of political orientations is unbalanced. This omission is the result of a simple typing error and the failure to proofread the questionnaire carefully enough. It is worth noting that this error occurred after hours of considered debate over the proper terms to be used in labeling different political orientations—especially the extremes. The most careful conceptualization can go for naught unless every step in the research process is taken with sufficient caution.

NOTE 6: There go the answer spaces across the page again. Since Question 15 contains a contingency question, making it awkward to place the answer spaces to the right, it would have been better to place those for Question 13 on the left.

NOTE 7: This is not a very good format for the contingency question. See Figure 7-3 earlier in this chapter for a better format. Also, note how crowded the questionnaire is at this point. There is a danger that many respondents would get confused and miss the contingency question altogether. Can you determine why the researchers crowded questions together so much here?

Figure 7-7 *(continued)*

questionnaire, you will find marginal notations (*Note 1* and so on). Whenever such a notation appears, you might try to figure out how the questionnaire could have been improved at that point. In the notes below the illustration questionnaire, we tell how we feel it could have been improved.

To improve your critical skills in questionnaire construction, you should also look for mistakes we have *not* marked. For an illustration of a questionnaire that is more social work–related, one that is also technically more sophisticated, we refer you to the Commission on Aging survey in Appendix D.

CONSTRUCTING COMPOSITE MEASURES

Some variables are too complex, or multifaceted, to be measured with just one item on a questionnaire. These variables are composites of various indicators, and accordingly they require composite or cumulative measures that combine several empirical indicators of the referent variable into a single measure. Examples of complex variables that social work researchers may find difficult to tap adequately with a single questionnaire item are marital satisfaction, level of social functioning, level of client satisfaction with services, practitioner attitudes about working with various target populations, quality of life, and attitudes about women or minorities. (In Chapter 5 we discussed how you might go about locating existing composite measures, and information about their reliability and validity, from published material.)

The composite or cumulative measures of complex variables are called *scales* and *indexes*. Indexes and scales enable us to represent complex variables with scores that provide greater potential for variance than would a single item. Analyzing one score derived from multiple items also is more efficient than analyzing each item separately. Consider, for example, the Child's Attitude Toward Mother scale, which we examined in Chapter 6. Instead of analyzing 25 responses of 1 to 5 dealing with different facets of children's attitudes toward their mothers, we are able to sum all 25 responses and obtain one score ranging from 25 to 125 to represent that multifaceted variable.

Indexes and scales typically provide ordinal measures of variables. In other words, they rank-order people (or other units of analysis) in terms of specific variables such as attitude toward mother, social functioning, and the like. That rank-order is determined by the overall score that combines all of the items on the scale.

Item Selection

The first step in constructing an index or scale is *item selection*. To begin, naturally, items should have *face validity*. If you want to measure self-esteem, for example, each of your items should appear *on its face* to indicate some aspect of self-esteem. You might conceive of concepts related to self-esteem, such as depression, but your self-esteem scale should include items reflecting only self-esteem, not items reflecting depression. Thus, if you are measuring self-esteem, you would not ask people if they feel lonely or blue just because you think that depression is related to self-esteem. Instead, you would reserve that question for a scale that measures depression and restrict the self-esteem scale to items pertaining to the favorableness of one's self-image. (You might have items asking people whether they feel they are smart, attractive, likable, competent, trustworthy, and so on.) This is known as *unidimensionality* in scale construction.

Items also should have adequate *variance*. If everyone gives the same response to a particular item, then that item would have no use in constructing a scale. Suppose, for example, that on a scale attempting to measure parental child-rearing attitudes no parents admitted to wanting to sexually abuse their children. Then that item would not be useful in distinguishing parents who are more likely to be abusive from those who are less likely to be abusive. To find out whether items have adequate variance, you would pretest the scale and then examine the range of responses to each item.

Ultimately, which items you select for a scale should depend on how those items influence the scale's *reliability* and *validity,* which are determined using procedures discussed in the preceding chapter. Items that have no relationship with other items on the same scale, or with an external criterion of the validity of the scale, should be discarded or modified.

Handling Missing Data

In virtually every study utilizing indexes and scales, some respondents fail to respond to some items. Sometimes they may just leave the item blank; at other times they may choose a "don't know" response. There are several ways to deal with this problem of missing data.

First, if all but a few respondents respond to every item, you may decide to exclude from the analysis the data from those few respondents whose index or scale contains some missing data. But this should not be done if it looks as if it might bias your remaining sample, such as by excluding most of the people who share a particular characteristic.

Second, you may sometimes have grounds for treating missing data as one of the available responses. For instance, if a questionnaire has asked respondents to indicate their participation in a number of activities by checking "yes" or "no" for each, many respondents may have checked some of the activities "yes" and left the remainder blank. In such a case, you might decide that a failure to answer meant "no" and score missing data in this case as though the respondents had checked the "no" space.

Third, a careful analysis of missing data may yield an interpretation of their meaning. In constructing a measure of political conservatism, for example, you may discover that respondents who

failed to answer a given question were generally as conservative on other items as those who gave the conservative answer. As another example, a recent study measuring religious beliefs found that people who answered "don't know" about a given belief were almost identical to the "disbelievers" in their answers about other beliefs. (*Note:* You should not take these examples as empirical guides in your own studies, but only as suggestive of ways to analyze your own data.) Whenever the analysis of missing data yields such interpretations, then, you may decide to score such cases accordingly.

You can handle this problem in a number of other ways. If an item has several possible values, you might assign the middle value to cases with missing data—for example, you could assign a 2 if the values are 0, 1, 2, 3, and 4. For a continuous variable such as age, you could similarly assign the mean to cases with missing data. Or missing data can be supplied by assigning values at random. All of these are conservative solutions in that they work against any relationships you may expect to find.

If you're creating an index out of several items, it sometimes works to handle missing data by using proportions based on what is observed. Suppose your index is composed of six indicators, and you have only four observations for a particular subject. If the subject has earned 4 points out of a possible 4, you might assign an index score of 6; if the subject has 2 points (half the possible score on four items), you could assign a score of 3 (half the possible score on six observations).

The choice of a particular method to be used depends so much on the research situation as to preclude the suggestion of a single "best" method or a ranking of the several we have described. Excluding all cases with missing data can bias the representativeness of the findings, but including such cases by assigning scores to missing data can influence the nature of the findings. The safest and best method would be to construct the scale or index using alternative methods and see whether the same findings follow from each. Understanding your data is the final goal of analysis anyway.

SOME PROMINENT SCALING PROCEDURES

As you might imagine from the lengthy list of reference volumes for existing scales, which we presented in Figure 5-3, scales can come in a seemingly endless variety of formats. Some scaling procedures are highly complex and require a tremendous expenditure of labor to develop. Because of the time and expense involved, some scaling formats that historically have been highly regarded by social scientists, such as Guttman scaling and Thurstone scaling, are rarely used these days by social work researchers operating within the constraints of more limited budgets and time restrictions. Less complex scales can be as simple as one-item scales that may have very little wording and that may be administered in a conversational format. For example, if you want to assess the moods of very young children (perhaps before and after receiving some form of treatment, like play therapy), you might present them with a handful of simple cartoonish faces, with a smiley face at one end of the continuum and a frowning, sad face at the other end. You would then ask them to select the face that best fit how they were feeling. Or you might assess how well your adult clients were responding to your intervention for anxiety by asking them to rate their anxiety on a scale from 1 to 10, with 1 representing no anxiety and 10 representing the worst anxiety imaginable.

Likert Scaling

Not all highly regarded scaling formats are extraordinarily expensive. The term **Likert scale,** for example, is associated with a question format that is frequently used in contemporary survey questionnaires. Basically, the respondent is presented with a *statement* in the questionnaire and is asked to indicate whether he or she "strongly agrees," "agrees," "disagrees," "strongly disagrees," or is "undecided." Modifications of the wording of the response categories (for example, "approve") may be used, of course.

The particular value of this format is the unambiguous *ordinality* of response categories. If respondents were permitted to volunteer or select such answers as "sort of agree," "pretty much agree," "really agree," and so forth, the researcher would find it impossible to judge the relative strength of agreement intended by the various respondents. The Likert format resolves this dilemma.

The Likert format also lends itself to a straightforward method of scale or index construction. Because identical response categories are used for several items intended to measure a given variable, each such item can be scored in a uniform manner. With five response categories, scores of 0 to 4 or 1 to 5 might be assigned, taking the direction of the items into account (for instance, assign a score of 5 to "strongly agree" for positive items and to "strongly disagree" for negative items). Each respondent would then be assigned an overall score representing the summation of the scores he or she received for responses to the individual items.

The Likert method is based on the assumption that an overall score based on responses to the many items reflecting a particular variable under consideration provides a reasonably good measure of the variable. These overall scores are not the final product of index or scale construction; rather, they are used in an *item analysis* to select the *best* items. Essentially, each item is correlated with the large, composite measure. Items that correlate highest with the composite measure are assumed to provide the best indicators of the variable, and only those items would be included in the index or scale ultimately used for analyses of the variable.

It should be noted that the uniform scoring of Likert-item response categories assumes that each

	Very Much	Somewhat	Neither	Somewhat	Very Much	
Interesting	☐	☐	☐	☐	☐	Boring
Simple	☐	☐	☐	☐	☐	Complex
Uncaring	☐	☐	☐	☐	☐	Caring
Useful	☐	☐	☐	☐	☐	Useless
			etc.			

Figure 7-8 Semantic Differential

item has about the same *intensity* as the rest. you should also realize that Likert-type items can be used in a variety of ways: you are by no means bound to the method described. Such items can be combined with other types of items in the construction of simple scales. However, if all the items being considered for inclusion in a composite measure are in the Likert format, the method we described should be considered.

Semantic Differential

As we've seen, Likert-type items ask respondents to agree or disagree with a particular position. The *semantic differential* format asks them to choose between two opposite positions. Here's how it works.

Suppose we are conducting an experiment to evaluate the effectiveness of this book on readers' appreciation of social work research. Let's say that we have created experimental and control groups as described in Chapter 9. Now we have the subjects report their feelings about social work research. A good way to tap those feelings would be to use a semantic differential format.

To begin, you must determine the *dimensions* along which each selection should be judged by subjects. Then you need to find two *opposite* terms, representing the polar extremes along each dimension. Let's suppose one dimension that interests you is simply whether subjects are interested in research. Two opposite terms in this case

could be "interesting" and "boring." Similarly, we might want to know whether they regarded research as "complex" or "simple," "caring" or "uncaring," and so forth.

Once we have determined the relevant dimensions and have found terms to represent the extremes of each, we might prepare a rating sheet to be completed by each subject. Figure 7-8 shows an example of what it might look like.

On each line of the rating sheet, the subject would indicate how he or she felt about social work research: whether it was interesting or boring, for instance, and whether it was "somewhat" that way or "very much" so. To avoid creating a biased pattern of responses to such items, it's a good idea to vary the placement of terms that are likely to be related to each other. Notice, for example, that "uncaring" and "useful" are on the left side of the sheet and "caring" and "useless" are on the right side. It is very likely that those who select "uncaring" would also choose "useless" as opposed to "useful."

CONSTRUCTING CULTURALLY SENSITIVE INSTRUMENTS

In Chapter 3 we discussed cultural insensitivity in research as an ethical problem and briefly identified some steps researchers can take to try to avoid it. In Chapter 6 we illustrated measurement errors that can result from cultural bias and interviewer insensitivity. We will conclude the current chapter by reexamining these issues in connection with the construction of culturally sensitive measurement instruments. We cannot assume that scales and indexes that appear to be reliable and valid when tested out with one culture will be reliable and valid when used with other cultures. In the United States, this issue is particularly relevant to the use of instruments that have been tested with whites and then used when conducting research with members of minority groups.

Language Difficulties

Constructing culturally sensitive instruments is particularly salient when some of our research subjects don't speak English well or at all. Three rather obvious steps to be taken under these circumstances are the use of *bilingual interviewers,* the *translating of the measures into the language of the respondents,* and *pretesting the measures* to see if they are understood as intended. But taking these steps will not guarantee success in attaining reliable and valid measurement. The translation process, for example, is by no means simple.

Yu, Zhang, and associates (1987) provide the following illustration of some of the complexities involved in translating instruments. They were trying to translate items on self-esteem from English to Chinese for a study being conducted in Shanghai. Their first problem involved whether to translate the instrument into Shanghainese, an unstandardized and unwritten language, or into a standard Chinese language. Another difficulty involved a set of questions that began with the words, "Think of a person who . . . ," such as when they asked "Think of a person who feels that he is a failure generally in life," or "Think of a person who feels he has much to be proud of." They would then ask, "Is this person very much like you, much like you, somewhat like you, very little like you, or not at all like you during the past year?" (1987:78). In their pretesting, Yu and Zhang discovered that most respon-

dents did not understand this form of questioning and frequently asked questions like, "Who is this person?" "What did you say his name is?" (1987:79).

Yu and Zhang consequently modified the questions but still encountered problems in their further pretesting. One problematic revised item read, "Have you ever felt that you had something to be proud of?" Yu and Zhang discovered that in the culture they were studying humility is an important virtue, and therefore they could not use a negative answer to this question as an indicator of self-esteem. Another revised item read, "Have you ever thought that you were a failure in life?" Many poor housewives responded with a blank look, asking, "What is a failure in life?" Living in a society where the communist government assigns jobs and salaries, and where almost no one gets fired and where income variations are minimal, they previously had not thought of life in terms of competitiveness and success or failure. Yu and Zhang also reported problems in culturally related suspicions that interviewers were part of a surveillance system, which could impede the validity of the information respondents provide.

One procedure that has been developed to deal with complexities in translating instruments from one language into another is called *back-translation.* This method begins with a bilingual person translating the instrument and its instructions to a target language. Then another bilingual person translates from the target language back to the original language (not seeing the original version of the instrument). Then the original instrument is compared to the back-translated version of it, and items with discrepancies are modified further. But back-translation is by no means foolproof. It does not guarantee the avoidance of cultural bias. For example, the reluctance among Chinese respondents to acknowledge pride is not a translation problem, but one of understanding unique cultural values and their implications for social desirability. Constructing culturally sensitive measurement instruments involves issues that go beyond resolving language difficulties.

Other Factors in Cultural Bias

Rogler (1989) provides several examples of the influence of cultural bias not involving language difficulties in connection to research in mental health. One involves a study conducted in Puerto Rico of how the schizophrenia of one spouse influences marital decision making. Questions commonly used to evaluate marital decision making in the United States—"where to go on vacation, which school the children should attend, the purchasing of insurance policies, and so on"—did not apply to impoverished Puerto Rican families who were "struggling to satisfy their most elementary needs for food, clothing, and housing" (1989:29).

In another example, Rogler discusses findings indicating that Puerto Ricans living in the Washington Heights section of Manhattan reported more psychiatric symptoms than did their counterparts sharing the same social class in other ethnic groups. Rogler cites other findings showing that the psychiatric symptom statements on the measuring scales were evaluated as less socially undesirable by Puerto Rican respondents than by respondents from other ethnic groups. In other words, the social desirability bias against admitting to psychiatric symptoms seemed to be influencing Puerto Rican respondents less than other respondents. Therefore, the finding of higher rates of psychiatric symptomatology among Puerto Ricans may have been invalid, a measurement error resulting from cultural differences in the social undesirability of particular scale responses.

To try to anticipate and avoid problems like these, Rogler recommends that researchers spend a period of *direct immersion in the culture* of the population to be studied before administering measures that were developed on other populations. To assess potential problems in the applicability of the measures, researchers should

interview knowledgeable informants in the study population and should use the *field observation methods* that we will discuss in Chapter 12. When Rogler and his associates did this, for example, they observed spiritualist mediums attempting to control the spirits of patients in a psychiatric hospital in Puerto Rico. This helped sensitize them to the importance of spiritualism in that culture, which influenced how they interpreted patient reports of evil spirits in their psychiatric measures.

Rogler's work also illustrates the importance of pretesting your instruments. In Chapter 6 we mentioned the importance of always testing your questionnaire in a dry run to see if your target population will understand it and not find it too unwieldy, even if you are not researching minorities. We think you can see from this discussion that such pretesting is particularly important when applying an instrument to a population other than the one for whom the instrument was initially developed. It was through pretesting, for example, that Rogler learned of the inapplicability of questions about vacations and insurance policies when studying decision making among impoverished Puerto Rican families.

Hill (1978) discussed the influence of cultural bias in connection to whites conducting interviews in low-income black communities where respondents rarely see whites. Whites who visit them may be perceived as outsiders or as representatives of white institutions that have some control over their lives. Their interview responses are therefore likely to reflect political expedience rather than their actual situations. Monette, Sullivan, and DeJong (1994) reviewed studies showing that when African Americans are interviewed by whites they are less likely to express dissatisfaction or resentment about racism and more likely to express positive feelings about whites. Likewise, when whites are interviewed by African Americans, they are more likely to express "pro-black" attitudes.

It is widely believed that cultural sensitivity will be enhanced when the people gathering the data are of the same ethnicity as the respondents. While this may be a good rule of thumb to follow whenever possible, it is not a foolproof guarantee that cultural bias will be completely avoided. When people are interviewed by "outsiders," they may have a tendency to exaggerate their views in one direction. When they are interviewed by someone of their own ethnicity, they may exaggerate in the other direction.

We'll end our discussion of cultural sensitivity by summarizing steps that you can take to enhance it. When developing measures to be used in research involving people whose culture is different from your own, you should:

1. Directly immerse yourself in the culture before selecting, constructing, or administering measures.

2. Try to find instruments that have been tested and found to be reliable and valid among people in that culture.

3. When such instruments cannot be found, and when existing instruments appear to have some problems related to cultural sensitivity, it is better to modify existing instruments to adapt them to the culture, or to construct new instruments that are more culturally sensitive, than to assume that the reliability and validity assessed in a different cultural context will transfer to the culture you are studying.

4. Utilize knowledgable informants in the study population (perhaps even hiring a consultant from that population) to assess potential problems in the cultural sensitivity of existing measures and/or to help you develop new measures.

5. When studying people who have difficulties speaking your language, use bilingual interviewers and translate the measures into the language of the respondents.

6. After translation is completed by one bilingual person, another bilingual person should back-translate from the target language back to the original language (not seeing the original version of the instrument). Then you should compare the original instrument to the back-translated version of it, noting discrepancies and further modifying items as needed.

7. Pretest the measures to see if they are understood as intended, and, if feasible, test their reliability and validity on the people in the culture you want to study.

8. If possible, use interviewers (or people to administer written instruments) who are of the same ethnicity as the respondents, but do not assume that this is a foolproof guarantee that cultural bias will be completely avoided. Respondents may exaggerate their views in the direction of what they perceive to be socially desirable in their own culture.

In implementing the above steps to enhance cultural sensitivity, be sure to remember that within each ethnic group there are a multiplicity of cultures. Do not assume, for example, that all Asian Americans or all Mexican Americans will need the same instruments or measurement approaches. They will need different instruments and approaches depending on factors such as how recently they immigrated to the United States or how acculturated they have become.

CONSTRUCTING QUALITATIVE MEASURES

Although much of the material in this chapter so far has been about quantitative measurement instruments, such as self-administered questionnaires and scales, constructing measurement instruments is a topic relevant to qualitative research methods as well. For example, we have indicated that qualitative methods can be used to learn about potential cultural biases in measurement instruments and how to avoid them. Also, much earlier in this chapter, we discussed guidelines for asking questions that are just as applicable to gathering information from respondents in qualitative studies as they are in quantitative studies. In either type of study, for instance, one should avoid wording that is biased, too complex, or not relevant to respondents.

At this point, however, we will examine some of the ways that instrument construction is different in qualitative measurement than it is in quantitative measurement. Let's begin by noting that, like quantitative research, qualitative research often involves gathering data by directly observing people in addition to asking them questions. In this chapter we are limiting the discussion to measures for asking people questions, not instruments used for recording direct observations. The latter types of instruments will be discussed in later chapters.

The chief difference between quantitative and qualitative measures for asking people questions is that quantitative measures are always highly structured, tend to use closed-ended questions primarily, and may be administered in either an interview or questionnaire format, whereas qualitative measures rely on interviews that are usually unstructured and that mainly contain open-ended questions with in-depth probes. In Chapter 12 we will discuss qualitative interviewing in greater detail; here we merely want to illustrate how the measures it uses contrast with quantitative measures.

Qualitative interviews can range from completely unstructured, informal conversational interviews that use no measurement instruments to highly structured, standardized interviews in which interviewers must ask questions in the exact order and with the exact wording in which they are written out in advance. In between these two extremes are semistructured interviews utilizing interview guides that list in outline form the topics and issues the interview should ask about, but that allow the interviewer to be flexible, informal, and conversational and to adapt the style of the interview and the sequencing and wording of questions to each particular interviewee.

Excerpts from an exemplary, highly structured standardized open-ended interview schedule are presented in Figure 7-9. This schedule has been used in a qualitative study of openness in adoption conducted by Ruth McRoy, a social work professor at the University of Texas at Austin, and Harold Grotevant, a professor of family social science at the University of Minnesota. Their entire schedule consists of 179 items. We think that the 46 items we have excerpted for Figure 7-9 will give you a sufficient illustration of what a superbly crafted standardized interview schedule looks like. It also illustrates some of the points we made about constructing measurement instruments that apply to both quantitative and qualitative research. Notice, for example, the open-endedness, neutrality, and logical arrangement and sequencing of the questions. Notice also where and how the schedule systematically instructs interviewers to probe for detail and clarification and how it provides parenthetical details to help interviewers clarify the point of the question for respondents who may initially have difficulty in answering. We'd also like you to notice its use of contingency questions. Finally, we suggest you compare this schedule with the questionnaire presented in Figure 7-7 to see the contrast between quantitative and qualitative inquiry in the way questions are asked and the much greater opportunity in qualitative inquiry to probe for in-depth meanings and subjective perspectives.

How might the McRoy/Grotevant instrument have appeared had it been in the form of an interview guide for a semistructured interview? Perhaps it would have been a brief outline of questions to ask about, such as the following one, which we have imagined based on some of the excerpts in Figure 7-9:

I. Background regarding adoption

   A. Prior expectations? Counseling?

   B. Adoption process? How it felt?

   C. Discussions with child? Relatives?

   D. Characteristics of child? Similarities and dissimilarities with parents?

   E. Anticipation of life changes and how prepared for?

McRoy/Grotevant Adoption Research
School of Social Work
2609 University Ave.
University of Texas at Austin
Austin, TX 78712   Code #: __ __ __ __ - __ - __ __
                     Interviewer: _____
                     Date: _____

ADOPTIVE PARENT INTERVIEW

Begin the interview process by reviewing with the parent
the number of adopted children s/he has, their names and
ages.

BACKGROUND REGARDING ADOPTION

   1. Could you begin by telling me a little bit about why
      you decided to adopt?

   2. Whom did you talk to about adoption before you
      reached your decision?
      What advice did you receive?

   3. What did you expect the adoption process to be like?

   4. Please explain the process you went through to adopt
      _____.

   5. How did you feel going through the process?
      .
      .
      .

  11. Do any of your friends have adopted children?
      (Probe: How have they and their experiences
      influenced your feelings?)
      .
      .
      .

  32. When did you tell _____ (child) s/he
      was adopted?

  33. Have you had any problems since your adoption?

  34. How old were you when _____ (child) was
      adopted?

SOURCE: Used by permission of Ruth McRoy.

Figure 7-9 Excerpts from a Standardized Open-Ended Interview Schedule on
Openness in Adoptions

35. How did your relatives react to your decision to adopt?

36. In what ways is _____ (child) like you (temperament, appearance)?

37. In what ways is _____ (child) dissimilar to you (temperament, appearance)?

38. Did you anticipate that the arrival of _____ (child) would mean making changes in your life style?
If so, what changes did you anticipate?

39. How did you and your spouse prepare for the arrival of _____ (child)? (e.g., reading, talking with each other or to others, preparing siblings, etc.)

40. Did you and your spouse talk about how your relationship might change?
How did you plan to handle the changes?
How did your relationship *actually* change after the adoption of your child?

41. Please describe the time around the arrival of _____ in your family.
How would you describe _____'s early behavior (Probe: pleasant, easy, fussy, difficult, etc.)?
What were some of the satisfactions and problems you encountered in the first 3 years?
What was your relationship like with _____ during those early years? (Probe for specific events and behaviors rather than global evaluations.)

KNOWLEDGE ABOUT DEGREES OF OPENNESS IN ADOPTION

42. What options did your adoption agency offer regarding open or closed adoptions (non-identifying information, photos of birthparents, continued sharing of information, meeting parents, ongoing contact, etc.)?

43. Had you heard of open adoptions before you came to _____ (agency)?

Figure 7-9 *(continued)*

44. If so, what did you think the term meant?

45. What does the term "semi-open adoption" mean to you?

46. What does the term "traditional or closed adoption" mean to you?

47. Describe the process you went through before deciding what form of openness you would choose?

48. What option did you choose?

49. Why did you choose this option?

50. What do you see as the advantages and the disadvantages of:
    a. traditional "closed" adoption

    b. semi-open adoption

    c. open adoption

IF FAMILY CHOSE A TRADITIONAL (CLOSED) ADOPTION, CONTINUE DIRECTLY ON TO THE *PINK* SECTION, PAGES *6–7*.

IF FAMILY CHOSE TO SHARE INFORMATION ONLY, NOW GO TO THE *GREEN* SECTION, PAGES *8–9*.

IF FAMILY CHOSE TO MEET THE BIRTHPARENTS, NOW GO TO THE *YELLOW* SECTION, PAGES *10–11*.

IF FAMILY RESPONDENT CHOSE TO HAVE ONGOING FACE TO FACE CONTACT, NOW GO TO THE *BLUE* SECTION, PAGES *12–14*.

IF FAMILY INITIALLY CHOSE SEMI-OPEN AND LATER CHANGED TO FULLY DISCLOSED, NOW GO TO THE *ORANGE* SECTION, PAGES *15–18*.

IF FAMILY CHOSE CONFIDENTIAL (CLOSED) ADOPTION [This section appears on pink paper]

51. How do you plan to talk with your child about adoption?

Figure 7-9 *(continued)*

(Or, for older children, How have you talked with your child about adoption?)

    a. Now?

    b. In middle childhood?

    c. In adolescence?

52. Does _____ (child) know what "birthmother" means?

53. What does _____ (child) call his/her birthmother?

54. What does _____ (child) call his/her birthfather?

55. How do you feel about this?

56. Does _____ (child) like to talk about his/her adoption?
Does s/he initiate conversations with you about it?

57. Does _____ (child) ever try to use his/her adoption as a lever to get his/her way? If so, please describe.

58. If there are other siblings in the household, do they ever try to use _____ (child's) adoption against him/her? If so, please describe.

   .
   .
   .

IF FAMILY CHOSE TO SHARE INFORMATION ONLY. . . . [This section appears on green paper]

   .
   .
   .

72. How do you feel after you have received a letter, picture, gift, etc. from the birthparents?

   .
   .

75. What impact do you think sharing information will have on:
a. your child?

Figure 7-9 *(continued)*

b. you and your spouse?

c. on birthparents?

d. on other children in the family (if applicable)?

    .

    .

    .

IF FAMILY CHOSE TO MEET BIRTHPARENTS . . . . [This
section appears on yellow paper]

82. Describe the circumstances of your *FIRST* meeting.
    Did it occur at placement or later?

    .

    .

    .

84. How did you feel about the birthparents?
    Has that feeling changed since then? If so how?

    .

    .

    .

87. How do you think the birthparents felt about you?

    .

    .

IF FAMILY CHOSE TO HAVE ONGOING CONTACT . . . . [This
section appears on blue paper]

  .

  .

  .

106. Do you plan to have continued contact? (Why or why
     not?)

    .

    .

    .

111. How would you describe your relationship with the
     birthparent(s)? (Probe: as a relative, friend,
     etc.)

    .

    .

    .

117. How do you feel after a visit? Have your feelings
     changed over time?

    .

    .

    .

Figure 7-9 *(continued)*

```
          IF FAMILY INITIALLY CHOSE A LESS OPEN OPTION AND LATER
          CHANGED TO A MORE OPEN OPTION . . . . [This section
          appears on orange paper]
          .
          .
          .
          136. Describe the changes that took place.

          137. How did you feel about the decision to change?
               .
               .
               .
          166. What is the most satisfying aspect of your
               relationship with your child's birthmother?

          167. What is the most difficult aspect of your
               relationship with your child's birthmother?
               .
               .
               .
          179. We've talked about quite a few things, but I wonder
               if there might be something that we have skipped
               which you might feel to be important to understand-
               ing you and your family. Is there anything that you
               would like to add to what we have discussed?
```

Figure 7-9 *(continued)*

II. Knowledge about degrees of openness in adoption
   A. Understandings of meanings and options prior to adoption?
   B. Advantages and disadvantages of each option anticipated?

III. Type of adoption chosen and issues
   A. How discussed and dealt with in family?
   B. Problems? Discomfort discussing? Manipulation? Other siblings?

IV. Issues involving birthparents
   A. Impact of communications on child? On parents? On birthparents? On other children?
   B. Impact of face-to-face meetings? Feelings each set of parents has about the other?

C. Degree of ongoing contact? Why?

V. Any changes in degree of openness over time?
   A. What type of changes?
   B. Impact?

As we end this chapter, we'd like to remind you that despite pointing out the differences between quantitative and qualitative measures for asking people questions, we've also identified some commonalities shared by the two approaches. We'd also like to reiterate that the same study can use both approaches; the two approaches need not be seen as mutually exclusive or in conflict with one another. We summarize these points in the box "A Comparison of Quantitative and Qualitative Measures to Asking People Questions."

A COMPARISON OF QUANTITATIVE AND QUALITATIVE APPROACHES TO ASKING PEOPLE QUESTIONS

	Quantitative Approaches	Qualitative Approaches
Similarities in Measurement Principles		
Try to use language that respondents will understand	always	always
Ask one question at a time; avoid double-barreled questions	always	always
Only ask questions that respondents are capable of answering and that are relevant to them	always	always
Avoid biased items and terms	always	always
Stylistic Differences		
Questionnaires or scales	often	rarely
Interviews	sometimes	usually
Same wording and sequence of questions for all respondents	always	rarely
Interviewer flexibility regarding wording, sequencing, and conversational style	never	very often
Open-ended questions	rarely	usually
Probes	rare and brief	frequent and in-depth
Closed-ended questions	usually	sometimes
Formality of interview	Relaxed, friendly demeanor, but professional tone and not overly casual	More likely to resemble a spontaneous, informal, friendly conversation
Complementary Functions		
Objectivity and consistency versus flexibility and subjective meanings	Develop measures to be administered to many respondents in ways that attempt to minimize random	Develop measures that allow for researcher flexibility and subjectivity in order to pursue

	Quantitative Approaches	Qualitative Approaches
	and systematic measurement error, but that may be at a superficial level, requiring an investigation of their validity	deeper, more valid levels of understanding of subjective meanings among fewer respondents
Generalizability versus in-depth, theoretical understanding	Verify, in a precise, statistical fashion, whether understandings emerging from qualitative measurement are generalizable	Develop a deeper theoretical understanding of the meanings of statistical findings emerging from quantitative measurement
Test hypotheses versus generating hypotheses and deeper understandings	Test hypotheses, perhaps generated from qualitative studies, generating new findings that might require further qualitative study to be sufficiently understood	Study phenomena whose meanings are not sufficiently understood, perhaps generating hypotheses for quantitative study

Main Points

• Questionnaires provide a method of collecting data by (a) asking people questions or (b) asking them to agree or disagree with statements representing different points of view.

• Questions may be open-ended (respondents supply their own answers) or closed-ended (they select from a list of answers provided them).

• Usually, short items in a questionnaire are better than long ones.

• Negative items and terms should be avoided in questionnaires because they may confuse respondents.

• In questionnaire items bias is the quality that encourages respondents to answer in a particular way to avoid or to support a particular point of view. Avoid it.

• Contingency questions are questions that should be answered only by people giving a particular response to some preceding question. The contingency question format is very useful in that it saves asking people to answer questions that have no meaning for them. For example, a ques-

tion about the number of times a person has been pregnant should be asked only of women.

• Matrix questions are those in which a standardized set of closed-ended response categories are to be used in answering several questionnaire items. This format can facilitate the presentation and completion of items.

• Single indicators of variables may not have sufficiently clear validity to warrant their use.

• Composite measures, such as scales and indexes, solve this problem by including several indicators of a variable in one summary measure.

• Both scales and indexes are intended as ordinal measures of variables.

• Face validity is the first criterion for the selection of indicators to be included in a composite measure; the term means that an indicator seems, on face value, to provide some measure of the variable.

• If different items are indeed indicators of the same variable, they should be related empirically to one another. If, for example, frequency of church attendance and frequency of prayer are both indicators of religiosity, people who attend church frequently should be found to pray more than those who attend church less frequently.

• Once an index or a scale has been constructed, it is essential that it be validated.

• Likert scaling is a measurement technique based on the use of standardized response categories (for instance, strongly agree, agree, disagree, strongly disagree) for several questionnaire items. The Likert format for questionnaire items is very popular and extremely useful.

• Scales and indexes that appear to be reliable and valid when tested with one culture may not be reliable and valid when used with other cultures.

• Constructing culturally sensitive instruments can involve the use of bilingual interviewers, translating, back-translation, pretesting, direct immersion in the culture of the population to be studied, and interviewing knowledgeable informants in the study population.

• Although qualitative and quantitative measurement approaches share certain principles, quantitative measures are always highly structured, tend to use closed-ended questions primarily, and may be administered in either an interview or questionnaire format, whereas qualitative measures rely on interviews that are usually unstructured and that mainly contain open-ended questions and in-depth probes.

Review Questions and Exercises

1. For each of the open-ended questions listed below, construct a closed-ended question that could be used in a questionnaire.

a. What was your family's total income last year?

b. How do you feel about increasing public spending on social welfare?

c. How important is learning theory in your approach to social work practice?

d. What was your main reason for studying to be a social worker?

e. What do you feel is the biggest problem facing this community?

2. Using the Likert format, construct a brief scale measuring client satisfaction with service delivery.

Additional Readings

Glock, Charles, Ringer, Benjamin, and Babbie, Earl, *To Comfort and to Challenge: A Dilemma of the Contemporary Church* (Berkeley: University of California Press, 1967). An empirical study illustrating composite measures. Because the construction of scales and indexes can be most fully grasped through concrete examples, this might be a useful study to examine. The authors use a variety of composite measures, and they are relatively clear about the methods used in constructing them.

Lazarsfeld, Paul, Pasanella, Ann, and Rosenberg, Morris (eds.), *Continuities in the Language of Social Research* (New York: Free Press, 1972), especially Section 1. An excellent collection of conceptual discussions and concrete illustrations. The construction of composite measures is presented within the more general area of conceptualization and measurement.

Miller, Delbert, *Handbook of Research Design and Social Measurement* (New York: Longman, 1983). An excellent compilation of frequently used and semistandardized scales. The many illustrations reported in Part 4 of the Miller book may be directly adaptable to studies or at least suggestive of modified measures. Studying the illustrations, moreover, may give a better understanding of the logic of composite measures in general.

Oppenheim, A. N., *Questionnaire Design and Attitude Measurement* (New York: Basic Books, 1966). A fine presentation on composite measures, with special reference to questionnaires. Oppenheim gives an excellent presentation of the logic and the skills of scale construction—the kinds of scales discussed in Chapter 7 of the present book and many not discussed here.

The Logic of Research Design

In Chapter 4 we indicated that social work research studies can be classified according to three major purposes: *exploration, description,* and *explanation.* The degree to which researchers need to build certain logical arrangements into their studies depends on which of these purposes are guiding their work.

We noted, for example, that if our purpose is limited to *exploring* a new area about which little is known—in the hope of generating new insights and hypotheses that will be studied more rigorously later on—it is appropriate to use flexible methods that yield tentative findings. Trying to tightly structure exploratory studies in order to permit conclusive logical inferences and generalizations to be made from the findings would not only be unnecessary but also undesirable. An inflexible methodology in an exploratory study would not permit researchers the latitude they need to probe creatively into unanticipated observations or into areas about which they lack the information needed to construct a design that would be logically conclusive.

But when our research purpose is *description* or *explanation,* then adhering to certain logical principles in the design of our research becomes much more important. *Descriptive* studies seek to portray accurately the characteristics of a population. These studies usually will attempt to make *generalizations* about the attributes of that population by studying a small part of (a sample drawn from) that population. As we implied in Chapter 4, the more confident we are that the part (sample) that we study is *representative* of the population, the more confident we can be in the *generalizations* we make about the population.

Explanatory studies also usually aim to generalize from a sample to a population. But what they seek to generalize focuses on causal processes occurring among variables, not simply on describing specific attributes. Explanatory studies therefore need to be concerned with those *logical arrangements* that permit us to make inferences about causality in the sample we observe as well as those logical arrangements that enable us to generalize our *causal inferences* to a larger population.

Two fundamental issues in descriptive and explanatory research, then, are the *generalizability* of research findings and the *logical validity* of the *causal inferences* made about those findings. In fact, these issues are also important in exploratory research in the sense that we need to be careful not to overgeneralize exploratory findings or draw unwarranted causal inferences from them. Part 3 of this book discusses the logical arrangements and considerations involved in designing research studies that will produce generalizable findings and valid inferences.

Chapter 8 on *sampling* deals with generalizability. As we'll see, it is possible for us to select a few people or things for observation and then apply what we observe to a much larger group of people or things than we actually observed. Chapters 9 and 10 deal not only with generalizability, but also with the validity of causal inferences.

In the prologue to this book we discussed the need to assess the effectiveness of social work practice and programs. We noted that this need stems from such forces as public skepticism about our effectiveness, increasing demands for accountability, and our own professional and humanitarian concern for the welfare of clients. Implicit in the term *effectiveness* is the notion of *causality*. That is, the extent to which we demonstrate our effectiveness depends on the degree to which we can *infer* that our services *caused* the desired *effect* that they sought to attain.

Whether we can logically infer causality depends on the way we design our research. In Part 2 we already addressed measurement errors. The material in that section is part of research design, and methodological errors regarding measurement certainly limit our ability to correctly infer anything from our findings. But even if our measurement and sampling procedures are impeccable, additional design issues will influence whether our findings permit *causal* inferences.

Chapters 9 and 10 will examine the logic of causal inference and show how different design arrangements bear upon our ability to infer cause and effect. They will address these issues primarily from the standpoint of evaluating the effectiveness of social work services. But they will also show that questions about causality and relevant design arrangements bear on other social work research questions in addition to the effectiveness of service delivery.

Chapter 9 addresses the criteria necessary for inferring causality and methodological impediments to causal inference. It focuses on various *group* designs, particularly *experiments* and *quasi-experiments,* their advantages and disadvantages, and how they attempt to enhance causal inferences. Chapter 10, in contrast, discusses *single-subject* designs. It shows how the logic of time-series designs can be applied to a single case and thus permits causal inferences to be made about the effects of a particular intervention on a particular case. Although the generalizability of this approach is limited, Chapter 10 will examine why single-subject designs have great potential utility to clinical practitioners, who can implement them as part of their clinical practice, and how the findings of single-subject designs can be aggregated and replicated to advance knowledge about the effectiveness of social work practice and programs.

What you learn in these chapters should help you appreciate the paradoxical complexities involved in selecting a research design or in assessing the value of studies whose designs are limited. On the one hand, you should be prepared to spot swiftly, with an acute skepticism, logical arrangements that do not permit sweeping generalizations or causal inferences to be made. On the other hand, you should be aware of the practical obstacles that make ideal logical arrangements infeasible and thus be able to appreciate the utility of some findings that may have to be interpreted cautiously.

The Logic of Sampling

What You'll Learn in This Chapter

Now we'll see how it's possible for social scientists
to select a few hundred or thousand people for
study—and discover things that apply to hundreds
of millions of people not studied.

INTRODUCTION

In November 1988, George Bush was elected president of the United States with 54% of the popular vote, as against 46% for Michael Dukakis. Prior to the election, a number of political polls had predicted a Bush victory. Let's see how well they predicted the election.

Here are the results of several national polls conducted in early November on the eve of the election. For purposes of comparability, we've assigned the "undecideds" proportionately to the percentages who chose one of the candidates.

	BUSH	DUKAKIS
Gallup Poll	56	44
ABC/Washington Post	55	45
CBS/New York Times	55	45
ACTUAL VOTE	**54**	**46**
CNN/Los Angeles Times	54	46
NBC/Wall Street Journal	53	47
Harris Poll	53	47

Although the poll estimates varied a bit, you can see how closely they were clustered around the actual election-day results. Now, how many interviews do you suppose it took each of these pollsters to come within a couple of percentage points in estimating the behavior of about ninety million voters? Fewer than 2000! In this chapter, we are going to find out how it's possible for social researchers to pull off such wizardry.

We've been talking a lot about observation in recent chapters. Those discussions have omitted the question of *what* or *who* will be observed. If you think about it for a minute, you'll see that a social researcher has a whole world of potential observations. Yet nobody can observe everything. A critical part of social research, then, is the decision about what will be observed and what won't. If you want to study voters, for example, which voters should you study? That's the subject of this chapter.

Sampling is the process of selecting observations. After a brief history of social scientific sampling, the key section of this chapter discusses the logic and the skills of **probability sampling.** As we'll see, probability sampling techniques—involving *random sampling*—allow a researcher to make relatively few observations and generalize from those observations to a much wider population. We'll examine the requirements for generalizability.

As you'll discover, random selection is a precise, scientific procedure; there is nothing haphazard about it. There are specific sampling techniques that allow us to determine and/or control the likelihood of specific individuals being selected for study. In the simplest example, flipping a coin to choose between two individuals gives each one exactly the same—50%—probability of selection. More complex techniques guarantee an equal probability of selection when substantial samples are selected from large populations.

Although probability sampling is precise, it is not always feasible to use probability sampling techniques. Consequently, social work research studies often use **nonprobability sampling.** Therefore, we'll take some time to examine a variety of nonprobability methods as well. Although not based on random selection, these methods have their own logic and can provide useful samples for social inquiry. We'll examine both the advantages and the shortcomings of such methods, and we'll see where they fit within the social scientific enterprise.

THE HISTORY OF SAMPLING

Sampling in social research has developed hand in hand with political polling. This is the case, no doubt, because political polling is one of the few opportunities social researchers have to discover the accuracy of their estimates. On election day, they find out how well or how poorly they did.

President Alf Landon

You may have heard about the *Literary Digest* in connection with political polling. The *Digest* was a popular news magazine published in the United States between 1890 and 1938. In 1920, *Digest* editors mailed postcards to people in six states, asking them who they were planning to vote for in the presidential campaign between Warren Harding and James Cox. Names were selected for the poll from telephone directories and automobile registration lists. Based on the postcards sent back, the *Digest* correctly predicted that Harding would be elected. In elections that followed, the *Literary Digest* expanded the size of its poll and made correct predictions in 1924, 1928, and 1932.

In 1936, the *Digest* conducted their most ambitious poll: Ten million ballots were sent to people listed in telephone directories and on lists of automobile owners. Over two million responded, giving Republican contender Alf Landon a stunning 57% to 43% landslide over incumbent President Franklin Roosevelt. The editors modestly cautioned:

> We make no claim to infallibility. We did not coin the phrase "uncanny accuracy" which has been so freely applied to our Polls. We know only too well the limitations of every straw vote, however enormous the sample gathered, however scientific the method. It would be a miracle if every State of the forty-eight behaved on Election Day exactly as forecast by the Poll.   (1936A:6)

Two weeks later, the *Digest* editors knew the limitations of straw polls even better: Voters gave Roosevelt a third term in office by the largest landslide in history, with 61% of the vote. Landon won only 8 electoral votes to Roosevelt's 523. The editors were puzzled by their unfortunate turn of luck.

A part of the problem surely lay in the 22% return rate garnered by the poll. The editors asked:

> Why did only one in five voters in Chicago to whom the *Digest* sent ballots take the trouble to reply? And

why was there a preponderance of Republicans in the one-fifth that did reply? . . . We were getting better cooperation in what we have always regarded as a public service from Republicans than we were getting from Democrats. Do Republicans live nearer to mail-boxes? Do Democrats generally disapprove of straw polls? (1936b:7)

A part of the answer to these questions lay in the sampling frame used by the *Digest:* telephone subscribers and automobile owners. Such a sampling design selected a disproportionately wealthy sample, especially coming on the tail end of the worst economic depression in the nation's history. The sample effectively excluded poor people, and the poor people predominantly voted for Roosevelt's New Deal recovery program.

President Thomas E. Dewey

The 1936 election also saw the emergence of a young pollster whose name was to become synonymous with public opinion. In contrast to the *Literary Digest,* George Gallup correctly predicted that Roosevelt would beat Landon. Gallup's success in 1936 hinged on his use of **quota sampling,** which we'll have more to say about later in the chapter. For now, you need only know that quota sampling is based on a knowledge of the characteristics of the population being sampled: what proportion are men, what proportion are women, what proportions are of various incomes, ages, and so on. People are selected to match the population characteristics: the right number of poor, white, rural men; the right number of rich, black, urban women; and so on. The quotas are based on those variables most relevant to the study. By knowing the numbers of people with various incomes in the nation, Gallup selected his sample so as to ensure the right proportion of respondents at each income level. Gallup and his American Institute of Public Opinion used quota sampling to good effect in 1936, 1940, and 1944—correctly picking the presidential winner each of those years.

Then, in 1948, Gallup and most political pollsters suffered the embarrassment of picking New York Governor Thomas Dewey over incumbent President Harry Truman. A number of factors accounted for the 1948 failure. First, most of the pollsters stopped polling in early October despite a steady trend toward Truman during the campaign. In addition, many voters were undecided throughout the campaign, and they went disproportionately for Truman when they stepped in the voting booth. More important for our present purposes, however, Gallup's failure rested on the unrepresentativeness of his samples.

Quota sampling—which had been effective in earlier years—was Gallup's undoing in 1948. Recall that this technique requires that the researcher know something about the total population (of voters in this instance). For national political polls, such information came primarily from census data. By 1948, however, a world war, producing a massive movement from country to city, had radically changed the character of the American population from what the 1940 census showed. City dwellers, moreover, were more likely to vote Democratic, hence the overrepresentation of rural voters also underestimated the number of Democratic votes.

Two Types of Sampling Methods

In 1948, a number of academic researchers had been experimenting with *probability sampling* methods. By and large, they were far more successful than those using quota samples. Today, probability sampling remains the primary method for selecting samples for social science research. To appreciate the logic of probability sampling, it is useful to distinguish it from *nonprobability sampling.* The bulk of this chapter will be devoted to probability sampling because it is currently the most respected and useful method. A smaller portion of this chapter will consider the various methods of nonprobability sampling.

We'll begin with a discussion of the logic of probability sampling and a brief glossary of sampling concepts and terminology. Then we'll look at the concept of sampling distribution: the basis of estimating the accuracy of findings based on samples. Following these theoretical discussions, we'll consider populations and sampling frames, focusing on practical problems of determining the target group of the study and the way to begin selecting a sample. Next, we'll examine the basic types of sample designs: simple random samples, systematic samples, stratified samples, and cluster samples. Finally, a short discussion and description of nonprobability sampling is presented.

THE LOGIC OF PROBABILITY SAMPLING

If all members of a population were identical in all respects—all demographic characteristics, attitudes, experiences, behaviors, and so on—there would be no need for careful sampling procedures. In such a case, any sample would indeed be sufficient. In this extreme case of homogeneity, in fact, one case would be sufficient as a sample to study characteristics of the whole population.

In fact, of course, the human beings who compose any real population are quite heterogeneous, varying in many ways. Figure 8-1 offers a simplified illustration of a heterogeneous population: The 100 members of this small population differ by sex and race. We'll use this hypothetical micropopulation to illustrate various aspects of sampling through the chapter.

A sample of individuals from a population, if it is to provide useful descriptions of the total population, must contain essentially the same variations that exist in the population. This is not as simple as it might seem, however.

Let's take a minute to look at some of the ways researchers might go astray. Then we will see how probability sampling provides an efficient method for selecting a sample that should adequately reflect variations that exist in the population.

Conscious and Unconscious Sampling Bias

At first glance, it may look as though sampling is a pretty straightforward matter. To select a sample of 100 university students, you might simply

44 white women   6 black women
44 white men   6 black men

Figure 8-1 A Population of 100 Folks

go to campus and interview the first 100 students you find walking around campus. This kind of sampling method is often used by untrained researchers, but it has serious problems.

Figure 8-2 illustrates what can happen when you simply select people who are convenient for study. Although women are only 50% of our micropopulation, those closest to the researcher (in the upper-right corner) happen to be 70% women; and although the population is 12% black, none were selected into the sample.

Moving beyond the risks inherent in simply studying people who are convenient, there are other potential problems. To begin, your own personal leanings or biases may affect the sample

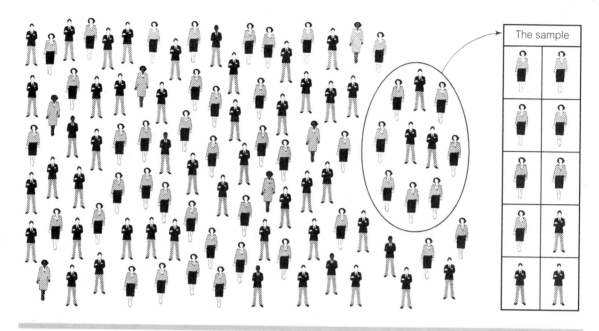

Figure 8-2 A Sample of Convenience: Easy, but Not Representative

selected in this manner; hence the sample would not truly represent the student population. Suppose you're a little intimidated by students who look particularly "cool," feeling they might ridicule your research effort. You might consciously or unconsciously avoid interviewing such people. Or, you might feel that the attitudes of "super-straight-looking" students would be irrelevant to your research purposes, and you avoid interviewing them.

Even if you sought to interview a "balanced" group of students, you wouldn't know the exact proportions of different types of students making up such a balance, and you wouldn't always be able to identify the different types just by watching them walk by.

Even if you made a conscientious effort to interview every tenth student entering the university library, you could not be sure of a *representative* sample, since different types of students visit the library with different frequencies. Your sample would overrepresent students who visit the library more often.

When we speak of "bias" in connection with sampling, this simply means those selected are not "typical" or "representative" of the larger populations they have been chosen from. This kind of bias is virtually inevitable when you pick people by a seat-of-your-pants approach.

Similarly, the "public-opinion call-in polls"— in which radio stations or newspapers ask people to call specified telephone numbers to register their opinions—cannot be trusted to represent general populations. At the very least, not everyone in the population will even be aware of the poll. This problem also invalidates polls by magazines and newspapers who publish coupons for readers to complete and mail in. Even among those who are aware of such polls, not all will express an opinion, especially if doing so will cost them a stamp, an envelope, or a telephone charge.

Ironically, the failure of such polls to represent all opinions equally was inadvertently acknowledged by Philip J. Perinelli (1986), staff manager of A.T.&T. Communications' DIAL-IT 900 Service, which offers the call-in poll facility to organizations. Perinelli attempted to counter criticisms by saying, "The 50-cent charge assures that only interested parties respond and helps assure also that no individual 'stuffs' the ballot box." We cannot determine general public opinion by considering "only interested parties." This excludes those who don't care 50-cents' worth, as well as those who recognize that such polls are not valid. Both types of people may have opinions and may even vote on election day. Perinelli's assertion that the 50-cent charge will prevent ballot-stuffing actually means that only the wealthy can afford to engage in that practice.

The possibilities for inadvertent sampling bias are endless and not always obvious. Fortunately there are techniques that let us avoid bias.

Representativeness and Probability of Selection

Although the term *representativeness* has no precise, scientific meaning, it carries a commonsense meaning that makes it a useful concept in the discussion of sampling. As we'll use the term here, a sample will be representative of the population from which it is selected if the aggregate characteristics of the sample closely approximate those same aggregate characteristics in the population. (Samples need not be representative in all respects; representativeness is limited to those characteristics that are relevant to the substantive interests of the study, although you may not know which are relevant.) If the population, for example, contains 50% women, then a representative sample would also contain "close to" 50% women. Later in this chapter we'll discuss "how close" in detail.

A basic principle of probability sampling is that *a sample will be representative of the population from which it is selected if all members of the population have an equal chance of being selected in the sample.* (We'll see shortly that the size of the sample selected also affects the degree of representativeness.) Samples that have this quality are often labeled EPSEM samples (equal probability of selection method). We'll discuss variations of this

principle later, but it is primary and forms the basis of probability sampling.

Moving beyond this basic principle, we must realize that samples—even carefully selected EPSEM samples—are seldom if ever *perfectly* representative of the populations from which they are drawn. Nevertheless, probability sampling offers two special advantages.

First, probability samples, although never perfectly representative, are typically *more representative* than other types of samples because the biases discussed in the preceding section are avoided. In practice, there is a greater likelihood that a probability sample will be representative of the population from which it is drawn than that a nonprobability sample will be.

Second, and more important, probability theory permits us to estimate the accuracy or representativeness of the sample. Conceivably, an uninformed researcher might, through wholly haphazard means, select a sample that nearly perfectly represents the larger population. The odds are against doing so, however, and we would be unable to estimate the likelihood that he or she has achieved representativeness. The probability sampler, on the other hand, can provide an accurate estimate of success or failure.

Following a brief glossary of sampling terminology, we'll examine the means the probability sampler uses to estimate the representativeness of the sample.

SAMPLING CONCEPTS AND TERMINOLOGY

The following discussions of sampling theory and practice use a number of technical terms. To make it easier for you to understand those discussions, it is important to quickly define these terms. For the most part, we'll employ terms commonly used in sampling and statistical textbooks so that readers may better understand those other sources.

In presenting this glossary of sampling concepts and terminology, we would like to acknowledge a debt to Leslie Kish and his excellent textbook

Survey Sampling. Although we have modified some of the conventions used by Kish, his presentation is easily the most important source of this discussion.

Element An *element* is that unit about which information is collected and that provides the basis of analysis. Typically, in survey research, elements are people or certain types of people. However, other kinds of units can constitute the elements for social work research: families, social clubs, or corporations might be the elements of a study. (*Note:* Elements and units of analysis are often the same in a given study, though the former refers to sample selection and the latter refers to data analysis.)

Population A *population* is the theoretically specified aggregation of study elements. Whereas the vague term *Americans* might be the target for a study, the delineation of the population would include the definition of the element *Americans* (for example, citizenship, residence) and the time referent for the study (Americans as of when?). Translating the abstract *adult New Yorkers* into a workable population would require a specification of the age defining *adult* and the boundaries of *New York*. Specifying the term *college student* would include a consideration of full-time and part-time students, degree candidates and non-degree candidates, undergraduate and graduate students, and similar issues.

Although researchers must begin with careful specification of their population, poetic license usually permits them to phrase their reports in terms of the hypothetical universe. For ease of presentation, even the most conscientious researcher normally speaks of "Americans" rather than "resident citizens of the United States of America as of November 12, 1992." The primary guide in this matter, as in most others, is that you should not mislead or deceive your readers.

Study Population A *study population* is that aggregation of elements from which the sample is actually selected. As a practical matter, you are seldom in a position to guarantee that every element meeting the theoretical definitions laid down actually has a chance of being selected in the sample. Even where lists of elements exist for sampling purposes, the lists are usually somewhat incomplete. Some students are always omitted, inadvertently, from student rosters. Some telephone subscribers request that their names and numbers be unlisted. The study population, then, is the aggregation of elements from which the sample is selected.

Often researchers decide to limit their study populations more severely than indicated in the preceding examples. National polling firms may limit their national samples to the 48 contiguous states, omitting Alaska and Hawaii for practical reasons. A researcher wishing to sample psychology professors may limit the study population to those who are serving in psychology departments, omitting those serving in other departments. (In a sense, we might say that these researchers have redefined their universes and populations, in which case they must make the revisions clear to their readers.)

Sampling Unit A *sampling unit* is that element or set of elements considered for selection in some stage of sampling. In a simple single-stage sample, the sampling units are the same as the elements. In more complex samples, however, different levels of sampling units may be used. For instance, you might select a sample of census blocks in a city, then select a sample of households on the selected blocks, and finally select a sample of adults from the selected households. The sampling units for these three stages of sampling are, respectively, census blocks, households, and adults, of which only the last of these are the elements. More specifically, the terms *primary sampling units, secondary sampling units,* and *final sampling units* are used to designate the successive stages.

Sampling Frame A **sampling frame** is the actual list of sampling units from which the sample, or some stage of the sample, is selected. In single-stage sampling designs, the sampling frame is simply a list of the study population (defined earlier). If a simple sample of students is selected from a student roster, the roster is the sampling frame. If the primary sampling unit for a complex population sample is the census block, the list of census blocks composes the sampling frame—either in the form of a printed booklet, a magnetic tape file, or some other computerized record.

In a single-stage sample design, the sampling frame is a list of the elements composing the study population. In practice, existing sampling frames often define the study population rather than the other way around. We often begin with a population in mind for our study; then we search for possible sampling frames. The frames available for our use are examined and evaluated, and we decide which frame presents a study population most appropriate to our needs.

The relationship between populations and sampling frames is critical and has not been given sufficient attention. A later section of this chapter will pursue this issue in greater detail.

Observation Unit   An *observation unit,* or unit of data collection, is an element or aggregation of elements from which information is collected. Again, the unit of analysis and unit of observation are often the same—the individual person—but that need not be the case. Thus the researcher may interview heads of households (the observation units) to collect information about all members of the households (the units of analysis).

Our task is simplified when the unit of analysis and the observation unit are the same. Often that is not possible or feasible, however, and in such situations we need to exercise some ingenuity in collecting data relevant to our units of analysis without actually observing those units.

Variable   As discussed earlier, a *variable* is a set of mutually exclusive attributes: gender, age, employment status, and so forth. The elements of a given population may be described in terms of their individual attributes on a given variable. Often social research aims to describe the distribution of attributes composing a variable in a population. Thus a researcher may describe the age distribution of a population by examining the relative frequency of different ages among members of the population.

A variable, by definition, must possess *variation;* if all elements in the population have the same attribute, that attribute is a *constant* in the population, rather than part of a variable.

Parameter   A *parameter* is the summary description of a given variable in a *population.* The mean income of all families in a city and the age distribution of the city's population are parameters. An important portion of social research involves the estimation of population parameters on the basis of sample observations.

Statistic   A *statistic* is the summary description of a given variable in a sample. Thus the mean income computed from a sample and the age distribution of that sample are statistics. Sample statistics are used to make estimates of population parameters.

Sampling Error   Probability sampling methods seldom, if ever, provide statistics exactly equal to the parameters that they are used to estimate. Probability theory, however, permits us to estimate the degree of error to be expected for a given sample design. *Sampling error* will be discussed in more detail later.

Confidence Levels and Confidence Intervals
The two key components of sampling error estimates are **confidence levels** and **confidence intervals.** We express the accuracy of our sample statistics in terms of a level of confidence that the statistics fall within a specified interval from the parameter. For example, we may say we are 95% confident that our sample statistics (for example, 50% favor Candidate X) are within plus or minus 5 percentage points of the population parameter.

As the confidence interval is expanded for a given statistic, our confidence increases, and we may say we are 99.9% confident that our statistic falls within ±7.5 percentage points of the parameter. We'll describe how sampling intervals and levels are calculated in the next section, which will make these two concepts even clearer.

PROBABILITY SAMPLING THEORY AND SAMPLING DISTRIBUTION

With definitions presented, we can now examine the basic theory of probability sampling as it applies to social research. We'll also consider the logic of sampling distribution and sampling error with regard to a **binomial variable**—a variable composed of two attributes.

Probability Sampling Theory

The ultimate purpose of sampling is to select a set of elements from a population in such a way that descriptions of those elements (statistics) accurately portray the parameters of the total population from which the elements are selected. Probability sampling enhances the likelihood of accomplishing this aim and also provides methods for estimating the degree of probable success.

Random selection is the key to this process. In random selection, each element has an equal chance of selection independent of any other event in the selection process. Flipping a perfect coin is the most frequently cited example: the "selection" of a head or a tail is independent of previous selections of heads or tails. Rolling a perfect set of dice is another example. Such images of random selection seldom apply directly to social research sampling methods, however. The social researcher more typically uses tables of random numbers or computer programs that provide a random selection of sampling units. As we'll see in Chapter 11, on survey research, computers can be used to select random telephone numbers for interviewing—called *random digit dialing*.

The reasons for using random selection methods—random-number tables or computer programs—are twofold. First, this procedure serves as a check on conscious or unconscious bias on the part of the researcher. The researcher who selects cases on an intuitive basis might very well select cases that would support his or her research expectations or hypotheses. Random selection erases this danger. More important, random selection offers access to the body of probability theory, which provides the basis for estimates of population parameters and estimates of error. Let's turn now to an examination of this latter aspect.

The Sampling Distribution of Ten Cases

To introduce the statistics of probability sampling, let's begin with a simple example of only ten cases.* Suppose there are ten people in a group, and each has a certain amount of money in his or her pocket. To simplify, let's assume that one person has no money, another has one dollar, another has two dollars, and so forth up to the person with nine dollars. Figure 8-3 presents the population of ten people.

Our task is to determine the average amount of money one person has: specifically, the *mean* number of dollars. If you simply add up the money shown in Figure 8-3, you'll find that the total is $45, so the mean is $4.50. Our purpose in the rest of this exercise is to estimate that mean without actually observing all ten individuals. We'll do that by selecting random samples from the population and using the means of those samples to estimate the mean of the whole population.

To start, suppose we were to select—at random—a sample of only *one* person from the ten. Depending on which person we selected, we'd estimate the group's mean as anywhere from $0 to $9. Figure 8-4 gives a graphic display of those ten possible samples.

The ten dots shown on the graph in Figure 8-4 represent the ten "sample" means we would get

---

*We want to thank Hanan Selvin for suggesting this method of introducing probability sampling.

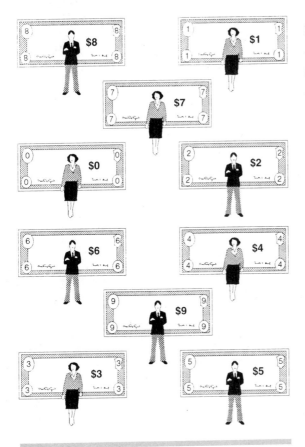

Figure 8-3 A Population of Ten People with $0–$9

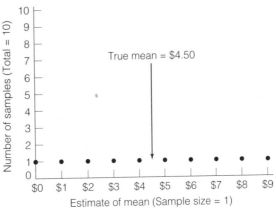

Figure 8-4 The Sampling Distribution of Samples of 1

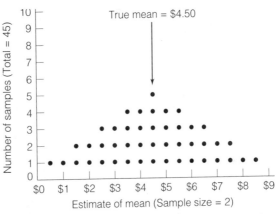

Figure 8-5 The Sampling Distribution of Samples of 2

as estimates of the population. The distribution of the dots on the graph is called the *sampling distribution*. Obviously, it would not be a very good idea to select a sample of only one, since we stand a very good chance of missing the true mean of $4.50 by quite a bit.

But what if we take samples of two each? As you can see from Figure 8-5, increasing the sample size improves our estimations. There are now 45 possible samples: $0/$1, $0/$2, . . . $7/$8, $8/$9. Moreover, some of those samples produce the same means. For example, $0/$6, $1/$5, and $2/$4 all produce means of $3. In Figure 8-5, the three dots shown above the $3 mean represent those three samples.

The 45 sample means are not evenly distributed, as you can see. Rather, they are somewhat clustered around the true value of $4.50. Only two samples deviate by as much as $4 from the true value ($0/$1 and $8/$9), whereas five of the samples would give the true estimate of $4.50; another eight samples miss the mark by only 50 cents (plus or minus).

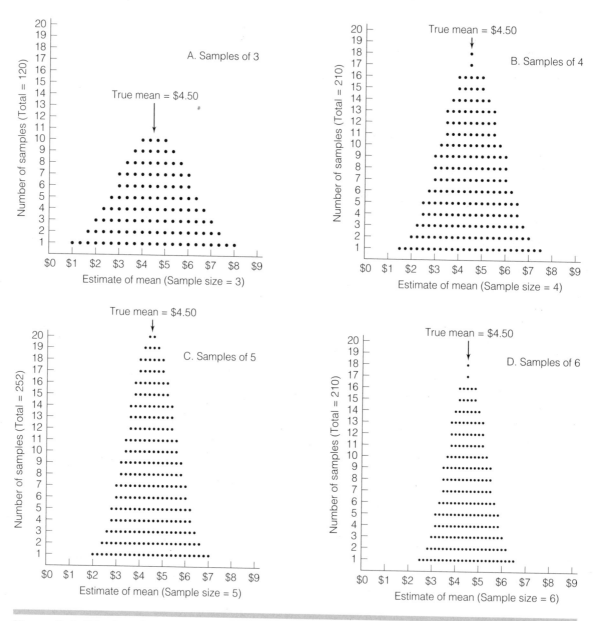

Figure 8-6   The Sampling Distributions of Samples of 3, 4, 5, and 6

Now suppose we select even larger samples. What do you suppose that will do to our estimates of the mean? Figure 8-6 presents the sampling distributions of samples of 3, 4, 5, and 6. Notice how the width of the distributions shrinks with each successive increase in sample size. Notice how an increasing proportion of sample means keeps getting closer and closer to the true mean and that even those sample means that are farthest away from the true mean keep

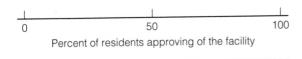

Figure 8-7 Range of Possible Sample Study Results

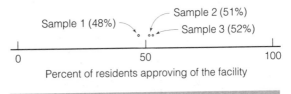

Figure 8-8 Results Produced by Three Hypothetical Studies

getting closer to the true mean as the sample size increases.

The progression of sampling distributions is clear. Every increase in sample size improves the distribution of estimates of the mean, and thus reduces the amount of *sampling error*. The limiting case in this procedure, of course, is to select a sample of ten. There would be only one possible sample (everyone) and it would give us the true mean of $4.50. In that case, there would be no sampling error.

Binomial Sampling Distribution

Let's turn now to a more realistic sampling situation and see how the notion of sampling distribution applies, using a simple example involving a population much larger than ten. Let's assume for the moment that we wish to study the adult population of a small town in a rural region to determine approval or disapproval of establishing in that town a community-based residential facility for formerly institutionalized, chronically mentally disabled individuals. The study population will be that aggregation of, say, 20,000 adults identified in the city directory: the sampling frame. The elements will be the town's adult residents. The variable under consideration will be attitudes toward the facility, a binomial variable: approve and disapprove. We'll select a random sample of, say, 100 residents for purposes of estimating the entire population of the town.

The horizontal axis of Figure 8-7 presents all *possible* values of this parameter in the population—from 0% approval to 100% approval. The

midpoint of the axis—50%—represents half the residents approving of the facility and the other half disapproving.

To choose our sample, we give each resident in the directory a number and select 100 random numbers from a table of random numbers. (How to use a table of random numbers is explained on pages 252–253, in the box titled "Using a Table of Random Numbers.") Then we interview the 100 residents whose numbers have been selected and ask for their attitudes toward the facility: whether they approve or disapprove. Suppose this operation gives us 48 residents who approve of the facility and 52 who disapprove. We present this statistic by placing a dot on the *x* axis at the point representing 48%.

Now let's suppose we select another sample of 100 residents in exactly the same fashion and measure their approval or disapproval of the facility. Perhaps 51 residents in the second sample approve of the facility. We place another dot in the appropriate place on the *x* axis. Repeating this process once more, we may discover that 52 residents in the third sample approve of the facility.

Figure 8-8 presents the three different sample statistics representing the percentages of residents in each of the three random samples who approved of the facility. The basic rule of random sampling is that such samples drawn from a population give estimates of the parameter that pertains in the total population. Each of the random samples, then, gives us an estimate of the percentage of residents in the town population who approve of the facility. Unhappily, however, we have selected three samples and now have three separate estimates.

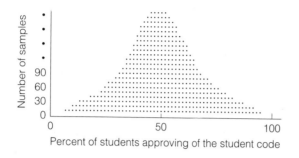

Figure 8-9 The Sampling Distribution

To retrieve ourselves from this dilemma, let's draw more and more samples of 100 residents each, question each of the samples concerning their approval or disapproval of the facility, and plot the new sample statistics on our summary graph. In drawing many such samples, we discover that some of the new samples provide duplicate estimates, as in the illustration of ten cases. Figure 8-9 shows the sampling distribution of, say, hundreds of samples. This is often referred to as a normal curve.

Note that by increasing the number of samples selected and interviewed, we have also increased the range of estimates provided by the sampling operation. In one sense we have increased our dilemma in attempting to guess the parameter in the population. Probability theory, however, provides certain important rules regarding the sampling distribution presented in Figure 8-9.

First, if many independent random samples are selected from a population, the sample statistics provided by those samples will be *distributed around the population parameter* in a known way. Thus, although Figure 8-9 shows a wide range of estimates, more of them are in the vicinity of 50% than elsewhere in the graph. Probability theory tells us, then, that the true value is in the vicinity of 50%.

Second, probability theory gives us a formula for estimating *how closely* the sample statistics are clustered around the true value. This formula con-

tains three factors: the parameter, the sample size, and the *standard error* (a measure of sampling error):

$$s = \sqrt{\frac{P \times Q}{n}}$$

Let's assume that the population parameter in the hypothetical small town is 50% approving of the facility and 50% disapproving. Recall that we have been selecting samples of 100 cases each. When these numbers are put into the formula, we find that the standard error equals .05, or 5%.

In probability theory, the standard error is a valuable piece of information because it indicates the extent to which the sample estimates will be distributed around the population parameter. If you are familiar with the standard deviation in statistics, you may recognize that the standard error, in this case, is the standard deviation of the sampling distribution. (The steps for computing the standard deviation are discussed on pages 470–472 in Chapter 15.)

Specifically, probability theory indicates that certain proportions of the sample estimates will fall within specified increments—each equal to one standard error—from the population parameter. Approximately 34% (.3413) of the sample estimates will fall within one standard error increment above the population parameter, and another 34% will fall within one standard error below the parameter. In our example, the standard error increment is 5%, so we know that 34% of our samples will give estimates of resident approval between 50% (the parameter) and 55% (one standard error above); another 34% of the samples will give estimates between 50% and 45% (one standard error below the parameter). Taken together, then, we know that roughly two-thirds

Symbols: P,Q = the population parameters for the binomial; if 60% of the residents approve of the facility and 40% disapprove, *P* and *Q* are 60% and 40% or .6 and .4. Note that *Q* = 1 − *P* and *P* = 1 − *Q.*
n = the number of cases in each sample.
s = the standard error.

(68%) of the samples will give estimates within ±5% of the parameter.

Moreover, probability theory dictates that roughly 95% of the samples will fall within plus or minus two standard errors of the true value, and 99.9% of the samples will fall within plus or minus three standard errors. In our present example, then, we know that only one sample out of a thousand would give an estimate lower than 35% approval or higher than 65%.

The proportion of samples falling within one, two, or three standard errors of the parameter is constant for any random sampling procedure such as the one just described, providing that a large number of samples are selected. The size of the standard error in any given case, however, is a function of the population parameter and the sample size. If we return to the formula for a moment, we note that the standard error will increase as a function of an increase in the quantity P times Q. Note further that this quantity reaches its maximum in the situation of an even split in the population. If $P = .5$, $PQ = .25$; if $P = .6$, $PQ = .24$; if $P = .8$, $PQ = .16$; if $P = .99$, $PQ = .0099$. By extension, if P is either 0.0 or 1.0 (either 0% or 100% approve of the facility), the standard error will be 0. If everyone in the population has the same attitude (no variation), then every sample will give exactly that estimate.

The standard error is also a function of the sample size—an *inverse* function. As the sample size increases, the standard error *decreases*. As the sample size increases, the several samples will be clustered nearer to the true value. Another rule of thumb is evident in the formula: because of the square root formula, the standard error is reduced by half if the sample size is *quadrupled*. In our present example, samples of 100 produce a standard error of 5%; to reduce the standard error to 2.5%, we must increase the sample size to 400.

All of this information is provided by established probability theory in reference to the selection of large numbers of random samples. If the population parameter is known and very many random samples are selected, we are able to pre-

dict how many of the samples will fall within specified intervals from the parameter. Be clear that this discussion only illustrates the *logic* of probability sampling. It does not describe the way research is actually conducted. Usually, we do not know the parameter: we conduct a sample survey to estimate that value. Moreover, we don't actually select large numbers of samples: we select only one sample. Nevertheless, the preceding discussion of probability theory provides the basis for inferences about the typical social research situation. Knowing what it would be like to select thousands of samples allows us to make assumptions about the one sample we do select and study.

Whereas probability theory specifies that 68% of that fictitious large number of samples would produce estimates falling within one standard error of the parameter, we turn the logic around and infer that any single random sample has a 68% chance of falling within that range. In this regard we speak of *confidence levels:* we are 68% confident that our sample estimate is within one standard error of the parameter. Or we may say that we are 95% confident that the sample statistic is within two standard errors of the parameter, and so forth. Quite reasonably, our confidence increases as the margin for error is extended. We are virtually positive (99.9%) that we are within three standard errors of the true value.

Although we may be confident (at some level) of being within a certain range of the parameter, we have already noted that we seldom know what the parameter is. To resolve this dilemma, we substitute our sample estimate for the parameter in the formula; lacking the true value, we substitute the best available guess.

The result of these inferences and estimations is that we are able to estimate a population parameter and also the expected degree of error on the basis of one sample drawn from a population. Beginning with the question "What percentage of the town population approves of the facility?" you could select a random sample of 100 residents and interview them. You might then report that your best estimate is that 50% of the population approve of the facility and that you are 95% confident that between 40% and 60% (plus or minus two standard errors) approve. The range from 40% to 60% is called the *confidence interval*. (At the 68% confidence level, the confidence interval would be 45% to 55%.)

The logic of confidence levels and confidence intervals also provides the basis for determining the appropriate sample size for a study. Once you have decided on the degree of sampling error you

can tolerate, you will be able to calculate the number of cases needed in your sample. Thus, for example, if you want to be 95% confident that your study findings are accurate within plus or minus five percentage points of the population parameters, you should select a sample of at least 400.

Table 8-1 is a convenient guide in this regard. The table also illustrates how, as sample sizes reach a certain point, further increases in sample size would yield diminishing returns in reducing

Table 8-1 Estimated Sampling Error

SAMPLE SIZE	BINOMIAL PERCENTAGE DISTRIBUTION				
	50/50	60/40	70/30	80/20	90/10
100	10	9.8	9.2	8	6
200	7.1	6.9	6.5	5.7	4.2
300	5.8	5.7	5.3	4.6	3.5
400	5	4.9	4.6	4	3
500	4.5	4.4	4.1	3.6	2.7
600	4.1	4	3.7	3.3	2.4
700	3.8	3.7	3.5	3	2.3
800	3.5	3.5	3.2	2.8	2.1
900	3.3	3.3	3.1	2.7	2
1000	3.2	3.1	2.9	2.5	1.9
1100	3	3	2.8	2.4	1.8
1200	2.9	2.8	2.6	2.3	1.7
1300	2.8	2.7	2.5	2.2	1.7
1400	2.7	2.6	2.4	2.1	1.6
1500	2.6	2.5	2.4	2.1	1.5
1600	2.5	2.4	2.3	2	1.5
1700	2.4	2.4	2.2	1.9	1.5
1800	2.4	2.3	2.2	1.9	1.4
1900	2.3	2.2	2.1	1.8	1.4
2000	2.2	2.2	2	1.8	1.3

sampling error and perhaps not be worth the additional data collection costs. For example, suppose 50% of our small town's population approve of the facility and 50% disapprove. Table 8-1 shows that increasing the sample size from 100 to 400 will reduce the estimated sampling error by five percentage points. But increasing it from 400 to 700 will reduce it by only 1.2 points, and increasing it from 700 to 1000 will reduce the estimated sampling error by only six-tenths of a point.

How to use this table: Find the intersection between the sample size and the approximate percentage distribution of the binomial in the sample. The number appearing at this intersection represents the estimated sampling error, at the 95% confidence level, expressed in percentage points (plus or minus). Example: In a sample of 400 respondents, 60% answer yes and 40% answer no. The sampling error is estimated at plus or minus 4.9 percentage points. The confidence interval, then, is between 55.1% and 64.9%. We would estimate (95% confidence) that the proportion of the total population who would say yes is somewhere within that interval.

This then is the basic logic of probability sampling. Random selection permits the researcher to link findings from a sample to the body of probability theory so as to estimate the accuracy of those findings. All statements of accuracy in sampling must specify both a confidence level and a confidence interval. The researcher may report that he or she is x% confident that the population parameter is between two specific values.

Here's how George Gallup (1984:7) described his sampling error in a newspaper report of a recent Gallup Poll regarding attitudes of children and parents:

> The adult findings are based on in-person interviews with 1520 adults, 18 and older, conducted in more than 300 scientifically selected localities across the nation during the period October 26–29. For results based on samples of this size, one can say with 95% confidence that the error attributable to sampling and other random effects could be three percentage points in either direction.

Or hear what the *New York Times* (1984:12) had to say about a poll they conducted among Democrats during the 1984 political campaigns:

> In theory, in 19 cases out of 20, the results from a poll such as this should differ by no more than three percentage points, in either direction, from what would have been obtained by interviewing all Democratic voters.

The next time you read statements like these in the newspaper, they should make more sense to you. Be wary, however, that such statements are sometimes made when they are not warranted, but you are now able to make that determination.

The foregoing discussion has considered only one type of statistic: the percentages produced by a *binomial* or **dichotomous variable.** The same logic, however, would apply to the examination of other statistics, such as mean income. Because the computations are somewhat more complicated in such a case, we have chosen to consider only binomials in this introduction.

You should be cautioned that the survey uses of probability theory as discussed previously are not wholly justified technically. The theory of sampling distribution makes assumptions that almost never apply in survey conditions. The number of samples contained within specified increments of standard errors, for example, assumes an infinitely large population, an infinite number of samples, and sampling with replacement. Moreover, the inferential jump from the distribution of several samples to the probable characteristics of one sample has been grossly oversimplified in the preceding discussion.

These cautions are offered to give you perspective. Researchers often appear to overestimate the precision of estimates produced by use of probability theory in connection with social research. As will be mentioned elsewhere in this chapter and throughout the book, variations in sampling techniques and nonsampling factors may further reduce the legitimacy of such estimates. Nevertheless, the calculations discussed in this section can be extremely valuable to you in understanding and evaluating your data. Although the calculations do not provide as precise estimates as some researchers might assume, they can be quite valid for practical purposes. They are unquestionably more valid than less rigorously derived estimates based on less rigorous sampling methods.

Most important, you should be familiar with the basic *logic* underlying the calculations. If you are so informed, you will be able to react sensibly to your own data and to those reported by others.

POPULATIONS AND SAMPLING FRAMES

The immediately preceding section has dealt with the theoretical model for social research sampling. Although it is necessary for the research consumer, student, and researcher to understand that theory, it is no less important that they appreciate the less-than-perfect conditions that exist in the field. The present section is devoted to a discussion of one aspect of field conditions that requires a compromise with regard to theoretical conditions and assumptions. Here we'll consider the congruence of or disparity between populations and sampling frames.

Simply put, a sampling frame is the list or quasi-list of elements from which a probability sample is selected. Here are some reports of sampling frames appearing in research journals:

> The data for this research were obtained from a random sample of parents of children in the third grade in public and parochial schools in Yakama County, Washington.
>
> (PETERSEN AND MAYNARD, 1981:92)

> The sample at Time 1 consisted of 160 names drawn randomly from the telephone directory of Lubbock, Texas.   (TAN, 1980:242)

> The data reported in this paper . . . were gathered from a probability sample of adults aged 18 and over residing in households in the 48 contiguous United States. Personal interviews with 1,914 respondents were conducted by the Survey Research

Center of the University of Michigan during the fall of 1975.

> (JACKMAN AND SCHEUER SENTER, 1980:345)

Properly drawn samples provide information appropriate for describing the population of elements composing the sampling frame—nothing more. It is necessary to make this point in view of the all-too-common tendency for researchers to select samples from a given sampling frame and then make assertions about a population similar to, but not identical to, the study population defined by the sampling frame.

For an example of an overgeneralized sampling frame, take a look at this report, which is discussing the drugs most frequently prescribed by American physicians:

> Information on prescription drug sales is not easy to obtain. But Rinaldo V. DeNuzzo, a professor of pharmacy at the Albany College of Pharmacy, Union University, Albany, NY, has been tracking prescription drug sales for 25 years by polling nearby drugstores. He publishes the results in an industry trade magazine, *MM&M.*
>
> DeNuzzo's latest survey, covering 1980, is based on reports from 66 pharmacies in 48 communities in New York and New Jersey. Unless there is something peculiar about that part of the country, his findings can be taken as representative of what happens across the country.
>
> (MOSKOWITZ, 1981:33)

The main thing that should strike you is the casual comment about whether there is anything peculiar about New York and New Jersey. There is. The lifestyle in these two states is hardly typical of the other 48. We cannot assume that residents in these large, urbanized, Eastern seaboard states necessarily have the same drug-use patterns as residents of Mississippi, Utah, New Mexico, and Vermont.

Does the survey even represent prescription patterns in New York and New Jersey? To determine that, we would have to know something about the manner in which the 48 communities and the 66 pharmacies were selected. We should be wary in this regard, in view of the reference to "polling nearby drugstores." As we'll see, there are several methods for selecting samples that ensure representativeness, and unless they are used, we should not generalize from the study findings.

Studies of organizations are often the simplest from a sampling standpoint because organizations typically have membership lists. In such cases, the list of members constitutes an excellent sampling frame. If a random sample is selected from a membership list, the data collected from that sample may be taken as representative of all members— *if all members are included in the list.*

Populations that can be sampled from good organizational lists include elementary school, high school, and university students and faculty; church members; factory workers; fraternity or sorority members; members of social, service, or political clubs; and members of professional associations.

The preceding comments apply primarily to local organizations. Often statewide or national organizations do not have a single, easily available membership list. There is, for example, no single list of Episcopalian church members. However, a slightly more complex sample design could take advantage of local church membership lists by first sampling churches and then subsampling the membership lists of those churches selected. (More about that later.)

Other lists of individuals may be especially relevant to the research needs of a particular study. Government agencies maintain lists of registered voters, for example, that might be used if you wanted to conduct a preelection poll or an in-depth examination of voting behavior—but you must ensure that the list is up to date. Similar lists contain the names of automobile owners, welfare recipients, taxpayers, business permit holders, licensed professionals, and so forth. Although it may be difficult to gain access to some of these lists, they provide excellent sampling frames for specialized research purposes.

Realizing that the sampling elements in a study need not be individual persons, we may note that the lists of other types of elements also exist: universities, businesses of various types, cities, academic journals, newspapers, unions, political clubs, professional associations, and so forth.

Telephone directories are frequently used for "quick and dirty" public opinion polls. Undeniably they are easy and inexpensive to use, and that is no doubt the reason for their popularity. And, if you want to make assertions about telephone subscribers, the directory is a fairly good sampling frame. (Realize, of course, that a given directory will not include new subscribers or those who have requested unlisted numbers. Sampling is further complicated by the inclusion in directories of nonresidential listings.) Unfortunately, telephone directories are all too often taken to be a listing of a city's population or of its voters. There are many defects in this reasoning, but the chief one involves a social-class bias. Poor people are less likely to have telephones; rich people may have more than one line. A telephone directory sample, therefore, is likely to have a middle- or upper-class bias.

The class bias inherent in telephone directory samples is often hidden. Preelection polls conducted in this fashion are sometimes quite accurate, perhaps because of the class bias evident in voting itself: poor people are less likely to vote. Frequently, then, these two biases nearly coincide, and the results of a telephone poll may come very close to the final election outcome. Unhappily, the pollster never knows for sure until after the election. And sometimes, as in the case of the 1936 *Literary Digest* poll, you may discover that the voters have not acted according to the expected class biases. The ultimate disadvantage of this method, then, is the researcher's inability to estimate the degree of error to be expected in the sample findings.

Street directories and tax maps are often used for easily obtained samples, but they may also suffer from incompleteness and possible bias. For example, in strictly zoned urban regions, illegal housing units are unlikely to appear on official records. As a result, such units would have no chance for selection, and sample findings could not be representative of those units, which are often poorer and more overcrowded than the average.

Review of Populations and Sampling Frames

Surprisingly little attention has been given to the issues of populations and sampling frames in social research literature. With this in mind, we've devoted special attention to them here. To further emphasize the point, here is a summary of the main guidelines to remember:

1. Findings based on a sample can be taken as representative only of the aggregation of elements that compose the sampling frame.

2. Often, sampling frames do not truly include all the elements that their names might imply. Omissions are almost inevitable. Thus a first concern of the researcher must be to assess the extent of the omissions and to correct them if possible. (Realize, of course, that the researcher may feel he or she can safely ignore a small number of omissions that cannot easily be corrected.)

3. Even to generalize to the population composing the sampling frame, it is necessary for all elements to have equal representation in the frame: Typically, each element should appear only once. Elements that appear more than once will have a greater probability of selection, and the sample will, overall, overrepresent those elements.

Other, more practical matters relating to populations and sampling frames will be treated elsewhere in this book. For example, the form of the sampling frame—such as a list in a publication, a 3 × 5 card file, mailing address plates, machine-readable cards, or magnetic tapes—can affect how easy it is to use. And ease of use may often take priority over scientific considerations: An "easier" list may be chosen over a "more difficult" one, even though the latter is more appropriate to the target population. We should not take a dogmatic position in this regard, but every researcher should

carefully weigh the relative advantages and disadvantages of such alternatives.

Other Considerations in Determining Sample Size

The importance of the foregoing material notwithstanding, decisions about sample size in social work research rarely involve estimating sampling error. Often, this is due to practical limitations. It may not be possible to obtain an adequate sampling frame for some populations of concern to social workers, such as the homeless, undocumented recent immigrants, and so on. Meager budgets for conducting research or time constraints may preclude conducting preliminary surveys to estimate population parameters. Inadequate resources also may force researchers simply to select the largest sample the budget will permit, knowing in advance that that maximum sample size will fall short of the number needed for a desired estimated sampling error.

In studies that have meager resources but seek to conduct multivariate analyses, the selected sample size often will be determined by multiplying the number of variables to be simultaneously analyzed by the minimum number of cases per variable required by the appropriate multivariate statistical procedure. For instance, a doctoral student who is conducting research for a dissertation, who seeks to conduct a multiple regression analysis of ten variables, and who is paying for the research out of his or her own shallow pocket, might choose a sample size of 100 because a common statistical rule-of-thumb requirement for multiple regression analysis is to have at least ten cases for each variable.

To further illustrate this point, imagine that you want to collect data on the living arrangements of people with chronic mental illness. What proportion live with their immediate family? In independent apartments? In transitional facilities? On the streets? To keep it simple, suppose you will look at only five categories of living arrangements. Also suppose that you want to see whether gender and ethnicity are related to living arrangements. You will have two categories for gender (male/female), and let's assume you will have five categories of ethnicity.

Now imagine what a table would look like if it showed how many men and women of each ethnicity had each living arrangement. One half of the table would be for men. It would contain a matrix of 25 cells: five columns for ethnicity (one column for each category you will examine) criss-crossing with five rows (one row for each category of living arrangement). The other half of the table would contain the same matrix of 25 cells for women. In all, then, you'd have a matrix containing 50 cells.

How large of a sample would you need to be able to make meaningful comparisons in your table containing 50 cells? Obviously, if your sample was small, consisting, say, of about 50 or less people, you'd have quite a few cells in your table that were empty or that contained only one person. With so many cells representing so few people it would be virtually impossible to make meaningful comparisons between men and women of various ethnicities. Even with a sample of 100 people, you'd have many cells containing too few people for meaningful comparisons. One rule of thumb is to select a sample that is five times as large as your number of cells. Using that rule, your sample size would need to be 250. Others prefer a ten-to-one ratio, which would require a sample size of 500 for a 50-cell table. Although there is not a single, mathematically pristine answer to this question, anticipating the number of cells to be used in your data analysis can be helpful in avoiding selecting a sample size that turns out to be too woefully inadequate.

Later on in this volume we will be discussing multivariate statistical procedures. We also will discuss experimental designs. We will see why experimental and some quasi-experimental designs are appropriate for evaluating the effectiveness of social work practice. It will be evident that it is usually unrealistic to expect clients selected to receive social work services to be drawn randomly from some large population. The basis for determining sample size in experimental and quasi-experimental studies has to do with statistical power analysis, another topic we will address later. At this point, for the sake of simplicity, we can say that statistical power analysis deals with determining how many cases must be assigned to different comparison groups in order to have an adequate statistical probability of detecting real differences among those groups.

TYPES OF SAMPLING DESIGNS

Up to this point, we have focused on **simple random sampling** (SRS). And, indeed, the body of statistics typically used by social researchers assumes such a sample. As we will see shortly, however, you have a number of options in choosing your sampling method, and you will seldom if ever choose simple random sampling. There are two reasons for that. First, with all but the simplest sampling frame, simple random sampling is not feasible. Second, and probably surprisingly, simple random sampling may not be the most accurate method available. Let's turn now to a discussion of simple random sampling and the other options available.

Simple Random Sampling

As noted, *simple random sampling* is the basic sampling method assumed in the statistical computations of social research. The mathematics of random sampling are especially complex, so we'll detour around them in favor of describing the ways of employing this method in the field.

Once a sampling frame has been established in accord with the preceding discussion, to use simple random sampling the researcher assigns a single number to each element in the list without skipping any number in the process. A table of

USING A TABLE OF RANDOM NUMBERS

In social research, it is often appropriate to select a set of random numbers from a table such as the one presented in Appendix E. Here's how to do that.

Suppose you want to select a simple random sample of 100 people (or other units) out of a population totaling 980.

1. To begin, number the members of the population: in this case, from 1 to 980. Now the problem is to select 100 random numbers. Once you've done that, your sample will consist of the people having the numbers you've selected. (*Note:* It's not essential to actually number them, as long as you're sure of the total. If you have them in a list, for example, you can always count through the list after you've selected the numbers.)

2. The next step is to determine the number of digits you will need in the random numbers you select. In our example, there are 980 members of the population, so you will need three-digit numbers to give everyone a chance of selection. (If there were 11,825 members of the population, you'd need to select five-digit numbers.) Thus, we want to select 100 random numbers in the range from 001 to 980.

3. Now turn to the first page of Appendix E. Notice there are several rows and columns of five-digit numbers, and there are several pages. The table represents a series of random numbers in the range from 00001 to 99999. To use the table for your hypothetical sample, you have to answer these questions:

a. How will you create three-digit numbers out of five-digit numbers?

b. What pattern will you follow in moving through the table to select your numbers?

c. Where will you start?

Each of these questions has several satisfactory answers. The key is to create a plan and follow it. Here's an example.

4. To create three-digit numbers from five-digit numbers, let's agree to select five-digit numbers from the table but consider only the left-most three digits in each case. If we picked the first number on the first page—10480—we would only consider the 104. (We could agree to take the digits furthest to the right, 480, or the middle three digits, 048, and any of these plans would work.) The key is to make a plan and stick with it. For convenience, let's use the left-most three digits.

random numbers (Appendix E) is then used to select elements for the sample. The box titled "Using a Table of Random Numbers" explains its use.

If your sampling frame is in a machine-readable form—cards or magnetic tape—a simple random sample can be selected automatically by computer. (In effect, the computer program numbers the elements in the sampling frame, generates its own series of random numbers, and prints out the list of elements selected.)

5. We can also choose to progress through the tables any way we want: down the columns, up them, across to the right or to the left, or diagonally. Again, any of these plans will work just fine so long as we stick to it. For convenience, let's agree to move down the columns. When we get to the bottom of one column, we'll go to the top of the next; when we exhaust a given page, we'll start at the top of the first column of the next page.

6. Now, where do we start? You can close your eyes and stick a pencil into the table and start wherever the pencil point lands. (I know it doesn't sound scientific, but it works.) Or, if you're afraid you'll hurt the book or miss it altogether, close your eyes and make up a column number and a row number. ("I'll pick the number in the fifth row of column 2.") Start with that number. If you prefer more methodological purity, you might use the first two numbers on a dollar bill, which are randomly distributed, to determine the row and column on which to start.

7. Let's suppose we decide to start with the fifth number in column 2. If you look on the first page of Appendix E, you'll see that the starting number is 39975. We have se-

lected 399 as our first random number, and we have 99 more to go. Moving down the second column, we select 069, 729, 919, 143, 368, 695, 409, 939, and so forth. At the bottom of column 2, we select number 104 and continue to the top of column 3: 015, 255, and so on.

8. See how easy it is? But trouble lies ahead. When we reach column 5, we are speeding along, selecting 816, 309, 763, 078, 061, 277, 988. . . . Wait a minute! There are only 980 students in the senior class. How can we pick number 988? The solution is simple: Ignore it. Any time you come across a number that lies outside your range, skip it and continue on your way: 188, 174, and so forth. The same solution applies if the same number comes up more than once. If you select 399 again, for example, just ignore it the second time.

9. That's it. You keep up the procedure until you've selected 100 random numbers. Returning to your list, your sample consists of person number 399, person number 69, person number 729, and so forth.

Figure 8-10 offers a graphic illustration of simple random sampling. Note that the members of our hypothetical micropopulation have been numbered from 1 to 100. Moving to Appendix E, we decide to use the last two digits of the first column and to begin with the third number from the top. This yields person number 30 as the first one selected into the sample. Number 67 is next, and so forth. (Person 100 would have been selected if '00' had come up in the list.)

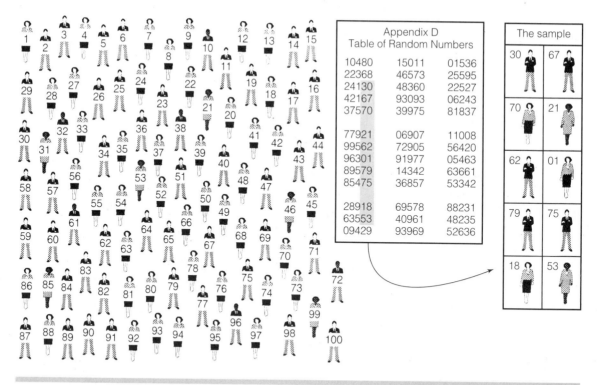

Figure 8-10 A Simple Random Sample

Systematic Sampling

Simple random sampling (SRS) is seldom used in practice. As we will see, it is not usually the most efficient sampling method, and it can be rather laborious if done manually. SRS typically requires a list of elements. When such a list is available, researchers usually employ **systematic sampling** rather than simple random sampling.

In *systematic sampling,* every *k*th element in the total list is chosen (systematically) for inclusion in the sample. If the list contains 10,000 elements and you want a sample of 1000, you select every tenth element for your sample. To ensure against any possible human bias in using this method, you should select the first element at random. Thus, in the preceding example, you would begin by selecting a random number between one and ten. The element having that number is included in

the sample, plus every tenth element following it. This method is technically referred to as *a systematic sample with a random start.* Two terms are frequently used in connection with systematic sampling. The **sampling interval** is the standard distance between elements selected in the sample: ten in the preceding sample. The sampling ratio is the proportion of elements in the population that are selected: 1/10 in the example.

$$\frac{\text{sampling}}{\text{interval}} = \frac{\text{population size}}{\text{sample size}}$$

$$\frac{\text{sampling}}{\text{ratio}} = \frac{\text{sample size}}{\text{population size}}$$

In practice, systematic sampling is virtually identical to simple random sampling. If the list of elements is indeed randomized before sampling, one might argue that a systematic sample drawn from that list is in fact a simple random sample. By now, debates over the relative merits of simple random sampling and systematic sampling have been resolved largely in favor of the simpler method: systematic sampling. Empirically, the results are virtually identical. And, as we will see in a later section, systematic sampling, in some instances, is slightly more accurate than simple random sampling.

There is one danger involved in systematic sampling. The arrangement of elements in the list can make systematic sampling unwise. Such an arrangement is usually called *periodicity*. If the list of elements is arranged in a cyclical pattern that coincides with the sampling interval, a grossly biased sample may be drawn. Two examples will illustrate.

In one study of soldiers during World War II, the researchers selected a systematic sample from unit rosters. Every tenth soldier on the roster was selected for the study. The rosters, however, were arranged in a table of organizations: sergeants first, then corporals and privates, squad by squad. Each squad had ten members. As a result, every tenth person on the roster was a squad sergeant. The systematic sample selected contained only sergeants. It could, of course, have been the case that no sergeants were selected for the same reason.

As another example, suppose we select a sample of apartments in an apartment building. If the sample is drawn from a list of apartments arranged in numerical order (for example, 101, 102, 103, 104, 201, 202, and so on), there is a danger of the sampling interval coinciding with the number of apartments on a floor or some multiple thereof. Then the samples might include only northwest-corner apartments or only apartments near the elevator. If these types of apartments have some other particular characteristic in common (for example, higher rent), the sample will be biased. The same danger would appear in a systematic sample of houses in a subdivision arranged with the same number of houses on a block.

In considering a systematic sample from a list, then, you should carefully examine the nature of that list. If the elements are arranged in any particular order, you should figure out whether that order will bias the sample to be selected and take steps to counteract any possible bias (for example, take a simple random sample from cyclical portions).

In summary, however, systematic sampling is usually superior to simple random sampling, in convenience if nothing else. Problems in the ordering of elements in the sampling frame can usually be remedied quite easily.

Stratified Sampling

In the two preceding sections, we discussed two methods of sample selection from a list: random and systematic. **Stratification** is not an alternative to these methods, but it represents a possible modification in their use.

Simple random sampling and systematic sampling both ensure a degree of representativeness and permit an estimate of the error present. Stratified sampling is a method for obtaining a greater degree of representativeness—for decreasing the probable sampling error. To understand why that is the case, we must return briefly to the basic theory of sampling distribution.

We recall that sampling error is reduced by two factors in the sample design. First, a large sample produces a smaller sampling error than a small sample. Second, a homogeneous population produces samples with smaller sampling errors than does a heterogeneous population. If 99% of the population agrees with a certain statement, it is extremely unlikely that any probability sample will greatly misrepresent the extent of agreement. If the population is split 50-50 on the statement, then the sampling error will be much greater.

Stratified sampling is based on this second factor in sampling theory. Rather than selecting your sample from the total population at large, you ensure that appropriate numbers of elements are drawn from homogeneous subsets of that population.

Suppose you seek to obtain a stratified sample of clients in a large social service agency in order to assess client satisfaction with the services they received. You suspect that ethnic minority clients might be relatively dissatisfied with services, and you want to ensure that they are adequately represented in the sample. Consequently, you might first organize your list of cases so that clients of the same ethnicity are grouped together. Then you would draw appropriate numbers from each ethnic group. In a nonstratified sample, representation by ethnicity would be subjected to the same sampling error as other variables. In a sample stratified by ethnicity, the sampling error on this variable is reduced to zero.

Even more complex stratification methods are possible. In addition to stratifying by ethnicity, you might also stratify by age group, by type of presenting problem, and so forth. In this fashion you might be able to ensure that your sample would contain the proper numbers of Hispanic children with behavior disorders, of black families experiencing marital discord, of elderly Asian American clients, and so forth.

The ultimate function of stratification, then, is to organize the population into homogeneous subsets (with heterogeneity between subsets) and to select the appropriate number of elements from each. To the extent that the subsets are homogeneous on the stratification variables, they may be homogeneous on other variables as well. If age group is related to type of presenting problem, a sample stratified by age group will be more representative in terms of presenting problem as well. If socioeconomic status is related to ethnicity, a sample stratified by ethnicity will be more representative in terms of socioeconomic status.

The choice of stratification variables typically depends on what variables are available. Gender can often be determined in a list of names. University lists are typically arranged by class. Lists of faculty members may indicate their departmental affiliation. Government agency files may be arranged by geographic region. Voter registration lists are arranged according to precinct.

In selecting stratification variables from among those available, however, you should be concerned primarily with those that are presumably related to variables that you want to represent accurately. Because gender is related to many variables and is often available for stratification, it is often used. Education is related to many variables, but it is often not available for stratification. Geographic location within a city, state, or nation is related to many things. Within a city, stratification by geographic location usually increases representativeness in social class, ethnic group, and so forth. Within a nation, it increases representativeness in a broad range of attitudes as well as in social class and ethnicity.

Methods of stratification in sampling vary. When you are working with a simple list of all elements in the population, two are predominant. One method is to sort the population elements into discrete groups based on whatever stratification variables are being used. On the basis of the relative proportion of the population represented by a given group, you select—randomly or systematically—a number of elements from that group constituting the same proportion of your desired sample size. For example, if elderly Hispanics compose 1% of the client population and you desire a sample of 1000 clients, you would select 10 elderly Hispanic clients.

The other method is to group cases as just described and then put those groups together in a continuous list. You would then select a systematic sample, with a random start, from the entire list. Given the arrangement of the list, a systematic sample would select proper numbers (within an error range of 1 or 2) from each subgroup. (*Note:* A simple random sample drawn from such a composite list would cancel out the stratification.)

Figure 8-11 offers a graphic illustration of stratified, systematic sampling. As you can see, we lined up our micropopulation according to sex and race. Then, beginning with a random start of "3", we've taken every tenth person thereafter: 3, 13, 23, . . . , 93.

Stratified sampling ensures the proper representation of the stratification variables to enhance

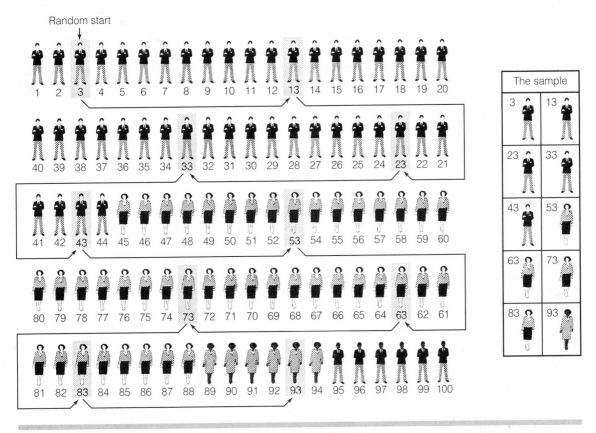

Figure 8-11 A Stratified, Systematic Sample with a Random Start

representation of other variables related to them. Taken as a whole, then, a stratified sample is likely to be more representative on a number of variables than a simple random sample. Although the simple random sample is still regarded as somewhat sacred, it should now be clear that you can often do better.

Implicit Stratification in Systematic Sampling

It was mentioned earlier that systematic sampling can, under certain conditions, be more accurate than simple random sampling. That is the case whenever the arrangement of the list creates an implicit stratification. As already noted, if a list of agency cases is arranged by ethnicity, then a systematic sample provides a stratification by ethnicity whereas a simple random sample would not.

In a study of students at the University of Hawaii, after stratification by school class the students were arranged by their student identification numbers. These numbers, however, were their social security numbers. The first three digits of the social security number indicate the state in which the number was issued. As a result, within a class, students were arranged by the state in which they were issued a social security number, providing a rough stratification by geographic origins.

You should realize, therefore, that an ordered list of elements may be more useful to you than an unordered, randomized list. This point has been stressed here in view of an unfortunate belief that lists should be randomized before systematic sampling. Only if the arrangement presents the problems discussed earlier should the list be rearranged.

Proportionate and Disproportionate Stratified Samples

So far we have been illustrating stratified random sampling with a uniform proportion of cases drawn from each homogeneous grouping. This is called *proportionate stratified sampling*. For example, if our overall sample is to be 10% of the population, we would draw 10% of each homogeneous group.

In some studies, however, it may be advisable to select a larger proportion of cases from some groups than from others. Suppose, for example, that the preceding client satisfaction survey is being conducted in an agency whose 1000 clients include 600 white clients, 300 black clients, 40 Hispanic clients, 30 Asian American clients, 20 Native American clients, and 10 clients whose ethnicity falls in a catchall "other" category. We could select 10% of the white and black clients and have 60 and 30 cases in each group. But if we selected 10% of the clients in the other groups, we would have only four Hispanics, three Asian Americans, two Native Americans, and one "other." There would be nothing wrong with this if all we sought to do was to come up with an overall satisfaction rating for the entire agency.

But what if we sought a detailed analysis about each ethnic group or sought to generalize about which ethnic groups were more satisfied or dissatisfied than others? Such an analysis would not be possible for groups represented by only a handful of cases. Therefore, we would have to take a larger proportion of the very small homogeneous groupings than of the larger ones. This is called *disproportionate stratified sampling*. This sampling procedure gives cases from specified small subgroups a disproportionately better chance of being selected than cases from larger subgroups.

For example we might select 10% of the white and black clients and 50% from each of the remaining groups. That would give us 20 Hispanics, 15 Asian Americans, 10 Native Americans, and 5 "other." This would permit us to undertake our detailed analyses. But if we also wanted to portray an overall agency composite of client satisfaction, we would have to weight the average satisfaction level of each ethnic group in accordance with its overall proportion in the agency population.

Suppose on a 1 (very dissatisfied) to 5 (very satisfied) scale the average rating of each group was as follows:

Table 8-2 Illustration of Disproportionate Stratified Sampling

ETHNIC GROUP	NUMBER OF CASES	AVERAGE RATING
White	60	4.0
Black	30	2.0
Hispanic	20	1.0
Asian American	15	3.0
Native American	10	1.0
Other	5	2.0

If the influence on the overall mean of the cases in the 50% groups were not adjusted in accordance with their true proportion in the population, the overall agency average satisfaction rating would be calculated as shown in Equation (1) Figure 8-12.

But the average rating of 2.75 would underestimate the true overall level of client satisfaction due to the disproportionate influence of the ethnic groups represented by 50% of their cases. To correct for this, we would weight the two 10%

$$\frac{(60 \times 4) + (30 \times 2) + (20 \times 1) + (15 \times 3) + (10 \times 1) + (5 \times 2)}{60 + 30 + 20 + 15 + 10 + 5} \tag{1}$$

$$= \frac{240 + 60 + 20 + 45 + 10 + 10}{140} = \frac{385}{140} = 2.75$$

$$\frac{(60 \times 4 \times 5) + (30 \times 2 \times 5) + (20 \times 1) + (15 \times 3) + (10 \times 1) + (5 \times 2)}{(60 \times 5) + 30 \times 5) + 20 + 15 + 10 + 5}$$

$$= \frac{1200 + 300 + 20 + 45 + 10 + 10}{300 + 150 + 20 + 15 + 10 + 5} \tag{2}$$

$$= \frac{1585}{500} = 3.17$$

SOURCE: Code of Ethics, Part I, Section E, p. 4. Silver Springs, MD: National Association of Social Workers, 1980.

Figure 8-12 Equations for Table 8-2

groups by multiples (weights) of 5 (to bring their influence up to an equivalent 50% representation), as shown in Equation (2) Figure 8-12.

Thus the true overall average rating of client satisfaction of 3.17 would be above the midpoint of 3.0 on the 1 to 5 rating scale, not below it as implied by the misleading 2.75 calculation. But saying this would not negate the accuracy or importance of calculations showing that ethnic minority clientele tend to be far less satisfied with services than is depicted by the overall rating.

MULTISTAGE CLUSTER SAMPLING

The preceding sections have dealt with reasonably simple procedures for sampling from lists of elements. Such a situation is ideal. Unfortunately, however, much interesting social research requires the selection of samples from populations that cannot be easily listed for sampling purposes. Examples would be the population of a city, state, or nation; all university students in the United States; and so forth. In such cases, the sample design must be much more complex. Such a design typically involves the initial sampling of groups of elements—clusters—followed by the selection of elements within each of the selected clusters.

Cluster sampling may be used when it is either impossible or impractical to compile an exhaustive list of the elements composing the target population. All church members in the United States would be an example of such a population. It is often the case, however, that the population elements are already grouped into subpopulations, and a list of those subpopulations either exists or can be created practically. Thus, church members in the United States belong to discrete churches, and it would be possible to discover or create a list of those churches. Following a cluster sample format, then, the list of churches would be sampled in some manner as discussed previously (for example, a stratified, systematic sample). Next, you would obtain lists of members from each of the selected churches. Each of the lists would then be sampled, to provide samples of church members for study. (For an example, see Glock, Ringer, and Babbie, 1967.)

Another typical situation concerns sampling among population areas such as a city. Although there is no single list of a city's population, citizens reside on discrete city blocks or census blocks. It is possible, therefore, to select a sample of blocks initially, create a list of persons living on each of the selected blocks, and subsample persons on each block.

In a more complex design, you might sample blocks, list the households on each selected block, sample the households, list the persons residing in each household, and, finally, sample persons within each selected household. This multistage sample design would lead to the ultimate selection of a sample of individuals but would not require the initial listing of all individuals in the city's population.

Multistage cluster sampling, then, involves the repetition of two basic steps: listing and sampling. The list of primary sampling units (churches, blocks) is compiled and, perhaps, stratified for sampling. Then a sample of those units is selected. The selected primary sampling units are then listed and perhaps stratified. The list of secondary sampling units is then sampled, and so forth.

Cluster sampling is highly recommended by its efficiency, but the price of that efficiency is a less accurate sample. A simple random sample drawn from a population list is subject to a single sampling error, but a two-stage cluster sample is subject to two sampling errors. First, the initial sample of clusters will represent the population of clusters only within a range of sampling error. Second, the sample of elements selected within a given cluster will represent all the elements in that cluster only within a range of sampling error. Thus, for instance, you run a certain risk of selecting a sample of disproportionately wealthy city blocks, plus a sample of disproportionately wealthy households within those blocks. The best solution to this problem lies in the number of clusters selected initially and the number of elements selected within each.

Typically, you'll be restricted to a total sample size; for example, you may be limited to conducting 2000 interviews in a city. Given this broad limitation, however, you have several options in designing your cluster sample. At the extremes you might choose one cluster and select 2000 elements within that cluster; or you might choose 2000 clusters and select one element within each. Of course, neither of these extremes is advisable, but a broad range of choices lies between them. Fortunately, the logic of sampling distributions provides a general guideline to be followed.

Recall that sampling error is reduced by two factors: an increase in the sample size and increased homogeneity of the elements being sampled. These factors operate at each level of a multistage sample design. A sample of clusters will best represent all clusters if a large number are selected and if all clusters are very much alike. A sample of elements will best represent all elements in a given cluster if a large number are selected from the cluster and if all the elements in the cluster are very much alike.

With a given total sample size, however, if the number of clusters is increased, the number of elements within a cluster must be decreased. In this respect, the representativeness of the clusters is increased at the expense of more poorly representing the elements composing each cluster, or vice versa. Fortunately, the factor of homogeneity can be used to ease this dilemma.

Typically, the elements composing a given natural cluster within a population are more homogeneous than are all elements composing the total population. The members of a given church are more alike than are all church members; the residents of a given city block are more alike than are all the residents of a whole city. As a result, relatively fewer elements may be needed to adequately represent a given natural cluster, although a larger number of clusters may be needed to adequately represent the diversity found among the clusters. This fact is most clearly seen in the extreme case of very different clusters composed of identical elements within each. In such a situation, a large number of clusters would adequately represent all its members. Although this extreme situation never exists in reality, it is closer to the truth in most cases than its opposite: identical clusters composed of grossly divergent elements.

The general guideline for cluster design, then, is to maximize the number of clusters selected while decreasing the number of elements within each cluster. It must be noted, however, that this scientific guideline must be balanced against an administrative constraint. The efficiency of cluster sampling is based on the ability to minimize the listing of population elements. By initially selecting clusters, you need list only the elements composing the selected clusters, not all elements in the entire population. Increasing the number of clusters, however, goes directly against this efficiency factor in cluster sampling. A small number of clusters may be listed more quickly and more cheaply than a large number. (Remember that all the elements in a selected cluster must be listed even if only a few are to be chosen in the sample.)

The final sample design will reflect these two constraints. In effect, you will probably select as many clusters as you can afford. Lest this issue be left too open-ended at this point, one rule of thumb may be presented. Population researchers conventionally aim for the selection of 5 households per census block. If a total of 2000 households is to be interviewed, you would aim at 400 blocks with 5 household interviews on each. Figure 8-13 presents a graphic overview of this process.

Before turning to more detailed procedures available to cluster sampling, it bears repeating that this method almost inevitably involves a loss of accuracy. The manner in which this appears, however, is somewhat complex. First, as noted earlier, a multistage sample design is subject to a sampling error at each stage. Because the sample size is necessarily smaller at each stage than the total sample size, the sampling error at each stage will be greater than would be the case for a single-stage random sample of elements. Second, sampling error is estimated on the basis of observed variance among the sample elements. When those

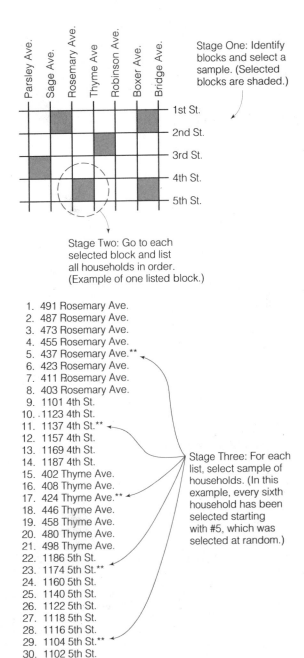

Figure 8-13 Multistage Cluster Sampling

elements are drawn from among relatively homogeneous clusters, the estimated sampling error will be too optimistic and must be corrected in the light of the cluster sample design.

Multistage Cluster Sampling, Stratification

Thus far, we have looked at cluster sampling as though a simple random sample were selected at each stage of the design. In fact, stratification techniques can be used to refine and improve the sample being selected.

The basic options available are essentially the same as those possible in single-stage sampling from a list. In selecting a national sample of churches, for example, you might initially stratify your list of churches by denomination, geographic region, size, rural or urban location, and perhaps by some measure of social class.

Once the primary sampling units (churches, blocks) have been grouped according to the relevant, available stratification variables, either simple random or systematic sampling techniques can be used to select the sample. You might select a specified number of units from each group or *stratum,* or you might arrange the stratified clusters in a continuous list and systematically sample that list.

To the extent that clusters are combined into homogeneous strata, the sampling error at this stage will be reduced. The primary goal of stratification, as before, is homogeneity.

There is no reason why stratification could not take place at each level of sampling. The elements listed within a selected cluster might be stratified before the next stage of sampling. Typically, however, that is not done. (Recall the assumption of relative homogeneity within clusters.)

Probability Proportionate to Size (PPS) Sampling

This section introduces a more sophisticated form of cluster sampling used in many large-scale survey sampling projects. In the preceding discussion, we talked about selecting a random or systematic sample of clusters and then a random or systematic sample of elements within each cluster selected. Notice that this produces an overall sampling scheme in which every element in the whole population has the same probability of selection.

Let's say we are selecting households within a city. If there are 1000 city blocks and we initially select a sample of 100, that means that each block has a 100/1000 or .1 chance of being selected. If we next select 1 household in 10 from those residing on the selected blocks, each household has a .1 chance of selection within its block. To calculate the overall probability of a household being selected, we simply multiply the probabilities at the individual steps in sampling. That is, each household has a 1/10 chance of its block being selected and a 1/10 chance of that specific household being selected if the block is one of those chosen. Each household, in this case, has a $1/10 \times 1/10 = 1/100$ chance of selection overall. Because each household would have the same chance of selection, the sample so selected should be representative of all households in the city.

There are dangers in this procedure, however. In particular, the varying sizes of blocks (measured in numbers of households) present a problem. Let's suppose that half the city's population resides in 10 densely packed blocks filled with highrise apartment buildings, and suppose that the rest of the population lives in single-family dwellings spread out over the remaining 900 blocks. When we first select our sample of 1/10 of the blocks, it is quite possible that we'll miss all of the 10 densely packed highrise blocks. No matter what happens in the second stage of sampling, our final sample of households will be grossly unrepresentative of the city, being composed only of single-family dwellings.

Whenever the clusters sampled are of greatly differing sizes, it is appropriate to use a modified sampling design called *probability proportionate to size*—PPS. This design (1) guards against the problem we've just described and (2) still produces a final sample in which each element has the same chance of selection.

As the name suggests, each cluster is given a chance of selection proportionate to its size. Thus, a city block with 200 households has twice the chance of selection as one with only 100 households. The method for doing this is demonstrated in the illustration that follows in the next section. Within each cluster, however, a fixed *number* of elements is selected, say, 5 households per block. Notice how this procedure results in each household having the same probability of selection overall.

Let's say that Household A is located on a block containing 100 households altogether, and Household B is located on a block containing 25 households. Suppose that we plan to select 5 households from whatever blocks are picked. This means that if the block containing Household A is picked, that household has a 5/100 chance of selection in the second stage of sampling. If the block containing Household B is picked, it has a 5/25 or 20/100 chance of being selected in the second stage of sampling. At the second stage of sampling, then, Household B has four times as good a chance of having its block selected in the first stage as did Household A. In the overall sampling design, then, both Household A and Household B have the same chance of being selected.

In a PPS sample design, the overall probability of selection for elements is calculated as follows:

1. The probability of a cluster being selected is equal to its proportional share of all the elements in the population times the number of clusters to be selected.

2. The probability of an element being selected within a cluster is equal to the number to be selected within each cluster divided by the number of elements contained within that particular cluster.

3. The overall probability of an element being selected equals (1) times (2).

Here's an example. Suppose a city is composed of 2000 blocks and 100,000 households and that we want to select 1000 households. That means

that each household should have a 1000/100,000 or .01 chance of selection. We decide to accomplish this by picking 200 blocks PPS and selecting 5 households on each of the blocks chosen.

Now consider a block containing 100 households. The block has a probability of selection equal to:

$$\begin{matrix} 200 \\ \text{blocks} \\ \text{to be} \\ \text{chosen} \end{matrix} \times \frac{\overset{100}{\text{(households on the block)}}}{\underset{\text{(households in the city)}}{100,000}} = .2$$

If that block is selected, each household has a second-stage probability of selection equal to:

$$\frac{5 \text{ (to be selected on each block)}}{100 \text{ (households on that block)}} = .05$$

Multiplying .2 times .05, we get an overall probability of selection equal to .01, as required.

Now let's consider a block with only 20 households on it. The block's chance of selection is only $200 \times 20/100,000$ or .04, much less than the earlier example. If this block is selected, however, each household has a chance of 5/20 or .25 of selection in the second stage. Overall, its probability of selection is .04 times .25, or .01: the same as the earlier case and as required by the overall sample design.

If you examine the method for calculating overall probabilities carefully, you'll see why the result is always going to be the same.

Example 1
$$200 \times 100/100,000 \times 5/100 = .01$$

Example 2
$$200 \times 20/100,000 \times 5/20 = .01$$

The only thing that differs in the two examples is the number of households on the blocks, and that number appears in both numerator and denominator, thus cancelling itself out. No matter what the block size, then, the overall probability of a household being selected will be equal to 200 times 5/100,000, or .01. See how neat and clean it is?

As a practical matter, PPS cluster sampling is never quite this neat in the field. For example, the estimates of the number of households on blocks are seldom totally accurate, so that blocks are given too high or too low probabilities of selection. There are several statistical solutions to this problem, however, although it's probably not necessary for you to know them for purposes of this introduction to sampling. Other problems arise because some households selected cannot be interviewed—either the people are never home or they refuse to be interviewed. Again, the structure of PPS sampling makes adjustments possible, so that the data collected from households that are selected and interviewed can be taken as representative of all households in the city.

We began this section on PPS sampling by pointing to the danger of missing very large blocks altogether. There is another benefit inherent in this more sophisticated design. If you recall the earlier discussion of homogeneity and heterogeneity, you'll remember that sampling is less of a problem if all the elements being selected are pretty much alike—that is, homogeneous. PPS sampling takes advantage of that fact in the sense that households composing a single city block or similar geographic groupings are likely to be quite similar to one another, as are the families residing in them. Specifically, the similarity of households on a block is greater than the similarity among households in a whole city. This means that it takes relatively few households on a single block to describe all the households on that block. As a rule of thumb, five is usually enough in the context of a large multistage cluster sample. Observing more than five households on a single block would improve the description of the block slightly, but the description of the city as a whole would be better improved by adding more blocks to the sample than adding more households on fewer blocks. Given that you can only interview, say, 1000 households altogether, it would be better to interview five each on 200 blocks than to interview 20 each

on 50 blocks. In addition to guarding against specific dangers, then, PPS sampling is an efficient use of limited resources.

ILLUSTRATION: SAMPLING SOCIAL WORK STUDENTS

Now let's use a hypothetical example to see what cluster sampling looks like in practice. The illustration that follows is less complex than the area probability samples that are employed in studies of geographic areas such as cities, states, or the nation. It is hypothetical because the recent social work research literature is devoid of studies using probability cluster sampling. Nonetheless, this example illustrates the applicability of cluster sampling to social work research and the various principles of this sampling approach.

Suppose you obtained a research grant from the National Institute of Mental Health to conduct a longitudinal study of how social work students change their attitudes about case management with the chronically mentally disabled during their social work education. There are approximately 100 graduate programs of social work in the United States and approximately 300 undergraduate programs. You will need to make several repeated site visits to each program selected for the study in order to collect longitudinal data from the students there. You desire a nationally representative sample of students, but your travel budget limits your site visits to 40 programs.

There is no national list of social work students, so a multistage sampling design is created. In the initial stage of sampling, programs are selected with probability proportionate to size (PPS), and then students are selected from each.

Selecting the Programs

The Council on Social Work Education publishes an annual report listing each social work education program and its enrollment size. This list constitutes the sampling frame for the first stage of sampling. It shows a nationwide total of approxi-

Table 8-3 Form Used in Listing Social Work Education Programs

PROGRAM	ENROLLMENT SIZE	CUMULATIVE ENROLLMENT
School A	200	200
School B	400	600
School C	100	700

mately 50,000 students, including 25,000 at the graduate level and 25,000 at the undergraduate level. Consequently, you decide to select 20 programs from each level for your study.

For your data analysis you desire a sample size of 1000 students, so you decide to select 25 students from each of the 40 participating programs. To accomplish this, you make two lists of programs: one for graduate programs and one for undergraduate programs. Each list identifies the enrollment size of each program and the cumulative enrollment of the programs on the list, as illustrated in Table 8-3.

The object at this point is to select a sample of 20 programs from each list in a way such that each would have a chance of selection proportionate to its enrollment size. To accomplish this, the cumulative totals are used to create ranges of numbers for each program equaling the number of students enrolled in that program. School A in Table 8-2 is assigned the numbers 1 through 200, School B is assigned 201 through 600, School C is assigned 601 through 700, and so forth.

By selecting 20 numbers for each list ranging between 1 and 25,000, it is possible to select 40 programs for the study. The 20 numbers could be selected in a systematic sample as follows. Set the sampling interval at 1250 (25,000/20). Select a random start at between 1 and 1250. Let's say the starting number randomly selected is 563. Since that number falls within the range of numbers assigned to School B (201 through 600), School B is selected.

Increments of 1250 (the sampling interval) are then added to the random starting number, and every school within whose range one of the resultant numbers appears is selected to participate in the study. It should be apparent that in this fashion, each school has a chance of selection directly proportionate to its enrollment size. A school enrolling 400 students has twice the chance of selection as a school with 200 and ten times the chance of selection as one with only 40 students.

Selecting the Students

Once the sample of programs is selected, a list of the students enrolled is obtained from each selected program. A sampling interval is then computed for each program based on its enrollment size and the number of students desired from each program (25). If a program enrolled 250 students, the sample interval, therefore, would be set at 10. A random number is selected and incremented by the sampling interval to select the sample of students from that school. This procedure is repeated for each school.

PROBABILITY SAMPLING IN REVIEW

The preceding discussions have been devoted to the key sampling method used in controlled survey research: probability sampling. In each of the variations examined, we have seen that elements are chosen for study from a population on a basis of random selection with known nonzero probabilities.

Depending on the field situation, probability sampling can be very simple, or it can be extremely difficult, time consuming, and expensive. Whatever the situation, however, it remains the most effective method for the selection of study elements. There are two reasons for this.

First, probability sampling avoids conscious or unconscious biases in element selection on the part of the researcher. If all elements in the population have an equal (or unequal and subsequently weighted) chance of selection, there is an excellent chance that the sample so selected will closely represent the population of all elements.

Second, probability sampling permits estimates of sampling error. Although no probability sample will be perfectly representative in all respects, controlled selection methods permit the researcher to estimate the degree of expected error in that regard.

In spite of the preceding comments, it is sometimes not possible to use standard probability sampling methods. Sometimes it isn't even appropriate to do so. In those cases, nonprobability sampling is used. The remainder of this chapter is devoted to a brief discussion of the different forms of nonprobability sampling available to you as a researcher.

NONPROBABILITY SAMPLING

Social work research is often conducted in situations in which it is not feasible to select the kinds of probability samples just described. Suppose you wanted to study homelessness: There is no list of all homeless individuals, nor are you likely to create such a list. Moreover, as we'll see, there are times when probability sampling wouldn't be appropriate if it were possible. In many such situations, nonprobability sampling procedures are called for, and we'll examine four types in this section: purposive or judgmental sampling, quota sampling, reliance on available subjects, and snowball sampling.

Purposive or Judgmental Sampling

Occasionally it may be appropriate for you to select your sample on the basis of your own knowledge of the population, its elements, and the nature of your research aims: in short, based on your judgment and the purpose of the study. Especially in the initial design of your questionnaire, you might wish to select the widest variety of respondents to test the broad applicability of questions. Although

the study findings would not represent any meaningful population, the test run might effectively uncover any peculiar defects in your questionnaire. This situation would be considered a pretest, however, rather than a final study.

In some instances, you may wish to study a small subset of a larger population in which many members of the subset are easily identified, but the enumeration of all of them would be nearly impossible. For instance, you might want to study the homeless. Many of the homeless might be visible in certain areas of town, such as near shelters, the Salvation Army facility, or other social welfare facilities. But it would not be feasible to define and sample all of them. In studying all or a sample of the most visible homeless individuals, you might collect data sufficient for your purposes, particularly if your study is exploratory. Thus, you might ask personnel in those facilities to use their judgment in handpicking cases that they think represent those segments of the homeless population with which they are familiar.

Suppose you are writing a grant proposal to secure funding for new social services to be targeted to the homeless, and the funding source requires that your proposal include a report of an assessment of the social service needs of the homeless in your community. Suppose, given your agency's meager resources and the nearness of the proposal submission deadline, you have neither the time nor money to conduct a communitywide survey of the homeless using probability sampling. One option would be to select a purposive sample of community leaders, experts, and professionals known for their work with and expertise on the problem of homelessness in your locality. You could use your knowledge of the community to handpick key people who, in your judgment, best represent the range of those persons in the best position to know of the needs of the homeless in your community, and then survey them as to their estimates of those needs.

Sometimes purposive sampling is employed not to select typical cases, but to select atypical ones. This is commonly done when we seek to compare opposite extremes of a phenomenon in order to generate hypotheses about it. For instance, in seeking to generate hypotheses about the etiology of mental illness, we might want to study certain children of mentally ill parents, contrasting the life experiences and other attributes of children who became diagnosably mentally ill and those who became extraordinarily healthy. Or, in seeking to gain insights into the attributes of effective practice, we may handpick for intensive study those cases with whom practitioners felt extremely successful and those cases with whom they felt extremely ineffectual. Rubin and associates (1983) used this sampling method in a study seeking to understand why some graduate schools of social work were experiencing sharp declines in the numbers of applications submitted to their Master's programs. Using available data listing the extent of the applications decline in each school, they studied those schools that had the largest and smallest declines. The two groups of schools seemed to be distinguished primarily by the extent and aggressiveness of their recruitment efforts. The authors therefore postulated that variance in recruitment efforts might help explain the variation in applications decline from school to school.

Quota Sampling

Quota sampling, mentioned earlier, is the method that helped George Gallup avoid disaster in 1936—and set up the disaster of 1948. Like probability sampling, quota sampling addresses the issue of representativeness, although the two methods approach the issue quite differently.

Quota sampling begins with a matrix describing the characteristics of the target population. You need to know what proportion of the population is male and what proportion female, for example, and for each sex, what proportions fall into various age categories, educational levels, ethnic groups, and so forth. In establishing a national quota sample, you would need to know what proportion of the national population is urban, eastern, male, under 25, white, working class,

and the like, and all the other permutations of such a matrix.

Once such a matrix has been created and a relative proportion assigned to each cell in the matrix, you collect data from persons having all the characteristics of a given cell. All the persons in a given cell are then assigned a weight appropriate to their portion of the total population. When all the sample elements are so weighted, the overall data should provide a reasonable representation of the total population.

Quota sampling has several inherent problems. First, the quota frame (the proportions that different cells represent) must be accurate, and it is often difficult to get up-to-date information for this purpose. The Gallup failure to predict Truman as the presidential victor in 1948 was due partly to this problem.

Second, biases may exist in the selection of sample elements within a given cell—even though its proportion of the population is accurately estimated. An interviewer, instructed to interview five persons meeting a given, complex set of characteristics, may still avoid persons living at the top of seven-story walk-ups, having particularly run-down homes, or owning vicious dogs.

In recent years, attempts have been made to combine probability and quota sampling methods, but the effectiveness of this effort remains to be seen. At present, you would be advised to treat quota sampling warily.

Reliance on Available Subjects

Relying on available subjects, such as stopping people at a street corner or some other location, can be an extremely risky sampling method, although it is used quite frequently. It is most justified when the researcher wants to conduct an experiment, study the characteristics of people passing the sampling point at specified times or when less risky sampling methods are not feasible. Even when use of this method is justified, it is imperative that the researcher exercise great caution in generalizing from his or her data to a larger population. Also, he or she should alert readers to the risks associated with this method.

Not everyone calls this method *relying on available subjects*. Some call it *availability sampling*. Others call it *convenience sampling* or *accidental sampling*. Regardless of what you call it, you should know that the way you perceive the utility of findings associated with this sampling method can vary a great deal, depending on the overall nature of the study and its findings. Let's look at some examples of possible studies using this method that illustrate that variance in potential utility. We'll begin with some examples illustrating very limited utility.

Suppose several students in a social work research course chose to do a team research project for that course by interviewing students in the course about their attitudes regarding private practice. The representativeness of the sample would be extremely dubious. Perhaps that research class was the only class whose scheduling did not conflict with an elective on psychoanalytic psychotherapy, and therefore students aspiring to become private practitioners of psychotherapy were more likely to take that research class. It is virtually impossible to anticipate all the possible biases that may render a particular accidental sample like this one atypical in one direction or another.

University researchers frequently conduct surveys limited to the students who happen to enroll in their classes. The ease and inexpense of such a method explains its popularity, but it seldom produces data of much general value. It may be useful to pretest a questionnaire, but such a sampling method should not be used for a study purportedly describing students as a whole.

Consider this report on the sampling design in an examination of knowledge and opinions about nutrition and cancer among medical students and family physicians:

> The fourth-year medical students of the University of Minnesota Medical School in Minneapolis comprised the student population in this study. The physician population consisted of all physicians attending a "Family Practice Review and Update" course sponsored by the University of Minnesota Department of Continuing Medical Education. (COOPER-STEPHENSON AND THEOLOGIDES, 1981:472)

After all is said and done, what will the results of this study represent? They do not provide a meaningful comparison of medical students and family physicians in the United States or even in Minnesota. Who were the physicians who attended the course? We can guess that they were probably more concerned about their continuing education than other physicians, but we can't say that for sure. Ultimately, we don't know what to do with the results of a study like this.

Despite their risks, some studies that rely on available subjects have great value. Consider, for instance, randomized experiments evaluating practice effectiveness. Experiments typically are conducted in agencies where the researcher happens to be employed or otherwise have access to clients. Experimental settings are not randomly selected (although it would be nice if they could be). Clients virtually never are randomly selected to participate in experiments (although, again, it would be nice if they could be). Rather, they must volunteer, and it's usually on the basis of which clients happen to be around needing an intervention, or happen to enter a program, at the time of the study. (Imagine the response you would likely get from people randomly selected from the general community if you asked them to participate in an experimental evaluation of an intervention aimed at preventing child abuse or at alleviating their family dysfunction or their emotional distress!)

Students often mistakenly equate random sampling with random assignment of subjects to experimental and control groups (which we'll discuss in the next chapter). Although random assignment and random sampling share some common features, they are not the same processes. Random sampling refers to using random procedures to select people from a larger population, with the aim of generalizing to that population.

Random assignment refers to randomly assigning a pool of subjects to two groups, so that the two groups initially are representative of each other. Random assignment offers no basis to presume that the experimental participants as a whole (that is, both groups combined) are representative of a larger population. Instead, random assignment is typically done with a convenience sample, and the people who happen to be available and willing to participate in an experiment may be atypical. That's one of the main reasons experimental results often have to be viewed with caution regarding the extent to which they can be generalized to settings or populations beyond the study conditions. We'll say a lot more about this in the next chapter, where you'll see how experiments can have great value despite their reliance on available subjects.

Experiments are not the only type of study that can have value despite relying on available subjects. Consider the following fictional scenario. Students in a research class in a prestigious school of social work in a large state university are assigned a semester-long group project in which they must design and carry out a research study in order to gain hands-on research experience. They have no money for the project, and precious little time. They decide that the best feasible project would be to survey all 150 second-year students about to graduate from their master's of social work (MSW) degree program. The survey consists of a brief questionnaire assessing student attitudes about working with clients who are infected with HIV/AIDS. They disseminate the questionnaire to every second-year student. Two-thirds of the students complete and return their questionnaire. Thus, they have a sample that relies on available subjects in two ways. First, the students in their particular school are selected for reasons of convenience only. Second, they must rely on the students who chose to complete and return their questionnaires.

This might sound like a study that may be a good learning experience for the students, but one whose findings are not likely to have much utility to the social work profession at large. But what if half of the respondents to their survey express unfounded fears and myths about the contagion of HIV/AIDS and say they would refuse to work with clients infected with it? Because of the sampling limitations, the researchers would not know whether the respondents were representative of the population of second-year MSW students in the nation or even in their program. But because they had a two-thirds response rate, and because half of that two-thirds expressed unwarranted fears of HIV/AIDS and an appalling refusal to work with people infected with it, they would know that at a minimum one-third of the students about to graduate from their program and enter professional social work practice felt that way. Even if their sample of respondents was unlike the non-respondents, therefore, they may have identified an important problem with implications for adding content on HIV/AIDS (and on professional ethics!) to their school's MSW curriculum.

But, you may well ask, what about generalizing their finding to the larger population of schools of social work? This particular school was selected on grounds of convenience, only. We cannot assume its students represent all social work students. While that may be true, known attributes about the school and its national prestige offer reasons to guess that its students are no more likely than students in most schools to be ignorant about HIV/AIDS or to refuse to work with clients infected with it. Consequently, it might be reasonable to suppose that if the problem is this severe in this particular highly regarded school, it's probably severe in a lot of other schools. Admittedly, this would be speculation. But the findings would probably have a great impact on social work educators, nonetheless. If nothing else, they'd at least want to survey their own students to see if the problem is as bad in their program as in the one originally surveyed. Therefore, even though the original survey could not be generalized to all schools, it would have made an important contribution in alerting social work educators to the potential seriousness of this problem and stimulating them to investigate it further.

Here's another fictional scenario that makes the same point in perhaps a more dramatic fashion. Suppose two patients with advanced stages of AIDS accidentally are given the same unintended combination of medications, after which both patients immediately become symptom free and test negatively for the disease. Six months later they continue to test negatively and appear to be in perfect health. Should health professionals, people with AIDS, their loved ones, and the general public be informed about these findings and the combination of medications involved, despite the fact that the sample was accidental and cannot be presumed to be representative? You bet they should!

Although the representativeness of samples that rely on available subjects should always be considered with great caution, your view of the value of studies using availability samples ultimately will depend on your knowledge about the population and your judgment about the studies' particular sampling procedures and findings. The foregoing fictional survey of all second-year students in a prestigious MSW program in a state university, for instance, is likely to have more value to social work educators in general than a survey of the same attitudes among students who happen to attend a debate on the need for more curriculum on HIV/AIDS in a small new program in a school with a fundamentalist religious affiliation. This is true even though both surveys would rely on available subjects.

Suppose you seek to estimate the likely enrollment in a proposed continuing education workshop on play therapy and you consider two sampling options, both of which rely on available subjects. One option is a convenience sample consisting of respondents to a survey of your school's social work alumni. The other option is a convenience sample consisting of practitioners who attend your school's upcoming continuing education workshops. There are two remaining workshops, one that focuses on treating abused children and one that focuses on early childhood development. If 80% of the practitioners attending these workshops express the need for a workshop on play therapy, you might understandably view that figure with caution, since the practitioners drawn to attend the two workshops with topics that are related to children and play therapy reasonably can be presumed to be more likely than the larger population of practitioners to work with children or have an interest in play therapy. It would be wrong to project that 80% of practitioners in general will want to enroll in a workshop on play therapy. On the other hand, if 80% of the respondents to your alumni survey express the need for a workshop on play therapy, you would have less reason to suspect a connection between views on that need and likeliness of being included in the sample. Although you'd still want to exercise caution in generalizing from your convenience sample, you'd have better grounds for supposing that a large number of practitioners is experiencing the need for and will enroll in a workshop on play therapy.

You may want to develop the workshop regardless of which of the above two availability samples you use. Even if you just rely on practitioners attending the two upcoming workshops, you may have useful information about whether there is sufficient demand for the play therapy workshop. Although these practitioners may not represent the larger population, they may be more representative of practitioners who actually attend continuing education workshops than are the typical respondents to your alumni survey. If you need an enrollment of at least 20 practitioners to justify offering the new workshop, and many more than 20 of the current workshop attendees say they will definitely come to the new workshop, you have reasonable grounds for proceding with your plans to develop the new workshop regardless of the larger representativeness of your convenience sample. In fact, you may have more confidence in current attendees who say they will attend the new workshop to follow through and actually attend it than in their counterparts in a larger convenience sample that is more representative of the broader practitioner population, but less representative of those practitioners who really follow through and attend workshops. Thus, your judgment about the availability sample and your knowledge of the population will influence the practical implications you derive from the findings regarding enrollment projections.

Like it or not, the reality is that the majority of studies you are likely to encounter in social work or in the human services in general will use nonprobability sampling techniques, usually due to practical limitations making probability samples unfeasible. Often the samples will have to rely on available subjects. Rather than dismiss all of these efforts as worthless, we recommend that you exercise good judgment and caution in ferreting out those studies and findings that appear to have some utility. We think you will find that many of them will equip you with important information that you previously lacked, information that either offers tentative guidelines for practice or ideas for further inquiry.

Snowball Sampling

Another nonprobability sampling technique, one that some consider to be a form of accidental sampling, is called *snowball sampling*. This procedure is most commonly used in qualitative field research, and we will discuss it further in the chapter on that type of methodology. Snowball sampling is appropriate when the members of a special population are difficult to locate. It thus might be appropriately used to find a sample of homeless individuals, migrant workers, undocumented immigrants, and so on. This procedure is implemented by collecting data on the few members of the target population that one is able to locate, and then asking those individuals to provide the information needed to locate other members of that population whom they happen to know. The term *snowball* refers to the process of accumulation as each located subject suggests other subjects. This sampling procedure also results in samples that have questionable representativeness and is used primarily for exploratory purposes.

GENDER BIAS AND SAMPLING

In recent years feminists have been sensitizing social researchers to the relationship of women's issues to research. For example, Chapter 5 presented a box dealing with the treatment of gender in operationalizing variables, excerpted from a pamphlet prepared by members of Committees on the Status of Women in Sociology. All aspects of the research process can be affected by gender bias, and sampling is one area where such bias can be particularly problematic. Even probability sampling can be affected by gender bias, for instance, when we inappropriately decide to exclude a particular gender from our sampling frame.

Perhaps the most commonly encountered gender bias problem in sampling is the unwarranted generalization of research findings to the population as a whole when one gender is not adequately represented in the research sample. (The same type of problem, by the way, is encountered when certain minority groups are inadequately represented in the sample but generalizations are made to the entire population.) Campbell (1983) reviewed the occurrence of gender biases in the gender-role research literature and identified a number of illustrations of this problem. For example, she cited studies on achievement motivation and on management and careers whose samples included only white, middle-class male subjects but whose conclusions did not specify that their generalizations were limited to individuals with those attributes. She was particularly critical of life-cycle research, as follows (p. 206):

Nowhere is the effect of bias on sampling more evident than in the popular and growing field of the life cycle or stages. Beginning with Erikson's . . . work on the "Eight Stages of Man" to Levinson's Seasons of a Man's Life . . . the study of life cycles has focused on male subjects. When women are examined, it is in terms of how they fit or don't fit the male model. Without empirical verification, women are said to go through the same cycles as men . . . or are said to go through cycles that are antithetical to men's. . . . Based on a survey of the literature on life cycles, Sangiuliano . . . concluded that "Mostly we (researchers) persist in seeing her (woman) in the reflected light of men." . . .

The inadequate representation of a particular gender in a sample can be much subtler than just excluding them entirely or including an insufficient proportion of them. It could also occur due to biased data collection procedures, even when the number of individuals of a particular sex is not the issue. For instance, Campbell notes that the Gallup poll interviews male subjects beginning at 6:00 P.M., while conducting most interviews with females between 4:00 and 6:00 P.M. Thus, Campbell argues that most professional women would not be home before 6:00 P.M. and are not adequately represented in the sample. If she is correct, then even if the overall proportion of women in the Gallup Poll seems to be sufficient, the views expressed by the women in the sample are not adequately representative of the views of the population of women.

As another example, if we wanted to generalize about gender-related differences in job satisfaction, we would not want to select our sample only from those work settings where professional or managerial positions go predominantly to men and where semiprofessional clerical jobs go predominantly to women.

There may be instances, however, when the exclusion of a particular gender from a study's sample is warranted or inescapable—instances where only one gender is relevant and where generalizations will be restricted to that gender. Thus, only one gender would be included in the sample of a survey of client satisfaction in a program whose clientele all happen to be of the same gender. For example, perhaps it is a group support program for battered women or for rape victims.

But we must be on guard not to let any gender-role biases improperly influence us to deem a particular gender irrelevant for a given study. For example, we should not be predisposed to restrict our samples to men when we study things like ag-gression, management, unemployment, or criminal behavior and to women when we study things like parenting, nurturing, or housekeeping.

Main Points

• A sample is a special subset of a population observed for purposes of making inferences about the nature of the total population itself.

• Although the sampling methods used earlier in this century often produced misleading inferences, current techniques are far more accurate and reliable.

• The chief criterion of the quality of a sample is the degree to which it is representative—the extent to which the characteristics of the sample are the same as those of the population from which it was selected.

• Probability sampling methods provide one excellent way of selecting samples that will be quite representative.

• The most carefully selected sample will almost never provide a perfect representation of the population from which it was selected. There will always be some degree of sampling error.

• Probability sampling methods make it possible for you to estimate the amount of sampling error that should be expected in a given sample.

• The chief principle of probability sampling is that every member of the total population must have some known nonzero probability of being selected into the sample.

• A sampling frame is a list or quasi-list of the members of a population. It is the resource used in the selection of a sample. A sample's representativeness depends directly on the extent to which a sampling frame contains all the members of the total population that the sample is intended to represent.

• Simple random sampling is logically the most fundamental technique in probability sampling, although it is seldom used in practice.

• Systematic sampling involves the selection of every *k*th member from a sampling frame. This method is functionally equivalent to simple random sampling, with a few exceptions, and it is a more practical method.

• Stratification is the process of grouping the members of a population into relatively homogeneous strata before sampling. This practice has the effect of improving the representativeness of a sample by reducing the degree of sampling error.

• Multistage cluster sampling is a more complex sampling technique that is frequently used in those cases in which a list of all the members of a population does not exist. An initial sample of groups of members (clusters) is selected first. Then, all the members of the selected cluster are listed, often through direct observation in the field. Finally, the members listed in each of the selected clusters are subsampled, thereby providing the final sample of members.

• Probability proportionate to size (PPS) is a special, efficient method for multistage cluster sampling.

• If the members of a population have unequal probabilities of selection into the sample, it is necessary to assign weights to the different observations made in order to provide a representative picture of the total population. Basically, the weight assigned to a particular sample member should be the inverse of its probability of selection.

• Purposive sampling is a type of nonprobability sampling method in which the researcher uses his or her own judgment in the selection of sample members. It is sometimes called a judgmental sample.

• Quota sampling is another nonprobability sampling method. You begin with a detailed description of the characteristics of the total population (quota matrix) and then select your sample members in such a fashion as to include different composite profiles that exist in the population. The representativeness of a quota sample depends in large part on the accuracy of the quota matrix as a reflection of the characteristics of the population.

• In general, nonprobability sampling methods are regarded as less reliable than probability sampling methods. On the other hand, they are often easier and cheaper to use.

Review Questions and Exercises

1. Review the discussion of the 1948 Gallup Poll that predicted that Thomas Dewey would defeat Harry Truman for president. Discuss some ways in which Gallup could have modified his quota sample design to have avoided the error.

2. Using Appendix D of this book, select a simple random sample of 10 numbers in the range from 1 to 9876. Describe each step in the process.

3. In a paragraph or two, describe the steps involved in selecting a multistage cluster sample of nursing home residents throughout the nation.

Additional Reading

Kish, Leslie, *Survey Sampling* (New York: Wiley, 1965). Unquestionably the definitive work on sampling in social research. Let's not beat around the bush: if you need to know something more about sampling than was contained in this chapter, there is only one place to go. Kish's coverage ranges from the simplest matters to the most complex and mathematical. He is both highly theoretical and downright practical. Easily readable and difficult passages intermingle as Kish exhausts everything you could want or need to know about each aspect of sampling.

CHAPTER

9

Causal Inference and Group Designs

What You'll Learn in This Chapter

This chapter examines the criteria for drawing
causal inferences from research findings
and the ways various designs attempt
to meet those criteria.

INTRODUCTION

As we noted earlier in this book, social workers and social work researchers often want to make inferences about cause and effect. We may be interested, for example, in specifying the causes of child abuse or in identifying the factors that explain why attendance at some community organization meetings is higher than at others. Or we might want to know what makes a particular child lose self-control at some times but not at others. Perhaps the most pressing causal issue facing the profession of social work today concerns the effectiveness of social work services. What *effects,* if any, are *caused* by social workers?

To answer these questions, we need to understand the logic of causal inference. Under what conditions may we infer that a change in the dependent variable was really caused by the independent variable and not something else? What are some of the most plausible rival explanations, and how do we rule them out? This chapter identifies appropriate and inappropriate criteria for inferring causality. It identifies various group designs—such as cross-sectional, experimental, and quasi-experimental designs—and the ways they attempt to ferret out causality.

We'll see that just because a dependent variable varies in a predictable fashion with variation in an independent variable, that's not a sufficient basis for inferring that the independent variable *caused* the dependent variable to change. Before we can make a *causal* inference, we have to determine which variable changed first. But even if we find that the independent variable changed first, we still must rule out various alternative plausible causes of the change in the dependent variable.

Our research study is said to have internal validity to the extent that it is able to sort out whether it was the independent variable versus the alternative causes that really explains why the dependent variable changed. The alternative explanations for the change are called *threats to internal validity.* After we examine some prominent threats to internal validity, we will see why and how **experimental designs** are thought to have

the most internal validity, and therefore thought to be the best way to determine whether one thing is really the cause of another.

Then we'll examine **quasi-experimental designs.** These are designs that are like experiments, that have less internal validity than experiments, but that often have adequate internal validity and are used when feasibility constraints make true experiments impossible to carry out. Along the way we'll also examine why experiments are so hard to carry out in most social work settings. In addition, we'll consider the important role that *qualitative research methods* can play in assessing how well experimental and quasi-experimental designs are being carried out and in assessing the meanings of experimental and quasi-experimental findings. Let's begin by examining criteria for inferring causality.

CRITERIA FOR INFERRING CAUSALITY

This section will discuss three specific criteria for causality as suggested by Paul Lazarsfeld (1959). *The first requirement in a causal relationship between two variables is that the cause precede the effect in time.* It makes no sense in science to imagine something being caused by something else that happened later on. A bullet leaving the muzzle of a gun does not cause the gunpowder to explode; it works the other way around.

As simple and obvious as this criterion may seem, we will discover endless problems in this regard in the analysis of social science data. Often, the time order connecting two variables is simply unclear. Suppose, for example, that a study finds that nuclear families containing a member suffering from schizophrenia are much more likely to be at lower levels of socioeconomic status than families without such members. Which comes first: the schizophrenia or the lower socioeconomic status? Does socioeconomic stress contribute to the onset of schizophrenia? Or does having a schizophrenic member reduce a family's ability to advance socioeconomically? Even when the time order seems essentially clear, exceptions can often be found. For instance, we would normally assume that the educational level of parents would be a cause of the educational level of their children. Yet some parents may return to school as a result of the advanced education of their own children.

Another example of this ambiguity can be found in a study by Rubin (1991), which evaluated the effectiveness of a support group intervention for battered women. One of the intervention goals was to help women still living with the batterer to leave him. One of the six women who participated in the study left her abusive husband the day before she attended her first support group meeting. Since the intended effect (leaving the batterer) preceded the hypothesized cause (attending the support group meetings), it would seem at first glance that the intervention could not have caused the intended effect. Indeed, it would seem more logical to suppose that attending the group meeting, rather than being the cause of the separation, was merely one of a variety of ways in which the woman was implementing a decision to separate—a decision that resulted from other forces.

On the other hand, one could argue that this woman's awareness of the support group, and her anticipation of being part of it, helped embolden her to leave. It is also conceivable that she anticipated being embarrassed by admitting to the group that she continued to live with the batterer, and wanting to make a good impression on the group helped contribute in some way to her decision to leave when she did. If either of these explanations seems plausible, it follows that without the intervention (that is, without the presence of the support group) the woman may not have left the batterer, even though she left him before attending the support group.

Because people sometimes change their behavior or cognitions in anticipation of events, such as when one's mood improves in anticipation of a joyful event or when one's spending increases in anticipation of a bonus or a tax rebate, we need to consider potential anticipatory effects when thinking about time order and causality.

The second requirement in a causal relationship is that the two variables be empirically correlated with one another. It would make no sense to say that exploding gunpowder causes bullets to leave muzzles of guns if, in observed reality, bullets did not come out after the gunpowder exploded.

Again, social science research has difficulties in regard to this seemingly obvious requirement. In the probabilistic world of explanation at least, there are few perfect correlations. Suppose a community survey finds that citizen opposition to establishing a community-based residential facility for the developmentally disabled increases with proximity to the proposed site of the facility. Most community residents living close to the proposed facility might oppose it, but some might support it. We are forced to ask, therefore, how great the empirical relationship must be for that relationship to be considered causal.

The third requirement for a causal relationship is that the observed empirical correlation between two variables cannot be explained away as being due to the influence of some third variable that causes both of them. For instance, you may observe that your left knee generally aches just before it rains, but this does not mean that your joints affect the weather. A third variable, relative humidity, is the cause of both your aching knee and the rain.

The box titled "Correlation and Causality" illustrates the point that correlation does not necessarily point to a particular causal relationship.

To review, most social researchers consider two variables to be causally related—that is, one causes the other—if (1) the cause precedes the effect in time, (2) there is an empirical correlation between them, and (3) the relationship is not found to be the result of the effects of some third variable on each of the two initially observed. Any relationship satisfying *all* these criteria is causal, and these are the only criteria.

INTERNAL VALIDITY

When we consider the extent to which a research study permits causal inferences to be made about relationships between variables, we reencounter the term *validity*. You may recall that when we were discussing measurement validity in Chapter 6, we referred to validity as the extent to which a measure really measures what it intends to measure. When discussing causal inference, however, the term *validity* is used differently. Two forms of validity that are important when considering causality are *internal validity* and *external validity*.

Internal validity refers to the confidence we have that the results of a study accurately depict whether one variable is or is not a cause of another. To the extent that the preceding three criteria for inferring causality are met, a study has internal validity. Conversely, to the extent that we have not met these criteria, we are limited in our grounds for concluding that the independent variable does or does not play a causal role in explaining the dependent variable.

External validity refers to the extent to which the causal relationship depicted in a study can be *generalized* beyond the study conditions. We will examine internal validity in depth at this point and return to the concept of external validity later in this chapter.

Ascertaining the internal validity of a study is a judgment call, one that we make based on how well we feel a particular study controlled for various threats to internal validity. Cook and Campbell (1979) recommend using the modifier "approximately" when referring to internal validity. There is no formula for calculating internal validity, and reasonable people may disagree over the extent to which a study seems to have it. To clarify this, let's examine some specific threats to internal validity.

Threats to Internal Validity

Campbell and Stanley (1963:5–6) and Cook and Campbell (1979:51–55) point to several threats to internal validity. Here are nine:

1. *History.* During the course of the research extraneous events may occur that will confound the results. The term *history* is tricky. The extraneous events need not be major news events that one would read about in a history book. *History* is used simply to refer to the fact that the extraneous events coincide in time with the manipulation of the independent variable. For example, suppose a study evaluates the effectiveness of social services in improving resident morale in a nursing home merely by measuring the morale of a group of residents before and after they receive social services. It is possible that some extraneous improvement in the nursing home environment, an improvement independent of the social services, was introduced between the before and after measures. That possibility represents a threat to the internal validity of the research because it, rather than the independent variable (social services), might cause the hypothesized improvement in the dependent variable (morale).

2. *Maturation or the passage of time.* People are continually growing and changing, whether they are a part of a research study or not, and those changes affect the results of the research. In the above nursing home illustration, for example, it would be silly to infer that because residents were physically frailer several years after receiving social services, the social services caused the physical deterioration. Maturation, through the aging process, would represent a severe threat to the internal validity of such a conclusion. But this threat to internal validity does not require that basic developmental changes occur; it also can refer simply to the effects of the passage of time. Suppose, for example, that a study to evaluate the effectiveness of a crisis counseling program for victims of rape merely assessed the mood state or social functioning of the victims before and after treatment. We might expect the rape victims' emotional moods or social functioning levels to be at their worst immediately in the aftermath of the trauma. With or without crisis counseling at that point, we might expect the mere passage of time to alleviate some portion of the terrible impact of the trauma, even if we assume that the long-term effects will still be devastating. Likewise, consider bereavement counseling: it would be silly to

CORRELATION AND CAUSALITY

by Charles Bonney, Department of Sociology, Eastern Michigan University

Having demonstrated a statistical relationship between a hypothesized "cause" and its presumed "effect," many people (sometimes including researchers who should know better) are only too eager to proclaim "proof" of causation. Let's take an example to see why "it ain't necessarily so."

Imagine you have conducted a study on college students and have found an inverse correlation between marijuana smoking (variable M) and grade point average (variable G)—that is, those who smoke tend to have lower GPAs than those who do not, and the more smoked, the lower the GPA. You might therefore claim that smoking marijuana lowers one's grades (in symbolic form, M → G), giving as an explanation, perhaps, that marijuana adversely affects memory, which would naturally have detrimental consequences on grades.

However, if an inverse correlation is all the evidence you have, a second possibility exists. Getting poor grades is frustrating; frustration often leads to escapist behavior; getting stoned is a popular means of escape; ergo, low grades cause marijuana smoking (G → M)!

Unless you can establish which came first, smoking or low grades, this explanation is supported by the correlation just as plausibly as the first.

Let's introduce another variable into the picture: the existence and/or extent of emotional problems (variable E). It could certainly be plausibly argued that having emotional problems may lead to escapist behavior, including marijuana smoking. Likewise it seems reasonable to suggest that emotional problems are likely to adversely affect grades. That correlation of marijuana smoking and low grades may exist for the same reason that runny noses and sore throats tend to go together—*neither* is the cause of the other, but rather, both are the consequences of some third variable ($E \rightleftharpoons {M \atop G}$). Unless you can rule out such third variables, this explanation too is just as well supported by the data as is the first (or the second).

Then again, perhaps students smoke marijuana primarily because they have friends who smoke, and get low grades because they are simply not as bright or well prepared or industrious as their classmates, and the fact that it's the same students in each case in your sample is purely coincidental. Unless your correlation is so strong and so consistent that mere coincidence becomes highly unlikely,

conclude that, just because the functioning level or mood of clients whose loved one died immediately before counseling was somewhat better after counseling, the bereavement counseling must have caused the improvement.

3. *Testing.* Often the process of testing will enhance performance on a test without any corresponding improvement in the real construct that the test attempts to measure. Suppose we want to see if a workshop helps social workers perform

this last possibility, while not supported by your data, is not precluded either.

Incidentally, this particular example was selected for two reasons. First of all, *every one* of the above explanations for such an inverse correlation has appeared in a national magazine at one time or another. And second, every one of them is probably doomed to failure because it turns out that, among college students, most studies indicate a *direct* correlation, i.e., it is those with higher GPAs who are more likely to be marijuana smokers! Thus, with tongue firmly in cheek, we may reanalyze this particular finding:

1. Marijuana relaxes a person, clearing away other stresses, thus allowing more effective study; hence, $M \rightarrow G$.

or

2. Marijuana is used as a reward for really hitting the books or doing well ("Wow, man! An 'A'! Let's go get high!"); hence, $G \rightarrow M$.

or

3. A high level of curiosity (E) is definitely an asset to learning and achieving high grades and may also lead one to investigate "taboo" substances; hence, $E \rightrightarrows {M \atop G}$.

or

4. Again coincidence, but this time the samples just happened to contain a lot of brighter, more industrious students whose friends smoke marijuana!

The obvious conclusion is this: if *all* of these are possible explanations for a relationship between two variables, then no *one* of them should be too readily singled out. Establishing that two variables tend to occur together is a *necessary* condition for demonstrating a causal relationship, but it is not by itself a *sufficient* condition. It is a fact, for example, that human birthrates are higher in areas of Europe where there are lots of storks, but as to the meaning of that relationship . . . !

better on their state licensure exam. We might construct a test that we think will measure the same sorts of things as are measured on the licensure exam and then administer that test to social workers before and after they take our workshop. If their scores on the exam improve, we might wish to attribute the improvement to the effects of our workshop. But suppose the social workers, after taking the first test, looked up answers to test items before our workshop began and then remembered those answers the next time they took the same test? They would then be able to score higher on the posttest without even attending our workshop and we therefore could not claim that taking our workshop caused their scores to improve.

4. *Instrumentation.* Thus far, we haven't said much about the process of measurement in pretesting and posttesting, and it's appropriate to remind you of the problems of measurement discussed earlier. If we use different measures of the dependent variable (say, different exams related to licensure), how can we be sure that they are comparable to each other? Perhaps exam scores will have improved simply because the posttest measure was an easier exam than the pretest measure. Or if ratings are being made by the researchers, their standards or their abilities may have changed over the course of the study.

5. *Statistical regression.* Sometimes it's appropriate to evaluate the effectiveness of services for clients who were referred because of their extreme scores on the dependent variable. Suppose, for example, that a new social work intervention to alleviate depression among the elderly is being pilot-tested in a nursing home for residents whose scores on a depression inventory indicate the most severe levels of depression. From a clinical standpoint it would be quite appropriate to provide the service to the residents who appear to be most in need of the service. But consider for a moment from a methodological standpoint what is likely to happen to the depression scores of the referred residents even without any intervention. In considering this we should take into account the fact that with repeated testing on almost any assessment inventory, an individual's scores on the inventory are likely to fluctuate somewhat from one administration to the next—not because the individual really changed, but because of the random testing factors that prevent instruments from having perfect reliability. For example, some of the residents referred because they had the poorest pretest scores may have been having an

atypically bad day at pretest and may typically score better on the inventory on an average day. Perhaps they didn't sleep well the night before the pretest, perhaps a chronic illness flared up that day, or perhaps a close friend or relative passed away that week.

When we provide services to only those people with the most extremely problematic pretest scores, the odds are that the proportion of service recipients with atypically bad pretest scores will be higher than the proportion of nonrecipients with atypically bad pretest scores. Conversely, those not referred because their pretest scores were better are likely to include some people whose pretest scores were atypically high (that is, people who were having an unusually good day at pretest). Consequently, even without any intervention, the group of service recipients is more likely to show some improvement in its average depression score over time than is the group that was not referred. There is a danger, then, that changes occurring because subjects started out in extreme positions will be attributed erroneously to the effects of the independent variable.

Statistical regression is a difficult concept to grasp. It might aid your understanding of this term to imagine or actually carry out the following amusing experiment, which we have adapted from Posavac and Carey (1985). Grab a bunch of coins—about 15 to 20 will suffice. Flip each coin six times and record the number of heads and tails you get for each coin. That number will be the pretest score for each coin. Now, refer each coin that had no more than two heads on the pretest to a social work intervention that combines task-centered and behavioral practice methods. Tell the referred coins (yes, go ahead and speak to them—but first make sure you are truly alone) that tails is an unacceptable behavior and that therefore its task is to try to come up heads more often. After you give each its task, flip it six more times, praising it every time it comes up heads. If it comes up tails, say nothing because you don't want to reward undesirable behavior.

Record, as a posttest, the number of heads and tails each gets. Compare the total number of posttest heads with the total number of pretest heads for the referred coins. The odds are that the posttest is higher. Now flip the nonreferred coins six times and record their posttest scores, but say nothing at all to them. We do not want them to receive the intervention. That way, we can compare the pretest-posttest change of the coins that received the intervention to what happened among those coins that did not receive the intervention. The odds are that the untreated coins did not show nearly as much of an increase in the number of heads as did the treated coins.

This experiment works almost every time. If you got results other than those described here, odds are that if you replicated the experiment you would get such results the next time. What do these results mean? Is task-centered/behavioral casework an effective intervention with coins? As social scientists, our minds are open to this possibility, but we doubt it. Rather, we believe these results illustrate that if we introduce the independent variable only to those referred on the basis of extreme scores, we can expect some improvement in the group solely because those scores will statistically regress to (which means they will move toward) their true score. In this case, the coins tend to regress to their true score of three (50%) heads and three (50%) tails. When the assessment is done on people, we can imagine their true score as being the mean score they would get if tested many times on many different days.

Of course, human behavior is more complex than the behavior of coins. But this illustration represents a common problem in the evaluation of human services. That is, because we are most likely to begin interventions for human problems that are inherently variable when those problems are at their most severe levels, we can expect some amelioration of the problem to occur solely because of the natural peaks and valleys in the problem and not necessarily because of the interventions.

6. *Selection biases.* Comparisons don't have any meaning unless the groups being compared are really *comparable.* Suppose we sought to evaluate the effectiveness of an intervention to promote positive parenting skills by comparing the level of improvement in parenting skills of parents who voluntarily agreed to participate in the intervention program with the level of improvement of parents who refused to participate. We would not be able to attribute the greater improvement among program participants to the effects of the intervention—at least not with a great deal of confidence about the internal validity of our conclusion—because other differences between the two groups might explain away the difference in improvement. For example, the participants may have been more motivated than program refusers to improve and thus may have been trying harder, reading more, and doing any number of things unrelated to the intervention that may really explain why they showed greater improvement. Selection biases are a common threat to the internal validity of social service evaluations because groups of service recipients and nonrecipients are often compared on outcome variables in the absence of prior efforts to see that the groups being compared were really equivalent to begin with. Perhaps this most typically occurs when individuals who choose to utilize services are compared with individuals who were not referred to those services or who chose not to utilize them.

7. *Experimental mortality.* Although the notion that some social experiments could kill subjects is not impossible to imagine, this problem refers to a more general and less extreme form of mortality. Often subjects will drop out of an experiment before it is completed, and the statistical comparisons and conclusions drawn can be affected by that.

Consider an evaluation comparing an intervention group with a group that did not receive the tested intervention; each group is to receive a pretest and posttest. Suppose that clients who receive the intervention but perceive no improvement in their target problem drop out of treatment and refuse to be posttested. At posttest the only intervention recipients left would be those who felt they were improving. Suppose the rate of perceived improvement among those not receiving the intervention is exactly the same as among those receiving the intervention, but, not having been disappointed, all of the nonrecipients agree to be posttested. The intervention recipients will be more likely to report improvement simply because of the attrition (experimental mortality) of recipients who perceived no improvement.

8. *Ambiguity about the direction of causal influence.* As we discussed earlier in this chapter, there is a possibility of ambiguity concerning the time-order of the independent and dependent variables. Whenever this occurs, the research conclusion that the independent variable caused the changes in the dependent variable can be challenged with the explanation that the "dependent" variable actually caused changes in the independent variable.

Suppose, for example, a study finds that clients who completed a substance abuse treatment program are less likely to be abusing substances than those who dropped out of the program. There would be ambiguity as to whether the program influenced participants not to abuse substances or whether the abstinence from substance abuse helped people complete the program.

9. *Diffusion or imitation of treatments.* Sometimes service providers or service recipients are influenced unexpectedly in ways that tend to diminish the planned differences in the way the independent variable is implemented among the groups being compared. For instance, suppose the effects of hospice services that emphasize palliative care and psychosocial support for the terminally ill are being compared to the effects of more traditional health care providers, who historically have been more attuned to prolonging life and thus have been less concerned with the unpleasant physical and emotional side effects of certain treatments. Over time traditional health care providers have been learning more about hospice care concepts, accepting them, and attempting to implement them in traditional health care facilities. With all this diffusion and imitation of hospice care by traditional health care providers,

failure to find differences in outcome between hospice and traditional care providers may have more to do with unanticipated similarities between hospice and traditional providers than with the lack of effectiveness of hospice concepts.

A similar problem complicates research evaluating the effectiveness of case management services. Many social workers who are not called case managers nevertheless conceptualize and routinely provide case management functions—such as outreach, brokerage, linkage, and advocacy—as an integral part of what they learned to be good and comprehensive direct social work practice. Consequently, when outcomes for clients referred to case managers are compared to the outcomes of clients receiving "traditional" social services, the true effects of case management as a treatment approach may be blurred by the diffusion of that approach among practitioners who are not called case managers. In other words, despite their different labels, the two treatment groups may not be as different in the independent variable as we think they are.

We can illustrate further the foregoing threats to internal validity by examining how they bear on some commonly used research designs. Although research consumers may disagree over approximately how well specific studies have controlled for particular threats to internal validity, it is usually possible to differentiate those studies whose internal validity is very low, those with very high internal validity, and those that merit a "mixed review." A large part of this assessment depends on which of the following types of designs a study employs. We'll begin with some designs that have a low degree of internal validity, which Campbell and Stanley (1963) have termed *preexperimental designs.*

Preexperimental Designs

As we noted earlier, to the extent that studies look only at the correlation between two variables without controlling for *threats to internal validity,* they have low internal validity. But some studies don't even establish correlation. Consider the **one-shot**

case study, for example. The shorthand notation for this design is

$$X \quad O$$

The X in this notation represents the introduction of a stimulus, such as an intervention. The O represents observation, which yields the measurement of the dependent variable. In this design, a single group of subjects is measured on a dependent variable after the introduction of a stimulus (that is, an intervention) without comparing the obtained results to anything else.

For instance, a service might be delivered and then the service recipients' social functioning might be measured. This design offers no way of ascertaining whether the observed level of social functioning is any higher (or lower!) than it was to begin with or any higher (or lower!) than it is among comparable individuals who received no service. This design, then—in addition to failing to assess correlation—fails to control for any of the threats to internal validity.

Even if time order is established and the hypothesized change is observed, we still have met only two of the three criteria for inferring causality. Meeting only these two criteria means that we cannot rule out the possibility that *extraneous variables* or *extraneous events* caused the observed change. Consider, for example, the *one-group pretest-posttest design*. The shorthand notation for this design is

$$O_1 \quad X \quad O_2$$

The subscripts 1 and 2 in this notation refer to the sequential order of the observations; thus, O_1 is the pretest before the intervention, and O_2 is the posttest after the intervention. This design assesses the dependent variable before and after the stimulus (intervention) is introduced. Thus, in the evaluation of the effectiveness of social services it would assess the outcome variable before and after services are delivered.

Although this design assesses correlation and controls for causal time order, it does not take into account factors other than the independent variable that might have caused the change be-

tween pretest and posttest results—factors usually associated with the following threats to internal validity: history, maturation, testing, and statistical regression.

Suppose, for example, that we assess the attitudes of social work students about social action strategies of community organization—strategies emphasizing tactics of confrontation and conflict (protests, boycotts, and so on)—before and at the end of their social work education. Suppose we find that over this time they became less committed to confrontational social action strategies and more in favor of consensual community development approaches.

Would such a finding permit us to infer that the change in their attitude was *caused* by their social work education? No, it would not. Other factors could have been operating during the same period and may be the ones that caused the change. For instance, perhaps the students matured and became more tolerant of slower, more incremental strategies for change (the threat to internal validity posed by *maturation or the passage of time*). Or perhaps certain events extraneous to their social work education transpired during that period and accounted for their change (the threat of *history*). For example, perhaps a series of protest demonstrations seemed to backfire and contribute to the election of a presidential candidate they abhorred, and their perception of the negative effects of these demonstrations made them more skeptical of social action strategies.

In another example of the one-group pretest-posttest design, suppose we assess whether a cognitive-behavioral intervention with abusive parents results in higher scores on a paper-and-pencil test of parenting skills and cognitions about childhood behaviors. In addition to wondering whether history and maturation might account for the improvement in scores, we would wonder about testing and statistical regression.

As to *testing*, perhaps taking the pretest influenced the parents to learn the correct, or socially desirable, responses to the test. The more desirable impression they conveyed at posttest, therefore, may have more to do with the effects of taking the two tests than with the effects of the intervention.

As to *statistical regression,* perhaps the parents were referred for treatment at a time when their parental functioning and attitudes about their children were at their worst. Even if the parenting skills and cognitions of these parents were quite unacceptable when they were at their best, improvement from pretest to posttest might simply reflect the fact that they were referred for treatment when they were at their worst and that therefore their scores couldn't help but increase somewhat due to regression toward their true average value before intervention.

A third preexperimental design is the **posttest-only design with nonequivalent groups** (Cook and Campbell, 1979). The shorthand notation for this design, which has also been termed the *static-group comparison design,* is

$$\frac{X \ O}{O}$$

This design assesses the dependent variable after the stimulus (intervention) is introduced for one group, and at the same time assesses the dependent variable for a second group that may not be comparable to the first group and that was not exposed to the independent variable. In the evaluation of the effectiveness of social services, this design would entail assessing clients on an outcome variable only after (not before) they receive the service being evaluated and comparing their performance with a group of clients who did not receive the service and who plausibly may be unlike the treated clients in some meaningful way.

Let's return, for example, to the preceding hypothetical illustration regarding evaluating the effectiveness of a cognitive-behavioral intervention with abusive parents. Using the posttest-only design with nonequivalent groups, rather than comparing the pretest and posttest scores of parents who received the intervention, we might compare their posttest scores to the scores of abusive parents who were not referred or who declined the intervention. We would hope to show that the

treated parents scored better than the untreated parents, since this would indicate a desired correlation between the independent variable (treatment status) and the dependent variable (test score). But this correlation would not permit us to infer that the difference between the two groups was caused by the intervention. The most important reason for this is the design's failure to control for the threat of *selection biases.* Without pretests, we have no way of knowing whether the scores of the two groups would have differed as much to begin with, before the treated parents began treatment. Moreover, it seems quite plausible that these two groups were not really equivalent in some important respects. The parents who were referred or who chose to participate may have been more motivated to improve or may have had more supportive resources than those who were not referred or who refused treatment.

It is not at all uncommon to encounter program providers who, after their program has been implemented, belatedly realize that it might be useful to get some evaluative data on its effectiveness and are therefore attracted to the posttest-only design with nonequivalent groups. In light of the expedience of this type of design, and in anticipation of the practical administrative benefits to be derived from positive outcome findings, they may not want to hear about selection biases and low internal validity. But we nevertheless hope you will remember the importance of these issues and tactfully discuss them with others when the situation calls for it.

Figure 9-1 graphically illustrates the three preexperimental research designs just discussed. See if you can visualize where the potentially confounding and misleading factors could intrude into each design.

As we end this discussion of preexperimental designs and prepare to move on to designs with higher levels of internal validity, a parting qualification is in order. When we say that a particular design has low internal validity, we are not saying that you should never use that design or that studies employing that design never have value. Remember, not all research studies strive to produce

1. THE ONE-SHOT CASE STUDY

Administer the experimental stimulus to a single group and measure the dependent variable in that group afterward. Make an intuitive judgment as to whether the posttest result is "high" or "low."

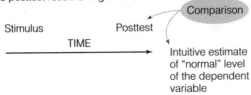

2. THE ONE-GROUP PRETEST-POSTTEST DESIGN

Measure the dependent variable in a single group, administer the experimental stimulus, and then remeasure the dependent variable. Compare pretest and posttest results.

3. THE STATIC-GROUP COMPARISON

Administer the experimental stimulus to one group (the experimental group), then measure the dependent variable in both the experimental group and a control group.

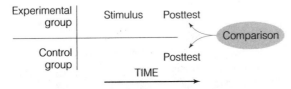

SOURCE: Adapted from Donald Campbell and Julian Stanley, *Experimental and Quasi-Experimental Designs for Research* (Chicago: Rand McNally, 1963), pp. 6–13. Copyright 1963 American Educational Research Association, Washington, D.C. Used by permission.

Figure 9-1 Three Preexperimental Research Designs

conclusive, causal inferences. Many studies have an exploratory or descriptive purpose.

Suppose, for example, that your agency has initiated a new, innovative intervention for a small target group about which little is known. It might be very useful to find out whether clients' posttest scores are better (or perhaps worse!) than their pretest scores in a one-group pretest-posttest design. You might implement that design on a pilot-study basis, purely for the purpose of generating tentative exploratory/descriptive information. Pilot studies like this are commonly produced in practice settings where stronger designs are not feasible and are often reported in practice-oriented journals. If the posttest scores are much better than at pretest, that might encourage you regarding the plausibility of the hypothesis that the intervention is effective, even if it does not allow you to claim that you verified conclusively that the intervention caused the desired effects. With such results, you would have established correlation and time order and may have provided a reasonable basis for continued testing of the intervention, including perhaps the seeking of resources for conducting a larger study with more internal validity. Two types of designs with higher levels of internal validity than preexperimental studies are *experimental* and *quasi-experimental* designs. First we'll look at experimental designs.

EXPERIMENTAL DESIGN

Experimental designs attempt to provide maximum control for threats to internal validity. They do so by giving the researchers greater ability to manipulate and isolate the independent variable. But this requires methodological arrangements that are rarely feasible to implement in real social work settings—arrangements that might have to be imposed in an artificial manner that might limit the generalizability of the study.

Although we commonly visualize the typical experimental setting to be a laboratory, experiments also can be conducted in agency (or field) settings. In social work, the most common use of experimental designs is to evaluate the effectiveness of our services or practice methods. The essential components of experiments involve (1) randomly assigning individuals to experimental and control groups, (2) introducing the independent variable (which typically is a program or intervention method) to the experimental group while withholding it from the control group, and (3) comparing the amount of experimental and control group change on the dependent variable.

For example, suppose we wanted to assess the effectiveness of an intervention used by gerontological social workers in nursing home facilities, an intervention that engages clients in a review of their life history in order to alleviate depression and improve morale. Rather than just comparing residents who requested the intervention with those who did not—which would constitute a pre-experimental approach because we could not assume the two groups were equivalent to begin with—an experimental approach would use a table of random numbers, or flip a coin, or use systematic sampling procedures to *randomly* assign each resident who agrees to participate and for whom the intervention is deemed appropriate to an experimental group (which would receive the intervention) or to a control group (which would not receive it). Observations on one or more indicators of depression and morale (the dependent variables) would be taken before and after the intervention is delivered, and to the extent that the experimental group's mood improves more than that of the control group, the findings would support the hypothesis that the intervention causes the improvement.

The preceding example illustrates the *classic experimental design,* also called the **pretest-posttest control group design.** This design is diagrammed in Figure 9-2. The shorthand notation for this design is

$$R \quad O_1 \quad X \quad O_2$$
$$R \quad O_1 \qquad O_2$$

The R in this design stands for random assignment of subjects to either the experimental group or the control group. The O_1's represent pretests, and the O_2's represent posttests.

Notice how this design controls for many threats to internal validity. If the improvement in mood were caused by history or maturation, there would

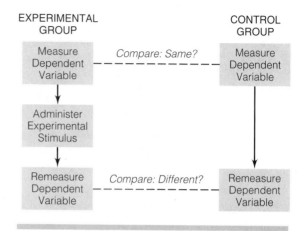

Figure 9-2 Diagram of Basic Experimental Design

be no reason the experimental group should improve any more than the control group. Likewise, because the residents were assigned on a randomized basis, there is no reason to suppose that the experimental group was any more likely to statistically regress to less extreme scores than was the control group. Random assignment also removes any reason for supposing that the two groups were different initially with respect to the dependent variable or to other relevant factors such as motivation or psychosocial functioning.

Notice also, however, that the pretest-posttest control group design does not control for the possible effects of testing and retesting. If we think that taking a pretest might have an impact on treatment effects, or if we think that it might bias their posttest responses, we might opt for an experimental design called the **posttest-only control group design.** The shorthand notation for this design is

$$R \quad X \quad O$$
$$R \qquad O$$

This design assumes that the process of random assignment removes any significant initial differences between experimental and control groups. This assumption of initial group equivalence permits the inference that any differences between the two groups at posttest reflect the causal impact of the independent variable.

If we would like to know the amount of pretest-posttest change but are worried about testing effects, we could employ a fancy design called the **Solomon four-group design.** The shorthand notation for this design is

$$
\begin{array}{llll}
R & O_1 & X & O_2 \\
R & O_1 & & O_2 \\
R & & X & O_2 \\
R & & & O_2
\end{array}
$$

This design, which is highly regarded by research methodologists but rarely used in social work studies, combines the classical experimental design with the posttest-only control group design. It does this simply by randomly assigning subjects to four groups instead of two. Two of the groups are control groups and two are experimental groups. One control group and one experimental group are pretested and posttested. The other experimental and control group are only posttested. If special effects are caused by pretesting, those effects can be discerned by comparing the two experimental group results with each other and the two control group results with each other.

Randomization

It should be clear at this point that the cardinal rule of experimental design is that the experimental and control groups must be *comparable*. Ideally, the control group represents what the experimental group would have been like had it not been exposed to the experimental stimulus. There is no way to guarantee that the experimental and control groups will be equivalent in all relevant respects. There is no way to guarantee that they will share exactly the same history and maturational processes or will not have any relevant differences prior to the introduction of the experimental stimulus. But there is a way to guarantee a high mathematical likelihood that their differences will be insignificant. That way is through random assignment to experimental and control groups, a process also known as *randomization*.

Randomization, or random assignment, is not the same as random sampling. The subjects to be randomly assigned are rarely randomly selected from a population. Instead, they are individuals who voluntarily agreed to participate in the experiment, a fact that limits the external validity of the experiment. Unlike random sampling, which pertains to *generalizability*, randomization is a device for increasing *internal* validity. It seeks not to ensure that the subjects are representative of a population, but rather to reduce the risks that experimental group subjects are not representative of control group subjects.

The principal technique of randomization simply entails using probability sampling procedures to assign subjects to experimental and control groups. Having recruited, by whatever means, the group of all subjects, the researchers might flip a coin to determine to which group each is assigned; or they may number all the subjects serially and assign them by selecting numbers from a random number table; or they may put the odd-numbered subjects in one group and put the even-numbered ones in the other.

Put within the framework of our earlier discussions of sampling, in randomization the subjects are a population from which we select two probability samples, each consisting of half the population. Because each sample reflects the characteristics of the total population, the two samples mirror each other. And, as we saw in Chapter 8, the *number* of subjects involved is important. In the extreme, if we recruited only two subjects and assigned, by the flip of a coin, one as the experimental subject and the other as the control, there would be no reason to assume that the two subjects are similar to each other. With larger numbers of subjects, however, randomization makes good sense.

Matching

The comparability of experimental and control groups can sometimes be achieved more directly through a **matching** process similar to the *quota sampling* methods discussed in Chapter 8. Matching can be done with or without randomization, but only when it is combined with randomization do you have a true experiment. Matching without randomization does not control for all possible biases in who gets assigned to which group. To illustrate matching with randomization, suppose 12 of your subjects are young white men. You might assign 6 of those at random to the experimental group and the other 6 to the control group. If 14 subjects are middle-aged black women, you might randomly assign 7 to each group. The overall matching process could be most efficiently achieved through the creation of a *quota matrix* constructed of all the most relevant characteristics. (Figure 9-3 provides a simplified illustration of such a matrix.) Ideally, the quota matrix would be constructed to result in an even number of subjects in each cell of the matrix. Then, half the subjects in each cell would go into the experimental group and half into the control group.

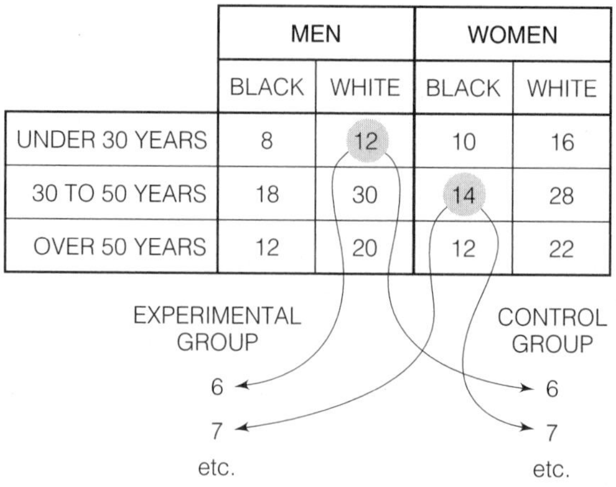

Alternatively, you might recruit more subjects than are required by your experimental design. You might then examine many characteristics of the large initial group of subjects. Whenever you discover a pair of very similar subjects, you might assign one at random to the experimental group and the other to the control group. Potential subjects who were unlike anyone else in the initial group might be left out of the experiment altogether.

Whatever method is used, the desired result is the same. The overall average description of the experimental group should be the same as that of the control group. For instance, they should have about the same average age, the same gender composition, the same racial composition, and so forth. As a general rule, the two groups should be comparable in terms of those variables that are likely to be related to the dependent variable under study. In a study of gerontological social work, for example, the two groups should be alike in terms of age, gender, ethnicity, and physical and mental health, among other variables. In

Figure 9-3 Quota Matrix Illustration

some cases, moreover, you may delay assigning subjects to experimental and control groups until you have initially measured the dependent variable. Thus, for instance, you might administer a questionnaire measuring subjects' psychosocial functioning and then match the experimental and control groups to assure yourself that the two groups exhibited the same overall level of functioning prior to intervention.

When considering the assignment of subjects to the experimental and control groups, you should be aware of two arguments in favor of randomization over matching without randomization. First, you may not be in a position to know in advance what the relevant variables are for the matching process. Second, there's a more technical reason for randomization. Most of the statistics used to evaluate the results of experiments assume randomization. Failure to design your experiment that way, then, makes your later use of those statistics less meaningful.

Providing Services to Control Groups

You may recall reading in Chapter 3 that the withholding of services from people in need raises ethical concerns. It also may be unacceptable to agency administrators, who fear bad publicity or the loss of revenues based on service delivery hours. It is therefore important to point out that when we discuss withholding the intervention being tested (that is, the independent variable) from the control group, we do not mean that people in the control group should be denied services. We simply mean that they should not be receiving the *experimental* intervention being tested during the period of the test.

When experiments are feasible to carry out in social work settings, control group members are likely to receive the usual, routine services provided by an agency. Experimental group members will receive the new, experimental intervention being tested, perhaps in addition to the usual, routine services. Thus, the experiment may determine whether services that include the new intervention are more effective than routine services, rather than attempting to ascertain whether the new intervention is better than no service. Moreover, control group members may be put at the top of a waiting list to receive the new intervention once the experiment is over. If the results of the experiment show that the tested intervention is effective, or at least is not harmful, it can then be offered to control group members. The researcher may also want to measure whether control group members change in the desired direction after they receive the intervention. The findings of this measurement can buttress the main findings of the experiment.

Measurement Bias and Blind Ratings

Despite the relatively superior internal validity of experimental designs, experiments may not control for all threats to validity. One common problem we mentioned earlier is experimental mortality. There is no foolproof design that can guarantee avoidance of this problem. Perhaps a more serious threat to the validity of social work experiments these days, however, is measurement bias. Although researchers evaluating the effectiveness of social work interventions and programs seem to be growing more aware of the need to control

for history, maturation, statistical regression, selection biases, and causal time order, many studies—experimental or otherwise—fail to include measurement procedures that control for potential biases toward "observing" greater improvement among clients receiving the tested service.

Whenever measurement of the dependent variable in experimental studies involves the use of research staff to supply ratings (either through direct observation or interviews), the individuals supplying the ratings should not know the experimental status of the subjects they are rating. In other words, they should be "blind" as to whether any given rating refers to someone who has received the experimental stimulus (or service) or someone who has not. Whenever you encounter the term *blind ratings* or *blind raters,* it means that the study has controlled for the potential—and perhaps unconscious—bias of raters toward perceiving results that would confirm the hypothesis. Likewise, whenever researchers fail to inform you that such ratings were blind, you should have some skepticism regarding the validity of the study. No matter how elegant the rest of a study's design might be, the value and validity of a study lacking blind ratings are suspect to the extent that results favoring the experimental groups were produced by biased raters.

The use of blind raters, unfortunately, is often not feasible in social work research studies. When we are unable to use blind raters, we should try to find alternative ways to avoid rater bias. For example, we might use validated self-report scales to measure the dependent variable, rather than rely on raters who may be biased. Sometimes we can use raters who are not blind, but who do not seem likely to be biased. We may, for instance, ask teachers to rate the classroom conduct of children receiving two different forms of social work intervention. The teachers may know which intervention each student is receiving, but may not have much technical understanding of the interventions or any reason to favor one intervention over another. Whenever we are conducting experimental research (or any other type of research), and we are unable to use blind raters or some other measurement alternative that we think is free of bias, we should try to use more than one measurement alternative, relying on the principle of triangulation, as was discussed in Chapter 6. If two or more measurement strategies, each of which is vulnerable to different biases, produce the same results, we can have more confidence in the validity of those results.

AN ILLUSTRATION OF A SOCIAL WORK EXPERIMENT

Thus far in this chapter the discussion has been chiefly technical. Therefore, at this point we want to give you an illustration of an actual social work experiment. This example will add a little more reality and life to the topic; it will also illustrate how experiments often deviate from conventional design arrangements but are still considered "true" experiments. For example, the design described in the following illustration is patterned after the classical pretest-posttest control group design, but instead of having one experimental group, it uses four experimental groups and one control group. Each experimental group receives a different intervention, and the experimental groups are compared with each other as well as with the control group. Another interesting aspect of this example is that the control group is not denied service; it receives the routine service instead of the experimental one.

Experiment on Cognitive-Behavioral Interventions with Parents at Risk of Child Abuse

Whiteman, Fanshel, and Grundy (1987) were interested in the effectiveness of different aspects of a cognitive-behavioral intervention aimed at reducing parental anger in the face of perceived provocation by children in families in which child abuse had been committed or in families at risk for child abuse. Underlying their inquiry were prior research findings suggesting that although child abuse is caused by complex multiple factors

and stressors, a common stressor that situationally may more immediately trigger the abusive act is the parent's anger resulting from perceived provocation by the child. Whiteman and associates postulated that abusive parents cognitively appraise the perceived provocation as a threat to their needs, values, or interests. Attaching this negative meaning to the situation, they become angry and physiologically tense. The ultimate abusive act then is an impulsive, maladaptive attempt to cope with stress.

The foregoing conceptual framework suggested testing out a composite package of cognitive-behavioral interventions that attempt to develop three coping skills: (1) giving a less negative meaning to the situation—seeing the child's behavior as resulting from factors other than malicious intent; (2) relaxation techniques to attenuate the intense pressure that results in impulsive, abusive behavior; and (3) problem-solving techniques to provide acceptable ways to prevent and ameliorate perceived provocations.

Fifty-five subjects participated in their experiment. Fifteen were identified child abusers being treated by a public agency in New York City. Forty were being treated by a private agency whose social workers had some indication that a child was in danger of parental maltreatment. The subjects were randomly assigned to four intervention groups and a control group that received no experimental intervention but instead continued to receive services from the referral agency.

The first intervention group received cognitive restructuring interventions dealing with the parents' perceptions, expectations, appraisals, and stresses. The second intervention group was trained in relaxation procedures. The third intervention group worked on problem-solving skills. The fourth intervention group received a treatment package composed of the three interventional modalities delivered separately to the first three intervention groups. Despite these variations, each intervention group stressed the same cognitive-behavioral intervention techniques and principles such as gradual skill acquisition, behavioral rehearsal, and recognition and reinforcement of progress. Also, each intervention was delivered over a brief treatment span of six sessions that took place in the clients' homes. The practitioners delivering the interventions were all social work doctoral students who had master's degrees in social work. Three were experienced clinicians.

The dependent variables in the experiment—the indicators of the effectiveness of the intervention—were measured by an assessment instrument that contained sections on parental anger and parental child-rearing attitudes and styles. This instrument was administered in tape-recorded pretest and posttest sessions in the clients' homes. The authors reported that the internal consistency reliability of the sections of the measurement instrument ranged from .66 to .90, but they did not report the instrument's validity.

The results revealed no significant differences among the experimental and control groups at pretest. At posttest, however, the treated (experimental group) subjects had significantly greater reductions in anger than the untreated (control group) subjects. The intervention group with the greatest reduction in anger was the one receiving the composite package of interventions that had been delivered separately to the other three intervention groups.

The posttest results on child-rearing attitudes and styles were less clearcut. Some intervention groups improved more than the control groups on some sections of the instrument, but the results were inconsistent across the different sections of the instrument. Analysis of the data on all intervention subjects as one overall experimental group, however, revealed significant improvements on two of the four sections of the instrument—those measuring parental empathy and responses to irritating behavior. (No significant improvement was found on sections measuring affection and discipline.)

In light of their findings, Whiteman and associates recommended that social workers use the composite intervention package in attempting to reduce anger and promote positive child-rearing attitudes among abusive or potentially abusive parents. Their results also indicated the impor-

tance of the problem-solving skills component in reducing anger, the importance of the cognitive restructuring component in improving child-rearing attitudes, and the relative unimportance of including the relaxation component in the intervention package.

The study by Whiteman and his colleagues demonstrates nicely the applicability of experimental design to social work practice. Among other things, it shows how clients can be randomly assigned to experimental and control groups without denying services to the control group subjects (who continued to receive the services provided by the referral agency). The preceding study also illustrates how experimental designs can control for many, but not necessarily all, threats to internal validity. Take a moment to review the threats we listed earlier in this chapter and consider which were and were not controlled in this experiment. You should be able to see that history, maturation, statistical regression, selection biases, and causal time order were controlled. But what about testing? Did taking the pretest sensitize clients to figuring out the socially acceptable answers at posttest? What about instrumentation? Did the treated clients improve in their anger, attitudes, and behavior when confronted with real-life stressful situations, or did they just learn during the six sessions what instrument answers were more acceptable to the clinicians and/or researchers? Remember, the authors reported the reliability of the instrument, but not its validity. Did it really assess their anger and attitudes, or did it assess their propensity to give socially desirable answers? Random assignment to experimental and control conditions won't resolve the preceding instrumentation questions, particularly when measurement is obtrusive, as is interviewing subjects in tape-recorded sessions.

Apparently experimental mortality was not a problem in the study under discussion, for the authors reported none. But what about diffusion or imitation of treatments? Notice that little was said about the nature of the services provided by the referral agencies. Did any of those services incorporate cognitive-behavioral treatment ideas resembling the tested intervention package? If so, might that have blurred the true effects of the tested intervention?

The study by Whiteman and associates also illustrates some problems regarding the artificiality and potentially limited generalizability of some experiments—problems associated with the term *external validity,* which we will discuss more fully later in this chapter. For example, can we generalize from the effects of doctoral students in a special, experimental setting to the likely effects of practitioners with lesser training working under less ideal circumstances, such as with larger caseloads? And would the intervention be as effective with clients who would refuse to participate in the experiment? You might also wonder about client attributes. Whiteman and his colleagues reported various statistics describing those attributes, which for the sake of brevity we omitted from our synopsis. Finally, you might wonder about research reactivity. To what extent do the special research procedures used, or experimental clients' awareness that they were receiving a special treatment, limit our ability to assume that the same effects would be attained under routine service delivery conditions outside of a research context?

In posing these questions, we are not attempting to denigrate the study. Indeed, it is one of the best recent examples of experimental research available in the social work literature! The purpose of these questions is to illustrate that no study—not even the best study—controls for all threats to validity. No single study ever "proves" anything. No matter how strong a study may be in some, or even most respects, we must remain vigilant in considering potential limitations and in understanding the need for replication in the scientific method.

QUASI-EXPERIMENTAL DESIGNS

It is often impossible to achieve random assignment of subjects to experimental and control groups. Agency administrators and practitioners may cite many reasons why it is not acceptable to withhold interventions from clients or prospective clients. For example, withholding services may seem unethical, may have unwanted fiscal implications, or may lead to complaints from consumers who feel deprived. These ethical concerns are not always warranted. In other sections of this book we discuss key assumptions underlying ethical concerns and some reasons why perpetually providing untested services may be more questionable ethically than withholding services that might be ineffectual or harmful.

But no matter how strong a case we may make for random assignment to experimental and control groups, our chances of getting it are usually quite slim. Even if we were able to convince an agency director of the merits of using an experimental design, chances are we would also have to convince the board members to whom the director reports. It might also be necessary to convince agency practitioners, whom the administrator does not want to alienate and who will refer subjects to the experiment.

Rather than forgo evaluation altogether in such instances, it is sometimes possible to create and execute alternative research designs that have less internal validity than "true" experiments but still provide a moderate amount of support for causal inferences. As we noted earlier, such designs are called *quasi-experimental* and are distinguished from "true" experiments primarily by the lack of random assignment of subjects to experimental and control groups. In this section, we'll describe some quasi-experimental designs that are applicable to social work research.

Nonequivalent Control Groups

Sometimes when it's not possible to create experimental and control groups by random assignment from a common pool, it is possible to find an existing "control" group that appears to be similar to the experimental group.

Suppose, for example, that you wish to evaluate the effects on depression of an intervention that gives nursing home residents pets. It is unlikely that you would be permitted to select randomly in any nursing homes those residents who will be given pets and those from whom pets would be withheld. You can probably imagine the administrative hassles that might erupt because some residents or their relatives feel they are being deprived. As an alternative to a true experimental design, then, you may be able to find two nursing homes that agree to participate in your research and that appear to be very similar in all respects relevant to internal validity. For example, the two homes might have about the same number and types of residents and staff, might provide the same level of care, and so on. In particular, you would want to make sure that the resident populations of the two homes were very similar in terms of age, socioeconomic status, mental and physical disabilities, psychosocial functioning, ethnicity, and so on. You could then introduce the intervention in one home, and use the other as a comparison group. (The term *comparison group* is used instead of *control group* when subjects are not assigned randomly.)

The two homes could be compared in a pretest to make sure that they really are equivalent on the dependent variable before introducing the independent variable. If their average depression scores are about the same, it would be reasonable to suppose that differences at posttest represent the effects of the intervention. Of course, such a causal inference would be even more credible had subjects been randomly assigned. But to the extent that you could provide convincing data as to the comparability of the two homes on plausible extraneous variables, your causal inference would be credible and your study would have value. The name of this commonly used quasi-experimental design is the **nonequivalent control groups design.** Its shorthand notation is

$$O_1 \quad X \quad O_2$$
$$O_1 \qquad O_2$$

You may note that the preceding notation is the same as the pretest-posttest control group design except that it lacks the R for random assignment.

Here's another example of this design, using an excerpt from an actual study in which two ju-

nior high schools were selected for purposes of evaluating a program aimed at discouraging tobacco, alcohol, and drug use.

> The pairing of the two schools and their assignment to "experimental" and "control" conditions was not random. The local Lung Association had identified the school where we delivered the program as one in which administrators were seeking a solution to admitted problems of smoking, alcohol, and drug abuse. The "control" school was chosen as a convenient and nearby demographic match where administrators were willing to allow our surveying and breath-testing procedures. The principal of that school considered the existing program of health education effective and believed that the onset of smoking was relatively uncommon among his students. The communities served by the two schools were very similar. The rate of parental smoking reported by the students was just above 40 percent in both schools. (MCALISTER ET AL., 1980:720)

Lacking random assignment of subjects into experimental and control groups, we might wonder if the two schools are comparable. But it helps to know that in the initial set of observations, the experimental and comparison (control) groups reported virtually the same (low) frequency of smoking. Over the 21 months of the study, smoking increased in both groups, but it increased less in the experimental group than in the control group, suggesting that the program had an impact on students' behavior.

Simple Time-Series Designs

Another commonly used set of quasi-experimental designs are called **time-series designs.** A particularly feasible time series design—feasible because it does not require a control group—is called the **simple interrupted time-series design.** The shorthand notation for this design is

$$O_1 \quad O_2 \quad O_3 \quad O_4 \quad O_5 \quad \times \quad O_6 \quad O_7 \quad O_8 \quad O_9 \quad O_{10}$$

Each O in the preceding notation represents a different observation point for measuring the dependent variable over time. No particular number

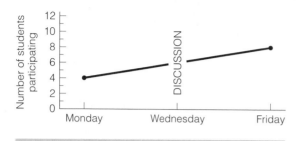

Figure 9-4 Two Observations of Class Participation: Before and After an Open Discussion

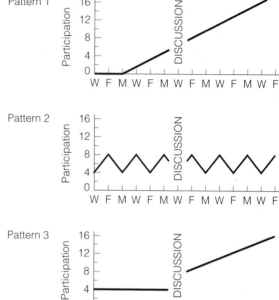

Figure 9-5 Three Patterns of Class Participation in a Longer Historical Perspective

of measurements is required, although the more the better. The above notation indicates that measurement of the dependent variable occurred at five points in time before the intervention was introduced and at another five points after that.

To illustrate the time-series design—studies of processes occurring over time—we will begin by asking you to assess the meaning of some hypothetical data. Suppose one of us comes to you with what he says is an effective technique for getting students to *participate* in classroom sessions of a course he is teaching. To prove his assertion, he tells you that on Monday, only four students asked questions or made a comment in class; on Wednesday he devoted the class time to an open discussion of a controversial issue raging on campus; and on Friday, when he returned to the subject matter of the course, eight students asked questions or made comments. In other words, he contends, the discussion of a controversial issue on Wednesday doubled classroom participation. This simple set of data is presented graphically in Figure 9-4.

Are you persuaded that the open discussion on Wednesday had the consequence he says it has? Probably you'd object that his data don't prove the case. Two observations (Monday and Friday) aren't really enough to prove anything. Ideally he should have had two separate classes with students assigned randomly to each, held an open discus-

sion in only one, and then compared the two on Friday. But he doesn't have two classes of randomly assigned students. Instead, he's been keeping a record of class participation throughout the semester for the one class. This record would allow you to conduct a time-series evaluation.

Figure 9-5 presents three possible patterns of class participation over time—both before and after the open discussion on Wednesday. Which of these patterns would give you some confidence that the discussion had the impact he contends it had?

If the time-series results looked like Pattern 1 in Figure 9-5, you'd probably conclude that the process of greater class participation had begun on the Wednesday before the discussion and had continued, unaffected, after the day devoted to the discussion. The long-term data seem to suggest that the trend would have occurred even without the discussion on Wednesday. Pattern 1, then, contradicts the assertion that the special discussion increased class participation.

Pattern 2 contradicts his assertion also. It indicates that class participation has been bouncing up and down in a regular pattern throughout the semester. Sometimes it increases from one class to the next, and sometimes it decreases; the open discussion on that Wednesday simply came at a time when the level of participation was due to increase. More to the point, we note that class participation decreased again at the class following the alleged postdiscussion increase.

Only Pattern 3 in Figure 9-5 supports his contention that the open discussion mattered. As we see, the level of discussion before that Wednesday had been a steady four students per class. Not only did the level of participation double following the day of discussion, but it continued to increase further afterward. Although these data do not protect us against the possible influence of some extraneous factor (he might also have mentioned that participation would figure into students' grades), they do exclude the possibility that the increase results from a process of maturation (indicated in Pattern 1) or from regular fluctuations (indicated in Pattern 2).

Multiple Time-Series Designs

A stronger form of time-series analysis (that is, one with greater internal validity) adds time-series analysis to the nonequivalent control group design. This form is called **multiple time-series designs.** Probably the most applicable multiple time-series design for social workers is the **interrupted time-series with a nonequivalent control group time-series design.** The shorthand notation for this design is

$$O_1 \ O_2 \ O_3 \ O_4 \ O_5 \ \times \ O_6 \ O_7 \ O_8 \ O_9 \ O_{10}$$
$$O_1 \ O_2 \ O_3 \ O_4 \ O_5 \ \ O_6 \ O_7 \ O_8 \ O_9 \ O_{10}$$

In this design both an experimental group and a nonequivalent control group (neither assigned randomly) are measured at multiple points in time before and after an intervention is introduced to the experimental group.

Carol Weiss (1972) presented a useful example of this design, one which compared time-series data from an "experimental" state to time-series data from four "control" states:

> An interesting example of multiple time series was the evaluation of the Connecticut crackdown on highway speeding. Evaluators collected reports of traffic fatalities for several periods before and after the new program went into effect. They found that fatalities went down after the crackdown, but since the series had had an unstable up-and-down pattern for many years, it was not certain that the drop was due to the program. They then compared the statistics with time-series data from four neighboring states where there had been no changes in traffic enforcement. Those states registered no equivalent drop in fatalities. The comparison lent credence to the conclusion that the crackdown had had some effect.   (1972:69)

Although this study design is not as good as one in which subjects are assigned randomly, it is nonetheless an improvement over assessing the experimental group's time-series performance without comparison to a control group. It is also an improvement over comparing an experimental and nonequivalent control group without the added benefit of time-series data. That's what makes these designs *quasi-experiments* instead of just fooling around. The key in assessing this aspect of evaluation studies is *comparability*, as the following example illustrates.

Rural development is a growing concern in the poor countries of the world and one that has captured the attention and support of many rich countries. Through national foreign assistance programs and through international agencies such as the World Bank, the developed countries are in the process of sharing their technological knowledge and skills with the developing countries. Such programs have had mixed results, however. Often, modern techniques do not produce the intended results when applied in traditional societies.

Rajesh Tandon and L. Dave Brown (1981) undertook an experiment in which technological training would be accompanied by instruction in village organization. They felt it was important for poor farmers to learn how to organize and exert collective influence within their villages—in getting needed action from government officials, for example. Only then would their new technological skills bear fruit.

Both intervention and evaluation were attached to an ongoing program in which 25 villages had been selected for technological training. Two poor farmers from each village had been trained in new agricultural technologies. Then they had been sent home to share their new knowledge with their fellow villagers and to organize other farmers into "peer groups" who would assist in spreading that knowledge. Two years later, the authors randomly selected two of the 25 villages (subsequently called Group A and Group B) for special training and 11 others as controls. A careful comparison of demographic characteristics showed the experimental and control groups to be strikingly similar to each other, suggesting they were sufficiently comparable for the study.

The peer groups from the two experimental villages were brought together for special training in organization building. The participants were given some information about organizing and making demands on the government, and they were also given opportunities to act out dramas similar to the situations they faced at home. The training took three days.

The outcome variables considered in the evaluation all had to do with the extent to which members of the peer groups initiated group activities designed to improve their situation. Six types were studied. "Active initiative," for example, was defined as "active effort to influence persons or events affecting group members versus passive response or withdrawal" (Tandon and Brown, 1981:180). The data for evaluation came from the journals that the peer group leaders had been keeping since their initial technological train-

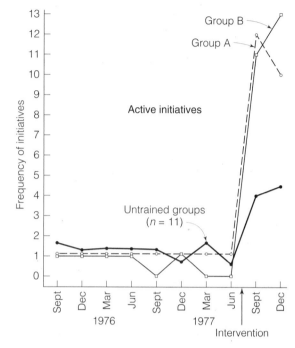

SOURCE: Rajesh Tandon and L. Dave Brown, "Organization-Building for Rural Development: An Experiment in India," *The Journal of Applied Behavioral Science* (April–June 1981):182.

Figure 9-6 Active Initiatives Over Time

ing. The researchers read through the journals and counted the number of initiatives taken by members of the peer groups. Two researchers coded the journals independently and compared their work to test the reliability of the coding process. Figure 9-6 compares the number of active initiatives by members of the two experimental groups with those coming from the control groups. Similar results were found for the other outcome measures.

Notice two things about the graph. First, there is a dramatic difference in the number of initiatives by the two experimental groups as compared with the eleven controls. This would seem to confirm the effectiveness of the special training program.

Second, notice that the number of initiatives also increased among the control groups. The researchers explain this latter pattern as a result of contagion. Because all the villages were near each other, the lessons learned by peer group members in the experimental groups were communicated in part to members of the control villages.

This example illustrates the strengths of multiple time-series designs where true experiments are inappropriate to the program being evaluated.

An Illustration of a Quasi-Experiment in Social Work

Earlier in this chapter, to breathe more life into the topic of experimental design, we presented an illustration of an actual social work experiment. We'll do the same thing here in respect to the topic of quasi-experimental designs. The study we'll summarize combined aspects of nonequivalent control groups designs and simple time-series designs.

One of the authors of this book (Rubin) contracted with a County Child Protective Service Agency to evaluate the effectiveness of their three-year, federally funded demonstration program that aimed to prevent foster care placement (and thus preserve families) of children of substance abusing parents referred for child abuse or neglect. The program sought to achieve its family preservation aims by having its staff provide both intensive case management intervention and the direct provision of child welfare services that emphasized things like role modeling, behavioral techniques, and the use of the relationship between worker and parents. Although the routine child protective services provided by other units in the agency were similar to the services in the demonstration program, two things set the demonstration program apart from the routine services: (1) federal funding enabled the demonstration program workers to have much lower caseloads and thus to see their clients much more frequently than the workers in the other units,

and (2) contracts with other agencies were established to improve the prospects that families in the demonstration program would receive a comprehensive spectrum of services to meet their multiple needs. Because random assignment to experimental and control groups was not acceptable to the agency, Rubin devised a quasi-experimental design. One component of the overall evaluation design was called the *overflow design*. The overflow design was a nonequivalent control group design, in that it sought to achieve comparability between groups of clients treated and not treated by the demonstration program without using random assignment to achieve that comparability. Instead of random assignment, the basis for determining which treatment condition each family received was whether the demonstration program's caseloads were full at the time of case assignment.

The demonstration program had much fewer workers than the rest of the agency, and could only serve about 42 active cases at any particular time. Consequently, it was expected that many substance abusing parents would be referred to the demonstration program when its caseloads were full and therefore would have to be referred back to the other units where they would receive the same routine services that all clients received before the onset of the demonstration program.

Despite lacking random assignment, this design would probably possess adequate internal validity, since it seemed unlikely that families who happen to be referred when caseloads are full would not be comparable to families who happen to be referred when caseloads are not full. It seemed reasonable to suppose that if demonstration program families had fewer placements of children out of the home than did comparison group families (in the overflow group) receiving the routine services, the difference could be attributable to the effects of the program rather than to extraneous differences between the two groups.

Nevertheless, while it seemed unlikely that the two groups would not be comparable, Rubin recognized that this was not the same degree of unlikeliness provided by random assignment. Rubin wondered, for example, whether those workers who refer the families would eventually become predisposed to referring only those cases in greater need to the demonstration program. This did not seem like a farfetched possibility, since the referring workers might want to see that the cases with the most need get the most intensive, most comprehensive services. Also, they might tire of having cases referred to the demonstration program referred back to them during overflow periods, and therefore might become predisposed not to refer cases to the demonstration program unless those cases were in unusually great need.

Another concern was the potential for diffusion or imitation of treatment effects (discussed earlier in this chapter as a threat to internal validity). There was reason to suppose that the workers in the routine units knew about the family preservation aims and methods of the demonstration program, that they might resent the extra resources and lower caseloads of the demonstration program workers, and that they might copy some of the demonstration program methods in an effort to prove that they could be just as effective at preserving families.

In light of these concerns, Rubin added a simple time-series component to the design. The time-series design examined agencywide out-of-home placements of children of referred substance abusing parents during the four six-month intervals immediately preceding the demonstration program and four six-month intervals after it began. Rubin reasoned that if diffusion or imitation of treatment effects was occurring, it would be reflected in a countywide (combining both the demonstration program cases and the routine service unit cases) reduction in out-of-home placements after the onset of the program, and that no differences may appear in the overflow design. He also reasoned that the same reduction might occur if the demonstration program was effective but its cases were in greater need than the cases

in the other units. The evaluation was completed at the same time that this is being written and has not yet been published (Rubin, in press). The results of the nonequivalent control group component (overflow design) provided relatively little support for the effectiveness of the demonstration program. However, the results of the simple time-series design component partially supported the program's effectiveness.

Discussions with agency workers provided some evidence to suggest that both of Rubin's concerns eventuated. Talks with some workers indicated that the diffusion and imitation of treatments may have been occurring to some extent. Perhaps more problematic was the revelation by one worker, at the conclusion of the project, that she had arranged (without telling the evaluators) to ensure that only the cases in greater need got referred to the demonstration project. While this revelation tended to invalidate the results of the nonequivalent control groups (overflow design) component of the evaluation, it did not invalidate the results of the time-series component, since the latter looked at the countywide impact of the program, not just the differences between the demonstration program clients and overflow clients.

It is important to note that the addition of the quasi-experimental time-series component would have had value even if a randomized experimental design had been feasible, because a randomized experimental design would have been just as vulnerable to diffusion and imitation of treatment effects as was the nonequivalent control groups design. Of course, a randomized experimental design would seem more likely to have avoided worker bias in case assignment. But even a randomized experimental design can be undermined by agency staff who covertly refuse to comply with the random assignment and, without informing the researcher, arrange for clients randomly assigned to one treatment condition to receive the other treatment condition. This illustration, therefore, leads us to a consideration of the many practical pitfalls that social work researchers face in attempting to carry out their best laid plans for experimental and quasi-experimental designs in social work agency settings.

PRACTICAL PITFALLS IN CARRYING OUT EXPERIMENTS AND QUASI-EXPERIMENTS IN SOCIAL WORK AGENCIES

As the foregoing example illustrates, carrying out valid, useful experimental or quasi-experimental research in social work takes more than developing a rigorous research design. Unlike experiments carried out in other disciplines, which tend to take place in laboratory settings or research clinics controlled by researchers, social work experiments tend to take place in agency settings controlled by people who are not researchers, who may not understand the requisites of experimental and quasi-experimental designs, and who may even resent and attempt to undermine the demands of the research design. Consequently, if you try to do this kind of research, it won't take you long to learn that in this business the various adages and two-word bumper sticker warnings about best laid plans going awry are particularly applicable.

Two social workers noted for their experimental research on the effectiveness of social work interventions for people with chronic mental illnesses and their families, Phyllis Solomon and Robert Paulson (1995), have delineated the many practical pitfalls encountered in attempting to implement this sort of research in service-oriented agencies. Here are some of the pitfalls they identified in their address to experienced researchers at the first National Conference of the Society of Social Work and Research.

Fidelity of the Intervention   The term *intervention fidelity* refers to the degree to which the intervention actually delivered to clients was delivered the way it was intended to be delivered. We often evaluate social work interventions that cannot be spelled out in step-by-step manuals. Instead, we rely on social work practitioners to implement general guidelines in skillful, creative, and idiosyncratic ways with each client. Some practitioners, however, might have better judgment than others. Some might misunderstand or misinterpret the intent of the intervention. This means that the intervention we think we are evaluating may not be implemented as intended to experimental group subjects, or that the services received by experimental and control group subjects may be more similar than we intended. Related reasons why interventions (the independent variables of experimental research) may not be implemented as intended include delays and start-up problems in implementing new programs, the use of staff who are inexperienced with or untrained in the new intervention, high initial staff turnover in new programs, organizational changes that impact the program, loss of staff enthusiasm over time, and ongoing supervision provided by agency supervisors who may not follow the research protocol.

Contamination of the Control Condition   Even if the experimental group receives the intervention as intended, the control condition can be contaminated by interaction of control group and experimental group members. Suppose, for example, an experiment in a school social work intervention assigns some students in the same school to either an experimental group, which receives the new intervention being tested, or a control group, which receives the routine services. The students in each group will interact in the school setting, and the improvements among the experimental group students may therefore have a beneficial spillover impact on the behavior of the control group students. If this happens, the two groups will not be as different on outcome measures (dependent variables) as was predicted, and we may therefore erroneously conclude that the new intervention did not make a difference. Solomon and Paulson suggest that contamination of the control condition can even occur if experimental and control group clients share the same agency waiting room.

Resistance to the Case Assignment Protocol

As was the case in the illustration of the quasi-experimental evaluation of the family preservation program using an overflow case assignment design, practitioners may resent having to assign cases to treatment conditions on the basis of research requirements rather than on the basis of their own professional judgment about the best service match for each client. Practitioners tend to believe that the services they are providing are effective, and consequently they may not be committed to adhering to the research protocol in case assignment, since they think they already "know" the answer to the research question. Believing they already know what services work best for what clients, they may feel compelled to violate the research protocol to make sure that the client receives the service they think that client should receive. Even if they are unsure as to what service works best for what client, they may pressure to enroll clients in the greatest need into the experimental condition due to the newness and innovative nature of that condition, or the fact that that condition offers more services than the control condition.

Client Recruitment and Retention

Difficulties in recruiting a sufficient number of clients to participate in the study can arise when the research must rely on referrals of clients from outside agencies. This can be particularly problematic when the research design precludes joint involvement by referred clients in the services provided by the referring agencies. This can result in the "dumping" by those agencies of cases they do not want to serve, perhaps because the dumped clients resist services or seem less likely to benefit from services. Moreover, the agencies may be reluctant to refer any clients, since that might adversely affect the referring agency's reimbursement, when that reimbursement is based on the amount of services provided directly by the referring agency. Referring agencies might also not understand, and might resent, having their referrals assigned to a control condition, particularly if that assignment means referring back control clients to the referral agency.

Moreover, difficulties in client recruitment and retention can arise from the clients' own reactions to case assignment procedures and measurement requirements. Clients may resent the use of randomized procedures to determine which service they receive, and therefore may opt not to participate. Some clients might agree to participate, but then change their minds after learning that they have not been assigned to the new, innovative, experimental condition. Other clients might take longer to drop out of the control or comparison condition; perhaps after being inconvenienced by completing the pretesting they will refuse to participate in the posttesting.

The above do not exhaust all the possible pitfalls you are likely to encounter if you attempt to carry out experimental or quasi-experimental research. They are simply some of the more common ones. A list of all the potential snafus would seem endless. The point here is twofold: (1) be prepared to encounter pitfalls like these, and (2) build into your design mechanisms for preventing, detecting, and dealing with these pitfalls before they ruin your study.

Mechanisms for Avoiding or Alleviating Practical Pitfalls

Solomon and Paulson recommend a number of mechanisms that might help you avoid or alleviate the pitfalls discussed above. One important suggestion is to engage agency staff members in the design of the research and to enlist their support in it from its inception. Although this may help reduce the likelihood or degree of their resistance to the research, it will not guarantee that their resistance is eliminated. We speak from experience on this, since this step was taken in the quasi-experimental evaluation of the family preservation demonstration program discussed earlier, in which the program staff ended up deviating from the case assignment protocol. You should not assume that agency staff support for the research protocol will endure as they begin to encounter daily practice concerns. Instead, you should build into the study ongoing mechanisms in which some research staff members are on site throughout the project interacting with program staff and monitoring whether they are complying with the research protocol and implementing the experimental and control conditions as intended.

This is one place in which **qualitative** research methods can come in handy as a valuable part of a **quantitative** research study. We've been mentioning qualitative methods throughout this book, and will give them much more attention when we get to Chapter 12. Qualitative methods offer a number of ways on-site research staff members can attempt to observe research implementation pitfalls. For example, they can interact formally or informally with agency staff members to identify compliance problems or learn how they are implementing the interventions. They can use videotapes or practitioner activity logs to assess intervention fidelity. They can also identify implementation problems by following along with (shadowing) practitioners in their daily activities. They can participate in in-service trainings or group supervision to identify discrepancies between the intended intervention and what agency trainers or supervisors are proscribing. The box titled "Qualitative Methods for Experimental or Quasi-Experimental Research" summarizes the ways qualitative research methods can be employed to help avoid or alleviate the many practical pitfalls that can be encountered in trying to carry out quantitative research studies employing experimental or quasi-experimental designs.

QUALITATIVE METHODS FOR EXPERIMENTAL OR QUASI-EXPERIMENTAL RESEARCH

It is not uncommon to hear researchers known primarily for their experimental or quasi-experimental quantitative findings say that almost all of their "quantitative" studies have included components that relied on qualitative methods. In this box we will list some prominent qualitative methods and the important functions they can serve in experimental and quasi-experimental studies. You can read more about these qualitative methods in Chapters 12 and 13. Many of the ideas for this box were derived from a presentation by Phyllis Solomon (University of Pennsylvania School of Social Work) and Robert I. Paulson (Portland State University School of Social Work) at the first annual conference of the Society for Social Work and Research, in Washington, D.C., April 11, 1995. Their presentation was titled "Issues in Designing and Conducting Randomized Human Service Trials."

Functions in Experimental and Qualitative Method	Quasi-Experimental Studies
Ethnographic shadowing (follow along and observe practitioners in their daily activities)	• Learn how they actually implement the intervention • Learn if the interventions and other aspects of the research protocol are being implemented as intended
Participant observation during training or group supervision	• Identify discrepancies between the intended intervention and what agency trainers or supervisors are actually proscribing
Participant observation during agency staff meetings	• Determine whether agency staff are complying with the research protocol and identify difficulties they are having with compliance
Informal conversational interviews with agency staff	• Identify compliance problems with the research protocol • Learn how they are actually implementing the interventions
Videotaping or audiotaping practitioner-client sessions	• Assess the fidelity of the intervention (Is it being implemented in a skillful manner, as intended?)
Practitioner activity logs	• Assess the fidelity of the intervention • Are the proper amounts and types of services being delivered to the clients for whom they were intended?
Event logs	• Identify major organizational and systems changes that may impede continued compliance with the research protocol
Focus groups	• Document the process of implementing the research design and interventions, and identify implementation problems • Develop possible explanations for unexpected, puzzling findings
Snowball sampling	• Recruit subjects from vulnerable or hard-to-find target populations
Semistructured, open-ended interviews (using interview guides) with prospective clients who refuse services or clients who prematurely terminate services	• Learn why they are unwilling to participate or why they dropped out so as to figure out ways to improve client recruitment and retention

Qualitative Method	Functions in Experimental and Quasi-Experimental Studies
Content analysis of agency documents and service delivery manuals	• Identify potential practical pitfalls that need to be planned for in developing the research design • Develop specificity about the services being evaluated • Did the proper amounts and types of services get delivered to the clients for whom they were intended?
Semistructured, open-ended interviews with practitioners or their clients following data analysis	• Develop possible explanations for unexpected, puzzling findings

Solomon and Paulson recommend additional mechanisms to help avoid or alleviate practical pitfalls. You might, for example, try to avoid contamination of the control condition by locating experimental and control conditions in separate buildings or agencies. You might try to promote the fidelity of the intervention by developing a treatment manual that very clearly and very specifically defines the components and steps of the experimental and control interventions. You might anticipate and alleviate client recruitment and retention problems by planning to recruit clients assertively on an ongoing basis throughout your study, rather than assume that your initial cohort will be large enough and will remain intact. Client recruitment and retention might also be enhanced by reimbursing clients for their participation, particularly for their time and efforts in pretesting and posttesting. The payment should be large enough to work as an incentive without being so great that it becomes coercive. The amount should fit the difficulties clients experience in participating. It should also fit their income levels and emotional states. You might want to increase the amount over time at each subsequent measurement point and give a bonus to clients who stay the distance and complete all the measurements throughout the study. The

amount should be enough to acknowledge to clients that their time is valued and that the measurement can be an imposition. The amount should also fit within your research budget. Paying clients $10 to complete pretests, $15 to complete posttests, and perhaps another $10 bonus to stay the distance is probably a reasonable amount.

It should be obvious to you by now, however, that conducting this sort of research does not come easily or cheaply. You will need to do careful planning and to obtain substantial resources to do it well. Otherwise, the practical pitfalls we have been discussing are likely to ruin carefully constructed designs that, on paper, seem to have impeccable internal validity. We will revisit this issue in Chapter 18, when we discuss political and logistical problems in evaluation research. Before we leave this chapter, we need to move beyond issues of internal validity, which have dominated our discussion to this point, and turn to the issue of external validity.

EXTERNAL VALIDITY

When a study has a high degree of internal validity, it allows causal inferences to be made about the sample and setting that were studied. But what about other settings and larger populations? Can we generalize the same causal inferences to them?

External validity refers to the extent to which we can *generalize* the findings of a study to settings and populations beyond the study conditions. Internal validity is a necessary but not sufficient condition for external validity. Before we can generalize a causal inference beyond the conditions of a particular study, we must have adequate grounds for making the causal inference under conditions of that study in the first place. But even when internal validity in a particular study is high, a number of problems may limit its external validity.

A major factor influencing external validity is the **representativeness** of the study sample, setting, and procedures. Suppose a deinstitutionalization program is implemented in an urban community. Suppose that there is strong support for the program among community residents, that it is well funded, and that there is a comprehensive range of noninstitutional community support resources accessible to the mentally ill residing in the community. Suppose, in turn, that the well-funded program can afford to hire high-caliber staff, give them small caseloads, and reward them amply for good work. Finally, suppose that an evaluation with high internal validity finds that the program improves the quality of life of the mentally ill.

Would those findings imply that legislators or mental health planners in other localities could logically conclude that a similar deinstitutionalization program would improve the quality of life of the mentally ill in their settings? Not necessarily. It would depend on the degree to which their settings, populations, and procedures match those of the studied program.

Suppose their community is rural, has fewer or more geographically dispersed community-based resources for the mentally ill, or has more neighborhood opposition to residences being located in the community. Suppose legislators view deinstitutionalization primarily as a cost-saving device

and therefore do not allocate enough funds to enable the program to hire or keep high-caliber staff or to give them caseload sizes that are small enough to manage adequately. And what about differences in the characteristics of the mentally ill target population? Notice that we have said nothing about the attributes of the clients in the tested program. Perhaps they were different in age, diagnosis, ethnicity, average length of previous institutionalization, and degree of social impairment than the intended target population in the communities generalizing from the study findings. To the extent that such differences apply, similar programs implemented in other settings might not have the same effects as did the program in the tested setting.

Would such differences mean that this study had low external validity? Not necessarily. On the one hand, we could say that a study has low external validity if its conditions are far removed from conditions that could reasonably be expected to be replicated in the "real" world. On the other hand, a study's external validity could be adequate even if there are many other settings to which it cannot be generalized. The point is that a study must be generalizable to some real-world settings and that it must represent that which it intends to represent. It does not have to represent every conceivable population or setting.

For example, a study evaluating a program of care for the profoundly and chronically disabled in rural settings does not need to be generalizable to the mildly or acutely disabled or to the disabled residing in urban settings in order to have external validity. It just has to be representative of those attributes that it intends to represent, no matter how narrowly it defines those attributes.

Problems in external validity abound in the literature evaluating social work practice and programs. One common problem limiting external validity is ambiguity or brevity in reportage. Many studies do not articulate in adequate detail the specific attributes of the clients who participated in the evaluated service. Many are vague about the attributes of the practitioners. Some studies generalize about the effectiveness of *professional* social work practitioners based on findings about the effectiveness of *student* practitioners. Some studies leave out important details about the evaluated clinical setting, such as caseload size and the like. Consequently, while it may be clear that the evaluated intervention did or did not cause the desired change among the studied clients—that is, that the study had high *internal* validity—it is often not clear to whom those findings can be *generalized*. Thus, some studies find services to be effective, but do not permit the generalization that those services would be effective outside of the study conditions. Likewise, some other studies find no support for the effectiveness of services, but do not permit the generalization that those services would be ineffective when implemented under other conditions.

Another common problem in external validity involves research **reactivity.** When clients know that they are participating in an experiment, such awareness may cause changes in the dependent variable that cannot be generalized outside of the experimental situation. For instance, if clients monitor their own problem behaviors as part of the data collection procedures, some or all of the improvement that occurs may be caused by the self-monitoring and consequently not be generalizable to clinical situations that don't involve the same data collection procedures. Thus, one way in which the client may react to the research procedures is by becoming more aware of the problem behaviors; consequently, they may become more vigilant in resolving them. Another way is through what are generally termed **placebo effects.** Placebo effects refer to changes caused not by the specific attributes of a particular intervention, but rather by the nonspecific attributes of any intervention or research procedure that makes clients feel that they are receiving something special. Awareness of receiving a special treatment or special attention might ameliorate client problems in ways (such as through the power of suggestion) that do not generalize outside of the special (and perhaps artificial) research environment.

If we are concerned about potential placebo effects and wish to control for them, we could employ an experimental design called the **placebo control group design.** The shorthand notation for this design is

$$
\begin{array}{cccc}
R & O_1 & X & O_2 \\
R & O_1 & & O_2 \\
R & O_1 & P & O_2
\end{array}
$$

This design randomly assigns clients to three groups: an experimental group and two different control groups. One control group receives no experimental stimulus, but the other receives a placebo (represented by the P in the preceding notation). Placebo group subjects would receive special attention of some sort other than the tested stimulus or intervention. Perhaps practitioners would meet with them regularly to show special interest in them and listen to them, but they would not apply any of the tested intervention procedures.

Placebo control group designs pose complexities from both a planning and interpretation standpoint, particularly when experimental interventions contain elements that resemble placebo effects. For example, in some interventions that emphasize constructs like "empathy" and "unconditional positive regard," it is difficult to sort out intervention effects from placebo effects. But when they are feasible to use, placebo control group designs provide greater control for threats to external validity than do designs that use only one control group.

Cross-Sectional Studies

Because most experimental and quasi-experimental research designs focus on controlling for threats to *internal* validity, they are highly desirable designs to utilize when we seek to derive causal inferences from our research. We have noted, however, that these designs are not flawless, and their *external* validity, in particular, often can be limited. Researchers who lack the means to conduct experimental or quasi-experimental designs, or who may be interested in studying larger, more representative samples, might opt to conduct cross-sectional studies, which we discussed briefly in Chapter 4.

Cross-sectional studies (also referred to as *correlational studies*) examine a phenomenon by taking a cross section of it *at one point in time*. For example, they might examine the plausibility of parent-child discord as a cause of childhood behavioral disorders by administering two measures to children at the same point: one that assesses the degree of parent-child discord and one that assesses whether the child has a behavioral disorder. If the two measures are highly and positively correlated—that is, if the probability of behavioral disorder is higher when the amount of parent-child discord is greater—the results support the *plausibility* of the supposition that the discord contributes to the causation of behavioral disorders.

But although the results are *consistent* with the notion that discord helps cause the disorder, they do not themselves demonstrate that the nature of the relationship is indeed causal. For instance, time order is not taken into account. Perhaps the causal order of the relationship is the other way around. That is, perhaps parent-child discord, rather than causing the behavioral disorder, increases as a result of the disorder. Also, the preceding correlation by itself does not rule out alternative variables that might cause both the discord and the behavioral disorder. For example, perhaps stressful life events produce both problems simultaneously.

Recognizing that simple correlations have relatively little internal validity, researchers using cross-sectional designs may attempt to rule out the plausibility of rival hypotheses by controlling for alternative variables through *multivariate statistical procedures*. They do this by collecting data on as many plausible alternative explanatory variables as they can and then analyzing all the variables simultaneously, using multivariate techniques like those discussed in Part 5 of this book. It would be premature to present those complex statistical methods at this point, but we will discuss them in Chapters 15 and 16. For now, it is sufficient to alert you to the fact that these multivariate procedures markedly enhance the internal validity of cross-sectional studies by enabling much greater control over alternative hypotheses, thereby increasing the plausibility of causal inferences drawn from cross-sectional data.

As we have seen, social work settings often do not permit the kinds of sophisticated methodological arrangements needed to manipulate variables and meet all the criteria for inferring causality in an ideal manner. Because of their feasibility, cross-sectional designs have always been popular in social work research, and with recent advances in multivariate statistical analysis, the internal validity of these designs is improving. Cross-sectional designs are also commonly used in descriptive and exploratory research.

Main Points

• There are three basic criteria for the determination of causation in scientific research: (1) the independent (cause) and dependent (effect) variables must be empirically related to each other, (2) the independent variable must occur earlier in time than the dependent variable, and (3) the observed relationship between these two variables cannot be explained away as being due to the influence of some third variable that causes both of them.

• Experiments are an excellent vehicle for the controlled testing of causal processes.

• The classical experiment tests the effect of an experimental stimulus on some dependent variable through the pretesting and posttesting of experimental and control groups.

• It is generally less important that a group of experimental subjects be representative of some larger population than that experimental and control groups be similar to one another.

• Randomization is the generally preferred method for achieving comparability in the experimental and control groups.

• Campbell and Stanley describe three forms of preexperiments: the one-shot case study, the one-group pretest-posttest design, and the posttest-only design with nonequivalent groups.

• Nine important threats to internal validity in experimental design are

a. history

b. maturation

c. testing

d. instrumentation

e. regression

f. selection

g. mortality

h. causal time order

i. diffusion or imitation of treatments

• The classical experiment with random assignment of subjects guards against most, but not all, threats to internal validity.

• Control groups in experiments in social work settings need not be denied services. They can receive alternate, routine services, and/or they can be put on a waiting list to receive the experimental intervention.

• Experiments also face problems of external validity: experimental findings may not reflect real life or generalize to other settings or populations.

• The interaction of testing with the stimulus is an example of external invalidity, and the classical experiment does not guard against that problem.

• The Solomon four-group design and other variations on the classical experiment can safeguard against some of the problems of external validity.

• Campbell and Stanley suggest that, given proper randomization in the assignment of subjects to the experimental and control groups, there is no need for pretesting in experiments, and this is reflected in the posttest-only control group design.

• Many experimental studies fail to include measurement procedures, such as blind raters, that control for researcher or practitioner bias toward perceiving results that would confirm the hypothesis.

• It is often impossible to randomly assign subjects to experimental and control groups in real agency settings, and quasi-experimental designs can provide credible, although less ideal, alternatives when experimental designs are not feasible.

• Three credible types of quasi-experimental designs are time-series designs, nonequivalent control groups, and multiple time-series designs.

• Cross-sectional studies with multivariate statistical controls can provide another credible alternative to experimental designs. When cross-sectional studies utilize representative samples, their external validity can be an advantage. When experimental studies have to rely on artificial arrangements or on atypical voluntary subjects, they may have the disadvantage of dubious external validity.

• Many practical pitfalls are likely to be encountered in attempting to implement experiments or quasi-experiments in service-oriented agencies. These pitfalls may compromise the fidelity of the interventions being evaluated, contaminate the control condition or the case assignment protocol, or hinder client recruitment and retention.

• The inclusion of various qualitative research methods as part of an experiment or quasi-experiment can aid in avoiding or alleviating many of the practical pitfalls.

Review Questions and Exercises

1. A newspaper article (Perlman, 1982) discussed arguments linking fluoridation to acquired immune deficiency syndrome (AIDS), citing this evidence: "While half the country's communities have fluoridated water supplies, and half do not, 90% of AIDS cases are coming from fluoridated areas and only 10% are coming from nonfluoridated areas." Discuss this in terms of what you have learned about the criteria of causation, indicating what other variables might be involved.

2. Pick six of the nine threats to internal validity discussed in the book and make up examples (not discussed in the book) to illustrate each.

3. Briefly sketch out an experimental or quasi-experimental design for testing out a new intervention in your fieldwork agency or in another social work agency with which you are familiar. Then conduct a qualitative (open-ended, semi-structured) interview with one or two direct-service practitioners and an administrator in that agency, asking them about the practical pitfalls you are likely to encounter in attempting to implement the design. If they identify numerous pitfalls, how do those pitfalls compare to the ones identified in this chapter? If they simply pat you on the back and say, "Great (hypothetical) study, no problem" (they know they don't really have to implement it), do you think they are leveling with you? Why or why not?

Additional Readings

Campbell, Donald, and Stanley, Julian, *Experimental and Quasi-Experimental Designs for Research* (Chicago: Rand McNally, 1963). An excellent analysis of the logic and methods of experimentation in social research. This book is especially useful in its application of the logic of experiments to other social research methods.

Cook, Thomas D., and Campbell, Donald T., *Quasi-Experimentation: Design and Analysis Issues for Field Settings* (Chicago: Rand McNally, 1979). An expanded and updated version of Campbell and Stanley.

Hirschi, Travis, and Selvin, Hanan, *Principles of Survey Analysis* (New York: Free Press, 1973), especially Part II. Excellent statements on causation within a practical framework. We can think of no better discussions of causation within the context of particular research findings than these. The book is readable, stimulating, and generally just plain excellent.

Kaplan, Abraham, *The Conduct of Inquiry* (San Francisco: Chandler, 1964). A philosopher's perspective on social research. Especially in his discussions of explanation (Part 9), Kaplan lays the logical foundation for an understanding of the nature and analysis of causal relationships in social science.

Lazarsfeld, Paul, Foreword in Hyman, Herbert, *Survey Design and Analysis* (New York: Free Press, 1955). A classic and still valid statement of causation in social science. In the context of the elaboration model, Lazarsfeld provides a clear statement of the criteria for determining causation.

Ray, William, and Ravizza, Richard, *Methods Toward a Science of Behavior and Experience* (Belmont, CA: Wadsworth, 1985). A comprehensive examination of social science research methods, with a special emphasis on experimentation. This book is especially strong in the philosophy of science.

Rosenberg, Morris, *The Logic of Survey Analysis* (New York: Basic Books, 1968). A clear and practical statement of how the social researcher addresses causation. In his opening chapter, Rosenberg discusses the general meaning of causal relationships. In the concluding two chapters, he describes the process through which a researcher may arrive at causal conclusions.

10

Single-Subject Designs

What You'll Learn in This Chapter

Here you'll see how direct service practitioners
can carry out experiments with an individual
client or client system in order to evaluate their
own effectiveness and the effectiveness of
particular interventions.

INTRODUCTION

In Chapter 9 we saw that when it is not possible to assign people to control groups, time-series designs can be used to evaluate the impact of programs or interventions on groups of individuals. By taking repeated measures of the dependent variable (the service or policy goal, or target problem that one seeks to change), treated groups can serve as their own controls. These repeated measures attempt to identify stable trends in the target problem. If marked deviations in these trends coincide with the introduction or withdrawal of the service or intervention, the plausibility of the hypothesis that changes in the dependent variable were caused by variation in the service or intervention (the independent variable) can be supported.

Key concepts here are multiple measurement points and unlikely coincidences. The more measurement points one has and the more stable the trends identified in that measurement, the easier it is to infer whether any changes in the target problem can be attributed to changes in the independent variable or to rival sources of change, such as maturation, history, or statistical regression. In other words, identifying stable trends through many repeated measures enhances the internal validity of evaluations that cannot utilize control groups by enabling the researcher to pinpoint precisely where change in the dependent variable occurs and whether those points coincide with changes in the independent variable. To the extent that changes in the dependent variable consistently occur only after the independent variable is introduced or withdrawn (and not at other times), a pattern of coincidences has been established that makes rival explanations such as maturation and history seem unlikely.

OVERVIEW OF THE LOGIC OF SINGLE-SUBJECT DESIGNS

Single-subject designs apply the logic of time-series designs to the evaluation of the impact of interventions or policy changes on individual cases or systems. Such designs involve obtaining repeated measures of a client system with regard to particular outcome indicators of a target problem. Repeated measures of the trend in the target problem are obtained before a particular intervention is introduced, and these repeated measures are continued after intervention is introduced to see if a sustained pattern of improvement in the target problem commences shortly after the onset of intervention.

The phase of repeated measures that occurs before intervention is introduced is called the *baseline*. Baselines are control phases—that is, they serve the same function as control groups do in group experiments. The data patterns collected during the baseline (control) phases are compared to the data patterns collected during the *intervention* (experimental) phases. To infer that an intervention is effective—that is, that improvements in the dependent variable can be attributed to the intervention and not to some rival explanation such as history or maturation—we look for shifts in the trend or pattern of the data that coincide with shifts between baseline and intervention phases.

Consider the graph in Figure 10-1, for example. We see a shift from a stable pattern of no consistent change in the target problem during baseline to a sustained trend of improvement in the target problem at the start of and throughout the intervention phase. Something other than the intervention may have caused that change, but that would be a big coincidence given the large number of repeated measures and the absence of any marked shift in the data pattern at any time other than after intervention begins.

Now, for the sake of contrast, consider the graph in Figure 10-2. Here we see virtually the same intervention data as in Figure 10-1, but after a trend during baseline that shows that the target problem was already improving during baseline at the same rate at which it continued to improve during intervention. Here we would conclude that something other than the intervention was probably causing the improvement, such

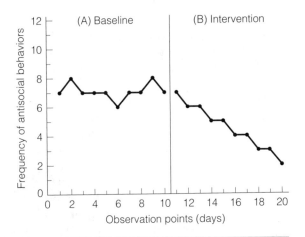

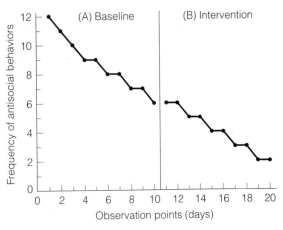

Figure 10-1 Graph of Hypothetical Single-Subject Design Outcome Supporting Effectiveness of Intervention (Basic AB Design)

Figure 10-2 Graph of Hypothetical Single-Subject Design Outcome Not Supporting Effectiveness of Intervention (Basic AB Design)

as maturation or the mere passage of time. This example illustrates how repeated measures during the baseline and intervention phases enable us to control for threats to internal validity that refer to processes that were under way before treatment begins. Without repeated measures in each phase—that is, with only one preintervention measure and one postintervention measure—we would have no way to detect such ongoing processes (for example, maturation, reactivity, regression toward the mean) and thus would need experimental and control groups.

But what about history? Perhaps a big coincidence really did occur regarding the illustration depicted in Figure 10-1. Perhaps a dramatic and helpful change took place in the client's social environment precisely when intervention began. History cannot be ruled out with results like those in Figure 10-1, but note how history seems less plausible than in simple pretest/posttest group designs that contain only two data points (one before intervention and one after) and in which longer periods of time usually separate the two data points. In single-subject designs we can pinpoint the day or the week when the stable pattern of improvement begins, and we can discuss

with the client what significant events or changes occurred at that point (other than the onset of intervention) to get a fairly good idea of whether history seems like a plausible explanation.

Single-subject designs can increase their control for history by having more than one baseline and intervention phase. We will examine how that is done in depth later in this chapter. For now let us consider the following illustration. Suppose a school social worker seeking to enhance the self-esteem and social functioning of an acting-out adolescent at high risk of dropping out of school monitors the student's disciplinary referrals and administers a standardized self-esteem scale on a weekly basis. Suppose further that the social worker decided to interrupt the intervention phase for a few weeks, perhaps to take a well-deserved vacation or perhaps to see whether the student could maintain the improvement without being dependent on lengthy treatment. If a graph of the student's repeated measures resembled the data patterns displayed in Figure 10-3, then the social worker would have reasonable grounds for inferring that it was probably the intervention, and not history, that accounted for the student's improved functioning.

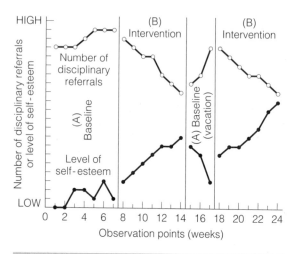

Figure 10-3 Graph of Hypothetical Single-Subject Design Outcome Supporting Effectiveness of Intervention (ABAB Design)

Such an inference is reasonable because the shifts in the data patterns, or trends, occurred on *three successive* occasions coinciding with the introduction or interruption of intervention and at no other time. With this many successive trend shifts the odds become extremely slim that other events are producing the desired change in the target problem and simply happen to coincide with variation in the independent variable. Thus the history hypothesis becomes farfetched.

$N = 1$

When the preceding logic of time-series analysis is applied to the evaluation of outcome with individual cases, the research designs can be termed "single-subject designs," "single-case designs," or "single-system designs." The latter two terms are favored by those who seek to remind us that client systems need not be individual subjects, but can include a family unit, a community, and so on. But the term "single-subject designs" is more commonly used and therefore will be used here—

with the caveat that it can apply to cases or systems that may involve more than one individual.

Regardless of what we call them, a distinguishing feature of these designs is that the sample size is one. Whether our unit of analysis is one individual, one family, one community, or one organization, the number of sampling elements is one. Consequently, one of the chief limitations of these designs is their dubious external validity. In Chapter 8 we discussed the precariousness of generalizing from samples that lacked adequate size or selection procedures. What, then, are we to think of a sampling approach that contains only one element? Although some dismiss these designs as little more than idiosyncratic case studies that cannot be generalized, a case can be made for their increased usage in social work.

SINGLE-SUBJECT DESIGNS IN SOCIAL WORK

Those who pooh-pooh single-subject designs because of their small sample size perhaps overlook the important role they have played in the history of behavioral research, beginning early in this century with laboratory research on animal behavior. Who, for example, would want to dismiss the importance of Pavlov's dog as a single-subject in the development of learning theory? As for research on *human* behavior, single-subject designs began to proliferate during the 1960s, when behavior modification studies burgeoned. Eventually recognition grew that single-subject designs could be used not only in behavioral modification studies, but also in the evaluation of any social service intervention for which target problems could be operationally defined in terms conducive to multiple, repeated measures. By the late 1970s a growing cadre of social work researchers and educators was advocating an increased emphasis on these designs as a way to integrate research and practice, increase the amount of practice-oriented research being produced, and ultimately advance the empirical base of social work practice.

As discussed earlier in this book, significant scientific advances do not necessarily require the use of large-scale studies that attempt to verify hypotheses. Important contributions also can be made by exploratory studies that use more flexible methods, including smaller samples, in efforts to discover new insights and generate hypotheses and theories for which generalizability can be tested later in more tightly controlled studies using larger, probability samples.

Single-subject experiments can identify with a high degree of internal validity those interventions that seem to work in one, perhaps idiosyncratic, context and can be tested for generalizability in subsequent studies. These subsequent studies might include larger scale experiments utilizing control groups, or they might be additional single-subject experiments that attempt to approximate replications of the original single-subject experiment in other contexts. For example, suppose a gerontological social worker finds, based on his or her results in a single-subject design, that reviewing life history with a particular client in a long-term care facility significantly improved the client's morale and diminished the client's depression. Gerontological social workers in similar facilities with similar clients could attempt to replicate the intervention and study. To the extent that they also replicate the results, then evidence would accumulate supporting the generalizability of the findings. Ultimately, this evidence may be sufficient to secure the more extensive degree of support needed to make feasible a larger scale experiment utilizing a control group. But even if a larger, control group experiment is never conducted, the accumulation of single-subject evidence will advance the scientific basis for continuing to deliver the tested intervention.

Accumulating findings of single-subject experiments has value not only in advancing the scientific basis of particular interventions or of a particular practitioner's effectiveness, but also in evaluating an entire agency or program. Suppose, for example, that a funding source calls for a program evaluation to determine whether a family service agency is providing effective services and thus merits continued or perhaps increased levels of support. Suppose further that administrative and ethical considerations rule out the possibility of utilizing a control group in the evaluation. One option might be to conduct a time-series design. But suppose target problems and service objectives vary substantially from case to case. The objective might be to reduce a child's antisocial behavior in one case, to decrease marital conflict in another, to prevent abusive parental behavior in a third, and so on. One option would be to conduct a separate single-subject experiment on each case or on a representative subset of cases and to use the idiosyncratic case objectives or target problems as the dependent variable in each experiment. The agency could then report not only the proportion of its cases that attain successful outcomes but, more important, the proportion of those outcomes that the logic of time-series analysis shows to have been caused specifically by receiving agency services.

A reverse process also can be cited to justify the value of single-subject designs. That is, individual practitioners or agencies may wonder whether interventions supported initially by group experiments in other settings will work as well in their particular, and perhaps idiosyncratic, context. For instance, suppose a few gerontological social workers first learned about reviewing life histories from an experiment reported in a gerontological social work journal, and they wondered whether they were capable of implementing the reported intervention as effectively and whether their particular clients would be able to benefit from it as much as those in the reported study, whose characteristics may have been inadequately specified or may have differed slightly from those of their clients. They could conduct single-subject experiments with one or more clients to answer these questions for themselves. Such experiments would reduce their doubt not only about the effectiveness of particular interventions with particular clients, but about their own effectiveness as clinical practitioners as well.

Use of Single-Subject Designs as Part of Social Work Practice

Single-subject designs can be implemented by some social work practitioners as part of their own clinical practice with some clients. Because these designs require only one case, the practitioner need not worry about amassing large samples or assigning clients to control groups. Each experiment contains idiosyncratic objectives applicable to an individual case—objectives that the practitioner would be attempting to help the client attain as a routine part of practice were no experiment to take place. Likewise, the practitioner would routinely want to monitor the client's progress in attaining those objectives. By taking repeated measures of changes in the target problem, the practitioner both monitors client progress (or lack thereof) and acquires a tool for a more systematic understanding of events or circumstances that may exacerbate or ameliorate the target problem. For example, suppose a child in a joint-custody arrangement is being treated for explosive and antisocial behaviors. Suppose further that the problematic behaviors tend to occur shortly before the child is about to go into the custody of one or the other parent. Repeated measures of the target behavior might help the practitioner chronologically identify this coincidence during the initial stages of service delivery, which in turn would help the practitioner better understand the causes of the target problem and develop an appropriate strategy to deal with it. Practitioners who spend considerable amounts of time unsystematically attempting to record and evaluate their practices might find conducting single-subject designs to be one way to make that effort more systematic and valid.

There are, however, practical obstacles to integrating single-subject designs as part of direct practice. These constraints make it unrealistic for many practitioners to utilize these designs, particularly when they are working in certain kinds of agency settings or with certain types of target problems. Client crises often do not allow practi-

tioners enough time to take repeated measures to identify baseline trends prior to implementing the intervention. In some settings heavy caseloads reduce the amount of time practitioners have to plan or conduct repeated measures during any phase. The practitioner's peers and supervisors in an agency may not recognize the value of researching one's own practice effectiveness, and therefore may not support it. Clients may resent the extensive self-monitoring procedures that these designs may require.

Despite these obstacles, social work practitioners should strive to implement single-subject designs whenever they can. Social work practice entails providing interventions or services that have not yet received adequate scientific testing concerning their beneficial or harmful effects on clients. In light of this, the question may not be whether each of us can afford the time needed to use single-subject methodology as part of our practices, but whether we (as a profession) can afford not to allocate the time. Given the profession's commitment to the social welfare of its clients and its aspirations to call its work truly professional, practitioners can conduct single-subject experiments when implementing untested interventions to see whether they are helping clients, harming them, or merely wasting scarce resources that could be put to better use.

Wasting scarce resources in the social welfare arena is not just a question of efficiency or public accountability. It is also a question of compassion and professional concern for clients. For if we are wasting our time and the client's time on ineffectual services, then we are not ameliorating suffering. Neither are we able to use that time to implement alternative services that might really help that client. By conducting single-subject designs as part of their practice, social work practitioners can obtain immediate feedback that will indicate whether they should modify the service program to better help (or perhaps stop hindering) specific clients.

The point here is not that practitioners would necessarily become researchers intent on publishing their findings. Rather, the point is that the use of scientific measurement procedures and single-subject design logic can be an important part of practice—simply in being a more compassionate, conscientious, and professional practitioner—and requires no aspirations to be a researcher or to publish scientific findings.

As one way to illustrate this point, consider the counseling technique termed "paradoxical intent." Stated simply, this technique instructs clients to try to make the target problem worse. It resembles lay notions of reverse psychology and is sometimes thought to help alleviate the target problem for individuals who resist the efforts of the change agent or whose excessive worry about improving the target problem impedes efforts to achieve the desired change. For example, clients whose anxiety about insomnia produces tension that makes it even more difficult to fall asleep might be instructed to keep their eyes open when they go to bed and to try not to close them no matter how tired they become. The technique of paradoxical intent is popular among some social workers who do a lot of counseling and family therapy, but it has not yet had ample empirical testing concerning its beneficial or harmful effects. Among the practitioners who use this technique and have sufficient time to use single-subject methodology, which are the more compassionate and professional: those who use single-subject design logic and scientific measurement procedures to monitor whether this intervention is helping clients, harming them, or wasting their time or those who are less systematic about monitoring the technique's effects?

Along the same lines, suppose you had a rare illness that required the use of one or more alternative medical treatments that had not yet been adequately tested. Which physician would you find more humane and want to treat you: one who used single-subject principles to monitor the positive and negative effects of each alternative treatment on you or one who simply applied the treatment with which he or she was most comfortable and then didn't burden you with a bunch of scientific testing?

But readers should not be misled by an overly rosy portrayal of the feasibility of conducting single-subject designs as part of their own practices; nor should they think that single-subject designs offer a panacea for resolving long-standing doubts about the effectiveness of social work practice. As will be seen shortly, conducting repeated measures of target problems in a way that attempts to provide data that are credible from the standpoint of reliability and validity can be a difficult and complex task. And delaying treatment until a stable trend of baseline measurements has been established (even when it's possible to do so) is a lot easier to recommend in a textbook or classroom lecture than it is to do when confronted by individuals who are suffering. Also, many client problems do not lend themselves to any sort of repeated measures. It is silly, for example, to conduct repeated measures to see whether a crisis intervention succeeded in helping a family whose house burned down find an emergency shelter. It either did or did not; one need not monitor variation in the degree of goal attainment to find out.

Their limitations notwithstanding, single-subject designs can be valuable tools for social work researchers, administrators, planners, and practitioners. Because most readers of this text are preparing for careers as social work practitioners, the rest of this chapter will treat the topic of single-subject designs primarily from the standpoint of conducting them as part of one's own practice. But this treatment will also provide information needed by researchers who seek to conduct single-subject designs or by administrators who will use them for agency evaluation, planning, and accountability.

MEASUREMENT ISSUES

Early decisions in planning a single-subject experiment involve identifying the target problem and goals and defining them in operational terms. These decisions influence the next phase of the research plan: developing a measurement and data collection plan.

Operationally Defining Target Problems and Goals

Identifying target problems is chiefly a practice consideration and is treated in depth in various texts on practice and assessment. It might involve gathering information from a broad spectrum of individuals who are connected to the client system and carefully considering the reliability and validity of information provided by alternative sources. It might involve the use of standardized assessment instruments, such as self-report scales. It might involve a process of partialization, in which problems are prioritized: the most urgent yet easily resolved problems are addressed first and the thornier, longer-term ones are tackled later. It might also involve establishing a contract in which client and practitioner agree on the problems to be tackled and how they will be monitored. Readers are referred to practice texts (Compton and Galaway, 1984; Reid and Epstein, 1972) for a thorough treatment of this topic from a practice standpoint.

From a research standpoint, the critical issue is defining the target problems in operational terms (that is, in precise and observable terms). Operational definitions were discussed at length in Chapter 5, and the same issues discussed there apply to single-subject designs. For some reason, however, it seems that practitioners are more likely to dispute the applicability of operational definitions when thinking about individual cases than when thinking about research in general. Some argue that it is impossible to define certain clinical constructs, such as level of social functioning, in specific and observable terms. This dispute inevitably gets resolved, however, in a dialogue like the one on prejudice discussed in Chapter 5. Ultimately most skeptics realize that clinicians or clients would never have selected a target problem in the first place if they had no way of observing, at least indirectly, its indicators. That is, they

would never choose to work toward improving client functioning in one area or another unless they already had some basis for observing certain indicators that convinced them that the level of functioning was unacceptably low.

Any problem that we would have reason to work on, therefore, could be operationally defined if we simply considered the specific indicators that led us to decide that it needed our attention. Consider the alternative. If it were possible to identify a problem that could not be defined in operational terms, on what grounds would the practitioner or client have decided that it required intervention, and how in the world would they ever decide whether the problem was or was not adequately resolved? Here we are not dealing just with a research issue, but with a practice issue, as well. Imagine, for example, trying to learn how to do clinical assessment or when to terminate interventions from a practice instructor who taught exclusively via presentations of his or her own cases, but who was unable to identify for students what he or she observed in each case that led him or her to work on one particular target problem in one case and a different problem in another, or what the instructor observed that led him or her to terminate the intervention in each case.

In considering operational definitions, some students note that practitioners might rely on the client's complaint that a particular problem requires attention. But even here practitioners are using an operational definition. That is, they are persuaded to work on a problem based upon their *observation* of the extent of the client's expressed difficulty or dissatisfaction with that problem. Thus, they could take repeated measures simply by having clients indicate daily on a brief scale the degree of difficulty they felt they experienced with the problem that day.

But saying that all identified target problems can be operationally defined does not mean that the selection of observable indicators is always a routine or easy decision. We often are confronted with knotty target problems that cannot be observed directly (for example, anxiety, depression, or self-esteem) and that require us to select and observe indirect indicators of the problem. There may be an extensive array of potential indicators, and selecting the wrong one might lead to incorrect conclusions later on. Take self-esteem, for example. Some self-report measures of self-esteem treat level of self-esteem as a fairly permanent personality trait, and consequently these measures are not sensitive to small, short-term changes in it. If the operational definition of the target problem were a score on such a scale, it might be very difficult to detect changes in self-esteem that represented meaningful improvements from a clinical standpoint.

Among the array of potential observable indicators of a target problem there may be positive indicators representing the absence of the problem or negative indicators that signify the presence of the problem. For instance, if the target problem concerned a client's depression, an operational definition might involve negative indicators like the frequency of crying spells or the frequency of self-derogatory remarks. The goal then would be a reduction in the observed indicators. The operational definition also might include positive indicators like the amount of time spent socially interacting with friends. If so, then the goal would be to increase those indicators. Practitioners might want to restrict their definition to positive indicators for clinical reasons, so that they and the client are not always thinking in negative terms about the problem. They might also choose to monitor several indicators of the problem or goal, perhaps including some that are positive as well as some that are negative.

What to Measure

Because of the need to obtain many repeated observations in single-subject experiments, the operational indicators should occur frequently enough to be measured on a regular basis. Direct-service practitioners working in a suicide prevention program, for example, might want to monitor the amount of sleep a client gets each day, the daily number of positive client self-cognitions, or weekly scores on a self-report depression inventory. They would probably not record an infrequent event like the number of suicide attempts each day or week because it would take too long to establish enough variation in the data pattern. On the other hand, a planner or administrator using single-subject methodology to evaluate the effectiveness of an entire suicide prevention program could appropriately monitor the number of reported suicides or suicide attempts each week in a populous area served by the program. Likewise, a practitioner working with an abusive parent might want to monitor the amount of time the parent plays with the child each day or the number of positive statements (praise, encouragement, and so on) from parent to child during weekly observation sessions, rather than record the daily or weekly incidence of serious abuse by the parent. But an administrator of a countywide program to prevent child abuse appropriately could monitor the countywide incidence of serious child abuse each week.

There is no strict rule concerning how many operational indicators one should measure. The fewer one measures, the greater the risk of failing to detect client improvement on indicators other than those being measured. For example, a case manager might be effective in motivating a chronically mentally ill client to take medication as prescribed and in securing more community support services. But if the case manager only measured the client's degree of psychopathology or the client's job-seeking behavior, he or she might get negative results and erroneously conclude that the intervention was not working. On the other hand, it is unwise to try to measure so many indicators that the data gathering process becomes unwieldy and overwhelms the client, practitioner, or both. Moreover, the greater the number of indicators that are monitored, the greater the risk that the data pattern of one or more of them will show improvement after intervention solely on the basis of chance fluctuations.

Triangulation

As a rule of thumb, two or three indicators are generally considered appropriate. This is usually a feasible approach on the one hand, and it meets the criterion of triangulation on the other. As discussed in Chapter 6, triangulation is a principle that applies to all types of research designs, not just single-subject experiments. It refers to situations in which researchers are confronted with a multiplicity of imperfect measurement options, each of which has some advantages and disadvantages. To maximize the chances that the hypothesized variation in the dependent variable will be detected, the researcher triangulates measures: more than one measurement option is used. (Despite its connotation of a triangle, triangulation does not require using three options, only more than one.)

In single-subject designs, triangulation does not necessarily mean that more than one target problem is to be measured. It means that more than one indicator of the same target problem is to be measured. For instance, a school social worker whose client is underachieving might want to monitor the amount of time the client spends on homework each night and teacher ratings of his or her class attentiveness and participation. Triangulation does not require that the social worker also monitor indicators of other problems, such as antisocial behaviors (fighting, disciplinary referrals, and so on). The practitioner may choose to monitor more than one problem, but the principle of triangulation does not require it. The principle of triangulation applies to all measurement options—not just what to measure—and we will consider it again in our discussion of data gathering.

DATA GATHERING

The options and decisions to be made in planning measurement and data collection in single-subject experiments are not unlike those confronting researchers designing other types of studies. Researchers must decide whether the data sources should be available records, interviews, self-report scales, or direct observations of behavior. The advantages and disadvantages of these sources are for the most part the same in single-subject experiments as those in other types of research.

Who Should Measure?

One issue involves who should do the measuring. When practitioners make measurements to evaluate their own practice, the risk of observer bias might be heightened, for it is only human to want to obtain findings that support our practice effectiveness and indicate that client suffering is being ameliorated. Perhaps even riskier is relying exclusively on clients to do the measuring themselves. Clients may be biased to perceive positive results not only to please themselves or to project a socially desirable image to the practitioner, but also to avoid disappointing the practitioner. Significant others (teachers, cottage parents, and so on) might be asked to monitor certain behaviors in the hope that they have less invested than the client or practitioner in seeing a positive outcome. But neither their objectivity nor their commitment to the study can be guaranteed. This is particularly important in light of the large amount of time and dedication that might be required to carefully and systematically monitor the client's behavior on a continuous basis. In light of the repeated measures required by single-subject designs and the strong potential for bias, there is no easy answer concerning who should do the measuring. Here, then, we return to the principle of triangulation and perhaps use all three of the preceding options to gather the data. In this context we see another advantage of triangulation—the opportunity it provides for assessing measurement reliability. To the extent that different data gatherers agree in their measures, we can have more confidence that the data are accurate.

Sources of Data

In considering alternative sources of data (available records, interviews, self-report scales, or direct behavioral observations), several issues are particularly salient in single-subject designs. Available records, for example, might enable the researcher or practitioner to obtain a retrospective baseline of pretreatment trends and therefore not have to delay treatment while collecting baseline data. This, of course, can occur only when we are fortunate enough to have access to existing records that contain carefully gathered, reliable data that happen to correspond to the way the target problem has been operationally defined in the single-subject experiment.

Self-report scales also merit special consideration in single-subject designs. On the one hand, they can be very convenient; repeated measures can be expedited by simply having clients complete a brief self-report scale each day where they live or each time the practitioner sees them. Self-report scales also ensure that the repeated measures are being administered and scored in a uniform fashion.

But on the other hand, the use of these scales carries some special risks in single-subject experiments. For one thing, clients might lose interest in completing them carefully over and over again. Perhaps a more serious risk, however, is the potential for the client to be biased to complete these scales with responses that convey a socially desirable impression. This risk would be greatest when the single-subject experiment is being conducted by practitioners to evaluate their own practice, because clients might be particularly predisposed to giving inaccurate responses in order to please the clinicians about their helpfulness or to make favorable impressions on them.

Reliability and Validity

Readers might wonder at this point whether these risks could be avoided by using standardized self-report scales with established high levels of reliability and validity. All other things being equal (such as relevance to the problem or client, sensitivity to change, and instrument length and complexity), of course it is better to use scales whose reliability and validity have been empirically supported, if such scales are available for the particular variable one seeks to measure. But the conditions under which the validity of standardized instruments is tested tend to contrast with single-subject experimental conditions in critical ways. Standardized instruments tend to be validated in large-scale assessment studies in which (1) the respondent is part of a large group of individuals who have no special, ongoing relationship with the researcher and who are by and large anonymous, (2) the instrument will not be completed more than one or two times by each respondent, and (3) a respondent's score on the instrument has no bearing on whether the respondent is benefitting from some service.

In contrast, when clients complete these instruments as part of single-subject experiments, they are not anonymous and they have a special relationship with a service provider. They may therefore be sensitive about the impression they are conveying and more intent on conveying a favorable impression than in a more anonymous situation. With each repeated completion of the instrument their answers may become less valid, perhaps due to carelessness or perhaps because they remember their previous answers. Finally, and perhaps most important, they may be keenly aware of the difference between nontreatment (baseline) phases and treatment phases; they may know that if the service is being effective, their scores should improve during the treatment phases. This awareness may predispose them to convey a more positive impression during the treatment phases. In light of these differences, we cannot assume that because a particular self-report instrument has empirically been shown in other contexts not to have serious validity problems due to social desirability biases, it will adequately avoid those biases in a single-subject experiment.

Direct Behavioral Observation

The large number of repeated measures in single-subject experiments also complicates the decision to use direct behavioral observations as the data source. This is particularly problematic when the experiment is being conducted as part of one's own practice because busy practitioners may lack the time needed to conduct the observations themselves or the resources needed to induce someone else to observe the client. To the extent that observation of the target problem can be limited to office or home visits, the difficulty of practitioner observation is reduced. But many target problems need to be observed on a more continuous basis. Barring the availability of a significant other (such as a teacher, relative, or cottage parent) willing to observe on a regular basis, we are commonly forced to rely on clients to observe themselves. The term for client self-observation is *self-monitoring*. If the dependent variable is the number of a certain type of thoughts or feelings that a client has during a particular period—phenomena that only the client could observe—then self-monitoring would be the only direct observation option.

The problem with self-monitoring is that in addition to its vulnerability to measurement bias (as discussed earlier), it is highly vulnerable to the problem of research reactivity. *Reactivity* occurs when the process of observing or recording the data—that is, the self-measurement process itself—brings about change in the target problem. For example, suppose a practitioner encourages a mother who has a conflictual relationship with her son to record each time she praises him and each time she scolds him. Regardless of what else the practitioner does, the mere act of recording may sensitize the mother to her tendency to scold her son too often and praise him too rarely, and this in turn may bring her to praise him more and scold him less.

From a clinical standpoint, of course, reactivity might not be such a bad idea. That is, self-monitoring can be used as a clinical tool to help

bring about the desired change. Indeed, it often is used that way. But when it is used as the only measurement procedure in research, it clouds the process of inferring whether the intervention alone brought about the change. This problem can be offset somewhat by the realization that if self-monitoring alone is bringing about the desired change, the change might be detected by noticing an improving trend in a graph of the pretreatment (baseline) data.

You might ask, then, what is the best way to try to avoid the above problems without sacrificing the use of direct observation? Answering this question is easy; the problem is getting the resources needed to do things the best way. First, we would again use the principle of triangulation; that is, we would have more than one person conduct the observations. Second, we would seek to include at least one observer who did not have a vested interest in the outcome of the study or the impression conveyed by the data and who therefore might be relatively unbiased. Third, we would assess the interrater reliability of the observers (how much their observations agree). And fourth, we would arrange for at least one of the observers to conduct the observations in a relatively unobtrusive manner.

Unobtrusive Versus Obtrusive Observation

Unobtrusively observing behavior means that the observer blends into the observation setting in such a way that the act of observing and recording is by and large not noticeable to those being observed (see Chapter 13). For example, a group worker attempting to reduce the amount of antisocial behavior by boys in a residential facility might ask a colleague who supervises their recreational activities to record in the notebook he or she always carries while supervising them the number of fights, arguments, and so on that the targeted boys get into.

The opposite of unobtrusive observation is obtrusive observation. Measurement is obtrusive to the extent that the subject is aware of the observation and is therefore vulnerable to research re-activity or to acting in an atypical manner in order to convey a socially desirable impression. Self-monitoring is perhaps the most obtrusive form of observation because the subject is not only the observee but also the observer. But there are many other forms of observation that can be so obtrusive that the credibility of the entire study is imperiled. Some of these examples can be deceptive because researchers or practitioners may take steps that at first glance seem to provide some degree of unobtrusiveness.

For example, the researcher/practitioner may observe the client through a one-way mirror, thinking that because the client cannot see him or her, the client is less aware of the observation. To a certain extent this is true. But consider the following wrinkle. After taking pretreatment (baseline) measures through a one-way mirror of a conflictual mother-son diad interacting, the practitioner introduces a task-centered intervention in which the practitioner and the mother agree that the mother's task will be to try to praise her son more when he is acting appropriately. The practitioner continues to monitor the interactions through a one-way mirror to see if the intervention will be effective in increasing the number of statements of praise as compared to the pretreatment baseline.

Although it is commendable that the practitioner made observations while not visible by the clients, it is wrong to suppose that the observations were truly unobtrusive or that the baseline and intervention phases were really comparable in their degree of obtrusiveness. In both phases the mother has some degree of awareness that on the other side of the mirror the practitioner is watching. And in the intervention phase she knows precisely which behavior (that is, praise) the practitioner is watching for, knowledge she did not have in the earlier, baseline phase.

Thus, the degree of obtrusiveness in both phases is compounded by the increased vulnerability to a social desirability bias during the intervention phase. And because the client is more in-clined to provide the socially desirable response during the intervention phase, the problem of obtrusiveness becomes a bigger threat to the credibility of the findings. In other words, the desired increase in praise very easily could have nothing to do with the efficacy of the intervention, but instead merely reflects the fact that after the intervention was introduced the client became more predisposed to put on a socially desirable performance—a performance that might have no correlation whatsoever to the way the mother interacts with her child in a natural setting or when the practitioner is not watching. You might think this example is farfetched, that no one would conduct single-subject research with such obvious potential measurement bias. But studies like this not only have been conducted; they have been published in our professional literature!

Data Quantification Procedures

Data gathered through direct observation in single-subject experiments can be quantified in terms of their *frequency, duration,* and/or *magnitude.* For example, the target problem of temper tantrums could be recorded in terms of the number of temper tantrums observed in a specified period (frequency), how long each tantrum lasted (duration), and/or how loud or violent it was (magnitude). Using the principle of triangulation, all three quantification procedures could be used simultaneously.

Another procedure combines both frequency and duration and may be used when it is impractical to record either frequency or duration alone. It is called *interval recording.* This method involves dividing an observation period into equal blocks of short time intervals and then recording whether or not the target behavior occurred at all during each interval. Suppose, for example, that a target problem of an intervention with conflictual spouses was operationally defined as the degree to which they interrupt each other when conversing. Suppose further that the observer was recording interruptions during a 30-minute period in which the couple was instructed to engage in a typical conversation. (Let's put obtrusiveness aside for now.) The interruptions might occur so rapidly that the observer would be overwhelmed trying to record each one in a frequency count. The interruptions might last so long that duration recording would be too fatiguing. With interval recording the observer would break the 30-minute session into equal intervals of perhaps one minute each. Then all that would be required would be to enter a check mark for each interval that contained at least one interruption.

But the direct observation of behavior does not always require continuous observation during lengthy sessions. *Spot-check* recording can be used to observe target behaviors that occur very often, that last a long time, or that are expected to occur during specified periods. For instance, suppose a social worker in a residential treatment facility for distressed adolescents introduces a behavioral modification intervention that seeks to increase the amount of school homework that residents do during specified study periods each evening. The social worker or a cottage parent could briefly glance at the study area each evening, varying the precise time of the observation from day to day, and quickly record whether or not specified individuals were studying (yes or no) or simply count how many were studying at that particular moment. Spot-checks thus not only have the advantage of being less time consuming, they also can be less obtrusive than continuous observation because the observer appears only briefly and at unexpected, intermittent times.

The Baseline Phase

The logic of single-subject designs requires taking enough repeated measures to make it unlikely that extraneous factors (such as changes in the client's environment) would account for improvements that take place in the target problem upon the onset of intervention. The logic also relies on comparing trends that are identified in the repeated measures to control for factors like maturation or statistical regression. Based on this logic, the internal validity of single-subject designs is enhanced when the baseline period has enough measurement points to show a stable trend in the target problem and enough points to establish the unlikelihood that extraneous events affecting the target problem will coincide only with the onset of intervention. Although the ideal number of baseline measurement points needed will vary depending on how soon a stable trend appears, it is reasonable to plan for somewhere between five and ten baseline measures. With some very stable baselines, one can begin to see trends with as few as three to five data points. But the more data points we have, the more confidence we can have in the stability of the observed trend and in the unlikelihood that extraneous events will coincide only with the onset of intervention.

The realities of practice do not always permit us to take an ideal number of baseline measures, however. For example, the client's problem might be too urgent to delay intervention any longer, even though the baseline trend appears unstable or is unclear. When an ideal baseline length is not feasible, we simply come as close to the ideal as the clinical and administrative realities permit.

A stable trend is one that shows the target problem to be occurring in a predictable and orderly fashion. The trend is identified by plotting the data points chronologically on a graph, drawing a line between each data point, and then observing whether the overall pattern is clearly increasing (Figure 10-4(A)), decreasing (Figure 10-4(B)), relatively flat (Figure 10-4(C)), or cyclical (Figure 10-4(D)). By contrast, Figure 10-4(E) provides an illustration of an unstable baseline in which no clear trend is obvious.

The meaning of increasing or decreasing baselines depends on the operational definition of the target problem. If it involves undesirable phenomena such as temper tantrums, then an increasing baseline trend would mean the problem is worsening, and a decreasing baseline would indicate improvement. If the operational definition

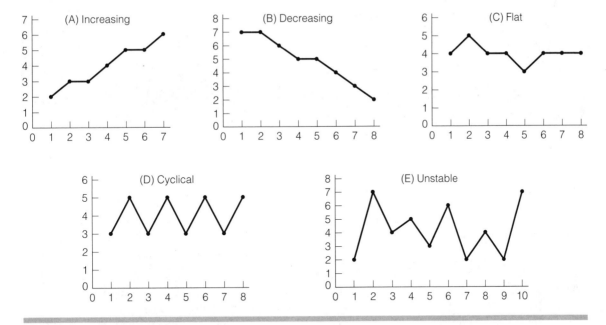

Figure 10-4 Alternative Baseline Trends

involves desirable indicators such as doing homework, then an increasing baseline would signify improvement and a decreasing baseline would signify deterioration.

When the baseline trend signifies improvement, even if it is stable, it may be advisable to continue collecting baseline measures until the improving trend levels off, as illustrated in Figure 10-5. If intervention is introduced at the peak of an improving baseline trend (before it levels off), it will be difficult to achieve a dramatic improvement in the trend. That is, the baseline trend would mean that the client was improving so steadily without any intervention that (1) even an effective intervention might not affect the rate of improvement, and (2) perhaps no intervention on that particular indicator was needed in the first place. In other words, introducing an intervention on the heels of an improving baseline introduces the risk of erroneously concluding that an intervention made no difference simply because the ongoing improvement process was already so steady.

We would also want to extend baseline measures beyond the point at which we initially planned to introduce the intervention if the baseline data collected up to that point were unstable (that is, if they failed to yield a predictable trend). As noted earlier, when we observe an unstable baseline we ideally would extend the baseline measures until a stable pattern appears. However, it was also noted that the constraints of practice do not always permit us to extend the baseline until a desirable trend is obtained. Other priorities, such as client suffering or endangerment, may take precedence over the internal validity of the research design. If so, then we simply do the best we can with what we have. Perhaps the intervention is so effective that even an unstable or improving baseline pattern will prove to be clearly worse than the intervention data pattern. Figure 10-6 shows an unstable baseline juxtaposed with two alternative intervention data patterns. One pattern illustrates the difficulty of interpreting outcome with an unstable baseline; the other

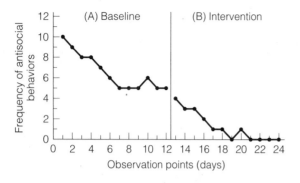

Figure 10-5 Graph of Hypothetical Outcome after Extending a Baseline with an Improving Trend (AB Design)

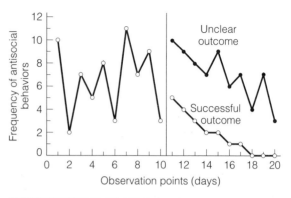

Figure 10-6 Graph of Two Hypothetical Outcomes with an Unstable Baseline (AB Design)

pattern illustrates that it is not necessarily impossible to do so.

In a similar vein, Figure 10-7 illustrates that even with an improving baseline it may be possible to obtain results that support the efficacy of the intervention.

We also might want to deviate from the planned time of completion of the baseline phase when, after the design is implemented, we learn that extraneous environmental changes that may have a potentially important effect on the target problem will coincide with the beginning of the intervention period. For example, if the client has a severe hay fever problem and the target behavior is something like interpersonal irritability or school performance, we would not want to introduce the intervention at the beginning or end of the hay fever season. If we learn of such a situation after the baseline phase has begun, one option would be to extend the baseline longer than initially planned so that it includes enough data points to identify a stable trend after the relevant environmental conditions have changed. Another option would be to withdraw the intervention for a short time later on and then reintroduce it, hoping that the hiatus from treatment would provide a second baseline whose beginning or end would not coincide with important environmental changes. (This latter op-

tion is called an ABAB design, and it will be examined in more depth shortly.)

Some believe that practitioners should employ single-subject practice evaluation procedures even when it is impossible to obtain an adequate baseline, such as when they cannot obtain more than one or two baseline data points. Some even believe in employing these procedures when it is impossible to obtain any baseline data whatsoever. Their rationale is that although the lack of an adequate baseline impedes the drawing of causal inferences, the rest of the data collected still enhance practice by providing a more scientific process for monitoring client progress. Not everyone agrees with this point of view, however. In light of the aforementioned practical difficulties in taking repeated measures, especially regarding the practitioner's ability to obtain measures that are not highly vulnerable to various sources of measurement error, you may question whether the likely benefit of these procedures justifies their costs in those instances when it is impossible to obtain an adequate baseline. If you do not think they are justified in such instances, remember that we are referring only to instances when obtaining an adequate baseline is impossible. When you can obtain an adequate baseline, then the argument for not employing these procedures is much weaker.

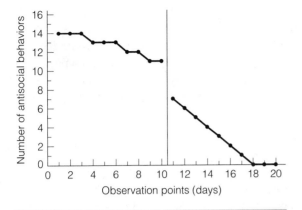

Figure 10-7 Graph of a Hypothetical Outcome Supporting Intervention Efficacy with an Improving Baseline (AB Design)

We would also like you to remember that if you do use these procedures even when you cannot obtain more than a couple of baseline data points, then your data do not provide a suitable basis for inferring about your efficacy. You may find that these procedures are quite valuable in enhancing your monitoring of client progress, but you should resist the temptation to claim that your data verify the effectiveness of your intervention.

We would also like to remind you that when you cannot delay intervention in order to take baseline measures, you should consider whether it is possible to obtain a useful retrospective baseline. A *retrospective baseline*, also called a *reconstructed baseline*, is one in which the baseline is reconstructed from the past. The two primary sources of data for a retrospective baseline are available records or the memory of the client (or significant others). An example of using available records would be obtaining school records on attendance, grades, detentions, and so on for a child with behavioral problems in school. An example of using memory, provided in a recent study by Nugent (1991), would be asking clients with anger control problems to recall how many

blowups they had during the previous week or two, and perhaps triangulating their data with the recollections of their spouse or parent. Bloom and Fischer (1982) offer the following two guidelines when relying on memory to reconstruct a baseline: (1) Use specific, identifiable events that are easy to recall (such as angry blowups, detention referrals, and so on) and therefore are less vulnerable to distortion than things that are harder to recall (such as feelings of inadequacy, anxiety, and so on), and (2) for the same reason, use only the immediate past, such as the past week or two—do not go back more than a month.

ALTERNATIVE SINGLE-SUBJECT DESIGNS

AB: The Basic Single-Subject Design

The simplest single-subject design includes one baseline phase (A) and one intervention phase (B), as illustrated in Figures 10-1, 10-2, 10-5, 10-6, and 10-7. This is a popular design among practitioner/researchers because it involves only one baseline phase and therefore poses the least conflict with service delivery priorities. But this design is weaker than single-subject designs that contain more baselines. With only one baseline, there is only one point at which the independent variable shifts from baseline to intervention. Consequently, only one unlikely coincidence can occur. Although taking many repeated measures reduces the plausibility that some extraneous event and not the intervention would explain a major shift in the data pattern of the dependent variable that occurs only after the onset of intervention, extraneous events are controlled much better when there are several shifts between baseline and intervention phases.

Despite its *relative* weakness, the AB design is still quite useful. More rigorous designs may not be feasible in many practice situations, and with enough repeated measures the AB design can provide some logical and empirical evidence concerning the effectiveness of interventions for which the impact on clients has not yet received enough scientific testing. Also, AB designs can be replicated, and if the results of various AB studies on the same intervention are consistent, then the evidence about the effectiveness of the intervention is strengthened. For instance, suppose several AB studies at different times and with different clients all find that the same type of target problem only begins to improve shortly after the same intervention is introduced. How credible is the argument that with every client an extraneous event could have coincided only with the onset of intervention and caused the improvement? AB designs are also useful in that they provide immediate feedback to practitioners that enables them to monitor variations in the target problem, explore with the client alternative explanations of changes, and modify service delivery if the need for modification is indicated by this information.

ABAB: Withdrawal/Reversal Design

To better control for extraneous events, the ABAB design adds a second baseline phase (A) and a second intervention phase (B). The second baseline phase is established by withdrawing the intervention for a while. After a stable trend is identified in the second baseline, the intervention is reintroduced. This design assumes that if the intervention caused the improvement in the target problem during the first intervention period, then the target problem will reverse toward its original baseline level during the second baseline (after the intervention is withdrawn). When the intervention is reintroduced, the target problem should start improving again. The basic inferential principle here is that if shifts in the trend or level of the target problem occur successively each time the intervention is introduced or withdrawn, then it is not plausible that some extraneous event and not the intervention is causing the change. Because the independent variable is changed

three times, there is more causal evidence than in the AB design. In other words, the number of unlikely successive coincidences that would have to occur in an ABAB design is three, as compared to one in the AB design.

There are two major problems with the ABAB design, problems that often can be resolved. One is a practical or ethical problem. Practitioners may feel that withdrawing an intervention that appears to be working is indefensible in light of the suffering or other costs the client may bear if conditions revert back to baseline. These concerns would be intensified with clients with dangerous problems or those particularly sensitive to setbacks. Practitioners may fear that withdrawal of the intervention would confuse or alienate the client and would perhaps hurt the practitioner-client relationship or in other ways impede future efforts when the intervention is reintroduced. These are important and valid concerns, and researchers should not fault practitioners who resist implementing ABAB designs because of these concerns.

But practitioners should not underestimate the opportunities they have for implementing ABAB designs without compromising intervention priorities. Occasionally there are natural breaks in the intervention phase when the practitioner attends a conference or takes a vacation, and these periods can be exploited to establish a second baseline (provided that the practitioner is not the only one observing and recording the extent of the target problem). Also, it is often consistent with good practice to withdraw an intervention temporarily at a point at which the target problem appears to have been overcome and then monitor whether the client can sustain his or her gains during the hiatus of treatment.

The other major, but potentially resolvable, problem with ABAB designs is that the assumption that the target problem can revert to baseline conditions may not be valid in many practice situations. Perhaps an intervention has had irreversible effects during the first intervention period. For instance, suppose the intervention involved social skills training, perhaps training individuals with mild developmental disabilities to interact at social gatherings or in the workplace. Once these skills are learned and the individuals are rewarded in the natural environment for using them, they may not need training to be reintroduced in order to sustain the gains they have made. Or suppose the intervention was to help an elderly woman become less isolated, lonely, and depressed. Suppose further that the intervention was environmentally oriented and focused on securing a better residence for her, one where she would be among peers with whom she could easily interact and become friends. If this intervention succeeded during the first B period, is it reasonable to suppose that she would lose her new friends or become depressed again because the practitioner withdrew the intervention (that is, efforts to change her environment, not the new residence)?

To reduce the chances that effects will be irreversible, in some situations we might want to keep the first intervention period relatively short. Then, as soon as the second baseline shows a trend toward reversal, we could reintroduce the intervention and hope to reestablish the improving trend that was briefly interrupted during the second baseline. Irreversible effects also may be less problematic if, despite the failure to obtain a reversal during the second baseline, we observed a new, improving trend during the second intervention period. Suppose, for example, that in the case of the depressed and lonely elderly woman we reintroduce the environmentally oriented intervention by getting her a pet and that this further alleviates her depression. This possibility is illustrated in Figure 10-8, in which we see a shift in the dependent variable each time intervention is introduced, but maintenance of the first intervention's gains occurs during the second baseline. Despite the absence of a reversal during the second baseline, the data's overall pattern would support the conclusion that it is the intervention and not some extraneous variable that accounts for the improvement and that the intervention's

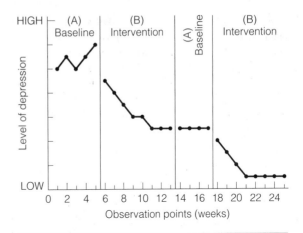

Figure 10-8 Graph of Hypothetical Outcome of ABAB Design Supporting Intervention Efficacy Despite Failure to Obtain a Reversal During Second Baseline

effects simply do not tend to reverse when the intervention is withdrawn.

But what do we conclude when the results of the ABAB design resemble those in Figure 10-9? Was the improvement that occurred only after the first introduction of the intervention caused by some extraneous event that happened to coincide with the introduction of the intervention? In other words, should we refrain from attributing the improvement to the effects of the intervention because no other changes occurred in the target problem the next two times the intervention was introduced or withdrawn? Or can we speculate that perhaps the intervention was so effective, or the nature of the target problem so irreversible, that only one shift in the trend or level of the target problem (that is, the shift at the onset of the first intervention phase) was possible? Depending on the nature of the target problem and what we learn from the client about extraneous events coinciding with changes in the design phases, it may be possible in some cases to decide which of these rival explanations seems to be the most plausible. But perhaps an even better way to resolve this dilemma is through replication. If results like those depicted in Figure 10-9 tend to be obtained consistently in future ABAB experiments on the same intervention, then the case for powerful or irreversible effects would be strengthened because there is no rational reason why extraneous events that cause shifts in the target problem should occur with every client only at those points at which intervention is first introduced.

Multiple-Baseline Designs

Multiple-baseline designs also attempt to control for extraneous variables by having more than one baseline and intervention phase. But instead of withdrawing the intervention to establish more than one baseline, multiple-baseline designs begin two or more baselines simultaneously. This is done by measuring different target behaviors in each baseline or by measuring the same target behavior in two different settings or across two different individuals. Although each baseline starts simultaneously, the intervention is introduced at a different point for each one. Thus, as the intervention is introduced for the first behavior, set-

ting, or individual, the others are still in their baseline phases. Likewise, when the intervention is introduced for the second behavior, setting, or individual, the third (if there are more than two) is still in its baseline phase.

The main logical principle here is that if some extraneous event, such as a significant improvement in the environment, coincides with the onset of intervention and causes the client's improved functioning, then that improvement will show up in the graph of each behavior, setting, or individual at the same time, even though some might still be in baseline. On the other hand, if the intervention is accountable for the improvement, then that improvement will occur on each graph at a different point that corresponds to the introduction of the intervention.

Figure 10-10 illustrates a hypothetical multiple-baseline design across three nursing home residents who feel an extreme sense of hopelessness. In this hypothetical illustration, the practitioner read a report of a group experiment by Mercer and Kane (1979), the findings of which supported the efficacy of reducing hopelessness in residents like these by giving them a houseplant to take care of. The practitioner begins taking baseline measures of hopelessness via a self-report scale for each resident at the same time. But he or she gives each resident a houseplant, along with instructions about caring for it, at three different times. Each resident's level of hopelessness, as reflected in the self-report scores, begins to decrease steadily only after the intervention is introduced. Therefore, it is not reasonable to suppose that some extraneous event, such as some other improvement in the overall environment of the nursing home, really caused the change.

But suppose the results looked like those in Figure 10-11. In Figure 10-11 we see that the steady improvement in hopelessness commenced for each resident at the same time that the first intervention (houseplant) was introduced. It is not plausible to infer that the plant was causing the improvement because two of the residents had not yet received theirs. Instead, it is more plausi-

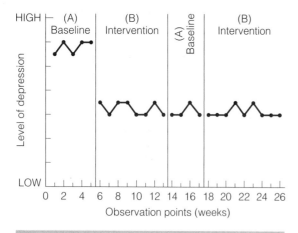

Figure 10-9 Graph of Hypothetical Outcome of ABAB Design with Unclear Results

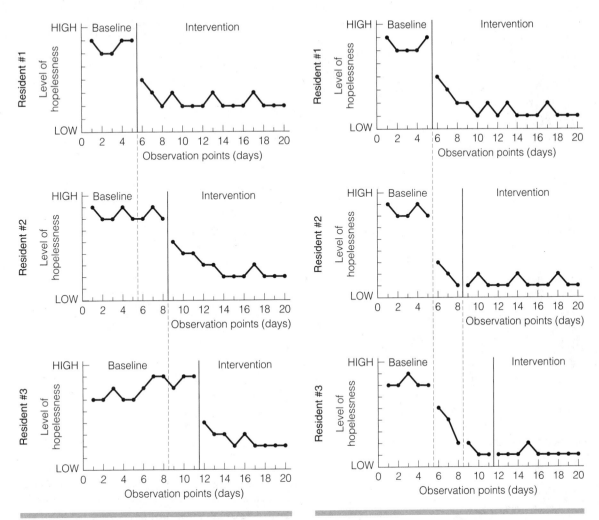

Figure 10-10 Graph of Hypothetical Outcome of Multiple Baseline Design Across Subjects Supporting Efficacy of Intervention

Figure 10-11 Graph of Hypothetical Outcome of Multiple-Baseline Design Across Subjects Illustrating Extraneous Variable as Plausible Cause of Improvement

ble to suppose that some extraneous improvement in the broader nursing home environment coincided with the onset of the intervention with the first resident and caused the improvement in all three. This illustrates how an AB design (with the first resident) could yield misleading findings due to its weaker control for history than occurs in multiple-baseline designs.

Figures 10-12 and 10-13 illustrate the same logical principles with multiple-baseline designs across target behaviors or settings. Both figures refer to a hypothetical case involving a boy referred to a residential treatment center because of his antisocial behaviors. There he participates in a cognitive-behavior modification intervention like the one reported by Taber (1981) that includes teaching him how to say things to himself to help stop himself from committing explosive, antisocial behaviors in situations in which he has been most vulnerable to losing control. In Figure 10-12, the first baseline ends and intervention begins as the client starts to rehearse the verbal self-instructions in connection to fighting. One week later he begins to rehearse in connection to impulsive, inappropriate shouting. The following week he starts rehearsing in connection to swearing.

The graphs in Figure 10-12 show that once the client begins rehearsing for fighting, a dramatic shift in the data pattern occurs for all three target behaviors at the same time. What caused this? Was it an extraneous event in the residential facility that happened to coincide with the end of the first baseline? Perhaps. But when multiple baselines are applied across different behaviors, a data pattern like this could also be caused by a rival explanation. This rival explanation is termed **generalization of effects.** Generalization of effects occurs when an intervention, although intended to apply to only one behavior or setting at a time, affects other target behaviors or settings that are still in the baseline phase as soon as it is applied to the first behavior or setting. In the current illustration, for instance, the rehearsals regarding fighting perhaps helped the boy simultaneously apply the verbal self-instructions to other behaviors that he knew got him into trouble.

Another way that generalization of effects could occur is when the intervention affects only one of the target behaviors, but the change in that behavior in turn changes the other behaviors. In the preceding illustration, for example, it is conceivable that the reduction in fighting gave the boy less to shout and swear about. The reduction in fighting also could have led to more positive feedback from peers and adults, and this improvement in his interpersonal relations (or the rewarding nature of the feedback) could have reduced his need to swear and shout or increased his desire to act appropriately.

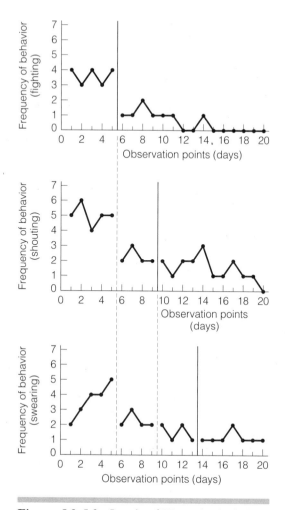

Figure 10-12 Graph of Hypothetical Outcome of Multiple Baseline Design Across Target Behaviors, with Unclear Results

The same sort of ambiguity in the data pattern appears in Figure 10-13. Here the three baselines end as the boy rehearses the verbal self-instructions across three different settings. At the end of the first baseline he rehearses in connection to school. At the end of the second he rehearses in connection to the cottage. At the end of the third he rehearses in connection to recreational activities. As

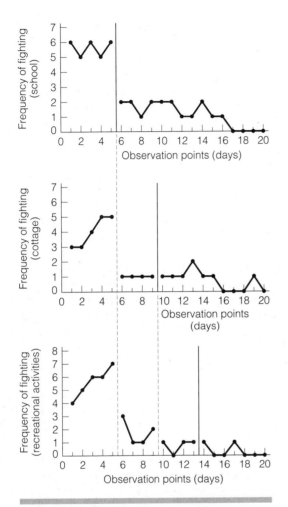

Figure 10-13 Graph of Hypothetical Outcome of Multiple-Baseline Design Across Settings, with Unclear Results

in Figure 10-12, we do not know whether the simultaneous improvement in all three settings at the end of the first baseline was due to an extraneous event or to generalization of effects.

How do we decide which rival explanation, history or generalization of effects, is the more plausible? We may be unable to do so. But, if it is feasible, we might try to replicate the experiment

with other clients. If we continue to get results like those in Figures 10-12 and 10-13, the generalization of effects hypothesis becomes more plausible, because it is not reasonable to suppose that some extraneous event would cause improvement in the target problem only at the point where the first baseline ends when clients were treated at different times.

But with some interventions it is difficult to conceive how they possibly could be applied to different behaviors or settings at different times. Suppose, for example, that the intervention involves family systems therapy in a case in which a child's poor functioning in various areas is theoretically thought to stem from problems in the parents' relationship with each other. If the practitioner seeks to resolve the target problem in the child by focusing intervention on the parental relationship, it may not be realistic to try apply the intervention to different behaviors or settings regarding the child. Moreover, to do so might be deemed clinically inappropriate because it would continue to focus the intervention on the child.

Multiple-Component Designs

Several designs can be used to analyze the impact of changes in the intervention. These designs are appropriate when we decide to modify an intervention that does not appear to be helping the client or when we seek to determine which parts of an intervention package really account for the change in the target problem. One such design is called the *changing intensity design*. This design includes several phases of the same intervention, but in each phase either the amount of intervention or the level of performance expected of the client is increased. The symbol for this design is $AB^1B^2B^3$. As a hypothetical illustration of this design, suppose a chronically mentally disabled individual is unable to maintain steady employment. The intervention package might include two components that are applied simultaneously: (1) social skills training to prepare him for job interviews and appropriate on-the-job behavior and (2) a reward for each real job interview he undergoes or each week he keeps his job. If during B^1 (the first intervention phase) an inadequate degree of improvement is observed, the amount of time the client spends in social skills training might be increased or the reward system might be intensified. When these changes are implemented, the second intervention phase, B^2, would commence. Suppose B^2 results in increased improvement, but at a level that still is not acceptable. A third intervention phase, B^3, might be initiated and might involve increasing the number of job interviews or the duration of employment expected of the client in order to earn the reward.

Consider the same client, and suppose that instead of introducing the social skills training and reinforcement schedules simultaneously, they were introduced separately. Suppose the social skills training was introduced first but yielded no improvement and that, in light of the lack of improvement, that intervention was terminated and the reinforcement schedule was tested in its place. So far we would have an ABC design, in which B was the social skills training phase and C was the reinforcement phase. Suppose there still was no improvement, so a case advocacy phase was initiated to investigate the possibility that we may need to convince prospective employers to consider hiring or be more tolerant of individuals whose illnesses impede their job-seeking skills or their on-the-job behavior. The case advocacy phase, then, would add a fourth component to the design and we would have an ABCD design.

The preceding two designs are flexible; they allow practitioners to change intervention plans as warranted by the data patterns observed in each successive phase. But they must be used cautiously due to limitations associated with *carry-over effects, order effects,* and *history.* Suppose that in the ABCD illustration a sustained pattern of improvement was obtained only during the D (case advocacy) phase as illustrated in Figure 10-14. It would be risky to conclude that for future

clients like this one all we needed to do was to provide the case advocacy and not the other two interventions. It is plausible that had we changed the D phase to the B phase for this client, we may not have had the same, positive results. Perhaps the client's social skills improved during the original B phase but those skills were insufficient in helping him stay employed because employers were either unwilling to risk hiring someone with a history of mental illness or because they were unwilling to tolerate any deviance whatsoever from any employees. It is conceivable that only with the addition of the case advocacy during the D phase did the improvement in social skills matter. Perhaps the case advocacy would have had no impact had it not been preceded by helping the client attain a level of social functioning that prospective employers could be convinced to tolerate. In other words, the case advocacy might not have worked without the order effects (that is, in coming after the social skills training, not before it) and the carry-over effects of the social skills training on the case advocacy efforts. And with respect to the limitation of history, we must recognize that as we continue to substitute new interventions for those whose data patterns do not adequately differ from baseline, we increase the odds that one of those substitutions eventually will coincide with an extraneous improvement in the client's environment.

One way to sort out the above possibilities would be to replicate the interventions with future clients, introducing them in a different sequence while measuring outcome in the same way. Ultimately, we might find that the intervention that was originally in the D phase produced the desired results only when it was introduced after the interventions in the original B or C phase.

Another option would be to start out with a more complex multiple component design that attempts, in advance, to control for the above limitations. There are a variety of such designs. Because their complexity limits their applicability to real social work practice settings, they will be

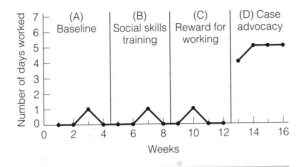

Figure 10-14 Graph of Hypothetical Outcome of Multiple-Component (ABCD) Design, with Unclear Results

mentioned only briefly here. One is the "construction design," A-B-A-C-A-BC-( ), in which the A phases represent baselines and the BC phase combines the B and C interventions. The phase indicated by the parentheses refers to the intervention or combination of interventions that appears to be most effective and is ultimately chosen. Another is the "strip design," A-BC-A-B-A-C-( ), which is like the construction design but in which the combined intervention (BC) is introduced first. Other possibilities include the "alternating intervention design," A-Randomized Alternation of B & C-(B or C), and the "interaction design," A-B-A-B-BC-B-BC. We recommend the following texts that deal exclusively with single-subject designs to readers who wish to pursue these complex designs in depth: Barlow and Hersen (1984), Bloom, Fischer and Orme (1995), and Jayaratne and Levy (1979).

DATA ANALYSIS

In analyzing the results of single-subject experiments, we ask the following three questions:

1. Is there a *visual* pattern in the graph(s) depicting a series of coincidences in which the level or trend of the target problem changes only after the intervention is introduced or withdrawn?

2. What is the *statistical* probability that the data observed during the intervention phase(s) merely are part of the normal, chance fluctuations in the target problem, fluctuations that we could have expected to occur had the baseline been extended and intervention not introduced?

3. If change in the target problem is associated with the tested intervention, is the amount of change important from a *substantive,* or *clinical,* standpoint?

These three questions refer to the visual, statistical, and substantive significance of the findings.

When we analyzed the meanings of each of the graphs illustrated in Figures 10-1 through 10-14, we dealt with *visual significance.* Visual significance is ascertained, not through the use of fancy statistics, but merely by "eyeballing" the data pattern, as the term "visual" implies. To the extent that we can see that shifts in the target problem either do not occur when intervention is introduced or occur just as often at other times, there is less visual significance. That is, in those instances there is less visual evidence for supposing that the intervention is affecting the target problem. To the extent that shifts in the level or trend of the target problem tend to coincide only with shifts in the independent variable (that is, with movement from one phase to another), then there is more visual significance and thus more logical support for supposing that the intervention is affecting the target problem.

Sometimes our visual analysis of the data will obviate the need for statistical analysis, particularly when the degree of visual significance (or lack thereof) is dramatic. Indeed, some single-subject methodologists cite evidence suggesting that when experienced researchers judge whether an outcome is visually significant, their conclusions are usually supported by subsequent statistical analyses (Jayaratne, Tripodi, and Talsma, 1988). Practitioners who tend to be immobilized by their anxiety about statistics, therefore, can implement single-subject designs in the hope that their visual analysis of the data will be sufficient.

There are times, however, when the changes in the level or trend of the target problem from one phase to the next are subtle or when we are not sure whether our visual analysis of the data is being influenced by our desire to see a favorable outcome. At these times it is helpful to augment our visual analysis with a statistical one.

Statistical and substantive significance mean the same thing in single-subject designs as they do in other sorts of research, and they will be discussed in depth, in connection to group designs, in Chapters 16 and 17. Alternative procedures for estimating statistical significance in single-subject design research will be covered in Appendix I. We recommend that you examine Appendix I after you read Chapters 16 and 17; however, if you already have a basic familiarity with the concepts of statistical and substantive significance, you may want to read Appendix I as soon as you finish this chapter.

Interpreting Ambiguous Results

Most of this chapter has used illustrations involving clearcut hypothetical data patterns to simplify conveying the logic of single-subject research regarding the differentiation of results that are visually significant from results that are not visually significant. Unfortunately, however, single-subject studies in the real world often obtain ambiguous results that are more difficult to interpret. Consider, for example, Figure 10-15, which shows the results from a study by Rubin (1991).

The data in Figure 10-15 were collected from a battered woman participating in an intervention geared to helping battered women live independently from their batterers. The data refer to thoughts, feelings, and behaviors associated with feeling better about oneself and doing things to become more independent. An increase in scores during the intervention phase, therefore, would indicate a desirable outcome.

As you can see, the data in the graph reveal a somewhat unstable baseline, followed by eleven days of intervention without any improvement in

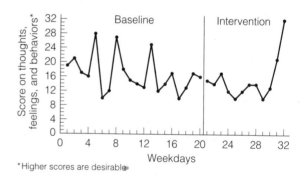

*Higher scores are desirable

SOURCE: Allen Rubin, "The Effectiveness of Outreach Counseling and Support Groups for Battered Women: A Preliminary Evaluation," *Research on Social Work Practice,* 1 (4), October 1991, p. 349. Reprinted by permission of Sage Publications, Inc.

Figure 10-15 Graph of Outcome of Group Treatment of a Battered Woman

scores, and then two days of dramatic improvement at the end of the study. (This case was part of a larger study involving additional clients, and feasibility constraints required that the data collection for this woman end after her 32nd data point.)

How would you interpret this graph? Do you think it reflects visual significance? One can be tempted to perceive visual significance in this graph, particularly if one is affiliated with the agency and wants the intervention to succeed. One might focus on the dramatic improvement toward the end of the baseline phase and argue that although it took a while before the intervention started having an effect, it eventually worked. One might further argue that this woman may have been denying her situation and that it therefore stands to reason that the intervention effects would not occur immediately at the onset of treatment. This argument is not unreasonable. Indeed, those taking a psychosocial approach to practice might not expect most clients to begin showing improvement on outcome indicators until intervention has been ongoing for quite a long time, due to such factors as resistance, denial, and so on.

We believe, however, that a more compelling argument can be made against perceiving visual significance in this graph, based on two major points. First, the increase in the scores at the end of the intervention period could be nothing more than a random, or perhaps cyclical, temporary blip up—just as there were a few blips up during the unstable baseline. We do not know how short lived the improvement will be. Second, even if the improvement is permanent, the fact that it did not occur sooner during intervention increases the plausibility that it could be due to history.

When we argue that this graph is not visually significant, we do not mean to imply that it shows that the intervention could not have caused the improvement—merely that this graph does not provide enough evidence to deem alternative explanations (such as history, and so on) much less plausible than the conclusion that the intervention did cause the improvement. We believe that it is possible that it simply took a while before the effects of the intervention began to be reflected in the outcome scores. However, saying that this is possible is a far cry from saying that the graph reflects in a visually significant way that this indeed is the most plausible explanation. In other words, saying that a graph is not visually significant does not mean that its interpretation is unambiguously negative. In this case, we believe the interpretation is ambiguous, and that in light of that ambiguity the graph lacks visual significance.

The foregoing example illustrates the ambiguity that can occur when intervention goes on for quite a while before any noticeable improvement occurs in the target problem. Sometimes, however, improvement in the target problem coincides nicely with the onset of the intervention, but then reverses sharply during the last data point or two. If the intervention and monitoring cannot be continued, it may be difficult to determine whether the intervention was effective. Perhaps the undesirable data points at the end of the intervention period indicate that the temporary improvement was due merely to a honeymoon period or to extraneous factors that coincided with the onset of the intervention. On the other hand, perhaps the undesirable data points at the end of the intervention period are themselves merely a result of extraneous forces causing a temporary blip in the context of meaningful, sustainable intervention effects. Ambiguous results can occur in many other ways, as well, particularly when there is instability in the data during baseline and/or during the intervention phase.

Aggregating the Results of Single-Subject Research Studies

At several points in this chapter we noted that the interpretation of ambiguous data patterns in single-subject research can be enhanced through the replication process. If, for example, improvement occurs late in the intervention phase of one study, we cannot rule out history as a plausible explanation. But if improvement occurs roughly at the same late point consistently across studies, it seems more plausible to argue that the intervention takes a while before showing desired effects than to argue that extraneous events are causing the improvement across different clients who begin intervention at different times. The same logic holds when we don't know whether the data pattern reflects irreversible intervention effects in an ABAB study or the generalization of effects in a multiple baseline study.

Above and beyond facilitating the interpretation of ambiguous data, replication can serve two additional important purposes in single-subject research. One of these purposes is to reduce doubt about the external validity of our findings. The more we can replicate a particular type of outcome across different clients, settings, and practitioners, the more confidence we develop (inductively) in our ability to generalize that outcome. The other purpose is to evaluate an entire service program. If, for example, an agency conducts a single-subject evaluation on a reasonably representative sample of its clients (such as every fifth client entering treatment during a particular time period), then it can assess its overall agency effectiveness by aggregating the results of each individual evaluation.

When we want to aggregate the results of various individual studies, either for the purpose of dealing with ambiguous findings or for the purpose of generalizing about the effectiveness of an intervention or an agency, we need a mechanism for making sense out of the variations in outcome from study to study. One such mechanism is to report the proportion of studies that had each type of outcome in which we are interested. For example, we would want to know the proportion of outcomes that were and were not visually significant, and we might want to know the proportion of studies with the same type of ambiguous data pattern. Thus, we might be able to say that an effective intervention was delivered in, say, 60% of our agency's cases. Or we might be able to say that in, say, 70% of our replications, a data pattern was found suggesting delayed intervention effects.

One problem here is the absence of systematic guidelines as to what specific percentages represent cutoff points regarding alternative interpretations. Should an agency, for example, be happy with a 50% effectiveness rate? A lower rate? Or is a higher effectiveness rate needed before it can claim to be effective in an overall, aggregated sense as a program? If a practitioner replicates an AB study across 10 clients and obtains visually significant results three times, should he or she conclude that the intervention was effective with three cases, or should the practitioner wonder whether some other factor (such as history) accounts for the data pattern in those three cases, since the visual significance was not replicated in the remaining seven cases? As the field of single-subject research matures, perhaps such guidelines will be developed. For now, however, there may be some value in merely describing the proportion of various outcomes being obtained in connection to a particular intervention, practitioner, or agency. As those outcomes accumulate, one can inductively look for patterns that might suggest hypotheses as to the conditions under which a particular practitioner, intervention, or agency is successful. This accumulation might also establish effectiveness rate norms to which the results of future aggregated evaluations can be compared.

In closing this chapter, we would like to note that the process of aggregating the results of single-subject studies illustrates how this type of research has the potential to go well beyond idiosyncratically evaluating intervention with a "single subject." Although we have identified a variety of feasibility problems in carrying out single-subject research, and we certainly do not see it as a panacea that everyone can use when other designs are not feasible, we hope that you will consider applying what you have learned in this chapter throughout your career as a professional social worker.

The Role of Qualitative Research Methods in Single-Case Evaluation

In Chapter 9 we saw that qualitative research methods can make valuable contributions when incorporated with quantitative methods in experimental and quasi-experimental designs. The same is true of single-subject designs, which are generally considered quantitative. One way qualitative methods can be helpful is in interpreting ambiguous quantitative results. When instability occurs at a particular point in the data pattern, for instance, we can employ qualitative interviews with the client and significant others to try to learn whether important extraneous events in the client's social environment coincided with the instability. If they did, we might be more inclined to attribute certain changes in the graphed data to extraneous forces, rather than consider them reflections of the effectiveness or ineffectiveness of the intervention. If qualitative interviewing fails to identify any extra-

QUALITATIVE METHODS FOR
SINGLE-CASE EVALUATION

As we did for group designs in the previous chapter, in this box we will list some prominent qualitative methods and the important functions they can serve in single-subject design evaluation studies. You can read more about these qualitative methods in Chapters 12 and 13.

Qualitative Method	Functions in Single-Case Evaluation
Informal conversational interviews with clients or significant others	• Identify extraneous events or forces connected with changes in the graphed data
	• Assess target problem and develop measurement and intervention plan
	• Assess what parts of the intervention client perceives to be most helpful and why
	• Corroborate the improvement (or lack thereof) self-reported or self-monitored by the client or by the significant other
Videotaping or audiotaping practitioner-client sessions	• Assess the fidelity of the intervention (Is it being implemented in a skillful manner, as intended?)
Event logs completed by client or significant others	• Assess where and when target problems occur and the circumstances that mediate it
	• Identify extraneous events occurring during baseline or intervention phases that might be helpful in interpreting whether changes that occur in the quantitative data are attributable to the intervention

neous forces that may explain the changes observed in the graph, the notion that those changes represent intervention effects becomes more plausible.

Another important role for qualitative interviewing in single-case evaluation is in assessment. Qualitative interviews with the client and with significant others can improve our understanding of the target problem, how to measure it, and how best to intervene. Qualitative interviews with significant others can be used to corroborate the improvement (or lack thereof) self-reported or self-monitored by the client. Qualitative interviews can also assess what parts of the intervention clients perceive to be most helpful and why. As we will see in Chapter 12, interviewing is not the only qualitative method useful in single-case evaluation.

Event logs completed by clients or their significant others also can be quite helpful in assessing where and when target problems occur and the circumstances that mediate it. Event logs can also help identify extraneous events occurring during baseline or intervention phases that might be helpful in interpreting whether changes that occur in the quantitative data are attributable to the intervention. The utility of qualitative methods as part of single-subject designs is summarized in the accompanying box titled "Qualitative Methods for Single-Case Evaluation."

Main Points

• Any target problem on which a practitioner would choose to focus can be defined in operational terms and then measured. If it could not be, then the practitioner would have had no basis for observing that it was an important problem in the first place.

• Taking many repeated measures and identifying stable trends in the data enhances the internal validity of single-subject designs by facilitating control for extraneous factors that affect the target problem.

• Baselines are control phases of repeated measures taken before an intervention is introduced. Baselines ideally should be extended until a stable trend in the data is evident.

• Including more than one baseline and intervention phase in a single-subject experiment strengthens the control of history through the principle of unlikely successive coincidences. This is done in ABAB designs and multiple-baseline designs.

• AB designs have the weakest control for history, but they are the most feasible designs and can provide useful information.

• When using designs with more phases than the AB design, caution needs to be exercised regarding possible carry-over effects, order effects, generalizability of effects, and the irreversibility of effects.

• The prime weakness of single-subject designs is their limited external validity. With a sample of one we are dealing with idiosyncratic conditions that cannot be generalized to other clients, practitioners, or settings. But this problem can be alleviated through replication.

• Single-subject designs can be used by practitioners to more scientifically and systematically monitor client progress or their own effectiveness.

• Single-subject designs have special measurement problems. Triangulating measures is therefore recommended. This means simultaneously using more than one imperfect measurement option.

• Special caution needs to be exercised in single-subject designs with regard to the measurement problems of reactivity, obtrusiveness, and social desirability bias.

• Single-subject design data should always be analyzed for their visual and practical significance.

• The visual as well as statistical results of single-subject research can be ambiguous; the replication process can help in resolving this ambiguity.

• The results of various single-subject studies can be aggregated by calculating the proportion of studies with specific types of outcomes.

Review Questions and Exercises

1. Select some aspect of your own behavior that you would like to improve (for example, smoke less, eat less, exercise more, study more, and so on) and develop a plan to improve it. Conduct a single-subject experiment and analyze the data to see if your plan is effective. Try to be aware of the degree to which you experience the measurement problems of reactivity and bias.

2. Think of a particular case or intervention that has piqued your curiosity about practice effectiveness. Design a single-subject experiment relevant to that case or intervention. Try to design it in a way that would be feasible to implement.

Additional Readings

Bloom, Martin, Fischer, Joel, and Orme, John G., *Evaluating Practice: Guidelines for the Accountable Professional*, 2nd ed. (Boston: Allyn and Bacon, 1995). This excellent, comprehensive text is an invaluable reference guide for social workers who plan to implement single-subject designs as a regular part of their practice. All important aspects of single-subject designs and ways to combine the roles of practitioner and researcher are covered in depth, and students often report that they learn a great deal about practice per se in this unique book.

Barlow, David H., and Hersen, Michael, *Single-Case Experimental Designs: Strategies for Studying Behavioral Change* (New York: Pergamon Press, 1984). This is an excellent and thorough text written from a more technical perspective than the Bloom and Fischer text. It is one of the most widely cited texts on single-subject designs.

Jayaratne, Srinika, and Levy, Rona L., *Empirical Clinical Practice* (New York: Columbia University Press, 1979). Here is a user-friendly introduction to scientifically based practice. It covers single-subject designs from the perspective of clinical practice and provides a step-by-step outline for incorporating them in practice. Reprints and critiques of published single-subject research studies help readers integrate the text.

PART

4

Quantitative and Qualitative Modes of Observation

11
Survey Research

12
Qualitative Research Methods

13
Unobtrusive Research: Quantitative and Qualitative Methods

The term *research design* refers to all of the decisions made about how a research study is to be conducted. In Part 3 we discussed the logic of research design. We saw in that section that research designs can be classified according to the logical arrangements that bear upon our ability to draw causal inferences from our research findings. Thus, for example, we can use experimental designs, quasi-experimental designs, preexperimental designs, cross-sectional designs, and so forth. Earlier, we noted that research designs can also be classified according to their purpose. Thus we distinguished among exploratory, descriptive, and explanatory designs. In Part 4, we'll look at yet another way research designs can be classified—according to the modes of observation they use.

Chapter 11 will describe survey research, one of the most popular research methods in social work. As we'll see, this type of research involves collecting data through asking people questions—either in self-administered questionnaires or through interviews.

Chapter 12 on qualitative research examines what is perhaps the most natural form of data collection used by social scientists: the direct observation of social phenomena in natural settings, which is also called field research. As we shall see, some field researchers go beyond mere observation to participate in what they are studying so as to get a more intimate view and fuller understanding.

Chapter 13 discusses three forms of unobtrusive data collection that take advantage of some of the data available all around us. Content analysis is a method of collecting social data through carefully specifying and counting social artifacts such as books, songs, speeches, and paintings. Without making any personal contact with people, you can use this method to examine a wide variety of social phenomena. The analysis of existing statistics offers another way of studying people without having to talk to them. Governments and a variety of private organizations regularly compile great masses of data, and these data can often be used with little or no modification to answer properly posed questions. Finally, historical documents are a valuable resource for social scientific analysis.

Before we turn to the actual descriptions of the several methods, two points should be made. First, you will probably discover you have been using these scientific methods quite casually in your daily life for as long as you can remember. You use some form of field research every day. You are using a crude form of content analysis every time you judge an author's motivation or orientation from his or her writings. You engage in at least casual experiments frequently. The chapters in Part 4 will show you how to improve your use of these methods so as to avoid the pitfalls of casual, uncontrolled observation.

Second, none of the data collection methods described in the following chapters is appropriate to all research topics and situations. We have tried to give you some ideas, early in each chapter, of when a given method might be appropriate. Still, it would not be possible to anticipate all the possible research topics that may one day interest you. As a general guideline, it is always best to use a variety of techniques in the study of any topic. Because each method has its weaknesses, the use of several methods can help fill in any gaps, and if the different, independent approaches to the topic all yield the same conclusion, that can constitute a form of replication.

Survey Research

What You'll Learn in This Chapter

Here you'll learn how to do mail, interview, and
telephone surveys. You'll need to recall the earlier
discussions of sampling and question wording.

INTRODUCTION

Survey research is a very old research technique. In the Old Testament, for example, we find:

> After the plague the Lord said to Moses and to Eleazar the son of Aaron, the priest, "Take a census of all the congregation of the people of Israel, from twenty old and upward. . . ."   (NUMBERS 26:1–2)

Ancient Egyptian rulers conducted censuses for the purpose of administering their domains. Jesus was born away from home because Joseph and Mary were journeying to Joseph's ancestral home for a Roman census.

A little-known survey was attempted among French workers in 1880. A German political sociologist mailed some 25,000 questionnaires to workers to determine the extent of their exploitation by employers. The lengthy questionnaire included items such as these:

> Does your employer or his representative resort to trickery in order to defraud you of a part of your earnings?
>
> If you are paid piece rates, is the quality of the article made a pretext for fraudulent deductions from your wages?

The survey researcher in this case was not George Gallup but Karl Marx (1880:208). Though 25,000 questionnaires were mailed out, there is no record of any being returned.

Tom Smith (1988) has traced the history of American political polling back to within 50 years of the nation's founding.

> Proto-straw polls appeared in the presidential election of 1824. These precursors to modern election polls originated out of a combination of short-term political changes associated with the end of the first American party system in general and the demise of the congressional caucus system of nomination in particular and long-term developments associated with growing democratization, centralization, and quantification.   (1988:21)

The precursors to surveys in social work were conducted in Europe in the mid-19th century. They focused on the earnings and expenditures of the working poor. Some were conducted to determine appropriate levels of relief grants; others were done to provide evidence for social reform. A prominent influence on the early use of surveys in social work was Charles Booth, a wealthy and politically conservative London shipowner who set out in 1886 to disprove claims by Marxists that one-fourth of the working class lived in severe poverty. Using his own money to fund the research, Booth and his assistants surveyed East London residents about many socioeconomic forces bearing upon their lives. It took 17 volumes, called *The Life and Labour of the People of London* (1891–1903), to report the study. Ironically, instead of disproving the Marxists' claims, Booth concluded that they had underestimated the proportion of people living in poverty. Booth even recommended some social welfare measures that he termed *limited socialism*.

Booth's work coincided with the emergence of early social reform efforts in the social work profession. As the 20th century began, muckraking journalists and novelists spurred public interest in surveys like Booth's, surveys that would document the muckraker's depictions of urban squalor and exploitation. The most famous of the social surveys to follow was called the *Pittsburgh Survey*, conducted from 1909 to 1914 by social workers and civic leaders to assess social conditions in Pittsburgh. Published in several volumes, the Pittsburgh survey exposed the deplorable social conditions in the city and helped stimulate major social reforms.

The Pittsburgh Survey's success demonstrated how survey methods can be used for social reform purposes and thus helped spark what was called "the Social Survey Movement" by social workers in cities throughout the United States. The surveys conducted as part of this "movement" were broad in scope, reporting vast amounts of data on industrial, economic, political, and social factors in one city at a time. The data were amassed for the purpose of arousing communities as to the need for social reform. In this connection, the surveys were often conducted and reported in a biased manner and began to be seen as propagandistic. By the 1920s, the credibility of these surveys was tarnished, and their popularity waned as the social reform era ended. But the movement had a lasting impact on the use of surveys in social work. It's early successes prompted social agencies to adopt narrower surveys, focusing on specialized agency concerns, as a regular function. Eventually, the utility of survey methods for a wide range of research purposes became recognized.

Today, survey research is perhaps the most frequently used mode of observation in the social sciences. You probably have been a **respondent** in a survey more than once, and it is quite possible that you have done a survey of your own. In a typical survey, the researcher selects a sample of respondents and administers a standardized questionnaire to them.

Several of the fundamental elements of survey research have already been covered in detail in this book, so you are already partially trained in this important research method. In Chapter 7, we examined the logic and techniques of questionnaire construction, so we won't repeat that in this chapter. Also, Chapter 8 has already covered the topic of sampling, referring most often to survey situations.

Given that you already know how to prepare a questionnaire and select a sample of people to answer it, this chapter will focus on the options available to you for the purpose of administering the questionnaire. How do you go about getting questionnaires answered? As you'll see, sometimes it's appropriate to have respondents complete questionnaires themselves, and other times it's more appropriate to have interviewers ask the questions and record the answers given. This latter technique can be used in face-to-face interviews or over the telephone. We'll examine all these possibilities and then compare their relative advantages and disadvantages.

The chapter concludes with a short discussion of **secondary analysis,** the analysis of survey data collected by someone else, perhaps for some purpose other than that of subsequent analyses. This use of survey results has become an important aspect of survey research in recent years, and it's especially useful for students and others with scarce research funds.

Let's begin by looking at the kinds of topics you could study using survey research.

TOPICS APPROPRIATE TO SURVEY RESEARCH

Surveys may be used for descriptive, explanatory, and exploratory purposes. They can be limited to one point in time, in cross-sectional surveys, or they can be repeated at different points in time, in longitudinal surveys. Surveys are chiefly used in studies that have individual people as the units of analysis. Although this method can be used for other units of analysis, such as groups or interactions, it is necessary that some individual persons are used as respondents or informants. Thus, it would be possible to undertake a survey in which divorces were the unit of analysis, but the survey questionnaire would need to be administered to the participants in the divorces (or to some other informants).

Survey research is probably the best method available to the social scientist interested in collecting original data for describing a population too large to observe directly. Careful probability sampling provides a group of respondents whose characteristics may be taken to reflect those of the larger population, and carefully constructed standardized questionnaires provide data in the same form from all respondents. The U.S. decennial **census** differs from surveys primarily in that all members of the U.S. population are studied rather than a sample. (The Census Bureau also conducts numerous sample surveys in addition to the decennial censuses.)

Surveys are also excellent vehicles for measuring attitudes and orientations in a large population. Public opinion polls—for example, Gallup, Harris, Roper, Yankelovich—are well-known examples of this use.

The popularity of public opinion polling—particularly political polling—has often made the research technique itself a subject of public discussion, as indicated in this sampling of newspaper headlines:

- "Polls' Divergence Puzzles Experts"
- "Why Trust the Polls?"
- "Networks Criticized on Polls"
- "First, You Take a Poll—Not Always"
- "Are Restraints Needed on Election Day Polls?"
- "Dilemma of Voter Polls: Suspense or Knowledge"
- "Pollsters Bicker on Why Landslide Caught Them"

Perhaps our favorite story in this genre appeared on May 20, 1985, in the *New York Times* under the headline "Pollsters Cite Surveys Indicating Confidence in Their Work." Adam Clymer began his report on the meetings of the American Association for Public Opinion Research this way:

> Two of the nation's leading polltakers say their surveys show that the public is pretty well satisfied with the accuracy and usefulness of public opinion polls. But as they discussed their findings with their colleagues, they sounded as if they did not trust their own results.

The public's opinion of public opinion research is further complicated by scientifically unsound "surveys" that nonetheless capture our attention because of the topics they cover and/or their "findings." A good recent example may be found in the "Hite Reports" on human sexuality. While enjoying considerable attention in the popular press, writer Shere Hite was roundly criticized by the research community for her data collection methods. For example, a 1987 Hite report was based on questionnaires completed by women around the country—but which women? Hite reported that she distributed some 100,000 questionnaires through various organizations, and around 4500 were returned.

Now 4500 and 100,000 are large numbers in the context of survey sampling. However, given Hite's research methods, her 4500 respondents didn't necessarily represent American women any more than the *Literary Digest*'s enormous 1936 sample represented the American electorate when their two million sample ballots indicated Alf Landon would bury FDR in a landslide.

For another recent example of a scientifically unsound "survey" we can cite a questionnaire that one of us received in the mail in September 1991. Perhaps you received it as well. It concerns an important topic: AIDS.

The cover letter accompanying the questionnaire informs the recipient that only *well-informed* people are being surveyed and the survey is being conducted by the American Foundation for AIDS Research. The letter goes on to inform the reader of the seriousness of the problem. The survey items on the questionnaire assess perceptions regarding whether the public adequately realizes the seriousness of the problem and needs more education about it, whether political leaders are providing enough funding to fight AIDS, and so on. Preceding most survey items is a paragraph providing information that could predispose the respondent to give certain responses desired by the surveyors. (The same kind of potentially biasing information is contained in the cover letter.)

For example, preceding an item asking whether respondents think the majority of Americans realize the seriousness of "this tragedy," is a paragraph informing respondents that the AIDS epidemic is a national emergency and citing figures indicating its rapid growth. Even if we agree that the surveyors are correct in their figures and in referring to the situation as a tragic epidemic and national emergency, we can criticize the soundness of their survey because prefacing their items with such statements probably encourages respondents to agree that we need to spend more money fighting AIDS and educating the public about it. In other words, they are fostering a *social desirability bias,* as we discussed in Chapter 6. This is in addition to a possible sampling bias, in surveying only "well-informed people."

To make matters worse, from a scientific standpoint at least, the questionnaire ends by asking respondents to contribute a charitable donation to their foundation and to enclose their check when they return the questionnaire. No matter how you feel about this foundation and the problem it is fighting, and even if you like this approach as a fundraising strategy for a noble cause, you should realize that this tactic probably discourages people from responding unless they are willing to contribute and that this tactic therefore probably stacks the deck toward receiving responses indicating the need to spend more on AIDS. Thus, from a scientific standpoint, the survey is unsound. (This example may also remind you of material discussed in Chapter 3, concerning the intentional use of biased research methods as a means to achieve humanitarian political aims.)

In short, there is a wide variation in the quality of survey research reported in the mass media, as well as in academic journals, and it's important to be able to separate the wheat from the chaff. This chapter has the purpose of assisting you in that task. Let's turn now to the three major methods for getting responses to questionnaires.

SELF-ADMINISTERED QUESTIONNAIRES

There are three main methods of administering survey questionnaires to a sample of respondents. This section will deal with the method in which respondents are asked to complete the questionnaires themselves—*self-administered* questionnaires—and the following sections will deal with

surveys that are administered by staff interviewers in face-to-face encounters or by telephone.

Although the mail survey is the typical method used in self-administered studies, there are several other common methods. In some cases, it may be appropriate to administer the questionnaire to a group of respondents gathered at the same place at the same time. A survey of students taking an introductory social work course might be conducted in this manner during class. High school students might be surveyed during homeroom period.

Some recent experimentation has been conducted with regard to the home delivery of questionnaires. A research worker delivers the questionnaire to the home of sample respondents and explains the study. Then the questionnaire is left for the respondent to complete, and the researcher picks it up later.

Home delivery and the mail can be used in combination as well. Questionnaires can be mailed to families, and then research workers visit homes to pick up the questionnaires and check them for completeness. In just the opposite method, questionnaires have been hand delivered by research workers with a request that the respondents mail the completed questionnaires to the research office.

On the whole, when a research worker either delivers the questionnaire, picks it up, or both, the completion rate seems higher than for straightforward mail surveys. Additional experimentation with this method is likely to point to other techniques for improving completion while reducing costs. Mail surveys are the typical form of self-administered survey, however, and the remainder of this section is devoted specifically to that type of study.

Mail Distribution and Return

The basic method for data collection through the mail has been transmittal of a questionnaire, accompanied by a letter of explanation and a self-addressed, stamped envelope for returning the questionnaire. You probably have received one or two in your lifetime. As a respondent, you are expected to complete the questionnaire, put it in the envelope, and return it. If, by any chance, you've received such a questionnaire and failed to return it, it would be extremely valuable for you to recall the reasons you had for not returning it—and keep those in mind any time you plan to send questionnaires to others. One big reason for not returning questionnaires is the complaint that it seems like too much trouble.

Anything you can do to make the job of completing and returning the questionnaire easier will improve your study. Imagine receiving a questionnaire that made no provisions for its return to the researcher. Suppose you had to (1) find an envelope, (2) write the address on it, (3) figure out how much postage it required, and (4) put the stamps on it. How likely is it that you would return the questionnaire?

To overcome this problem, researchers have developed a number of ways to make the return of questionnaires easier. One development is a *self-mailing* questionnaire, requiring no return envelope. The questionnaire is designed so that when it is folded in a particular fashion, the return address appears on the outside. That way, the respondent doesn't have to worry about losing the envelope.

A few brief comments are in order here on the postal options available to you. You have options for mailing questionnaires out and for getting them returned. On outgoing mail, your choices are essentially between first-class postage and bulk rate. First is more certain, but bulk rate is far cheaper. (Consult your local post office for rates and procedures.) On return mail, your choice is between postage stamps and business-reply permits. Here, the cost differential is more complicated. If you use stamps, you pay for them whether people return their questionnaires or not. With the business-reply permit, you pay for only those that are used, but you pay an additional surcharge of about a nickel. This means that stamps are cheaper if a lot of questionnaires are returned, but business-reply permits are cheaper if fewer are returned (and you won't know in advance how many will be returned).

There are many other considerations involved in choosing among the several postal options. Some researchers, for example, feel that the use of postal stamps communicates more "humanness" and sincerity than bulk rate and business-reply permits. Others worry that respondents will steam off the stamps and use them for some purpose other than returning the questionnaires. Because both bulk rate and business-reply permits require establishing accounts at the post office, you'll probably find stamps much easier in small surveys.

Cover Letter

An important factor influencing response rates to mailed surveys is the quality of the cover letter that accompanies the questionnaire. The cover letter is usually the first thing prospective respondents read, and consequently it should be constructed in a way that will motivate them to respond and alleviate any resistance they may have about participating in the survey.

To motivate individuals to respond, you should explain the purpose and importance of the survey in terms that the prospective respondent can understand. You should obtain endorsement or sponsorship of the study from organizations or persons who are esteemed by prospective respondents and then identify those organizations or persons in the cover letter. You should explain why each individual's response is important to the success of the study and to solving a problem that respondents care about.

To alleviate resistance to participating, you should assure the anonymity of responses, explain how the sample was selected, and indicate how long it takes to complete the questionnaire (the quicker, the better).

Figure 11-1 is a cover letter that accompanied a 1975 survey of mental health practitioners. It illustrates the elements just discussed for motivating participation and reducing resistance.

Monitoring Returns

The mailing of questionnaires sets up a new research question that may prove valuable to the study. As questionnaires are returned, you should not sit back idly but should undertake a careful recording of the varying rates of return among respondents.

An invaluable tool in this activity will be a return rate graph. The day on which questionnaires were mailed should be labeled Day 1 on the graph, and every day thereafter the number of returned questionnaires should be logged on the graph. Because this is a minor activity, it is usually best to compile two graphs. One should show the number returned each day—rising, then dropping. Another should report the cumulative number or percentage. In part, this activity provides you with gratification, for you get to draw a picture of your successful data collection. More important, however, it is your guide to how the data collection is going. If you plan follow-up mailings, the graph provides a clue about when such mailings should be launched. (The dates of subsequent mailings should be noted on the graph.)

As completed questionnaires are returned, each should be opened, scanned, and assigned an identification number. These numbers should be assigned serially as the questionnaires are returned—even if other identification (ID) numbers have already been assigned. Two examples should illustrate the important advantages of this procedure.

Let's assume you are studying attitudes toward day-care programs for preschool children. In the middle of the data collection, let's say the news media begins covering accusations of sexual abuse in day-care programs. By knowing the date of that public disclosure and the dates when questionnaires have been received, you will be in a position to determine the effects of the disclosure. (Recall the discussion of history in connection with experiments.)

In a less sensational way, serialized ID numbers can be valuable in estimating nonresponse

biases in the survey. Barring more direct tests of bias, you may wish to assume that those who failed to answer the questionnaire will be more like respondents who delayed answering than like those who answered right away. An analysis of questionnaires received at different points in the data collection might then be used for estimates of sampling bias. For instance, if the level of client satisfaction with agency services decreases steadily through the data collection, with those replying right away reporting higher satisfaction and those replying later reporting lower satisfaction, you might tentatively conclude that those who failed to answer at all have lower satisfaction yet. Although it would not be advisable to make statistical estimates of bias in this fashion, you could take advantage of approximate estimates.

If respondents have been identified for purposes of follow-up mailing, then preparations for those mailings should be made as the questionnaires are returned. The case study later in this chapter will discuss this process in greater detail.

Follow-up Mailings

Follow-up mailings may be administered in a number of ways. In the simplest, nonrespondents are simply sent a letter of additional encouragement to participate. A better method, however, is to send a new copy of the survey questionnaire with the follow-up letter. If potential respondents have not returned their questionnaires after two or three weeks, the questionnaires probably have been lost or misplaced. Receiving a follow-up letter might encourage them to look for the original questionnaire, but if they can't find it easily, the letter may go for naught.

The methodological literature on follow-up mailings strongly suggests that it is an effective method for increasing return rates in mail surveys. In general, the longer a potential respondent delays replying, the less likely he or she is to do so at all. Properly timed follow-up mailings, then, provide additional stimuli to respond.

Dear Colleague:

Enclosed is a brief questionnaire that attempts to identify how MH/MR practitioners view aftercare treatment for patients discharged from state hospitals. This questionnaire has been mailed to all practitioners in the Allegheny County MH/MR service delivery system. The present survey is being conducted with the approval of the Allegheny County MH/MR Board, as well as with the endorsement of the administrators in each of the eleven Allegheny County catchment area centers.

Although many practitioners are being surveyed, <u>your participation is critical to the success of the study</u>. Since each unreturned questionnaire reduces the generalizability of the study, a very high response rate is necessary to accurately identify your views and lend value to the study.

Please be assured that <u>your responses are completely anonymous</u>. Although county administrators have approved this survey, it is independent from them. In fact, there is no way whatsoever for anyone, including myself, to identify who returned any given questionnaire. Also, there are no correct or incorrect responses in the survey. As a service provider, your views are important, regardless of their nature. The findings of the survey, which will be shared with all Allegheny County practitioners, will be reported on a large group basis only.

Therefore, in the interest of contributing to the knowledge base of mental health practice and to the success of this survey, would you kindly take about <u>30 minutes</u> from your already busy schedule to complete the enclosed questionnaire and return it in the enclosed stamped, self-addressed envelope. Also, upon returning the questionnaire, would you please mail the enclosed stamped postcard, which merely serves to identify those persons who did respond. The postcard will be used for follow-up contacts to non-respondents. It provides no knowledge of any person's responses and in no way affects the anonymity of the separately returned questionnaire.

Please try to return these materials as soon as possible and no later than May 21, 1975. If you have any questions, please contact me at the above address. Thank you.

Sincerely,

Allen Rubin
Principal Investigator

Figure 11-1 A Sample Cover Letter

The effects of follow-up mailings will be seen in the response rate curves recorded during data collection. The initial mailings will be followed by a rise and subsequent subsiding of returns; the follow-up mailings will spur a resurgence of returns; and more follow-ups will do the same. In practice, three mailings (an original and two follow-ups) seem the most efficient.

The timing of follow-up mailings is also important. Here the methodological literature offers less precise guides, but it has been our experience that two or three weeks is a reasonable space between mailings. (This period might be increased by a few days if the mailing time—out and in—is more than two or three days.)

When researchers conduct several surveys of the same population over time, they will be able to develop more specific guidelines in this regard. The Survey Research Office at the University of Hawaii conducts frequent student surveys and has been able to refine the mailing and remailing procedure considerably. Indeed, a consistent pattern of returns has been found, which appears to transcend differences of survey content, quality of instrument, and so forth. Within two weeks after the first mailing, approximately 40% of the questionnaires are returned; within two weeks after the first follow-up, an additional 20% are received; and within two weeks after the final follow-up, an additional 10% are received. (These response rates all involved the sending of additional questionnaires, not just letters.) There are no grounds for assuming that a similar pattern would appear in surveys of different populations, but this illustration should indicate the value of carefully tabulating return rates for every survey conducted.

If the individuals in the survey sample are not identified on the questionnaires, it may not be possible to remail only to nonrespondents. In such a case, you should send your follow-up mailing to all members of the sample, thanking those who may have already participated and encouraging those who have not to do so. (The case study reported in a later section of this chapter describes another method that may be used in an anonymous mail survey.)

Acceptable Response Rates

A question that new survey researchers frequently ask concerns the percentage return rate that should be achieved in a mail survey. It should be pointed out here that the body of inferential statistics used in connection with survey analysis assumes that all members of the initial sample complete and return their questionnaires. Since this almost never happens, response bias becomes a concern, with the researcher testing (and hoping for) the possibility that the respondents look essentially like a random sample of the initial sample, and thus a somewhat smaller random sample of the total population. (For more detailed discussions of response bias, you might want to read Donald [1960] and Brownlee [1975].)

Nevertheless, overall **response rate** is one guide to the representativeness of the sample respondents. If a high response rate is achieved, there is less chance of significant response bias than if a low rate is achieved. But what is a *high* response rate? A quick review of the survey literature will uncover a wide range of response rates. Each of these may be accompanied by a statement like "This is regarded as a relatively high response rate for a survey of this type." (A U.S. senator made this statement regarding a poll of constituents that achieved a 4% return rate.) Even so, it's possible to state some rules of thumb about return rates. A response rate of at least 50% is usually considered adequate for analysis and reporting. A response of at least 60% is *good*. And a response rate of 70% is *very good*. You should bear in mind, however, that these are only rough guides; they have no statistical basis, and a demonstrated lack of response bias is far more important than a high response rate.

As you can imagine, one of the more persistent discussions among survey researchers concerns ways of increasing response rates. You'll recall that this was a chief concern in the earlier discussion of options for mailing out and receiving questionnaires. Survey researchers have developed a number of ingenious techniques addressing this problem. Some have experimented with novel formats. Others have tried paying respondents to participate. The problem with paying, of course, is that it's expensive to make meaningfully high payment to hundreds or thousands of respondents, but some imaginative alternatives have been used. Some researchers have said, "We want to get your two-cents worth on some issues, and we're willing to pay"—enclosing two pennies. Another enclosed a quarter, suggesting that the respondent make some little child happy.

Don Dillman (1978) has undertaken an excellent review of the various techniques survey researchers have used to increase return rates on mail surveys, and he evaluates the impact of each. More important, Dillman stresses the necessity of paying attention to all aspects of the study—what he calls the "Total Design Method"—rather than one or two special gimmicks.

A Case Study

The steps involved in the administration of a mail survey are many and can best be appreciated in a walk-through of an actual study. We'll conclude this section, then, with a detailed description of the University of Hawaii student survey mentioned earlier. As you'll see shortly, the study does not represent the theoretical ideal for such studies, but in that regard it serves present purposes all the better. The study was conducted by the students in a graduate seminar in survey research methods.

By way of general overview, approximately 1100 students were selected from the university registration tape through a stratified, systematic sampling procedure. For each student selected, six self-adhesive mailing labels were printed by a computer.

By the time we were ready to distribute the questionnaires, it became apparent that our meager research funds were inadequate to cover several mailings to the entire sample of 1100 students. (Questionnaire printing costs were higher than anticipated.) As a result, a systematic two-thirds sample of the mailing labels was chosen, yielding a subsample of 770 students.

Earlier, we had decided to keep the survey anonymous in the hope of encouraging more candid responses to some sensitive questions. (Later surveys of the same issues among the same population indicated this anonymity was unnecessary.) Thus, the questionnaires would carry no identification of students on them. At the same time, we hoped to reduce the follow-up mailing costs by mailing only to nonrespondents.

To achieve both of these aims, a special postcard method was devised. Each student was mailed a questionnaire that carried no identifying marks, plus a postcard addressed to the research office—with one of the student's mailing labels affixed to the reverse side of the card. The introductory letter asked the student to complete and return the questionnaire—assuring anonymity—and to return the postcard simultaneously. Receiving the postcard would tell us that the student had returned his or her questionnaire—without indicating *which* questionnaire it was. This procedure would then facilitate follow-up mailings.

The 32-page questionnaire was printed in booklet form (photo-offset and saddle-stitched). A three-panel cover permitted the questionnaire to be returned without an additional envelope.

A letter introducing the study and its purposes was printed on the front cover of the booklet. It explained why the study was being conducted (to learn how students feel about a variety of issues), how students had been selected for the study, the importance of each student's responding, and the mechanics of returning the questionnaire.

Students were assured that their responses to the survey would be anonymous, and the postcard method was explained. A statement followed about the auspices under which the study was being conducted, and a telephone number was provided for those who might want more information about the study. (About five students called for information.)

By printing the introductory letter on the questionnaire, we avoided the necessity of enclosing a separate letter in the outgoing envelope, thereby simplifying the task of assembling mailing pieces.

The materials for the initial mailing were assembled in the following steps. (1) One mailing label for each student was stuck on a postcard. (2) Another label was stuck on an outgoing manila envelope. (3) One postcard and one questionnaire were placed in each envelope—with a glance to ensure that the name on the postcard and on the envelope were the same in each case.

These steps were accomplished through an assembly line procedure involving several members of the research team. Although the procedure was somewhat organized in advance, it took a certain amount of actual practice before the best allocation of tasks and persons was discovered.

It is also worth noting that the entire process was delayed several days while the initial batch of manila envelopes was exchanged for larger ones. This delay could have been avoided if we had walked through the assembly process in advance.

The distribution of the survey questionnaires had been set up for a bulk rate mailing. Once the questionnaires had been stuffed into envelopes, they were grouped by zip codes, tied in bundles, and delivered to the post office.

Shortly after the initial mailing, questionnaires and postcards began arriving at the research office. Questionnaires were opened, scanned, and assigned identification numbers as described earlier in this chapter. For every postcard received, a search was made for that student's remaining labels, and they were destroyed.

After a period of two or three weeks, all the remaining mailing labels were used to organize a follow-up mailing. The assembly procedures described previously were repeated with one exception. A special, separate letter of appeal was included in the mailing piece. The new letter indicated that many students had returned their questionnaires already, but that it was very important for all others to do so as well.

The follow-up mailing stimulated a resurgence of returns, as expected, and the same logging procedures were continued. The returned postcards told us which additional mailing labels to destroy. Unfortunately, time and financial pressures made it impossible to undertake a third mailing, as had been initially planned, but the two mailings resulted in an overall return rate of 62%.

We trust this illustration will give you a fairly good sense of what's involved in the execution of mailed self-administered questionnaires—a very popular survey method. Let's turn now to another method of conducting surveys.

INTERVIEW SURVEYS

The **interview** is an alternative method of collecting survey data. Rather than asking respondents to read questionnaires and enter their own answers, researchers send interviewers to ask the questions orally and record respondents' answers. Interviewing is typically done in a face-to-face encounter, but telephone interviewing, as we'll see, follows most of the same guidelines. Also, most interview surveys require more than one interviewer, although you might undertake a small-scale interview survey yourself. Portions of this section will discuss methods for training and supervising a staff of interviewers assisting you on the survey.

The Role of the Interviewer

There are a number of advantages in having a questionnaire administered by an interviewer rather than the respondent. To begin, interview surveys typically attain higher response rates than mail surveys. A properly designed and executed interview survey ought to achieve a completion rate of at least 80% to 85%. (Federally funded surveys often require one of these response rates.) Respondents seem more reluctant to turn down an interviewer standing on their doorstep than they are to throw away a mail questionnaire.

Within the context of the questionnaire, the presence of an interviewer generally decreases the number of "don't knows" and "no answers." If minimizing such responses is important to the study, the interviewer can be instructed to probe for answers ("If you had to pick one of the answers, which do you think would come closest to your feelings?").

Interviewers can also provide a guard against confusing questionnaire items. If the respondent clearly misunderstands the intent of a question or indicates that he or she does not understand, the interviewer can clarify matters, thereby obtaining relevant responses. (Such clarifications must be strictly controlled, however, through formal *specifications*. See "Coordination and Control.")

Finally, the interviewer can observe as well as ask questions. For example, the interviewer can note the respondent's race if this is considered too delicate a question to ask. Similar observations can be made regarding the quality of the dwelling, the presence of various possessions, the respondent's ability to speak English, the respondent's general reactions to the study, and so forth. In one survey of students, respondents were given a short, self-administered questionnaire to complete—concerning sexual attitudes and behavior—during the course of the interview. While a student completed the questionnaire, the interviewer made detailed notes regarding the dress and grooming of the respondent.

Before leaving this example, there is an ethical issue that should be raised. Some researchers have objected that such practices violate the spirit of the agreement by which the respondent has allowed the interview. Although ethical issues seldom are open and shut in social research, it is important for you to be sensitive to that aspect of research. We have examined ethical issues in detail in Chapter 3.

Survey research is of necessity based on an unrealistic *stimulus-response* theory of cognition and behavior. It must be assumed that a questionnaire item will mean the same thing to every respondent, and every given response must mean the same when given by different respondents. Although this is an impossible goal, as illustrated in the box "How Much Is 'Very'?," survey questions are drafted to approximate the ideal as closely as possible. The interviewer must also fit into this ideal situation. The interviewer's presence should not affect a respondent's perception of a question or the answer given. The interviewer, then, should be a *neutral* medium through which questions and answers are transmitted.

If this goal is successfully accomplished, different interviewers will obtain exactly the same responses from a given respondent. (Recall earlier discussions of reliability.) This neutrality has a special importance in area samples. To save time and money, a given interviewer is typically assigned to complete all the interviews in a particular geographic area—a city block or a group of nearby blocks. If the interviewer does anything to affect the responses obtained, then the bias thus interjected might be interpreted as a characteristic of that area.

Let's suppose that a survey is being done to determine attitudes toward low-cost housing, to help in the selection of a site for a new government-sponsored development. An interviewer assigned to a given neighborhood might—through word or gesture—communicate his or her own distaste for low-cost housing developments. Respondents might therefore tend to give responses generally in agreement with the interviewer's own position. The results of the survey would indicate that the neighborhood in question strongly resisted construction of the development in its area whereas their apparent resistance might only reflect the interviewer's attitudes.

General Rules for Interviewing

The manner in which interviews ought to be conducted will vary somewhat by survey population and will be affected somewhat by the nature of the survey content as well. Nevertheless, it is possible

HOW MUCH IS "VERY"?

by Keith Crew, Department of Sociology, University of Kentucky

One summer not long ago, I spent some time interviewing rural and small-town Appalachian residents for a large survey project. The person who trained and pretested me on the interview schedule related the following experience, which she had while interviewing in the same area on a previous survey. Many of the questions on the interview schedule were Likert-type items ranging from "very much" to "very little" or "very good" to "very poor." The problem was that in the colloquial language of the region, the word "very" apparently has an idiomatic usage which is closer to what we mean by "fairly" or even "poorly." For instance, if you inquired about someone's health and they responded that they were doing "very well,"

they do not mean that their health is excellent, but quite the contrary, that they are just getting along.

One assumption of surveys, which seems so obvious that it is usually ignored, is that the researcher and the respondent are speaking the same language. In this case, the sponsors of the survey (who shall remain nameless) refused to consider the difference in language usage: they told their interviewers to code "very well" if that was what the respondent said. In other words, in many cases the coded response was quite likely the exact opposite of the respondent's opinion; furthermore, since we are discussing a regional-cultural variation it is not really "legit" to simply toss it into the category of "random error."

to provide some general guidelines that apply to most if not all interviewing situations.

Appearance and Demeanor As a general rule, the interviewer should dress in a fashion similar to that of the people he or she will be interviewing. A richly dressed interviewer will probably have difficulty getting good cooperation and responses from poorer respondents. And a poorly dressed interviewer will have similar difficulties with richer respondents.

To the extent that the interviewer's dress and grooming differ from those of the respondents, it should be in the direction of cleanliness and neatness in modest apparel. If cleanliness is not next

to godliness, it appears to be next to neutrality. Although middle-class neatness and cleanliness may not be accepted by all sectors of American society, they remain the primary norm and are more likely to be acceptable to the largest number of respondents.

Dress and grooming are typically regarded as signals to a person's attitudes and orientations. At the time this is being written, wearing torn jeans, green hair, and a razor-blade earring may communicate—correctly or incorrectly—that you are politically radical, sexually permissive, favorable to drug use, and so forth.

In demeanor, interviewers should be pleasant if nothing else. Because they will be prying into the respondent's personal life and attitudes, they must communicate a genuine interest in getting to know the respondent without appearing to spy. They must be relaxed and friendly without being too casual or clinging. Good interviewers also have the ability to determine very quickly the kind of person the respondent will feel most comfortable with, the kind of person the respondent would most enjoy talking to. There are two aspects of this. Clearly, the interview will be more successful if the interviewer can become the kind of person the respondent is comfortable with. Second, since respondents are asked to volunteer a portion of their time and to divulge personal information about themselves, they deserve the most enjoyable experience the researcher and interviewer can provide.

Familiarity with Questionnaire   If an interviewer is unfamiliar with the questionnaire, the study suffers and an unfair burden is placed on the respondent. The interview is likely to take more time than necessary and be generally unpleasant. Moreover, the interviewer cannot acquire familiarity by skimming through the questionnaire two or three times. It must be studied carefully, question by question, and the interviewer must practice reading it aloud.

Ultimately, the interviewer must be able to read the questionnaire items to respondents without error, without stumbling over words and phrases. A good model for interviewers is the actor reading lines in a play or motion picture. The lines must be read as naturally as though they constituted a natural conversation, but that conversation must follow exactly the language set down in the questionnaire.

By the same token, the interviewer must be familiar with the specifications prepared in conjunction with the questionnaire. Inevitably some questions will not exactly fit a given respondent's situation, and the interviewer must determine how the question should be interpreted in that situation. The specifications provided to the interviewer should give adequate guidance in such cases, but

the interviewer must know the organization and contents of the specifications well enough to refer to them efficiently. It would be better for the interviewer to leave a given question unanswered than to spend five minutes searching through the specifications for clarification or trying to interpret the relevant instructions.

Following Question Wording Exactly   Earlier we discussed the significance of question wording for the responses obtained. A slight change in the wording of a given question may lead a respondent to answer yes rather than no.

Even though you have very carefully phrased your questionnaire items to obtain the information you need and to ensure that respondents will interpret items precisely as you intend, all this effort will be wasted if interviewers rephrase questions in their own words.

Recording Responses Exactly   Whenever the questionnaire contains open-ended questions—those soliciting the respondent's own answer—it is very important that the interviewer record that answer exactly as given. No attempt should be made to summarize, paraphrase, or correct bad grammar.

This exactness is especially important because the interviewer will not know how the responses are to be coded before processing. Indeed, the researchers may not know the coding until they have read a hundred or so responses. For instance, the questionnaire might ask respondents how they feel about the traffic situation in their community. One respondent might answer that there are too many cars on the roads and that something should be done to limit their numbers. Another might say that more roads are needed. If the interviewer recorded these two responses with the same summary—"congested traffic"—the researchers would not be able to take advantage of the important differences in the original responses.

Sometimes, the respondent may be so inarticulate that the verbal response is too ambiguous to permit interpretation. However, the interviewer may be able to understand the intent of the response through the respondent's gestures or tone. In such a situation, the exact verbal response should still be recorded, but the interviewer should add marginal comments giving both the interpretation and the reasons for arriving at it.

More generally, researchers can use any marginal comments explaining aspects of the response not conveyed in the verbal recording, such as the respondent's apparent uncertainty in answering, anger, embarrassment, and so forth. In each case, however, the exact verbal response should also be recorded.

Probing for Responses Sometimes respondents will respond to a question with an inappropriate answer. For example, the question may present an attitudinal statement and ask the respondent to strongly agree, agree somewhat, disagree somewhat, or strongly disagree. The respondent, however, may reply: "I think that's true." The interviewer should follow this reply with: "Would you say you strongly agree or agree somewhat?" If necessary, interviewers can explain that they must check one or the other of the categories provided. If the respondent adamantly refuses to choose, the interviewer should write in the exact response given by the respondent.

Probes are more frequently required in eliciting responses to open-ended questions. For instance, in response to a question about traffic conditions, the respondent might simply reply, "Pretty bad." The interviewer could obtain an elaboration on this response through a variety of probes. Sometimes the best probe is silence; if the interviewer sits quietly with pencil poised, the respondent will probably fill the pause with additional comments. (This technique is used effectively by newspaper reporters.) Appropriate verbal probes might be "How is that?" or "In what ways?" Perhaps the most generally useful probe is "Anything else?"

It is frequently necessary to probe for answers that will be sufficiently informative for analytic purposes. In every case, however, it is imperative that such probes be completely *neutral*. The probe must not in any way affect the nature of the subsequent response. Whenever you anticipate that a given question may require probing for appropriate responses, you should present one or more useful probes next to the question in the questionnaire. This practice has two important advantages. First, you will have more time to devise the best, most neutral probes. Second, all interviewers will use the same probes whenever they are needed. Thus, even if the probe is not perfectly neutral, all respondents will be presented with the same stimulus. This is the same logical guideline discussed for question wording. Although a question should not be loaded or biased, it is essential that every respondent be presented with the same question, even a biased one.

Coordination and Control

Most interview surveys require the assistance of several interviewers. In the large-scale surveys, of course, such interviewers are hired and paid for their work. As a student researcher, you might find yourself recruiting friends to assist you in interviewing. Whenever more than one interviewer is involved in a survey, it is essential that efforts be carefully controlled. There are two aspects of this control: training interviewers and supervising them after they begin work.

Interviewers should be trained in a group, rather than individually. The latter approach will inevitably result in more superficial training.

The interviewer training session should begin with the description of what the study is all about. Even though the interviewers may be involved only in the data-collection phase of the project, it will be useful to them to understand what will be done with the interviews they conduct and what purpose will be served. Morale and motivation are usually low when interviewers do not know what is going on.

The training on how to interview should begin with a discussion of general guidelines and procedures, such as those discussed earlier in this chapter. Then you should turn to the questionnaire itself. The whole group should go through the questionnaire together—question by question. Do not simply ask if anyone has any questions about the first page of the questionnaire. Read the first question aloud, explain the purpose of the question, and then entertain any questions or comments the interviewers may have. Once all their questions and comments have been handled, go on to the next question in the questionnaire.

It is always a good idea to prepare what are called **specifications** to accompany an interview questionnaire. Specifications are explanatory and clarifying comments about handling of difficult or confusing situations that may occur with regard to specific questions in the questionnaire. When you are drafting the questionnaire, you should try to think of all the problem cases that might arise—the bizarre circumstances that might make a question difficult to answer. The survey specifications should provide detailed guidelines on how to handle such situations. As an example, such a simple matter as age might present problems. Suppose a respondent says he or she will be 25 next week. The interviewer might not be sure whether to take the respondent's current age or the nearest one. The specifications for that question should explain what should be done. (Probably, you would specify that age as of last birthday should be recorded in all cases.)

If you have prepared a set of specifications, you should go over them with the interviewers when you go over the individual questions in the questionnaire. Make sure your interviewers fully understand the specifications as well as the questions themselves and the reasons for them.

This portion of the interviewer training is likely to generate a number of troublesome questions from your interviewers. They will ask: "What should I do if . . . ?" In such cases, you should never give a quick answer. If you have specifications, be sure to show how the solution to the problem could be determined from the specifications. If you do not have specifications

prepared, show how the preferred handling of the situation fits within the general logic of the question and the purpose of the study. Giving offhand, unexplained answers to such questions will only confuse the interviewers, and they will probably not take their work very seriously. If you do not know the answer to such a question when it is asked, admit it and ask for some time to decide on the best answer. Then think out the situation carefully and be sure to give all the interviewers your answer, explaining your reasons.

Once you have gone through the whole questionnaire, you should conduct one or two demonstration interviews in front of everyone. Preferably, *you* should interview someone else. Realize that your interview will be a model for those you are training, and make it good. It would be best, moreover, if the demonstration interview were done as realistically as possible. Do not pause during the demonstration to point out how you have handled a complicated situation: Handle it, and then explain later. It is irrelevant if the person you are interviewing gives real answers or takes on some hypothetical identity for the purpose, just so long as the answers are consistent.

After the demonstration interviews, you should pair off your interviewers and have them practice on each other. When they have completed the questionnaire, have them reverse roles and do it over again. Interviewing is the best training for interviewing. As your interviewers are practicing on each other, you should try to wander around, listening in on the practice so that you will know how well they are doing. Once the practice is completed, the whole group should discuss their experiences and ask any other questions they may have.

The final stage of the training for interviewers should involve some "real" interviews. Have them conduct some interviews under the actual conditions that will pertain to the final survey. You may want to assign them people to interview, or perhaps they may be allowed to pick people themselves. Do not have them practice on people you have selected in your sample, however. After each interviewer has completed three to five interviews, have him or her check back with you. Look over the completed questionnaires to see if there is any evidence of misunderstanding. Again, answer any questions that individual interviewers may have. Once you are convinced that a given interviewer knows what to do, assign some actual interviews—using the sample you have selected for the study.

It is essential that you continue supervising the work of interviewers over the course of the study. It is probably unwise to let them conduct more than 20 or 30 interviews without seeing you. You might assign 20 interviews, have the interviewer bring back those questionnaires when they are completed, look them over, and assign another 20 or so. Although that may seem overly cautious, you must continually protect yourself against misunderstandings that may not be evident early in the study.

If you are the only interviewer in your study, these comments may not seem relevant to you. That is not wholly the case, however. You would be advised, for example, to prepare specifications for potentially troublesome questions in your questionnaire. Otherwise, you run the risk of making ad hoc decisions during the course of the study that you will later regret or forget. Also, the emphasis that has been placed on practice applies equally to the one-person project and to the complex funded survey with a large interviewing staff.

TELEPHONE SURVEYS

Throughout the early history of survey research, interview surveys were always conducted face-to-face, typically in the respondent's household. As the telephone became virtually omnipresent in American society, however, researchers began experimenting with that new vehicle for survey interviewing.

For years telephone surveys had a rather bad reputation among professional researchers. Telephone surveys are limited by definition to people who have telephones. Years ago, then, this method

produced a substantial social-class bias by excluding poor people from the surveys. This was vividly demonstrated by the *Literary Digest* fiasco of 1936. Even though voters were contacted by mail, the sample was partially selected from telephone subscribers—who were hardly typical in a nation just recovering from the Great Depression.

Over time, however, the telephone has become a standard fixture in almost all American homes. The Census Bureau (1992:551) estimates that 93.6% of all households had telephones in 1991, so the earlier form of class bias has been substantially reduced.

A related sampling problem involved unlisted numbers. If the survey sample was selected from the pages of a local telephone directory, it would totally omit all those people—typically richer—who requested that their numbers not be published. This potential bias has been erased through a technique that has advanced telephone sampling substantially: *random-digit dialing*, which we'll examine later.

Telephone surveys have many advantages that underlie the growing popularity of this method. Probably the greatest advantages are money and time, in that order. In a face-to-face, household interview, you may drive several miles to a respondent's home, find no one there, return to the research office, and drive back the next day—possibly finding no one there again. It's cheaper and quicker to let your fingers make the trips.

When interviewing by telephone, you can dress any way you please without affecting the answers respondents give. And, sometimes respondents will be more honest in giving socially disapproved answers if they don't have to look you in the eye. Similarly, it may be possible to probe into more sensitive areas, though that is not necessarily the case. (People are, to some extent, more suspicious when they can't see the person asking them questions—perhaps a consequence of "surveys" aimed at selling magazine subscriptions and time-share condominiums.)

Telephone surveys can give you greater control over data collection if several interviewers are engaged in the project. If all the interviewers are calling from the research office, they can get clarification from the person in charge whenever problems occur, as they inevitably do. Alone in the boondocks, an interviewer may have to wing it between weekly visits with the interviewing supervisor.

Finally, another important factor involved in the growing use of telephone surveys has to do with personal safety and concerns for the same. Don Dillman (1978:4) describes the situation this way:

> Interviewers must be able to operate comfortably in a climate in which strangers are viewed with distrust and must successfully counter respondents' objections to being interviewed. Increasingly, interviewers must be willing to work at night to contact residents in many households. In some cases, this necessitates providing protection for interviewers working in areas of a city in which a definite threat to the safety of individuals exists.

Concerns for safety thus work two ways to hamper face-to-face interviews. Potential respondents may refuse to be interviewed, fearing the stranger-interviewer. And the interviewers themselves may be in danger. All this is made even worse by the possibility of the researchers being sued for huge sums if anything goes wrong.

There are still problems involved in telephone interviewing. As we've already mentioned, the method is hampered by the proliferation of bogus "surveys," which are actually sales campaigns disguised as research. If you have any questions about any such call you receive, by the way, ask the interviewer directly whether you've been selected for a survey only or if a sales "opportunity" is involved. It's also a good idea, if you have any doubts, to get the interviewer's name, phone number, and company. Hang up if they refuse to provide any of these.

The ease with which people can hang up is, of course, another shortcoming of telephone surveys. Once you've been let inside someone's home for an interview, they are unlikely to order you out of the house in mid-interview. It's much easier to terminate a telephone interview abruptly, saying something like, "Whoops! Someone's at the door. I gotta go." or "OMIGOD! The pigs are eating my Volvo!" (That sort of thing is much harder to fake when you're sitting in their living room.)

Computer Assistance

In Chapter 14 of this book, we'll be looking at some of the ways computers have influenced the conduct of social research—particularly in the area of data processing and analysis. Computers are also changing the nature of telephone interviewing. In the years to come, you will hear a great deal about something called *CATI: computer-assisted telephone interviewing*. Although there are variations in practice, here's what it can look like.

Imagine an interviewer wearing a telephone-operator headset, sitting in front of a computer terminal and its video screen. The central computer randomly selects a telephone number and dials it. (This avoids the problem of unlisted telephone numbers.) On the video screen is an introduction ("Hello, my name is . . .") and the first question to be asked ("Could you tell me how many people live at this address?").

When the respondent answers the phone, the interviewer says hello, introduces the study, and asks the first question displayed on the screen. When the respondent answers the question, the interviewer types that answer into the computer terminal—either the verbatim response to an open-ended question or the code category for the appropriate answer to a closed-ended question. The answer is immediately stored in the central computer. The second question appears on the video screen, is asked, and the answer is entered into the computer. Thus, the interview continues.

This is not science fiction but is being used increasingly by academic, government, and commercial survey researchers. Much of the development work for this technique has occurred at the University of California's Survey Research Center in Berkeley, sometimes in collaboration with the U.S. Department of Agriculture and other government agencies.

J. Merrill Shanks and Robert Tortora (1985:4) have reviewed some of the ways in which they have integrated computers into the survey process. In addition to what was evident in the preceding scenario, the computer is a valuable tool in the development of questionnaires: drafting, testing, revising, and formatting. The logistics of the interviewing process (for example, training, scheduling, and supervising interviewers) can be managed by computer. As we'll see in Chapter 14, coding open-ended responses is also well-suited to the computer, as is the prevention and/or correction of errors.

Shanks and Tortora go beyond CATI, however, to talk about *computer-assisted survey methods* more generally. Many of the same techniques discussed previously can be applied to face-to-face household interviews.

The development of portable microcomputers now permits an interviewer to set up shop in the respondent's home, reading questions off the screen and recording the answers as described previously. In addition, it is sometimes appropriate to adapt the computer to self-administered questionnaires. In some situations, respondents can be asked to sit at computer terminals and enter their own answers to the questions that appear on the screen.

The development of computer technology in connection with data collection is one of the most exciting things happening today in survey research. Although it is particularly relevant to telephone interviewing, its potential extends much further.

COMPARISON OF THE THREE METHODS

We've now seen there are a number of ways in which you can collect survey data. Although we've touched on some of the relative advantages and disadvantages of each, let's take a minute to compare them more directly.

Self-administered questionnaires are generally cheaper and quicker than interview surveys.

These considerations are likely to be important for an unfunded student wishing to undertake a survey in connection with a term paper or a thesis. Moreover, if you use the self-administered mail format, it costs no more to conduct a national survey than a local one; the cost difference between a local and a national interview survey (either face-to-face or by telephone) would be far greater. Also, mail surveys typically require a small staff: One person can conduct a reasonable mail survey alone, although you should not underestimate the work involved.

Self-administered surveys are also more appropriate in dealing with especially sensitive issues if the surveys offer complete anonymity. Respondents are sometimes reluctant to report controversial or deviant attitudes or behaviors in interviews but are willing to respond to an anonymous self-administered questionnaire.

Interview surveys have many advantages, also. For instance, they generally produce fewer incomplete questionnaires. Although respondents may skip questions in a self-administered questionnaire, interviewers are trained not to do so. The computer offers a further check on this in CATI surveys. Interview surveys, moreover, have typically achieved higher completion rates than self-administered ones. In an analysis of response rates to 517 surveys, John Goyder (1985) has concluded that the difference in response rates between interview and mail surveys has decreased in recent times and that the earlier differences were primarily a function of more extensive follow up in the case of interview surveys.

Although self-administered questionnaires may be more effective in dealing with sensitive issues, interview surveys are definitely more effective in dealing with complicated ones. Prime examples would be the enumeration of household members and the determination of whether a given household address contained more than one housing unit. Although the concept housing unit has been refined and standardized by the Bureau of the Census and interviewers can be trained to deal with the concept, it is extremely difficult to communicate in a self-administered questionnaire. This advantage of interview surveys pertains more generally to all complicated contingency questions.

With interviewers, it is possible to conduct a survey based on a sample of addresses or phone numbers rather than on names. An interviewer can arrive at an assigned address or call the assigned number, introduce the survey, and even—following instructions—choose the appropriate person at that address to respond to the survey. By contrast, self-administered questionnaires addressed to "occupant" receive a notoriously low response.

Finally, interviewers questioning respondents face-to-face are able to make important observations aside from responses to questions asked in the interview. In a household interview, they may note the characteristics of the neighborhood, the dwelling unit, and so forth. They may also note characteristics of the respondents or the quality of their interaction with the respondents—whether the respondent had difficulty communicating, was hostile or seemed to be lying, and so forth.

Ultimately, you must balance all these advantages and disadvantages of the three methods in relation to (1) your research needs and (2) your resources.

STRENGTHS AND WEAKNESSES OF SURVEY RESEARCH

Like other modes of observation in social scientific research, surveys have special strengths and weaknesses. It is important to know these in determining whether the survey format is appropriate to your research goals.

Surveys are particularly useful in describing the characteristics of a large population. A carefully selected probability sample in combination with a standardized questionnaire offers the possibility of making refined descriptive assertions about a student body, a city, a nation, or other large population. Surveys determine unemployment rates, voting intentions, and the like with uncanny accuracy. Although the examination of official documents—such as marriage, birth, or death records—can provide equal accuracy for a few topics, no other method of observation can provide this general capability.

Surveys—especially self-administered ones—make very large samples feasible. Surveys of 2000 respondents are not unusual. A large number of cases is very important for both descriptive and explanatory analyses. Whenever several variables are to be analyzed simultaneously, it is essential to have a large number of cases.

Because surveys make large samples feasible, their findings may be more generalizable than the findings of experiments. This advantage in external validity, however, is offset by the limited internal validity of surveys, particularly cross-sectional surveys (surveys conducted at one point in time). Experiments tend to offer more internal validity for inferring about what caused what among the sample and within the experimental context, but they also tend to offer limited external validity for generalizing beyond the experimental sample or context. Thus, if a rigorously designed experiment finds that giving ten elderly persons a pet improves their moods, we would probably be uncertain as to the generalizability of that causal inference to elderly people in general, particularly those who have different attributes than the experimental sample or who are living in different kinds of settings. A cross-sectional survey of the moods of thousands of elderly people, on the other hand, will tell us in general whether elderly people with pets have better moods than elderly people without pets. It wouldn't, however, tell us whether having pets caused their moods to improve. Perhaps being less depressed in the first place is what leads to getting a pet.

The survey would also enable us to analyze multiple variables simultaneously; thus, we could see whether the relationship applied to elderly people of different ethnicities, different income levels, different living arrangements, different levels of dependency, and so on. But we'd still be uncertain as to causality. By conducting a longitudinal survey—for example, assessing the same elderly folks' moods and pet situations over time—we'd be in a better position to speculate about causality. That is, we could ascertain whether the moods were changing before or after the pets were obtained, but we'd still have less internal validity than in an experiment. Despite the uncertainty about causality, the high level of generalizability of the findings to the population as a whole, as well as to various subgroups of the population, in their natural settings, is an advantage of surveys that few experiments can offer.

In one sense, surveys are flexible. Many questions may be asked on a given topic, giving you considerable flexibility in your analyses. Although experimental design may require you to commit yourself in advance to a particular operational definition of a concept, surveys let you develop operational definitions from actual observations.

Finally, standardized questionnaires have an important strength in regard to measurement generally. Earlier chapters have discussed the ambiguous nature of most concepts: They have no ultimately real meanings. One person's religiosity is quite different from another's. Although you must be able to define concepts in ways most relevant to your research goals, you may not find it easy to apply the same definitions uniformly to all subjects. The survey researcher is bound to this requirement by having to ask exactly the same questions of all subjects and having to impute the same intent to all respondents giving a particular response.

Survey research has a number of weaknesses. First, the requirement for standardization just mentioned often seems to result in the fitting of round pegs into square holes. Standardized questionnaire items often represent the least common denominator in assessing people's attitudes, orientations, circumstances, and experiences. By designing questions that will be at least minimally appropriate to all respondents, you may miss what is most appropriate to many respondents. In this sense, surveys often appear superficial in their coverage of complex topics. Although this problem can be partly offset through sophisticated analyses, it is inherent in survey research.

Similarly, survey research can seldom deal with the *context* of social life. Although questionnaires can provide information in this area, the survey researcher can seldom develop the feel for the total life situation in which respondents are thinking and acting that, say, the participant observer can (see Chapter 12).

Although surveys are flexible in the sense mentioned earlier, they are inflexible in other ways. Studies involving direct observation can be modified as field conditions warrant, but surveys typically require that an initial study design remain unchanged throughout. As a field researcher, for example, you can become aware of an important new variable operating in the phenomenon you are studying and begin making careful observations of it. The survey researcher would likely be unaware of the new variable's importance and could do nothing about it in any event.

Finally, surveys are subject to the artificiality mentioned earlier in connection with experiments. Finding out that a person gives conservative answers to a questionnaire does not necessarily mean the person is conservative; finding out that a person gives prejudiced answers to a questionnaire does not necessarily mean the person is prejudiced. This shortcoming is especially salient in the realm of action. Surveys cannot measure social action; they can only collect self-reports of recalled past action or of prospective or hypothetical action. There are two aspects of this problem. First, the topic of study may not be amenable to measurement through questionnaires. Second, the act of studying that topic—an attitude, for instance—may affect it. A survey respondent may have given no thought to whether the governor should be impeached until asked for his or her opinion by an interviewer. He or she may, at that point, form an opinion on the matter.

Survey research is generally weak on validity and strong on reliability. In comparison with field research, for example, the artificiality of the survey format puts a strain on validity. As an illustration, people's opinions on issues seldom take the form of strongly agreeing, agreeing, disagreeing, or strongly disagreeing with a specific statement. Their survey responses in such cases, then, must be regarded as approximate indicators of what we have in mind initially in framing the questions. This comment, however, needs to be held in the context of earlier discussions of the ambiguity of *validity* itself. To say something is a valid or an invalid measure assumes the existence of a "real" definition of what is being measured, and many scholars now reject that assumption.

Reliability is a clearer matter. Survey research, by presenting all subjects with a standardized stimulus, goes a long way toward eliminating unreliability in observations made by the researcher. Moreover, careful wording of the questions can also reduce significantly the subject's own unreliability.

As with all methods of observation, a full awareness of the inherent or probable weaknesses of survey research can partially resolve them in some cases. Ultimately, though, you are on the safest ground when you can use a number of different research methods in studying a given topic. The box titled "Combining Survey Research Methods and Qualitative Research Methods" illustrates this point. In so doing, it also illustrates the point we've been repeating throughout this text regarding the complementarity of quantitative and qualitative methods.

COMBINING SURVEY RESEARCH METHODS AND QUALITATIVE RESEARCH METHODS

By combining qualitative research methods with survey research methods, we can benefit from the strengths of survey research while we offset its weaknesses regarding superficiality, missing social context, inflexibility, artificiality, and questionable validity. The book *Qualitative Methods in Family Research*, edited by Jane Gilgun and two associates (1992), includes a chapter by Mark Rank that advocates for the blending of qualitative and quantitative methods and shows the benefits of it in a study of childbearing among welfare recipients.

Rank was interested in the debate over whether welfare programs like Aid to Families with Dependent Children (AFDC) encourage women to have more children by increasing the payments when additional children are born. He began his study with qualitative interviews and fieldwork observations (like the ones to be described in Chapter 12) at various agencies serving welfare recipients and in neighborhoods where many recipients lived. The people he observed and talked to in these settings did not agree with the stereotype of women choosing to bear more children so their public assistance payments would increase. Instead, they believed that most women receiving welfare wanted to get off welfare and did not want any more children.

Were their beliefs accurate? To find out, Rank conducted a secondary analysis of survey data from the data bases of the Wisconsin (Rank's state) Department of Health and Social Services and the U.S. Bureau of the Census. His quantitative analysis supported his preliminary qualitative findings. Women on welfare had a "substantially lower fertility rate than women in the general population" (1992:289). Even when Rank controlled for various demographic variables, women on welfare still had a much lower fertility rate.

Rank then wondered what accounts for his dramatic findings. To find out, he and his assistant conducted in-depth qualitative interviews with 50 families on welfare. The open-ended, semistructured interviews were conducted face-to-face in the respondents' homes, were tape-recorded, and lasted up to three hours. None of the nonpregnant women they interviewed wanted to have another child in the near future. They consistently cited financial and social forces that are not conducive to having more children. Virtually all of them expressed wanting to get off of welfare, and they appeared to recognize that the meager increase in payments for having more children was far outweighed by the increase in economic, social, and psychological costs that would come with having more children. Rank concluded that his quantitative and qualitative data reinforced each other and enhanced the validity of his findings, findings that challenged the assumption of conservative and neoliberal policy analysts that welfare payments encourage women to have more children.

Whereas Rank's work began with qualitative observations, two studies in which one of the authors of this text (Rubin) has been involved illustrate the value of employing qualitative methods after survey methods yield enigmatic findings. In the first, students in his doctoral research seminar in 1982 conducted a class project involving the secondary analysis of survey data from the Council on Social Work Education in an effort to identify variables that might explain why some schools of social work were experiencing much larger declines in applications to their master's degree programs than were others during that era of nationwide declines in applications to MSW programs. Their main finding was highly unexpected and puzzling. The schools with the worst declines in applications were more likely to have doctoral programs and greater prestige.

To try to figure out what accounted for these suprising findings the students conducted semistructured, open-ended qualitative telephone interviews with administrators in those schools with the most severe and least severe declines. What they learned was that the schools with the least severe declines tended to have initiated aggressive recruitment efforts to people who ordinarily would not have applied to their programs due to pragmatic obstacles (like geographic distance, jobs, and so on) and had developed nontraditional outreach programs that often involved modifications in their curriculum standards. Administrators in the more prestigious schools experiencing the most severe declines expressed an unwillingness to alter their curriculum standards in order to keep up enrollments. Thus, the qualitative data uncovered a different meaning to the more superficial, and perplexing, survey data that seemed to portray the more prestigious schools as somehow losing their attractiveness to prospective applicants.

In a more recent class project, students in Rubin's doctoral seminar surveyed graduate and undergraduate social work students about their views regarding parenting and mental illness, using a self-administered scale developed for the survey. Much to their surprise, they found that students with more fieldwork or other experience in working with parents of people suffering from mental illness were somewhat less likely to emphasize biological factors in the etiology of mental illness and somewhat more likely to view mental illness as a result of parental or family dysfunction. This was surprising in light of the growing accumulation of research evidence supporting biological factors in etiology and treatment and pointing to the need to support families and not treat them as having caused the illness.

It was clear to the doctoral seminar students, therefore, that their survey results were superficial. In discussing their meaning, some wondered whether many of the surveyed students with more experience in this area might be getting that experience in programs using outdated approaches where they are supervised by professionals who have not been keeping up with current research and who might be fond of expressing 1970s-style family systems theory stereotypes like, "Crazy people come from crazy families."

While this potential explanation seemed plausible to some, most of the seminar students remained mystified by the results. All the students agreed, however, that before their survey results could have much value, a qualitative inquiry would be needed, one that would use open-ended and in-depth interviews with students and field instructors to probe the meaning of the views depicted by the survey instrument.

SECONDARY ANALYSIS

As a mode of observation, survey research involves the following steps: (1) questionnaire construction, (2) sample selection, and (3) data collection, through either interviewing or self- administered questionnaires. It should now be apparent that surveys are usually major undertakings. It is not unusual for a large-scale survey to take several months or even more than a year to progress from conceptualization to having data in hand. (Smaller-scale surveys can, of course, be done more quickly.) At the same time, however, it is possible for you to pursue your particular social research interests—analyzing survey data from, say, a national sample of 2000 respondents—while avoiding the enormous expenditure of time and money such a survey entails. *Secondary analysis* makes such work possible.

With the development of computer-based analyses in social research, it has become easily possible for social researchers to *share* their data with one another. Data also may be obtained from various agencies that regularly conduct large-scale surveys, such as the Bureau of the Census, the National Institute of Mental Health, or the Council on Social Work Education.

Suppose, for example, that you are concerned about a potential problem in social work education and want to research it. Perhaps you have noticed that female faculty members tend to occupy the lower ranks in your school or that they are unlikely to have administrative positions. You might want to assess, on a national basis, whether women and men of equivalent backgrounds differ in regard to such variables as rank, academic responsibilities, salary, and scholarly productivity.

Conducting a nationwide survey of social work faculty members would be quite costly and time-consuming. Even if you could get the resources to conduct the survey, you would have to worry

368 / CHAPTER 11 / SURVEY RESEARCH

about the potential problem of nonresponse. As an alternative to conducting the survey yourself, you could purchase—for far less money than the cost of conducting a survey—a copy of all the data for a given year on the population of social work faculty members already collected by the Council on Social Work Education in its annual statistical canvass, which includes the information you seek to analyze and which uses faculty members as the unit of analysis.

Beginning in the 1960s, the potential for secondary analysis was developed on an international scale. A consortium of research centers collaborated with one another to form a network of *data archives,* each of which would collect and administer data sets from various parts of the United States and the world. Decks of punch cards and magnetic tapes were shelved the way books are shelved in a conventional library, and the holdings were available for broad circulation and use. Whereas library books are loaned, however, the data sets are reproduced and sold. You get to keep your copy and use it again and again for as long as you find new things to study.

The advantages of secondary analysis are obvious and enormous: it is cheaper and faster than doing original surveys, and, depending on who did the original survey, you may benefit from the work of topflight professionals. There are disadvantages, however. The key problem involves the recurrent question of validity. When one researcher collects data for one particular purpose, you have no assurance that those data will be appropriate to your research interests. Typically, you'll find that the original researcher asked a question that "comes close" to measuring what you are interested in, but you'll wish the question had been asked just a little differently—or that another, related question had also been asked. Your question, then, is whether the question that was asked provides a valid measure of the variable you want to analyze.

Notice that this problem resembles closely one of the key problems in the analysis of existing statistics. Recall that Stouffer had to ask whether out-of-state marriages provided a valid measure

of what he was calling, on theoretical grounds, impulsive marriages. As with existing statistics, this dilemma in secondary analysis can be lessened through replication. Perhaps a particular set of data does not provide a totally satisfactory measure of what interests you. But there are other sets of data available. Even if no one set of data provides totally valid measures, you can build up a weight of evidence by analyzing all the possibilities. If each of the imperfect measures points to the same research conclusion, you will have developed considerable support for its accuracy.

In this book, the discussion of secondary analysis has a special purpose. As we continue our examination of modes of observation in social research, you should have developed a full appreciation of the range of possibilities available to you in finding the answers to questions about social life. There is no single method of getting information that unlocks all puzzles. Yet there is no limit to the ways you can find out about things. And, more powerfully, you can zero in on an issue from several independent directions, gaining an even greater mastery of it.

Main Points

• Survey research, a popular social research method, is the administration of questionnaires to a sample of respondents selected from some population.

• Survey research is especially appropriate for making descriptive studies of large populations; survey data may be used for explanatory purposes as well.

• Questionnaires may be administered in three basically different ways: Self-administered questionnaires may be completed by the respondents themselves; interviewers may administer questionnaires in face-to-face encounters, reading the items to respondents and recording the answers; or interviewers may conduct telephone surveys.

• It is generally advisable to plan follow-up mailings in the case of self-administered questionnaires: send new questionnaires to respondents who fail to respond to the initial appeal.

• A proper monitoring of questionnaire returns will provide a good guide to when a follow-up mailing is appropriate.

• The essential characteristic of interviewers is that they be neutral; their presence in the data collection process must not have any effect on the responses given to questionnaire items.

• Interviewers must be carefully trained to be familiar with the questionnaire, to follow the question wording and question order exactly, and to record responses exactly as they are given.

• A probe is a neutral, nondirective question designed to elicit an elaboration on an incomplete or ambiguous response given in an interview in response to an open-ended question. Examples would include: "Anything else?" "How is that?" "In what ways?"

• The advantages of a self-administered questionnaire over an interview survey are economy, speed, lack of interviewer bias, and the possibility of anonymity and privacy to encourage more candid responses on sensitive issues.

• Surveys conducted over the telephone have become more common and more effective in recent years, and computer-assisted telephone interviewing (CATI) techniques are especially promising.

• The advantages of an interview survey over a self-administered questionnaire are fewer incomplete questionnaires and fewer misunderstood questions, generally higher return rates, and greater flexibility in terms of sampling and special observations.

• Survey research in general has advantages in terms of economy and the amount of data that can be collected. The standardization of the data collected represents another special strength of survey research.

• Survey research has the weaknesses of being somewhat artificial and potentially superficial. It is difficult to gain a full sense of social processes in their natural settings through the use of surveys.

• Secondary analysis refers to the analysis of data collected earlier by another researcher for some purpose other than the topic of the current study.

Review Questions and Exercises

1. Construct a set of contingency questions for use in a self-administered questionnaire that would solicit the following information:

a. Is the respondent employed?

b. If unemployed, is the respondent looking for work?

c. If the unemployed respondent is not looking for work, is he or she retired, a student, or a homemaker?

d. If the respondent is looking for work, how long has he or she been looking?

2. Find a questionnaire printed in a magazine or newspaper (for a reader survey, for example). Bring the questionnaire to class and critique it. Critique other aspects of the survey design.

Additional Readings

Babbie, Earl, *Survey Research Methods* (Belmont, CA: Wadsworth, 1973). A comprehensive overview of survey methods. (You thought we'd say it was lousy?) This textbook, although overlapping somewhat with the present one, covers aspects of survey techniques that are omitted here.

Bradburn, Norman M., and Sudman, Seymour, *Polls and Surveys: Understanding What They Tell Us* (San Francisco: Jossey-Bass, 1988). These veteran survey researchers answer questions about their craft that are commonly asked by the general public.

Dillman, Don A., *Mail and Telephone Surveys: The Total Design Method* (New York: Wiley, 1978). An excellent review of the methodological literature on mail and telephone surveys. Dillman makes many good suggestions for improving response rates.

Hyman, Herbert, *Secondary Analysis of Sample Surveys* (New York: Wiley, 1972). A comprehensive overview of secondary analysis. Hyman examines the role of this method within the broader context of social scientific inquiry, discusses methods of secondary analysis, and provides many illustrations.

Kiecolt, E. Jill, and Nathan, Laura E., *Secondary Analysis of Survey Data* (Beverly Hills, CA: Sage, 1985). An excellent overview of the major sources of data for secondary analysis and guidelines for taking advantage of them.

Rossi, Peter, Wright, James, and Anderson, Andy (eds.), *Handbook of Survey Research* (New York: Academic Press, 1983). A useful reference book on various aspects of survey design and execution.

Smith, Tom W., "The First Straw? A Study of the Origins of Election Polls," *Public Opinion Quarterly*, 1990, Vol. 54 (Spring: 21–36). This article examines the early history of American political polling, with special attention to the media reactions to the polls.

Stouffer, Samuel, *Communism, Conformity, and Civil Liberties* (New York: Wiley, 1955). An old but classic survey. This massive survey examined the impact of (Joe) McCarthyism on the attitudes of both the general public and community leaders, asking whether the repression of the early 1950s affected support for civil liberties.

Qualitative Research Methods

What You'll Learn in This Chapter

You'll improve your ability to observe social life in
its natural setting—where the action is. You'll
learn how to prepare for the field, how to
observe, how to conduct intensive qualitative
interviews, how to take notes, and how to analyze
what you observe.

INTRODUCTION

Earlier, we said that you had been doing social research all your life. That should become even clearer to you now as we turn to qualitative research methods. Commonly used qualitative research methods include *participant observation, direct observation,* and *unstructured* or *intensive interviewing.* The term *field research* is often used to include all these methods, and we will use it that way in this chapter. (Thus, we will be using *field research* and *qualitative research* somewhat interchangeably, since they are often used interchangeably in the research literature.)

Field research probably seems like the most obvious way to learn about something: just go and watch it happen, experience it, perhaps even participate in it. While these are "natural" activities, we'll see that they are also skills to be learned and honed. That's what this chapter is all about.

Many of the observation methods discussed in this book are designed to produce data appropriate for *quantitative* (statistical) analysis. Thus, surveys provide data from which to calculate the percentage unemployed in a population, mean incomes, and so forth. Field research more typically yields *qualitative* data: observations not easily reduced to numbers. For example, a field researcher may note the "defiant dignity" of homeless people who refuse to utilize squalid shelters or the "fatalism" of chronically unemployed men who hang out together, without being able to express either the dignity or the fatalism as numerical quantities or degrees.

Occasionally, people use the term *qualitative data* interchangeably with *nominal* data. That is, they use it to refer to data reported in the qualitative categories of nominal variables like gender, ethnicity, and so on. That's *not* how we are using the term, however. When we refer to qualitative data, we are referring to data gathered by participant observation, direct observation, case studies, intensive interviewing, and similar methods. Although nominal measurements are often used in qualitative research, they can also be used for quantitative purposes—for instance, by assessing the percentage of cases in various "qualitative" categories.

Field research is both very old and very new in social science. Social researchers have used many of the techniques we'll discuss in this chapter for centuries. Within the social sciences, anthropologists are especially associated with this method and have contributed to its development as a scientific technique. It should be noted that something similar to this method is used by many people who might not, strictly speaking, be regarded as social science researchers. Newspaper reporters are one example; direct-practice social workers are another.

It bears repeating that all of us constantly use field research. In a sense, we do field research whenever we observe or participate in social behavior and try to understand it, whether at an unemployment office, in a doctor's waiting room, on an airplane, or anywhere. Whenever we report our observations to others, we are reporting field research. The purpose of this chapter is to discuss this method in some detail, provide a logical overview of the method, and suggest some of the specific skills and techniques that make scientific field research more useful than the casual observation we all engage in.

Field observation differs from some other models of observation in that it is not only a data collecting activity. Frequently, perhaps typically, it is a theory-generating activity as well. As a field researcher you will seldom approach your task with precisely defined hypotheses to be tested. More typically, you will attempt to make sense out of an ongoing process that cannot be predicted in advance—making initial observations, developing tentative general conclusions that suggest particular types of further observations, making those observations and thereby revising your conclusions, and so forth. The alternation of induction and deduction discussed in Part 1 of this book is perhaps nowhere more evident and essential than in good field research.

THE TERMINOLOGY OF QUALITATIVE INQUIRY

If you read much of the literature on qualitative inquiry—either reports of qualitative research or texts about how to do it—you are likely to encounter what Lofland and Lofland (1995:6) call a "terminological jungle." In this jungle, authors often use different labels for research approaches that can seem awfully similar. We'll briefly examine some important terms here before moving on to the qualitative (field) research methods that tend to cut across all of these labels.

Grounded Theory

Glaser and Strauss (1967) coined the term *grounded theory* to refer to an inductive process of discovering theory from data. Contrasting grounded theory with theory generated from deductive reasoning from a priori assumptions, they argued that theories generated from, and *grounded* in, observations of the empirical world had a better chance of being useful and valid than logico-deductive theories. In their view, researchers become insensitive to new perspectives when their observations are guided exclusively by a specific preconceived theory.

Although grounded theory emphasizes an inductive process, it can also incorporate deductive processes. It does this through the use of *constant comparisons*. As researchers detect patterns in their inductive observations, they develop concepts and working hypotheses based on those patterns. Then they seek out more cases and conduct more observations and compare those observations against the concepts and hypotheses developed from the earlier observations.

Their selection of new cases is guided by *theoretical sampling* concepts. Theoretical sampling begins by selecting new cases that seem to be similar to the case(s) that generated previously detected concepts and hypotheses. Once the researcher perceives that no new insights are being generated from observing similar cases, a different type of case is selected, and the same process is repeated (selecting additional cases similar to this new type of case until no new insights are being generated). This cycle of exhausting similar cases and then seeking a different category of cases can be repeated until the researcher believes that further seeking of new types of cases will not alter the findings.

Grounded theorists use basically the same field observation methods that are used by other qualitative researchers—methods that we'll be discussing shortly, such as participant observation and open-ended interviewing.

To illustrate the use of constant comparisons in the grounded theory process, imagine that you are seeking to discover the key components of effective community-based social work intervention aimed at forestalling relapse among young adults who have had schizophrenia. You might begin with open-ended interviews of several practitioners who have excellent reputations for their clinical effectiveness in this area. Perhaps you'd ask those practitioners to recall their most successful cases and to discuss the interventions they employed with those cases.

Let's suppose that you perceive a common pattern across every interview—a pattern in which each practitioner mentions the use of social skills training in the rehabilitation of the young adults and communication skills training in helping their parents cope with them. You might therefore develop a working hypothesis that the use of such behavioral interventions distinguishes effective from ineffective practice in this area.

To better ground your hypothesis in the empirical world, you might interview several additional practitioners with good clinical reputations to see if the same patterns are generated. If those interviews fail to generate new insights, you might re-interview the practitioners, but with a different case sampling approach. This time you might ask them to discuss the interventions they employed with their least successful cases. Suppose a few of them mention the same behavioral interventions that they mentioned with their most successful cases—the same behavioral interventions to which your working hypothesis refers. This would force you to modify your hypothesis. You might probe to uncover other aspects of their practice with their least successful cases—aspects that might help explain why the same interventions that seemed to work well with other cases did not work with these cases.

Let's suppose that these probes generate another common pattern—a pattern in which each of the least successful clients failed or refused to take their prescribed medications. Based on this observation, your modified working hypothesis might combine medication monitoring interventions with behavioral interventions in distinguishing effective practice.

Continuing the grounded theory process, you would interview additional practitioners and ask about different types of cases. For example, you might learn of some parents who did not benefit from the communications skills training because the practitioner did not adequately develop a therapeutic alliance with them before introducing that training. This might lead you to modify your working hypothesis further, perhaps by adding the prerequisite that family intervention be delivered in the context of a supportive relationship with the practitioner, one in which the parents understand that they are not being blamed for their child's illness.

At this point you might realize that all of your cases have involved clients who live with their parents. Therefore, you might conduct interviews in reference to successful and unsuccessful cases in which the clients did not live with their parents. You might learn that with clients who do not live with their parents, effective practice also requires a lot of attention to securing suitable living arrangements and does not involve family communication skills training. Further sampling might identify many cases involving a dual diagnosis of schizophrenia and substance abuse. You might have to modify your hypothesis to include some substance abuse interventions geared for this target population.

By the time you have completed the grounded theory process, you will have interviewed many different practitioners (perhaps including some with poor clinical reputations) and asked about many additional types of cases. This additional empirical grounding will probably have led you to add many more modifications to your hypothesis. Some modifications might deal with practitioner attributes, such as empathy, warmth, and diagnostic skill. Some modifications might deal with client attributes, such as the need for different types of interventions depending on client degree of impairment, social support resources, and so on. Other modifications might deal with the full gamut of case management functions.

Gilgun (1991) sees a number of parallels between the grounded theory method and what social workers do in direct practice—particularly regarding clinical assessment. Both methods start where the case is and focus on the perceptions of the informant. Both try to understand the case in a wider environmental context. Both combine induction and deduction and the constant comparison method in formulating working hypotheses based on observations and then modifying those hypotheses in light of further observations. Both try to avoid imposing preconceived ideas or theories on cases. Both rely heavily on open-ended interviewing and use largely the same interviewing skills (as will be evident later in this chapter, when we discuss qualitative interviewing). The process of using notes and memos in grounded theory resembles the social worker's use of process recording and problem-oriented case recordkeeping. Both attempt "to keep a balance between being in tune with clients and maintaining an analytic stance" (1991:17). Both like to conduct observations in natural settings, such as in the home or community.

Ethnography

Although essentially all qualitative inquiry is consistent with the grounded theory approach, it is usually given a different label. Sometimes it is called *naturalistic research,* to convey the emphasis on observing the details of everyday life as they naturally unfold in the real world. Sometimes it is called *ethnographic research,* or *ethnography,* to emphasize the study of a culture from the point of view of the people who inhabit that culture.

Conducting ethnographic research in social work, for example, might involve studying the culture of a public welfare agency from the point of view of the workers or clients in that agency, or the culture of the homeless poor from the point of view of people who are homeless and poor. Sometimes researchers do not purport to be studying an entire culture, and therefore do not call their research ethnography, but nevertheless refer to the field research methods they use—the methods we will be discussing in this chapter as field or qualitative research methods—as *ethnographic methods.*

Some ethnographic researchers have coined the term *ethnomethodology* in reference to studies that focus on the use of norms, labeling, linguistic expressions, understandings, and assumptions that people use to "make sense of their everyday activities" and "behave in socially acceptable ways" (Patton, 1990:88). Ethnomethodologists also create unusual situations in an effort to understand how groups attempt to make sense of what is happening (Patton, 1990).

John Lofland (1995) speaks more specifically of *analytic ethnography* in an article aimed at delineating the key elements in a research strategy used by many field researchers.

Generic Propositions   Lofland argues that analytic ethnographers are committed ultimately to the establishment of general propositions regarding the patterns of human social life. Some of those patterns are descriptive (for example, the frequency of certain events) and some are explanatory (for instance, what causes certain kinds of behavior).

Unfettered Inquiry   Despite diverse views about what is or is not a "proper" subject for social science inquiry, Lofland suggests field researchers basically side with the view that anything is fair game.

Deep Familiarity To the extent possible you place yourself in the position of those you wish to understand. Lofland (1995:45) quotes Erving Goffman describing this process by saying, "You are close to them while they are responding to what life does to them. I feel that the way this is done is not, of course, just to listen to what they talk about, but to pick up their minor grunts and groans as they respond to their situation." Goffman suggests such researchers are not so much interviewers or listeners as *witnesses*.

Emergent Analysis As discussed above in terms of "grounded theory," Lofland argues that theory emerges in the course of analyzing observations; it does not precede observation in the form of hypotheses.

True Content Confronting postmodern suggestions that there is no "true" reality, Lofland says that analytic ethnographers proceed as though it existed anyway, developing and using techniques that will accurately capture what is "really" going on.

New Content In contrast to the natural sciences tradition of replicating findings, Lofland says that analytic ethnographers aim at the creation of new observations and/or new analyses with each research effort.

Developed Treatment Here Lofland speaks of a balance between the presentation of data from observations and the elaboration of theoretical concepts that can represent and make sense of those data.

Lofland recognizes that some field researchers would quibble with some details in his characterization of analytic ethnography and some would even disagree with some fundamentals. Nonetheless, his description provides a good sense of what is typically meant by ethnography in field research.

Phenomenology

Sometimes the more philosophical term, *phenomenology,* is used to emphasize a focus on people's subjective experiences and interpretations of the world. This type of focus tends to apply to all qualitative inquiry, and therefore the term *phenomenology* might also be used to convey the philosophical assumptions underlying ethnography, ethnomethodology, or other terms for qualitative inquiry.

One form of phenomenology is *heuristic inquiry*. In heuristic inquiry researchers shed an effort to be detached observers and actually experience firsthand the phenomenon they are studying, using *introspection* to examine their own thoughts and feelings while experiencing that phenomenon. In social work, for example, a researcher might stay in a shelter for the homeless to better understand the meaning of that experience to the homeless and perhaps to better understand why some homeless people refuse to use shelters.

A related philosophical term that you might encounter is *hermeneutics*. Hermeneutics emphasizes the process of interpretation, in which researchers seek to detect patterns from voluminous, and perhaps chaotic, details. Although these researchers attempt to make logical sense out of observed details, this interpretive process relies on the art and skill of the researcher, not on the application of specifiable logical rules of data analysis. Because this process is relatively amorphous and vulnerable to the influence of subjective perspectives, researchers who engage in this approach to research should take into account the perspectives they bring to the research, as well as the perspectives of those they observe, when they interpret and report the meaning of what they observe.

An important phenomenological principle in qualitative research is the German term *verstehen,* which means "understanding." Qualitative inquiry involves the attempt to understand those we observe from *their* own perspective—to understand *their* feelings, *their* views of reality, and the special meanings of what we observe to them. Thus, *verstehen* corresponds closely to a social work practice concept you may know about—*empathy*. Direct-service practitioners attempt to use empathy to understand their clients in much the same way that *verstehen* is used in qualitative inquiry.

Before we leave this section on terminology, we want to remind you of the overlapping way these terms are used in many reports of qualitative research studies. Don't be surprised, for example, if you encounter a study reported as ethnographic research that uses grounded theory in a naturalistic investigation guided by phenomenological inquiry using heuristic observation methods and a hermeneutic approach to data interpretation. If you read such a study, we can, based on our own introspection, empathize with you, and we hope this chapter will help you in your *verstehen* of it.

TOPICS APPROPRIATE TO FIELD RESEARCH

One of the key strengths of field research is the comprehensiveness of perspective it gives the researcher. By going directly to the social phenomenon under study and observing it as completely as possible, you can develop a deeper understanding of it. This mode of observation, then, is especially, though not exclusively, appropriate to research topics that appear to defy simple quantification. The field researcher may recognize several nuances of attitude and behavior that might escape researchers using other methods.

Somewhat differently, field research is especially appropriate to the study of those topics for which attitudes and behaviors can best be understood within their natural setting. Experiments and surveys may be able to measure behaviors and attitudes in somewhat artificial settings, but not all behavior is best measured this way. For example, field research provides a superior method for studying the experience of being an inpatient in a state psychiatric hospital.

Finally, field research is especially appropriate to the study of social processes over time. Thus, the field researcher might be in a position to examine the rumblings and final explosion of a riot as events actually occur rather than trying to reconstruct them afterward.

Other good uses of field research methods would include protest demonstrations, agency board meetings, labor negotiations, public hearings, interactions between social workers and clients, or similar events taking place within a relatively limited area and time. Several such observations must be combined in a more comprehensive examination across time and space.

In their *Analyzing Social Settings* (1995: 101–113), John Lofland and Lyn Lofland discuss several appropriate kinds of foci for field research. They call them *thinking topics*.

1. *Practices*. This refers to various kinds of behavior.

2. *Episodes*. Here the Loflands include a variety of events such as divorce, crime, and illness.

3. *Encounters*. This involves two or more people meeting and interacting in immediate proximity with one another.

4. *Roles*. Field research is also appropriate to the analysis of the positions people occupy and the behavior associated with those positions: occupations, family roles, ethnic groups.

5. *Relationships*. Much social life can be examined in terms of the kinds of behavior appropriate to pairs or sets of roles: mother-son relationships, friendships, and the like.

6. *Groups*. Moving beyond relationships, field research can also be used to study small groups, such as friendship cliques, athletic teams, and work groups.

7. *Organizations.* Beyond small groups, field researchers also study formal organizations, such as hospitals or schools.

8. *Settlements.* It is difficult to study large societies such as nations, but field researchers often study smaller scale "societies" such as villages, ghettos, and neighborhoods.

9. *Social Worlds.* There are also ambiguous social entities with vague boundaries and populations, which are nonetheless proper subjects for social scientific study: "the sports world," "Wall Street," and the like.

10. *Lifestyles or Subcultures.* Finally, social scientists sometimes focus on ways that large numbers of people adjust to life: groups such as a "ruling class" or an "urban underclass."

In all these social settings, field research can reveal things that would not otherwise be apparent. It does this by probing social life in its natural setting. Although some things can be studied adequately in questionnaires or in the laboratory, others cannot. And direct observation in the field lets you observe subtle communications and other events that might not be anticipated or measured otherwise.

THE VARIOUS ROLES OF THE OBSERVER

In this chapter, we use the term *field research* rather than the frequently used term *participant observation* because field researchers need not always participate in what they are studying, though they usually will study it directly at the scene of the action. Raymond Gold (1969:30–39) has discussed four different positions on a continuum of roles that field researchers may play in this regard: *complete participant, participant-as-observer, observer-as-participant,* and *complete observer.* Gold described the *complete participant* as follows:

The true identity and purpose of the complete participant in field research are not known to those whom he observes. He interacts with them as naturally as possible in whatever areas of their living interest him and are acceptable to him in situations in which he can play or learn to play requisite day-to-day roles successfully. (1969:33)

The complete participant, in this sense, may be a genuine participant in what he or she is studying (for example, a participant in a protest demonstration) or may pretend to be a genuine participant. In any event, if you are acting as the complete participant, you let people see you *only* as a participant, not as a researcher.

Clearly, if you are not a genuine participant in what you are studying, you must learn to behave as though you were. If you are studying a group made up of uneducated and inarticulate people, it would not be appropriate for you to talk and act like a university professor or student.

Here let us draw your attention to an *ethical* issue, one on which social researchers themselves are divided. Is it ethical to deceive the people you are studying in the hope that they will confide in you as they will not confide in an identified researcher? Do the interests of science—the scientific values of the research—offset such ethical considerations? Although many professional associations have addressed this issue, the norms to be followed remain somewhat ambiguous when applied to specific situations.

Related to this ethical consideration is a scientific one. No researcher deceives his or her subjects solely for the purpose of deception. Rather, it is done in the belief that the data will be more valid and reliable, that the subjects will be more natural and honest if they do not know the researcher is doing a research project. If the people being studied know they are being studied, they might modify their behavior in a variety of ways. First, they might expel the researcher. Second, they might modify their speech and behavior to appear more respectable than would otherwise be the case. Third, the social process itself might be radically changed. Students making plans to burn down the university administration building, for example, might give up the plan altogether once they learn that one of their group is a social scientist conducting a research project.

On the other side of the coin, if you are a complete participant, you may affect what you are studying. To play the role of participant, you must *participate*. Yet your participation may importantly affect the social process you are studying. Suppose, for example, that you are asked for your ideas about what the group should do next. No matter what you say, you will affect the process in some fashion. If the group follows your suggestion, your influence on the process is obvious. If the group decides not to follow your suggestion, the process by which the suggestion is rejected may affect what happens next. Finally, if you indicate that you just don't know what should be done next, you may be adding to a general feeling of uncertainty and indecisiveness in the group.

Ultimately, *anything* the participant observer does or does not do will have some effect on what is being observed; it is simply inevitable. More seriously, what you do or do not do may have an *important* effect on what happens. There is no complete protection against this effect, though sensitivity to the issue may provide partial protection.

Because of these several considerations, ethical and scientific, the field researcher frequently chooses a different role from that of complete participant. In Gold's terminology, you might choose the role of *participant-as-observer*. In this role, you would participate fully with the group under study, but you would make it clear that you were also undertaking research. If you were a member of the volleyball team, for example, you might use that position to launch a study in the sociology of sports, letting your teammates know what you were doing. There are dangers in this role also, however. The people being studied may shift much of their attention to the research project rather than focusing on the natural social process, and the process being observed may no longer be typical. Or, conversely, you yourself

may come to identify too much with the interests and viewpoints of the participants. You may begin to "go native" and lose much of your scientific detachment.

The *observer-as-participant* is one who identifies himself or herself as a researcher and interacts with the participants in the social process but makes no pretense of actually being a participant. A good example of that would be a newspaper reporter learning about a social movement—for instance, the unionization of migrant farm workers. The reporter might interview leaders and also visit workers where they live, watch strawberry picking, go with an injured worker to the hospital, and so on.

The *complete observer*, at the other extreme, observes a social process without becoming a part of it in any way. The subjects of study might not realize they are being studied because of the researcher's unobtrusiveness. Sitting at a bus stop to observe jaywalking behavior at a nearby intersection would be an example. Although the complete observer is less likely to affect what is being studied and less likely to "go native" than the complete participant, he or she is also less likely to develop a full appreciation of what is being studied. Observations may be more sketchy and transitory.

Fred Davis (1973) characterized the extreme roles that observers might play as "the Martian" and "the Convert." The latter involves the observer delving deeper and deeper into the phenomenon under study, running the risk that anthropologists refer to as "going native." We'll examine this further in the next section.

On the other hand, you may be able to most fully grasp the "Martian" approach by imagining that you were sent to observe life on Mars (assuming life forms had been found there). Probably you would feel yourself inescapably separate from the Martians. Some social scientists adopt this degree of separation when observing cultures or social classes different from their own.

Ultimately, different situations require different roles for the researcher. Unfortunately, there are no clear guidelines for making this choice, and you must rely on your understanding of the situation and your own good judgment. In making your decision, however, you must be guided by both methodological and ethical considerations. Because these often conflict with one another, your decision will frequently be a difficult one, and you may find sometimes that your role limits your study.

RELATIONS TO SUBJECTS

Having introduced the different roles you might play in connection with your field research observations, we're now going to focus more specifically on how you may relate to the subjects of your study and to their points of view. In the previous section, we've opened up the possibility of pretending to occupy social statuses you don't really occupy. Now let's consider how you would think and feel in such a situation.

Let's suppose you have decided to study a religious cult that has enrolled many people in your neighborhood or in a neighborhood you have social work responsibilities for. You might study the group by joining it or pretending to join it. Take a moment to ask yourself what the difference is between "really" joining and "pretending" to join. The main difference is one of whether you actually take on the beliefs, attitudes, and other points of view shared by the "real" members. If the cult members believe that Jesus will come next Thursday to destroy the world and save the members of the cult, do you believe that or do you simply pretend to believe it?

Traditionally, social scientists have tended to emphasize the importance of "objectivity" in such matters. In this example, that injunction would be to avoid getting swept up in the beliefs of the group. Without denying the advantages associated with such objectivity, social scientists today also recognize the benefits to be gained by immersing themselves in the points of view they are studying, gaining what Lofland and Lofland

(1995:61) refer to as *insider understanding.* Ultimately, you will not be able to understand the thoughts and actions of the cult members unless you are able to *adopt their points of view as true*—even if you only do so on a temporary basis. In a sense, you need to *believe* that Jesus is coming Thursday night to fully appreciate the phenomenon you've set out to study.

Adopting an alien point of view is an uncomfortable prospect for most people. It's one thing to learn about the strange views that others may hold—and sometimes you probably have difficulty even tolerating those views—but to take them on as your own is ten times worse. Robert Bellah (1970, 1974) has offered the term *symbolic realism* in this regard, indicating the need for social researchers to treat the beliefs they study as worthy of respect rather than as objects of ridicule. If you seriously entertain this prospect, you may appreciate why William B. Shaffir and Robert A. Stebbins (1991:1) concluded that "fieldwork must certainly rank with the more disagreeable activities that humanity has fashioned for itself."

There is, of course, a danger involved in adopting the points of view of the people you are studying. When you abandon your objectivity in favor of adopting the views you are studying, you lose the possibility of seeing and understanding the phenomenon within frames of reference unavailable to your subjects. On the one hand, accepting the belief that the world will end Thursday night allows you to appreciate aspects of that belief available only to believers; stepping outside that view, however, makes it possible for you to consider some reasons why people might adopt such a view. You may discover that some reached that state as a consequence of personal traumas (such as unemployment or divorce), while others were brought into the fold through their participation in particular social networks (for instance, their whole bowling team joined the cult). Notice that the cult members might disagree with those "objective" explanations, and you might not come up with them to the extent that you were operating legitimately within the group's views.

There is, of course, a dilemma here. There are important advantages in both postures, even though they seem mutually exclusive. It is, in fact, possible to assume both postures. Sometimes you can simply shift viewpoints at will. When appropriate, you can fully assume the beliefs of the cult; later, you can step outside those beliefs (more accurately, you step inside the viewpoints associated with social science). As you become more adept at this kind of research, you may lose the sense of switching between viewpoints. Many field researchers find it is possible to hold contradictory viewpoints simultaneously, even though it is impossible to say much more about it than that.

When one of us (Babbie) was studying trance channelers—people who allow spirits to occupy their bodies and speak through them—he found it was possible to participate fully in channeling sessions without becoming alienated from conventional social science. Rather than "believing" in the reality of channeling, Babbie found it possible to suspend beliefs in that realm: neither believing it to be genuine (like most of the other participants) nor disbelieving it (like most scientists). Put differently, Babbie was open to either possibility. Notice how this differs from our normal need to "know" whether such things are legitimate or not.

The problem we've just been discussing could be seen to appear at a psychological level, occurring mostly inside the researcher's head. There is a corresponding problem at a social level. When you become deeply involved in the lives of the people you are studying, you are likely to be moved by their personal problems and crises. Imagine, for example, that one of the cult members becomes ill and needs a ride to the hospital. Should you provide transportation? Sure. Suppose someone wants to borrow money to buy a stereo. Should you loan it? Probably not. Suppose they need the money for food?

There are no black-and-white rules for resolving situations such as these. However, we want to warn you that such problems arise and you will need to deal with them, regardless of whether you have revealed yourself to be a researcher or not. Such problems do not tend to arise in other types of research—surveys or experiments, for example—but they are part and parcel of participant observation.

PREPARING FOR THE FIELD

Suppose for the moment that you have decided to undertake field research on a grassroots community organization. Let's assume further that you are not a member of that group, that you do not know a great deal about it, and that you will identify yourself to the participants as a researcher. This section will discuss some of the ways you might prepare yourself before undertaking direct observation of the group.

As is true of all research methods, you would be well advised to begin with a search of the relevant literature, filling in your knowledge of the subject and learning what others have said about it. Because library research is discussed at length in Appendix A, we won't say anything further at this point.

In the next phase of your research, you may wish to make use of informants (discussed in Chapter 8, on sampling). You might wish to discuss the community group with others who have already studied it or with anyone else likely to be familiar with it. In particular, you might find it useful to discuss the group with one of its members. Perhaps you already know a member, or you can meet someone who is. This aspect of your preparation is likely to be more effective if your relationship with the informant extends beyond your research role. In dealing with members of the group as informants, you should take care that your initial discussions do not compromise or limit later aspects of your research. Realize that the impression you make on the member-informant, the role you establish for yourself, may carry over into your later effort. For example, creating the initial impression that you may be a spy for an opposing group is unlikely to facilitate later observations of the group.

You should also be wary about the information you get from informants. Although they may have more direct, personal knowledge of the subject under study than you, what they "know" is probably a mixture of fact and point of view. Members of the community group in our example are unlikely to give you completely unbiased information (nor would members of opposing groups). Before making your first contact with the group, then, you should be already quite familiar with it, and you should understand the general, theoretical context within which it exists.

There are a variety of ways to establish your initial contact with the people you plan to study. How you do it will depend, in part, on the role you intend to play. Especially if you are to take on the role of complete participant, you must find a way of developing an identity with the people to be studied. If you wish to study dishwashers in a restaurant, the most direct method would be to get a job as a dishwasher. In the case of the community organization, you might simply join the group. Many of the social processes appropriate to field research are sufficiently open to make your contact with the people to be studied simple and straightforward. If you wish to observe a mass demonstration, just be there. If you wish to observe patterns in jaywalking, hang around busy streets.

Whenever you wish to make a more formal contact with the people and wish to identify yourself as a researcher, you must be able to establish a certain rapport with them. You might contact a participant with whom you feel comfortable and gain that person's assistance. If you are studying a formal group, you might approach the group leaders. Or you may find that one of your informants who has studied the group can introduce you.

While you will probably have many options in making your initial contact with the group, you should realize that your choice can influence your subsequent observations. Suppose, for example, that you are studying a community clinic and begin with high-level administrators. First, your initial impressions of the clinic are going to be shaped by the administrators' views, which will be quite different from those of patients or staff. This initial impression may influence the way you subsequently observe and interpret—even though you are unaware of the influence.

Second, if the administrators approve of your research project and encourage patients and staff to cooperate with you, the latter groups will probably look on you as somehow aligned with the administration, which can affect what they say to you. Nurses might be reluctant to tell you about their plans to organize through the Teamsters Union, for example.

In making direct, formal contact with the people you want to study, you will be required to give them some explanation of the purpose of your study. Here again, you face an ethical dilemma. Telling them the complete purpose of your research might lose their cooperation altogether or importantly affect their behavior. On the other hand, giving only what you believe would be an acceptable explanation may involve outright deception. Realize in all this that your decisions—in practice—may be largely determined by the purpose of your study, the nature of what you are studying, observations you wish to use, and other such factors.

Previous field research offers no fixed rule—methodological or ethical—to follow in this regard. Your appearance as a researcher, regardless of stated purpose, may result in a warm welcome from people flattered that a scientist finds them important enough to study. Or it may result in your being totally ostracized or worse. (Do not, for example, burst into a meeting of an organized crime syndicate and announce that you are writing a term paper on organized crime.)

SAMPLING IN FIELD RESEARCH

Chapter 8 of this book discussed the logic and techniques involved in probability sampling in social research. Although the general principles of representativeness in that context should be remembered in field research, controlled sampling techniques are normally inappropriate, and nonprobability sampling techniques are more likely to be used. This section will discuss the matter of sampling as it typically applies in field research.

To begin, the population and the units of analysis in the field research project may be somewhat ambiguous. In studying the community group mentioned previously, are you interested in studying that group only, the members of the group, social action in general, or what? If you are studying three juvenile gangs in a particular city, are the gangs, the individual juveniles, or the city your units of analysis? Are you interested only in describing the gangs, or does your interest extend to juvenile peer relations in general? It is important that you ask yourself what population you wish to make general assertions about when you are finished with your research. The answer to this question will not always be obvious to you, and it may change over the course of your research. A limited initial concern may be expanded later as you conclude that certain of the phenomena you are observing apply well beyond your specific subjects of study. Although this general issue may not be easy to resolve in practice, sensitivity to it should help clarify your goals and methods.

The concept of sampling in connection with field research is more complicated than for the kinds of research dealt with in the earlier chapters. Field researchers attempt to observe everything within their field of study; thus, in a sense, they do not sample at all. In reality, of course, it is impossible to observe everything. To the extent that field researchers observe only a portion of what happens, then, what they do observe is a de facto sample of all the possible observations that might have been made. If several people are shouting support for the speaker in a community meeting, those shouts the researcher hears and understands represent a sample of all such shouts. Or if a researcher observes acts of violence during a riot, the observed acts are a sample of all such

acts of violence. You will seldom be able to select a controlled sample of such observations, but you should bear in mind the general principles of representativeness and interpret your observations accordingly.

Sometimes, however, you will be in a position to sample among possible observations. If you are studying the development of a grassroots community organization over time, for instance, you may choose to interview different members of that organization by listing all the members and then selecting a probability sample. This might not be the best method of sampling for your purposes, however. McCall and Simmons (1969) suggest three types of nonprobability sampling methods that are specifically appropriate to field research: the *quota* sample, the *snowball* sample, and *deviant* cases.

To begin, if the group or social process under study has fairly clearly defined categories of participants, some kind of **quota sample** might be used: persons representing all different participation categories should be studied. (Review Chapter 8 for a more detailed discussion of quota sampling as a general procedure.) In the study of a formal group, for instance, you might wish to interview both leaders and nonleaders. In studying a community organization, it might be useful to interview both radical and more moderate members of that group. In general, whenever representativeness is desired, you should use quota sampling and interview both men and women, young people and old people, and the like.

Second, McCall and Simmons mention the **snowball sample**—a technique that begins with a few relevant subjects you've identified and expands the sample through referrals. If you wish to learn the pattern of recruitment to a community organization over time, you might begin by interviewing fairly recent recruits, asking them who introduced them to the group. You might then interview the persons named, asking them who introduced *them* to the group. You might interview *those* persons in turn, asking, in part, who introduced them. In studying a loosely structured group, you might ask one of the participants who he or she believes to be the most influential members of the group. You might interview those people and, in the course of the interviews, ask who they believe to be the most influential. In each of these examples, your sample would "snowball" as each of your interviewees suggested others.

Finally, McCall and Simmons draw attention to the importance of **deviant case sampling.** Often, our understanding of fairly regular patterns of attitudes and behaviors is further improved by examining cases that do not fit into the regular pattern. You might gain important insights into the nature of group morale as exhibited at a meeting by interviewing people who did not appear to be caught up in the emotions of the crowd or by interviewing people who did not attend the meeting at all.

Deviant cases are unusual in some respect. Suppose, for example, you are interested in conducting a case study of several case management programs to describe the diversity of case management practice and to generate hypotheses about factors that influence the case management process. If you suspect that the nature of case management may vary considerably depending on the size of the case manager's caseload, you might want to select a couple of programs known for their extremely high caseloads and a couple known for their extremely low caseloads.

For another example, suppose you seek to generate hypotheses about the extent of family involvement in nursing home care. You might want to study intensively several families who are known by nursing home staff as being the most highly involved in the care of their relative and several who are known to be the least involved.

Perhaps, however, you might suspect that extreme or deviant cases are so unusual that they provide a distorted portrayal of the phenomenon you want to study. If so, Patton (1990) suggests that you consider using *intensity sampling*. In intensity sampling you would select cases that are more or less intense than usual, but not so unusual that they would be called deviant. Thus,

rather than selecting families that are most and least involved in nursing home care, you might select families known to be more or less involved than most families, but that are not so involved or so uninvolved that they represent aberrations whose information might be misleading or not particularly useful.

Suppose, for example, you are studying case management processes in a county mental health program where the case managers' average caseload size is 200 cases, and in a federally funded model mental health program in a different locality with an average caseload size of 2 cases. The former program may be in a state with no real commitment to case management, where funding is abysmally low, and where "case manager" may be a meaningless label it uses for the sake of appearing to comply with current trends without spending any more money. "Case management" in that program would be a misnomer, and the "case managers" in that program would have so little time to spend on any case that studying what they do might not provide a particularly rich source of information about the case management process. The latter program, as well, might not be a rich source of information. It may be so well endowed as a model program that it bears no resemblance to case management programs elsewhere, programs whose caseload sizes tend to range between 20 and 40 cases. Case managers in the model program may have so much time to spend on each case that they perform functions that go far beyond what case managers normally do even in good case management programs. Consequently, rather than select these extreme programs for study, you might select an *intensity sample* of programs with average caseload sizes of about 20 and about 40.

Another strategy that can perhaps be viewed as a form of extreme case sampling is *critical incidents sampling*. The critical incidents technique is particularly useful for generating hypotheses about social work practice effectiveness. A critical incident is one in which something of special importance seemed to happen—something either positive or negative—that might offer valuable new insights about how we can improve practice.

One way you could apply this technique would be to ask direct-service practitioners to identify the cases that, in their judgment, turned out to be their best successes or their worst failures. Then you could interview them intensively about each of the cases they identify, seeking to detect commonalities in what different practitioners did with their most successful cases and commonalities in what they did with their least successful cases. From these patterns you could suggest hypotheses for further study about the attributes that might distinguish successful and unsuccessful practice.

Another option that Patton identifies is *maximum variation sampling*. This strategy aims to capture the diversity of a phenomenon within a small sample to be studied intensively. By observing a phenomenon under heterogeneous conditions we are likely to generate more useful insights about it. Thus, if you want to study case management processes, you might select some programs with high, medium, and low caseload sizes; some in urban, suburban, and rural areas; some that are old, some that are new; and so on.

On the other hand, you might opt for a *homogeneous sample*. Suppose you are interested in studying how case managers attempt to handle role overload. You would probably want to restrict your sample to programs in which the case managers' caseload sizes were unusually large.

Earlier in this chapter, when we discussed grounded theory, we mentioned *theoretical sampling*. We indicated that theoretical sampling begins by selecting new cases that seem to be similar to the case(s) that generated previously detected concepts and hypotheses, but that once the researcher perceives that no new insights are being generated from observing similar cases, a different type of case is selected, and the same process is repeated until the observation of different types of cases seems to be generating no new insights. Theoretical sampling thus combines elements of homogeneous sampling and deviant case sampling. (In our earlier example of the grounded theory process, we actually combined theoretical sampling with the critical incidents technique.)

The types of nonprobability sampling strategies and samples that we've been discussing can all be called **purposive sampling** and **purposive samples.** In purposive sampling—unlike probability sampling—you select a sample of observations that you believe will yield the most comprehensive understanding of your subject of study, based on the intuitive feel for the subject that comes from extended observation and reflection. You can use purposive sampling procedures to select deviant cases or critical cases, but you can also use them to try to obtain a fairly representative portrayal of the phenomenon you are studying.

In a study of homelessness, you might wish to make observations on a number of different locations in the city. You could pick the sample of locations through standard probability methods; or, more likely, you could use a rough quota system, observing busy areas and deserted ones, or including samples from different times of day. In a study of the way nursing home staff and residents interact, you would observe different kinds of nursing homes and different areas of each home, for example. You might even seek to study deviant cases within a representative sample of larger groupings, such as applying the critical incidents technique across a representative sample of agencies. Although controlled probability sampling is seldom used in field research, understanding its principles and logic (as discussed in Chapter 8) is likely to produce more effective intuitive sampling in field research.

In field research, bear in mind two stages of sampling. First, to what extent are the total situations *available* for observation representative of the more *general* class of phenomena you wish to describe and explain? Are the three juvenile gangs you are observing representative of all gangs? Second, are your *actual* observations within those total situations representative of all the *possible* observations? Have you observed a representative sample of the members of the three gangs? Have

STUDYING EVERYDAY LIFE

by Robert Kubey, Department of Communication, Rutgers University

A number of methods have been developed that allow research subjects to report on their behavior while they are still in the field and going about their normal everyday activities. While one can learn about the daily behavior of people by having them fill out questionnaires or answer questions over the phone, it is often more valid to have respondents report on their behavior as it is actually happening or shortly thereafter.

One method is to ask subjects to keep a diary, but one in which they report on specific types of activities. Radio stations were among the first to use diaries in field research by having radio listeners keep track of which radio programs they listened to each day. The results from such diaries were then used to set advertising rates by demonstrating the true reach and popularity of a station. The A. C. Nielsen Company, which is well known for the mechanical "audimeter" device that records only when a household's television set is turned on and the channel to which it is turned—not who

specifically is watching it—also used diaries in order to collect detailed demographic data on the kinds of people who watch certain sorts of television programs.

Early radio and advertising researchers also pioneered a field method using the telephone. Researchers would simply phone households at random and ask what radio program they were then listening to in order to measure radio program popularity.

Alexander Szalai (1972) and John Robinson (1977) have honed the use of the diary to a fine art in their studies of how people use time around the world. They can tell you, for example, how many hours a day the average Bulgarian housewife spends shopping, when a Peruvian man is most likely to go to sleep each night, and how much time Americans spend working.

Other researchers are less interested in time use and more interested in how people experience everyday life and what they think about from moment to moment. One of the more popular methods to study subjective

---

you observed a representative sample of the interactions that have taken place? Even when controlled probability sampling methods are impossible or inappropriate, the logical link between representativeness and generalizability still holds. The logic of sampling and generalizability is basic in social research and is illustrated in a different context in the accompanying box titled "Studying Everyday Life."

Having discussed specific techniques that may be used for sampling in field research, we conclude with the injunction offered by Lofland and Lofland (1995:16):

Your overall goal is to collect the *richest possible data*. Rich data mean, ideally, a wide and diverse range of information collected over a relatively prolonged period of time. Again, ideally, you achieve

experience now in use is called the Experience Sampling Method (ESM) (Larson and Csikszentmihalyi, 1983).

If you were a subject in an ESM study, you'd be given an electronic paging device (beeper) and some small booklets of self-report forms. Then, you'd be signaled at random intervals, usually about eight times each day, for the period of a week. Every time you heard the beeper, you'd fill out a self-report form indicating where you were, who you were with, what you were doing, and how you were feeling on a series of mood adjectives using a semantic differential scale (see Chapter 7 of this book).

The ESM has been used around the world in a wide variety of ways. Some researchers have used it to study how people feel doing different activities and to help determine which daily activities are most psychologically rewarding (Csikszentmihalyi and Kubey, 1981). Others have used it to study the mood swings associated with psychological disorders such as bulimia and schizophrenia.

A similar random signaling technique called "thought sampling" has been used to find out what people think and fantasize about, how often they do it, and the conditions that provoke certain thoughts and fantasies.

When you think about it, the possibilities for adapting ESM to social research topics are endless.

References

Csikszentmihalyi, Mihaly, and Robert Kubey. 1981. "Television and the Rest of Life: A Systematic Comparison of Subjective Experience," *Public Opinion Quarterly,* Vol. 45, 317–328.

Larson, Reed, and Mihaly Csikszentmihalyi. 1983. "The Experience Sampling Method," in H. T. Reis (ed.), *Naturalistic Approaches in Studying Social Interaction.* New Directions for Methodology of Social and Behavioral Sciences, no. 15. San Francisco: Jossey-Bass.

Robinson, John. 1977. *How Americans Use Time: A Social-Psychological Analysis of Everyday Behavior.* New York: Praeger.

Szalai, Alexander. 1972. *The Use of Time: Daily Activities of Urban and Suburban Populations in Twelve Countries.* The Hague: Mouton.

this through direct, face-to-face contact with, and prolonged immersion in, some social location or circumstance. (emphasis in the original)

QUALITATIVE INTERVIEWING

In part, field research is a matter of going where the action is and simply watching and listening. You can learn a lot merely by being attentive to what's going on. At the same time, as we've already indicated, field research can involve more active inquiry. Sometimes it's appropriate to ask people questions and record their answers. Your on-the-spot observations of a full-blown riot will lack something if you don't know why people are rioting. Ask somebody.

We have already discussed interviewing in Chapter 11, on survey research. The interviewing you will do in connection with field observation, however, is different enough to demand a separate treatment here. In surveys, questionnaires are always structured and commonly use many closed-ended questions, but in field research interviews will be almost entirely open-ended and are likely to be unstructured.

Patton (1990) identifies three forms of qualitative, open-ended interviewing:

1. The informal conversational interview.
2. The general interview guide approach.
3. The standardized open-ended interview.

(1990:280)

Informal Conversational Interviews

An *informal conversational interview* is an unplanned and unanticipated interaction between an interviewer and a respondent that occurs naturally during the course of fieldwork observation. It is the most open-ended form of interviewing. When this type of interviewing occurs, the person with whom you are talking may not even think of the interaction as an interview.

When you conduct an informal conversational interview you should be extremely flexible so that you can pursue relevant information in whatever direction seems appropriate. Your questions should be generated naturally and spontaneously from what you happen to observe at a particular point in a particular setting or from what individuals in that setting happen to say to you. In other words, this is the type of interviewing that will occur spontaneously when you are conducting fieldwork observations and want to maximize your understanding of what you are observing and what the people whom you are observing think about what is happening.

Because you cannot anticipate the situation beforehand, you conduct informal conversational interviews with no predetermined set of questions. Nonetheless, it is important for you to use your skills in asking questions and listening—skills that you probably learned as part of your social work practice training.

Lofland and Lofland (1995:56–57) suggest that investigators adopt the role of the "socially acceptable incompetent" when interviewing. You should offer yourself as someone who does not understand the situation you find yourself in and must be helped to grasp even the most basic and obvious aspects of that situation.

> A naturalistic investigator, almost by definition, is one who does not understand. She or he is "ignorant" and needs to be "taught." This role of watcher and asker of questions is the quintessential *student* role. (Lofland and Lofland, 1995:56; emphasis in the original)

Asking questions and noting answers is a natural process for us all, and it seems simple enough to add that to your bag of tricks as a field researcher. Be a little cautious, however. There is a danger that, to paraphrase comedian Flip Wilson, "what you ask is what you get."

As we've already discussed in Chapter 7, question wording is a tricky business. All too often, the way we ask questions subtly biases the answers we get. Sometimes we put our respondent under pressure to look good. Sometimes we put the question in a particular context that completely precludes the most relevant answers.

Suppose you want to find out why a group of youths in a residential facility for emotionally distressed children is running amok. You might be tempted to focus your questioning on how the youths feel about the disciplinary style of their cottage parents. Although you may collect a great deal of information about their attitudes toward their cottage parents, they may be rioting for some other reason. Or perhaps most are simply joining in for the excitement. Properly done, informal conversational interviewing would enable you to find out.

One of the special strengths of this type of interviewing is its flexibility in the field. It allows you to respond to things you see or hear that you could not anticipate. The answers evoked by your initial questions should shape your subsequent ones. It doesn't work, in this situation, merely to ask preestablished questions and record the answers. You need to ask a question, hear the answer, interpret its meaning for your general inquiry, frame another question either to dig into the earlier answer in more depth or to redirect the person's attention to an area more relevant to your inquiry. In short, you need to be able to listen, think, and talk almost at the same time.

The discussion of *probes* in Chapter 11 provides a useful guide to getting answers in more depth without biasing later answers. Learn the skills of being a good listener. Be more interested than interesting. Learn to say things like "How is that?" "In what ways?" "How do you mean that?" "What would be an example of that?" Learn to look and listen expectantly, and let the person you are interviewing fill in the silence.

At the same time, you can't afford to be a totally passive receiver in the interaction. You'll probably have some general (or specific) questions in mind based on what you are observing, and you will have to learn the skills of subtly directing the flow of conversation.

There's something you can learn here from the Far Eastern martial arts. The aikido master never resists an opponent's blow but rather accepts it, joins with it, and then subtly redirects it in a more appropriate direction. You should master a similar skill for interviewing. Don't try to halt your respondent's line of discussion, but learn to take what he or she has just said and branch that comment back in the direction appropriate to your purposes. Most people love to talk to anyone who's really interested. Stopping their line of conversation tells them you aren't interested; asking them to elaborate in a particular direction tells them you are.

Consider this hypothetical example in which you are interested in why college students chose their majors.

You: What are you majoring in?

Resp: Engineering.

You: I see. How did you come to choose engineering?

Resp: I have an uncle who was voted the best engineer in Arizona in 1981.

You: Gee, that's great.

Resp: Yeah. He was the engineer in charge of developing the new civic center in Tucson. It was written up in most of the engineering journals.

You: I see. Did you talk to him about your becoming an engineer?

Resp: Yeah. He said that he got into engineering by accident. He needed a job when he graduated from high school, so he went to work as a laborer on a construction job. He spent eight years working his way up from the bottom, until he decided to go to college and come back nearer the top.

You: So is your main interest in civil engineering, like your uncle, or are you more interested in some other branch of engineering?

Resp: Actually, I'm leaning more toward electrical engineering—computers in particular. I started messing around with microcomputers when I was in high school, and my long-term plan is. . . .

Notice how the interview first begins to wander off into a story about the respondent's uncle. The first attempt to focus things back on the student's own choice of major failed. The second attempt succeeded. Now the student is providing the kind of information you're looking for. It's important for you to develop the ability to "control" conversations in that fashion.

Because informal conversational interviewing is so much like normal conversations, it is essential that you keep reminding yourself that you are not having a normal conversation. In normal conversations, each of us wants to come across as an interesting, worthwhile person. If you'll watch yourself the next time you are chatting with someone you don't know too well, you may find that much of your attention is spent on thinking up interesting things to say—contributions to the conversation that will make a good impression. Often, we don't really hear each other because we're too busy thinking of what we'll say next. As an interviewer, the desire to appear interesting is counterproductive to your job. You need to make the other person seem interesting, by being interested. (Do this, by the way, and people will actually regard you as a great conversationalist.)

Interviewing needs to be an integral part of your whole field research process. Later, we'll stress the need to review your notes every night—making sense out of what you've observed, getting a clearer feel for the situation you're studying, and finding out what you should pay more attention to in further observations.

In this same fashion, you need to review your notes on informal conversational interviews, detecting all the things you should have asked but didn't. Start asking those things the next time an applicable informal conversational interview emerges. As with all other aspects of field research, informal conversational interviewing improves with practice. Fortunately, it is something you can practice any time you want. Practice on your friends.

Interview Guide Approach

Besides including the unplanned interviews that emerge spontaneously in the conduct of field observations, qualitative inquiry can include the use of interviews that are planned in advance and that are therefore more structured than informal conversational interviews. Although all qualitative interviewing is open-ended and allows respondents to express their own perspectives in their own words, qualitative interviewing strategies can vary in the extent to which the sequencing and wording of the open-ended questions is predetermined.

Highly structured strategies attempt to ensure that all respondents are asked the same questions, in the same sequence, to maximize comparability of responses and to ensure that complete data are gathered from each person on all relevant questions. Greater structure can also reduce interviewer biases and inconsistencies in the way different interviewers conduct their interviews. More structure also eases the researcher's task of organizing and analyzing interview data and helps readers of the research report to judge the quality of the interviewing methods and instruments employed.

The downside to the highly structured approach, however, is that it reduces the natural, conversational nature of the interview and the interviewer's flexibility to follow up on important unanticipated circumstances or responses. Patton (1990) suggests that one way to provide more structure than in the completely unstructured informal conversational interview, but still maintain a relatively high degree of flexibility, is to use the interview guide strategy.

An *interview guide* lists in outline form the topics and issues that the interviewer should cover in the interview, but allows the interviewer to adapt the sequencing and wording of questions to each particular interview. Thus, the interview guide ensures that different interviewers will cover the same material and keep focused on the same predetermined topics and issues, while at the same time remaining conversational and free to probe into unanticipated circumstances and responses. Interview guides will vary in the extent of detail they provide. How much detail you provide in your guide will depend on the extent to which you are able to anticipate the important topics and issues in advance and how much detail you think your interviewers need in order to ensure that they will all cover the same material in a thorough fashion (Patton, 1990).

Suppose, for example, that you want to use intensive interviews of social workers in a qualitative evaluation of an in-service training program aimed at improving their own interviewing skills in conducting clinical assessments. A relatively brief interview guide might list a handful or so of broad question areas to ask about, such as:

1. What interviewing training activities and assignments did the trainee do in the program?

2. In what areas of interviewing, if any, does the trainee feel more or less skillful as a result of the program?

3. What service functions, if any, does the trainee feel better (or worse) prepared to provide as a result of the training?

4. Has the program influenced the trainee's career plans, and if so, how?

5. What did the trainee like and dislike most about the program? What are its strengths and weaknesses, and what changes, if any, does the trainee suggest?

A more detailed interview guide for the same type of evaluation might look something like the following rough example:

I. Overall impression of program
    A. Likes? Dislikes?
    B. Strengths? Weaknesses?
    C. Suggested changes?
    D. Perceived influence of program on trainee?
        1. Service functions prepared to provide
        2. Career plans
        3. Interviewing skills, in general

II. Activities in program
    A. Readings?
    B. Written experiential assignments?
    C. Role plays?
    D. Peer or instructor feedback?
    E. Instructor modeling of interview skills?

III. Progress made or not made in specific areas of interviewing
    A. Beginning the interview
        1. Meeting and greeting clients
        2. Introductions
        3. Putting client at ease
        4. Explaining purpose of interview
        5. Obtaining client's reason for coming
    B. Physical attending
        1. Eye contact
        2. Posture
        3. Intermittent positive gestures
        4. Appropriately relaxed and professionally comfortable?
    C. Verbal attending
        1. Nonjudgmental prompts
        2. Brief pauses before responding
        3. Appropriate paraphrasing
        4. Encouraging client to talk
        5. Sensitivity to differences in culture/ethnicity
        6. Conveying empathy and warmth
        7. Speaking in a natural, spontaneous, genuine manner
    D. Exploring the problem
        1. Taking social histories
        2. Examining problem from different perspectives
        3. Assessing situational and systemic factors
    E. Questioning and probing
        1. Asking clear and succinct questions
        2. Asking questions in an unbiased manner
        3. Asking exploratory questions in an open-ended manner
        4. Interspersing closed- and open-ended questions
        5. Pursuing important details with neutral probes
        6. Knowing not to bombard with too many questions
        7. Logical sequencing of questions
        8. Sensitivity to privacy concerns

In addition to facilitating your learning about the use of detailed interview guides, we hope this illustrative guide will be useful to you as you think about developing your own skills as a qualitative interviewer and as an interviewer in your social work practice roles.

Regardless of how detailed you make your interview guide, you should make sure that your interviewers are completely familiar with its contents and purposes before they begin any interviews. If they are not, the interview will not flow smoothly and your efforts to ensure that all the material is covered in the context of a natural, conversational interview will be imperiled.

Interviewers also have to be prepared to decide when and when not to follow up in a neutral probing manner on unanticipated topics that emerge during the interview, depending on their importance to the respondent and to the purpose of the research. Thus, interviewers should be trained carefully before embarking on any interviews. (See our discussion of coordination and control in Chapter 11 for information on the training of interviewers.)

Standardized Open-Ended Interviews

As we just mentioned, sometimes you will want to ensure that all interviews are conducted in a consistent, thorough manner—with a minimum of interviewer effects and biases. When this is your aim, the most appropriate strategy is to conduct standardized open-ended interviews. This strategy also may be needed when resource limitations leave you with insufficient time to pursue less structured strategies in a comprehensive way with large numbers of respondents, or when you are tracking individuals over time and therefore want to reduce the chances that changes observed over time are being caused by changes in the way interviews are being conducted.

In light of these concerns, the standardized open-ended interview consists of questions that are "written out in advance exactly the way they are to be asked in the interview" (Patton, 1990:285). Great care goes into the wording of the questions and their sequencing. Probes are

to be limited to where they are indicated on the interview schedule, although some studies employing highly skilled interviewers may permit more flexibility in probing than other studies using this strategy. We presented excerpts from an exemplary standardized open-ended interview schedule in Exhibit 7-2, way back in Chapter 7, on constructing measurement instruments. You may want to take another look at those excerpts at this point to see how a standardized open-ended interview schedule compares to an interview guide.

RECORDING OBSERVATIONS

Because of the in-depth, open-endedness of qualitative interviews, recording responses poses quite a challenge to the interviewer. The aims and philosophical roots of qualitative inquiry mandate that the respondent's answers should be recorded as fully as possible. Recording them verbatim is ideal. A tape recorder, therefore, is an essential tool of the qualitative interviewer. Not only does it ensure verbatim recording, but it frees interviewers to keep their full attention focused on respondents, to communicate that they are listening to what is being said, and to probe into important cues.

Noting these advantages of tape recording, Patton (1990) nevertheless urges interviewers using tape recorders to take some notes while they interview in order to refer back to something important said earlier in the interview or to occasionally jot down summary points or key phrases to facilitate later analysis of the tape. He also suggests that note taking (done in moderation) helps pace the interview and lets respondents know that you find what they are saying important.

Tape recorders, however, are not applicable for a great deal of the data gathering in field research, particularly data gathered as a result of observation outside the interview context. And even in interviews, tape recorders cannot capture all the relevant aspects of social processes. Therefore, other basic tools of field research include a notebook—or *field journal*—and a pencil. The greatest advantage of the field research method is the presence of an observing, thinking researcher on the scene of the action. If possible, you should take notes on your observations *as you observe*. When that is not possible, you should write down your notes as soon as possible afterward.

Your notes should include both your empirical observations and your interpretations of them. You should record what you "know" has happened and what you "think" has happened. It is important, however, that these different kinds of notes be identified for what they are. For example, you might note that Person X spoke out in opposition to a proposal made by a group leader, that you *think* this represents an attempt by Person X to take over leadership of the group, and that you *think* you heard the leader comment to that effect in response to the opposition.

Just as you cannot hope to observe everything, neither can you record everything you do observe. Just as your observations represent a de facto sample of all possible observations, your notes represent a sample of your observations. Rather than recording a random sample of your observations, you should, of course, record the most important ones.

Some of the most important observations can be anticipated before beginning the study; others will become apparent as your observations progress. Sometimes your note taking can be made easier if you prepare standardized recording forms in advance. In a study of the homeless, for instance, you might anticipate the characteristics of homeless individuals that are the most likely to be useful for analysis—age, gender, social class, ethnicity, psychiatric history, and so forth—and prepare a form in which actual observations can be recorded easily. Or you might develop a symbolic shorthand in advance to speed up recording. For studying citizen participation at a community meeting, you might want to construct a numbered grid representing the different sections of the meeting room; then you would be able to record the location of participants easily, quickly, and accurately.

None of this advance preparation should limit your recording of unanticipated events and aspects of the situation. Quite the contrary, speedy handling of anticipated observations can give you more freedom to observe the unanticipated.

Every student is familiar with the process of taking notes. And as we said earlier, everybody is somewhat familiar with field research in general. Like *good* field research, however, good note taking requires more careful and deliberate attention and involves some specific skills. Some guidelines follow. You can learn more about this in John Lofland and Lyn Lofland's *Analyzing Social Settings* (1995:91–96), mentioned earlier in the chapter.

First, don't trust your memory any more than you have to; it's untrustworthy. If this sounds too unkind, try this experiment. Recall the last few movies you saw that you really liked. Now, name five of the actors or actresses. Which had the longest hair? Which was the most likely to start conversations? Which was the most likely to make suggestions that others followed? ("Quick! Bring the wagons into a circle!") Now, if you didn't have any trouble answering any of those questions (and think you outsmarted us), how sure are you of your answers? Would you be willing to bet $100 that a panel of impartial judges would observe what you recall? If you are absolutely certain of your answers, what color shoes was your methods instructor wearing three class meetings ago? Gotcha! Even if you pride yourself on having a photographic memory, it's a good idea to take notes either during the observation or as soon afterward as possible. If you are taking notes during observation, do it unobtrusively, since people are likely to behave differently if they see you taking down everything they say or do.

Second, it's usually a good idea to take notes in stages. In the first stage, you may need to take sketchy notes (words and phrases) to keep abreast of what's happening. Then get off by yourself and rewrite your notes in more detail. If you do this soon after the events you've observed, the sketchy notes should allow you to recall most of the details. The longer you delay, the less likely it is you'll recall things accurately and fully.

We know this method sounds logical, and you've probably made a mental resolve to do it that way if you're ever involved in field research. Let us warn you, however, that you'll need some self-discipline to keep your resolution in practice. Careful observation and note taking can be tiring, especially if it involves excitement or tension and if it extends over a long period of time. If you've just spent eight hours straight observing and making notes on how people have been coping with a disastrous flood, your first thought afterward is likely to be directed toward getting some sleep, dry clothes, or a drink. You may need to take some inspiration from newspaper reporters who undergo the same sorts of hardships, then write their stories and meet their deadlines.

Third, you will inevitably wonder *how much* you should record. Is it really worth the effort to write out all the details you can recall right after the observation session? The general guideline here is yes. Generally, in field research you can't be really sure of what's important and what's unimportant until you've had a chance to review and analyze a great volume of information, so you should even record things that don't seem important at the outset. They may turn out to be significant after all. Also, the act of recording the details of something "unimportant" may jog your memory on something that is important.

You should realize that most of your field notes will not be reflected in your final report on the project. Put more harshly, most of the notes you take will be "wasted." But take heart: even the richest gold ore yields only about 30 grams of gold per metric ton, meaning that 99.997% of the ore is wasted. Yet that 30 grams of gold can be hammered out to cover an area 18 feet square—the equivalent of about 685 book pages. So take a ton of notes, and plan to select and use only the gold.

Like other aspects of field research (and all research for that matter), proficiency comes with practice. The nice thing about field research is

you can begin practicing now and can continue practicing in almost any situation. You don't have to be engaged in an organized research project to practice observation and recording. You might start by volunteering to take the minutes at committee meetings, for example.

DATA PROCESSING

The preceding section of this chapter dealt with the ways you, as a field researcher, would make observations and record them. Now, we're going to look at what you might do with those recorded observations afterward. In large part, this discussion will focus on the process of *filing* and organizing. We'll give you a brief overview of the process, but before actually undertaking a project you'd do well to study some of the specific techniques field researchers have developed. Again, an excellent source of nitty-gritty, detailed suggestions is John and Lyn Lofland's *Analyzing Social Settings* (1995:181–203).

Rewriting Your Notes

Hot on the trail of some social phenomenon, you are likely to end a day of observations with a mass of scribbled notes in your notebook, on the backs of envelopes, or on wine-stained cocktail napkins. Depending on how late in the day or night you complete your observations, you may be tempted to set the notes aside and sleep on them. Don't. Field researchers can't work on a 9 to 5 schedule, and it is vital that you rewrite your notes as soon as possible after making a set of observations.

It's far better to type up your full notes than to write them longhand. They'll be more legible, and as your typing improves it will be faster than longhand. If you can use a computer for this purpose, that's better yet, and we'll discuss the possibilities computers offer. First, let's see what you can do with a typewriter and paper.

Use your notes as a stimulus to recreate as many details of the day's experiences as possible.

Your goal should be to produce typed notes as comprehensive and detailed as you would have taken in the first place if it had been possible to record everything that seemed potentially relevant. If you regard your scribbled on-the-spot notes as a trigger for your memory, you'll see the importance of retyping each night, and you'll have a clear sense of how to proceed.

Also, you should make at least two copies of your notes, whether carbons, photocopies, or dittos. When you analyze your data and prepare your report, you will need to be able to cut and paste without losing information. With at least two copies, you can cut up one and have the other as a backup. Let's see next how you will use the multiple copies of your typed notes.

Creating Files

Your typed notes will probably represent a more-or-less chronological record of your observations in the project, and you should be sure to include notations of the dates and times you made them. You should keep one complete set of notes in this form. It will serve as a master file you can fall back on to establish the chronological order of events later on and to get more copies of certain notes if you need them. You don't need to store your master file in a bank safe-deposit box (unless you're studying organized crime), but you should take care of it.

The copies of your typed notes are for cutting up, underlining, scribbling on, circling, and filing. So far in this chapter, we have focused on making observations. A mass of raw observations, however, doesn't tell us much of general value about social life. Ultimately, you must analyze and interpret your observations, discerning *patterns* of behavior, finding the underlying *meaning* in the things you observed. The organization and filing of your notes is the first step in discovering that meaning.

Files can be organized in endless ways, so we'll suggest some possibilities you might otherwise overlook. As you undertake your own research project, however, you'll find that deciding what files to create is a part of your analysis of the data.

As a start, you should create some background files. If you are studying the women's movement, for instance, it would be useful to have a separate file on its history. You'll probably begin the file with notes from your initial reading about the movement: When and where did it begin? How many people were in it initially? What have been the major events in the history of the movement? What were the dates? Although you'll probably begin this file before making observations in the field, you should plan to add to it over the course of your study because you'll be continually learning more about the history of your subject. You'll probably want to create a biographical file, too. Who are the key figures in the movement? You may want to have separate files for the most important figures. In any event, you should keep all the information on a particular individual together. That will allow you to get a fuller sense of the person, and it may also help you to understand the links between diverse events.

Lest you forget, you should also create a bibliographical file to keep track of all the things you will have read in the course of your study. When you write your report, you will want to make references to what other people have written, and it will be both wasteful and frustrating if you have to return continually to the library to relocate sources.

The creation of background files represents a rather straightforward housekeeping function, but the creation of *analytic* files depends more on the nature of what you are studying and what you "see" in what you observe. As you begin to develop a sense of the different aspects of what you're observing, you'll want to establish files to deal with those different aspects.

Suppose, for example, that you begin to sense that the movement you're studying has a psychological significance for the people participating in it. You'll want to establish a file for data relating to that aspect. You might do that as follows. Write "Psychological Significance" on a manila file folder. Every time you find an entry in your notes that's relevant to the psychological aspect of the movement—perhaps a participant will tell you that the movement has enhanced her assertiveness—you should cut out that entry (recall the multiple copies?) and stick it in the file folder.

Perhaps one of your interests in the movement concerns the varying degrees of social action considered, proposed, or engaged in by movement members. Sometimes they seem willing to compromise; at other times they are more oriented toward confrontation and conflict. Perhaps you will want to explain why those differences occur. Create a file on "Degrees of Confrontation" and clip and file all relevant entries from your notes.

We could continue endlessly with illustrations of the kinds of analytical files you might want to create, but we think you've gotten a sense of what's involved. We can't give you a blueprint of what files will be appropriate in your project— you get to do that. We should add, however, that the creation of analytic files is a continuous process. Do not create a filing system at the beginning of the project and stick doggedly to it throughout. Stay flexible and keep modifying the system as new topics appear to be relevant.

The flexibility of your filing system suggests another important step in the data processing of field research notes and other materials. As you modify your view of how best to organize your files, you should frequently review the materials already filed to see if certain notes should be moved to a newly created file. Sometimes it will work to merely *cross-reference* your notes. You can jot a note to yourself indicating that the notes on X in File A are also relevant to the topic in File G. Stick the jotted note in File G.

Using Computers

You may think of computers primarily in connection with the statistical analysis of quantitative data. However, computers also have a powerful contribution to make to field research and other forms of qualitative research. Although this po-

tential is just now being realized, we'd like to give you some sense of what you can expect as well as what you can do right now.

To begin, any standard word processing system is a vast improvement over the cut-and-paste technology available for typewritten material. Once you've entered your field notes into the computer, you can make complete or partial copies effortlessly, excerpting and reorganizing your notes any number of ways.

Word processing systems can search through your notes for specific words and phrases. Enter the word *shout* in such a search routine, and the computer will show you each time that string of letters appears in your notes: "shout," "shouting," "shouted," and so on. If you anticipate this tactic when you enter your notes, in fact, you can be even more effective. In addition to the narratives and analyses you might normally write, jot in key code words relevant to your study. For instance, you might type in the word *demographics* every time your notes discuss the makeup of the groups you are observing.

Once you've entered your notes into the computer, you can review and reprocess them endlessly. Let's say you didn't take our advice about entering code words when you first typed up the notes, or perhaps you didn't anticipate some of the variables you now wish you had noted. You can go back and enter such codes easily.

In addition to the benefits you can get from standard word processing systems, there are numerous computer programs designed specifically for use in qualitative research. The first popular program for this purpose was Ethnograph, and in more recent years Nudist has become extremely popular. Some of the other programs used by qualitative researchers at present include: Aspects, ATLAS/ti, Cofta, Computer-Mediated Dialog Simulation, Context, DragonDictate, Graphics COPE, HyperResearch, Intext, Kurzweil Voice, Kwalitan, SALT (Systemic Analysis of Language Transactions), Sonar Professional, Textpack, Top Grade, VBPro, and WinWord. Our purpose in providing this list is to document the fact that computers are no longer seen as only appropriate for quantitative research.

There is an Internet *listserv* (electronic discussion group) established to "increase awareness and debate about Computer Assisted Qualitative Data Analysis Software": qual-software@mailbase.ac.uk. If you have access to the Internet, you can subscribe to this listserv, originating in the United Kingdom, and keep up to date on new developments. (See Appendix H, on "Social Work Research and Cyberspace.") Given the pace of technological change, it is inevitable that our discussion in this book will be somewhat out of date by the time you read it. You can also explore this topic further through Weitzman and Miles (1995).

Many of the programs, like Ethnograph, can be applied to field notes entered in a standard word processing system. Once you have created a file of your notes using a word processing system, you can ask Ethnograph to number all lines of that file. Sitting with a printed copy of the numbered notes, you would make marginal notations coding portions in terms of variables you are interested in. You could mark each of the places that contain demographic descriptions, for example, or those that deal with emotional states of those you observed. You could mark all the places that have to do with group leadership, social action, or gender discrimination.

Once you've coded the printed notes, you use the program again to enter the codes into your computer file, using codewords and line numbers. That complete, the program is prepared to bring together all your notes on any particular topic or set of topics. Using a program like Ethnograph in conjunction with your word processor's built-in ability to search for specific words and phrases makes data processing in field research much easier and more powerful than previously. Moreover, we can expect that such programs will get better in the years to come.

As we've indicated, the creation and use of analytic files is part and parcel of the interpretation of your data. Let's turn now to that topic specifically.

DATA ANALYSIS

Throughout the previous discussions, we have omitted a direct discussion of the most critical aspects of field research: how you determine what is important to observe and how you formulate your analytic conclusions on the basis of those observations. We have indicated that observations and analysis are interwoven processes in field research. Now it is time to say something about that interweaving. In addressing this topic, we are returning to an early discussion of *inductive logic*. Field research is one topic in which that mode of reasoning is especially evident and important.

As perhaps the most general guide, you look especially for *similarities* and *dissimilarities*. (That just about covers everything you are likely to see.) On the one hand, you look for those patterns of interaction and events that are generally common to what you are studying. In sociological terms, you look for *norms* of behavior. What behavior patterns do all the participants in a situation share? Do all jaywalkers check for police officers before darting across the street? Do all the participants in a campus political rally join in the same forms of supportive behavior during speeches? Do all the participants in a religious revival meeting shout "hallelujah!" at the appropriate times? Do all prostitutes dress seductively? In this sense, then, the field researcher is especially attuned to the discovery of *universals*. As you first notice these, you become more deliberate in observing whether they are truly universal in the situation you are observing. If they are essentially universal, you ask why that should be the case. What function do they serve, for example? This explanation may suggest conditions under which the "universals" would not appear, and you may look around for those conditions in order to test your expectations.

On the other hand, the field researcher is constantly alert to *differences*. You should be on the watch for deviation from the general norms you may have noted. Although most of the participants in a religious revival meeting murmur "hallelujah" throughout the leader's sermon, you may note a few who do not. Why do they deviate from the norm? In what other ways are they different from the other participants?

Sometimes you will find aspects of behavior for which there is no easily identifiable norm. How do different people handle the problem of standing in a line for tickets at a movie theater? Some stare into space, some strike up conversations with strangers, some talk to themselves, some keep standing on tiptoes to see if the line is really moving, some keep counting their money, some read, and so forth. An important part of a field researcher's initial task in such situations is to create a classification of behaviors: an organized list of the variety of types. Having done that, you then seek to discover other characteristics associated with those different types of behavior. Are the "rich-looking" or "poor-looking" moviegoers more likely to recount their money? Do men strike up more conversations with strangers than women? Do old people talk to themselves more than young people? Your purpose is to discover general patterns.

John Lofland and Lyn Lofland (1995: 127–145) suggest six different ways of looking for patterns in the topic of your research. Let's suppose you are interested in analyzing child abuse in a particular neighborhood. Here are some of the ways you might make sense out of your observations.

1. *Frequencies.* How often does child abuse occur among families in the neighborhood under study? Realize there may be a difference between the frequency and what people are willing to tell you.

2. *Magnitudes.* What are the levels of abuse? How brutal is it?

3. *Structures.* What are the different types of abuse: physical, mental, sexual? Are they related in any particular manner?

4. *Processes.* Is there any order among the elements of structure? Do abusers begin with mental abuse and move on to physical and sexual abuse, or do they occur along a variety of paths?

5. *Causes.* What are the causes of child abuse? Is it more common in particular social classes, different religious or ethnic groups? Does it occur more often during good times or bad?

6. *Consequences.* How does child abuse affect the victims, both in the short term and the long term? What changes does it cause in the abusers?

To the field researcher, the formulation of theoretical propositions, the observation of empirical events, and the evaluation of theory are typically all part of the same ongoing process. Although your actual field observations may be preceded by deductive theoretical formulas, you seldom if ever merely test a theory and let it go at that. Rather, you develop theories, or generalized understandings, over the course of your observations. You ask what each new set of empirical observations represents in terms of general social scientific principles. Your tentative conclusions, so arrived at, then provide the conceptual framework for further observations. In the course of your observations of citizen participation, for example, it may strike you that whenever a well-dressed and important-looking person expresses an opinion, others tend to agree. Having noticed this apparent pattern, you might pay more attention to this aspect of the phenomenon, thereby testing more carefully your initial impression. You might later observe that your initial impression held true only when the "leader" was also middle-aged, for example, or perhaps only when he or she was of a particular ethnicity. These more specific impressions would simultaneously lead you to pay special attention to the new variables and require that you consider what general principle might be underlying the new observations.

An inherent advantage of field research is that interaction between data collection and data analysis affords a greater flexibility than is typical for other research methods. Survey researchers, for instance, must at some point commit themselves to a questionnaire, thus limiting the kind of data that will be collected. If subsequent analyses indicate that they have overlooked the most important variable of all, they are out of luck. The field researcher, on the other hand, can continually modify the research design as indicated by the observations, the developing theoretical perspective, or changes in what he or she is studying.

This advantage in field research comes at the price of an accompanying danger. As you develop theoretical understanding of what you are observing, there is a constant risk that you will observe only those things that support your theoretical conclusions. You'll recall that this problem has already been discussed in connection with selective perception.

This danger may be at least partially avoided in a number of ways. First, you can augment your qualitative observations with quantitative ones. If you expect religious proselytization to be greater under some conditions than others, you might formulate a concrete operational definition of proselytization and begin counting under the different conditions. For example, you might note the number of group members who raised this topic, the number of members assigned to the task, or perhaps the number of new converts added to the group. Even rough quantifications such as these might provide a safeguard against selective perception and misinterpretation.

Second, we should recall that one of the norms of science is its intersubjectivity. As a field researcher, then, you might enlist the assistance of others as you begin to refine your theoretical conclusions. In the case of religious conversion, for instance, you might ask colleagues to attend several meetings of the group over time and indicate their observations about the relative stress placed on proselytization in each of the meetings.

Finally, as with all such problems, sensitivity and awareness may provide sufficient safeguards. Merely by being aware of the problem, you may be able to avoid it.

This last comment points to a more general aspect of field research analysis. *Introspection*—examining your own thoughts and feelings—is a natural and crucial process for understanding what you observe. Because you will have been observing social life close up and all its details, you should be able to put yourself in the place of those you are studying—George Herbert Mead called this "taking the role of the other"—and ask yourself how you would have felt and behaved. Can you imagine yourself acting the way the person you observed acted? Why do you suppose you would have done that?

Introspection, then, can protect against many of the pitfalls of inquiry. When leavened with some role taking, it can give you insights into what you see going on around you. And as you'll recall from our earlier discussion, sometimes participant observation puts you in a position to directly experience the phenomenon under study, rather than having to imagine how others might think or feel.

In all social science research methods, there is a large gap between understanding the skills of data analysis and actually using those skills effectively. Typically, experience is the only effective bridge across the gap. This situation applies more to field research than to any other method. It is worth recalling the parallel between the activities of the scientist and those of the investigative detective. Although fledgling detectives can be taught the technical skills and can be given general guidelines, insight and experience separate good detectives from mediocre ones. The same is true of field researchers.

To assist you further in logical reasoning in your analysis of field research (and other) data, the next section contains a brief examination of some errors people commonly make in logic. We trust these examples will help steer you away from such mistakes and alert you to such mistakes in the reasoning of others. The box titled "Are Black Children Undernourished?" gives you another opportunity to sharpen your critical-reasoning skills.

ARE BLACK CHILDREN UNDERNOURISHED?

Here's an example of faulty reasoning to help you refine your analytic skills. In the midst of national concern over the persistence of hunger in America, President Reagan appointed a 13-member Task Force on Food Assistance to determine the nature and extent of the problem and to recommend government action. One of the panel's members, Dr. George Graham, attracted considerable attention by indicating his belief that the problem of malnutrition among children had been exaggerated—especially with regard to black children. He was quoted as stating his view thusly:

"National data show that black children are now taller than white children—obviously, they must be getting more to eat," he said yesterday, echoing comments he made Wednesday. "If you think that blacks as a group are undernourished, look around at the black athletes on television—they're a pretty hefty bunch."

As you can see, Dr. Graham cites two pieces of evidence—one statistical, one impressionistic—to support his thesis that black Americans are no more likely to suffer malnutrition than other Americans. Are you convinced by his arguments? If not, how would you respond? Think about it, and then continue reading.

DRAWING CONCLUSIONS: SOME LOGICAL PITFALLS

Although no one can give you a neat set of logical rules for analyzing qualitative data, we want to draw your attention to an excellent book—Howard Kahane's *Logic and Contemporary Rhetoric* (1992)—that outlines many of the errors people commonly make. Here are some of the pitfalls to keep in mind, based primarily on those described by Kahane.

Provincialism   All of us look at the world through glasses framed by our particular histories and current situations. There is always a danger, then, that the field researcher—or any researcher for that matter—will interpret people's behavior so that it makes sense from the researcher's own point of view. For example, a Christian researcher may see things in Christian terms, a socialist within

socialist terms, and so forth. This problem is particularly evident in cross-cultural research.

Going Native   The opposite extreme of provincialism is *going native*, a term used primarily in conjunction with ethnography. It occurs when researchers overidentify with the culture they are observing and consequently lose their own sense of identity and analytic stance. A difficult challenge for field researchers is the need to avoid provincialism while maintaining an objective focus on the research concepts and working hypotheses being explored. Field researchers should try to understand how the behavior of the people they observe is connected to the worldview of those people, but they should not abandon their ability to critically assess what they observe, to relate it to theoretical perspectives, and to seek out and remain open to new observations that may modify prior interpretations. Social work practi-

First, Graham says black children are taller, on the average, than white children. But does this mean "they must be getting more to eat"? What other factors might affect height? If you said "genetics," you can go to the head of the class. Racial and ethnic groups differ in average height. Consider the African Watusi tribesmen, for example. These poor cattle-herders of Burundi and Rwanda are noted for their spectacular height, commonly over seven feet tall. It would be absurd to conclude that they must eat more than Americans.

Second, how about the black athletes on television? Does their heftiness mean that black Americans as a whole must be getting a lot to eat? In this instance, you might have asked whether the black athletes are typical of all black Americans. Of course not. They are no more typical of blacks in general than white athletes are typical of all white Americans. Otherwise, we would need to look at Japanese Sumo wrestlers and conclude that the Japanese people in general must be bigger and better fed than Americans.

Source: "Big Changes Made in Hunger Report," *San Francisco Chronicle*, 30 December 1983, p. 10.

tioners are taught essentially the same sort of thing when they learn how to empathize with clients without overidentifying with them.

When field research reports are written, they should reflect a critical search for alternative interpretations. If you read a report that doesn't reflect such a search, you might wonder whether the author overidentified in some way with what he or she observed. You might also wonder about some of the remaining pitfalls to be discussed.

Emotional Reactions   Gilgun (1991) points out that overidentification and a loss of an analytic stance can also occur when the researcher reacts emotionally to research observations. Social work researchers commonly investigate issues about which they have strong personal reactions or ideological views—issues such as homelessness, child abuse, and wife battering or rape. Gilgun suggests that the risks associated with this pitfall can be lessened by working in teams, since the emotional reactions of one investigator can be dealt with by other team members.

Hasty Conclusion   Researchers as well as other people are susceptible to drawing hasty conclusions. Whenever the researcher offers an interpretation of data, be sure to evaluate the "weight" of evidence leading to that interpretation. Is the conclusion essentially inevitable given the data lying behind it, or are other conclusions just as reasonable?

Questionable Cause   Whenever it seems to you that X caused Y, ask yourself if that is necessarily the case. What else could have caused Y? Kahane (1992:63) gives several economic examples. If a business goes bankrupt, people often conclude that the company's president lacked business skills—even when the bankruptcy occurred during a severe recession marked by a great many business failures.

Suppressed Evidence Field researchers amass a great deal of information through direct observations, interviews, library work, and so on. To reach conclusions requires dismissing information as much as selecting it. On the whole, the researcher will dismiss information that is "not relevant" but that is obviously a matter of judgment.

In particular, take note of any of your observations that do not figure in the conclusions, as well as observations not mentioned that you can reasonably assume were made. If a researcher concludes that members of a neo-Nazi group opposed blacks out of a fear of economic competition, for example, we would expect that most members were working class or lower middle class. But if the researcher has not indicated the occupations of the members, you might well wonder about the conclusion.

False Dilemma Research conclusions, like nonscientific opinions, often represent the selection of one position from among alternatives. Selecting one often seems to rule out all others, but this need not be the case. Kahane offers this example: "Economics, not biology, may explain male domination." This bold assertion seems to rule out the influence of politics, education, custom, religion, and a host of other possibilities.

> This statement suggests that there are just two possibilities: either biology explains male dominance (note the begged question!), or economic success does. And it suggests that the second possibility, economic success, "may" (weasel word) be the true explanation of male domination. Yet there are many other possibilities, such as social custom, religious conviction, and various *combinations* of economic and biological factors. By tempting us to think of the cause of male domination as either economics or biology, the quote leads us to overlook other possibilities and thus to commit the fallacy of *false dilemma*. (1992:42)

Be wary of this pitfall in reading the works of others, but also be wary of falling into it yourself.

We suspect these few examples of logical pitfalls will have sharpened your critical faculties somewhat, and we encourage you to read Kahane's book for more guidance and insights. As with observation, note taking, filing, and the other skills of field research, your ability to reason logically will also improve with practice.

CASE STUDIES

If you read much of the social work or social science literature on qualitative inquiry, you are likely to see the term *case study* used as a qualitative research method. Robert Yin, in his excellent book *Case Study Research* (1985), defines a case study as an empirical inquiry that:

- Investigates a contemporary phenomenon within its real-life context; when
- the boundaries between phenomenon and context are not clearly evident; and in which
- multiple sources of evidence are used.

(1985:23)

Yin points out that a common flaw in the literature is the belief that case studies use only qualitative methods, or that "case study" is a qualitative method (one that might be used mistakenly as a synonym for "ethnography" or "participant observation"). But the mode of observation used is not what distinguishes a case study. Instead, case studies are distinguished by their exclusive focus on a particular case (or several cases in a multiple-case study) and their utilization of a full variety of evidence regarding that case, including, perhaps, some evidence gathered by the use of quantitative research methods.

Sources of evidence might include existing documents, observations, and interviews. Evidence might also be sought by surveying people about the case or perhaps manipulating some variables (such as when we employ single-subject designs as described in Chapter 10). Many different types of units of analysis can comprise the "case" in case study research. (You may recall our discussion of different units of analysis in Chapter 4.) Thus, the case might be an individual, a program, a decision, an organization, a neighborhood, an event, or something else.

For example, a case study might be conducted to understand why a state decided to close down several of its institutions for the mentally or developmentally disabled, how it implemented that decision, what unanticipated problems occurred in the aftermath of the closings, and so on. Or a case study might be on a particular client, perhaps employing a single-subject evaluation of intervention with that client as part of the case study.

As with single-subject designs (and even with many group experiments, for that matter), the logical focus in case studies is not on statistical generalization to other cases (or external validity). Instead, the focus is on what Yin calls *analytical generalization,* which involves connecting case study findings to a particular theory. This is done by showing how the weight of the various sources of evidence gathered in the case study is consistent with a theory. This is not an adequate test of the theory, because it is only one case, but the accumulation of consistent results in the replication process can serve as a useful test of the theory, in the same way that replications of single-subject or group experiments are utilized.

The rationale for using the case study method typically is the availability of a special case that seems to merit intensive investigation. For example, suppose a particular state is the first to implement a massive program of deinstitutionalization. You might want to conduct a case study of that event and its impact as a way of informing similar policy considerations in other states. Another example might be the first effort to provide case management services in a rural area. A case study might identify implementational problems and the ways they were handled—information that could be of great value to program planners in other rural regions.

Here is one more example. Suppose you theorize that people who volunteer in social service agencies do so primarily to meet egoistic needs that are not being fulfilled in their other life roles, even though they might say they are doing it for altruistic reasons. You might decide to select an agency where your theory might get its stiffest test, with the rationale that if it seems to hold up in that agency, it would probably hold up anywhere. Maybe, for example, you would study volunteers who work with terminally ill patients in a hospice program, believing that such a program offers the greatest likelihood of finding people whose real, underlying motives really are as altruistic as they say they are.

Qualitative Methods in Case Studies Evaluating Practice Effectiveness

The application of the case study method that perhaps is of greatest interest to social workers is when the case being studied is an individual, group, or family engaged in social work treatment. In the past, much of our profession's "practice wisdom" was generated by clinical case studies of clients. That method fell out of favor in the 1960s and 1970s, as skepticism grew about the objectivity and validity of qualitative case studies about one's own clients, accompanied by a demand for evidence generated from studies with experimental controls for internal validity.

Today, however, a new wave of enthusiasm has emerged for qualitative methods in general, as well as for the incorporation of qualitative methods into experimental research. Thus, an experiment evaluating the effectiveness of a program or intervention might utilize qualitative methods to assess problems in the implementation of the program or intervention—information that may help suggest ways to improve future outcomes or which may show that a program or intervention with a negative outcome was never implemented properly in the first place.

Of special interest to practitioners is the trend toward using a case study approach that combines qualitative and quantitative methods while using single-subject designs to evaluate one's own practice effectiveness. When we discussed single-subject designs in Chapter 10, for instance, we noted that it is often difficult to detect from the graphed quantitative results whether an improvement in the target behavior was caused by the intervention or by some extraneous event(s). Intensive qualitative (clinical) interviewing of the client, as well as the client's significant others, can help identify what other important changes in the client's social environment may have coincided with changes in the quantitative data on the target behavior. If the qualitative information indicates that important extraneous events did indeed coincide with the quantitative changes, then the notion that the intervention is responsible for those changes will be less plausible. On the other hand, if intensive interviewing reveals no such extraneous coincidences, then it becomes more plausible to view changes in the target behavior as intervention effects.

A recent study by William Nugent (1991) illustrates a case study combining qualitative methods and a single-subject design. Nugent evaluated the effectiveness of a cognitive-behavioral intervention he used in treating a woman whose severe outbursts of anger were disrupting her family life. His quantitative data showed that, according to the client's self-recorded frequency of daily outbursts, the client had an outburst almost every day during phases when she was not in treatment, but that frequency fell to only about once every ten days during treatment phases.

Nugent employed the qualitative method of informal conversational interviews (discussed earlier in this chapter) to buttress his quantitative findings. He used these interviews with the client before implementation of the intervention to understand the client's difficulty dealing with anger. After implementing the intervention he used these interviews to assess how she was implementing the cognitive-behavioral exercises she was taught and to obtain her subjective perspective on what was happening to the target problem and why. He also

interviewed the client's husband in a qualitative fashion to obtain his perspective on changes in the pattern of the client's angry outbursts.

The qualitative data generated from these interviews corroborated the quantitative results and identified what aspects of the cognitive-behavioral exercises the client perceived to be most helpful and why and how she perceived them to be helpful. As it turned out, the client modified the cognitive-behavioral exercises she was using about five days into the intervention period and felt that that modification helped her a lot. Thus, the intervention that apparently produced the successful outcome was not exactly what Nugent had intended it to be. If he had not utilized qualitative interviews in his study, he would not have known that.

Client Logs

Interviewing is not the only qualitative method that practitioners can use to evaluate their own practice. Another method involves the use of client logs, which Bloom and Fischer (1982) describe as journals that clients keep of events relevant to their problems. The logs can be utilized to record quantitative data about target behaviors as well as qualitative information about critical incidents.

Bloom and Fischer illustrate different logs for different purposes. For example, an exploratory log might be used to obtain beginning assessment information about a problem and might therefore involve recording where and when a critical incident occurs, what happened, who was present, the situational context (that is, a staff meeting, over dinner, and so on), what the client wanted, and the client's cognitive and behavioral reaction to the incident. A slightly different type of log might be used later in assessment—one that refers to the occurrence of the specified target problem only and that seeks to identify the conditions under which the problem tends to be better or worse.

Client logs can also be useful in recording extraneous events occurring during the baseline and intervention phases when quantitative outcome data are being collected. The information on these logs can help the practitioner determine whether some important extraneous change may have coincided with the improvement in the target problem during the intervention phase, and this determination will illuminate inferences about whether it was really the intervention or something else that produced the change. Although we indicated earlier that qualitative interviews can also provide this information, a log can help to avoid distortions of memory that might occur in an interview. This may be particularly important with regard to the exact dates when critical incidents occurred; for example, the client may not remember accurately whether an incident occurred during the baseline phase or early during the intervention phase. Likewise, for assessment purposes, knowing whether the improvement may have begun a day or so before the critical incident occurred would be crucial in drawing inferences about that incident's bearing on the target problem.

We refer you to the Bloom and Fischer text if you would like to see detailed illustrations of several types of logs. All of these logs, however, are easy to construct. You can head the first column as the date, the next column as the time of day, and then have subsequent column headings for the place, the activity, who was present, what happened, events that led up to or followed the problem, the client's cognitive and behavioral reaction, and so on. Alternatively, you can use a simplified version that has fewer columns—it's up to you to judge what best fits the client, the problem, and the log's purpose.

Whatever approach you use, however, make sure that there are lined rows in each column with plenty of open-ended space for the clients to record their qualitative observations. Also, be sure to explain the log carefully to the client, including the log's purpose and value, how it is to be used, the need to restrict entries to brief summaries of critical incidents only, and the importance of recording incidents as soon as possible after they

occur (to reduce memory distortions). Bloom and Fischer also suggest practicing making entries with the client using hypothetical situations.

ILLUSTRATIONS OF QUALITATIVE STUDIES

The creative, malleable, and open-ended nature of qualitative research makes it harder to be as specific and precise about how to gather and interpret qualitative data than is the case with quantitative research. Compared to quantitative research, there are fewer strict rules to determine whether qualitative research is being done appropriately or whether qualitative data are being interpreted correctly. Books on qualitative methodology often refer to qualitative inquiry as a craft or a mindset and suggest that the best way to learn about the many ways of doing it may be through involvement in a diversity of exemplary qualitative studies. Therefore, let's now examine some lengthier illustrations of qualitative inquiry in action. We hope these descriptions will give you a clearer sense of the diverse and creative ways you might use qualitative methods in your own examination of social welfare problems. We'll head each illustration by identifying the qualitative methods it exemplifies and the substantive research topic examined.

Participant Observation and Informal Conversational Interviews: Studying the Homeless Poor

As research associates of the Community Service Society of New York City, Ellen Baxter and Kim Hopper (1982) embarked in 1979 on an investigation of the habitats of homeless individuals in New York City. They originally envisioned their research as part of a larger study of the living conditions of the chronically mentally disabled. Their early observations, however, revealed that the homeless population was far too heterogeneous and the origins of homelessness too diverse to limit their study to the mentally disabled. Displaying the flexibility of field researchers, they modified their focus to include more than the mentally disabled. Their chief concern was "to document how the homeless meet and resolve daily problems of survival in an often hostile environment" (1982:395). They conducted their observations wherever the homeless might sleep, stake out a domain, be fed, or receive services—at

> . . . park benches, street corners, doorways, subways, train stations, bus and ferry terminals, missions and flophouses, publicly and privately operated shelters, food programs, and emergency rooms. The terrain was initially mapped out through interviews with individuals and groups . . . serving, researching, or advocating on behalf of the homeless. In the course of our own field work, additional sites were periodically discovered and investigated, including hallways and stairwells in occupied buildings, abandoned buildings, the piers along the East and Hudson rivers, alleyways, and heating vents—often with the homeless serving as guides. (1982:395)

They also found some homeless individuals in such out-of-the-way refuges as the steam tunnels running under Park Avenue and loading docks in commercial districts that are unused at night. Had they not used a qualitative approach, they would not have been able to anticipate such locations, and consequently they would not have found as diverse a sample.

They typically began their observations by initiating conversation with the offer of food, coffee, cigarettes, or change, and they introduced themselves as researchers on homelessness. But after encountering resistance, they again displayed flexibility; they began delaying this information awhile and describing their work in simpler terms, such as that of writers doing a story on homelessness.

In addition to their direct observations and interviews with the homeless, Baxter and Hopper interviewed others who work with or are connected with homeless people. And on some occasions, they posed as homeless individuals themselves, such as when they entered public shelters to stay overnight. This enabled them to gain insights that would have been difficult to gain from the outside. For example, they were able to discover that from the standpoint of the homeless, service refusal appears to have a more rational meaning than it does to professionals or to the public. The latter groups view service refusal as a reflection of defects in character or judgment, disinterest in being helped, or preference to live on the street. But observations Baxter and Hopper made indicated that whenever services were offered, they were not adequate to accommodate the number of homeless individuals who sought to use them. Refusal of service seemed rational in light of the deplorable conditions they observed in the public shelters, conditions that sometimes made living in the streets and parks seem more attractive to them. In the public shelters Baxter and Hopper observed overcrowding, lack of sanitation, and inadequate security—conditions that "would not meet federal regulations for prison cells" (1982:398). Among other things, they noted the few toilets and showers that were often filthy or out of order, louse-infested mattresses and linens, the pilfering of clothing, the threat of violence, and fears of catching some dread disease.

But despite observing how service refusal can have an element of rationality, Baxter and Hopper also observed the harshness and toll of life on the streets, where the homeless are hungry, cold, socially isolated, and deprived of sleep. They observed how this strain can disorient individuals who were not mentally ill before they became homeless, and they noted that clinicians generally do not understand this because they generally see the homeless only after their desperate straits have taken a toll on their mental health. Through their immersion with the homeless, they also gained insights about the deeper meanings of other aspects of homelessness. For example, they observed the protective function of appearing bizarre and filthy and of having a noxious odor, which can protect homeless women by repelling men on the prowl. (Baxter and Hopper added, however, that foulness of appearance is virtually unavoidable, given the scarcity of toilets and bathing and laundry facilities.)

In light of these insights—insights that have escaped others—Baxter and Hopper concluded that the presumption of incompetence on the part of the homeless was a self-fulfilling prophecy because the homeless are eager to receive decent and humane care in those rare instances when such care is available. Despite the great hardships of living on the streets, that decision can have the deeper meaning of salvaging a sense of defiant dignity and self-determination for the homeless in the face of the deplorable conditions of the shelters available to them. Baxter and Hopper ended their report with several proposals intended to make more and better services available to the homeless, to make it more rational for them to utilize those services, and to enhance the efforts of social workers to help the homeless.

Grounded Theory and Informal Conversational Interviews: Stages of Homelessness

A more recent qualitative study of homelessness was reported by John Belcher (1991), a social work professor at the University of Maryland at Baltimore. Belcher was interested in the pathways people travel as they drift from one stage of homelessness to another. Using the grounded theory method of Glaser and Strauss (1967), Belcher and two colleagues conducted three rounds of informal conversational interviews over a three-month period with 40 homeless men and women in Baltimore, whom they identified using snowball sampling in facilities for the homeless. To gain the trust of respondents and to reduce their anxiety about the interviews, Belcher and his colleagues eschewed carrying paper and pencil, bringing interview guides, or arranging specific interview times. They did not, however, pose as homeless persons, and they told the respondents who they were.

Their interview process began with an initial orienting interview, after which the researchers recorded responses into a case file for the respondent. All the files were then reviewed in an attempt to identify common themes. A second interview was then conducted with the same respondents (after locating them), guided by a set of questions that the researchers developed and kept in mind based on the themes identified from the first set of interviews. After these interviews responses were again recorded in the case files. Patterns that were detected from responses to both rounds of interviews enabled the researchers to formulate working hypotheses, which they checked out with respondents in the third round of interviews. These hypotheses were then revised in light of the responses to the third interview.

The researchers used triangulation in the study by verifying important interview responses with other sources. If, for example, a respondent reported being ejected from a particular shelter, the researchers cross-checked this information with the operator of that shelter.

The process just described led to the postulation that homeless individuals tend to drift downward through three stages of homelessness. In the first stage they are living below the poverty line and move in and out of intense poverty. Their living arrangements fluctuate episodically, in line with fluctuations in their economic plight—sometimes they reside in a tenuous home and at other times double up with friends or family. They are anxious and fearful, may abuse substances somewhat, have a network of informal supports, and are connected to service providers.

In the second stage, they have been homeless for an extended period, but less than a year. They abuse substances more commonly, experience deterioration in their social relationships, are beginning to lose hope, but still do not identify with the community of homeless individuals.

In the third stage, they have been homeless for about a year or more, see themselves as part of the homeless community, have lost hope, abuse substances, stay in shelters, have no social relationships, and are extremely suspicious of and shun members of mainstream society. All their limited energies are focused on surviving on the street; the rest of the world is meaningless to them.

If the preceding hypothesis is true, homeless individuals drift downward through the stages as they lose income, relationships, and hope. When they drift into the lower two stages, Belcher suggests, it becomes harder to intervene effectively to help them escape homelessness. Consequently, Belcher recommends strategies to deal with homelessness that are preventive in nature, including social change efforts for long-term prevention and expanding welfare benefits to temporarily prevent homelessness.

Field Research: Life in the Streets

A modern classic field research study is Elliot Liebow's *Tally's Corner* (1967). Liebow, an anthropology graduate student, was hired to work on an ongoing study of child-rearing practices among low-income families in the District of Columbia. His task was to do fieldwork among low-income adult males to fill out the picture created by numerous interviews with families. Liebow prepared for the fieldwork through a series of meetings with the project staff, learning the kinds of materials that were needed. He read the reports already written on the project. Then, one day,

> . . . having partially digested the project literature, I told the director that I was ready to get started. He suggested a neighborhood that might be "a good place to get your feet wet." His instructions were: "Get out there and make like an anthropologist."
> (1967:245)

Arriving in the suggested neighborhood, Liebow discovered a white police detective scuffling with an angry black woman. Approaching two black male onlookers, Liebow asked them what happened. They answered cautiously. The conversation continued, warming somewhat as each expressed negative feelings about the police. Eventually convinced that Liebow was not himself a police officer, one of the men spent the next several hours talking to him over coffee.

Liebow revealed his identity as a researcher and the purpose of his research from the start. Though recognized as an "outsider," he was accepted as a friend, and he became more and more a part of the street corner life as the research progressed. Liebow soon found himself deeply involved in the lives of his subjects. He reports:

> I went to three different jails during this time, sat through one murder trial and two hearings in judges' chambers, testifying at one of them. I went to bondsmen's offices, to the United Employment Services, to the Blessed Martin de Porres Hostel (for homeless men) and into several private homes.
> (1967:245)

Whenever his new friends ran afoul of the law, Liebow's legal advice was sought and respected. He reports that he stayed in close touch with the project director about this participation, weighing the consequences of his actions for his research. There was certainly a danger that his own participation would change the character of the events and situations he had set out to study in the first place. Liebow's description of his record keeping nicely illustrates the procedures described earlier in this chapter:

> Throughout this period, my field observations were focused on individuals: what they said, what they did, and the contexts in which they said them or did them. I sought them out and was sought out by them.
>
> My field notes contain a record of what I saw when I looked at Tally, Richard, Sea Cat and the others. I have only a small notion—and one that I myself consider suspect—of what they saw when they looked at me.
> (1967:248)

Ultimately, Liebow was able to gain a personal experience of street corner life in a black, urban ghetto that few white people have. To an unusual extent, he was able to see and understand the men as they saw and understood themselves. He was able to learn their views and experiences of family life, employment, and—more to the point—unemployment.

Case Study Interviews: Caring for Persons with AIDS (PWAs)

Linda Matocha (1992) is a nursing professor interested in the effects of caregiving on family caregivers of persons with AIDS (PWAs). By exploring those effects, she hoped to enrich our understanding of the strengths, resources, adaptations, and needs of family caregivers—with the aim of deriving useful implications for formulating effective interventions and policies.

Her prior two years of work with PWAs and their families, as well as her knowledge of the literature, led her to identify four initial domains of interest: physical needs, psychological needs, economic needs, and social needs. Matocha selected eight families for study, two for each of four illness phases. (She says little about how these eight families were selected from a larger pool beyond saying that they reflected real-world differences in demographic characteristics, modes of transmission of the disease, and family relationships.)

She conducted at least three in-depth interviews with the PWAs and the primary caregivers they identified. The interviews ran from two to eight hours each. Matocha used no instruments to guide the interviews. She began each interview with one question: "Tell me your story. Start wherever you would like" (1992:73). She followed with open-ended questions as the interviews progressed. She recorded and responded to significant nonverbal communications in addition to verbal ones. She experienced and displayed strong emotions during the interviews: crying, laughing, and sharing other emotions with the participants. This, she felt, helped build trust and open the families up more. She helped the caregivers in her study when needed, providing respite, transportation, and so on, and she attended the funerals of the PWAs.

Data were entered in four types of logs: a condensed log; a more detailed log, which also included Matocha's own thoughts; a running log in which data would be analyzed according to the grounded theory method; and a log of problems she encountered doing the research. Matocha describes her caregivers as compassionate, optimistic advocates for the PWAs. As to the physical domain, the caregivers' health deteriorated on learning of the AIDS diagnosis. Several weeks after that their health tended to improve, but it would deteriorate again when the health of the PWA became unstable. The pre-AIDS level of health of the caregivers gradually returned after the death of the PWA.

Psychologically, learning of the diagnosis and attempting to cope with it was stressful for the caregivers. An additional toll was taken as they began to anticipate the demands of caregiving, the death of the PWA, and living without the PWA. As the health of the PWA became unstable, stress piled up. As with physical health, the pre-AIDS level of psychological well-being of the caregivers gradually returned after the death of the PWA.

Socially, the caregivers felt isolated and stigmatized during the newly diagnosed phase, feeling that they must keep the diagnosis a secret from family and friends. Their social interaction improved several weeks later, but they again became isolated when the demands of caregiving controlled their lives as the PWA's health deteriorated. After the death of the PWA their social lives returned to normal.

Matocha was surprised with the economic effects she observed. They were less than she expected and seemed to affect middle-class participants more than poor ones. She also did not anticipate a fifth domain of effects of caregiving: spiritual effects.

Matocha derives a number of practice-relevant implications from her observations. Caregivers often feel overwhelmed and need to talk with others about their situations and to vent their emotions. They need to tell the secret of the diagnosis and liberate themselves from the stigma. They need advice about finances and making wills. They need to learn to have fun without feeling guilty.

Like this synopsis of her study, and like many reports of qualitative studies, Matocha's report is light on precision in describing methodological details and heavier on findings that give us a sense of what it's like to walk in the shoes of her participants. Matocha admits to potential problems of reliability and to letting her own thoughts and feelings affect the results. She recognizes the need for replication by others. But she feels that those limitations come with the territory when you seek to obtain an in-depth understanding of how people experience sensitive issues at different points in their natural environments and private lives. In fact, Matocha's candid display of strong emotions during her interviews, and her personal involvement in helping her study participants, can be seen from the standpoint of qualitative inquiry not as limitations but as desired methodological procedures required for "gaining access to private spheres" and learning about secrets, loyalties, traditions, and sensitive habits that would otherwise remain inaccessible to the researcher (Daly, 1992:4–5). If there is something in Matocha's findings that gives you new ideas or a deeper sense of the problem she studied, you may feel that despite the tentativeness of your new insights due to the (arguably inescapable) limitations in Matocha's methodology, her study was quite valuable.

Feminist Research: The Positive Outcomes of Caregiving

Katherine Allen and Alexis Walker, two professors who work in the area of family studies, took a different tack than Matocha in studying family caregiving. Calling themselves feminist social scientists, Allen and Walker wanted "to set the record straight" about the relationships between dependent elderly mothers and their caregiving daughters (1992:199). The previous research on caregiving, they felt, focused too much on the negative consequences of caregiving and neglected the positive consequences. They believed that the previous research left unheard the voices of the care receivers themselves and did not adequately portray the positive side of "women's caring labor," especially feminine concerns for nurturing and the sensitivity by the mothers and their daughters to the impact of caregiving or care receiving on their intergenerational partners.

In reporting their methodology, Allen and Walker distinguished feminist research from other types of research not by its method, but by its worldview. Indicating that their ultimate aim in doing the research was to achieve social change, they stated that "conducting feminist research is an experience of resistance" (1992: 201). They selected 29 white mother-daughter pairs for their semistructured interviews. These 29 were selected from 222 pairs who volunteered to take part in the study after reading newspaper articles about it. Allen and Walker did not specify in precise terms all the details about their sampling criteria and procedures for selecting these 29 from the larger set of 222. They did, however, point out that they restricted their sample of mothers to those who exhibited physical impairments but no cognitive impairments. This is an important restriction, since Allen and Walker themselves acknowledge that the outcomes of caregiving are different when care receivers suffer from dementia.

The interviews were conducted in respondents' homes. The study data consisted of extensive, verbatim notes on the women's comments. Allen and Walker exemplified the postmodern approach to feminist research in acknowledging that "as women, feminists, and daughters, we brought to our work certain prejudgments that helped to construct the way in which we analyzed the data" (1992:205). They further acknowledged: "Data were read repeatedly and screened for statements that reflected positive comments and anecdotes about caregivers or care receivers and the experience of providing or receiving care" (1992:206). Inevitably, virtually all social research is influenced to some degree by the paradigms of the investigators. In acknowledging these things, Allen and Walker can be commended for being upfront about it.

In light of their selective sampling and observational procedures, you probably will not be surprised to learn that Allen and Walker found what they were looking for: positive comments by both mothers and daughters about the outcomes of caregiving. These outcomes included the mutual enjoyment of companionship, the gratification of knowing their intergenerational partner cared for and was concerned about them, and the awareness that their intergenerational partner appreciated them.

Allen and Walker appropriately emphasized caution in generalizing from their findings, pointing out the limited representativeness of their sample and the fact that they paid attention only to positive outcomes. They justified the latter limitation by suggesting that without it the positive aspects of caregiving would continue to be ignored and an overfocus on the negative aspects would continue. Implicitly, they also justified it through their feminist worldview and their social action agenda.

How you feel about that justification, their study as a whole, and whether their study is more appropriately called research and science versus social action and ideology probably depends on the extent to which you share their view of feminism and their postmodern worldview. You may or may not identify with that worldview, and you may or may not be skeptical about their findings, but in either case you should know that the Allen and Walker study is an exemplary illustration of the kind of inquiry associated with their worldview. Even if you have reservations about calling this type of work scientific research, you should understand that many postmodern and feminist scholars these days value work like this and are conducting studies like it, some of which you are likely to encounter as your education and career progress. We would recommend that even if you are skeptical about this kind of inquiry you might want to do what Allen and Walker did: don't focus exclusively on the negatives; see what useful ideas you can gain. Regardless of the scientific merits of their work, if Allen and Walker succeeded in helping you consider some possible aspects of caregiving that you had previously over-

looked, then whether you buy their ideas as facts or mere possibilities, their work will have had value for you. But you should be sure to remember their sampling restrictions, and the selective nature of their observations, when you think about applying or generalizing their ideas.

Life History: Sexual Abuse and Delinquent Girls

Robin Robinson (1994), as part of her dissertation in social welfare at Brandeis University, conducted a different kind of qualitative study guided by feminist theory that, like the Allen and Walker study, sought to give voice to her informants without questioning the veracity of their accounts. Her goal was to describe the significant events in the life stories of delinquent girls as told to her in oral history interviews. In particular, she was interested in life experiences that led to delinquent behaviors resulting in their referral for social services.

She interviewed 30 girls, whom she randomly selected from purposively selected areas thought to be representative of Massachusetts. Robinson embarked on her study with the notion that a history of sexual abuse might be prevalent among this population of girls and that abuse might be a key factor in leading them to delinquent behaviors. Rather than operationally define *sexual abuse,* however, she relied on the girls' own subjective experiences and perceptions. Robinson looked for cues suggestive of possible incidents of sexual abuse, and when she felt there was a cue she encouraged the girls to elaborate on the nature of the abuse and how they experienced it.

She began each interview with an open-ended question: "Tell me about your family?" (1994: 81). In addition to observing their verbal responses during the interviews, Robinson took note of the girls' facial expressions, body language, and overall affect. The interviews were unstructured and conversational, although Robinson slowly and gently probed when the girls mentioned or hinted at sensitive events difficult for them to talk about. The girls discussed many painful and traumatic life events—including betrayal by parents, miscarriages and abortions, suicide attempts, and others—but Robinson focused on sexual abuse as the key event, noting that 23 of the 30 girls reported having been sexually abused. Ten of the girls reported being victimized by more than one person. Robinson's report cites various excerpts from her interviews, giving readers a sense of the girls' experiences of the abuse in their own voices. From this information, and guided by her theoretical framework and feminist perspective, Robinson concluded that correctional systems and social agencies should begin to view these girls not just as offenders, but as victims of horrendous experiences who need services specifically geared to sexual abuse.

Robinson's study provides another excellent illustration of the differences between quantitative and qualitative methods and the differences between positivism and postmodern or feminist inquiry. Positivist, quantitative researchers would have begun with an operational definition of sexual abuse. They, and even some qualitative researchers who are not postmodernists, may have considered the possibility that the reports of sexual abuse by some girls may not have been entirely accurate. They may have wondered about the influence of the interviewer's feminist perspective and preconceptions about sexual abuse on what was said by the girls or perceived by the interviewer. They may have wondered about possible reasons why the girls may be intentionally or unintentionally distorting what really happened. To deal with these possibilities, they may have used triangulated measures, including interviewing the girls' families and the use of multiple interviewers who were not instructed to try to find sexual abuse.

Had Robinson done all these things, however, she would have violated the norms of postmodern, feminist inquiry. As was the case with the Allen and Walker study, your reaction to Robinson's study probably will depend on the degree to which you share her worldview. If you share her worldview, you probably will not question her methods, findings, or conclusions. But even if you don't share her worldview and are skeptical about her methods, you should recognize that they are exemplary within the context of her epistemological orientation. And even if you have reservations about the generalizability of her findings, you can still deem them an important new perspective to be considered seriously and pursued further.

These six brief accounts of qualitative studies scarcely do justice to the projects they describe, but they should give you a more concrete view of what qualitative inquiry entails and its diversity. All of the original reports are interesting and eminently readable, so you might like to read them for yourself. These six illustrations do not exhaust the limitless ways to do qualitative research or all the qualitative methods commonly used. In subsequent chapters we'll be discussing and illustrating additional qualitative methods.

THE STRENGTHS AND WEAKNESSES OF FIELD RESEARCH

It's time now to wrap up our discussion of field research and move on to some of the other methods available to social researchers. We'll conclude the chapter by assessing the relative strengths and weaknesses of this particular method. This examination will be somewhat longer than those of earlier chapters because we'll spend part of the time comparing field research with experiments and surveys.

Depth of Understanding

As we've already indicated, field research is especially effective for studying the subtle nuances of attitudes and behaviors and for examining social processes over time. For these reasons, the chief strength of this method lies in the depth of understanding it may permit. Although other research methods may be challenged as "superficial," that charge is seldom lodged against field research.

Let's review a couple of field research examples to see why this is so.

"Being there" is a powerful technique for gaining insights into the nature of human affairs. Listen, for example, to what this nurse reports about the impediments to patients' coping with cancer:

> Common fears that may impede the coping process for the person with cancer can include the following:
>
> —Fear of death—for the patient, and the implications his or her death will have for significant others.
> —Fear of incapacitation—because cancer can be a chronic disease with acute episodes that may result in periodic stressful periods, the variability of the person's ability to cope and constantly adjust may require a dependency upon others for activities of daily living and may consequently become a burden.
> —Fear of alienation—from significant others and health care givers, thereby creating helplessness and hopelessness.
> —Fear of contagion—that cancer is transmissible and/or inherited.
> —Fear of losing one's dignity—losing control of all bodily functions and being totally vulnerable.
>
> (GARANT 1980:2167)

Observations and conceptualizations such as these are valuable in their own right. In addition, they can provide the basis for further research—both qualitative and quantitative.

Now listen to what Joseph Howell (1973) has to say about "toughness" as a fundamental ingredient of life on Clay Street, a white, working-class neighborhood in Washington, D.C.

> Most of the people on Clay Street saw themselves as fighters in both the figurative and literal sense. They considered themselves strong, independent people who would not let themselves be pushed around. For Bobbi, being a fighter meant battling the welfare department and cussing out social workers and doctors upon occasion. It meant spiking Barry's beer with sleeping pills and bashing him over the head with a broom. For Barry it meant telling off his boss and refusing to hang the door, an act that led to his being fired. It meant going through the ritual of a duel with Al. It meant pushing Bubba around and at times getting rough with Bobbi. June and Sam had less to fight about, though if pressed they both hinted that they, too, would fight. Being a fighter led Ted into near conflict with Peg's brothers, Les into conflict with Lonnie, Arlene into conflict with Phyllis at the bowling alley, etc.
>
> (1973:292)

Even though you haven't heard the episodes Howell refers to in this passage, you have the distinct impression that Clay Street is a tough place to live. That "toughness" comes through far more powerfully than would a set of statistics on the median number of fistfights occurring during a specified period of time.

These examples point to the greater depth of meaning that qualitative methods can tap in concepts, such as liberal and conservative, that is generally unavailable to surveys and experiments. Instead of defining concepts, field researchers will commonly give some detailed illustrations.

Flexibility is another advantage of field research. In this method, you may modify your research design at any time, as discussed earlier. Moreover, you are always prepared to engage in field research, whenever the occasion arises, whereas you could not as easily initiate a survey or an experiment.

Field research can be relatively inexpensive. Other social scientific research methods may require expensive equipment or an expensive research staff, but field research typically can be undertaken by one researcher with a notebook and pencil. This is not to say that field research is never expensive. The nature of the research project, for example, may require a large number of trained observers. Expensive recording equipment may be needed. Or the researcher may wish to undertake participant observation of interactions in expensive Paris nightclubs.

Field research has a number of weaknesses as well. First, being qualitative rather than quantitative, it seldom yields precise descriptive statements about a large population. Observing casual political discussions in laundromats, for instance, would not yield trustworthy estimates of the future voting behavior of the total electorate. Nevertheless, the study could provide important insights into the process of political attitude formation.

More generally, the conclusions drawn from qualitative field research are often regarded as suggestive rather than definitive. This is due to certain problems and subjectivity and generalizability.

Subjectivity

Suppose you were to characterize your best friend's political orientations based on everything you know about him or her. Clearly your assessment of that person's politics is not superficial. The measurement you arrived at would appear to have considerable validity. We can't be sure, however, that someone else would characterize your friend's politics the same way you did, even with the same amount of observation.

Field research measurements—although in-depth—are also often very personal. How others judge your friend's political orientation depends very much on their own orientation, just as your judgment would depend on your political orientation. Conceivably, then, you would describe your friend as middle-of-the-road, although others might perceive him or her as a fire-breathing radical.

Be wary, therefore, of any purely descriptive measurements in field research. If a researcher reports that the members of a club tend to be conservative, know that such a judgment is unavoidably linked to the researcher's own politics. You can be more trusting, however, of comparative evaluations: identifying who is more conservative than whom, for example. Even if we had different political orientations, we would probably agree pretty much in ranking the relative conservatism of the members of a group.

In any event, study the characterizations offered by field researchers to get a full sense yourself of what the people characterized are like. Even if you disagree with the researcher, you will be able to get some value out of the research he or she has done.

In a sense, we've been talking about the issue of generalizability. Let's look at that more directly now.

Generalizability

One of the chief goals of science is generalization. Social scientists study particular situations and events in order to learn about social life in general. Usually, nobody would be interested in knowing about the specific subjects observed by the researcher. Who cares, after all, how George Gallup's sample of 1500 voters are going to vote? We are interested only if their voting intentions can be generalized to the total electorate. (This was the key issue in Chapter 8, on sampling.)

Generalizability is a problem for field research. It crops up in three forms. First, as we've already suggested, the personal nature of the observations and measurements made by the researcher can produce results that would not necessarily be replicated by another, independent researcher. If the observation depends in part on the particular observers, then it becomes more valuable as a source of insight than as proof or truth.

Second, because field researchers get a full and in-depth view of their subject matter, they can reach an unusually comprehensive understanding. By its very comprehensiveness, however, this understanding is less generalizable than results based on rigorous sampling and standardized measurements. Let's say you set out to fully understand how your city council operates. You study each of the members in great depth, learning about their ideological positions, how they came to public life, how they got elected, who their friends and enemies are. You could learn about their family lives, seeing how personal feelings enter into their public acts. After such an in-depth study, you could probably understand the actions of the council really well. But would you be able to say much about city councils in general? Surely your study would have provided you with some general insights, but you wouldn't be able to carry over everything you learned from the specific to the general. Having mastered the operations of the Dayton City Council, you might not be able to say much about Cleveland's. You should, however, be in a position to organize a great study of the Cleveland City Council.

In reviewing reports of field research projects, you should determine where and to what extent the researcher is generalizing beyond his or her specific observations to other settings. Such generalizations may be in order, but you need to judge that. Nothing in this research method guarantees it.

Finally, there is often a problem of generalizability even within the specific subject matter being observed. As an illustration, let's imagine you were interested in learning about Scientology. Suppose you were particularly interested in their recruitment practices: How does the group attract new members, what kinds of people are attracted, and so on? One way to find the answers to such questions would be for you to express interest in the church yourself. Talk to members; attend meetings and retreats. In this fashion, you'd be able to get a firsthand experience of what you wanted to study. You could observe the way you were treated after expressing interest, and you could observe the treatment of other newcomers. By getting to know the other people who were considering joining the church, you would get an idea of the kinds of people who were joining.

Here's the problem of generalizability. Although you might talk to a number of church members, you couldn't be sure how "typical" they were. You might end up talking only to people assigned the job of talking to potential recruits. Or perhaps you make your contact through your English class and meet mostly members majoring in the humanities and none majoring in the sciences.

The potentials for biased sampling are endless. The same would apply to the new recruits you got to know. They might not be typical of new recruits in general.

RESEARCH ETHICS IN FIELD RESEARCH

We introduced the topic of research ethics in Chapter 3 and pointed out that there are a wide range of ethical issues to be faced in connection with any form of social research. Yet field research, by bringing researchers into direct and often intimate contact with their subjects, seems to raise these concerns dramatically.

As a reminder of the importance of ethical concerns in social research, we've reported below some of the problems mentioned by Lofland and Lofland (1995:63):

- Is it ethical to talk to people when they do not know you will be recording their words?

- Is it ethical to get information for your own purposes from people you hate?

- Is it ethical to see a severe need for help and not respond to it directly?

- Is it ethical to be in a setting or situation but not commit yourself wholeheartedly to it?

- Is it ethical to develop a calculated stance toward other humans, that is, to be strategic in your relations?

- Is it ethical to take sides or to avoid taking sides in a factionalized situation?

- Is it ethical to "pay" people with trade-offs for access to their lives and minds?

- Is it ethical to "use" people as allies or informants in order to gain entree to other people or to elusive understandings?

This completes our primary chapter on qualitative research methods, a chapter that focused on field research. But we have not yet finished discussing this important type of research. We'll return to qualitative inquiry in the next chapter, which discusses qualitative as well as quantitative unobtrusive methods. There we'll examine a social work study that used intensive qualitative interviewing and a qualitative data analysis strategy. We'll also discuss the qualitative method of historical and comparative analysis.

We'll mention qualitative research again in the final chapter of this book, in regard to program evaluation. The other upcoming chapters of this book (Chapters 14 through 17), however, will focus on quantitative approaches to data analysis. In Chapter 1 we discussed the necessity of having both qualitative and quantitative approaches to inquiry, and their complementarity. The same chord was struck in Chapter 2 in connection to inductive and deductive theory construction. In that connection, we hope you will keep in mind that the amount of content on qualitative methods relative to the amount on quantitative methods that you will encounter in the remaining chapters (as well as in the preceding chapters) just has to do with pedagogical factors. The greater attention given to quantitative methods does not reflect the way we view the relative importance of these two equally valuable approaches to empirical inquiry.

Main Points

• Field research is a social research method that involves the direct observation of social phenomena in their natural settings.

• You may or may not identify yourself as a researcher to the people you are observing. Identifying yourself as a researcher may have some effect on the nature of what you are observing, but concealing your identity may involve deceit.

• You may or may not participate in what you are observing. Participating in the events may make it easier for you to conceal your identity as a researcher, but participation is likely to affect what is being observed.

• Because controlled probability sampling techniques are usually impossible in field research, a rough form of quota sampling may be used in the attempt to achieve better representativeness in observations.

• Snowball sampling is a method through which you develop an ever-increasing set of sample observations. You ask one participant in the event under study to recommend others for interviewing, and each of the subsequently interviewed participants is asked for further recommendations.

• Often, the careful examination of deviant cases in field research can yield important insights into the "normal" patterns of social behavior.

• Qualitative interviewing tends to be open-ended and unstructured. Three forms of qualitative, open-ended interviewing are: the informal conversational interview, the general interview guide approach, and the standardized open-ended interview.

• The field journal is the backbone of field research, because that is where the researcher records his or her observations. Journal entries should be detailed, yet concise. If possible, observations should be recorded as they are made; otherwise, they should be recorded as soon afterward as possible.

• Field research is a form of qualitative research, although it is sometimes possible to quantify some of the observations being recorded.

• In field research, observation, data processing, and analysis are interwoven and cyclical processes.

• Some of the logical pitfalls of data analysis are provincialism, hasty conclusions, questionable causes, suppressed evidence, and false dilemmas.

• Case studies are often referred to as a qualitative method, even though they often utilize quantitative modes of observation and analysis. Case studies are distinguished by their exclusive focus on a particular case and their utilization of a full variety of evidence regarding that case.

• Some case studies combine qualitative methods with single-subject experiments to evaluate practice effectiveness.

• Commonly used qualitative methods in these studies involve intensive interviews and client logs.

• The process of data analysis is largely a search for patterns of similarities and differences—followed by an interpretation of those patterns.

• Compared with surveys and experiments, field research measurements generally tap more depth of meaning but have less reliability, and field research results cannot be generalized as safely as those based on rigorous sampling and standardized questionnaires.

Review Questions and Exercises

1. Think of some group or activity you participate in or are very familiar with. In two or three paragraphs, describe how an outsider might effectively go about studying that group or activity. What should he or she read, what contacts should be made, and so on?

2. To show that you appreciate the different strengths and weaknesses of experiments, surveys, and field research, give brief descriptions of two studies especially appropriate to each method. Be sure each study would be most appropriately studied by the method you match it with.

Additional Readings

Berg, Bruce, *Qualitative Research Methods for the Social Sciences,* 2nd ed. (Boston: Allyn & Bacon, 1995). In contrast to omnibus research texts, this one focuses specifically on innovative techniques for the collection and analysis of qualitative data.

Douglas, Jack, *Creative Interviewing* (Beverly Hills, CA: Sage, 1985). This book provides some excellent guidance on the pitfalls of in-depth interviewing and on how to avoid those pitfalls.

Denzin, Norman K., and Lincoln, Yvonna S., *Handbook of Qualitative Research* (Thousand Oaks, CA: Sage, 1994). This compendium of readings provides a wide range of papers about doing qualitative research, primarily utilizing postmodern and naturalistic paradigms. This book will give you more information on various qualitative methods, interpreting qualitative data, and perspectives on positivist and alternative paradigms, written primarily from the viewpoints of authors who prefer alternatives to positivist and postpositivist approaches to human inquiry.

Emerson, Robert M. (ed.), *Contemporary Field Research* (Boston: Little, Brown, 1988). A diverse and interesting collection of articles on how field research contributes to understanding, the role of theory in such research, personal and relational issues that emerge, and ethical and political issues.

Gilgun, Jane, Daly, Kerry, and Handel, Gerald (eds.), *Qualitative Methods in Family Research* (Thousand Oaks, CA: Sage, 1992). A useful compendium of qualitative studies on families, with relevance to social work practice, illustrating the use of qualitative interviewing, case studies, life history interviews, participant observation, and document analysis.

Glaser, Barney G., and Strauss, Anselm L., *Discovery of Grounded Theory: Strategies for Qualitative Research* (Chicago: Aldine, 1967). This classic on grounded theory is perhaps one of the most commonly cited and most highly recommended books on the inductive philosophy of qualitative inquiry, strategies for conducting it, and analyzing qualitative data.

Gubrium, Jaber F., and Silverman, David (eds.), *The Politics of Field Research: Sociology Beyond Enlightenment* (Newbury Park, CA: Sage, 1989). A set of essays dealing with the issue of bias in scientific observation "against the commonplace view that Science, Reason, and enlightened intervention are the straightforward hallmarks of Progress in the resolution of social problems" (p. 1).

Johnson, Jeffrey C., *Selecting Ethnographic Informants* (Newbury Park, CA: Sage, 1990). The author discusses the various strategies that apply to the task of sampling in field research.

Lofland, John, *Doomsday Cult: A Study of Conversion, Proselytization, and Maintenance of Faith* (Englewood Cliffs, NJ: Prentice Hall, 1966). Another excellent illustration of field research methods in practice. This study examines the dynamic development of a deviant religious movement still active today. A shorter report of this study may be found in John Lofland and Rodney Stark, "Becoming a World-Saver: Conversion to a Deviant Perspective," *American Sociological Review,* Vol. 30 (December 1965) 862–875.

Lofland, John, and Lofland, Lyn, *Analyzing Social Settings,* 3rd ed. (Belmont, CA: Wadsworth, 1995). An unexcelled presentation of field research methods from beginning to end. This eminently readable little book manages successfully to draw the links between the logic of scientific inquiry and the nitty-gritty practicalities of observing, communicating, recording, filing, reporting, and everything else involved in field research. In addition, the book contains a wealth of references to field research illustrations.

McCall, George, and Simmons, J. L. (eds.), *Issues in Participant Observation: A Text and Reader* (Reading, MA: Addison-Wesley, 1969). An excellent collection of important articles dealing with field research. The 32 selections cover most aspects of field research, both theoretical and practical. Moreover, many of the selections provide illustrations of actual research projects.

Miles, Matthew B., and Huberman, A. Michael, *Qualitative Data Analysis,* 2nd ed. (Thousand Oaks, CA: Sage, 1994). If you ever do a qualitative study and find yourself overwhelmed with masses of unstructured data and at sea as to how to analyze or report the data, this soucebook will come in handy. It provides many practical illustrations of alternative ways to reduce, display, and draw verifiable conclusions from qualitative data.

Patton, Michael Quinn, *Qualitative Evaluation and Research Methods,* 2nd ed. (Newbury Park, CA: Sage, 1990). This text provides a comprehensive treatment of qualitative inquiry, with a special focus on its use in program evaluation. It covers conceptual issues in qualitative inquiry; the design of qualitative studies; and the analysis, interpretation, and reporting of qualitative data.

Reissman, Catherine (ed.), *Qualitative Studies in Social Work Research* (Thousand Oaks, CA: Sage, 1994). A useful compendium of qualitative research studies relevant to social welfare policy and social work practice. It illustrates the application of grounded theory to research on social work and health, narrative methods in studying traumatized target groups, and the benefits of subjectivity in qualitative research.

Shaffir, William B., and Stebbins, Robert A. (eds.), *Experiencing Fieldwork* (Newbury Park, CA: Sage, 1991). A fine collection of fieldworker accounts of the field research enterprise. It offers an especially strong treatment of researchers' relationships with their subjects.

Silverman, David, *Interpreting Qualitative Data* (Newbury Park, CA: Sage, 1993). This book brings together theoretical concerns, data collection techniques, and the process of making sense of what is observed.

Unobtrusive Research: Quantitative and Qualitative Methods

What You'll Learn in This Chapter

This chapter will present overviews of three unobtrusive methods of social inquiry: content analysis, analysis of existing statistics, and historical/comparative analysis. Each method allows researchers to study things from afar without influencing them in the process.

INTRODUCTION

So far in this book we have discussed most of the major sources of data and modes of observation social work researchers use. Previous chapters have discussed the use of questionnaires, interviews, indexes and self-report scales, secondary analysis of existing databases, and qualitative methods of direct observation and participant observation. In addition, the chapter on single-subject designs in Part 3 included material on the techniques and issues involved in quantitative methods of direct behavioral observation.

In examining the advantages and disadvantages of alternative modes of observation, we have confronted problems associated with some degree of intrusion by researchers into whatever they are studying. We have discussed, for example, social desirability biases that may influence what people tell us or how they behave when they know we are observing them. Likewise, we have discussed the problem of reactivity, which occurs when our quantitative or qualitative research procedures change the things we are studying.

Our discussion of direct behavioral observation in single-subject designs (Chapter 10) noted that the problems of reactivity and social desirability bias are associated with modes of observation that are *obtrusive*. We further noted that observation is obtrusive to the extent that those we are observing are aware of our observation. Conversely, we noted that observation is *unobtrusive* to the extent that those being observed are unaware of it. Although we have discussed ways to minimize our obtrusiveness, such as blending into the natural environment when conducting direct observation of behavior, most observation methods are not totally exempt from that danger.

The one mode of observation that best avoids being obtrusive is the use of available records. By *available records,* we do not mean just compilations of statistical data, although such compilations would be included as a prime example of available records. The term has a much broader meaning and includes an almost endless array of possible data sources, such as agency case records and practitioner process notes, reports or editorials in newspapers or on TV, minutes of board meetings, agency memoranda and annual reports, books or professional journal articles, legal opinions or laws relevant to social welfare, administrative rulings, and so on.

Three major advantages associated with the method of using available records are its unobtrusiveness, its expedience (it usually costs less and takes less time than do other methods of data collection), and our ability to study phenomena that have occurred in the past. In light of these advantages, this chapter will examine three methods of analyzing available records: content analysis, analysis of existing statistics, and historical/comparative analysis. To set the stage for our examination of these three research methods, we want to draw your attention to an excellent book that should sharpen your senses about the potential for unobtrusive measures in general. It is, among other things, the book from which we take the term *unobtrusive measures*.

A COMMENT ON UNOBTRUSIVE MEASURES

In 1966, Eugene J. Webb and three colleagues published an ingenious little book on social research (revised in 1981) that has become a classic. It focuses on the idea of *unobtrusive* or *nonreactive* research. Webb and his colleagues have played freely with the task of learning about human behavior by observing what people inadvertently leave behind them. Want to know what exhibits are the most popular at a museum? You could conduct a poll, but people might tell you what they thought you wanted to hear or what might make them look more intellectual and serious. You could stand by different exhibits and count the viewers that came by, but people might come over to see what you were doing. Webb and his colleagues suggest you check the wear and tear on the floor in front of various exhibits.

Those where the tiles have been worn down the most are probably the most popular. Want to know which exhibits are popular with little kids? Look for mucus on the glass cases. To get a sense of the most popular radio stations, you could arrange with an auto mechanic to check the radio dial settings for cars brought in for repair.

The possibilities are limitless. Like an investigative detective, the social researcher looks for clues, and clues of social behavior are all around you. In a sense, everything you see represents the answer to some important social scientific question—all you have to do is think of the question.

Although problems of validity and reliability crop up in unobtrusive measures, a little ingenuity can either handle them or put them in perspective. We encourage you to look at Webb's book. It's enjoyable reading, and it should be a source of stimulation and insight for you in taking on social inquiry through the use of the data that already exist. For now, let's turn our attention to three unobtrusive methods often used by social scientists.

CONTENT ANALYSIS

Content analysis is a way of transforming qualitative material into quantitative data. It may be applied to virtually any form of communication, not just available records. It consists primarily of coding and tabulating the occurrences of certain forms of content that are being communicated. For example, we might analyze social work course syllabi to see if certain types of faculty members or schools have more content on ethnic minorities than do others. Or we might examine presentations at social work conferences at different times in our profession's history, perhaps counting the number of references to psychoanalytic concepts or to ecological or social reform concepts to see if the popularity of different professional orientations or conceptual frameworks has shifted over time. Or we might tabulate how often various types of issues are mentioned in the minutes of community organization meetings. Is the amount of citizen participation reflected in the minutes related to the frequency with which certain types of issues appear in the minutes? Content analysis research can have great applicability to direct social work practice. In his text on *Effective Casework Practice,* Joel Fischer (1978) calls the practitioner-client relationship the keystone of casework practice and identifies practitioner empathy, warmth, and genuineness as the three core conditions of an effective helping relationship. The field first learned of the importance of these conditions from an extensive body of content analysis research studies, which were reviewed by Marsden (1971). In these studies, written and taped excerpts from therapy sessions were rated according to the degree to which the core relationship conditions were observed. The findings tended to indicate that the more these three conditions were present, the better the clinical process and outcome. Some topics are more appropriately addressed by content analysis than by any other method of inquiry. Suppose for a moment that you're interested in how mentally ill individuals are portrayed on television. Perhaps the National Alliance for the Mentally Ill plans to mount a campaign to educate the public about the nature of mental illness, alleviate fears about the mentally ill, and offset stereotypes about them. Suppose one facet of the campaign is aimed at the television medium and seeks to reduce the extent to which TV programs portray mentally ill individuals as violent or dangerous. Suppose further that you seek to evaluate the impact of that facet of the campaign on TV programming, and you will utilize a time-series design to assess whether the campaign seems to be reducing the extent to which mentally ill individuals are portrayed in television shows as violent or dangerous. Content analysis would be the best mode of observation for your time-series study.

Briefly, here's what you would do. First, you'd develop an operational definition of your dependent variable: the extent to which mentally ill individuals are portrayed as violent or dangerous.

The section on coding later in this chapter will help you do that. Next you'd have to decide what to watch. Probably you would decide (1) what stations to watch, (2) for what days or period, and (3) at what hours. Then, you'd stock in some snacks and start watching, classifying, and recording. Once you had completed your observations, you'd be able to analyze the data you collected and determine whether mentally ill individuals were being portrayed less violently after the campaign than before it.

Content analysis, then, is particularly well suited to the study of communications and to answering the classic question of communications research: "Who says what, to whom, why, how, and with what effect?" As a mode of observation, content analysis requires a considered handling of the *what,* and the analysis of data collected in this mode, as in others, addresses the *why* and *with what effect.*

SAMPLING IN CONTENT ANALYSIS

In the study of communications, as in the study of people, it is often impossible to observe directly all you are interested in. In your study of television portrayals of the mentally ill, we'd advise against attempting to watch everything that's broadcast. It wouldn't be possible, and your brain would probably short-circuit before you got close to discovering that for yourself. Usually, then, it's appropriate to sample. Let's begin by looking again at units of analysis and then review some of the sampling techniques that might be applied to them in content analysis.

Units of Analysis

You'll recall from Chapter 4 that determining appropriate units of analysis—the individual units about which or whom descriptive and explanatory statements are to be made—can be a complicated task. For example, if we wished to compute the average family income, the individual family would be the unit of analysis. But we would have to ask individual members of families how much money they make. So individuals would be the units of observation, and the individual family would still be the unit of analysis. Similarly, we may wish to compare crime rates of different cities in terms of their sizes, geographic regions, racial composition, and other differences. Even though the characteristics of these cities are partly a function of the behaviors and characteristics of their individual residents, the cities would ultimately be the units of analysis.

The complexity of this issue is often more apparent in content analysis than in other research methods. That is especially the case when the units of observation differ from the units of analysis. A few examples should clarify this distinction.

Let's suppose we want to find out whether criminal law or civil law makes the most distinctions between men and women. In this instance, individual laws would be both the units of observation and the units of analysis. We might select a sample of a state's criminal and civil laws and then categorize each law by whether or not it makes a distinction between men and women. In this fashion, we would be able to determine whether criminal or civil law differentiates most by gender.

Somewhat differently, we might wish to determine whether states that enact laws distinguishing among different racial groups are also more likely than other states to enact laws distinguishing between men and women. Although the examination of this question would also involve the coding of individual acts of legislation, the unit of analysis in this latter case is the individual state, not the law. It is essential that this issue be clear, for sample selection depends largely on what the unit of analysis is. If individual writers are the units of analysis, the sample design should select all or a sample of the writers appropriate to the research question. If books are the units of analysis, we should select a sample of books, regardless of their authors.

We are not suggesting that sampling should be based solely on the units of analysis. Indeed, we may often subsample—select samples of subcategories—for each individual unit of analysis. Thus, if writers are the units of analysis, we might (1) select a sample of writers from the total population of writers, (2) select a sample of books written by each writer selected, and (3) select portions of each selected book for observation and coding.

Finally, let's look at a trickier example: the study of television portrayals of the mentally ill. What is the unit of analysis? Is it the TV show? Each instance that an individual with mental illness is portrayed? Perhaps a given TV show contains several portrayals of different mentally ill individuals, some of whom are portrayed more violently than others. You would have to decide whether each TV show was to be given one overall score, whether each mentally ill person in it would be given a separate score, or perhaps some other option.

In designing the sample, you would need to establish the universe to be sampled from. In this case, what TV stations will you observe? What will be the period of the study—which days and what hours of those days will you observe? Then, how many programs do you want to observe and code for analysis?

Now you're ready to design the sample selection. As a practical matter, you wouldn't have to sample among the different stations if you had assistants—each of you could watch a different channel during the same time period. But let's suppose you are working alone. Your final sampling frame, from which a sample will be selected and watched, might look something like this:

- Jan. 7, Channel 2, 7–9 P.M.
- Jan. 7, Channel 4, 7–9 P.M.
- Jan. 7, Channel 9, 7–9 P.M.
- Jan. 7, Channel 2, 9–11 P.M.
- Jan. 7, Channel 4, 9–11 P.M.
- Jan. 7, Channel 9, 9–11 P.M.
- Jan. 8, Channel 2, 7–9 P.M.
- Jan. 8, Channel 4, 7–9 P.M.

- Jan. 8, Channel 9, 7–9 P.M.
- Jan. 8, Channel 2, 9–11 P.M.
- Jan. 8, Channel 4, 9–11 P.M.
- Jan. 8, Channel 9, 9–11 P.M.
- Jan. 9, Channel 2, 7–9 P.M.
- Jan. 9, Channel 4, 7–9 P.M.
- and so on.

Notice that we've made several decisions for you in the illustration. First, we have assumed that channels 2, 4, and 9 are the ones appropriate to your study. We've assumed that you found the 7 to 11 P.M. prime time hours to be the most relevant and that two-hour periods would do the job. We picked January 7 out of the hat for a starting date. In practice, of course, all these decisions should be based on your careful consideration of what would be appropriate to your particular study.

Once you have become clear about your units of analysis and the observations appropriate to those units and have created a sampling frame like the one we've illustrated, sampling is simple and straightforward. The alternative procedures available to you are the same ones described earlier in Chapter 8: random, systematic, stratified, and so on.

Sampling Techniques

In content analysis of written prose, sampling may occur at any or all of the following levels: words, phrases, sentences, paragraphs, sections, chapters, books, writers, or the contexts relevant to the works. Other forms of communication may also be sampled at any of the conceptual levels appropriate to them.

Any of the conventional sampling techniques discussed in Chapter 8 may be used in content analysis. We might select a *random* or *systematic* sample of agency memoranda, of state laws passed regarding the rights of mental patients, or of the minutes of community organization meetings. We might number all course syllabi in a school of social work and then select a random sample of 25.

Stratified sampling is also appropriate to content analysis. To analyze the editorial policies of American newspapers, for example, we might first group all newspapers by region of the country, size of the community in which they are published, frequency of publication, or average circulation. We might then select a stratified random or systematic sample of newspapers for analysis. Having done so, we might select a sample of editorials from each selected newspaper, perhaps stratified chronologically.

Cluster sampling is equally appropriate to content analysis. Indeed, if individual editorials were to be the unit of analysis in the previous example, then the selection of newspapers at the first stage of sampling would be a cluster sample. In an analysis of political speeches, we might begin by selecting a sample of politicians; each politician would represent a cluster of political speeches. The study of TV portrayal of the mentally ill described previously is another example of cluster sampling.

It should be repeated that sampling need not end when we reach the unit of analysis. If novels are the unit of analysis in a study, we might select a sample of novelists, subsamples of novels written by each selected author, and a sample of paragraphs within each novel. We would then analyze the content of the paragraphs for the purpose of describing the novels themselves.

Let us turn now to a more direct examination of analysis that has been mentioned frequently in the previous discussions. At this point, *content analysis* will refer to the coding or classification of material being observed. Part 5 will deal with the manipulation of those classifications to draw descriptive and explanatory conclusions.

CODING IN CONTENT ANALYSIS

Content analysis is essentially a coding operation. Communications—oral, written, or other—are coded or classified according to some conceptual framework. Thus, for example, newspaper editorials may be coded as liberal or conservative. Radio broadcasts might be coded as propagandistic or not. Novels might be coded as pro–social welfare or not. Political speeches might be coded as to whether or not they impugn the character of welfare recipients or the homeless. Recall that terms such as these are subject to many interpretations, and the researcher must specify definitions clearly.

Coding in content analysis involves the logic of conceptualization and operationalization as these have been discussed in Chapter 5. In content analysis, as in other research methods, you must refine your conceptual framework and develop specific methods for observing in relation to that framework.

Manifest and Latent Content

In the earlier discussions of field research, we found that the researcher faces a fundamental choice between *depth* and *specificity* of understanding. Often, this represents a choice between *validity* and *reliability,* respectively. Typically, field researchers opt for depth, preferring to base their judgments on a broad range of observations and information, even at the risk that another observer might reach a different judgment of the situation. But survey research—through the use of standardized questionnaires—represents the other extreme: total specificity, even though the specific measures of variables may not be fully satisfactory as valid reflections of those variables. The content analyst has more of a choice in this matter.

Coding the **manifest content**—the visible, surface content—of a communication more closely approximates the use of a standardized questionnaire. To determine, for example, how sexist certain books are, you might simply count the number of times male pronouns are used in conjunction with generalized prestigious roles (such as referring to the role of some nonspecified physician as "his" role) or the average number of such uses per page. This strictly quantitative method would have the advantage of ease and *reliability* in coding and of letting the reader of the research report know precisely how sexist language was measured. It would have a disad-

vantage, on the other hand, in terms of *validity*. Surely the term *sexist book* conveys a richer and deeper meaning than the number of times male pronouns are used.

Alternatively, you may take a more qualitative approach by coding the **latent content** of the communication: its underlying meaning. In the present example, you might read an entire book or a sample of paragraphs or pages and make an overall assessment of how sexist the book is. Although your total assessment might well be influenced by the inappropriate appearance of male pronouns, it would not depend fully on the frequency with which such words appeared.

Clearly, this second method seems better designed for tapping the underlying meaning of communications, but its advantage comes at a cost of reliability and specificity. Especially if more than one person is coding the novel, somewhat different definitions or standards may be used. A passage that one coder regards as sexist may not seem sexist to another. Even if you do all of the coding yourself, there is no guarantee that your definitions and standards will remain constant throughout the enterprise. Moreover, the reader of your research report would be generally uncertain about the definitions you have used.

Wherever possible, the best solution to this dilemma is to use *both* methods. A given unit of observation should receive the same characterization from both methods to the extent that your coding of manifest and latent content has been reasonably valid and reliable. If the agreement achieved by the two methods is fairly close, though imperfect, the final score might reflect the scores assigned in the two independent methods. If, on the other hand, coding manifest and latent content produces gross disagreement, you would be well advised to reconsider your theoretical conceptualization.

Conceptualization and the Creation of Code Categories

For all research methods, conceptualization and operationalization typically involve the interaction of theoretical concerns and empirical observations. If, for example, you believe some newspaper editorials to be liberal and others to be conservative, ask yourself why you think so. Read some editorials, asking yourself which are liberal and which are conservative. Was the political orientation of a particular editorial most clearly indicated by its manifest content or by its tone? Was your decision based on the use of certain terms (for example, *pinko, right-winger,* and so on) or on the support or opposition given to a particular issue or political personality?

Both inductive and deductive methods should be used in this activity. If you are testing theoretical propositions, your theories should suggest empirical indicators of concepts. If you have begun with specific empirical observations, you should attempt to derive general principles relating to them and then apply those principles to the other empirical observations.

Throughout this activity, you should remember that the operational definition of any variable is composed of the attributes included in it. Such attributes, moreover, should be mutually exclusive and exhaustive. A newspaper editorial, for instance, should not be described as both liberal and conservative, though you should probably allow for some to be middle-of-the-road. It may be sufficient for your purposes to code novels as being erotic or nonerotic, but you may also want to consider that some could be antierotic. Paintings might be classified as representational or not, if that satisfied your research purpose, or you might wish to further classify them as impressionistic, abstract, allegorical, and so forth.

Realize further that different levels of measurement may be used in content analysis. You may, for example, use the nominal categories of liberal and conservative for characterizing newspaper editorials, or you might wish to use a more refined ordinal ranking, ranging from extremely liberal to extremely conservative. It is important that you bear in mind, however, that the level of measurement implicit in your coding methods—nominal, ordinal, interval, or ratio—does not necessarily reflect the nature of your variables. If

the word *love* appeared 100 times in Novel A and 50 times in Novel B, you would be justified in saying that the word *love* appeared twice as often in Novel A, but not that Novel A was twice as erotic as Novel B. Similarly, if person A agrees with twice as many anti-Semitic questionnaire statements as person B, that does not make person A twice as anti-Semitic.

No coding scheme should be used in content analysis until it has been carefully pretested. You should decide what manifest or latent contents of communications will be regarded as indicators of the different attributes composing your research variables. Then write down these operational definitions and use them in the actual coding of several units of observation. If you plan to use more than one coder in the final project, each should independently code the same set of observations, so that you can determine the extent of agreement produced. In any event, you should take special note of any difficult cases: observations not easily classified using the operational definition. Finally, you should review the overall results of the pretest to ensure they will be appropriate to your analytic concerns. If, for example, all the pretest newspaper editorials have been coded as liberal, you may want to reconsider your definition of that attribute.

As with other types of quantitative research, it is not essential that you commit yourself in advance to a specific definition of each concept. Often you will do better to devise the most appropriate definition of a concept on the basis of your subsequent quantitative analyses. In the cases of erotic novels, for example, you might count separately the frequency with which different erotic words appear. This procedure would allow you to determine, during your later analysis, which words or combinations of words provided the most useful indication of your variable.

Counting and Recordkeeping

If you plan to evaluate your content analysis data quantitatively, your coding operation must be amenable to data processing.

Table 13-1   An Abbreviated Sample Tally Sheet

SOCIAL WORKER ID	NUMBER OF CASE RECORDS EVALUATED	SUBJECTIVE EVALUATION*	NUMBER OF CASE RECORDS WITH ENVIRONMENTAL TARGET PROBLEMS	NUMBER OF CASE RECORDS WITH ENVIRONMENTAL INTERVENTIONS	NUMBER OF CASE RECORDS WITH ASSESSMENTS FOCUSING ON STUDENT PSYCHOPATHOLOGY
001	37	2	10	6	25
002	26	4	25	24	2
003	44	3	30	23	14
004	30	1	0	0	30

*1—Counseling only; 2—Slightly environmental; 3—Moderately environmental; 4—Very environmental.

First, the end product of your coding must be *numerical*. If you are counting the frequency of certain words, phrases, or other manifest content, that will necessarily be the case. Even if you are coding latent content on the basis of overall judgments, it will be necessary to represent your coding decision numerically: 1 = very liberal, 2 = moderately liberal, 3 = moderately conservative, and so on.

Second, it is essential that your recordkeeping clearly distinguishes between your units of analysis and your units of observation, especially if these two are different. The initial coding, of course, must relate to your units of observation. If novelists are your units of analysis, for instance, and you wish to characterize them through a content analysis of their novels, your primary records will represent novels. You may then combine your scoring of individual novels to characterize each novelist.

Third, when counting, it normally is important to record the *base* from which the counting is done. It would tell us little that inappropriate male pronouns appeared 87 times in a book if we did not know about how many words there were in the book altogether. The issue of observation base is most easily resolved if *every* observation is coded in terms of one of the attributes making up a vari-

able. Rather than simply counting the number of liberal editorials in a given collection, for example, code each editorial by its political orientation, even if it must be coded "no apparent orientation."

Let's suppose that we want to study the practice of school social workers. More specifically, suppose we seek to learn whether school social workers today are more likely to intervene with family members and school personnel than in the past and whether in the past they were more likely to restrict their intervention to counseling the troubled student.

One possible approach would be to use school social workers as the units of analysis and to rank the practice orientation reflected in the assessment and process notes in a sample of case records for each social worker sampled. Table 13-1 illustrates a portion of a tally sheet that might utilize a four-point scale to code the orientation of each social worker. In the first column each social worker in the sample has been assigned an identification number to facilitate mechanized data processing. The second column identifies the number of case records coded for each social worker, important information because it is necessary to calculate the percentage of case records with particular attributes.

The next column in Table 13-1 is for assigning a subjective overall assessment of the social worker's orientation. (Such assignments might later be compared with the several objective measures.) Other columns provide space for recording the number of case records that reflect specific interventions, target problems, or assessment notions. In a real content analysis there would be spaces for recording additional information in the case records, such as client attributes, dates of service, social worker attributes, and so on.

QUANTITATIVE AND QUALITATIVE EXAMPLES OF CONTENT ANALYSIS

Let's look at two examples of content analysis in action in social work. Each will involve qualitative material. The first will illustrate the transformation of qualitative material into quantitative data. The second keeps a qualitative focus throughout.

A Quantitative Illustration: The Changing Self-Image of Social Work

Two social workers, James Billups and Maria Julia (1987), wanted to see whether and how the self-image of modern social work has been changing since the formation of the National Association of Social Workers (NASW) in 1955. They decided to study this issue by conducting a content analysis of social work practice position vacancy descriptions that appeared in 1960, 1970, and 1980.

An early task confronting Billups and Julia involved choosing the sources of vacancy descriptions that they would analyze. They thought it would make the most sense to use the publication put out by NASW that carries the most position vacancy descriptions in social work. For the years 1960 and 1970 that source was the journal *Social Casework*. Subsequently, NASW made its *NASW News* the prime source for position vacancy announcements. Accordingly, Billups and Julia decided to use *Social Casework* as their source for 1960 and 1970 and *NASW News* as their source for 1980.

Each of these publications was issued ten times per year, and each issue contained a very large number of position vacancy descriptions. Because of their resource constraints, Billups and Julia did not want to analyze every one of the thousands of descriptions published over the three years of interest. As was explained in Chapter 8, with such a large population it is not necessary to study the entire population of descriptions in order to describe them accurately. Probability sampling techniques enable us to obtain accurate descriptions of a population based on a small fraction of that population. Billups and Julia selected a systematic random sample of 506 position vacancy descriptions, which accounted for 10% of the population of descriptions published in 1960, 1970, and 1980.

Next Billups and Julia had to formulate a standard definition of dimensions of practice that they would look for in the position vacancy descriptions. They decided that they would examine *manifest* content only (not latent content). They defined dimensions of practice according to the following four major components: (1) position title (such as administrator, caseworker, clinical social worker, therapist, and so on); (2) principal field of practice where the work would take place (such as family and child welfare, mental health, and so forth); (3) major practice responsibilities (such as casework, group work, direct or indirect practice, and so on); and (4) required or preferred education and experience. These four components were broken down into mutually exclusive and exhaustive subcategories. Standardized coding instructions were developed, which were used by two coders. The intercoder reliability was assessed, and it was acceptable.

Billups and Julia found marked changes in the position vacancy announcements over the years. There was a dramatic drop in the mention of method-specific titles and responsibilities, for example. Whereas almost half of the announcements in 1960 mentioned the term *casework* or *caseworkers,* almost none did in 1980. Replacing the method-specific terms were terms like *social worker, direct practice, clinical social workers, therapists,* and so on.

Other sizable changes were observed in the fields of practice mentioned in the announcements. Whereas the family and child welfare field was mentioned by almost 60% of the announcements in 1960, in 1980 it was only 21%. The largest growth was observed in the fields of mental health, aging, corrections, rehabilitation, industrial social work, and substance abuse.

In interpreting these changes, Billups and Julia call attention to two possible contrasting trends. On the one hand, the reduction in the use of method-specific titles like *casework* and *group work* might signify "a growing expectation that more social work practitioners will need to assume both a holistic view of problems and a broader repertoire of approaches to practice" than in the past (1987:21). On the other hand, decreases in public welfare fields and increases in the use of terms like *therapist* might signify abandonment of the very poor and a narrower approach to practice imitating the roles of other clinical professions.

A Qualitative Illustration:
Adoption Revelation and Communication

The foregoing Billups and Julia study illustrates a quantitative approach to content analysis, in that it transformed manifest qualitative material into quantitative categories. But some approaches to content analysis keep a strict qualitative focus throughout, and report qualitative material only in qualitative terms, without transforming the material into quantitative data. An example of this approach in social work is a study by Ruth McRoy and her associates (1990) on adoption revelation.

The researchers thought that the relatively high frequency of psychiatric treatment referrals of adopted children might indicate problems in the process of revealing to children that they were adopted. They decided to explore this issue by looking for patterns among case illustrations of problematic and nonproblematic revelations of

adoption. Their nonprobability sample (an availability sample) consisted of 50 adoptive families whose adopted child was in residential treatment facilities and who had been adopted before the age of two.

Intensive, open-ended interviews were conducted with the parents, adopted child, and caseworker for each family. The interviews were tape recorded and transcribed verbatim. A content analysis was then performed on the information on the tapes. (Thus, this study did not use an unobtrusive content analysis as a way of collecting data; it used intensive interviews for that purpose. The content analysis was applied after the data were collected.)

Like many qualitative research reports, this one did not provide much detail as to methodological procedures—details that would enable the reader to assess the validity of its conclusions. As we discussed in Chapter 12, qualitative approaches eschew such structure in favor of more flexible approaches that permit deeper probing into subjective meanings—probes that usually seek to generate new insights more than they seek to test hypotheses.

McRoy and her associates present the results of their content analysis of their interview data primarily in the form of lengthy quotes that they incorporated into composite case illustrations. In one case illustration, for example, a girl was not told by her parents that she was adopted until she was ten years old. The quotation shows that she refused to believe them, that she was traumatized by the revelation. In two other case illustrations, boys who learned of being adopted when they were five reacted with anger or mistrust.

One theme that seemed to cut across the case illustrations was the need for social workers working with adoptive families to deal with issues concerning how, when, and by whom children are informed of their adoption. Social workers need to encourage adoptive parents to be the first to inform the child of the adoption.

Another recurrent theme indicated the need for ongoing communication between parents and the child regarding the adoption and the need to express empathy and understanding regarding the child's ongoing questions about his or her background and the reasons for being placed for adoption. The evidence for this conclusion is presented in several quotes that illustrate how learning of being adopted seemed to trigger problems in some families but not in others. In one, a daughter describes how she became rebellious against her parents when she found out at age ten what adoption really means. The problem became exacerbated, in her view, when her parents seemed to have difficulty discussing the adoption with her and were not always truthful with her about aspects of the adoption. Other quotes are provided from cases involving better communication where the children reported experiencing less discomfort with the adoption issue.

These illustrations of content analysis in action should give you a clearer picture of the procedures and potential that characterize this research method. Let's conclude the discussion of content analysis with an overview of its particular strengths and weaknesses.

STRENGTHS AND WEAKNESSES OF CONTENT ANALYSIS

Probably the greatest advantage of content analysis is its economy in terms of both time and money. A single college student could undertake a content analysis, whereas undertaking a survey, for example, might not be feasible. There is no requirement for a large research staff; no special equipment is required. As long as you have access to the material to be coded, you can undertake content analysis.

Safety is another advantage of content analysis. If you discover you have botched a survey you may be forced to repeat the whole research project with all the attendant costs in time and money. If you botch your field research, it may be impossible to redo the project; the event under study may no longer exist. In content analysis, it is usually easier to repeat a portion of the study than it is for other research methods. You might be required, moreover, to recode only a portion of your data rather than to repeat the entire enterprise.

Also important, content analysis permits you to study processes occurring over long periods of time. You might focus on the imagery of blacks conveyed in American novels of 1850 to 1860, for example, or you might examine changing imagery from 1850 to present.

Finally, content analysis has the advantage, mentioned at the outset of the chapter, of being *unobtrusive*. That is, the content analyst seldom has any effect on the subject *being studied*. Because the books have already been written, the case records already recorded, the speeches already presented, content analyses can have no effect on them. This advantage is not present in all research methods.

Content analysis has disadvantages as well. For one thing, content analysis is limited to the examination of *recorded* communications. Such communications may be oral, written, or graphic, but they must be recorded in some fashion to permit analysis.

Content analysis, as we have seen, has both advantages and disadvantages in terms of validity and reliability. For validity, problems are likely unless you happen to be studying communication processes per se. For instance, did the drop in the mention of terms like *casework* in the Billups and Julia study necessarily mean that practitioners were becoming more holistic in their practice and using a broader repertoire of intervention approaches? Is it conceivable that the only thing that changed was the labels being used to describe the same forms of practice—that the field was merely using more fashionable terminology for the same old practices?

Although validity is a common problem with content analysis, the concreteness of materials studied in quantitative approaches to content analysis strengthens the likelihood of reliability. You can always code and recode and even recode again if you want, making certain that the coding is consistent. In field research, by contrast, there's probably nothing you can do after the fact to ensure greater reliability in observation and categorization. Let's move from content analysis now and turn to a related research method: the analysis of existing data. Although numbers rather than communications are the substance analyzed in this case, we think you'll see the similarity to content analysis.

ANALYZING EXISTING STATISTICS

Frequently it is possible or necessary to undertake social scientific inquiry through the use of official or quasi-official statistics. Recall, for example, Samuel Stouffer's study of the consequences of the Great Depression on the family, which used government statistics on marriages, divorces, and the like. This resembles secondary analysis, in which you obtain a copy of someone else's data and undertake your own statistical analysis. In this section, we're going to look at ways of using the data analyses others have already done. Before getting into the nuts and bolts of this research method, we'd like to point out that existing statistics should always be considered at least a supplemental source of data. If you were planning a survey of political attitudes, for instance, you would do well to examine and present your findings within a context of voting patterns, rates of voter turnout, or similar statistics relevant to your research interest. Or, if you were doing evaluation research on the impact on employee productivity of an industrial social work program, probably statistics on absenteeism, sick leave, and so on would be interesting and revealing in connection with the data your own research would generate. Existing statistics, then, can very often provide a historical or conceptual context within which to locate your original research.

Existing statistics can also provide the main data for a social scientific inquiry. In contrast to the structure of preceding discussions, we want to begin here with an illustration: Durkheim's classic study, *Suicide* (1897). Then we'll look at some of the special problems this method presents in terms of units of analysis, validity, and reliability. We'll conclude the discussion by mentioning some useful sources of data.

Studying Suicide

Why do people kill themselves? Undoubtedly every suicide case has a unique history and explanation, yet all such cases could no doubt be grouped according to certain common causes, such as depression, disgrace, and other kinds of personal problems. French sociologist Emile Durkheim had a slightly different question in mind when he addressed the matter of suicide, however. He wanted to discover the environmental conditions that encouraged or discouraged it, especially social conditions.

The more he examined the available records, the more patterns of differences became apparent to Durkheim. All of these patterns interested him. One of the first things to attract his attention was the relative *stability* of suicide rates. Looking at several countries, he found suicide rates to be about the same year after year. He also discovered that a disproportionate number of suicides occurred during the hot summer months, leading him to hypothesize that temperature might have something to do with suicide. If that were the case, suicide rates should be higher in the southern European countries than in the temperate ones. However, Durkheim discovered that the highest rates were found in countries in the central European latitudes, so temperature couldn't be the answer.

He explored the role of age (35 was the most common suicide age), gender (men outnumbered women around four to one), and numerous other factors. Eventually, a general pattern emerged from different sources.

In terms of the stability of suicide rates over time, for instance, Durkheim found the pattern was not *totally* stable. He found spurts in the rates during times of political turmoil, which occurred in a number of European countries around 1848. This observation led him to hypothesize that suicide might have something to do with "breaches in social equilibrium." Put differently, social stability and integration seemed to be a protection against suicide.

This general hypothesis was substantiated and specified through Durkheim's analysis of a different set of data. The different countries of Europe had radically different suicide rates. The rate in Saxony, for example, was about ten times that of Italy, and the relative ranking of various countries persisted over time. As Durkheim considered other differences in the various countries, he eventually noticed a striking pattern: predominantly Protestant countries had consistently higher suicide rates than Catholic ones. The predominantly Protestant countries had 190 suicides per million population; mixed Protestant-Catholic countries, 96; and predominantly Catholic countries, 58 (Durkheim, 1897:152). It was possible, Durkheim reasoned, that some other factor, such as level of economic and cultural development, might explain the observed differences. If religion had a genuine effect on suicide, the religious difference would have to be found *within* given countries. To test this idea, Durkheim first noted that the German state of Bavaria had both the most Catholics and the lowest suicide rates in that country, whereas heavily Protestant Prussia had a much higher suicide rate. Not content to stop there, however, Durkheim examined the provinces composing each of those states. Table 13-2 shows what he found.

As you can see, in both Bavaria and Prussia, provinces with the highest proportion of Protestants also had the highest suicide rates. Increasingly, Durkheim became confident that religion played a significant role in the matter of suicide.

Returning eventually to a more general theoretical level, Durkheim combined the religious findings with the earlier observation about increased suicide rates during times of political turmoil. Put most simply, Durkheim suggested that many suicides are a product of *anomie*, "normlessness," or a general sense of social instability and disintegration. During times of political strife, people might feel that the old ways of society were collapsing. They would become demoralized and depressed, and suicide was one answer to the severe discomfort. Seen from the other direction, social integration and solidarity—reflected in personal feelings of being part of a coherent, enduring social whole—would offer protection against depression and suicide. That was where the religious difference fit in. Catholicism, as a far more structured and integrated religious system, would give people a greater sense of coherence and stability than would the more loosely structured Protestantism.

From these theories, Durkheim created the concept of *anomic suicide* and, more important, he added the concept of *anomie* to the lexicon of the social sciences. Please realize we have given you only the most superficial picture of Durkheim's classic study, and we think you'd enjoy looking through the original. In any event, this study gives you a good illustration of the possibilities for research contained in the masses of data regularly gathered and reported by government agencies.

Units of Analysis

As we have already seen in the case of *Suicide,* the unit of analysis involved in the analysis of existing statistics is often *not* the individual. Thus, Durkheim was required to work with political-geographic units: countries, regions, states, and cities. The same situation would probably appear if you were to undertake a study of crime rates, accident rates, disease, and so forth. By their nature, most existing statistics are aggregated: they describe groups.

The aggregate nature of existing statistics can present a problem, though not an insurmountable one. As we saw, for example, Durkheim wanted to determine whether Protestants or Catholics were more likely to commit suicide.

Table 13-2   Suicide Rates in Various German Provinces, Arranged in Terms of Religious Affiliation

RELIGIOUS CHARACTER OF PROVINCE	SUICIDES PER MILLION INHABITANTS	RELIGIOUS CHARACTER OF PROVINCE	SUICIDES PER MILLION INHABITANTS
Bavarian Provinces (1867–1875)*		Pomerania	171.5
		Average	264.6
Less than 50% Catholic		*68% to 89% Protestant*	
Rhenish Palatinate	167	Hanover	212.3
Central Franconia	207	Hesse	200.3
Upper Franconia	204	Bradenberg and Berlin	296.3
Average	192	East Prussia	171.3
50% to 90% Catholic		Average	220.0
Lower Franconia	157	*40% to 50% Protestant*	
Swabia	118	West Prussia	123.9
Average	135	Silesia	260.2
Over 90% Catholic		Westphalia	107.5
Upper Palatinate	64	Average	163.6
Upper Bavaria	114	*28% to 32% Protestant*	
Lower Bavaria	19	Posen	96.4
Average	75	Rhineland	100.3
		Hohenzollern	90.1
Prussian Provinces (1883–1890)		Average	95.6
More than 90% Protestant			
Saxony	309.4		
Schleswig	312.9		

* *Note:* The population below 15 years has been omitted.

Source: Adapted from Emile Durkheim, *Suicide* (Glencoe, Ill.: Free Press, 1897, 1951), p. 153.

None of the records available to him indicated the religion of those people who committed suicide, however. Ultimately, then, it was not possible for him to say whether Protestants committed suicide more often than Catholics, though he *inferred* as much. Because Protestant countries, regions, and states had higher suicide rates than Catholic countries, regions, and states, he drew the obvious conclusion.

There's danger in drawing that kind of conclusion, however. It is always possible that patterns of behavior at a group level do not reflect corresponding patterns on an individual level. Such er-

rors are said to be due to an *ecological fallacy*, which was discussed in Chapter 4. It was possible, for example, that it was Catholics who committed suicide in the predominantly Protestant areas. Perhaps Catholics in predominantly Protestant areas were so badly persecuted that they were led into despair and suicide. Then it would be possible for Protestant countries to have high suicide rates without any Protestants committing suicide.

Durkheim avoided the danger of the ecological fallacy in two ways. First, his general conclusions were based as much on rigorous, theoretical deductions as on the empirical facts. The

CONSTRUCTING INDICATORS OF QUALITY OF LIFE

by Ira M. Wasserman, Department of Sociology, Eastern Michigan University

Within the social sciences there has been a recent concern with constructing quality of life indicators for various political-geographical areas (e.g., states, standard metropolitan statistical areas). Studies of this type (Liu 1973, 1975; Smith 1973) have differentiated various topical areas related to the overall quality of life of a population within a political boundary (e.g., health, education, economics, public safety, individual status) and have then proceeded to select individual indicator measures of these categories which are then equally aggregated together to form an overall measure for that area. The overall quality of life for the political region is then computed by equally weighting the various topical measures. For example, Liu (1973:18) measures the health and welfare index for American states by the use of such individual variables as the number of physicians, dentists, and nurses per 100,000 population, as well as by the number of admissions to mental hospitals in the state per 100,000 population. Employing the previous variables, as well as other selected variables, he then constructed a health and welfare index for the 50 states, weighting each of the selected variables equally. He then constructed an overall quality of life index for the fifty states by aggregating together equally the 11 topical indices which he had differentiated.

As Gehrmann (1978) has demonstrated, there are a number of methodological difficulties with this type of index construction. First, the quality of life index for the various topical areas will be a function of the individual variables selected for the various topical areas. For example, in his construction of indices Liu (1973) tended to select input variables (e.g., physicians per capita, which is an input into the health system), while Smith (1973) tended to select output variables (e.g., mortality per capita, which is an output of any health system in an area). Also, it is possible that the selected variables may have no policy relation to the topical area. For example, hospital beds or physicians per capita may not be a good indicator of the

correspondence between theory and fact made a counterexplanation, such as the one we just made up, less likely. Second, by extensively retesting his conclusions in a variety of ways, Durkheim further strengthened the likelihood that they were correct. Suicide rates were higher in Protestant countries than in Catholic ones; higher in Protestant regions of Catholic countries than in Catholic regions of Protestant countries; and so forth. The

replication of findings added to the weight of evidence in support of his conclusions.

Problems of Validity

Whenever you base your research on an analysis of data that already exist, you are obviously limited to what exists. Often, the existing data don't

health quality of life in an area if these facilities are used by a national population (e.g., location of the Mayo Clinic in Minnesota or the location of Veterans Hospitals in various large metropolitan areas). Thus, even though the measure may be relatively high for a given geographical area, it may not reflect the health facilities available to the population in the area, since the individuals from many other areas may use these facilities quite extensively. A second methodological difficulty with the construction of quality of life indices is the aggregation of the selected variables, i.e., the problem of weighting of the individual variables. For example, health facilities and climate are variables that are likely to be weighted high by individuals over 60, but are likely to be given a lower weighting by individuals under 60. In the construction of quality of life indices the manner in which the population of an area is likely to weight the various individual variables must be taken into account in constructing the overall measure.

In summary, the construction of objective quality of life indicators has been hindered by the inability of social investigators to solve key methodological problems. First, no consensus has developed concerning the individual variables that are to be selected for the construction of the various indices. Second, no consensus has been developed concerning the manner in which the various selected variables are to be aggregated together employing some weighting scheme.

References

Gehrmann, Friedhelm. 1978. "'Valid' Empirical Measurement of Quality of Life?" *Social Indicators Research* 5 (January): 73–109.

Liu, Ben-Chieh. 1973. *The Quality of Life in the United States, 1970: Index, Ratings, and Statistics.* Kansas City, MO: Midwest Research Institute.

Liu, Ben-Chieh. 1975. *Quality of Life Indicators in U.S. Metropolitan Areas, 1970: A Comprehensive Assessment.* Washington, DC: Environmental Protection Agency.

Smith, David M. 1973. *The Geography of Social Well-Being in the United States: An Introduction to Territorial Social Indicators.* New York: McGraw-Hill Book Company.

cover exactly what you are interested in, and your measurements may not be altogether valid representations of the variables and concepts you want to draw conclusions about.

Two characteristics of science are used to handle the problem of validity in analysis of existing statistics: logical reasoning and replication. As an example of logical reasoning, you'll recall that Durkheim was not able to determine the religion of persons who committed suicide. He did know the predominant religions of the regions whose suicides he studied, reasoning that most of the suicides in a predominantly Protestant region would be Protestants.

Replication can be a general solution to problems of validity in social research. Recall the earlier discussion of the interchangeability of indicators. Crying in sad movies isn't necessarily a valid measure of compassion, so if women cry more than men, that doesn't prove they are more compassionate. Neither is putting little birds back in their nests a valid measure of compassion, so that wouldn't prove women to be more compassionate. And giving money to charity could represent something other than compassion, and so forth. None of these things, taken alone, would prove that women were more compassionate than men. But if women appeared more compassionate than men by all these measures, that would create a weight of evidence in support of the conclusion. In the analysis of existing statistics, a little ingenuity and reasoning can usually turn up several independent tests of your hypothesis, and if all the tests seem to confirm it, the weight of evidence supports the view you are advancing.

Problems of Reliability

The analysis of existing statistics depends heavily on the quality of the statistics themselves: Are they accurate reports of what they claim to report? That can be a substantial problem sometimes because the weighty tables of government statistics are sometimes grossly inaccurate.

Because a great deal of the research into crime is dependent on official crime statistics, this body of data has come under critical evaluation. The results have not been too encouraging. Suppose, for purposes of illustration, that you were interested in tracing the long-term trends in marijuana use in the United States. Official statistics on the numbers of people arrested for selling or possessing it would seem to be a reasonable measure of use. Right? Not necessarily.

To begin, you face a hefty problem of validity. Before the passage of the Marijuana Tax Act in 1937, grass was legal in the United States, so arrest records would not give you a valid measure of use. But even if you limited your inquiry to the post-1937 era, you would still have problems of reliability stemming from the nature of law enforcement and crime recordkeeping.

Law enforcement, for example, is subject to various pressures. A public outcry against marijuana, led perhaps by a vocal citizens' group, often results in a police "crackdown on drug trafficking"—especially if it occurs during an election or budget year. A sensational story in the press can have a similar effect. In addition, the volume of other business facing police has an effect on marijuana arrests.

Lois DeFleur (1975) has traced the pattern of drug arrests in Chicago between 1942 and 1970 and has demonstrated that the official records present a far more accurate history of police practices and political pressure on police than a history of drug use. On a different level of analysis, Donald Black (1970) and others have analyzed the factors influencing whether an offender is actually arrested by police or let off with a warning. Ultimately, official crime statistics are influenced by whether specific offenders are well or poorly dressed, whether they are polite or abusive to police officers, and so forth. Consider unreported crimes, sometimes estimated to be as much as ten times the number of crimes known to police, and the reliability of crime statistics gets even shakier.

These comments concern crime statistics at a local level. Often it is useful to analyze national crime statistics, such as those reported in the FBI's annual *Uniform Crime Reports*. Additional problems are introduced at the national level. Different local jurisdictions define crimes differently. Also, participation in the FBI program is voluntary, so the data are incomplete.

Finally, the process of recordkeeping affects the records that are kept and reported. Whenever a law enforcement unit improves its recordkeeping system—computerizing it, for example—the apparent crime rates always increase dramatically. That can happen even if the number of crimes committed, reported, and investigated does not increase.

Your first protection against the problems of reliability in the analysis of existing statistics is awareness—knowing that the problem may exist. Investigating the nature of the data collection and tabulation may enable you to assess the nature and degree of unreliability so that you can judge its potential impact on your research interest. If you also use logical reasoning and replication, as discussed previously, you can usually cope with the problem.

Sources of Existing Statistics

It would take a whole book just to list the sources of data available for analysis. In this section, we'll mention a few sources and point you in the direction of finding others relevant to your research interest.

One valuable book you can buy is the annual *Statistical Abstract of the United States,* published by the U.S. Department of Commerce. It includes statistics on the individual states and (less extensively) cities as well as on the nation as a whole. You can learn the number of work stoppages in the country year by year, residential property taxes of major cities, the number of water pollution discharges reported around the country, the number of business proprietorships in the nation, and hundreds of other such handy bits of information.

Federal agencies—the Departments of Labor, Agriculture, Transportation, and so forth—publish countless data series. To find out what's available, go to your library, find the government documents section, and spend a few hours browsing through the shelves. You'll come away with a clear sense of the wealth of data available for your insight and ingenuity. World statistics are available through the United Nations. Its *Demographic Yearbook* presents annual vital statistics (births, deaths, and other data relevant to population) for the individual nations of the world. Other publications report a variety of other kinds of data. Again, a trip to your library is the best introduction to what's available.

The amount of data provided by nongovernment agencies is as staggering as the amount your taxes buy. Chambers of commerce often publish data reports on business, as do private consumer groups. Ralph Nader has information on automobile safety, and *Common Cause* covers politics and government. And, as mentioned earlier, George Gallup publishes reference volumes on public opinion as tapped by Gallup Polls since 1935.

Perhaps the best source of existing statistics for social workers is the *Social Work Almanac,* published by the National Association of Social Workers. The *Almanac,* which first appeared in 1992, is compiled by Leon Ginsberg, a social work professor at the University of South Carolina. It includes parts of other reports mentioned above, which were selected for the *Almanac* because of their relevance to social workers. The *Almanac* presents statistics on the U.S. population demographics, problems of children, crime and delinquency, education, health and mortality, the elderly, economic assistance to the poor, housing, homelessness, and professional issues in social work.

The availability of existing statistics makes it possible to create some fairly sophisticated measures. The box on "Suffering Around the World" describes an analysis published by the Population Crisis Committee.

Most recently, the availability of data by electronic means has vastly expanded the game. Now it's possible to download data sets using File Transfer Protocol (ftp) or the World Wide Web. These new possibilities are discussed at length in Appendix H, "Social Work Research and Cyberspace."

It is tempting to continue listing data sources, but you probably have already gotten the idea. We suggest you visit the government documents section the next time you're at your college library. You'll be amazed by the data waiting for your analysis. The lack of funds to support expensive data collection is no reason for not doing good and useful research.

Illustrations of the Analysis of Existing Statistics in Research on Social Welfare Policy

Two studies of social welfare policy illustrate the applicability to social work of analyzing existing statistics. They also illustrate some of the problems that have already been discussed in using this method.

SUFFERING AROUND THE WORLD

In 1992, the Population Crisis Committee, a nonprofit organization committed to combating the population explosion, undertook to analyze the relative degree of suffering in nations around the world. Every country with a population of one million or more was evaluated in terms of the following ten indicators—with a score of 10 on any indicator representing the highest level of adversity:

- life expectancy
- daily per capita calorie supply
- percentage of the population with access to clean drinking water
- proportion of infant immunization
- rate of secondary school enrollment
- gross national product
- inflation
- number of telephones per 1000 people
- political freedom
- civil rights

Here's how the world's nations ranked in terms of these indicators. Remember, high scores are signs of overall suffering.

Extreme Human Suffering:
93 - Mozambique
92 - Somalia
89 - Afghanistan, Haiti, Sudan
88 - Zaire
87 - Laos
86 - Guinea, Angola
85 - Ethiopia, Uganda
84 - Cambodia, Sierra Leone
82 - Chad, Guinea-Bissau
81 - Ghana, Burma
79 - Malawi
77 - Cameroon, Mauritania
76 - Rwanda, Vietnam, Liberia
75 - Burundi, Kenya, Madagascar, Yemen

High Human Suffering:
74 - Ivory Coast
73 - Bhutan, Burkina Faso, Central African Republic
71 - Tanzania, Togo
70 - Lesotho, Mali, Niger, Nigeria
69 - Guatemala, Nepal
68 - Bangladesh, Bolivia, Zambia
67 - Pakistan
66 - Nicaragua, Papua–New Guinea, Senegal, Swaziland, Zimbabwe

In one study, Martha Ozawa (1989) investigated whether the Aid to Families with Dependent Children Program has contributed to the dramatic rise in illegitimate birth rates among adolescents. Ozawa hypothesized that a high AFDC payment and a high AFDC acceptance rate increases the illegitimacy rate of births to adolescents. Her reasoning was that more generous payments and higher acceptance rates make it easier for the childbearing adolescent to establish her own household and to avoid an unwanted marriage. In this connection, Ozawa envisioned positive aspects of the adolescent's decision to raise a child alone rather than to marry. She emphasized that she was not studying the decision to bear a child in order to receive AFDC (she

65 - Iraq
64 - Gambia, Congo, El Salvador, Indonesia, Syria
63 - Comores, India, Paraguay, Peru
62 - Benin, Honduras
61 - Lebanon, China, Guyana, South Africa
59 - Egypt, Morocco
58 - Ecuador, Sri Lanka
57 - Botswana
56 - Iran
55 - Suriname
54 - Algeria, Thailand
53 - Dominican Republic, Mexico, Tunisia, Turkey
51 - Libya, Colombia, Venezuela
50 - Brazil, Oman, Philippines

Moderate Human Suffering:
49 - Solomon Islands
47 - Albania
45 - Vanuatu
44 - Jamaica, Romania, Saudi Arabia, Seychelles, Yugoslavia (former)
43 - Mongolia
41 - Jordan
40 - Malaysia, Mauritius
39 - Argentina

38 - Cuba, Panama
37 - Chile, Uruguay, North Korea
34 - Costa Rica, South Korea, United Arab Emirates
33 - Poland
32 - Bulgaria, Hungary, Qatar
31 - Soviet Union (former)
29 - Bahrain, Hong Kong, Trinidad and Tobago
28 - Kuwait, Singapore
25 - Czechoslovakia, Portugal, Taiwan

Minimal Human Suffering:
21 - Israel
19 - Greece
16 - United Kingdom
12 - Italy
11 - Barbados, Ireland, Spain, Sweden
8 - Finland, New Zealand
7 - France, Iceland, Japan, Luxembourg
6 - Austria, Germany
5 - United States
4 - Australia, Norway
3 - Canada, Switzerland
2 - Belgium, Netherlands
1 - Denmark

cited prior research showing that adolescents do not bear infants out of wedlock in order to receive AFDC payments). Instead, she was studying the impact of AFDC on the adolescent's decision whether to marry or to raise the child alone.

Ozawa's unit of analysis was the state. Her dependent variable was the state's rate of illegitimacy among women aged 19 and under. Her independent variables included the state AFDC benefit level and the state AFDC acceptance rate. (These were not the only independent variables she studied, but for the purpose of simplifying this illustration we'll keep focused on the two primary ones.)

Analyzing U.S. National Center for Health Statistics, Ozawa showed that the national adolescent illegitimacy rate rose 70% between 1970 and

1982. To assess the impact of AFDC on those rates, she obtained government data published by the Bureau of the Census, the Committee on Ways and Means, and the Social Security Administration. Her results supported her hypothesis; pregnant adolescents in states with higher AFDC payments and higher acceptance rates were less likely to marry than those in states with lower AFDC payments and lower acceptance rates.

In developing policy implications from her findings, Ozawa urged policymakers to understand the positive aspects of the decision not to marry and to consider "granting AFDC payments to low-income, unmarried adolescent mothers regardless of the economic backgrounds of their parents" (1988:11).

In another study, Claudia Coulton and her associates (1990) were concerned that economic forces in the United States during the 1980s were concentrating poor people in deteriorating central urban neighborhoods where they were becoming further isolated from economic opportunities and increasingly exposed to adverse social and physical conditions associated with extreme poverty. Coulton and her associates postulated that published research that had already documented this trend was based primarily on national census data that might have underestimated the problem, because income estimates from the 1980 census were for income earned in 1979 and thus did not reflect the impact of the recession that began late in 1979 and continued into the early 1980s.

To study this phenomenon in depth, as well as several related statistical phenomena that we won't go into here, Coulton and her associates decided to limit their study to one urban area: Cleveland, Ohio. They recognized that this decision would limit the generalizability of their findings but believed that others could replicate their study in other cities to see if the same patterns could be observed.

Coulton and her associates prefaced their study by noting that poverty rates rose sharply in the 1980s and that to the extent that poverty was be-

coming more geographically concentrated, it was becoming more difficult for poor people to reach jobs located in the suburbs. Workers who could afford to move closer to suburban jobs were induced to do so, and this further concentrated the poverty of the inner city neighborhood they left behind and reduced the opportunity of those left behind to find jobs close to home (to which they could travel). As the neighborhood deteriorated, the worsening social environment conceivably might have had harmful effects on the individuals left behind—particularly the youths—as they became increasingly exposed to such problems as teen pregnancy, delinquency, school dropout, and so on.

The research team used a variety of sources of existing statistics for Cleveland, including data from the Center for Regional Economic Issues located at Case Western Reserve University; birth and death information reported by the Ohio Department of Health (which provided data on low birthweight, infant death rate, teen birthrate, and illegitimacy rates); crime rate data from the Federal Bureau of Investigation; juvenile delinquency data from the Cuyahoga County Juvenile Court; drug arrest rates from the Cleveland Police Department; and housing value data from the Housing Policy Research Program of Cleveland State University.

The existing statistics analyzed by Coulton and her associates showed that by 1988 nearly 50% of Cleveland's poor people lived in neighborhoods of concentrated poverty, compared with 21% in 1970. (The researchers defined high-poverty areas as census tracts where more than 40% of the population lives in a household below the poverty threshold.) Thus, poor people were becoming more spatially isolated from the rest of society and less likely to encounter nonpoor people in their neighborhoods. The statistics on poverty-related physical and social problems that Coulton and her associates analyzed indicated that as poor people were becoming more concentrated in high-poverty areas, the social and physical problems to which they were being exposed were deteriorating rapidly, particularly for people living in "emerging poverty areas," areas that lost many blue-collar workers in the early 1980s and that consequently became poverty areas since 1980. Noting the importance of the person-in-environment framework for social work practice and the special vulnerability of poor children living in high poverty neighborhoods, Coulton and her associates recommended that social workers need to consider interventions at the environmental level:

> Social workers need practice models that combine their traditional approaches to service delivery with economic redevelopment of distressed parts of the city and mechanisms that reestablish connections between central city residents and distant, suburban job locations. Barriers to these connections are geographic but also involve social networks, information channels, and psychological distance. As poor neighborhoods become increasingly adverse environments due to economic and social decline, programs and interventions are needed that will disrupt their growing isolation from the mainstream.
>
> (1990:15)

In addition to providing an excellent illustration of the creative analysis of a variety of sources of existing statistics, the study by Coulton and her associates offers a splendid example of the relevance of research (and policy!) to social work practice.

HISTORICAL/COMPARATIVE ANALYSIS

In this final section of the chapter, we examine historical/comparative research, a method that differs substantially from those previously discussed, though it overlaps somewhat with field research, content analysis, and the analysis of existing statistics.

The discussion of longitudinal and time-series research designs in earlier chapters notwithstanding, our examination of research methods to date has focused primarily on studies anchored in one point in time and in one locale, whether a particular small group or a nation. This focus, although accurately portraying the main emphasis of contemporary social work research, conceals the fact that social scientists are also interested in tracing the development of social forms over time and comparing those developmental processes across cultures.

Historical/comparative analysis is usually considered a qualitative method, one in which the researcher attempts to master many subtle details. The main resources for observation and analysis are historical records. While a historical/comparative analysis might include content analysis, it is not limited to communications. The method's name includes the word *comparative* because most social scientists—in contrast to historians, who may simply describe a particular set of events—seek to discover common patterns that recur in different times and places.

Many historical writings can be found in the social work literature. Biographies of social work pioneers comprise a large segment of these writings. Another segment contains case studies tracing the development of social welfare policies and programs. Less common, but perhaps more useful for informing current practice, are studies that are more comparative in their efforts to seek recurring patterns that help explain the past and imply possible lessons for the present. An excellent example of the latter type of study, one with particular relevance to social work research, is Sidney Zimbalist's (1977) book *Historic Themes and Landmarks in Social Welfare Research*, which was developed from his doctoral dissertation.

Based on his analysis of social work research studies published between the late 19th century and the mid-1960s, Zimbalist identified a recurring cycle in which social work researchers exhibited an excessive tendency to go overboard in overzealously embracing the latest wave of research. Rather than take a balanced and critical outlook regarding the range of research approaches available, considering both their strengths and weaknesses and the conditions under which each is most appropriate, social work researchers tended to faddishly embrace promising new approaches as a panacea for the profession's research needs.

Zimbalist detected this cycle in early research on the causes of poverty and the measurement of its prevalence, the embracing of the social survey movement at the beginning of the 20th century, on up through the study of the multiproblem family in the mid-1960s.

Zimbalist's work appears prophetic. Soon after it was published, many in the profession zealously embraced single-subject methodology as a panacea for the profession's need to develop a better empirical base for practice and to resolve longstanding gaps between research and practice. Today, we are more aware of the limitations of single-subject methodology and, while we continue to see its utility alongside the gamut of other research methods, we are less likely to focus on it as a cure-all for the profession's research ills. We may also be witnessing today the emergence of a new cycle, as many advocate abandoning "obsolete" quantitative methods in favor of qualitative methods. Thus, Zimbalist's work goes beyond describing the past and gives us a framework for understanding current controversies in social work research.

Another excellent example of historical/comparative research that offers lessons for the present is a study by Morrissey and Goldman (1984) on recurrent cycles of reform in the care of the chronic mentally ill. Morrissey and Goldman identify parallels between the recent deinstitutionalization movement and Dorothea Dix's 19th-century crusade to build state hospitals to provide asylum and sanctuary to individuals too sick to fend for themselves in communities that did not want them. In Dix's era, the reform intended to make care more humane by shifting its locus from the community to the hospital. In today's era of deinstitutionalization, the reform intended to make care more humane by shifting its locus from the hospital to the community. But today we hear of large numbers of mentally ill individuals who are homeless or in jails and who are living in squalor—many of the same conditions that prompted Dix's crusade over a century ago.

Morrissey and Goldman show how both reforms failed for the same reason: each merely shifted the locus of care without garnering enough public fiscal support to ensure that the new locus of care would ultimately be any more humane than the old one. Without adequate financing, Dix's intended humane sanctuaries for the mentally ill too often became overcrowded, inhumane "snake-pits" where sick individuals who could not afford expensive private care could be warehoused and forgotten. Without adequate financing, the noble intentions of the deinstitutionalization movement have for too many individuals led to community-based conditions as bad as in the back wards of state hospitals.

One lesson for today from this research is that if we seek to ensure more humane care for the long-term mentally ill, we must go beyond conceptualizing idealized programs or notions about where to provide care; the real issue is convincing the public to allocate adequate fiscal support for that care. Without the latter, our reformist efforts may be doomed to repeat the unintended consequences of previous reforms.

Sources of Historical/Comparative Data

As we saw in the case of existing statistics, there is no end of data available for analysis in historical research. To begin, historians may have already reported on whatever it is you want to examine, and their analyses can give you an initial grounding in the subject, a jumping-off point for more in-depth research. Ultimately, you will usually want to go beyond others' conclusions and examine some "raw data" and draw your own conclusions. These vary, of course, according to the topic under study. Raw data might, for example, include old letters or diaries, sermons or lectures, and so forth.

In discussing procedures for studying the history of family life, Ellen Rothman points to the following sources:

In addition to personal sources, there are public records which are also revealing of family history. Newspapers are especially rich in evidence on the educational, legal, and recreational aspects of family life in the past as seen from a local point of view. Magazines reflect more general patterns of family life; students often find them interesting to explore for data on perceptions and expectations of mainstream family values. Magazines offer several different kinds of sources at once: visual materials (illustrations and advertisements), commentary (editorial and advice columns), and fiction. Popular periodicals are particularly rich in the last two. Advice on many questions of concern to families—from the proper way to discipline children to the economics of wallpaper—fills magazine columns from the early nineteenth century to the present. Stories that suggest common experiences or perceptions of family life appear with the same continuity.   (1981:53)

Organizations generally document themselves, so if you are studying the development of some organization you should examine its official documents: charters, policy statements, speeches by leaders, and so on.

Often, official government documents provide the data needed for analysis. To better appreciate the history of race relations in America, A. Leon Higginbotham, Jr. (1978) examined some 200 years of laws and court cases involving race. Himself the first black American appointed a federal judge, Higginbotham found that the law, rather than protecting blacks, was the embodiment of bigotry and oppression. In the earliest court cases, there was considerable ambiguity over whether blacks were indentured servants or, in fact, slaves. Later court cases and laws clarified the matter— holding blacks to be something less than human.

Many of the source materials for historical research can be found in academic libraries. Specialized librarians may be available to help you locate obscure documents. Skills in using the library, therefore, are essential if you wish to conduct historical research. (We will discuss using the library in Appendix A.)

Two broad types of source materials are *primary* sources and *secondary* sources. Primary sources provide firsthand accounts by someone present at an event. Examples are diaries, letters, organizational bylaws, the minutes of a meeting, the orally reported memory of an eyewitness, and so on. Secondary sources describe past phenomena based on primary sources. Thus, if you cite a book on the history of Lyndon Johnson's Great Society social welfare programs in his war on poverty, you are using a secondary source. But if you go to the LBJ Presidential Library in Austin, Texas and cite letters, laws, and official documents from that period that you find there, you are using primary sources.

A danger in working exclusively with secondary sources is that you may merely repeat the mistakes contained in those sources and fail to give yourself the opportunity to provide a new, independent perspective on past events. But primary sources can be flawed as well. For example, an eyewitness could have been biased or may experience faulty memory.

Stuart (1981) argues that people who author primary sources based on events that they witnessed probably had a vested interest in those events. He cites an example of bias in the statistical reports of the populations of Native Americans on reservations by Indian agents in the late 19th century. Some agents exaggerated the population size in order to obtain more supplies for their reservations from the federal government's Office of Indian Affairs. A television biography of Lyndon Johnson, aired by the Public Broadcasting System, relied heavily on primary sources such as people who worked on Johnson's White House staff. His decision not to run for reelection in 1968 was portrayed largely in terms of his dismay over the tragedy of the war in Vietnam and his desire to find a way to negotiate an end to it. Unmentioned in the historical documentary was the fact that he announced his decision not to run on the eve of the Wisconsin primary election, when political polls there predicted that Senator Eugene McCarthy would beat him by a

"READING AND EVALUATING DOCUMENTS"

by Ron Aminzade and Barbara Laslett, University of Minnesota

The purpose of the following comments is to give you some sense of the kind of interpretive work that historians do and the critical approach they take toward their sources. It should help you to appreciate some of the skills that historians develop in their efforts to reconstruct the past from residues, to assess the evidentiary status of different types of documents, and to determine the range of permissible inferences and interpretations. Here are some of the questions historians ask about documents:

1. Who composed the documents? Why were they written? Why have they survived all these years? What methods were used to acquire the information contained in the documents?

2. What are some of the biases in the documents and how might you go about checking or correcting them? How inclusive or representative is the sample of individuals, events, etc. contained in the document? What were the institutional constraints and the general organizational routines under which the document was prepared? To what extent does the document provide more of an index of institutional activity than of the phenomenon being studied? What is the time lapse be-

large margin in that primary, and when newspaper articles spoke of the pending humiliation of an incumbent president of Johnson's stature being rejected by the voters of his own party. Was that omission due to overreliance on primary sources who were close to, and fond of, Lyndon Johnson? We can only surmise.

In conducting historical research, then, you should keep some cautions in mind. As we saw in the case of existing statistics, you cannot trust the accuracy of records—official or unofficial, primary or secondary. You need always be wary of bias in your data sources. If all your data on a pioneer social worker are taken from people who worked for that social worker, you are unlikely to get a well-rounded view of that person. If all of your data on the development of a social movement are taken from activists in the movement itself, you are unlikely to gain a well-rounded view

of the movement. The diaries of affluent, friendly visitors of the Charity Organization Societies of a century ago may not give you an accurate view of life among the immigrant poor whom they visited during those times.

As a final illustration of this point, suppose you conduct historical research in an effort to understand the chief forces at play that led to massive discharges from state hospitals as part of the deinstitutionalization movement in mental health. If you rely only on the reports of the staff of state mental health bureaucracies, you may be led to believe that those discharges were primarily a humanitarian response to advances in psychopharmacology and concern for the civil liberties of the mentally ill. You might not discover that the greatest number of discharges occurred long after the discovery of psychotropic drugs in the mid-1950s. Instead, they came in the mid-1970s,

tween the observation of the events documented and the witnesses' documentation of them? How confidential or public was the document meant to be? What role did etiquette, convention, and custom play in the presentation of the material contained within the document? If you relied solely upon the evidence contained in these documents, how might your vision of the past be distorted? What other kinds of documents might you look at for evidence on the same issues?

3. What are the key categories and concepts used by the writer of the document to orga-

nize the information presented? What are the selectivities or silences that result from these categories of thought?

4. What sort of theoretical issues and debates do these documents cast light upon? What kinds of historical and/or sociological questions do they help answer? What sorts of valid inferences can one make from the information contained in these documents? What sorts of generalizations can one make on the basis of the information contained in these documents?

---

when fiscal crises in state governments prompted state officials to recognize that by discharging patients from state hospitals to community facilities, the costs of caring for the mentally ill could be passed on from the state to the federal government (Morrissey and Goldman, 1984).

Your protection against these dangers in historical research lies in *corroboration*. If several sources point to the same set of "facts," your confidence in them might reasonably increase. Thus, when conducting historical research you should try not to rely on a single source or on one type of source. Try to obtain data from every relevant source you can find, and be sure to seek sources that represent different vested interests and different points of view. The box titled "Reading and Evaluating Documents" provides additional suggestions regarding the use of historical documents and what to make of them.

The critical review that Aminzade and Laslett urge for the reading of historical documents can serve you more generally in life than just in the pursuit of historical/comparative research. Consider applying some of the boxed questions with regard to presidential press conferences, advertising, or (gasp!) college textbooks. None of these offers a direct view of reality; all have human authors and human subjects.

Analytic Techniques

As a qualitative research method, historical/comparative research treats hypotheses differently from the way quantitative methods do when seeking to formulate explanations. Rather than sticking with a hypothesis throughout an entire study that has been rigidly designed in advance to test it, historical researchers are likely to continually revise and reformulate their hypotheses throughout the process of examining, analyzing, and synthesizing the historical documents they encounter.

Because historical/comparative research is a fluid qualitative method, there are no easily listed steps to follow in the analysis of historical data. Max Weber used the German term *verstehen*—understanding—in reference to an essential quality of social research (a term we discussed briefly in Chapter 12). Weber meant that the researcher must be able to take on, mentally, the circumstances, views, and feelings of those being studied to interpret their actions appropriately. More recently, social scientists have adopted the term *hermeneutics* (another term we mentioned in Chapter 12) for this aspect of social research. Originally a Christian theological term referring to the interpretation of spiritual truth in the Bible, *hermeneutics* has been secularized to mean the art, science, or skill of interpretation.

Whereas the conclusions drawn from quantitative research methods can rest, in part, on numerical calculations—*x* is either greater than *y* or it isn't—hermeneutic conclusions are harder to pin down and more subject to debate. But hermeneutics involves more than mere opinions. Albert Einstein described the foundation of science this way:

> Science is the attempt to make the chaotic diversity of our sense-experience correspond to a logically uniform system of thought. In this system single experiences must be correlated with the theoretic structure in such a way that the resulting coordination is unique and convincing. (1940:487)

The historical/comparative researcher must find patterns among the voluminous details describing the subject matter of study. Often the "theoretic structure" Einstein mentioned takes the form of what Weber called ideal types: conceptual models composed of the essential characteristics of social phenomena. Thus, for example, Weber himself did considerable research on bureaucracy. Having observed numerous actual bureaucracies, Weber (1925) detailed those qualities essential to bureaucracies in general: jurisdic-

tional areas, hierarchically structured authority, written files, and so on. Weber did not merely list characteristics common to all the actual bureaucracies he observed. Rather, he needed to fully understand the essentials of bureaucratic operation to create a theoretical model of the "perfect" (ideal type) bureaucracy.

Often historical/comparative research is informed by a particular theoretical paradigm. Thus Marxist scholars may undertake historical analyses of particular situations—such as the history of Hispanic minorities in the United States—to determine whether they can be understood in terms of the Marxist version of conflict theory.

Although historical/comparative research is regarded as a qualitative rather than quantitative technique, historians often make use of quantitative methods. For example, historical analysts often use time-series (see Chapter 9) data to monitor changing conditions over time, such as data on population, crime rates, unemployment, infant mortality rates, and so forth. When historical researchers rely on quantitative data, their reports will rely on numbers, graphs, statistical trends, and the like to support their conclusions. When they rely on qualitative methods, their reports will contain less quantitative data and instead will cite narrative material in their sources to illustrate the recurring patterns that they think they have detected.

So far, we have discussed *comparative analysis* in conjunction with historical research in the sense of comparing processes over time. But, as we mentioned earlier, comparative research can also compare processes across cultures. *Cross-cultural studies* are scarce in the social work literature. This is unfortunate in light of the value of the cross-cultural work that we mentioned in Chapter 3 in connection to cultural sensitivity. Cross-cultural studies can use most of the quantitative or qualitative research methods that are discussed in this book.

This concludes our discussion of unobtrusive research methods. As you can see, social scientists have a variety of ways to study social life without having any impact on what they study.

Main Points

• Unobtrusive measures are ways of studying social behavior without affecting it in the process.

• Content analysis is a social research method appropriate for studying human communications. Besides being used to study communication processes, it may be used to study other aspects of social behavior.

• Units of communication, such as words, paragraphs, and books, are the usual units of analysis in content analysis.

• Standard probability sampling techniques are appropriate in content analysis.

• Manifest content refers to the directly visible, objectively identifiable characteristics of a communication, such as the specific words in a book, the specific colors used in a painting, and so forth. That is one focus for content analysis.

• Latent content refers to the meanings contained within communications. The determination of latent content requires judgments on the part of the researcher.

• Coding is the process of transforming raw data—either manifest or latent content—into standardized, quantitative form.

• A variety of government and nongovernment agencies provide aggregate data for studying aspects of social life.

• The ecological fallacy refers to the possibility that patterns found at a group level differ from those that would be found on an individual level; thus we can be misled when we analyze aggregated data for the purpose of understanding individual behavior.

• The problem of validity in connection with the analysis of existing statistics can usually be handled through logical reasoning and replication.

• Existing statistics often have problems of reliability, and it is necessary to use them with caution.

• Social scientists also use historical/comparative methods to discover patterns in the histories of different cultures.

• Hermeneutics refers to interpreting social life by mentally taking on the circumstances, views, and feelings of the participants.

• An ideal type is a conceptual model composed of the essential qualities of a social phenomenon.

Review Questions and Exercises

1. In two or three paragraphs, outline a content analysis design to determine whether the Republican or the Democratic party is more supportive of public spending on social welfare. Be sure to specify units of analysis, sampling methods, and the relevant measurements.

2. Social scientists often contrast the sense of "community" in villages, small towns, and neighborhoods from life in large, urban societies. Try your hand at constructing an ideal type of community, listing its essential qualities.

Additional Readings

Baker, Vern, and Lambert, Charles, "The National Collegiate Athletic Association and the Governance of Higher Education," *Sociological Quarterly,* 1990, Vol. 31:3, pp. 403–421. A historical analysis of the factors producing and shaping the NCAA.

Ginsberg, Leon, *Social Work Almanac* (Washington, DC: ASW Press, 1992). This is perhaps the best source of existing statistics for social workers, since it contains over 200 tables and figures selected for their relevance to social workers and social service delivery.

Isaac, Larry W., and Griffin, Larry J., "A Historicism in Time-series Analyses of Historical Process: Critique, Redirection, and Illustrations for U.S. Labor History," *American Sociological Review,* 1989, Vol. 54 (December: 873–890).

Øyen, Else, ed., *Comparative Methodology: Theory and Practice in International Social Research* (Newbury Park, CA: Sage, 1990). Here are a variety of viewpoints on different aspects of comparative research. Appropriately, the contributors are from many different countries.

U.S. Bureau of the Census, *Statistical Abstract of the United States, 1995, National Data Book and Guide to Sources* (Washington, DC: U.S. Government Printing Office, 1995). This is absolutely the best book bargain available (present company excluded). Although the hundreds of pages of tables of statistics are not exciting bedtime reading—the plot is a little thin—it is an absolutely essential resource volume for every social scientist.

Webb, Eugene T., Campbell, Donald T., Schwartz, Richard D., Sechrest, Lee, and Grove, Janet Belew, *Nonreactive Measures in the Social Sciences* (Boston: Houghton Mifflin, 1981). A compendium of unobtrusive measures. Includes physical traces, a variety of archival sources, and observation. Good discussion of the ethics involved and the limitations of such measures.

Weber, Robert Philip, *Basic Content Analysis* (Newbury Park, CA: Sage, 1990). Here's an excellent beginner's book for the design and execution of content analysis. Both general issues and specific techniques are presented.

P A R T

Analysis of Data

14
Processing Data

15
Interpreting Descriptive Statistics and Tables

16
Inferential Data Analysis: Part 1

17
Inferential Data Analysis: Part 2

In this part of the book, we'll be discussing several aspects of what is the most exciting portion of the research process: the analysis of data and the development of generalized understanding about social phenomena. In the chapters composing Part 5, we'll examine the steps that separate observation from the final reporting of findings.

Chapter 14 addresses the quantification of the data collected through the modes of observation discussed in Part 4. Today, many social science data are analyzed by machine: computers and other data processing devices. Chapter 14 provides a brief overview of some of the equipment involved and describes the processes required to convert observations into forms suitable for machine processing.

The first discussion on the logic of data analysis is presented in Chapter 15. We'll begin with an examination of methods of analyzing and presenting the data related to a single variable. Then we'll turn to the relationship between two variables and learn how to construct and read simple percentage tables. After that we will examine tables containing more than two variables and see how the analysis of multivariate tables, by controlling for alternative explanations, enhances our ability to interpret the causal implications of observed relationships.

Chapters 16 and 17 provide an introduction to statistical procedures that social work researchers commonly use to guide decisions concerning whether they can generalize beyond their own study about the relationships they observe in their findings, the causal processes that underlie the observed relationships, and the strengths of those relationships. The emphasis of these chapters is on understanding the logic of inferential statistics, rather than procedures for computing them. This chapter also examines the criteria that are used to decide when to use each of the various statistical procedures, mistakes that are commonly made in using or interpreting them, and controversies about their use.

Processing Data

What You'll Learn in This Chapter

Now that you've amassed a volume of
observations, you are about to learn how to
transform them into a form appropriate to
computer analysis. Here you will be introduced to
a technology that has immense value in social
work research and is emerging as a valuable tool
in direct social work service.

INTRODUCTION

Despite the widespread use of computers throughout our society today, their utility in social work practice has only begun to be recognized. Until recently, social welfare agencies used computers almost exclusively for clerical and fiscal functions, not to facilitate direct service (Boyd, Hylton, and Price, 1978). In 1986, however, Henry Miller reviewed more current applications of computer technology to social work and identified several innovations of value to social work practitioners.

The most straightforward way computers can aid social work practitioners is in helping social work administrators in managing social welfare agencies. In addition to facilitating day-to-day fiscal management, computers enable administrators, supervisors, and others to have at their fingertips analyses of agency or practitioner caseloads, trends in those caseloads, service delivery activities, interagency activities, and so on.

Computers also are being used as an assessment aid in direct-service delivery. Miller (1986) cites several examples. Public welfare social workers may have to decide how many hours to allocate for homemaker services for aged or disabled clients. Child welfare workers may have to select from a variety of alternatives the best placement for a particular child. Computer programs being used to aid in such direct-practice decisions are called decision support systems (DSS). The DSS program uses data on previously served clients similar to the one in question to identify the alternative most likely to fit the current client. The purpose of the DSS is not to make the decision for the practitioner, but to supplement the memory of the practitioner, who may decide to override the "recommendation" of the DSS. Computers also can be used to facilitate the work of case management practitioners to track client progress and activities across a maze of service deliverers.

Clinical practitioners can use their own microcomputers to store and retrieve treatment plans and case notes. They can also use interactive assessment programs that guide assessment interviews and offer diagnostic and treatment planning suggestions based on the clinical information entered.

Nurius and Hudson (1988), for example, describe the Clinical Assessment System (CAS) program, which contains 20 clinical measures of a wide range of client intrapersonal and interpersonal problems that social workers commonly encounter. The program automatically calculates and records the scores of these measures and interprets the scores for the social worker. Practitioners also can use the CAS to monitor client progress on graphs like those discussed in Chapter 10 in connection with using single-subject designs to evaluate your own practice. The practitioner merely needs to enter each score on the target problem over the course of treatment, and the CAS provides graphs and statistics that help the practitioner judge client progress and the need to modify treatment plans.

But despite the preceding advances, you are taking this course at a time when the computer's contribution to social work practice and research is still being discovered. This chapter will introduce you to that contribution.

The purpose of this chapter is to describe methods of converting social work data into a *machine-readable* form—a form that can be read and manipulated by computers and similar machines used in data processing. If you were conducting a research project at more or less the same time as you are reading the chapters of this book, your data, at this point, would be in the form of completed questionnaires, content analysis code sheets, or the like. At the completion of the stage covered in this chapter, those data would have been recorded on microcomputer floppy disks, cassettes, punch cards, or some other device that can be read by a machine.

Given the rapid pace of computer development and dissemination today, we can't anticipate the kind of equipment you may have available to you for your use. As a result, we're going to provide you with an overview of several stages in the evolution of computers in social research. That way, we should say something about whatever you have to work with. Moreover, it's useful for you to know about the earlier equipment and techniques because they sometimes reveal the logic of data analysis more clearly than today's advanced equipment and techniques.

COMPUTERS IN SOCIAL RESEARCH

For our purposes, the history of computing in social research began in 1801, more than half a century prior to the birth of modern social work. That's the year a Frenchman, Joseph-Marie Jacquard, created a revolution in the textile industry that was to have an impact in the most unlikely corners of life.

To facilitate the weaving of intricate patterns, Jacquard invented an automatic loom that took its instructions from punched cards. As a series of cards passed through the loom's "reader," wooden pegs poked through the holes punched in the cards, and the loom translated that information into weaving patterns. To create new designs, Jacquard needed merely to punch the appropriate holes in new cards, and the loom responded accordingly.

The point to be recognized here is that *information* (for example, a desired weaving pattern) could be *coded* and *stored* in the form of holes punched in a card and subsequently *retrieved* by a machine that read the holes and took action based on the meanings assigned to those holes.

The next step in our selective computer history takes place in the United States during the 1890 census. As you may know, the U.S. Constitution mandates a complete census of the nation's population every 10 years, beginning with the 1790 enumeration of just under 4 million Americans. As the new nation's population grew, however, so did the task of measuring it. The 1880 census enumerated a population of over 62 million—but it took the Census Bureau 9 years to finish its tabulations. Clearly, a technological breakthrough was required before the 1890 census was conducted. The bureau sought suggestions.

A former Census Bureau employee, Herman Hollerith, had an idea. Hollerith had worked on the 1880 census. As a young engineering instructor at MIT, he proposed to adapt the Jacquard card to the task of counting the nation's population. As local tallies were compiled, they would be punched into cards. Then a tabulating machine of Hollerith's creation would read the cards and determine the population counts for the entire nation.

Hollerith's system was tested in competition with other proposals and found to be the fastest. As a result, the Census Bureau rented $750,000 worth of equipment from Hollerith's new Tabulating Machine Company, and the 1890 population total was reported within six weeks, in contrast to the nine years required for the 1880 census. Hollerith's Tabulating Machine Company, incidentally, continued to develop new equipment, merged with other pioneering firms, and was eventually renamed the International Business Machines Corporation: IBM. By the 1950s, punched cards—commonly called *IBM cards*—were being adapted for the storage and retrieval of social research data, and they are still used, although rarely, for that purpose.

Enter Computers

Most data analyses today are conducted with computers, ranging from large mainframe computers to small personal microcomputers. The computer—through manipulation programs—performs intricate computations and provide sophisticated presentations of the results. It can be programmed to examine several variables simultaneously and to compute a variety of statistics. Data stored on magnetic disks or tapes can be read much faster than was ever possible with the early punched cards. Computers can calculate complex statistics a good deal faster and more accurately than humans.

There are a number of computer programs available today for the analysis of social work data. Appendix G of this book gives some information and instructions about the use of one of the more popular of these: SPSS. If you can get a sense of how SPSS works, you will understand the general logic of using computer programs to carry out data analyses.

Possibly, you will have some other computer program available to you: ABtab, AIDA, A.STAT, BMDP, CRISP, DAISY, DATA-X, Dynacomp, INTER-STAT, MASS, MicroCase, Microquest, Microstat, Micro-SURVEY, Minitab, POINT FIVE, P-STAT, SAM, SAS, SNAP, Statgraf, Statpak, StatPro, STATS PLUS, Statview, Survey Mate, SYSTAT, STAT80, STATA, SURVTAB, TECPACS, to name just a few. Whatever program you use, the basic logic of data storage and analysis is the same.

Until the late 1970s, all computer analyses were performed on large, expensive computers— sometimes called *mainframe* computers—maintained by centralized computer centers, and most analyses still are. To make use of such facilities, you need to supply the data for analysis and the instructions for the analysis you want. Your instructions might take the form of an SPSS setup, as mentioned earlier and described more fully in Appendix G. And you might take your data to the computer center in the form of cards or a magnetic tape, or you might simply reference a data set maintained in the center's data library. (Your instructor will tell you how to do this if you are to do this type of computer analysis in the course.)

In recent years, two developments have improved the process described here. *Remote job entry* systems place card readers and printers near the researchers and allow them to submit jobs and receive their results at locations some distance from the computer center. Your departmental office may have such equipment; requests and results are sent to and from the computer center over coaxial cables.

Time sharing is a further advance. In a sense, computers have always operated on a time-sharing basis—several users sharing the same computer. Initially, however, computer facilities were shared in a serial fashion: the computer would run your job, then ours, then someone else's. The current, more sophisticated computer, however, can perform several different tasks simultaneously. It can read our request, analyze yours, and print out someone else's all at the same time. In fact, the tremendous speed of computers makes it possible to sandwich small operations (which may take only thousandths of a second) in the middle of larger jobs. This capacity has made it possible for computers to handle requests from hundreds of users simultaneously, often giving the impression that each has the computer's complete attention. Such interactions with the computer typically use *computer terminals*—typewriter devices that either print on paper or display their operations on video monitors that look like television screens.

Time sharing through the use of computer terminals supports a variety of uses. Text-editing programs allow users to write, edit, and print out reports. Or, if your computer center supports a time-sharing system, you'll probably find a variety of video games stored somewhere in the system.

For our present purposes, we want to discuss the use of time sharing for social work data analysis. Here's a common pattern. Your data are maintained by the computer center, either on tape or disk. You request a particular analysis by inputting your instructions on a terminal. Once you have prepared the entire set of instructions, you type a final instruction (which will vary from computer to computer) requesting that the job be run. The computer then takes over, eventually producing your results, either for pick-up at the center or printed out on your terminal.

The use of computer time sharing in social research became even more practical with the development of portable computer terminals no larger than small, portable typewriters. Such terminals communicate with the computer over standard telephone lines. Thus, you can take a portable terminal home or on a trip around the world. To use it, you dial a special number on your regular phone. The computer answers—usually with a shrill tone.

Early telecommunications required you to fit the telephone receiver into two rubber cups—called an *acoustical coupler*—on the terminal, and this device is still used in some circumstances. For the most part today, however, *modems*—either built into the computer or contained in an external device—can be connected directly into a standard telephone jack. Once connected, anything you type on the terminal is transmitted over telephone lines to the computer. It does what you ask and sends the results back to your terminal.

Time-sharing systems can also connect you to nationwide computer networks such as *CompuServe, America Online,* or *Prodigy.* Today, the *Internet* is rapidly becoming a vital research and communication tool for academics and others. The current revision of this textbook, for example, involved countless communications with colleagues around the world. Research and teaching examples were found in electronic forums. Portions of the manuscript were sent electronically for review and comment.

The possible uses of such networks are mind-boggling, and presently available services only scratch the surface of their potential. You can, for example, dial a special number and connect with a computer that will allow you to search rapidly through past editions of the *New York Times* and locate articles on some topic of interest to you. If you wish, you can have the articles printed out on your terminal. (Appendix A—on library use—describes other variations on this facility.) Or, you can leave messages in the network, to be picked up by other users.

More relevant to our current discussion, computer networks make it possible for a researcher sitting at home in California to get a copy of a data set maintained on a computer in Massachusetts and to analyze those data using a program maintained on a computer in Texas. The results of the analysis would be returned to the user in California, and the results could also be stored for examination by a colleague in Michigan. We don't mean to suggest that this procedure is commonplace today, but it is likely to become commonplace early in your research career. And before the end of your career, you'll look back on all that as primitive.

Microcomputers

The most useful and exciting development to date has been the *microcomputer,* and you've probably had some personal experience with them. These machines are small, complete computers, not much larger than a typewriter (or even smaller). Operations are displayed on some type of video-display screen. Information is stored on 5.25-inch "floppy disks," or 3.5-inch diskettes—round sheets of magnetic tape encased in cardboard or plastic. Most microcomputers today use "hard disks" that store data in the hundreds of millions of bytes.

Microcomputers have already proven effective in a variety of tasks. This book, for example, was written on a microcomputer. In addition, the same machine can be used for all your correspondence, scheduling your time and printing daily appointments and to-do lists, maintaining your checkbook, handling your personal telephone directory, and performing other tasks too numerous to list. When traveling, you can check into a hotel, unplug the regular telephone in your room, plug in your computer, and be in touch with people and computers around the country. When you want a break from writing, you can play chess with the computer or save the world from alien invaders.

As the memory capacity of microcomputers has mushroomed, data analysis programs have been developed to bring the examination of social science data within the capability of micros. Nor is the technological evolution complete. Introducing a special issue of *Sociological Methods & Research* on "Microcomputers and Social Research," David R. Heise wrote:

> Microcomputers are cheap, reliable, portable, computationally powerful, and easy to use. This profile makes them significantly different from mainframe computers and guarantees wide diffusion. By the

end of the decade, microcomputers will have changed the way social scientists do research, the way they teach courses, and the way they work in applied settings. Microcomputers also will create new topics for social analysis as the microcomputer revolution reaches diverse sectors of society.

(1981:395)

The microcomputer revolution has progressed so rapidly that it's easy to lose sight of how much things have changed in a relatively short time. When one of us (Babbie) was a graduate student at the University of California (Berkeley) just 30 years ago, the Survey Research Center had an IBM 1620 computer, which occupied approximately the same space as six or seven refrigerators. Its memory capacity was 24K, or approximately 24,000 characters worth of information. The IBM 1620 served the needs of 30–40 active researchers, who published numerous books and articles each year.

This book has been written partly on a battery-operated laptop microcomputer about the size of a metropolitan telephone directory. Its memory is 16 megabytes: 667 times as much memory as the old 1620. The pocket calculator used to calculate that figure is smaller than a pack of cards and has a memory 2.67 times that of the huge machine that served the needs of 30–40 researchers at the Survery Research Center only 30 years ago!

Now you have an overview of the role played by computers in social research. The remainder of this chapter will discuss the steps (and options) involved in converting data into forms amenable to computer analysis. We'll discuss the coding process and enumerate the several methods of transforming data into a machine-readable form.

CODING

For computers to work their magic, they must be able to read the data you've collected in your research. Moreover, computers are at their best with numbers. If a survey respondent tells you that he or she thinks the biggest problem facing social service delivery in El Paso, Texas, today is "immigration from Mexico," the computer can't understand that response. You must translate: a process called **coding.** The discussion of content analysis in Chapter 13 dealt with the coding process in a manner very close to our present concern. Recall that the content analysis must develop methods of assigning individual paragraphs, editorials, books, songs, and so forth with specific classifications or attributes. In content analysis, the coding process is inherent in data collection or observation.

When other research methods are used, it is often necessary to engage in a coding process after the data have been collected. For example, open-ended questionnaire items result in nonnumerical responses, which must be coded before analysis. Or a field researcher might wish to undertake a **quantitative analysis** based on qualitative field notes. You might wish, for example, to quantify the open-ended interviews you conducted with participants in some event under study.

As with content analysis, the task here is one of reducing a wide variety of idiosyncratic items of information to a more limited set of attributes composing a variable. Suppose, for example, that a survey researcher has asked respondents, "What is your occupation?" The responses to such a question would vary considerably. Although it would be possible to assign each separate occupation reported a separate numerical code, this procedure would not facilitate analysis, which typically depends on several subjects having the same attribute.

The occupation variable has a number of preestablished coding schemes (none of them very good, however). One such scheme distinguishes professional and managerial occupations, clerical occupations, semi-skilled occupations, and so forth. Another scheme distinguishes among different sectors of the economy: manufacturing, health, education, commerce, and so forth. Still others combine both.

The occupational coding scheme chosen should be appropriate to the theoretical concepts being examined in the study. For some studies, coding all occupations as either white-collar or blue-collar might be sufficient. For others, self-employed and not self-employed might be sufficient. Or a peace researcher might wish to know only whether the occupation was dependent on the defense establishment or not.

Although the coding scheme ought to be tailored to meet particular requirements of the analysis, one general rule of thumb should be kept in mind. If the data are coded so as to maintain a great deal of detail, code categories can always be combined during an analysis that does not require such detail. (Appendix G describes how to do this in SPSS.) If the data are coded into relatively few, gross categories, however, there is no way during analysis to recreate the original detail. Thus, you would be well advised to code your data in somewhat more detail than you plan to use in the analysis.

Of course, if your data are in the form of numerical responses, then those data can be entered in raw form exactly as respondents report them. For example, if a response to an item on age indicates that the respondent is 65 years old, then 65 is entered in the columns on age.

Developing Code Categories

There are two basic approaches to the coding process. First, you may begin with a relatively well-developed coding scheme, derived from your research purpose. Thus, as suggested earlier, the peace researcher might code occupations in terms of their relationship to the defense establishment. Or let's suppose that you have been engaging in participant observation of an emerging new neighborhood organization. You have been keeping very careful notes of the reasons new members have given for joining. Perhaps you have developed the impression that new members seem to regard the organization as a substitute for a family. You might, then, review your notes

carefully—coding each new member's comments in terms of whether this aspect of the organization was mentioned. You might also code their comments in terms of their own family status: whether they have a family or not.

If you are fortunate enough to have assistance in the coding process, your task would be to refine your definitions of code categories and to train your coders so that they will be able to assign given responses to the proper categories. You should explain the meaning of the code categories you have developed and give several examples of each. To ensure that your coders fully understand what you have in mind, it would be useful for you to code several cases. Then your coders should be asked to code the same cases, without knowing how you coded them, and your coders' work should be compared with your own. Any discrepancies will indicate an imperfect communication of your coding scheme to your coders. Even if there is perfect agreement between you and your coders, however, you should still *check-code* for at least a portion of the cases throughout the coding process.

If you are not fortunate enough to have assistance in coding, it is still important to obtain some verification of your own reliability as a coder. Nobody is perfect, especially a researcher hot on the trail of a finding. In your study of an emerging neighborhood organization, let's suppose you have the impression that people who do not have a regular family will be more likely to regard the new organization as a family substitute. The danger is that whenever you discover a subject who reports no family, you will unconsciously try to find some evidence in the subject's comments that the organization is a family substitute. If at all possible, then, you should try to get someone else to code some of your cases to see if that person would make the same assignments you made. (Note how this relates to the characteristic of *intersubjectivity* in science.)

The second approach to coding is appropriate whenever you are not sure initially how your data should be coded—you do not know what variables they represent among your subjects of study. Suppose, for example, that you have asked, "Do you feel a woman has a right to an abortion for any reason she may have?" Although you might anticipate some responses, it is unlikely that you could anticipate the full range of variation in responses. In such a situation, it would be useful to prepare a list of perhaps 50 or 100 actual responses to this open-ended question. You could then review that list, noting the different dimensions that those responses reflect. Perhaps you would find that several of the responses contained references to civil liberties. Perhaps a number of the negative responses referred to religious beliefs.

Once you have developed a coding scheme based on the list of 50 or 100 responses, you should ensure that each of the listed responses fits into one of the code categories. Then you would be ready to begin coding the remaining responses. If you have coding assistance, the previous comments regarding the training and checking of coders would apply here; if you do not, the comments on having your own work checked apply.

Like the set of attributes composing a variable, and like the response categories in a closed-ended questionnaire item, code categories should be both exhaustive and mutually exclusive. Every piece of information being coded should fit into one and only one category. Problems arise whenever a given response appears to fit equally into more than one code category, or when it fits into none.

CODEBOOK CONSTRUCTION

The end product of the coding process is the conversion of data items into numerical codes. These codes represent attributes composing variables, which in turn are assigned card and column locations within a data file. A **codebook** is a document that describes the locations of variables and lists the code assignments to the attributes composing those variables. A codebook serves two essential functions. First, it is the primary guide used in the coding process. Second, it is your guide for locating variables and interpreting punches in your data file during analysis. If you decide to correlate two variables as a part of your analysis of your data, the codebook tells you where to find the variables and what the punches represent.

Exhibit 14-1 illustrates how a portion of a codebook could be constructed from several items of a hypothetical questionnaire. The questions deal with the gender, age, educational degree, and primary job responsibility of social work practitioners. Also illustrated in Exhibit 14-1 is a data matrix showing how data would appear after being entered and stored in a computer. The codebook tells us that we can find the information on social workers' gender in column 1, their age in columns 2 and 3, their degree in column 4, and their primary job responsibility in column 5.

CODING AND DATA ENTRY OPTIONS

Not long ago, nearly all data entry took the form of manual keypunching, with cards either analyzed by unit-record equipment or read into computers for more complex analyses. Recent years have brought major advances in data entry. Through the use of computer terminals and microcomputers, data are now typically keyed directly into data files stored on computer disks. As before, however, this is intimately related to coding, and there are a number of methods for effecting that link. Let's look at a few of those possibilities.

Transfer Sheets

The traditional method of data processing involves the coding of data and the transfer of code assignments to a *transfer sheet* or *code sheet*. Such sheets were traditionally ruled off in 80 columns, corresponding to the data card columns, but they can be adapted to other data configurations appropriate to the data entry method. (Exhibit 14-2

QUESTIONNAIRE ITEMS:

1. What is your gender?
   _____ Male
   _____ Female

2. What is your age?
   _____ Years

3. What is your highest professional degree in social work?
   _____ Baccalaureate
   _____ Masters
   _____ Doctorate
   _____ Other (specify: _____)

4. What is your primary job responsibility in your current social
   work position?
   _____ Direct service provider
   _____ Supervisor
   _____ Administrator
   _____ Planner
   _____ Other (specify: _____)

CODEBOOK:

Column	Variable	Codes—Categories
1	Gender	1—Male 2—Female 0—No answer
2–3	Age	Enter raw number 00—No answer
4	Degree	1—Baccalaureate 2—Masters 3—Doctorate 4—Other 0—No answer
5	Responsibility	1—Direct service 2—Supervisor 3—Administrator 4—Planner 5—Other 0—No answer

Data matrix after computer entry for five cases who are female, aged
34, with Masters degrees, and direct service providers:

```
23421
23421
23421
23421
23421
```

Exhibit 14-1   Illustration of Codebook and Data Matrix for Portion of a
Hypothetical Questionnaire

01	02	03	04	05	06	07	08	09	10		71	72	73	74	75	76	77	78	79	80
0	0	1	3	7	8	9	3	1	1		4	5	2	1	1	7	8	7	1	2
0	0	2	4	2	4	2	4	1	2		2	2	5	1	1	2	8	2	2	2
0	0	3	6	6	1	2	3	1	1		1	3	6	2	1	3	9	2	2	3
0	0	4	5	3	4	4	2	2	1		1	4	1	0	3	6	0	4	2	1

Exhibit 14-2   A Partial Coding Transfer Sheet

provides an illustration.) Coders write numbers corresponding to the desired code categories in the appropriate columns of the sheets. The code sheets are then used for keying data into computer files. This is still a useful technique when particularly complex questionnaires or other data source documents are being processed.

Edge-Coding

Edge-coding does away with the need for code sheets. The outside margin of each page of a questionnaire or other data source document is left blank or is marked with spaces corresponding to variable names or numbers. Rather than transferring code assignments to a separate sheet, the codes are written in the appropriate spaces in the margins. The edge-coded source documents are then used for data entry.

Direct Data Entry

If the questionnaires have been adequately designed, you can often enter data directly into the computer without using separate code sheets or even edge-coding. The precoded questionnaire would contain indications of the columns and the punches to be assigned to questions and responses, and data can be entered directly. When the direct-entry method is to be used, it is essential that documents be *edited* before data entry. An editor should read through each to ensure that every question has been answered (enter a

99 or some other standard code for "missing data") and to clarify any unclear responses. If most of the document is amenable to direct entry (for example, closed-ended questions presented in a clear format), it is also possible to code a few open-ended items and still enter data directly. In such a situation, you should enter the code for a given question in a specified location near the question to ease the data entry job.

The layout of the document is extremely important for effective direct data entry. If most of the question and response categories are presented on the right side of the page but one set is presented on the left side, those entering the data frequently miss the deviant set. (*Note:* Many respondents will make the same mistake, so a questionnaire carefully designed for data entry will be more effective for data collection as well.)

For content analysis and similar situations in which coding takes place during data collection, it makes sense to record the data in a form amenable to direct entry. Perhaps a precoded form would be appropriate, or, in some cases, the data might be recorded directly on transfer sheets.

Data Entry by Interviewers

The most direct data entry method in survey research has already been discussed in Chapter 11: Computer-Assisted Telephone Interviewing or *CATI*. As you'll recall, interviewers with telephone headsets sit at computer terminals, which display the questions to be asked and type in the respondents' answers. In this fashion, data are entered directly into data files as soon as they are generated. Closed-ended data are ready for immediate analysis. Open-ended data can be entered as well, but they require an extra step.

Let's say the questionnaire asks respondents, "What would you say is the greatest problem facing America today?" The computer terminal would prompt the interviewer to ask that question. Then, instead of expecting a simple numerical code as input, it would allow the interviewer to type in whatever the respondent said: for example, "crime in the streets, especially the crimes committed by. . . ." Subsequently, coders would sit at computer terminals, retrieving the open-ended responses one-by-one and assigning numerical codes as discussed earlier in this chapter.

Coding to Optical Scan Sheets

Sometimes data entry can be achieved effectively through the use of an *optical scanner*. This machine reads black pencil marks on a special code sheet and creates data files to correspond with those marks. (These sheets are frequently called *op-sense* or *mark-sense* sheets.) It is possible for coders to transfer coded data to such special sheets by blacking in the appropriate spaces. The sheets are then fed into an optical scanner and data files are created automatically.

Although an optical scanner provides greater accuracy and speed to manual data entry, it has disadvantages as well. Some coders find it very difficult to transfer data to the special sheets. It can be difficult to locate the appropriate column, and once the appropriate column is found, the coder must search for the appropriate space to blacken.

Second, the optical scanner has relatively rigid tolerances. Unless the black marks are sufficiently black, the scanner may make mistakes. (You will have no way of knowing when this has happened until you begin your analysis.) Moreover, if the op-sense sheets are folded or mutilated, the scanner may refuse to read them at all.

Direct Use of Optical Scan Sheets

It is sometimes possible to use optical scan sheets a little differently and possibly avoid the difficulties they may offer coders. Persons asked to complete questionnaires may be asked to record their responses directly on such sheets. Either standard sheets can be provided with instructions on their use, or special sheets can be prepared for the particular study. Questions can be presented with the several answer categories, and the respondents can be asked to blacken the spaces provided beside the answers they choose. If such sheets are properly laid out, the optical scanner can read and enter the answers directly. This method may be even more feasible in recording experimental observations or in compiling data in a content analysis.

DATA CLEANING

Whichever data processing method you have used, you will now have a set of machine-readable data that purport to represent the information collected in your study. The next important step is the elimination of errors: "cleaning" the data.

No matter how, or how carefully, the data have been entered, some errors are inevitable. Depending on the data processing method, these errors may result from in correct coding, incorrect reading of written codes, incorrect sensing of blackened marks, and so forth.

Two types of cleaning should be done: *possible-code* cleaning and *contingency* cleaning.

Possible-Code Cleaning

For any given variable, there is a specified set of legitimate attributes, translated into a set of possible codes. In the variable gender, there will be perhaps three possible codes: 1 for male, 2 for female, and 0 for no answer. If a case has been coded 7, say, in the column assigned to gender, it is clear that an error has been made.

Possible-code cleaning can be accomplished in two different ways. First, you may have access to modern computer programs that can check for errors as the data are being entered. If you tried to enter a 7 for gender, for example, the computer might beep and refuse the erroneous code. Some computer programs are designed to test for illegitimate codes in data files that weren't checked during data entry.

If you do not have access to these kinds of computer programs, you can achieve a possible-code cleaning by examining the distribution of responses to each item in your data set. Thus if you find your data set contains 350 people coded 1 on gender (for female) and 400 people coded 2 (for male) and one person coded 7, you'll suspect the 7 is an error.

Whenever you discover errors, the next step is to locate the appropriate source document (for example, a questionnaire), determine what code should have been entered, and make the necessary correction.

Contingency Cleaning

Contingency cleaning is more complicated. The logical structure of the data may place special limits on the responses of certain respondents. For example, a questionnaire may ask for the number of children women have had. All female respondents, then, should have a response coded (or a special code for failure to answer), whereas no male respondent should have an answer recorded (or should only have a special code indicating the question is inappropriate to him). If a given male respondent is coded as having borne three children, either an error has been made and should be corrected or your study is about to become more famous than you ever dreamed.

Contingency cleaning is typically accomplished through computer programs that require a rather complicated set of if-then statements. In some cases, the programs that support direct data entry can be instructed to check automatically for

proper contingencies, just as they check for legitimate codes.

Although data cleaning is an essential step in data processing, it may be safely avoided in certain cases. Perhaps you will feel you can safely exclude the very few errors that appear in a given item—if the exclusion of those cases will not significantly affect your results. Or, some inappropriate contingency responses may be safely ignored. If some men have been given motherhood status, you can limit your analysis of this variable to women. However, you should not use these comments as rationalizations for sloppy research. "Dirty" data will almost always produce misleading research findings.

Main Points

• The quantification of data is necessary in order to permit subsequent statistical manipulations and analyses.

• The observations describing each unit of analysis must be transformed into standardized, numerical codes for retrieval and manipulation by machine.

• A given variable is assigned a specific location in the data storage medium: in terms of punch card columns or variable numbers in a disk file, for example. That variable is assigned the same location in all the data files containing the data describing the different cases about which observations were made.

• The attributes of a given variable are represented by different codes in the locations assigned to that variable.

• A codebook is the document that describes the locations assigned to different variables and the codes assigned to represent different attributes.

• Data entry can be accomplished in a variety of ways. Increasingly, data are keyed directly into computer disk files.

• A transfer sheet is a special coding sheet on which numerical codes are recorded. These transfer sheets are then used for data entry.

• Edge-coding is an alternative to the use of transfer sheets. The numerical coding is done in the margins of the original documents—such as questionnaires—instead of on transfer sheets.

• Optical scan sheets or mark-sense sheets may be used in some research projects to save time and money in data processing. These are the familiar sheets used in examinations on which answers are indicated by black marks in the appropriate spaces. Optical scanners are machines that read the black marks and transfer the same information to data files.

• Possible-code cleaning refers to the process of checking to see that only those codes assigned to particular attributes—possible codes—appear in the data files. This process guards against one class of data processing error.

• Contingency cleaning is the process of checking to see that only those cases that *should* have data on a particular variable do in fact have such data. This process guards against another class of data processing error.

Review Questions and Exercises

1. Create a codebook—with column and code assignments—for the following questions in a case record:

a. Does the client attend a sheltered workshop?
   Yes   If yes, which one?
                Workshop A   Workshop B
   No

b. Client's level of disability:
   Mild
   Moderate
   Severe or profound
   Other:

c. Most important target problem:
   Social skills
   Vocational
   Social environmental support system
   Personal hygiene
   Housekeeping skills
   Psychopathology
   Self-esteem
   Residential living arrangements
   Family stress
   Other:

2. Create another codebook—with column and code assignments—for the following questions in a community survey:

a. What do you feel is the most important problem facing this community today?

b. In the spaces provided below, please indicate the three community problems that most concern you by putting a 1 beside the one that most concerns you, a 2 beside your second choice, and a 3 beside your third choice.
   Crime
   Traffic
   Drug abuse
   Pollution
   Prejudice and discrimination
   Inflation
   Unemployment
   Housing shortage

Additional Readings

Butterfield, William (ed.), "Computers for Social Work Practitioners." This special issue of the *Practice Digest* (National Association of Social Workers, Vol. 6, Winter 1983) is a good place for social workers to begin examining the possible applications of computer technology to their practice. They might also examine a new journal from Haworth Press: ***Computers in Human Services.***

Fielding, Nigel G., and Lee, Raymond M. (eds.), *Using Computers in Qualitative Research* (Newbury Park, CA: Sage, 1991). While computers are primarily associated with quantitative research, this set of articles shows how powerfully they can be used with qualitative methods.

Hall, Larry D., and Marshall, Kimball P., *Computing for Social Research: Practical Approaches* (Belmont, CA: Wadsworth, 1992). An excellent introduction to computer hardware and software, It could be useful to you whether you continue in social research or not.

Heise, David (ed.), *Microcomputers in Social Research* (Beverly Hills, CA: Sage, 1981). This special issue of *Sociological Methods and Research* examines the role of the microcomputer in several areas of social research, including anthropology, urban planning, social-psychophysiology, and simulations of social systems. Contains some how-to discussions also.

Madron, Thomas Wm., Tate, C. Neal, and Brookshire, Robert G., *Using Microcomputers in Research* (Newbury Park, CA: Sage, 1985). This book examines many different ways in which social researchers can profit from microcomputers, including data gathering, analysis, and writing, to name a few.

Saris, Willem E., *Computer-Assisted Interviewing* (Newbury Park, CA: Sage, 1991). Here's an up-to-date review of the *CADAC* (computer-assisted data collection) options available for modern social researchers.

Schwartz, M. (ed.), *Using Computers in Clinical Practice* (New York: Haworth Press, 1984). Different uses of computers in direct-service delivery. Applications in such areas as clinical assessment, child therapy, and so on.

Interpreting Descriptive Statistics and Tables

What You'll Learn in This Chapter

You'll come away from this chapter able to
perform a number of simple yet powerful ways to
manipulate data for the purpose of reaching
research conclusions.

INTRODUCTION

In this chapter we embark on a topic that intimidates many social work students: statistical analysis. Students who believe that they are weak in math often let their anxiety get in the way of learning this material, making it seem more difficult than it really is. Years of teaching this material to apprehensive students has taught us that even those students with the greatest initial anxiety typically learn to comprehend this material quite well, especially when it is presented in a manner geared to their aptitudes—which we intend to do in this chapter.

So relax; no matter how apprehensive you may feel, we assure you that your feelings are not at all uncommon. Most of your classmates are probably just as apprehensive as you are. If you can just put your anxieties on hold for a while (perhaps through deep breathing exercises, or some other anxiety management technique), we think you will find this material understandable, relevant, and maybe even somewhat enjoyable.

We'll start by looking at tables and statistics that describe one variable at a time. This is called univariate analysis. Then we'll look at tables and statistics that describe relationships among variables. This is called bivariate or multivariate analysis, depending on how many variables are examined simultaneously. When you finish this chapter, you will be prepared to consider inferential statistics, which deal with whether the data in a particular study or sample can be generalized beyond that study or sample. That topic will be the focus of Chapters 16 and 17.

DESCRIPTIVE STATISTICS

Descriptive statistics is a method for presenting quantitative descriptions in a manageable form. Scientific research often involves the collection of large masses of data. Suppose we had surveyed 2000 people, asking each of them 100 questions—not an unusually large study. We would now have a staggering 200,000 answers! No one could possibly read all those 200,000 answers and reach any meaningful conclusions about them. Thus, much scientific analysis involves the *reduction* of data from unmanageable details to manageable summaries.

Consider, for example, the raw data matrix created from a hypothetical set of case records from a social service agency. Table 15-1 presents a partial data matrix. Notice that each of the rows in the matrix represents a case (or other unit of analysis), each column represents a variable, and

Table 15-1 Partial Raw Data Matrix

	GENDER	AGE	ETHNICITY	EDUCATION	INCOME	PRESENTING PROBLEM	SERVICE PROVIDED	PROGRESS RATING
Case 1	1	3	2	2	4	1	3	0
Case 2	1	4	1	2	4	4	1	1
Case 3	2	2	2	5	5	2	4	2
Case 4	1	5	2	4	4	3	2	2
Case 5	2	3	1	7	8	6	1	5
Case 6	2	1	3	3	3	5	5	1

each cell in the matrix represents the coded attribute or value a given case has on a given variable. The first column in Table 15-1 represents a client's gender. Let's say a "1" represents male and "2" represents female. That means that clients 1 and 2 are male, 3 is female, and so forth.

In the case of age, client 1's "3" might mean 30–39 years old, client 2's "4" might mean 40–49. However age had been coded (see Chapter 14), the code numbers shown in Table 15-1 would describe each of the clients represented there.

Notice that the data have already been reduced somewhat by the time a data matrix like this one has been created. If age had been coded as just suggested, the specific answer "33 years old" has already been reduced to the category "30–39." Overall, the case records may have given us 60 or 70 different ages, but we have now reduced them to 6 or 7 categories.

Now let's look at some additional ways of summarizing data. We'll begin with measures that summarize one variable at a time.

UNIVARIATE ANALYSIS

Univariate analysis is the examination of the distribution of cases on only one variable at a time. We'll begin with the logic and formats for the analysis of univariate data.

Distributions

The most basic format for presenting univariate data is to report all individual cases; that is, to list the attribute for each case under study in terms of the variable in question. Suppose you are interested in the ages of clients served by your agency, and suppose hundreds of clients have been served. (Your data might have come from agency records.) The most direct manner of reporting the ages of clients would be to list them: 63, 57, 49, 62, 80, 72, 55, and so forth. Such a report would provide your reader with the fullest details of the data, but it would be too cumbersome for most purposes. You could arrange your data in a somewhat more manageable form without losing any of the detail by reporting that 5 clients were 38 years old, 7 were 39, 18 were 40, and so forth. Such a format would avoid duplicating data on this variable.

For an even more manageable format—with a certain loss of detail—you could report clients' ages as *marginals,* which are **frequency distributions** *of grouped data:* 246 clients under 45 years of age, 517 between 45 and 50 years of age, and so forth. In this case, your reader would have fewer data to examine and interpret, but he or she would not be able to reproduce fully the original ages of all the clients. Thus, for example, the reader would have no way of knowing how many clients were 41 years of age.

The preceding example presented marginals in the form of raw numbers. An alternative form would be the use of *percentages.* Thus, for example, you could report that x% of the clients were under 45, y% were between 45 and 50, and so forth. (See Table 15-2.) In computing percentages, you frequently must make a decision about the *base* from which to compute: the number that represents 100%. In the most straightforward

Table 15-2 An Illustration of a Univariate Analysis

AGES OF AGENCY CLIENTS (HYPOTHETICAL)	
Under 35	9%
36–45	21
46–55	45
56–65	19
66 and older	6
	100% = (433)
No data =	(18)

examples, the base is the total number of cases under study. A problem arises, however, whenever some cases have missing data. Let's assume, for example, that you have conducted a survey in which respondents were asked to report their ages. If some respondents failed to answer that question, you have two alternatives. First, you might still base your percentages on the total number of respondents, reporting those who failed to give their ages as a percentage of the total. Second, you could use the number of persons giving an answer as the base from which to compute the percentages. You should still report the number who did not answer, but they would not figure in the percentages.

The choice of a base depends wholly on the purposes of the analysis. If you wish to compare the age distribution of your survey sample with comparable data describing the population from which the sample was drawn, you will probably want to omit the "no answers" from the computation. Your best estimate of the age distribution of all respondents is the distribution for those answering the question. Since "no answer" is not a meaningful age category, its presence among the base categories would confuse the comparison of sample and population figures. (See Table 15-2 for an example.)

Central Tendency

Beyond simply reporting marginals, you may choose to present your data in the form of summary averages or measures of *central tendency*. Your options in this regard are the **mode** (the most frequent attribute, either grouped or ungrouped), the arithmetic **mean,** or the **median** (the *middle* attribute in the ranked distribution of observed attributes). Here's how the three averages would be calculated from a set of data.

Suppose that you are analyzing the case records of an adolescent residential facility whose clients range in age from 13 to 19, as indicated in the accompanying table.

AGE	NUMBER
13	3
14	4
15	6
16	8
17	4
18	3
19	3

Now that you've seen the actual ages of the 31 clients, how old would you say they are in general, or on the average? Let's look at three different ways you might answer that question.

The easiest **average** to calculate is the *mode,* the most frequent value. As you can see, there were more 16-year-olds (8 of them) than any other age, so the modal age is 16, as indicated in Figure 15-1.

Figure 15-1 also demonstrates the calculation of the mean. There are three steps: (1) multiply each age by the number of clients who have that age, (2) total the results of all those multiplications, and (3) divide that total by the number of clients. As indicated in Figure 15-1 the mean age in this illustration is 15.87.

The *median* represents the "middle" value: half are above it, half below. If we had the *precise ages* of each client (for example, 17 years and 124 days), we'd be able to arrange all 31 subjects in order by age, and the median for the whole group would be the age of the middle subject.

As you can see, however, we do not know precise ages; our data constitute "grouped data" in this regard: three people who are not precisely the same age have been grouped in the category "13 years old," for example.

Figure 15-1 illustrates the logic of calculating a median for grouped data. Because there are 31

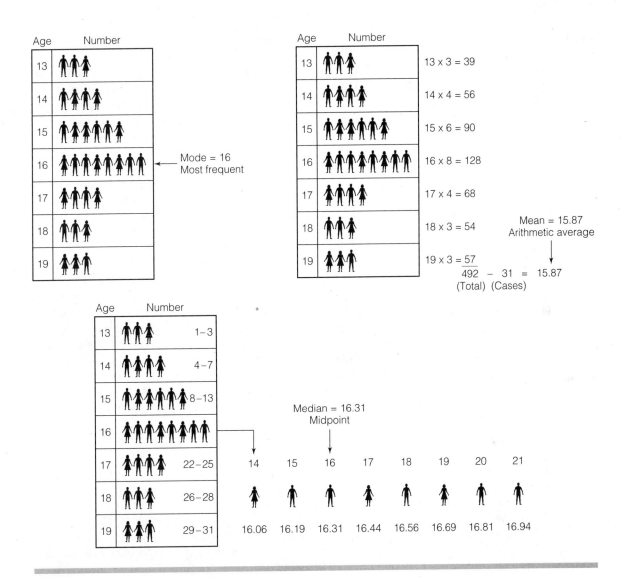

Figure 15-1 Three "Averages"

clients altogether, the "middle" client would be number 16, if they were arranged by age—15 would be younger and 15 would be older. Look at the bottom portion of Figure 15-1, and you'll see that the middle person is one of the eight 16-

year-olds. In the enlarged view of that group, we see that number 16 is the third from the left.

Because we do not know the precise ages of the clients in this group, the statistical convention here is to assume they are evenly spread along the width of the group. In this instance, the *possible* ages of the clients go from 16 years and no days to 16 years and 364 days. Strictly speaking, the range, then, is 364/365 days. As a practical matter, it's sufficient to call it 1 year.

If the eight clients in this group were evenly spread from one limit to the other, they would be one-eighth of a year apart from each other—a 0.125-year interval. Look at Figure 15-1 and you'll see that if we place the first client half the interval from the lower limit and add a full interval to the age of each successive client, the final one is half an interval from the upper limit.

What we have done, therefore, is calculate, hypothetically, the precise ages of the eight clients—assuming their ages were spread out evenly. Having done that, we merely note the age of the middle client—16.31—and that is the median age for the group. Whenever the total number of clients is an even number, of course, there is no middle case. In that case, you merely calculate the mean of the two values it falls between. Suppose there were one more 19-year-old, for example. The midpoint in that case would fall between number 16 and number 17. The mean, in that case, would be calculated as $(16.31 + 16.44)/2 = 16.38$.

In the research literature, you will find both means and medians presented. Whenever means are presented, you should be aware that they are susceptible to extreme values: a few very large or very small numbers. For example, the 1980 mean per capita gross national product (GNP) for the United States was $9700, contrasted, for example, with $190 for Sri Lanka, $3470 for Ireland, and $7920 for Australia. The tiny oil sheikdom for Kuwait, however, had a mean per capita GNP of $14,890, yet most residents of that country are impoverished, as may be inferred from the fact that their infant mortality rate was three times that of the United States in 1980 and their life expectancy at birth was 18 years less. The high mean per capita GNP in Kuwait reflects the enormous petro-wealth of a few (Population Reference Bureau, 1980).

Dispersion

Averages have the special advantage to the reader of reducing the raw data to the most manageable form: a single number (or attribute) can represent all the detailed data collected in regard to the variable. This advantage comes at a cost, of course, because the reader cannot reconstruct the original data from an average. This disadvantage of averages can be somewhat alleviated through the reporting of summaries of the **dispersion** of responses. The simplest measure of dispersion is the *range:* the distance separating the highest from the lowest value. Thus, besides reporting that our clients have a mean age of 15.87, we might also indicate that their ages ranged from 13 to 19.

There are many other measures of dispersion. In reporting intelligence test scores, for example, you might determine the *interquartile range,* the range of scores for the middle 50% of subjects. If the highest one-fourth had scores ranging from 120 to 150, and if the lowest one-fourth had scores ranging from 60 to 90, you could report that the interquartile range was 90 to 120, or 30, with a mean score of, let's say, 102.

A somewhat more sophisticated measure of dispersion, but one that is used very widely, is the **standard deviation.** The logic of this measure was discussed in Chapter 8 as the standard error of a sampling distribution. In that chapter (more precisely, in Figure 8-9) we saw what a normal curve looks like. It is symmetrical and has a shape resembling a bell. (It is sometimes called a bell-shaped curve or simply a bell curve.) When we can assume that our data have a normal distribution (that is, when they are distributed in the shape of a normal curve), then approximately 34% (.3413) of our sample data will fall within one standard deviation above the mean, and another 34% will fall within one standard deviation below the mean, as illustrated in Figure 15-2. That leaves almost one-third of the sample values falling more than one standard deviation away from the mean (approximately 16% more than one standard deviation above the mean and approximately 16% more

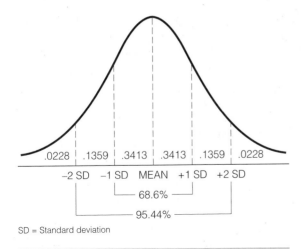

.0228 | .1359 | .3413 | .3413 | .1359 | .0228

−2 SD −1 SD MEAN +1 SD +2 SD

└──── 68.6% ────┘

└──────── 95.44% ────────┘

SD = Standard deviation

Figure 15-2 Standard Deviation Proportions of the Normal Curve

than one standard deviation below the mean). Knowing this, we can get a sense of how far away from the mean the values in our data are falling by calculating the standard deviation.

For example, suppose a large state mental health department's mean caseload size for its case managers working with people with long-term mental disorders is 28, and its standard deviation is 2. If we assume a normal distribution of caseload size, then we know that approximately 68% of case managers have caseload sizes between 26 and 30 (with about 34% between 26 and 28 and 34% between 28 and 30). We would also know that about 16% had caseload sizes of less than 26 and that about 16% had caseload sizes of more than 30. Since the case management research literature tends to recommend that caseload sizes should not be far in excess of 30 (Rubin, 1987), we might portray that state's caseload size as conforming reasonably well to what is recommended.

Suppose another state reports a mean caseload size of 25, but with a standard deviation of 15. Although that state's mean of 25 is lower than the first state's mean of 28, approximately 16% of its

case managers have caseload sizes in excess of 40 (25 plus 1 standard deviation of 15), and about 34% have caseload sizes somewhere between 25 and 40 (as compared to 28 and 30 for the first state). Therefore, despite the lower mean in the second state, we might portray the first state's case management caseload sizes more favorably, since far fewer of its case managers were dispersed far above the mean (or far above the recommended caseload size).

Now that we see the value in knowing the standard deviation (and not just relying exclusively on statistics that portray central tendency), let's examine how you calculate it.

Normally when you calculate a standard deviation you have a very large number of cases, but to keep the calculations simple here, we'll do it for only ten cases. Let's illustrate this calculation with hypothetical data for the first state we described. Let's assume the ten values for caseload size are those listed in column A in Table 15.3.

The first step in calculating the standard deviation is to calculate the mean for column A: that is, the mean of the values in your sample. The mean for the figures in column A is 28, as shown in column B. The next step is to subtract the mean from each value in your sample. That difference is listed in column C. After that, we must square each deviation listed in column C. Those squares are listed in column D. Next, we must add up all those squares, which in our hypothetical example comes to 40. The next step is to divide that sum of squares by the number of cases in our sample, which here is 10. Forty divided by 10 is 4. The final step is to obtain the square root of that dividend. The square root of 4 is 2, so our standard deviation is 2.

Continuous and Discrete Variables

The calculations just described are not appropriate for all variables. To understand this, we must examine two types of variables: *continuous* and *discrete*. Age is a continuous, ratio variable; it increases steadily in tiny fractions instead of

Table 15-3 How to Calculate
Standard Deviation

A	B	C	D
SAMPLE VALUE (CASELOAD SIZE)	MEAN	DEVIATION (DIFFERENCE BETWEEN MEAN AND SAMPLE VALUE)	DEVIATION SQUARED
25	28	–3	9
26	28	–2	4
26	28	–2	4
27	28	–1	1
27	28	–1	1
28	28	0	0
30	28	2	4
30	28	2	4
30	28	2	4
31	28	3	9

Sum = 280

n = 10

Mean = 28

Sum of Squares = 40

Standard deviation = $\sqrt{\dfrac{40}{10}}$ $\sqrt{4}$ = 2

jumping from category to category as does a discrete variable such as gender or military rank. If discrete variables were being analyzed—a nominal or ordinal variable, for example—some of the techniques discussed here would not be applicable. Strictly speaking, medians, means, and standard deviations should be calculated only for interval and ratio data, respectively. If the variable in question were gender, for example, raw number or percentage marginals would be appropriate and useful analyses. Calculating the mode would

be a legitimate, though not very revealing, analysis, but reports of mean, median, or dispersion summaries would be inappropriate. Although researchers can sometimes learn something of value by violating rules like these, you should only do so with caution.

There are, however, numerous "gray-area" situations regarding the calculation of averages. Suppose, for example, that you were assessing client satisfaction with the services they received by asking them to rate those services on a 4-point scale: 4 = very satisfied, 3 = satisfied, 2 = dissatisfied, and 1 = very dissatisfied. You should note that this would be an ordinal-level measurement because there is no reason to believe that the distance from rating 1 (very dissatisfied) to rating 2 (dissatisfied) is the same as the distance between rating 2 and rating 3 (satisfied), and so on. Consequently, calculating the mean rating or the standard deviation for a large number of clients would be technically questionable because such calculations would treat these ordinal-level ratings as if they were real values.

Yet such technical violations are commonly found and can be useful. A mean score across all clients may not have a precise mathematical meaning regarding client satisfaction, but it could be useful in comparing large numbers of ratings across client subgroups. For example, suppose the mean rating from ethnic minority clients was 1.4, as compared to a mean rating of 3.2 from white clients. Despite its imprecise meaning, this comparison would provide a clear and useful indication that the two groups do not express the same levels of satisfaction and that the reasons for the difference ought to be assessed and dealt with. (We make similar comparisons all the time, by the way, when we discuss students' grade-point averages!)

The key here is *utility*. If you find that a researcher's statistical calculations are useful in revealing the nature of social affairs, then you should be somewhat lenient in the application of statistical techniques to data that do not warrant them. The other edge of this sword, however, is the danger of being lulled into thinking that the results represent something truly precise. In this case, for example, you might question the utility and appropriateness of carrying the means and standard deviations out to three decimal points.

Detail Versus Manageability

In presenting univariate—and other—data, you will be constrained by two often conflicting goals. On the one hand, you should attempt to provide your reader with the fullest degree of detail regarding those data. On the other hand, the data should be presented in a manageable form. As these two goals often go directly counter to each other, you will find yourself continually seeking the best compromise between them. One useful solution is to report a given set of data in more than one form. In the case of age, for example, you might report the marginals on ungrouped ages *plus* the mean age and standard deviation.

"Collapsing" Response Categories

Textbook examples of tables are often simpler than tables appearing in published research reports or in your own analyses of data. For example, we have already addressed the problem of missing data (that is, "no answer" to a particular question). Another common problem occurs when a table has so many rows or columns that it is difficult to detect any meaningful pattern in it.

As an illustration of this point, consider Table 15-4, which reports data collected in a 1982 survey of entering masters students specializing in direct practice in eight schools of social work (Rubin and Johnson, 1984). The section of the questionnaire that generated these data asked entering students to rate the extent to which each of 16 client groups or case situations appealed to them as they considered what they would like to do in their professional practice after graduation. (You might find the results interesting, and perhaps surprising, in view of the kinds of target populations and problems traditionally thought to distinguish social work practice from that of other helping professions.)

As you review the table, you may find that there are so many numbers that it is difficult to determine the exact order of appeal of the client groups or case situations, which are listed in alphabetical order. One way to simplify the **interpretation** of these data is to combine or "collapse" the response categories, which in this case appear in the columns. There is usually more than one way to do this. For example, in this instance we might collapse the six columns into three columns or perhaps into two columns. To wind up with three columns, we would combine "extreme" and "substantial," "moderate" and "a little," and "very slight" and "none." To wind up with two columns, we would combine "extreme," "substantial," and "moderate" into one column and combine "a little," "very slight," and "none" into the other column.

Table 15-5 uses the latter alternative, collapsing the data into two columns. It also illustrates another technique to simplify table interpretation for the reader. Whereas Table 15-4 listed the rows in alphabetical order, Table 15-5 lists them in order of the frequency with which students find them at least moderately appealing to work with. Notice how much easier it is to understand and interpret the data in Table 15-5.

As you can see from this introductory discussion of univariate analysis, this seemingly simple matter can be rather complex. The lessons of this section, in any event, will be important as we move now to a consideration of subgroup comparisons and bivariate analyses.

SUBGROUP COMPARISONS

Univariate analyses *describe* the units of analysis of a study and, if they are a sample drawn from some larger population, allow us to make descriptive inferences about the larger population. Bivariate and multivariate analyses are aimed primarily at *explanation*. Before turning to explanation, however, we should consider the case of subgroup description.

Table 15-4 Appeal Ratings of Sixteen Client Groups or Case Situations

CLIENT GROUP OR CASE SITUATION	APPEAL RATING (PERCENTAGES)					
	EXTREME	SUBSTANTIAL	MODERATE	A LITTLE	VERY SLIGHT	NONE
Abused or neglected children	19	35	28	9	5	4
Abusive parents	10	28	34	15	8	5
Adult criminal offenders	4	15	23	14	26	18
Alcohol or substance abusers	12	23	26	22	12	5
Clients experiencing a turbulent adolescence	30	34	21	8	4	2
College students in emotional crisis	24	29	25	11	6	6
Hospital-discharge planning in health care	9	15	19	16	19	21
Juvenile status offenders	14	22	30	13	13	8
People wanting to adopt a child	17	18	24	17	14	9
People who are depressed	17	38	27	9	7	2
People with marital or family problems	39	37	14	7	2	1
People in poverty needing subsistence resources	7	18	29	17	21	9
The aged	10	11	27	19	23	10
The chronically mentally disabled discharged from state hospitals	6	10	19	19	22	24
The developmentally disabled	5	17	24	20	25	9
The physically disabled	3	15	19	26	25	12

Often it's appropriate to describe subsets of cases, subjects, or respondents. Table 15-6, for example, presents income data for men and women separately. In addition, the table presents the ratio of women's median income to that of men, showing that women in the labor force earn a little over half what men earn.

In some situations, the researcher presents subgroup comparisons purely for descriptive purposes. More often, the purpose of subgroup descriptions is comparative: Women earn less than men. In the present case, it is assumed that there is something about being a woman that results in the lower incomes. When we compare incomes of blacks and whites, a similar assumption is made. In such cases, the analysis is based on an assumption of *causality:* one variable causing another, as in gender causing income.

Table 15-5   Collapsing Extreme Categories from Table 15-4

CLIENT GROUP OR CASE SITUATION	APPEAL RATING (PERCENTAGES)	
	MODERATE OR HIGHER	A LITTLE OR LOWER
People with marital or family problems	90	10
Clients experiencing a turbulent adolescence	86	14
People who are depressed	82	18
Abused or neglected children	82	18
College students in emotional crisis	78	22
Abusive parents	72	28
Juvenile status offenders	66	34
Alcohol or substance abusers	61	39
People wanting to adopt a child	59	41
People in poverty needing subsistence resources	54	46
The aged	48	52
The developmentally disabled	46	54
Hospital-discharge planning in health care	43	57
Adult criminal offenders	42	58
The physically disabled	37	63
The chronically mentally disabled discharged from state hospitals	35	65

BIVARIATE ANALYSIS

In contrast to univariate analysis, subgroup comparisons constitute a kind of **bivariate analysis** in that two variables are involved. As we noted earlier, the purpose of univariate analysis is purely descriptive. The purpose of subgroup comparisons is also largely descriptive—independently describing the subgroups—but the element of comparison is added. Most bivariate analysis in social research adds another element: relationships between the variables themselves. Thus, while univariate analysis and subgroup comparisons focus on describing the *people* (or other

units of analysis) under study, bivariate analysis focuses on the *variables*.

Notice, then, that Table 15-7 could be regarded as an instance of subgroup comparison: It independently describes the attitudes of men and women toward sexual equality. It shows—comparatively and descriptively—that the women under study are more supportive of equality than the men.

The same table, seen as an *explanatory* bivariate analysis, tells a somewhat different story. It suggests that the variable gender has an effect on the variable *attitude toward gender equality*. The attitude is seen as a dependent variable that is

Table 15-6 Median Earnings of Year-Round, Full-Time Civilian Workers with Earnings by Sex: 1967 to 1977

YEAR	WOMEN'S EARNINGS	MEN'S EARNINGS	RATIO OF WOMEN'S TO MEN'S EARNINGS
1977	$8,618	$14,626	.59
1976	8,622	14,323	.60
1975	8,449	14,175	.60
1974	8,565	14,578	.59
1973	8,639	15,254	.57
1972	8,551	14,778	.58
1971	8,369	14,064	.60
1970	8,307	13,993	.59
1969	8,227	13,976	.59
1968	7,763	13,349	.58
1967	7,503	13,021	.58

Source: Adapted from the U.S. Bureau of the Census, "A Statistical Portrait of Women in the United States: 1978," Series P-23, No. 100, p. 73.

Table 15-7 "Do you approve or disapprove of the proposition that men and women should be treated equally in all regards?"

	MEN	WOMEN
Approve	63%	75%
Disapprove	37	25
	100%	100%
	(400)	(400)
No answer =	(12)	(5)

partially determined by the *independent variable,* gender. Explanatory bivariate analyses, then, involve the "variable language" introduced in Chapter 2. In a subtle shift of focus, we are no longer talking about men and women as different subgroups but of gender as a variable: a variable that has an influence on other variables. The logic of interpreting Table 15-7 is as follows:

1. Women generally are accorded an inferior status in American society: Thus they should be more supportive of the proposed equality of the sexes.

2. A respondent's sex should therefore affect (cause) his or her response to the questionnaire item: Women should be more likely to approve than men.

3. If the male and female respondents in the survey are described separately in terms of their responses, a higher percentage of the women should approve.

The data presented in Table 15-7 confirm this reasoning. Of the women, 75% approve of gender equality as compared to 63% of the men.

Adding the logic of causal relationships among variables has an important implication for the construction and reading of percentage tables. One of the chief bugaboos for new data analysts is deciding on the appropriate "direction of percentaging" for any given table. In Table 15-7, for example, we have divided the group of subjects into two subgroups—men and women—and then described the attitudes of each subgroup. That is the correct method for constructing this table.

Notice, however, that it would have been possible—though inappropriate—to construct the table differently. We could have first divided the subjects into those approving of gender equality and those disapproving of it, and then we could have described each of those subgroups in terms of the percentages of men and women in each. This method would make no sense in terms of explanation, however.

Table 15-7 suggests that your gender will affect how you feel about gender equality. Had we used the other method of construction, the table would suggest that your attitude toward gender equality affects whether you are a man or a woman—which makes no sense; your attitude cannot determine your gender.

There is another, related problem that complicates the lives of new data analysts. How do you read a percentage table? There is a temptation to read Table 15-7 as follows: "Of the women, 75% approved and only 25% disapproved; therefore being a woman makes you more likely to approve." That is not the correct way to read the table, however. The conclusion that gender—as a variable—has an effect on attitudes must hinge on a comparison between men and women. Specifically, we note that *women are more likely than men* to approve of gender equality: comparing the 75% with the 63%. Suppose, for example, that 100% of the men approved. Regardless of the fact that women approved 3 to 1, it wouldn't make sense to say that being a woman increased the likelihood of approval. In fact, the opposite would be true in such a case. The comparison of subgroups, then, is essential in reading an explanatory bivariate table.

In constructing and presenting Table 15-7, we have used a convention called *percentage down*. This term means that you can add the percentages down each column to total 100%. You read this form of table across a row. For the row labeled "approve," what percentage of the men approve? What percentage of the women approve?

The direction of percentaging in tables is arbitrary, and some researchers prefer to percentage across. They would organize Table 15-8 so that "men" and "women" were shown on the left side of the table, identifying the two rows, and "approve" and "disapprove" would appear at the top to identify the columns. The actual numbers in the table would be moved around accordingly, and each row of percentages would total 100%. In that case, you would read the table down a col-

umn, still asking what percentage of men and women approved. The logic and the conclusion would be the same in either case; only the form would be different.

In reading a table that someone else has constructed, therefore, you need to find out in which direction it has been percentaged. Usually that will be apparent in the labeling of the table or in the logic of the variables being analyzed. As a last resort, however, you should add the percentages in each column and each row. If each of the columns totals 100%, the table has been percentaged down. If the rows total 100% each, it has been percentaged across. The rule of thumb, then, is as follows:

1. If the table is percentaged down, read across.
2. If the table is percentaged across, read down.

Percentaging a Table

Figure 15-3 reviews the logic by which we create percentage tables from two variables. We've used the same variables as in the previous example—gender and attitudes toward equality for men and women—but we have reduced the numbers to make the illustration more manageable.

Here's another example, from a study by Rubin and Shuttlesworth (1983) on engaging families as support resources in nursing-home care—an issue that is highly relevant to gerontological social work. Rubin and Shuttlesworth were concerned that efforts to improve nursing-home care by increasing family involvement in the treatment process might be hindered by ambiguity among nursing-home staff and relatives of residents as to whether relatives or staff members were responsible for specific tasks.

To assess the degree of that ambiguity, Rubin and Shuttlesworth surveyed staff members and relatives of residents in two nursing homes. Their survey instrument listed 100 tasks in nursing-home care and asked respondents to indicate who they believed was primarily responsible for each task: the staff, the family, or both equally responsible.

A. Some men and women who either favor (=) sexual equality or don't (≠) favor it.

B. Separate the men and the women (the independent variable).

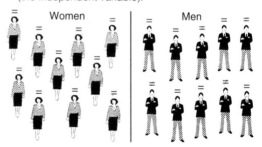

C. Within each gender group, separate those who favor equality from those who do not (the dependent variable).

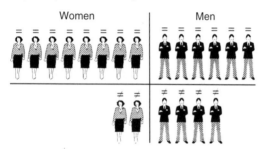

D. Count the numbers in each cell of the table.

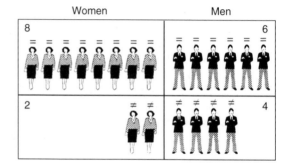

E. What percentage of the women favor equality?

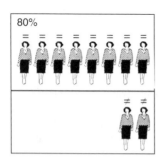

F. What percentage of the men favor equality?

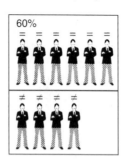

G. Conclusions

While a majority of both men and women favored sexual equality, women were more likely than men to do so.

Thus, gender appears to be one of the causes of attitudes toward sexual equality.

	Women	Men
Favor equality	80%	60%
Don't favor equality	20%	40%
Total	100%	100%

Figure 15-3   Percentaging a Table

Table 15-8 presents the data on one of the tasks, dealing with keeping books and magazines available for the residents. It tells us that there were 134 relatives in the sample. Of these, 14% deemed this task to be primarily the staff's responsibility, 38% deemed it a joint responsibility, and 48% deemed it primarily the family's responsibility. Of the 56 staff members in the sample, 29% considered this task to be primarily the staff's responsibility, 57% considered it a joint responsibility, and 14% considered it primarily the family's responsibility.

Thus, the data in Table 15-8 indicate that relatives are more likely than staff members to consider keeping books and magazines available to be the responsibility of the family. This is determined by noting that a larger percentage (48%) of the relatives deem that task as primarily a family responsibility than do staff members (14%). We might note, as well, that more staff members than relatives judged that task to be primarily the staff's responsibility (29% compared to 14%). Note that the independent variable in this table is the respondent group (staff member or relative), since that might affect one's role expectations regarding specific tasks, rather than role expectations affecting whether the respondent is a relative or a staff member.

Rubin and Shuttlesworth derived several alternative plausible implications from their data. Perhaps the most noteworthy one is that nursing-home staff members might underestimate the willingness of family members to take primary responsibility for nontechnical tasks in nursing-home care. If so, they reasoned, then those staff members also might not be communicating sufficient support for family involvement in directly providing certain aspects of nontechnical care. Consequently, Rubin and Shuttlesworth developed various recommendations for staff training and family-staff communication to help avoid this problem.

Constructing and Reading Tables

Before introducing multivariate analysis, let's review the steps involved in the construction of explanatory bivariate tables:

1. The cases are divided into groups according to their attributes of the independent variable.

2. Each of these subgroups is then described in terms of attributes of the dependent variable.

3. Finally, the table is read by comparing the independent variable subgroups with one another in terms of a given attribute of the dependent variable.

Let's repeat the analysis of gender and attitudes toward gender equality following these steps. For the reasons just outlined, gender is the independent variable; attitudes toward gender equality constitute the dependent variable. Thus, we proceed as follows:

1. The cases are divided into men and women.

2. Each gender subgrouping is described in terms of approval or disapproval of gender equality.

3. Men and women are compared in terms of the percentages approving of gender equality.

Table 15-8 Whom do nursing-home staff members and relatives consider to be primarily responsible for keeping books and magazines available for the resident?

PRIMARY RESPONSIBILITY	RESPONDENT GROUP	
	RELATIVES	STAFF MEMBERS
Nursing-Home Staff	14%	29%
Joint Responsibility	38	57
Family	48	14
100% =	(134)	(56)

In the example of family versus staff responsibility for nursing-home care tasks, the respondent group is the independent variable, and who respondents deem responsible for the task is the dependent variable. The table would be constructed as follows:

1. Divide the respondents into subgroups according to whether they are relatives or staff members.

2. Describe each subgroup of respondents in terms of the percentages who deem the task to be primarily a staff responsibility, a joint responsibility, or a family responsibility.

3. Compare the two subgroups in terms of the percentages responding in each category of responsibility.

Bivariate Table Formats

Tables such as those we've been examining are commonly called **contingency tables**: values of the dependent variable are contingent upon values of the independent variable. While contingency tables are very common in social work research, their format has never been standardized. As a result, a variety of formats will be found in research literature. As long as a table is easy to read and interpret, there is probably no reason to strive for standardization. However, there are a number of guidelines that should be followed in the presentation of most tabular data.

1. A table should have a heading or a title that succinctly describes what is contained in the table.

2. The original content of the variables should be clearly presented—in the table itself if at all possible, or in the text with a paraphrase in the table. This information is especially critical when a variable is derived from responses to an attitudinal question because the meaning of the responses will depend largely on the wording of the question.

3. The attributes of each variable should be clearly indicated. Complex categories will have

to be abbreviated, but the meaning should be clear in the table and, of course, the full description should be reported in the text.

4. When percentages are reported in the table, the base upon which they are computed should be indicated. It is redundant to present all of the raw numbers for each category because these could be reconstructed from the percentages and the bases. Moreover, the presentation of both numbers and percentages often makes a table confusing and more difficult to read.

5. If any cases are omitted from the table because of missing data ("no answer," for example), their numbers should be indicated in the table.

MULTIVARIATE ANALYSIS

Multivariate tables are constructed from several variables. They are constructed on the basis of a more complicated subgroup description by following essentially the same steps just outlined for bivariate tables. Instead of one independent variable and one dependent variable, however, we will have more than one independent variable. Instead of explaining the dependent variable on the basis of a single independent variable, we'll seek an explanation through the use of more than one independent variable.

Let's return to the example of attitudes toward gender equality. Suppose we believed age would also affect such attitudes, that young people would approve of gender equality more than older people. As the first step in table construction, we would divide the total sample into subgroups based on the various attributes of *both* independent variables simultaneously: young men, old men, young women, and old women. Then the several subgroups would be described in terms of the dependent variable, and comparisons would be made. Table 15-9 is a hypothetical table that might result.

Following the convention presented here, this table has also been percentaged down, and therefore should be read across. The interpretation of this table warrants several conclusions.

1. Among both men and women, younger people are more supportive of gender equality than older people. Among women, 90% of those under 30 and 60% of those 30 and older approve.

2. Within each age group, women are more supportive than men. Among those respondents under 30, 90% of the women approve, compared with 78% of the men. Among those 30 and over, 60% of the women and 48% of the men approve.

3. As measured in the table, age appears to have a stronger effect on attitudes than gender. For both men and women, the effect of age may be summarized as a 30 percentage point difference. Within each age group, the percentage point difference between men and women is 12.

4. Age and gender have independent effects on attitudes. Within a given attribute of one independent variable, different attributes of the second still affect attitudes.

5. Similarly, the two independent variables have a cumulative effect on attitudes. Young women are most supportive, and older men are the least supportive.

A section on the *elaboration model* later in this chapter will examine the logic of multivariate analysis in much greater detail. Before we conclude this section, however, it will be useful to note an alternative format for presenting such data.

Several of the tables presented in this chapter are somewhat inefficient. When the dependent variable—attitude toward gender equality—is dichotomous (two attributes), knowing one attribute permits the reader to easily reconstruct the other. Thus, if we know that 90% of the women under 30 approve of gender equality, then we know automatically that 10% disapprove. So reporting the percentages of those who disapprove is unnecessary. On the basis of this recognition, Table 15-9 could be presented in the alternative format of Table 15-10.

In Table 15-10, the percentages approving of gender equality are reported in the cells representing the intersections of the two independent variables. The numbers presented in parentheses below each percentage represent the number of

Table 15-9 Multivariate Relationship: Attitude, Sex, and Age "Do you approve or disapprove of the proposition that men and women should be treated equally in all regard?"

	UNDER 30		30 AND OVER	
	WOMEN	MEN	WOMEN	MEN
Approve	90%	78%	60%	48%
Disapprove	10	22	40	52
	100%	100%	100%	100%
	(200)	(200)	(200)	(200)
No Answer =	(2)	(10)	(3)	(2)

Table 15-10 Simplification of Table 15-9 "Do you approve or disapprove of the proposition that men and women should be treated equally in all regards?"

	PERCENTAGE WHO APPROVE	
	WOMEN	MEN
Under 30	90	78
	(200)	(200)
30 and over	60	48
	(200)	(200)

cases upon which the percentages are based. Thus, for example, the reader knows that there are 200 women under 30 years of age in the sample, and 90% of those approved of gender equality. This shows, moreover, that 180 of those 200 women approved, and that the other 20 (or 10%) disapproved. This new table is easier to read than the former one, and it does not sacrifice any detail.

Here is a somewhat more complicated multivariate table, drawn from the social science literature on self-perception. This example represents an attempt by Morris Rosenberg (1965) to shed some light on self-esteem among adolescent boys. As we see in Table 15-11, Rosenberg examined the simultaneous impact of three variables on self-esteem:

1. *Gender distribution of siblings:* Do the subjects live in families in which girls outnumber boys or in which boys either equal or outnumber girls?

Table 15-11 Self-Esteem of Adolescent Boys in Relation to Sex Distribution of Siblings, Ordinal Position, and Grades

Self-Esteem	RESPONDENT IN FIRST HALF OR MIDDLE OF FAMILY GRADES			RESPONDENT IN LAST HALF OF FAMILY (YOUNGER MINORITY) GRADES		
	A–B	C	D–F	A–B	C	D–F
	NO BROTHERS OR BROTHERS IN THE MINORITY					
High	56%	45%	41%	46%	60%	64%
Medium	20%	27%	27%	19%	18%	18%
Low	24%	28%	32%	35%	22%	18%
Total percent	100%	100%	100%	100%	100%	100%
Number	(79)	(104)	(41)	(26)	(65)	(22)
	BROTHERS IN THE MAJORITY OR EQUAL					
High	51%	40%	29%	42%	44%	30%
Medium	26%	27%	18%	32%	33%	20%
Low	23%	32%	53%	26%	23%	50%
Total percent	100%	99%	100%	100%	100%	100%
Number	(168)	(240)	(102)	(78)	(86)	(56)

Source: Adapted from Morris Rosenberg, *The Logic of Survey Analysis* (New York: Basic Books, 1968), p. 214.

Note: Study is of families with three or more children.

2. *Ordinal position:* Are the subjects older or younger than others within their families?

3. *Grades:* What kinds of grades do the subjects get in school?

Let's see what Table 15-11 tells us about self-esteem. To simplify matters, let's focus on the percentages of adolescent boys who are high in self-esteem. To determine the impact of the gender distribution of siblings, we compare the top rows of percentages in the two halves of the table: 56% to 51%, 45% to 40%, 41% to 29%, 46% to 42%, 60% to 44%, and 64% to 30%. What pattern do you notice in all those comparisons? In each case, the boys living in families with a sister majority (top half of table) are more likely to have high self-esteem than boys similar to them in every other regard except sibling gender distribution. Living in a sister majority family seems to promote higher self-esteem. Although consistent, the differences are not uniform, however. Overall, the gender distribution of siblings seems to matter most for boys who get bad grades in school. There are only small differences among those with good grades.

How about ordinal position? Is self-esteem affected by whether boys are older or younger within their set of brothers and sisters? To find out, we make a different set of comparisons, comparing the right and left halves of the table: 56% to 46%, 45% to 60%, 41% to 64% (in the top half of the table), 51% to 42%, 40% to 44%, and 29% to 30% (in the bottom half). Once again, we are comparing groups of boys who are similar to each other except for their ordinal position. There doesn't seem to be much of a pattern in this set of comparisons. Although the various comparisons reveal differences in self-esteem, we cannot conclude that there is a consistent relationship between ordinal position and high self-esteem. Sometimes the older boys have higher self-esteem; sometimes the younger ones do.

Finally, what effect do grades have on self-esteem? We would probably suspect that good grades would result in high self-esteem and bad grades in low self-esteem. Let's see if that's true. Here the relevant comparisons are among the three grade groupings in each of the four parts of the table: 56% to 45% to 41%, 46% to 60% to 64%, 51% to 40% to 29%, and 42% to 44% to 30%. Is our suspicion confirmed by the data?

Grades seem to have the expected effect on self-esteem among those boys who are older than their brothers and sisters, but we find a very different pattern among the younger minority brothers. For Rosenberg, the latter set of data pointed to

> . . . the possibility that the younger-minority boy might be characterized by a particular type of self-esteem, namely, unconditional self-acceptance. While the self-esteem of others appeared to be influenced by their level of academic performance, the self-esteem of the younger-minority boy appeared to be relatively impervious to it. It might thus be that the self-esteem of the younger-minority boy was so firmly established in the family by the interest and affection of his father, mother, and older sisters that it was relatively independent of later extra-familial experiences. (1968:214)

THE ELABORATION MODEL

As you can see from the previous examples, multivariate analysis can be used to elaborate on a relationship between two variables. This process, commonly referred to as the *elaboration model,* helps us to better understand and interpret the *explanatory* and *causal* implications of empirical relationships that we observe between two variables through the simultaneous introduction of additional variables. As you will see, this model of analysis is particularly useful when we are unable to conduct true experiments that permit causal inferences, especially when we have used a cross-sectional, or survey, design. For reasons discussed earlier in Chapter 9, feasibility constraints give us few opportunities to conduct true experimental research. When experimental control for plausible extraneous variables or rival explanations is not possible, we can attempt to control for them *statistically,* through the use of multivariate analysis.

To restate the elaboration process, we use multivariate analysis to better understand the causal meaning of a relationship (or lack of a relationship) between two variables, and we do this by studying the effects on the original relationship that are produced by introducing other variables. This process can lead to the following types of interpretations (elaborations) of the original relationship that we observed:

1. The original relationship might be *replicated.* That is, it would appear to be essentially the same in the multivariate analysis as it was in the bivariate analysis.

2. The original relationship might be *explained away as spurious.* That is, two variables that were related in a bivariate analysis are no longer related when one or more extraneous variables are controlled for in a multivariate analysis.

3. The original relationship might be *interpreted* based on multivariate control. That is, additional variables might help explain why the independent variable is related to the dependent variable.

4. The multivariate analysis might *specify* the conditions under which the original relationship tends to diminish or increase. That is, the original relationship might hold for some, but not all categories of the additional variable(s) being controlled. When this happens, the additional variables being controlled are called *distorter variables,* because they distort the true relationship between the independent and dependent variables.

5. Two variables that were not related in the bivariate analysis, or that were weakly related in it, might be strongly related after extraneous variables, called *suppressor variables,* are controlled in the multivariate analysis.

To clarify this process further and to get some more practice at interpreting multivariate tables,

let's look at a hypothetical example regarding the evaluation of case management services for discharged psychiatric patients. Social work is the most prominent professional affiliation among case managers, and social work roles such as linkage and advocacy (among others) comprise the case manager's efforts to help discharged psychiatric patients get the services they need in a timely and appropriate fashion. In our hypothetical example, case management effectiveness will be indicated by rehospitalization rates. This is a controversial and probably inadequate indicator of case management effectiveness, for reasons we shall discuss shortly, but its problems make it a useful indicator to use in our example.

Hypothetical Illustration of the Elaboration Process: Case Management Evaluation

Suppose you assess the effectiveness of a case management program serving psychiatric patients being discharged to diverse communities. You decide to use rehospitalization rates as the indicator of case management effectiveness, comparing the rehospitalization rate of the first 200 discharged patients who receive case management services to the rehospitalization rate of the first 200 discharged patients who receive other, more traditional, forms of service. Suppose you find that of the 200 case-managed patients, 50% (100 patients) are rehospitalized, whereas only 40% (80 patients) of the patients who are not case-managed are rehospitalized. In other words, the case-managed patients seem to fare worse in avoiding rehospitalization than do the others, making case management not only look ineffective, but perhaps somewhat harmful. This hypothetical result is illustrated in Table 15-12.

You might wonder whether these results are misleading. Perhaps case management really is beneficial, but discovering its true relationship to rehospitalization rates requires controlling for some extraneous variable. You might begin to search for that extraneous variable by supposing that case managers with masters degrees might be

Table 15-12 Hypothetical Relationship Between Case Management Provision and Rehospitalization

REHOSPITALIZED?	CASE-MANAGED	NOT CASE-MANAGED
Yes	50%	40%
No	50	60
	100%	100%
	(200)	(200)

more effective than those with baccalaureate degrees. Perhaps the poor bivariate results you obtained can be attributed to the large number of case managers who lack graduate-level professional training. If so, then the rehospitalization rates for patients assigned to practitioners with masters degrees should be lower.

You could test this supposition in a multivariate analysis like the one illustrated in Table 15-13. First, you would divide your sample into subsets on the basis of the extraneous variable being controlled (which, in this illustration, is the degree level of the practitioner—baccalaureate or masters). Then you would recompute the relationship between your independent and dependent variables (that is, between case management provision and rehospitalization rate) separately for each subset (each category) of the variable being controlled. If, as a result of this elaboration process, your findings were like those in Table 15-13, you would conclude that the original relationship was replicated—that the higher rehospitalization rate of case-managed patients was not affected by controlling for practitioner degree level.

But suppose you then realize that you have overlooked another, possibly more relevant, extraneous variable. You wonder whether the bivariate relationship between case management provision and rehospitalization rate can be explained away by the fact that the patients with the most chronic impairments are both more likely to be rehospitalized and to be referred for case management. That is, you suppose that the extraneous variable, type of impairment, accounts for the variation in both the independent and dependent variables, and that without their

Table 15-13 Original Relationship Replicated: Hypothetical Data Relating Case Management Provision to Rehospitalization, Controlling for Practitioner's Degree

	BACCALAUREATE DEGREE		MASTERS DEGREE	
REHOSPITALIZED?	CASE-MANAGED	NOT CASE-MANAGED	CASE-MANAGED	NOT CASE-MANAGED
Yes	50%	40%	50%	40%
No	50	60	50	60
	100%	100%	100%	100%
	(100)	(100)	(100)	(100)

relationship to the extraneous variable, the original bivariate relationship would disappear. For the sake of simplicity, let's assume that you operationally define type of impairment in terms of the number of times patients have been hospitalized for psychiatric reasons—if more than once, you might call them chronic; otherwise, you might call them acute.

You would test this supposition by constructing a multivariate table in the same manner as we constructed Table 15-13. Only this time, you would control for a different extraneous variable, type of impairment. This process is illustrated in Table 15-14. Unlike the outcome in Table 15-13, if your results resembled those in Table 15-14, you would conclude that the original bivariate relationship was spurious—that the type of impairment, which preceded both your independent and dependent variables, explains away the original relationship between case management provision and rehospitalization rate.

The basis for this conclusion is the observation that for patients with the same type of impairment, there is virtually no difference in rehospitalization rates between those who do and those who do not receive case management. For the acute subset, those patients who were and were not case-managed had rehospitalization rates of between 36% and 38%. For the subset whose impairments were deemed chronic, both groups of patients had a rehospitalization rate of between 53% and 55%.

Also notice how the acute subset of patients had both a lower rate of case management and a lower rehospitalization rate, whereas the chronic subset of patients had both a higher rate of case management and a higher rehospitalization rate. Thus, this table shows that the chronically impaired patients simply were much more likely to receive case management and that it is their greater impairment, and not the impact of case management, that accounts for the higher rehospitalization rate among case-managed patients.

To better understand the logic of this analysis, it might help if you reexamine Table 15-12 and compare it to Table 15-14. Try to see how Table 15-12 could be constructed from the data in Table 15-14 simply by removing the extraneous variable (type of impairment) controlled for in Table 15-14. For example, multiply 38% (.38) times 40, which equals 15. Add that to 53% (.53) times 160, which equals 85. Fifteen plus 85 equals 100, and

Table 15-14 Original Relationship Spurious: Hypothetical Data Relating Case Management Provision to Rehospitalization, Controlling for Type of Impairment

REHOSPITALIZED?	ACUTE IMPAIRMENT		CHRONIC IMPAIRMENT	
	CASE-MANAGED	NOT CASE-MANAGED	CASE-MANAGED	NOT CASE-MANAGED
Yes	38%	36%	53%	55%
No	62	64	47	45
	100%	100%	100%	100%
	(40)	(160)	(160)	(40)

40 plus 160 equals 200. Thus, 100 of the 200 case-managed patients, or 50%, were rehospitalized, just as indicated in Table 15-12. You can use the same process to see how the data for patients who were not case-managed in the two tables are in agreement.

So far in our hypothetical example we have shown how the original relationship, in the direction of higher rehospitalization rates for case-managed patients, was *explained away as spurious* when type of impairment was controlled. But what if you suspect that there really is a relationship between case management provision and rehospitalization rates—and that the true impact of case management on rehospitalization rates is being distorted by a variable that you haven't controlled for.

Let's suppose, then, that you decide to control for one more variable: adequacy of community-based care. Your rationale is that perhaps case-managed patients ought to have higher rehospitalization rates when they are discharged to communities that are unwilling or inadequately prepared to care for them humanely. You might therefore suppose that case management effectiveness is indicated by higher rehospitalization rates in unreceptive or inadequately prepared communities where patients are more likely to require rehospitalization and by lower rehospitalization rates in communities that are willing and able to provide humane care. (You might operationally define adequacy of community-based care in terms of resident attitudes, the availability of various essential services, and so on.) In other words, because case managers are responsible for seeing that client needs are met, they might be effecting higher rehospitalization rates for clients needing rehospitalization and lower rates in communities where humane care does not require rehospitalization.

Table 15-15 illustrates hypothetical data that would support your supposition. This table shows that the adequacy of community-based care is a *distorter variable* that was distorting the true relationship between case management provision and rehospitalization rates. This table also illustrates how multivariate analyses might *specify* the conditions under which the original bivariate relationship might diminish or increase. According to this hypothetical table, when community-based care is adequate, case-managed clients have

Table 15-15 Original Relationship Specified by Controlling for Distorter Variable: Hypothetical Data Relating Case Management Provision to Rehospitalization, Controlling for Adequacy of Community-Based Care

REHOSPITALIZED?	ADEQUATE CARE		INADEQUATE CARE	
	CASE-MANAGED	NOT CASE-MANAGED	CASE-MANAGED	NOT CASE-MANAGED
Yes	10%	30%	90%	50%
No	90	70	10	50
	100%	100%	100%	100%
	(100)	(100)	(100)	(100)

only one-third the rehospitalization rate of clients that were not case-managed. But when community-based care is inadequate, case-managed clients are almost twice as likely to be rehospitalized as are clients that are not case-managed.

Again, we urge you to try to see how the data in Table 15-15 are consistent with the data in Table 15-12. For example, for the case-managed clients, 10% (.10) times 100 (in the adequate care subset) plus 90% (.90) times 100 (in the inadequate care subset) equals 100 rehospitalized patients, or 50% (.50) times the total of 200 case-managed clients.

So far we have used the same bivariate table to illustrate replicating the bivariate relationship, explaining it away as spurious, and specifying the conditions under which the original relationship holds for some, but not all categories of a distorter variable. To illustrate the remaining two functions in the elaboration process, those involving interpretation and suppressor variables, we'll need to change the numbers a bit in the hypothetical bivariate relationship.

To illustrate suppressor variables, we'll begin by examining the hypothetical data in Table 15-16, showing that case managed patients are no less likely to be rehospitalized than patients who are not case managed. Specifically, the rehospitalization rate is 50% for both groups of patients. But suppose you suspect that type of impairment is

operating as a suppressor variable; that is, it is suppressing the true effectiveness of case management. You could control for type of impairment in the same way that we illustrated in Table 15-14, the only difference being that whereas before we were controlling it to explain away as spurious the relationship in which receiving case management was associated with a greater rehospitalization rate, here we are controlling it to see if receiving case management is more strongly associated with lower rehospitalization rates than is indicated in the bivariate table.

Essentially, then, we are going through the same process as in Table 15-14, using the same variables, except in this case we are showing how multivariate control can find a relationship where there originally was none, while in Table 15-14 we were showing how multivariate control can find no relationship where there originally was one.

Looking at Table 15-17, you can see that 75% of the case managed patients (150 out of 200) had a chronic impairment, and 60% of them were rehospitalized (90 out of 150). Only 25% of the patients not receiving case management (50 out of 200) had a chronic impairment, and 80% of them were rehospitalized (40 out of 50). Thus, for patients with chronic impairments, the case management rehospitalization rate of 60% was better than the 80% rate for those not receiving case management. Looking at the patients with acute impairments, we see that again the 20% rehospitalization rate for those receiving case management (10 out of 50) was better than the 40% rehospitalization rate for those not receiving case management (60 out of 150). In sum, because case managed patients were more likely to have chronic impairments, and because people with chronic impairments were more likely to need rehospitalization, type of impairment was operating as a suppressor variable, causing the bivariate relationship to be less than the true relationship between receiving case management and rehospitalization rate.

We have thus shown how multivariate control can change the original bivariate relationship be-

Table 15-16 Hypothetical Relationship Between Case Management Provision and Rehospitalization

REHOSPITALIZED?	NUMBER CASE-MANAGED	NUMBER NOT CASE-MANAGED
Yes	100	100
No	100	100
Total	200	200

Table 15-17   Original Relationship Strengthened When Suppressor Variable Controlled: Hypothetical Data Relating Case Management Provision to Rehospitalization, Controlling for Type of Impairment

| | ACUTE IMPAIRMENT | | CHRONIC IMPAIRMENT | |
REHOSPITALIZED?	CASE-MANAGED	NOT CASE-MANAGED	CASE-MANAGED	NOT CASE-MANAGED
Yes	10	60	90	40
No	40	90	60	10
Total	50	150	150	50

tween independent and dependent variables. But so far our interest in the variables being controlled has not gone beyond seeing what their control does to the relationship between the independent and dependent variables. We have looked to the controlled variables to see if the bivariate relationship changes, but we have not looked to them to help us interpret why or how the bivariate relationship exists. When we control variables for the purpose of interpretation, we look at how the bivariate relationship changes not for the purpose of concluding that the original bivariate data were misleading, but to understand the basis for the relationship and the mechanisms through which it occurs.

For example, imagine that a bivariate table shows that 300 case managed patients have a 30% rehospitalization rate, versus a 60% rehospitalization rate for 300 patients not receiving case management. Suppose we want to better understand why and how case management practitioners achieve lower rehospitalization rates, and identify the processes that account for the difference. Perhaps we think the chief factor influencing case management's superior outcome might be the case manager's better success in getting patients to take their psychotropic medications consistently as prescribed by their psychiatrist. To test

this possibility, we might obtain data like the hypothetical data in Table 15-18.

In Table 15-18 we see that two-thirds (200 of the 300) case managed patients took their medications, whereas only one-third of the other patients did so. We also see that among the patients who took their medications the rehospitalization rate was 10% for case-managed patients (20 out of 200) and 30% for the others (30 out of 100). Among the patients who did not take their medications, however, the rehospitalization rate was 70% for case-managed patients (70 out of 100) and 75% for the others (150 out of 200). Thus we can see that the superior effectiveness of case management was influenced by how successful case managers were in attaining medication taking. When medications were taken, the case management rehospitalization rate was only 10% and is one-third of the 30% rate for the others. But when medications were not taken, the case management rehospitalization rate shot up to 70%, and was only slightly better than the 75% rate for the others.

At this point you may be wondering whether the results in Table 15-18 are merely another illustration of specification, in which the original relationship diminishes or increases when we control for a distorter variable. Why, you may wonder,

Table 15-18   Interpretation of Original Relationship: Hypothetical Data Relating Case Management Provision to Rehospitalization, Controlling for Medication Compliance

REHOSPITALIZED?	MEDICATIONS TAKEN		MEDICATIONS NOT TAKEN	
	CASE-MANAGED	NOT CASE-MANAGED	CASE-MANAGED	NOT CASE-MANAGED
Yes	20	30	70	150
No	180	70	30	50
Total	200	100	100	200

are we calling this something else; specifically, why are we calling this interpretation? The answer is in the way we are conceptualizing the causal ordering of the variables. In this hypothetical example we are not conceptualizing medication taking as something that influences the occurence of case management. When we show that case management effectiveness changes according to medication taking, we are not saying that the original relationship is wrong or misleading. Instead, we are conceptualizing medication taking as something that case managers influence, as something that helps us understand why the original relationship exists. We are saying that a chief way in which case managers achieve lower rehospitalization rates is by achieving medication taking. We can look at the hypothetical results and see that 200 of the 300 case-managed patients (two-thirds) were taking their medications, whereas only one-third of the other patients were doing so.

We are not, however, saying that everyone doing a study like this or looking at these results would conceptualize things in the same way we are. Suppose the decision to refer patients to a case manager was influenced by a preexisting assessment of whether or not they were taking their medications before referral, perhaps with the strange idea that case management services should only be provided to patients already at higher levels of motivation and functioning. Under those circumstances, medication taking would be seen as a distorter variable whose control changed the meaning or meaningfulness of the original relationship, not as a variable that helps us understand why the original relationship exists and is meaningful and the mechanisms by which case managers achieve their lower rates.

Students often experience difficulty with this type of distinction in the elaboration model, commonly finding the terminology to be fuzzy and confusing. If that's how you are experiencing it, we would encourage you not to worry too much about terminology like specification versus interpretation or whether or not to call a particular variable a distorter variable, an extraneous variable, or a whatchimicallit variable. Although we think the terminology is useful and important, we think it is far more important that you see the need to conceptualize variables that might change or help you better understand bivariate relationships and that you are able to construct and interpret the multivariate tables that control for those variables, regardless of how you classify those variables.

Descriptive Statistics and Qualitative Research

The material you have been reading in this chapter clearly applies more to quantitative than to qualitative research. But it is not irrelevant to qualitative research. It is a mistake to believe that the distinction between qualitative and quantitative research is only about whether counting takes place or whether statistics are used. As we end this chapter, we want to call your attention again to the complementarity between quantitative and qualitative research methods, as we have at the end of previous chapters. How on earth, you may wonder, can we connect all this statistical material to qualitative research methods? Actually, it's pretty easy.

Researchers interpreting descriptive statistics often find that some of those statistics imply the need for a qualitative inquiry to better understand their meaning. Researchers conducting qualitative studies rarely report elaborate statistical analyses, but they often find that counting some things is an inescapable part of detecting patterns or developing a deeper understanding of the phenomenon they are studying.

Suppose you are conducting a qualitative inquiry to gain a deeper understanding of what it is like to have a sleep disorder. Would your understanding of what it feels like to have the disorder be more or less superficial if, in addition to qualitative observations, you counted some things like the mean number of hours the people you observed slept and the proportion of nights they didn't sleep at all? You wouldn't want to rely on the numbers alone, and you certainly would want to emphasize how the individuals with the disorder subjectively and perhaps idiosyncratically felt about their lack of sleep, but, at the same time, knowing whether we are talking about someone who almost never sleeps versus

someone who sleeps on average a handful of hours per night—perhaps with wild swings from night to night (that is, high dispersion)—gives us a more informed basis to consider their experience. If you tell us their lack of sleep makes it hard for them to concentrate at work, for example, our ability to sense what that must be like for them might be enhanced if we know they are averaging only about one hour of sleep per night.

Here's an example that starts with a quantitative inquiry. Suppose you are administering a child welfare program aimed at improving parenting and preserving families. Your program's funding level is influenced by descriptive statistics about the number of days children spend in out-of-home placements and scores on a scale measuring risk of child abuse. On both measures you find that the agency mean is mediocre and that the standard deviation is huge.

This prompts you to examine closely the univariate frequency distribution of each variable, and you find that in each distribution, most cases are not clustered near the mean. Instead, about one-third are way above the mean and about one-third are way below the mean. You recognize the need to probe into the meaning of these findings, to try to discover what is going on differently with the very successful and terribly unsuccessful cases, realizing that your mean is misleading and that what you find might imply ways to improve outcomes among cases like the ones that currently have unsuccessful outcomes.

If you had some solid hunches about what is accounting for the difference between the successful and unsuccessful cases, you might enter additional variables quantitatively, following an elaboration model format. However, you don't have a clue. So you decide to conduct a qualitative investigation, employing a couple of social work doctoral students seeking hands-on practicum experience in doing qualitative research in an agency setting. They begin by interviewing practitioners qualitatively, probing into their ideas and recollections about what the practitioners did differently with their most and least successful cases. They also pour through case records in an unstructured, open-ended fashion looking for patterns that might distinguish the two sets of cases. Quickly they find that almost all of the cases with the very worst outcomes had been assigned to three particular practitioners, and almost all of the cases with the very best outcomes had been assigned to three other practitioners.

Nobody knows what might explain the differences in outcome between the two sets of practitioners, so the students decide to observe the six practitioners with extreme outcomes in a qualitative fashion, in both their office sessions and home visits with clients. After collecting and analyzing a considerable amount of qualitative information, they begin to notice differences in the ways the two sets of practitioners work with parents. The practitioners with the more successful outcomes seem to be more prone toward providing services in the parents' homes, listening to parents empathically and helping them obtain needed resources, educating the parents about child development and child rearing, and teaching specific parenting skills. The ones with less successful outcomes seem to spend less time with parents, make fewer home visits, be less responsive to the concrete needs for resources parents express, and spend more time moralizing to them.

The students conducting the qualitative observations recognize that their insights and report will be more meaningful if they can describe the extent of the differences they so far have been observing qualitatively. For example, to just say one group did something more or less than another group is less meaningful in terms

of the qualitative goal of developing a richer understanding of the phenomenon than saying that the successful practitioners averaged three home visits to each client per week as compared to the unsuccessful ones seeing clients only once a month and only in their office.

So they begin including in their qualitative journal log of observational notes such quantitative information as the number and length of home visits versus office sessions, the number of times the practitioner obtains a resource, the number of empathic versus moralizing statements, and the amount of time spent teaching about parenting. We are not saying that these quantitative indicators are the only things or the main things the students will record. They will continue to record qualitative information, such as obtaining the clients' subjective perspectives on how they experience the practitioner's services. Moreover, the quantitative measures will have emerged from an analysis of the qualitative material collected earlier. Eventually, their report might stimulate others to conduct quantitative, hypothesis-testing studies seeing if the patterns emerging from this qualitative study can be generalized beyond these six practitioners and their clients. And, as the never-ending process in the scientific search for understanding continues, those quantitative studies might stimulate future qualitative inquiries in efforts to discover the meanings of their findings. And so on.

Now let's consider a hypothetical example of a purely qualitative study. Perhaps you decide to pursue a Ph.D. degree in social work, for which you must produce a research dissertation. You decide to conduct a qualitative study like the one that Elliott Liebow (1994) conducted, seeking to portray the lives of homeless women. Your methodology relies on observation and informal conversational interviews with a small group of homeless women whom you come to know at a shelter and a soup kitchen where you volunteer to help and befriend them. Perhaps you begin to find, as Liebow did, that what may seem irrational or aimless to most people might be rational and purposeful from the perspective of the homeless women. For example, perhaps you find that a reason they express for neglecting personal hygiene is to make oneself repulsive to men who are abusive and thus prevent victimization while sleeping in dangerous settings. If you begin to detect a pattern regarding this explanation for neglecting personal hygiene, you might find yourself inescapably wondering how many of the homeless women you meet this explanation applies to. Was the first woman who expressed a rational explanation for neglecting personal hygiene the only one who felt this way? Indeed, it is hard to imagine how you could detect such a "pattern" in the first place without

some awareness of the proportion of your observations that fit the pattern. In this connection, reports of qualitative studies commonly comment about the proportion of observations that fit various qualitative categories. The researchers probably won't couch those comments in the context of formal tables of frequency distributions, particularly since they tend to deal with relatively small amounts of numbers. They may couch their quantitative allusions in imprecise terms like "most" or "few" or "often," but if you read many reports of qualitative research you are likely to find quite a few instances where the researcher obviously counted something. This point, and the more formal use of descriptive statistics in qualitative studies, is elaborated in the box "Do Qualitative Researchers Count?"

DO QUALITATIVE RESEARCHERS COUNT?

Some people unfortunately think in black and white or stereotypical ways about quantitative and qualitative studies and the investigators who conduct them. In their most extreme forms, these stereotypes may portray quantitative researchers as inchworms who can do nothing but count and qualitative researchers as never counting anything and perhaps having some kind of math phobia. Those who think qualitative researchers never count anything or never use statistics might find their stereotypes dispelled by reading two recent compendiums of qualitative studies edited or coedited by social work professors. The two books are: *Qualitative*

Studies in Social Work Research, edited by Catherine Reissman (Sage, 1994), and *Qualitative Methods in Family Research*, edited by Jane Gilgun, Kerry Daly, and Gerald Handel (Sage, 1992). Taking the latter volume first, we found that in 9 of the 16 studies the researchers alluded to doing some counting. In four studies the counting was mentioned only in imprecise terms (which we'll italicize), as exemplified by the following excerpts:

"Participants *often* prescribed to more than one personal theory . . . members of couples *frequently* shared the same . . . theories" (p. 54).

"Caregivers were *often* optimistic. . . . Weight *loss* or *gain*, sleep disturbances, and *reduced* exercise were characteristic of this phase" (p. 75).

"Caregivers *often* spend a *great deal* of time at the bedside of the PWA [person with AIDS]" (p. 77).

". . . retirement—*with few exceptions*—has meant *husbands' retirement*" (p. 274).

In five of the studies, the counting clearly involved the use of some descriptive statistics, reported in precise terms, usually in connection to describing study participants. Here are some excerpts:

"The average age of the elders was 65, with a range of 48 to 83 . . . one-quarter were unsure of their marital status" (p. 90).

"The mean age of the sample was 31 for husbands and 30 for wives. The mean length of marriage was 6 years. The couples had experienced a fertility problem for a mean average of 5 years" (p. 107).

"The mean age of daughters in the study was 55 years, although there was a range from 33 to 72. More than half (52%) were married, although 21% were widowed and 14% were divorced" (p. 204).

One of the studies, by Mark Rank (1992), used qualitative methods to try to explain quantitative data indicating that women on welfare have a low fertility rate. The quantitative data are presented in two tables, one of which displays the number and proportion of births in relation to six separate time periods. The other shows the relationship between fertility rates and five demographic variables for different populations.

The Reissman volume contains 10 qualitative studies, 4 of which report some quantitative data, along similar lines as in the Gilgun et al. book. One of the studies, by Denise Burnette (1994), uses a multivariate frequency table to portray her sample of elderly people. Her narrative further describes her sample in terms of means and proportions for various demographic characteristics. Later in her report she refers to a *median* of 13 years of long-term illness, the proportion who were cognitively intact, the amount of hours spent watching television, the proportion speaking with friends and relatives at least four times a week, and people in the lowest *quartile* or *quintile* of poor health.

The editors of the above two volumes have made valuable contributions to the social work research literature. Their work illustrates the diversity in qualitative research, its complementarity with quantitative research, and the ways descriptive data are and can be used in qualitative studies. Oh, and by the way, for anyone who's had any doubts about it, they've shown that qualitative researchers—in more ways than one—do indeed count!

Main Points

• Descriptive statistics is a method for presenting quantitative descriptions in a manageable form.

• Univariate analysis is the analysis of a single variable.

• The full original data collected with regard to a single variable are, in that form, usually impossible to interpret. Data reduction is the process of summarizing the original data to make them more manageable, all the while maintaining as much of the original detail as possible.

• A frequency distribution shows the number of cases having each of the attributes of a given variable.

• Grouped data are created through the combination of attributes of a variable.

• *Averages* (the mean, median, and mode) reduce data to an easily manageable form, but they do not convey the detail of the original data.

• Measures of dispersion give a summary indication of the distribution of cases around an average value.

• One commonly used measure of dispersion is the standard deviation.

• To undertake a subgroup comparison: (a) divide cases into the appropriate subgroups, (b) describe each subgroup in terms of a given variable, and (c) compare those descriptions across the subgroups.

• Bivariate analysis is nothing more than a different interpretation of subgroup comparisons: (a) divide cases into subgroups in terms of their attributes on some *independent variable,* (b) describe each subgroup in terms of some *dependent variable,* (c) compare the dependent variable descriptions of the subgroups, and (d) interpret any observed differences as a statistical association between the independent and dependent variables.

• As a rule of thumb in interpreting bivariate percentage tables: (a) "percentage down" and "read across" in making the subgroup comparisons, or (b) "percentage across" and "read down" in making subgroup comparisons.

• Multivariate analysis is a method of analyzing the simultaneous relationships among several variables and may be used to more fully understand the relationship between two variables.

• The elaboration model is a method of multivariate analysis appropriate to social work research.

• The elaboration model is primarily a logical model that can illustrate the basic logic of other multivariate methods.

• The basic steps in elaboration are as follows: (a) a relationship is observed to exist between two variables, (b) a third variable is held constant in the sense that the cases under study are subdivided according to the attributes of that third variable, (c) the original two-variable relationship is recomputed within each of the subgroups, and (d) the comparison of the original relationship with the relationships found within each subgroup provides a fuller understanding of the original relationship itself.

• A suppressor variable is one that conceals the relationship between two other variables.

• A distorter variable distorts the true nature of the relationship between two other variables.

• The use of descriptive statistics often can enrich a qualitative study, and it is not uncommon to find some quantitative data included in reports of qualitative research.

Review Questions and Exercises

1. Using the hypothetical data in the following table, construct and interpret tables showing

a. The bivariate relationship between age and attitude toward transracial adoption.

b. The bivariate relationship between ethnicity and attitude toward transracial adoption.

c. The multivariate relationship linking age, ethnicity, and attitude toward transracial adoption.

2. Construct multivariate tables using hypothetical data on a social work research question of interest to you. Illustrate in your tables the elaboration logic of replication, interpretation, explanation, and specification.

Additional Readings

Hirschi, Travis, and Selvin, Hanan, ***Delinquency Research: An Appraisal of Analytic Methods*** (New York: Free Press, 1967). Excellent logical discussions and concrete examples. This book examines the empirical research in the field of delinquency from a rigorously logical perspective. Critiques of specific research examples often set the stage for important and insightful general discussions of elaboration and other aspects of the logic of scientific inquiry.

Lazarsfeld, Paul, Pasanella, Ann, and Rosenberg, Morris (eds.), ***Continuities in the Language of Social Research*** (New York: Free Press, 1972). An excellent and classic collection of conceptual discussions and empirical illustrations. Section II is especially relevant, although the logic of elaboration runs throughout most of the volume.

Rosenberg, Morris, ***The Logic of Survey Analysis*** (New York: Basic Books, 1968). The most comprehensive statement of elaboration available. Rosenberg presents the basic paradigm and goes on to suggest logical extensions of it. It is difficult to decide which is more important, this aspect of the book or the voluminous illustrations. Both are simply excellent, and this book serves an important instructional purpose.

Weinbach, Robert, and Grinnell, Richard, ***Statistics for Social Workers*** (New York: Longman, 1987). A "user-friendly" introduction to statistics, filled with social work examples and geared to those who are not mathematically oriented.

Ziesel, Hans, ***Say It with Figures*** (New York: Harper & Row, 1957). An excellent discussion of table construction and other elementary analyses. Although several years old, this is still perhaps the best available presentation of that specific topic. It is eminently readable and understandable and has many concrete examples.

Inferential Data Analysis: Part 1

What You'll Learn in This Chapter

Here you'll learn about statistical procedures
frequently used in social work research to guide
decisions about what can be generalized about the
relationships we observe in our findings.

INTRODUCTION

In Chapter 15 we discussed procedures for presenting and descriptively analyzing data. When we analyze data for descriptive purposes, our focus is limited to the data we have collected on our study's sample. Descriptive analysis does not provide a basis for generalizing beyond our particular study or sample. Even the results of bivariate or multivariate analyses that show relationships between different variables in our study do not provide sufficient grounds for inferring that those relationships exist in general or have any theoretical meaning.

But we seldom conduct research just to describe our samples per se; in most instances, our purpose is to make assertions about the larger population from which our sample has been selected or about the causal processes in general that explain why we have observed a particular relationship in our data. This chapter will examine the statistical measures used for making such inferences and their logical bases.

CHANCE AS A RIVAL HYPOTHESIS

In earlier chapters of this book we considered in depth many potential sources of error impinging on our ability to make inferences about the relationships we observe in our findings. For example, we discussed various sorts of bias, threats to internal validity, and the need to control for extraneous variables. These sources of error, if not adequately controlled, represent rival hypotheses, or alternative explanations, to the interpretations we seek to draw from our data. Thus, if our data indicate the hypothesized relationship between our independent and dependent variables but we haven't controlled for a critical extraneous variable that plausibly might explain away as spurious the relationship we think we observe, a rival hypothesis containing that extraneous variable represents a plausible alternative explanation of our findings.

Another rival hypothesis, one that we haven't yet discussed, is *chance*. Chance has to do with *sampling error*, a concept covered in Chapter 8 (on sampling theory). It also pertains to the luck of the draw when randomly assigning subjects to groups. No matter how rigorous our random assignment or sampling methods may be, there is always the chance that, just due to the luck of the draw, the data we obtain may be a fluke and not representative of any broader population or causal processes.

For example, suppose we conduct the perfect experiment to evaluate the effectiveness of a social service, an experiment that is flawless in every conceivable way. When we randomly assign individuals to experimental and control groups, no matter how impeccable our random assignment procedures may be, there is always a chance that a large majority of the individuals who are going to improve with or without any treatment will get assigned to the experimental group and that a large majority of those whose problems are the most intransigent will get assigned to the control group. And it can work the other way around, too—the most difficult cases could be assigned to the treatment group and the others to the control group. Although random assignment minimizes the probability of such imbalances, it does not guarantee that they will never occur simply due to chance.

Flukes in random sampling or random assignment need not be dramatic, like an all-or-nothing occurrence, to threaten the validity of our inferences. Suppose you are conducting an experiment to evaluate the effectiveness of an intervention to prevent future incidents of child abuse or neglect by parents who have been referred for being abusive or neglectful. Let's assume that the intervention being evaluated is utterly ineffectual and worthless. Let's further assume that 26 parents will be randomly assigned to the treatment (experimental) group and another 26 to the control group. Thus, your sample size is 52.

Finally, let's assume that with or without receiving the worthless intervention, half of the 52 parents will recidivate and half will not. That is, half will be found to have been abusive or neglectful again during the test period. We will call that half the recidivists. What do you suppose the odds are that the 26 recidivists will be divided evenly between your experimental and control groups? Actually, the odds of that happening are less than 50-50. The chances are greater that the random assignment will have some other result; perhaps 14 or 15 recidivists will be assigned to one group and 12 or 11 to the other. Or maybe it will even be a split of 16/10, 17/9, and so on. It is even possible, albeit extremely unlikely, to have a 26/0 split.

This does not mean that the 13/13 even split is less likely to occur than any other particular split. To the contrary, no other singular split is as likely to occur as the 13/13 split. It just means that the odds are better than even that one of the other 26 possible splits will occur. In other words, if you add the odds of getting a 14/12 split, a 15/11 split, and so on until all possible splits other than 13/13 are included, the sum of all those odds will be greater than the chances of getting a perfectly even 13/13 split.

You can demonstrate this to yourself quickly and easily, without any mathematical gymnastics. All you need is a deck of cards. We'll designate each red card as a recidivist and each black one as a nonrecidivist. Begin by shuffling the deck, so that the cards are randomly ordered. Next, deal (that is, randomly assign) the 52 cards alternately into two equal piles of 26, and see whether either pile has exactly 13 red cards and 13 black ones. Finally repeat this little exercise a couple of times. Did you get a 13/13 split each time? It's possible, but not very likely. (Of course, in a real study you wouldn't know who the recidivists would be or how many there would be before random assignment. You would learn that later, toward the end of the study. But in our hypothetical example, because we are assuming that the intervention has no effects whatsoever, we can just designate in advance those who will eventually recidivate for reasons having nothing to do with the intervention.)

Whenever we randomly assign people to groups or randomly select a sample, we utilize a process that is the same as putting each person's name on a card, shuffling the cards, and then dealing them into one or more piles. The point of this exercise is that when we subsequently collect data from the people (in each "pile"), the odds are that we are going to observe some relationships that are not generalizable or theoretically meaningful—relationships that inescapably result simply from the luck of the draw.

If, for example, you randomly dealt 12 red cards into one pile on your left and 14 into another pile on your right, you would attribute the difference to luck—you would not infer that the position of the pile (left or right) in a general sense affects the likelihood of its getting red cards. Thus, if in a real study we find that our experimental group of 26 cases had a 46% rate of recidivism (or 12 out of 26) and our control group had a 54% rate of recidivism (or 14 out of 26), we must take into account the likelihood that the difference had more to do with the luck of the draw, or chance, than with the impact of the tested intervention.

This example illustrates that a study of an independent variable that has absolutely no effect whatsoever on the tested dependent variable has a good chance of obtaining findings that show some relationship—albeit perhaps quite weak—between the two variables. And this point applies to *all* types of explanatory research designs, not just experimental ones. Every time we seek to *infer* whether the relationships we have observed have some theoretical meaning or can be *generalized* beyond our sample, we must take into account the role that *chance,* or *sampling error,* plays as a potential explanation of our findings.

Refuting Chance

In light of what we have said so far in this chapter, it may appear that we face a dilemma whenever we seek to infer whether relationships can be generalized in a theoretical sense or to a population. If any relationship, no matter how dramatic, conceivably could have resulted from the luck of the draw, how are we to decide where to draw the line between findings that can and cannot be generalized? In other words, how are we to decide whether the relationship we have observed verifies our hypothesis or, alternatively, merely resulted by chance?

Suppose, for example, that the recidivism rate in our experimental group is lower than the recidivism rate in our control group. How much lower must it be in order to infer that the intervention, and not chance, is probably responsible for the difference? Would a difference of 1% be enough—say 49% of treated cases recidivate, as compared to 50% of control cases? No? Well, then how about a 2% difference—say 48% compared to 50%? Still not impressed? Where would you draw the line? When asked this question, students often look perplexed. Some say 5%. Others say 10%. Many shrug.

Fortunately, there is a solution to this dilemma, one that enables us to infer, for any particular relationship we observe in our sample, whether that relationship is strong enough to confirm our hypothesis and thus be generalized. That solution involves testing to see if the relationship we have observed is statistically significant.

STATISTICAL SIGNIFICANCE

Testing for statistical significance means calculating the probability, or odds, of finding due to chance a relationship at least as strong as the one we have observed in our findings. That probability will fall somewhere between 0 and 1.0. For example, if the probability is .05, it means that 5 times out of 100, or 1 in 20, we can expect to obtain a relationship at least as strong as the observed one just due to the luck of the draw. If the probability is .10, then we can expect to obtain that strong a relationship 10 times out of 100, or 1 in 10, just due to the luck of the draw, and so on.

There are many alternative ways to calculate statistical significance; the correct method for any given study depends on several considerations that we will address later. But the most important thing for you to understand at this point is that all of the methods for calculating statistical significance, no matter how different their mathematical assumptions and formulas may be, ultimately yield the same thing—a probability between 0 and 1.0 that the observed relationship was obtained simply due to chance.

Theoretical Sampling Distributions

Tests of statistical significance ascertain the probability that observed relationships can be attributed to sampling error, or chance, by using theoretical sampling distributions. When you test for the statistical significance of your data, you will not have to confront a theoretical sampling distribution; your computer will already take that distribution into account and will calculate for you the probability that the relationship in question was obtained due to chance. But it is nevertheless important that you understand the underlying logic of theoretical sampling distributions in order to truly understand—and take the magic out of—statistical significance.

Just as there are different methods for calculating statistical significance, there are different types of sampling distributions that pertain to different types of data. For example, one type of sampling distribution pertains to sampling error that occurs when drawing a random sample from a population, and another type pertains to the chance variations that occur when using randomization to subdivide a given pool of subjects into subgroups. But the underlying logic of these distributions is similar. For the sake of simplicity, we'll focus our illustrations in this chapter on the latter type of sampling distribution that pertains to random assignment in experimental designs.

The logic of this type of theoretical sampling distribution can be illustrated in an uncomplicated fashion by returning to our hypothetical example involving a deck of cards in which the red cards represent recidivists and the black cards represent nonrecidivists. Suppose we have just concluded a real experiment in which 12 (46%) of 26 treated cases recidivated, as compared to 14 (54%) of 26 untreated cases. We would want to know the odds that our lower recidivism rate for treated cases was due to the luck of the draw in randomly assigning cases to the two groups. Even though our experiment was a real one, one way to calculate those odds could involve using a deck of cards. We would begin by writing the name of each of the 26 recidivists, including both the treated and the untreated ones, on a separate red card. Then we would do the same on black cards for the nonrecidivists.

Next, we would shuffle the cards thoroughly, randomly assign (deal) them to two piles of 26 cards each, and record the red/black ratio in each pile. Then we would gather up the cards, reshuffle thoroughly, and repeat the entire process, again recording the randomly obtained ratio at the end. We would continue to do this again and again thousands of times, cumulatively tabulating the number of times that each red/black ratio occurred. At some point, perhaps after days of fanatical shuffling and dealing, we would see that continuing this merriment any further would be pointless; we already would have tabulated so many outcomes that any additional outcomes would not essentially alter the proportions we had already established for each possible outcome.

In other words, if a particular ratio had occurred 100 times after 1000 deals, we could say with confidence that the odds of that outcome occurring due to chance were 1 in 10, or .10. Even if we were to continue the process and get that particular ratio on the next two deals, its probability would remain essentially unchanged at 102 divided by 1002, or .102 (which with rounding off would still be .10).

So at that point we would stop our shuffling and calculate the proportion of times that, just due to the luck of the draw, we obtained an outcome signifying a relationship at least as large as the one we observed in our real study. That is, we

would add the proportion of 12/14 splits to that of 11/15 splits to that of 10/16 splits, and so on. The list of proportions that we calculated for the various outcomes would be our theoretical sampling distribution.

Table 16-1 displays the **theoretical sampling distribution** that we would obtain for this particular example.

Fortunately, the authors did not have to spend days shuffling and dealing cards to obtain this distribution; one of us did it in minutes on a computer using software that contains statistical procedures that calculated the chi-square significance test (corrected for small sample size).

To use Table 16-1, find the row that corresponds to the outcome we happened to obtain in our real experimental findings. We noted earlier that our hypothetical findings had 12 recidivists in the treated group and 14 in the untreated group. By locating that outcome in the theoretical sampling distribution, we can identify the probability associated with it. We find in Table 16-1 that the probability of obtaining that particular outcome due to chance is .377, and the cumulative probability of finding a difference between the two groups at least as large as the one we found in our experiment is .782. In other words, if we randomly assign 26 recidivists and 26 nonrecidivists into two equally sized groups an infinite number of times, then for every 1000 assignments, 782 would produce differences between the two groups at least as large as the difference we found in our experiment, and 377 would produce the exact difference we found. Thus, mere chance produces relationships at least as large as the one we observed in our hypothetically real study 78.2% of the time. That means that we have a 78.2% likelihood of obtaining, just due to the luck of the draw, a difference between the two groups equal to or greater than 12 recidivists out of 26 cases in one group and 14 recidivists out of 26 cases in the other.

This would tell us that the relationship we observed in our actual findings is probably explained by chance and not the effects of the tested

Table 16-1   Theoretical Sampling Distribution for Randomly Assigning
26 Recidivists and 26 Nonrecidivists in Two Groups of 26 Cases Per Group

OUTCOME	PROBABILITIES (ROUNDED OFF TO NEAREST ONE-THOUSANDTH)	
(DIVISION OF RECIDIVISTS BETWEEN THE TWO GROUPS)	PROBABILITY OF EACH PARTICULAR OUTCOME	CUMULATIVE PROBABILITY
26/0 or 0/26	.000	.000
1/25 or 25/1	.000	.000
2/24 or 24/2	.000	.000
3/23 or 23/3	.000	.000
4/22 or 22/4	.000	.000
5/21 or 21/5	.000	.000
6/20 or 20/6	.000	.000
7/19 or 19/7	.002	.002
8/18 or 18/8	.011	.013
9/17 or 17/9	.039	.052
10/16 or 16/10	.114	.166
11/15 or 15/11	.239	.405
12/14 or 14/12	.377	.782
13/13 or 13/13	.218	1.000

intervention. This does not mean that we have "proven" that the relationship was due to the luck of the draw. Our hypothesis could still be true. Likewise, it is conceivable that if the entire population of abusive or neglectful parents were to receive the tested intervention, 46% of them would recidivate, as compared to 54% if none received the tested intervention. All we can say at this point, based on our particular results with a sample of 52 people, is that we cannot reasonably rule out chance as a plausible rival hypothesis because findings at least as dramatic as ours occur 78.2% of the time when the only thing affecting the distribution of outcomes in the two groups is the luck of the draw.

As we mentioned before, fortunately we do not have to create a theoretical sampling distribution every time we seek to assess the probability that the relationships we observe in our findings were caused by chance. Statistical procedures, called **tests of statistical significance,** handle this for us. Indeed, once we have entered our data into a computer, we can hit a few keys and find out in the batting of an eye the probability that our observed relationship was caused by chance. But it is important to understand that statistical significance tests calculate that probability on the basis of the same theoretical sampling distribution logic that we have just described. Just why that understanding is important should become clearer as we continue our discussion of statistical significance testing.

Significance Levels

Up to now we have addressed the logic underlying procedures to calculate the odds that a particular relationship that we observed in our findings can be attributed to chance and not to the general veracity of our research hypothesis. But we still have not indicated *where one draws the line* between findings that should and should not be attributed to chance. Obviously, if the probability that chance explains the relationship is very high, say near or above .50 (that is, 50-50 odds), it would be unthinkable to rule out chance as a plausible rival explanation. But just how low must its probability be before we can risk ruling out its plausibility? Even if it were as low as .25 would we dare say that a rival hypothesis that is true as often as one out of every four times is not plausible?

No matter where we happen to draw the line between findings that will and will not be attributed to chance, we deem a finding to be **statistically significant** when its probability of occurring due to chance is at or below a cutoff point that we select in advance—before we analyze our data. Thus, if we draw the line at .05, then we deem a relationship to be statistically significant if it occurs due to chance no more than 5 times out of 100 randomized trials (or 5 out of 100 deals of the deck). Drawing the line at .05 thus would mean that a relationship with, say, a .06 probability of being caused by chance would be deemed statistically *not significant,* whereas anything less than .05 would be deemed statistically *significant.* In short, we call a relationship statistically significant when the probability that it is explained by chance is at or below a point that we have identified in advance as so low that we are willing to risk refuting chance as a plausible rival hypothesis.

In other words, when we call a relationship statistically significant, we say that it can be generalized beyond our sample and that it reflects more than chance covariation. If we assess statistical significance using a theoretical sampling distribution pertaining to random sampling from a population, significance refers to generalizing from the sample to the population. If, on the other hand, the sampling distribution is based on random assignment of cases, significance pertains to generalizing about causal processes.

Traditionally, social scientists, including social work researchers, have settled on .05 as the most commonly used cutoff point to separate findings that are not deemed to be significant from those that are. Those findings that fall in the zone beyond the cutoff point, and which are therefore considered to be statistically significant, comprise the critical region of the theoretical sampling distribution. The cutoff point is called the **level of significance.** When it is set at .05, it is signified by the expression: $p \leq .05$. This means that any probability equal to or less than .05 will be deemed statistically significant. Researchers usually just report it as less than .05 ($p < .05$) because the probability rarely equals .05 exactly. A probability that is even a tiny bit above .05, say at .051 for example, would be considered to be greater than .05—outside of the critical region—and therefore statistically not significant.

Returning to the theoretical sampling distribution illustrated in Table 16-1, how big a difference in recidivism between our experimental and control groups would we need in order to have statistical significance at the .05 level? To answer this question, we look at the column of cumulative probabilities until we find the cutoff point between values above .05 and below .05. Thus, we see that we would need to have no more than 8 recidivists in one of the groups (and at least 18 in the other) in order for the difference to be statistically significant. Likewise, we see that any difference that is less extreme than an 8 to 18 split has a probability greater than .05 and would therefore be deemed not significant. Thus, even if our experimental group had a 35% recidivism rate (9 out of 26) and our control group's recidivism rate was much higher, at 65% (17 out of 26), using the .05 level of significance we would not be able to refute the plausibility of chance as a rival hypothesis. However, had we established in advance .10 as our level of significance, then a 9/17 split would be statistically significant because its cumulative probability of .052 is less than .10.

It is critical to bear in mind that the .05 level of significance is *not* dictated by mathematical theory. It is *not sacred*. Not all studies use that level. Some studies use a lower level, perhaps at .01, although that almost never happens in social work research. A strong case can be made for using a higher level, perhaps around .10, under certain conditions, especially when our sample is small, for reasons to be discussed later.

Before moving on, we should point out the importance of selecting your significance level *before* you conduct your data analysis. Doing so after the analysis has been completed would put you in the position of deciding the criterion of significance in light of the knowledge of which criteria would make your findings significant or not. Even if you have a great deal of integrity, it would be difficult to rule out the possibility that, perhaps unintentionally, your selection of a significance level was biased by your a priori knowledge of what each significance level would mean regarding the significance of your findings. Moreover, what if every researcher were in this position? We all may be confident of our own intellectual honesty and capacity to remain unbiased, but we would probably be uncomfortable if everyone else was selecting significance levels in light of whichever level would make their findings "significant."

One-Tailed and Two-Tailed Tests

In the preceding example, you may have wondered why the theoretical sampling distribution illustrated in Table 16-1 lumped together the probability of getting a split of *either* 12 recidivists in our experimental group and 14 in our control group or 14 recidivists in the experimental group and 12 in the control group. Because we were evaluating the effectiveness of an intervention aimed at *preventing* recidivism, why would we consider the probability of chance producing a 14/12 or worse split—in which the experimental group's recidivism would be greater (worse) than the control group's? Why not just limit the probabilities of interest to those for relationships in which the experimental group's outcome (recidivism) is better (lower) than the control group's?

The reason why the positive and negative outcomes were lumped together in our distribution was that we did not say that our hypothetical study was interested in finding out only whether the effects of the evaluated intervention are beneficial. We stated that we were evaluating its effectiveness, but we did not foreclose on the possibility of finding that it is harmful. And if our findings were to turn out in the harmful direction, we would want to know whether those findings allow us to generalize that the intervention is indeed harmful or whether the results were just a fluke caused by the luck of the draw. Consequently, we would be interested in the probabilities of finding either a positive or negative relationship due to chance.

Hypotheses that do not specify whether the predicted relationship will be positive or negative are called *nondirectional* hypotheses. When testing nondirectional hypotheses, we use *two-tailed* tests of significance. For any particular relationship that we find, regardless of whether it is positive or negative, two-tailed tests of significance add together the probability of finding a relationship that strong in the positive direction to that of finding one in the negative direction. Using a two-tailed test in our example, we found that the probability of getting a relationship at least as large as a 12/14 or 14/12 split in *either* direction was .782. That figure adds the probability of getting 12 or fewer recidivists in one group to the probability of getting 12 or fewer recidivists in the other group. Thus, the probability of getting only 12 or fewer recidivists in the experimental group, and not including the probability of the reverse results, is one-half of .782, or .391.

We say a test has "two tails" because we are interested in extreme, unlikely values in the sampling distribution for both positive and negative relationships. To illustrate this point, we have modified the sampling distribution that appeared in Table 16-1. The revised version appears in Table 16-2. Notice how instead of lumping positive and negative outcomes together, Table 16-2 is symmetrical, with the positive outcomes and their probabilities in the top half and their negative counterparts in the bottom half. Notice also that each probability is one-half the amount it was in Table 16-1.

The "two tails" in this distribution consist of those values at either end (top or bottom) of the table that are in our *critical region* for claiming statistical significance. Because we are using a two-tailed test of significance—that is, because we are interested in both positive and negative outcomes—we would have to add together the probabilities we find in each tail to identify our cutoff points. In other words, we would add the two *tails* together.

Thus, although the probability in this distribution of having 9 or fewer recidivists in the experimental group is less than .05 (at .026), that finding

Table 16-2 Theoretical Sampling Distribution (Showing Each Tail) for Randomly Assigning 26 Recidivists and 26 Nonrecidivists into Two Groups of 26 Cases Per Group

OUTCOME (DIVISION OF RECIDIVISTS/ NONRECIDIVISTS BETWEEN THE TWO GROUPS)		CUMULATIVE PROBABILITY	OUTCOME (DIVISION OF RECIDIVISTS/ NONRECIDIVISTS BETWEEN THE TWO GROUPS)		CUMULATIVE PROBABILITY
GROUP 1	GROUP 2		GROUP 1	GROUP 2	
0/26	26/0	.0000	14/12	12/14	.3910
1/25	25/1	.0000	15/11	11/15	.2025
2/24	24/2	.0000	16/10	10/16	.0830
3/23	23/3	.0000	17/9	9/17	.0260
4/22	22/4	.0000	18/8	8/18	.0065
5/21	21/5	.0000	19/7	7/19	.0010
6/20	20/6	.0002	20/6	6/20	.0002
7/19	19/7	.0010	21/5	5/21	.0000
8/18	18/8	.0065	22/4	4/22	.0000
9/17	17/9	.0260	23/3	3/23	.0000
10/16	16/10	.0830	24/2	2/24	.0000
11/15	15/11	.2025	25/1	1/25	.0000
12/14	14/12	.3910	26/0	0/26	.0000
13/13	13/13	.5000			

would not be significant because, when added to the probability of having 9 or fewer recidivists in the control group, it exceeds .05 (that is, .026 plus .026 equals .052). The figures in Table 16-1, then, reflect the probabilities that pertain to a two-tailed test after adding the two tails together (as shown in Table 16-2). Our significance level in Table 16-2 would still be .05, but two cutoff points—points designating the two tails— would identify the critical region of results that would be deemed statistically significant. One "significant" tail would consist of outcomes with 8 or fewer recidivists in the experimental group, and the other "significant" tail would consist of outcomes with 8 or fewer recidivists in the control group. The probability for each tail would be .0065, but after add ing the two tails together the probability becomes .013.

But suppose we had stipulated in advance that we were only interested in whether the effects of the intervention were positive. Then we would have formulated a *directional* hypothesis. Directional hypotheses predict whether a relationship will be positive or negative. When we test a directional hypothesis, we can use a *one-tailed* test of significance. But this choice restricts our options. That is, we will be able to infer whether the relationship we find can be generalized in the predicted direction only. If our findings turn out to be in the opposite direction, we cannot reverse gears and use a two-tailed test and then claim the same level of significance. Consequently, many social scientists recommend that two-tailed tests should usually be used even when the hypothesis is directional.

To illustrate the use of one-tailed tests, let's apply a one-tailed test of significance to the data in Table 16-2. Because we are only interested in generalizing about positive intervention effects— effects associated with lower recidivism in the experimental group—any finding in the opposite direction will simply be interpreted as not supporting the hypothesis and will not be generalized. Consequently, we would establish our cutoff point at the top "tail" of the distribution only, and in essence would be assessing the probability

of getting a certain result or *better* due to chance. Thus, still using the .05 level of significance, we would now be able to generalize outcomes in which the experimental group had 9 or fewer recidivists because the cumulative probability for that outcome in the one, preselected tail of the distribution is .026 (that is, $p < .05$).

Suppose, however, after having planned to use a one-tailed test with our directional hypothesis, we found 17 recidivists in the experimental group and only 9 in the control group. Wanting to alert others to the potentially harmful effects of the tested intervention, suppose we then reversed gears and used a two-tailed test. What would our significance level be if we were to claim this finding to be statistically significant? It would not be .05, for we were prepared to call the other tail significant with its cumulative probability of .026. In order to deem this finding significant, then, our real significance level would have to be at .052 or higher. But if a significance level higher than .05 is acceptable, then why didn't we initially plan to use it in our anticipated one-tailed test? If we choose to use it now, are we not deceiving ourselves and others and in effect merely manipulating the selection of a significance level to fit our findings?

One way to resolve this dilemma would be to report the two-tailed probability of the finding— calling it not significant—and informing readers that you used a one-tailed test in the other direction with a .05 significance level. If the tested intervention is in widespread use, you might want to alert readers of the unexpected and potentially worrisome direction of this finding and urge them to replicate your evaluation. Readers would then be informed adequately to make their own decision about how to respond to your findings. But it would be inappropriate to cite your findings as a basis for inferring that the tested intervention is indeed harmful.

The Null Hypothesis

Now that you know what directional and nondirectional hypotheses are, let's consider another type of hypothesis called the **null hypothesis**—a term that you might understandably think was coined by impish statisticians out to make mischief. But you will encounter this term frequently as you produce, utilize, and participate in research studies, and it is important that you understand it.

Throughout this chapter we have been referring to chance as a rival hypothesis. When we refer to that rival hypothesis, we call it the *null* hypothesis. Simply put, the null hypothesis postulates that the relationship being statistically tested is explained by chance—that it does not really exist in a population or in a theoretical sense—even though it may seem to be related in our particular findings. Thus, when our findings are shown to be statistically significant, we reject the null hypothesis because the probability that it is true—that our results were caused by chance—is less than our level of significance. So, if our results are statistically significant at the .05 level of significance, we would conclude that the null hypothesis has only a .05 probability of being true, and we would therefore reject it.

What makes this term tricky is that whenever we are rejecting the null hypothesis, we are supporting the plausibility of our research hypothesis (assuming that we are predicting that two variables are related and that we are not seeking to show that they are unrelated). Conversely, whenever we *fail to reject* the null hypothesis, we are *failing to support* our research hypothesis.

So why bother having a null hypothesis? Weren't we managing just fine by referring to chance as a rival hypothesis? Although we could probably get along well enough without this term, it actually does serve one particularly important function. It reminds us that our level of statistical significance does not pertain to the probability that our research hypothesis is true. All that it tells us is the probability that the observed relationship was caused by chance—that is, the probability that the *null* hypothesis is true. Suppose our results are significant at the .05 level. That would indicate that the null hypothesis has only a .05 probability

of being true, but it absolutely would *not* tell us that our research hypothesis therefore has a .95 probability of being true.

Remember, chance is only one of many rival hypotheses that could account for our findings. Others that we mentioned at the beginning of this chapter are biases, threats to internal validity, extraneous variables, and so on. We need to remain vigilant about this, lest we allow low statistical probability levels to gull us into thinking that we can ignore the methodological strengths and weaknesses of a particular study. Indeed, what surer way to see to it that your findings will be statistically significant than to introduce certain biases into the methodology—for example, rigging the measurement so that you get findings that will support your hypothesis? Thus, by using the term *null hypothesis* we remind ourselves that the only hypothesis whose likely truth conforms to our significance level is a statistical hypothesis, not our research hypothesis.

The term *null hypothesis* also facilitates our consideration of other potential errors connected to statistical significance testing, errors that we will examine next.

Type I and Type II Errors

Every time we make a decision about the statistical significance of a tested relationship, we risk making an error. If we decide to reject the null hypothesis, we risk making one type of error. If we do not reject the null hypothesis, we risk making another type of error. This is true because we are dealing with probabilities, not certainties.

Remember that our significance level only tells us the *probability* that the null hypothesis is false. Although we may reject as *implausible* a null hypothesis with a probability of .05, we never reject it as *impossible*. There is always some chance, however slight, that a statistically significant relationship really was caused by chance. In other words, we may have gotten a rare and very lucky draw in the random assignment or in random sampling. With a .05 significance level, we can expect to get such a lucky draw once for every 20 tests of statistical significance that we perform.

The error that is risked when we have statistically significant results—and therefore reject the null hypothesis—is called a **Type I error.** A Type I error occurs if the null hypothesis we have rejected as implausible is really true. When we reject the null hypothesis, we have no way of knowing whether we are actually committing a Type I error; all we know is the probability that we are doing so. That probability is equivalent to our significance level. At the .05 level of significance, therefore, we take a .05 risk of committing a Type I error when we reject the null hypothesis.

The only way we can avoid risking a Type I error is by failing to reject the null hypothesis. However, whenever we do that we automatically risk making a **Type II error.** A Type II error occurs if we fail to reject a false null hypothesis. Remember, just because the probability that the tested relationship can be attributed to chance is greater than our significance level, that *does not guarantee* that it was caused by chance. If our significance level is .05 and the probability that our result was due to chance is .06, then we fail to reject the null hypothesis—even though the probability that the null hypothesis is true is only .06!

Thus, findings that are not significant do not mean that our research hypothesis has been proven to be false. They just mean that we lack the level of probability we require before we will rule out chance as a plausible explanation for our findings. Consequently, if our probability level falls short of being statistically significant but is close to significant, then rather than claim to have disproven our hypothesis, we would probably alert readers to the low, albeit nonsignificant, probability level and encourage them to replicate our research in this area. It could be that our research hypothesis really is true, but we had too small a sample, or too unlucky a draw, to verify it at a statistically significant level. (We will explain the role of sample size in this issue shortly.)

Table 16-3 summarizes the relationships between Type I errors and Type II errors. It is provided to help you visualize the impossibility of avoiding the risk of both a Type I and Type II error simultaneously. Whenever we lower our significance level in order to reduce the risk of committing a Type I error, we automatically increase the risk of making a Type II error. Conversely, whenever we raise our significance level in order to reduce the risk of committing a Type II error, we increase the risk of committing a Type I error.

Social scientists tend to accept a much lower risk of making a Type I error than a Type II error. This probably is connected to their desire to obtain statistically significant results and their consequent wish to offset any biases that might result from that desire. Thus, by taking a .05 or lower risk of incorrectly supporting their own hypotheses, they project an impressive image of scientific caution and objectivity.

But just because so many social scientists conform to this convention does not mean that Type I errors are necessarily more serious than Type II errors, especially when human suffering is at stake. Deciding which type of error is more serious requires making value judgments, and the choice will vary depending on the nature and context of the research question. To illustrate this point, let's return to our hypothetical example involving the prevention of recidivism among abusive parents, again using the theoretical sampling distribution illustrated in Table 16-2. Recall that a 9/17 split had a probability of .052 with a two-

Table 16-3 Type of Error Risked Related to Decision About Null Hypothesis

	DECISION REGARDING NULL HYPOTHESIS	
TYPE OF ERROR	REJECT	NOT REJECT
Type I	Risked	Not Risked
Type II	Not Risked	Risked

tailed test and therefore was not significant at the .05 level. Consequently, at that significance level we would decide to risk committing a Type II error and would be unwilling to take a .052 risk of committing a Type I error.

Would we be justified in that decision? Reasonable people might disagree about this issue, but what if we had very little evidence that any alternative interventions effectively prevent child abuse? If nothing else works and there is no evidence that the intervention produces noxious side effects, which error has worse human consequences: recommending an intervention that really has no effect on child abuse, or failing to recommend one that really does reduce the incidence of child abuse? As you think about this, realize that if our hypothetical 9/17 results could be generalized, it would mean that the intervention lowers the child abuse rate from 65% (17 out of 26 cases in the untreated control group) to 35% (9 out of 26 treated cases). That's prevention of a substantial amount of suffering and other damage. On the other hand, if the null hypothesis is true, then the use of this intervention by others would result in a lot of wasted resources that could have been spent seeking more effective ways to deal with this serious problem.

Of course, one way to resolve this dilemma is through replication. Another way is by increasing our sample size. In fact, we would probably recommend that the preceding results warrant replicating our study with a larger sample. As we will see next, increasing our sample size provides a way to reduce the risk of committing a Type II error without having to increase the risk of committing a Type I error.

The Influence of Sample Size

As we discussed in Chapter 8 (on sampling), the larger our sample, the less sampling error we have. When we reduce sampling error, we reduce the probability that the relationships we observe in our findings can be attributed to it. Consequently, the same relationship that was too weak

to be significant with a smaller sample can, without changing in magnitude, become statistically significant with a larger sample. In other words, it is safer to generalize findings from large samples than from small ones, and even a very weak relationship might warrant generalization if it was found in a very large sample.

For example, in a study of the salaries of social work faculty members in 1980, Rubin (1981) found that after controlling for several extraneous variables, the mean salary was $26,638 for men and $26,157 for women. With a very large sample size of 1067 faculty members, Rubin found that the $481 difference between the mean salaries of men and women was statistically significant at the .01 level.

To illustrate the effects of sample size further, let's again go back to our hypothetical example on evaluating an intervention to prevent child abuse. Only this time we'll vary the sample size, relying in part on examples of hypothetical data presented by Blalock (1972).

To begin, suppose that we assigned only five cases to each group, and found that 2 of the 5 treated parents recidivated as compared to 3 of the 5 untreated controls. Although 3/5 represents a 60% recidivism rate, and 2/5 is only 40%, with these small samples the role of chance is so great that it would be ludicrous to take such percentages seriously. If we were to double our sample size to 10 cases per group and found the same recidivism rates (that is, 4 out of 10 versus 6 out of 10), our results still would not be significant at the .05 level.

But if we found the same rates (that is, the same relationship) with 50 cases in each group (20 out of 50 versus 30 out of 50), then the probability of the null hypothesis being true would be less than .05, and we would reject it at that level of significance. And if we doubled the sample size to 100 per group, and still found the same 40% versus 60% rates, the probability of the null hypothesis being true would fall to below .01.

To help solidify your understanding of this point, let's compare one more pair of hypothetical results for the preceding example. Suppose we assigned 50 cases to each group and found 24 (48%) treated recidivists and 26 (52%) untreated recidivists. That outcome would not be significant at the .05 level. But suppose we found the exact same relationship with 5000 cases in each group. That would entail 2400 (48%) treated recidivists and 2600 (52%) untreated recidivists. For that finding, the probability of the null hypothesis being true would be less than .001!

MEASURES OF ASSOCIATION

When we assess statistical significance, we ask only one question: "Can a relationship be inferred to exist in a theoretical sense or in a broader population?" We do not assess how strong the relationship is. It is tempting to treat significance levels as indicators of the relative strength of different relationships—that is, to assume that a relationship that is significant at the .001 level is stronger than one that is significant at the .05 level. But such an assumption would be incorrect.

We just saw how sample size can influence statistical significance. We saw that a 40% recidivism rate among treated cases versus a 60% recidivism rate among controls would be significant at the .05 level for 50 cases per group, whereas a 48% versus a 52% recidivism rate would be significant at the .001 level for 5000 cases per group. Therefore, the stronger relationship is not necessarily the one with the lower probability of a Type I error.

It is also tempting to think that because significance testing doesn't tell us how strong a relationship is, it might be okay to bypass significance testing and just deal with measures of the strength of relationships. But that, too, would be inappropriate. Some strong relationships can be caused by chance. If 0% of two treated cases recidivate, as compared to 100% of two untreated cases, generalizing that strong relationship would be no more appropriate than inferring that two coins were biased if you flipped two heads with one and two tails with the other. In short, significance testing is an essential first step in interpreting a relationship, but it only tells us the probability that a relationship was caused by chance. It does not tell us its strength.

Let's look now at how we measure the strength of a relationship. We'll refer to the statistical procedures for doing so as *measures of association*. We can begin by recognizing that we have already been discussing measures of association when we cite differences in percentages between two dichotomous variables like recidivism and the provision of treatment. It is intuitively obvious that a 40% versus a 60% recidivism rate signifies a stronger relationship than a 48% versus a 52% rate. But when we are dealing with variables that have more than two categories or those that are at ordinal or interval/ratio levels of measurement, we need some other kind of summarizing statistic. (But in our discussion of measures of association we will commonly refer back to our recidivism example, which uses two dichotomous variables, just to simplify the discussion—that is, to illustrate strength of relationship concepts in intuitively obvious terms.)

Some commonly used measures of association yield values that range from zero, which signifies no relationship whatsoever, to 1.0, which signifies a perfect relationship. A value of −1.0 also would signify a perfect relationship. The minus sign in front of a relationship magnitude statistic does not mean the relationship is weaker than one with a plus sign. The minus sign only means that the variables are negatively (inversely) related (as one goes up, the other goes down). The closer the value is to zero, the less able we are to predict the relative value of one variable by knowing the other.

For example, if two groups had exactly the same recidivism rate, then knowing whether a particular case was in one group or the other would not affect our calculation of the odds that that case will recidivate. We might be able to predict the odds from the overall recidivism rate for cases in either group, but knowing what group the case was in would not influence our prediction one way or the other. Thus, the relationship magnitude would be zero.

On the other hand, if one group had a 0% recidivism rate and the other group had a 100% recidivism rate, then knowing which group a case was in would enable us to predict with 100% accuracy whether that case will recidivate. The relationship magnitude would be 1.0, a perfect relationship.

Table 16-4 illustrates two perfect relationships and one two-by-two table showing a relationship magnitude of zero. The two-by-two table at the top shows no relationship, and the relationship magnitude therefore would be zero because the two groups have exactly the same recidivism rates. The fact that there are fewer recidivists than nonrecidivists (that is, the recidivism rate is 40%) may be an important descriptive finding. But since each group has the same 40% recidivism rate, knowing what group a case is in offers nothing toward predicting whether that case will recidivate, and therefore the relationship magnitude is zero.

In the second two-by-two table, the relationship magnitude is 1.0 because none of the experimental group cases recidivated whereas all of the control group cases did. Thus, knowing which group a case was in would be all we needed to know to predict with perfect accuracy whether or not the case will recidivate.

The same degree of predictability is evident in the third example, but this time there is a minus sign in front of the 1.0 because as one variable increases, the other decreases. The relationship magnitude is –1.0 because each additional session of treatment attended, without exception, reduces the number of incidents of verbal abuse observed by the same amount each time. It is a perfect relationship because knowing the number of sessions one attends is all we need to know to predict with perfect accuracy the number of incidents of verbal abuse observed. The minus sign is not pejorative and does not signify a weaker relationship; it simply means that an increase in one variable is associated with a decrease in the other variable.

Table 16-4 Illustrations of Relationship Magnitudes of Zero, 1.0, and –1.0

EXAMPLE OF A RELATIONSHIP MAGNITUDE OF ZERO:

	Experimental Group	Control Group
Recidivists	40	40
Nonrecidivists	60	60

EXAMPLE OF A RELATIONSHIP MAGNITUDE OF 1.0:

	Experimental Group	Control Group
Recidivists	0	100
Nonrecidivists	100	0

EXAMPLE OF A RELATIONSHIP MAGNITUDE OF –1.0:

CASE NUMBER	NUMBER OF TREATMENT SESSIONS ATTENDED	NUMBER OF INCIDENTS OF VERBAL ABUSE OBSERVED
1	1	14
2	2	12
3	3	10
4	4	8
5	5	6
6	6	4
7	7	2
8	8	0

So far we have contrasted a perfect relationship (with a magnitude of 1.0 or –1.0) with no relationship (zero magnitude). But what about something in between? How about, for example, a 40% recidivism rate for treated cases versus a 60% one for controls? In that case, knowing that a case was in the treatment group would predispose us to predict nonrecidivism and knowing the case was in the control group would predispose us to predict recidivism. But if we predicted recidivism for every control case and nonrecidivism for every treated case, we would be wrong 40% of the time. That's a lot of errors. But with an overall recidivism rate of 50% (which would be the case with an equal number of cases in the 40% and 60% groups), we would be wrong 50% of the time if we tried to predict recidivism for each case without knowing which group each case was in. Thus, knowing which group a case was in would reduce our percentage of errors from 50% to 40%, or a proportional reduction in error of .20. (The .20 is derived from the fact that if we express the .10 reduction from .50 to .40 in proportional terms, then .10 is 20%, or .20, of .50.)

In short, if there is some relationship between our variables, it means that knowing the value for one variable will reduce the number of errors we make in predicting the value for the other variable. And the stronger the relationship is, the more our prediction errors will be reduced. The term for this process is *proportionate reduction of error* (PRE). Some of the measures of association that we will now examine are based on the PRE framework, and some are not. But each measure yields a statistic ranging from zero to 1.0 (or –1.0). The stronger the relationship, the closer the statistic will be to 1.0 (or –1.0) and the greater will be the reduction of uncertainty. The weaker the relationship, the closer the statistic will be to zero and the less will be the reduction of uncertainty.

Which measure of association should be used depends primarily on the level of measurement of your variables. As we identify each measure we will not discuss its computational formula or things of that sort. At the end of this chapter we'll refer you to some excellent statistics texts for that information. Rather than overwhelm you with mathematics here, we want to make sure you understand the conceptual meaning and utility of these statistics and when to use each; their calculation can be

handled by computer. But we do encourage you to study statistics further when you finish this text. Comprehension of the mathematical derivations of statistics (and their calculation) helps in understanding their meaning. But to deal with the more advanced mathematical content here, we think, would present too much too soon and interfere with your comprehension of the basics.

When both your independent and dependent variables are at the *nominal level of measurement*, some common measures of association are *lambda, Yules' Q, phi*, and *Cramer's V*. Phi and Cramer's V can be squared like correlation coefficients, which we shall address shortly. Like the remaining measures of association we will be examining, both phi and Cramer's V can range from zero to 1.0.

Which to use (phi or Cramer's V) depends only on whether both of your variables are dichotomous. If they are, then you can use phi. If either variable has more than two categories, then Cramer's V should be used. (Certain computer programs, like the one we'll discuss in Appendix G, automatically choose between V or phi, as indicated by the number of categories per variable.)

Let's examine a practical example involving the use of phi and Cramer's V. During the early 1980s Rubin and Shuttlesworth (1983) conducted several studies on role ambiguity in the subdivision of tasks between nursing-home staff members and relatives of residents. They listed various tasks in caring for the nursing-home residents and asked staff members and relatives to indicate whether they thought each task was primarily the responsibility of the staff or the family. Thus, they assessed two variables at the nominal level of measurement: (1) whether the respondent was a staff member or a relative and (2) who the respondent thought was responsible for the listed task.

One item asked who respondents thought was responsible for keeping the resident's clothing inventory up to date. In one of their studies, 54% of nursing-home administrators, as compared to 35% of relatives, thought this task was primarily the responsibility of the nursing-home staff. The phi for this statistically significant relationship was .41. Each group believed itself to be primarily responsible for the task. The same type of result was found for other nontechnical tasks.

A practice implication of this finding was the need to engage nursing-home administrators and family members in interactions to clarify their respective responsibilities and ensure that nursing-home staff members recognized and supported family willingness to be more involved in nontechnical care tasks. Suppose instead of comparing relatives to staff, the study had compared administrators, nurses, social workers, and other direct-care staff members. Then, instead of a two-by-two table, there would be a four-by-two table, which contained four rows (one for each category of staff) and two columns (whether the staff member viewed the family or staff as primarily responsible for the task). Because the row variable would have more than two categories, Cramer's V would be used instead of phi.

When both your independent and dependent variables are at the *ordinal level of measurement,* three commonly used measures of association are *gamma, Spearman's rho,* and *Kendall's tau.* Which to use depends on how you wish to treat ties in the ordinal ranks, and there is no clearcut basis for recommending any one of these measures. Whichever is used, the statistic will range from zero to 1.0 and can be interpreted in terms of uncertainty reduction. Readers are referred to Blalock (1972) for a more technical comparison of these three statistics.

Suppose you asked social workers in nursing homes to rate as excellent, good, fair, or poor both the quality of relationship between residents and their nearest relative as well as the degree of involvement of that relative in the care of the resident. To assess the strength of that association you would use gamma, rho, or tau, because each of the two variables is a rating (excellent to poor) at the ordinal level of measurement.

When both variables are at the *interval or ratio level of measurement,* the most commonly used measure of association is *Pearson's product-moment correlation (r).* In fact, with this level of measurement in both variables, r is used for both the purpose of statistical significance testing and for the purpose of measuring the strength of association. (We will say more about statistical significance testing purposes later.) When we square the correlation coefficient and thus obtain r^2, we obtain a value that equals the *proportion of variance in the dependent variable that is explained by the independent variable.* Thus, if $r = .7$, then $r^2 = .49$, which means that about half the variation in the dependent variable has been explained.

To illustrate the use of the product-moment r, let's return to the nursing-home studies conducted by Rubin and Shuttlesworth. In one study (1982) they summed up the number of tasks that each relative said was the primary responsibility of the family. That sum was at the ratio level of measurement because it had a precise numerical meaning with a true zero point. (In other words, relatives could say that no tasks were their responsibility, or that any other number of the listed tasks were their responsibility—which was different from just looking at their nominal response of "yes" or "no" to one particular task.)

Rubin and Shuttlesworth used the product-moment r statistic to assess the strength of association between the number of tasks viewed as the family's responsibility and the number of times the respondent visited the resident. The statistically significant r of .47 suggested that respondents' survey responses tended to be corroborated by their visitation frequency, a finding that supported the validity of the measurement instrument.

When we are measuring the association between a *nominal independent variable and an interval or ratio-level dependent variable,* two commonly used statistics are *eta* and the *point-biserial correlation coefficient.* The latter is used when your nominal variable is dichotomous, such as when comparing a treatment group with a control group. The former (eta) is used when comparing more than two categories of a nominal independent variable with an interval or ratio-level dependent variable. Again, these statistics range from zero to 1.0 and can be squared and interpreted in terms of uncertainty reduction.

Had Rubin and Shuttlesworth wanted to assess the magnitude of the association between the summed number of tasks viewed as the family's responsibility (a ratio-level measure) and whether the respondent was a relative or a staff member (a dichotomous nominal-level measure), they would have used the point-biserial correlation coefficient.

Effect Size

Statistics that portray the strength of association between variables are often referred to by the term **effect size.** The use of this term is particularly common in clinical outcome research. The relationship magnitude statistics that we've been discussing so far (phi, rho, r, point-biserial correlation coefficient, and so on) are all effect-size statistics. So are some others that we haven't yet discussed, but which we will address shortly. Effect-size statistics portray the strength of association found in any study, no matter what outcome measure is used, in terms that are comparable across studies. Thus, they enable us to compare the effects of different interventions across studies using different types of outcome measures.

To illustrate this function in clinical outcome research, suppose two different studies are conducted, each of which is an experimental evaluation of the effectiveness of a different approach to treating male batterers. The first evaluates a cognitive-behavioral approach and finds that the experimental group subjects receiving the tested treatment averaged two physically abusive incidents per subject during a posttreatment follow-up period, as compared to a mean of three physically abusive incidents for control subjects. The second study evaluates a psychosocial approach. Instead of using the ratio-level outcome measure of number of abusive incidents, it uses the nominal measure of whether or not any physical abuse occurred during the follow-up period. It finds

that 40% of experimental subjects were abusive, as compared to 60% of control subjects. Suppose that the findings of each study are statistically significant.

How can we judge which of the two interventions had the stronger effects? Comparing their outcomes as just stated is a bit like comparing apples and oranges since they used different types of outcome indicators. Effect size statistics help alleviate this problem. The point-biserial correlation coefficient for the first study can be compared to the phi statistic for the second study. Although their calculations are different, each has the same meaning. The intervention with the larger effect size is the one that explained more of the variation in its dependent variable. In other words, the intervention with the larger effect size had stronger effects on the particular outcome variable being assessed in connection to it (assuming that internally valid designs that permit causal inferences were used).

Not everyone who reports the foregoing measures of association (phi, r, and so on) refers to them as the "effect size." Some do; many don't. For example, one author might say, "The effect size was substantial, since phi .50," whereas another author might simply say, "The relationship was strong, since phi .50."

But there is another type of effect size statistic that is always referred to as the "effect size" since it has no other name. This statistic, abbreviated as ES (E for effect and S for size), is used when interval or ratio-level data permit dividing the difference between the means of the experimental and control groups by the standard deviation.

Different approaches to calculating ES vary as to whether the standard deviation that is used in the calculation is that of the control group, the pooled standard deviation of the two groups combined, or an estimate of the standard deviation of the population to which a study is attempting to generalize. To simplify our discussion, we'll just use the approach involving the standard deviation of the control group, which is probably the most commonly used method (Fischer, 1990). In this approach, the effect size formula is as follows:

$$ES = \frac{(\text{experimental group mean}) - (\text{control group mean})}{(\text{control group standard deviation})}$$

To illustrate the use of the preceding formula, let's return to the hypothetical example of two studies, each of which evaluates the effectiveness of a different approach to treating male batterers. Only this time let's assume that each uses a ratio-level measure of outcome. Let's say that the first study assesses the mean number of physically abusive incidents and finds an experimental group mean of 2, a control group mean of 3, and a standard deviation of 1. Its effect size would be as follows:

$$ES = \frac{2 - 3}{1} = -1.0$$

When calculating ES this way, we interpret the plus or minus sign in the dividend according to whether a reduction in the outcome measure represents a desirable or undesirable effect. In the preceding example, it represents a desirable effect since we were seeking to reduce physical abuse. We would therefore report the ES as 1.0 (not − 1.0), because the minus sign in reporting ES is used only to indicate undesirable effects (in the opposite direction of what was sought). We would interpret this ES of 1.0 by observing that the experimental group's mean was 1 standard deviation better than the control group's mean. In a normal curve, only 16% of the cases have values at least 1 standard deviation better than the mean, and 84% of the cases have less desirable values. Therefore, if we assume a normal distribution of control group scores, then an ES of 1.0 indicates that the mean outcome for experimental subjects was better than 84% of the outcomes for control subjects. You can interpret any ES in this manner by using the Z-table commonly found in introductory texts on descriptive statistics. Z-tables show what proportion of a normal curve is found above and below z scores. This ES formula produces a z score, since z scores tell how far a score is from a mean in standard deviation units. In Appendix J of this text you will find a Z-table that displays some ES values along with the corresponding percentage of outcomes for control subjects that is worse than the mean outcome for experimental subjects for each ES value.

Let's say that the second study in our hypothetical example assesses the mean number of verbally and physically abusive incidents combined (unlike the first study, which assessed only physical abuse) and has a longer posttreatment measurement period than in the first study. Suppose the second study finds an experimental group mean of 20, a control group mean of 26, and a standard deviation of 10. Its effect size would be as follows:

$$ES = \frac{20 - 26}{10} = -.60$$

Although the two studies quantified outcome in different ways—one dealing with much larger numbers than the other—dividing by the standard deviation makes the results of the two studies comparable. The preceding results indicate that the cognitive-behavioral intervention evaluated in the first study had stronger effects on its outcome measure than the psychosocial intervention evaluated in the second study had on its outcome measure.

At this point you may be wondering whether the relative strength depicted in the preceding outcomes may have been different if, instead of reporting the ES statistic, our hypothetical authors had reported effect size in terms of the point-biserial correlation coefficient or some other measure of association. The answer is "no." Either approach would have shown the stronger effect size in the first study. In fact, some texts provide formulas and tables that enable us to translate one effect size statistic into another.

For example, an ES of .60 always equals a correlation of .287, and an ES of 1.0 always equals a correlation of .447. Which to use depends primarily on whether you want to envision mean group differences in terms of standard deviation units on a normal curve. You should be familiar with both approaches to effect size so that you will not be mystified when you encounter studies that report effect sizes in different ways.

An important word of caution is needed here. Notice that we have been careful not to say that effect size statistics indicate which intervention had "better" outcomes. We have said that effect size statistics indicate which intervention had stronger effects on its particular outcome variable and which explained more variation in its outcome variable, but this is very different than saying which intervention had a *better* outcome.

Suppose one intervention has an ES of 1.0 in respect to reducing *less severe* forms of verbal spouse abuse during a *brief* postintervention measurement period, and another has an ES of .6 with respect to *extremely severe* physical spouse abuse during a *lengthy* postintervention measurement period. Conceivably, the latter intervention is more valuable than the former, despite its lower ES, since its ES was assessed in connection to a more severe form of spouse abuse and over a longer period. The process of deciding which intervention is preferable involves value judgments and other considerations that we will examine in the next two sections. Effect size is only one of several important issues to consider in that process.

Strong, Medium, and Weak Effect Sizes

It is often useful to interpret our effect sizes in terms such as "weak, medium, or strong." That way, they take on added meaning relative to other research findings and other explanations. But interpreting some effect sizes can be a tricky business. For example, an *r* of .30 when squared equals .09, indicating that the independent variable is explaining 9% of the variation in the dependent variable.

We often have a reflexive tendency to attach the same meanings to these percentages as we attach to our exam scores, seeing percentages above 70% or 80% as strong and anything much lower as weak. Although these benchmarks may be applicable to studies of measurement reliability, using them as general guideposts to distinguish strong and weak relationships is incorrect.

As an illustration of this point, consider research on the causes of mental illness. There is a large, diverse array of factors that can contribute to the causation of mental illness, factors about which there remains great scientific uncertainty. If a study were to find that 20% of the variation in whether or not an individual becomes mentally ill is explained by one factor, then there would probably be widespread agreement that this was a very "strong" relationship relative to other findings in this field of study. Indeed, it might be called a major discovery.

For another example, let's return to our hypothetical child-abuse illustration. Suppose our experiment found a 40% recidivism rate for 100 treated cases and a 60% recidivism rate for 100 untreated cases. We would find that for this relationship the phi statistic would equal .20. Squaring phi, we would conclude that 4% ($.20 \times .20 = .04$) of the variation in recidivism is explained by whether or not the intervention was provided. Because we would have explained only 4% of the variation in recidivism, would we conclude that this was a weak relationship? While we might not all give the same answer to that question, we probably would agree that there is no one mathematically correct answer to it. Four percent may seem small at first glance, but what about the fact that our intervention reduced the child-abuse recidivism rate by 20%, which is a 33% reduction because 20% is one-third of 60%? Also, what if prior experimental research had found that alternative interventions had a weaker or even no impact on recidivism rates?

Consider also the fact that if our hypothetical experiment were to find a 35% recidivism rate for treated cases versus a 65% recidivism rate for untreated cases, then calculating the relationship magnitude would reveal that only 9% of the variation in recidivism rates is being explained. Yet the recidivism rate for untreated cases would nearly double the rate for treated cases. Clearly then, a percentage (such as 9%) that may seem small in contexts like a grade on a test or as a reliability coefficient is not necessarily small in the context of explaining variation in some dependent variables.

In this connection, Cohen (1977) argues that an ES of about .5, in which about 6% of the dependent variable variance is explained, should be considered to be of medium strength, noting that .06 is the percentage of variation in height explained by age group if we compare 14- and 18-year-old girls. It also applies to the difference in mean IQ between clerical and semiskilled workers. Cohen also argues that an ES of .8, in which about 14% of variation is explained, should be considered strong, noting that that amount applies to the difference in the mean IQ between college graduates and persons with only a 50-50 chance of passing in a high school academic curriculum.

Cohen deems as weak an ES of about .2, in which about 1% of dependent variable variance is explained. Yet Rosenthal and Rubin (1982) point out that a new intervention that improves a treatment success rate from 45% to 55% would have a correlation of only .10, which, when squared, indicates that only 1% of the variance in outcome is explained by whether or not the new intervention was received. Noting that the increase from .45 to .55 might be very important when the increase is in such outcome indicators as survival rates or cure rates, they argue that the value of some interventions with "weak" effect sizes is often underestimated.

Recently some researchers have begun to develop *empirical* guidelines for interpreting the relative strength of relationship magnitude statistics. In one classic study, Smith and Glass (1977) calculated the mean ES of nearly 400 controlled evaluations of counseling and psychotherapy and found it to be .68, which is equivalent to an r of .32 and an r^2 of .10 (which means that on average 10% of dependent variable variance was explained). Several years later Haase, Waechter, and Solomon (1982) found that the median strength-of-association value for research reported during the 1970s in the *Journal of Counseling Psychology* was .08, meaning that on average 8% of dependent variable variance is explained by the independent variable. Earlier, Hamblin (1971) estimated a comparable figure of .10 for sociological research. In 1985 Rubin and Conway reported analogous figures based on their survey of the social work research literature. For the social work research literature as a whole, the median relationship magnitude statistic was .13; for evaluations of the effectiveness of clinical interventions, it was approximately .10. Thus, if a future evaluation of the effectiveness of a clinical social work intervention finds a statistically significant relationship in which the intervention explains more than 10% of the variance in the dependent variable, then that relationship can be said to be stronger than the average statistically significant relationship found in clinical social work outcome research.

More recently, Lipsey (1990) reported 102 mean effect sizes calculated in studies that reviewed psychological, educational, and behavioral treatment effectiveness research. The midpoint of these 102 mean effect sizes was .45, which corresponds to an r^2 of .05. This is lower than the figures found for psychotherapy, counseling, and clinical social work interventions and is closer to the figure for medium effects suggested earlier by Cohen.

The preceding findings on average effect sizes can provide approximate benchmarks that can be useful in interpreting effect sizes in future research. It seems reasonable to say that interventions whose effect sizes explain approximately 5% to 10% of outcome variance are about as effective as the average intervention reported in published evaluations. Before squaring, the correlation coefficients of these "average" interventions would be in the neighborhood of .23 to .32. Their ES would be about .45 to .68.

But it is important that we reiterate the caution that an intervention's effect size, alone, does not indicate its value. An intervention with a stronger effect size is not necessarily "better" than an intervention with a weaker effect size. For example, an intervention that reduces the rate of child abuse or school dropout among high-risk individuals from 55% to 45% may be more valuable to society than an intervention that reduces the annual turnover rate among Big Brother/Big Sister volunteers from 60% to 40%. Or, returning to an example we used earlier, an intervention that reduces the rate of extreme physical abuse from 55% to 45% might be deemed more valuable than an intervention that reduces the rate of mild verbal abuse from 65% to 35%. Determining which intervention is "better" or more valuable involves considering the substantive significance of research findings, an issue which we shall take up next.

Substantive Significance

Measures of the strength of a relationship do not automatically indicate the **substantive significance** of that relationship. By the substantive significance of a relationship we mean its *importance* from a *practical standpoint*. No matter how strong a relationship may be—no matter how well it compares to an average effect size or how close to 1.0 it may be in a measure of association—we still can ask whether it constitutes a substantively important or a trivial finding.

Let's consider this issue in connection to the child abuse example we used earlier in this chapter. Suppose one intervention makes the difference between a 35% and a 65% recidivism rate. Assuming that the finding was statistically significant, how substantively significant is that finding? That is, how much practical importance does it have for the field? Suppose another experiment finds that a different intervention with the same target population makes a statistically significant difference

between a 20% recidivism rate and an 80% rate. Assuming that the two interventions were equal in terms of cost, time, and so on, determining which was the more substantively significant finding would seem to be a fairly straightforward process, and we would choose the one with the 20% recidivism rate. That is, because everything else but relationship magnitude was of equal importance, the stronger relationship would be the more substantively significant relationship.

But suppose a different experiment finds that after five years of daily psychoanalysis that costs $500 per week, 80% of treated abusive parents as compared to 20% of untreated parents say they agree with Freud's ideas. Which intervention would you find to be more valuable if you were providing services to that target population: the one that made a 30% difference in child-abuse recidivism, or the one that made a 60% difference in agreement with Freud's ideas? We hope you would deem the weaker relationship involving the intervention that reduced child abuse by 30% to have more substantive significance than the stronger relationship pertaining to attitudes about a theory. (Not that there is anything wrong with psychoanalysis per se; we would say the same thing about any theory in this practical context.)

The preceding admittedly extreme hypothetical comparison illustrates that there is not an automatic correspondence between the strength of a relationship and that relationship's substantive significance. It is important to know how much variation in the dependent variable is explained by the independent variable and how that figure compares to the amount of variation previously explained in other, comparable studies that used comparable variables. But not all studies are comparable in practical importance.

Therefore, after we have ascertained the statistical significance of a relationship and measured the strength of the association, we must make subjective value judgments in order to gauge the substantive significance of that relationship—value judgments that might take into consideration such intangibles as the importance of the variables and problem studied, whether the benefits of implementing the study's implications are worth the costs of that implementation, what prior knowledge we have about the problem studied and how to alleviate it, and so on. If we judge that the study addresses a trivial problem, assesses trivial variables, reports results that imply actions whose costs far outweigh their benefits, or yields findings that add nothing to what is already known, then we might deem observed relationships to be trivial even if they explain a relatively large amount of variation in the dependent variable. To reiterate, it is necessary to consider all three issues: statistical significance, strength of relationship, and substantive significance.

Main Points

• Inferential statistics help rule out chance as a plausible explanation of our findings; thus, combined with our consideration of design issues, they help us decide whether we can generalize, based on our findings, about populations or theoretical processes.

• Statistical significance testing identifies the probability that our findings can be attributed to chance. Chance, or sampling error, represents a rival hypothesis for our findings—a purely statistical hypothesis called the null hypothesis.

• Tests of statistical significance utilize theoretical sampling distributions, which show what proportion of random distributions of data would produce relationships at least as strong as the one observed in our findings. The theoretical sampling distribution thus shows the probability that observing the relationship we observed was due to the luck of the draw when and if no such relationship really exists in a population or in a theoretical sense.

• The probability that the observed relationship could have been produced by chance is compared to a preselected level of significance. If that probability is equal to or less than that level of significance, then the finding is deemed statistically significant and the plausibility of the null hypothesis (chance) is refuted.

• Social researchers traditionally tend to use .05 as the level of significance, but that is merely a convention. A higher or lower level can be justified depending on the research context. When .05 is used, a finding that is significant at the .05 level is one that could not be expected to result from the luck of the draw, or sampling error, more than 5 times out of 100.

• When testing directional hypotheses we can use one-tailed tests of significance. These locate the critical region of significant values at one, predicted end of the theoretical sampling distribution.

• When testing nondirectional hypotheses, we must use two-tailed tests of significance. These place the critical regions at both ends of the theoretical sampling distribution.

• Type I errors occur when we reject a true null hypothesis. Type II errors occur when we accept a false null hypothesis. Every decision based on statistical significance testing risks one error or the other.

• Increasing sample size reduces the risk of a Type II error, but the larger the sample, the greater the likelihood that weak relationships will be statistically significant.

• Measures of association, such as correlation coefficients and analogous statistics (phi, rho, Cramer's V, gamma, eta, and so on), assess how strong a relationship is. The stronger the relationship, the closer the measure of association statistic will be to 1.0 or −1.0. The weaker the relationship, the closer it will be to zero. Many measures of association are based on a proportionate reduction of error (PRE) model and tell us how much error in predicting attributes of a dependent variable is reduced by knowledge of the attribute of the independent variable. Many measure of association statistics can be squared to indicate the proportion of variation in the dependent variable that is explained by one or more independent variables.

• Statistics that portray the strength of association between variables are often referred to by the term *effect size*. Effect-size statistics might refer to proportion of dependent variable variation explained or to the difference between the means of two groups divided by the standard deviation.

• Statistical significance, relationship strength, and substantive significance must not be confused with one another. Statistically significant relationships are not necessarily strong or substantively meaningful. Strong relationships are not necessarily substantively significant, and some seemingly weak relationships in which only a small percentage of dependent variable variance is explained can have great substantive significance. The substantive significance of a finding pertains to its practical or theoretical value or meaningfulness; it cannot be assessed without making value judgments about the importance of the variables or problem studied, what the finding adds to what is already known or not known about alleviating a problem, and so on.

Review Questions and Exercises

1. Here are some really silly hypotheses you can test at the beginning of class or while relaxing in the student lounge:

a. Firstborns are more likely to have an odd number of letters in their first name than later-borns.

b. Firstborns are more likely to have an odd number of letters in their middle name than later-borns.

c. Firstborns are more likely to have an odd number of letters in their last name than later-borns.

d. Firstborns are more likely to be brunettes than later-borns.

If you test these hypotheses among about 20 or 30 students and find that for one or more of the hypotheses the proportions are not exactly equal for firstborns and later-borns, what does that signify? What would it mean if you tested the statistical significance of your results and found that the probability of getting the results due to chance, or sampling error, was .04? Would you conclude that the hypothesis was really true and could be generalized? Or would you conclude that despite the significance it would be wrong to generalize. If the latter, what type of error would you be making if you generalized? Should you use a one- or two-tailed test of significance?

2. Deal a deck of cards into two piles of four cards per pile. Do this 20 times, subtracting the number of red cards in the left-hand pile from the number in the right-hand pile each time. After each deal, record the difference in the percentage of red cards between the two piles. Construct a theoretical sampling distribution based on those 20 differences in percentages. Next, repeat this process, but this time deal out 20 cards in each pile. Compare the two sampling distributions. Which has the greater degree of dispersion (that is, the greater degree of sampling error)?

Suppose each red card represents a student who stayed in school and each black card represents a dropout. If the left-hand pile represents high-risk students who received school social work services, and the right-hand pile represents their control group counterparts, what do these two theoretical sampling distributions illustrate regarding the influence of sample size on statistical significance? What do they illustrate about the importance of refuting the plausibility of chance?

Additional Readings

Blalock, Hubert M., Jr., **Social Statistics** (New York: McGraw-Hill, 1972). An excellent introductory textbook. One of our favorites. It is clear, well organized, and understandable. Describes statistical methods frequently used by social workers and offers guidelines for when to use each.

Jendrek, Margaret Platt, *Through the Maze: Statistics with Computer Applications* (Belmont, CA: Wadsworth, 1985). An innovative, practical introduction to social statistics. Jendrek explains the logic of various statistical techniques and then illustrates how the reader can calculate them with simple computer programs or through the use of systems such as SPSS^x.

Weinbach, Robert W., and Grinnell, Richard, *Statistics for Social Workers* (New York: Longman, 1991). Another excellent introductory statistics textbook. This one attempts to simplify complicated statistical concepts and procedures, tries to avoid mathematical terms, and is filled with social work examples.

Inferential Data Analysis: Part 2

What You'll Learn in This Chapter

Continuing our discussion of statistical analysis,
we'll examine the probability of avoiding Type II
errors, the use of meta-analysis, the functions
of alternative statistical tests and what is
involved in selecting them, and problems
and issues in the use of inferential statistics.

INTRODUCTION

Now that you understand the concept of statistical significance and the need to consider relationship strength and substantive significance as well, let's cover some additional, more advanced material on inferential statistics. We'll begin by looking at how you can assess the probability of avoiding Type II errors.

STATISTICAL POWER ANALYSIS

In Chapter 16 we defined Type I and Type II errors and discussed the importance of both types of errors. We noted that tests of statistical significance assess the probability of making Type I errors. We indicated that researchers can reduce the probability of making a Type II error by increasing their sample size, but we did not discuss how you can assess exactly how much of a risk of making a Type II error they take in any particular study. Assessing that risk is very important, but we saved that topic for this chapter because an understanding of measures of association and effect size is required in order to assess the risk of making Type II errors. Assessing the probability of making Type II errors is called **statistical power analysis.** Statistical power analysis is an often-neglected, but terribly important, area of inferential statistics. It can be an extremely complex topic from a mathematical standpoint, and most introductory research or statistics texts in the social sciences barely mention it. But recognition is growing of the importance of this topic and the erroneous conclusions that are risked by its frequent neglect in social research studies. We think it is essential that you have a conceptual grasp of this topic so that you will be able to use available power tables to guide decision making about sample size and your interpretation of findings that are not statistically significant. For a more thorough treatment of this topic, including its mathematical underpinnings, we refer you to an outstanding book titled *Statistical Power Analysis for the Behavioral Sciences* by Jacob Cohen (1988).

Statistical power analysis deals with the probability of avoiding Type II errors. That is, it assesses the probability of *correctly* rejecting a null hypothesis that is *false*. Recall that statistical significance testing tells us only the probability of *incorrectly* rejecting a null hypothesis that is *true*. In other words, significance testing tells us only the probability of committing a Type I error, whereas power analysis deals with the probability of committing a Type II error.

Historically, social scientists, including social work researchers, have virtually ignored the probability of committing Type II errors in reporting their studies. They routinely accept a .05 risk of a Type I error regardless of, and seemingly unaware of, the risk of committing a Type II error. Implicitly, they seem to assume that Type I errors are the only ones really worth worrying about. In a review of social work research, for example, Orme and Combes-Orme (1986), performing their own calculations on the results reported in the studies they reviewed, found that almost half of the studies took greater than a .20 risk of committing a Type II error for relationships equivalent to a correlation of .30—relationships of medium strength in which $r^2 = .09$. That magnitude of relationship would be found, for instance, if 35% of treated cases as compared to 65% of untreated cases recidivated. Thus, some studies that conclude that tested interventions or programs are ineffective might be incorrectly labeling as failures interventions or programs that in reality have substantively important effects.

It's our guess that the neglect of this issue can be understood largely as a function of the neglect of statistical power analysis in the education of researchers, the self-perpetuating tradition of neglect of it in the literature, the mistaken notion that Type I errors are always many times more serious than Type II errors, and the incorrect perception that it is not feasible to estimate and reduce the risk of committing Type II errors. Assuming that we already have sufficiently illustrated the importance of Type II errors, let's look now at the feasibility of estimating and reducing the probability of committing them.

Mathematically calculating the risk of committing a Type II error is far too advanced a topic for this book, and we refer you to Cohen's text for that material. Fortunately, however, we can estimate that risk without performing calculations. We can do this simply by examining statistical power tables that Cohen constructed based on such calculations. What we find in statistical power tables is the power of statistical significance tests for varying levels of significance, sample sizes, and relationship magnitudes. Cohen's book provides such tables for various types of significance tests.

Drawing from the figures in Cohen's tables, Table 17-1 displays the power of testing the significance of correlation coefficients at the .05 and .10 levels of significance for small, medium, and large effect sizes. This table can be used to plan a research study even if your significance test does not involve correlation coefficients because the figures in Cohen's tables for other types of significance tests are approximately the same as in Table 17-1. If you desire more precision, we encourage you to obtain Cohen's book and examine his (more detailed) tables.

In using Table 17-1 to plan a research study, the first step is to choose a significance level. (If you choose the .01 level, you will need to examine the tables in Cohen's book.) The next step is to estimate the strength of the correlation (which is one form of effect size) between your independent and dependent variables that you expect exists in the population. The columns in the table pertain to small ($r = .10$; $r^2 = .01$), medium ($r = .30$; $r^2 = .09$), and large ($r = .50$; $r^2 = .25$) effect sizes. (If you want to assess the power for a different effect size—say .20, .40, or larger than .50—you will need to consult Cohen's book. But you probably will be satisfied using Table 17-1, as you will see.)

Of course, you have no way of knowing before collecting your data what the effect size in the population really is, or if a relationship exists at all, but you can identify a figure that approximates your expectations. For example, earlier we noted that Rubin and Conway (1985) identified an r^2 of .10 as the average strength of significant relationships found in clinical social work outcome research. (You may recall that this effect size corresponds to the medium ES of .60 when using means and the standard deviation to calculate effect size.) Therefore, if that is your area of study and you expect that your hypothesis is true, you might expect to find an r^2 of about .10. Thus, you would use one of the columns for medium effect size in Table 17-1.

Each figure in that column is the probability (imagine a decimal point before each figure) of correctly rejecting the null hypothesis for a .30 population r at different levels of sample size. The different sample sizes are listed in the column headed "Sample Size."

Recall our earlier discussion of the effects of sample size on statistical significance. Note how the probability of rejecting the null hypothesis increases as sample size increases. For example, if your sample size is only 10 cases, and your significance level is .05, your probability of correctly rejecting the null hypothesis is only .13. That is, your statistical power would be only .13. That would mean that you would have a probability of 1.00 minus .13, or .87, of incorrectly accepting a false null hypothesis. The latter probability of .87 would be your probability of committing a Type II error.

But if your sample size is 40 cases, then your power would be .48. Still, however, you would have a .52 probability (1.00 − .48 = .52) of committing a Type II error. In order to have a .20 probability of committing a Type II error (Cohen recommends .20 as a maximum), your power would have to be .80 (which we find by subtracting .20 from 1.00). To obtain at least that level of power your sample size would have to be 90 cases. (More precisely, your power for 90 cases would be .83. If you consult Cohen's book, you will find that 84 cases will give you a power of exactly .80.) If you want your probability of committing a Type II error to equal your probability

Table 17-1 Power of Test of Significance of Correlation
Coefficient by Level of Significance, Effect Size, and Sample Size[a]

SAMPLE SIZE[a]	.05 SIGNIFICANCE LEVEL			.10 SIGNIFICANCE LEVEL[b]			SAMPLE SIZE[a]
	EFFECT SIZE			EFFECT SIZE			
	SMALL	MEDIUM	LARGE	SMALL	MEDIUM	LARGE	
	$r = .10$ $r^2 = .01$	$r = .30$ $r^2 = .09$	$r = .50$ $r^2 = .25$	$r = .10$ $r^2 = .01$	$r = .30$ $r^2 = .09$	$r = .50$ $r^2 = .25$	
10	06	13	33	11	22	46	10
20	07	25	64	13	37	75	20
30	08	37	83	15	50	90	30
40	09	48	92	16	60	96	40
50	11	57	97	18	69	98	50
60	12	65	99	20	76	99	60
70	13	72	*	22	82	*	70
80	14	78		23	86		80
90	16	83		25	90		90
100	17	86		27	92		100
200	29	99		41	*		200
300	41	*		54			300
400	52			64			400
500	61			72			500
600	69			79			600
700	76			84			700
800	81			88			800
900	85			91			900
1000	89			94			1000

[a]The figures in this table are approximately the same as for tables on chi-square tests (with a 2 by 2 table) and t-tests. For t-tests, the number of cases in each group, added together, would approximate the sample size in this table.

[b]The figures at each level of significance are for a two-tailed test; however, the power figures at the .10 level approximate the power of one-tailed tests at the .05 level.

*Power values below this point exceed .995.

The figures for this table were derived from tables in Cohen, Jacob, *Statistical Power Analysis for the Behavioral Sciences,* 2nd ed., Lawrence Erlbaum Associates, Inc. 1988.

of committing a Type I error (that is, to be at .05), your statistical power will have to be .95, and to obtain that level of power you will need a sample size of more than 100 cases (140 cases is the precise figure in Cohen's book).

In short, by using this table, you can select a sample size that will provide you with the level of risk of a Type II error that you desire. But what if it is impossible to obtain a sample that big? Suppose you plan to survey all the social workers in a rural area where the population of social workers numbers only 50. Table 17-1 indicates that your statistical power is only .57 for $n = 50$, $r = .30$, and a significance level of .05. Thus, your probability of committing a Type II error would be .43 (1.00 – .57). It's probably not worth all the expense and effort to do a study when you know in advance that even if your research hypothesis is true you are taking almost a 50-50 risk of coming up with an incorrect conclusion, despite the fact that your risk of a Type I error is only .05. In that case, because you cannot increase your sample size, one reasonable alternative would be to lower your risk of committing a Type II error by increasing your risk of committing a Type I error.

For example, you might decide to raise your significance level from .05 to .10. Then you would consult the column under the .10 significance level in Table 17-1. In the column for a medium effect size and a .10 significance level, you would find that your power would be .69 (as compared to .57 for the .05 significance level) for $n = 50$. Thus, by raising the risk of a Type I error to .10, you would reduce the probability of a Type II error to .31 (1.00 – .69). You might still conclude that that is too great a risk to warrant doing the study. But if you did decide to pursue it, taking risks of .10 and .31 for the two types of errors might make more sense than taking risks of .05 and .43.

Ideally, of course, you would find some way to increase your sample size—perhaps by including another geographic area in the study—in order to have an acceptably low risk for both types of errors. Also, whatever you decided to do about your study and its sample size would be decided in light of the risks involved. It is mind-boggling to imagine that many researchers are implementing studies without taking statistical power analysis into account; consequently, they don't know the odds that they are spinning their wheels trying to confirm hypotheses that, even if true, have a low probability of being supported.

Imagine, for example, that you are evaluating the effectiveness of a school social work program in an inner-city high school that you think will reduce dropout rates from 55% to 45%. As we indicated in Chapter 16, this reduction would correspond to a correlation of .10 (.01 when squared), which in Table 17-1 is found in the column for a small effect size. To have statistical power of .80 (and therefore a .20 probability of committing a Type II error) you would need a sample size of approximately 800 cases if you chose a .05 significance level, or about 600 cases if you chose a .10 significance level.

Although statistical power analysis has its greatest utility when conducted on an a priori basis—that is, while your study is still being designed—it also has value on a post hoc basis after you fail to reject the null hypothesis. When reporting null findings, it is important to inform readers of the probability that, in failing to reject the null hypothesis, you are committing a Type II error. This is true regardless of whether your power analysis was conducted before or after your study. Before readers dismiss your hypothesis as one that failed to be confirmed, they should be informed of the probability that your failure to support it resulted from a Type II error. The importance of this is perhaps most obvious when new interventions are being tested for problems for which we know of no other effective interventions.

Before leaving this topic, let's reiterate a point made earlier in order to clarify an aspect of statistical power analysis that may seem confusing. How can statistical power analysis tell us in advance the probability of incorrectly failing to reject a false null hypothesis when we have no way of determining in advance whether the null hypothesis is false or true? The answer to this question is that statistical power analysis does not tell us in advance the odds that we *will* reject a false null hypothesis; the probability it gives us tells us only the odds that we will reject the null hypothesis *if it really happens to be false*. In other words, when using statistical power analysis, we begin by saying, "*Suppose* the null hypothesis really is false and that a relationship of a certain strength (we also specify the particular strength that we are assuming) really does exist in the population. *If that is so*, what is the probability that we will obtain findings that are statistically significant were we to use a given sample size and significance level?"

META-ANALYSIS

In light of the preceding material on both Type I and Type II errors, you would be correct in supposing that relying exclusively on the results of any one study to guide you in your practice can be precarious. Any one study might be making a Type I or a Type II error. One study with a very small sample, for example, might obtain statistically insignificant results for an intervention with a moderate effect size. Another study of the same intervention, but with a much larger sample, might obtain statistically significant results with a smaller effect size.

If you have ever reviewed the research literature on a particular topic (perhaps as part of your work in preparing a term paper), you know that different studies tend to come up with different findings about the same topic or research question. One study, for example, might find that case management has strong effects, while a second study might find that it has weak effects. Several studies might find that case management has medium effects, while some might find that it has no effects. Another study might even find that it has harmful effects.

Different studies tend to come up with contrasting findings for a variety of reasons, not all of which are statistical reasons. Differences in re-

search design and the ways data are collected is one common reason. In studies of intervention efficacy, different studies might come up with contrasting findings because they operationalize the intervention in different ways, because they differ with respect to the background characteristics of the client groups comprising their samples, or because they used different ways to measure outcome. Sometimes studies that seem almost identical come up with different findings simply due to sampling error and chance fluctuations.

It is not easy to draw conclusions from a bewildering array of inconsistent findings across different studies on the same topic. And yet it may be of great utility to try to figure out some way to make some general statement about how effective an intervention seems to be in light of all the studies taken as a whole. Suppose, for example, you are planning a new service delivery program and are torn between emphasizing case management services versus an alternative service delivery approach. You review the research literature evaluating the effectiveness of each approach, hoping to learn whether one approach by and large tends to be more effective than the other. If you were able to conclude that in light of all the studies case management tended to have an effect size of ES = .70, while the alternate approach tended to have an ES of .25, you might find that to be an important reason for favoring a case management approach in your planning deliberations.

A method for simplifying the process of drawing conclusions from a bewildering array of inconsistent findings across different studies on the same topic is called **meta-analysis.** Although the term *meta-analysis* sounds complicated, its underlying meaning is not. It simply involves calculating the mean effect size across previously completed research studies on a particular topic. Meta-analysis emerged in the late 1970s, when Smith and Glass (1977) reported their classic meta-analysis (which we mentioned earlier) showing that the mean ES of nearly 400 controlled evaluations of counseling and psychotherapy was .68. In other words, Smith and Glass read the many studies, recorded the ES found in each study, added up all the ES's, and then divided the sum by the number of ES's they recorded to determine the average ES across all the studies.

Meta-analyses need not be limited to the calculation of mean effect sizes; some statistically complex meta-analytic procedures can be used to calculate the statistical significance of an overall set of results aggregated across various studies. The latter procedures are less commonly used than those that just focus on aggregating effect sizes (Fischer, 1990).

Fischer (1990) found more than 300 meta-analyses conducted during the 1980s on such topics as psychotherapy in general, cognitive therapy, family therapy, deinstitutionalization, and so on. Almost all of these meta-analyses were done in fields related to social work, but only two were found in social work per se: one on social work practice in mental health (Videka-Sherman, 1988) and one on adolescent drug prevention programs (Tobler, 1986).

In his excellent review of meta-analysis, Fischer identifies its benefits. One of the most important benefits is something we have already been discussing: By providing mean effect sizes, meta-analysis gives us benchmarks that are useful in considering the relative strengths of effectiveness of various interventions. A related benefit of meta-analysis is its ability to identify relationships across studies. For example, in addition to calculating overall mean effect sizes for broad intervention approaches, we can see how the mean effect size varies depending on various clinical or methodological factors.

Despite these benefits, meta-analysis has many critics and is a very controversial procedure. One of the most serious criticisms is that researchers conducting meta-analyses might lump together studies that are methodologically strong with those that have serious methodological limitations and treat their results equally in the analysis. Thus, if two studies with very weak internal validity report effect sizes of 1.0 for a particular intervention, and one very strong experiment reports an effect size of zero for the same intervention, a

mean effect size of .67 will be reported in the meta-analysis (1 + 1 + 0, divided by 3). Critics argue that this is misleading because the finding of the methodologically strong study may be the only one that is valid, and therefore the only one that should guide the selection of practice interventions.

An example of this controversy appeared in the social work literature in the late 1980s. Lynn Videka-Sherman (1988), in her meta-analysis of social work practice effects in treating chronic mentally ill clients, reported that shorter-term treatments produced better effect sizes than longer-term treatments. This conclusion irked Gerard Hogarty, a social worker who had devoted his career to experimental research on the treatment of individuals with chronic mental illness. Hogarty had pointed out time and again in his research findings, and in reviewing the experimental research of his colleagues, that chronic mental illness tends to be a lifelong affliction requiring long-term care.

In his critique of Videka-Sherman's meta-analysis, Hogarty (1989) argued that Videka-Sherman's finding resulted largely from her inclusion of one study whose methodology did not apply to the comparison of short- versus long-term treatment effects. That study used a cross-sectional design and found that service users were much more likely to be rehospitalized than nonusers, with a very large negative effect size of −1.97. A negative ES indicates harmful effects. If one study finds a negative ES of −1.97, and another study finds a beneficial positive ES of +1.97, the mean ES of the two studies will be 0 (no effects). Hogarty argued that this finding was due to a selectivity bias, in which the treatment users were more impaired than the nonusers, and that Videka-Sherman was wrong to view the individuals who had no treatment as having had shorter term treatment than the more severely impaired individuals who received some treatment.

Hogarty went on to show how Videka-Sherman's meta-analysis would have had the opposite conclusion if it had included only studies with strong experimental controls. In criticizing this and various other findings of the Videka-

Sherman meta-analysis, Hogarty argued that "effect sizes from the better designed studies frequently were overwhelmed [in calculating mean effect sizes and correlations between effect size and treatment factors] by effect sizes from reports of lower quality that unduly influenced judgments of effective practice" (1989:363).

In attempting to handle the preceding criticism, some meta-analysts have rated the methodological quality of studies and then used that rating as a factor in their meta-analyses. The reliability and validity of those ratings, however, is open to question. Rather than include studies of varying methodological quality, and then rating their quality, some meta-analysts simply exclude studies with poor methodologies. However, there is no guarantee that their methodological judgment will be adequate in this regard (Fischer, 1990).

Another potential pitfall in meta-analysis involves sampling bias. Fischer (1990) explains how sampling bias can result from two problems: (1) the reviewer may have missed some important studies (as Hogarty claimed that Videka-Sherman did) and (2) much research is not published. The latter problem may make meta-analysis particularly vulnerable to coming up with biased findings because studies that do not support the effectiveness of tested interventions may be less likely to be submitted for, or accepted for, publication than are studies with positive results. Therefore, studies with positive findings may be more likely to be identified by meta-analysts than are studies with negative findings.

In light of all these problems, therefore, perhaps the best advice to readers of meta-analyses, at least for the time being, is "caveat emptor!" ("let the buyer beware!").

SELECTING A TEST OF STATISTICAL SIGNIFICANCE

As we mentioned early in the previous chapter, there are many alternative ways to calculate statistical significance. In fact, new tests are continually being developed, and it is unrealistic to expect to have a deep understanding of all of them. In this section we will focus on the criteria for selecting from among the tests that are commonly used in social work research. Our treatment of this topic will be kept to the conceptual level. We will not delve into the computational formulas or mathematical derivations of each statistical test.

Like measures of association, significance testing can be calculated by using computers. Our priority here will be knowing which test to run on the computer, not learning how to do the calculations yourself. But, again, we encourage you to pursue your studies in this area beyond this book and to examine the texts we'll recommend at the end of this chapter. The more you learn about the mathematical derivations and calculations associated with each test of significance, the richer will be your conceptual understanding of each test.

The prime criteria influencing the selection of a statistical significance test are: (1) the level of measurement of the variables, (2) the number of variables included in the analysis (bivariate or multivariate) and the number of categories in the nominal variables, (3) the type of sampling methods used in data collection, and (4) the way the variables are distributed in the population to which the study seeks to generalize. Depending on a study's attributes regarding these criteria, a selection will be made between two broad types of significance tests: *parametric tests* and *nonparametric tests*.

The term *parametric test* is derived from the word *parameter*. A parameter is a summary statistic that describes an entire population, such as the mean age of all abusive parents in the United States or the standard deviation in their income. **Parametric tests** assume that at least one of the variables being studied has an interval- or ratio-level of measurement, that the sampling distribution of the relevant parameters of those variables is normal, and that the different groups being compared have been randomly selected and are independent of one another. Commonly used parametric tests include the *t-test, analysis of variance,* and *Pearson's product-moment correlation.*

Nonparametric tests, on the other hand, have been created for use when not all of the assumptions of parametric statistics can be met. Most do not require an interval or ratio level of measurement and can be used with nominal- or ordinal-level data that are not distributed normally. Some do not require independently selected samples. The most commonly used nonparametric test is *chi-square*.

The *chi-square* statistical test is used when we are treating both our independent and dependent variables as nominal-level, such as in our hypothetical example in Chapter 16 relating the provision of treatment (yes or no) to child abuse recidivism (yes or no). It was used to calculate the probabilities displayed in Tables 16-1 and 16-2. The chi-square test assesses the extent to which the frequencies you observe in your table of results differ from what you would expect to observe if the distribution was created by chance.

Thus, if 100 recidivists and 100 nonrecidivists were randomly divided between two groups, we would expect to observe 50 recidivists and 50 nonrecidivists in each group. The greater the deviation between that expected split and the observed split, the greater will be the value of the chi-square statistic. For example, if we observed a 40/60 split for treated cases and a 60/40 split for control cases for a sample size n of 200, the computer would calculate a chi-square value of 8.0 and would indicate that that value is significant at the .01 level.

Whether a particular chi-square value is statistically significant depends on something called *degrees of freedom*. The number of degrees of freedom you have depends on how many categories are in each variable, and it is equal to one less than the number of categories in one variable times one less than the number of categories in the other variable. This may be written as $(r - 1)(c - 1)$, where r is the number of categories in the row variable and c is the number of categories in the column variable. Once you know chi-square is 8.0, or whatever value it happens to be, you must look that value up in a table that shows what chi-

square values are significant for what degrees of freedom. Appendix F shows that for one degree of freedom (df), which we would have in our recidivism example (2 row categories minus 1 times 2 column categories minus 1), we would need a chi-square value of at least 6.6349 to be significant at the .01 level. Because our chi-square value of 8.0 exceeds that figure, our finding would be statistically significant at .01. If you have access to a statistical computer program, your computer will take everything into account and determine the significance for you. You won't need to calculate chi-square or degrees of freedom or to consult a table of chi-square values. But it is still useful to know what steps the computer is taking for you, and we again encourage you to consult one of the statistics texts we'll recommend later in order to develop a deeper understanding of these processes.

Now let's review the commonly used parametric tests we mentioned above. We'll start with the **t-test.** The *t*-test is appropriate for use when we have a dichotomous nominal independent variable (that is, a variable with only two categories, such as when we compare treated and untreated cases) and an interval- or ratio-level dependent variable. Thus, if we were comparing treated and untreated cases in terms of the number of abusive incidents, we would use the *t*-test instead of chi-square because the number of abusive incidents, unlike the nominal variable of recidivism (yes/no), is at the ratio level of measurement.

When you use the *t*-test, your computer will calculate a *t* value based on a complicated formula that divides the difference between the means of the two groups on the dependent variable by an estimate of the standard deviation of the theoretical sampling distribution, which itself must be calculated using a complicated formula that takes into account the sample size and standard deviation of each group in your sample. Despite the complexity of the formula, the function of the *t*-test ultimately is the same as any other significance test: to ascertain the probability that the observed relationship was due to sampling error, or chance. And like other significance tests, once you calculate the t value, you must take into account the degrees of freedom and then locate in a table of t values the probability that your finding was due to the luck of the draw. In a t-test, the degrees of freedom will equal your total sample size (summing across both groups) minus 2. Thus, for our example of two groups of 100 abusive parents each, our degrees of freedom would be 198 (200 − 2). Also like other significance tests, your computer will take all of this into account and determine the probability of a Type I error for you. Once you run your computer program, all you have to do is look at that probability figure to know whether or not the relationship is statistically significant.

Another parametric test is **analysis of variance,** abbreviated ANOVA. This test uses the same logic as the t-test and, if used when a t-test could have been used, will generate the same probability value as the t-test. ANOVA can be used to test for the significance of bivariate and multivariate relationships. When testing bivariate relationships, the only difference between it and the t-test is that the t-test can be applied only when the nominal independent variable is dichotomous. ANOVA, on the other hand, can be used when the independent variable has more than two categories. (The dependent variable still must be interval- or ratio-level.)

Thus, if instead of just comparing one treatment group to one control group we wish to compare the outcomes of three or more different treated or untreated groups, we would use ANOVA instead of the t-test. Its formula is even more complicated than the t-test's formula. It produces a statistic called the F value, which one compares to a table of significant F values, just as one does with other statistical tests. Ultimately, we want to know, based on that F value, the probability that the differences between our groups (on an interval- or ratio-level dependent variable) are due to chance. ANOVA will ascertain that by comparing those *between* group differences to the variation *within* each group. Again, our computer

will tell us the probability that the null hypothesis is true, just as it will when we use any other significance test.

Each of the preceding two parametric tests, the t-test and ANOVA, apply when the independent variable is nominal. The other commonly used parametric test, the *Pearson product-moment correlation* (r), is used when both the independent and dependent variables are at the interval or ratio level of measurement. We discussed this statistic in Chapter 16 as a measure of association and alerted you to the fact that it can also be used in testing for statistical significance.

When testing r for statistical significance we ask: assuming there is no correlation between these two variables in the population (that is, $r = 0$), what is the probability of finding the correlation we found in a randomly drawn sample from that population as big as the sample we randomly selected? In other words, what is the probability that the null hypothesis ($r = 0$) is true for the entire population and that the correlation we found in our sample occurred just because of the luck of the draw, or sampling error? To find this probability, we look at a table showing what r values (between 0.0 and 1.0) are statistically significant for different sample sizes and different levels of significance. That table of significant values is constructed applying a complicated extension of the ANOVA formula for independent variables with indefinitely large numbers of categories. Again, our computer will not only calculate r for us, but it will also tell us the probability that the null hypothesis (that is, the hypothesis that $r = 0$ for the population) is true. In other words, with the push of a few buttons we will learn both the strength of the observed relationship and whether or not it is statistically significant.

Multivariate Analyses

So far, our discussion of statistical inference has been kept at the bivariate level. Inferential statistical tests also have been developed for **multivariate analyses.** A commonly used extension of correlational analysis for multivariate inferences is *multiple regression analysis.* Multiple regression analysis shows the overall correlation between each of a set of independent variables and an interval- or ratio-level dependent variable. That multiple correlation is symbolized by a capital R, which is the multiple correlation coefficient. As with bivariate correlational analysis, by squaring R we find the proportion of variance that is explained in the dependent variable. But whereas r^2 represents the proportion of variation explained by one independent variable, R^2 represents the proportion of variation explained by the entire set of independent variables.

For example, Rubin and Thorelli (1984) reported a multiple regression analysis that sought to explain variation in the duration of service among social service volunteers. Their analysis included 22 variables that might explain duration of service, including such factors as the volunteer's gender, age, ethnicity, socioeconomic status, family obligations, residential mobility, prior experiences, reasons for volunteering, and benefits expected from volunteering. The R value for the entire set of 22 variables was .56, which means that 31% (.56 squared equals .31) of the variation in duration of service was explained by all 22 variables acting in concert.

Multiple regression also calculates a statistic called the *standardized regression coefficient,* or *beta weight,* for each predictor variable. The higher the beta weight, the greater is the relative effect of the particular predictor variable on the dependent variable when all other predictor variables are controlled. Multiple regression also tests the statistical significance of each beta weight, thus identifying which particular predictor variables are *significantly* related to the dependent variable *after controlling for all other predictor variables.*

In the Rubin and Thorelli study the only significant predictor variable, and the one with the highest beta weight, was the extent of psychic benefits (such as client gratitude, volunteers' sense that they made a big difference in someone's life, and so on) that volunteers expected to derive from their volunteer work. The less they expected, the longer they lasted as volunteers. That variable alone—when the effects of all the other 21 predictor variables were controlled—explained 18% of the variation in duration of service. Thus, its partial correlation coefficient was .43 (the square root of .18). The proportion of variation in duration of service attributable to all the other 21 variables combined was only 13%.

Partial correlation coefficients have the same meaning and uses as their bivariate counterparts, with one prime difference: they measure the association between two variables after other, extraneous variables have been controlled. That is, they express the degree of a relationship at constant levels of the extraneous variables that are controlled. Their significance can be assessed as well, just as with bivariate correlations.

A multivariate statistic that is analogous to multiple regression analysis, but which is designed for use when the dependent variable is dichotomous, is called *discriminant function analysis.* Discriminant function analysis produces the same sorts of statistics as does multiple regression analysis. The statistics have different names from the ones used in multiple regression analysis, but their inferential uses are essentially the same.

In their 1988 article in the *Schizophrenia Bulletin,* Bartko and his associates provide an excellent discussion of the functions of multiple regression analysis and related multivariate statistics—a discussion geared to mental health practitioners who are consumers of research but who lack a strong background in statistics. They use Venn diagrams, reproduced in Figures 17-1 and 17-2, to illustrate the logic of multiple regression analysis.

In Figure 17-1 we see three overlapping circles. The middle circle represents the variance of a dependent variable, which we'll call variable Y. The other two circles represent two independent variables, X_1 and X_2, which are each associated with the dependent variable, Y, but not with each other. Each of the circles for the two independent variables shares a relatively large area of variance with circle Y. For the purpose of simplicity, each

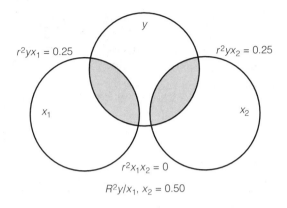

Figure 17-1 Illustration of Two Predictor Variables X_1 and X_2 Correlating with the Response-Dependent Variable Y but Not with Each Other, Resulting in a Larger R^2

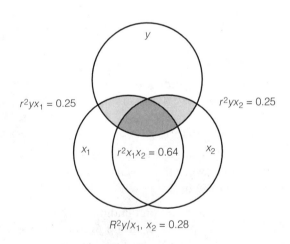

Figure 17-2 Illustration of Two Predictor Variables X_1 and X_2 Correlating with the Response-Dependent Variable Y and with Each Other, Resulting in a Lower R^2

SOURCE FIG. 17-1, 17-2: J. J. Bartko et al., "Statistical Issues in Long-Term Follow Up Studies," *Schizophrenia Bulletin*, 14(4), 1988, pp. 575–587. Used by permission of the National Institute of Mental Health.

has been made to share 25% of the variance of Y. Thus, X_1 and X_2 each has a correlation (r) of .50 with Y, which when squared (r^2) indicates that each accounts for 25% of the variance in Y. Together, the two independent variables cumulatively account for 50% of the variance in Y, which we get by adding the two shaded areas of Y, each of which is 25% of Y. In other words, we are saying that the two independent variables combined have a Multiple R^2 of .50, meaning that they explain half of the variation in Y and that the other half is unaccounted for (that is, it is due to other factors not studied).

Figure 17-2 resembles Figure 17-1, but with an important difference: this time the circles for the independent variables overlap with each other in addition to their overlap with Y. In this example, therefore, there is a relationship between the two independent variables. Both X_1 and X_2 have a .50 correlation with Y, and they have a .64 correlation with each other. If we look only at the bivariate correlation of X_1 with Y or X_2 with Y, we would say that either variable, when examined alone in relation to Y, explains 25% of the variation in Y. But because X_1 and X_2 in this case also overlap with each other, the multiple R^2 of Y with the two independent variables is not simply a sum of the r^2 of X_1 with Y and the r^2 of X_2 with Y. We must subtract the area of three-way overlap between X_1, X_2, and Y, which is represented by the darkest shading. Using multiple regression calculations we would find that when the darkest area of three-way overlap is subtracted, the multiple R^2 of Y with X_1 and X_2 drops to .28. Because of the large overlap (correlation) between X_1 and X_2, in other words, those two variables together account for only an additional 3% of the variation in Y beyond the 25% that each alone accounted for.

Suppose our multiple regression analysis added a third variable, one that overlapped with the lighter shaded area of X_2 and Y. To the extent that that variable had three-way overlap with X_2 and Y, it would further reduce the importance of X_2 as a factor in explaining Y. In other words, the importance of X_2 in explaining Y—which seemed quite important with a bivariate r of .50—would diminish as the other variables were controlled.

Additional Nonparametric Tests

As we said at the outset of our discussion of significance tests, there are so many statistical tests—and so many new ones continually being developed—that it is unrealistic to try to be very knowledgeable about all of them. Earlier we discussed the most commonly used ones in social work research. Before leaving this topic we'll just briefly identify some of the other types of tests that you might encounter. We again encourage you to consult the texts we'll recommend at the end of this chapter if you wish to become more knowledgeable about these tests.

Occasionally you will encounter situations or studies in which a nonparametric test other than chi-square is needed. For example, sometimes our sample size is too small to use the chi-square test. A test that is like chi-square, but which was designed for use when the sample is too small for chi-square, is called the *Fisher's exact test*.

Another example pertains to before-and-after designs in which the same sample is used for the "before" and "after" data on the same nominal variable and the two groups of data being compared (that is, the "before" data and the "after" data) are related. This violates one of the assumptions of the chi-square test. In its place, therefore, the *McNemar nonparametric test*, which was designed for such situations, can be used.

Other nonparametric tests have been designed for use with ordinal data. These include the *Mann-Whitney U test*, the *median test*, the *Kolmogorov-Smirnov two-sample test*, and the *Wilcoxon sign test*. Textbooks covering nonparametric statistics, as well as some statistical software manuals for computers, will tell you more about when to use each of these tests. As with all the other statistical tests we've discussed, ultimately your computer can do all your calculations and provide you with the probability that the observed relationship was due to chance. No matter which test you use, that probability level will have the same meaning as the one we have been discussing throughout this chapter and the previous chapter.

COMMON MISUSES AND MISINTERPRETATIONS OF INFERENTIAL STATISTICS

Inferential statistics are commonly misused and misinterpreted by the producers and consumers of social research. These errors are common across social science disciplines, not just in social work research. In this section we will summarize those errors, most of which we already alluded to in the earlier sections of this chapter and the previous chapter.

Our discussion of statistical power analysis identified one common mistake in the use and interpretation of inferential statistics: *the failure to consider statistical power*. This error can have one or more of the following unfortunate consequences:

1. Conducting a study with a sample size so small that the probability of obtaining statistically significant results, even if the null hypothesis is false, is so small that the study is not worth doing.

2. Wasting resources by selecting a sample size that is much larger than needed to have an adequate level of statistical power.

3. Failing to interpret null findings (insignificant findings) in light of statistical power and consequently overlooking the probability that a Type II error accounts for the lack of support for the research hypothesis.

A related error is the *mistaken notion that failure to reject the null hypothesis means the same thing as verifying it*. Results that fall short of statistical significance may still have a relatively low probability of having been caused by chance, or sampling error. This is especially problematic with near-significant results and low statistical power.

Conversely, it is incorrect to interpret a rejection of the null hypothesis (that is, when results are statistically significant) as a confirmation of the research hypothesis. *The null hypothesis is a statistical hypothesis only.* As such, it deals only with chance as a rival hypothesis, not with alternate explanations associated with measurement error or errors in the research design. In this connection, you should not be so impressed by the sophistication of a study's statistical analysis or the significance and strength of its findings that you become less vigilant about nonstatistical sources of methodological error and bias. Do not let fancy-schmancy *statistical procedures camouflage serious nonstatistical methodological limitations.* To draw appropriate inferences from a study, we must consider how all facets of its methodology bear upon our ability to generalize from its findings, not just the role of chance.

Even when a relationship is statistically significant and a study's methodology is relatively flawless, *we must remember to distinguish between statistical significance and relationship strength.* Failing to make this distinction is an error commonly made by both the producers and consumers of research. A statistically significant relationship is not necessarily a strong one, and weak relationships can be statistically significant given a large enough sample size.

A related error commonly made by both producers and consumers of research alike is the *failure to distinguish substantive significance from either statistical significance or relationship strength.* Statistically significant relationships may or may not be meaningful from a substantive, or practical, standpoint. Even when statistically significant relationships are strong, they may contain variables that are substantively trivial.

Let's look now at an error that we haven't yet mentioned in this or the previous chapter, but one that has become quite worrisome in this high-tech

computer age. Now that researchers can complete many different inferential analyses of their data just by pressing a few buttons on a computer keyboard, they have become increasingly vulnerable to unwittingly *inflating the probability of committing a Type I error by conducting multiple bivariate tests of significance.* Suppose, for example, that a research team separately tests 20 different bivariate relationships using the .05 level of significance each time. Suppose further that they find that only one of the relationships is statistically significant at the .05 level. Should they reject the null hypothesis? The answer to this question is no, they shouldn't. Here's why.

When we set our significance level at .05, we are recognizing that for every 100 statistically significant relationships observed, 5 are produced by chance. It also means that for every 100 tests of hypothesized relationships that do not really exist in a population or in a theoretical sense, 5 will turn out to be statistically significant in our findings just due to the luck of the draw. As explained earlier, that's what we mean when we recognize that with statistically significant findings we take a .05 risk of committing a Type I error. Five out of 100 equals one out of 20. Thus, if we run 20 separate significance tests, we can expect to find about one that will be "significant" due just to chance.

To illustrate the preceding point, imagine that a voluntary social welfare organization where you work sponsors a "Las Vegas Night" to raise funds, and you volunteer to operate a roulette wheel with 20 numbers on it. Suppose the payoff odds for betting on the correct number are 15 to 1. (The odds favor the house in order to raise funds!) Suppose some jokers come along and insist that they be able to spin the wheel 20 times instead of once to try to win a 15 to 1 payoff on their one bet. You wouldn't let them because you intuitively recognize that the odds apply to one spin of the wheel only. The odds that their number will come up get better the more spins they take, and after 20 spins you would expect that their number probably will come up at least once. The precise probability that their number would come up once in 20 spins is .64 (better than 50-50).

For exactly the same reason, researchers take more than a .05 risk of committing a Type I error if they run multiple, separate significance tests of bivariate relationships. For every 20 separate tests they run at the .05 level of significance, the probability of committing a Type I error with just one "significant" finding is really .64, not .05. The more separate bivariate tests they run, the greater is their real probability of committing a Type I error. The .05 level applies only to the case in which only one test is run.

This does not mean that researchers should never test more than one relationship per study. It just means that if they wish to test more than one, they must recognize and deal with the potential this has for inflating their real risk of committing a Type I error. Perhaps the simplest way to resolve this problem is to use what is termed the *Bonferroni adjustment*. This involves reducing your significance level by dividing it by the number of separate bivariate tests of significance being run. Thus, if your initial significance level is .05, and you want to run 20 bivariate tests, you would divide .05 by 20, and then use the dividend of .0025 as your significance level for each test.

Another way to overcome this problem is by selecting one of the appropriate advanced, multivariate tests of significance that tests various hypotheses simultaneously and adjusts for the multiple comparisons in calculating the probability of committing a Type I error. Earlier we mentioned two such tests: multiple regression analysis and discriminant function analysis. (Other advanced tests, such as multivariate analysis of variance, are beyond the scope of this book, but research reports will usually inform the reader if any was used to avoid inflating the probability of committing a Type I error.)

A risky alternative would be to conduct the multiple bivariate tests and hope that so many of them are statistically significant that the probability of that happening due to chance is still quite slim (like seeing your number come up in the majority of spins of the roulette wheel). A less risky alternative would be to interpret the "significant" bivariate findings, not as verification of the tested relationships, but rather as a basis for hypothesizing that the "significant" relationships exist. Then we could see if the significance of that reduced number of relationships is indeed replicated in a subsequent study. In other words, you could conduct multiple significance testing with an exploratory purpose: to generate those hypotheses that merit further testing.

But *one of the worst sins* that can be committed after conducting an analysis of many different variables in order to discover which variables are significantly related is to turn around after completing such a "fishing expedition" and claim that the "significant" relationships were the hypotheses that were really being tested in the first place and to then interpret the findings as a verification of those hypotheses.

The various errors that can be made in the use and interpretation of inferential statistics offer another reason to consider the complementarity of quantitative and qualitative methods (which we have been discussing at the end of most previous chapters). This point is illustrated in the box "Type III Errors and the Role of Qualitative Inquiry."

TYPE III ERRORS AND THE ROLE
OF QUALITATIVE INQUIRY

In this chapter as well as the previous one you've been reading a lot about Type I and Type II errors, and you may have trouble keeping them straight. Here's a simple mnemonic device for keeping them straight.

Associate the issue with the words, *gullible* and *skeptical*, in alphabetical order. Type I: you gullibly conclude that the statistically significant relationship in your data is genuine, when it was really due to chance. Thus, you might gullibly conclude that listening to Barry Manilow music causes delinquency when a weird sampling fluke (that is, chance) produces a significant difference in which most of the particular delinquents you happen to study say they listen to his music regularly while most of the nondelinquents respond, "Barry who?" (You mistakenly reject a true null hypothesis.) Type II: You skeptically conclude that there is no genuine relationship, when there really is one. Thus, you might skeptically conclude that eighth-graders are not more likely to listen to gangsta rap music than are senior citizens because the probability that your results were due to chance was slightly above the .05 level. (You therefore fail to reject a false null hypothesis.) Now that you can keep Type I and Type II errors straight, we want to add a third: Type III errors. A Type III error means asking the wrong research question, or solving the wrong research problem, in the first place (Miller and Crabtree, 1994). One common way quantitative studies commit Type III errors—a way particularly germane to inferential statistics—is by testing the wrong hypothesis or by operationally defining a variable in

the hypothesis in the wrong way. Here's a hypothetical example to illustrate Type III errors and the role of qualitative inquiry in dealing with them or avoiding them. Suppose you are studying *caregiver burden*, a term that refers to the toll taken on people who care for loved ones suffering from chronic, debilitating illnesses like Alzheimer's disease (AD), AIDS, or profound mental illness. Suppose you postulate that the weaker the informal support systems (close relatives, close friends, and so on) nearby to give caregivers emotional encouragement and respite, the greater the degree of caregiver burden that will be experienced. You conduct a cross-sectional study and find that a moderate and statistically significant relationship exists between your two variables. Because your findings are statistically significant, you are risking a Type I error, but not a Type II error. Then a colleague points out that the caregiver burden scale you used to operationally define your dependent variable has items in it that quantify the strength of the informal support system. In other words, the operational definitions of the two variables overlapped, and your hypothesis therefore was really a tautology, a foregone and irrelevant conclusion, since the strength of the informal support system was quantified in both your independent and dependent variable. You have committed what some call a Type III error, and your statistically significant finding has little value to the field. Some qualitative methodologists argue that you would have been less likely to complete an entire study on the wrong variables had your study been more open-ended, flexible, and inductive. A qualitative approach, they argue, would enable you to learn incrementally about the most relevant variables and their deeper meanings and would enable you to adjust your inquiry as you go along, rather than be stuck throughout the entire study with the operational definition you selected in advance.

Suppose you are planning to develop a support group intervention in which caregivers can meet weekly to receive information you provide, discuss their situation, and give each other suggestions and emotional support. You are wondering whether the nature of the intervention needs to vary depending upon the type of illness the loved one has. Relatedly, you are wondering whether each group should consist exclusively of caregivers whose loved ones have the same type of illness. You conduct a cross-sectional survey and find no statistically significant differences across illness types in the degree of caregiver burden (using the same caregiver burden scale as above). You decide, based on these findings, not to individually tailor the intervention to specific illness types. You wonder whether in failing to reject the null hypothesis you may be committing a Type II error. You discuss this with your colleague (an insomniac who lately has been reading up on qualitative inquiry at bedtime), and she suggests that you need to worry more about a Type III error than a Type II error. "Just because the different groups have the same amount of burden," she says, "doesn't imply that the nature of the burden or its deeper meaning is the same across different illness types."

You decide to follow her suggestion and conduct an in-depth qualitative inquiry, relying on open-ended interviews, with a handful of caregivers in each illness type. You find that your colleague was right; although each group

seems to be experiencing comparable *levels* of burden, its deeper *meanings* are different for each group. The caregivers of people with AD, for example, are more likely to be burdened by the physical demands of caregiving and by the conflicting emotions they experience in having to care for someone who can't remember who they are or appreciate their sacrifice. The caregivers of people with mental illness are more likely to be emotionally burdened by the blame they feel implicit in some mental health professionals' views that their family dysfunction is in part responsible for the illness. The caregivers of persons with AIDS are more likely to be burdened by the shame they irrationally feel about their loved one's illness and the need to keep the illness a secret from their friends and relatives, due to society's unjustified stigmatization of people with AIDS and those in close contact with them. These findings convince you to individually tailor the intervention to specific illness types, the opposite implication of your quantitative findings.

Suppose you evaluate the effectiveness of your support group intervention for persons with AIDS, assessing whether their burden scale score decreases after intervention more than a comparison group. Suppose the difference in the decrease between the two groups is in the predicted direction, seems to be of a meaningful magnitude, but is not statistically significant. Again you wonder about a Type II error, especially since you had a small sample, and again your colleague reminds you of Type III errors. In this instance, the Type III concern has to do with the fact that the burden scale you used was developed for caregivers in general, and has nothing in it about stigma.

A qualitative inquiry with participants in both groups, again relying on open-ended interviews, might help you resolve your doubt about both Type II and Type III errors. Suppose, for example, the participants in the comparison group discussed experiencing the same high levels of stigma throughout the study period, whereas virtually all of the participants who had received your interevention talked about how the support group empowered them to no longer keep the nature of their loved one's illness a secret from friends and relatives. Suppose they said that although the physical burden of caregiving was still the same, and although the tragic impending loss of their loved one at such a young age continued to exert a serious emotional toll on them, they experienced the support group as immensely helpful in lifting the extreme stigma that had been burdening them.

Qualitative data like these would tell you that perhaps the support group intervention was more effective than depicted by your quantitative data, since the quantitative measure did not address stigma. Thus, you might strongly suspect that a Type III error would be made by relying exclusively on the quantitative data. Moreover, the qualitative evidence in which support group recipients reported feeling immensely helped in overcoming social stigma might give you further reason to suppose that your intervention really was effective, and that a serious Type II error would be committed were you to dismiss or ignore its potential effectiveness. Of course, a better scenario would have been to conduct your qualitative interviews in a pilot study before designing your quantitative analysis. Had you done so, you may have anticipated the need to include a measure of stigma in your quantitative evaluation and, consequently, have come up with more meaningful and conclusive quantitative findings.

CONTROVERSIES IN THE USE OF INFERENTIAL STATISTICS

When we think of statistics, we tend to think of mathematics and logic—topics that we tend to associate with right and wrong answers. Consequently, neophyte researchers are often surprised to learn that there are some basic issues in the use of inferential statistics about which even the foremost authorities on statistics disagree. As you read professional journals, you will occasionally notice a study that used a statistical procedure that seems to violate certain statistical assumptions—perhaps applying a parametric test when the data seem to warrant a nonparametric test. Sometimes you will notice intense debates among authors about the appropriateness of the statistical procedure used by one of them.

A thorough treatment of unresolved statistical issues that continue to be debated by statistics luminaries would require material far too advanced and lengthy for the purposes of this text. But in this concluding section of this chapter, we do want to introduce you to the chief issues being debated in a way that will help you to avoid feeling so overwhelmed by these debates that they immobilize your utilization of inferential analyses.

A common theme cutting across various ongoing controversies in inferential analysis involves the violation of assumptions that underlie some or all of the tests of statistical significance. Where one stands in these controversies seems to be connected to whether one thinks statistical significance is supposed to provide a sufficient and precise proof of the probability of error in generalizing from a sample to a population or whether it is viewed less rigidly as merely a first step—just one approximate guideline—in considering what can and cannot be inferred.

At one extreme are those who believe that statistical significance is irrelevant and misleading unless all of the assumptions of the chosen significance test have been met, including the assumption of perfectly random sampling or random assignment. For example, if a study that did not use random sampling (or even if random sampling was used but there were some missing data on one of the variables being tested) were to report statistically significant findings at the .05 level, members of this camp would argue that because the sampling was not strictly random, we really have no basis for saying that there is a .05 probability that the findings are generalizable to the population.

If we agree that the point of significance testing is to provide *sufficient* grounds for making precise inferences about the probability of correctly generalizing from a sample to a population, then it is difficult to dispute the preceding argument. But another camp makes the distinction between inference based on statistical tests of significance and inference based on design issues. Members of this camp see testing for statistical significance as a first step in the inferential process, but it is not a sufficient step. Design issues—issues regarding sampling techniques, measurement error, and so on—must also be considered. Those with this point of view do not expect significance tests to "prove" that the precise probability that the research hypothesis is true is the significance level. Rather, the significance level is interpreted only as the probability that the *null* hypothesis is true—that the result can be attributed to chance. Having ruled out chance, our inferential analysis is far from over. We must then use our informed judgment about other obstacles to the generalizability of our findings—obstacles connected to flaws in the overall research design.

If we have the more rigid and ambitious expectations—that statistical inference is considered sufficient and the significance level must reflect the exact probability that our research hypothesis can be correctly generalized to a population—then any violation of statistical assumptions may be unacceptable. But if we view the significance level as merely a useful guideline for an appropriate cutoff point for dismissing the plausibility of chance, recognize that a host of design issues must also be considered, and consider that even the best significance level is no more than a judgment call, then it is easier to live with violations of the statistical assumptions of significance tests.

Ironically, those with the more ambitious expectations of statistical significance tests may be the ones least likely to use them and most likely to fault others for using them. This is because feasibility constraints in social work research make it so difficult to meet all the assumptions of statistical significance tests, especially regarding perfectly random sampling with no missing data whatsoever on tested variables. In light of this reality, others argue that there is no reasonable alternative to combining inference based on statistical significance and inference based on design.

Another issue over which statisticians disagree has to do with applying tests of significance when data have been gathered from an entire population rather than a sample. Some argue that significance testing applies only to generalizations about a population based on statistics gained from a sample. Their central point is that with an entire population, unlike a sample, we have no sampling error. Therefore, testing to see if our findings can be attributed to sampling error is both inappropriate and unnecessary. Any relationships we observe in our findings, no matter how weak, can be generalized to the population because our data came from the entire population. The relationships observed in population data may vary with regard to their strength and substantive significance, but they are automatically significant in the statistical sense and thus can be generalized, for because there is no sampling error there is no probability of a Type I error.

Others, however, argue that there are some instances when significance testing with populational data is both necessary and appropriate. Those who advance this point of view do not deny the essential logic of the preceding point of view, but rather cite an exception to it. That exception occurs when we seek to go beyond learning whether two variables are related in a population in a descriptive sense and wish to infer the likelihood that the independent variable really helps us to explain the variation in the dependent variable. When the latter is the case, then significance testing might be done with population data in order to form inferences that one seeks to make about the *causal processes* that explain the dependent variable.

The function of significance testing with population data is not to see whether the observed relationship really exists in the population as a whole, but instead to determine the likelihood that its existence in the population is merely a function of random processes (as opposed to being evidence of some theoretical process). Blalock (1972) uses an example involving the 50 United States to illustrate this point. We'll borrow from his example and modify it somewhat to make it more relevant to social work.

Suppose a study of all 50 states finds that AFDC (Aid to Families with Dependent Children) payments are higher in those states whose names have an even number of letters than in those states whose names have an odd number of letters. If so, we wouldn't need significance testing in order to generalize this finding to the population of states. But who would argue therefore that having an even number of letters in a state's name plausibly plays a causal role in increasing AFDC payments and should be taken into account in developing theory about social welfare policy? Any time we look for a relationship in population data we are subdividing the population into various subsets according to the categories of our independent variable, not unlike dealing a population (deck) of 52 cards into two

or more piles. The odds are that we will find some differences on a dependent variable between some subsets, no matter how inane our independent variable may be. For example, after we randomly subdivide a deck of cards there may be no theoretical reason to suppose that one pile of cards will have, say, more hearts or diamonds or kings or queens than another pile. But nevertheless it is extremely unlikely that we would find no differences between the two piles. In the same sense, if we look for relationships in a population, the odds are that we will find some, just due to chance covariation among some of the variables. Significance testing identifies the probability that relationships observed in a population could have been generated by random processes (like shuffling and dealing a deck of cards), and therefore it enhances our consideration of the plausibility of the notion that the relationships we find reflect causal processes and therefore have potential theoretical value.

One's expectations about the role of statistical tests of significance and the precise meaning of the level of significance will influence one's stances about other statistical issues, as well. For example, some statisticians prefer parametric tests of significance over nonparametric tests even when the characteristics of the variables being tested call for the use of nonparametric tests. They may justify their preference based on the greater statistical power associated with parametric tests. Realizing that there is nothing sacred about the .05 level of significance—or any other level that might be chosen—they would prefer to trade precision in the probability of committing a Type I error in order to reduce their probability of committing a Type II error. Thus, if their findings are significant at the .05 level, they would recognize that their probability of making a Type I error is not exactly .05 because their data did not meet all the assumptions of parametric tests.

Whatever course of action researchers choose, the best statistical option would be debatable, and no mathematical formula will resolve the debate.

When analyzing your own data—so long as you understand the meaning and limitations of statistical inference as explained in these last two chapters—we encourage you to use whatever procedure you judge to be best in light of what you have learned and not to let these controversies immobilize you. Likewise, when you encounter research done by others that seems to be methodologically rigorous, we encourage you not to disregard it just because its inferential statistics violate some assumptions. Just as a sophisticated statistical analysis should not cause us to overlook design flaws, a debatable statistical analysis alone should not be sufficient grounds for disregarding the potential utility of an otherwise well-designed study.

Remember, the replication process ultimately should be used to verify the generalizations made in any particular study. Some would even argue that if the same finding is consistently replicated in study after study, then whether or not it is statistically significant in any or all of those studies is beside the point. Significant or not, it is unlikely that we would make a Type I or a Type II error in generalizing about the same finding replicated again and again. It might be the case that a persistent design flaw explains the result, but we would have a pretty good idea about the plausibility of chance as an explanation.

For example, suppose four studies all fail to get significant results at the .05 level, but for each one the probability of making a Type I error is .10. The probability of that happening due to chance four consecutive times is (.10) (.10) (.10) (.10), or .0001. Although each result by itself is not significant, the consistent replication of the same finding might reasonably predispose us to rule out chance as the explanation.

In fact, those who argue against using statistical significance tests unless all assumptions are met might also argue that the preceding type of replication would yield the same inferences even if none of the studies bothered to test the significance of their findings or to report the probability of committing a Type I error. For example, if

every study of a particular intervention finds that treated cases have a recidivism rate that is approximately 30% less than the recidivism rate of untreated cases, then after a large number of replications with the same result (assuming that we can rule out flaws in the research designs) we don't need to know whether any of the findings were statistically significant in order to infer that that particular intervention seems to reduce the recidivism rate by about 30%.

This concludes our chapters on data analysis. If some of the points in these chapters were too technical for you, don't be discouraged; you probably have a lot of company. You don't need to totally understand all of this material in order to contribute significantly to the research process or to utilize research intelligently. But if you would like to pursue some of these topics further, we encourage you to study the additional readings we will list shortly. And if you wish to peruse illustrations of how social workers have debated the statistical controversies we've been discussing these last few pages, we refer you to articles in the *Social Service Review* by Cowger (1984, 1985, 1987), by Rubin (1985a), and by Glisson (1987).

Main Points

• Statistical power analysis calculates the probability of avoiding a Type II error. It does so by calculating the probability of committing a Type II error and subtracting that probability from 1.0. The remainder is the statistical power. By consulting statistical power tables (in which the calculations have already been done for us) in planning our study, we can learn what sample size or significance level will be ideal in order to have the level of statistical power we desire. When we test hypotheses without first consulting statistical power tables, we risk having a low likelihood of obtaining findings that would support those hypotheses even if those hypotheses are true.

- Meta-analysis is a procedure for calculating the mean effect size across previously completed research studies in a particular field.

- There are many different tests of statistical significance, and the most appropriate one to use will depend primarily on the level of measurement of your variables, the number of variables in the analysis, sampling procedures, and the way the variables are distributed in the population. All of these tests ultimately will tell you the probability of committing a Type I error.

- Unresolved debates among authorities on inferential statistics pertain to the conditions under which significance tests can be used justifiably in light of the fact that some of their underlying assumptions are not being met.

Review Questions and Exercises

1. Find several explanatory research articles on a problem area that concerns you in a social work journal or an interdisciplinary journal. Bring them to class and critique them from the following standpoints:

a. If the null hypothesis was not rejected, did the author adequately address statistical power issues and the probability of committing a Type II error? If correlations are reported, locate in Table 17-1 the closest column heading to each correlation. Then locate the row corresponding to the sample size used in the study. Then locate the row/column intercept to identify the statistical power for a two-tailed test at the .05 significance level. Was that level of power adequate in your judgment (assuming a two-tailed test at the .05 significance level)?

b. If the null hypothesis was rejected, did the author seem to confuse statistical significance with relationship strength or substantive significance? Was any measure of association used? Or did the author stop the analysis once

statistical significance was assessed? How would you interpret the substantive significance of the findings?

2. Examine one of the articles (Fischer, 1973; Wood, 1978; Reid and Hanrahan, 1982; Rubin, 1985b) that reviewed practice effectiveness research, as discussed in the Prologue to this book. Consider the sample size (combining all experimental and control groups) of each reviewed study that failed to reject the null hypothesis (that is, each study that failed to support the effectiveness of the evaluated program or intervention). If the evaluated program or intervention really was correlated at the .30 level with the outcome variable, what probability would each of the studies have had of accepting the false null hypothesis (that is, of committing a Type II error)? This can be answered by using Table 17-1, as described in 1a above. Discuss the implications of this for social work practice.

Additional Readings

Bloom, Martin, Fischer, Joel, and Orme, John G. *Evaluating Practice: Guidelines for the Accountable Professional,* 2nd ed. (Boston: Allyn and Bacon, 1995). At the end of Chapter 10 we originally recommended this excellent, comprehensive text on the use of single-subject designs in evaluating one's own practice. We are mentioning it again here because it has several very helpful chapters on statistical approaches to the analysis of single-subject design data.

Cohen, Jacob, *Statistical Power Analysis for the Behavioral Sciences,* 2nd ed. (Lawrence Erlbaum Associates, Inc., 1988). The most thorough and clear explanation of statistical power analysis we know of. Filled with tables that simplify the determination of statistical power to guide decisions about sample size and significance levels in planning research. Cohen offers guidelines on relationship strength and elaborates on distinctions among statistical significance, relationship strength, and substantive significance. Mathematical formulas and derivations are also provided, along with excellent illustrative examples. Very readable—a must reference for serious researchers. Consumers of research, too, will find value in Cohen's simple formulas for calculating relationship strength when authors report only statistical significance.

Lipsey, Mark W., *Design Sensitivity: Statistical Power for Experimental Research* (Newbury Park, CA: Sage, 1990). Here is another excellent book on statistical power analysis. It also discusses meta-analysis and the impact of research design attributes on statistical power. Some of the material in this book is a bit advanced for students who do not have a strong background in statistics, but we recommend it highly.

Morrison, Denton, and Henkel, Ramon (eds.), *The Significance Test Controversy: A Reader* (Chicago: Aldine-Atherton, 1970). A compilation of perspectives—pro and con—on tests of statistical significance. The question of the validity, utility, or significance of tests of statistical significance reappears periodically in social science journals. Each reappearance is marked by an extended exchange between different points of view. This collection of such articles offers an excellent picture of the persistent debate.

The Social Context
of Research

This book concludes with a deeper examination of the social context of social work research. Because this topic is so important in social work research, we began examining it much earlier and continued to touch on it in many of the preceding chapters. In Chapter 3, for example, we discussed the ethics and politics of social work research and showed how ethical and political considerations can require that we compromise our plans to conduct scientifically "flawless" studies. We saw the importance of various, often subtle, ethical problems and the need to judge whether the long-term benefits of a study really outweigh the potential harm it may do by using ethically questionable research methods. In Chapter 4 we saw how practical, administrative constraints can require additional compromises.

In Chapter 18, we'll see how the term *program evaluation* overlaps heavily with social work research—much of what we call social work research could also be called program evaluation research. Consequently, this chapter deals less with the methods of program evaluation—methods we've been discussing all along—than with the ways the social context of program evaluation influences the implementation of the research methods and designs that you've studied in the preceding chapters. We'll also look at different types of program evaluation as well as steps program evaluators can take in order to alleviate resistance to program evaluation research.

Program Evaluation

What You'll Learn in This Chapter

This final chapter examines a use of social research that has grown rapidly during the last few decades: program evaluation. In addition to learning about different types and methods of program evaluation, you'll see how vested interests can influence the ways evaluation research is conducted and utilized, and you'll learn what evaluators can do about the highly politicized atmosphere in which program evaluation research is conducted.

INTRODUCTION

In recent years a field of research has grown that has heightened sensitivity to the political context of social research. This field is called *evaluation research,* or *program evaluation*. It refers to the purpose of research rather than to any specific research methods. Its purpose is to assess and improve the conceptualization, design, planning, administration, implementation, effectiveness, efficiency, and utility of social interventions and human service programs (Rossi and Freeman, 1982). Toward that end, program evaluation systematically applies many quantitative and qualitative research designs and methods—experiments, surveys, participant observation, and so forth.

At the start of this book we distinguished social work research from basic social scientific research by its purpose, citing the former's focus on practical knowledge that social workers need to solve the problems they confront in their practice and that agencies need to guide their efforts to alleviate human suffering and promote social welfare. In light of that focus, program evaluation—when applied to social welfare settings and issues—is conceptually very similar to social work research, and many of the research studies conducted by social workers have a program evaluation purpose. Because program evaluation has more to do with the purposes of research than with specific research methods, this chapter will focus more on the implications of those purposes for carrying out research than on particular methodologies or designs. Although we will examine some methodological material, it is important to recognize that throughout this book we have been discussing research methods that can be applied for program evaluation purposes.

HISTORICAL OVERVIEW

Although the growth of program evaluation is a fairly recent phenomenon, planned social evaluation is really quite old. Some authors have traced it back to 2200 B.C. in China and connected it with personnel selection (Shadish et al., 1991). Whenever people have instituted a social reform for a specific purpose, they have paid attention to its actual consequences, even if they have not always done so in a conscious, deliberate, or systematic fashion or called what they were doing program evaluation. In the mid-19th century, for example, the reform movement for more humane care of the mentally ill, led by Dorothea Dix, succeeded in getting states to build more public mental hospitals. Some superintendents of state mental hospitals contributed to such hospitals' growth by citing data that, they contended, indicated that state hospitals were succeeding in curing mental illness (Grob, 1973). Those superintendents were discharging 90% or more of their patients and claiming that this meant that they were achieving 90% to 100% cure rates! At that time notions of rehospitalization, relapse, and chronicity were not in vogue, and the superintendents therefore temporarily got away with using discharge from the state hospital as an operational definition of recovery from mental illness, although they didn't use the term *operational definition*. (Here we begin to see the importance of the political context of program evaluation, a theme that will pervade this chapter.)

More systematic approaches to program evaluation can be traced back to the beginning of the 20th century. Early efforts evaluated schools that used different teaching approaches, comparing educational outcomes by examining student scores on standardized tests. Several decades later experimental program evaluation studies examined the impact of worker morale on industrial productivity and the impact of public health education programs on hygienic practices. In the 1940s, after New Deal social welfare programs were implemented, studies examined the effects of work relief versus direct relief, the effects of public housing, and the effects of treatment programs on juvenile delinquency. Program evaluation received additional impetus during World War II, with studies such as Stouffer's (1949, 1950) research on soldier morale and the impact of personnel and propaganda policies on morale. After the war, large public expenditures were committed to programs attempting to improve housing, public health, attitudes toward minorities, and international problems in health, family planning, and community development. As expenditures grew, so did interest in data on the results of these programs.

Program evaluation became widespread by the late 1950s as efforts increased to alleviate or prevent social problems such as juvenile delinquency and to test out innovations in psychotherapy and new psychopharmacological discoveries. By the late 1960s textbooks, professional journals, national conferences, and a professional association on evaluation research emerged. This explosion of interest in program evaluation continued during the 1970s, as the public increasingly demanded evidence regarding the return on its investment in various programs to combat poverty, child abuse, substance abuse, crime and delinquency, mental illness, and so on. But by the late 1970s, after public funding for these programs waned, declines began in the funding of studies to evaluate them. This trend toward reduced funding of program evaluation accelerated during the 1980s, as federal evaluation offices were hit hard by the budget cuts of the Reagan administration (Shadish et al., 1991).

Although the government today provides less funding for program evaluation than it did before the 1980s, we still live in an "age of accountability," as liberals and conservatives alike demand that programs be more accountable to the public regarding whether they are really delivering what they promise to deliver. In fact, the need to evaluate may be greater when program funding is scarce than when it is abundant, since the scarcity of funds may intensify concerns that we not waste what little funds we have on ineffectual programs. In this connection, it is a mistake to assume that only fiscal conservatives—those reluctant to spend money on social programs—are the ones expressing skepticism about what "bang the pub-

lic is getting for its buck." Individuals of all political persuasions have this interest, including human service professionals who fiercely support increased social welfare spending but who are dedicated to finding better ways to help people and do not want to see scarce welfare resources squandered on programs that don't really help their intended target populations. In fact, a major group that has historically been a force in favor of greater accountability consists of consumer rights advocates concerned about whether clients—the consumers of our services—are being served properly.

As a result of these forces, and despite recent funding cuts, program evaluation today has become ubiquitous in the planning and administration of social welfare policies and programs. In fact, instead of having a program evaluator position, an agency might assign responsibility for program evaluation activities to personnel called planners or program analysts (Posavac and Carey, 1985). Funding sources still require both a program evaluation component as a prerequisite for approving grant applications and supportive evaluative data as a basis for renewing funding. But this requirement has been a mixed blessing. On the one hand, the requirement that programs evaluate their efforts induces agency personnel to support more research that could help us improve policies and programs and find better ways to help people. On the other hand, this requirement means that agency personnel and others have vested interests in the findings of that research.

THE POLITICS OF PROGRAM EVALUATION

Because the findings of evaluation research can provide ammunition to the supporters or opponents of a program, intense political pressure is introduced into the program evaluation process. Vested interests can impede the atmosphere for free, scientific inquiry. Instead of pursuing truth as scientifically as possible to improve human well-being, program evaluation efforts may be implemented in ways that fit perceived program maintenance needs. Sometimes this means that there will be intense pressure to design the research or to interpret its findings in ways that are likely to make the program look good. Other times it may simply mean that the program evaluation is conducted in the cheapest, most convenient way possible, guided by the belief that funding sources don't pay much attention to the quality of the research and just want to be able to say that the programs they fund have been evaluated. Consequently, it is naive to suppose that when administrators hire someone to be responsible for program evaluation activities or to conduct a specific evaluation, they will pick the person most qualified from a scientific, research methodology standpoint.

Political considerations—that the evaluation will be done to favor vested interests—may be a much higher priority. Indeed, it probably is not overly cynical to suppose that commitment to conducting the most scientific study possible sometimes will threaten administrators and be perceived as a problem. They are unlikely to admit as much; rather, they may call individuals with a devotion to methodological rigor "too ivory towerish and out of touch with the real world." (And sometimes they are correct—if zeal for methodological rigor blinds researchers and makes them insensitive to realistic feasibility constraints that make some methodological compromises appropriate and unavoidable.) Consequently, it's not unusual to see agencies fill program evaluation positions with people who lack any special proficiency in or dedication to research design, but who instead are good computer jocks—high-tech bureaucrats who can grind out evaluative data that will put the program in a favorable light and who will not make waves about academic issues like the internal or external validity of the evaluation.

When you are in a position in your career to participate in, conduct, or utilize program evaluations, you should not be naive about the potential influence of vested interests on the integrity or quality of evaluations. We will spend much of this chapter discussing that influence, because it is, in large part, what distinguishes program evaluation from other forms of social research. Nevertheless, it would be misleading to imply that *all* program evaluation is corrupt. Agency administrators and others with vested interests often have sufficient integrity and professional concern for learning the best ways to help clients that they are able to put their vested interests aside and act in a manner that fosters the most objective, scientific evaluation possible. While it may be naive to assume that all (or even most) evaluations will be immune from the political pressures applied by those with vested interests, it would be overly cynical to assume that all evaluations are politically biased. After you finish this chapter, we hope that your view of the politics of program evaluation is a savvy one—that you will be vigilant about the potential for the corrupting influence of vested interests, yet aware that despite this potential many objective and useful program evaluation studies have been done in the past and are likely to be done in the future.

In-House Versus External Evaluators

When program evaluators work for the agency being evaluated, they are called in-house evaluators. Program evaluators also might work for external agencies, such as government or regulating agencies and private research consultation firms (which often bid for government grants to evaluate programs receiving public funds). University faculty members also may secure research grants to evaluate programs or may simply wish to conduct applied research as part of their scholarly duties.

In-house evaluators are often thought to have certain advantages over external evaluators. They may have greater access to program information and personnel, more knowledge about program processes that might bear on the design of an evaluation or the meaning of findings, and more sensitivity to the research needs of the program and to the realistic obstacles to the feasibility of certain research designs or methods. They might also be more likely to be trusted by program personnel and consequently to receive better cooperation and feedback from them. But the flip side of the coin is that their commitment to the program, to their superiors, or to the advancement of their own careers might make them less objective and independent than external evaluators.

But it would be naive to suppose that external evaluators are never subjected to the same kinds of political considerations as are in-house evaluators. External evaluators may have strong incentives to get and stay in the good graces of the personnel of the program being evaluated. If they alienate those personnel, the quality of their evaluation may be imperiled by the lack of cooperation with the research agenda. In fact, one criterion for choosing the recipient of a program evaluation grant might be the quality of the relationship the evaluator has with the program and the potential of that relationship for securing cooperation from program participants.

Also, it is incorrect to assume that external sponsors of the evaluation are always more objective than in-house personnel. Perhaps the sponsors of the evaluation want to stop funding the program and need negative evaluation results to justify the cessation of funding to their own constituents. On the other hand, the sponsors might fret that negative results would make them (the sponsors) look bad and in turn threaten their own fundraising efforts.

One of the authors of this text (Rubin) has worked on several program evaluations that illustrate these points. In one, Congress allocated funds for demonstration programs with the stipulation that the funded programs be evaluated by external evaluators. But Congress did not stipulate anything further about the nature of the evaluation designs or how the external evaluators were to be selected. At a meeting in Washington, the federal bureaucrats encouraged recipients of their funding to utilize simple preexperimental designs and simplistic measures of program effects that are likely to generate favorable results. For example, they advocated simply assessing whether there was a 10% reduction in out-of-home placements of children from the year preceding the funded project's onset to the year after its implementation. They dismissed the need for design controls for threats to internal validity or for statistical controls for chance fluctuations. (Apparently, the bureaucrats were concerned with having Congress continue to fund their programs in the future.)

In an informal conversation at the meeting, one program evaluator, whose job security depended on securing contracts from programs to be their external evaluator, confided that he would not propose rigorous designs because he believed that such designs would scare off programs whose contracts he needed. Instead, he would propose uncontrolled, preexperimental pretest-posttest designs, using outcome measures that were vulnerable to practitioner bias and easy for programs to administer to their practitioners. He seemed to be having great success at the meeting, claiming to have secured "external" evaluation contracts from four program administrators who went to the meeting before selecting an evaluator.

Fiscal concerns impacted not only the evaluation designs employed, but led to attempts to influence the way findings were interpreted, since it was believed that the prospects for future funding are enhanced by obtaining favorable evaluation outcomes. This influence can be exerted in various ways, some more subtle than others. Evaluators can be told, for example, that if the program has a successful outcome, spinoff programs are likely to be funded, and the evaluator can receive the contract to be the "external" evaluator in those spinoff programs. Assuming additional program development further down the road, external evaluators may realize that staying in the good graces of the folks whose programs are being evaluated, and producing desired conclusions for those programs, can have significant long-term benefits for the evaluator's own job security, income, and career.

Another way to influence evaluators is by creating headaches for them when their evaluations are written in a manner program administrators do not like. External evaluators quickly learn, for example, that if they produce reports that reflect favorably on the evaluated program, program staff members are extremely unlikely to mobilize efforts to discredit the credibility of the evaluation or the competence of the evaluator. And they also learn that if their reports are not as positive as program staff desire, especially if those staff are worried about the impact of the evaluation findings on future funding, such mobilization efforts are likely to ensue, and the evaluator's standing with his or her employing agency might be seriously tarnished. A weak study with positive findings is unlikely to be attacked by program staff who stand to benefit by those findings. However, a strong study with a few relatively minor flaws is likely to be vilified by program staff who see the findings as threatening their funding prospects.

These things happen not just because there are good guys and bad guys. They happen because many program staff work hard to secure scarce funding for programs they believe are helping people. These program staff members may believe that even if we are unsure of the effectiveness of their programs we should keep investing funds in them and trying to improve them. Negative findings, they may fear, will simply lead to funding cutbacks with no opportunity to improve on current efforts. Some might argue, from a more cynical perspective, that some staff members are also concerned with enhancing the fiscal well-being of their own agency and the status of their own jobs. There probably is a good deal of truth in both points of view, keeping individual differences in mind.

Another illustration of these points occurred during the mid-1970s, when the Council on Social Work Education (CSWE) was awarded a research grant by the social work training unit of the National Institute of Mental Health (NIMH) to evaluate the community mental health curriculum of schools of social work. A prime purpose of the evaluation was to describe the different ways graduate schools of social work were implementing their NIMH training grants. At that time almost every master's degree program in social work was receiving many thousands of dollars annually to prepare students for practice in the field of community mental health, and the research project sought to identify community mental health curriculum innovations fostered by the NIMH grants.

The researchers were able to identify innovative community mental health curricula in some schools. But based on data gathered over a two-year period during multiple site visits to participating schools, they concluded that most schools of social work had initiated no curriculum innovations associated specifically with community mental health. Instead, their NIMH grant funds enabled them to expand their traditional curriculum, and they justified that practice on the grounds that everything that has always been taught in a school of social work is related to community mental health.

We might anticipate that faculty members and administrators in schools of social work would be upset with the preceding conclusion, which was included in the report of the evaluation (Rubin, 1979), because school personnel might fear that it would threaten continuation of NIMH funding for programs that used the funds to expand their regular programs without developing any special mental health curriculum. At the same time, we might also anticipate that the NIMH social work training staff would appreciate the candor of the report, thinking that they then could use the report to distinguish schools making appropriate use of NIMH funding from those that were not and to influence the latter schools to be more accountable to them. But as it turned out, according to CSWE administrators, the NIMH staff expressed more consternation about the findings than did anyone else.

Their fear was that bureaucrats in other units of NIMH—units that were in competition with social work for federal funds—could use the report as ammunition in their efforts to secure a bigger slice of the funding pie for their units at the expense of social work training. If that were to happen, not only would schools of social work receive less funding, but the staff of the social work training unit would lose status in the bureaucracy and see their own budget reduced.

So, you see, the web of politics in program evaluation can be widespread, and sometimes the external groups sponsoring an evaluation are not as independent and objective as we might suppose. In the foregoing example, the NIMH social work training staff were quite eager to get a report that would portray schools of social work as doing wonderfully innovative things with their NIMH funds, a report that they could then use to justify their own performance in allocating funds and monitoring their usage and in order to argue for more funding for their unit. And in choosing CSWE to conduct the evaluation, it is reasonable to suppose that they fully expected that a glowing report would be forthcoming because CSWE is funded and governed by representatives of schools of social work and because one of the main goals of CSWE is to lobby for greater funding for social work education. In fact, the CSWE administrative staff expressed displeasure with the report and tried to influence its author, a CSWE staff member, to modify the interpretation of the findings in order to depict more favorably the benefits of NIMH funding for schools of social work.

Utilization of Program Evaluation Findings

As the preceding discussion illustrates, the findings of program evaluation studies can affect jobs, programs, and investments. Beliefs and values are at stake as well. Consequently, political and ideological forces can influence whether and how program evaluation findings are utilized.

As president, Richard Nixon appointed a blue-ribbon national commission to study the consequences of pornography. After a diligent, multi-faceted evaluation, the commission reported that pornography didn't appear to have any of the negative social consequences often attributed to it. Exposure to pornographic materials, for example, didn't increase the likelihood of sex crimes. You might have expected liberalized legislation to follow from the research. Instead, the president said the commission was wrong.

Less dramatic examples of the failure to follow the implications of evaluation research could be listed almost endlessly. Undoubtedly every evaluation researcher can point to studies he or she conducted—studies providing clear research results and obvious policy implications—that were ignored.

There are three important reasons why the implications of evaluation research results are not always put into practice. First, the implications may not always be presented in a way that nonresearchers can understand. Second, evaluation results sometimes contradict deeply held beliefs. That was certainly the case with the pornography commission just mentioned. If everybody *knows* that pornography is bad, that it causes all manner of sexual deviance, it is likely that research results to the contrary will have little immediate impact. By the same token, people thought Copernicus was crazy when he said the earth revolved around the sun. Anybody could tell the earth was standing still. The third barrier to the use of evaluation results is *vested interests*.

Suppose a group of practitioners in a family service agency, after receiving extensive training (and indoctrination) in a new model of family therapy, succeeds in convincing their colleagues and superiors in the agency to let them form a new unit specializing in service delivery based on that model of family therapy. They are convinced that their services will be effective, and forming the new unit has significantly enhanced their prestige and autonomy in the agency. How do you think they are going to feel when your evaluation suggests that their program doesn't work? It is unlikely that they'll fold up their tent, apologize for misleading people, and return willingly to their old routines. It's more likely that they'll point out inescapable limitations in your research, call it misleading or worthless, and begin intense lobbying with colleagues and superiors to have the program continue.

Logistical Problems

The social context of program evaluation affects not only the utilization of the outcomes of evaluative studies but also the logistics involved in their implementation. *Logistics* refers to getting subjects to do what they're supposed to do, getting research instruments distributed and returned, and other seemingly unchallenging tasks. These tasks are more challenging than you would guess!

Motivating Sailors   When Kent Crawford and his colleagues (1980) set out to find a way to motivate "low performers" in the U.S. Navy, they found out just how many problems can occur. The purpose of the research was to test a three-pronged program for motivating sailors who were chronically poor performers and often in trouble aboard ship. First, a workshop was to be held for supervisory personnel, training them in effective leadership of low performers. Second, a few supervisors would be selected and trained as special counselors and role models—people the low performers could turn to for advice or just as sounding boards. Finally, the low performers themselves would participate in workshops aimed at training them to be more motivated and effective in their work and in their lives. The project was to be conducted aboard a particular ship, with a control group selected from sailors on four other ships.

To begin, the researchers reported that the supervisory personnel were not exactly thrilled with the program.

> Not surprisingly, there was considerable resistance on the part of some supervisors toward dealing with these issues. In fact, their reluctance to assume ownership of the problem was reflected by "blaming" any of several factors that can contribute to their

personnel problem. The recruiting system, recruit training, parents, and society at large were named as influencing low performance—factors that were well beyond the control of the supervisors.
>
> (CRAWFORD ET AL., 1980:488)

Eventually, the reluctant supervisors came around and "this initial reluctance gave way to guarded optimism and later to enthusiasm" (1980:489). The low performers themselves were even more of a problem, however. The research design called for pretesting and posttesting of attitudes and personalities, so that changes brought about by the program could be measured and evaluated.

> Unfortunately, all of the LPs (Low Performers) were strongly opposed to taking these so-called personality tests and it was therefore concluded that the data collected under these circumstances would be of questionable validity. Ethical concerns also dictated that we not force "testing" on the LPs.
>
> (CRAWFORD ET AL., 1980:490)

As a consequence, the researchers had to rely on interviews with the low performers and on the judgments of supervisors for their measures of attitude change. The subjects continued to present problems, however.

Initially, the ship's command ordered 15 low performers to participate in the experiment. Of the 15, however, one went into the hospital, another was assigned duties that prevented participation, and a third went over the hill (absent without leave). Thus, the experiment began with 12 subjects. But before it was completed, 3 more subjects completed their enlistments and left the Navy, and another was thrown out for disciplinary reasons. The experiment concluded, then, with 8 subjects. Although the evaluation pointed to positive results, the very small number of subjects warrants caution in any generalizations from the experiment.

The special, logistical problems of evaluation research grow out of the fact that it occurs within the context of uncontrollable daily life.

Administrative Control   As suggested in the previous example, the logistical details of an evaluation project are often under the control of program administrators. Let's suppose you're evaluating whether conjugal visits would improve morale among prison inmates. On the fourth day of the program, a male prisoner knocks out his wife, dresses up in her clothes, and escapes. Although you might be tempted to assume that his morale was greatly improved by escaping, that turn of events would complicate your study design in many ways. Perhaps the warden will terminate the program altogether, and where's your evaluation then? Or, if the warden is braver, he or she may review the files of all those prisoners you selected randomly for the experimental group and veto the "bad risks." There goes the comparability of your experimental and control groups. As an alternative, stricter security measures may be introduced to prevent further escapes, and the security measures may have a dampening effect on morale. So the experimental stimulus has changed in the middle of your research project. Some of the data will reflect the original stimulus, other data will reflect the modification. Although you'll probably be able to sort it all out, your carefully designed study has become a logical snakepit.

Maybe you've been engaged to evaluate the effect of race relations lectures on prejudice in the Army. You've carefully studied the soldiers available to you for study, and you've randomly assigned some to attend the lectures and others to stay away. The rosters have been circulated weeks in advance, and at the appointed day and hour, the lectures begin. Everything seems to be going smoothly until you begin processing the files: the names don't match. Checking around you discover that military field exercises, KP duty, and a variety of emergencies required some of the experimental subjects to be elsewhere at the time of the lectures. That's bad enough, but then you learn that helpful commanding officers sent others to fill in for the missing soldiers. And whom do you suppose they picked to fill in? Soldiers who didn't have anything else to do or who couldn't be trusted to do anything important. You might learn this bit of information a week or so before the deadline for submitting your final report on the impact of the race relations lectures.

These are some of the logistical problems confronting evaluation researchers. It is important that you be familiar with the problems to understand why some research procedures may not measure up to the design of the classical experiment. As you read reports of evaluation research, however, you'll find that—all our earlier comments notwithstanding—it is possible to carry out controlled social research in conjunction with real-life experiments.

Now let's look at some of the steps that program evaluators can take to prevent or minimize logistical problems and to promote the utility and ultimate use of their findings.

Planning an Evaluation and Fostering Its Utilization

Posavac and Carey (1985) propose a number of steps that they postulate will help program evaluators anticipate and deal with potential logistical problems and potential resistance to an evaluation and its utilization. As a first step, they recommend learning as much as possible about the *stakeholders*—those with vested interests in the evaluation whose beliefs, income, status or careers, and workload might be affected by the evaluation. To promote their identification with the evaluation and their support of it during the data collection phase, it is essential that they be involved in a meaningful way in planning the evaluation. Service recipients are also stakeholders and therefore should be included in the planning.

It also is important at the outset to find out who wants the evaluation, why they want it, and who doesn't want it. If, for example, program sponsors want the evaluation but program personnel either don't know about it or don't want it, the evaluator should try to make the program personnel more comfortable with the evaluation to foster their cooperation in collecting and interpreting data. One way to do this, of course, is by involving them as stakeholders, and by sharing mutual incremental feedback throughout all phases of the evaluation. Then, involvement should begin early in the planning of the evaluation, not just after the research design is ready to be implemented. In addition to fostering cooperation with the evaluation, involving personnel in the planning is thought to improve the chances for identifying those daily organizational realities that might pose logistical obstacles to alternative research designs or data collection methodologies.

As a final step in engaging program personnel in planning the evaluation, Posavac and Carey recommend obtaining their feedback regarding a written proposal that reflects their input. The purpose of presenting them with the proposal is to make certain that they agree with evaluators about the components of the evaluation and the nature of the program being evaluated. In addition, by reconsidering everything in a final, written package, they might see logistical problems not apparent in earlier discussions.

Planning an evaluation is a two-way street. It should consider not only potential problems posed by stakeholders, but also potential problems stemming from mistakes the evaluator might make in designing the evaluation. For example, involving decision makers who are likely to utilize the research helps ensure that evaluators will address questions relevant to their decision-making needs rather than questions that are trivial or of interest only to audiences not in a position to act on the research findings. Also, without adequate input from program personnel, evaluators might choose or develop the wrong data collection instruments, such as self-report scales that clients might not understand or be willing to complete. Conceivably the attainment of program objectives might need to be measured idiosyncratically for each client because each client has unique needs and target problems. If so, practitioners might convince evaluators to assess goal attainment through an aggregation of single-subject designs rather than through a group experiment that assesses all clients with the same outcome measures.

Evaluators also might not understand the unrealistic burden that their data collection procedures might place on practitioners already strained trying to meet heavy paperwork requirements without sacrificing the quality of service they are providing to their many clients.

The cooperation of program personnel might be fostered further by assuring them that they will get to see and respond to a confidential draft of the evaluation report before it is finalized and disseminated to other stakeholders. While they should not be made to feel that they will be able to censor the report, they should be assured that their suggestions will be taken seriously. By meeting with key personnel to discuss the report, evaluators can point out and clarify implications of the findings that personnel might find particularly useful for improving the program. And this should be done in a timely fashion—not after it is too late for certain decisions to be made.

Finally, the evaluator can foster the utilization of the evaluation report by tailoring its form and style to the needs and preferences of those in a position to utilize it. Clear, succinct, and cohesive composition always helps, as does careful typing and a neat, uncluttered layout. The briefer and neater the report, the more likely busy administrators and practitioners are to read it carefully. When adapting the report to an audience of program personnel, do not present every peripheral finding. And do not present negative findings bluntly and tactlessly. If program objectives are not being attained, couch the findings in language that recognizes the yeoman efforts and skills of program personnel and that does not portray them as inadequate. Try not to convey a message of success or failure, but rather provide suggestions for developing new programs or improving existing ones. Try to alert program personnel in the planning stage that all reports bring some good news and some bad news and that the focus will be less on judging the value of the program than on identifying feasible ways to improve it. And make sure that sufficient attention is given to realistic, practical implications of the findings.

A note of caution is in order here. We are not implying that if you follow all the steps we have proposed that you are certain to avoid problems in the way program personnel respond to a proposed evaluation or its findings. These steps are recommended as ways to reduce the likelihood of encountering those problems or the severity of those problems if they do arise. But even if you follow all the proposed steps, under certain circumstances you may still encounter serious problems with program personnel. If, for example, they feel their funding is threatened by your findings, they may still seek to discredit your evaluation, even if you went by the book in dealing with them. As to logistical problems, you may find the best-laid plans go awry when unforeseen circumstances influence program personnel to make unanticipated changes. If you are lucky, they will discuss in advance the changes they are considering, which will enable you to learn about these changes in a timely way and interact with program personnel in a way that helps protect the viability and utility of the evaluation. This is most likely to occur if you have been allocated enough resources to be on site at the program on a daily basis. If, however, your resources are insufficient to have a frequent on-site presence and ongoing interaction with program personnel, you may find out about program changes that wreak havoc on the planned evaluation too late to salvage the evaluation. Do not presume that evaluation plans made months earlier will remain at the forefront of the minds of program personnel as they encounter unexpected difficulties in operating their programs. Moreover, even if they do remember the evaluation plans, they may not realize that the program changes they are considering will impact the evaluation.

For instance, in a family preservation program that one of us (Rubin) evaluated, the program personnel did not realize that by increasing the treatment duration from three months to one year, they would influence the planned program evaluation by reducing the sample size by 75% (and thus drastically cutting its statistical power)! Neither did they think to inform the evaluation

staff of this decision, which was made several months after the project and its evaluation began and which additionally bore on the timing of the posttests. Nor did they realize that their postimplementation decision to start referring comparison group clients to a comparable family preservation intervention program would affect the internal validity of the study design. And to make matters worse, the program administrator, who after a lengthy planning discussion had agreed to a careful, detailed plan for ensuring the equivalence of the family preservation group and the comparison group, decided to assign all the clients with the most serious problems to her program, and the clients with the least serious problems to the comparison group. She assigned clients on that basis for three years and did not inform the evaluator of that until she saw undesirable outcome results at the completion of the evaluation. All this happened despite the fact that the evaluator followed all the evaluation planning steps recommended in this book. He did not, however, have the resources needed to have an evaluator on site often enough to learn about these changes in advance. Live and learn!

PURPOSES OF PROGRAM EVALUATION

So far in this chapter we have been discussing the politics of program evaluation primarily in connection to assessing the effectiveness of programs in attaining their formal goals. Asking whether a program is achieving a successful outcome is perhaps the most significant evaluative question we could ask, and it probably is the question that immediately comes to mind when we think about program evaluation. It may also be the most politically charged question because it bears so directly on key vested interests, such as those associated with funding. But as we noted at the beginning of this chapter, program evaluation can have other purposes and other research questions that, although they may ultimately have some bearing on program outcome, focus on issues in the conceptualization, design, planning, administration, and implementation of interventions and programs.

At this point, then, we are going to look at the different purposes of program evaluation. We will do so with particular attention to methodological issues, but you will see that political considerations keep cropping up as we compare these alternative purposes of program evaluation. We will classify three broad purposes of program evaluation: whether the evaluation seeks to assess (1) the ultimate success of programs, (2) problems in how programs are being implemented, or (3) information needed in program planning and development.

Before we elaborate on each of these purposes, we would like to introduce you to two terms that have been commonly used to classify these alternative purposes in the program evaluation literature: summative and formative evaluations. *Summative evaluations* are concerned with the first of the three purposes, involving the ultimate success of a program and decisions about whether it should be continued or chosen in the first place from among alternative options. The results of a summative evaluation convey a sense of finality. Depending on whether the results imply that the program succeeded, the program may or may not survive. *Formative evaluations,* on the other hand, are not concerned with testing the success of a program. They focus instead on obtaining information that is helpful in planning the program and in improving its implementation and performance (Posavac and Carey, 1985). Summative evaluations will generally be quantitative in approach. Formative evaluations may use quantitative methods, qualitative methods, or both. As you will see, these types or purposes of program evaluation are not mutually exclusive. Rather, they complement one another, and some evaluations can cover more than one of these purposes, such as when an evaluation finds that a program failed to attain its goals because it was never properly implemented in the first place.

We'll begin by looking at the evaluation of program outcome and efficiency. You will see that even within this one type of program evaluation there are competing views about how to proceed.

Evaluating Outcome and Efficiency

Evaluations of program outcome and efficiency may assess whether the program is effectively attaining its goals, whether it has any unintended harmful effects, whether its success (if any) is being achieved at a reasonable cost, and how the ratio of its benefits to its cost compares with the benefits and costs of other programs with similar objectives.

This approach to evaluation, sometimes called the *goal attainment model* of evaluation, refers to the formal goals and mission of the program—whether it is achieving what its funders or the general public want it to achieve. Typically, in designing goal attainment evaluations the *formal* goals of the program will be specified as dependent variables and operationally defined in terms of measurable indicators of program success. The focus is on maximizing the *internal validity* of the evaluation design to rule out bias and other plausible rival explanations of outcome and to be able to determine whether the particular outcomes observed were really *caused* by the program.

Thus, evaluations of goal attainment strive to use the most internally valid *experimental* design possible and to use rigorous, objective, quantitative measures. Ideally, program participants, such as service recipients, will make up the experimental group, and their counterparts who do not participate or who receive an alternate program will make up the control or comparison group. Alternatively, *quasi-experimental* designs that do not require a control group, such as time-series or single-subject designs, will be used. In short, this approach to program evaluation primarily applies the principles discussed in Chapters 9 and 10 of this book in order to infer causal connections between program efforts and indicators of program outcome. An example of this type of evaluation—one that received some notoriety in concluding that a popular program had unintended harmful effects—is illustrated in the box titled "Evaluating Criminal Justice Programs."

EVALUATING CRIMINAL JUSTICE PROGRAMS

by R. John Kinkel, Department of Sociology, University of Michigan at Flint

In 1979, millions of Americans had the opportunity to watch the Oscar-winning film *Scared Straight* on national television. Developed at Rahway State Prison, New Jersey, the film dramatized the sordid side of prison life to young toughs in hopes of "scaring" the juvenile offenders out of future criminal behavior. The film's narrator, Peter Falk, claimed the program was 90% successful; 9 out of 10 juveniles who took part in the program went "straight." A recent evaluation of the program came up with some different figures.

Professor James Finckenauer, Rutgers University School of Criminal Justice, was hired by the New Jersey Department of Corrections to undertake a rigorous evaluation of the *Scared Straight* program (officially known as the Juvenile Awareness Project). *Scared Straight* was a curious combination of juveniles, criminal justice operatives, and prison inmates working on a joint endeavor. For about three years juveniles (some delinquent and others, volunteers) were sent for grueling two-hour sessions inside the Rahway maximum security prison. Once inside, the youths were ushered into a room with a group of convicts who were serving sentences of 25 years or more. The convicts went through their well-practiced routine for berating the juveniles' tough-guy postures. The convicts impressed the kids with the sordid side of prison life: the loss of privacy, individuality, and the constant threat of assault and homosexual slavery. The *Scared Straight* program became so popular that it was adopted in one form or another by a large number of states as well as some provinces in Canada.

Finckenauer's study began in December 1977. He used a small but representative sample of juveniles from nine different agencies that refer kids to the project. The first part of the evaluation focused on nine different measures of attitudes concerning crime, law, justice, police, punishment, and obeying the law. The results of the testing showed no appreciable difference between the experimental and control groups in terms of attitude change—not a good sign if one were anticipating dramatic behavioral change. But the big question still remained: Did *Scared Straight* deter future delinquent behavior?

The results of Finckenauer's six-month follow-up study of juvenile offenders showed that the experimental group (supposedly scared straight!) had a success rate lower than the control group.

Each juvenile's court record was tracked: any further recorded offense was counted as evidence of failure. A significantly higher proportion of the juveniles who *did not attend*

No matter how rigorous the assessment of outcome, the evaluation may be deemed incomplete unless it also assesses the costs of obtaining the outcome. In other words, how *efficient* is the program in achieving its outcome? Suppose, for example, that an evaluation of a case management program to prevent rehospitalization of the chronically mentally ill concludes that the pro-

Two Reports of the *Scared Straight* Program

	TWO VIEWS OF REALITY		
	FALK'S FACTS	FINCKENAUER'S FIGURES	
Program	*Scared Straight*	*Scared Straight*	
Time frame of analysis	3 months	6 months	
Type of sample	Not representative	Representative	
Sample size	17	81	
Control group	No	Yes*	
Success rate	90%	Experimental	Control
		59%	89%

*Random assignment plus subjects were comparable on key demographic variables: age, sex, race, criminal history.

the *Scared Straight* program did better at avoiding crime than their juvenile delinquent counterparts. The success rate of the control group was 89% whereas the outcome of the experimental group was only 59% effective. Furthermore, the juveniles in the experimental group committed more serious crimes than the control group. Finckenauer speculates that a "delinquency-fulfilling prophecy" was at work. By demeaning and belittling the young "tough guys," the convicts may have compelled them to go out and prove they were not impressed.

Evaluation research can provide some sobering facts for policy makers and citizens alike after the initial rave reviews of a program have worn off—endorsements of movie stars notwithstanding.

Reference
James Finckenauer, *Evaluation of Juvenile Awareness Project: Reports 1 and 2* (Newark, NJ: Rutgers School of Criminal Justice, 1979).

gram successfully reduces the number of days patients are hospitalized. Suppose further that the total number of days hospitalized for 50 case-managed patients during the course of the evaluation is 400, as compared to 500 for 50 controls. In other words, the case management program made a difference of 100 fewer hospitalized days. So far, so good. But suppose the extra cost of providing the case management services during the study period was $50,000. Thus, each day of hospitalization saved by providing case management was costing $500 (which we get by dividing $50,000 by 100). If the cost of hospital care was less than $500 per day per patient, then some might conclude that despite the program's effectiveness, it was not an efficient way to care for the mentally ill.

Such questions of efficiency tend to be purely economic and may not take into account important value judgments, such as those dealing with the worth of humanistic benefits reaped by service recipients. The costs of the preceding hypothetical program to the public at large may seem high, but some might believe that those costs are justified by the improved quality of life experienced by patients when they reside in the community. Thus, once again we see the social and political context of program evaluation. Different stakeholders might disagree about whether a particular benefit of a program is worth the extra cost, depending on which stakeholder is bearing the cost and which is reaping the benefit. And many benefits, such as improved health or an individual's self-esteem, cannot be valued in dollars.

But it is nevertheless useful to assess program efficiency. Even if humanistic considerations lead us to believe that a less efficient program is still the most desirable option, at least we could make that decision in light of the ratio of costs to benefits. And sometimes assessing efficiency helps us to determine which alternative program provides more humanistic benefits. Suppose, for example, that an alternative type of case management program that costs $25,000 for 50 cases results in 425 hospitalized days for the same study period as the case management program that resulted in 400 hospitalized days. Although the $25,000 program had a slightly worse outcome, its costs were only half that of the $50,000 program. That means that an allocation of $50,000 would enable us to provide the cheaper program to twice as many cases as the more expensive program. Therefore, assuming that a finite level of funding

does not permit us to provide the more expensive program to most of the target population, the slightly less effective but much more efficient program might yield greater humanistic benefits.

Cost-Effectiveness and Cost-Benefit Analyses

The two major approaches to assessing the efficiency of a program are called **cost-effectiveness analysis** and **cost-benefit analysis.** In cost-effectiveness analysis, the only monetary considerations are the costs of the program itself; the monetary benefits of the program's effects are not assessed. In cost-benefit analysis, in addition to monetizing program costs, an effort is made to monetize the program's outcome.

In the foregoing case management example, we would be conducting a cost-effectiveness analysis if we limited our focus to the program-cost-per-day of hospitalization prevented. Thus, if we report that one program costs $500 per hospitalized day prevented, and another program costs $300 per hospitalized day prevented, we have reported the findings of a cost-effectiveness analysis. If, on the other hand, we had attempted to monetize outcome by assessing the societal benefits of the program in terms such as the increased economic productivity of the individuals receiving case management, we would have been conducting a cost-benefit analysis. Borrowing from White (1988), we can illustrate the difference between cost-benefit and cost-effectiveness analyses with the following example. Suppose two alternative school social work interventions are evaluated, each of which aims to reduce the dropout rate of youths at inner-city high schools. Existing data, reported prior to the study, have shown that the graduation rate in the targeted high schools is only 50%. Intervention A costs $50,000, is utilized by 100 students, and 75 of the 100 graduate from high school. Intervention B costs $40,000, is utilized by 100 students, and 60 of them graduate from high school. Based on the previously established 50% graduation rate, one would expect 50 of every 100 students to graduate. Since 75 of 100 (75%) participating in Intervention A graduated, a cost-effectiveness analysis would find that Intervention A had the effect of adding 25 graduates at a cost of $50,000, or $2000 per additional graduate. Intervention B was $10,000 cheaper to implement ($40,000 is $10,000 less than the $50,000 cost of Intervention A), but had the effect of adding only ten graduates for the $40,000, which comes to $4000 per additional graduate. Thus, Intervention A is more cost effective, because $2000 per additional graduate is a better cost-effectiveness ratio than $4000 per additional graduate.

Notice that so far we have not estimated the monetary value of graduating from high school, an estimate that would be required if we were conducting a cost-benefit analysis. Suppose we did conduct such an analysis and found that the projected increased career earnings of the high school graduates was $50,000 per graduate and that the government would have to spend $10,000 less on social services and welfare benefits to each high school graduate, as compared to each dropout. Adding those two figures together, we could estimate that the monetary benefit per additional graduate is $60,000. Since Intervention B had the effect of adding ten graduates, we could conclude that its monetized outcome was ten times $60,000, or $600,000. That figure would be far in excess of the intervention's $40,000 cost, so we could argue that the intervention is worth funding—that it is cost-beneficial because the dollar value of benefits resulting from the intervention exceed the dollar value costs of providing the intervention.

Note that we could draw this conclusion without ever comparing Intervention B to Intervention A. Of course, were we to estimate the cost benefit of Intervention A, we would find that Intervention A's monetized outcome would be even more cost-beneficial (with benefits equaling 25 times $60,000, or $1,500,000) than Intervention B's. Cost-benefit analyses need not ask whether one program's benefits-to-costs ratio is better than another program's. They may just look at one program and ask whether its monetized benefits exceed its monetary costs.

Assessing the costs of a program can be highly complex. It requires technical expertise in cost accounting and deals with such accounting concepts as variable versus fixed costs, incremental versus sunk costs, recurring versus nonrecurring costs, hidden versus obvious costs, direct versus indirect costs, future costs, opportunity costs, and so forth (Posavac and Carey, 1985). Because program evaluators often lack that expertise, they often do not include cost-effectiveness or cost-benefit analyses as part of their evaluations. The cost accounting concepts just mentioned go beyond the scope of this text, but we will recommend some texts at the end of this chapter for further study of this topic.

Because cost-effectiveness analysis attempts to monetize only program costs and not program outcomes, it involves fewer cost accounting complexities and fewer questionable monetizing assumptions than does cost-benefit analysis. When we attempt to monetize the outcome of health and welfare programs, we get into difficult value issues, such as attaching a dollar figure to the value of human lives. White (1988) offers the example of neonatal intensive care units to illustrate this point.

Although intensive care units for very low birthweight babies are not cost-beneficial, every major hospital in this country spends hundreds of thousands of dollars providing them. The same point applies to the frail elderly. No matter what the costs are for nursing homes or other programs of care for the frail elderly, the monetized benefits of those programs—such as through increased earning capacity—are not going to exceed the program costs. We do not put a dollar value on the quality of life benefits that we seek to provide the frail elderly.

Likewise, when hospice programs attempt to alleviate the pain and suffering of the terminally ill, they cannot monetize that benefit in terms of dollars that the outcome of their care generates through increased earning capacity. Because of the values problem in attempting to reduce benefits to monetary terms, as well as the difficulty in foreseeing and monetizing all the costs and benefits that might be attributable to a program's outcome, cost-effectiveness analyses are generally considered less controversial and more doable than are cost-benefit analyses. Still, excellent cost-benefit analyses can be found. An illustration of an excellent cost-benefit analysis done in an evaluation of a community support program for the mentally ill (Weisbrod et al., 1980) is presented in Table 18-1. It should give you a better sense of the complexities involved in monetizing program costs and outcomes.

Problems and Issues in Evaluating Goal Attainment

When people don't like a message they receive, they often blame the messenger. In the same vein, when they don't like the findings of an outcome evaluation, they often blame the evaluation's methodology. It is commonly perceived that over the years evaluations of program outcomes have had far more negative findings, indicating program failure, than positive findings. It is also widely believed that studies with negative findings tend not to be utilized because of the vested interests at stake. And expectations that rigorous, experimental outcome studies tend to produce negative findings have made administrators wary of such studies and reluctant to authorize them. One common complaint is that all these studies do is tell us that we are failing; they don't show us how to do things better.

One important criticism of the traditional approach to evaluating goal attainment correctly points out that the determination of program goals and their measurable indicators can be hazardous. Sometimes the mission of a program is stated in grandiose terms that no one really takes seriously—terms articulated for political reasons or to convince legislators or others that a program should be funded. Consequently, it is argued that finding negative outcomes in evaluations of the attainment of those goals is a foregone conclusion—that evaluations are doomed to keep coming up with negative findings if they keep taking formally stated goals seriously.

In addition to their grandiosity, formal goals are often stated so vaguely that different evaluators may find it impossible to agree on what they really mean in terms of specific, observable indicators of success. The Head Start program in the War On Poverty is often cited as a case in point. Its formal mission was to offset the effects of poverty in order to enhance the opportunities of children. That's a noble mission, but what are its operational indicators? Evaluative researchers have disagreed over whether the focus of the outcome measures should be on indicators of learning readiness, academic achievement, emotional development and self-esteem, classroom conduct, delinquency later in life, physical health and nutrition, resource redistribution, or something else. The possibilities seem endless, and often program personnel themselves cannot agree on what specific indicators of success are implied by their program's mission statement.

Consequently, when evaluators choose a few operational indicators of success, they risk missing areas in which the program really is succeeding. If so, then their negative findings may be misleading and may endanger the continuation of programs that are succeeding in other, equally important ways. In light of these problems, some argue that the evaluation of outcome ought to be abandoned altogether and replaced by evaluations of program processes. Others argue that, even with these problems, outcome studies at least tell us some things about what is and is not being attained, which is better than having no information at all about program outcomes, particularly if appropriate caution is exercised in acting upon the findings.

Some suggest keeping the goal attainment model, but with some adjustments. One idea has been to ignore the formal goals or mission statement of a program and simply measure every conceivable indicator of outcome that the evaluators think has some potential of being affected by it. But the feasibility of such undisciplined fishing

Table 18-1 Costs and Benefits per Patient in Experimental (E) and Control (C) Groups for 12 Months After Admission

CATEGORY	GROUP		
	C	E	E–C
COSTS			
I. Direct treatment costs			
A. Mendota Mental Health Institute (MMHI)			
Inpatient	$3096	$ 94	$–3002*
Outpatient	42	0	–42*
B. Experimental Center Program	0	4704	4704†
Total	$3138	$4798	$ 1660†
II. Indirect treatment costs			
A. Social service agencies			
1. Other hospitals (not MMHI)			
University hospitals	$ 147	$ 239	$ 92*
Madison General Hospital	417	87	–330*
St. Mary's Hospital	152	17	–135
Methodist Hospital	220	39	–181
Out-of-town hospitals	808	264	–544*‡
Total	$1744	$ 646	$–1098
2. Sheltered workshops (Madison Opportunity Center Inc. and Goodwill Industries)	$ 91	$ 870	$ 779*‡
3. Other community agencies			
Dane County Medical Health Center	55	50	–5
Dane County Social Services	41	25	–16*
State Department of Vocational Rehabilitation	185	209	24§
Visiting Nurse Service	0	23	23*
State Employment Service	4	3	–1‖
B. Private medical providers	22	12	–10‡¶
Total	$2142	$1838	$ –304†
III. Law enforcement costs			
A. Overnights in jail	$ 159	$ 152	$ –7‡
B. Court contacts	17	12	–5‡
C. Probation and parole	189	143	–46
D. Police contacts	44	43	–1‡
Total	$ 409	$ 350	$ –59†

*Significant at the $P < .05$ level.

†Significance not tested because the number is a sum of means.

‡These data are derived from agency or patient reports on the number of contacts. Patient reports were used only when it was not possible or was excessively costly to obtain the relevant information from the agency. Estimates of the cost per contact were obtained from the agency.

§Data from the Department of Vocational Rehabilitation (DVR) were available only for the 28-month study period as a whole, a period that included the follow-up period after the experiment. The per-patient costs are 12/28, or 43% of the 28-month cost and reflect the average cost for one year. The figures reflect some double counting because much of the DVR expenditures went for payments to other agencies that are included in the Cost section (category II). However, we have been able to account for and to exclude DVR payments to the sheltered workshops, which comprise by far the major source of double counting.

‖Significant at the $P < .10$ level.

¶These figures include fees for physicians, psychologists, and nurses but exclude any associated laboratory fees.

Table 18-1   *(continued)*

CATEGORY	GROUP		
	C	E	E–C
COSTS			
IV. Maintenance costs			
A. Cash payments			
1. Governmental (including administration)			
Social Security (supplemental security income, retirement, survivors and disability)	$ 557	$ 269	$ –288*
Aid for Dependent Children	446	167	–279*
Unemployment Compensation	19	55	36#
Welfare	33	43	10
Other costs (including supervised residences)	43	0	–43*
Total	$1098	$ 534	$ –564†
2. Private	102	197	95#
3. Experimental Center payments	0	202	202†
4. Patient payments	…	…	…
B. In kind food and lodging costs, by source			
1. Private (from family, Salvation Army, etc.)	287	102	–185
2. Government and Experimental Center	0	0	0
Total Measured Maintenance Costs	$1487	$1035	$ –452†
V. Family burden costs			
A. Lost earnings due to patient	$ 120	$ 72	–48**††
B. Other costs (see VI, physical illness and emotional strain)	…	…	…
Total Costs for Which Monetary Estimates Have Been Made	$7296	$8083	$ 797†
VI. Other family burden costs			
A. See V, lost earnings	…	…	…
B. No. of families reporting physical illness due to patient	25	14	–11**
C. Percent of family members experiencing emotional strain due to patient	48	25	–23**‡‡
VII. Burdens on other people (eg, neighbors, co-workers)	…	…	…

#These data are derived from patient reports and as such are subject to misreporting. In some cases, individual spot-checks were made with the agency in question; agencies that were not able to provide us with information on all patients were sometimes able to provide it on the spot-check basis.

**These figures are derived from interviews conducted four months after admission with 22 families (34%) of E-group patients and 18 families (27%) of C-group patients. The other families were not interviewed because: they lived outside of Dane County (23%), the subject or the family refused consent (18%), the relative could not be contacted (21%), or miscellaneous reasons (8%). The questionnaire examined the families' experience in the two weeks preceding the interview only, and these figures were projected to an annual average. The reduced sample size and the single interview yielded data that must be interpreted with caution.

††These figures were derived by multiplying the number of days family members missed work because of the patient by a daily wage of $24 (or $3 an hour).

‡‡This figure is based on interviewers' assessments.

§§The earnings do not include the value of fringe benefits, if there were any.

Table 18-1   *(continued)*

CATEGORY	GROUP		
	C	E	E–C
COSTS			
VIII. Illegal activity costs, average			
A. No. of arrests	1.0	0.8	–0.2[#]
B. No. of arrests for felony	0.2	0.2	0.0[#]
IX. Patient mortality costs (% of group dying during year)			
A. Suicide	1.5	1.5	0.0
B. Natural causes	0.0	4.6	4.6
BENEFITS			
I. Earnings[§§]			
A. From competitive employment	$1136	$2169	$1033*[#]
B. From sheltered workshops	32	195	163*[#]
Total Benefits for Which Monetary Estimates Have Been Made	$1168	$2364	$1196[†]
II. Labor market behavior			
A. Days of competitive employment per year	77	127	50[#]
B. Days of sheltered employment per year	10	89	79[#]
C. Percent of days missed from job	3	7	4[#]
D. No. of beneficial job changes	2	3	1[|||]
E. No. of detrimental job changes	2	2	0[|||]
III. Improved consumer decision making			
A. Insurance expenditures	$ 33	$ 56	$ 23[#]
B. Percent of group having a savings account	27	34	7
IV. Patient mental health (see Table 2)	…	…	…
VALUED BENEFITS MINUS VALUED COSTS			
Valued benefits	$ 1168	$ 2364	$ 1196
Valued costs	7296	8093	797
Net (Benefits Minus Costs)	$–6128	$–5729	$ 399[†]

\|\|\|These figures reflect our judgments, which were based on examination of patient reports.

Source: Weisbrod, Burton A.; Test, Mary Ann; and Stein, Leonard I. "Alternative to Mental Hospital Treatment: II. Economic Benefit-Cost Analysis," *Archives of General Psychiatry,* vol. 37, April 1980, 400–405. (Table appears on pp. 401–402.) Copyright © 1980, American Medical Association. Used by permission.

expeditions for endless potential indicators may be dubious. Also, as discussed in Chapter 17, when a large number of dependent variables are assessed independently of one another, the risk of a Type I error is inflated. An alternative suggestion, therefore, has been to assess official program goals as well as a limited number of additional goals that seem to be the most plausible in light of the social science theories upon which the program is based. But this suggestion, too, may be somewhat (albeit less) vulnerable to inflating the risk of a Type I error, and it offers no guarantee that the most important effects of the program will be detected.

Monitoring Program Implementation

As we noted a few pages ago, some programs have unsuccessful outcomes simply because they are not being implemented properly. Suppose an AIDS prevention program develops a public education leaflet and decides to evaluate its effectiveness in a small pilot distribution in a particular high school. Suppose the program personnel deliver the leaflets to the vice principal of the school, who agrees to disseminate them to all students. Suppose that for some reason—unanticipated opposition by the principal or the PTA, mere oversight, or whatever—the leaflets never get disseminated. Or perhaps they get disseminated in an undesirable way. Maybe instead of handing them out to every student in a school assembly, the vice principal merely deposits them in each teacher's mailbox with a vague message encouraging them to distribute the leaflets to their students. Maybe some teachers distribute the leaflets but most do not.

Suppose further that the program personnel never learn that the leaflets were not disseminated as intended. The implications of this turn of events would be quite serious. Because few or no students would have received the leaflet in the first place, the intervention was never implemented as planned and it had no chance to succeed. No matter what indicators of outcome were

chosen, the leaflet dissemination effort would be doomed to fail. But it would fail not because it was a bad idea or an ineffectual leaflet but because it was never really tried. If the evaluators had merely conducted an outcome study and had not assessed whether and how the program got implemented, they would be in danger of abandoning a public education intervention that, if only implemented properly, might effectively prevent the spread of AIDS.

This example illustrates that no matter how well an outcome evaluation is designed, if it is not supplemented by an evaluation of program implementation, then it risks not identifying or misinterpreting the meaning of negative results. In turn, no matter how highly we value outcome studies, there is a clear need for the evaluation of program implementation. And familiarity with organizational goal theory helps us realize just how important implementation evaluations can be.

Even when we can be sure that we have properly identified the *formal, official* goals of a program and their operational indicators, we cannot assume that those goals are the real priority of program personnel responsible for attaining them. Program personnel at all levels tend over time to become preoccupied with daily routines and with their own agendas—that is, with *unofficial* goals pertaining to organizational maintenance, personal prestige and career advancement, bureaucratic rules and procedures, and the like. As these unofficial goals displace official, formal goals, they may result in activities that are either irrelevant to or at odds with the attainment of the official goals.

Thus, for example, administrators of family service agencies may secure federal poverty funds not because they are devoted to fighting poverty, but because those funds will help balance agency budgets and enhance the agency board evaluation of the administrators' performance. Suppose the administrators propose to use the funds so that the agencies can reach out to more poverty-stricken individuals and thus try to engage them in receiving the agencies' direct services. Once they've received the funds, however, there is no guarantee that the agencies will try to reach poor clients as diligently as they promised in their grant applications. Even if the administrators sincerely sought to do so, they might run into unanticipated resistance by direct-service practitioners who think that such efforts would be an unrewarding and improper use of their therapeutic talents and who prefer to continue serving the kind of clientele with whom they are familiar and comfortable.

Consider the implications for program evaluation in the foregoing hypothetical example. Suppose a nationwide outcome study were done to see if the federal funding of direct social services to the poor resulted in a reduction in poverty or a reduction in various psychosocial problems among the poor. If the family service agencies, due to their own internally directed objectives, never really tried very hard to serve poor clients, then the outcome would in all likelihood be negative. But it would be wrong to conclude from such results that the provision of direct services to the poor is an ineffective way to help them deal with the problems of poverty, because the services never reached enough poor people in the first place.

For the same reasons, one can see from this example the importance of evaluating program implementation even without any evaluation of program outcome. If an evaluation of agency caseload attributes found that the agencies never implemented the program as planned—that poor people were not being served—then who needs an outcome evaluation? And those results would be quite useful. Instead of just depicting the program as a success or failure, it would identify what went wrong and could help policymakers consider ways to improve the program's implementation. In addition, simply monitoring program implementation would help keep the agency accountable to its funders. Ultimately, of course, they would want to know the outcome of the program. But, in the meantime, just knowing how the program is being implemented is invaluable.

Evaluations of program implementation are not necessarily concerned only with the question of whether a program is being implemented as planned. There are many other possible questions that examine how best to implement, as well as maintain, the program. Here are just a few of the important questions that can be researched without getting into questions of outcome:

- Which fundraising strategy yields the most funds?
- What proportion of the target population is being served?
- What types of individuals are we not reaching?
- Why are so many targeted individuals refusing services?
- What satellite clinic locations are reaching the most clients?
- What types of practitioners seem to have the best attitudes about working with certain underserved target populations?
- Do practitioners in specialized units have better attitudes than those in multipurpose units?
- How skillful are various types of practitioners in their clinical interventions?
- In what areas do they seem least prepared and in need of continuing education?
- How are staff reacting to new agency procedures? What difficulties are they experiencing with them?
- Are clients satisfied with services? Why or why not?
- Why do so many drop out of treatment prematurely?

Process Evaluation

A term closely aligned with monitoring program implementation is called *process evaluation*. Process evaluations ask many of the same questions as indicated above in connection with monitoring program implementation, and they focus on identifying strengths and weaknesses in program processes and recommending needed improvements. Often agency administrators will ask evaluators to conduct outcome evaluations of their programs while those programs are still in their infancy and have not yet had enough time to identify and resolve start-up bugs and other problematic processes in implementation. These administrators may be in a hurry for outcome data because they are under intense pressure from funding sources to prove their success at goal attainment. Seasoned evaluators, however, may try to persuade them to table any outcome evaluation until a process evaluation has been completed, so that outcome data are collected only after the program has been debugged. The administrators may or may not have the time or resources to conduct a process evaluation first, then an outcome evaluation. In contrast, other administrators, perhaps under less external pressure, may be content just to have the process evaluation, asking not whether their program works, but how to make it work better.

All the methodologies covered in the foregoing chapters of this book can be applied to evaluate program implementation. The most appropriate methodology to use depends on the nature of the research question. Surveys utilizing questionnaires or scales might be used to assess staff, client, or community attitudes that affect program implementation decisions. Available records might be analyzed to assess whether the attributes of clients being served match program priorities regarding the intended target population. Experimental or quasi-experimental designs might be used to assess the effectiveness of alternative fundraising strategies, to measure the impact of different organizational arrangements on staff attitudes, to determine which outreach strategies are most successful in engaging hard-to-reach prospective clients in treatment, and so on. Process evaluations, however, tend to rely heavily on qualitative methods. Open-ended qualitative interviewing, for instance, might be the best way to learn how staff are reacting to new agency procedures and the unanticipated difficulties they are experiencing with them. Qualitative interviewing might also work best for discovering the reasons

clients cite for service dissatisfaction or for refusing or prematurely terminating service delivery. Participant observation might be used to assess how staff relate to clients or to one another. In some studies, evaluators have posed as clients and observed how staff members behaved and the ways their behavior affected clients.

Evaluation for Program Planning: Needs Assessment

Thus far we have been discussing the evaluation of programs that have already been implemented. But the term *program evaluation* also connotes diagnostic evaluation. Just as clinical practitioners evaluate client problems and needs during a preintervention assessment period to develop the best treatment plan, program evaluators may assess a program's target population in order to enhance program planning. They might assess the extent and location of the problems the program seeks to ameliorate, as well as the target population's characteristics, problems, expressed needs, and desires. This information is then used to guide program planning and development concerning such issues as what services to offer, how to maximize service utilization by targeted subgroups, where to locate services, and so on.

For example, suppose you are planning a new statewide program to help the homeless. What would you need to know to guide your planning? You might want to find out how many homeless people there are in the state. How many are there in specific locations in the state? What are the reasons for each individual's homelessness, and how many people are there for each reason? How many choose to be homeless? How many seem to be homeless because of mental illness or substance abuse? How many are homeless because they lost their jobs and cannot find work? How long have they been homeless? How many of the homeless are in different ethnic groups, and how many are recent immigrants or do not speak English? What proportion of the homeless consists of children and entire family units? What special problems do the children experience in such matters as education, health, nutrition, self-esteem, and so on? What special problems and needs are expressed by the adult homeless, those with emotional disorders, and others? These are just a few of the diagnostic questions you might ask; the answers will help you suggest what interventions to develop, where to locate them, how to staff them, and so on.

The process of systematically researching diagnostic questions like the ones just mentioned is called **needs assessment.** The term *needs assessment* is widely used to cover all sorts of techniques for collecting data for program planning purposes and has become essentially synonymous with evaluation for program planning.

Before examining specific alternative techniques of needs assessment, it is important to recognize a thorny conceptual issue that complicates the definition of needs. That issue pertains to whether needs are defined in *normative* terms or in terms of *demand*. If needs are defined normatively, then a needs assessment would focus on comparing the objective living conditions of the target population with what society, or at least that segment of society concerned with helping the target population, deems acceptable or desirable from a humanitarian standpoint. Normatively defining the needs of the homeless, for instance, might lead you to conclude that certain housing or shelter programs need to be developed for individuals living in deplorable conditions on the streets, even if those individuals don't express any dissatisfaction with their current homelessness.

If needs are defined in terms of demand, however, only those individuals who indicate that they feel or perceive the need themselves would be considered to be in need of a particular program or intervention. Thus, in this homelessness example, individuals who prefer to be homeless might not be counted as in need of the program. Defining needs in terms of demand can be tricky. Perhaps individuals express no need for a planned program because they don't understand how the planned program will help them or because they have come to expect that every time a social program is provided to them it is stigmatizing or unacceptable to them in some other way. Thus, in assessing whether the homeless need a new shelter program, many homeless individuals might express no need for the program and might even disdain the idea because they have no reason to believe that the new program really will be more acceptable to them than the filthy, crowded, dangerous shelters they already refuse to use.

The need for undergraduate social work education programs provides another example of the complexities involved regarding normative needs and felt needs. Many argue that the number of social work programs and social work majors that our society needs should be gauged by social welfare labor force needs. That is, the need for social work education would be defined in terms of the job market demand to hire social work majors to fill social worker positions. If the number of graduates with social work majors exceeds labor force demands for social workers, those defining need in terms of demand would see this situation as a problem and argue that we ought to reduce social work enrollments. But those who define needs normatively might disagree, arguing that even if social work majors don't get social work jobs, even if there is no demand for their services, our society is still improved by having more social work majors. The rationale would be that social work education, even if it does not lead to a job, helps prepare better citizens who are more understanding of social welfare problems and needs and who will be more likely to contribute to societal efforts to alleviate social welfare problems. In other words, they would argue that our society needs more social work majors even if it does not recognize that need and is not prepared to utilize them.

How we define needs affects the choice of specific techniques to assess them. For example, if we define needs normatively, we might be able to establish the need for a particular program by analyzing existing statistics. Thus, if census data showed a relatively high number of unmarried teenage mothers in a particular area, we might be predisposed to conclude that more family planning or child-rearing education services are needed in that area. But if we take demand into account, we might want to supplement the census information by conducting a survey of teenage mothers to determine the conditions, if any, under which they would actually utilize the particular services that we are contemplating.

The specific techniques for conducting a needs assessment are usually classified in five categories: (1) the key informants approach, (2) the community forum approach, (3) the rates under treatment approach, (4) the social indicators approach, and (5) the community survey approach. Let's look at each of these approaches.

Key Informants   The key informant approach utilizes questionnaires or interviews to obtain expert opinions from individuals presumed to have special knowledge about the target population's problems and needs, as well as about current gaps in service delivery to that population. The key informants selected to be surveyed might include leaders of groups or organizations that are in close contact with the target population and that have special knowledge of its problems. It might also include practitioners who work closely with the target population.

In assessing the needs of the homeless, for instance, key informants might include professionals working in public shelters or soup kitchens; researchers or other personnel addressing homelessness as part of their work for local planning agencies; neighborhood leaders in communities where the homeless tend to congregate; administrators and case managers in community mental health programs; public officials advocating legislation to help deal with the problem of homelessness; leaders of citizen advocacy groups on behalf of the poor, homeless, or mentally ill; law enforcement officials who have been dealing with the problem; and so on.

The prime advantage of the key informants approach is that a sample can be obtained and surveyed quickly, easily, and inexpensively. Also, conducting the survey can provide the fringe benefits of building connections with key community resources concerned about the problem and of giving your program some visibility. The chief disadvantage of this method, however, is that your information is not coming directly from the target population; the quality of that information depends on the objectivity and depth of knowledge underlying the expressed opinions.

To illustrate this disadvantage, consider the following possible pitfalls in an assessment of homelessness. Perhaps key informants affiliated with public shelters are unaware of those individuals who refuse to utilize the shelters, their reasons for doing so, and the unique problems they have. Perhaps advocates for poverty legislation will be likely to downplay needs associated with the mentally ill homeless because they see homelessness primarily as an economic problem and do not want to foster the notion that people are homeless due to defects in character or due to a voluntary preference. Perhaps mental health officials will be biased toward exaggerating mental illness as the cause of homelessness, or perhaps their bias will be to downplay the problem of homelessness among the mentally ill because that problem may reflect negatively on deinstitutionalization policies they have implemented. Perhaps neighborhood leaders where the homeless tend to congregate may be biased toward perceiving the need for services that get the homeless out of their neighborhood. In light of pitfalls like these, it is important that the representativeness of the key informant sample be maximized by using sampling procedures that are as scientific as possible. But even that is no guarantee that these pitfalls will be sufficiently minimized.

Community Forum   The community forum approach involves holding a meeting in which concerned members of the community can express their views and interact freely regarding needs. Although this approach offers a number of nonscientific advantages—such as its feasibility, its ability to build support and visibility for the sponsoring agency, and its ability to provide an atmosphere in which individuals can consider the problem in depth and be stimulated by what others have said to consider things they might otherwise have overlooked—from a scientific standpoint this approach is risky.

Those who attend such meetings might not be representative of the people in the best position to know about the needs of the target population and of those whose views are relatively unbiased. Instead, those with vested interests or with a particular ax to grind are likely to be overrepresented. The views expressed at such meetings are expressed publicly, and therefore strong social pressures might inhibit certain individuals from speaking at all or from expressing minority viewpoints. In light of these problems, rather than hold an open meeting for anyone to attend, it may be advisable to hold a series of closed meetings, each for a different, preselected homogeneous group.

Rates Under Treatment   The rates under treatment approach attempts to estimate the need for a service and the characteristics of its potential clients, based on the number and characteristics of clients already using that service. This method makes most sense when the rates under treatment are examined in a community other than, but similar to, a target community that does not yet provide the service in question. The assumption is that if the two communities really are comparable, the size and characteristics of the target population in the community without the service will parallel the size and characteristics of those already being treated in the comparison community.

A prime data collection method in this approach is the secondary analysis of case records from the comparison community. The prime advantages of the rates under treatment approach are its quickness, easiness, inexpensiveness, and unobtrusiveness. Its prime disadvantage is that it assesses only that portion of the target population that is already using services, and thus it pertains primarily to demand and may underestimate normative need. In fact, it may even underestimate demand because the number of individuals who want to utilize the service may exceed the caseload capacity in the comparison community. Moreover, many who want to use that type of service may choose not to use the one offered in the comparison community due to something undesirable in the way it is being provided.

Another disadvantage of this approach is that the records and data in the comparison community may be unreliable or biased. Accurate record-keeping may be a low priority in many agencies in the comparison community, particularly if service delivery demands leave little time for it. Also, agencies may exaggerate the number of clients served or their needs for services in order to look good to funding sources or others to whom they are accountable. One way this can happen is by multiple counting of the same individual across different agencies serving the target population. Another way is by recording one unit of service delivered to a family of four in such a manner that others might think that four units of service were provided to four different members of the target population. These inaccuracies often are not intentional.

Social Indicators   Another type of needs assessment that makes use of existing statistics is the social indicators approach. But this approach does not look at just treatment statistics; it examines aggregated statistics that reflect conditions of an entire population. For example, infant mortality rates (the number of infants who die during their first year of life) can be an indicator of the need for prenatal services in a particular community. Such rates could also be examined to identify communities that have the greatest need for these services. Likewise, rates of reported child abuse in a community can be used as an indicator of that community's need for a newly developed abuse prevention program. School dropout rates can indicate the need for a school district to begin hiring school social workers. Using social indicators is unobtrusive and can be done quickly and inexpensively. But those advantages need to be weighed against potential problems in the reliability of a particular existing database. Also, the utility of this approach depends on the degree to which the existing indicators can be assumed to reflect future service utilization patterns accurately. As we noted, the social indicators approach to needs assessment relies on the utilization of existing statistics. You may recall that Chapter 13 discussed the methodological issues involved in using existing statistics as well as some prominent sources for finding existing statistics. If you plan to conduct a needs assessment using the social indicators approach, you may want to reexamine that material.

Surveys of Communities or Target Groups

The most direct way to assess the characteristics and perceived problems and needs of the target group is to survey its members. This usually involves surveying a sample drawn from the population, although it is not inconceivable that when feasible a census of the entire target group might be undertaken.

Surveying members of target groups to assess their needs involves the application of the principles and techniques of sampling (Chapter 8) and survey research (Chapter 11). Ideally, probability sampling techniques should be used when we want to maximize the representativeness of the sample. But exceptions to this can be made—for instance, when it is impossible to obtain a sampling frame, as when attempting to survey the homeless. In such cases, qualitative sampling approaches may be more appropriate than quantitative ones.

Data collection methods might use highly structured, *quantitative* questionnaires or semi-structured, *qualitative* interviews, depending on the nature of the target group and what is already known or not known about its possible needs. For example, in assessing the need for additional day-care facilities for low-income parents, the needs assessment might include questions about the number of preschool-age children living with respondents, current child-care arrangements, whether and when respondents would use a new day-care facility, what respondents expect it to provide, what respondents would do differently to further their own education or careers were a day-care facility provided, respondents' demographic attributes, and so on.

The advantages and disadvantages of the direct survey approach parallel those in surveys in general. Evaluators ought to be particularly mindful of the potential biases associated with low response rates, social desirability, and acquiescent response sets. Suppose, for example, that the survey is conducted by mail. Those who bother to respond cannot be assumed to represent those who do not respond. In all likelihood, the respondents will feel a greater need for the program than the nonrespondents, and they are likely to differ in other ways as well. Suppose the questions are phrased only in general terms concerning whether a particular service ought to be available. Respondents might be predisposed to agree. Why not agree with the provision of a new service if no mention is made about its costs or whether the respondent would actually use it? But if respondents who agree that a service sounds nice are asked if they think it is worth its costs or whether they intend to use it, they might respond negatively.

Thus, the advantages of this method—its directness and its potential for ascertaining how prospective service consumers perceive their need for and likely utilization of programs—need to be weighed against potential biases in measurement or in response rates. Of course, what you have learned in this book about sampling, measurement, and surveys might enable you to design a needs assessment survey that adequately minimizes those biases. But doing so would be time consuming and expensive, and feasibility constraints might require that one or more of the foregoing four approaches to needs assessment be used instead.

Like research methods in general, each of the five approaches to needs assessment has its own advantages and disadvantages. Ideally, then, we should combine two or more approaches to needs assessment to get a more complete picture of normative needs, felt needs, and demand for prospective services.

Focus Groups

A qualitative research method often used for needs assessment, or for collecting other forms of program evaluation data, involves the use of *focus groups*. In a focus group, a small group of people (some recommend 12–15 people; others recommend no more than 8) are brought together in a room to engage in a guided discussion of a specified topic. When used for needs assessment, the discussants may be key informants, referral sources, service consumers or potential consumers, or community residents. They will be selected for the focus group on the basis of their relevancy to the topic being discussed. For example, if the topic pertains to prospective consumer utilization of a new service an agency is considering, the participants may be referral sources, current service consumers, or perhaps a sample of community residents in targeted neighborhoods. If the topic concerns consumer satisfaction with agency services, the participants may be drawn from current consumers.

Typically, focus group participants are chosen without using probability sampling methods. Purposive sampling (as in using key informants) or reliance on available subjects is much more common. It is also common to convene more than one focus group; relying on only one group is generally considered too risky, since any one particular group may be atypical.

Despite the risks inherent in generalizing from focus groups, they offer some advantages that agency personnel and program evaluators may value. They are inexpensive, generate speedy results, and offer flexibility for probing. The group dynamics that occur in focus groups can bring out aspects of the topic that evaluators may not have anticipated and that may not have emerged in individual interviews. Imagine, for example, that you, as a consumer in a social work education program, are being asked about your satisfaction with the program and how it might be improved to offer better services. Suppose you are responding to a structured questionnaire or a structured interview with closed-ended questions about your degree of satisfaction with the classroom course offerings, field practicums, audiovisual or computer resources, the quality of the teaching, advisement, instructor accessibility, and so forth. Your responses would be limited to checking off things like "moderately satisfied, slightly dissatisfied," and so on to program attributes anticipated by those who designed the survey. Suppose the survey questionnaire also contains some open-ended items asking you to think of anything else you particularly liked or disliked about the program or recommendations you have for improving it. You may or may not give a great deal of thought to these open-ended items, and even if you give them considerable thought you may not think of some things that others may think of and with which you would agree.

Now suppose that you were being asked about these things not in a structured survey format but in a focus group. Instead of asking you to check off your degree of satisfaction with this or that, or to come up by yourself with new ideas for improvements, the focus group leader would ask you and some of your cohorts to engage in a sort of bull-session discussion about your satisfaction or dissatisfaction with the program and how it could be improved. Chances are, if one or more of your colleagues began expressing dissatisfaction with something with which you also were dissatisfied, you might feel more comfortable in expressing the extent of your own dissatisfaction and its sources. As the members of the focus group interact about these issues, new ideas might be stimulated that would not have occurred to you in an individual interview or in completing a questionnaire. For instance, someone might say, "Gee, I sure wish the program offered an elective course on interventions connected to death and dying." This might spark someone else to say, "Yeah, and I would have loved to take a course on play therapy." Neither of these ideas may have occurred to you as an individual survey respondent, but on hearing them in a focus group you might respond, "Wow, I had assumed that the faculty knew best what courses were and were not appropriate to offer in a school of social work, but if those two courses were offered I sure would have taken them both. They sound like they would have prepared me with specific practice intervention competencies more than a lot of the other electives offered!" This might spur other group participants, who like you may not have thought of these courses in the context of an individual survey, to indicate that they too would love to take these two courses. And perhaps a few other prospective elective courses would be identified that students would find highly relevant to practice and that would be heavily enrolled in. At the same time, these comments might prompt the group members to focus more on preparation for practice competency as their chief source of dissatisfaction with the program, and a rich discussion might ensue identifying issues, potentially popular elective courses, and other ways to improve the program that would not have been anticipated or identified by many respondents in a survey. Instead of only one or two prospective new elective courses being identified by one or two isolated individuals in a survey, the focus group might identify a larger number of new courses and show which would generate the most excitement and the largest potential enrollments.

That said, however, it is important to remember that focus groups have disadvantages as well. As we mentioned above, the representativeness of focus group members is questionable. Perhaps those who agree to participate or who are the most vocal are the ones with the biggest axes to grind about the program, the ones most satisfied with the program, or the ones most eager to curry favor with program providers. While the group dynamics can bring out information that would not have emerged in a survey, those dynamics can also create pressures for people to say things that may not accurately reflect their true feelings or their prospective deeds. Whereas some individuals feeling dissatisfied with a program may feel more comfortable about expressing that dissatisfaction if others express it first, the same individuals may be less likely to express their dissatisfaction if those who speak up first express great satisfaction with the program. If a couple of members show enthusiasm for a prospective service, others may feel group pressure to say they, too, would utilize the service, even though, in reality, they would not utilize it. In light of these dynamics, special knowledge about group dynamics and special groupwork skills are needed to moderate focus groups. Another disadvantage is that the data emerging from focus groups are likely to be much more voluminous and less systematic than structured survey data. Analyzing focus group data, therefore, can be more difficult, tedious, and subject to the biases of the evaluator. And the analysis becomes more difficult to the extent that multiple focus groups yield inconsistent open-ended data. Thus, focus groups, like any other qualitative or quantitative research method, have certain advantages and disadvantages and are best used in combination with other research methods.

THREE MODELS OF PROGRAM EVALUATION PRACTICE

Shadish et al. (1991) have conceptualized a typology of three models of program evaluation practice—a typology that addresses many of the issues that have been covered in this chapter.

The first model that they identify resembles the goal attainment model discussed earlier, and it is called the *manipulable solution model of evaluation practice*. This model posits that the greatest priority in program evaluation is to serve the *public* interest, not the interests of stakeholders who have vested interests in a program. Advocates of this model believe that *summative* evaluations, which test out *whether* programs really work—whether they are effective in delivering the public benefits they promise—are more important than finding out how and why they work.

In this connection, proponents of this model of program evaluation ideally would like to see a sort of "experimenting society" (Campbell, 1971) in which multiple alternative solutions to the social problems the public seeks to ameliorate are tested for their effectiveness. Multiple solutions are tested (instead of just one program) in order to increase the chances of finding one that works and in order to see which solution works best. Thus, maximizing internal validity in order to reduce uncertainty about program effects is preferred over flexible (perhaps qualitative) research methods geared to discovering how to improve a program.

In contrast to the manipulable solution model is the *generalizable explanation model of evaluation practice* (Shadish et al., 1991). Those who advocate this model believe that many solutions will be effective and that their effects will differ under different conditions. A program may be effective under certain conditions but may have opposite effects under different conditions. For example, in earlier chapters we discussed Gerard Hogarty's research, which found that social casework can be effective in the treatment of individuals suffering from schizophrenia when that casework is combined with pharmacotherapy, but that its effects are harmful when it is not combined with pharmacotherapy. In a review of the research on case management effectiveness, Rubin (1992) found that the outcomes associated with case management vary from study to study and hypothesized that this variation may be influenced by the way case management is defined and the service delivery conditions under which it is implemented. For instance, case managers who have light caseloads and work in well-endowed service delivery systems may be much more effective than those with heavier caseloads and more fragmented service delivery systems. Simply finding that a case management program in one area is effective does not mean that that program is the solution for a different area.

The generalizable explanation model is less concerned with internal validity than with external validity, seeking more to identify multiple variables that bear on differential program outcomes in different settings than to test program effects in one randomized experiment. This model also emphasizes problems in the implementation of identified solutions.

The third model of program evaluation identified by Shadish et al. (1991) is the *stakeholder service model of evaluation practice*. Proponents of this model argue that evaluations will be more likely to be utilized, and thus have a greater impact on social problems, when they are tailored to the information needs of stakeholders closely involved in the programs being evaluated. Some proponents of this model focus on program managers as the stakeholders to whom evaluations should be geared, since the managers have more control over social programs than do other stakeholders. Other proponents of this model emphasize a broader focus that includes stakeholders such as the intended clients, service providers, and board members of a program. Proponents of the stakeholder model agree that the purpose of program evaluation is not to generalize findings to other sites, but rather to restrict the focus to the particular program under study. They also agree that stakeholders (not the evaluator) should play the key role in making decisions as to the design and purpose of the evaluation (in light of the evaluator's informed input). They criticize proponents of the other two models as being too concerned with theory and methodology at the expense of the practical information needs of real people with real problems that require immediate action. Although it is not inconceivable that some stakeholders might desire a summative evaluation, *formative* evaluations tend to be associated with this model.

Critics of the stakeholder model contend that stakeholders may seek information that is not relevant to ameliorating social problems—asking questions that are uninformed, lack general value, and are geared to the stakeholder's own vested interest. They further contend that political and economic priorities will compromise the integrity of the evaluation, and that sacrificing methodological principles in order to be more responsive to the need for immediate answers geared to the concerns of stakeholders may result in producing inaccurate, and possibly misleading, information.

Shadish and his associates point out that these three models of program evaluation practice are not mutually exclusive. For example, the manipulable solution model blends into the generalizable explanation model when its adherents implement simultaneous replications of experiments in different settings, or when they conduct meta-analyses. (Meta-analysis was discussed in Chapter 17.) Likewise, some stakeholders, such as congressional committees, may have social problem solving as their chief priority. As is the case with social work practitioners choosing among models of direct social work practice, it is perhaps best not to adhere dogmatically to just one model of program evaluation practice. Evaluators might be better advised to apply certain aspects of each model selectively, depending on the evaluator's situation. For example, if you work as an in-house evaluator for a social service agency, it may be extremely unwise for you to ignore some of the advantages of the stakeholder model. If, on the other hand, you are an external evaluator concerned primarily with testing a proposed solution to a social problem, it may not make sense to sacrifice that priority in pursuit of the immediate information needs of program managers. At the same time, however, you may be well advised to engage stakeholders in the evaluation planning process (in line with some of the principles discussed earlier in this chapter) and to recognize the potential contextual issues that may limit the generalizability of your results.

AN ILLUSTRATION OF A QUALITATIVE APPROACH TO EVALUATION RESEARCH

In several places throughout this text we have reiterated the view that quantitative and qualitative approaches to empirical inquiry are equally important. And in this, our final chapter, we have noted that program evaluations can use both quantitative and qualitative methods. This point is reinforced in the box titled "Combining Quantitative and Qualitative Methods in Program Evaluation." Yet we suspect that most of the contents in this chapter on program evaluation probably relate more to quantitative studies than to qualitative ones. We also suspect that the same can be said about the book as a whole, despite our efforts to say quite a bit about qualitative methods. This is due in part to the chapters needed to explain statistical analysis (in Part 5). Therefore, we think it fitting that we end both this chapter and this book with another illustration of qualitative research, one that shows how qualitative methods can be used in program evaluation.

The illustration we'll use was reported by Robert Bogdan and Steven Taylor (1990), two qualitatively oriented researchers who have been conducting evaluation research since the early 1970s on policy issues connected to the institutionalization and deinstitutionalization of people with developmental disabilities (people who are often labeled mentally retarded). Their work led them to question the policy of institutionalization and to become strong advocates for deinstitutionalization and the integration of people with disabilities into the community. However, their review of qualitative studies that documented the plight of disabled people who have been transferred from dehumanized institutions to dehumanized conditions in the community raised questions about how to improve the integration of this target population into the community.

Bogdan and Taylor believe that many quantitatively oriented outcome evaluations on the effects of deinstitutionalization have asked the wrong question, which Bogdan and Taylor call the "Does it work?" question. In their apparent orientation to the stakeholder service model of evaluation practice, Bogdan and Taylor note that community-based practitioners, like human service practitioners in general, believe in their work. They are not skeptical about what they do and therefore find no value in evaluative studies that merely tell whether a particular program was or was not effective. When "Does it work?" studies produce pessimistic results, they attribute the findings to the unfortunate prevalence of poorly funded, poor-quality community-based programs.

Moreover, they tend to see community integration as a moral question, similar to the issue of slavery. Bogdan and Taylor draw an analogy between asking about the effectiveness of policies and programs that free people from institutions and asking about the effectiveness of policies that freed slaves in the Civil War era, pointing out that slavery would not be justified were outcome studies to find that freed slaves were encountering difficulties in community integration. We, by the way, find this analogy debatable, but we share it with you so that you can see how the values of Bogdan and Taylor have influenced their work. Even if you disagree with their analogy, you might admire their candor about their values and about how values influenced the questions they asked. (Do you recall our discussion way back in Chapter 3 on the issue of whether research is ever truly value free?)

Rather than study whether community integration works, Bogdan and Taylor asked, "What does integration mean?" (notice the qualitative orientation to meanings) and "How can integration be accomplished?" Bogdan and Taylor saw these questions as more optimistic ones than asking whether community integration works. They also saw these questions as more responsive to practitioner/stakeholder needs, not only because practitioners are optimistic about what they do, but because they are more interested in formative information about how better to accomplish

their aims than they are in summative outcome conclusions.

Their focus on discovering insights about what community integration means and how better to achieve it led them to eschew probability sampling and to use instead qualitative strategies that employed aspects of snowball sampling, extreme case sampling, and critical incidents sampling (all of which were discussed in Chapter 12). Bogdan and Taylor were not interested in studying typical, or average, programs. They were not interested in representativeness. Instead, they sought to identify exemplary programs that were reputed to be doing well in achieving community integration. Their sampling efforts toward identifying exemplary programs employed a variety of techniques, "including announcements in professional newsletters, national mailings, and reviews of the professional literature" (1990:187). They also contacted a number of key informants who could tell them which agencies they felt were doing a good job and who could also identify other key informants who might know of additional exemplary programs. The key informants included disability rights activists, university-based researchers, and leaders of parent and professional groups.

Bogdan and Taylor conducted in-depth, open-ended phone interviews with officials in each program that was identified in their snowball sample. The purpose of these interviews was to obtain information that would help them whittle the sample down to eight agencies that promised to yield the most comprehensive understanding of what community integration means and how best to achieve it. Their interview questions attempted to probe into what the programs were doing, how well they seemed to be doing it, and how sincere they seemed to be in their efforts. These questions, as well as some routine questions about agency characteristics, enabled the researchers to select a sample of agencies that all seemed exemplary, but that varied in geographic location, services offered, and administrative arrangements.

The reason for the small sample size was that each agency in the sample was studied intensively, including a series of visits by the researchers over a three-year period. To gain entry into the agencies, and to foster their enthusiastic cooperation with the study, the researchers honestly told agency staff that their agency had been nominated as innovative or exemplary. This not only flattered administrators but helped them realize that their participation provided an opportunity to gain national visibility as a model program. Bogdan and Taylor report that this ironically seemed to lead many officials and staff to talk more openly about their problems than they otherwise might have done.

Each agency site visit lasted several days, during which the researchers employed a grounded theory approach involving triangulated qualitative data collection methods such as direct observation, intensive interviewing, and document analysis. The interviews were conducted with staff, clients and their family members, and representatives of other agencies in the vicinity. The site visits yielded thousands of pages of field notes and interview transcripts (and probably none of the inferential statistics with which we tried to captivate you in our previous two chapters).

Bogdan and Taylor's prime approach to data presentation is through case studies. The case studies are prepared after each agency visit. They provide an agency overview, describe the innovative agency policies that seem to be fostering community integration, and provide illustrative case examples of how agency innovations are perceived to be impacting people's lives. When applicable, they also report agency problems and dilemmas. The case study "stories" of the agencies are then disseminated to the field as a whole through short articles in relevant newsletters, articles that focus on the positive aspects of the visited agencies. The articles attempt to disseminate state-of-the-art descriptions to provide readers with new ideas that they may be able to adapt in their efforts to improve community integration in their own agencies.

With this positive, "optimistic," qualitative approach that focuses on process, Bogdan and Taylor believe they are producing research that will have greater utility to the field, and ultimately do more to improve the well being of disabled individuals, than they would if they were producing quantitative studies of outcome. Although many may disagree as to whether their particular approach is more valuable than other particular approaches to research and evaluation, we think few will fail to appreciate the value of their approach as one of a variety of valuable ways to use research in our efforts to improve practice, alleviate human suffering, and promote social welfare.

As we end this discussion of program evaluation, we also finish the final chapter of this book. Throughout this book we have shown how decisions in the design of social work research inescapably involve trade-offs. There is no one perfect way to do research, and no study is ever immune to potential error. No matter how sophisticated a study's research design or data analysis procedures may be, no study ever "proves" anything. Researchers simply do the best they can, within the feasibility constraints they face, to add something to the profession's knowledge base. We will always need to replicate studies and conduct new ones. Using the scientific method in social work—or in any other discipline—means that what we think we know is always open to question. If we really care about helping people, we will keep an open mind and attempt to improve our knowledge base. Social work research, like social work practice, is a problem-solving process. In attempting to provide practitioners with the knowledge they need to solve the problems they encounter, social work research can be seen as inescapably connected to social work practice. Ultimately, the success of our profession and the welfare of our clients will be affected by the degree to which social work practitioners take a scientific outlook and support the social work research enterprise. We hope that what you have learned in this book will help you to do both.

COMBINING QUANTITATIVE AND QUALITATIVE METHODS IN PROGRAM EVALUATION

Evaluative Function	Quantitative Methods	Qualitative Methods
Planning an evaluation		Open-ended interviews with stakeholders
		Content analysis of program documents
		Participant observation of program activities
Needs assessment	Survey of key informants, target group, or community	Community forum
	Rates under treatment	Focus groups
	Social indicators	
Process evaluation (Monitoring program implementation and identifying needed improvements)	Staff and client surveys	Case studies of model programs
	Analysis of agency records on amounts of various types of service delivery and to whom	Focus groups of program staff and service consumers
		Open-ended interviews with staff about unofficial goals and implementation problems
		Participant observation of service provision, staff training and staff meetings
		Open-ended interviews with service consumers
		Content analysis of staff meeting documents or practitioner entries in client records

Evaluative Function	Quantitative Methods	Qualitative Methods
		Videotaping or audiotaping service provision to assess practitioner skill or compliance with recommended procedures
Evaluating goal attainment	Experimental and quasi-experimental designs, combined with process evaluation to determine the nature of the program that did or did not attain its goals	Supplement outcome evaluation with foregoing process evaluation methods to ascertain the nature of the successful program or to learn whether the unsuccessful program was really implemented as intended
Evaluating efficiency	Cost-effectiveness analysis	
	Cost-benefit analysis	

Main Points

• Program evaluation applies different research methods and designs in order to assess and improve the conceptualization, design, planning, administration, implementation, effectiveness, efficiency, and utility of social interventions and human service programs.

• Although people have always in some way evaluated the reforms they have instituted, systematic and scientific approaches to program evaluation are a 20th-century phenomenon that has burgeoned during the last few decades as increased social welfare spending spawned an "age of accountability."

• The importance of program evaluation in funding decisions creates a highly political atmosphere in which stakeholders with vested interests can impede free scientific inquiry.

• Political considerations can affect not only in-house evaluators, but can also bias external evaluators who seem to be more independent. Even

funding sources and other external sponsors of an evaluation can have a stake in its outcome and may try to influence it for political reasons.

• Political and ideological forces can influence not only the methodology and interpretation of evaluative research, but also whether and how its findings get utilized. It cannot be assumed that the implications of evaluation research will necessarily be put into practice, especially if they conflict with official interests or points of view.

• The social context of program evaluation studies also affects the logistics involved in implementing them.

• A number of steps have been proposed to help evaluators alleviate potential problems in the logistics of their studies, as well as to alleviate resistance to them and to their utilization. These steps involve learning as much as possible about the stakeholders and their vested interests in the evaluation, involving them in a meaningful way in all phases of planning and performing the evaluation, maintaining ongoing mutual feedback between them and the evaluator, and tailoring the evaluation and its reportage to their needs and preferences as much as possible without sacrificing scientific objectivity.

• Although the evaluation of program outcome is one of the first things that comes to mind when people think of program evaluation, other important foci of evaluation research address research questions concerned with planning new programs and monitoring their implementation.

• Evaluations of program outcome should strive to enhance causal inference by using the most internally valid experimental or quasi-experimental design possible.

• The assessment of efficiency asks whether program outcomes are being achieved at a reasonable cost and applies the principles of cost accounting to calculate the ratio of program benefits to costs. But deciding whether the benefits of a program justify its costs ultimately means going beyond purely economic considerations and involves making value judgments about humanistic benefits.

• Evaluating program outcome, or goal attainment, is complicated by ambiguities in determining the specific outcome indicators implied by official organizational goals, by the intentionally grandiose nature of some statements of organizational missions, and by the displacement of official goals by unofficial ones.

• Some programs have unsuccessful outcomes not because they are wrong in theory, but because they were never implemented as intended. Outcome evaluations, therefore, ought to be supplemented by evaluations that monitor program implementation. Monitoring implementation can help resolve problems early on, help keep agencies accountable, and help identify the best ways to implement and maintain programs.

• The most common focus in evaluation for program planning is the assessment of need. Needs can be defined normatively or in terms of demand.

• Five approaches to needs assessment include surveying key informants, holding a community forum, examining rates under treatment, analyzing social indicators, and conducting a direct survey of the community or target group. Each approach is imperfect; each has its own unique advantage and disadvantages. Ideally, a needs assessment will combine more than one approach.

• Different models of program evaluation practice have been conceptualized. These models vary according to whether the focus of the evaluation is on (1) testing, on behalf of the public interest, whether solutions to social problems really work; (2) assessing variations in program outcome and implementation under different conditions and across different settings; and (3) obtaining immediate information addressing the concerns of stakeholders in a particular program.

Review Questions and Exercises

1. Interview an administrator and some practitioners at a social welfare agency, perhaps the one in which you have your field placement. What evaluations, if any, have been conducted at the agency, with what outcomes? Were the findings utilized? Why or why not? Try to identify the stakeholders and their vested interests regarding those evaluations and findings. If no evaluation has ever been conducted, why not? Are politically or ideologically based resistances involved?

2. In the same or another agency, construct skeletal plans for evaluating program implementation and outcome. What resistances or logistical problems to the evaluation might be anticipated? How would the evaluation be useful to decision makers? What difficulties did you encounter in trying

to translate the formal mission statement of the agency into observable indicators of outcome?

3. Consider a social problem that is currently receiving a lot of media attention in your community. Design a needs assessment study regarding that problem or a specific service you have in mind for alleviating it. Assume a data collection budget of $5000 and a six-month deadline for designing and completing the assessment.

4. Find a research article in a social work journal that describes a study conducted for the purpose of evaluating program outcome. A good example would be the study by Boone et al., "The Impact of Early and Comprehensive Social Work Services on Length of Stay," *Social Work in Health Care,* Fall 1981, pp. 1–9. See if you can identify the stakeholders in the research, and critique the article from the standpoint of whether it showed how potential biases associated with vested interests were controlled for.

Additional Readings

Bennet, Carl A., and Lumsdaine, Arthur A. (eds.), *Evaluation and Experiment* (New York: Academic Press, 1975). Packed with illustrative examples, this reader digs into a number of special aspects of evaluation research. About every problem you are likely to hit is discussed in the book.

Evaluation Studies Review Annual. Sage Publications puts out a new review annually; each year has different editors and contains some of the best articles on program evaluation that have been published. This is an excellent source in which to find examples of exemplary program evaluation studies, debates on methodological issues, and analyses of the political context of program evaluation. The contents vary in level of difficulty; some are most relevant to more experienced program evaluators, but many are relevant to all students interested in this topic.

Posavac, Emil J., and Carey, Raymond G., *Program Evaluation: Methods and Case Studies* (Englewood Cliffs, NJ: Prentice Hall, 1985). As our various references to this book throughout the chapter suggest, it is an excellent basic text for the beginning program evaluator.

Rossi, Peter H., and Freeman, Howard E., *Evaluation: A Systematic Approach* (Beverly Hills, CA: Sage, 1982). Here is another good basic text on program evaluation to which we've referred in this chapter.

Shadish, William R., Cook, Thomas D., and Leviton, Laura C., *Foundations of Program Evaluation: Theories of Practice* (Newbury Park, CA: Sage, 1991). This unique book is a must for serious students of program evaluation who seek a conceptually advanced treatment of this topic. It develops a typology of models of program evaluation and a conceptual framework to critically analyze theories of program evaluation. Using that framework, it compares the work of seven of the field's foremost theorists and develops recommendations for a new theory of program evaluation.

Weiss, Carol, *Evaluation Research* (Englewood Cliffs, NJ: Prentice Hall, 1972). Here's a quicker and easier introduction to evaluation research. In a short paperback, the author gives a good overview of the method and points you toward aspects you might want to learn more about. It is an especially good beginning if you don't have any prior experience in social research in general. This introduction may let you discover that you'd like to get some experience.

Using the Library

INTRODUCTION

Throughout this book we have been assuming that you will be reading reports of social work research. In this appendix, we want to talk a little about how you'll find reports to read.

As we've indicated repeatedly, you live in a world filled with social science research reports. Your daily newspaper, magazines, professional journals, alumni bulletins, club newsletters—virtually everything you pick up to read may carry reports dealing with a particular topic. Usually, you'll pursue that interest through your library. Although we'll give you just a brief overview here, you can get more information in an excellent little book—Alden Todd's *Finding Facts Fast* (Berkeley, CA: Ten Speed Press, 1979).

GETTING HELP

When you want to find something in the library, your best friend is the reference librarian, who is specially trained to find things in the library. Sometimes it's hard to ask people for help, but you'll do yourself a real service to make an exception in this case.

Some libraries have specialized reference librarians—for the social sciences, humanities, government documents, and so forth. Find the one you need and tell him or her what you're interested in. The reference librarian will probably put you in touch with some of the many available reference sources.

REFERENCE SOURCES

You have probably heard the expression *information explosion*. Your library is one of the main battlefields. Fortunately, a large number of reference volumes offer a guide to the information that's available.

Books in Print This volume lists all the books currently in print in the United States—listed separately by author and by title. Out-of-print books can often be found in older editions of *Books in Print*.

Readers' Guide to Periodical Literature This annual volume with monthly updates lists articles published in many journals and magazines. Because the entries are organized by subject matter, this is an excellent source for organizing your reading on a particular topic. Exhibit A-1 presents a sample page from the *Readers' Guide*.

In addition to these general reference volumes, you'll find a great variety of specialized references. A few are listed as examples.

- Social Work Abstracts
- Sociological Abstracts
- Psychological Abstracts

128   READERS' GUIDE TO PERIODICAL LITERATURE

MUSIC–*cont.*
Study and teaching
See also
Guitar—Study and teaching
Themes, motives, etc.
See also
Automobiles in music
Theory
See also
Atonality
Japan
The Japanese and Western music. L. Futoransky. il *The Courier (Unesco)* 40:38+ D '87
MUSIC, AMERICAN
See also
Jazz music
MUSIC, ELECTRONIC
See also
Comuters—Musical use
Musical instruments, Electronic
MUSIC AND STATE
Viewpoint [government subsidies of opera] J. L. Poole. *Opera News* 52:4 F 13 '88
Soviet Union
Gorbachev sets the beat for Soviet rock. il *U.S. News & World Report* 104:8-9 F 8 '88
MUSIC AND THE BLIND
Call him Doc [D. Watson] F. L. Schultz. il pors *Country Journal* 15:44-53 F '88
MUSIC AND THE HANDICAPPED
See also
Guitarists, Handicapped
MUSIC CORPORATION OF AMERICA *See* MCA, Inc.
MUSIC CRITICS AND CRITICISM
See also
Opera reviews
MUSIC FESTIVALS
Austria
Bregenz. H. Koegler. il *Opera News* 52:38 F 13 '88
Germany (West)
Bayreuth. J. H. Sutcliffe. il *Opera News* 52:36 Ja 30 '88
Great Britain
Buxton. E. Forbes. *Opera News* 52:40–1 F 13 '88
Italy
Torre del Lago [Puccini Festival] M. Hamlet-Metz. *Opera News* 52:38-40 F 13 '88
Pennsylvania
Philadelphia [American Music Theater Festival] R. Baxter. *Opera News* 52:34 Ja 30 '88
MUSICAL COMEDIES, REVUES, ETC. *See* Musicals, revues, etc.
MUSICAL INSTRUMENTS, ELECTRONIC
It's alive with the sound of—well, just about everything [Synclavier synthesizer] L. Helm. il *Business Week* p75 F 8 '88
MUSICAL INSTRUMENTS INDUSTRY
See also
New England Digital Corporation
MUSICALS, REVUES, ETC.
Choreography
See Choreography
Reviews
Single works
Anything goes
Dance Magazine il 62:52-7 Ja '88. J. Gruen
Cabaret
Dance Magazine 62:73-4 Ja '88. H. M. Simpson
The chosen
The Nation 246:175 F 6 '88. T. M. Disch
Into the woods
Dance Magazine 62:64 Ja '88. K. Grubb
Oil City Symphony
The Nation 246:175-6 F 6 '88. T. M. Disch
The phantom of the opera
Life il 11:88-92 F '88. M. Stasio
Maclean's il 101:51 F '88. L. Black
New York il 21:89-90 F 8 '88. J. Simon
The New Yorker 63:97-8 F 8 '88. M. Kramer
Newsweek il por 111:68-70+ F 8 '88. J. Kroll
Rolling Stone il p26 F 25 '88. D. Handelman
Time il 131:83-4 F 8 '88. W. A. Henry
Stage setting and scenery
High-tech magic: follow that gondola [Phantom of the opera] J. Kroll. il *Newsweek* 111:70 F 8 '88
Writing
Changing the face of Broadway [A. Lloyd Webber] M. Stasio. il pors *Life* 11:88-92 F '88
MUSICIANS
See also
Drugs and musicians

Rock musicians
MUSKE, CAROL, 1945-
Skid [poem] *The New Yorker* 63:38 F 8 '88
MUSLIMS
See also
Islam
Afghanistan
Beyond the Afghan stalemate. L. Komisar. il *The New Leader* 71:5-6 Ja 11-25 '88
Middle East
The Islamic resurgence: a new phase? R. Wright. bibl f *Current History* 87:53-6+ F '88
MUTATION
See also
Transposons
MUTUAL FUNDS *See* Investment trusts
MUTUALISM (BIOLOGY) *See* Symbiosis
MUZIEKTHEATER (AMSTERDAM, NETHERLANDS)
See Opera houses
MYASTHENIA GRAVIS
Suzanne Rogers: "I looked at my face and thought, 'Who'd hire a freak?'". A. W. Petrucelli. pors *Redbook* 170:104+ F '88
MYCOBACTERIAL DISEASES
See also
Tuberculosis
MYCOTOXINS *See* Toxins and antitoxins

N

N. W. AYER & SON, INC.
Ayer to the throne [Burger King ad campaign] B. Kanner. il *New York* 21:24+ F 29 '88
NADIS, STEVEN J.
Robot observatories. il *Omni (New York, N.Y.)* 10:24+ Ja '88
NAEP *See* National Assessment of Educational Progress
NAKAGAMI, KENJI, 1946-
about
Two contemporary writers. D. Palmé. *The Courier (Unesco)* 40:44 D '87
NAKED SHORT SELLING *See* Securities—Short selling
NANDINA
Nandina does the unexpected. il *Southern Living* 23:50 Ja '88
NAPLES (ITALY)
Music
See also
Opera—Italy
NARCOTIC ADDICTS *See* Drug abuse
NARCOTICS LAWS AND REGULATIONS
See also
Boats in narcotics regulation
Robots in narcotics regulation
Austria
A five-year penalty call [Czech hockey legend J. Bubla serving prison sentence for smuggling heroin] J. Holland. il por *Macleans's* 101:6 F 8 '88
Colombia
Battling the drug lords [Attorney General C. Hoyos murdered] E. Tolmie. il *Maclean's* 101:26 F 8 '88
Day of the assassins [Attorney General C. Hoyos murdered] M. S. Serrill. il por *Time* 131:42 F 8 '88
How cocaine rules the law in Colombia [assassination of Attorney General C. Hoyos] C. A. Robbins. il *U.S. News & World Report* 104:28-9 F 8 '88
Murderers of Medellin [assassination of Colombia's Attorney General C. Hoyos] F. Willey. il *Newsweek* 111:33 F 8 '88
NARCOTICS TRADE
See also
Boats in narcotics regulation
Narcotics laws and regulations
Robots in narcotics regulation
Teen drug dealers: uncovering the real story. W. White and K. Dickerson. il *Teen* 32:36-9+ F '88
Panama
The dictator in the dock [M. A. Noriega] N. Cooper. il pors *Newsweek* 111:33 F 22 '88
Drugs, money and death [cover story; special section] il pors map *Newsweek* 111:32-6+ F 15 '88
More bad news for Noriega. N. Cooper. il por *Newsweek* 111:37 F 8 '88
Noriega's money machine [aides testify before Senate subcommitttee] M. S. Serrill. il *Time* 131:39-40 F 22 '88

Exhibit A-1 A Page from the *Readers' Guide to Periodical Literature*

- Social Science Index
- Social Science Citation Index
- Popular Guide to Government Publications
- New York Times Index
- Facts on File
- Editorial Research Reports
- Business Periodicals Index
- Monthly Catalog of Government Publications
- Public Affairs Information Service Bulletin
- Education Index
- Applied Science and Technology Index
- A Guide to Geographic Periodicals
- General Science Index
- Biological and Agricultural Index
- Nursing and Applied Health Index
- Nursing Studies Index
- Index to Little Magazines
- Popular Periodical Index
- Biography Index
- Congressional Quarterly Weekly Report

- Library Literature
- Bibliographic Index

USING THE STACKS

For serious research, you should learn to use the stacks, where most of the library's books are stored. In this section, we'll give you some information about finding books in the stacks.

The Card Catalog

Your library's card catalog is the main reference system for finding out where books are stored. Each book is described on three separate 3 × 5 cards. The cards are then filed in three alphabetic sets. One set is arranged by author, another by title, and the third by subject matter.

If you want to find a particular book, you can look it up in either the author file or the title file. If you only have a general subject area of interest, you should thumb through the subject catalog. Exhibit A-2 presents a sample card in the card catalog.

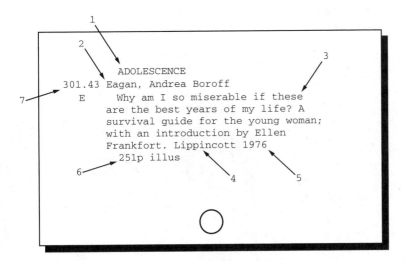

SOURCE: Lilian L. Shapiro, *Teaching Yourself in Libraries* (New York: H. W. Wilson, 1978), pp. 3–4.

Exhibit A-2 Sample Subject Catalog Card

1. Subject heading (always in capital letters)

2. Author's name (last name, first name)

3. Title of the book

4. Publisher

5. Date of publication

6. Number of pages in the book plus other information. (Here we are told that the book contains illustrations.)

7. Call number. (This is needed to find a nonfiction book on the library shelves. A book of fiction generally carries no number and is found in alphabetical order by the author's name.)

Library of Congress Classification

Here's a useful strategy to use when you're researching a topic. Once you've identified the call number for a particular book in your subject area, go to the stacks, find that book, *and* look over the other books on the shelves near it. Because the books are arranged by subject matter, this method will help you locate relevant books you didn't know about.

Alternatively, you may want to go directly to the stacks and look at books in your subject area. In most libraries, books are arranged and numbered according to a subject matter classification developed by the Library of Congress. The following is a selected list of Library of Congress categories.

Library of Congress Classifications (partial)

A GENERAL WORKS

B PHILOSOPHY, PSYCHOLOGY, RELIGION

B-BD	Philosophy
BF	Psychology
BL-BX	Religion

C HISTORY-AUXILIARY SCIENCES

D HISTORY (except America)

DA-DR	Europe
DS	Asia
DT	Africa

E-F HISTORY (America)

E	United States
E51-99	Indians of North America
E185	Negroes in the United States
F101-1140	Canada
F1201-3799	Latin America

G GEOGRAPHY-ANTHROPOLOGY

G-GF	Geography
GC	Oceanology and oceanography
GN	Anthropology
GV	Sports, amusements, games

H SOCIAL SCIENCES

HB-HJ	Economics and business
HM-HX	Sociology

J POLITICAL SCIENCE

JK	United States
JN	Europe
JQ	Asia, Africa
JX	International relations

K LAW

L EDUCATION

M MUSIC

N FINE ARTS

NA	Architecture
NB	Sculpture
NC	Graphic arts
ND	Painting
NE	Engraving
NK	Ceramics, textiles

P LANGUAGE AND LITERATURE

RE	English language
PG	Slavic language
PJ-PM	Oriental language
PN	Drama, oratory, journalism
PQ	Romance literature
PR	English literature
PS	American literature
PT	Germanic literature

Q SCIENCE

QA	Mathematics
QB	Astronomy
QC	Physics

QD	Chemistry
QE	Geology
QH-QR	Biology

R MEDICINE

| RK | Dentistry |
| RT | Nursing |

S AGRICULTURE—PLANT AND ANIMAL
 INDUSTRY

T TECHNOLOGY

| TA-TL | Engineering |
| TR | Photography |

U MILITARY SCIENCE

V NAVAL SCIENCE

Z BIBLIOGRAPHY AND LIBRARY SCIENCE

ABSTRACTS

Social work researchers and practitioners will find particular value in publications that present summaries of books and articles that help them locate a great many references easily and effectively. These summaries are often prepared by the original authors. As you find relevant references, you can track down the original works and see the full details.

In social work, the most relevant publication of these summaries is *Social Work Abstracts* (which up until several years ago, used to be called *Social Work Research & Abstracts*). Exhibit A-3 contains a sample page from that reference. Publications such as *Dissertation Abstracts International, Sociological Abstracts, Psychological Abstracts, SAGE Urban Studies Abstracts,* and *Public Administration Abstracts* might also contain references relevant to particular research topics in social work.

COMPUTERIZED LIBRARY FILES

It seems certain that, in the years to come, you'll be finding library materials increasingly by computer. For example, you'll sit at a computer terminal, type the title of a book, and in seconds see a video display of a catalog card. If you wanted to

explore the book further, you could type an instruction at the terminal and see an abstract of the book, or perhaps the whole book. Alternatively, you might type a subject name and see a listing of all the books and articles written on that topic. You could skim through the list and indicate which ones you wanted to see.

Although this may seem pretty futuristic, it's closer at hand than you may think. computer network systems such as The Source, CompuServe, and others already allow microcomputer owners to locate and retrieve articles from the *New York Times,* United Press International, and many other similar information sources by connecting their microcomputers over telephone lines to a central computer perhaps thousands of miles away.

Many college libraries now have access to the Educational Resources Information Center (ERIC). This computer-based system allows you to search through hundreds of major educational journals to find articles published in the subject area of your interest (within the field of education). Once you identify the articles you are interested in, the computer will print out abstracts of those articles.

Taking the long view, it would be a good idea for you to begin familiarizing yourself with such computer-based systems now, since you are likely to be using them a great deal in the future. Ultimately, you may do all your library searching from your own home, using your own computer.

PROFESSIONAL JOURNALS

Despite the exciting advances occurring in computer-based systems and the great practical value of publications containing abstracts, it would be a mistake to rely exclusively on them for the purpose of locating journal articles pertinent to your interests. There is no guarantee that every reference of value to you will get identified in a computer search or a publication of abstracts. In particular, there is the problem of the time lag between the publication of an article and the appearance of its abstract in a publication of abstracts or a computerized system.

1498, Andrews, S., & Wikler, L. Developmental disabilities. Health and Social Work, 6(4, Supplement): 628-685, 1981.

School of Social Work, Univ. of Nebraska, Omaha

Social work practice with the developmentally disabled has been expanding and is recognized as an area of specialty interest. Opportunities for formal training in this specialty have also expanded, but the significant gains of the last decade are severely threatened by current economic and human service policies of the government. (Journal abstract, edited)

1499, Barstow, L. F. Working with cancer patients in radiation therapy. Health and Social Work, 7(1): 35–40, 1982.

Radiation therapy can be a source of stress to the cancer patient. Specific fears related to the word "radiation," to the greater isolation of radiation therapy departments, and to possible side effects should be addressed to help patients and families deal more effectively with the overall ramifications of their life with cancer. Social workers established a program in a radiation therapy clinic to help patients deal with these specific stresses of treatment. The program concentrated on individual casework with patients and families. The social worker's initial focus was to evaluate psychosocial needs and then to facilitate solutions. Group work was also an important part of the program. A number of group modalities were tried until one was found that seemed to meet the most needs. (Author abstract, edited)

1500, Berkman, B., Henley, B. Medical and surgical services in acute-care hospitals. Health and Social Work, 6(4, Supplement): 22S–27S, 1981.

Social Work in Health Care Program, Massachusetts General Hospital Institute of Health Professions, Boston

Practitioners on medical and surgical units of acute-care general hospitals represent the greatest number of social workers in health. Drawing on a recent survey of thirty-nine hospitals in New England to characterize social work practice in this specialty interest area, the discussion reveals that patients served by social workers average longer lengths of stay than patients not referred to social work. The patients referred are older, are more ill, are more incapacitated, and concomitantly have more psychosocial problems. The social work method primarily used with medical and surgical inpatients is short-term casework, which emphasizes two types of intervention—emotional support and advocacy. (Author abstract, edited)

1501, Burnell, G. M., & Taylor, P. H. Psychoeducational programs for problems in living. Health and Social Work, 7(1): 7–13, 1982.

Dept. of Psychiatry, Kaiser-Permanente Medical Center, Santa Clara, Calif.

In a two-year demonstration project, the investigators tested the feasibility of offering a psychoeducational program as an adjunct to psychotherapy for patients with problems related to daily living. Fourteen patients were identified as needing support according to the Heimler Scale of Social Functioning. These patients then attended a six-week stress management course and reported improvement in stress-related symptoms by the last session. A substantial percentage of the eighty-five participants who attended courses in both January and March of the program's first year reported high satisfaction with course content and suggestions made by counselors and health educators. In-

creased awareness of the role of psychoeducational programs in deflecting the overuse of medical services should facilitate their implementation by health providers. (Author abstract, edited)

1502. Caputi, M. A., A 'quality of life' model for social work practice in health care. Health and Social Work, 7(2): 103–10, 1982.

School of Social Work, Univ. of Wisconsin, Madison

Traditionally, medicine has defined the quality of care in terms of the appropriate application of its technology in the diagnosis and treatment of illness. This definition, however, neglects the impact of the psychosocial correlates associated with the onset of illness and its effects on the individual and family unit throughout the medical care process. This omission fails to recognize the complementarity between the technical and psychosocial aspects of care. This discussion provides a new definition of the quality of care that includes both components. The redefinition serves as the basis for the social work-initiated "quality of life" model of interprofessional practice. The goal of this three-phased model is to enhance the patient's and the family's coping skills through facilitating communication with health professionals. By increasing access to and use of medical and psychosocial information, patients can become active participants in the treatment of their illness and make better-informed choices. (Author abstract, edited)

1503, Clement, J., & Klingbell, K. S. The emergency room. Health and Social Work, 6(4, Supplement): 83S–90S, 1981.

Dept. of Social Work, Harborview Medical Center, Seattle, Wash.

Amid wholesale cutbacks in social service programs, emergency room social work remains a fast-growing field. Little has been published about this specialty interest area, however, and no school of social work offers a graduate program in it. A ten-year-old program of emergency room social work in a major teaching hospital that can serve as a model for comparable programs is described. (Journal abstract, edited)

1504. Cleveland, T. S., Where are we going with specialty interest groups? Health and Social Work, 6(4, Supplement): 9S–12S, 1981.

Social Work Services, Martin Luther King, Jr. General Hospital, Los Angeles, Calif.

Several reasons for the proliferation of specialty interest groups in health practice are examined. They include (1) the fragmentation of roles between social workers in practice and in academic positions, (2) accreditation standards for various programs that mandate the involvement of social workers, (3) social workers' desires for a voice in the policy arena, (4) the impact of the medical profession on the delivery of social services, (5) the role demands on social workers in health settings and the limited preparation of social workers for these roles, (6) the need for continuing education in social work, (7) the fragmented way in which standards for social work practice have emerged, and (8) the long-standing division between "medical" and "psychiatric" social workers. To counter the trend of proliferating specialty interest groups, social workers must present uniform definitions of health and mental health practice based on social work's holistic view of clients.

Exhibit A-3 A Page from *Social Work Research & Abstracts* (now called *Social Work Abtracts*)

Unless you examine recent issues in professional journals that are the most relevant to your particular interest, therefore, you may be taking too great a risk that you will miss some important, recently published article that could have a profound impact upon what you choose to do and how you choose to do it. For example, perhaps someone just published a study exactly like the one you are planning. If so, you may or may not want to proceed with your study. You might wish to revise it in some way in order to build upon the recently published study or to avoid some methodological problem discussed in that study that you had not previously considered.

Examining recent issues of journals is probably less time consuming than you might imagine. These issues ought to be available in the section of your library that contains unbound current periodicals. Once you locate the recent issues—about the last two years ought to suffice—of the relevant journals, it should take only a few minutes to thumb through the tables of contents looking for titles that have some potential bearing on your topic. Once you spot a relevant title, turn to the page on which the article begins. There you will find an abstract of the article, which, like the abstracts appearing in publications of abstracts, takes only seconds to read in order to determine if the article is sufficiently pertinent to warrant reading in greater detail.

If you are uncertain about the professional journals that are pertinent to your topic, you might want to examine the list of journals reviewed in several issues of *Social Work Abstracts*. Each issue contains a list of the journals reviewed for that issue. You might also want to get help with this from your reference librarian, mentioned earlier. Just as a beginning idea of some of the journals you might wish to review—this list is far from complete—here is a list of some of the major journals by problem area:

Social Work (Covers Various Problem Areas)
Social Work
Journal of Social Service Research
Social Service Review

Social Work Research
Research on Social Work Practice

Aging and the Aged
Journal of Gerontological Social Work
Journal of Gerontology
The Gerontologist

Alcoholism and Drug Addiction
Advances in Alcohol and Substance Abuse
Journal of Studies on Alcohol

Crime and Delinquency
Adolescence
Canadian Journal of Criminology
Youth and Society

Family and Child Welfare
Adoption and Fostering
Child Care Quarterly
Child Services Review
Child Welfare
Children Today
Family Process
Family Therapy
Journal of Family Issues
Journal of Marital and Family Therapy

Health
Health and Social Work
Journal of Health and Social Behavior
Social Work in Health Care

Mental Health
American Journal of Orthopsychiatry
Archives of General Psychiatry
Community Mental Health Journal
Hospital and Community Psychiatry
Schizophrenia Bulletin

Mental Retardation
American Journal of Mental Deficiency
Journal of Mental Deficiency Research
Mental Retardation

School Social Work
School Social Work Journal
Social Work in Education

Social Policy and Action
Public Welfare
Social Policy

Other
Behavior Modification
Behavior Therapy
Cognitive Therapy and Research
Community Development Journal
Journal of Applied Behavior Analysis
Journal of Applied Behavioral Science
Journal of Jewish Communal Service
Social Work with Groups

Additional Readings

Bart, Pauline, and Frankel, Linda, **The Student Sociologist's Handbook,** 3rd edition (Glenview, IL: Scott, Foresman, 1981). A survival kit for doing social research. Contains a step-by-step guide for writing research papers; chapters on periodicals, abstract and indexing services, bibliographies, bibliographic aids, and other secondary sources; and a complete guide to governmental and non-governmental sources of data. Special section on gender roles and women's studies.

Becker, Leonard, and Gustafson, Clair, **Encounter with Sociology: The Term Paper** (San Francisco: Boyd and Fraser, 1976). An excellent guide for writing term and research papers in the social sciences. Contains some good discussion of methodological issues to consider as well.

Li, Tze-chung, **Social Science Reference Sources: A Practical Guide** (Westport, CT: Greenwood Press, 1980). Lists and describes all types of references materials, including databases and archives as well as published sources. Organized into two parts: social sciences in general and by discipline.

The Research Report

INTRODUCTION

This book has considered the variety of activities that compose the *doing* of social research. In this appendix, we'll turn to an often neglected subject: reporting the research to others. (We touched on this subject briefly in Chapter 4 when we provided an overview of the research process.) Unless the research is properly communicated, all the efforts devoted to previously discussed procedures will go for naught.

Before proceeding further on this topic, we should suggest one absolutely basic guideline. Good social scientific reporting requires good English (unless you are writing in a foreign language). Whenever we ask the "figures to speak for themselves," they tend to remain mute. Whenever we use unduly complex terminology or construction, communication is reduced. Every researcher should read and reread (at approximately three-month intervals) an excellent small book by William Strunk, Jr. and E. B. White, *The Elements of Style*.* If you do this faithfully, and if even 10% of the contents rub off, you stand a good chance of making yourself understood and your findings appreciated.

_____
*William Strunk, Jr., and E. B. White, 3rd ed. (New York: Macmillan, 1979). The following is another useful reference on writing: H. W. Fowler, *A Dictionary of Modern English Usage* (New York: Oxford University Press, 1965).

Scientific reporting has several functions, and it is a good idea to keep these in mind. First, the report communicates to an audience a body of specific data and ideas. The report should provide those specifics clearly and with sufficient detail to permit an informed evaluation. Second, the scientific report should be viewed as a contribution to the general body of professional knowledge. While remaining appropriately humble, you should always regard your research report as an addition to what we know about social work. Finally, the report should serve the function of stimulating and directing further inquiry.

SOME BASIC CONSIDERATIONS

Despite these general guidelines, different reports serve different purposes. A report appropriate for one purpose might be wholly inappropriate for another. This section of this appendix deals with some of the basic considerations in this regard.

Audience

Before drafting your report, you must ask yourself who you hope will read it. Normally, you should make a distinction between professional colleagues and general readers. If written for the former, you may make certain assumptions about their existing knowledge and may perhaps summarize certain points rather than explaining them in detail. Similarly, you may appropriately use more technical language than would be appropriate for a general audience.

At the same time, you should remain always aware that any science or profession is composed of factions or cults. Terms and assumptions acceptable to your immediate colleagues may only confuse other professionals. That applies with regard to substance as well as techniques. The social worker who is reporting a study on cognitive-behavioral interventions to an audience of colleagues who are not familiar with those interventions, for example, should explain previous findings in more detail than would be necessary if he or she were addressing an audience of social workers specializing in cognitive-behavioral interventions.

Form and Length of Report

We should begin this subsection by saying that our comments apply to both written and oral reports. These two forms, however, will affect the nature of the report.

It is useful to think about the variety of reports that might result from a research project. To begin, you may wish to prepare a short *research note* for publication in an academic or technical journal. Such reports should be approximately one to five pages in length (typed, double-spaced) and should be concise and direct. In a small amount of space, you will not be able to present the state of the field in any detail, and your methodological notes must be somewhat abbreviated as well. Basically, you should tell the reader why you feel a brief note is justified by your findings, then tell what those findings are.

Often, researchers must prepare reports for the sponsors of their research. These may vary greatly in length, of course. In preparing such a report, however, you should bear in mind the audience for the report—scientific or lay—and their reasons for sponsoring the project in the first place. It is both bad politics and bad manners to bore the sponsors with research findings that have no interest or value to them. At the same time, it may be useful to summarize the ways in which the research has advanced basic scientific knowledge (if it has).

Working papers or monographs are another form of research reporting. Especially in a large and complex project, it will be useful to obtain comments on your analysis and the interpretation of your data. A working paper constitutes a tentative presentation with an implicit request for comments. Working papers can also vary in length, and they may present all of the research findings of the project or only a portion of them. Because your professional reputation is not at stake in a working paper, you should feel free to present tentative interpretations that you cannot altogether justify—identifying them as such and asking for evaluations.

Many research projects result in papers delivered at professional meetings. Often, these serve the same purpose as working papers. You are able to present findings and ideas of possible interest to your colleagues and ask for their comments. Although the length of professional papers may vary depending on the organization of the meetings, we'd encourage you to say too little rather than too much. Although a working paper may ramble somewhat through a variety of tentative conclusions, conference participants should not be forced to sit through an oral unveiling of the same. Interested listeners can always ask for more details later, and uninterested ones can gratefully escape.

Probably the most popular research report is the article published in an academic journal. Again, lengths vary, and you should examine the lengths of articles previously published by the journal in question. As a rough guide, however, 20 typed pages is as good as any. A subsequent section on the organization of the report is primarily based on the structure of a journal article, so we will say no more at this point, except to indicate that student term papers should be written on this model. As a general rule, a term paper that would make a good journal article would also make a good term paper.

A book, of course, represents the most prestigious form of research report. It has all the advantages of the working paper—length, detail—but it should be a more polished document. Because the publication of research findings as a book gives those findings an appearance of greater substance and worth, you have a special obligation to your audience. Although you will still hope to receive comments from colleagues, possibly leading you to revise your ideas, you must realize that other readers may be led to accept your findings uncritically.

Aim of the Report

Earlier in this book, we considered the different *purposes* of social research projects. In preparing your report, you should keep these different purposes in mind.

Some reports may focus primarily on the *exploration* of a topic of interest. Inherent in this aim is the tentativeness and incompleteness of the conclusions. You should clearly indicate to your audience the exploratory aim of the study and point to the shortcomings of the particular project. An important aspect of an exploratory report is to point the way to more refined research on the topic.

Many studies have a *descriptive* purpose, and the research reports from such studies will have a descriptive element. You should carefully distinguish for the reader those descriptions that apply only to the sample and those that are inferred to the population. Whenever inferential descriptions are to be made, you should give your audience some indication of the probable range of error in those descriptions.

Many reports have an *explanatory* aim; you wish to point to causal relationships among variables. Depending on the probable audience for your report, you should carefully delineate the rules of explanation that lie behind your computations and conclusions, and as in the case of de-

scription, you must give your readers some guide to the relative certainty of your conclusions.

Finally, some research reports may have the aim of *proposing action*. For example, the researcher of prejudice may wish to suggest ways in which prejudice may be reduced, on the basis of the research findings. This aim often presents knotty problems, however, because your own values and orientations may interfere with your proposals. Although it is perfectly legitimate for your proposals to be motivated by personal values, you must ensure that the specific actions you propose are warranted by your data. Thus, you should be especially careful to spell out the logic by which you move from empirical data to proposed action.

ORGANIZATION OF THE REPORT

Although the organization of reports differs somewhat on the basis of form and purpose, it is possible to suggest a general format for presenting research data. The following comments apply most directly to a journal article, but with some modification they apply to most forms of research reports.

Purpose and Overview

It is always helpful to the reader if you begin with a brief statement of the purpose of the study and the main findings of the analysis. In a journal article, this overview may sometimes be given in the form of an *abstract* or *synopsis*.

Some researchers find this difficult to do. For example, your analysis may have involved considerable detective work, with important findings revealing themselves only as a result of imaginative deduction and data manipulation. You may wish, therefore, to lead the reader through the same exciting process, chronicling the discovery process with a degree of suspense and surprise. To the extent that this form of reporting gives an accurate picture of the research process, we feel it has considerable instructional value. Nevertheless, many readers may not be interested in following your entire research account, and not knowing the purpose and general conclusions in advance may make it difficult for them to understand the significance of the study.

An old forensic dictum says: "Tell them what you're going to tell them; tell them; and tell them what you told them." You would do well to follow this dictum in the preparation of research reports.

Review of the Literature

Because every research report should be placed in the context of the general body of scientific knowledge, it is important to indicate where your report fits in that picture. Having presented the general purpose of your study, you should then bring the reader up to date on the previous research in the area, pointing to general agreements and disagreements among the previous researchers.

In some cases, you may wish to challenge previously accepted ideas. You should carefully review the studies that had led to the acceptance of those ideas, then indicate the factors that have not been previously considered or the logical fallacies present in the previous research.

When you are concerned with resolving a disagreement among previous researchers, you should organize your review of the literature around the opposing points of view. You should summarize the research supporting one view, then summarize the research supporting the other, and finally suggest the reasons for the disagreement.

To an extent, your review of the literature serves a bibliographic function for readers, indexing the previous research on a given topic. This can be overdone, however, and you should avoid an opening paragraph that runs three pages, mentioning every previous study in the field. The comprehensive bibliographic function can best be served by a bibliography at the end of the report,

and the review of the literature should focus only on those studies that have direct relevance to the present study.

Avoiding Plagiarism

Whenever you are reporting on the work of others, it is important that you be clear about who said what. It is essential that you avoid *plagiarism:* the theft of another's words and/or ideas—whether intentional or accidental—and the presentation of those words and ideas as your own. Because this is a common and sometimes unclear problem for college students, let's take a minute to examine it in some detail. Here are the main ground rules regarding plagiarism:

• You cannot use another writer's exact words without using quotation marks and giving a complete citation, which indicates the source of the quotation such that your reader could locate that quotation in its original context. As a rule of thumb, taking a passage of eight or more words without citation is a violation of federal copyright laws.

• It is also not acceptable to edit or paraphrase another's words and present the revised version as your own work.

• Finally, it is not even acceptable to present another's *ideas* as your own—even if you use totally different words to express those ideas.

The following examples should clarify what is or is not acceptable in the use of another's work.

The Original Work:

Laws of Growth.

Systems are like babies: once you get one, you have it. They don't go away. On the contrary, they display the most remarkable persistence. They not only persist; they grow. And as they grow, they encroach. The growth potential of systems was explored in a tentative, preliminary way by Parkinson, who concluded that administrative systems maintain an average growth of 5 to 6 percent per annum regardless of the work to be done. Parkinson was right so far as he goes, and we must give him full honors for initiating the serious study of this important topic. But what Parkinson failed to perceive, we now enunciate—the general systems analogue of Parkinson's Law.

The System Itself Tends to Grow At 5 To 6 Percent Per Annum

Again, this Law is but the preliminary to the most general possible formulation, the Big-Bang Theorem of Systems Cosmology.

Systems Tend To Expand To Fill The Known Universe*

Now let's look at some of the *acceptable* ways you might make use of Gall's work in a term paper.

Acceptable: John Gall, in his work on *Systemantics,* draws a humorous parallel between systems and infants: "Systems are like babies: once you get one, you have it. They don't go away. On the contrary, they display the most remarkable persistence. They not only persist; they grow."†

Acceptable: John Gall warns that systems are like babies. Create a system and it sticks around. Worse yet, Gall notes, systems keep growing larger and larger.‡

Acceptable: It has also been suggested that systems have a natural tendency to persist, even grow and encroach (Gall, 1975: 12). [*Note:* This format requires that you give a complete citation in your bibliography.]

Here now, are some *unacceptable* uses of the same material, reflecting some common errors.

Unacceptable: In this paper, I want to look at some of the characteristics of the social systems we create in our organizations. First, systems are like babies: once you get one, you have it. They don't go away. On the contrary, they display the most remarkable persistence. They not only persist; they grow. [It is unacceptable to directly quote someone else's materials without using quotation marks and giving a full citation.]

Unacceptable: In this paper, I want to look at some of the characteristics of the social systems we create in our organizations. First, systems are a lot like children: once you get one, it's yours. They don't go away; they persist. They not only persist, in fact: they grow. [It is unacceptable to edit another's work and present it as your own.]

Unacceptable: In this paper, I want to look at some of the characteristics of the social systems we create in our organizations. One thing I've noticed is that once you create a system, it never seems to go away. Just the opposite, in fact: they have a tendency to grow. You might say systems are a lot like children in that respect. [It is unacceptable to paraphrase someone else's ideas and present them as your own.]

Each of the preceding unacceptable examples is an example of plagiarism, and they represent a serious offense. Admittedly, there are some "gray areas." Some ideas are more or less in the public domain, not "belonging" to any one person. Or you may reach an idea on your own that someone else has already put in writing. If you have a question about a specific situation, discuss it with your instructor in advance.

We have discussed this topic in some detail since it is important that you place your research in the context of what others have done and said, and yet the improper use of their materials is a serious offense. Mastering this matter, however, is a part of your "coming of age" as a scholar.

Study Design and Execution   A research report containing interesting findings and conclusions can be very frustrating when the reader is unable to determine the methodological design and execution of the study. The worth of all scientific findings depends heavily on the manner in which the data were collected and analyzed.

---

*John Gall, *Systemantics: How Systems Work and Especially How They Fail,* New York: Quadrangle, 1975, pp. 12–14. Note: Gall previously gave a full citation for Parkinson.

†John Gall, *Systemantics: How Systems Work and Especially How They Fail,* New York: Quadrangle, 1975, p. 12.

‡John Gall, *Systemantics: How Systems Work and Especially How They Fail,* New York: Quadrangle, 1975, p. 12.

In reporting the design and execution of a survey, for example, you should always include the following: the population, the sampling frame, the sampling method, the sample size, the data collection method, the completion rate, and the methods of data processing and analysis. Comparable details should be given if other methods are used. The experienced researcher is able to report these details in a rather short space, without omitting anything required for the reader's evaluation of the study.

Analysis and Interpretation

Having set the study in the perspective of previous research and having described the design and execution of it, you should then present your data. The following major section will provide further guidelines in this regard. For now, a few general comments are in order.

The presentation of data, the manipulations of those data, and your interpretations should be integrated into a logical whole. It is frustrating to the reader to discover a collection of seemingly unrelated analyses and findings with a promise that all the loose ends will be tied together later in the report. Every step in the analysis should make sense—at the time it is taken. You should present your rationale for a particular analysis, present the data relevant to it, interpret the results, then indicate where that result leads next.

Summary and Conclusions

Following the forensic dictum mentioned earlier, we believe it is essential to summarize the research report. You should avoid reviewing every specific finding but you should review all of the significant ones, pointing once more to their general significance.

The report should conclude with a statement of what you have discovered about your subject matter and where future research might be directed. A quick review of recent journal articles will probably indicate a very high frequency of the concluding statement "It is clear that much more research is needed." This is probably always a true conclusion, but it is of little value unless you can offer pertinent suggestions about the nature of that future research. You should review the particular shortcomings of your own study and suggest ways in which those shortcomings might be avoided by future researchers. You also should draw implications for social welfare policy and program development, social work practice, and, if appropriate, social work education. Make sure that the implications that you develop are supported by your findings; do not use this section of the report as a license to make unsupported editorial pronouncements.

GUIDELINES FOR REPORTING ANALYSES

The presentation of data analyses should provide a maximum of detail without being cluttered. You can accomplish that best by continually examining your report to see whether it achieves the following aims.

Quantitative data should be presented in such a way to permit recomputations by the reader. In the case of percentage tables, for example, the reader should be able to collapse categories and recompute the percentages. Readers should be given sufficient information to permit them to compute percentages in the table in the opposite direction from your own presentation.

All aspects of the analysis should be described in sufficient detail to permit a secondary analyst to replicate the analysis from the same body of data. This means that he or she should be able to create the same indexes and scales, produce the same tables, arrive at the same regression equations, obtain the same factors and factor loadings, and so forth. That will seldom be done, of course, but if the report is presented in such a manner as to make it possible, the reader will be far better equipped to evaluate the report.

A final guide to the reporting of methodological details is that the reader should be in a position to completely replicate the entire study independently. It should be recalled from an earlier discussion that replicability is an essential norm of science generally. A single study does not prove a point; only a series of studies can begin to do so. Unless studies can be replicated, there can be no meaningful series of studies.

We have previously mentioned the importance of integrating data, analysis, and interpretations in the report. A more specific guideline can be offered in this regard. Tables, charts, and figures, if any, should be integrated into the text of the report—appearing near that portion of the text discussing them. Sometimes students describe their analyses in the body of the report and place all the tables in an appendix at the end. This procedure greatly impedes the reader. As a general rule, it is best to (1) describe the purpose for presenting the table, (2) present it, and (3) review and interpret it.

Be explicit in drawing conclusions.

Although research is typically conducted for the purpose of drawing general conclusions, you should carefully note the specific basis for such conclusions. Otherwise you may lead your reader into accepting unwarranted conclusions.

Point to any qualifications or conditions warranted in the evaluation of conclusions. Typically, you are in the best position to know the shortcomings and tentativeness of your conclusions, and you should give the reader the advantage of that knowledge. Failure to do so can misdirect future research and result in a waste of research funds.

We will conclude with a point made at the outset of this appendix, since it is extremely important. Research reports should be written in the best possible literary style. Writing lucidly is easier for some people than for others, and it is always harder than writing poorly. You are again referred to the Strunk and White volume. Every researcher would do well to follow this procedure: Write. Read Strunk and White. Revise. Reread Strunk and White. Revise again. That will be a difficult and time-consuming endeavor, but so is science.

A perfectly designed, carefully executed, and brilliantly analyzed study will be altogether worthless unless you are able to communicate your findings to others. This appendix has attempted to provide some general and specific guidelines toward that end. The best guides are logic, clarity, and honesty. Ultimately, there is probably no substitute for practice.

A Consumer's Guide to Social Work Research

There may have been times when you felt that neither this course nor this textbook were really appropriate for you. You may find it difficult to believe right now that you'll ever engage in the execution of social work research. But even if you aren't fully prepared to undertake major research projects on your own, you have become what we sometimes call the "informed consumer." Even if you never conduct a major project of your own, you are able to evaluate the research of others. This is not an insignificant ability because you are going to be exposed to social work research throughout your career as a social worker. No social work research studies are perfectly flawless. As you read reports of research in our professional journals, it is very important, therefore, that you be able to separate the wheat from the chaff.

In this appendix we'll offer some consumer tips for you to use in reviewing reports of social work research in the years to come. In part, these guidelines serve as a review of the territory we've covered in the book. It's fine for you to use this section as a review of the book, but realize that our primary purpose here is to strengthen your abilities to evaluate research rather than to design and execute it. As a consequence, we've skipped over several topics of the book and focused only on those in which consumer skills are particularly germane. We will organize the consumer's guide pretty much along the same lines as the rest of the book, however.

So, whenever you are confronted with what "research shows," here are some of the questions you might want to ask. Not all of the questions apply to all studies, but this list ought to give you enough questions to choose from.

PROBLEM FORMULATION AND RESEARCH DESIGN

• What was the purpose of the study: exploration, description, explanation, or a combination?

• Was the research formulated with sufficient linkage to prior literature? Does it address an important research question that is articulated clearly?

• Who conducted the research? Who paid for it? What motivated the study? If the study's conclusions happen to correspond to the interests of the sponsor or researcher, that doesn't disqualify those conclusions, but you want to be especially wary.

• What was the unit of analysis? Was it appropriate to the purpose of the study? Are the conclusions drawn from the research appropriate to the unit of analysis? For example, have the researchers studied cities and ended up with assertions about individuals?

- Is this a cross-sectional or longitudinal study? Be especially wary of longitudinal assertions being made on the basis of cross-sectional observations.

- If longitudinal data have been collected, be sure that comparable measurements have been made at each point in time. If survey data are involved, for example, have the same questions been asked each time? If the report compares, say, crime or poverty rates, be sure they have been defined the same way each time. (Definitions of "poverty" frequently change, for example.)

- Did the study commit any ethical violations? If so, did the benefits of the study outweigh and justify those violations?

MEASUREMENT

- What are the names of the concepts under study?

- Has the researcher delineated different dimensions of the variable? Have those distinctions been kept straight in the analysis and reporting?

- What indicators have been chosen as measures of those dimensions and concepts? Is each indicator a valid measure of what it is intended to measure? What else could the indicator be a measure of? Is it a reliable measure? Has the reliability been tested?

- What is the level of measurement of each variable: nominal, ordinal, interval, or ratio? And is it the appropriate level?

- Have composite measurements been used: indexes, scales, or typologies? If so, is it appropriate to the purpose of the study? Has it been constructed correctly?

SAMPLING

- Was it appropriate to study a sample or should all elements have been studied?

- If sampling was called for, were probability sampling methods appropriate or would a purposive, snowball, or quota sample have been appropriate? Has the appropriate sample design been used?

- What is the population the researcher wants to draw conclusions about?

- What is the researcher's purpose? If it is description, then rigorous probability sampling methods are called for.

- If a probability sample has been selected, what sampling frame has been used? Is it an appropriate representation of the population that interests the researcher? What elements of the population have been omitted from the sampling frame and what extraneous elements have been included?

- What specific sampling techniques have been used: simple random sampling, systematic sampling, or cluster sampling? Has the researcher stratified the sampling frame prior to sampling? Have the stratification variables been chosen wisely: that is, are they relevant to the variables under study?

- How large a sample was selected? What was the completion rate: that is, what percent of the sample responded? Are there any likely differences between those who responded and those who didn't?

- If the study tested a hypothesis, did the sample size provide adequate statistical power to reduce the probability of committing a Type II error?

- Even assuming that the respondents are representative of those selected in the sample, what is the sampling error to be expected from a sample of this size?

- Has the researcher tested for representativeness: comparing the sex distribution of the population and of respondents, for example, or their ages, ethnicity, education, or income?

- Ultimately, do the individuals (or other unit of analysis) studied represent the larger population from which they were chosen? That is to say, do conclusions drawn about the sample tell us anything meaningful about populations or about life in general?

EXPERIMENTS

• What is the primary dependent variable in the experiment? What effect is the experimenter trying to achieve, for example?

• What is the experimental stimulus or stimuli?

• What other variables are relevant to the experiment? Have they been measured?

• For each variable, check carefully how it has been defined and measured. Consider potential problems of validity and reliability.

• Has a proper control group been used? Have subjects been assigned to the experimental and control groups through random selection or by matching? Has it been done properly? Has the researcher provided any evidence of the initial comparability of experimental and control group subjects?

• Have there been pretest and posttest measurements of the dependent variable?

• What is the chance of a placebo (or "Hawthorne") effect in the experiment? Has any attention been given to the problem? Does the study use a double-blind design, for example?

• Are there any problems of internal validity: history, maturation, testing, instrumentation, statistical regression, selection biases, experimental mortality, ambiguous causal direction, diffusion or imitation?

• With regard to external validity, how has the experimenter ensured that the findings will apply to life in the real world or to other social work practice settings?

SURVEY RESEARCH

• Check all the relevant questions regarding sampling.

• What questions have been asked of respondents? What was the precise wording of the questions? Be wary of researchers who merely paraphrase the questions.

• If closed-ended questions have been asked, were the answer categories provided appropriate, exhaustive, and mutually exclusive?

• If open-ended questions were asked, how have the answers been categorized? Has the researcher guarded against his or her own bias creeping in during the coding of open-ended responses?

• Are all the survey questions clear and unambiguous? Could they have been misinterpreted by respondents? If so, what might the given answers mean instead of what the researcher has assumed?

• Are respondents capable of answering the questions asked? If not, they may answer anyway but their answers may not mean anything.

• Are any of the questions double-barreled? Look for conjunctions like *and* and *or.* Are respondents being asked to agree or disagree with two ideas when they might like to agree with one and disagree with the other?

• Do the questions contain negative terms? If so, respondents may have misunderstood them and answered inappropriately.

• Is there a danger of social desirability in any of the questions? Is any answer so right or so wrong that respondents may have answered on the basis of what people would think of them?

• As a general rule, it is a good idea to test all questionnaire items by asking them of yourself to see how you would answer. Any difficulty you might have in answering might also apply to others. Then, try to assume different points of view (for example, liberal versus conservative, religious versus unreligious) and ask how the questions might sound to someone with that point of view.

• If the researcher has conducted a secondary analysis of previously collected data, you should determine the quality of the researchers who originally collected the data. Also, are the data available for analysis appropriate to the current purposes? Do the questions originally asked reflect adequately on the variables now being analyzed?

FIELD RESEARCH

• What are the main variables in this study? How have they been defined and measured? Do you see any problems of validity?

• How about reliability? Would another researcher observing the same events classify things the same?

• Is there any chance that the classification of observations has been influenced by the way those classifications will affect the research findings and/or the researcher's hypotheses?

• If descriptive conclusions have been drawn— for example, "the group's standards were quite conservative"—what are the implicit standards being used?

• How much can the study's findings be generalized to a broader sector of society? What claims has the researcher made in this regard? What is the basis for such claims?

• If people have been interviewed, how were they selected? Do they represent all appropriate people?

• How much did the researcher participate in the events under study? How might that participation have affected the events themselves?

• Did the researcher reveal his or her identity as a researcher? If revealed, what impact could that have had on the behavior of those being observed?

• Does the research indicate any personal feelings—positive or negative—about those being observed? If so, what effect might that have in what was observed and the conclusions drawn from it?

• Has the researcher's own cultural identity or background clouded his or her interpretation of what has been observed?

ANALYZING EXISTING STATISTICS

• Who originally collected the data being reanalyzed? Were there any flaws in the data collection methods? What was the original purpose of data collection? Would that affect the data collected?

• What was the unit of analysis of the data? Is it appropriate to the current research question and the conclusions being drawn? Is there a danger of the ecological fallacy?

• When were the data collected? Are they still appropriate to current concerns?

• What are the variables being analyzed in the current research? Were the definitions used by the original researchers appropriate to current interests?

DATA ANALYSIS

• What statistical techniques have been used in the analysis of data and are they appropriate to the levels of measurement of the variables involved?

• Has the researcher undertaken all relevant analyses? Have all appropriate variables been examined? Would it have been important, for example, to replicate the results among men and women separately?

• Is it possible that the correlation observed between two variables might have been caused by a third, extraneous variable, making the observed relationship spurious?

• Have tests of statistical significance been used? If so, have they been interpreted correctly? Has statistical significance been confused with substantive significance?

• Does a particular research finding really make a difference? Does it matter? Is an observed difference between subgroups, for example, a large or meaningful one? Are there any implications for action? Not all findings need to have policy implications, but it's one yardstick to use in reviewing research.

• Has the researcher gone beyond the actual findings in drawing conclusions and implications?

• Are there logical flaws in the analysis and interpretation of data?

DATA REPORTING

• Has the researcher placed this particular project in the context of previous research on the topic? Does this research add to, modify, replicate, or contradict previous studies?

• In general, has the researcher reported the details of the study design and execution fully? Are there parts of the report that seem particularly vague or incomplete in the reporting of details?

• Has the researcher reported any flaws or shortcomings in the study design or execution? Are there any suggestions for improved research on the topic in the future?

Commission on Aging Survey

COMMISSION ON AGING SURVEY

Respondent # _____

Respondent's Name: _____

Respondent's Address: _____
Street _____
City/Town _____

Telephone:

Name of Interviewer: _____

Number of Visits

	1	2	3	4	5
Date					
Time Started					
Time Ended					
Time Spent					
Result*					
Appointment Date and Time					

*Codes:
1. Interview completed.
2. Interview partly completed—Appointment made.
3. Appointment made for interview later.
4. Refusal—No interview obtained.
5. No one at home.
6. Eligible respondent not home.
7. Other (SPECIFY) _____

Field Supervisor: _____ Date: _____
Editor: _____ Date: _____
Coder: _____ Date: _____
Keypuncher: _____ Date: _____

Serial Number

RESPONDENT'S IDENTIFYING INFORMATION

Name:

Address:

Census Tract Number:

Telephone:

Social Security Number:

Birthdate:

Marital Status: [ ] Single
[ ] Married
[ ] Divorced
[ ] Separated
[ ] Widowed

Interviewer's Name:

Date of Interview:

I. SATISFACTORY HOME AND COMMUNITY ENVIRONMENT

(1) To begin the interview, we would like to learn something about your current living arrangements. First, do you live alone or do you share your quarters with other people?

[ ] Live alone
[ ] Share quarters — 21/

   1a. Who do you live with?

      [ ] Spouse
      [ ] Children: Number ___
      [ ] Grandchildren: Number ___
      [ ] Other relatives: Number ___
      [ ] Unrelated persons: Number ___ 22-26/

   1b. How many people is that altogether?

      ___ 27/

(2) Do you own or rent these living quarters?

[ ] Own
[ ] Rent — 28/

   2a. Do you own it fee simple, leasehold, or do you have other arrangements?

      [ ] Fee simple
      [ ] Leasehold
      [ ] Other (specify) ___ 29/

(3) How long have you been living in these quarters?

___ 30-31/
(enter number of years)

(4) If you had your choice, do you think you (and your husband/wife) would prefer living alone or with other people (other than your husband/wife)?

[ ] Prefer living alone
[ ] Prefer living with others — 32/

(5) How many rooms do you have in these quarters, other than bathrooms, halls, lanais, and so forth?

___ 33/
34/b

I. SATISFACTORY HOME AND COMMUNITY ENVIRONMENT

(6) Do you have a private bathroom or do you share it with other people (other than your husband/wife)?

[ ] Private bathroom
[ ] Shared bathroom — 35/

(7) Is there a telephone readily available for your use?

[ ] Yes
[ ] No — 36/

(8) Do you have hot and cold running water?

[ ] Yes
[ ] Cold only
[ ] Neither — 37/

(9) Do you find the temperature in your home:

[ ] Usually comfortable
[ ] Usually uncomfortable
[ ] About half and half — 38/

(10) Do you have enough windows for adequate light on most days?

[ ] Yes
[ ] No — 39/

(11) Do you have enough electric lighting in all rooms, in some rooms only, or not enough in any room?

[ ] Enough in all rooms
[ ] Enough in some only
[ ] Not enough in any
[ ] No electrical lighting — 40/

(12) Generally speaking, how would you rate the physical condition of your living quarters—such things as plumbing, the roof, the floor, windows, and so forth? Would you describe it as:

[ ] Excellent
[ ] Good
[ ] Fair
[ ] Poor — 41/

42/b

I. SATISFACTORY HOME AND COMMUNITY ENVIRONMENT

(13) Would you say that the size of your living quarters is:

[ ] Too large
[ ] Too small
[ ] Just about right

43/_____

(14) How well do you think your present home satisfies your current needs for comfort, convenience, and safety?

[ ] Very well
[ ] Fairly well
[ ] Not too well
[ ] Not at all

44/_____

(15) Would you say that you find such things as home maintenance, keeping up repairs, and general housework:

[ ] Difficult
[ ] Sometimes difficult
[ ] Never a problem

45/_____

(16) Do you have a room where you can usually go and shut the door to be alone if you want to?

[ ] Yes
[ ] No

46/_____

(17) Does noise from either outside or other parts of the building in which you live bother you? (IF YES Would you say *often* or only *sometimes?*)

[ ] No
[ ] Sometimes
[ ] Often

47/_____

(18) For each of the following, please tell me if it represents a big problem for you, a slight problem, or no problem.

	Big Prob.	Slight Prob.	No Prob.	
a. Pests such as mice, rats, and so forth.	[ ]	[ ]	[ ]	48-52/
b. Insects	[ ]	[ ]	[ ]	
c. Refuse collection	[ ]	[ ]	[ ]	
d. Overcrowding in stores, restaurants, and so forth	[ ]	[ ]	[ ]	
e. Air pollution	[ ]	[ ]	[ ]	

53/b

I. SATISFACTORY HOME AND COMMUNITY ENVIRONMENT

(19) All things considered, how do you feel about staying in these quarters to moving somewhere else? Would you say you:

[ ] Would definitely prefer to stay here
[ ] Would probably prefer to stay here
[ ] Would probably prefer to move elsewhere
[ ] Would definitely prefer to move elsewhere
[ ] Don't know

54/_____

(20) Since you have lived here, would you say that the neighborhood has changed for the better, for the worse, or stayed about the same?

[ ] For the better
[ ] Stayed about the same
[ ] For the worse

55/_____

(21) How attached are you to your neighborhood? Would you say you:

[ ] Are very attached
[ ] Are fairly attached
[ ] Have no real feeling
[ ] Do not like it and would like to move

56/_____

(22) How good do you think your neighborhood is for the older people to live?

[ ] A good place
[ ] A fair place
[ ] A poor place

57/_____

(23) Generally speaking are the following places or people a convenient distance from where you live? (If the respondent is not in need or does not care about being near these things such as a bank, park, etc., then mark "N.A.") (Let the respondent decide convenience)

	Yes	No	N.A.	
a. Friends	[ ]	[ ]	[ ]	58-66/
b. Relatives	[ ]	[ ]	[ ]	
c. Church	[ ]	[ ]	[ ]	
d. Stores	[ ]	[ ]	[ ]	
e. Medical facilities	[ ]	[ ]	[ ]	
f. Bank	[ ]	[ ]	[ ]	
g. Park	[ ]	[ ]	[ ]	
h. Other recreational facilities	[ ]	[ ]	[ ]	
i. Restaurant	[ ]	[ ]	[ ]	

67-80/b

II. PERSONAL HEALTH, SAFETY, AND PHYSICAL WELL-BEING

ID No.: 1-5/

(1) Here is a list of health problems that people often have. I'll read them and you tell
me if you have any of them. First, a list of conditions which usually continue to
require care or treatment or restrict activities:
(Interviewer: check "Yes" or "No" for each item.)

6/2

	Yes	No
a. Diabetes	[ ]	[ ]
b. High blood pressure	[ ]	[ ]
c. Heart trouble	[ ]	[ ]
d. Stroke	[ ]	[ ]
e. Arthritis	[ ]	[ ]
f. Cancer	[ ]	[ ]
g. Paralysis or Parkinson's disease	[ ]	[ ]
h. Glaucoma (cataracts) or other eye trouble not relieved by glasses	[ ]	[ ]

7-14/

(2) How many days have you been sick to the point of being unable to carry on your
regular activities during the *last four weeks*?

[ ] No days (Interviewer: check "Not sick" on Question 3 and go on to
Question 4.)
[ ] 1 to 7 days
[ ] 8 to 14 days
[ ] 15 to 21 days
[ ] 22 days or more

15/

(3) While you were sick during this time, were you mostly:

[ ] (Not sick)
[ ] Just at home
[ ] In bed at home
[ ] In the hospital

16/

(4) For doing each of the following activities, please tell me if you have no difficulty, can
do it with some difficulty, or if you cannot do it.

17-19/

	No Difficulty	Some Difficulty	Cannot Do It
a. Going up and down stairs	[ ]	[ ]	[ ]
b. Getting about the house	[ ]	[ ]	[ ]
c. Washing and bathing	[ ]	[ ]	[ ]

20/b

II. PERSONAL HEALTH, SAFETY, AND PHYSICAL WELL-BEING

(4) (cont.)

	No Difficulty	Some Difficulty	Cannot Do It
d. Dressing and putting on shoes	[ ]	[ ]	[ ]
e. Getting out of the house	[ ]	[ ]	[ ]
f. Watching television	[ ]	[ ]	[ ]
g. Feeding yourself	[ ]	[ ]	[ ]

21-24/

(5) Please tell me whether you currently need each of the following health aids, and if
so, whether you currently have it?

	Need?		If YES: do you have it?	
	Yes	No	Yes	No
a. Eyeglasses	[ ]	[ ]	[ ]	[ ]
b. Hearing aid	[ ]	[ ]	[ ]	[ ]
c. False teeth	[ ]	[ ]	[ ]	[ ]
d. Cane or crutch	[ ]	[ ]	[ ]	[ ]
e. Leg brace	[ ]	[ ]	[ ]	[ ]
f. Special shoes	[ ]	[ ]	[ ]	[ ]
g. Truss or abdominal brace	[ ]	[ ]	[ ]	[ ]
h. Wheelchair	[ ]	[ ]	[ ]	[ ]
i. Other health aids	[ ]	[ ]	[ ]	[ ]

25-33/

34-42/b

II. PERSONAL HEALTH, SAFETY, AND PHYSICAL WELL-BEING

(6) Have you had a medical checkup in the last year?

[ ] Yes
[ ] No
→ Was there any special reason why you didn't get a checkup?

43/ ___

44/ ___

(7) Have you had all the immunizations and inoculations you think you should have?

[ ] Yes
[ ] No
[ ] Don't know
→ Which additional ones do you think you should have?

45/ ___

46/ ___

47/b

II. PERSONAL HEALTH, SAFETY, AND PHYSICAL WELL-BEING

(8) During the past year have you been injured in any of the following kinds of accidents?

	Yes	No
a. An automobile accident	[ ]	[ ]
b. Falling in the home	[ ]	[ ]
c. An injury on the job	[ ]	[ ]
d. Other	[ ]	[ ]

48-51/ ___

(9) Are you currently registered for Medicare?

[ ] Yes
[ ] No

52/ ___

(10) Are you a member of any health care program such as Kaiser, HMSA, Blue Cross, or some program like that?

[ ] Yes
[ ] No

→ IF YES: Which program do you belong to?

[ ] Kaiser
[ ] HMSA
[ ] Blue Cross
[ ] Other ___

53/ ___

54/ ___

(11) Now I will list to you some groups of food. Would you please tell me how often you eat something from each of the groups. That is, do you eat something from the group almost every day, sometimes, or almost never?

a. Milk, cheese, ice cream, or anything else made out of milk.

[ ] Almost every day
[ ] Sometimes
[ ] Almost never

55/ ___

b. Any kind of meat, including beef, veal, pork, lamb, poultry, or fish, eggs, dry beans, peas, tofu, or nuts.

[ ] Almost every day
[ ] Sometimes
[ ] Almost never

56/ ___

57/b

II. PERSONAL HEALTH, SAFETY, AND PHYSICAL WELL-BEING

(11) (cont.)

c. Any fruit or vegetable or juice.

[ ] Almost every day
[ ] Sometimes
[ ] Almost never

58/____

d. Any kind of food made of bread or cereal, or rice.

[ ] Almost every day
[ ] Sometimes
[ ] Almost never

59/____

(12) Do you take vitamin pills every day or almost every day?

[ ] Yes
[ ] No

60/____

(13) In general, would you say your appetite is poor, fair, or good?

[ ] Poor
[ ] Fair
[ ] Good

61/____

(14) Has your appetite been like this only recently, during the past year, or most of your life?

[ ] Recently
[ ] Past year
[ ] Most of life

62/____

(15) Would you say you have been gaining weight, staying the same, or losing weight over the past two years?

[ ] Gaining
[ ] Losing
[ ] Staying the same

63/____

(16) Do you have trouble buying foods that you like?

[ ] Yes
[ ] No
[ ] Sometimes

64/____

65-80/b

ID No.: 1-5/

III. ECONOMIC SATISFACTION

Now we would like to learn just a little about your financial situation.

(1) To begin, could you tell me whether you (and your husband/wife) are responsible for managing your day-to-day finances such as buying food and clothing, paying the rent or mortgage payments, and so forth, or are your finances handled by someone else?

[ ] Handled by respondent
[ ] Handled by someone else

6/3

(1a) Who is responsible for handling your finances?

7/____

(1b) Do you receive any financial support from your children or other relatives?

[ ] Yes
[ ] No

8/____

(2) During the past year did you (or the person handling your finances) receive any income from the following sources?

	Yes	No
Wages	[ ]	[ ]
Income from a business or professional practice	[ ]	[ ]
Income from farming	[ ]	[ ]
Social Security	[ ]	[ ]
Retirement payments or pensions	[ ]	[ ]
Interest on savings or dividends	[ ]	[ ]
Others	[ ]	[ ]

9/____

10-16/

(3) Could you tell me approximately how much income you (and the person responsible for your finances) had from all sources during the past year?

$ _____

17-21

(4) How many people were supported by that income?

22-23

24/b

III. ECONOMIC SATISFACTION

(5) Do you currently have a job?

[ ] Yes   [ ] No

IF YES

(5a) Do you work full-time or part-time?

[ ] Full-time
[ ] Part-time

IF NO

(5b) Would you like a job if you could find work you liked and could do?

[ ] Yes
[ ] No

(6) How well do you think your income and assets satisfy your needs:

[ ] Very well
[ ] Well
[ ] Adequately
[ ] Barely
[ ] Poorly

IF ANSWER IS "POORLY" OR "BARELY" TO 6 ABOVE:

(6a) How much more money do you and your family need each month to live comfortably?

[ ] Less than $50
[ ] $50 to $99
[ ] $100 to $149
[ ] $150 or more

25/___

26/___

27/___

28/___

29/___

30/b

IV. INTELLECTUAL AND SOCIAL SATISFACTION

(1) How often did you visit in person with a member of your family last week?

[ ] Every day
[ ] A few times
[ ] Once
[ ] Not at all
[ ] No family nearby

(2) How often did you visit in person with friends or neighbors last week?

[ ] Every day
[ ] A few times
[ ] Once
[ ] Not at all

(3) About how often last week did you talk to friends, relatives, business contacts, or others on the telephone?

[ ] Every day
[ ] Several times
[ ] Once
[ ] Not at all

(4) Of all your neighbors, about how many do you know well enough to visit with?

[ ] 5 or more
[ ] 3 or 4
[ ] 1 or 2
[ ] None

(5) Do you have as much contact as you would like with a person you feel close to—somebody that you can trust and confide in?

[ ] Yes
[ ] No

(6) Do you think that you see enough of your friends, relatives, and neighbors?

[ ] Yes
[ ] No

31/___

32/___

33/___

34/___

35/___

36/___

37/b

APPENDIX

Random Numbers

10480	15011	01536	02011	81647	91646	69179	14194	62590	36207	20969	99570	91291	90700
22368	46573	25595	85393	30995	89198	27982	53402	93965	34095	52666	19174	39615	99505
24130	48360	22527	97265	76393	64809	15179	24830	49340	32081	30680	19655	63348	58629
42167	93093	06243	61680	07856	16376	39440	53537	71341	57004	00849	74917	97758	16379
37570	39975	81837	16656	06121	91782	60468	81305	49684	60672	14110	06927	01263	54613
77921	06907	11008	42751	27756	53498	18602	70659	90655	15053	21916	81825	44394	42880
99562	72905	56420	69994	98872	31016	71194	18738	44013	48840	63213	21069	10634	12952
96301	91977	05463	07972	18876	20922	94595	56869	69014	60045	18425	84903	42508	32307
89579	14342	63661	10281	17453	18103	57740	84378	25331	12566	58678	44947	05585	56941
85475	36857	53342	53988	53060	59533	38867	62300	08158	17983	16439	11458	18593	64952
28918	69578	88231	33276	70997	79936	56865	05859	90106	31595	01547	85590	91610	78188
63553	40961	48235	03427	49626	69445	18663	72695	52180	20847	12234	90511	33703	90322
09429	93969	52636	92737	88974	33488	36320	17617	30015	08272	84115	27156	30613	74952
10365	61129	87529	85689	48237	52267	67689	93394	01511	26358	85104	20285	29975	89868
07119	97336	71048	08178	77233	13916	47564	81056	97735	85977	29372	74461	28551	90707
51085	12765	51821	51259	77452	16308	60756	92144	49442	53900	70960	63990	75601	40719
02368	21382	52404	60268	89368	19885	55322	44819	01188	65255	64835	44919	05944	55157
01011	54092	33362	94904	31273	04146	18594	29852	71585	85030	51132	01915	92747	64951
52162	53916	46369	58586	23216	14513	83149	98736	23495	64350	94738	17752	35156	35749
07056	97628	33787	09998	42698	06691	76988	13602	51851	46104	88916	19509	25625	58104
48663	91245	85828	14346	09172	30168	90229	04734	59193	22178	30421	61666	99904	32812
54164	58492	22421	74103	47070	25306	76468	26384	58151	06646	21524	15227	96909	44592
32639	32363	05597	24200	13363	38005	94342	28728	35806	06912	17012	64161	18296	22851
29334	27001	87637	87308	58731	00256	45834	15398	46557	41135	10367	07684	36188	18510
02488	33062	28834	07351	19731	92420	60952	61280	50001	67658	32586	86679	50720	94953
81525	72295	04839	96423	24878	82651	66566	14778	76797	14780	13300	87074	79666	95725
29676	20591	68086	26432	46901	20849	89768	81536	86645	12659	92259	57102	80428	25280
00742	57392	39064	66432	84673	40027	32832	61362	98947	96067	64760	64584	96096	98253
05366	04213	25669	26422	44407	44048	37937	63904	45766	66134	75470	66520	34693	90449
91921	26418	64117	94305	26766	25940	39972	22209	71500	64568	91402	42416	07844	69618
00582	04711	87917	77341	42206	35126	74087	99547	81817	42607	43808	76655	62028	76630
00725	69884	62797	56170	86324	88072	76222	36086	84637	93161	76038	65855	77919	88006
69011	65795	95876	55293	18988	27354	26575	08625	40801	59920	29841	80150	12777	48501
25976	57948	29888	88604	67917	48708	18912	82271	65424	69774	33611	54262	85963	03547
09763	83473	73577	12908	30883	18317	28290	35797	05998	41688	34952	37888	38917	88050
91567	42595	27958	30134	04024	86385	29880	99730	55536	84855	29080	09250	79656	73211
17955	56349	90999	49127	20044	59931	06115	20542	18059	02008	73708	83517	36103	42791
46503	18584	18845	49618	02304	51038	20655	58727	28168	15475	56942	53389	20562	87338
92157	89634	94824	78171	84610	82834	09922	25417	44137	48413	25555	21246	35509	20468
14577	62765	35605	81263	39667	47358	56873	56307	61607	49518	89656	20103	77490	18062
98427	07523	33362	64270	01638	92477	66969	98420	04880	45585	46565	04102	46880	45709
34914	63976	88720	82765	34476	17032	87589	40836	32427	70002	70663	88863	77775	69348
70060	28277	39475	46473	23219	53416	94970	25832	69975	94884	19661	72828	00102	66794
53976	54914	06990	67245	68350	82948	11398	42878	80287	88267	47363	46634	06541	97809
76072	29515	40980	07391	58745	25774	22987	80059	39911	96189	41151	14222	60697	59583
90725	52210	83974	29992	65831	38857	50490	83765	55657	14361	31720	57375	56228	41546
64364	67412	33339	31926	14883	24413	59744	92351	97473	89286	35931	04110	23726	51900
08962	00358	31662	25388	61642	34072	81249	35648	56891	69352	48373	45578	78547	81788
95012	68379	93526	70765	10592	04542	76463	54328	02349	17247	28865	14777	62730	92277
15664	10493	20492	38391	91132	21999	59516	81652	27195	48223	46751	22923	32261	85653

16408	81899	04153	53381	79401	21438	83035	92350	36693	31238	59649	91754	72772	02338
18629	81953	05520	91962	04739	13092	97662	24822	94730	06496	35090	04822	86774	98289
73115	35101	47498	87637	99016	71060	88824	71013	18735	20286	23153	72924	35165	43040
57491	16703	23167	49323	45021	33132	12544	41035	80780	45393	44812	12515	98931	91202
30405	83946	23792	14422	15059	45799	22716	19792	09983	74353	68668	30429	70735	25499
16631	35006	85900	98275	32388	52390	16815	69298	82732	38480	73817	32523	41961	44437
96773	20206	42559	78985	05300	22164	24369	54224	35083	19687	11052	91491	60383	19746
38935	64202	14349	82674	66523	44133	00697	35552	35970	19124	63318	29686	03387	59846
31624	76384	17403	53363	44167	64486	64758	75366	76554	31601	12614	33072	60332	92325
78919	19474	23632	27889	47914	02584	37680	20801	72152	39339	34806	08930	85001	87820
03931	33309	57047	74211	63445	17361	62825	39908	05607	91284	68833	25570	38818	46920
74426	33278	43972	10119	89917	15665	52872	73823	73144	88662	88970	74492	51805	99378
09066	00903	20795	95452	92648	45454	09552	88815	16553	51125	79375	97596	16296	66092
42238	12426	87025	14267	20979	04508	64535	31355	86064	29472	47689	05974	52468	16834
16153	08002	26504	41744	81959	65642	74240	56302	00033	67107	77510	70625	28725	34191
21457	40742	29820	96783	29400	21840	15035	34537	33310	06116	95240	15957	16572	06004
21581	57802	02050	89728	17937	37621	47075	42080	97403	48626	68995	43805	33386	21597
55612	78095	83197	33732	05810	24813	86902	60397	16489	03264	88525	42786	05269	92532
44657	66999	99324	51281	84463	60563	79312	93454	68876	25471	93911	25650	12682	73572
91340	84979	46949	81973	37949	61023	43997	15263	80644	43942	89203	71795	99533	50501
91227	21199	31935	27022	84067	05462	35216	14486	29891	68607	41867	14951	91696	85065
50001	38140	66321	19924	72163	09538	12151	06878	91903	18749	34405	56087	82790	70925
65390	05224	72958	28609	81406	39147	25549	48542	42627	45233	57202	94617	23772	07896
27504	96131	83944	41575	10573	08619	64482	73923	36152	05184	94142	25299	84387	34925
37169	94851	39117	89632	00959	16487	65536	49071	39782	17095	02330	74301	00275	48280
11508	70225	51111	38351	19444	66499	71945	05422	13442	78675	84081	66938	93654	59894
37449	30362	06694	54690	04052	53115	62757	95348	78662	11163	81651	50245	34971	52924
46515	70331	85922	38329	57015	15765	97161	17869	45349	61796	66345	81073	49106	79860
30986	81223	42416	58353	21532	30502	32305	86482	05174	07901	54339	58861	74818	46942
63798	64995	46583	09785	44160	78128	83991	42865	92520	83531	80377	35909	81250	54238
82486	84846	99254	67632	43218	50076	21361	64816	51202	88124	41870	52689	51275	83556
21885	32906	92431	09060	64297	51674	64126	62570	26123	05155	59194	52799	28225	85762
60336	98782	07408	53458	13564	59089	26445	29789	85205	41001	12535	12133	14645	23541
43937	46891	24010	25560	86355	33941	25786	54990	71899	15475	95434	98227	21824	19585
97656	63175	89303	16275	07100	92063	21942	18611	47348	20203	18534	03862	78095	50136
03299	01221	05418	38982	55758	92237	26759	86367	21216	98442	08303	56613	91511	75928
79626	06486	03574	17668	07785	76020	79924	25651	83325	88428	85076	72811	22717	50585
85636	68335	47539	03129	65651	11977	02510	26113	99447	68645	34327	15152	55230	93448
18039	14367	61337	06177	12143	46609	32989	74014	64708	00533	35398	58408	13261	47908
08362	15656	60627	36478	65648	16764	53412	09013	07832	41574	17639	82163	60859	75567
79556	29068	04142	16268	15387	12856	66227	38358	22478	73373	88732	09443	82558	05250
92608	82674	27072	32534	17075	27698	98204	63863	11951	34648	88022	56148	34925	57031
23982	25835	40055	67006	12293	02753	14827	23235	35071	99704	37543	11601	35503	85171
09915	96306	05908	97901	28395	14186	00821	80703	70426	75647	76310	88717	37890	40129
59037	33300	26695	62247	69927	76123	50842	43834	86654	70959	79725	93872	28117	19233
42488	78077	69882	61657	34136	79180	97526	43092	04098	73571	80799	76536	71255	64239
46764	86273	63003	93017	31204	36692	40202	35275	57306	55543	53203	18098	47625	88684
03237	45430	55417	63282	90816	17349	88298	90183	36600	78406	06216	95787	42579	90730
86591	81482	52667	61582	14972	90053	89534	76036	49199	43716	97548	04379	46370	28672
38534	01715	94964	87288	65680	43772	39560	12918	86537	62738	19636	51132	25739	56947

Abridged from *Handbook of Tables for Probability and Statistics,* Second Edition, edited by William H. Beyer (Cleveland: The Chemical Rubber Company, 1968). Used by permission of The Chemical Rubber Company.

Distribution of Chi-Square

Probability

df	.99	.98	.95	.90	.80	.70	.50
1	.0^{3}157	.0^{3}628	.00393	.0158	.0642	.148	.455
2	.0201	.0404	.103	.211	.446	.713	1.386
3	.115	.185	.352	.584	1.005	1.424	2.366
4	.297	.429	.711	1.064	1.649	2.195	3.357
5	.554	.752	1.145	1.610	2.343	3.000	4.351
6	.872	1.134	1.635	2.204	3.070	3.828	5.348
7	1.239	1.564	2.167	2.833	3.822	4.671	6.346
8	1.646	2.032	2.733	3.490	4.594	5.527	7.344
9	2.088	2.532	3.325	4.168	5.380	6.393	8.343
10	2.558	3.059	3.940	4.865	6.179	7.267	9.342
11	3.053	3.609	4.575	5.578	6.989	8.148	10.341
12	3.571	4.178	5.226	6.304	7.807	9.034	11.340
13	4.107	4.765	5.892	7.042	8.634	9.926	12.340
14	4.660	5.368	6.571	7.790	9.467	10.821	13.339
15	5.229	5.985	7.261	8.547	10.307	11.721	14.339
16	5.812	6.614	7.962	9.312	11.152	12.624	15.338
17	6.408	7.255	8.672	10.085	12.002	13.531	16.338
18	7.015	7.906	9.390	10.865	12.857	14.440	17.338
19	7.633	8.567	10.117	11.651	13.716	15.352	18.338
20	8.260	9.237	10.851	12.443	14.578	16.266	19.337
21	8.897	9.915	11.591	13.240	15.445	17.182	20.337
22	9.542	10.600	12.338	14.041	16.314	18.101	21.337
23	10.196	11.293	13.091	14.848	17.187	19.021	22.337
24	10.856	11.992	13.848	15.659	18.062	19.943	23.337
25	11.524	12.697	14.611	16.473	18.940	20.867	24.337
26	12.198	13.409	15.379	17.292	19.820	21.792	25.336
27	12.879	14.125	16.151	18.114	20.703	22.719	26.336
28	13.565	14.847	16.928	18.939	21.588	23.647	27.336
29	14.256	15.574	17.708	19.768	22.475	24.577	28.336
30	14.953	16.306	18.493	20.599	23.364	25.508	29.336

continued

Source: We are grateful to the Literary Executor of the late Sir Ronald A. Fisher, F. R. S., to Dr. Frank Yates, F. R. S., and to Longman Group Ltd., London, for permission to reprint Table IV from their book *Statistical Tables for Biological, Agricultural, and Medical Research* (6th Edition, 1974).

For larger values of df, the expression $\sqrt{2\chi^2} - \sqrt{2df - 1}$ may be used as a normal deviate with unit variance, remembering that the probability of χ^2 corresponds with that of a single tail of the normal curve.

Probability

df	.30	.20	.10	.05	.02	.01	.001
1	1.074	1.642	2.706	3.841	5.412	6.635	10.827
2	2.408	3.219	4.605	5.991	7.824	9.210	13.815
3	3.665	4.642	6.251	7.815	9.837	11.341	16.268
4	4.878	5.989	7.779	9.488	11.668	13.277	18.465
5	6.064	7.289	9.236	11.070	13.388	15.086	20.517
6	7.231	8.558	10.645	12.592	15.033	16.812	22.457
7	8.383	9.803	12.017	14.067	16.622	18.475	24.322
8	9.524	11.030	13.362	15.507	18.168	20.090	26.125
9	10.656	12.242	14.684	16.919	19.679	21.666	27.877
10	11.781	13.442	15.987	18.307	21.161	23.209	29.588
11	12.899	14.631	17.275	19.675	22.618	24.725	31.264
12	14.011	15.812	18.549	21.026	24.054	26.217	32.909
13	15.119	16.985	19.812	22.362	25.472	27.688	34.528
14	16.222	18.151	21.064	23.685	26.873	29.141	36.123
15	17.322	19.311	22.307	24.996	28.259	30.578	37.697
16	18.841	20.465	23.542	26.296	29.633	32.000	39.252
17	15.511	21.615	24.769	27.587	30.995	33.409	40.790
18	20.601	22.760	25.989	28.869	32.346	34.805	42.312
19	21.689	23.900	27.204	30.144	33.687	36.191	43.820
20	22.775	25.038	28.412	31.410	35.020	37.566	45.315
21	23.858	26.171	29.615	32.671	36.343	38.932	46.797
22	24.939	27.301	30.813	33.924	37.659	40.289	48.268
23	26.018	28.429	32.007	35.172	38.968	41.638	49.728
24	27.096	29.553	33.196	36.415	40.270	42.980	51.179
25	28.172	30.675	34.382	37.652	41.566	44.314	52.620
26	29.246	31.795	35.563	38.885	42.856	45.642	54.052
27	30.319	32.912	36.741	40.113	44.140	46.963	55.476
28	31.391	34.027	37.916	41.337	45.419	48.278	56.893
29	32.461	35.139	39.087	42.557	46.693	49.588	58.302
30	35.530	36.250	40.256	43.773	47.962	50.892	59.703

A Learner's Guide to SPSS 6.1[1]

Jeffrey M. Jacques, Ph.D.
Department of Sociology and Criminal Justice
Florida A&M University

INSTRUCTIONAL GOALS

By the time you complete this appendix and do all the suggested exercises, you will know:

- When to use SPSS
- How to use basic SPSS 6.1 files created by others
- Which basic SPSS commands to use when performing statistical analysis such as:

    1. Univariate analysis
    2. Scaling
    3. Bivariate analysis
    4. Multivariate analysis

- How to create your own SPSS files
- How to build basic SPSS system files
- How to build an enhanced SPSS system file

---

*My thanks to the people who critiqued earlier versions of this Appendix. I would particularly like to thank my long-time colleague Emmit Hunt at Florida A&M University and Kenneth Jacques, a sociology major, at The Florida State University.

[1]In the text, I shall use SPSS to stand for SPSS 6.1. Most of the later versions use a similar interface while earlier versions use a command line interface typically hidden from the user. In any case, SPSS^X, SPSS, SPSS for Windows, SPSS for Windows95, or SPSS PC+ produce similar statistical outputs that require appropriate interpretations. By the way, all procedures were tested with SPSS Version 6.1 for Windows and SPSS for the Macintosh editions.

INTRODUCTION

This Learner's Guide has been developed specifically for students and faculty who have an interest in understanding how to approach data analysis using state-of-the-art micro-computer technology. We shall concentrate on how best to use the computer and the powerful statistical/analytic software of SPSS: The Statistical Package for the Social Sciences, Version 6.1. We only assume here that you have a basic understanding of how to use your computer—whether it be an IBM/MS–DOS compatible, an Apple Macin-tosh/PowerPC, or a Unix-based system—and the graphic user interface (GUI) common among computers with a Windows-like environment.

In this Learner's Guide we shall emphasize the basic approach and practical skills that any professional might be expected to use routinely during his or her career. We shall examine carefully how best to evaluate and understand data collected by others as well as how best to work with data you or I might collect. Additionally, as a sophisti-cated consumer, your knowledge of the procedures outlined below will better prepare you to interpret the analytic work reported by others. Most importantly, you will have developed the basic skills in how to approach data analysis by becoming the researcher—by using your skills, your computer, and the sophisticated software of SPSS.

Strange as it may seem, the best place to begin a discussion of when to use the com-puter is not at the computer. Nor is a discussion of the software the best approach. The best place to start is with a clear understanding of what you wish to find out. The com-puter and SPSS are simply tools that can be used to help you: (1) summarize your data, (2) create appropriate tables and graphs, (3) examine relationships among vari-ables, (4) perform tests of statistical significance based on your hypotheses, and (5) de-velop fairly sophisticated models. Indeed, because the computer and SPSS are extremely fast, you will be able to examine data and relationships among variables in a variety of ways heretofore unimagined. The basic point is this: if you understand your research questions thoroughly, then your computer and SPSS can be very helpful when it comes to manipulating large amounts of data, finding patterns, and testing hypotheses.

One or two comments about what this appendix will not do. This appendix will not make you an expert at using your computer system or SPSS. We assume here that you have developed basic expertise working with Windows, Windows95, MacOS, etc. Nor will you become an SPSS consultant—well, not at first. SPSS software includes hun-dreds of commands, procedures, and options within these procedures. What this Learner's Guide will do is to emphasize the most often used commands and procedures, outline how best to approach a research study by using your hardware and software, show you the basic commands of SPSS, and show you step by step how to use the com-puter and SPSS, Version 6.1 to facilitate the analysis of data.

The Example

To help illustrate each step of the analytic-computer process, we shall use the results from the General Social Survey,[2] most often called the GSS. The GSS has been an on-

---

[2]Davis, James Allan, and Smith, Tom W. *General Social Surveys, 1972–1994.* Principal Investigator, James A. Davis; Director and Co-Principal Investigator, Tom W. Smith. NORC ed. Chicago: National Opinion Re-

going survey of social indicators of the American population since 1972. Since that time, data were collected by carefully trained interviewers from a national multistage probability sample of approximately 1500 English-speaking persons, 18 years of age or over, who were living in non-institutional settings within the continental United States. Thus, data have been collected from more than 30,000 American adults over a 23-year period. The publisher provides a subset of these samples: 300 cases for each of the years of 1973, 1978, 1983, 1988, and 1993. Thus, a total of 1500 cases and more than 50 variables have been provided to all instructors who adopted this text. You can use your copy of this data set to follow the examples below. In addition, you can go beyond these examples and examine relationships among other variables found on this same data file. Doing the suggested exercises on this data set will improve your mastery of SPSS.

One continuing focus of the GSS surveys was abortion—how Americans view the conditions under which women have the right to obtain a legal abortion. It is a topic that provokes strong feelings on both sides of the issue. At one extreme, it is argued, "Americans with a conscience" believe that reproductive rights are "issues of life and death for women, not mere matters of choice. NOW supports access to safe and legal abortion, to effective birth control, to reproductive health and education. We oppose attempts to restrict these rights through legislation, regulation (like the gag rule) or Constitutional amendment."[3] Similarly, "Americans with a conscience," it is argued from the other side, believe that life begins at conception, that the developing fetus experiences sleep and wakefulness and awareness, and that it is morally and religiously abhorrent to take a life, particularly while that life is growing in the womb.[4]

While each group has eloquently stated their position, the overall research questions for us to explore include:

- How frequently are such views held? or Where do most Americans stand on the right of women to obtain a legal abortion?
- What are the descriptive characteristics of people associated with each position?
- Why do people hold these divergent attitudes?

Your previous work in research methods has included a discussion of the need to operationalize important concepts. The GSS survey research team at the National Opinion Research Center (NORC), University of Chicago, chose to operationalize Americans' attitudes toward legal abortion by including a total of seven questions. They included the following statement and questions:

Please tell me whether or not *you* think it should be possible for a pregnant woman to obtain a *legal* abortion:

1. If there is a strong chance of serious defect in the baby?
2. If she is married and does not want any more children?

search Center, producer, 1994; Storrs, CT: The Roper Center for Public Opinion Research, University of Connecticut, distribution. 1 data file (32,380 logical records) and 1 codebook (1,073 pp).

[3]NOW statement on reproductive rights. National Organization for Women 10/83. Revised 1/95. http://www.now.org:80/general.html#Reproductive, May, 1996.

[4]See ProLife News at http://hebron.ee.gannon.edu/~frezza/AboutPLN.html, May, 1996, and related documents.

3. If the woman's own health is seriously endangered by the pregnancy?

4. If the family has a very low income and cannot afford any more children?

5. If she became pregnant as a result of rape?

6. If she is not married and does not want to marry the man?

7. If the woman wants it for any reason?[5]

To each of these statements, thousands of GSS respondents could answer: "Yes," "No," "Don't Know," or simply refuse to respond. Most people responded "Yes" or "No" to most questions. Thus it is possible to use these data to explore where most Americans stand on the issue of access to legal abortion services.

In addition to attitudes toward abortion and many other topical areas of interest (e.g., crime, welfare, government, etc.), the GSS survey team collected background information on respondents: income, occupational prestige, marital status, age, education, sex, race, family status and number of children, religious affiliation and church attendance patterns, and political party membership and political views. (Although the GSS includes more than 2000 variables, we shall restrict our analysis to these background variables and the seven attitude questions on abortion rights.) Thus we can describe the characteristics of Americans and their associated views toward legal abortion as well as attempt to explain why various attitudes are held.

Our study provides an opportunity to test the general hypothesis that in America, attitudes toward legal abortion can be explained, in part, by the life experiences and social categories of Americans. More specifically, we can examine the following questions:

1. What are the current views of Americans toward a woman's right to a legal abortion?

2. Were there significant changes in Americans' attitudes toward a woman's right to a legal abortion over the last two decades?

3. Are there significant differences among people from different racial groups, gender categories, age groups, or religious organizations on the variables used to measure attitudes toward legal abortion?

4. Are there significant differences between people with different familial experiences (e.g., marital status, having children) on the variables used to measure attitudes toward legal abortion?

5. Are there significant correlations between the variables of income or education with attitudes toward legal abortion?

6. Is there any substantial difference between how those who identify with the Democratic or Republican party view a woman's right of access to a legal abortion? What about self-described political views—conservatism or liberalism—and their relationship to attitudes toward a woman's right to a legal abortion?

7. What variable, or combinations of variables, are the best predictors of Americans' attitudes toward legal abortion?

---

[5]This question was added in 1977. The previous six items were included in each survey year.

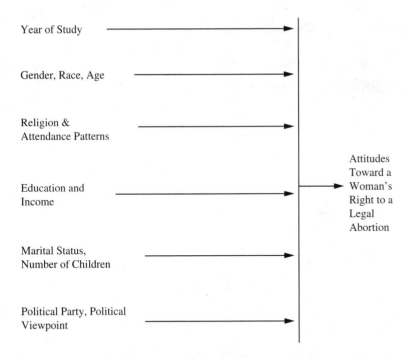

Figure 1 Working Model of Legal Abortion Attitude Study

A short summary of the model of this research project may be found in Figure 1. This model, and our research questions, will guide our examination of the GSS data set and our use of the computer via SPSS.

WORKING WITH THE GENERAL SOCIAL SURVEY (GSS) DATA

By now you have probably mastered the fundamentals of how to structure a research project, how to develop an instrument, and how to select your sample. Here's where you get a chance to start your examination of the data collected by the National Opinion Research Center and reported in the GSS.

Go ahead and boot your computer[6]—turn on the monitor, the CPU, and all related equipment. When the screen lights up, find and launch SPSS Version 6.1. After some

---

[6]If you are planning to use your college's computer lab, this is a good time to find out about your college's resources and which version of SPSS you will be using. If you don't know about your college's computer lab, ask your teacher or a fellow student. Then, get the help you need by telling the computer personnel what you plan to do. They will probably set up an account for you and give you documentation on how to use your college's system and how to access SPSS. Unfortunately, there is no single standard for all computer sites. So, take your time and find out.

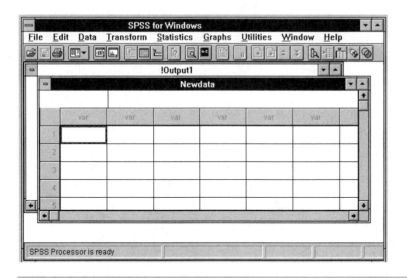

Figure 2 Initial Display Screen for SPSS 6.1

time and a few clicks and clanks of the hard drive, your screen should look like that of Figure 2.

When you launch successfully SPSS 6.1, you will see a screen similar to that of Figure 2. It will have a menu bar with the typical options of "File," "Edit," etc. across the top, a row of icons that perform many of the same functions as those listed in the menu bar immediately below, and at least two layers of windows.[7] At the bottom you will see the status bar, which will provide changing information about what SPSS is doing. When SPSS is ready for your command(s), the status bar will report: "SPSS Processor is ready" in the lower left part of your SPSS window.

Most of the screen is reserved for your data, input or syntax window, and output window. For now, we'll work with two basic windows. In the foreground you will see a data editor window, which will display the "active file" or "working file" data in a series of rows—typically one row for each respondent—and a series of columns—typically one column for each variable (e.g., YEAR, SEX, RACE, etc.). In the background will be the output window for displaying textual outputs—the results of all commands you use. We'll examine this soon.

To load the GSS file, simply use your mouse to choose from the menu bar at the top of the screen:

File ➤
   Open . . .

and then choose from the selection box GSS7393s.sav if you wish to work with the smaller (fewer variables as required by SPSS 6.1 for Windows Student Version), or

---

[7]The number of layers will depend on the preferences you set in the Preference option of the Edit menu.

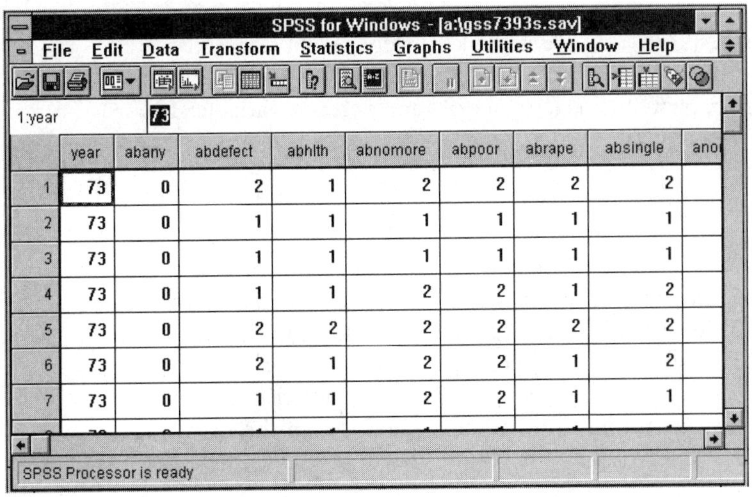

Figure 3 Display Screen with GSS Loaded for SPSS

GSS7393.sav if you choose to work with the larger file and any standard SPSS version. As illustrated in Figure 3, variable names (year, abany, abdefect, age, race, sex, etc.) appear at the top of each column and each row includes the response of each GSS respondent.

You can examine additional variables by using the arrow graphics at the end of the scroll bar at the bottom of the data editor display window and you can examine additional respondents' data by using the arrows at the end of the scroll bar at the right of the display window. A simple press on any of the arrow graphics at each corner of the scroll bars will give a slightly different view of the data set. Try it. To get back to the original display, press the arrow at the opposite location of the same scroll bar or, from the menu bar, choose:

Data ➤
   Go to Case . . .

and enter a 1 in the space provided. A simple press of the return key will bring the display to the first case of the data set.

WORKING WITH SOMEONE ELSE'S DATA

Initial Activities: Step 1

The first goal of working with someone else's data is to understand what has been provided. Most data sets come with a complete codebook—a complete listing of all the variables (what each variable name means, e.g., abany = "[O]btain a legal abortion: If the woman wants it for any reason"), the codes used for each attribute (e.g., 1 = "Yes," 2 = "No"), and how those who did not respond, or were not asked, were coded (e.g., 0 or blank for "Never Asked/Not Applicable," 8 for "Don't Know," or 9 "No answer.")

When no such codebook is provided, you can see a roster of variables, one variable at a time, by using:

Utilities ➤
   Variables . . .

which will provide an information or dialogue box. In this dialogue box, the left-hand side will list all the variables in the working file and the associated variable information to its right. As you select each variable in its picker box by using your mouse and "clicking" on the variable of interest, the summary information will change at the right. Try it.

To get a complete list of all variables used by SPSS, you can create a dictionary of what is included in the data set by using the File Info subcommand. From the menu bar at the top of the screen, choose:

Utilities ➤
   File Info

and you will get a complete roster of all the variables in your active file written to the output window. Your output, in the output window, will include a report that will have a format similar to this:

```
ABANY    ABORTION IF WOMAN WANTS FOR ANY REASON                    2
            Print Format: F1
            Write Format: F1
            Missing Values: 0, 8, 9

            Value    Label
                0 M  NAP
                1    YES
                2    NO
                8 M  DK
                9 M  NA
```

Pretty much what you would expect. The name of the variable is listed first (e.g., ABANY) and its corresponding label next ("ABORTION IF A WOMAN WANTS FOR ANY REASON"). The number to the far right is the variable position in the file—in this case, the variable ABANY is the second variable in this data set. Immediately below the variable label is a roster of how SPSS will handle the data when printed or written to another file (in both cases, "F1" indicates a numeric display one character wide). Missing values (e.g., 0, 8, 9) are those values that will be excluded when statistical summaries and analyses are calculated. More important, all values, and their associated labels, are listed next. A "0" is used for "Not Applicable," "1" for "Yes," and "2" for "No." Note that between the values and labels (e.g., 0, 8, and 9) is the capital letter "M" for "missing values" designation, again. You can now examine the remaining variables and clearly see what is included in this file.

Exercise 1: If you do have access to a computer, SPSS, and the GSS data set, try these commands (Utilities ➤ File Info) yourself. When the !Untitled Output Window is the front most active window, you can scroll—using the scroll bar at your far right—to see the dictionary for each of the variables. You can print a copy of this dictionary, assuming that you are connected to a printer, by choosing from the menu bar, File and then Print. This is always a good first step. If you do not have access to this equipment, look at the end of this appendix for a complete roster of GSS codebook information.

Basic Working and System Files   Now that we have the data entered into an active SPSS file we must tell the computer how to manipulate the data. This is where we will use SPSS commands that instruct SPSS what to do with the data our GSS data set.

SPSS Commands   While you will be selecting most of your procedures from a menu system, you need to know how SPSS is generating the commands. Each time you select a menu item or its submenu component, SPSS is building an SPSS command. SPSS commands are composed of at least two parts—the first is the command name or keyword(s) (e.g., LIST, FREQUENCIES, etc.) while the second is the specifications (typically a list of your variables on which you wish to execute this command). Thus, SPSS generates, behind the scenes, appropriate information that it then processes using your data to know which file management or statistical procedures you wish to execute. For example, when we requested Utilities ➤ File Info we created a command, DISPLAY DICTIONARY,[8] which SPSS then executed to produce the roster of all variables and their elements.

Similarly, to produce a roster of the data actually in the file we could choose from the menu bar:

Statistics ➤
   Summarize ➤
      List Cases . . .

which would then bring up a dialog box like that of Figure 4.

All of this is used to produce a standard list output from an English-like command that actually looks something like this:

```
LIST VARIABLES = YEAR, SEX, RACE.
```

We'll have more to say about this later. But for now, it is important to remember that command names (i.e., LIST) come first, the subcommand of VARIABLES= follows

---

[8]If DISPLAY DICTIONARY is not listed on the !OUTPUT window and you are using the SPSS standard version, go to the

Edit ➤
   Preferences ➤
      Output . . .

and then select (place an X in the box by clicking on it) the box labeled "Display" in the "Command" options in the upper left corner.

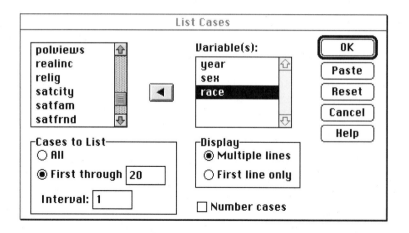

Figure 4   LIST CASES Dialog Box

closely, while the specifications or variable names (i.e., YEAR, SEX, RACE)—that which is specific about your study—follow immediately after the subcommand.

You say that you are using SPSS 6.1, so why bother to know this? Good question. You will find knowing how to structure SPSS commands is an important asset when we start working with complex commands that are not easily developed using the menu system. Similarly, if you make an error developing a command, you may find it easier to fix your errors using the syntax window than by trying to re-create complex commands using the menu system. In addition, SPSS is in fact writing these commands in this format to a separate file, typically titled spss.jnl, which you may find useful when you are working in a production environment. Speaking of a production environment, you can save your commands in a file for later use under a separate file name and then "re-use" them with different data that use the same variables or variable names as often as you wish.[9]

Data Cleaning and Error Checking: Step 2

Whether you plan to enter the data for this study yourself—to be discussed later—or are using data entered by others, it is always a good idea to check the veracity of the data. Most people take considerable care in entering the data from any study. Even the most careful data entry person will make a few errors—especially after entering several hundreds of data values.

One approach to error checking is to examine the data set directly. From the "File Info" command you have a roster of variables and labels for valid values and missing values. You can, with the LIST command produce a roster of values for each and every variable. By checking both rosters you can identify data entry errors. For example, the attributes for the variable SEX has been assigned "1" for "Male" and "2" for "Female"

---

[9]Alas, this option is not available if you are using the SPSS 6.1: Student Version.

Table 1 Output from LIST VARIABLES=YEAR, SEX, RACE Command

```
YEAR SEX RACE
 73   1    1
 73   2    1
 73   2    1
 73   2    1
 73   1    1
 73   2    1
 73   1    1
 73   2    1
 73   1    1
 73   2    1
 73   2    1
 73   1    1
 73   1    1
 73   1    1
 73   2    1
 73   1    1
 73   1    1
 73   2    1
 73   1    1
 73   2    1
Number of cases read:   20    Number of cases listed:   20
```

as the only valid entries. Any values other than these would be due to data entry errors. Thus, a value of 3 entered for the variable of SEX would be an invalid value and should be changed to the correct value, when known, or to a standard missing value.

The LIST Command   While this is only useful if you are working with a relatively small file, the LIST CASES command will list the values for each variable for each respondent. If you wish a complete listing of all the variables and the values for each person in the study, you would include the following commands. Choose, from the menu bar:

Statistics ➤
   Summarize ➤
      List Cases . . .

You will then be given a dialog box, as seen in Figure 4. Simply select the variables of interest to you—choose from those listed in the left box, press the ➤ button to transfer them to the Variable(s): box, and, when finished, press "OK." By default, SPSS 6.1 will give you a complete listing of all cases in your output window. To see all the results simply use the scroll bar at the right of the output window. Point the arrow of the mouse at the box in the scroll bar, hold the mouse button down, and then drag the mouse up to see earlier pages.

To restrict the number of cases—say, to 20 cases—simply choose the option in the lower left portion of the screen and enter 20 in the "First through" box. Then click the "OK" button. A typical output would look like Table 1.

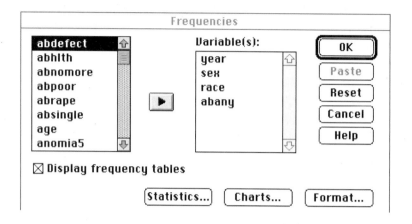

Figure 5 FREQUENCIES Dialog Box

A Better Approach: FREQUENCIES A better approach for checking data entry errors, as well as getting a first peek at the variables of interest, involves running the procedure, FREQUENCIES. This procedure will produce a summary table of values for each variable. Since you know from your codebook/dictionary the valid maximum and minimum values for each variable, any reported value(s) outside this range would indicate a data entry error.

In SPSS 6.1, make sure that you have loaded an active file by going to the menu bar and selecting

Window ➤
　　GSS7393s.sav. (or whatever your file name is)

This will bring the data set window to the foreground. Now, point and click the mouse at menu option:

Statistics ➤
　　Summarize ➤
　　　　Frequencies . . .

This will open a dialog box for the FREQUENCIES command where you can identify each of the variables of interest. Once you choose a variable of interest, press the ➤ button[10] in the middle of the dialog box to move the selected variable to the "Variable(s):" box. See Figure 5.

Repeat this for as many variables with which you wish to work. A simple press of the "OK" button will force SPSS 6.1 to write the results to your !OUTPUT window. (Click on the "!output" window, or select it from the window command of the menu bar, to see these results.) See Table 2 for an example of a typical output window.

---

[10]Alternately, you can double-click on the variable name and SPSS will transfer it to the Variable(s) box for processing.

Table 2 Typical FREQUENCIES Output

YEAR   GSS YEAR FOR THIS RESPONDENT

Value Label	Value	Frequency	Percent	Valid Percent	Cum Percent
	73	300	20.0	20.0	20.0
	78	300	20.0	20.0	40.0
	83	300	20.0	20.0	60.0
	88	300	20.0	20.0	80.0
	93	300	20.0	20.0	100.0
		-------	-------	-------	
	Total	1500	100.0	100.0	

Valid cases   1500   Missing cases   0

- -

SEX   RESPONDENTS SEX

Value Label	Value	Frequency	Percent	Valid Percent	Cum Percent
MALE	1	590	39.3	39.3	39.3
FEMALE	2	910	60.7	60.7	100.0
		-------	-------	-------	
	Total	1500	100.0	100.0	

Valid cases   1500   Missing cases   0

- -

RACE   RACE OF RESPONDENT

Value Label	Value	Frequency	Percent	Valid Percent	Cum Percent
WHITE	1	1320	88.0	88.0	88.0
BLACK	2	146	9.7	9.7	97.7
OTHER	3	34	2.3	2.3	100.0
		-------	-------	-------	
	Total	1500	100.0	100.0	

Valid cases   1500   Missing cases   0

- -

ABANY   ABORTION IF WOMAN WANTS FOR ANY REASON

Value Label	Value	Frequency	Percent	Valid Percent	Cum Percent
YES	1	448	29.9	38.1	38.1
NO	2	728	48.5	61.9	100.0
NAP	0	300	20.0	Missing	
DK	8	22	1.5	Missing	
NA	9	2	.1	Missing	
		-------	-------	-------	
	Total	1500	100.0	100.0	

Valid cases   1176   Missing cases   324

Alternately, you can type in the syntax window[11] the FREQUENCIES command. It is easy to enter. Minimally, it consists of:

FREQUENCIES VARIABLES=variable_name(s).

You can identify each variable name.[12]

FREQUENCIES VARIABLES= YEAR SEX RACE.

and then execute the command. This command will create the same results and write them to your !OUTPUT window.

In either case, a comparison between the values reported in the value column of each table and the values listed in your dictionary will enable you to capture invalid entries.

If you do find a data entry error, here's how to find and fix an error fast. Let's assume that your Frequencies procedure produced a table for the variable of SEX with mostly "1"s—"males," and "2"s—"females," and one "3." You know that the value of "3" is an invalid value and you wish to change the data in the file. Just select the first cell under the variable name SEX in the Data Editor window. Now, from the menu bar, choose:

Edit ➤
   Search For Data . . .

and enter the value 3 in the text box titled:"Search." A simple press on the button "Search Forward" would identify the offending entry and place you in the appropriate row and cell. If you know the correct value, type over the incorrect value in the Data Editor window and "Save" the corrected information. If you don't know the correct value, enter an appropriate missing value (e.g., 0, 8, or 9—that which is defined as a missing value in the codebook or dictionary). Fast, simple, and neat.

Whichever SPSS version you have chosen to use, the output should confirm that all the values recorded for the variables are appropriate.

Take a minute and examine closely Table 2. It provides a quick "first look" at the pattern of response across the 1500 sampled Americans as reported in this GSS data subset. The file includes an equal number of respondents/cases (i.e., 300 cases) from each year of study (i.e., 1973, 78, 83, 88, and 93); more white respondents than any other racial designation—88% were "white," 9.7% reported "Black" and 2.3% reported

---

[11]The syntax window is simply a third window. It provides an opportunity to key-in SPSS commands by by-passing the menu system—which is used to generate these same commands. It is often much more efficient to use the syntax window than the menu system. If no syntax window is open and you are using the SPSS 6.1 standard version, do:

Edit ➤
   Preferences . . .

and then click on the box "Open a syntax window at start-up to run SPSS commands."

[12]Or you may be able to use the FREQUENCIES command and the keyword, ALL, by writing the command line in the "!untitled syntax" window. This command substitutes for naming each and every variable in your active file. Then run the command.

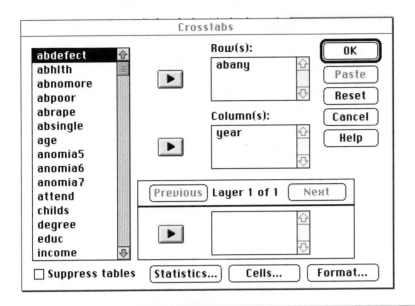

Figure 6 CROSSTABS Dialog Box

"Other"; and more female than male respondents—590 were male (39.3%) while 910 were female (60.7%). All these variables had no missing data.

Of these same 1500 cases, 1176 answered the question on "Abortion for any reason" with "valid" responses (responding either "Yes"—448 or "No"—728) while two respondents did not answer, 22 "Didn't know," and 300 were classified as "Not Applicable"—NAP. Thus, of all 1500 respondents, 29.9% said "Yes" while 48.5% said "No;" of those who gave a valid response, 38.1% said "Yes" while 61.9% said "No." SPSS nicely provides both ways of looking—including and excluding missing cases—at the response pattern.

One More Approach: Crosstabs   The CROSSTABS procedure is useful for creating tabular displays of two variables at a time. This is especially important when you wish to confirm that the respondents had consistent patterns across a set of descriptive variables. For example, we noted earlier that for the variable of ABANY, 300 cases were classified "NAP" and treated as missing. We may use the SPSS procedure, CROSSTABS, to find out if there is a pattern.

Using SPSS 6.1, choose:

Statistics ➤
   Summarize ➤
      Crosstabs . . .

which opens a dialog box like that of Figure 6.

Table 3 Typical CROSSTABS Output: ABANY BY YEAR

```
ABANY   ABORTION IF WOMAN WANTS FOR ANY REASON
by  YEAR   GSS YEAR FOR THIS RESPONDENT

                       YEAR                        Page 1 of 1
              Count |
                    |
                    |                                Row
                    |    78|    83|    88|    93| Total
ABANY        -------+------+------+------+------+
                 1  |   109|    99|   104|   136|   448
     YES         |     |      |      |      |  38.1
             +------+------+------+------+
                 2  |   185|   198|   186|   159|   728
      NO         |     |      |      |      |  61.9
             +------+------+------+------+
            Column    294    297    290    295   1176
            Total    25.0   25.3   24.7   25.1  100.0

Number of Missing Observations:  324
```

Select ABANY and press the ➤ key on top and closest to the keyword "Row(s)." Scroll down so you can select YEAR and press the ➤ key nearest the word column. A press on the OK button will produce a table like that of Table 3.

Or, the CROSSTAB command may be entered from the syntax window:

CROSSTABS TABLES=varlist BY varlist

For looking at the ABANY response pattern by YEAR, the minimal CROSSTABS command becomes:

CROSSTABS TABLES=ABANY BY YEAR

Using either procedure produces a table. Note that in the lower right hand corner of Table 3, 1176 cases are reported. Not surprisingly, 448 "Yes" and 728 "No" responses were recorded—look across the rows of the table. Similarly slightly less than 300 responses were noted for each of the listed years—look down each column—labeled 78, 83, 88, and 93. All this is consistent with our earlier FREQUENCIES run. But note that there is no column for 1973, even though 1973 was listed earlier. Thus, the 300 cases we found as "NAP" when we ran the FREQUENCIES command have been identified as occurring in 1973—the missing year of the data.

There are other useful crosstabs when searching for incongruities in the data. Let's assume that we are interested in the joint distribution of race by sex over the life of the study, as well as looking at race and sex for each year. To start with we would choose:

Statistics ➤
    Summarize ➤
        Crosstabs . . .

(If there are entries in the Row(s) and Column(s) boxes, press reset.) Now, select the variable of SEX for Row(s) and RACE for Column(s). A press of OK will produce a table similar to the first table in Table 6. Most (88%) of the respondents were white with more than half of these being "FEMALE"—910 versus 590 for "MALE."

Return to your CROSSTABS dialog box and now, in the bottom entry box, choose the variable YEAR. A press of the "OK" button produces a series of tables—one for each year. See Table 4. By inspection of each year (i.e., YEAR GSS YEAR FOR THIS RESPONDENT, Value = 73, 78, 83, 88, or 93) we can see that each table includes 300 cases (as we would expect from what we learned from the FREQUENCIES run) and that the distribution of these data are pretty consistent across the years. This completes Table 4. Take a minute and review it carefully.

One more use of CROSSTABS should be noted. When more than one variable has been used to measure the same concept, or related concepts, we have an opportunity to check the reliability, and thus the veracity, of these variables and make a judgment about the entire data set. We have that opportunity here: data were collected about educational background using two variables—(1) number of years of education, and (2) earned degree. Using the complete 1972–1994 GSS data set, it is interesting to examine this joint distribution. See Table 5.

Each row indicates the number of years of completed education (i.e., 0 through 20 years) while each column reports the highest earned degree (i.e., less than H.S., High School, Junior College, Bachelor, and Graduate degrees). Of the 31,664 randomly sampled respondents, 31,510 answered queries on both variables—number of years of education and highest earned degree. Just as we could find using FREQUENCIES, respondents more often reported 12 years of education (32.7%) than any other year, with 16 years of education being second most common (10.4%). Not surprisingly, the most often reported earned degree was earning a high school diploma (51.4%). Inspection of the body of the table indicates that 10,004 of the 31,510 respondents completed 12 years of education and earned a high school diploma. No surprises here. Similarly, those who held a degree from a junior college (N=1172) most often had 14 years of education (778 of the 1172 respondents) while those with a baccalaureate degree (N=3766) typically reported 16 years of education (2863 of the 3766 respondents). Such data make sense and support our assessment of reliability.

But clearly some of the response patterns do not make logical sense. A few respondents reported 15, 16, or 17 years of education but never earned a degree: that is 12 people reported 15 years of education, 7 people reported 16 years of education, and 2 people reported 17 years of education but none of these same people reported earning any educational degree(s). Additional data incongruities should be examined. While some respondents may have earned a H.S. diploma early with only 10 or 11 years of school—perhaps earning a H.S. degree via a GED program—it is unlikely that those eight people who had completed only eight years of school had, in fact, earned a H.S. diploma. It is even more unlikely that the five respondents who reported 11, 12, or 13 years of education earned a baccalaureate degree. While most people reported their education in a reliable manner, some people likely "fudged" their educational information. You may find these respondents and change their data to a missing code or, as you will learn later, simply tell SPSS to ignore these respondents.

Table 4 Typical CROSSTABS Output: RACE, SEX, AND YEAR*

```
SEX   RESPONDENTS SEX   by   RACE   RACE OF RESPONDENT

                      RACE                 Page 1 of 1
             Count |
                   |WHITE     BLACK     OTHER
                   |                               Row
                   |     1 |     2 |     3 | Total
  SEX        -------+-------+-------+-------+
              1 |   532 |    49 |     9 |   590
    MALE        |       |       |       |       | 39.3
                +-------+-------+-------+
              2 |   788 |    97 |    25 |   910
    FEMALE      |       |       |       |       | 60.7
                +-------+-------+-------+
            Column   1320     146      34     1500
            Total    88.0     9.7     2.3    100.0

Number of Missing Observations:   0
---------------------------------------------------------------------
SEX   RESPONDENTS SEX   by   RACE   RACE OF RESPONDENT
Controlling for..
YEAR   GSS YEAR FOR THIS RESPONDENT   Value = .73

                      RACE                 Page 1 of 1
             Count |
                   |WHITE     BLACK     OTHER
                   |                               Row
                   |     1 |     2 |     3 | Total
  SEX        -------+-------+-------+-------+
              1 |   119 |     9 |     1 |   129
    MALE        |       |       |       |       | 43.0
                +-------+-------+-------+
              2 |   149 |    20 |     2 |   171
    FEMALE      |       |       |       |       | 57.0
                +-------+-------+-------+
            Column    268      29       3      300
            Total    89.3     9.7     1.0    100.0

SEX   RESPONDENTS SEX   by   RACE   RACE OF RESPONDENT
Controlling for..
YEAR   GSS YEAR FOR THIS RESPONDENT   Value = 78

                      RACE                 Page 1 of 1
             Count |
                   |WHITE     BLACK     OTHER
                   |                               Row
                   |     1 |     2 |     3 | Total
  SEX        -------+-------+-------+-------+
              1 |    99 |    12 |     1 |   112
    MALE        |       |       |       |       | 37.3
                +-------+-------+-------+
              2 |   172 |    15 |     1 |   188
    FEMALE      |       |       |       |       | 62.7
                +-------+-------+-------+
            Column    271      27       2      300
            Total    90.3     9.0      .7    100.0
---------------------------------------------------------------------
```

*Partial Output - 1983, 1988, and 1993 not included in this table.

Table 5 CROSSTABS Output: EDUCATION BY DEGREE

DEGREE BY EDUCATION

Count		LT HIGH SCHOOL 0	HIGH SCHOOL 1	JUNIOR COLLEGE 2	BACHELOR 3	GRADUATE 4	Row Total
EDUC	0	90	1				91 0.3
	1	31					31 0.1
	2	71					71 0.2
	3	164					164 0.5
	4	234					234 0.7
	5	292	1				293 0.9
	6	474					474 1.5
	7	668					668 2.1
	8	1967	8				1975 6.3
	9	1132	133				1265 4
	10	1552	191				1743 5.5
	11	1638	380		1		2019 6.4
	12	297	10004	2	3	3	10309 32.7
	13	56	2266	37	1		2360 7.5
	14	26	2054	778	16	6	2880 9.1
	15	12	899	263	42	6	1222 3.9
	16	7	190	71	2863	135	3266 10.4
	17	2	32	13	515	243	805 2.6
	18		18	5	212	593	828 2.6
	19		4	1	66	280	351 1.1
	20	1	9	2	47	402	461 1.5
Column Total		8714 27.7	16190 51.4	1172 3.7	3766 12	1668 5.3	31510 100

Number of Missing Observations: 154

Exercise 2: Why not take some time, load your SPSS file and try the summarize commands of FREQUENCIES and CROSSTABS. After you re-create the tables noted above, try other variables, commands, and optional subcommands. When using the CROSSTABS command, make sure that you examine carefully the joint distribution of DEGREE and EDUCation. Which data appear reasonable? Which data appear unreasonable? Why? If you find some errors, make appropriate corrections and save your file using a new file name.

Useful Descriptive Statistics: Step 3

The third step when working with files prepared by others is to develop a clear picture of who were the respondents. Thus, a brief demographic descriptive profile should be gleaned from the data. There are several SPSS procedures that are very efficient tools for this purpose—some of which you have begun to master already. They include, FREQUENCIES, DESCRIPTIVES, and CROSSTABS. You have mastered the procedures FREQUENCIES and CROSSTABS so that you could find errors in the data set. Now, we can use these same procedures to develop a clear description of the characteristics of the respondents.

The use of the FREQUENCIES procedure takes a moment of thought. It is a powerful procedure that will list all values of each variable as well as all possible summary statistics (i.e., measures of central tendency—mean, median, mode, measures of dispersion—range, variance, standard error, and the shape of the distribution—skewness and kurtosis). This is at once an asset as well as a liability. While it makes sense to make such calculations for interval level variables (e.g., age, number of years of completed education, etc.), it makes less sense for ordinal level variables (e.g., degree, church/synagogue attendance) and no sense for nominal level variables with three or more categories (e.g., race, religion, etc.).

Thus, while you can ask SPSS to compute such summary descriptive statistics for each and every numeric variable—even variables that use numerals as descriptive codes, SPSS assumes that you have the sophistication to know when to use each summary statistic. Here's a rule of thumb based on the earlier text discussion of levels of measurement:

IF THE VARIABLE IS MEASURED AT THE	THEN USE THE MEASURE(S) OF CENTRAL TENDENCY OF:
NOMINAL LEVEL	MODE & reported percents
ORDINAL LEVEL	+ MEDIAN
INTERVAL & RATIO LEVEL	+ MEAN, Standard Dev

Now, to execute the Frequencies command, choose:

Statistics ➤
   Summarize ➤
      Frequencies . . .

and select each of the nominal level variables (e.g., RACE, SEX, MARITAL, RELIG). Your output should look like that of Table 6.

Table 6 SUMMARY STATS: STANDARD FREQUENCIES

```
FREQUENCIES VARIABLES=,race,sex, relig, marital.*
```

SEX   RESPONDENTS SEX

Value Label	Value	Frequency	Percent	Valid Percent	Cum Percent
MALE	1	590	39.3	39.3	39.3
FEMALE	2	910	60.7	60.7	100.0
	Total	1500	100.0	100.0	

Valid cases   1500   Missing cases   0

RACE   RACE OF RESPONDENT

Value Label	Value	Frequency	Percent	Valid Percent	Cum Percent
WHITE	1	1320	88.0	88.0	88.0
BLACK	2	146	9.7	9.7	97.7
OTHER	3	34	2.3	2.3	100.0
	Total	1500	100.0	100.0	

Valid cases   1500   Missing cases   0

RELIG   RS RELIGIOUS PREFERENCE

Value Label	Value	Frequency	Percent	Valid Percent	Cum Percent
PROTESTANT	1	910	60.7	60.7	60.7
CATHOLIC	2	392	26.1	26.2	86.9
JEWISH	3	36	2.4	2.4	89.3
NONE	4	124	8.3	8.3	97.6
OTHER	5	36	2.4	2.4	100.0
NA	9	2	.1	Missing	
	Total	1500	100.0	100.0	

Valid cases   1498   Missing cases   2

MARITAL   MARITAL STATUS

Value Label	Value	Frequency	Percent	Valid Percent	Cum Percent
MARRIED	1	886	59.1	59.1	59.1
WIDOWED	2	132	8.8	8.8	68.0
DIVORCED	3	164	10.9	10.9	78.9
SEPARATED	4	49	3.3	3.3	82.2
NEVER MARRIED	5	267	17.8	17.8	100.0
NA	9	2	.1	Missing	
	Total	1500	100.0	100.0	

Valid cases   1498   Missing cases   2

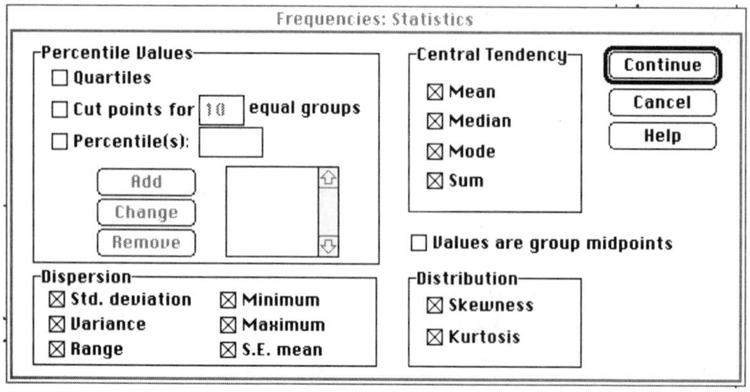

Figure 7 FREQUENCIES:STATISTICS Dialog Box

When working with interval level variables, add summary statistics. Following standard practice, choose:

Statistics ➤
  Summarize ➤
    Frequencies . . .

A press of the STATISTICS . . . command button at the bottom of the FREQUENCIES dialog box presents a roster of summary statistics options. See Figure 7.

Select all the statistics of interest. When finished, press the "Continue" button (it will return you to the original dialog box) and then the "OK" button. Your output should look like that of Table 7. In addition to the standard frequencies distribution, you now have appropriate summary statistics with which to, well, summarize the data.

Here's an interesting wrinkle. If you had asked for a variable with many values (e.g., age or income), you would have had pages of output for each variable. SPSS provides a useful solution to this problem—a FORMAT dialog box. It may be selected from the lower right corner of the FREQUENCIES dialog box (Figure 8).

Once displayed, choose the "Best Fit" option. SPSS produces a single-page summary output, as seen in Table 8. Note the differences between the Table 6 and Table 7—the inclusion of summary statistics; then examine close the difference between these two tables and Table 8—the format of the output. In constructing the output for the variable of AGE, SPSS produced a condensed three-column format on a single page.

In these FREQUENCIES commands, we have specified which variables we wish to use rather than using the expression: FREQUENCIES VARIABLES=ALL in the syntax window. This is appropriate since we wish to have summary statistics computed only when the variable of interest was measured at the metric level, (e.g., age, education, etc.).

Sometimes it is not necessary to report data using frequency distributions; rather, the summary statistics may be sufficient. You have two quick ways of producing such summaries. First, you can continue to use the FREQUENCIES command, just un-select

Table 7 FREQUENCIES WITH SUMMARY STATS

FREQUENCIES VARIABLES = EDUC DEGREE/STATISTICS=ALL

EDUC   HIGHEST YEAR OF SCHOOL COMPLETED

Value Label	Value	Frequency	Percent	Valid Percent	Cum Percent
	0	4	.3	.3	.3
	1	1	.1	.1	.3
	2	2	.1	.1	.5
	3	9	.6	.6	1.1
	4	13	.9	.9	1.9
	5	12	.8	.8	2.7
	6	22	1.5	1.5	4.2
	7	25	1.7	1.7	5.9
	8	89	5.9	5.9	11.8
	9	56	3.7	3.7	15.6
	10	77	5.1	5.1	20.7
	11	94	6.3	6.3	27.0
	12	519	34.6	34.7	61.7
	13	104	6.9	6.9	68.6
	14	137	9.1	9.2	77.8
	15	54	3.6	3.6	81.4
	16	156	10.4	10.4	91.8
	17	36	2.4	2.4	94.2
	18	44	2.9	2.9	97.1
	19	22	1.5	1.5	98.6
	20	21	1.4	1.4	100.0
DK	98	2	.1	Missing	
NA	99	1	.1	Missing	
	Total	1500	100.0	100.0	

Mean	12.369	Std err	.082	Median	12.000
Mode	12.000	Std dev	3.180	Variance	10.113
Kurtosis	.975	S E Kurt	.126	Skewness	-.318
S E Skew	.063	Range	20.000	Minimum	.000
Maximum	20.000	Sum	18517.000		

Valid cases   1497   Missing cases   3

DEGREE   RS HIGHEST DEGREE

Value Label	Value	Frequency	Percent	Valid Percent	Cum Percent
LT HIGH SCHOOL	0	390	26.0	26.0	26.0
HIGH SCHOOL	1	781	52.1	52.1	78.2
JUNIOR COLLEGE	2	61	4.1	4.1	82.2
BACHELOR	3	183	12.2	12.2	94.5
GRADUATE	4	83	5.5	5.5	100.0
NA	9	2	.1	Missing	
	Total	1500	100.0	100.0	

Mean	1.191	Std err	.029	Median	1.000
Mode	1.000	Std dev	1.119	Variance	1.253
Kurtosis	.387	S E Kurt	.126	Skewness	1.093
S E Skew	.063	Range	4.000	Minimum	.000
Maximum	4.000	Sum	1784.000		

Valid cases   1498   Missing cases   2

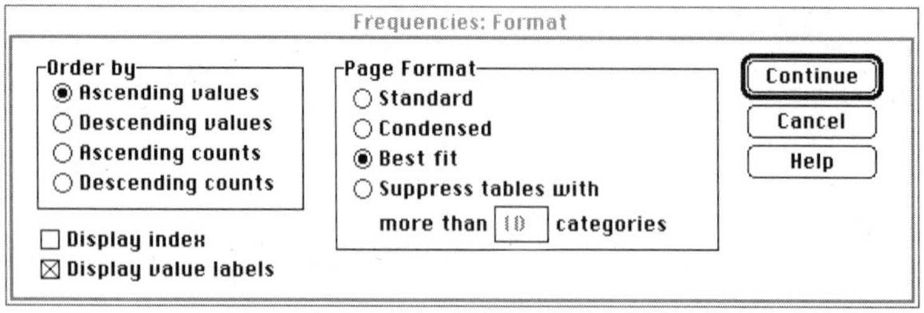

Figure 8 FREQUENCIES:FORMAT Dialog Box

"Display frequency tables." A click of the mouse in the box to the left of this subcommand will instruct SPSS to not display the table but still report all selected summary statistics.

A second SPSS alternative to summarize interval level variables is to use the DESCRIPTIVES . . . command.

Statistics ➤
  Summarize ➤
    Descriptives . . .

You will see the standard dialog selection box. You can choose which variables and which summary statistics you wish to have SPSS calculate. Which summary statistics? Well, a click on the Options . . . button will enable you to select all appropriate summary statistics—basically from the same roster as that found in the FREQUENCIES command.

Note that DESCRIPTIVES may be much more efficient and produce the same results[13] as found in the FREQUENCIES command. See Table 9.

Note also that if you are not completely familiar with your data set there is some danger in using this command. For example, you may not know if a value was not declared as a missing value and that value, as well as all the respondents who chose that value, were included in the calculations of the reported summary statistics. This is the case for the variables of INCOME, which uses coded values for income intervals, and the code of 13 for those persons who "refused" to answer the question. Similarly, the variable of PARTYID uses an ordinal scale of valid values that range from 0—"Strong Democrat" through 6—"Strong Republican." Unfortunately for the unsuspecting, the value 7 is not classified as missing and is used to indicate "Other Party." Thus, I recommend that you run your FREQUENCIES commands first, examine carefully all parts of the output, and then use the DESCRIPTIVES command to summarize appropriately selected variables.

---

[13]Okay, for those who look carefully, there are some minor difference in the reported summary statistics. This is due to rounding-off procedures.

Table 8 FREQUENCIES WITH SUMMARY STATS CONDENSED FORMAT

FREQUENCIES VARIABLES=age/format=onepage/statistics=all.

AGE   AGE OF RESPONDENT

Value	Freq	Pct	Cum Pct	Value	Freq	Pct	Cum Pct	Value	Freq	Pct	Cum Pct
18	9	1	1	42	32	2	54	66	20	1	87
19	21	1	2	43	30	2	56	67	14	1	88
20	22	1	3	44	25	2	58	68	19	1	89
21	23	2	5	45	19	1	59	69	7	0	90
22	35	2	7	46	22	1	61	70	15	1	91
23	38	3	10	47	27	2	62	71	16	1	92
24	32	2	12	48	18	1	64	72	10	1	92
25	38	3	15	49	27	2	66	73	13	1	93
26	45	3	18	50	20	1	67	74	14	1	94
27	49	3	21	51	21	1	68	75	14	1	95
28	29	2	23	52	16	1	69	76	7	0	96
29	43	3	26	53	19	1	71	77	11	1	96
30	38	3	28	54	25	2	72	78	13	1	97
31	37	2	31	55	22	1	74	79	5	0	98
32	27	2	33	56	17	1	75	80	5	0	98
33	38	3	35	57	18	1	76	81	6	0	98
34	31	2	37	58	20	1	77	82	8	1	99
35	38	3	40	59	18	1	79	83	5	0	99
36	37	2	42	60	18	1	80	84	2	0	99
37	35	2	45	61	17	1	81	85	3	0	99
38	26	2	46	62	19	1	82	86	3	0	100
39	31	2	48	63	19	1	84	87	3	0	100
40	33	2	51	64	15	1	85	89	2	0	100
41	23	2	52	65	16	1	86				

M I S S I N G   D A T A

Value	Freq	Value	Freq	Value	Freq
99	7				

Mean	43.759	Std err	.445	Median	40.000
Mode	27.000	Std dev	17.197	Variance	295.729
Kurtosis	-.728	S E Kurt	.127	Skewness	.537
S E Skew	.063	Range	71.000	Minimum	18.000
Maximum	89.000	Sum	65332.000		

Valid cases   1493   Missing cases   7

Table 9 SUMMARY STATS: DESCRIPTIVES

```
DESCRIPTIVES VARIABLES=,race,sex, relig, marital.

Number of valid observations (listwise) =      1486.00
```

Variable	Mean	Std Dev	Minimum	Maximum	Valid N	Label
CHILDS	1.95	1.84	0	8	1497	NUMBER OF CHILDREN
SIBS	3.98	3.16	0	26	1498	NUMBER OF BROTHERS AN
EDUC	12.37	3.18	0	20	1497	HIGHEST YEAR OF SCHOO
AGE	43.76	17.20	18	89	1493	AGE OF RESPONDENT

Other Useful Statistical Descriptive Measures You have already mastered CROSSTABS. But here are some additional uses, especially when you are working with longitudinal data. For example, a roster of the demographic variable of sex by year is important. We know that there will be differences—at least due to sampling error. Comparing differences is facilitated by using percents. We can request CROSSTABS to provide cell counts and percentages (percents based on row totals, column totals, or total sample size) in the CROSSTABS display dialog box.

Following our usual practice, choose:

Statistics ➤
   Summarize ➤
      Crosstabs . . .

which opens a dialog box like that of Figure 6. Now, press the "Cells" button along the bottom of this dialog box. From here select the "Observed" option in "Counts" and the "Column" option in "Percentages."[14] See Figure 9.

A press of the "Continue" button returns us to the crosstabs dialog box. We can now select the "statistics" button and choose the "chi square" option in the upper left portion of this dialog box. A press of "Continue" and then "OK" runs the CROSSTABS procedure and produces an output like that of Table 10.

Note that below each table cell count is the reported percentage for that column. Of the 300 sampled respondents in 1973, 50% were male and 50% were female. In 1978 42.7% of the GSS sampled respondents were male while 57.3% were female. (Examine Table 10 for the remaining years.) Thus, there were some differences in the distribution

---

[14]If you have access to the syntax window, you can enter the command:

  CROSSTABS

  /TABLES= sex BY year

  /CELLS= COUNT COLUMN

  /STATISTICS.

quickly and easily. Go ahead and execute this command to get the same results without going through so many menu steps.

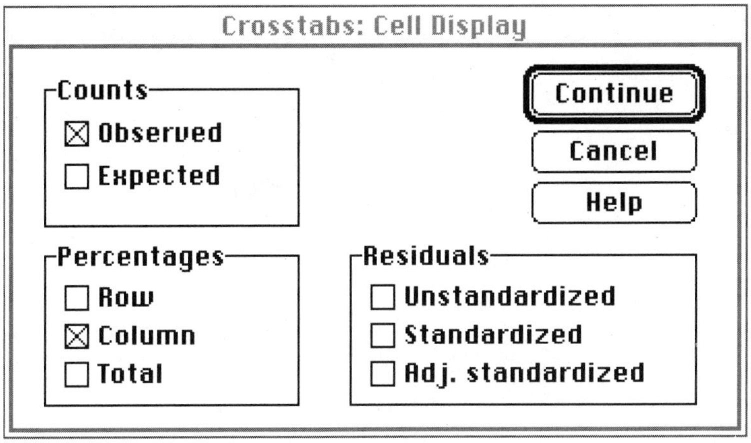

Figure 9 CROSSTABS Cell Display Dialog Box

of sex across the sampled years; however, these differences were not large enough—chi square$_{(4\ df)}$ = 8.27965, p = .082—to be considered statistically significant.

The final procedure of interest useful in summarizing these demographic comparisons is the procedure MEANS. It is particularly useful when you wish to use the average value to summarize variables such as age, educational years, and so on. It is found in the menu bar under:

Statistics ➤
    Compare Means ➤
        Means . . .

which brings forward the Means dialog box as seen in Figure 10.

A press of the "OK" button executes the MEANS procedure. We can now examine the output. See Table 11 for any trend in the demographic variables of age or education over the life of the study.

We could have just as easily entered the MEANS command in the syntax window. It takes the form of:

```
MEANS TABLES= var_list BY var_list.
```

or

```
MEANS TABLES= AGE, EDUC BY YEAR.
```

This follows the standard SPSS format and enables a simple comparison of averages across each category of the independent variable—in this case we are using YEAR as though it were an independent variable. Thus, as seen in Table 11, the average age of all the sample respondents was 44.4, while the average ages of 43.7, 42.6, 43.9, 46.1, and 45.5 years were found for the 1973, 78, 83, 88, and 93 sample years, respectively. Thus, there was not a large difference in the average ages across the study years. See Table 11.

Table 10 CROSSTABS Output: SEX BY YEAR

```
CROSSTABS
 /TABLES= sex BY year
 /CELLS= COUNT COLUMN
 /STATISTICS.

SEX   RESPONDENTS SEX  by  YEAR  GSS YEAR FOR THIS RESPONDENT

                    YEAR                               Page 1 of 1
             Count  |
             Col Pct|
                    |                                     Row
                    |   73|   78|   83|   88|   93| Total
 SEX        --------+-----+-----+-----+-----+-----+
                 1  |  150|  128|  135|  122|  119|   654
    MALE          |  50.0| 42.7| 45.0| 40.7| 39.7|  43.6
                  +-----+-----+-----+-----+-----+
                 2  |  150|  172|  165|  178|  181|   846
   FEMALE         |  50.0| 57.3| 55.0| 59.3| 60.3|  56.4
                  +-----+-----+-----+-----+-----+
             Column  300   300   300   300   300   1500
             Total  20.0  20.0  20.0  20.0  20.0  100.0


      Chi-Square                 Value          DF        Significance
  -------------------         ----------        ----      ------------


 Pearson                       8.27965           4           .08185
 Likelihood Ratio              8.25918           4           .08253
 Mantel-Haenszel test for      6.26385           1           .01232
     linear association

 Minimum Expected Frequency -  130.800

 Number of Missing Observations:  0
```

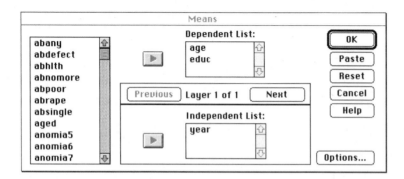

Figure 10 MEANS Dialog Box

Table 11 SUMMARY STATS: MEANS AGE EDUCATION BY YEAR

```
-> MEANS
->    TABLES=age BY year
->    /TABLES= educ  BY year
->    /CELLS MEAN STDDEV COUNT
->    /FORMAT= LABELS
->    /STATISTICS ANOVA LINEARITY.
```

```
                    - - Description of Subpopulations - -
Summaries of    AGE         AGE OF RESPONDENT
By levels of    YEAR        GSS YEAR FOR THIS RESPONDENT
```

Variable	Value Label	Mean	Std Dev	Cases
For Entire Population		44.3728	17.4967	1494
YEAR	73	43.7215	16.9727	298
YEAR	78	42.6333	17.8177	300
YEAR	83	43.8930	17.7199	299
YEAR	88	46.1342	18.2645	298
YEAR	93	45.4916	16.5402	299

```
  Total Cases = 1500
Missing Cases = 6 or    .4 Pct
```

```
                    - - Description of Subpopulations - -
Summaries of    EDUC        HIGHEST YEAR OF SCHOOL COMPLETED
By levels of    YEAR        GSS YEAR FOR THIS RESPONDENT
```

Variable	Value Label	Mean	Std Dev	Cases
For Entire Population		12.3031	3.1409	1498
YEAR	73	11.5251	3.0159	299
YEAR	78	12.0133	3.4262	300
YEAR	83	12.5800	3.0988	300
YEAR	88	12.3344	2.9461	299
YEAR	93	13.0600	2.9988	300

```
  Total Cases = 1500
Missing Cases = 2 or    .1 Pct
```

```
                    - - Analysis of Variance - -
Dependent Variable    EDUC        HIGHEST YEAR OF SCHOOL COMPLETED
    By levels of      YEAR        GSS YEAR FOR THIS RESPONDENT
```

Value Label	Mean	Std Dev	Sum of Sq	Cases
73	11.5251	3.0159	2710.5619	299
78	12.0133	3.4262	3509.9467	300
83	12.5800	3.0988	2871.0800	300
88	12.3344	2.9461	2586.5552	299
93	13.0600	2.9988	2688.9200	300
Within Groups Total	12.3031	3.1021	14367.0637	1498

Source	Sum of Squares	d.f.	Mean Square	F	Sig.
Between Groups	401.3422	4	100.3355	10.4267	.0000
Linearity	344.4543	1	344.4543	35.7951	.0000
Dev. from Linearity	56.8879	3	18.9626	1.9706	.1165

```
                      R =  .1527    R Squared =  .0233
Within Groups         14367.0637      1493       9.6229
                    Eta =  .1649    Eta Squared =  .0272
```

Some differences do appear across the years on other variables, however. For example, the variable of EDUC, the number of years of education, does change over the years—increasing from 11.5 years in 1973 to 13.06 years by 1993. Using the MEANS command and the subcommand STATISTICS enables examining the data using ANOVA and testing for LINEARITY. The typical adult American was more likely to have completed high school and attended college than in earlier years.

The great advantage in using CROSSTABS and MEANS over FREQUENCIES is that you not only get the summary totals for all respondents (e.g., look at the "Total" column and row line on the CROSSTABS output and the "Summaries For Entire Population" row on the MEANS output), but you also get information for each attribute of your "independent" variable.

Indeed, CROSSTABS and MEANS are sufficiently powerful to include several levels of variables. You can enter these levels in the appropriate dialog box if you are using the menu bar or by entering additional BY keywords directly into the command. For example, you might wish to know the religious affiliation of respondents for each study year by race and sex. Here's a simple embellishment of the CROSSTABS command:

CROSSTABS TABLES=RELIG BY YEAR BY RACE BY SEX.

Or, you may wish to know the average level of educational attainment of the respondents for each study year by sex within each race category. Your MEANS procedure becomes:

MEANS TABLES=EDUC BY YEAR BY RACE BY SEX.

You may include up to four levels of control using the BY keyword. Of course, the more BY keywords, the more complex the output and the fewer cases in any unique cell. This does give you a brief picture, however, of the power of SPSS.

Well, as the saying goes, this is "just a first look" about the retrieving data set demographic statistics and how to use basic tabular summary and simple comparative procedures of SPSS.

Exercise 3:   Take some time, load your SPSS file and try the commands of FREQUENCIES, CROSSTABS, and MEANS. After you re-create the tables noted above, try other variables, commands, and optional subcommands.

Some Useful Graphic Techniques   While statistical tables are solid communication devices for those interested in social science data, graphic presentations of such data often make a visceral impact on the reader. SPSS has a wealth of graphic options, some of which exist within statistical commands—e.g., FREQUENCIES—while others may be accessed through the graphic routines. Most graphics are best created, not surprisingly, from the graph menu:

Graphs ➤

From here you can choose from a variety of graph types, including bar, line, area, hi-lo, scatterplots, etc. In addition, most of these have a variety of additional choices; there are three choices of bar and line charts, two for area charts and four for scatterplots.

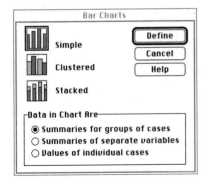
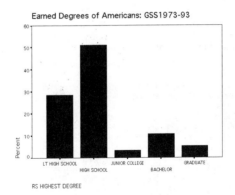
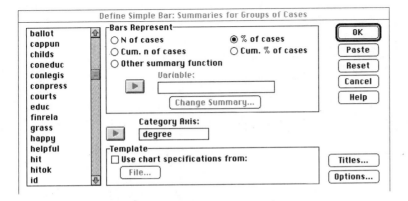

Figure 11 Bar Graph Dialog Boxes and Bar Graph

Within each of these choices you control the types of data with which you are working—summaries across a single variable, comparing variables, etc. I think you get the
point. One of the great advances of SPSS 6.1 over earlier versions has been the addition
of powerful graphic capabilities. We'll illustrate only a few here. You can try these, and
others, too.

Perhaps a good place to start is with the descriptive data on education. We can create, at first, a simple graph and then improve upon presenting the changes in educational achievement we noted earlier. The command sequence:

Graphs ➤
  Bar . . .

begins the process. Choosing within this dialog box the options of "simple" and "Summaries for groups of cases" are the default choices—how convenient. A press of the
"Define" button lists the variables from which we may choose and how we wish to display the results—what the bars represent and how to display the data. See Figure 11 for
the dialog box and selections. A press on the "Titles . . ." yields an opportunity to key

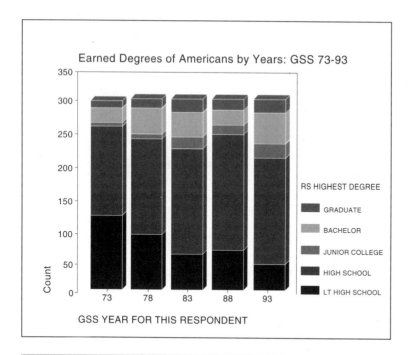

Figure 12 Stacked Bar Graph

in an appropriate title and de-selecting, in the "Options . . ." button; "display groups defined by missing data" will complete the bar graph. (If you miss these options, you can further modify the graph once it is displayed.)

A more complex bar graph may be seen in Figure 12. Let's work with the variables of degree and year since we are interested in tracing the changes in educational achievement over the last 20 years. We will again choose

Graphs ➤
    Bar . . .

but here we shall select the icon for "Stacked bars." A press of the "Define" button gives us the opportunity to select—bar represents—"N of cases," the "category axis:" defined by the variable of YEAR and "defined stacks by:" DEGREE. Again, entering a "Title . . ." and eliminating the inclusion of missing data from the "Options . . ." buttons are no problem. Once displaced, we can further improve on the graphic appeal by choosing to make each bar three-dimensional—choose from the menu bar:

Carousel ➤
    Edit . . .

then, from the new menu bar:

Attributes ➤
    Bar Style

and then 3D-effect.

A click of the mouse button on the "Apply All" button and the stacked bar chart will include an interesting 3-D look. Finally, we can reduce the amount of white space at the top of each bar by setting the axis display limit between 0 and 350 with 50 for major divisions and tick marks—labels listed on the vertical axis. This is accomplished in:

Chart ➤
   Axis

Now choose scale and then change the appropriate values. When finished, it will look like Figure 12—actually it will look better on the screen than in print.

From this graph it is easy to see that since 1973, the number of Americans who had yet to earn at least a high school diploma decreased substantially over the last twenty years. In addition, by 1993, the number of Americans earning a baccalaureate degree was substantially greater than those in earlier years. Such graphs make a visually strong case when you "look at data" and when you need to present your findings to others.

Of course, you are expected to know which graphs are appropriate for which data types—bar charts for categorical data (race or sex status), histograms for continuous data (age), scatterplots for two continuous variables (income and degree), and so on. Since you can easily modify the chart, add titles, determine the number of tick marks, use the grid lines, use labels rather than values of the variables, add footnotes, determine what to do with missing values, etc., you should examine several ways to graphically summarize data—you can present the data as simply as you wish or as complicated by combining multiple variables. So, do the exercise below.

Exercise 4:   Take some time, go ahead and load the data set and try various graphic routines and options within each. After you re-create these simple bar graphs, try other techniques by choosing from the gallery options alternate graphic types with the "Replace" button.

Well, what have we found out about the GSS respondents, and therefore most Americans, across the last 20-odd years?

For most years, the typical respondents were white (88%), female (60.7%), and Protestant (60.7%). A substantial minority, 31%, of the respondents were members of other faiths—typically, Catholic(26.2%)—while few (8.3%) reported no religious membership. They attended church—typically, on a monthly basis. While the average age was 44 years old, most adult respondents were between the ages of 27 and 61. Most respondents were married in each of the sampled years, although proportionately fewer Americans were married in 1993 (52.5%) than in 1973 (60.7%). They had a median family income, in 1986 dollars, of $24,000 per year, approximately, across the study years. Finally, they typically defined their political views as "moderate." You say that you don't see how I know this. Try running the procedures outlined above with the background variables included in our data file. Now, compare your results with mine.

Before You Run the Race, Make Sure It's Worth the Effort: Step 4

We now have a brief look at the respondents and how they answered each of the demographic questions of interest. A reasonable social scientist would want to convince

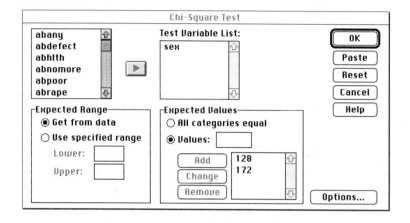

Figure 13 Chi-Square Test Dialog Box

himself/herself that the data set is, in fact, reasonably representative of the population from which it was selected. This is especially true when you are working with data collected by others. Using some of these same demographic variables, we can compare the distribution of our GSS subset to the larger data set. For example, I know from examining the GSS codebook and original file[15] the number and proportion of women and men in each of the survey years. In 1993, 57.3% of the 1606 respondents were women and 42.7% were men. If our data subset sampling procedure were exactly on target, then we would have expected to find 172 women (57.3% * 300) and 128 men (42.7% * 300) in our subsample. We have already noted that the number of men and women in our 1993 subsample was 186 women and 114 men. Are these differences between what we would expect to find and what we in fact found likely due to sampling error, or do they reflect a bias in the sampling process? Read on. . . .

We can use SPSS to examine this question.

Data ➤
    Select Cases . . . ➤
        If

and select just those cases from the 1993 sample by entering the expression: YEAR = 93. SPSS will indicate all other cases are to be excluded (note the slash drawn through the row numbers to the left of each row) from further analysis—at least until you re-select "all cases" from the same menu. Now, select

Statistics ➤
    Nonparametric Tests ➤
        Chi square . . .

You should see a dialog box, albeit incomplete, like that of Figure 13.

---

[15]See earlier Davis and Smith reference.

Just choose the variable SEX from the variable list and then choose the "Values:" option within the "Expected Values" box. In this box, enter 128 and press the "Add" button. Then enter 172 and press the "Add" button again. (Note that these values must be entered in the appropriate order—since men have a coded value of "1" while women have a code of "2," the expected number of men must be entered before the expected number of women.) Your chi-square test dialog box should now look exactly like that of Figure 13. A press on the "OK" button is all that is needed to invoke the SPSS command. The results—chi square$_{(1\ df)}$ = 2.6708, sig = .1022—indicate no significant difference between our GSS subsample and the total 1993 data set on the variable of sex.

Of course you could write in the syntax window the following commands:

```
TEMPORARY.
SELECT IF (YEAR EQ 93).
NPAR TEST
 /CHISQUARE = sex
 /EXPECTED = 128 172
 /MISSING ANALYSIS.
```

and then run them, directly producing the same tabular results.

Why not try these calculations yourself. A quick trip to the library will give you access to the complete GSS codebook. Choose one or two other demographic variables and make your own comparison between our subsample data and the larger data set. Then, if you have Internet skills, examine *Census* summary statistics and compare the original GSS demographic variables distribution to *Census* summary statistics for 1980 and 1990. What do you conclude about the veracity of the GSS?

Making a Class Act Work for You: COMPUTE, IF, and RECODE

All of us like to work with data that are easy to use and easy to understand. Data transformation commands are useful tools in "fixing" data values. What needs to be fixed? Well, here are some examples. When doing data entry we sometimes take the easy way out and use coded values for class intervals rather than entering the actual values. NORC personnel are no different. For example, they chose for the variable of income to enter a 5 for all respondents whose total family income was between $5,000 through $5,999 rather than the actual amount. These codes may be easily entered but they are less easy to interpret.

We may find that it is to our advantage to change the codes of some variables rather than use the original codes entered by others or us—for example, changing the coding of a variable that is a dichotomy (e.g., SEX) from "1" and "2" to "0" and "1" since the values "0" and "1" are preferable when interpreting mean scores. Additionally, we may wish to more easily summarize a variable with many attributes by aggregating several attributes into just a few categories. Finally, we may wish to create new variables from those already in our study so that we can better target answers to our research questions (e.g., combining the two variables of RACE and SEX into a single variable of RACE-SEX). Below is a brief discussion of some useful data transformation commands.

Converting Coded Values to Useful and Real Values: RECODE   RECODE is a simple procedure that enables us to convert easily the current values of any variable to new values. It has a standard SPSS form:

```
RECODE varname (old value = new value) . . . (old value = new value).
```

We can, for example, RECODE the variable of SEX with the command:

```
RECODE SEX (2=0).
```

or RECODE the variable of RACE:

```
RECODE RACE (2=0).
```

or do both at the same time:

```
RECODE SEX, RACE (2=0).
```

Converting variables such as SEX or RACE to a dichotomy of codes "0" (for "Female" or "Black") and "1" (for "Male" or "White") will enhance our calculating and reporting statistical findings.[16] Mean values calculated on "0" and "1" will yield a value that can be interpreted as the proportion of respondents that were coded "1." Read on. Right now, let's return to the RECODE procedure.

Those whose code on the variable of SEX or RACE was "2" are now assigned a value of "0." (To exclude those who were neither African-American nor white can be accomplished with a MISSING VALUES command—the value "3" can be declared as a missing value):

```
MISSING VALUES RACE (3).
```

Those persons coded "3" can then be excluded easily from most further analyses.[17]

While it may not be apparent from this example, you may RECODE several variables with the same statement. Using our GSS survey, we can tell SPSS to treat all variables that measured abortion attitudes similarly:

```
RECODE abany,abdefect,abhlth,abnomore,abpoor,abrape,absingle
(0=99)(1=1)(2=0)(ELSE=99).
```

Those who were coded in the original data set with a value of "0" will now have a code of "99." Those coded with a "1" = "Yes" will retain the value, those with a value of "2" = "No" will now have a code of "0," and those with any other code, "ELSE,"

---

[16]We could have just as easily coded the variables of SEX as "0" for "Male" and "1" for "Female" or the variable of RACE as "0" for "White" and "1" for "Black." The only impact will be in how we describe and interpret the analysis.

[17]If you wish to keep the current variable of RACE and create a new variable, such as NRACE, just add the expression INTO NRACE. Thus your command should look like this:
```
RECODE RACE (1=1)(2=0)(3=3) INTO NRACE.
```

will have a value of "99." Now, if we reassign the missing values from "0" to "99" with the command

```
MISSING VALUES abany,abdefect,abhlth,abnomore,abpoor,abrape,
absingle (99).
```

all respondents coded "99" who did not answer these questions will be treated as missing. Those persons who answered "Yes" will continue to have a coded value of "1" while those who answered "No" will have a coded value of "0." (This will become more meaningful when we examine the issue of developing a scale of the items used to measure abortion.)

It is often useful or necessary to RECODE values to "true" values. The original values of INCOME, for example, went from 1 through 13 with 1 through 12 indicating valid values. A value of 1 indicated total family income of less than $1000, a 2 indicated $1000 through $2999, etc. One of the nice facilities of SPSS is the ability to easily reassign the entered values of our data file to some other, more appropriate, data values. Rather than continue to work with these coded values of "1," "2," "3," etc., we can have SPSS store the "true" values. What are the "true" values? Well, if we take the average of each class interval:

$$(\$1,000 + \$2,999) / 2 \sim \$2,000$$
$$(\$3,000 + \$3,999) / 2 \sim \$3,500$$
$$(\$4,000 + \$4,999) / 2 \sim \$4,500$$

and choose a reasonable beginning (say, $500) and ending (say, $40,000) values, then we can have SPSS store the "true" values rather than the entered coded values.[18] This is accomplished with the RECODE command. The format of this RECODE command is:

```
RECODE INCOME (1=500)(2=2000)(3=3500)(4=4500)(5=5500)
               (6=6500)(7=7500)(8=9000)(9=12500)(10=17500)
               (11=22500)(12=40000)(13=0).
```

Note the standard form of the expressions used above (i.e., use of blanks, open and closed parentheses, and equal signs). Note also that no commas were used. These subcommands would be entered into the syntax window and then executed.

Several other options exist when working with the RECODE command and old values. For example, you could RECODE a range of values—say, (2 THRU 4=2)—in a single command segment rather than listing each of these values separately. If I am interested in combining the MARITAL statuses of divorced, separated, and widowed into one category—"previously married"—I could key:

```
RECODE MARITAL (2,3,4 = 2).
```

---

[18]The NORC staff were nice enough to recognize this problem and have included an additional variable, REALINC. It not only uses midpoint values but takes into account the effect of time by standardizing family income to 1986 dollars across all respondents who were included in the 1973–1993 surveys.

or, I could have used

RECODE MARITAL (2 thru 4 = 2).

and then changed the value labels—the labels assigned to each attribute—by entering in the syntax window the command:

VALUE LABELS MARITAL 1 "Married" 2 "Previously Married".

If you wish to use the dialog boxes in SPSS, then the Recode command will be found by choosing:

Transform ➤
  Recode ➤
    "Into same variables . . ."

from the menu bar. Then choose the variable of SEX. Press on the "Old and New Values . . ." button at the bottom of the dialog box. When the new dialog box appears, enter the old value of "2" and the new value "0" in their appropriate text boxes. Click on the "Add" button and 2 —> 0 appears in the "Old —> New" box. A click on the "Continue" button returns to the previous dialog box; a press on the OK button with your mouse will execute the Recode command. In a minute or two you will see the changed data in the Data Editor window—all those who had a value of "2" are now coded as "0" for this variable. By clicking on the variable name MARITAL in the data editor window you will be able to change the value labels as listed above.

More complex recoding requires just a little more work. The variable of RACE may serve as a good example. Here we wish to recode the variable so that we are working with a "dummy" variable—using the "0" for "African-Americans" and "1" for "White"— and exclude all others. Since we are treating the values quite differently we shall, in this example, create a new variable, NRACE, using the codes as noted above. Thus, choose from the menu bar:

Transform ➤
  Recode ➤
    "Into different variables . . ."

and then select the variable of RACE. In the "Output Variable" box, type the name of the new variable, NRACE, and its label, "New Race Variable." Now press the "Change" button. As before, a press of the "Old and New Values . . ." button brings up the new screen (Figure 14).

Enter a "1" in "Old Value," and a "1" in "New Value," and press the "Add" button. (A 1 —> 1 will appear in the "Old —> New:" box.) Enter a "2" in the "Old Value" and a "0" in the "New Value" boxes and press the "Add" button again. Finally, enter "3" in the "Old Value" and choose, in the "New Value" box, the "System-missing" option. Press the "Add" button. The second part of Figure 14 should be your guide.

(To include a value label for these newly assigned values—for example, in the variable of SEX, the value of "0"—double-click on the variable name, SEX, or NRACE in the data editor window. [If you would rather work with NRACE, you will find the vari-

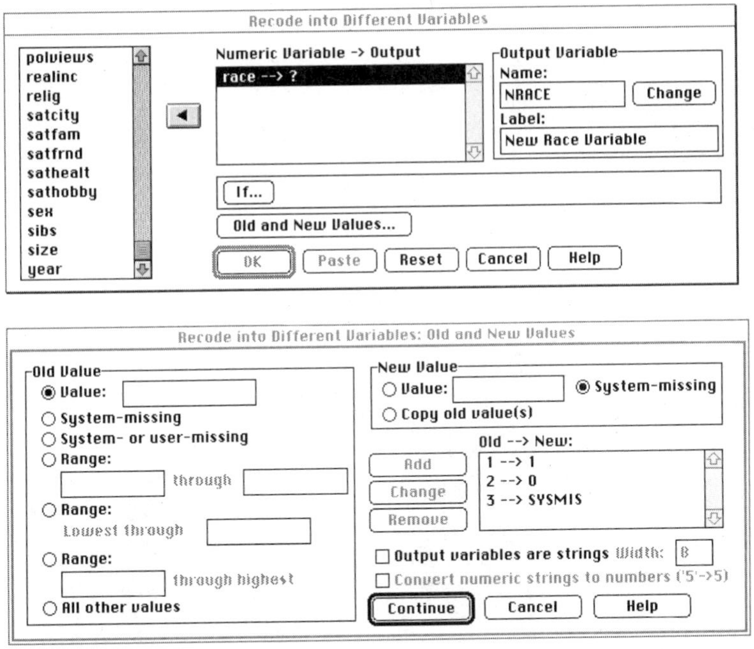

Figure 14 RECODE Variable Dialog Box

able, NRACE, added at the end of your list of variables in the data editor window.] A variable dialog box, like that seen in Figure 15, will appear. Simply choose the option, "Labels . . .", and enter, for the variable of SEX, a "0" in the "Value:" box and "FE-MALE" in the "LABEL" box. A simple press of the "Add" button, "Continue" button, and then the "OK" button will change the value labels assigned to the variable of SEX. Executing the FREQUENCIES command will convince you that the change in data values and labels has been made successfully.)

Working with Valid Values and Creating New Variables: COMPUTE and IF Commands   We already noted the use of the RECODE procedure to transform and store a coded value into a "true" value as well as create a new variable with many of the same values of another variable. Well, we can sometimes do this more efficiently with the COMPUTE and IF procedures. When we are working with interval and ratio level data, the COMPUTE statement will enable us to manipulate the data in the variable with all the typical mathematical operators. We can add (+), subtract (−), multiply values (*), and divide (/) values and variables. In addition, there is a large array of functions, including: (1) arithmetic functions (e.g., round to nearest integer, take the square root, etc.), (2) statistical functions (e.g., sum the values stored in several variables, calculate the mean across several variables, etc.), (3) logical functions (test to see

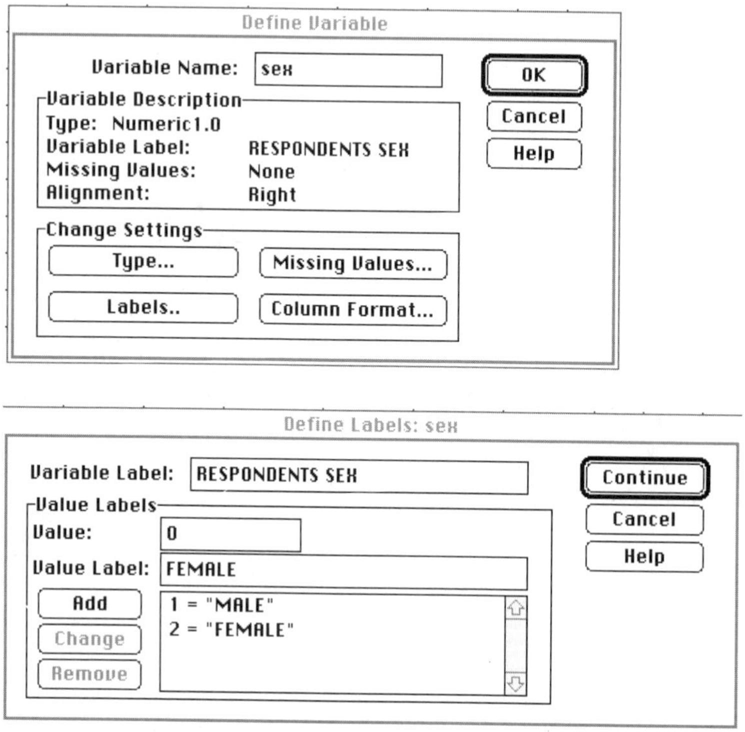

Figure 15 DEFINE Variable Dialog Box

if a value is in a specific range of values), and more. The simple format of the COMPUTE procedure is:

```
COMPUTE targetvariable = oldvariable operator oldvariable.
```

For example:

```
COMPUTE ABORTION = abany + abdefect + abhlth +
abnomore + abpoor + abrape + absingle.
```

This procedure statement tells SPSS to create a new variable, ABORTION, and store in this new variable the sum total of values for each respondent in ABANY, ABDEFECT, ABHLTH, etc.

You may be wondering what happens to people who did not answer all the questions. You will recall that we have declared MISSING VALUES for all these variables. When SPSS encounters a value previously defined as missing for the old variable (e.g., ABANY, ABDEFECT, etc.) it assigns the target variable (e.g., ABORTION) as missing, too. Therefore, those who did not respond to all the abortion rights questions will be treated as missing values. This makes logical sense since you do not know what their

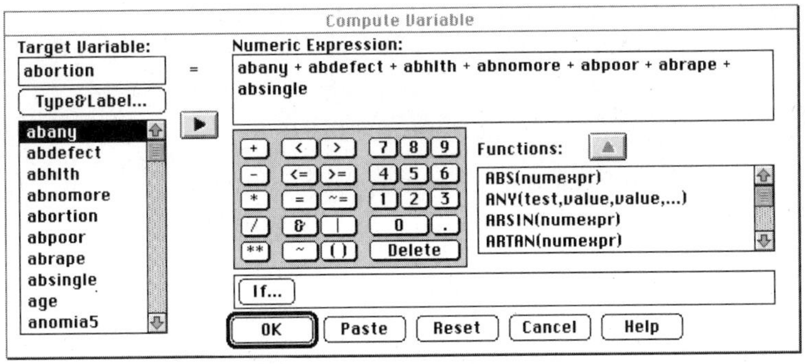

Figure 16 COMPUTE Variable Dialog Box

overall scale score would be unless you knew how each person responded to each and every one of the items.

If, however, you wished to include all people who answered at least five of the seven questions, then you could use the expression:

```
COMPUTE ABORTION = SUM.5(abany, abdefect, abhlth,
    abnomore, abpoor, abrape, absingle).
```

or, even better,

```
COMPUTE ABORTION = MEAN.5(abany, abdefect, abhlth,
    abnomore, abpoor, abrape, absingle).
```

If you are wish to use the dialogue process,[19] go ahead and try the

Transform ➤
   Compute

option. You will see a new dialog box with the variables at the left and all the operational and mathematical functions listed. (The functions will be in a scroll box.) You will be able to create this command by typing a new variable name in the appropriate text box—"Target Variable." Now, select the variable (e.g., ABANY), then the function ("+"), and then select the next variable (e.g., ABDEFECT). Repeat the process until all the variables have been selected. Press "OK" and SPSS will add this variable to your variable list. See Figure 16.

---

[19]If you are using the Student Version with the GSS, you will have to make room for each and every new variable. (Remember, the Student Version is limited to 50 variables.) Simply select variables that you are not going to use. Now, choose Edit from the menu bar and then cut. SPSS will eliminate these variables and you will now have the necessary room with which to work.

If you created this new summary variable, you might wish to give it a variable label. This is simple. From the syntax window, use the expression:

```
VARIABLE LABELS
  ABORTION 'SUM OF ALL ANSWERS TO EACH ABORTION QUESTION'.
```

or, from the dialog box, choose the "Type&Label" button. (Since this is an index and each of the values has a meaning, there is no need to use the VALUE LABELS command.)

Before we conclude this section, it is interesting to note that you can combine the COMPUTE command with IF statements to create new variables and assign appropriate values. The IF command enables you to use a logical expression—that is, a test condition—before you assign a value to a target variable. It takes the form of:

```
IF (logical expression) targetvariable = value.
```

Logical expressions test to see if a condition is true. You may use, for example, such phrases as RACE EQ 1. This logical expression contains a variable name, RACE; a logical operator, EQ (equal, or =); and a test value, 1. If the first part of the command is "true," then the second part of the command (targetvariable = value) is performed. More on this later.

For now, it is important to note that you may work with several logical expressions and have several logical expressions linked to each other as long as you include the appropriate logical operator(s) such as: AND, OR, NOT. Additionally, you have several alternate operators available. They include:

```
EQ or = Equal to              NE or <> Not equal to
LT or < less than             LE or <= Less than or equal to
GT or > greater than          GE or >= greater than or equal to
```

Here's one example. Let us assume that we wish to create a new variable that combines the variables of RACE and SEX. That is, we wish to be able to work with a variable that identifies African-Am. males, African-Am. females, white males, and white females. We can combine our COMPUTE and IF statement to create this new variable (RACESEX) by using the original values for RACE and SEX and using the command set of:

```
COMPUTE RACESEX=9.
IF (RACE EQ 1 AND SEX EQ 1)RACESEX=1.
IF (RACE EQ 1 AND SEX EQ 2)RACESEX=2.
IF (RACE EQ 2 AND SEX EQ 1)RACESEX=3.
IF (RACE EQ 2 AND SEX EQ 2)RACESEX=4.
```

The COMPUTE statement first creates a new variable, RACESEX, and assigns everyone a value of "9." The IF statements then check the RACE and SEX value codes for each respondent. If a respondent was white (RACE EQ 1) and male (SEX EQ 1), then his RACESEX code would be "1"; if the respondent was African-Am. (RACE EQ 2) and female (SEX EQ 2), then her RACESEX code would be reassigned from a value of "9" to the value of "4." Similarly, if the respondent was white (RACE EQ 1) and female (SEX EQ 2), then she would have her RACESEX code reassigned to the value of "2." Only where both conditions were true would SPSS change the assigned value of "9" to some other value.

To help keep track of this new variable and its values, we can use our labeling procedures:

```
VARIABLE LABELS  RACESEX, 'RACE AND SEX IDENTIFIER'.
VALUE LABELS    RACESEX  1 'WH-MALE' 2 'WH-FEMALE'
                         3 'AA-MALE' 4 'AA-FEMALE'.
```

and our MISSING VALUES procedure:

```
MISSING VALUES  RACESEX (9).
```

Of course, you would want to check any earlier RECODE changes made to these variables (i.e., have you already changed the coded values of RACE and/or SEX?) so that these statements use the most current and correct codes.

You now know how to better improve your data set by RECODEing variable values to their "true" value, treating dichotomies as 0 and 1 to improve interpretations, COMPUTE new variables, and create new variables with COMPUTE and IF statements. Once you get these values and variables just as you wish, make sure that you SAVE the file by using the "Save As" option in the File menu. Just use the dialog box to give it a new file name and you will have a saved copy—with all relevant changes—on your disk as well as the original file.

Exercise 5: Here's your chance to modify or create additional variables with which you wish to work. Take a few moments. Identify which variables are coded values that should really be changed to "true" values. If you are conducting your own study, then think back to your study goals. Ask yourself what combination of variables, if any, are needed to more adequately examine your hypotheses. Now, go ahead and use your RECODE, COMPUTE, and IF statements to make the necessary changes. Then, go ahead and label these, when necessary. Last, but not least, make sure that you save these changes in a new file that you can use later.

Developing a Scale You may be wondering why we spent so much time on how to use the data transformation commands of RECODE, COMPUTE, IF, and MISSING VALUES. We did so because we are interested in developing an appropriate scale that will give us a reliable measure of respondents' attitudes toward the right of women to obtain a legal abortion.

Our first step in developing such a scale is to use these recoded items and examine the typical response patterns. To do this, we can use the menu bar and select the appropriate procedures, or, in the syntax window, we can run the procedures you mastered earlier, RECODE, MISSING VALUES, and DESCRIPTIVES with the commands:

```
RECODE abany,abdefect,abhlth,abnomore,abpoor,abrape,absingle
    (0=99)(1=1)(2=0)(ELSE=99).

MISSING VALUES abany,abdefect,abhlth,abnomore,abpoor,abrape,
  absingle (99).
```

```
DESCRIPTIVES
  VARIABLES = abany,abdefect,abhlth,abnomore,abpoor,abrape,
  absingle.
```

Or, better,

```
DESCRIPTIVES
  VARIABLES =abdefect,abhlth,abnomore,abpoor,abrape,absingle
  /MISSING = LISTWISE /SORT = MEAN (D).
```

Thus, our first look at our variable of interest, attitudes toward the right of women to obtain a legal abortion, lists all items. The "mean" value, given that we have now re-coded the variable values to 0 and 1, tells us the proportion of persons who said "yes" to each of the questions. Thus, most respondents supported the right of a women to obtain an abortion if: (1) her health is seriously endangered (91%), (2) she was raped (83%), or (3) there is a strong chance of serious defect in the baby (82%). Clearly, there is much less agreement on abortion rights when other reasons are considered. We'll have more to say about these results later. For now, see Table 12.

Our DESCRIPTIVES analysis was only a reasonable first step. Since we are interested in a stable summary variable to measure abortion rights, we shall need to explore creating a scale or index. The principles of creating scales and indices are discussed elsewhere in this text. We recall from that discussion, all items should: (1) have sufficient data for all variables, (2) be logically related, (3) be reasonably correlated, and (4) be sufficiently diverse in their response pattern. Finally, (5) an index should have a sufficient range of scores. For our data, we recognize that we meet several of these criteria. There are two glaring exceptions. First, as we noted earlier, the item querying Americans that used the variable "any reason"—ABANY—was not asked in 1973. This explains why the number of cases fell substantially from 1500 cases. ABANY will not be part of this scale, although it could be used in other analyses and other scales measuring abortion attitudes from 1978 through 1993. Second, there is more than 90% agreement among Americans about the right of access to an abortion for women whose health is endangered. ABHLTH will be excluded from this analysis, too.

SPSS provides a procedure called RELIABILITY[20] for testing the internal consistency of any scale. We can execute the RELIABILITY procedure[21] with the following basic commands:

---

[20]If you are limited to the SPSS for Windows, Student Version, you will not be able to run the RELIABILITY procedure. You will, however, be able to run DESCRIPTIVES and CORRELATIONS. Use these procedures to choose the best combination of items for your scale.

[21]To use the RELIABILITY procedure correctly, we must first make sure that all the variables are coded in the same direction. Let's assume that you are studying political attitudes and you ask people to respond to ten statements, as was done in the 1985 GSS survey, using the options of "Strongly Agree, Agree, Disagree, and Strongly Disagree." In entering the data you assign a code of 1 for Strongly Agree, 2 for Agree, etc. You now recognize that some of the items were phrased in a positive direction while others were phrased in a negative direction. For example,

Taking everything into account, the world is getting better.

The public has little control over what politicians do in office.

Clearly these two statements are in opposite directions. Thus, each item must be coded so that the higher the score indicates a greater belief in the variable of interest. If you "Strongly Agree" to the first statement, then

Table 12 SUMMARY STATS:DESCRIPTIVES

```
-> RECODE abany,abdefect,abhlth,abnomore,abpoor,abrape,absingle
->     (0=99)(1=1)(2=0)(ELSE=99).
-> MISSING VALUES abany,abdefect,abhlth,abnomore,abpoor,abrape,absingle (99) .
-> DESCRIPTIVES
->    VARIABLES = abany,abdefect,abhlth,abnomore,abpoor,abrape,absingle.
```

Number of valid observations (listwise) =   1076.00
Valid

Variable	Mean	Std Dev	Minimum	Maximum	N	Label
ABANY	.38	.49	0	1	1176	ABORTION IF WOMAN WAN
ABDEFECT	.82	.39	0	1	1481	STRONG CHANCE OF SERI
ABHLTH	.91	.28	0	1	1483	WOMANS HEALTH SERIOUS
ABNOMORE	.44	.50	0	1	1478	MARRIED—WANTS NO MOR
ABPOOR	.49	.50	0	1	1482	LOW INCOME—CANT AFFO
ABRAPE	.83	.37	0	1	1471	PREGNANT AS RESULT OF
ABSINGLE	.45	.50	0	1	1479	NOT MARRIED

```
-> DESCRIPTIVES VARIABLES = abdefect,abhlth,abnomore,abpoor,abrape,absingle
->    /MISSING = LISTWISE /SORT = MEAN (D).
```

Number of valid observations (listwise) =   1374.00

Variable	Mean	Std Dev	Minimum	Maximum	Label
ABHLTH	.91	.29	0	1	WOMANS HEALTH SERIOUSLY END
ABRAPE	.83	.37	0	1	PREGNANT AS RESULT OF RAPE
ABDEFECT	.82	.39	0	1	STRONG CHANCE OF SERIOUS DE
ABPOOR	.51	.50	0	1	LOW INCOME—CANT AFFORD MOR
ABNOMORE	.47	.50	0	1	MARRIED—WANTS NO MORE CHIL
ABSINGLE	.46	.50	0	1	NOT MARRIED

*Note the differences between these two commands. The first produces a simple descriptive listing for each variable in the ordered listed on the command. The second produces the same statistics but eliminates all those persons who missed any question, sorts the variables by mean score, and prints the results in descending order. Note also that the variable, ABANY, was not included in the second DESCRIPTIVES command since the question was not asked in 1973.

---

you should have a high score (4) rather than a low score (1) as entered. We can RECODE this first item so that the code of 1 indicates "Strongly Disagree" while the code of 4 indicates "Strongly Agree." The second item is already coded in the correct direction—if you "agreed" to this statement, it would indicate that you felt that you had little control, rather than a lot of control; "disagree" responses would indicate greater political efficacy. Thus, using the RECODE facility, we can instruct SPSS to make the values assigned to each variable indicate a higher level of agreement. The RECODE statement is:

```
RECODE ITEM1 (1=4)(2=3)(3=2)(4=1).
```

Now higher scores on each variable indicate a belief in greater control of the political system. Thus, you may now run the RELIABILITY procedure with confidence.

```
RELIABILITY VARIABLES =
    abdefect,abnomore,abpoor,abrape,absingle
    /SCALE (abortion) =
    abdefect,abnomore,abpoor,abrape,absingle
    /SUMMARY means corr total
    /STATISTICS descriptive corr scale.
```

Or, after several iterations of finding the "best variables," the complete command becomes:

```
-> RELIABILITY VARIABLES =
->     abdefect,abnomore,abpoor,abrape,absingle
->     /SCALE (abortn1) =
->     abdefect,abnomore,abpoor,abrape,absingle,
->     /SCALE (abortn2) =
->     abnomore,abpoor,abrape,absingle,
->     /SCALE (abortn3) =
->     abnomore,abpoor,absingle,
->     /SUMMARY means corr total
->     /STATISTICS descriptive corr scale..
```

This will produce a complete RELIABILITY output like that of Table 13. Note that the output is divided into four major sections. The first section is a complete list of each of the declared variables to be included in the scale. In addition, you will find the mean, standard deviation and number of cases summary—just as we did with the DESCRIPTIVES command. Since all our data are coded 0 and 1, the mean values are simply the proportion of respondents who scored "high" or "yes" on each item.

You have probably noticed that the number of cases was substantially reduced from our initial 1500 (Americans who responded between 1973 and 1993) to 1391 cases. Any respondent who did not have a value of 0 or 1 was treated as a missing case. All those respondents who did not respond to one or more items were excluded from this analysis.

The second section reports a simple correlation matrix of all items and summarizes the scale statistics. If all five items were included, then the summary scale mean and standard deviation values, the item means and standard deviation values, and inter-item correlation statistics would be reported correctly. That is, if we kept all five items and added all the values of each item, our scale mean would be 3.06 with a standard deviation of 1.82. These reported data and summary statistics will become more useful when you complete the item selection process.

The third section, item-total statistics, is most important when building a scale or index. It helps you to identify which items or variables are contributing to your overall internal consistency score. Notice especially the column titled "alpha if item deleted." Notice also the computed and reported alpha (internal consistency) value (i.e., alpha = .8558) reported in the last section of the output. Now, return to the last column of section 3. Examine the variable of ABDEFECT. If this item, ABDEFECT, was deleted from the scale, the alpha value would improve to .8578. Thus, SCALE (abortn2) is

Table 13 RELIABILITY

```
-> RELIABILITY VARIABLES =
->     abdefect,abnomore,abpoor,abrape,absingle
->     /SCALE (abortn1) =
->     abdefect,abnomore,abpoor,abrape,absingle,
->     /SCALE (abortn2) =
->     abnomore,abpoor,abrape,absingle,
->     /SCALE (abortn3) =
->     abnomore,abpoor,absingle,
->     /SUMMARY means corr total
->     /STATISTICS descriptive corr scale..
```

```
****** Method 2 (covariance matrix) will be used for this analysis ******
R E L I A B I L I T Y   A N A L Y S I S   -   S C A L E   (A B O R T N 1)
```

		Mean	Std Dev	Cases
1.	ABDEFECT	.8160	.3877	1391.0
2.	ABNOMORE	.4615	.4987	1391.0
3.	ABPOOR	.5018	.5002	1391.0
4.	ABRAPE	.8267	.3786	1391.0
5.	ABSINGLE	.4565	.4983	1391.0

Correlation Matrix

	ABDEFECT	ABNOMORE	ABPOOR	ABRAPE	ABSINGLE
ABDEFECT	1.0000				
ABNOMORE	.4025	1.0000			
ABPOOR	.4061	.7552	1.0000		
ABRAPE	.6159	.4010	.4252	1.0000	
ABSINGLE	.4129	.7873	.7487	.4043	1.0000

```
        N of Cases =    1391.0
```

Statistics for Scale	Mean	Variance	Std Dev	N of Variables
	3.0625	3.3004	1.8167	5

Item Means	Mean	Minimum	Maximum	Range	Max/Min	Variance
	.6125	.4565	.8267	.3702	1.8110	.0367

Inter-item Correlations	Mean	Minimum	Maximum	Range	Max/Min	Variance
	.5359	.4010	.7873	.3863	1.9634	.0274

Item-total Statistics

	Scale Mean if Item Deleted	Scale Variance if Item Deleted	Corrected Item- Total Correlation	Squared Multiple Correlation	Alpha if Item Deleted
ABDEFECT	2.2466	2.4967	.5334	.4152	.8578
ABNOMORE	2.6010	1.9767	.7666	.6848	.7990
ABPOOR	2.5607	1.9817	.7587	.6425	.8014
ABRAPE	2.2358	2.5113	.5382	.4186	.8568
ABSINGLE	2.6060	1.9756	.7685	.6797	.7985

```
Reliability Coefficients     5 items
Alpha =   .8558              Standardized item alpha =   .8524
```

(continued)

Table 13 (*continued*)

```
R E L I A B I L I T Y   A N A L Y S I S   -   S C A L E   (A B O R T N 2)

Item-total Statistics
              Scale          Scale        Corrected
              Mean           Variance     Item-           Squared        Alpha
              if Item        if Item      Total           Multiple       if Item
              Deleted        Deleted      Correlation     Correlation    Deleted
ABNOMORE      1.7850         1.3286        .7998           .6840          .7754
ABPOOR        1.7448         1.3355        .7880           .6420          .7808
ABRAPE        1.4198         1.8884        .4469           .2018          .9065
ABSINGLE      1.7901         1.3314        .7974           .6775          .7765

Reliability Coefficients     4 items
Alpha =   .8578          Standardized item alpha =    .8504


R E L I A B I L I T Y   A N A L Y S I S   -   S C A L E   (A B O R T N 3)
ABSINGLE          .7873         .7487       1.0000

       N of Cases =      1391.0
                                                  N of
Statistics for       Mean    Variance   Std Dev  Variables
      Scale          1.4198   1.8884    1.3742       3

Item Means           Mean    Minimum   Maximum   Range    Max/Min   Variance
                     .4733    .4565     .5018     .0453    1.0992    .0006
Inter-item
Correlations         Mean    Minimum   Maximum   Range    Max/Min   Variance
                     .7637    .7487     .7873     .0386    1.0516    .0003

Item-total Statistics
              Scale          Scale        Corrected
              Mean           Variance     Item-           Squared        Alpha
              if Item        if Item      Total           Multiple       if Item
              Deleted        Deleted      Correlation     Correlation    Deleted
ABNOMORE      .9583          .8716         .8248           .6823          .8563
ABPOOR        .9180          .8882         .7954           .6328          .8810
ABSINGLE      .9633          .8756         .8197           .6751          .8605

Reliability Coefficients     3 items
Alpha =   .9065          Standardized item alpha =    .9065
```

*Note this is a subset of the complete run. You may wish to run the procedure yourself to see the complete listing.

created and run without the variable of ABDEFECT in the equations. ABDEFECT is suppressing the internal consistency value, which will improve to .8578 and may be omitted from all remaining iterations. We continue this process of eliminating variables until the reported value of alpha can not be improved by eliminating any additional variables. Thus, in the final section, the final and "best"—most internally consistent—scale includes the three items of:

1.	ABNOMORE	MARRIED—WANTS NO MORE CHILDREN
2.	ABPOOR	LOW INCOME—CANT AFFORD MORE CHILDREN
3.	ABSINGLE	NOT MARRIED

Note that in our final iteration, the alpha value was .9065. This would be considered a reasonably reliable scale since its internal consistency alpha value is beyond .9. Our mean additive scale score for this scale across the 1391 respondents who answered all the questions about the rights of women to obtain a abortion is 1.42 with a standard deviation of 1.37. Average inter-item correlations was .7637—a relatively high figure further reflecting consistency in response across the three selected items.

I now know, at least tentatively, which items to include in my scale. A simple COMPUTE statement can be used to create an additive **ABORTION** index value for each respondent with the expression:

```
COMPUTE abortion=SUM.3(abnomore,abpoor,absingle).
```

or, even better, with an average computation across these three items:

```
COMPUTE abortion=MEAN.3(abnomore,abpoor,absingle).[22]
```

We shall include anyone who answered all three items—since there are so few items with which to work. It should be pointed out that with so few items we have a restricted range of possible scale values. A three dichotomous items scale produces a maximum of four unique values whether you sum the values of each item or calculate the mean score across the three items for each respondent. If we used all five of the best legal abortion items, the number of possible unique values becomes six (because those who said "No" to each question would have a scale score of "0"). This expression would be:

```
COMPUTE abortion=MEAN.5(abdefect,abnomore,abpoor,abrape,
  absingle).
```

or we could calculate the average score across all five items for each respondent who answered at least four of the five items with the expression:

```
COMPUTE abortion=MEAN.4(abdefect,abnomore,abpoor,abrape,
  absingle).
```

In the "real world" of social research, you would want to calculate findings using a variety of sets of indices and check to make sure that each index led you to similar conclusions. For our illustrative work here, we shall use the three-item scale.

We now may examine more closely Americans' attitudes toward a legal abortion and how they have changed over these twenty-one years; we may determine what relationships exist, if any, between this summary scale and other variables such as those listed in our initial hypotheses—sex, race, education, political attitudes, etc. We can then examine the "best fit" multivariate model.

---

[22]If SPSS creates the variable in your Data Editor window but no data appear, choose

Transform ➤

   Run Pending Transformations

Exercise 6: Here's your chance to create a scale or index. You may wish to run the same items, or you may wish to use other items that are logically related to each other (i.e., the five life satisfaction items). In either case, identify which variables need RE-CODEing, if any, and do it. Then, run the RELIABILITY procedure and determine the "best" scale. Once you find your "best" scale, go ahead and use your COMPUTE command to implement the scale for each case in your study.

A Closer Look at Summarizing the Variable of Interest: Attitudes Toward Legal Abortion

We have the opportunity to summarize our newly created variable, ABORTN3. A good place to start is with our standby, FREQUENCIES. Once we enter our COMPUTE statement:

```
COMPUTE abortion=MEAN.3(abnomore,abpoor,absingle).
```

we can enter the usual command sequence of:

Statistics ➤
  Summarize ➤
    Frequencies . . .

A press of the STATISTICS . . . command button at the bottom of the FREQUEN-CIES dialog box presents a roster of summary statistics options that we can select. Now, press the "CHARTS . . ." button and select "Bar Charts." A click on "Continue" and "OK" buttons will produce a table and chart like that of Figure 17.

While most Americans are in clear agreement about the legal rights of women to abortion access in issues of health of the mother, rape, and birth defect of the unborn, Americans are clearly divided on the remaining criteria. Thus, most Americans either accepted all (37.7%), or rejected all (42.9%), of the remaining criteria for legal access—legal access based on (1) poverty, (2) marital status, and (3) choice of married women. Relatively few (18.1%) Americans fell in between these two extreme positions. Similarly, the summary statistics of mean (.46) and standard deviation (.458) show clearly the degree of disagreement among Americans. See Figure 17.

Exercise 7: Here's your chance to create a scale or index. You may wish to run the same items, or you may wish to use other items that are logically related to each other. In either case, identify which variables need RECODEing, if any, and do it. Then, run the RELIABILITY procedure and determine the "best" scale. Once you find your "best" scale, go ahead and use your COMPUTE command to implement the scale for each case in your study.

Working with Valid Cases In looking at the tabular displays and summary statistics we have produced so far, it is probably clear to you that not everyone answered all the questions of interest. We know from the RELIABILITY procedure that 61 people did not answer at least one of the three useful items about abortion. Additionally, if you ran the FREQUENCIES, CROSSTABS, MEANS, or DESCRIPTIVES commands on

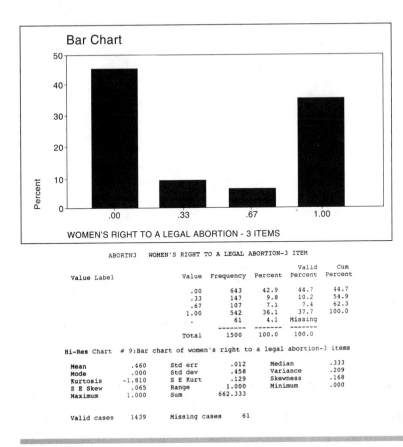

ABORTN3   WOMEN'S RIGHT TO A LEGAL ABORTION-3 ITEM

Value Label	Value	Frequency	Percent	Valid Percent	Cum Percent
	.00	643	42.9	44.7	44.7
	.33	147	9.8	10.2	54.9
	.67	107	7.1	7.4	62.3
	1.00	542	36.1	37.7	100.0
	.	61	4.1	Missing	
	Total	1500	100.0	100.0	

Hi-Res Chart # 9:Bar chart of women's right to a legal abortion-3 items

Mean	.460	Std err	.012	Median	.333
Mode	.000	Std dev	.458	Variance	.209
Kurtosis	-1.810	S E Kurt	.129	Skewness	.168
S E Skew	.065	Range	1.000	Minimum	.000
Maximum	1.000	Sum	662.333		

Valid cases   1439   Missing cases   61

Figure 17 Summary of Abortion Attitudes—3-Item Index

other variables you have noted that they too had "missing cases." For example, while only a few respondents did not report their age or years of education, income data, RE-ALINC, was less likely to be reported—116 missing observations. For our data set, one-third of the cases were missing on the variable of political views—POLVIEWS. Thus, we shall have to omit some people and/or some variables from further analysis.

At this point, let's assume that you are interested in those persons who were either African-American or white, and responded to the questions on abortion.

To select a subset of cases, you can use the menu bar. Choose the:

Data ➤
   Select Cases . . .

option. Once chosen from the menu, a Select Cases dialog box will appear. From here you can choose logical conditions for each variable. Just choose the option, "If condition is satisfied." and then press the "If" button. A new dialog box will appear where you can create the expression—for example:

```
((RACE EQ 1 OR RACE EQ 2) AND
NOT SYSMIS(ABORTION))
```

or

```
((race = 1 or race = 2) and not SYSMIS(abortion))[23]
```

which is equivalent to commands you would type in the syntax window, such as:

```
SELECT IF (RACE EQ 1 OR RACE EQ 2).
SELECT IF NOT MISSING(abortion).
```

You can add additional parameters as you see fit. Once you decide on the final selection criteria, implement the file command and save this new subset of data under its own file name using the "Save As . . ." option in the File menu.

Exercise 8:   If you are working with the GSS, then this is your chance to reduce substantially the cost of using SPSS as well as improve response time. Go ahead and create a new system file with just those cases of interest.

Now that we have created the subset of data with which we shall work, we can run the tabular and summary statistics we noted before, thus getting a clearer picture of the characteristics of people in our analysis. I encourage you to re-run these earlier procedures with the selected cases across all your variables in your or our GSS study.

Exercise 9:   After creating this modified file, execute the descriptive procedures in a variety of ways. Try further work with the graphics options. Remember to first consider the level of measurement of each variable, and then determine the most appropriate statistics and graphing techniques.

Bivariate Analysis

Now that we know that we may have faith in the reliability of our scale, we can begin to explore several of the research questions we listed earlier.

- Are there significant changes over the last two decades in Americans' attitudes toward legal abortion?
- Are there significant differences among people from different racial groups, gender categories, or religious groups on the variables used to measure attitudes toward legal abortion?
- Are there significant differences between people with different familial experiences (e.g., marital status, having children) on the variables used to measure attitudes toward legal abortion?

A useful analytic tool to address these questions is the CROSSTABS procedure. The general format of the CROSSTABS command in SPSS is:

---

[23]This assumes that you have saved a file with the new variable "ABORTION."

```
CROSSTABS TABLES= varlist, varlist BY varlist. . .varlist
/CELLS list
```

To this command, we will add the statistics option, which has the form:

```
/STATISTICS list.
```

Thus, if we wished to examine the relationship between the variables of legal abortion rights and change over time, religion, race, or sex we could do so with the following command sequence:

```
CROSSTABS TABLES= ABORTN3 BY YEAR, RELIG, RACE, SEX, RACESEX
/CELLS COUNT, COLUMN
/STATISTICS CHISQ, LAMBDA, GAMMA, ETA, CORR.
```

Alternately, we could simply select:

Statistics ➤
   Summarize ➤
      Crosstabs . . .

and then enter the appropriate variables, choose the Statistics option and appropriate bivariate summary statistics, and run the routine.

In either case, in addition to producing standard contingency tables that will list: (1) each variable, related values, and labels; (2) the number of cases for each value of each variable; and (3) the number of cases for each intersection of the variable pair, this CROSSTABS procedure will produce important summary statistics of: chi square, lambda, eta, gamma, and Pearsonian r.

The chi-square measure will enable us to test if the observed differences in the sample are sufficiently large for us to conclude that such differences exist in the population. Table 14 includes one of these outputs, attitudes toward legal abortion by year. The data illustrates well that there has been a significant change over the years—with a higher proportion of respondents supporting the rights of access to a legal abortion among the 1973 (43.4%) and 1993 (42.3%) respondents than at other times (35.1%, 31.4%, and 37.5% in 1978, 1983, and 1988, respectively).

When you are examining variables where there are relatively few cases for certain attributes and you are using the CROSSTABS command, it is often prudent to aggregate such categories and re-assign the value labels. Here I recommend the following:

```
RECODE ABORTN3 (0=0)(.3 THRU .7 = 1)(1=2).
VALUE LABEL ABORTN3 0 "AGAINST" 1 "SOMETIMES" 2 "FOR".
```

and for the variable of religion:

```
RECODE RELIG (3 THRU 5=3).
VALUE LABEL RELIG 1 'PROTESTANT' 2 'CATHOLIC' 3 'JEW/NONE/
OTHER'.
```

Since persons of the Jewish faith and those classified as "Other" religions had similar attitudes toward abortion as those with "No" religious affiliation, you may wish to combine them into a single category. Now, execute the command:

Table 14 Abortion Attitudes by Year

```
-> TITLE "BIVARIATE STATISTICS".
-> GET FILE="Jeff's HD:SPSS 6.1:GSS7393s.sav".
-> RECODE abany,abdefect,abhlth,abnomore,abpoor,abrape,absingle
->       (0=99)(1=1)(2=0)(ELSE=99).
-> MISSING VALUES abany,abdefect,abhlth,abnomore,abpoor,abrape,absingle (99) .
-> COMPUTE abortn3=MEAN.3(abnomore,abpoor,absingle).
-> VARIABLE LABEL ABORTN3 "WOMEN'S RIGHT TO A LEGAL ABORTION-3 ITEMS".
-> SELECT IF ((race  = 1 or race  = 2) AND NOT SYSMIS(ABORTN3)).
-> CROSSTABS TABLES= ABORTN3 BY YEAR
->   /CELLS COUNT, COLUMN
->   /STATISTICS CHISQ, LAMBDA, GAMMA, ETA, CORR.
```

```
                    YEAR                          Page 1 of 1
           Count  |
           Col Pct|
                  |                                   Row
                  |   73|   78|   83|   88|   93| Total
ABORTN3   --------+------+------+------+------+------+
           .00    |  114|  120|  142|  132|  116|   624
                  | 39.6| 42.1| 49.5| 48.5| 42.3|  44.4
                  +------+------+------+------+------+
           .33    |   26|   37|   24|   27|   29|   143
                  |  9.0| 13.0|  8.4|  9.9| 10.6|  10.2
                  +------+------+------+------+------+
           .67    |   23|   28|   31|   11|   13|   106
                  |  8.0|  9.8| 10.8|  4.0|  4.7|   7.5
                  +------+------+------+------+------+
           1.00   |  125|  100|   90|  102|  116|   533
                  | 43.4| 35.1| 31.4| 37.5| 42.3|  37.9
                  +------+------+------+------+------+
           Column    288   285   287   272   274   1406
           Total    20.5  20.3  20.4  19.3  19.5  100.0
```

Chi-Square	Value	DF	Significance
Pearson	29.30427	12	.00355
Likelihood Ratio	29.91794	12	.00287
Mantel-Haenszel test for linear association	.90135	1	.34242

Minimum Expected Frequency -   20.506

Approximate Statistic	Value	ASE1	Val/ASE0	Significance
Lambda :				
symmetric	.03053	.01508	2.00405	
with ABORTN3 dependent	.01407	.01963	.71166	
with YEAR dependent	.04204	.01691	2.43871	
Goodman & Kruskal Tau :				
with ABORTN3 dependent	.00705	.00311		.00308 *2
with YEAR dependent	.00523	.00186		.00347 *2
Gamma	-.02961	.03183	-.93031	
Pearson's R	-.02533	.02696	-.94936	.34260 *4
Spearman Correlation	-.02434	.02700	-.91220	.36182 *4
Eta :				
with ABORTN3 dependent	.08191			
with YEAR dependent	.06736			

*2 Based on chi-square approximation
*4 VAL/ASE0 is a t-value based on a normal approximation, as is the significance
Number of Missing Observations: 0

```
CROSSTABS TABLES= ABORTN3 BY RELIG
 /CELLS COUNT, COLUMN
 /STATISTICS CHISQ, LAMBDA, GAMMA, ETA, CORR.
```

The output becomes much easier to read and interpret. See Table 15. While more people were opposed to women having access to a legal abortion than were "for" such access, attitudes varied according to religious beliefs, although not quite as skewed as the public may believe. Both in the case of Protestants (47.6%) and Catholics (50.1%), more respondents were "against" such legal access while those who were of other faiths, or had no report of other religious memberships (68.5%), were much more likely to report that they were "for" the right of such legal access. These differences were statistically reliable and likely reflect important basis for differences of opinions.

The statistics lambda, gamma, eta, and Pearsonian r values are all measures of association. The use of each depends on the level of measurement of each variable. Use the following table to help you decide which measure(s) of association is most appropriate for your study:

DEPENDENT VARIABLE LEVEL OF MEASUREMENT	INDEPENDENT VARIABLE LEVEL OF MEASUREMENT		
	NOMINAL	ORDINAL	INTERVAL/ RATIO
Nominal	Lambda	Lambda	Lambda
Ordinal	Lambda	Gamma	Gamma
Interval/ratio	Eta	Eta/Gamma	Pearson's r

Note: Some people argue that you can treat ordinal-level variables that are not very skewed and that have relatively few categories as interval-level data—"metric-level data"—and use Pearson's r values.

In the current table, ABORTN3 BY RELIG, the variable of religious affiliation was measured at the nominal level and the variable of abortion attitudes may be treated as measured at the ordinal or interval level. Thus, you could argue reasonably that knowledge of respondents' religion reduces our errors in predicting attitudes toward abortion more than 20% (i.e., Gamma = .22 reduction in error; Eta, with Abortion as the dependent variable = .247 ~ 6.1% reduction in error). We will have more to say about this idea later.

One of the nicer features of using SPSS is the power it gives you to examine variable relationships using dependent, independent, and control variables. For example, you may be interested in comparing attitudes toward abortion by race controlling for sex—that is, comparing black and white men with each other and then comparing black and white women with each other. This could be accomplished easily by substituting the current CROSSTABS command with:

```
CROSSTABS TABLES=ABORTN3 BY RACE BY SEX.
```

```
(Don't forget optional CELL and STATISTICS commands.)
```

Table 15 Abortion Attitudes by Religious Affiliation

```
\\\\\\ - see previous tables for preliminary commands
-> TEMPORARY.
-> RECODE ABORTN3 (0=0)(.3 THRU .7 = 1)(1=2).
-> VALUE LABEL ABORTN3 0 "AGAINST" 1 "SOMETIMES" 2 "FOR".
-> RECODE RELIG (3 THRU 5=3).
-> VALUE LABEL RELIG 1 'PROTESTANT' 2 'CATHOLIC' 3 'JEW/NONE/OTHER'.
-> CROSSTABS TABLES= ABORTN3 BY RELIG
->    /CELLS COUNT, COLUMN
->    /STATISTICS CHISQ, LAMBDA, GAMMA, ETA, CORR.

ABORTN3  WOMEN'S RIGHT TO A LEGAL ABORTION-3 ITEM
by  RELIG  RS RELIGIOUS PREFERENCE
```

		RELIG			Page 1 of 1
Count		PROTESTA	CATHOLIC	JEW/NONE	
Col Pct		NT		/OTHER	Row
		1	2	3	Total
ABORTN3					
AGAINST	.00	408	183	31	622
		47.6	50.1	17.1	44.3
SOMETIMES	1.00	154	69	26	249
		17.9	18.9	14.4	17.7
FOR	2.00	296	113	124	533
		34.5	31.0	68.5	38.0
Column		858	365	181	1404
Total		61.1	26.0	12.9	100.0

Chi-Square	Value	DF	Significance
Pearson	88.39841	4	.00000
Likelihood Ratio	89.34234	4	.00000
Mantel-Haenszel test for linear association	45.00578	1	.00000

```
Minimum Expected Frequency -   32.100
```

Approximate

Statistic	Value	ASE1	Val/ASE0	Significance
Lambda :				
symmetric	.07003	.00873	7.62296	
with ABORTN3 dependent	.11893	.01494	7.62296	
with RELIG dependent	.00000	.00000		
Goodman & Kruskal Tau :				
with ABORTN3 dependent	.04023	.00767		.00000 *2
with RELIG dependent	.01934	.00432		.00000 *2
Gamma	.21985	.04025	5.28859	
Pearson's R	.17910	.02586	6.81646	.00000 *4
Spearman Correlation	.14230	.02660	5.38305	.00000 *4
Eta :				
with ABORTN3 dependent	.24712			
with RELIG dependent	.18107			

```
*2 Based on chi-square approximation
*4 VAL/ASE0 is a t-value based on a normal approximation, as is the significance

Number of Missing Observations:  2
```

Note that the intervening or control variable, in this case SEX, must be listed after an additional BY keyword. (You may have up to four levels of control variables or a maximum of five BY keywords.) This command will produce a separate table for males and for females where each table will enable you to compare black and white respondents' abortion attitude scores for that sex attribute. Of course, you could easily compare all four groups with the RACESEX variable.

```
CROSSTABS TABLES=ABORTN3 BY RACESEX.
```

And then you might wish to examine the RACESEX variable for each year as well as across all years with the command:

```
CROSSTABS TABLES=ABORTN3 BY RACESEX/ABORTN3 BY RACESEX BY YEAR.
```

Pretty easy; pretty neat. . . .

Exercise 10:   Now go ahead and run the appropriate CROSSTABS procedures on the data for other variables. Go ahead and try it out. Then, take a few moments and think about how best to interpret what your outputs mean and the similarities and/or differences between the results across the different survey years.

Our variable of interest, ABORTION, provides us with the opportunity to use two other related hypotheses testing measures—the T-test and ANOVA or Analysis of Variance. The T-test is used to compare the mean values of a dependent variable (e.g. ABORTION) when there are only two attributes of an independent variable (e.g., SEX, or as we have done here, RACE). The T-test may be invoked from the menu bar with:

Statistics ➤
   Compare Means ➤
      Independent Samples T-test . . .

which will produce a dialog box like that of Figure 18. Once you select each and every dependent variable used to measure respondents' attitudes toward abortion and place them in the "Test Variable(s):" box, a simple click on the independent variable, SEX, will produce:

sex(? ?)

SPSS is asking for you to indicate the values that will define the two groups. A press of the "Define Groups . . ." will bring the subdialog box—as seen in the second part of Figure 18. Selecting the original values of "1" and "2" will complete the building of the T-test expression. A press of "Continue" and then "OK" will invoke the T-tests. See Figure 18.

The procedure statement for invoking the T-test directly from the syntax window is straightforward. It takes the form:

```
T-TEST GROUPS = varname (val1,val2)
 /VARIABLES = varlist.
```

After the procedure name, the word GROUPS must appear if you wish to run a test of independent samples. (The keyword PAIRS is used when working with related

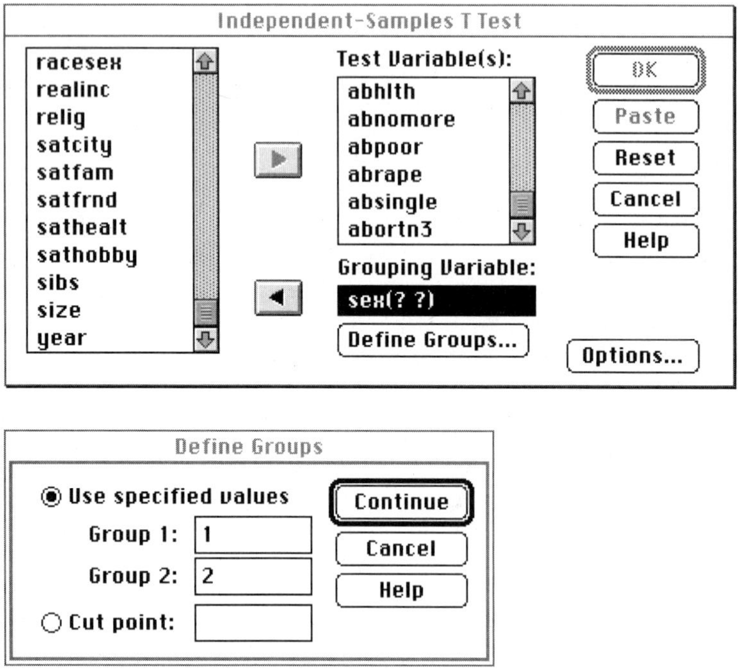

Figure 18 T-Test Dialog Box

samples.) Since a T-TEST can compare only two groups at a time, you are asked to specify which two values of an independent variable are appropriate. The VARIABLES keyword provides you an opportunity to list which dependent variable(s) you wish to test. For example, in our study, the following T-TEST procedure works well:

```
T-TEST GROUPS = SEX(1,2)/VARIABLES = ABORTION.
```

or, we can test all the items as well as the summary scale score with the command:

```
T-TEST GROUPS = SEX(0,1)
  /VARIABLES=abany abdefect abhlth abnomore abpoor abrape
  absingle.
```

That is, SPSS is to execute the T-test on each of our ABORTION items as well as our index scale score by comparing males and females. Note that no STATISTICS subcommand is needed. See Table 16.

The output from the T-TEST procedure is segmented by variables and types of information. For each dependent variable, SPSS reports descriptive statistics (number of cases, mean, etc.) for each grouping in the first part of the output. An F-value is then calculated. It will help you to determine which T-test value to use. The average difference on the three-item abortion index variable between males and females was .0567. Test for equality of variances is reported next. (If the F-value is not significant, then use

Table 16 Abortion Attitudes by Sex

```
\\\\\\\ - see previous tables for preliminary commands
-> TEMPORARY.
-> RECODE ABORTN3 (0=0)(.3 THRU .7 = 1)(1=2).
-> VALUE LABEL ABORTN3 0 "AGAINST" 1 "SOMETIMES" 2 "FOR".
-> RECODE RELIG (3 THRU 5=3).
-> VALUE LABEL RELIG 1 'PROTESTANT' 2 'CATHOLIC' 3 'JEW/NONE/OTHER'.
 -> T-TEST
->    GROUPS=sex(1 2)
->    /VARIABLES = abortn3.
```

```
t-tests for Independent Samples of SEX     RESPONDENTS SEX
                               Number
Variable                       of Cases    Mean        SD    SE of Mean
-----------------------------------------------------------------
ABORTN3  WOMEN'S RIGHT TO A LEGAL ABORTION-3 ITEM

MALE                            561       .4973       .456      .019
FEMALE                          845       .4406       .457      .016
-----------------------------------------------------------------

          Mean Difference = .0567

          Levene's Test for Equality of Variances: F= .031   P= .860


          t-test for Equality of Means                          95%
Variances  t-value      df    2-Tail Sig   SE of Diff     CI for Diff
-----------------------------------------------------------------
Equal       2.28      1404         .023        .025      (.008, .106)
Unequal     2.28   1201.05         .023        .025      (.008, .106)
```

the pooled variance T-value.) For our study, there was a significant difference between female and male mean values (T-value $_{[1,404 \text{ df}]}$ = 2.28, sig = .023), although this difference is numerically not large (.0567). For these respondents, you can run each of the specific abortion questions. In addition, you can now run the T-test procedure for the variable of RACE, if you wish, by simply substituting the variable name SEX with RACE. But, what if you wish to compare all four race/sex categories?

If you wish to compare more than two groups at the same time, then you will need to use the Analysis of Variance, ANOVA, procedure. SPSS has several such procedures. The procedure that best fits our needs here is called ONEWAY. Not surprisingly, it is a one-way analysis of variance test. In addition to calculating appropriate sums of squares and F-values, it will report tests for homogeneity of variance, allow you to make a priori contrast comparisons of any combination of groups, and make a posteriori comparisons as well:

Statistics ➤
    Compare Means ➤
        Oneway ANOVA . . .

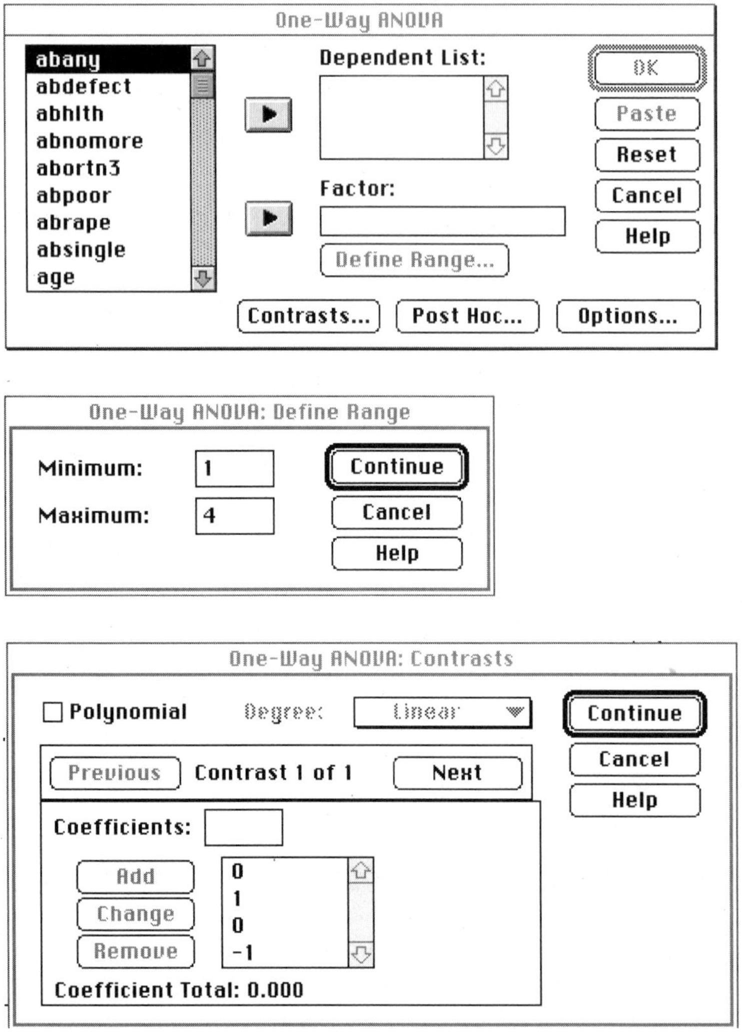

Figure 19 One-Way ANOVA Dialog Box

which will bring forward an ANOVA dialog box like that of Figure 19.

Once you choose ABORTN3 as the "Dependent List:" variable and RACESEX as the "Factor" or independent variable, you will have to "Define the Range . . .". See the second dialog box. This is where you would enter the values of 1—"Minimum:" and 4 "Maximum:". A press on the "Continue" button returns to the original dialog box with the values of 1 and 4 present next to variable of RACESEX.

For the sake of illustration, let us assume that we wish to compare the race-sex groups (black male, black female, white male, and white female) on our ABORTION variable. Additionally, we wish to test the hypothesis that black females and white females were different from one another. Finally, we would like to find out if there are any other differences. Thus, we shall use the subcommands of "Contrasts . . ." for the a priori comparison of African American females with white females. A press on the "Contrasts . . ." button produces the third dialog box in Figure 19. For each of the RACESEX attributes a value in the "Coefficients:" box must be keyed. These values must be keyed in the same order as the attributes and must, when completed, total to 0.000. Thus, to select the two female groups for a priori comparison, one must enter the values of 0, 1, 0, –1.

To select the multiple comparison procedure across all RACESEX categories, select the "Post Hoc . . ." button and then select the "Duncan's multiple range test." A press of the "Continue" button returns the original One-Way dialog box. A press of "OK" executes the ANOVA procedure. Finally, additional important summary statistics and labels may be requested from the "Options . . ." button. Choose both available summary statistics and choose also the display label option.

Here is the general format, if you wish to enter this command via the syntax window:

```
ONEWAY varlist BY varname (min,max)
    /CONTRASTS wt wt wt wt
    /RANGES test
    /FORMAT LABELS
    /STATISTICS list.
```

Or, the procedure command would look like this:

```
ONEWAY ABORTION BY RACESEX (1,4)
    /CONTRAST= 0 1 0 -1
    /RANGES=DUNCAN
    /FORMAT LABELS
    /STATISTICS ALL
    /MISSING ANALYSIS.
```

Table 17 illustrates this output. First, SPSS produces the standard analysis of variance F-test table. Then, for each group, it produces summary descriptive information (e.g., counts, mean, standard deviation, etc.).

The second section of the output reports the contrasts. These are basically T-tests. Several contrasts may be run at any one time. Here we were just interested in running African-American females vs. white females. Note that a reliable difference was found.

The third section of the output reports the tests for homogeneity of variance. To help determine how much confidence you can have in your F-value, tests for homogeneity of variances are performed. (Generally, if these are significant, then you cannot have a great deal of faith in your direct ANOVA output.)

The final section of the ONEWAY output is the a posteriori comparisons. Our procedure indicated that we wished to run the DUNCAN test. Note the organization of the summary table and the placement of stars where homogeneous subsets were found.

Quite a clearer pattern emerges when examining the variable of marital status. Those persons whose current marital status was "Never Married" (mean on abortion scale = .5638) were quite different from both of the other aggregates (those persons "Married," mean = .4458 or "Previously Married," mean = .4254). See Table 18. These differences were statistically reliable: $F_{(2,1401)} = 7.9381$; sig = 0004. (We cannot determine directly

Table 17 Abortion Attitudes by Race and Sex

```
\\\\\\ - see previous tables for preliminary commands
ONEWAY ABORTION BY RACESEX (1,4)
   /CONTRAST= 0 1 0 -1
   /RANGES=DUNCAN
   /FORMAT LABELS
   /STATISTICS ALL
   /MISSING ANALYSIS .

              - - - - O N E W A Y  - - - -

      Variable  ABORTN3   WOMEN'S RIGHT TO A LEGAL ABORTION-3 ITEM
      By Variable  RACESEX  RACE AND SEX IDENTIFIER

                           Analysis of Variance
                              Sum of        Mean        F       F
        Source       D.F.    Squares      Squares     Ratio   Prob.
Between Groups         3     2.0909        .6970      3.3444   .0186
Within Groups       1402   292.1771        .2084
Total               1405   294.2681

                                    Standard   Standard
Group      Count    Mean   Deviation    Error    Minimum   Maximum   95 Pct Conf Int for Mean

WH-MALE      513    .4964     .4584      .0202     .0000    1.0000      .4567 TO   .5362
WH-FEMAL     750    .4529     .4600      .0168     .0000    1.0000      .4199 TO   .4859
AA-MALE       48    .5069     .4402      .0635     .0000    1.0000      .3791 TO   .6348
AA-FEMAL      95    .3439     .4251      .0436     .0000    1.0000      .2573 TO   .4305

Total       1406    .4633     .4576      .0122     .0000    1.0000      .4393 TO   .4872

            Fixed Effects Model            .4565      .0122                         .4394 to   .4871

            Random Effects Model                      .0302                         .3671 to   .5595

Random Effects Model - estimate of between component variance    1.808E-03

      Variable  ABORTN3   WOMEN'S RIGHT TO A LEGAL ABORTION-3 ITEM
      By Variable  RACESEX  RACE AND SEX IDENTIFIER

Contrast Coefficient Matrix

             WH-MALE    AA-MALE
                  WH-FEMAL    AA-FEMAL

Contrast 1    .0    1.0    .0    -1.0
```

Table 17 (continued)

		Pooled Variance Estimate				Separate Variance Estimate		
	Value	S. Error	T Value	D.F.	T Prob.	S. Error	T Value	D.F.	T Prob.
Contrast 1	.1090	.0497	2.193	1402.0	.028	.0467	2.333	123.6	.021

Levene Test for Homogeneity of Variances

Statistic	df1	df2	2-tail Sig.
7.7343	3	1402	.000

Variable   ABORTN3   WOMEN'S RIGHT TO A LEGAL ABORTION-3 ITEM
By Variable RACESEX   RACE AND SEX IDENTIFIER

Multiple Range Tests: Duncan test with significance level .05

The difference between two means is significant if
MEAN(J)-MEAN(I) >= .3228 * RANGE * SQRT(1/N(I) + 1/N(J))
with the following value(s) for RANGE:

Step	2	3	4
RANGE	2.78	2.92	3.01

(*) Indicates significant differences which are shown in the lower triangle

```
                A W
                A H W A
                - - H A
                F F - -
                E E M M
                M M A A
                A A L L
                L L E E

Mean    RACESEX
.3439   AA-FEMAL
.4529   WH-FEMAL   *
.4964   WH-MALE    *
.5069   AA-MALE
```

Table 18 Abortion Attitudes by Marital Status

```
-> TITLE "BIVARIATE STATISTICS".
-> GET
->   FILE="Jeff's HD:SPSS 6.1:GSS7393s.sav".
-> EXECUTE.
-> RECODE abany,abdefect,abhlth,abnomore,abpoor,abrape,absingle
->   (0=99)(1=1)(2=0)(ELSE=99).
-> MISSING VALUES abany,abdefect,abhlth,abnomore,abpoor,abrape,absingle (99) .
-> COMPUTE abortn3=MEAN.3 (abnomore,abpoor,absingle) .
-> VARIABLE LABEL ABORTN3 "WOMEN'S RIGHT TO A LEGAL ABORTION-3 ITEMS".
-> SELECT IF ((race = 1 or race = 2) AND NOT SYSMIS(ABORTN3)).
-> RECODE MARITAL (1=1)(2,3,4 = 2)(5=3).
-> VALUE LABELS MARITAL
->   1 "Married" 2 "Prev-Married" 3 "Nev-Married".
-> ONEWAY
->   abortn3 BY MARITAL(1 3)
->   /RANGES=DUNCAN
->   /HARMONIC NONE
->   /FORMAT LABELS
->   /STATISTICS ALL
->   /MISSING ANALYSIS .
```

- - - - - O N E W A Y - - - - -

Variable ABORTN3   WOMEN'S RIGHT TO A LEGAL ABORTION-3 ITEM
By Variable MARITAL MARITAL STATUS
Analysis of Variance

Source	D.F.	Sum of Squares	Mean Squares	F Ratio	F Prob.
Between Groups	2	3.2936	1.6468	7.9381	.0004
Within Groups	1401	290.6446	.2075		
Total	1403	293.9382			

Group	Count	Mean	Standard Deviation	Standard Error	Minimum	Maximum	95 Pct Conf Int for Mean
Married	833	.4458	.4562	.0158	.0000	1.0000	.4148 TO .4768
Prev-Mar	315	.4254	.4542	.0256	.0000	1.0000	.3750 TO .4757
Nev-Marr	256	.5638	.4548	.0284	.0000	1.0000	.5078 TO .6198
Total	1404	.4627	.4577	.0122			.4388 TO .4867
Fixed Effects Model			.4555	.0122			.4389 to .4866
Random Effects Model				.0416			.2838 to .6417

Random Effects Model - estimate of between component variance   3.63E-03

Table 18 (*continued*)

```
Variable  ABORTN3    WOMEN'S RIGHT TO A LEGAL ABORTION-3 ITEM
  By Variable  MARITAL    MARITAL STATUS

Levene Test for Homogeneity of Variances

     Statistic    df1     df2     2-tail Sig.
       .1903       2      1401       .827

- - - - O N E W A Y - - - - - -

     Variable  ABORTN3    WOMEN'S RIGHT TO A LEGAL ABORTION-3 ITEM
       By Variable  MARITAL    MARITAL STATUS

Multiple Range Tests:  Duncan test with significance level .05

The difference between two means is significant if
  MEAN(J)-MEAN(I)  >= .3221 * RANGE * SQRT(1/N(I) + 1/N(J))
with the following value(s) for RANGE:

Step      2      3
RANGE    2.78   2.92
(*) Indicates significant differences which are shown in the lower triangle

                                       P  N
                                       r  M  e
                                       e  a  v
                                       v  r  -
                                       -  r  M
                                          M  i  a
                                          a  e  r
                                          r  d  r

 Mean      MARITAL
 .4254     Prev-Mar
 .4458     Married
 .5638     Nev-Marr    *  *
```

from this output if these observed abortion attitude scale differences of "Never Married" persons vs. the other groups were due to marital status differences or, perhaps, age. This is an interesting question requiring multivariate techniques—to be explored soon.)

Exercise 11: Here's your chance to run appropriate T-TEST and ONEWAY procedures. Take a few minutes and try them on your data or on the data for any specific year of respondents.

In addition to comparing ascribed status groups (e.g., males vs. females, African-Am. vs. whites), we indicated an interest in determining the relationship, if any, between attitudes toward abortion and the explanatory variables of socio-economic status and political philosophy. We noted two general research questions.

- Are there significant correlations between the variables of income, age, or education with attitudes toward legal abortion?
- Is there any substantial difference between how those who identify with the Democratic or Republican parties view a woman's right of access for a legal abortion? What about self-described political views—conservatism or liberalism—and their relationship to attitudes toward a woman's right to a legal abortion?

Testing for significant associations between variable sets is easy with SPSS. You have several options, including the command CORRELATION. From the menu bar select:

Statistics ➤
   Correlate ➤
      Bivariate . . .

These choices invoke the bivariate correlation dialogue boxes as seen in Figure 20.

To test this first correlate question, simply select the variables of abortn3 age, educ, degree, realinc, etc. from the picker box and make sure that each of the following have been selected: (1) Pearson (correlation coefficient), (2) Two tailed (test of significance),[24] (3) and Display actual significance levels. A click on the "Options . . ." brings forward the window in which you can select: (1) Means and standard deviations and (2) "Exclude cases pairwise." This final optional choice will include as many cases as possible for each variable. If you had chosen "listwise," the variable with the least number of actual cases (POLVIEWS) would serve as the standard for the maximum number of cases available—fewer than 1000 cases for each variable pair would then be used.

The format of the CORRELATION command, when using the syntax window, is straightforward:

```
CORRELATION varlist WITH varlist.
```

or

```
CORRELATION age educ realinc abortn3.
```

---

[24]If you have hypothesized the direction of the relationship between variable pairs, then change this option to "One tailed" test of significance.

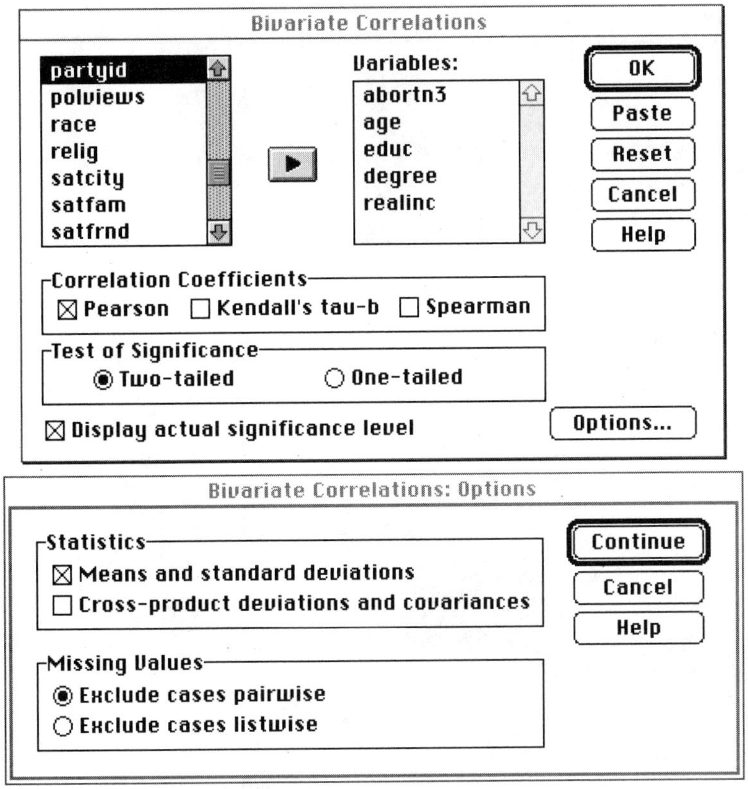

Figure 20 Bivariate Correlation Dialog Box

or we can take advantage of several options and get a more complete output with the command:

```
CORRELATION
    /VARIABLES= abortn3 age educ degree realinc partyid
    polviews
    /PRINT=TWOTAIL SIG
    /STATISTICS DESCRIPTIVES
    /MISSING=PAIRWISE.
```

SPSS will provide the usual summary statistics and, more important, Pearson's "Correlation Coefficients" values, the number of valid cases, and the level of statistical significance for each pair. In this case, I have requested two-tailed tests of significance. The report is printed in matrix format so that you or I can inspect the correlations between not only my variable of interest (abortn3) and explanatory variables, but also the correlations between each pair of explanatory variables. In addition, by including the STATISTICS subcommand, SPSS will provide a list of the mean and standard deviation values for each variable. See Table 19.

Table 19 Bivariate Correlations Output

```
-> TITLE "BIVARIATE STATISTICS".
-> GET FILE="Jeff's HD:SPSS 6.1:GSS7393s.sav".
-> EXECUTE.
-> RECODE abany,abdefect,abhlth,abnomore,abpoor,abrape,absingle
->     (0=99)(1=1)(2=0)(ELSE=99).
-> MISSING VALUES abany,abdefect,abhlth,abnomore,abpoor,abrape,absingle (99) .
-> COMPUTE abortn3=MEAN.3(abnomore,abpoor,absingle).
-> VARIABLE LABEL ABORTN3 "WOMEN'S RIGHT TO A LEGAL ABORTION-3 ITEMS".
-> SELECT IF ((race  = 1 or race  = 2) AND NOT SYSMIS(ABORTN3)).
-> RECODE PARTYID(7=9).
-> CORRELATIONS
->     /VARIABLES= abortn3 age educ degree realinc partyid polviews
->     /PRINT=TWOTAIL SIG
->     /STATISTICS DESCRIPTIVES
->     /MISSING=PAIRWISE .
```

Variable	Cases	Mean	Std Dev
ABORTN3	1406	.4633	.4576
AGE	1400	43.3371	17.0944
EDUC	1404	12.4224	3.1384
DEGREE	1404	1.2066	1.1207
REALINC	1300	30600.3038	25983.5471
PARTYID	1386	2.6890	1.9900
POLVIEWS	944	4.1970	1.3392

- - Correlation Coefficients - -

	ABORTN3	AGE	EDUC	DEGREE	REALINC	PARTYID	POLVIEWS
ABORTN3	1.0000	-.0814	.2286	.1972	.1196	-.0517	-.2211
	(1406)	(1400)	(1404)	(1404)	(1300)	(1386)	(944)
	P= .	P= .002	P= .000	P= .000	P= .000	P= .054	P= .000
AGE	-.0814	1.0000	-.2228	-.1387	-.0902	.0427	.1175
	(1400)	(1400)	(1398)	(1398)	(1296)	(1380)	(939)
	P= .002	P= .	P= .000	P= .000	P= .001	P= .113	P= .000
EDUC	.2286	-.2228	1.0000	.8571	.3604	.1012	-.0592
	(1404)	(1398)	(1404)	(1402)	(1298)	(1384)	(943)
	P= .000	P= .000	P= .	P= .000	P= .000	P= .000	P= .069
DEGREE	.1972	-.1387	.8571	1.0000	.3766	.1006	-.0593
	(1404)	(1398)	(1402)	(1404)	(1300)	(1384)	(944)
	P= .000	P= .000	P= .000	P= .	P= .000	P= .000	P= .069
REALINC	.1196	-.0902	.3604	.3766	1.0000	.1059	.0117
	(1300)	(1296)	(1298)	(1300)	(1300)	(1282)	(875)
	P= .000	P= .001	P= .000	P= .000	P= .	P= .000	P= .730
PARTYID	-.0517	.0427	.1012	.1006	.1059	1.0000	.2813
	(1386)	(1380)	(1384)	(1384)	(1282)	(1386)	(937)
	P= .054	P= .113	P= .000	P= .000	P= .000	P= .	P= .000
POLVIEWS	-.2211	.1175	-.0592	-.0593	.0117	.2813	1.0000
	(944)	(939)	(943)	(944)	(875)	(937)	(944)
	P= .000	P= .000	P= .069	P= .069	P= .730	P= .000	P= .

(Coefficient / (Cases) / 2-tailed Significance)   " . " is printed if a coefficient cannot be computed

From these data (reading the first column of results from Table 21) it is clear that there is a significant, albeit small, correlation between the variable of attitudes toward legal access to abortion and age (r = −.0814)—the higher the age of respondents, the less willing to support access to a legal abortion; educational attainment as measured by the number of years of completed schooling (r = .2286) or the earned degree (r = .1972)—the greater the education, the more willing to support access; and income (r = .1196) standardized on 1986 dollar values.

Examining the relationship between political party affiliation (PARTYID), political liberalism/conservatism (POLVIEWS), and abortion attitudes takes only a second or two longer. Here you must recall that NORC personnel used the values of zero through 6 for "Strong Democrat" to "Strong Republican." They used also a value of "7" to indicate "other party" affiliation. You will need to recode the value "7" to a missing value before adding these variables to your "/VARIABLES=" roster and invoking the CORRELATION procedure. (No such problem exists with the variable POLVIEWS.)

Some will be surprised to find that there is no large correlation (r = −.0517, p = .054) between the level of political party identification and attitude toward abortion. However, political views, at least as was measured by the degree of self-identified liberalism (i.e., measured on a seven-point scale from extremely liberal—"1"—to extremely conservative—"7") was significantly correlated (r = −.2211; p < .001) with the attitude toward the right of women to obtain a legal abortion—those with greater levels of self-described conservatism held less "liberal" views on the right of access to a legal abortion.

In examining the table further it is important to note that almost all of the socioeconomic explanatory variables were significantly correlated with each other: for example, the variables of EDUC and DEGREE (r = .8571), REALINC and DEGREE (r = .3766), AGE and EDUC (r = −.2228). This is what one would reasonably expect. See the remaining matrix items in Table 21. Finally, on some of these variables and variable pairs (e.g., ABORTN3 with REALINC and POLVIEWS) there were many missing cases—the number of cases falls from 1406 cases to 1196 cases and 944 cases, respectively. Thus, we now know that considerable care would be required to include all these variables in any multivariate model.

Just as there are graphic forms and summary statistics for describing a single distribution, SPSS provides procedures for producing scatterplots as well as summary correlation/regression statistics. In SPSS 6.1, you can produce attractive scatterplots. Here's how. From the menu choose:

Graphs ➤
    Scatter . . .

From the Scatterplot dialog box choose:

Simple

and then press the "Define" button. From the Simple Scatterplot dialog box choose which variables you wish to plot in the usual manner: for example, choose DEGREE for the Y-Axis and EDUC for the X-Axis. A click on the "OK" button will produce an appropriate scatterplot similar to that of the first part of Figure 21.

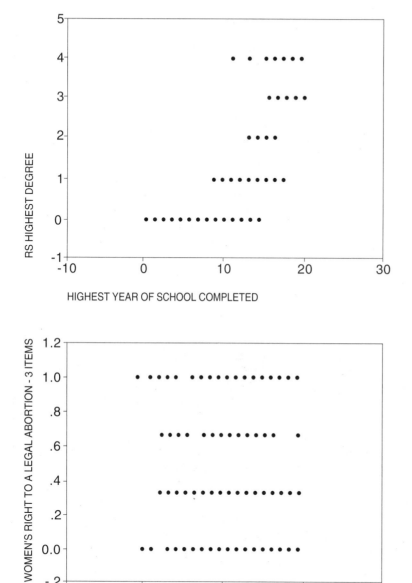

Figure 21 Scatterplot of Degree on Education; and Attitudes Toward a Legal Abortion on Educational Achievement

To create a new graph, re-select from the menu bar:

Graphs ➤
  Scatter . . .

and "Define." To remove the variable "DEGREE," select it and then press the left arrow button to its left. Now, select the variable ABORTN3 and press the right arrow key for the Y-Axis variable selection. A press of the "OK" button will complete the process and invoke the creation of the new graph. (You can try additional sets of variables, at your convenience.)

Running the REGRESSION procedure will produce similar summary CORRELATION measures as well as the values for appropriate prediction equations. You don't know how to do this? Read on.

Regression Analysis

While examining correlation values is important, it is only part of the story. It is also important to be able to express the mathematical relationship between, and among, variables. The SPSS REGRESSION procedure provides useful tools to examine such relationships. It may be invoked from the menu bar by selecting:

Statistics ➤
  Regression . . . ➤
    Linear . . .

(While several options have been provided, here we shall concentrate on the most often used standard, simple linear regression.) When the Linear Regression dialog box appears, like that of Figure 22, choose ABORTN3 for your "Dependent:" variable and "EDUC" for your "Independent(s):" variable.

Choosing the "Statistics . . ." option provides an opportunity to produce summary descriptive statistics, too.

Of course, you could have just as easily entered the commands directly in the syntax window. The command would look like this:

```
REGRESSION VARIABLES = ABORTN3 EDUC
    /DESCRIPTIVES MEAN STDDEV CORR SIG N
    /STATISTICS COEFF OUTS CI R ANOVA
    /DEPENDENT abortn3
    /METHOD=ENTER educ.
```

In either case, there are no surprises here. The format of the REGRESSION command is consistent with the procedures just discussed. Once the command name is given, and the optional subcommands entered, the keywords DEPENDENT and METHOD enable you to identify your dependent variable and independent variable, respectively. (We will have more to say about these commands in the next section of this Learner's Guide.) Of course, SPSS will assume you know enough about the levels of measurement of these variables so that the variables you include and the statistics computed are meaningful.

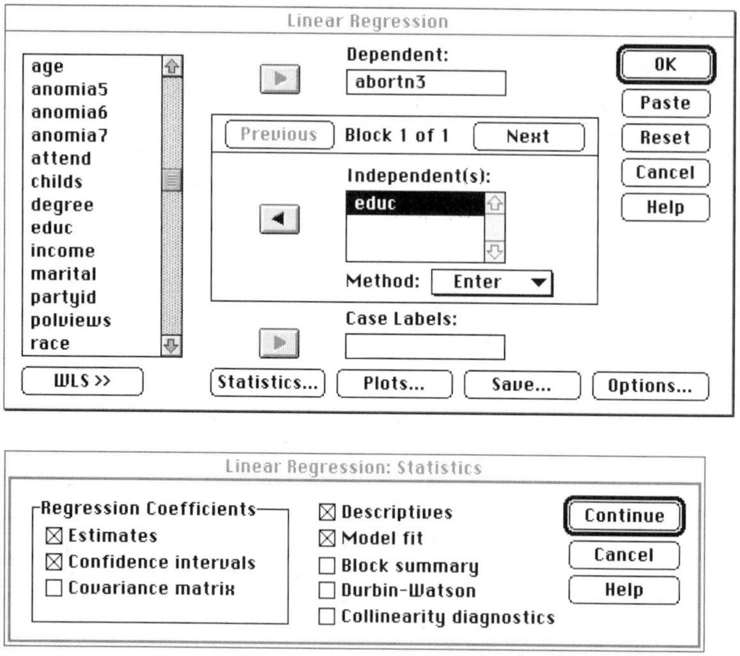

Figure 22 Dialog Box for Linear Regression

The output will look like that of Table 20. The output is divided into several major parts. The first part is a simple summary of descriptive statistics while the second part reports the bivariate correlation statistics. The third part reports how well the variables are correlated (Multiple R = .22856), how much of the variation in the dependent variable was accounted for by the independent variable(s) (R-Squared = .05224) and whether or not these values are statistically significant by using a standard ANOVA table ($F_{(1,1402 \text{ df})}$ = 77.27953, Signif F = .000).

The final part of the output provides the estimates for making prediction. In this case, your model for predicting ABORTN3 scale scores from knowledge of EDUC would be:

```
Predicted abortn3 values = -.049880 +.033330 * EDUC
```

Such a model would reduce our errors in predicting abortion scale scores by slightly more than 5%. Other variables, such as church/synagogue ATTENDance may have more explanatory power. Try one or more.

To draw a linear line on your scatterplot graph, simply calculate the appropriate predicted values for abortion scale scores, plot the points, and then connect them on the graph. That is, choose simple values for education (e.g., "0" years of education, then "20" years of education) and calculate predicted abortion values (e.g., –.05 and .617, respectively). Thus, as you might expect, those with little education were, as a group, estimated to have very little support for legal access while those with more education

Table 20 Regression Output

```
-> TITLE "BIVARIATE STATISTICS".
-> GET FILE="Jeff's HD:SPSS 6.1:GSS7393s.sav".
-> EXECUTE.
-> RECODE abany,abdefect,abhlth,abnomore,abpoor,abrape,absingle
->      (0=99)(1=1)(2=0)(ELSE=99).
-> MISSING VALUES abany,abdefect,abhlth,abnomore,abpoor,abrape,absingle (99) .
-> COMPUTE abortn3=MEAN.3(abnomore,abpoor,absingle).
-> VARIABLE LABEL ABORTN3 "WOMEN'S RIGHT TO A LEGAL ABORTION-3 ITEMS".
-> SELECT IF ((race  = 1 or race  = 2) AND NOT SYSMIS(ABORTN3)).
-> REGRESSION
->    /DESCRIPTIVES MEAN STDDEV CORR SIG N
->    /MISSING LISTWISE
->    /STATISTICS COEFF OUTS CI R ANOVA
->    /CRITERIA=PIN(.05) POUT(.10)
->    /NOORIGIN
->    /DEPENDENT abortn3
->    /METHOD=ENTER educ  .
```

```
* * * *   M U L T I P L E   R E G R E S S I O N   * * * *

Listwise Deletion of Missing Data

          Mean  Std Dev  Label

ABORTN3    .464    .458  WOMEN'S RIGHT TO A LEGAL ABORTION-3 ITEM
EDUC     12.422   3.138  HIGHEST YEAR OF SCHOOL COMPLETED

N of Cases =  1404

Correlation, 1-tailed Sig:

          ABORTN3      EDUC

ABORTN3    1.000       .229
             .          .000

EDUC        .229      1.000
            .000          .
```

```
* * * *   M U L T I P L E   R E G R E S S I O N   * * * *

Equation Number 1    Dependent Variable..   ABORTN3  WOMEN'S RIGHT TO A LEGAL A

   Descriptive Statistics are printed on Page     2

Block Number  1.  Method:  Enter       EDUC

Variable(s) Entered on Step Number  1..    EDUC      HIGHEST YEAR OF SCHOOL COMPLETED

Multiple R           .22856    Analysis of Variance
R Square             .05224                     DF    Sum of Squares   Mean Square
Adjusted R Square    .05157    Regression         1         15.35050      15.35050
Standard Error       .44569    Residual        1402        278.48774        .19864

                              F =      77.27953    Signif F =  .0000

---------------------------- Variables in the Equation ----------------------------

Variable            B        SE B     95% Confdnce Intrvl B       Beta      T  Sig T

EDUC           .033330    .003791     .025892     .040767      .228564   8.791 .0000
(Constant)     .049880    .048577    -.045411     .145171                1.027 .3047

End Block Number    1   All requested variables entered.
```

estimated to have very little support for legal access while those with more education were, as a group, estimated to have higher levels of support for legal abortion access.

Exercise 12: Bivariate correlation procedures are particularly useful when you are beginning to look for relationships among variable pairs. Take a few minutes and try these procedures on other variables or on your data set.

Multivariate Statistics Using Regression Analysis

The best known and most widely used multivariate technique is multiple regression. It is simply the logical extension of the simple linear model that we encountered earlier. The REGRESSION procedure is a powerful tool that works well with two, three, or more independent variables. It can be used to find the best linear fit among several independent or explanatory variables and a single dependent variable, as long as each of these variables can be treated as though they were measured at the metric level. This is not a problem with most of our variables (e.g., EDUC, AGE, and CHILDS). Other explanatory variables we shall have to RECODE to reflect a dichotomy using the values of 0 and 1 for SEX and RACE. (This is often referred to as creating a "dummy" variable.)

```
RECODE RACE (2=0).
VAR LABELS RACE "Proportion White".
RECODE SEX (2=0).
VAR LABELS SEX "Proportion Male".
```

All these variables may be treated as interval-level variables.

With only a little more energy, we can create from other important nominal-level variables (e.g., religion and marital status) other appropriate dichotomous variables that use our standard values of 0 and 1. Here are the appropriate commands for creating variables for each religion:

```
COMPUTE PROTEST=0.
IF (RELIG EQ 1)PROTEST=1.
COMPUTE CATHOLIC=0.
IF (RELIG EQ 2)CATHOLIC=1.
COMPUTE JEWISH=0.
IF (RELIG EQ 3)JEWISH=1.
COMPUTE OTHR=0.
IF (RELIG EQ 5)OTHR=1.
```

Now, people who reported a typical religious affiliation, or for that matter an atypical religious membership, will have a code of 1 for that "religion." See above. If they were not a member of that religion, they will have a code of 0. Note that the attribute "NONE" appears to be missing. Actually, it will be included in each of the other values and serve as the reference point for each variable. Simple enough.

Similarly, separate variables for each marital status attribute may be created with the command sequence:

```
COMPUTE married=0.
IF (marital eq 1)married=1.
COMPUTE widow=0.
IF (marital eq 2)widow=1.
COMPUTE divorce=0.
IF (marital eq 3)divorce=1.
COMPUTE separat=0.
IF (marital eq 4)separat=1.
```

Note that those coded as "Never Married" do not have a separate variable but are, again, included in the analysis as a reference point.

You may recall from our earlier analysis that the average score on these abortion items were not related, in a linear manner, to the year in which the survey was taken. Thus it would be inappropriate to include a single variable, "YEAR." Rather, we can create a series of four variables from the five years of study. While which year we use as a reference point is arbitrary, it is often easiest to interpret findings if you know which attribute was associated with the lowest score. If you recall, those persons responding in 1988 had the lowest average ABORT3 score. It makes logical sense to not include it as a separately listed variable. Here are the commands:

```
COMPUTE YR73=0.
IF (YEAR EQ 73)YR73=1.
COMPUTE YR78=0.
IF (YEAR EQ 78)YR78=1.
COMPUTE YR88=0.
IF (YEAR EQ 88)YR88=1.
COMPUTE YR93=0.
IF (YEAR EQ 93)YR93=1.
```

Certainly easy enough. . . .

Once all non-metric level variables have been handled in this manner, we can implement the REGRESSION procedure. The general form of a more complete REGRESSION procedure for SPSS is:

```
REGRESSION
 /CRITERIA = DEFAULTS PIN(value) POUT(value)
 /DESCRIPTIVES=DEFAULTS VARIANCE COV SIG N
 /VARIABLES = varlist
 /STATISTICS = DEFAULTS CHA HISTORY
 /DEPENDENT = variable
 /method (single option of FORWARD, STEPWISE, etc.)
 /RESIDUALS=DEFAULTS
 /SCATTERPLOT (select temporary variable names).
```

As you can see, SPSS provides a great deal of options and is extremely versatile. It can be used to find the best predictors of any interval level variable. Here's one way to run it with our data.

```
REGRESSION
 /DESCRIPTIVES
 /STATISTICS=DEFAULTS CHA HISTORY
 /VARIABLES= ABORTN3,
     RACE,SEX,AGE,
     EDUC,
     MARRIED TO SEPARAT
     CHILDS,
     PROTEST TO OTHR
     ATTEND,
     YR73 TO YR93
     PARTYID
 /DEPENDENT=ABORTN3
 /STEPWISE
 /RESIDUALS
 /SCATTERPLOT(*PRED,*RESID) .
```

This command is not that difficult to decipher since it is an embellishment upon the bivariate example noted above. First, the DESCRIPTIVES keyword will, again, produce means and standard deviation values for each variable as well as a zero-order correlation matrix of all the variables listed in the VARIABLES= statement. Of course, if you wish, you could request SPSS to compute and display the values for variance (use the option, VARIANCE), and the covariance matrix (use the option, COV), as well as other related statistics.

The VARIABLES=[25] specification enables you to specify which variables are included in your run. There is nothing really new here since all listed variables must be spelled as they were spelled earlier when they were declaring. See above. Additionally, you will note that we used the TO convention to identify all the variables we just created; from MARRIED to SEPARATed, from PROTEST (Protestant) to OTHR (other religious affiliation), and from YR73 to YR93. Since these variables are contiguous we can use the TO convention rather than listing each one.

The DEPENDENT= specification subcommand is the easiest of all REGRESSION subcommands. It enables you to identify which variable is to be treated as the dependent variable. You therefore see the variable name ABORTN3. That's all there is to using it.

Optionally, we can request that the REGRESSION procedure be run as an ENTER, FORWARD, BACKWARD, REMOVE, or STEPWISE procedure. Basically, the ENTER command enters all the variables simultaneously while the FORWARD subcommand causes SPSS to enter all the independent variables one at a time and check the F-value and criterion (PIN) tests. The BACKWARD subcommand enters all the

---

[25]You may have noticed that I did not include the variables of DEGREE or POLVIEWS. DEGREE was well correlated with EDUC so I have already included the important information. By not including POLVIEWS I do not exclude all the 1973 data. If you wish to include POLVIEWS, recognize that your analysis will be restricted to 1978 and later data.

variables at once and then begins removing the least powerful explanatory variables one at a time. The STEPWISE subcommand enters each independent variable one at a time, starting with the most powerful predictor, and then finds the second best predictor, the third best predictor, etc., on each new step. In the STEPWISE procedure, entry of an additional independent variable is based on the value of the partial correlation coefficients—those with the largest partial correlation coefficients are entered first. Additional predictor variables are entered, or are removed if they are no longer useful, until all the variables are in the equation or the limits set in the CRITERIA subcommand (default is .05 for entry of any variable) have been reached. Each entry of a new independent variable is treated as a new step, and all equation summary statistics—assuming the STATISTICS subcommand is present (e.g., Multiple R, R-squared, ANOVA, etc.), equation coefficients (e.g., slope, BETA values, significance, etc.), and summary data of those variables not in the equation (e.g., partial correlations, significance, etc.)—are recalculated. See Table 23.

The STATISTICS keyword can cause SPSS to output more than those statistics outlined above. By including the option CHA, a summary of R^2 CHAnges is printed as well as the F-value and significance level. The HISTORY option prints a final summary report at the end of all the steps.

Many researchers argue that it is essential to examine the residuals in order to make sure that they have not violated several of the basic multiple regression statistical assumptions. Well, SPSS is particularly strong in helping you to summarize and identify the RESIDUALS. This is accomplished by outputs that include histograms, normal probability plots, outliers, and test for the residuals.

You may be interested in having SPSS produce a scatterplot using the predicted values and the residual values as variables, or for that matter a variety of other scatterplots. That's exactly what you get with the SCATTERPLOT subcommand. See Table 21.

As you can see, REGRESSION is an enormously powerful procedure that provides a substantial amount of information. The first part of the output lists summary descriptive statistics for each variable across all cases for which there were data on all variables—thus we have 1363 cases out of the 1500 sampled cases for whom we have data on each and every variable in our data set. Simple mean and standard deviation values are reported here. Note that by choosing carefully descriptive SPSS variable names for each of the dummy variables, we did not need to enter variable labels and are easily able to interpret the meaning of these summary stats (i.e., .594 of the 1363 respondents were MARRIED, .083 were WIDOWed, etc.)

The second part of the standard output is a simple correlation matrix where the Pearson r values for each variable pair are presented. The correlation between ABORTN3 and RACE—proportion white—was .045; between ABORTN3 and SEX—proportion male—was .059; etc.

The heart of the REGRESSION output begins in the third section by reporting what is happening on each step of the analysis. Part three was designed to first list summary information and then summary statistics—particularly useful statistics such as "Multiple R," R-Squared, significance levels, etc. for the variables included in the equation at this step of the analysis. You ask which variables? They are listed in the section titled "Variables in the Equation." In addition to the values of the slopes, "b" and standardized

Table 21 Multiple Regression Output

```
* * * *   M U L T I P L E   R E G R E S S I O N   * * * *
```

Listwise Deletion of Missing Data

	Mean	Std Dev	Label
ABORTN3	.464	.458	WOMEN'S RIGHT TO A LEGAL ABORTION-3 ITEM
RACE	.898	.303	Proportion White
SEX	.397	.489	Proportion Male
AGE	43.337	17.067	AGE OF RESPONDENT
EDUC	12.415	3.135	HIGHEST YEAR OF SCHOOL COMPLETED
MARRIED	.594	.491	
WIDOW	.083	.276	
DIVORCE	.110	.313	
SEPARAT	.032	.177	
YR73	.201	.401	
YR78	.205	.404	
YR88	.199	.399	
YR93	.189	.392	
CHILDS	1.944	1.837	NUMBER OF CHILDREN
PROTEST	.611	.488	
CATHOLIC	.262	.440	
JEWISH	.023	.151	
OTHR	.021	.142	
ATTEND	3.856	2.696	HOW OFTEN R ATTENDS RELIGIOUS SERVICES
PARTYID	2.684	1.989	POLITICAL PARTY AFFILIATION

N of Cases =   1363

Correlation:

	ABORTN3	RACE	SEX	AGE	EDUC	MARRIED	WIDOW	DIVORCE	SEPARAT	YR73	YR78	YR88	YR93
ABORTN3	1.000	.045	.059	-.082	.228	-.050	-.063	.016	-.031	.061	-.004	-.030	.029
RACE	.045	1.000	.040	.031	.104	.131	.005	-.013	-.130	.000	.015	-.008	-.041
SEX	.059	.040	1.000	-.016	.056	.075	-.151	-.041	-.005	.038	-.029	-.036	-.009
AGE	-.082	.031	-.016	1.000	-.223	.010	.456	.007	-.031	-.035	-.005	.038	.053
EDUC	.228	.104	.056	-.223	1.000	.000	-.165	.012	-.041	-.098	-.089	.057	.105
MARRIED	-.050	.131	.075	.010	.000	1.000	-.364	-.426	-.221	.079	.049	-.068	-.055
WIDOW	-.063	.005	-.151	.456	-.165	-.364	1.000	-.106	-.055	-.038	-.001	.030	.018
DIVORCE	.016	-.013	-.041	.007	.012	-.426	-.106	1.000	-.064	-.059	-.010	.030	.052
SEPARAT	-.031	-.130	-.005	-.031	-.041	-.221	-.055	-.064	1.000	.012	-.021	-.008	.018
YR73	.061	.000	.038	-.035	-.098	.079	-.038	-.059	.012	1.000	-.254	-.250	-.242
YR78	-.004	.015	-.029	-.005	-.089	.049	-.001	-.010	-.021	-.254	1.000	-.253	-.245
YR88	-.030	-.008	-.036	.038	.057	-.068	.030	.030	-.008	-.250	-.253	1.000	-.241
YR93	.029	-.041	-.009	.053	.105	-.055	.018	.052	.018	-.242	-.245	-.241	1.000

Table 21 (*continued*)

CHILDS	-.159	-.086	-.062	.331	-.210	.241	.121	.006	.087	.072	.024	-.001	-.075
PROTEST	-.095	-.130	-.067	.122	-.088	.009	.076	.040	-.042	-.069	.035	-.006	.059
CATHOLIC	-.080	.135	-.013	-.065	.021	.047	-.016	-.060	.004	.063	-.029	.013	-.066
JEWISH	.171	.052	.043	.012	.157	.029	-.047	.023	-.028	-.043	-.031	-.004	-.038
OTHR	.034	-.002	-.052	-.009	.068	-.007	-.044	.015	.032	.005	-.009	.019	-.022
ATTEND	-.335	-.084	-.102	.142	.043	.118	.039	-.069	-.055	-.019	-.047	.018	.001
PARTYID	-.048	.217	.000	.047	.097	.040	.049	-.036	-.042	-.051	-.024	.034	.048

	CHILDS	PROTEST	CATHOLIC	JEWISH	OTHR	ATTEND	PARTYID
ABORTN3	-.159	-.095	-.080	.171	.034	-.335	-.048
RACE	-.086	-.130	.135	.052	-.002	-.084	.217
SEX	-.062	-.067	-.013	.043	-.052	-.102	.000
AGE	.331	.122	-.065	.012	-.009	.142	.047
EDUC	-.210	-.088	.021	.157	.068	.043	.097
MARRIED	.241	.009	.047	.029	-.007	.118	.040
WIDOW	.121	.076	-.016	-.047	-.044	.039	.049
DIVORCE	.006	.040	-.060	.023	.015	-.069	-.036
SEPARAT	.087	-.042	.004	-.028	.032	-.055	-.042
YR73	.072	-.069	.063	-.043	.005	-.019	-.051
YR78	.024	.035	-.029	-.031	-.009	-.047	-.024
YR88	-.001	-.006	.013	-.004	.019	.018	.034
YR93	-.075	.059	-.066	-.038	-.022	.001	.048
CHILDS	1.000	.030	.076	-.072	-.029	.130	-.035
PROTEST	.030	1.000	-.747	-.194	-.182	.090	-.102
CATHOLIC	.076	-.747	1.000	-.092	-.086	-.146	-.063
JEWISH	-.072	-.194	-.092	1.000	-.022	-.080	-.100
OTHR	-.029	-.182	-.086	-.022	1.000	.004	-.003
ATTEND	.130	.090	-.146	-.080	.004	1.000	.062
PARTYID	-.035	-.102	-.063	-.100	-.003	.062	1.000

693

(*continued*)

Table 21 (*continued*)

```
* * * *   M U L T I P L E   R E G R E S S I O N   * * * *

Equation Number 1   Dependent Variable..   ABORTN3   WOMEN'S RIGHT TO A LEGAL A

Descriptive Statistics are printed on Page   3

Block Number  1.  Method:  Stepwise   Criteria   PIN  .0500   POUT  .1000

Variable(s) Entered on Step Number  1..   ATTEND   HOW OFTEN R ATTENDS RELIGIOUS SERVICES
```

		Analysis of Variance		
Multiple R	.33507		DF	Sum of Squares	Mean Square
R Square	.11227	R Square Change	.11227		
Adjusted R Square	.11162	F Change	172.12338	Regression	1	32.01918	32.01918
Standard Error	.43131	Signif F Change	.0000	Residual	1361	253.17948	.18602

```
                                          F =   172.12338    Signif F =  .0000
```

------------ Variables in the Equation ------------

Variable	B	SE B	Beta	T	Sig T
ATTEND	-.056865	.004334	-.335067	-13.120	.0000
(Constant)	.683212	.020392		33.503	.0000

------------ Variables not in the Equation ------------

Variable	Beta In	Partial	Min Toler	T	Sig T
RACE	.017070	.018053	.993004	.666	.5056
SEX	.025167	.026572	.989611	.980	.3271
AGE	-.035766	.037578	.979967	-1.387	.1657
EDUC	.243421	.258111	.998112	9.853	.0000
MARRIED	-.011147	.011749	.986126	-.433	.6649
WIDOW	-.049664	.052671	.998499	-1.945	.0520
DIVORCE	-.007412	.007848	.995227	-.289	.7723
SEPARAT	-.049527	.052487	.996982	-1.938	.0528
YR73	.054412	.057740	.999623	2.133	.0331
YR78	-.020224	.021441	.997777	-.791	.4292
YR88	-.023547	.024987	.999662	-.922	.3568
YR93	.029040	.030822	.999998	1.137	.2557
CHILDS	-.117541	.123689	.983027	-4.597	.0000
PROTEST	-.064968	.068672	.991839	-2.538	.0112
CATHOLIC	-.031951	.033550	.978773	-1.238	.2159
JEWISH	.145301	.153723	.993629	5.737	.0000
OTHR	.035338	.037506	.999985	1.384	.1665
PARTYID	-.026903	.028498	.996138	-1.051	.2933

Table 21 (*continued*)

Equation Number 1   Dependent Variable..   ABORTN3   WOMEN'S RIGHT TO A LEGAL A

Variable(s) Entered on Step Number 2..   EDUC   HIGHEST YEAR OF SCHOOL COMPLETED

Multiple R   .41402
R Square   .17141
Adjusted R Square   .17019
Standard Error   .41684

R Square Change   .05914
F Change   97.07194
Signif F Change   .0000

Analysis of Variance

	DF	Sum of Squares	Mean Square
Regression	2	48.88631	24.44316
Residual	1360	236.31235	.17376

F =   140.67269   Signif F =   .0000

------------- Variables in the Equation -------------

Variable	B	SE B	Beta	T	Sig T
EDUC	.035535	.003607	.243421	9.853	.0000
ATTEND	-.058661	.004193	-.345645	-13.990	.0000
(Constant)	.248983	.048279		5.157	.0000

----------- Variables not in the Equation -----------

Variable	Beta In	Partial	Min Toler	T	Sig T
RACE	-.009465	-.010300	.981363	-.380	.7042
SEX	.010373	.011316	.985968	.417	.6766
AGE	.022438	.023736	.927216	.875	.3816
MARRIED	-.009912	-.010813	.984239	-.399	.6902
WIDOW	-.009386	-.010160	.970420	-.375	.7080
DIVORCE	-.011044	-.012102	.993266	-.446	.6555
SEPARAT	-.040068	-.043917	.995283	-1.621	.1053
YR73	.078945	.086295	.988573	3.193	.0014
YR78	.001037	.001134	.990174	.042	.9667
YR88	-.037423	-.041039	.994919	-1.514	.1302
YR93	.003627	.003962	.987178	.146	.8839
CHILDS	-.067301	-.071544	.936374	-2.644	.0083
PROTEST	-.042877	-.046713	.983454	-1.724	.0849
CATHOLIC	-.025101	-.027270	.976604	-1.006	.3147
JEWISH	.108746	.117522	.967728	4.363	.0000
OTHR	.018835	.020643	.993466	.761	.4467
PARTYID	-.050451	-.055068	.987189	-2.033	.0422

(*continued*)

Table 21 (*continued*)

Equation Number 1   Dependent Variable..   ABORTN3   WOMEN'S RIGHT TO A LEGAL A

Variable(s) Entered on Step Number   5..   CHILDS   NUMBER OF CHILDREN

Multiple R	.43876		
R Square	.19251	R Square Change	.00441
Adjusted R Square	.18954	F Change	7.41702
Standard Error	.41196	Signif F Change	.0065

Analysis of Variance

	DF	Sum of Squares	Mean Square
Regression	5	54.90433	10.9808
Residual	1357	230.29433	.16971

F =   64.70431   Signif F = .0000

------------- Variables in the Equation -------------

Variable	B	SE B	Beta	T	Sig T
EDUC	.032054	.003711	.219575	8.638	.0000
YR73	.087604	.028076	.076752	3.120	.0018
CHILDS	-.017136	.006292	-.068795	-2.723	.0065
JEWISH	.309085	.075079	.102310	4.117	.0000
ATTEND	-.055325	.004202	-.325989	-13.167	.0000
(Constant)	.287772	.052608		5.470	.0000

------------- Variables not in the Equation -------------

Variable	Beta In	Partial	Min Toler	T	Sig T
RACE	-.016743	-.018424	.913577	-.679	.4975
SEX	-.002065	-.002277	.918604	.084	.9332
AGE	.043774	.044729	.843097	1.649	.0994
MARRIED	-.004969	-.005321	.882664	-.196	.8447
WIDOW	-.002285	-.002492	.901188	.092	.9269
DIVORCE	-.006802	-.007534	.920891	-.277	.7815
SEPARAT	-.032248	-.035652	.920792	-1.314	.1892
YR78	-.026233	-.027988	.910547	1.031	.3027
YR88	-.017851	-.019217	.919743	-.708	.4792
YR93	.025104	.026957	.915214	.993	.3209
PROTEST	-.019816	-.021475	.916521	-.791	.4291
CATHOLIC	-.018794	-.020547	.920982	-.757	.4493
OTHR	.020339	.022563	.916636	.831	.4061
PARTYID	-.038016	-.041730	.911633	-1.538	.1243

End Block Number   1   PIN =   .050 Limits reached.

696

Table 21 (*continued*)

```
* * * *   M U L T I P L E   R E G R E S S I O N   * * * *

Equation Number 1    Dependent Variable..  ABORTN3    WOMEN'S RIGHT TO A LEGAL A

            Summary table
            -------------

Step  MultR   Rsq  AdjRsq  F(Eqn)   SigF  RsqCh    FCh  SigCh        Variable  BetaIn  Correl
  1  .3351  .1123  .1116  172.123   .000  .1123  172.123  .000  In:  ATTEND   -.3351  -.3351  HOW OFTEN R ATTENDS RELIGIOUS
  2  .4140  .1714  .1702  140.673   .000  .0591   97.072  .000  In:  EDUC      .2434   .2284  HIGHEST YEAR OF SCHOOL COMPLE
  3  .4276  .1829  .1811  101.369   .000  .0114   19.033  .000  In:  JEWISH    .1087   .1711
  4  .4337  .1881  .1857   78.654   .000  .0052    8.771  .003  In:  YR73      .0729   .0609
  5  .4388  .1925  .1895   64.704   .000  .0044    7.417  .007  In:  CHILDS   -.0688  -.1592  NUMBER OF CHILDREN

* * * * * * * * * * * * * * * * * * * * * * * * * * * * * * *

Residuals Statistics:

           Min     Max    Mean  Std Dev     N
*PRED    -.0763  1.1887   .4657   .2019   1388
*RESID  -1.0165  1.0763  -.0008   .4113   1388
*ZPRED  -2.6908  3.6101   .0090  1.0056   1388
*ZRESID -2.4674  2.6127  -.0019   .9985   1388

Total Cases =    1406

Durbin-Watson Test =  1.86825
```

(*continued*)

Table 21 (*continued*)

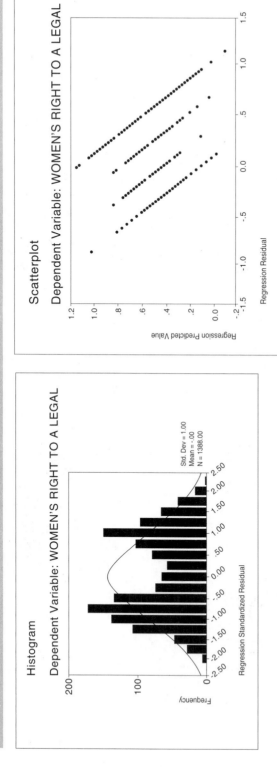

Histogram

Dependent Variable: WOMEN'S RIGHT TO A LEGAL

Std. Dev = 1.00
Mean = -.00
N = 1388.00

Scatterplot

Dependent Variable: WOMEN'S RIGHT TO A LEGAL

NOTE: This is only a partial output. Nor would this be the final work on the model. It does, however, well illustrate the power of SPSS.

698

slopes, "Beta," T-value, and significance value will be reported for each variable. The last major section of part three—either to its right or immediately following—will report a roster of "Variables not in the Equation." Useful information included here are the values for partial correlations—the correlation between each variable and the dependent variable given that other variables have been entered earlier, and related statistics. In the STEPWISE method you will have an additional page of part three output for each significant variable to be entered into the predictive equation. Once all variables, or all significant variables, have been entered, the typical end statement of part 3 will appear "End Block Number 1 PIN = .050 Limits reached."

Part 4 and 5, when requested, provide a simple summary of what happened at each step and a calculation for the Durban-Watson test, which checks for problems of multicolinearity among the explanatory variables. As noted earlier, a series of graphs summarizing a variety of calculations are then provided.

If you remember, way back at the beginning of this Appendix, we said that we were interested in finding the best predictors of attitudes toward the rights of women to obtain a legal abortion across the last 20 years of American history. We herein reported the STEPWISE method and standard CRITERIA for independent variable entry and removal across the 1500 cases—well, across the 1363 cases for whom we had data on each variable. While we had many independent variables in our original research model (see Figure 1 and our VARIABLES= list in Table 21), only a few variables were found to be "good"—in this case, significant beyond .05—predictors. Not surprisingly, the best predictor (r = −.335)—and entered on step one of the REGRESSION procedure—was church ATTENDance. It was entered first and explained approximately 11% of the variation in the abortion index scores for our data set. See part 3 of Table 21. Next, the variable of EDUCation—number of years of education—was entered since it had the largest partial correlation value (partial r = .258) of all variables yet to be entered into the equation. Note that the report on step 2, both variables, ATTEND and EDUC, are "Variables in the Equation." Education accounted for another 6% of the variation in our abortion index. Note also that SPSS output provides access to important comparative (use of Beta) and equation (use of "B" or slope) information at the left of each table. Summary stats (e.g., partial r, t statistics, significance level, etc.) are provided to the right under the heading of "Variables not in the Equation" for all those variables yet to be included in our "best predictors" model. The variable of JEWISH added 1% while the variables of YR73 and number of CHILDren, when entered sequentially, accounted for an additional .5% of explained variation each. All the remaining variables (e.g., sex, race, political party identification, etc.) did not add substantially to accurately predicting attitudes toward abortion, once these five variables were identified. Thus, our "best" predictor model accounted for slightly less than 20% of the variation in how our sampled Americans responded to our legal access to abortion index.

Our best simple equation, based on these respondents, becomes:

```
Predicted value of Abortion Index Value = .288 + .032*EDUC
                                         + .088*YR73
                                         - .017*CHILD
                                         + .309*JEWISH
                                         - .055*ATTEND
```

Thus, higher education, being Jewish, and being a 1973 respondent were associated with greater support for legal access to abortion services, while having more children and attending church more regularly was associated with less support for legal access to such services. To calculate the predicted value of support of such services from knowledge of these variables, simply substitute in the equation with the value for the variable (e.g., if respondent's number of years was 12, then multiply 0.32 by 12; if respondent was not in 1973 sample, then enter a 0 for YR73). Complete the process and then do the math to calculate a value. A single value will provide an indication of where people with similar characteristics would fall on this index.

However, examining the residuals indicates a need for some further work before finalizing the "best" equation. Of course, another form of this abortion scale—with additional or different items or perhaps across different years—might have produced different findings. . . .

Exercise 13:   If you are a hearty soul, this is your chance to try a multiple regression run. Simply follow your instincts and try the REGRESSION procedure using the minimum REGRESSION commands. Then, go ahead and try some of the options listed earlier. Don't worry, you can't hurt the computer or damage the software. Once you've mastered this command, try variations: try it on the GSS 1983 or 1993 data set only, use different explanatory variables, substitute DEGREE for EDUC and add POLVIEWS. You might even wish to see how well the regression equation built with your GSS 1988 sample "fits" the GSS 1993 sample data—just how good are models built on earlier data sets for predicting more recent attitudes? Or try other item sets (e.g., Life Satisfaction five-item scale or attitudes toward expenditures on national problems such as drugs, education, environment, etc.). In any case, feel free to explore! Examine Table 22 to see the complete list of the commands I used in this Learner's Guide. It will serve as a beginning reference for your independent work.

WORKING WITH DATA YOU COLLECT

Here's a postscript designed explicitly for those of you who wish to work with your own data, raw data, or data that must be imported from other files. If you are working on your own research project you have probably collected more data than you know what to do with. The question here is to find a way to effectively transfer the data so that you may work with them effectively using SPSS.

The reality of doing social research includes not only the design and implementation of good research methods and data collection techniques, but also the management and analysis of the collected data. With the use of your computer, and SPSS, you shall be able to manage the data in a fast, efficient, and cost-effective manner.

Getting the Data to the Computer: Step 1

SPSS 6.1 provides a Data Editor window that will enable you to enter your data into an SPSS file with all the appropriate labels and formats. If you have created a data file using Excel or another spreadsheet program, or word processing software, you can tell SPSS to read these files, too.

Table 22 Summary of Command Files

```
TITLE "BIVARIATE STATISTICS".
GET
  FILE="Jeff's HD:SPSS 6.1:GSS7393s.sav".
EXECUTE.

RECODE abany,abdefect,abhlth,abnomore,abpoor,abrape,absingle
    (0=99)(1=1)(2=0)(ELSE=99).
MISSING VALUES abany,abdefect,abhlth,abnomore,abpoor,abrape,absingle (99) .
COMPUTE abortn3=MEAN.3(abnomore,abpoor,absingle).
VARIABLE LABEL ABORTN3 "WOMEN'S RIGHT TO A LEGAL ABORTION-3 ITEMS".

COMPUTE RACESEX=9.
IF (RACE EQ 1 AND SEX EQ 1)RACESEX=1.
IF (RACE EQ 1 AND SEX EQ 2)RACESEX=2.
IF (RACE EQ 2 AND SEX EQ 1)RACESEX=3.
IF (RACE EQ 2 AND SEX EQ 2)RACESEX=4.
VARIABLE LABELS  RACESEX, 'RACE AND SEX IDENTIFIER'.
VALUE LABELS    RACESEX  1 'WH-MALE' 2 'WH-FEMALE'
                                  3 'AA-MALE' 4 'AA-FEMALE'.
MISSING VALUES   RACESEX (9).

SELECT IF ((race  = 1 or race  = 2) AND NOT SYSMIS(ABORTN3)).

CROSSTABS TABLES= ABORTN3 BY YEAR
 /CELLS COUNT, COLUMN
 /STATISTICS CHISQ, LAMBDA, GAMMA, ETA, CORR.

TEMPORARY.
RECODE ABORTN3 (0=0)(.3 THRU .7 = 1)(1=2).
VALUE LABEL ABORTN3 0 "AGAINST" 1 "SOMETIMES" 2 "FOR".
RECODE RELIG (3 THRU 5=3).
VALUE LABEL RELIG 1 'PROTESTANT' 2 'CATHOLIC' 3 'JEW/NONE/OTHER'.
CROSSTABS TABLES= ABORTN3 BY YEAR, RELIG,RACE,SEX, RACESEX
 /ABORTN3 BY RACESEX BY YEAR
 /CELLS COUNT, COLUMN
 /STATISTICS CHISQ, LAMBDA, GAMMA, ETA, CORR.

T-TEST
   GROUPS=sex(1 2)
   /VARIABLES= abortn3.

T-TEST
   GROUPS=sex(1 2)
   /VARIABLES=abany abdefect abhlth abnomore abpoor abrape absingle abortn3.
  /CRITERIA=CIN(.95) .

ONEWAY
  abortn3 BY racesex(1 4)
   /CONTRAST= 0 1 0 -1
   /RANGES=DUNCAN
   /HARMONIC NONE
   /FORMAT LABELS
   /STATISTICS ALL
   /MISSING ANALYSIS .
```

(continued)

Table 22 (*continued*)

```
RECODE MARITAL (1=1)(2,3,4 = 2)(5=3).
VALUE LABELS MARITAL
   1 "Married" 2 "Prev-Married" 3 "Nev-Married".
ONEWAY
  abortn3 BY MARITAL(1 3)
    /CONTRAST= 0  1  0  -1
    /RANGES=DUNCAN
    /HARMONIC NONE
    /FORMAT LABELS
    /STATISTICS ALL
    /MISSING ANALYSIS .

RECODE PARTYID(7=9).
CORRELATIONS
    /VARIABLES= abortn3 age educ degree realinc partyid polviews
    /PRINT=TWOTAIL SIG
    /STATISTICS DESCRIPTIVES
    /MISSING=PAIRWISE .

REGRESSION VARIABLES = ABORTN3 EDUC
    /DESCRIPTIVES MEAN STDDEV CORR SIG N
    /STATISTICS COEFF OUTS CI R ANOVA
    /DEPENDENT abortn3
    /METHOD=ENTER educ  .


TITLE "MULTIVARIATE STATISTICS".
GET
  FILE="Jeff's HD:SPSS 6.1:GSS7393s.sav".
EXECUTE.

RECODE abany,abdefect,abhlth,abnomore,abpoor,abrape,absingle
    (0=99)(1=1)(2=0)(ELSE=99).
MISSING VALUES abany,abdefect,abhlth,abnomore,abpoor,abrape,absingle (99) .
COMPUTE abortn3=MEAN.3(abnomore,abpoor,absingle).
VARIABLE LABEL ABORTN3 "WOMEN'S RIGHT TO A LEGAL ABORTION-3 ITEMS".

SELECT IF ((race  = 1 or race  = 2) AND NOT SYSMIS(ABORTN3)).

RECODE RACE (2=0).
VAR LABELS RACE "Proportion White".
RECODE SEX (2=0).
VAR LABELS SEX "Proportion Male".

COMPUTE PROTEST=0.
IF (RELIG EQ 1)PROTEST=1.
COMPUTE CATHOLIC=0.
IF (RELIG EQ 2)CATHOLIC=1.
COMPUTE JEWISH=0.
IF (RELIG EQ 3)JEWISH=1.
COMPUTE OTHR=0.
IF (RELIG EQ 5)OTHR=1.
```

Table 22 (*continued*)

```
COMPUTE married=0.
IF (marital eq 1)married=1.
COMPUTE widow=0.
IF (marital eq 2)widow=1.
COMPUTE divorce=0.
IF (marital eq 3)divorce=1.
COMPUTE separat=0.
IF (marital eq 4)separat=1.

COMPUTE YR73=0.
IF (YEAR EQ 73)YR73=1.
COMPUTE YR78=0.
IF (YEAR EQ 78)YR78=1.
COMPUTE YR88=0.
IF (YEAR EQ 88)YR88=1.
COMPUTE YR93=0.
IF (YEAR EQ 93)YR93=1.

RECODE PARTYID(7=9).

REGRESSION
 /DESCRIPTIVES
 /STATISTICS=DEFAULTS CHA HISTORY
 /VARIABLES= ABORTN3,
    RACE,SEX,AGE,
    EDUC,
    MARRIED TO SEPARAT
    YR73 TO YR93
    CHILDS,
    PROTEST TO OTHR
    ATTEND,
    PARTYID
 /DEPENDENT=ABORTN3
 /STEPWISE
 /RESIDUALS
 /SCATTERPLOT(*PRED,*RESID).
```

It's not hard to do, but several steps are required. Taking prudent care at this point is to your advantage. An example will help. Let us assume that you are conducting your own study of attitudes toward abortion and you select 20 people to respond to your survey. Let us assume further that you restrict your study to examining the impact of ascribed status characteristics (e.g., gender, race, and age) on abortion attitudes as measured by the GSS. Your questionnaire might look like Table 23.

You now have several options in creating a data file. Here are three of the many options available to you. First, you may use the traditional SPSS approach of a standard structured text file. Second, you might use any of the standard spreadsheet software packages (e.g., Excel, Lotus 1-2-3, Quatro Pro, etc.) for your data entry task. Third, you may use the Data Editor feature of SPSS. Each alternative has its strengths and

Table 23 Output from Display Command

                                                              I.D. #_____
                              STUDENT SURVEY

Hello, my name is Jeff Jacques and I am a student enrolled in Research
Methods. As part of the course requirement I am conducting a brief study of
student attitudes toward abortion. Please take a moment and consider when,
in your judgment, a woman should have the right to obtain a legal abortion.
You do not need to put your name on this survey--all information is
anonymous. Just take a few moments and CIRCLE the most appropriate answer.

Please CIRCLE whether or not you think it should be possible for a pregnant
woman to obtain a legal abortion:

    1. If there is a strong chance of serious   1.Yes   2.No   9. Don't Know
       defect in the baby?
    2. If she is married and does not want   1.Yes   2.No   9. Don't Know
       any more children?
    3. If the woman's own health is   1.Yes   2.No   9. Don't Know
       seriously endangered by the pregnancy?
    4. If the family has a very low income   1.Yes   2.No   9. Don't Know
       and cannot afford any more children?
    5. If she became pregnant as a result   1.Yes   2.No   9. Don't Know
       of rape?
    6. If she is not married and does not   1.Yes   2.No   9. Don't Know
       want to marry the man?
    7. If the woman wants it for any reason?   1.Yes   2.No   9. Don't Know

Background Items
    8. Sex   1. Male   2. Female
    9. Race   1. Black   2. White   3. Other
   10. Date of Birth   19____

Thanks for your help!

---

weaknesses. The best data entry procedure is to find what is easiest and most comfortable for you. Here we shall emphasize working with the Data Editor window of SPSS, so let's just scan the other techniques first.

If You Plan to Work with a Standard Text File . . .   If you are planning to use a standard fixed file format that may be created with any standard text editor or word processor, just remember that each record or line in the file represents each respondent. The number of "columns" you use on each record is determined by the number of variables and the width of each variable. Thus, if you plan to follow the GSS convention, the first six "columns" of each record or line will contain the IDNUMBER for each and every respondent—starting with 960001. Each question on abortion uses only one column, so all respondents' answers to question number 1, "If there is a strong chance of serious defect in the baby?" shall be recorded in seventh column for every respondent.

Table 24 Text File of My Survey

```
           1         2
12345678901234567901

96000122222222111931
96000211111111121965
96000311222222321969
96000411111111111931
96000511221222121955
96000611221222121919
96000711111111121949
96000811111222121948
96000911111111121959
96001011001200220221961
96001111111111221969
96001222222122121920
96001311222112121928
96001411211122121926
96001522222222121923
96001611111111111913
96001711221122121931
96001811222122111973
96001911111111121971
96002011211122121958
```

Note that these data are the same as that presented earlier.

(That's why the file is sometimes called a fixed format file.) Similarly, column 8 will be used to record respondents' answers to question 2, "If she is married and does not want any more children?" See Table 24.

You may be asking yourself how one would know what to enter for each value of each variable. You will find in Table 25 a copy of a codebook based on a subset of the GSS questionnaire and the questionnaire we created in Table 23. If you plan to use this data entry method, then examine closely Table 25. Note that the data for most variables required only one column, but IDNUMBER and year of birth, YRBIRTH, required more than one column. We therefore assigned the first six columns to IDNUMBER and four columns, 16–19, to YRBIRTH. Each record (or line of Table 24) contained the data for each variable in the same columnar format. Because we have such a consistent file structure, we will be able to tell SPSS how to read the variables and how to tell which variables are single-digit numbers and which require more than a single digit or column.

In the TABLE 5 subset of variables from the GSS, I have included information about the actual GSS format on this codebook. The original GSS codebook will serve as a good example for your work. You would find that the complete data set, the physical location of each variable (i.e., beginning and ending column number), what each variable was called, and the description of each variable name and values would be consistent with the information provided in Table 25 for our subset of variables.

Table 25 My Variable Codebook

GSS VARIABLE NAME	GSS QUEST'N NO.	DESCRIPTION	CODES/VALUES Survey	My REC/COL'S	GSS FORMAT VALUES	MISSING
IDNUMBER		Identifier squence	960001-96XXXX	1-6	1-6	
ABDEFECT	206A	If there is a strong chance of serious defect in the baby		7-13	780	8. Don't know
ABNOMORE	206B	If she is married and does not want any more children	All items used the following categories: 1. Yes 2. No		781 782	9. No answer BK. NA
ABHLTH	206C	If the woman's own helath is seriously endangered by the pregnancy				
ABPOOR	206D	If the family has a very low income and cannot afford any more children.			783	
ABRAPE	206E	If she became pregnant as a result of rape.			784	
ABSINGLE	206F	If she is not married and does not want to marry the man.			785	
ABANY	206G	The woman wants it for any reason.			786	
SEX	20	Sex	1. Male 2. Female	14	109	
RACE	21	Race	1. White 2. African American 3. Other	15	110	9
YRBIRTH	9	Date of Birth/AGE		16-17	92-93	9. No answer

GSS format for RECords and COLumns were based on The General Social Surveys, 1972-1994 Cumulative Codebook, 1995, Storrs, CT: The Roper Center for Public Opinion Research, 1995.

If You Plan to Work with a Spreadsheet File . . .   If you plan to use a spreadsheet package, then enter the data so that each row contains all the data for each respondent and each column contains a variable. We might use column A for IDNUMBER, column B for the first question about a "Serious defect in the baby," column C for the second question, "She does not want any more children," etc. If we use row 1 for the variable names, then data for the first respondent will begin in row 2, data for the second respondent will begin in row 3, etc. Thus, the fourth respondent's answer to question 3—a "Yes," which was coded as a value of 1—will be found in cell D5. Similarly, all the responses to each item by each respondent may be placed in their appropriate cell locations.

Once you enter all the data, make sure that you Save the file for further use. Typically, this command can be found under the File menu on most spreadsheet applications.

Using SPSS Version 6.1 Data Editor   First, make sure that the Data Editor Window—the window with the rows and columns—is in the foreground. If we use this short survey data set, you can begin entering the responses made by the first person in row 1 (e.g., 960001 for the IDNUMBER). (As soon as you begin to type, the values you type will appear in the data editor bar, and with a press of the tab key, the top of the column will change from "var" to "var00001" and the row number 1 will be darkened.) You are now ready to enter the data for the respondents' answer to the first question on abortion, "Serious defect in the baby." Just enter the value 2 in the second column. (Again, the column label at the top will change—"var" will change to "var00002.") You continue this process of entering data until all the data for each variable for the first respondent are entered. When you are ready to enter the data for the second respondent, simply use the arrow keys or the scroll bars to find the cell located at "var00001" and row 2. Or make this cell the active cell by moving the mouse to point to it and then click on it. Now, enter the data for the second respondent as you did the first; enter 9600002, tab key, 1, tab key, 1, etc. Simply continue this process until all the data have been entered. By the way, if you make an error, just choose the cell in which the error occurs and re-enter the correct data. The old data will be replaced with the correct data.

Once all the data have been entered, make sure that you save the data. Take your mouse, point at the word File, click the mouse button, and choose Save Data. Type an appropriate file name (e.g., MYDATA.SAV) and you will be able to access these data when you are ready to begin your analysis.

Exercise 14:   If you are working on a new project, you need to determine how you will complete your data entry activity. Choose and implement any one of the three methods noted above. In addition, with whichever method you choose, you should develop a codebook for your study—even if you do not need to list beginning and ending physical locations. You may use the codebook format of Table 25. When you finish developing a complete codebook, enter your data.

Finding Out About Your Computer Site: Step 2

If you are planning to use your college's computer lab, this is a good time to find out about your college's resources and which version of SPSS you will be using. If you don't know about your college's computer lab, ask your instructor or a friend. Then, get the help you need by telling the computer personnel what you plan to do; that is, that you plan to enter data, create files, and use SPSS to perform the analysis. They will probably set up an account for you and give you documentation on how to use your college's system, including: how to create a file, how to enter data into a file, how to correct any data entry errors, and—most important—how to access and use SPSS.

Unfortunately, there is no single standard for all computer sites or a single standard for all text editors, word processors, and spreadsheets. If you have yet to master these applications, you will have to get help from colleagues and university personnel. Just remember, if you are not using the SPSS Data Editor system, your goal is to get the data set created so that every card image, record, or line of data in the data file represents the responses from one respondent and that every response for the same variable is entered in the same fields or columns across all the respondents' records. Careful data entry takes time and effort. But, it will save you hours when you reach the data analysis stage. Take the time to do it right, and don't be reluctant to talk to the necessary people.

Reading the Data with SPSS Commands: Step 3

Now that you know the major parts of an SPSS command and how variable names are defined correctly, let's get started by telling the computer how to read your data. Indeed, until you give SPSS the essential information on how to read your data file, you will not be able to manipulate any of your variables or produce even the simplest reports.

If You Worked with a Spreadsheet File . . .   If you entered the data into any standard spreadsheet file with the variable names in the first row and saved it as a Lotus 1-2-3 or an Excel file, then choose:

File ➤
  Open . . .

and select your data file from the picker box remembering to select "Read variable names" from the spreadsheet option box, or a simple expression in the syntax window, such as:

```
GET TRANSLATE /FILE "MYSTUDY.XLS"26
     /TYPE XLS /FIELDNAMES.
```

Either set of steps will read your data successfully and create an "active" SPSS file. GET TRANSLATE tells SPSS that it should go out and retrieve the data from another file. /FILE "MYSTUDY.XLS" indicates the file's name and /TYPE XLS indicates, not surprisingly, the file type—in this case an Excel file. (There are many file types SPSS may read successfully but not all types are available in all versions of SPSS. So check the documentation that came with your version.) Finally, the specification /FIELDNAMES makes it clear to treat the first row in the spreadsheet file as variable names rather than data; the data will begin in the second read row. (Simply remember to choose the "Spreadsheet Options: Read variable Names" box if you are using the menu bar approach.)

---

[26]By the way, if you are using the Macintosh and plan to use your word processor, make sure that "smart quotes" is turned off.

Once you execute this command and have the Data Editor window as the active window, you can save all the variable names and the data in a single SPSS system file. The command is straightforward:

File ➤
  Save Data . . .

or

```
SAVE OUTFILE = 'filename'.
```

or

```
SAVE OUTFILE = 'MYSTUDY.SAV'.
```

Just run this command with the correct file name, and extension where needed. We'll be able to retrieve all the data and appropriate variable names from SPSS in all future work.

If You Worked with a Standard Data File . . .   For fixed formatted text files, the information on how to read the data is processed through the menu items of:

File ➤
  Read ASCII Data . . .

Not surprisingly, a dialog box will ask you to identify the file with your data. (Note that "Fixed" file type is the default and already selected for you.) Once the data file has been identified, a "Define Fixed Variables" dialog box appears. From the codebook, simply key in the variable name (e.g., IDNUMBER, ABDEFECT, etc.), "Start column:" (e.g., 1, 7, 8), and, if more than one column is needed, "End column:" (e.g., 6). (You do one variable at a time.) A press of the Add button builds the DATA LIST command; a press of "OK" executes the DATA LIST command to read the file using your newly entered format.

Did I say the DATA LIST command? The SPSS menu/dialog system is simply creating a DATA LIST command. If you wish to enter it directly in the syntax window, your DATA LIST command would look like this:

```
DATA LIST FILE="MYSTUDY"
 / IDNUMBER 1-6
     ABDEFECT 7, ABHLTH 8, ABNOMORE 9, ABPOOR 10,
     ABRAPE 11, ABSINGLE 12, ABANY 13,
     RACE 14, SEX 15, YRBIRTH 16-19.
```

IF, however you were reading the 1994 version of the GSS and you wished to examine similar variables, then your command would be:

```
DATA LIST FILE="MYSTUDY"
 /1 IDNUMBER 1-6
  AGE 92-93, SEX 109, RACE 110
  ABDEFECT ABHLTH ABNOMORE ABPOOR ABRAPE ABSINGLE ABANY
  780-786.
```

In both cases, the words DATA LIST are the procedure name, and are, therefore, re-quired—that's how SPSS knows how to read the data file. The FILE="MYSTUDY"[27] identifies the data file name you used. This enables SPSS to keep track of where to find the data. The /1 tells SPSS to read the first record. If you have a multi-record data set such that /2 would indicate to SPSS to read the second record, /10 would indicate that SPSS should read the tenth record, and so on.

In either case where the DATA LIST command is appropriate, I have identified the column(s) where SPSS may find each variable. For example, in our short classroom sur-vey answers to ABDEFECT may be found in column 7, answers to ABHLTH may be found in column 8, etc. Note that I left a single blank between the variable name (e.g., ABDEFECT) and the column (i.e., 7) where the data for that variable may be found. (Without a blank between the variable name and the variable column identifier, SPSS would not know that I had finished the variable name and was trying to indicate the column locations of the values. Look again at the other variables used to gather data on attitudes toward abortion.)

If the variable took more than a single column, I followed the variable name with a space, then the beginning column number, a dash, and then the ending column num-ber. For example, the variable of year of birth, YRBIRTH, was entered as a four-digit field in columns 16 and 19 with the expression YRBIRTH 16-19. Similarly, IDNUM-BER used six columns, one through six. I used the expression IDNUMBER 1-6.

If you need more than one record to complete your DATA LIST command—that is, to list all your variables and column identifiers—just start on the next record and skip at least one space. SPSS continues working with the same procedure command.

If your study includes data values with a decimal point but you used a text editor where you chose not to enter decimal points, we can tell SPSS to store these data as a real number (e.g., values that include a decimal point) by modifying our DATA LIST command record to read:

```
VARIABLENAME column number (2)
```

The (2) tells SPSS to place a decimal point two columns from the right-most value. For example, student grade point average (GPA) may have been part of your study. It might be declared with:

```
GPA 11-13 (2)
```

SPSS will read the values from columns 11 through 13 (e.g., 250, 300, 350, etc.) and convert them to real numbers (e.g., 2.50, 3.00, 3.50, etc.) by placing a decimal point in the appropriate place.

Similarly, SPSS can handle alphabetic values for a variable (e.g., STATE). In the parentheses you simply place an A. The (A) follows the column identifiers for that vari-able. Using the postal service two-character abbreviations for STATE (e.g., CA for Cal-ifornia, FL for Florida, etc.), we can define the variable name and characteristics with:

```
STATE 20-21 (A)
```

---

[27]It's always a good idea to check with your computer site on how best to reference data files, especially if you are using a different SPSS version and/or a different hardware platform.

Thus, STATE would be read as alpha-numeric characters from columns 20 through 21 of each record of the data file.

You will find, however, that declaring and using alphabetic values will limit your ability to manipulate and analyze the data. So, try to use only numeric values when creating your data file.

Here is another way to create the DATA LIST command for our short classroom study. These records are precisely equivalent to our earlier SPSS DATA LIST command.

```
DATA LIST FILE="MYSTUDY"
 / IDNUMBER 1-6
     ABDEFECT ABHLTH ABNOMORE ABPOOR ABRAPE ABSINGLE ABANY
     7-13,
     RACE 14, SEX 15, YRBIRTH 16-19.
```

SPSS is smart enough to figure out that it needs to equally divide all the variables with the number of columns available. In this case, SPSS will assign the data stored in column 7 to ABDEFECT, the data stored in column 8 to ABHLTH, the data stored in column 9 to ABNOMORE, etc. Alternately, if we were flexible, we might have used the expression:

```
     ABORT1 TO ABORT7 7-13,
```

When you have a large number of variables, all of which cover the same type(s) of information and each variable has the same column width, then you may use the TO convention.

Once you run your DATA LIST procedure, you can save all the variable names in the usual manner.

If You Worked with the Data Editor Window in SPSS 6.1 . . .   If you are working in SPSS 6.1, then you can easily convert "var00001" or "var00002" to a more meaningful variable name:

- Move the mouse so that the pointer is at var00001. (Note that the arrow is replaced with a + sign.)
- Double-click the mouse button.
- In the Define Variable dialog box, type the new name, e.g. IDNUMBER. (We'll examine the other options listed in this dialog box shortly.)
- Point and click on the "OK" button.

You should now see IDNUMBER rather than var00001 as the header for the first column. Repeat each of the steps listed above so that you are using reasonable descriptive variable names for each variable in your study. Remember the simple rules for variable names. Include every variable. Each variable name must: (1) be unique, (2) start with an alphabetic character, (3) have no more than eight characters, and (4) not use a reserved keyword (e.g., EQ, ALL, LE, etc.) or have as part of its name reserved special characters.

Once you make these changes, you can save all the descriptive variable names and the data in a single SPSS file. The process is straightforward—choose

File ▶
    Save Data . . .

Exercise 15:   If you are working on your own project or have to analyze someone else's data, then this is the time to try to create appropriate variable names. Take a few minutes and do so now. After doing the activities outlined above, SAVE the work using the appropriate procedures.

SPSS with a Little Class: Step 4

From this point you can begin to examine the data set with the typical SPSS commands used for descriptive summaries. But, before you do this, you may wish to add a little class.

To help you and the reader more clearly and fully understand what he or she is looking at, it is useful to label each of the variables and associated values—particularly those variables that may not be clearly understood. While the reader may have no trouble figuring out that the variable name RACE stands for respondent's race, or SEX stands for the respondent's sex, the reader may not be clear what the variable names of ABDEFECT, ABNOMORE mean. Similarly, when procedures are executed and results displayed for categorical variables such as sex, a value of 1 or 2 is not very meaningful unless you know that 1 is a code for "Male" and 2 is a code for "Female." SPSS will print out on your output the label for each variable name and each value when you use the appropriate optional commands.

If you wish to use the standard SPSS 6.1 interface to accomplish this task, recall from our earlier discussion of variable names that we noted that you could change any variable name with another by double-clicking the current variable name listed at the top of the column of the Data Editor window. In doing so, a "Define Variable" dialog box was activated. In addition to giving you the opportunity to change the variable name, it presented an opportunity to "Change Settings" including "Labels." By pointing at and clicking the mouse on the "Labels" button, you can enter the variable label and associated value labels, one at a time. In this version of SPSS, you may enter a variable label up to 120 characters long—although most of the time SPSS will only report the first 50 or so characters. So choose your variable labels carefully so that you and any reader of your output will find it easy to understand the variable under study.

To assign a label for a value in any variable, simply use this dialog box, enter the value in the "Value text box," enter a value in the "Value:" text box, and enter a label in the "Value Label" text box. Click on the "Add" button. The value label is added to the list. Repeat this procedure to add additional values and their associated labels. When you complete all the entries for this variable, then click on the "Continue" button, click "OK," and repeat these steps for the next variable.

Let us assume that you have a number of variables that use the same Value Labels (e.g., all the abortion questions use "1" for "YES" and "2" for "NO"). SPSS provides a nice option for this situation in that you can use templates. Simply select each of the continuous variables in the data window by pointing the mouse at the first variable, holding the mouse button down, and dragging across the other similarly structured variables. Now, choose:

DATA ➤
    Templates . . .

A template dialog box should now be open. Simply point and click your mouse on the "DEFINE" button. Then enter the Value Labels as you did above remembering to point and click on the "Add" button, or press the ALT-A keys simultaneously, as you complete each value label. In the Apply box, activate the "Value labels" option. Voilá.

Alternately you could be using the following commands from the syntax window:

```
VARIABLE LABELS varname 'label'.
```

For example, the following statements may be used for our survey of attitudes toward legal abortion:

```
VARIABLE LABELS IDNUMBER, 'RESPONDENT ID'
 /ABDEFECT  'STRONG CHANCE OF SERIOUS DEFECT'
 /ABHLTH 'WOMANS HEALTH SERIOUSLY ENDANGERED'
 /ABNOMORE  'MARRIED—WANTS NO MORE CHILDREN'
 /ABPOOR 'LOW INCOME—CANT AFFORD MORE CHILDREN'
 /ABRAPE 'PREGNANT AS RESULT OF RAPE'
 /ABSINGLE 'NOT MARRIED'
 /ABANY  'ABORTION IF WOMAN WANTS FOR ANY REASON'
 /RACE'RACE OF RESPONDENT'
 /SEX 'SEX OF RESPONDENT'.
```

Note that the command name, VARIABLE LABELS, is needed only once and the specifications—variable names and labels—are spaced properly. All the variable labels are identified by the variable name used in the DATA LIST command, a comma, and then the label for each is enclosed in single quote marks. So that SPSS may separate each variable from another, a slash "/" is placed at the beginning of each new variable label. So that SPSS knows that it is finished with the VARIABLE LABELS command, a period (.) is placed at the end of the last variable label.

As we have indicated, you can help the reader master the material more quickly by labeling not only the variable name, but also the values for certain variables. While it is not necessary to label every value for every variable (i.e., variables such as YRBIRTH or AGE require no value label since the numeric values are self-evident), such variables as RACE or SEX, which use coded values, should be labeled. Similarly, whenever you use codes for response categories—1 for "Yes," 2 for "No," etc., such as we did for our seven attitude questions—you should report what these value codes mean. This may be easily accomplished with the command:

```
VALUE LABELS varname, value 'label' value 'label'...value
'label'.
```

For example, returning to our short classroom study, here are several forms of the value label command:

```
VALUE LABELS RACE,     1 'WHITE'  2 'AFRICAN-AM'
                       3 'OTHER'
 /SEX,                 1 'MALE'   2 'FEMALE'
 /ABDEFECT TO ABANY    1 'YES'    2 'NO'
                       8 'DONT KNOW'   9 'NA'.
```

Note that the command name, VALUE LABELS, begins in column 1 and is followed by a space, the specifications of a variable name, its value, a single quote mark, the label, and then an ending single quote mark. Additional values and labels for the same variable follow the same format. Note also that when all the values and their labels for the variable have been entered, then for each new variable a slash "/" is entered. The values and the value labels then follow in the same manner.

By the way, when several variables use the same values and labels for each value, you may list all the variable names together, and then their values and labels. Of course, the use of the TO convention can be very helpful when several variables are listed one right after the other (e.g., ABDEFECT TO ABANY 1 'YES' 2 'NO', etc.).

What to Do When You Don't Know—MISSING VALUES: Step 5

Let's face it. Not everyone will answer every question. Some people are reluctant to tell you how much money they make or when they were born. When this occurs, or when you don't know what the valid value should be, you can tell the computer to ignore it. (Remember, we indicated in our codebook what we would do when we did not have a valid response.) Now, here's our chance to tell SPSS which variables will have which MISSING VALUES. It follows the usual command format of the procedure commands.

In SPSS 6.1, the "Missing Values . . ." command is part of the "Define Variable" and template dialog boxes. You would access this command just as you did the "Value Labels" command noted above.

Alternately, you could enter the following commands in the syntax window:

```
MISSING VALUES varname (value).
```

Here's the SPSS command for our study on attitudes toward legal abortion:

```
MISSING VALUES ABDEFECT TO ABANY (0 8 9)
     /RACE, YRBIRTH (9) .
```

It is important to note that when we have several contiguous variables, one right after another, all that have the same missing value, we can use the TO convention. Also note that when we change the value we shall choose as missing, a slash is placed between the value and the next variable name. Of course, we use the exact variable name that we assigned in our earlier statements.

Why use a MISSING VALUES command? Well, remember the FREQUENCIES output. Compare the columns and VALID PERCENT in tables which have "missing data." SPSS is smart enough to know to omit the person who did not answer the question before it computes each of these VALID PERCENTS. Similarly SPSS is also smart enough to know that the CUMulative PERCENT column should contain only those values based on valid responses.

Again, it is your responsibility to remember to save your work on a regular basis—especially after making substantive changes to your data file. All data and associated variable definitions, value labels, and missing values will be accessed automatically when you remember to save your data file.

Exercise 16:   Here's your chance to help others read your results more easily. (Actually, it will probably help you remember what each variable name and value mean, too.) Take a few minutes and develop appropriate VARIABLE LABELS and VALUE LABEL procedures for your study. Then, check the veracity of the data with the LIST and FREQUENCIES procedures. Once you have convinced yourself that you are working with a valid data set, create a new SPSS SYSTEM FILE.

CONCLUSIONS

Don't despair. It's not that hard. If you have been doing the exercises and working with the GSS data, then you have probably mastered many of the basics. If you have just looked through this Appendix, then go back to the first page and start reading the text and doing the exercises.

This is a good time to point out the steps we took in working with our GSS data set. Indeed, these steps are equally applicable to just about any study.

1. Know your research questions and specify your hypotheses in light of the data you collected.
2. Specify the information and statistical procedures you need to use.
3. Develop a codebook—either an original or use your DISPLAY command.
4. Build the data file and command files to create an SPSS file, if necessary.
5. Check and/or Clean the data.
6. Enhance your SPSS file.
7. Run your SPSS descriptive procedures.
8. Develop and test your scale.
9. Re-run your descriptive procedures with just those cases to be included in your final analysis.
10. Run your SPSS bivariate procedures.
11. Run your SPSS multivariate procedures.

Perhaps most important, take a few moments after each step and consider what you did, how it relates back to your study, and what patterns you can discover among the variables.

I would be remiss if I didn't point out that we have only scratched the surface of SPSS. If you would like to read more about this package, I recommend the SPSS manuals. If you are going to use SPSS in any continuing way, you will find them extremely useful. I know that I have.

Table 26 Display Dictionary of All Variables

08 Jun 96 SPSS 6.1 for the Power Macintosh   Page 1

```
-> SET
->    FORMAT=F8.2 PRINTBACK=ON ERRORS=ON MESSAGES=OFF HEADER=BLANK
->    BOX=X'1314151617181911121C1D' HISTOGRAM=X'1F' BLOCK=X'1E' WIDTH=80
->    LENGTH=59 JOURNAL "Jeff's HD:SPSS 6.1:Jeff" JOURNAL ON WORKSPACE=512 .

-> GET
->    FILE="Jeff's HD:SPSS 6.1:gss".

-> EXECUTE .

-> DISPLAY DICTIONARY.
```


List of variables on the working file

Name   Position

YEAR   GSS YEAR FOR THIS RESPONDENT   1
          Print Format: F2
          Write Format: F2

ID   RESPONDENT ID NUMBER   2
          Print Format: F4
          Write Format: F4

AGE   AGE OF RESPONDENT   3
          Print Format: F2
          Write Format: F2
          Missing Values: 0, 98, 99

          Value   Label

            98 M   DK
            99 M   NA

ATTEND   HOW OFTEN R ATTENDS RELIGIOUS SERVICES   4
          Print Format: F1
          Write Format: F1
          Missing Values: 9

          Value   Label

             0   NEVER
             1   LT ONCE A YEAR
             2   ONCE A YEAR
             3   SEVRL TIMES A YR
             4   ONCE A MONTH
             5   2-3X A MONTH
             6   NRLY EVERY WEEK
             7   EVERY WEEK
             8   MORE THN ONCE WK
             9 M   DK,NA

Table 26 (*continued*)

CHILDS   NUMBER OF CHILDREN   5
          Print Format: F1
          Write Format: F1
          Missing Values: 9

          Value   Label

              8   EIGHT OR MORE
              9 M   NA

DEGREE   RS HIGHEST DEGREE   6
          Print Format: F1
          Write Format: F1
          Missing Values: 7, 8, 9

          Value   Label

              0   LT HIGH SCHOOL
              1   HIGH SCHOOL
              2   JUNIOR COLLEGE
              3   BACHELOR
              4   GRADUATE
              7 M   NAP
              8 M   DK
              9 M   NA

EDUC   HIGHEST YEAR OF SCHOOL COMPLETED   7
          Print Format: F2
          Write Format: F2
          Missing Values: 97, 98, 99

          Value   Label

             97 M   NAP
             98 M   DK
             99 M   NA

FINRELA   OPINION OF FAMILY INCOME   8
          Print Format: F1
          Write Format: F1
          Missing Values: 8, 9

          Value   Label

              1   FAR BELOW AVERAGE
              2   BELOW AVERAGE
              3   AVERAGE
              4   ABOVE AVERAGE
              5   FAR ABOVE AVERAGE
              8 M   DK
              9 M   NA

Table 26 (*continued*)

| INCOME | TOTAL FAMILY INCOME | 9 |

Print Format: F2
Write Format: F2
Missing Values: 0, 98, 99

Value		Label
0	M	NAP
1		LT $1000
2		$1000 TO 2999
3		$3000 TO 3999
4		$4000 TO 4999
5		$5000 TO 5999
6		$6000 TO 6999
7		$7000 TO 7999
8		$8000 TO 9999
9		$10000 - 14999
10		$15000 - 19999
11		$20000 - 24999
12		$25000 OR MORE
13		REFUSED
98	M	DK
99	M	NA

| MARITAL | MARITAL STATUS | 10 |

Print Format: F1
Write Format: F1
Missing Values: 9

Value		Label
1		MARRIED
2		WIDOWED
3		DIVORCED
4		SEPARATED
5		NEVER MARRIED
9	M	NA

| MAWORK | MOTHERS EMPLOYMENT SINCE MARRIAGE | 11 |

Print Format: F1
Write Format: F1
Missing Values: 0, 8, 9

Value		Label
0	M	NAP
1		YES
2		NO
8	M	DK
9	M	NA

Table 26 (*continued*)

```
MEMNUM      NUMBER OF MEMBERSHIPS                                        12
            Print Format: F2
            Write Format: F2
            Missing Values: -1, 98, 99

            Value    Label

               -1 M  NAP
               98 M  DK
               99 M  NA


PAPRES16    FATHERS OCCUPATIONAL PRESTIGE SCORE (1970)                   13
            Print Format: F2
            Write Format: F2
            Missing Values: 0

            Value    Label

                0 M  DK,NA,NAP


PARTYID     POLITICAL PARTY AFFILIATION                                  14
            Print Format: F1
            Write Format: F1
            Missing Values: 8, 9

            Value    Label

                0     STRONG DEMOCRAT
                1     NOT STR DEMOCRAT
                2     IND,NEAR DEM
                3     INDEPENDENT
                4     IND,NEAR REP
                5     NOT STR REPUBLICAN
                6     STRONG REPUBLICAN
                7     OTHER PARTY
                8 M   DK
                9 M   NA


POSTLIFE    BELIEF IN LIFE AFTER DEATH                                   15
            Print Format: F1
            Write Format: F1
            Missing Values: 0, 8, 9

            Value    Label

                0 M   NAP
                1     YES
                2     NO
                8 M   DK
                9 M   NA
```

Table 26 (*continued*)

```
PRESTIGE   RS OCCUPATIONAL PRESTIGE SCORE   (1970)                    16
           Print Format: F2
           Write Format: F2
           Missing Values: 0


           Value     Label


               0 M   DK,NA,NAP


RACE       RACE OF RESPONDENT                                         17
           Print Format: F1
           Write Format: F1


           Value     Label


               1     WHITE
               2     BLACK
               3     OTHER


REALINC    FAMILY INCOME IN CONSTANT $                                18
           Print Format: F6
           Write Format: F6
           Missing Values: 0, 999999, 999998


           Value     Label


               0 M   NAP
          999998 M   DONT KNOW
          999999 M   NA


REGION     REGION OF INTERVIEW                                        19
           Print Format: F1
           Write Format: F1
           Missing Values: 0


           Value     Label


               0 M   NOT ASSIGNED
               1     NEW ENGLAND
               2     MIDDLE ATLANTIC
               3     E. NOR. CENTRAL
               4     W. NOR. CENTRAL
               5     SOUTH ATLANTIC
               6     E. SOU. CENTRAL
               7     W. SOU. CENTRAL
               8     MOUNTAIN
               9     PACIFIC


RELIG      RS RELIGIOUS PREFERENCE                                    20
           Print Format: F1
           Write Format: F1
           Missing Values: 8, 9
```

Table 26 (*continued*)

```
              Value    Label
                 1     PROTESTANT
                 2     CATHOLIC
                 3     JEWISH
                 4     NONE
                 5     OTHER
                 8 M   DK
                 9 M   NA


SEX           RESPONDENTS SEX                                      21
              Print Format: F1
              Write Format: F1

              Value    Label

                 1     MALE
                 2     FEMALE


SIBS          NUMBER OF BROTHERS AND SISTERS                       22
              Print Format: F2
              Write Format: F2
              Missing Values: 98, 99

              Value    Label

                98 M   DK
                99 M   NA


SIZE          SIZE OF PLACE IN 1000S                               23
              Print Format: F4
              Write Format: F4
              Missing Values: -1

              Value    Label

                -1 M   NOT ASSIGNED


TVHOURS       HOURS PER DAY WATCHING TV                            24
              Print Format: F2
              Write Format: F2
              Missing Values: -1, 98, 99

              Value    Label

                -1 M   NAP
                98 M   DK
                99 M   NA


ZODIAC        RESPONDENTS ASTROLOGICAL SIGN                        25
              Print Format: F2
              Write Format: F2
              Missing Values: 0, 98, 99
```

Table 26 (*continued*)

```
            Value      Label

              0 M    NAP
              1      ARIES
              2      TAURUS
              3      GEMINI
              4      CANCER
              5      LEO
              6      VIRGO
              7      LIBRA
              8      SCORPIO
              9      SAGITTARIUS
             10      CAPRICORN
             11      AQUARIUS
             12      PISCES
             98 M    DK
             99 M    NA
```

```
ABANY     ABORTION IF WOMAN WANTS FOR ANY REASON               26
          Print Format: F1
          Write Format: F1
          Missing Values: 0, 8, 9

            Value      Label

              0 M    NAP
              1      YES
              2      NO
              8 M    DK
              9 M    NA
```

```
ABDEFECT  STRONG CHANCE OF SERIOUS DEFECT                      27
          Print Format: F1
          Write Format: F1
          Missing Values: 0, 8, 9

            Value      Label

              0 M    NAP
              1      YES
              2      NO
              8 M    DK
              9 M    NA
```

```
ABHLTH    WOMANS HEALTH SERIOUSLY ENDANGERED                   28
          Print Format: F1
          Write Format: F1
          Missing Values: 0, 8, 9

            Value      Label

              0 M    NAP
              1      YES
              2      NO
              8 M    DK
              9 M    NA
```

Table 26 (*continued*)

ABNOMORE   MARRIED—WANTS NO MORE CHILDREN   29
            Print Format: F1
            Write Format: F1
            Missing Values: 0, 8, 9

            Value   Label

              0 M   NAP
              1   YES
              2   NO
              8 M   DK
              9 M   NA

ABPOOR   LOW INCOME—CANT AFFORD MORE CHILDREN   30
            Print Format: F1
            Write Format: F1
            Missing Values: 0, 8, 9

            Value   Label

              0 M   NAP
              1   YES
              2   NO
              8 M   DK
              9 M   NA

ABRAPE   PREGNANT AS RESULT OF RAPE   31
            Print Format: F1
            Write Format: F1
            Missing Values: 0, 8, 9

            Value   Label

              0 M   NAP
              1   YES
              2   NO
              8 M   DK
              9 M   NA

ABSINGLE   NOT MARRIED   32
            Print Format: F1
            Write Format: F1
            Missing Values: 0, 8, 9

            Value   Label

              0 M   NAP
              1   YES
              2   NO
              8 M   DK
              9 M   NA

Table 26 (*continued*)

```
AGED        SHOULD AGED LIVE WITH THEIR CHILDREN                    33
            Print Format: F1
            Write Format: F1
            Missing Values: 0, 8, 9

            Value     Label

                0 M   NAP
                1     A GOOD IDEA
                2     A BAD IDEA
                3     DEPENDS
                8 M   DK
                9 M   NA


ANOMIA5     LOT OF THE AVERAGE MAN GETTING WORSE                    34
            Print Format: F1
            Write Format: F1
            Missing Values: 0, 8, 9

            Value     Label

                0 M   NAP
                1     AGREE
                2     DISAGREE
                8 M   DK
                9 M   NA


ANOMIA6     NOT FAIR TO BRING CHILD INTO WORLD                      35
            Print Format: F1
            Write Format: F1
            Missing Values: 0, 8, 9

            Value     Label

                0 M   NAP
                1     AGREE
                2     DISAGREE
                8 M   DK
                9 M   NA


ANOMIA7     OFFICIALS NOT INTERESTED IN AVERAGE MAN                 36
            Print Format: F1
            Write Format: F1
            Missing Values: 0, 8, 9

            Value     Label

                0 M   NAP
                1     AGREE
                2     DISAGREE
                8 M   DK
                9 M   NA
```

Table 26 (*continued*)

```
CAPPUN     FAVOR OR OPPOSE DEATH PENALTY FOR MURDER                    37
           Print Format: F1
           Write Format: F1
           Missing Values: 0, 8, 9

           Value     Label

              0 M   NAP
              1     FAVOR
              2     OPPOSE
              8 M   DK
              9 M   NA


CONEDUC    CONFIDENCE IN EDUCATION                                     38
           Print Format: F1
           Write Format: F1
           Missing Values: 0, 8, 9

           Value     Label

              0 M   NAP
              1     A GREAT DEAL
              2     ONLY SOME
              3     HARDLY ANY
              8 M   DK
              9 M   NA


CONLEGIS   CONFIDENCE IN CONGRESS                                      39
           Print Format: F1
           Write Format: F1
           Missing Values: 0, 8, 9

           Value     Label

              0 M   NAP
              1     A GREAT DEAL
              2     ONLY SOME
              3     HARDLY ANY
              8 M   DK
              9 M   NA


CONPRESS   CONFIDENCE IN PRESS                                         40
           Print Format: F1
           Write Format: F1
           Missing Values: 0, 8, 9

           Value     Label

              0 M   NAP
              1     A GREAT DEAL
              2     ONLY SOME
              3     HARDLY ANY
              8 M   DK
              9 M   NA
```

Table 26 (*continued*)

COURTS   COURTS DEALING WITH CRIMINALS   41
           Print Format: F1
           Write Format: F1
           Missing Values: 0, 8, 9

           Value   Label

             0 M   NAP
             1   TOO HARSH
             2   NOT HARSH ENOUGH
             3   ABOUT RIGHT
             8 M   DK
             9 M   NA

GRASS   SHOULD MARIJUANA BE MADE LEGAL   42
           Print Format: F1
           Write Format: F1
           Missing Values: 0, 8, 9

           Value   Label

             0 M   NAP
             1   LEGAL
             2   NOT LEGAL
             8 M   DK
             9 M   NA

HAPPY   GENERAL HAPPINESS   43
           Print Format: F1
           Write Format: F1
           Missing Values: 0, 8, 9

           Value   Label

             0 M   NAP
             1   VERY HAPPY
             2   PRETTY HAPPY
             3   NOT TOO HAPPY
             8 M   DK
             9 M   NA

HELPFUL   PEOPLE HELPFUL OR LOOKING OUT FOR SELVES   44
           Print Format: F1
           Write Format: F1
           Missing Values: 0, 8, 9

           Value   Label

             0 M   NAP
             1   HELPFUL
             2   LOOKOUT FOR SELF
             3   DEPENDS
             8 M   DK
             9 M   NA

Table 26 (*continued*)

```
HIT        EVER PUNCHED OR BEATEN BY ANOTHER PERSON              45
           Print Format: F1
           Write Format: F1
           Missing Values: 0, 8, 9

           Value    Label

              0 M   NAP
              1     YES
              2     NO
              8 M   DK
              9 M   NA


HITOK      EVER APPROVE OF MAN PUNCHING ADULT MALE               46
           Print Format: F1
           Write Format: F1
           Missing Values: 0, 8, 9

           Value    Label

              0 M   NAP
              1     YES
              2     NO
              8 M   DK
              9 M   NA


NATCRIME   HALTING RISING CRIME RATE                             47
           Print Format: F1
           Write Format: F1
           Missing Values: 0, 8, 9

           Value    Label

              0 M   NAP
              1     TOO LITTLE
              2     ABOUT RIGHT
              3     TOO MUCH
              8 M   DK
              9 M   NA


NATDRUG    DEALING WITH DRUG ADDICTION                           48
           Print Format: F1
           Write Format: F1
           Missing Values: 0, 8, 9

           Value    Label

              0 M   NAP
              1     TOO LITTLE
              2     ABOUT RIGHT
              3     TOO MUCH
              8 M   DK
              9 M   NA
```

Table 26 (*continued*)

```
NATEDUC    IMPROVING NATIONS EDUCATION SYSTEM                        49
           Print Format: F1
           Write Format: F1
           Missing Values: 0, 8, 9

           Value     Label

               0 M   NAP
               1     TOO LITTLE
               2     ABOUT RIGHT
               3     TOO MUCH
               8 M   DK
               9 M   NA

NATENVIR   IMPROVING & PROTECTING ENVIRONMENT                        50
           Print Format: F1
           Write Format: F1
           Missing Values: 0, 8, 9

           Value     Label

               0 M   NAP
               1     TOO LITTLE
               2     ABOUT RIGHT
               3     TOO MUCH
               8 M   DK
               9 M   NA

NATFARE    WELFARE                                                   51
           Print Format: F1
           Write Format: F1
           Missing Values: 0, 8, 9

           Value     Label

               0 M   NAP
               1     TOO LITTLE
               2     ABOUT RIGHT
               3     TOO MUCH
               8 M   DK
               9 M   NA

OWNGUN     HAVE GUN IN HOME                                          52
           Print Format: F1
           Write Format: F1
           Missing Values: 0, 8, 9

           Value     Label

               0 M   NAP
               1     YES
               2     NO
               3     REFUSED
               8 M   DK
               9 M   NA
```

Table 26 (*continued*)

POLHITOK   EVER APPROVE OF POLICE STRIKING CITIZEN   53
           Print Format: F1
           Write Format: F1
           Missing Values: 0, 8, 9

           Value   Label

               0 M   NAP
               1   YES
               2   NO
               8 M   DK
               9 M   NA

POLVIEWS   THINK OF SELF AS LIBERAL OR CONSERVATIVE   54
           Print Format: F1
           Write Format: F1
           Missing Values: 0, 8, 9

           Value   Label

               0 M   NAP
               1   EXTREMELY LIBERAL
               2   LIBERAL
               3   SLIGHTLY LIBERAL
               4   MODERATE
               5   SLGHTLY CONSERVATIVE
               6   CONSERVATIVE
               7   EXTRMLY CONSERVATIVE
               8 M   DK
               9 M   NA

PORNINF   MATERIALS PROVIDE INFO ABOUT SEX   55
           Print Format: F1
           Write Format: F1
           Missing Values: 0, 8, 9

           Value   Label

               0 M   NAP
               1   YES
               2   NO
               8 M   DK
               9 M   NA

PORNOUT   MATERIALS PROVIDE OUTLET   56
           Print Format: F1
           Write Format: F1
           Missing Values: 0, 8, 9

           Value   Label

               0 M   NAP
               1   YES
               2   NO
               8 M   DK
               9 M   NA

Table 26 (*continued*)

```
PORNRAPE   MATERIALS LEAD TO RAPE                              57
           Print Format: F1
           Write Format: F1
           Missing Values: 0, 8, 9

           Value    Label

             0 M   NAP
             1     YES
             2     NO
             8 M   DK
             9 M   NA


RACLIVE    ANY OPP. RACE IN NEIGHBORHOOD                       58
           Print Format: F1
           Write Format: F1
           Missing Values: 0, 8, 9

           Value    Label

             0 M   NAP
             1     YES
             2     NO
             8 M   DK
             9 M   NA


SATCITY    CITY OR PLACE R LIVES IN                            59
           Print Format: F1
           Write Format: F1
           Missing Values: 0, 8, 9

           Value    Label

             0 M   NAP
             1     VERY GREAT DEAL
             2     GREAT DEAL
             3     QUITE A BIT
             4     A FAIR AMOUNT
             5     SOME
             6     A LITTLE
             7     NONE
             8 M   DK
             9 M   NA


SATFAM     FAMILY LIFE                                         60
           Print Format: F1
           Write Format: F1
           Missing Values: 0, 8, 9

           Value    Label

             0 M   NAP
             1     VERY GREAT DEAL
             2     GREAT DEAL
             3     QUITE A BIT
```

Table 26 (*continued*)

```
         4     A FAIR AMOUNT
         5     SOME
         6     A LITTLE
         7     NONE
         8  M  DK
         9  M  NA
```

SATFIN   SATISFACTION WITH FINANCIAL SITUATION   61
        Print Format: F1
        Write Format: F1
        Missing Values: 8, 9

```
         Value    Label

         1     SATISFIED
         2     MORE OR LESS
         3     NOT AT ALL SAT
         8  M  DK
         9  M  NA
```

SATFRND   FRIENDSHIPS   62
        Print Format: F1
        Write Format: F1
        Missing Values: 0, 8, 9

```
         Value    Label

         0  M  NAP
         1     VERY GREAT DEAL
         2     GREAT DEAL
         3     QUITE A BIT
         4     A FAIR AMOUNT
         5     SOME
         6     A LITTLE
         7     NONE
         8  M  DK
         9  M  NA
```

SATHEALT   HEALTH AND PHYSICAL CONDITION   63
        Print Format: F1
        Write Format: F1
        Missing Values: 0, 8, 9

```
         Value    Label

         0  M  NAP
         1     VERY GREAT DEAL
         2     GREAT DEAL
         3     QUITE A BIT
         4     A FAIR AMOUNT
         5     SOME
         6     A LITTLE
         7     NONE
         8  M  DK
         9  M  NA
```

Table 26 (*continued*)

```
SATHOBBY   NON-WORKING ACTIVITIES,HOBBIES                          64
           Print Format: F1
           Write Format: F1
           Missing Values: 0, 8, 9

           Value     Label

              0 M   NAP
              1     VERY GREAT DEAL
              2     GREAT DEAL
              3     QUITE A BIT
              4     A FAIR AMOUNT
              5     SOME
              6     A LITTLE
              7     NONE
              8 M   DK
              9 M   NA


SATJOB     JOB OR HOUSEWORK                                        65
           Print Format: F1
           Write Format: F1
           Missing Values: 0, 8, 9

           Value     Label

              0 M   NAP
              1     VERY SATISFIED
              2     MOD. SATISFIED
              3     A LITTLE DISSAT
              4     VERY DISSATISFIED
              8 M   DK
              9 M   NA


XMOVIE     SEEN X-RATED MOVIE IN LAST YEAR                        66
           Print Format: F1
           Write Format: F1
           Missing Values: 0, 8, 9

           Value     Label

              0 M   NAP
              1     YES
              2     NO
              8 M   DK
              9 M   NA
```

Social Work Research and Cyberspace

A new resource is rapidly becoming a powerful tool for social workers and other social scientists. Soon it will be indispensable. Since the Internet, the World Wide Web, and other elements of the "information superhighway" are changing month by month, we'll simply cover some basics that may be a useful introduction for readers who are new to cyberspace. Our aim is to orient you sufficiently for you to ask for help more effectively. We'll talk about three topics: e-mail, gophers, and the World Wide Web.

E-MAIL

The most common use of the Internet at present is as a substitute for telephonic and postal communications. E-mail is a hybrid of those two modes. Like a letter, you type out your communication on a computer. Then, rather than putting the letter in an envelope and mailing it, you send it over telephone lines. The recipient receives your message with their computer.

You will need a computer account at your school or through some other provider if you are to use e-mail or any of the other systems described in this appendix. If you can't obtain an account through your school, you may want to consider joining a commercial online service such as America Online, Bitnet, CompuServe, Delphi, Genie, MCI Mail, or Prodigy. While subscribers to the same commercial service can communicate easily with each other, they can also communicate with other portions of the Internet. We'll illustrate how that's done.

Once you are connected, you send messages consisting of the following elements: a message (just like a note, memo, or letter), a title (a fairly short heading to identify the message—for example, "Travel Plans"), and the address to which you wish to send the message. The sender's address is attached to the message automatically.

Let's look a little more carefully at the address where you want to send the message. Each e-mail address contains three basic elements:

```
<name>@<server>.<type>
```

First, the name is usually fairly straightforward. Names are assigned when an account is opened. Ours are "arubin" and "babbie," for example. Thus an e-mail address is typically a name at ("@") a location of a certain type.

Second, the type of account is also fairly simple. A series of abbreviations indicate the type of installation giving the person access to the net. Some common types used in the United States are:

edu   an educational institution

com   a commercial provider such as CompuServe or a company

org   a nonprofit organization, such as NPR

gov   a government office

net   a regional provider

bit   Bitnet

In place of these abbreviations, the address may be a country abbreviation. Here are some examples:

ar   Argentina

au   Australia

ca   Canada

cn   China

de   Germany

eg   Egypt

fr   France

gh   Ghana

jp   Japan

mx   Mexico

sg   Singapore

uk   United Kingdom

za   South Africa

The middle portion of the address (the server, the local computer), varies greatly. In the case of America Online, it is simply "aol." An example of an America Online address might be:

JDoe@aol.com

CompuServe uses a two-part account number in place of a name and "CompuServe" as the server. An example might be:

76424.156@CompuServe.com

Some educational servers are pretty straightforward. For example, babbie@chapman.edu is the address of one of us (you figure it out) who teaches at Chapman University. The other of us can be reached at arubin@mail.utexas.edu, indicating the University of Texas at Austin. "Mail" specifies a location to the computer in Austin.

When people give their addresses, they tend to pronounce the "@" as "at" and call periods "dots." Hence, Babbie would tell you his internet address is "babbie-at-chapman-dot-e-d-u".

In addition to originating messages, most e-mail systems make it easy for you to REPLY to a message you receive. When you do that, the computer automatically addresses your reply to the original sender and attaches your address as well. It may also automatically reprint the original message as a part of your reply, often identifying lines with ">" marks.

Including the original message (or part of it) can be used to remind the original sender of what you are responding to. Sometimes, you can break up the original message, interspersing your responses to the different parts of it. Here's a brief example:

Original Message:
```
Pat:
Let's go to the movies Saturday night.
I'd prefer to go in your car if that's okay.
Let me know by Thursday.
Cheers, Jan
```

Automatic Reply Format:
```
>Pat:
>Let's go to the movies Saturday night.
>I'd prefer to go in your car if that's okay.
>Let me know by Thursday.
>Cheers, Jan
```

Edited Reply:
```
Jan:
>Let's go to the movies Saturday night.
   Sure, that's great. What do you want to see?
>I'd prefer to go in your car if that's okay.
   My car's in the shop. How about yours?
See ya, Pat
```

Since it's possible to REPLY to a REPLY, you may find yourself engaged in an unfolding conversation.

When replying to a message, it's generally a bad idea to resend the entire message you received. Just include those portions (if any) that are useful in framing your response. If you resend everything, you may make the recipient wade through a lengthy document looking for your comment.

In the evolving conventions of e-mail, CAPITAL letters are used as the equivalent of shouting or emphasis and should be used sparingly. For example, you might say, "I MUST get a new computer before I go nuts," but putting your whole message in capitals is the equivalent of screaming.

Now and then, you may encounter capital letters that make no sense—for example, BTW, IMHO, and so on. These are some of the abbreviations being used in the evolving Internet culture. Here are only a few of those you may come across:

BTW	By the way
FYI	For your information
IMHO	In my humble opinion
IMNSHO	In my not so humble opinion
FAQ	Frequently asked questions
RTFM	Read the f———g manual

Since you can't communicate facial expressions or tones of voice in typed messages, some conventions have been developed to handle that lack. For example, you can include emotional references in your statements, such as "It really made my day <grin> when you reminded me the exam is Monday."

As a more creative solution, Internetters have been establishing an ever-growing set of *emoticons* to indicate emotions in print. Here are some examples. You need to tip your head 90 degrees to the left to get the point.

:-)	happy person
8-)	happy person with glasses
:-(	unhappy person
:-O	surprised person
:-p	person sticking out tongue

You can probably think up some new emoticons and introduce them to the world of the Internet.

```
    - - -
 /  0   0  \
      o
   \_/
```

LISTSERVS

In addition to person-to-person e-mail, you may find some of the thousands of electronic conversations, called *listservs*, useful. A number of them are appropriate to social research methods.

For example, METHODS is a listserv created for people teaching social research methods, though anyone can join. About 600 people from around the world belong as we write these words. Any of the subscribers can send a message to the list, and that message will appear in the mailboxes of all the other subscribers. If another subscriber wants to REPLY, that reply will also appear in the mailboxes of all subscribers. As a consequence, methods instructors have been able to discuss common problems and share solutions.

To subscribe to a listserv, you will send an e-mail message to the computer that manages that list. In the case of METHODS, you

send a message to: listserv@unmvma.unm.edu

do not put a title on the message

send this message: subscribe methods Joe Doe

substituting your name for "Joe Doe."

Once you have subscribed, you can send messages addressed to:

methods@unmvma.unm.edu

This is a standard format, although there are some variants and exceptions. To subscribe to any of the lists below, send a subscribing message by substituting "listserv" for the name of the list and use the name of the list in the body of the message, as illustrated in the case of METHODS above. Then you can send messages to the list using the address shown below.

There is no charge for subscribing to listservs. You don't have to participate in the conversations; you can just listen if you want. And you can unsubscribe any time. Here are some other listservs you might find interesting.

socwork@uafsysb.uark.edu
    social work list

abuse-l@ubvm.cc.buffalo.edu
    child abuse

evalten@sjuvm.stjohns.edu
    evaluation and statistics

outcometen@sjuvm.stjohns.edu
    outcome of mental health interventions

homeless@csf.colo.edu
    homelessness discussion
    Note: send subscription to listproc@csf.colo.edu
        instead of to "listserv"

femsw-l@moose.uvm.edu
    feminist social work
    Note: send subscription to listproc@moose.uvm.edu
        instead of to "listserv"

child-maltreatment-research-l@cornell.edu
    child abuse research
    Note: send subscription to listproc@cornell.edu
        instead of to "listserv"

scwk-l@ist01.ferris.edu
    student social work

por@gibbs.oit.unc.edu
   public opinion research

social-theory@mailbase.ac.uk
   social theory

qualrs-l@uga.cc.uga.edu
   qualitative research

qual-software@mailbase.ac.uk
   software for qualitative social research

cjust-l@cunyvm.cuny.edu
   criminal justice discussion

demographic-list@coombs.anu.edu.au
   demography list out of Australia

   Note: send subscription to majordomo@coombs.anu.edu.au
      instead of to "listserv'

familysci@ukcc.uky.edu
   family science discussion

ipe@csf.colorado.edu
   international political economy discussion

ncs-l@umdd.umd.edu
   National Crime Survey discussion

qualnet@chimera.sph.umn.edu
   qualitative research discussion

uncjin-l@albnyvm1
   United Nations Criminal Justice Information Network

sos-data@unc.edu
   social science data discussion

These are only a few of the listservs of interest to social work researchers. Moreover, the number is increasing daily. In the spirit of a snowball sample, however, you will find that subscribing to one list will bring you references to others, and if you subscribe to them, they'll bring further references. Without a doubt, there is more useful information available to you than you will be able to collect and read.

GOPHERS AND FTP

Imagine that a friend wrote a computer program or created a document that they wanted to share with you. Probably they would put a copy of the file on a disk and give it to you, so that you could load it into your computer. Now imagine that you have tens of thousands of friends around the globe doing just that. Obviously they can't put all those files on disks and send them to you. That's the function of *gophers,* which can execute a *file transfer protocol* (ftp).

Programs like Turbogopher or MacIP are designed to connect you to computers around the world. All you need (other than an ftp program) is the address ("host name") of an available computer. Perhaps the computer at your school can be accessed via a gopher.

Since this is a little more involved than sending e-mail or subscribing to a listserv, you should get local assistance in connecting to a gopher site. Once you are connected with the distant computer, you will find yourself looking at a directory of files available there. Your job is to select a file at the distant computer and copy it to your own computer. While it may require a little trial and error, you'll find the gopher program is designed to assist you in making the copies. (It will probably involve clicking a button labeled "Copy.")

The files available on computers around the world include text documents, computer games, check record programs, data analysis programs, and so on. You won't be able to appreciate the volume and variety of materials available to you except by checking it out for yourself.

WORLD WIDE WEB

Perhaps the most exciting aspect of the net today is the World Wide Web. It is something like the network of ftp sites—sources of information scattered around the world—but it is much easier to access information, and the presentation format is much fancier.

To access the Web, you will need a program like NetScape. Then you will be able to enter Web URL addresses (typically beginning "http://") and go visit. As you will discover, nearly every Web location will contain buttons you can click, which will take you to other, related locations.

For example, you can visit Chapman University by going to:

```
http://www.chapman.edu/
```

Once there, you will discover a variety of options, including a list of Chapman's academic programs. Click the "Wilkinson College" button and you will be presented with, among other things, a list of the divisions comprising the college. Click "Social Science" and then "Sociology." Now you will be able to get a list of the department "Faculty." Click that and then "Babbie" to get a picture of one of this book's authors. (Don't be fooled by the tie.)

If you had chosen "Political Science Department" instead of "Sociology," you would discover buttons that will take you to "The White House" or "The House of Representatives." This illustrates the interconnectedness of the various locations in the World Wide Web.

Here are just a few Web locations to get you started.

Books
```
.gopher://ftp.std.com/11/obi/book
http://www.bookwire.com/links/readingroom/readingroom.html
```

Europe
http://www.cec.lu/

Foundations
http://www.yahoo.com/Business_and_Economy/Organizations/
Foundations/

Jokes
http://www.misty.com/laughweb/lweb.html

Movie Reviews
gopher://spinaltap.micro.umn.edu:70/11/fun/Movies

New York Times Digest
http://nytimesfax.com/times.pdf

Population Data
http://opr.princeton.edu/pi/pindex.htm
http://opr.princeton.edu/archive/archive.html
http://www.pop.psu.edu/

Public Opinion Data
http://cspo.queensu.ca:8080/cspo.html

St. Petersburg (Russia)
http://www.spb.su/

Social Science Research Resources
http://www.carleton.ca/~cmckie/research.html
http://coombs.anu.edu.au/CoombsHome.html
http://www.indiana.edu:80/~csrwww/
http://www.uib.no/nsd/nsd-eng.html
http://www.pitt.edu/~ian/ianres.html
http://sosig.esrc.bris.ac.uk/
http://dawww.essex.ac.uk/othserv.html
http://ssdc.ucsd.edu/
http://www.yahoo.com/Social_Science/
http://www.yahoo.com/Society_and_Culture/Social_Work/

Social Work Issues

Abortion
http://www.yahoo.com/Society_and_Culture/Abortion_Issues/

Children
http://www.yahoo.com/Society_and_Culture/Children/

Civil Rights
http://www.yahoo.com/Society_and_Culture/Civil_Rights/

Crime
http://www.yahoo.com/Society_and_Culture/Crime/

Disabilities
http://www.yahoo.com/Society_and_Culture/Disabilities/

Gender Issues
http://www.yahoo.com/Society_and_Culture/Gender_Issues/

Homelessness
http://www.yahoo.com/Society_and_Culture/Homelessness/

Human Rights
http://www.yahoo.com/Society_and_Culture/Human_Rights/

Hunger
http://www.yahoo.com/Society_and_Culture/Hunger/

Minorities
http://www.yahoo.com/Society_and_Culture/Minorities/

Seniors
http://www.yahoo.com/Society_and_Culture/Seniors/

Sexuality
http://www.yahoo.com/Society_and_Culture/Sexuality/

Social Work Programs

University of Maryland School of Social Work
http://ssw01.ab.umd.edu/welcome.htm

University of Texas at Austin School of Social Work
http://www.utexas.edu/depts/sswork/

University of Windsor School of Social Work
http://www.uwindsor.ca/faculty/socsci/socwk/index.html

U.S. Government

Central Intelligence Agency (CIA)
http://www.ic.gov/

National Science Foundation
http://stis.nsf.gov/

The White House
http://www.whitehouse.gov/

U.S. Census Bureau
http://www.census.gov/

U.S. Department of Education
http://www.ed.gov/

U.S. House of Representatives
http://www.house.gov/

World Factbook

http://www.ic.gov/94fact/fb94toc/fb94toc.html

World History

http://neal.ctstateu.edu/history/world_history/
world_history.html

One of the most useful Web locations for social work students, faculty, and practitioners is *The Social Work Networker*. You can access it by going to:

http://pages.nyu.edu/~mfh0446/

Once you access the *Networker*, you will be welcomed to "a one stop index for all essential social work resources." It will offer you many different topics to click, and after you click a topic you will find many additional subtopics. For example, if you are looking for information on advocacy and public policy, you will find 12 options to click. One of them is "Welfare and Families." If you click that, you will be presented with a list of options covering "news articles, reports, and other information about the national debate over welfare reform and family issues."

If you are job hunting, you can click the "Job Opportunities" topic. That will bring up additional options, such as one that provides an extensive list of job openings for social workers in the health field. If you are looking for information about practice with a specific target population, you can go to "Populations Served." You will find background information and literature references connected to programs, policy issues, assessment, and interventions regarding addictions, different age groups, ethnic groups, and various psychosocial problems and diagnostic classifications. If you are looking for listserv discussion groups for social workers, you can click "THE LIST: Discussion lists for Social Workers" and find approximately 50 such discussion groups.

The *Networker* has many other useful features. One is called "The GROHOL Mental Health Page." Click it and you will find numerous options, such as "Page One at Psych Central." Clicking that brings access to articles, surveys, professional papers, and more. Under professional papers, for example, you may click "Treatment Manuals," which offers references for manuals for treatments that have been tested scientifically and found to be effective for various problems such as depression, marital discord, chronic mental illness, bulimia, posttraumatic stress disorder, and others.

Another feature that students in particular may value is "THE NEW SOCIAL WORKER Online." Clicking it gives you access to a magazine for social work students as well as recent graduates, covering such items as getting a job, choosing the right graduate school or field placement, and others. We encourage you to access *The Social Work Networker* and explore these and many other features it offers.

Inferential Statistics
and Single-Subject Designs

INTRODUCTION

When we discussed single-subject designs in Chapter 10, our focus was on analyzing their visual significance. We mentioned statistical significance but felt that you would need to understand the statistical material in subsequent chapters in order to best comprehend the application of inferential statistics to single-subject design data. Therefore, we indicated that we would return to that topic in this appendix.

STATISTICAL SIGNIFICANCE IN SINGLE-SUBJECT DESIGNS

Statistical significance means the same thing in single-subject designs as it does in other sorts of research, and it refers to the probability that differences in data patterns between baseline and intervention phases could have occurred merely by chance. Human behavior tends to fluctuate from one observation point to the next. For example, our social functioning from one day to the next can be influenced by a host of random factors, such as whether a telephone call in the early morning (a wrong number, perhaps) ruined our sleep the night before. Changes from the baseline to the intervention period in single-subject designs could have occurred as part of these normal fluctuations.

It often is difficult to figure out what accounts for these variations, which leads some to speculate about biorhythms, hormones, or the effects of the full moon. Because we are unable to predict or explain these fluctuations, it is important to recognize that due just to the luck of the draw an individual may have more good-functioning days during one phase than during another. When we test for statistical significance, we assess the probability, or odds, that such random fluctuations could account for the observed differences in our dependent variable that correspond to differences in our independent variable. That is, what are the odds that the increase in the number of relatively good-functioning data points during the intervention period had nothing to do with the intervention, but instead resulted merely from fate dealing a better hand (such as fewer undetectable negative conditions) during the intervention phase than during the baseline phase?

When applying inferential statistics to single-subject designs, we assume that the baseline sample of observations represents the overall data pattern of the target problem (including its normal fluctuations) that can be expected to continue during the intervention phase if the target problem remains unaffected by the intervention. We then calculate the probability that our intervention phase results are merely a continuation of the baseline distribution—that the obvious differences (if there are any) between the two phases are within the range of fluctuations that can be expected to occur due to chance.

If our calculations indicate a probability level at or below our significance level (let's say our significance level is .05), it means that for every 100 additional baselines we took at random, no more than 5 of the 100 data patterns would deviate from our original baseline as much as our intervention data did. (This assumes that our particular baseline really represents the long-range, expected pattern of the target problem.) With a probability of .05 or less, we would in turn conclude that the change in the data pattern probably was not due to random fluctuations, but rather to our intervention or some significant extraneous event. On the other hand, if the probability exceeded .05, the findings would not be deemed statistically significant and we would be reluctant to rule out random fluctuations as the explanation of the difference between the baseline and intervention data. (Here one should remember the importance of both Type I and Type II errors. These errors mean that attaining statistical significance does not totally eliminate the possibility that the data patterns were caused by chance fluctuations and that failure to attain it does not eliminate the possibility that the data patterns were not in fact due to random fluctuations.)

To suppose that a statistically significant change in the data pattern can be attributed to the intervention, we must have visual significance in the first place (as discussed in Chapter 10). If we do not—that is, if the shift in the data pattern begins to occur at some time other than soon after the onset of intervention—we cannot attribute even a statistically significant change to the intervention. For example, suppose that at the sixth observation point in a ten-point baseline, a sudden and dramatic improvement takes place in the level of the target problem and that that level is sustained throughout the intervention phase. Even if the data points during the intervention phase as a whole were significantly higher overall than those during baseline, it would be illogical to suppose that the intervention caused the increase because the shift in level happened before the intervention was introduced. In other words, statistical significance permits us to reject the hypothesis of random fluctuations (the null hypothesis), but such significance in this instance does not mean that the nonrandom event that caused the change was our particular independent variable. When adequate visual significance is lacking, history, maturation, and related threats to internal validity remain plausible causes of statistically significant changes (as discussed in Chapter 10).

ALTERNATIVE PROCEDURES FOR CALCULATING STATISTICAL SIGNIFICANCE

Some statistical procedures for analyzing single-subject data are more controversial than others. Unfortunately, the least controversial ones require so many repeated measures that they are rarely relevant to social work applications. Three procedures are generally considered to be the most relevant to social work practitioners. Although they are among the more controversial procedures, they can be used as "rules of thumb," and

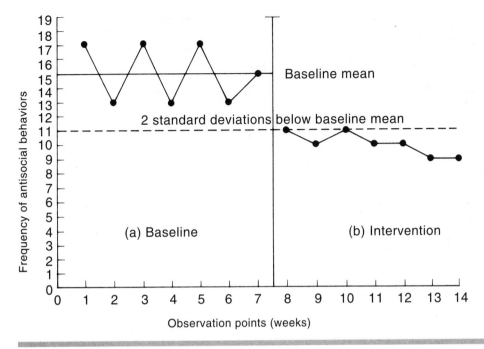

Figure I-1 Hypothetical Results to Illustrate Two Standard Deviation Procedure

their calculations do not require much statistical aptitude or an unrealistically large number of data points. Deciding which procedure to use in analyzing a particular set of data is based primarily on whether the data points are dichotomous and, if not, whether a pronounced trend is evident in the baseline data.

Two Standard Deviation Procedure

The two standard deviation procedure can be used if the data points are not dichotomous and the baseline trend is relatively flat or cyclical. Because this procedure only compares the levels of the baseline to those of the intervention data points and does not take into account whether the directions of their trends are different, it should not be used when there is a pronounced trend in the baseline. The procedure requires nondichotomous data because it involves the calculation of quantitative statistics, such as the mean and standard deviation. It also requires that there be some variation in the baseline data. (That is, all the data points cannot be the same number; if they were all the same, the standard deviation would be zero and the procedure would be meaningless.) The procedure assumes that if we were to extend the baseline indefinitely, ultimately 95% of our observations would be less than two standard deviations away from the baseline mean, which is the case in the normal curve.

This procedure involves the following computational steps. We will illustrate these steps using the data in Figure I-1.

1. Calculate the mean of the baseline observations.

$$\frac{17 + 13 + 17 + 13 + 17 + 13 + 15}{7} = 15$$

2. Subtract the baseline mean from each baseline score and square the difference.

$17 - 15 = 2 \quad 2^2 = 4$

$13 - 15 = -2 \quad (-2)^2 = 4$

$17 - 15 = 2 \quad 2^2 = 4$

$13 - 15 = -2 \quad (-2)^2 = 4$

$17 - 15 = 2 \quad 2^2 = 4$

$13 - 15 = -2 \quad (-2)^2 = 4$

$15 - 15 = 0 \quad 0^2 = 0$

3. Sum the above squares.

$4 + 4 + 4 + 4 + 4 + 4 = 24$

4. Divide the above sum of squares by the number of data points in your baseline minus one.

$$\frac{24}{(7 - 1)} = 4$$

5. The standard deviation is the square root of the dividend calculated in step 4.

Square root of 4 = 2

6. Since we are interested in the distance that is two standard deviations away from the mean, multiply the standard deviation by 2.

$2 \times 2 = 4$

7. Add and subtract the number representing two standard deviations to/from the baseline mean.

$15 + 4 = 19$

$15 - 4 = 11$

8. Examine the intervention data points. If the average intervention score is at least two standard deviations away from the baseline mean, or if at least two consecutive intervention data points go beyond two standard deviations away from the baseline mean, the change is statistically significant at the .05 level. A significant change could indicate that the intervention had beneficial or harmful effects, depending on whether the intervention data points are above or below the baseline mean and which direction is desired.

$$\text{Intervention mean} = \frac{11 + 10 + 11 + 10 + 10 + 9 + 9}{7} = 10$$

Since 10 is more than two standard deviations from 15, the change is significant.

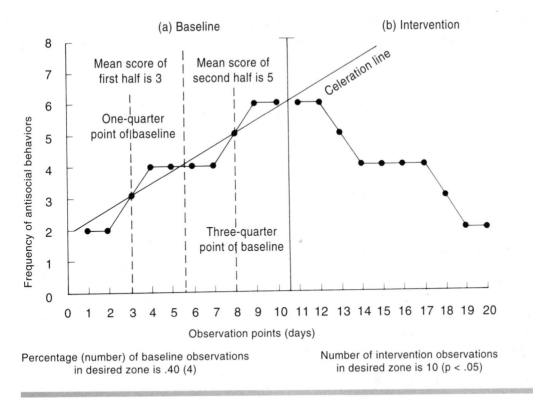

Figure I-2 Hypothetical Results to Illustrate Celeration Line Approach

Celeration Line Approach

When the baseline data have a pronounced slope that does not permit the use of the two standard deviation procedure, we usually can use the celeration line approach. This approach takes into account the direction in which the baseline data are moving (that is, the slope, or trend, of the baseline) in the determination of statistical significance. It assumes that if we were to extend the baseline, the data would continue increasing or decreasing at the same rate that they did during baseline. It involves constructing a line to estimate the slope of the baseline, extending that (celeration) line into the intervention period, and then comparing the proportion of data points above or below the celeration line during baseline to the proportion during the intervention phase.

The procedure involves the following computational steps, which have been suggested by Gingerich and Feyerherm (1979), and which are illustrated in Figure I-2.

1. Construct a chronological graph of the baseline scores.

2. Divide the baseline in half chronologically. (If there are an odd number of baseline data points, do not include the middle point in either half.)

3. Calculate the mean score of each half.

4. Plot the mean of each half at the chronological halfway point of each half (the one-quarter and three-quarter points of the overall baseline).

5. Draw a straight line connecting the two points plotted in step 4.

6. Extend the above line from the beginning of the baseline to the end of the intervention period. This is the celeration line.

7. Calculate the percentage of baseline observations that fall in the desired zone. The desired zone is above the celeration line if we are looking for an increase in the data points and below the celeration line if we are looking for a decrease.

8. Count the total number of data points in the intervention period.

9. Count the number of data points that fall in the desired zone during the intervention period. (See step 7 for the definition of desired zone.)

10. Examine the cell entries in Table I-1 to see if the proportion of data points in the desired zone is significantly greater during intervention than during baseline.

In using Table I-1 to analyze the data in Figure I-2, we would select the row that begins with .40 in the first column since the proportion of baseline observations in the desired zone is .40. We would then skip over to the column headed "10" since the total number of observations during intervention is 10. The cell entry for row .40 and column 10 is 8, which means that at least 8 observations need to be in the desired zone during intervention for the change to be statistically significant. The data in Figure I-2 show 10 observations in the desired zone. Because 10 exceeds 8, the change is statistically significant.

Notice that the data pattern in Figure I-2 has both visual and statistical significance. (As we discussed in Chapter 10, data have visual significance when there is a clear shift in the data pattern coinciding with the onset of intervention.) But would the calculations indicate statistical significance if the two standard deviation procedure had been used instead of the celeration line approach? Remember, the two standard deviation procedure considers only changes in the level of the data, not the slope of the data. In this illustration, the visual significance has to do with a change in the trend, or slope, of the data, not their level. The average score during the intervention period is the same as the average score during baseline. The change between baseline and intervention involves only the direction in which the target problem is moving. That is, following a steady deterioration during baseline, a steady improvement begins when intervention is introduced. Had we used the two standard deviation procedure, which would have been inappropriate due to the pronounced slope during baseline, the calculations would have indicated no significant change from baseline to intervention, an erroneous conclusion.

Proportion/Frequency Procedure

The third statistical procedure has its primary utility when our data are dichotomous. Dichotomous data are plotted as either "yes" or "no" on a graph and therefore cannot be used to plot slopes or calculate means or standard deviations. For example, the data may refer to whether or not an individual smoked a cigarette, had an alcoholic beverage, or slept a desired number of hours during a given day. This procedure uses the same binomial distribution tables (see Table I-1) that are used with the celeration line approach. The computational steps using this procedure are also very similar to those in the celeration line approach. When our data are dichotomous, the main computational difference between the two approaches is that with the proportion/frequency approach, instead of plotting a celeration line, we simply draw a line straight across the graph separating the yes's from the no's. Then we follow the same steps in the celeration line approach: we determine the proportion of observations above or below the line and use Table I-1 in the same way to see if the baseline and intervention proportions differ significantly. This process is illustrated in Figure I-3. This time the results are not statistically significant, however. With .40 observations in the desired zone during baseline and a total of 10 observations during intervention, we would need at least 8 observations in the desired zone during intervention for the change to be statistically significant. But we only had 7. (This procedure also can be used with continuous data, but with such data its calculations are more problematic and its use is more controversial.)

SUBSTANTIVE SIGNIFICANCE

In research using single-subject designs, just as in other forms of research, it is important to go beyond statistical significance and to consider substantive significance. (Some single-subject design literature refers to substantive significance as "clinical significance" or "practical significance.")

Changes can be visually or statistically significant but still fall short of the degree of change desired by the client, practitioner, or society. For example, an intervention might be effective in helping a smoker reduce the number of cigarettes he or she smokes each day but fail to help the client quit smoking entirely. Neither client nor practitioner might be satisfied with this outcome, even if it is visually and statistically significant. As another example, a case management intervention might help ex-mental patients reside in the community for a period that is long enough from the standpoint of statistical or visual significance but not long enough to convince the public that the case management program is worth its costs in terms of reduced hospitalization expenses. If an intervention is deemed not significant from a practical standpoint because the client and/or others are not satisfied with the magnitude of change that has occurred, then even if it is statistically significant the practitioner might search for a better intervention.

Polster and Lynch (1985) discuss a dramatic example of this point. A boy with a history of starting an average of seven fires per week was referred to a social worker. After one month of the social worker's intervention the target problem was reduced from an average of seven fires per week to two per week. Although this reduction might be statistically and visually significant, it lacks substantive significance. Two fires per week is still unacceptable; no fires may be the only level that is significant from a practical standpoint.

Table I-1 Table Showing the Number of Observations of a Specified Type (for Example, a Desired Behavior) During the Intervention Period That Are Necessary to Represent a Significant *Increase* at the .05 Level over the Proportion of Like Observations During the Baseline Period*

NUMBER OF OBSERVATIONS IN THE INTERVENTION PERIOD

PROPORTION OF OBSERVATIONS IN THE BASELINE PERIOD	4	6	8	10	12	14	16	18	20	24	28	32	36	40	44	48	52	56	60	64	68	72	76	80	84	88	92	96	100
.05	2	2	3	3	3	3	3	4	4	4	4	5	5	5	6	6	6	7	7	7	8	8	8	8	9	9	9	10	10
.10	3	3	3	4	4	4	5	5	5	6	7	7	8	8	9	9	10	10	11	12	12	13	13	14	14	15	15	16	16
1/8	3	3	4	4	5	5	5	6	6	7	8	8	9	10	10	11	12	12	13	14	14	15	15	16	17	17	18	19	19
.15	3	3	4	4	5	5	6	6	7	8	8	9	10	11	12	12	13	14	15	15	16	17	18	18	19	20	21	21	22
1/6	3	4	4	5	5	6	6	7	7	8	9	10	11	12	13	13	14	15	16	17	18	18	19	20	21	22	22	23	24
.20	3	4	5	5	6	6	7	8	8	9	10	11	12	13	14	15	16	17	18	19	20	21	22	23	24	25	26	27	28
.25	4	4	5	6	7	7	8	9	9	11	12	13	14	16	17	18	19	20	22	23	24	25	26	27	29	30	31	32	33
.30	4	5	6	6	7	8	9	10	10	12	13	15	16	18	19	21	22	24	25	26	28	29	30	32	33	35	36	37	39
1/3	4	5	6	7	8	9	9	10	11	13	15	16	18	19	21	22	24	26	27	29	30	32	33	35	36	38	39	41	42
.35	4	5	6	7	8	9	10	11	12	13	15	17	18	20	22	23	25	27	28	30	31	33	35	36	38	39	41	42	44
3/8	4	5	6	7	8	9	10	11	12	14	16	18	19	21	23	25	26	28	30	31	33	35	36	38	40	42	43	45	47
.40	4	5	6	8	9	10	11	12	13	15	16	18	20	22	24	26	28	29	31	33	35	37	38	40	42	44	46	47	49

Table I-1 (*continued*)

NUMBER OF OBSERVATIONS IN THE INTERVENTION PERIOD

PROPORTION OF OBSERVATIONS IN THE BASELINE PERIOD	4	6	8	10	12	14	16	18	20	24	28	32	36	40	44	48	52	56	60	64	68	72	76	80	84	88	92	96	100
.45	4	6	7	8	9	10	11	13	14	16	18	20	22	24	26	28	30	32	34	36	38	40	42	44	46	48	50	52	54
.50	—	6	7	9	10	11	12	13	15	17	19	22	24	26	28	31	33	35	37	40	42	44	46	48	51	53	55	57	59
.55	—	6	8	9	10	12	13	14	16	18	21	23	26	28	31	33	35	38	40	43	45	48	50	52	55	57	59	62	64
.60	—	6	8	9	11	12	14	15	17	19	22	25	27	30	33	35	38	41	43	46	48	51	54	56	59	61	64	66	69
5/8	—	—	8	10	11	13	14	16	17	20	23	25	28	31	34	36	39	42	45	47	50	53	55	58	61	63	66	69	71
.65	—	—	8	10	11	13	14	16	17	20	23	26	29	32	35	38	40	43	46	49	52	54	57	60	63	65	68	71	74
2/3	—	—	8	10	12	13	15	16	18	21	24	27	30	32	35	38	41	44	47	50	53	55	58	61	64	67	70	72	75
.70	—	—	—	10	12	13	15	17	18	21	24	28	31	34	37	40	43	46	49	52	55	58	61	64	67	70	73	75	78
.75	—	—	—	—	12	14	16	17	19	22	26	29	32	35	39	42	45	48	51	55	58	61	64	67	70	74	77	80	83
.80	—	—	—	—	—	14	16	18	20	23	27	30	34	37	40	44	47	51	54	57	61	64	67	71	74	77	81	84	87
5/6	—	—	—	—	—	—	—	18	20	24	27	31	34	38	42	45	49	52	56	59	63	66	69	73	76	80	83	87	90
.85	—	—	—	—	—	—	—	—	20	24	28	31	34	38	42	46	49	53	56	60	63	67	70	74	78	81	85	88	92
7/8	—	—	—	—	—	—	—	—	—	24	28	32	36	39	43	47	50	54	57	61	65	68	72	76	79	83	86	90	94
.90	—	—	—	—	—	—	—	—	—	—	—	32	36	40	44	47	51	54	58	62	66	69	73	77	80	84	88	91	95
.95	—	—	—	—	—	—	—	—	—	—	—	—	—	—	—	—	52	56	60	64	68	72	76	79	83	87	91	95	99

Tables of the Cumulative Binomial Probability Distribution—By the staff of the Harvard Computational Laboratory, Harvard University Press, 1955. This table constructed under the direction of Dr. James Norton, Jr., Indiana University—Purdue University at Indianapolis, 1973.

From the *Paradox of Helping: Introduction to the Philosophy of Scientific Practice* by Martin Bloom (New York: Macmillan, 1975). This table is reproduced by permission of the author and the publisher.

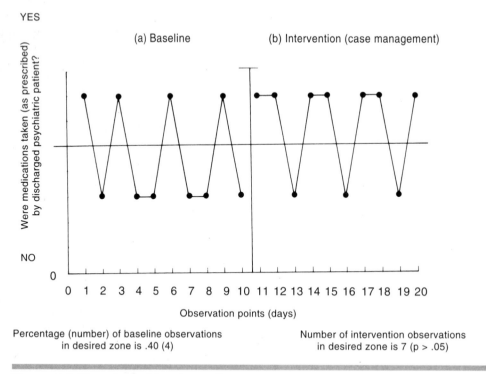

Figure I-3 Hypothetical Results to Illustrate Proportion/Frequency Procedures

As we discussed in Chapter 16, substantive significance is not calculated with a formula; it is primarily a subjective matter involving value judgments. Just as with other forms of research, in single-subject designs we must remember not to confuse the statistical and visual significance of an outcome with its strength or meaningfulness. Visual and statistical significance help us make decisions about whether a particular change really was caused by a particular intervention; they do not tell us whether we should be satisfied with the amount of change that occurred.

LIMITATIONS OF STATISTICAL SIGNIFICANCE IN SINGLE-SUBJECT DESIGNS

In Chapter 10 we noted that single-subject studies in the real world often obtain ambiguous graphs that are difficult to interpret from the standpoint of visual significance. For example, the baseline data may be unstable or the improvement in the intervention data may not begin until treatment has been going on for some time. Attempting to resolve this ambiguity simply by asking whether the differences between the two phases are statistically significant can be misleading.

If your results are statistically significant, that does not mean that the intervention caused the change. It means only that something other than chance probably accounts for the difference between the phases. That something might be history, and your lack of visual significance prevents you from concluding that the intervention is the most plausible explanation of the statistical difference.

If your results are not statistically significant, on the other hand, that does not give you more reason for ruling out the possibility that the intervention might be effective, but with delayed effects. The latter might still be possible in that the improvement occurred too late in the study to obtain enough "improved" data points during intervention to show a statistically significant difference.

Low Statistical Power

A particularly troublesome statistical problem in this area of research is the very low statistical power of most single-subject studies. Here we are not referring to the fact that these studies lack enough cases to have external validity. Instead, we are referring to the small number of data points in most single-subject research. From the standpoint of statistical power, the number of data points in single-subject research is analogous to the sample size in group research. That's because the luck of the draw pertains not to the sampling or random assignment of people, but to the sampling of observations.

Suppose, for example, that we monitor angry outbursts for only 4 days; we have 2 days with no outbursts and 2 days with five outbursts per day. Just due to luck, we have a fairly decent chance of having the 2 days with five outbursts fall in the baseline period and the 2 days with no outbursts fall in the intervention period. In contrast, suppose we monitor outbursts for 20 days that include 10 low-outburst days and 10 high-outburst days. The odds that all the high-outburst days will fall in baseline and that all the low-outburst days will fall in intervention—just due to the luck of the draw—are much, much lower than if we observe for only a total of 4 days. Therefore, our statistical power will be higher with 20 days of observation than with only 4.

When a study does not have a large number of data points, its chances of getting statistically significant results are slim even if it is evaluating an effective intervention. To assess the approximate statistical power of a single-subject design study, we can consult Table 17-1 (in Chapter 17), using the total number of data points across the two phases as our sample size. That table shows that when one has 20 data points, one has only about a 25% chance of obtaining statistically significant results at the .05 significance level when evaluating a moderately effective intervention. Even with 40 data points one's chances of obtaining statistically significant results are still less than 50-50.

One way to get a feel for the importance of statistical power is to reexamine Table I-1. Suppose your proportion of observations in the desired zone during baseline was .30. You would then use the row that begins with .30 to find how many observations in the desired zone during intervention that you would need in order to have statistical significance. Notice that if you had a total of only four observations in your intervention period, all four of them (100% of them) would have to be in the desired zone in order to have statistical significance. If you had a total of ten observations in your intervention period, however, only 60% (or six) would have to be in the desired zone in order to have statistical significance.

We suggest that you now look at the very last figure in that row, the one corresponding to a total of 100 intervention data points. Here you can see that only 39 (39%) are needed for statistical significance. Thus, an improvement from 30% in baseline to just 39% in intervention is significant with 100 intervention data points, whereas you would have had to double your proportion of desired observations (from .30 to .60) with 10 intervention data points. That is statistical power in action.

Since most single-subject studies, especially those conducted by practitioners, have about 20 or fewer data points, you should be careful not to let the lack of statistical significance carry too much weight when interpreting findings that are visually significant, especially when the degree of change seems meaningful from a practical, or clinical, standpoint (that is, when the degree of change seems substantively significant).

As we discussed earlier, when you have low statistical power you take a big, and perhaps unreasonable, risk of committing a Type II error. Therefore, when your graph is visually significant, but not statistically significant, you might want to put a lot of stock in your effect size.

EFFECT SIZE

As we noted in Chapter 16, the effect size statistic depicts how strong the effects of an intervention are. Effect size (ES) is easy to calculate when your data fit the two standard deviation approach for calculating statistical significance (that is, when your data are not dichotomous and when the baseline trend lacks a pronounced slope). The formula is the same as in group research, except that you use your baseline mean and standard deviation where the other formula uses the control group's, and you use your intervention mean instead of the experimental group mean. Thus, you subtract the baseline mean from the intervention mean and then divide the difference by the standard deviation of the baseline. You would already have calculated each of these figures when computing the two standard deviation procedure, so calculating effect size should be a very easy additional step.

In fact, the two standard deviation procedure essentially involves calculating your ES and then deeming significant any ES at or above 2.0. It is interesting to note that an ES of 2.0 is quite large. Many group research studies obtain statistically significant results with much lower ES's—about .60 on average. Apparently those who devised the two standard deviation rule-of-thumb procedure felt that a large ES was needed for significance in light of the low statistical power of most single-subject evaluation conducted by practitioners. Although they may be correct about that, you should nevertheless be mindful of the important risk of a Type II error if you obtain visually significant results and a relatively large ES (say, close to .60 or higher) that falls short of 2.0.

To illustrate this issue, suppose you conducted a study assessing the effectiveness of a cognitive-behavioral intervention to reduce angry blowups, as was done by Nugent (1991). Suppose the baseline mean was an average of two blowups per day and that during intervention, the mean fell to one blowup per day. Suppose further that the baseline standard deviation was one, indicating that although the baseline mean was two, a considerable portion of the baseline data points fell above and below that mean of two.

The two standard deviation procedure would indicate that your intervention mean (one) was only one standard deviation away from your baseline mean (two). This would not indicate statistical significance since that procedure requires that the intervention data reach two standard deviations away from your baseline mean. But your ES would be 1.0, which is considered large relative to published findings on the effects of clinical interventions in general (as we discussed in Chapter 16). If your graph showed visual significance, you might observe that based on your visual analysis, the intervention seems to be cutting the mean number of blowups in half (from two to one), and this might seem like a clinically meaningful change to you.

Because of your lack of statistical significance, you cannot rule out chance, or random fluctuations, as the explanation for your results. All you can do is note that because you have so few data points, you are unable to conduct a powerful test of statistical significance and that therefore replications are needed to assess the generalizability of your results and to see whether they were a fluke. You would not be able to claim that your large ES means that your intervention (and not chance) caused the reduction in blowups. But the large ES would mean that if your intervention did cause the change, it is a relatively powerful intervention—one that, in light of the high risk of a Type II error, should not be dismissed just because the data were not statistically significant.

We have limited our discussion of effect size in single-subject research to data patterns that fit the two standard deviation procedure. Calculating effect size is a lot more mathematically complex when your data require the celeration line or proportion/frequency procedure. The same issues of statistical power and Type II errors apply for those procedures as well. However, instead of attempting to calculate effect size when using those procedures, we suggest you simply focus on the change in the percentage of desired observations from baseline to intervention. If that amount of change seems to be substantively significant, and your graph is visually significant, the risk of a Type II error becomes extremely important, and the possibility that your intervention has strong effects should continue to be investigated in future research.

For example, suppose during 10 days of baseline a sixth-grade boy clowns around in class on 6 days. That would mean that 40% (4 out of 10 days) of the baseline observations were in the desired zone (not clowning). Suppose during 10 days of intervention with you (the school social worker), he clowns around only 3 days. That would mean an increase from 40% to 70% (7 out of 10 days) of observations in the desired zone. Looking that outcome up in Table I-1, you can see that with .40 in baseline and 10 observations in intervention, you need 8 intervention observations in the desired zone to have statistical significance. You had 1 fewer (7), and therefore do not have statistical significance. But with only 20 data points, your statistical power was only .25 (as shown in Table 17-1 in Chapter 17), and your probability of a Type II error in undertaking this study was therefore .75. Thus, it would be foolish (and perhaps tragic) to dismiss the potential efficacy of your intervention merely on the basis of significance testing—particularly in light of the fact that the proportion of days the boy clowned around during intervention (3) was half of what it was in baseline (6).

Again, you cannot generalize this finding, or claim that the change was not due to chance, but you should not dismiss the potential importance of the intervention either. The best conclusion might be to say that you have some tentative evidence that this intervention might be powerful, but that replication is needed to rule out chance as a plausible explanation and to see if the results generalize beyond this one case.

Because of the low statistical power of most single-subject studies, and the consequent high probability of Type II errors, it is important to try to replicate those studies and to aggregate their effect sizes. If, across replications, we consistently get results that are visually significant and that have clinically meaningful effect sizes, but that are not statistically significant in any individual study, we can interpret those replicated results to reflect an effective intervention, and we can attribute the lack of statistical significance to the low statistical power associated with having a small number of data points.

One mechanism for aggregating results across various single-subject studies involves calculating the mean ES (effect size). Using this mechanism, you would simply add up the ES of every study and then divide the sum by the number of studies. If your average (mean) ES turned out to be near or above the mean ES reported in various meta-analyses (.60 to .68 for comparing means, dividing by the baseline standard deviation), you might have reason to feel pretty good about the effectiveness of your intervention, assuming that the visual significance of the graphs was replicated fairly consistently.

Another purpose for aggregating effect sizes is to evaluate an entire service program. If, for example, an agency conducts a single-subject evaluation on a reasonably representative sample of its clients (such as every fifth client entering treatment during a particular time period), it can assess its overall agency effectiveness by aggregating the results of each individual evaluation. In addition to reporting the proportion of outcomes that were and were not visually significant, the agency could report its mean effect size as a way to estimate the degree of impact its services are making (assuming the visual analysis and research methodology permit inferences that agency services were indeed the cause of the observed effects).

Proportion Under Normal Curve Exceeded by ES Values

Assuming a normal distribution of control group scores, the figures in this table display the proportion of outcomes for control subjects that is worse than the mean outcome for experimental subjects for each specified ES value. For example, an ES of 1.0 means that the mean outcome for experimental subjects is one standard deviation better than the mean outcome for control subjects. In this table you can see that that particular ES (that is, 1.0, or one standard deviation) means that the average experimental subject's outcome was better than 84% of the outcomes for control subjects.

To simplify this table, we have not listed every possible ES value. If you want to find precise normal curve figures for exact ES values not listed in the table, you can consult the Z-table commonly found in introductory texts on descriptive statistics. Z-tables show what proportion of a normal curve is found above and below z scores. The ES values in this table are the same as z scores.

Below is a figure illustrating the meaning of the values in the table. It shows a normal curve. This normal curve represents the theoretical sampling distribution of outcomes for the population of people not receiving the experimental intervention. The shaded area under the curve represents the proportion of outcomes that is exceeded in the desired direction by (worse than) the experimental group mean. The unshaded area is the proportion of outcomes that is better than the experimental group mean. For negative effect sizes, the unshaded portion will be greater than the shaded portion, meaning that the experimental group did worse than the control group (indicating harmful intervention effects). For positive effect sizes, the shaded portion will be greater than the unshaded portion, indicating beneficial treatment effects.

(a) Positive ES

(b) Negative ES

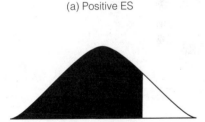

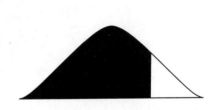

	POSITIVE ES VALUES		NEGATIVE ES VALUES
ES	PROPORTION UNDER NORMAL CURVE EXCEEDED	ES	PROPORTION UNDER NORMAL CURVE EXCEEDED
3.0	.9987	− 3.0	.0013
2.8	.9974	− 2.8	.0026
2.6	.9953	− 2.6	.0047
2.4	.9918	− 2.4	.0082
2.2	.9861	− 2.2	.0139
2.0	.9772	− 2.0	.0228
1.8	.9641	− 1.8	.0359
1.6	.9452	− 1.6	.0548
1.5	.9332	− 1.5	.0668
1.4	.9192	− 1.4	.0808
1.3	.9032	− 1.3	.0968
1.2	.8849	− 1.2	.1151
1.1	.8643	− 1.1	.1357
1.0	.8413	− 1.0	.1587
0.9	.8159	− 0.9	.1841
0.8	.7881	− 0.8	.2119
0.7	.7580	− 0.7	.2420
0.6	.7257	− 0.6	.2743
0.5	.6915	− 0.5	.3085
0.4	.6554	− 0.4	.3446
0.3	.6179	− 0.3	.3821
0.2	.5793	− 0.2	.4207
0.1	.5398	− 0.1	.4602
0.0	.5000		

Glossary

analysis of variance   A form of data analysis in which the variance of a dependent variable is examined for the whole sample and for separate subgroups created on the basis of some independent variable(s). See Chapter 17.

area probability sample   A form of multistage *cluster sample* in which geographic areas such as census blocks or tracts serve as the first-stage sampling unit. Units selected in the first stage of sampling are then listed—all the households on each selected block would be written down after a trip to the block—and such lists would be subsampled. See Chapter 8.

attributes   Characteristics of persons or things. See *variables* and Chapter 1.

available records   A source of data for a study, in which the information of concern has already been gathered by others before the study commences. For example, an evaluation of a statewide dropout prevention program may use available school records on dropout rates.

average   An ambiguous term generally suggesting typical or normal. The *mean, median,* and *mode* are specific examples of mathematical *averages*. See Chapter 15.

bias   (1) That quality of a measurement device that tends to result in a misrepresentation of what is being measured in a particular direction. For example, the questionnaire item "Don't you agree that the president is doing a good job?" would be *biased* in that it would generally encourage more favorable responses. See Chapter 6 for more on this topic. (2) The thing inside you that makes other people or groups seem consistently better or worse than they really are.

binomial variable   A variable that has only two attributes is binomial. *Gender* would be an example, having the attributes *male* and *female*.

bivariate analysis   The analysis of two variables simultaneously for the purpose of determining the empirical relationship between them. The construction of a simple percentage table or the computation of a simple correlation coefficient would be examples of *bivariate analyses*. See Chapter 15 for more on this topic.

census   An enumeration of the characteristics of some population. A census is often similar to a survey, with the difference that the *census* collects data from *all* members of the population and the survey is limited to a sample.

cluster sample   A multistage sample in which natural groups (*clusters*) are sampled initially, with the members of each selected group being subsampled afterward. For example, you might select a sample of U.S. colleges and universities from a directory, get lists of the students at all the selected schools, then draw samples of students from each. This procedure is discussed in Chapter 8. See also *area probability sample*.

codebook   The document used in data processing and analysis that tells the location of different data items in a data file. Typically, the codebook identifies the locations of data items and the meaning of the codes used to represent different attributes of variables. See Chapter 14 for more discussion and illustrations.

coding   The process whereby raw data are transformed into standardized form suitable for machine processing and analysis. See Chapter 14.

cohort study   A study in which some specific group is studied over time although data may be collected from different members in each set of observations. A study of the professional careers of students earning their social work degrees in 1990, in which questionnaires were sent every five years, for example, would be a cohort study. See Chapter 4.

conceptualization The mental process whereby fuzzy and imprecise notions (*concepts*) are made more specific and precise. So you want to study *prejudice*. What do you mean by *prejudice*? Are there different kinds of prejudice? What are they? See Chapter 4.

confidence interval The range of values within which a population parameter is estimated to lie. A survey, for example, may show 40% of a sample favoring Candidate A (poor devil). Although the best estimate of the support existing among all voters would also be 40%, we would not expect it to be exactly that. We might, therefore, compute a *confidence interval* (for example, from 35 to 45%) within which the actual percentage of the population probably lies. Note that it is necessary to specify a *confidence level* in connection with every *confidence interval*. See Chapter 8.

confidence level The estimated probability that a population parameter lies within a given *confidence interval*. Thus, we might be 95% *confident* that between 35% and 45% of all voters favor Candidate A. See Chapter 8.

conflict paradigm A view of social life that focuses on the attempts of individuals or groups to dominate one another or avoid being dominated. Marxist sociology is one example of the conflict paradigm.

construct validity The degree to which a measure relates to other variables as expected within a system of theoretical relationships. See Chapter 6.

content validity The degree to which a measure covers the range of meanings included within the concept. See Chapter 6.

contingency question A survey question that is to be asked only of *some* respondents, determined by their responses to some other question. For example, all respondents might be asked whether they belong to the Cosa Nostra, and only those who said yes would be asked how often they go to company meetings and picnics. The latter would be a *contingency question*. See Chapter 7 for illustrations of this topic.

contingency table A format for presenting the relationships among variables—in the form of percentage distributions. See Chapter 15 for several illustrations of it and for guides to making it.

control group In experimentation, a group of subjects to whom *no* experimental stimulus is administered and who should resemble the experimental group in all other respects. The comparison of the *control group* and the experimental group at the end of the experiment points to the effect of the experimental stimulus. See Chapter 9.

control variable A variable that is held constant in an attempt to further clarify the relationship between two other variables. Having discovered a relationship between education and prejudice, for example, we might hold gender constant by examining the relationship between education and prejudice among men only and then among women only. In this example, gender would be the *control variable*. See Chapter 15 to find out how important the proper use of control variables is in analysis.

cost-benefit analysis An assessment of program efficiency in which an attempt is made to monetize the benefits associated with a program's outcome, to see if those monetary benefits exceed program costs. See Chapter 18.

cost-effectiveness analysis An assessment of program efficiency in which the only monetary considerations are the costs of the program; the monetary benefits of the program's effects are not assessed. Cost-effectiveness analysis looks at the cost per unit of outcome, without monetizing the outcome. See Chapter 18.

criterion-related validity The degree to which a measure relates with some external criterion. For example, the validity of the college board is shown in their ability to predict the college success of students. See Chapter 6.

critical region Those values in the statistically significant zone of a theoretical sampling distribution. See Chapter 16.

cross-sectional study A study based on observations representing a single point in time. Contrasted with a *longitudinal study*.

curvilinear relationship A relationship between two variables that changes in nature at different values of the variables. For example, a curvilinear relationship might exist between amount of social work practice experience and practice effectiveness, particularly if we assume that practitioners with a moderate amount of experience are more effective than those with none and at least as effective as those nearing retirement.

deduction The logical model in which specific expectations of *hypotheses* are developed on the basis of general principles. Starting from the general principle that all deans are meanies, you might anticipate that *this* one won't let you change courses. That anticipation would be the result of *deduction*. See also *induction* and Chapter 2.

dependent variable That variable that is assumed to *depend* on or be caused by another (called the *independent variable*). If you find that income is partly a function of amount of formal education, income is being treated as a *dependent variable*.

descriptive statistics Statistical computations describing either the characteristics of a sample or the relationship among variables in a sample. *Descriptive statistics* merely summarize a set of sample observations, whereas *inferen-*

tial statistics move beyond the description of specific observations to make inferences about the larger population from which the sample observations were drawn.

deviant case sampling   A type of nonprobability sampling in which cases selected for observation are those thought not fitting the regular pattern. For example, the deviant cases might exhibit a much greater or lesser extent of something. See Chapter 12.

dichotomous variable   A variable having only two categories. See also *binomial variable.*

dimension   A specifiable aspect or facet of a concept.

direct behavioral observation   A source of data, or type of data collection, in which researchers watch what people do, rather than rely on what they say about themselves or what others say about them.

dispersion   The distribution of values around some central value, such as an *average*. The *range* is a simple example of a measure of *dispersion*. Thus, we may report that the *mean* age of a group is 37.9, and the range is from 12 to 89.

ecological fallacy   Erroneously drawing conclusions about individuals based solely on the observation of groups.

effect size   A statistic that portrays the strength of association between variables. Effect size statistics might refer to proportion of dependent variable variation explained or to the difference between the means of two groups divided by the standard deviation. See Chapter 16.

EPSEM   *Equal probability of selection method.* A sample design in which each member of a population has the same chance of being selected into the sample. See Chapter 8.

experimental design   A research method involving the rigorous controlling of an **independent variable,** called a "stimulus," in order to test hypotheses regarding the impact of that stimulus. This is accomplished by the establishment of nearly identical groups; the stimulus is applied to one (the *experimental group*) and withheld from the other (the *control group*).

external invalidity   Refers to the possibility that conclusions drawn from experimental results may not be generalizable to the "real" world. See Chapter 9 and also *internal invalidity.*

external validity   Refers to the extent to which we can generalize the findings of a study to settings and populations beyond the study conditions.

extraneous variable   See *control variable.*

external validity   Refers to the extent to which we can generalize the findings of a study to settings and populations beyond the study conditions. See Chapter 9.

face validity   That quality of an indicator that makes it seem a reasonable measure of some variable. That the frequency of church attendance is some indication of a person's religiosity seems to make sense without a lot of explanation. It has *face validity.*

frequency distribution   A description of the number of times the various attributes of a variable are observed in a sample. The report that 53% of a sample were men and 47% were women would be a simple example of a *frequency distribution*. Another example would be the report that 15 of the cities studied had populations under 10,000; 23 had populations between 10,000 and 25,000, and so forth.

generalizability   That quality of a research finding that justifies the inference that it represents something more than the specific observations on which it was based. Sometimes this involves the *generalization* of findings from a sample to a population. Other times it is a matter of concepts: if you are able to discover why people commit burglaries, can you *generalize* that discovery to other crimes as well?

generalization of effects   A rival explanation in multiple-baseline designs that occurs when an intervention that is intended to apply to only one behavior or setting affects other behaviors or settings that are still in baseline. See Chapter 10.

generalize   To infer that the findings of a particular study represent causal processes or apply to settings or populations beyond the study conditions.

Hawthorne effect   A term coined in reference to a series of productivity studies at the Hawthorne plant of the Western Electric Company in Chicago, Illinois. The researchers discovered that their presence affected the behavior of the workers being studied. The term now refers to any impact of research on the subject of study. See Chapter 9.

hypothesis   An expectation about the nature of things derived from a theory. It is a statement of something that ought to be observed in the real world if the theory is correct. See *deduction* and also Chapters 2 and 3.

hypothesis testing   The determination of whether the expectations that a hypothesis represents are, indeed, found to exist in the real world. See Chapters 2 and 4.

idiographic   (1) An approach to explanation in which you attempt to explain a single case fully, using as many idiosyncratic, explanatory factors as may be necessary. You might explain why your Uncle Ed is such a bigot by talking about what happened to him that summer at the beach, what his college roommate did to him, etc. This kind of explanation won't necessarily help us understand bigotry in general, but we'd feel we really understood your Uncle Ed. By contrast, see *nomothetic*.

independent variable   A variable whose values are *not* problematical in an analysis but are taken as simply given. An *independent variable* is presumed to cause or determine a *dependent variable*. If we discover that religiosity is partly a function of gender—women are more religious than men—gender is the *independent variable* and *religiosity* is the dependent variable. Note that any given variable might be treated as *independent* in one part of an analysis and dependent in another part of the analysis. *Religiosity* might become an *independent variable* in the explanation of crime.

index   A type of composite measure that summarizes several specific observations and represents some more general dimension. See Chapter 7.

induction   The logical model in which general principles are developed from specific observations. Having noted that Jews and Catholics are more likely to vote Democratic than Protestants are, you might conclude that religious minorities in the United States are more affiliated with the Democratic Party and explain why. That would be an example of *induction*. See also *deduction* and Chapter 2.

inferential statistics   The body of statistical computations relevant to making inferences from findings based on sample observations to some larger population. See also *descriptive statistics* and Chapters 16 and 17.

informant   Someone well versed in the social phenomenon that you wish to study and who is willing to tell you what he or she knows. If you were planning participant observation among the members of a religious sect, you would do well to make friends with someone who already knows about them—possibly a member of the sect—who could give you some background information about them. Not to be confused with a *respondent*.

internal consistency reliability   A practical and commonly used approach to assessing reliability that examines the homogeneity of a measurement instrument by dividing the instrument into equivalent halves and then calculating the correlation of the scores of the two halves. See Chapter 6.

internal invalidity   Refers to the possibility that the conclusions drawn from experimental results may not accurately reflect what went on in the experiment itself. See Chapter 9 and also *external invalidity*.

internal validity   The degree to which an effect observed in an experiment was actually produced by the experimental *stimulus* and not due to other factors.

interobserver reliability   See *interrater reliability*.

interpretation   A technical term used in connection with the elaboration model. It represents the research outcome in which a *control variable* is discovered to be the mediating factor through which an *independent variable* has its effect on a *dependent variable*. See Chapter 15.

interpretivism   An approach to social research that focuses on gaining an empathic understanding of how people feel inside, seeking to interpret individuals' everyday experiences, deeper meanings and feelings, and idiosyncratic reasons for their behaviors.

interrater reliability   The extent of consistency among different observers in their judgments, as reflected in the percentage of agreement or degree of correlation in their independent ratings.

interrupted time-series with a nonequivalent control group time-series design   The most common form of multiple time-series design, in which an experimental group and a control group are measured at multiple points in time before and after an intervention is introduced to the control group. See Chapter 9.

intersubjectivity   That quality of science (and other inquiries) whereby two different researchers, studying the same problem, arrive at the same conclusion. Ultimately, this is the practical criterion for what is called *objectivity*. We agree that something is "objectively true" if independent observers with different subjective orientations conclude that it is "true." See Chapter 2.

interval measure   A level of measurement describing a variable whose attributes are rank-ordered and have equal distances between adjacent attributes. The Fahrenheit temperature scale is an example of this, since the distance between 17° and 18° is the same as that between 89° and 90°. See also *nominal measure, ordinal measure,* and *ratio measure*. See Chapter 6.

interview   A data collection encounter in which one person (an interviewer) asks questions of another (a *respondent*). *Interviews* may be conducted face to face or by telephone. See Chapters 11 and 12 for more information on interviewing.

inverse relationship   See *negative relationship*.

judgmental sample   A type of *nonprobability sample* in which you select the units to be observed on the basis of your own *judgment* about which ones will be the most useful or representative. Another name for this is *purposive sample*. See Chapter 8 for more details.

latent content   As used in connection with content analysis, the underlying meaning of communications as distinguished from their *manifest content*. See Chapter 12.

level of significance   In the context of *tests of statistical significance,* the degree of likelihood that an observed, empirical relationship could be attributable to sampling error. A relationship is *significant* at the .05 *level* if the likelihood of its being only a function of sampling error is no greater than 5 out of 100. See Chapter 16.

Likert scale   A type of composite measure developed by Rensis Likert in an attempt to improve the levels of measurement in social research through the use of standardized response categories in survey *questionnaires. Likert* items are those using such response categories as strongly agree, agree, disagree, and strongly disagree. Such items may be used in the construction of true *Likert scales* and may also be used in the construction of other types of composite measures. See Chapter 7.

longitudinal study   A study design involving the collection of data at different points in time, as contrasted with a *cross-sectional study.*

manifest content   In connection with content analysis, the concrete terms contained in a communication, as distinguished from *latent content.* See Chapter 12.

matching   In connection with experiments, the procedure whereby pairs of subjects are *matched* on the basis of their similarities on one or more variables, and one member of the pair is assigned to the experimental group and the other to the *control group.* See Chapter 9.

mean   An *average,* computed by summing the values of several observations and dividing by the number of observations. If you now have a grade point average of 4.0 based on 10 courses, and you get an F in this course, your new grade point (mean) average will be 3.6.

median   Another *average,* representing the value of the "middle" case in a rank-ordered set of observations. If the ages of five men are 16, 17, 20, 54, and 88, the *median* would be 20. (The *mean* would be 39.)

meta-analysis   A procedure for calculating the average strength of association between variables (that is, the mean effect size) across previously completed research studies in a particular field. See Chapter 16.

mode   Still another *average,* representing the most frequently observed value or attribute. If a sample contains 1000 Protestants, 275 Catholics, and 33 Jews, *Protestant* is the *modal* category. See Chapter 15 for more thrilling disclosures about averages.

multiple time-series designs   A form of time-series analysis in which both an experimental group and a non-equivalent control group are measured at multiple points in time before and after an intervention is introduced to the experimental group. See Chapter 9.

multivariate analysis   The analysis of the simultaneous relationships among several variables. Examining simultaneously the effects of age, sex, and social class on religiosity would be an example of *multivariate analysis.* See Chapters 15 and 17.

needs assessment   Systematically researching diagnostic questions for program planning purposes. For example, community residents might be surveyed in order to assess their need for new child care services. See Chapter 18.

negative relationship   A relationship between two variables in which one variable increases in value as the other variable decreases in value. For example, we might expect to find a negative relationship between the level of utilization of community-based aftercare services and rehospitalization rates.

nominal measure   A level of measurement describing a variable whose different attributes are *only* different, as distinguished from *ordinal, interval,* or *ratio* measures. Gender would be an example of a nominal measure. See Chapter 6.

nomothetic   An approach to explanation in which you attempt to discover factors that can offer a general, though imperfect, explanation of some phenomenon. For example, we might note that education seems to reduce prejudice in general. Even though we recognize some educated people are prejudiced and some uneducated people are not, we have learned some of what causes prejudice or tolerance in general. By contrast, see *idiographic.*

nonequivalent control group design   A quasi-experimental design in which the researcher finds two existing groups that appear to be similar and measures change on a dependent variable before and after an intervention is introduced to one of the groups. See Chapter 9.

nonparametric tests   Tests of statistical significance that have been created for use when not all of the assumptions of parametric statistics can be met. Chi-square is the most commonly used nonparametric test. See Chapters 16 and 17.

nonprobability sample   A sample selected in some fashion other than those suggested by probability theory. Examples include *judgmental (purposive), quota,* and *snowball samples.* See Chapters 8 and 12.

nonsampling error   Those imperfections of data quality that are a result of factors other than sampling error. Examples include misunderstandings of questions by respondents, erroneous recordings by interviewers and coders, keypunch errors, and so forth.

null hypothesis   In connection with *hypothesis testing* and *tests of statistical significance,* that *hypothesis* that suggests there is no relationship between the variables under study.

You may conclude that the two variables *are* related after having statistically rejected the *null hypothesis*.

objectivity Doesn't exist. See *intersubjectivity*.

one-group pretest-posttest design A preexperimental design, with low internal validity, that assesses a dependent variable before and after a stimulus is introduced, but does not attempt to control for alternative explanations of any changes in scores that are observed. See Chapter 9.

one-shot case study A preexperimental research design, with low internal validity, that simply measures a single group of subjects on a dependent variable at one point in time after they have been exposed to a stimulus. See Chapter 9.

operational definition The concrete and specific *definition* of something in terms of the *operations* by which observations are to be categorized. The *operational definition* of "earning an A in this course" might be "correctly answering at least 90% of the final exam questions." See Chapter 5.

operationalization One step beyond *conceptualization*. *Operationalization* is the process of developing *operational definitions*.

ordinal measure A level of measurement describing a variable whose attributes may be *rank-ordered* along some dimension. An example would be *socioeconomic status* as composed of the attributes high, medium, low. See also *nominal measure, interval measure,* and *ratio measure*. See Chapter 6.

panel studies Longitudinal studies in which data are collected from the same sample (the panel) at several points in time. See Chapter 4.

paradigm (1) A model or frame of reference that shapes our observations and understandings. For example, "functionalism" leads us to examine society in terms of the functions served by its constituent parts, whereas "interactionism" leads us to focus attention on the ways people deal with each other face to face and arrive at shared meanings for things. (2) Almost a quarter.

parallel-forms reliability Consistency of measurement between two equivalent measurement instruments. See Chapter 6.

parametric tests Tests of statistical significance that assume that at least one of the variables being studied has an interval or ratio level of measurement, that the sample distribution of the relevant parameters of those variables is normal, and that the different groups being compared have been randomly selected and are independent of one another. Commonly used parametric tests are the *t*-test, analysis of variance, and the Pearson product-moment correlation. See Chapter 17.

placebo control group design An experimental design that controls for placebo effects by randomly assigning subjects to an experimental group and two control groups and exposing one of the control groups to a stimulus designed to resemble the special attention that subjects in the experimental group receive. See *placebo effects*.

placebo effects Changes in a dependent variable that are caused by the awareness of subjects in an experimental group that they are receiving something special. These changes would not occur if they received the experimental stimulus without that awareness. See Chapter 9.

positive relationship A relationship between two variables in which one variable increases in value as the other variable increases in value (or one decreases as the other decreases). For example, we might expect to find a positive relationship between rate of unemployment and extent of homelessness.

positivism A paradigm introduced by August Comte, which held that social behavior could be studied and understood in a rational, scientific manner—in contrast to explanations based in religion or superstition. Sometimes this view is extended to an assumption that human beings act rationally in their daily lives. Whereas one or another version of positivism has dominated most of social science history, it is now coming under increased challenge.

postmodernism An extreme form of *interpretivism* that rejects the notion of an objective social reality.

postpositivism A view stressing that observation and measurement cannot be as purely objective as the postivistic image of science implies.

posttest-only control group design A variation of the classical experimental design that avoids the possible testing effects associated with pretesting by testing only after the experimental group receives the stimulus, based on the assumption that the process of random assignment provides for equivalence between the experimental and control groups on the dependent variable prior to the exposure to the stimulus. See also *pretest-posttest control group design*.

posttest-only design with nonequivalent groups A preexperimental design involving two groups that may not be comparable, in which the dependent variable is assessed after the independent variable is introduced for one of the groups. See Chapter 9.

PPS *Probability proportionate to size*. This refers to a type of multistage *cluster sample* in which clusters are selected, not with equal probabilities (see *EPSEM*) but with *probabilities proportionate* to their *sizes*—as measured by the number of units to be subsampled. See Chapter 8.

pretest-posttest control group design   The classical experimental design in which subjects are assigned randomly to an experimental group that is exposed to a stimulus and to a control group that is not exposed to the stimulus. Each group is tested on the dependent variable before and after the experimental group is exposed to the stimulus. See Chapter 9.

probability sample   The general term for a sample selected in accord with *probability* theory, typically involving some random-selection mechanism. Specific types of *probability samples* include *area probability sample, EPSEM, PPS, simple random sample,* and *systematic sample.* See Chapters 8.

probe   A technique employed in interviewing to solicit a more complete answer to a question. It is a nondirective phrase or question used to encourage a respondent to elaborate on an answer. Examples include "Anything more?" and "How is that?" See Chapters 11 and 12 for a discussion of interviewing.

purposive sample   See *judgmental sample* and Chapter 12.

purposive sampling   Selecting a sample of observations that the researcher believes will yield the most comprehensive understanding of the subject of study, based on the researcher's intuitive feel for the subject that comes from extended observation and reflection. See Chapters 8 and 12.

qualitative analysis   The nonnumerical examination and interpretation of observations for the purpose of discovering underlying meanings and patterns of relationships. This is most typical of field research and historical research. See Chapter 12.

qualitative methods   Researcher methods that emphasize depth of understanding and the deeper meanings of human experience, and that are used with the aim of generating theoretically richer, albeit more tentative, observations. Commonly used qualitative methods include participant observation, direct observation, and unstructured or intensive interviewing. See Chapters 1, 12, and 13.

quantitative analysis   The numerical representation and manipulation of observations for the purpose of describing and explaining the phenomena that those observations reflect. See Chapter 14 especially, and also the remainder of Part 5.

quantitative methods   Research methods that emphasize precise, objective, and generalizable findings.

questionnaire   A document containing *questions* and other types of items designed to solicit information appropriate to analysis. *Questionnaires* are used primarily in sur-

vey research and also in experiments, field research, and other modes of observation. See Chapters 7 and 11.

quota sample   A type of *nonprobability sample* in which units are selected into the sample on the basis of prespecified characteristics, so that the total sample will have the same distribution of characteristics as are assumed to exist in the population being studied. See Chapter 8.

r^2 The proportion of variation in the dependent variable that is explained by the independent variable. See Chapter 16.

random error   A measurement error that has no consistent pattern of effects and that reduces the reliability of measurement. For example, asking questions that respondents do not understand will yield inconsistent (random) answers. See Chapter 6.

randomization   A technique for assigning experimental subjects to experimental and *control groups: randomly.* See Chapter 9.

range   A measure of *dispersion* composed of the highest and lowest values of a variable in some set of observations. In your class, for example, the *range* of ages might be from 17 to 37.

ratio measure   A level of measurement describing a variable whose attributes have all the qualities of *nominal, ordinal,* and *interval measures* and in addition are based on a "true zero" point. Age would be an example of a *ratio* measure. See Chapter 6.

reactivity   A process in which change in a dependent variable is induced by research procedures. See Chapter 9.

recursive   The "doubling-back" quality whereby the result of a process affects the process that caused it. For example, learning what causes a particular social problem may lead to new social policies that alter the social problem as we understood it.

reductionism   A fault of some researchers: a strict limitation (reduction) of the kinds of concepts to the considered relevant to the phenomenon under study.

reification   The process of regarding as real things that are not real.

reliability   That quality of measurement method that suggests that the same data would have been collected each time in repeated observations of the same phenomenon. In the context of a survey, we would expect that the question "Did you attend church last week?" would have higher reliability than the question "About how many times have you attended church in your life?" This is not to be confused with *validity.* See Chapter 6.

replication Generally, the duplication of an experiment to expose or reduce error. It is also a technical term used in connection with the elaboration model, referring to the elaboration outcome in which the initially observed relationship between two variables persists when a *control variable* is held constant. See Chapters 9, 10, and 15. See Chapter 1 and *intersubjectivity*.

representativeness That quality of a sample of having the same distribution of characteristics as the population from which it was selected. By implication, descriptions and explanations derived from an analysis of the sample may be assumed to *represent* similar ones in the population. *Representativeness* is enhanced by *probability sampling* and provides for *generalizability* and the use of *inferential statistics*. See Chapter 8.

respondent A person who provides data for analysis by responding to a survey *questionnaire*.

response rate The number of persons participating in a survey divided by the number selected in the sample, in the form of a percentage. This is also called the completion rate or, in self-administered surveys, the return rate: the percentage of *questionnaires* sent out that are returned. See Chapter 11.

sampling frame That list or quasi-list of units composing a population from which a sample is selected. If the sample is to be *representative* of the population, it is essential that the *sampling frame* include all (or nearly all) members of the population. See Chapter 8.

sampling interval The standard distance between elements selected from a population for a sample. See Chapter 8.

sampling ratio The proportion of elements in the population that are selected to be in a sample. See Chapter 8.

scale A type of composite measure composed of several items that have a logical or empirical structure among them. See Chapter 7.

secondary analysis A form of research in which the data collected and processed by one researcher are reanalyzed—often for a different purpose—by another. This is especially appropriate in the case of survey data. Data archives are repositories or libraries for the storage and distribution of data for *secondary analysis*.

self-report scales A source of data in which research subjects all respond in writing to the same list of written questions or statements that has been devised to measure a particular construct. For example, a self-report scale to measure marital satisfaction might ask how often one is annoyed with one's spouse, is proud of the spouse, has fun with the spouse, and so on.

simple interrupted time-series design A quasi-experimental design in which no comparison group is utilized and which attempts to develop causal inferences based on a comparison of trends over multiple measurements before and after an intervention is introduced. See Chapter 9.

simple random sample A type of *probability sample* in which the units composing a population are assigned numbers, a set of *random* numbers is then generated, and the units having those numbers are included in the sample. Although probability theory and the calculations it provides assume this basic sampling method, it is seldom used for practical reasons. An equivalent alternative is the *systematic sample* (with a random start). See Chapter 8.

snowball sample A *nonprobability sampling* method often employed in field research. Each person interviewed may be asked to suggest additional people for interviewing. See Chapters 8 and 12.

Solomon four-group design An experimental design that assesses testing effects by randomly assigning subjects to four groups, introducing the stimulus to two of the groups, conducting both pretesting and posttesting on one group that receives the stimulus and one group that does not, and conducting posttesting only on the other two groups. See Chapter 9.

specification Generally, the process through which concepts are made more specific. It is also a technical term used in connection with the elaboration model, representing the elaboration outcome in which an initially observed relationship between two variables is replicated among some subgroups created by the *control variable* and not among others. In such a situation, you will have *specified* the conditions under which the original relationship exists: for example, among men but not among women. See Chapter 15.

standard deviation A descriptive statistic that portrays the dispersion of values around the mean. It is the square root of the averaged squared differences between each value and the mean. See Chapter 15.

static-group comparison design A cross-sectional design for comparing different groups on a dependent variable at one point in time. The validity of this design will be influenced by the extent to which it contains multivariate controls for alternative explanations for differences among the groups. See Chapter 9.

statistical power analysis Assessment of the probability of avoiding Type II errors. See Chapter 17.

statistical significance A general term referring to the *un*likeliness that relationships observed in a sample could be attributed to sampling error alone. See *tests of statistical significance* and Chapter 16.

stratification The grouping of the units composing a population into homogenous groups (or *strata*) before sampling. This procedure, which may be used in conjunction with *simple random, systematic,* or *cluster sampling,* improves the *representativeness* of a sample, at least in terms of the *stratification* variables. See Chapter 8.

substantive significance The importance, or meaningfulness, of a finding from a practical standpoint.

systematic error An error in measurement with a consistent pattern of effects. For example, when child welfare workers ask abusive parents whether they have been abusing their children, they may get answers that are consistently untrue due to a systematic bias on the part of parents who do not want to admit to abusive behavior. This is in contrast to *random error,* which has no consistent pattern of effects. See Chapter 6.

systematic sample A type of *probability sample* in which every *k*th unit in a list is selected for inclusion in the sample: for example, every 25th student in the college directory of students, *k* is computed by dividing the size of the population by the desired sample size and is called the sampling interval. Within certain constraints, *systematic sampling* is a functional equivalent of *simple random sampling* and usually easier to do. Typically, the first unit is selected at random. See Chapter 8.

***t*-test** A test of the statistical significance of the difference between the means of two groups. See Chapter 17.

test-retest reliability Consistency, or stability, of measurement over time. See Chapter 6.

tests of statistical significance A class of statistical computations that indicate the likelihood that the relationship observed between variables in a sample can be attributed to sampling error only. See *inferential statistics* and Chapter 16.

theoretical sampling distribution The distribution of outcomes produced by an infinite number of randomly drawn samples or random subdivisions of a sample. This distribution identifies the proportion of times that each outcome of a study could be expected to occur due to chance. See Chapter 16.

time-series designs A set of quasi-experimental designs in which multiple observations of a dependent variable are conducted before and after an intervention is introduced. See Chapter 9.

trend studies Longitudinal studies that monitor a given characteristic of some population over time. An example would be annual canvasses of schools of social work to identify trends over time in the number of students specializing in direct practice, generalist practice, and administration and planning. See Chapter 4.

triangulation The use of more than one imperfect data collection alternative in which each option is vulnerable to different potential sources of error. For example, instead of relying exclusively on a client's self-report of how often a particular target behavior occurred during a specified period, a significant other (teacher, cottage parent, and so on) is asked to monitor the behavior as well.

Type I error An error that we risk whenever we reject the null hypothesis. It occurs when we reject a true null hypothesis. See Chapter 16.

Type II error An error that we risk whenever we fail to reject the null hypothesis. It occurs when we fail to reject a false null hypothesis.

units of analysis The *what* or *whom* being studied. In social science research, the most typical units of analysis are individual people. See Chapter 4.

univariate analysis The analysis of a single variable for purposes of description. *Frequency distributions, averages,* and measures of *dispersion* would be examples of *univariate analysis,* as distinguished from *bivariate* and *multivariate analysis.* See Chapter 15.

validity A descriptive term used of a measure that accurately reflects the concept that it is intended to measure. For example, your IQ would seem a more *valid* measure of your intelligence than would the number of hours you spend in the library. It is important to realize that the ultimate *validity* of a measure can never be proven. Yet, we may agree to its relative *validity, content validity, construct validity, internal validation,* and *external validation.* This must not be confused with *reliability.* See Chapter 6.

variables Logical groupings of *attributes.* The variable gender is made up of the attributes *male* and *female.*

weighting A procedure employed in connection with sampling whereby units selected with unequal probabilities are assigned weights in such a manner as to make the sample *representative* of the population from which it was selected. See Chapter 8.

Bibliography

Acker, J., Barry, K., and Esseveld, J.: 1983 "Objectivity and Truth: Problems in Doing Feminist Research," *Women's Studies International Forum, 6,* 423–435.

Adler, Patricia A., and Adler, Peter: 1994 "Observational Techniques," in Norman K. Denzin and Yvonna S. Lincoln (eds.), *Handbook of Qualitative Research.* Thousand Oaks, CA: Sage, pp. 377–392.

Allen, Katherine R., and Walker, Alexis J.: 1992 "A Feminist Analysis of Interviews with Elderly Mothers and Their Daughters," in Jane Gilgun, Kerry Daly, and Gerald Handel (eds.), *Qualitative Methods in Family Research.* Thousand Oaks, CA: Sage, pp. 198–214.

Altheide, David L., and Johnson, John M.: 1994 "Criteria for Assessing Interpretive Validity in Qualitative Research," in Norman K. Denzin and Yvonna S. Lincoln (eds.), *Handbook of Qualitative Research.* Thousand Oaks, CA: Sage, pp. 485–499.

Aneshenshel, Carol S., Becerra, Rosina M., Fiedler, Eve P., and Schuler, Roberleigh A.: 1989 "Participation of Mexican American Female Adolescents in a Longitudinal Panel Survey," *Public Opinion Quarterly, 53* (Winter), 548–562.

Asch, Solomon E.: 1958 "Effects of Group Pressure upon the Modification and Distortion of Judgments," in Eleanor E. Maccoby, Theodore M. Newcomb, and Eugene L. Hartley (eds.), *Readings in Social Psychology,* 3rd ed. New York: Holt, Rinehart and Winston, pp. 174–183.

Babbie, Earl R.: 1966 "The Third Civilization," *Review of Religious Research* (Winter), 101–102.
1985 *You Can Make a Difference.* New York: St. Martin's Press.

Banfield, Edward: 1968 *The Unheavenly City: The Nature and Future of Our Urban Crisis.* Boston: Little, Brown.

Barlow, David H., and Hersen, Michel: 1984 *Single Case Experimental Designs: Strategies for Studying Behavior Change,* 2nd ed. New York: Pergamon Press.

Bartko, John J., Carpenter, William T., and McGlashan, Thomas H.: 1988 "Statistical Issues in Long-Term Follow-Up Studies," *Schizophrenia Bulletin, 14* (4), 575–587.

Baxter, Ellen, and Hopper, Kim: 1982 "The New Mendicancy: Homeless in New York City," *American Journal of Orthopsychiatry, 52* (3), 393–407.

Belcher, John: 1991 "Understanding the Process of Social Drift Among the Homeless: A Qualitative Analysis," paper presented at the Research Conference on Qualitative Methods in Social Work Practice Research, Nelson A. Rockefeller Institute of Government, State University of New York at Albany, N.Y., August 24.

Bellah, Robert N.: 1970 "Christianity and Symbolic Realism," *Journal for the Scientific Study of Religion, 9,* 89–96.
1974 "Comment on the Limits of Symbolic Realism," *Journal for the Scientific Study of Religion, 13,* 487–489.

Beveridge, W. I. B.: 1950 *The Art of Scientific Investigation.* New York: Vintage Books.

Billups, James O., and Julia, Maria C.: 1987 "Changing Profile of Social Work Practice: A Content Analysis," *Social Work Research and Abstracts, 23* (4), 17–22.

Black, Donald: 1970 "Production of Crime Rates," *American Sociological Review, 35* (August), 733–748.

Blalock, Hubert M.: 1972   *Social Statistics*. New York: McGraw-Hill.

Blaunstein, Albert, and Zangrando, Robert (eds.): 1970   *Civil Rights and the Black American*. New York: Washington Square Press.

Bloom, Martin, and Fischer, Joel: 1982   *Evaluating Practice: Guidelines for the Accountable Professional*. Englewood Cliffs, NJ: Prentice Hall.

Blythe, Betty J., and Briar, Scott: 1987   "Direct Practice Effectiveness," *Encyclopedia of Social Work*, 18th ed. Silver Spring, MD: National Association of Social Workers, vol. 1, pp. 399–408.

Bogdan, Robert, and Taylor, Steven J.: 1990   "Looking at the Bright Side: A Positive Approach to Qualitative Policy and Evaluation Research," *Qualitative Sociology, 13*(2), 183–192.

Booth, C.: 1970   *The Life and Labour of the People of London*. New York: AMS Press. (Original work published 1891–1903)

Botein, B.: 1965   "The Manhattan Bail Project: Its Impact in Criminology and the Criminal Law Process," *Texas Law Review, 43*, 319–331.

Boyd, L., Hylton, J., and Price, S.: 1978   "Computers in Social Work Practice: A Review," *Social Work, 23*(5), 368–371.

Breuer, Josef, and Freud, Sigmund: [1895] 1957   "Studies in Hysteria," in *The Standard Edition of the Complete Psychological Works of Sigmund Freud*, vol. 2. London: Hogarth Press.

Briar, Scott: 1973   "Effective Social Work Intervention in Direct Practice: Implications for Education," in *Facing the Challenge: Plenary Session Papers from the 19th Annual Program Meeting*, Council on Social Work Education, pp. 17–30.
1987   "Direct Practice: Trends and Issues," *Encyclopedia of Social Work*, 18th ed. Silver Spring, MD: National Association of Social Workers, vol. 1, pp. 393–398.

Brownlee, K. A.: 1975   "A Note on the Effects of Nonresponse on Surveys," *Journal of the American Statistical Association, 52*(227), 29–32.

Buckingham, R., Lack, S., Mount, B., MacLean, L., and Collins, J.: 1976   "Living with the Dying," *Canadian Medical Association Journal, 115*, 1211–1215.

Burnette, Denise: 1994   "Managing Chronic Illness Alone in Late Life: Sisyphus at Work," in Catherine Reissman (ed.), *Qualitative Studies in Social Work Research*. Thousand Oaks, CA: Sage, pp. 5–27

Campbell, D. T.: 1971   ·"Methods for the Experimenting Society," paper presented at the meeting of the Eastern Psychological Association, New York, and at the meeting of the American Psychological Association, Washington, DC.

Campbell, Donald, and Stanley, Julian: 1963   *Experimental and Quasi-Experimental Designs for Research*. Chicago: Rand McNally.

Campbell, Patricia B.: 1983   "The Impact of Societal Biases on Research Methods," in Barbara L. Richardson and Jeana Wirtenberg (eds.), *Sex Role Research*. New York: Praeger, pp. 197–213.

Carmines, Edward G., and Zeller, Richard A.: 1979   *Reliability and Validity Assessment*. Beverly Hills, CA: Sage.

Census Bureau: See U.S. Bureau of the Census.

Chaffee, Steven, and Sun Yuel Choe: 1980   "Time of Decision and Media Use During the Ford-Carter Campaign," *Public Opinion Quarterly* (Spring), 53–69.

Chronicle of Higher Education: "Scholar Who Submitted Bogus Article to Journals May Be Disciplined," November 2, 1988, pp. A1, A7.

Cohen, Jacob: 1977   *Statistical Power Analysis for the Behavioral Sciences*. New York: Academic Press.

Coleman, James: 1966   *Equality of Educational Opportunity*. Washington, DC: U.S. Government Printing Office.

Compton, Beulah R., and Galaway, Burt: 1984   *Social Work Processes*. Homewood, IL: Dorsey Press.

Comstock, Donald: 1980   "Dimensions of Influence in Organizations," *Pacific Sociological Review* (January), 67–84.

Cook, Thomas D., and Campbell, Donald T.: 1979   *Quasi-Experimentation: Design and Analysis Issues for Field Settings*. Chicago: Rand McNally.

Cooper-Stephenson, Cynthia, and Theologides, Athanasios: 1981   "Nutrition in Cancer: Physicians' Knowledge, Opinions, and Educational Needs," *Journal of the American Dietetic Association* (May), 472–476.

Coulton, Claudia, Pandey, Shanta, and Chow, Julia: 1990   "Concentration of Poverty and the Changing Ecology of Low-Income, Urban Neighborhoods: An Analysis of the Cleveland Area," *Social Work Research and Abstracts, 26*(4), 5–16.

Cowger, Charles D.: 1984   "Statistical Significance Tests: Scientific Ritualism or Scientific Method?" *Social Service Review, 58*(3), 358–372.

1985 "Author's Reply," *Social Service Review,* 59(3), 520–522.

1987 "Correcting Misuse Is the Best Defense of Statistical Tests of Significance," *Social Service Review,* 61(1), 170–172.

Crawford, Kent S., Thomas, Edmund D., and Fink, Jeffrey J.: 1980 "Pygmalion at Sea: Improving the Work Effectiveness of Low Performers," *Journal of Applied Behavioral Science* (October–December), 482–505.

Cummerton, J.: 1983 "A Feminist Perspective on Research: What Does It Help Us to See?" Paper presented at the Annual Program Meeting of the Council on Social Work Education, Fort Worth, Texas.

Dahlstrom, W. Grant, and Welsh, George S.: 1960 *An MMPI Handbook.* Minneapolis: University of Minnesota Press.

Dallas Morning News: "Welfare Study Withholds Benefits from 800 Texans," February 11, 1990, p. 1.

Daly, Kerry: 1992 "The Fit Between Qualitative Research and Characteristics of Families," in Jane Gilgun, Kerry Daly, and Gerald Handel (eds.), *Qualitative Methods in Family Research.* Thousand Oaks, CA: Sage, pp. 3–11.

Davis, Fred: 1973 "The Martian and the Convert: Ontological Polarities in Social Research," *Urban Life, 2*(3): 333–343.

DeFleur, Lois: 1975 "Biasing Influences on Drug Arrest Records: Implications for Deviance Research," *American Sociological Review* (February), 88–103.

De Maria, W.: 1981 "Empiricism: An Impoverished Philosophy for Social Work Research," *Australian Social Work, 34,* 3–8.

Denzin, Norman K., and Lincoln, Yvonna S.: 1994 *Handbook of Qualitative Research.* Thousand Oaks, CA: Sage, 1994.

Dillman, Don A.: 1978 *Mail and Telephone Surveys: The Total Design Method.* New York: Wiley.

Donald, Marjorie N.: 1960 "Implications of Nonresponse for the Interpretation of Mail Questionnaire Data," *Public Opinion Quarterly, 24*(1), 99–114.

DuBois, B.: 1983 "Passionate Scholarship: Notes on Values, Knowing and Method in Feminist Social Science," in G. Bowles and R. Duelli-Klein (eds.), *Theories of Women's Studies.* London: Routledge & Kegan Paul, pp. 105–116.

Duelli-Klein, R.: 1983 "How to Do What We Want to Do: Thoughts About Feminist Methodology," in G. Bowles and R. Duelli-Klein (eds.), *Theories in Women's Studies.* London: Routledge & Kegan Paul, pp. 88–104.

Durkheim, Emile: [1893] 1964 *The Division of Labor in Society,* George Simpson (trans.). New York: Free Press.

[1897] 1951 *Suicide.* Glencoe, IL: Free Press.

Eichler, Margrit: 1988 *Nonsexist Research Methods.* Boston: Allen & Unwin.

Einstein, Albert: 1940 "The Fundamentals of Theoretical Physics," *Science* (May 24), 487.

England, Suzanne E.: 1994 "Modeling Theory from Fiction and Autobiography," in Catherine K. Reissman (ed.), *Qualitative Studies in Social Work Research.* Thousand Oaks, CA: Sage, pp. 190–213.

Epstein, Irwin: 1985 "Quantitative and Qualitative Methods," in Richard M. Grinnell (ed.), *Social Work Research and Evaluation.* Itasca, IL: Peacock, pp. 263–274.

Fischer, Joel: 1973 "Is Social Work Effective: A Review," *Social Work, 18*(1), 5–20.

1978 *Effective Casework Practice: An Eclectic Approach.* New York: McGraw-Hill.

1990 "Problems and Issues in Meta-Analysis," in Lynn Videka-Sherman and William J. Reid (eds.), *Advances in Clinical Social Work Research.* Silver Spring, MD: NASW Press, pp. 297–325.

Gage, N.: 1989 "The Paradigm Wars and Their Aftermath: A 'Historical' Sketch of Research and Teaching Since 1989," *Educational Research, 18,* 4–10.

Gallup, George: 1984 "Where Parents Go Wrong," *San Francisco Chronicle* (December 13), p. 7.

Garant, Carol: 1980 "Stalls in the Therapeutic Process," *American Journal of Nursing* (December), 2166–2167.

Gilgun, Jane: 1991 "Hand into Glove: The Grounded Theory Approach and Social Work Practice Research," paper presented at the Research Conference on Qualititative Methods in Social Work Practice Research, Nelson A. Rockefeller Institute of Government, State University of New York at Albany, N.Y., August 24.

Gilgun, Jane, Daly, Kerry, and Handel, Gerald (eds.): 1992 *Qualitative Methods in Family Research.* Thousand Oaks, CA: Sage.

Gingerich, W., and Feyerherm, W.: 1979 "The Celeration Line Technique for Assessing Client Change," *Journal of Social Service Research, 3*(1), 99–113.

Giuli, Charles A., and Hudson, Walter W.: 1977 "Assessing Parent-Child Relationship Disorders in Clinical Practice: The Child's Point of View," *Journal of Social Service Research, 1*(1), 77–92.

Glaser, Barney, and Strauss, Anselm: 1967 *The Discovery of Grounded Theory.* Chicago: Aldine.

Glisson, Charles: 1987 "Author's Reply," *Social Service Review, 61*(1), 172–176.

Glock, Charles Y., Ringer, Benjamin B., and Babbie, Earl R.: 1967 *To Comfort and to Challenge.* Berkeley: University of California Press.

Goffman, Erving: 1961 *Asylums: Essays on the Social Situation of Mental Patients and Other Inmates.* Chicago: Aldine.
1963 *Stigma: Notes on the Management of a Spoiled Identity.* Englewood Cliffs, NJ: Prentice Hall.
1974 *Frame Analysis.* Cambridge, MA: Harvard University Press.

Gold, Raymond L.: 1969 "Roles in Sociological Field Observation," in George J. McCall and J. L. Simmons (eds.), *Issues in Participant Observation.* Reading, MA: Addison-Wesley, pp. 30–39.

Goldstein, Eda G.: 1995 "Psychosocial Approach," *Encyclopedia of Social Work,* 19th ed. Washington, DC: National Association of Social Workers, *3,* pp. 1948–1954.

Gottlieb, Naomi, and Bombyk, M.: 1987 "Strategies for Strengthening Feminist Research," *Affilia* (Summer), 23–35.

Goyder, John: 1985 "Face-to-Face Interviews and Mailed Questionnaires: The Net Difference in Response Rate," *Public Opinion Quarterly, 49,* 234–252.

Graham, Laurie, and Hogan, Richard: 1990 "Social Class and Tactics: Neighborhood Opposition to Group Homes," *Sociological Quarterly, 31*(4), 513–529.

Graham, Mary: 1989 "One Toke Over the Line," *New Republic, 200*(16), 20–21.

Grob, Gerald N.: 1973 *Mental Institutions in America.* New York: Free Press.

Haase, Richard F., Waechter, Donna M., and Solomon, Gary S.: 1982 "How Significant Is a Significant Difference? Average Effect Size of Research in Counseling Psychology," *Journal of Counseling Psychology 29*(2), 59–63.

Hamblin, Robert L.: 1971 "Mathematical Experimentation and Sociological Theory: A Critical Analysis," *Sociometry, 34,* 4.

Heineman, M. B.: 1981 "The Obsolete Scientific Imperative in Social Work Research," *Social Service Review, 55,* 371–397.

Hempel, Carl G.: 1952 "Fundamentals of Concept Formation in Empirical Science," *International Encyclopedia of United Science,* vol. 2, no 7. Chicago: University of Chicago.

Higginbotham, A. Leon, Jr.: 1978 *In the Matter of Color: Race and the American Legal Process.* New York: Oxford University Press.

Hill, R. R.: 1978 "Social Work Research on Minorities: Impediments and Opportunities," paper presented at the National Conference on the Future of Social Work Research, San Antonio, Texas, October.

Hirschi, Travis, and Selvin, Hanan: 1973 *Principles of Survey Analysis.* New York: Free Press.

Hogarty, Gerard: 1979 "Aftercare Treatment of Schizophrenia: Current Status and Future Direction," in H. M. Pragg (ed.), *Management of Schizophrenia.* Assen, The Netherlands: Van Gorcum, pp. 19–36.
1989 "Metaanalysis of the Effects of Practice with the Chronically Mentally Ill: A Critique and Reappraisal of the Literature," *Social Work, 34*(4), 363–373.

Homans, George C.: 1971 "Reply to Blain," *Sociological Inquiry, 41* (Winter), 23.

Horowitz, Irving Louis: 1967 *The Rise and Fall of Project Camelot.* Cambridge, MA: MIT Press.

Howell, Joseph T.: 1973 *Hard Living on Clay Street.* Garden City, NY: Doubleday Anchor.

Hudson, Walter W.: 1982 *The Clinical Measurement Package.* Homewood, IL: Dorsey Press.

Hughes, Michael: 1980 "The Fruits of Cultivation Analysis: A Reexamination of Some Effects of Television Watching," *Public Opinion Quarterly* (Fall), 287–302.

Humphreys, Laud: 1970 *Tearoom Trade: Impersonal Sex in Public Places.* Chicago: Aldine.

Jackman, Mary R., and Scheuer Senter, Mary: 1980 "Images of Social Groups: Categorical or Qualified?" *Public Opinion Quarterly, 44,* 340–361.

Jayaratne, Srinika, and Levy, Rona L.: 1979 *Empirical Clinical Practice.* New York: Columbia University Press.

Jayaratne, Srinika, Tripodi, Tony, and Talsma, Eugene: 1988 "The Comparative Analysis and Aggregation of Single Case Data," *Journal of Applied Behavioral Science, 1*(24), 119–128.

Jensen, Arthur: 1969 "How Much Can We Boost IQ and Scholastic Achievement?" *Harvard Educational Review, 39*, 273–274.

Johnston, Hank: 1980 "The Marketed Social Movement: A Case Study of the Rapid Growth of TM," *Pacific Sociological Review* (July), 333–354.

Jones, James H.: 1981 *Bad Blood*. New York: Free Press.

Jones, Lovell: 1991 "The Impact of Cancer on the Health Status of Minorities in Texas," paper presented to the Texas Minority Health Strategic Planning Conference, July.

Kahane, Howard: 1992 *Logic and Contemporary Rhetoric*, 2nd ed. Belmont, CA: Wadsworth.

Kaplan, Abraham: 1964 *The Conduct of Inquiry*. San Francisco: Chandler.

Kelly, A.: 1978 "Feminism and Research," *Women's Studies International Quarterly, 1*, 226.

Kendall, Patricia L., and Lazarsfeld, Paul F.: 1950 "Problems of Survey Analysis," in Robert K. Merton and Paul F. Lazarsfeld (eds.), *Continuities in Social Research: Studies in the Scope and Method of "The American Soldier."* New York: Free Press.

Kish, Leslie: 1965 *Survey Sampling*. New York: Wiley.

Kronick, Jane C.: 1989 "Toward a Formal Methodology of Document Analysis in the Interpretive Tradition," paper presented at the meeting of the Eastern Sociological Society, Baltimore, MD.

Kuhn, Thomas: 1970 *The Structure of Scientific Revolutions*, 2nd ed. Chicago: University of Chicago Press.

Ladd, Everett C., and Ferree, G. Donald: 1981 "Were the Pollsters Really Wrong?" *Public Opinion* (December-January), 13–20.

Lasch, Christopher: 1977 *Haven in a Heartless World*. New York: Basic Books.

Lazarsfeld, Paul: 1959 "Problems in Methodology," in Robert K. Merton (ed.), *Sociology Today*. New York: Basic Books.

Levin, Jack, and Spates, James: 1970 "Hippie Values: An Analysis of the Underground Press," *Youth and Society, 2*, 59–72. Reprinted in M. Patricia Golden (ed.), *The Research Experience*. Itasca, IL: Peacock, 1976.

Liebow, Elliot: 1967 *Tally's Corner*. Boston: Little, Brown.

Literary Digest: 1936a "Landon, 1,293,669: Roosevelt, 972,897," October 31, pp. 5–6.
1936b "What Went Wrong with the Polls?", November 14, pp. 7–8.

Lofland, John: 1995 "Analytic Ethnography: Features, Failings, and Futures," *Journal of Contemporary Ethnography, 24*(1), 30–67.

Lofland, John, and Lofland, Lyn H.: 1995 *Analyzing Social Settings*, 3rd ed. Belmont, CA: Wadsworth.

Luker, K.: 1984 *Abortion and the Politics of Motherhood*. Berkeley: University of California Press.

Marsden, Gerald: 1971 "Content Analysis Studies of Psychotherapy: 1954 through 1968," in Allen E. Bergin and Sol L. Garfield (eds.), *Handbook of Psychotherapy and Behavior Change: An Empirical Analysis*. New York: Wiley.

Marx, Karl: [1867] 1967 *Capital*. New York: International Publishers.
1880 *Revue Socialist* (July 5). Reprinted in T. B. Bottomore and Maximilien Rubel (eds.), *Karl Marx: Selected Writings in Sociology and Social Philosophy*. New York: McGraw-Hill, 1956.

Matocha, Linda K.: 1992 "Case Study Interviews: Caring for Persons with AIDS," in Jane Gilgun, Kerry Daly, and Gerald Handel (eds.), *Qualitative Methods in Family Research*. Thousand Oaks, CA: Sage, pp. 66–84.

McAlister, Alfred, Perry, Cheryl, Killen, Joel, Slinkard, Lee Ann, and Maccoby, Nathan: 1980 "Pilot Study of Smoking, Alcohol, and Drug Abuse Prevention," *American Journal of Public Health* (July), 719–721.

McCall, George J., and Simmons, J. L. (eds.): 1969 *Issues in Participant Observation*. Reading, MA: Addison-Wesley.

McRoy, Ruth G.: 1981 *A Comparative Study of the Self-Concept of Transracially and Inracially Adopted Black Children*. Dissertation, University of Texas at Austin.

McRoy, Ruth G., Grotevant, Harold D., Ayers Lopez, Susan, and Furuta, Ann: 1990 "Adoption Revelation and Communication Issues: Implications for Practice," *Families in Society, 71*(9), 550–557.

McWirter, Norris: 1980 *The Guinness Book of Records*. New York: Bantam.

Mercer, Susan, and Kane, Rosalie A.: 1979 "Helplessness and Hopelessness Among the Institutionalized Aged," *Health and Social Work, 4*(1), 91–116.

Mies, M: 1983 "Toward a Methodology for Feminist Research," in G. Bowles and R. Duelli-Klein (eds.), *Theories of Women's Studies.* London: Routledge & Kegan Paul, pp. 117–139.

Milgram, Stanley: 1963 "Behavioral Study of Obedience," *Journal of Abnormal and Social Psychology, 67,* 371–378.
1965 "Some Conditions of Obedience and Disobedience to Authority," *Human Relations, 18,* 57–76.

Miller, Henry: 1986 "The Use of Computers in Social Work Practice: An Assessment," *Journal of Social Work Education, 22*(3), 52–60.

Miller, William L., and Crabtree, Benjamin F.: 1994 "Clinical Research," in Norman K. Denzin and Yvonna S. Lincoln (eds.), *Handbook of Qualitative Research.* Thousand Oaks, CA: Sage, pp. 340–352.

Monette, Duane R., Sullivan, Thomas J., and DeJong, Cornell R.: 1994 *Applied Social Research: Tool for the Human Services,* 3rd ed. Fort Worth, TX: Harcourt Brace.

Morgan, Lewis H.: 1870 *Systems of Consanguinity and Affinity.* Washington, DC: Smithsonian Institution.

Morrissey, J., and Goldman, H.: 1984 "Cycles of Reform in the Care of the Chronically Mentally Ill," *Hospital and Community Psychiatry, 35*(8), 785–793.

Morse, Janice M.: 1994 "Designing Funded Qualitative Research," in Norman K. Denzin and Yvonna S. Lincoln (eds.), *Handbook of Qualitative Research.* Thousand Oaks, CA: Sage.

Moskowitz, Milt: 1981 "The Drugs That Doctors Order," *San Francisco Chronicle* (May 23), 33.

Moss, Kathryn E.: 1988 "Writing Research Proposals," in Richard M. Grinnell, Jr. (ed.), *Social Work Research and Evaluation,* 3rd ed. Itasca, IL: Peacock, pp. 429–445.

Moynihan, Daniel: 1965 *The Negro Family: The Case for National Action.* Washington, DC: U.S. Government Printing Office.

Murray, Charles: 1984 *Losing Ground.* New York: Basic Books.

Murray, Charles, and Herrnstein, Richard J.: 1994 *The Bell Curve.* New York: Free Press.

Myrdal, Gunnar: 1944 *An American Dilemma.* New York: Harper & Row.

Neuman, W. Lawrence: 1994 *Social Research Methods: Qualitative and Quantitative Approaches.* Needham Heights, MA: Allyn & Bacon.

New York Times: "Method of Polls in Two States," June 6, 1984, p. 12.
"Test of Journals Is Criticized as Unethical," September 27, 1988, pp. 21, 25.
"Charges Dropped on Bogus Work," April 4, 1989, p. 21.

Nie, Norman H., Hull, C. Hadlai, Jenkins, Jean G., Steinbrenner, Karing, and Bent, Dale H.: 1975 *Statistical Package for the Social Sciences.* New York: McGraw-Hill.

Nugent, William R.: 1991 "An Experimental and Qualitative Analysis of a Cognitive-Behavioral Intervention for Anger," *Social Work Research and Abstracts, 27*(3), 3–8.

Nurius, P. S., and Hudson, W. W.: 1988 "Computer-Based Practice: Future Dream or Current Technology?" *Social Work, 33*(4), 357–362.

Oakley, A.: 1981 "Interviewing Women: A Contradiction in Terms," in H. Roberts (ed.), *Doing Feminist Research.* London: Routledge & Kegan Paul.

Orme, John G., and Combs-Orme, Terri D.: 1986 "Statistical Power and Type II Errors in Social Work Research," *Social Work Research & Abstracts, 22*(3), 3–10.

Ozawa, Martha N.: 1989 "Welfare Policies and Illegitimate Birth Rates Among Adolescents: Analysis of State-by-State Data," *Social Work Research and Abstracts, 24*(2), 5–11.

Parsons, Talcott, and Shils, Edward A.: 1951 *Toward a General Theory of Action.* Cambridge, MA: Harvard University Press.

Patton, Michael Quinn: 1990 *Qualitative Evaluation and Research Methods,* 2nd ed. Newbury Park, CA: Sage.

Perinelli, Phillip J.: 1986 "No Unsuspecting Public in TV Call-In Polls," *New York,* February 14, letter to the editor.

Perlman, David: 1984 "Fluoride, AIDS Experts Scoff at Nelder's Idea," *San Francisco Chronicle,* September 6, p. 1.

Petersen, Larry R., and Maynard, Judy L.: 1981 "Income, Equity, and Wives' Housekeeping Role Expectations," *Pacific Sociological Review* (January), 87–105.

Polansky, Norman A.: 1975 *Social Work Research.* Chicago: University of Chicago Press.

Polansky, Norman A., Lippitt, Ronald, and Redl, Fritz: 1950 "An Investigation of Behavioral Contagion in Groups," *Human Relations, 3,* 319–348.

Polster, Richard A., and Lynch, Mary A.: 1985 "Single-Subject Designs," in Richard M. Grinnell (ed.), *Social Work Research and Evaluation.* Itasca, IL: Peacock, pp. 381–431.

Population Reference Bureau: 1980 "1980 World Population Data Sheet," (a poster) prepared by Carl Haub and Douglas W. Heisler. Washington, DC: Population Reference Bureau.

Posavac, Emil J., and Carey, Raymond G.: 1985 *Program Evaluation: Methods and Case Studies.* Englewood Cliffs, NJ: Prentice Hall.

Powell, Elwin H.: 1958 "Occupation, Status, and Suicide: Toward a Redefinition of Anomie," *American Sociological Review, 23,* 131–139.

Public Opinion: 1984 "See How They Ran" (October–November), pp. 38–40.

Rank, Mark: 1992 "The Blending of Qualitative and Quantitative Methods in Understanding Childbearing Among Welfare Recipients," in Jane Gilgun, Kerry Daly, and Gerald Handel (eds.), *Qualitative Methods in Family Research.* Thousand Oaks, CA: Sage, pp. 281–300.

Ransford, H. Edward: 1968 "Isolation, Powerlessness, and Violence: A Study of Attitudes and Participants in the Watts Riots," *American Journal of Sociology, 73,* 581–591.

Rasinski, Kenneth A.: 1989 "The Effect of Question Wording on Public Support for Government Spending," *Public Opinion Quarterly, 53,* 388–394.

Reid, William J., and Epstein, Laura: 1972 *Task Centered Casework.* New York: Columbia University Press.

Reid, William J., and Hanrahan, Patricia: 1982 "Recent Evaluations of Social Work: Grounds for Optimism," *Social Work, 27*(4), 328–340.

Reinharz, Shulamit: 1992 *Feminist Methods in Social Research.* New York: Oxford University Press.

Reissman, Catherine (ed.):1994 *Qualitative Studies in Social Work Research.* Thousand Oaks, CA: Sage.

Robinson, Robin A.: 1994 "Private Pain and Public Behaviors: Sexual Abuse and Delinquent Girls," in Catherine Reissman (ed.), *Qualitative Studies in Social Work Research.* Thousand Oaks, CA: Sage, pp. 73–94.

Rodwell, Mary K.: 1987 "Naturalistic Inquiry: An Alternative Model for Social Work Assessment," *Social Service Review, 61*(2), 232–246.

Roethlisberger, F. J., and Dickson, W. J.: 1939 *Management and the Worker.* Cambridge, MA: Harvard University Press.

Rogler, Lloyd H.: 1989 "The Meaning of Culturally Sensitive Research in Mental Health," *American Journal of Psychiatry, 146*(3), 296–303.

Rosenberg, Morris: 1965 *Society and the Adolescent Self-Image.* Princeton, NJ: Princeton University Press.

1968 *The Logic of Survey Analysis.* New York: Basic Books.

Rosenhan, D. L.: 1973 "On Being Sane in Insane Places," *Science, 179,* 240–248.

Rosenthal, Robert, and Rubin, Donald: 1982 "A Simple, General Purpose Display of Magnitude of Experimental Effect," *Journal of Educational Psychology, 74*(2), 166–169.

Rossi, Peter H., and Freeman, Howard E.: 1982 *Evaluation: A Systematic Approach.* Beverly Hills, CA: Sage.

Rothman, Ellen K.: 1981 "The Written Record," *Journal of Family History* (Spring), 47–56.

Royse, David: 1988 "Voter Support for Human Services," *ARETE, 13*(2), 26–34.

1991 *Research Methods in Social Work.* Chicago: Nelson-Hall, p. 237.

Rubin, Allen: 1979 *Community Mental Health in the Social Work Curriculum.* New York: Council on Social Work Education.

1981 "Reexamining the Impact of Sex on Salary: The Limits of Statistical Significance," *Social Work Research & Abstracts, 17*(3), 19–24.

1985a "Practice Effectiveness: More Grounds for Optimism," *Social Work, 30*(6), 469–476.

1985b "Significance Testing with Population Data," *Social Service Review, 59*(3), 518–520.

1987 "Case Management," *Encyclopedia of Social Work,* 18th ed. Silver Spring, MD: National Association of Social Work, vol. 1, pp. 212–222.

1991 "The Effectiveness of Outreach Counseling and Support Groups for Battered Women: A Preliminary Evaluation," *Research on Social Work Practice, 1*(4), 332–357.

1992 "Is Case Management Effective for People with Serious Mental Illness? A Research Review," *Health and Social Work, 17*(2), 138–150.

In press "The Family Preservation Evaluation from Hell: Implications for Program Evaluation Fidelity," *Children and Youth Services Review.*

Rubin, Allen, and Conway, Patricia G.: 1985 "Standards for Determining the Magnitude of Relationships in Social Work Research," *Social Work Research & Abstracts, 21*(1), 34–39.

Rubin, Allen, Conway, Patricia G., Patterson, Judith K., and Spence, Richard T.: 1983 "Sources of Variation in Rate of Decline to MSW Programs," *Journal of Education for Social Work, 19*(3), 48–58.

Rubin, Allen, and Johnson, Peter J.: 1982 "Practitioner Orientations Toward the Chronically Disabled: Prospects for Policy Implementation," *Administration in Mental Health, 10,* 3–12.
1984 "Direct Practice Interests of Entering MSW Students," *Journal of Education for Social Work, 20*(2), 5–16.

Rubin, Allen, and Shuttlesworth, Guy E.: 1982 "Assessing Role Expectations in Nursing Home Care," *ARETE, 7*(2), 37–48.
1983 "Engaging Families as Support Resources in Nursing Home Care: Ambiguity in the Subdivision of Tasks," *Gerontologist, 23*(6), 632–636.

Ruckdeschel, Roy A., and Faris, B. E.: 1981 "Assessing Practice: A Critical Look at the Single-Case Design," *Social Casework, 62,* 413–419.

Sacks, Jeffrey J., Krushat, W. Mark, and Newman, Jeffrey: 1980 "Reliability of the Health Hazard Appraisal," *American Journal of Public Health* (July): 730–732.

Saletan, William, and Watzman, Nancy: 1989 "Marcus Welby, J.D." *New Republic, 200*(16), 22.

Sandelowski, M., Holditch-Davis, D. H., and Harris, B. G.: 1989 "Artful Design: Writing the Proposal for Research in the Naturalistic Paradigm," *Research in Nursing and Health, 12,* 77–84.

Schwartz, M.: 1984 *Using Computers in Clinical Practice.* New York: Haworth Press.

Schuerman, John: 1989 "Editorial," *Social Service Review, 63*(1), 3.

Selltiz, Claire, Wrightsman, Lawrence S., and Cook, Stuart W.: 1976 *Research Methods in Social Relations.* New York: Holt, Rinehart and Winston.

Shadish, William R., Cook, Thomas D., and Leviton, Laura C.: 1991 *Foundations of Program Evaluation.* Newbury Park, CA: Sage.

Shanks, J. Merrill, and Tortora, Robert D.: 1985 "Beyond CATI: Generalized and Distributed Systems for Computer-Assisted Surveys," prepared for the Bureau of the Census, First Annual Research Conference, Reston, VA, March 20–23.

Simon, Cassandra E., McNeil, John S., Franklin, Cynthia, and Cooperman, Abby: 1991 "The Family and Schizophrenia: Toward a Psychoeducational Approach." *Families in Society, 72*(6), 323–333.

Smith, Mary Lee, and Glass, Gene V.: 1977 "Meta-analysis of Psychotherapy Outcome Studies," *American Psychologist, 32*(9), 752–760.

Smith, Tom W.: 1988 "The First Straw? A Study of the Origins of Election Polls," *Public Opinion Quarterly, 54* (Spring), 21–36.

Solomon, Phyllis, and Paulson, Robert I.: 1995 "Issues in Designing and Conducting Randomized Human Service Trials," paper presented at the National Conference of the Society for Social Work and Research, Washington, DC.

Srole, Leo: 1956 "Social Integration and Certain Corollaries: An Exploratory Study," *American Sociological Review, 21,* 709–716.

Stouffer, Samuel: [1937] 1962 "Effects of the Depression on the Family," reprinted in Samuel A. Stouffer, *Social Research to Test Ideas.* New York: Free Press.

Stouffer, Samuel, et al.: 1949, 1950 *The American Soldier,* 3 vols. Princeton, NJ: Princeton University Press.

Strachan, Angus M.: 1986 "Family Intervention for the Rehabilitation of Schizophrenia: Toward Protection and Coping." *Schizophrenia Bulletin, 12*(4), 678–698.

Stuart, Paul: 1981 "Historical Research," in Richard M. Grinnell, *Social Work Research and Evaluation.* Itasca, IL: Peacock, pp. 316–332.

Taber, Sara M.: 1981 "Cognitive-Behavior Modification Treatment of an Aggressive 11-Year-Old Boy," *Social Work Research & Abstracts, 17*(2), 13–23.

Takeuchi, David: 1974 "Grass in Hawaii: A Structural Constraints Approach," M.A. thesis, University of Hawaii.

Tan, Alexis S.: 1980 "Mass Media Use, Issue Knowledge and Political Involvement," *Public Opinion Quarterly, 44,* 241–248.

Tandon, Rajesh, and Brown, L. Dave: 1981 "Organization-Building for Rural Development: An Experiment in India," *Journal of Applied Behavioral Science* (April-June), 172–189.

Taylor, James B.: 1977   "Toward Alternative Forms of Social Work Research: The Case for Naturalistic Methods," *Journal of Social Welfare, 4,* 119–126.

Thomas, W. I., and Znaniecki, Florian: 1918   *The Polish Peasant in Europe and America.* Chicago: University of Chicago Press.

Tobler, N. S.: 1986   "Meta-Analysis of 143 Adolescent Drug Prevention Programs: Quantitative Outcome Results of Program Participants Compared to a Control or Comparison Group," *Journal of Drug Issues, 4,* 537–567.

Turk, Theresa Guminski: 1980   "Hospital Support: Urban Correlates of Allocation Based on Organizational Prestige," *Pacific Sociological Review* (July), 315–332.

Turner, Jonathan: 1974   *The Structure of Sociological Theory.* Homewood, IL: Dorsey Press.

U.S. Bureau of the Census: 1979   *Statistical Abstract of the United States.* Washington, DC: U.S. Government Printing Office.

U.S. Bureau of the Census: 1992   *Statistical Abstract of the United States.* Washington, DC: U.S. Government Printing Office.

U.S. Department of Labor (Bureau of Labor Statistics): 1978   *The Consumer Price Index: Concepts and Content Over the Years,* Report 517. Washington, DC: U.S. Government Printing Office.

Videka-Sherman, Lynn: 1988   "Metaanalysis of Research on Social Work Practice in Mental Health," *Social Work, 33*(4), 325–338.

Votaw, Carmen Delgado: 1979   "Women's Rights in the United States," United States Commission of Civil Rights, Inter-American Commission on Women. Washington, DC: Clearinghouse Publications, p. 57.

Walster, Elaine, Piliavian, Jane, and Walster, G. William: 1973   "The Hard-to-Get Woman," *Psychology Today* (September), 80–83.

Webb, Eugene, Campbell, Donald T., Schwartz, Richard D., and Sechrest, Lee: 1981   *Nonreactive Research in the Social Sciences.* Chicago: Rand McNally.

Weber, Max: [1925] 1946   "Science as a Vocation," in Hans Gerth and C. Wright Mills (trans., eds.), *From Max Weber: Essays in Sociology.* New York: Oxford University Press.

Weinbach, Robert, and Grinnell, Richard: 1987   *Statistics for Social Workers.* New York: Longman.

Weisbrod, Burton A., Test, Mary Ann, and Stein, Leonard I.: 1980   "Alternative to Mental Hospital Treatment: II. Economic Benefit-Cost Analysis," *Archives of General Psychiatry, 37*(4), 400–408.

Weiss, Carol H.: 1972   *Evaluation Research.* Englewood Cliffs, NJ: Prentice Hall.

Weitzman, Eben, and Miles, Matthew: 1995   *Computer Programs for Qualitative Data Analysis.* Newbury Park, CA: Sage.

White, Karl R.: 1988   "Cost Analyses in Family Support Programs," in Heather B. Weiss and Francine H. Jacobs (eds.), *Evaluating Family Programs.* New York: Aldine De Gruyter, pp. 429–443.

White, Ralph: 1951   *Value-Analysis: The Nature and Use of the Method.* New York: Society for the Psychological Study of Social Issues.

Whiteman, Martin, Fanshel, David, and Grundy, John F.: 1987   "Cognitive-Behavioral Interventions Aimed at Anger of Parents at Risk of Child Abuse," *Social Work, 32*(6), 469–474.

Whittaker, James K.: 1987   "Group Care for Children," *Encyclopedia of Social Work,* 18th ed. Silver Spring, MD: National Association of Social Workers, vol. 1, pp. 672–682.

Wilson, Jerome: 1989   "Cancer Incidence and Mortality Differences of Black and White Americans: A Role for Biomarkers," in Lovell Jones (ed.), *Minorities and Cancer.* New York: Springer-Verlag.

Wood, Katherine M.: 1978   "Casework Effectiveness: A New Look at the Research Evidence," *Social Work, 23*(6), 437–458.

Yin, Robert K.: 1984   *Case Study Research: Design and Methods.* Beverly Hills, CA: Sage.

Yinger, J. Milton, et al.: 1977   *Middle Start: An Experiment in the Educational Enrichment of Young Adolescents.* London: Cambridge University Press.

York, James, and Persigehl, Elmer: 1981   "Productivity Trends in the Ball and Roller Bearing Industry," *Monthly Labor Review* (January), 40–43.

Yu, Elena S. H., Ming-Yuan, Zhang, et al.: 1987   "Translation of Instruments: Procedures, Issues, and Dilemmas," in W. T. Lui (ed.), *A Decade Review of Mental Health Research, Training, and Services,* Pacific/Asian American Mental Research Center, pp. 101–107.

Zimbalist, Sidney E.: 1977   *Historic Themes and Landmarks in Social Welfare Research.* New York: Harper & Row.

Index

IN-BOOK SURVEY

At Brooks/Cole, we are excited about creating new types of learning materials that are interactive, three-dimensional, and fun to use. To guide us in our publishing/development process, we hope that you'll take just a few moments to fill out the survey below. Your answers can help us make decisions that will allow us to produce a wide variety of videos, CD-ROMs, and Internet-based learning systems to complement standard textbooks. If you're interested in working with us as a student Beta-tester, be sure to fill in your name, telephone number, and address. We look forward to hearing from you!

In addition to books, which of the following learning tools do you currently use in your counseling/human services/social work courses?

_____ **Video** _____ in class _____ school library _____ own VCR

_____ **CD-ROM** _____ in class _____ in lab _____ own computer

_____ **Macintosh disks** _____ in class _____ in lab _____ own computer

_____ **Windows disks** _____ in class _____ in lab _____ own computer

_____ **Internet** _____ in class _____ in lab _____ own computer

How often do you access the Internet? _____

My own home computer is:

_____ Macintosh _____ DOS _____ Windows _____ Windows 95

The computer I use in class for counseling/human services/social work courses is:

_____ Macintosh _____ DOS _____ Windows _____ Windows 95

If you are NOT currently using multimedia materials in your counseling/human services/social work courses, but can see ways that video, CD-ROM, Internet, or other technologies could enhance your learning, please comment below:

_____

_____

_____

Other comments (optional): _____

_____

Name _____

Address _____

Telephone number (optional): _____

You can fax this form to us at (408) 375-6414; e-mail to: info@brookscole.com or detach, fold, secure, and mail.

FOLD HERE

NO POSTAGE
NECESSARY
IF MAILED
IN THE
UNITED STATES

B U S I N E S S   R E P L Y   M A I L

FIRST CLASS   PERMIT NO. 358   PACIFIC GROVE, CA

POSTAGE WILL BE PAID BY ADDRESSEE

ATTN: ___MARKETING_____

**Brooks/Cole Publishing Company
511 Forest Lodge Road
Pacific Grove, California 93950-9968**

FOLD HERE